Microsoft® Access® 2010

ILLUSTRATED

Complete

Lisa Friedrichsen

COURSE TECHNOLOGY
CENGAGE Learning™

Australia • Brazil • Japan • Korea • Mexico • Singapore • Spain • United Kingdom • United States

COURSE TECHNOLOGY
CENGAGE Learning™

Microsoft® Access® 2010—Illustrated Complete

Lisa Friedrichsen

Vice President, Publisher: Nicole Jones Pinard

Executive Editor: Marjorie Hunt

Associate Acquisitions Editor: Brandi Shailer

Senior Product Manager: Christina Kling Garrett

Associate Product Manager: Michelle Camisa

Editorial Assistant: Kim Klasner

Director of Marketing: Cheryl Costantini

Senior Marketing Manager: Ryan DeGrote

Marketing Coordinator: Kristen Panciocco

Contributing Authors: Barbara Clemens, Carol Cram, Elizabeth Eisner Reding

Developmental Editors: Lisa Ruffolo, Jeanne Herring, Pam Conrad

Content Project Manager: Melissa Panagos

Copy Editor: Mark Goodin

Proofreader: Vicki Zimmer

Indexer: BIM Indexing and Proofreading Services

QA Manuscript Reviewers: John Frietas, Serge Palladino, Susan Pedicini, Jeff Schwartz, Chris Scriver, Danielle Shaw, Marianne Snow, Susan Whalen

Print Buyer: Fola Orekoya

Cover Designer: GEX Publishing Services

Cover Artist: Mark Hunt

Composition: GEX Publishing Services

© 2011 Course Technology, Cengage Learning

ALL RIGHTS RESERVED. No part of this work covered by the copyright herein may be reproduced, transmitted, stored or used in any form or by any means graphic, electronic, or mechanical, including but not limited to photocopying, recording, scanning, digitizing, taping, Web distribution, information networks, or information storage and retrieval systems, except as permitted under Section 107 or 108 of the 1976 United States Copyright Act, without the prior written permission of the publisher.

Trademarks:

For product information and technology assistance, contact us at
Cengage Learning Customer & Sales Support, 1-800-354-9706
For permission to use material from this text or product, submit all requests online at **www.cengage.com/permissions**
Further permissions questions can be emailed to
permissionrequest@cengage.com

Some of the product names and company names used in this book have been used for identification purposes only and may be trademarks or registered trademarks of their respective manufacturers and sellers.

Microsoft and the Office logo are either registered trademarks or trademarks of Microsoft Corporation in the United States and/or other countries. Course Technology, Cengage Learning is an independent entity from Microsoft Corporation, and not affiliated with Microsoft in any manner.

Library of Congress Control Number: 2010934629

ISBN-13: 978-0-538-74717-2
ISBN-10: 0-538-74717-X

Course Technology
20 Channel Center Street
Boston, MA 02210
USA

Cengage Learning is a leading provider of customized learning solutions with office locations around the globe, including Singapore, the United Kingdom, Australia, Mexico, Brazil, and Japan. Locate your local office at:
international.cengage.com/region

Cengage Learning products are represented in Canada by Nelson Education, Ltd.

To learn more about Course Technology, visit **www.cengage.com/coursetechnology**

To learn more about Cengage Learning, visit **www.cengage.com**

Purchase any of our products at your local college store or at our preferred online store **www.cengagebrain.com**

Printed in the United States of America
1 2 3 4 5 6 7 8 9 18 17 16 15 14 13 12 11 10

Brief Contents

Contents

Office 2010

Access 2010

Preface

Welcome to *Microsoft Access 2010—Illustrated Complete*. If this is your first experience with the Illustrated series, you'll see that this book has a unique design: each skill is presented on two facing pages, with steps on the left and screens on the right. The layout makes it easy to learn a skill without having to read a lot of text and flip pages to see an illustration.

This book is an ideal learning tool for a wide range of learners—the "rookies" will find the clean design easy to follow and focused with only essential information presented, and the "hotshots" will appreciate being able to move quickly through the lessons to find the information they need without reading a lot of text. The design also makes this a great reference after the course is over! See the illustration on the right to learn more about the pedagogical and design elements of a typical lesson.

What's New In This Edition

- **Fully Updated.** Highlights the new features of Microsoft Access 2010 including the new Backstage view, new database templates, enhanced datasheet formatting tools, and the enhanced interface features. A new appendix covers cloud computing concepts and using Microsoft Office Web Apps. Examples and exercises are updated throughout.
- **Maps to SAM 2010.** This book is designed to work with SAM (Skills Assessment Manager) 2010. SAM Assessment contains performance-based, hands-on SAM exams for each unit of this book, and SAM Training provides hands-on training for skills covered in the book. Some exercises are available in SAM Projects, which is auto-grading software that provides both students and instructors with immediate, detailed feedback (SAM sold separately.) See page xii for more information on SAM.

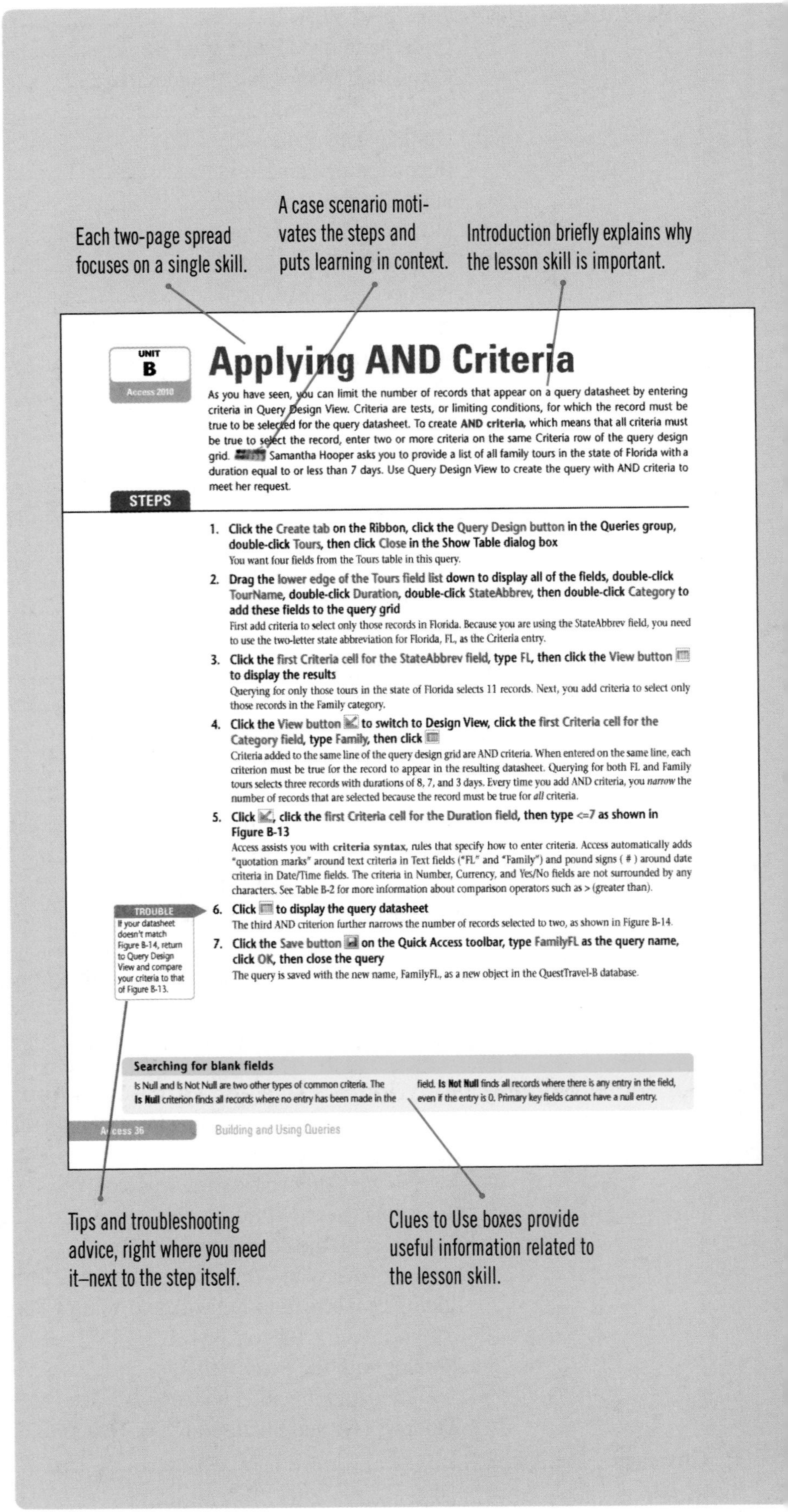

Each two-page spread focuses on a single skill.
A case scenario motivates the steps and puts learning in context.
Introduction briefly explains why the lesson skill is important.
UNIT B
Access 2010
Applying AND Criteria
As you have seen, you can limit the number of records that appear on a query datasheet by entering criteria in Query Design View. Criteria are tests, or limiting conditions, for which the record must be true to be selected for the query datasheet. To create AND criteria, which means that all criteria must be true to select the record, enter two or more criteria on the same Criteria row of the query design grid. Samantha Hooper asks you to provide a list of all family tours in the state of Florida with a duration equal to or less than 7 days. Use Query Design View to create the query with AND criteria to meet her request.
STEPS
1. Click the Create tab on the Ribbon, click the Query Design button in the Queries group, double-click Tours, then click Close in the Show Table dialog box
You want four fields from the Tours table in this query.
2. Drag the lower edge of the Tours field list down to display all of the fields, double-click TourName, double-click Duration, double-click StateAbbrev, then double-click Category to add these fields to the query grid
First add criteria to select only those records in Florida. Because you are using the StateAbbrev field, you need to use the two-letter state abbreviation for Florida, FL, as the Criteria entry.
3. Click the first Criteria cell for the StateAbbrev field, type FL, then click the View button to display the results
Querying for only those tours in the state of Florida selects 11 records. Next, you add criteria to select only those records in the Family category.
4. Click the View button to switch to Design View, click the first Criteria cell for the Category field, type Family, then click
Criteria added to the same line of the query design grid are AND criteria. When entered on the same line, each criterion must be true for the record to appear in the resulting datasheet. Querying for both FL and Family tours selects three records with durations of 8, 7, and 3 days. Every time you add AND criteria, you narrow the number of records that are selected because the record must be true for all criteria.
5. Click , click the first Criteria cell for the Duration field, then type <=7 as shown in Figure B-13
Access assists you with criteria syntax, rules that specify how to enter criteria. Access automatically adds "quotation marks" around text criteria in Text fields ("FL" and "Family") and pound signs (#) around date criteria in Date/Time fields. The criteria in Number, Currency, and Yes/No fields are not surrounded by any characters. See Table B-2 for more information about comparison operators such as > (greater than).
TROUBLE
If your datasheet doesn't match Figure B-14, return to Query Design View and compare your criteria to that of Figure B-13.
6. Click to display the query datasheet
The third AND criterion further narrows the number of records selected to two, as shown in Figure B-14.
7. Click the Save button on the Quick Access toolbar, type FamilyFL as the query name, click OK, then close the query
The query is saved with the new name, FamilyFL, as a new object in the QuestTravel-B database.
Searching for blank fields
Is Null and Is Not Null are two other types of common criteria. The Is Null criterion finds all records where no entry has been made in the field. Is Not Null finds all records where there is any entry in the field, even if the entry is 0. Primary key fields cannot have a null entry.
Access 36
Building and Using Queries
Tips and troubleshooting advice, right where you need it–next to the step itself.
Clues to Use boxes provide useful information related to the lesson skill.

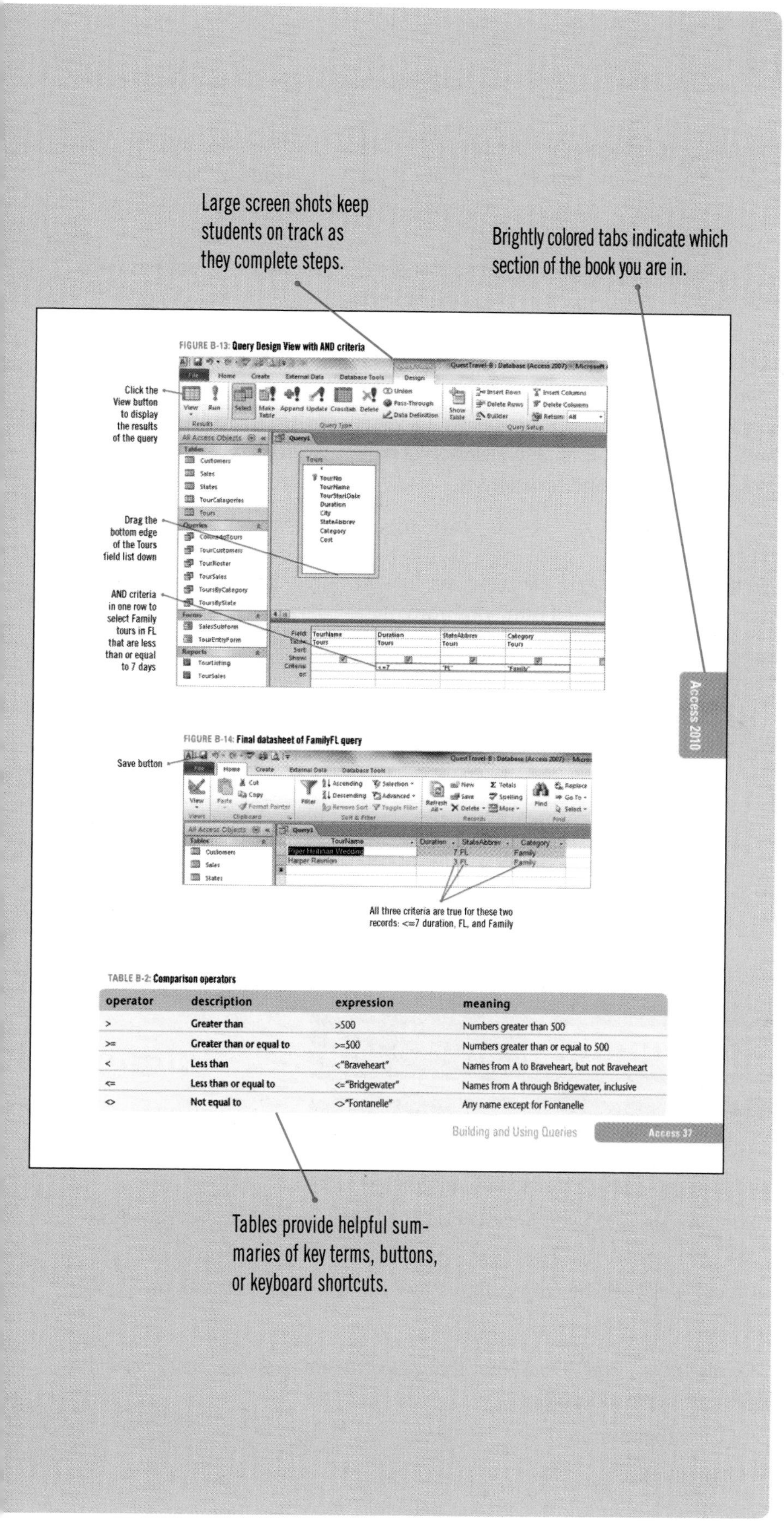
Large screen shots keep students on track as they complete steps.
Brightly colored tabs indicate which section of the book you are in.
FIGURE B-13: Query Design View with AND criteria
Click the View button to display the results of the query
Drag the bottom edge of the Tours field list down
AND criteria in one row to select Family tours in FL that are less than or equal to 7 days
Access 2010
FIGURE B-14: Final datasheet of FamilyFL query
Save button
All three criteria are true for these two records: <=7 duration, FL, and Family
TABLE B-2: Comparison operators
operator | description | expression | meaning
> | Greater than | >500 | Numbers greater than 500
>= | Greater than or equal to | >=500 | Numbers greater than or equal to 500
< | Less than | <"Braveheart" | Names from A to Braveheart, but not Braveheart
<= | Less than or equal to | <="Bridgewater" | Names from A through Bridgewater, inclusive
<> | Not equal to | <>"Fontanelle" | Any name except for Fontanelle
Building and Using Queries
Access 37
Tables provide helpful summaries of key terms, buttons, or keyboard shortcuts.

Assignments

The lessons use Quest Specialty Travel, a fictional adventure travel company, as the case study. The assignments on the light yellow pages at the end of each unit increase in difficulty. Assignments include:

- **Concepts Review** consist of multiple choice, matching, and screen identification questions.
- **Skills Reviews** are hands-on, step-by-step exercises that review the skills covered in each lesson in the unit.
- **Independent Challenges** are case projects requiring critical thinking and application of the unit skills. The Independent Challenges increase in difficulty, with the first one in each unit being the easiest. Independent Challenges 2 and 3 become increasingly open-ended, requiring more independent problem solving.
- **SAM Projects** is live-in-the-application autograding software that provides immediate and detailed feedback reports to students and instructors. Some exercises in this book are available in SAM Projects. (Purchase of a SAM Projects pincode is required.)
- **Real Life Independent Challenges** are practical exercises in which students create documents to help them with their everyday lives.
- **Advanced Challenge Exercises** set within the Independent Challenges provide optional steps for more advanced students.
- **Visual Workshops** are practical, self-graded capstone projects that require independent problem solving.

About SAM

SAM is the premier proficiency-based assessment and training environment for Microsoft Office. Web-based software along with an inviting user interface provide maximum teaching and learning flexibility. SAM builds students' skills and confidence with a variety of real-life simulations, and SAM Projects' assignments prepare students for today's workplace.

The SAM system includes Assessment, Training, and Projects, featuring page references and remediation for this book as well as Course Technology's Microsoft Office textbooks. With SAM, instructors can enjoy the flexibility of creating assignments based on content from their favorite Microsoft Office books or based on specific course objectives. Instructors appreciate the scheduling and reporting options that have made SAM the market-leading online testing and training software for over a decade. Over 2,000 performance-based questions and matching Training simulations, as well as tens of thousands of objective-based questions from many Course Technology texts, provide instructors with a variety of choices across multiple applications from the introductory level through the comprehensive level. The inclusion of hands-on Projects guarantee that student knowledge will skyrocket from the practice of solving real-world situations using Microsoft Office software.

SAM Assessment

- Content for these hands-on, performance-based tasks includes Word, Excel, Access, PowerPoint, Internet Explorer, Outlook, and Windows. Includes tens of thousands of objective-based questions from many Course Technology texts.

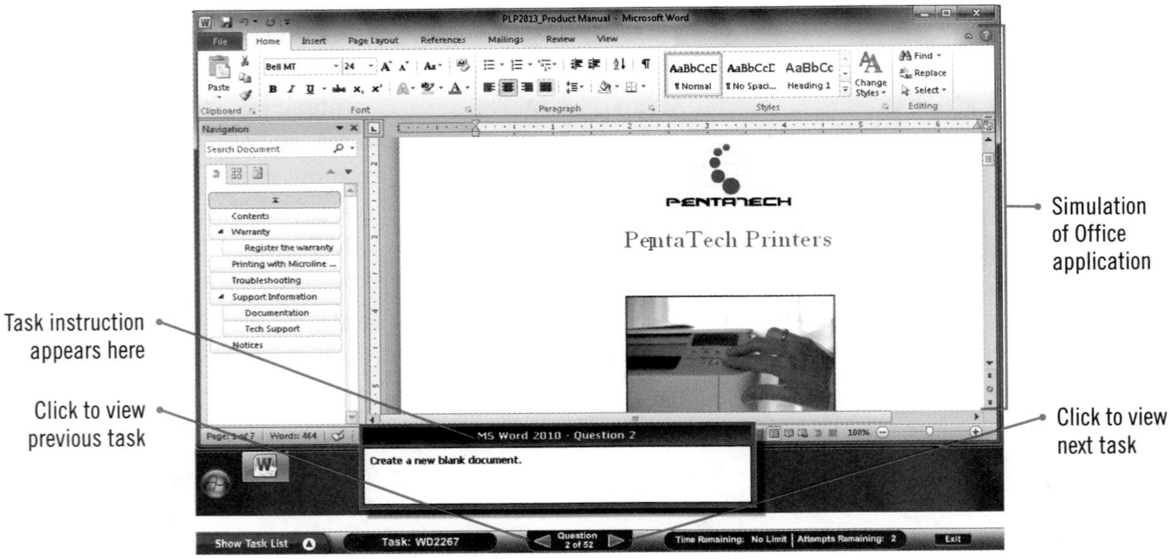

SAM Training

- Observe mode allows the student to watch and listen to a task as it is being completed.
- Practice mode allows the student to follow guided arrows and hear audio prompts to help visual learners know how to complete a task.
- Apply mode allows the student to prove what they've learned by completing a task using helpful instructions.

SAM Projects

- Live-in-the-application assignments in Word, Excel, Access, and PowerPoint that help students be sure they know how to effectively communicate, solve a problem, or make a decision.
- Students receive detailed feedback on their project within minutes.
- Additionally, teaches proper file management techniques.
- Ensures that academic integrity is not compromised, with unique anti-cheating detection encrypted into the data files.

Instructor Resources

The Instructor Resources CD is Course Technology's way of putting the resources and information needed to teach and learn effectively into your hands. With an integrated array of teaching and learning tools that offer you and your students a broad range of technology-based instructional options, we believe this CD represents the highest quality and most cutting-edge resources available to instructors today. The resources available with this book are:

- **Instructor's Manual**—Available as an electronic file, the Instructor's Manual includes detailed lecture topics with teaching tips for each unit.
- **Sample Syllabus**—Prepare and customize your course easily using this sample course outline.
- **PowerPoint Presentations**—Each unit has a corresponding PowerPoint presentation that you can use in lecture, distribute to your students, or customize to suit your course.
- **Figure Files**—The figures in the text are provided on the Instructor Resources CD to help you illustrate key topics or concepts. You can create traditional overhead transparencies by printing the figure files. Or you can create electronic slide shows by using the figures in a presentation program such as PowerPoint.
- **Solutions to Exercises**—Solutions to Exercises contains every file students are asked to create or modify in the lessons and end-of-unit material. Also provided in this section, there is a document outlining the solutions for the end-of-unit Concepts Review, Skills Review, and Independent Challenges. An Annotated Solution File and Grading Rubric accompany each file and can be used together for quick and easy grading.
- **Data Files for Students**—To complete most of the units in this book, your students will need Data Files. You can post the Data Files on a file server for students to copy. The Data Files are available on the Instructor Resources CD-ROM, the Review Pack, and can also be downloaded from cengagebrain.com. For more information on how to download the Data Files, see the inside back cover.

  Instruct students to use the Data Files List included on the Review Pack and the Instructor Resources CD. This list gives instructions on copying and organizing files.
- **ExamView**—ExamView is a powerful testing software package that allows you to create and administer printed, computer (LAN-based), and Internet exams. ExamView includes hundreds of questions that correspond to the topics covered in this text, enabling students to generate detailed study guides that include page references for further review. The computer-based and Internet testing components allow students to take exams at their computers, and also saves you time by grading each exam automatically.

Content for Online Learning.

Course Technology has partnered with the leading distance learning solution providers and class-management platforms today. To access this material, visit www.cengage.com/webtutor and search for your title. Instructor resources include the following: additional case projects, sample syllabi, PowerPoint presentations, and more. For additional information, please contact your sales representative. For students to access this material, they must have purchased a WebTutor PIN-code specific to this title and your campus platform. The resources for students might include (based on instructor preferences): topic reviews, review questions, practice tests, and more.

Acknowledgements

Instructor Advisory Board

We thank our Instructor Advisory Board who gave us their opinions and guided our decisions as we updated our texts for Microsoft Office 2010. They are as follows:

Terri Helfand, Chaffey Community College

Barbara Comfort, J. Sargeant Reynolds Community College

Brenda Nielsen, Mesa Community College

Sharon Cotman, Thomas Nelson Community College

Marian Meyer, Central New Mexico Community College

Audrey Styer, Morton College

Richard Alexander, Heald College

Xiaodong Qiao, Heald College

Student Advisory Board

We also thank our Student Advisory Board members, who shared their experiences using the book and offered suggestions to make it better: **Latasha Jefferson**, Thomas Nelson Community College, **Gary Williams**, Thomas Nelson Community College, **Stephanie Miller**, J. Sargeant Reynolds Community College, **Sarah Styer**, Morton Community College, **Missy Marino**, Chaffey College

Author Acknowledgements

Lisa Friedrichsen This book is dedicated to my students, and all who are using this book to teach and learn Access. Thank you. Also, thank you to all of the professionals who helped me create this book.

Read This Before You Begin

Frequently Asked Questions

What are Data Files?

A Data File is a partially completed Access database or another type of file that you use to complete the steps in the units and exercises to create the final document that you submit to your instructor. Each unit opener page lists the Data Files that you need for that unit.

Where are the Data Files?

Your instructor will provide the Data Files to you or direct you to a location on a network drive from which you can download them. For information on how to download the Data Files from cengagebrain.com, see the inside back cover. **Note**: These Access data files are set to automatically compact when they are closed. This requires extra free space on the drive that stores your databases. We recommend that your storage device (flash drive, memory stick, hard drive) always have at least 30 MB of free space to handle these processes.

What software was used to write and test this book?

This book was written and tested using a typical installation of Microsoft Office 2010 Professional Plus on a computer with a typical installation of Microsoft Windows 7 Ultimate.

The browser used for any Web-dependent steps is Internet Explorer 8.

Do I need to be connected to the Internet to complete the steps and exercises in this book?

Some of the exercises in this book require that your computer be connected to the Internet. If you are not connected to the Internet, see your instructor for information on how to complete the exercises.

What do I do if my screen is different from the figures shown in this book?

This book was written and tested on computers with monitors set at a resolution of 1024 × 768. If your screen shows more or less information than the figures in the book, your monitor is probably set at a higher or lower resolution. If you don't see something on your screen, you might have to scroll down or up to see the object identified in the figures.

The Ribbon—the blue area at the top of the screen—in Microsoft Office 2010 adapts to different resolutions. If your monitor is set at a lower resolution than 1024 × 768, you might not see all of the buttons shown in the figures. The groups of buttons will always appear, but the entire group might be condensed into a single button that you need to click to access the buttons described in the instructions.

COURSECASTS **Learning on the Go. Always Available...Always Relevant.**

Our fast-paced world is driven by technology. You know because you are an active participant—always on the go, always keeping up with technological trends, and always learning new ways to embrace technology to power your life. Let CourseCasts, hosted by Ken Baldauf of Florida State University, be your guide into weekly updates in this ever-changing space. These timely, relevant podcasts are produced weekly and are available for download at http://coursecasts.course.com or directly from iTunes (search by CourseCasts). CourseCasts are a perfect solution to getting students (and even instructors) to learn on the go!

UNIT
A
Windows 7

Getting Started with Windows 7

Files You Will Need:
No files needed.

The Windows 7 operating system lets you use your computer. Windows 7 shares many features with other Windows programs, so once you learn how to work with Windows 7, you will find it easier to use the programs that run on your computer. In this unit, you learn to start Windows 7 and work with windows and other screen objects. You work with icons that represent programs and files, and you move and resize windows. As you use your computer, you will often have more than one window on your screen, so it's important that you learn how to manage them. As you complete this unit, you create a simple drawing in a program called Paint to help you learn how to use buttons, menus, and dialog boxes. After finding assistance in the Windows 7 Help and Support system, you end your Windows 7 session. As a new Oceania tour manager for Quest Specialty Travel (QST), you need to develop basic Windows skills to keep track of tour bookings.

OBJECTIVES

- Start Windows 7
- Learn the Windows 7 desktop
- Point and click
- Start a Windows 7 program
- Work with windows
- Work with multiple windows
- Use command buttons, menus, and dialog boxes
- Get help
- Exit Windows 7

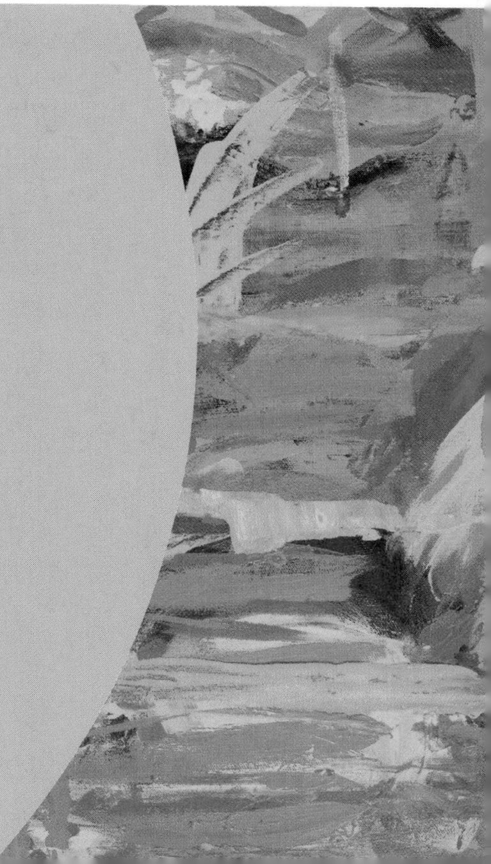

UNIT
A
Windows 7

Starting Windows 7

Windows 7 is an **operating system**, which is a program that lets you run your computer. A **program** is a set of instructions written for a computer. When you turn on your computer, the Windows 7 operating system starts automatically. If your computer did not have an operating system, you wouldn't see anything on the screen when you turn it on. For each user, the operating system can reserve a special area called a **user account** where each user can keep his or her own files. If your computer is set up for more than one user, you might need to **log in**, or select your user account name when the computer starts. If you are the only user on your computer, you won't have to select an account. You might also need to enter a **password**, a special sequence of numbers and letters each user can create. A password allows you to enter and use the files in your user account area. Users cannot see each others' account areas without their passwords, so passwords help keep your computer information secure. After you log in, you see a welcome message, and then the Windows 7 desktop. You will learn about the desktop in the next lesson. Your supervisor, Evelyn Swazey, asks you to start learning about the Windows 7 operating system.

STEPS

1. **Push your computer's power button, which might look like or , then if the monitor is not turned on, press its power button to turn it on**

   On a desktop computer, the power button is probably on the front panel. On a laptop computer it's most likely at the top of the keys on your keyboard. After a few moments, a Starting Windows message appears. Then you might see a screen that lets you choose a user account, as shown in Figure A-1.

> **TROUBLE**
> If you do not see a screen that lets you choose a user account, go to Step 3.

2. **Click a user name if necessary**

   The name you click represents your user account that lets you use the computer. The user account may have your name assigned to it, or it might have a general name, like Student, or Lab User. A password screen may appear. If necessary, ask your instructor or technical support person which user account and password you should use.

> **TROUBLE**
> If you clicked the wrong user in Step 2, change to the correct user by clicking the Switch user button on the password screen.

3. **Type your password if necessary, using uppercase and lowercase letters as necessary, as shown in Figure A-2**

   Passwords are **case sensitive**, which means that if you type any letter using capital letters when lowercase letters are needed, Windows will not allow you to access your account. For example, if your password is "book", typing "Book" or "BOOK" will not let you enter your account. As you type your password, its characters appear as a series of dots on the screen. This makes it more difficult for anyone watching you to see your password, giving you additional security.

> **TROUBLE**
> If you type your password incorrectly, you see "The user name or password is incorrect." Click OK to try again. To help you remember, Windows shows the Password Hint that you entered when you created your password.

4. **Click the Go button**

   You see a welcome message, and then the Windows 7 desktop, shown in Figure A-3.

FIGURE A-1: Selecting a user name

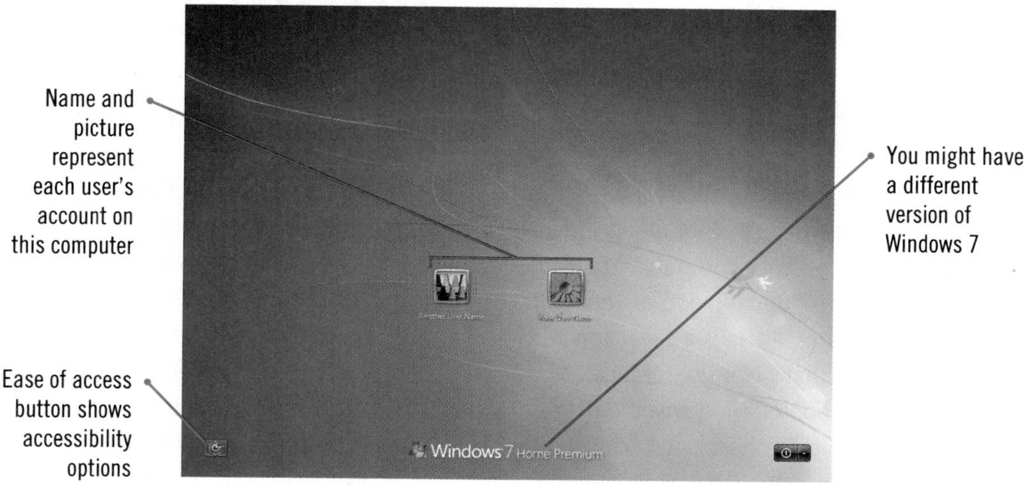
Name and picture represent each user's account on this computer
You might have a different version of Windows 7
Ease of access button shows accessibility options
Windows 7 Home Premium

FIGURE A-2: Password screen

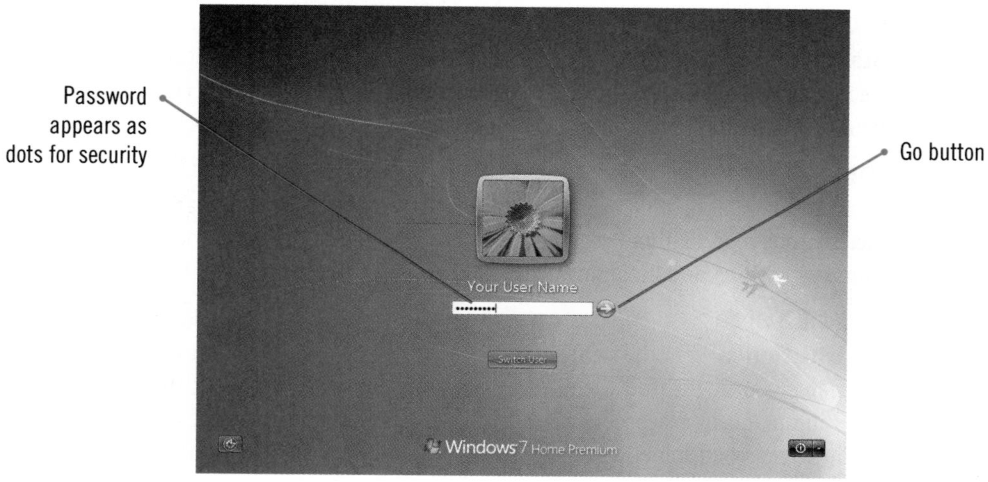
Password appears as dots for security
Go button
Your User Name
Switch User
Windows 7 Home Premium

FIGURE A-3: Windows 7 desktop

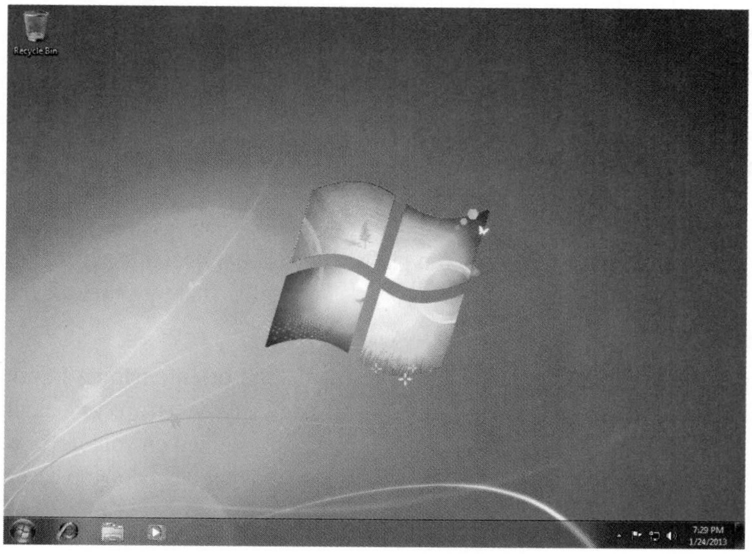
Recycle Bin
7:29 PM
1/24/2013

UNIT
A
Windows 7

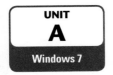

Learning the Windows 7 Desktop

After Windows 7 starts up, you see the Windows 7 desktop. The **desktop** consists of a shaded or picture background with small graphics called icons. **Icons** are small images that represent items such as the Recycle Bin on your computer. You can rearrange, add, and delete desktop icons. Like an actual desktop, the Windows 7 desktop acts as your work area. You can use the desktop to manage the files and folders on your computer. A **file** is a collection of stored information, such as a letter, video, or program. A **folder** is a container that helps you organize your files, just like a cardboard folder on your desk. If you're using a new installation of Windows, the desktop might show only a Recycle Bin icon in the upper-left corner and the **taskbar**, the horizontal bar at the bottom of your screen. Evelyn asks you to explore the Windows 7 desktop to begin learning how to communicate with your computer.

DETAILS

Windows 7 computers show these desktop elements. Refer to Figure A-4.

- **Start button**
  The **Start button** is your launching point when you want to communicate with your computer. You can use the Start button to start programs, to open windows that show you the contents of your computer, and to end your Windows session and turn off your computer.

- **Taskbar**
  The **taskbar** is the horizontal bar at the bottom of the desktop. The taskbar contains the Start button as well as other buttons representing programs, folders, and files. You can use these buttons to immediately open programs or view files and programs that are on your computer.

QUICK TIP

If your taskbar is a different color than the one in Figure A-4, your computer might have different settings. This won't affect your work in this chapter.

- **Notification area**
  The **notification area** at the right side of the taskbar contains icons that represent informational messages and programs you might find useful. It also contains information about the current date and time. Some programs automatically place icons here so they are easily available to you. The notification area also displays pop-up messages when something on your computer needs your attention.

- **Recycle Bin**
  Like the wastepaper basket in your office, the **Recycle Bin** is where you place the files and folders that you don't need anymore and want to delete. All objects you place in the Recycle Bin stay there until you empty it. If you put an object there by mistake, you can easily retrieve it, as long as you haven't emptied the bin.

- **Desktop background**
  The **desktop background** is the shaded area behind your desktop objects. You can change the desktop background to show different colors or even pictures.

You might see the following on your desktop:

- **Icons and shortcuts**
  On the desktop background, you can place icons called **shortcuts**, which you can double-click to access programs, files, folders, and devices that you use frequently. That way, they are immediately available to you.

- **Gadgets**
  Gadgets are optional programs that present helpful or entertaining information on your desktop. They include items such as clocks, current news headlines, calendars, picture albums, and weather reports. Some gadgets come with Windows 7 and you can easily place them on your desktop. You can download additional gadgets from the Internet. Figure A-5 shows a desktop that has a desktop background picture and shortcuts to programs, folders, and devices, as well as four gadgets.

FIGURE A-4: **Windows 7 desktop after a new Windows installation**

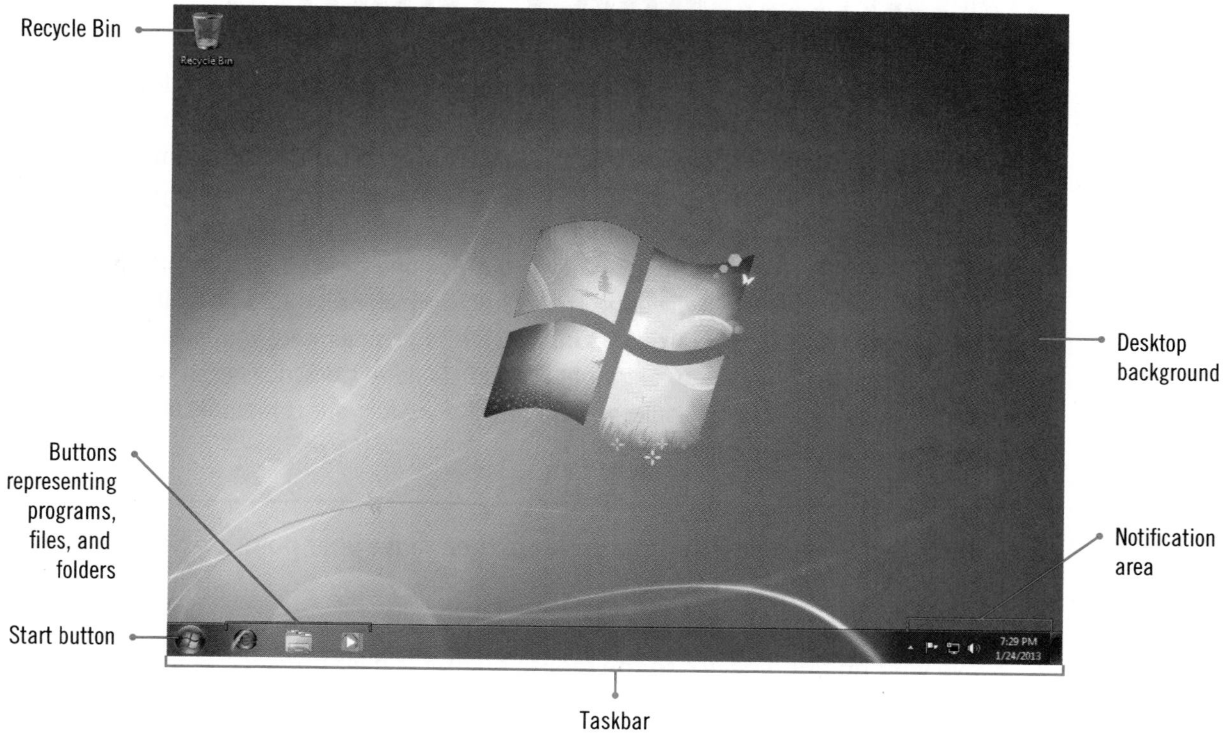
Recycle Bin
Recycle Bin
Desktop background
Buttons representing programs, files, and folders
Notification area
Start button
7:29 PM
1/24/2013
Taskbar

FIGURE A-5: **Windows 7 desktop with shortcuts, gadgets, and a picture background**

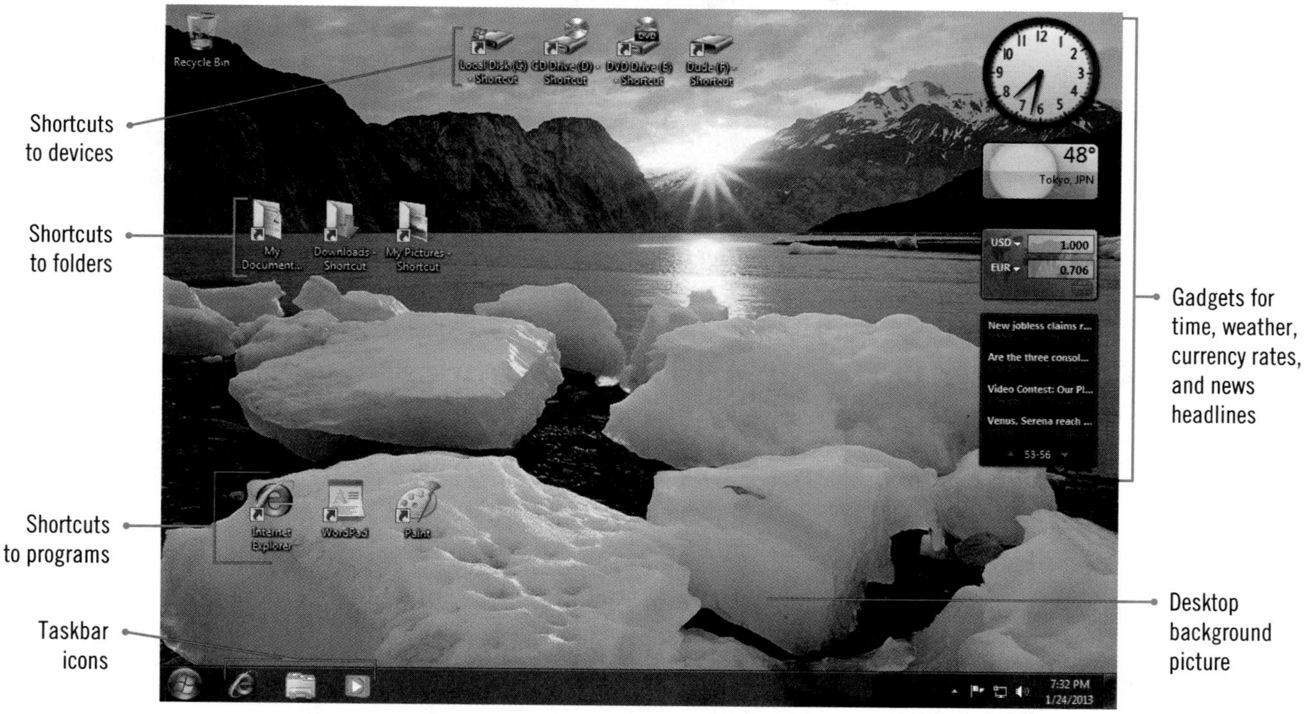
Recycle Bin
Shortcuts to devices
Shortcuts to folders
Gadgets for time, weather, currency rates, and news headlines
Shortcuts to programs
Desktop background picture
Taskbar icons
48°
Tokyo, JPN
USD
1.000
EUR
0.706
New jobless claims r...
Are the three consol...
Video Contest: Our Pl...
Venus, Serena reach ...
53-56
Internet Explorer
WordPad
Paint
7:32 PM
1/24/2013

What if my desktop looks different from these figures?

If you are using a computer that has been used by others, a different version of Windows 7, or a computer in a school lab, your desktop might be a different color, it might have a different design on it, or it might have different shortcuts and gadgets. Your Recycle Bin might be in a different desktop location. Don't be concerned with these differences. They will not interfere with your work in these units.

UNIT A
Windows 7

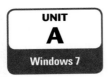

Pointing and Clicking

After you start Windows 7 and see the desktop, you can communicate with Windows using a pointing device. A **pointing device** controls the movement of the mouse pointer on your computer screen. The **mouse pointer** is a small arrow or other symbol that moves on the screen. The mouse pointer's shape changes depending on where you point and on the options available to you when you point. Your pointing device could be a mouse, trackball, touchpad, pointing stick, on-screen touch pointer, or a tablet. Figure A-6 shows some common pointing devices. A pointing device might be attached to your computer with a wire, connect wirelessly using an electronic signal, or it might be built into your computer. There are five basic **pointing device actions** you use to communicate with your computer: pointing, clicking, double-clicking, dragging, and right-clicking. Table A-1 describes each action. As you prepare to work on your tour schedule, you communicate with your computer using the basic pointing device actions.

STEPS

1. **Locate the mouse pointer on the desktop, then move your pointing device left, right, up, and down**
   The mouse pointer moves in the same direction as your pointing device.

2. **Move your pointing device so the mouse pointer is over the Recycle Bin**
   You are pointing to the Recycle Bin. The pointer shape is the **Select pointer**. The Recycle Bin icon becomes **highlighted**, looking as though it is framed in a box with a lighter color background and a border.

QUICK TIP
Use the tip of the pointer when pointing to an object.

3. **While pointing to the Recycle Bin, press and quickly release the left mouse button once, then move the pointer away from the Recycle Bin**
   Click a desktop icon once to **select** it, and then the interior of the border around it changes color. When you select an icon, you signal Windows 7 that you want to perform an action. You can also use pointing to identify screen items.

4. **Point to (but do not click) the Internet Explorer button on the taskbar**
   The button border appears and an informational message called a **ScreenTip** identifies the program the button represents.

5. **Move the mouse pointer over the time and date in the notification area in the lower-right corner of the screen, read the ScreenTip, then click once**
   A pop-up window appears, containing a calendar and a clock displaying the current date and time.

TROUBLE
You need to double-click quickly, with a fast click-click, without moving the mouse. If a window didn't open, try again with a faster click-click.

6. **Place the tip of the mouse pointer over the Recycle Bin, then quickly click twice**
   You **double-clicked** the Recycle Bin. A window opens, showing the contents of the Recycle Bin, shown in Figure A-7. The area near the top of the screen is the **Address bar**, which shows the name of the item you have opened. If your Recycle Bin contains any discarded items, they appear in the white area below the Address bar. You can use single clicking to close a window.

7. **Place the tip of the mouse pointer over the Close button in the upper-right corner of the Recycle Bin window, notice the Close ScreenTip, then click once**
   The Recycle Bin window closes. You can use dragging to move icons on the desktop.

QUICK TIP
You'll use dragging in other Windows 7 programs to move folders, files, and other objects to new locations.

8. **Point to the Recycle Bin icon, press and hold down the left mouse button, move the pointing device (or drag your finger over the touchpad) so the object moves right about an inch, as shown in Figure A-8, then release the mouse button**
   You dragged the Recycle Bin icon to a new location.

9. **Repeat Step 8 to drag the Recycle Bin back to its original location**

FIGURE A-6: **Pointing devices**

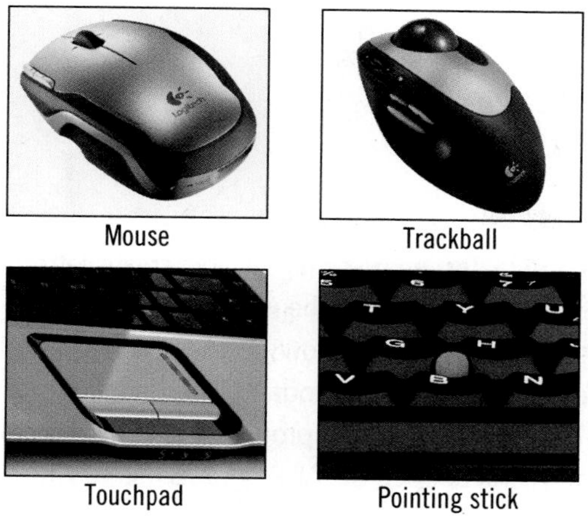

FIGURE A-7: **Recycle Bin window**

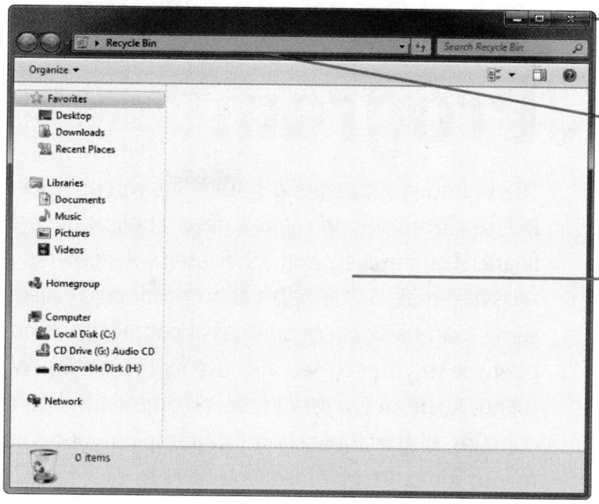

FIGURE A-8: **Dragging the Recycle Bin icon**

TABLE A-1: **Five pointing device actions**

action	how to	use for
Pointing	Move the pointing device to position the tip of the pointer over an object, option, or item	Highlighting objects or options, or displaying informational boxes called ScreenTips
Clicking	Quickly press and release the left mouse button once	Selecting objects or commands, opening menus or items on the taskbar
Double-clicking	Quickly press and release the left mouse button twice	Opening programs, folders, or files represented by desktop icons
Dragging	Point to an object, press and hold down the left mouse button, move the object to a new location, then release the mouse button	Moving objects, such as icons on the desktop
Right-clicking	Point to an object, then press and release the right mouse button	Displaying a shortcut menu containing options specific to the object

Using right-clicking

For some actions, you click items using the right mouse button, known as right-clicking. You can **right-click** almost any icon on your desktop to open a shortcut menu. A **shortcut menu** lists common commands for an object. A **command** is an instruction to perform a task, such as emptying the Recycle Bin. The shortcut menu commands depend on the object you right-click. Figure A-9 shows the shortcut menu that appears if you right-click the Recycle Bin. Then you click (with the left mouse button) a shortcut menu command to issue that command.

FIGURE A-9: **Right-click to show shortcut menu**

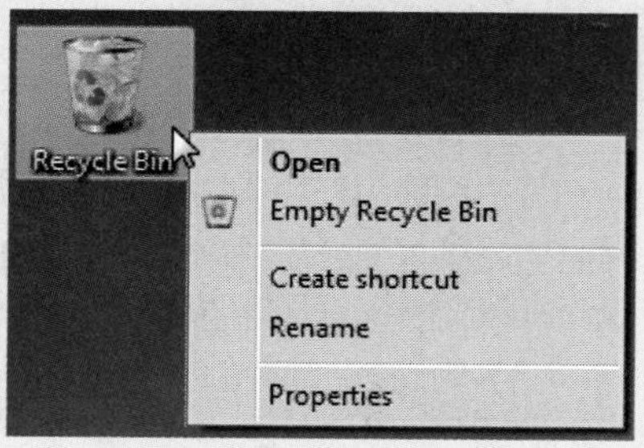

UNIT A

Windows 7

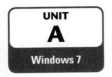

Starting a Windows 7 Program

The Windows 7 operating system lets you operate your computer and see the programs and files it contains. But to do your work, you'll need application programs. **Application programs** let you create letters, financial summaries, and other useful documents as well as view Web pages on the Internet and send and receive e-mail. Some application programs, called **accessories**, come with Windows 7. (See Table A-2 for some examples of accessories that come with Windows 7.) To use an application program, you must start (or open) it so you can see and use its tools. With Windows 7 you start application programs using the Start menu. A **menu** is a list of related commands. You use the Start menu to open the All Programs menu, which contains all the application programs on your computer. You can see some programs on the All Programs menu; some are in folders you have to click first. To start a program, you click its name on the All Programs menu. Evelyn asks you to explore the Paint accessory program for creating brochure graphics.

STEPS

1. **Click the Start button on the taskbar in the lower-left corner of screen**

   The Start menu opens, showing frequently used programs on the left side. The gray area on the right contains links to folders and other locations you are likely to use frequently. It also lets you get help and shut down your computer. See Figure A-10. Not all the programs available on your computer are shown.

2. **Point to All Programs**

   This menu shows programs installed on your computer. Your program list will differ, depending on what you (or your lab) have installed on your machine. Some program names are immediately available, and others are inside folders.

3. **Click the Accessories folder**

   A list of Windows accessory programs appears, as shown in Figure A-11. The program names are indented to the right from the Accessories folder, meaning that they are inside that folder.

4. **Move the pointer over Paint and click once**

   The Paint program window opens on your screen, as shown in Figure A-12. When Windows opens an application program, it starts the program from your computer's hard disk, where it's permanently stored. Then it places the program in your computer's memory so you can use it.

5. **If your Paint window fills the screen completely, click the Restore Down button in the upper-right corner of the window**

   If your Paint window doesn't look like Figure A-12, point to the lower-right corner of the window until the pointer becomes ⤡, then drag until it matches the figure.

Searching for programs and files using the Start menu

If you need to find a program, folder, or file on your computer quickly, the Search programs and files box on the Start menu can help. Click the Start button, then type the name of the item you want to find in the Search programs and files box. As you type, Windows 7 lists all programs, documents, e-mail messages, and files that contain the text you typed in a box above the Search box. The items appear as links, which means you only have to click the hand pointer on the item you want, and Windows 7 opens it.

FIGURE A-10: **Start menu**

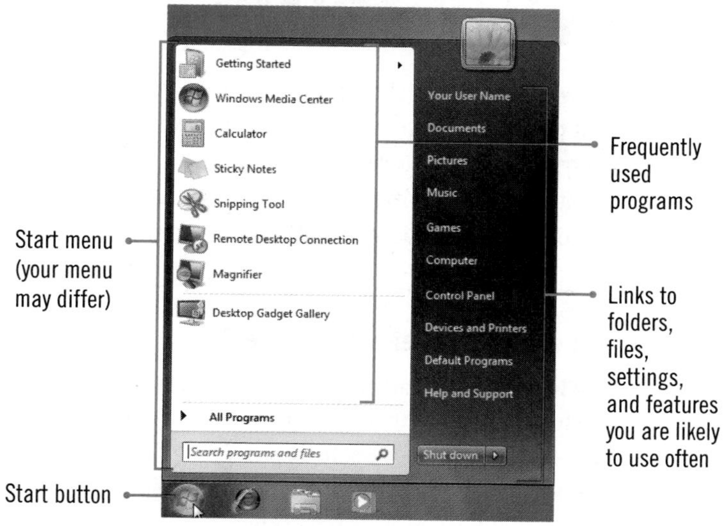

FIGURE A-11: **Accessories folder on All Programs menu**

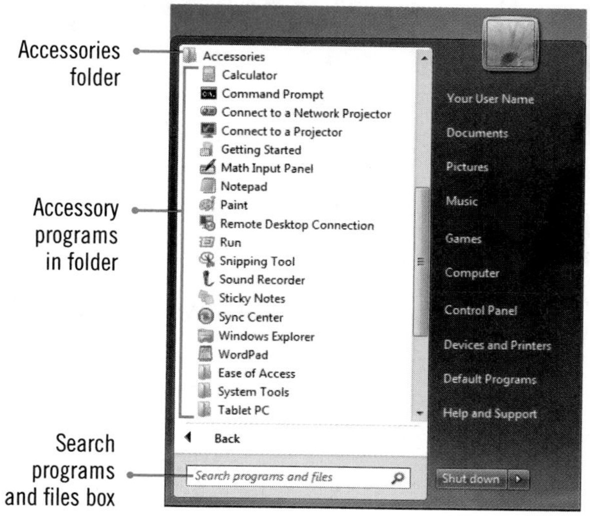

FIGURE A-12: **Paint program window**

TABLE A-2: **Some Windows 7 Accessory programs**

accessory program name	use to
Math Input Panel	Interpret math expressions handwritten on a tablet and create a formula suitable for printing or inserting in another program
Notepad	Create text files with basic text formatting
Paint	Create and edit drawings using lines, shapes, and colors
Snipping Tool	Capture an image of any screen area that you can save to use in a document
Sticky Notes	Create short text notes that you can use to set reminders or create to-do lists for yourself
Windows Explorer	View and organize the files and folders on your computer
WordPad	Type letters or other text documents with formatting

UNIT A

Windows 7

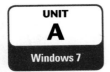

Working with Windows

When you start an application program, its **program window** opens, showing you the tools you need to use the program. A new, blank file also opens. In the Paint program, you create a drawing that you can save as a file and print. All windows in the Windows 7 operating system have similar window elements. Once you can use a window in one program, you can then work with windows in many other programs. As you develop your tour marketing plans, you work with the open Paint window using Windows 7 elements.

DETAILS

Many windows have the following common elements. Refer to Figure A-13:

- At the top of every open window, you see a **title bar**, a transparent or solid-colored strip that contains the name of the program and document you opened. This document has not been saved, so it has the temporary name "Untitled." On the right side of the title bar, you see three icons.

  The **Minimize button** temporarily hides the window, making it a button on the taskbar. The program is still running, but its window is hidden until you click its taskbar button to display it again. The **Maximize button** enlarges the window to fill the entire computer screen. If a window is already maximized, the Maximize button changes to the **Restore Down button**. Restoring a window reduces it to the last nonmaximized size. The **Close button** closes the program. To use it later, you need to start it again.
- Many windows have a **scroll bar** on the right side and/or on the bottom of the window. You click the scroll bar elements to show parts of your document that are hidden below the bottom edge or off to the right side of the screen. See Table A-3 to learn the parts of a scroll bar.
- Just below the title bar, at the top of the Paint window, is the **Ribbon**, a strip that contains tabs. **Tabs** are pages that contain buttons that you click to perform actions. The Paint window has two tabs, the Home tab and the View tab. Tabs are divided into **groups** of command buttons. The Home tab has five groups: Clipboard, Image, Tools, Shapes, and Colors. Some programs have **menus**, words you click to show lists of commands, and **toolbars**, containing program buttons.
- The **Quick Access toolbar**, in the upper-left corner of the window, lets you quickly perform common actions such as saving a file.

QUICK TIP

If your Ribbon looks different from Figure A-13, your window is a little narrower. A narrow window collapses some buttons so you can only see group names. In that case, you might need to click a group name to see buttons.

STEPS

1. **Click the Paint window Minimize button**

   The program is now represented only by its button on the taskbar. See Figure A-14. The taskbar button for the Paint program now has a gradient background with blue and white shading. Taskbar buttons for closed programs have a solid blue background.
2. **Click the taskbar button representing the Paint program**

   The program window reappears.
3. **Drag the Paint scroll box down, notice the lower edge of the Paint canvas that appears, then click the Paint Up scroll arrow until you see the top edge of the canvas**

   In the Ribbon, the Home tab is in front of the View tab.
4. **Point to the View tab with the tip of the mouse pointer, then click the View tab once**

   The View tab moves in front of the Home tab and shows commands for viewing your drawings. The View tab has three groups: Zoom, Show or hide, and Display.
5. **Click the Home tab**
6. **Click the Paint window Maximize button**

   The window fills the screen and the Maximize button becomes the Restore Down button.
7. **Click the Paint window's Restore Down button**

   The Paint window returns to its previous size on the screen.

TROUBLE

If your screen resolution is set higher than 1024 × 768, you might not see a scroll box. You can continue with the lesson.

QUICK TIP

To quickly restore down the selected window, press and hold down the Windows key and then press the down arrow key.

FIGURE A-13: **Paint program window elements**

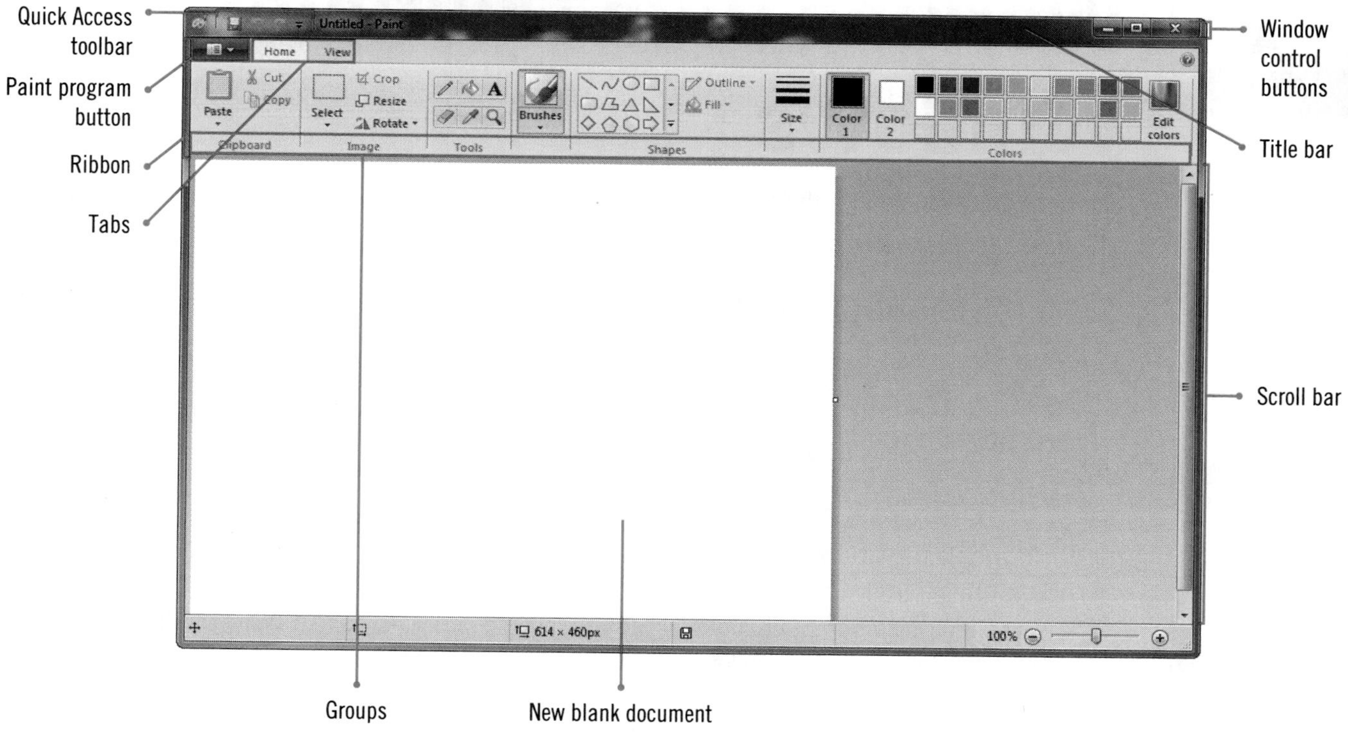

FIGURE A-14: **Taskbar showing Paint program button**

TABLE A-3: **Parts of a scroll bar**

name	looks like	use for
Scroll box	(Size may vary)	Drag to scroll quickly through a long document
Scroll arrows		Click to scroll up or down in small amounts
Shaded area	(Above and below scroll box)	Click to move up or down by one screen

Using the Quick Access toolbar

On the left side of the title bar, the Quick Access toolbar lets you perform common tasks with just one click. The Save button saves the changes you have made to a document. The Undo button lets you reverse (undo) the last action you performed. The Redo button reinstates the change you just undid. Use the Customize Quick Access Toolbar button to add other frequently used buttons to the toolbar, move the toolbar below the Ribbon, or hide the Ribbon.

UNIT A Windows 7

Working with Multiple Windows

Windows 7 lets you work with more than one program at a time. If you open two or more programs, a window opens for each one. You can work with each open program window, going back and forth between them. The window in front is called the **active window**. Any other open window behind the active window is called an **inactive window**. For ease in working with multiple windows, you can move, arrange, make them smaller or larger, minimize, or restore them so they're not in the way. To resize a window, drag a window's edge, called its **border**. You can also use the taskbar to switch between windows. See Table A-4 for a summary of taskbar actions. Keeping the Paint program open, you open the WordPad program and work with the Paint and WordPad program windows.

STEPS

1. **With the Paint window open, click the Start button, point to All Programs, click the Accessories folder, then click WordPad**

   The WordPad window opens in front of the Paint window. See Figure A-15. The WordPad window is in front, indicating that it is the active window. The Paint window is the inactive window. On the taskbar, the gradient backgrounds on the WordPad and Paint program buttons on the taskbar tell you that both programs are open. You want to move the WordPad window out of the way so you can see both windows at once.

2. **Point to a blank part of the WordPad window title bar, then drag the WordPad window so you can see more of the Paint window**

3. **Click once on the Paint window's title bar**

   The Paint window is now the active window and appears in front of the WordPad window. You can make any window active by clicking it. You can use the taskbar to do the same thing. You can also move among open program windows by pressing and holding down the [Alt] key on your keyboard and pressing the [Tab] key. A small window opens in the middle of the screen, showing miniature versions of each open program window. Each time you press [Tab], you select the next open program window. When you release [Tab] and [Alt], the selected program window becomes active.

4. **On the taskbar, click the WordPad window button**

   The WordPad window is now active. When you open multiple windows on the desktop, you may need to resize windows so they don't get in the way of other open windows. You can use dragging to resize a window.

5. **Point to the lower-right corner of the WordPad window until the pointer becomes ⤡, then drag up and to the left about an inch to make the window smaller**

   Windows 7 has a special feature that lets you automatically resize a window so it fills half the screen.

6. **Point to the WordPad window title bar, drag the window to the left side of the screen until the mouse pointer reaches the screen edge and the left half of the screen turns a transparent blue color, then release the mouse button**

   The WordPad window "snaps" to fill the left side of the screen.

7. **Point to the Paint window title bar, then drag the window to the right side of the screen until it snaps to fill the right half of the screen**

   The Paint window fills the right side of the screen. The Snap feature makes it easy to arrange windows side by side to view the contents of both at the same time.

8. **Click the WordPad window Close button then click the Maximize button in the Paint window's title bar**

   The WordPad program closes, so you can no longer use its tools unless you open it again. The Paint program window remains open and fills the screen.

QUICK TIP
To click an inactive window to make it active, click its title bar, window edge, or a blank area. To move a window, you must drag its title bar.

QUICK TIP
To instantly minimize all inactive windows, point to the active window's title bar, and quickly "shake" the window back and forth. This feature is called Aero Shake.

TROUBLE
Point to any edge of a window until you see the ⇔ or ⇕ pointer and drag to make it larger or smaller in one direction only.

FIGURE A-15: WordPad window in front of Paint window

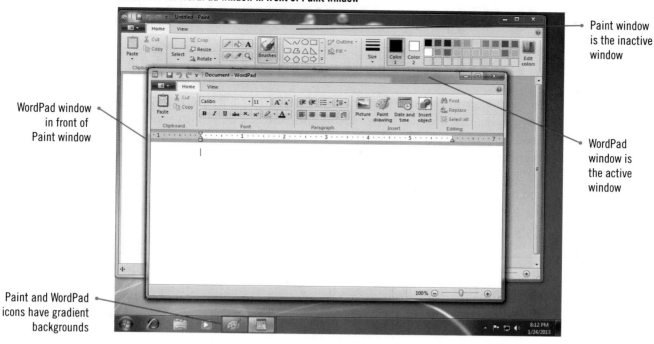

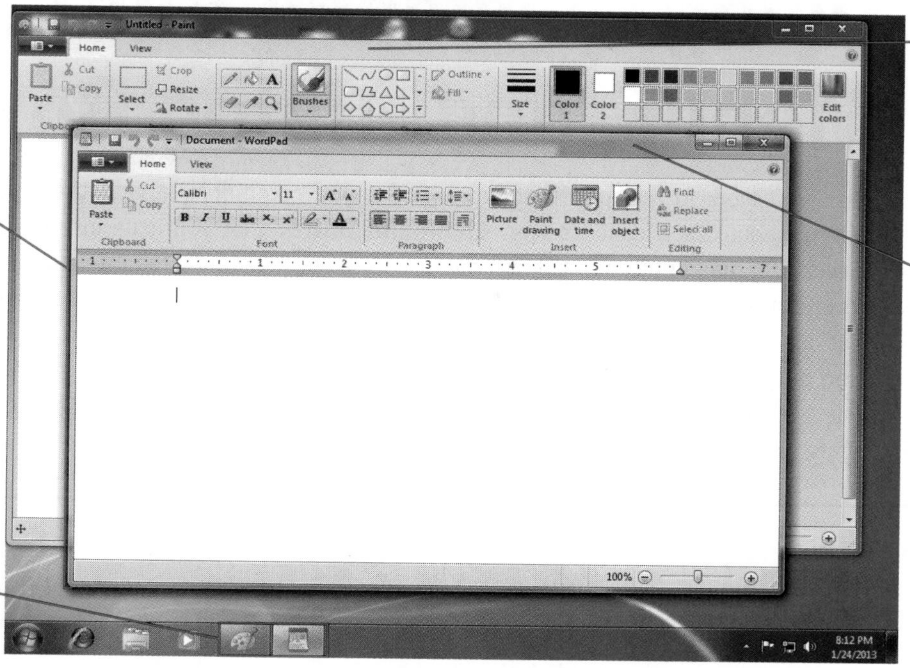

TABLE A-4: Using the Windows taskbar

to	do this
Add buttons to taskbar	Drag a program name from the Start menu over the taskbar, until a ScreenTip reads Pin to Taskbar
Change order of taskbar buttons	Drag any icon to a new taskbar location
See a list of recent documents opened in a taskbar program	Right-click taskbar program button
Close a document using the taskbar	Point to taskbar button, point to document name in jump list, then click Close button
Minimize all open windows	Click Show desktop button to the right of taskbar date and time
Redisplay all minimized windows	Click Show desktop button to the right of taskbar date and time
Make all windows transparent (Aero only)	Point to Show desktop button to the right of taskbar date and time
See preview of documents in taskbar (Aero only)	Point to taskbar button for open program

Switching windows with Windows Aero

Windows Aero is a set of special effects for Windows 7. If your windows have transparent "glass" backgrounds like those shown in the figures in this book, your Aero feature is turned on. Your windows show subtle animations when you minimize, maximize, and move windows. When you arrange windows using Aero, your windows can appear in a three-dimensional stack that you can quickly view without having to click the taskbar. To achieve this effect, called **Aero Flip 3D**, press and hold [Ctrl][⊞], then press [Tab]. Press [Tab] repeatedly to move through the stack, then press [Enter] to enlarge the document in the front of the stack. In addition, when you point to a taskbar button, Aero shows you small previews of the document, photo, or video—a feature called **Aero Peek**. Aero is turned on automatically when you start Windows, if you have an appropriate video card and enough computer memory to run Aero. If it is not on, to turn on the Aero feature, right-click the desktop, left-click Personalize, then select one of the Aero Themes.

UNIT A

Windows 7

Using Command Buttons, Menus, and Dialog Boxes

When you work in an open program window, you communicate with the program using command buttons, menus, and dialog boxes. **Command buttons** let you issue instructions to modify program objects. Command buttons are sometimes organized on a Ribbon into tabs, and then into groups like those in the Paint window. Some command buttons have text on them, and others only have icons that represent what they do. Other command buttons reveal **menus**, lists of commands you can choose. And some command buttons open up a **dialog box**, a window with controls that lets you tell Windows what you want. Table A-5 lists the common types of controls you find in dialog boxes. You use command buttons, menus, and dialog boxes to communicate with the Paint program.

STEPS

QUICK TIP
If you need to move the oval, use the keyboard arrow keys to move it left, right, up, or down.

TROUBLE
Don't be concerned if your object isn't exactly like the one in the figure.

1. **In the Shapes group on the Home tab, click the Rectangle button**
2. **In the Colors group, click the Gold button, move the pointer over the white drawing area, called the canvas, then drag to draw a rectangle a similar size to the one in Figure A-16**
3. **In the Shapes group, click the Oval button, click the Green color button in the Colors group, then drag a small oval above the rectangle, using Figure A-16 as a guide**
4. **Click the Fill with color icon in the Tools group, click the Light turquoise color button in the Colors group, click inside the oval, click the Purple color button, then click inside the rectangle, and compare your drawing to Figure A-16**
5. **In the Image group, click the Select list arrow, then click Select all, as shown in Figure A-17**

   The Select menu has several menu commands. The Select all command selects the entire drawing, as indicated by the dotted line surrounding the white drawing area.
6. **In the Image group, click the Rotate or flip button, then click Rotate right 90°**
7. **Click the Paint menu button just below the title bar, then click Print**

   The Print dialog box opens, as shown in Figure A-18. This dialog box lets you choose a printer, specify which part of your document or drawing you want to print, and choose how many copies you want to print. The **default**, or automatically selected, number of copies is 1, which is what you want.

TROUBLE
If you prefer not to print your document, click Cancel.

8. **Click Print**

   The drawing prints on your printer. You decide to close the program without saving your drawing.
9. **Click , click Exit, then click Don't Save**

TABLE A-5: Common dialog box controls

element	example	description
Text box	132	A box in which you type text or numbers
Spin box	1	A box with up and down arrows; click arrows or type to increase or decrease value
Option button		A small circle you click to select the option
Check box		Turns an option on when checked or off when unchecked
List box	Select Printer Add Printer Dell Laser Printer 3000cn PCL6 Fax	A box that lets you select an option from a list of options
Command button	Save	A button that completes or cancels the selected settings

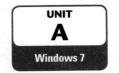

FIGURE A-16: **Rectangle and oval shapes with fill**

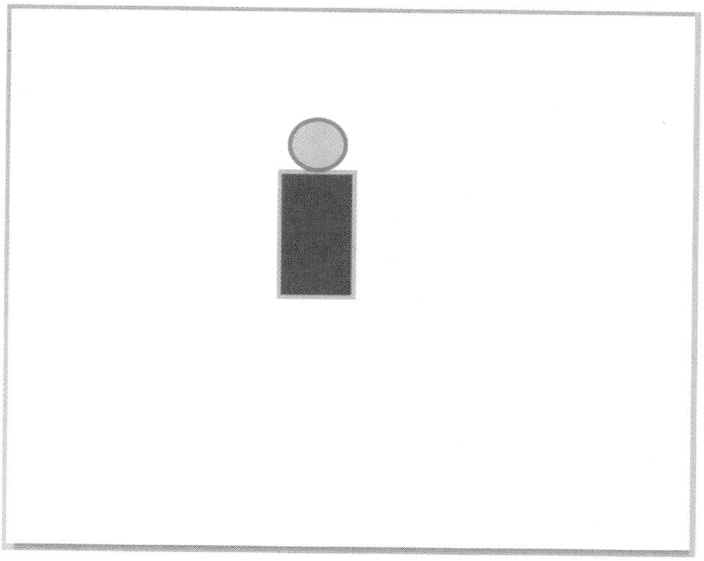

FIGURE A-17: **Select list arrow**

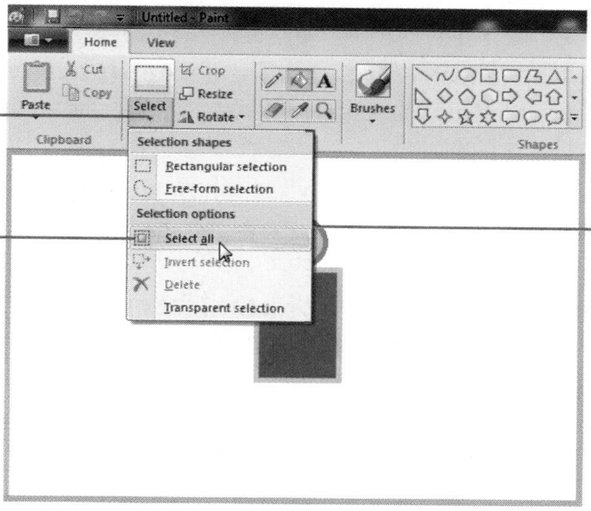

FIGURE A-18: **Print dialog box**

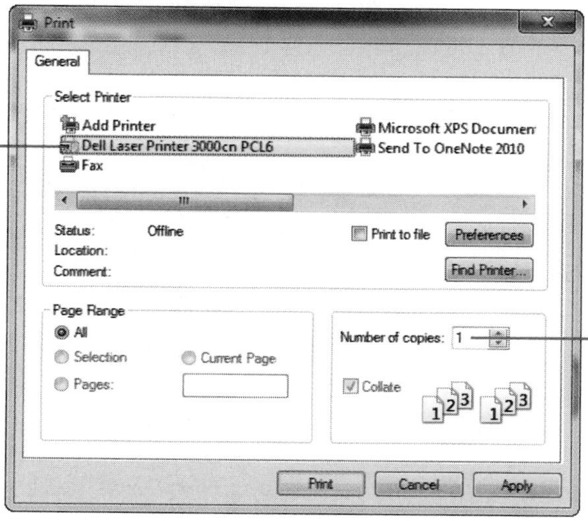

UNIT A

Windows 7

Getting Help

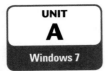

As you use Windows 7, you might feel ready to learn more about it, or you might have a problem and need some advice. You can open the Windows 7 Help and Support to find information you need. You can browse Help and Support topics by clicking a category, such as "Learn about Windows Basics." Within this category, you see more specific categories. Each category has topics in blue or purple text called **links** that you can click to learn more. You can also search Help and Support by typing one or more descriptive words called **keywords**, such as "taskbar," to ask Windows to find topics related to your keywords. The Help toolbar contains icons that give you more Help options. Table A-6 describes the Help toolbar icons. You use Windows 7 help to learn more about Windows and the WordPad accessory.

STEPS

TROUBLE

If your computer is not connected to the Internet, you will see an alert at the top of the Help window. You can continue with the steps in this lesson.

1. **Click the Start button, then on the right side of the Start menu, click Help and Support**

   The Windows Help and Support window opens, as shown in Figure A-19. A search box appears near the top of the window. Three topics appear as blue or purple text, meaning that they are links. Below them, you see descriptive text and a link to a Web site that contains more information about Windows.

2. **Under Not sure where to start?, position the hand pointer over Learn about Windows Basics, then click once**

   Several categories of Windows Basics topics appear, with links under each one.

3. **Under Desktop fundamentals, click The desktop (overview)**

   Help and Support information about the desktop appears, divided into several categories. Some of the text appears as a blue or purple link.

QUICK TIP

If you are using a mouse with a scroll wheel, you can use the scroll wheel to scroll up and down. If you are using a touchpad, the right side of your touch-pad might let you scroll.

4. **Drag the scroll box down to view the information, then drag the scroll box back to the top of the scroll bar**

   You decide to learn more about the taskbar.

5. **Under The desktop (overview), click the blue or purple text The taskbar (overview), then scroll down and read the information about the taskbar**

QUICK TIP

Search text is not case sensitive. Typing wordpad, Wordpad, or WordPad finds the same results.

6. **Click in the Search Help text box, type wordpad, then click the Search Help button**

   A list of links related to the WordPad accessory program appears. See Figure A-20.

7. **Click Using WordPad, scroll down if necessary, then click Create, open, and save documents**

8. **Scroll down and view the information, clicking any other links that interest you**

9. **Click the Close button in the upper-right corner of the Windows Help and Support window**

   The Windows Help and Support window closes.

TABLE A-6: Help toolbar icons

help toolbar icon	name	action
	Help and Support home	Displays the Help and Support Home page
	Print	Prints the currently-displayed help topic
	Browse Help	Displays a list of Help topics organized by subject
Ask	**Ask**	Describes other ways to get help
Options	**Options**	Lets you print, browse, search, set Help text size, and adjust settings

FIGURE A-19: **Windows Help and Support window**

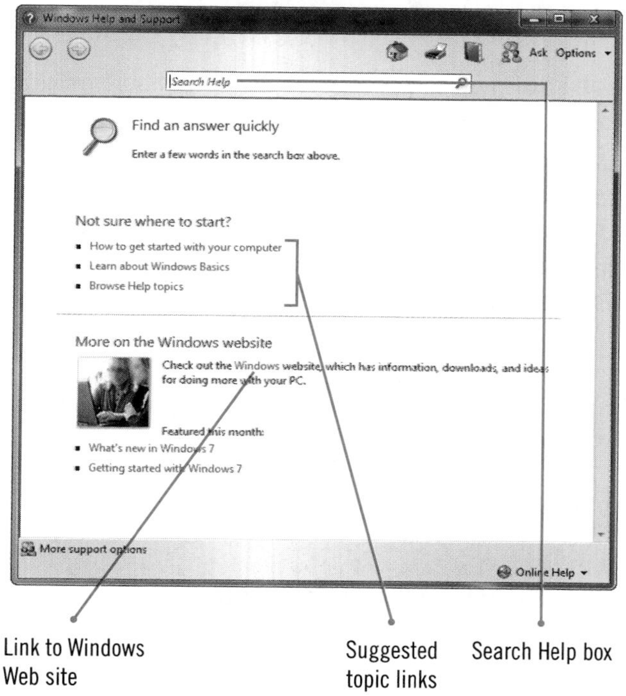

FIGURE A-20: **Results of a search on WordPad**

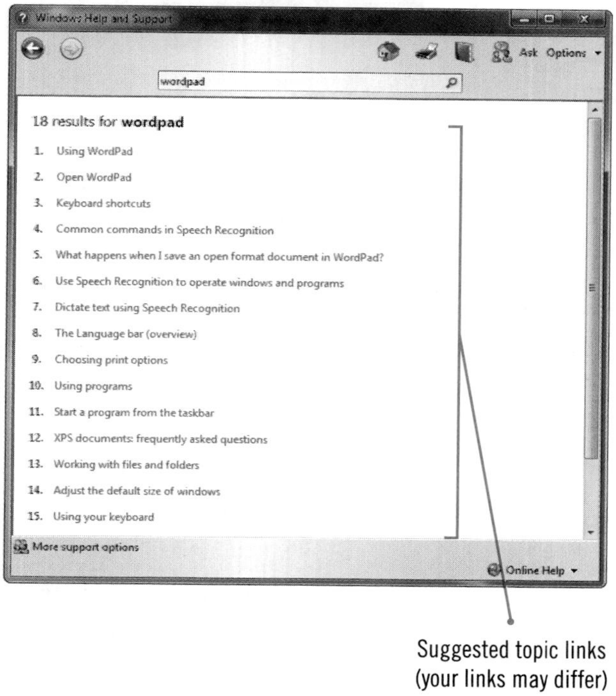

Finding other ways to get help

As you use Windows 7, you might want more help than you can find by clicking links or searching. You will find many other methods in the Windows Help and Support Home window. Click the Windows website link to locate blogs (Web logs, which are personal commentaries), downloads, Windows 7 video tours, and other current Windows 7 resources. Click the Ask button in the Help and Support window toolbar to learn about **Windows Remote Assistance**, which lets you connect with another computer, perhaps that of a trusted friend or instructor, so they can operate your computer using an Internet connection. The same window lets you open Microsoft Answers. **Microsoft Answers** is a website the lets you search **forums** (electronic gathering places where anyone can add questions and answers on computer issues), Microsoft help files, and even on-screen video demonstrations about selected topics.

UNIT A

Windows 7

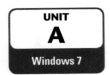

Exiting Windows 7

When you finish working on your computer, save and close any open files, close any open programs, close any open windows, and exit (or **shut down**) Windows 7. Table A-7 shows several options for ending your Windows 7 sessions. Whichever option you choose, it's important to shut down your computer in an orderly way. If you turn off or unplug the computer while Windows 7 is running, you could lose data or damage Windows 7 and your computer. If you are working in a computer lab, follow your instructor's directions and your lab's policies for ending your Windows 7 session. You have examined the basic ways you can use Windows 7, so you are ready to end your Windows 7 session.

STEPS

1. **Click the Start button on the taskbar**

   The lower-right corner of the Start menu lets you shut down your computer. It also displays a menu with other options for ending a Windows 7 session.

2. **Point to the Power button list arrow, as shown in Figure A-21**

   The Power button menu lists other shutdown options.

3. **If you are working in a computer lab, follow the instructions provided by your instructor or technical support person for ending your Windows 7 session. If you are working on your own computer, click Shut down or the option you prefer for ending your Windows 7 session**

4. **After you shut down your computer, you may also need to turn off your monitor and other hardware devices, such as a printer, to conserve energy**

TROUBLE

If a previous user has customized your computer, your button and menu commands might be in different locations. For example, the Power button may show "Restart," and "Shut down" may appear on the menu.

Installing updates when you exit Windows

Sometimes, after you shut down your machine, you might find that your machine does not shut down immediately. Instead, Windows might install software updates. If your power button shows this yellow icon, that means that Windows will install updates on your next shutdown. If you see a window indicating that updates are being installed, do not unplug or press the power switch to turn off your machine. Allow the updates to install completely. After the updates are installed, your computer will shut down, as you originally requested.

FIGURE A-21: **Shutting down your computer**

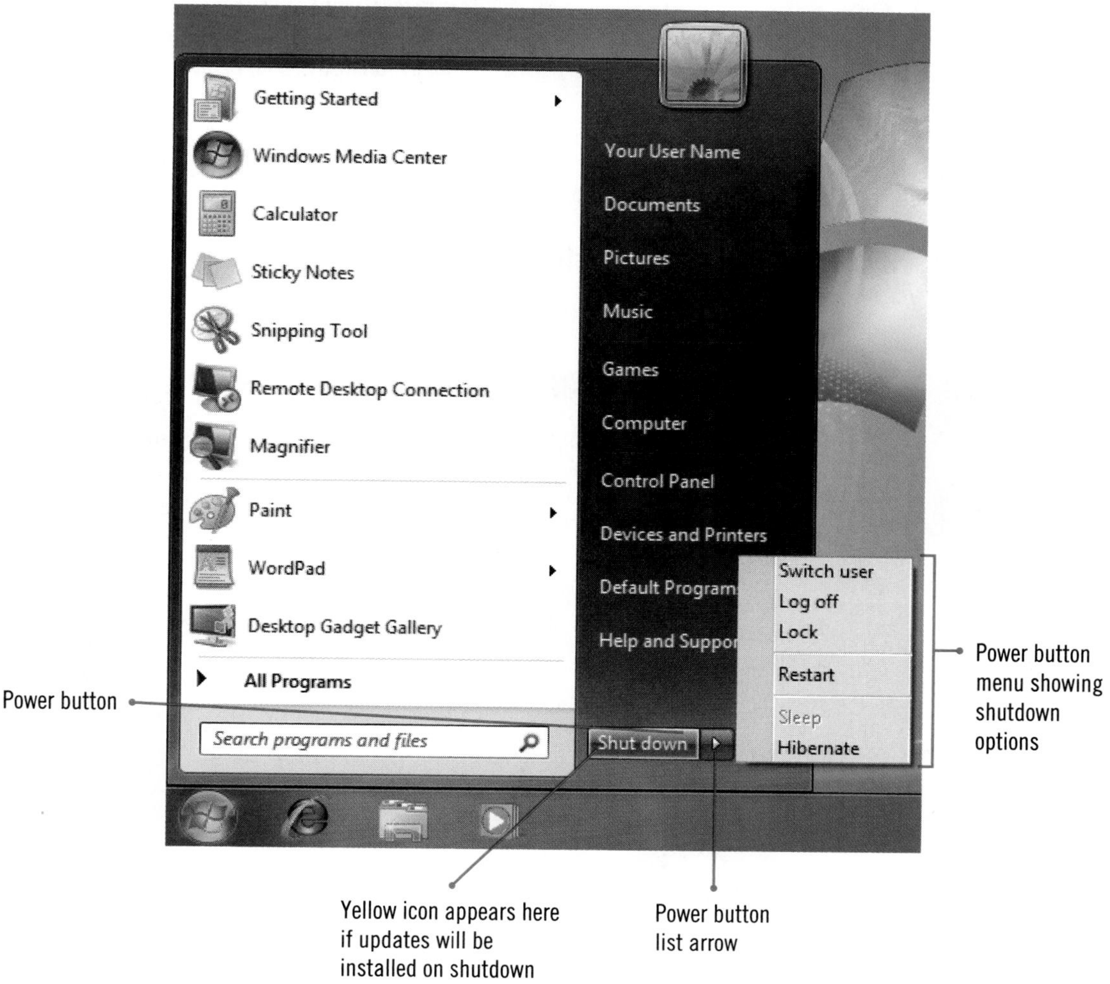

TABLE A-7: **Options for ending a Windows 7 session**

option	description	click
Shut down	Completely turns off your computer	Start button, Shut down
Switch user	Locks your user account and displays the Welcome screen so another user can log on	Start button, Power button list arrow, Switch user
Log off	Closes all windows, programs, and documents, then displays the Log in screen	Start button, Power button list arrow, Log off
Lock	Locks computer so only current user (or administrator) can use it	Start button, Power button list arrow, Lock
Restart	Shuts down your computer, then restarts it	Start button, Power button list arrow, Restart
Sleep	Puts computer in a low-power state while preserving your session in the computer's memory	Start button, Power button list arrow, Sleep
Hibernate	Turns off computer drives and screens but saves image of your work; when you turn machine on, it starts where you left off	Start button, Power button list arrow, Hibernate

Practice

Concepts Review

For current SAM information, including versions and content details, visit SAM Central (http://samcentral.course.com). If you have a SAM user profile, you may have access to hands-on instruction, practice, and assessment of the skills covered in this unit. Since various versions of SAM are supported throughout the life of this text, check with your instructor for the correct instructions and URL/Web site for accessing assignments.

Label the elements of the Windows 7 window shown in Figure A-22.

FIGURE A-22

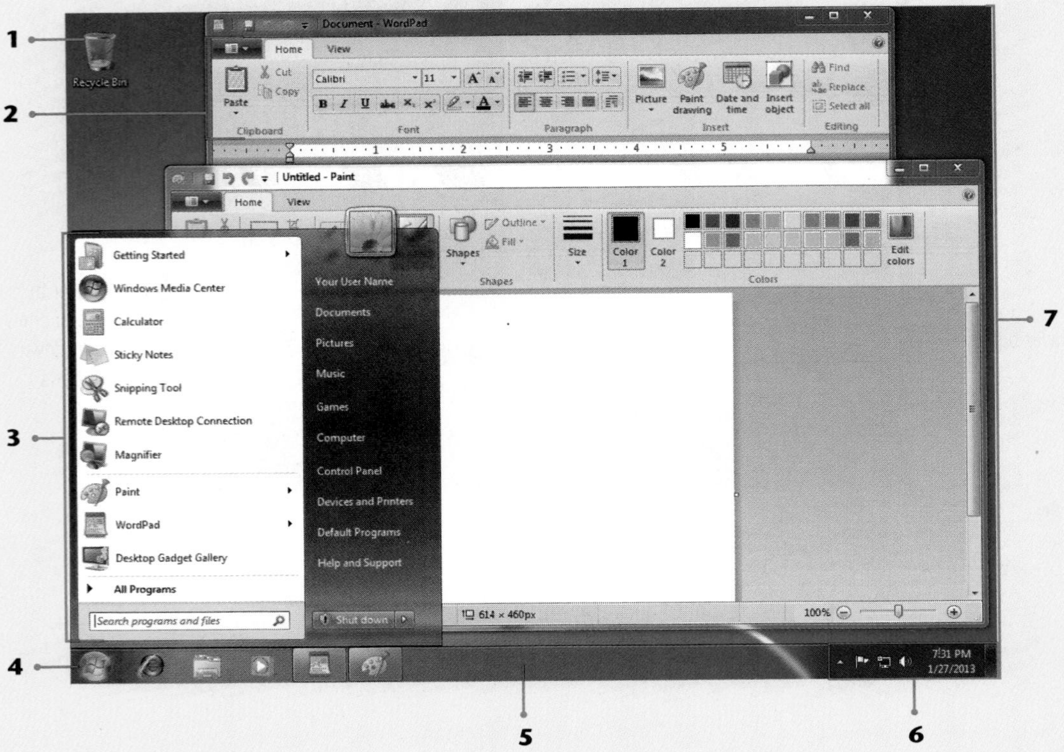

Match each term with the statement that best describes it.

8. Accessory	**a.** A sequence of numbers and letters users create to keep information secure
9. Keyword	**b.** The window in front of other windows
10. Trackball	**c.** Horizontal strip at bottom of screen that contains buttons
11. Active window	**d.** A pointing device
12. Password	**e.** Application program that comes with Windows 7
13. Operating system	**f.** Descriptive word you use to search Windows Help and Support
14. Taskbar	**g.** A program necessary to run your computer

Select the best answer from the list of choices.

15. What part of a window shows the name of the program you opened?

a. Title bar
b. Scroll bar
c. Ribbon
d. Quick Access toolbar

16. You use the Maximize button to:

- **a.** Restore a window to a previous size.
- **b.** Expand a window to fill the entire screen.
- **c.** Temporarily hide a window.
- **d.** Scroll down a window.

17. Which of the following is not an accessory program?

- **a.** Snipping Tool
- **b.** Paint
- **c.** WordPad
- **d.** Windows 7

18. Which button do you click to reduce an open window to a button on the taskbar?

- **a.** Maximize button
- **b.** Restore Down button
- **c.** Minimize button
- **d.** Close button

19. Right-clicking is an action that:

- **a.** Starts a program.
- **b.** Requires a password.
- **c.** Displays a shortcut menu.
- **d.** Opens the taskbar.

20. The Windows 7 feature that shows windows with transparent "glass" backgrounds is:

- **a.** Paint.
- **b.** Aero.
- **c.** Taskbar.
- **d.** Sticky Notes.

21. Windows 7 is a(n):

- **a.** Accessory program.
- **b.** Application program.
- **c.** Operating system.
- **d.** Gadget.

Skills Review

1. Start Windows 7.

- **a.** If your computer and monitor are not running, press your computer's and your monitor's power buttons.
- **b.** If necessary, click the user name that represents your user account.
- **c.** Enter a password if necessary, using correct uppercase and lowercase letters.

2. Learn the Windows 7 desktop.

- **a.** Examine the Windows 7 desktop to identify the Start button, the taskbar, the notification area, the Recycle Bin, the desktop background, desktop icons, and gadgets, if any.

3. Point and click.

- **a.** On the Windows desktop, select the Recycle Bin.
- **b.** Open the Start menu, then close it.
- **c.** Open the clock and calendar on the right side of the taskbar.
- **d.** Click the desktop to close the calendar.
- **e.** Open the Recycle Bin window, then close it.

4. Start a Windows 7 program.

- **a.** Use the Start button to open the Start menu.
- **b.** Open the All Programs menu.
- **c.** On the All Programs menu, open the Accessories folder.
- **d.** Open the WordPad accessory.

5. Work with Windows.

- **a.** Minimize the WordPad window.
- **b.** Redisplay it using a taskbar button.
- **c.** In the WordPad window, click the WordPad button in the Ribbon, then click the About WordPad command. (*Hint*: The WordPad button is next to the Home tab.)
- **d.** Close the About WordPad window.
- **e.** Maximize the WordPad window, then restore it down.
- **f.** Display the View tab in the WordPad window.

Skills Review (continued)

6. Work with multiple windows.

- **a.** Leaving WordPad open, open Paint.
- **b.** Make the WordPad window the active window.
- **c.** Make the Paint window the active window.
- **d.** Minimize the Paint window.
- **e.** Drag the WordPad window so it automatically fills the left side of the screen.
- **f.** Redisplay the Paint window.
- **g.** Drag the Paint window so it automatically fills the right side of the screen.
- **h.** Close the WordPad window, maximize the Paint window, then restore down the Paint window.

7. Use command buttons, menus, and dialog boxes.

- **a.** In the Paint window, draw a red triangle, similar to Figure A-23.
- **b.** Use the Fill with color button to fill the triangle with a gold color.
- **c.** Draw a green rectangle just below the triangle.
- **d.** Use the Fill with color button to fill the green triangle with a light turquoise color.
- **e.** Fill the drawing background with purple and compare your drawing with Figure A-23.
- **f.** Use the Select list arrow and menu to select the entire drawing, then use the Rotate or flip command to rotate the drawing left 90°.
- **g.** Close the Paint program without saving the drawing.

FIGURE A-23

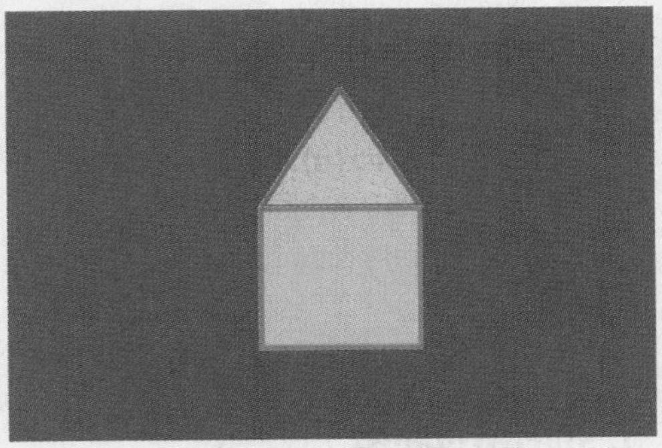

8. Get help.

- **a.** Open the Windows Help and Support window.
- **b.** Open the "How to get started with your computer" topic.
- **c.** Open the "First week tasks" topic, click a link called "Create a user account", then read the topic information.
- **d.** In the Search Help text box, search for help about user accounts.
- **e.** Find the link that describes what a user account is and click it.
- **f.** Read the topic, then close the Windows Help and Support window.

9. Exit Windows 7.

- **a.** Shut down your computer using the Shut down command or the command for your work or school setting.
- **b.** Turn off your monitor.

Independent Challenge 1

You work for Will's Percussion, an Oregon manufacturer of drums and drumsticks. The company ships percussion instruments and supplies to music stores and musicians in the United States and Canada. The owner, Will, gives seminars at drummer conventions on how to avoid repetitive stress injuries to the hands and arms. He knows this can also be a big problem for computer users as well, so he asks you to research the topic and write some guidelines for the company's employees.

- **a.** Start your computer, log on to Windows 7 if necessary, then open Windows Help and Support.
- **b.** Click the Learn about Windows Basics link.
- **c.** In the Learn about your computer section, read the topic about using your mouse.
- **d.** At the bottom of the topic, read the Tips for using your mouse safely.
- **e.** Using pencil and paper, write a short memo to Will listing, in your own words, the most important tips for avoiding soreness or injury when using a mouse. Close the Windows Help and Support window, then exit Windows.

Independent Challenge 2

You are the new manager for Katharine Anne's Designs, a business that supplies floral arrangements to New York businesses. The company maintains four delivery vans that supply flowers to various locations. Katharine asks you to investigate how the Windows 7 Calculator accessory can help her company be a responsible energy consumer.

Independent Challenge 2 (continued)

a. Start your computer, log on to Windows 7 if necessary, then open the Windows 7 accessory called Calculator.
b. Drag the Calculator window to place it in the lower-left corner of the desktop just above the taskbar.
c. Minimize the Calculator window, then redisplay it.
d. Click to enter the number 87 on the Calculator.
e. Click the division sign (/) button.
f. Click the number 2.
g. Click the equals sign button (=), and write the result shown in the Calculator window on a piece of paper. See Figure A-24.
h. Click the Help menu in the Calculator window, then click View Help. In the Using Calculator window, determine the three ways of entering calculations in the Calculator. Write the three methods on your handwritten list.
i. Close the Help window.

FIGURE A-24

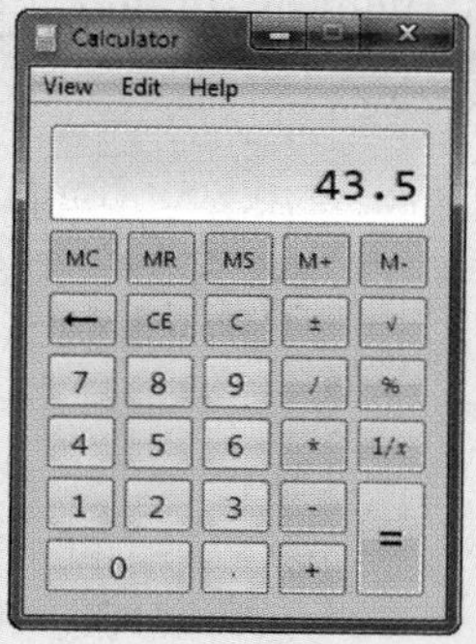

Advanced Challenge Exercise

ACE

- Open the View menu on the Calculator window, and click Date calculation.
- Click the list arrow under Select the date calculation you want, then click Calculate the difference between two dates.
- Write how Katharine's business might use this to calculate the length of time it takes a customer to pay an invoice.
- Click the View menu, point to Worksheets, then click Fuel economy (mpg).
- Click in the Distance (miles) text box and enter 100; click in the Fuel used (gallons) text box and type 5, then use the Calculate button to calculate the mileage.
- Write a short paragraph on how Katharine can use this feature to help calculate her van mileage.
- Click the View menu and return to the Basic view.
- Try to click the Calculator window's Maximize button. Note the result and add this fact to your document.

j. Close the Calculator, then exit Windows.

Independent Challenge 3

You are the office manager for Peter's Pet Shipping, a service business in Vancouver, BC that specializes in air shipping of cats and dogs to Canada and the northern United States. It's important to know the temperature in the destination city, so that the animals won't be in danger from extreme temperatures when they are unloaded from the aircraft. Peter has asked you to find a way to easily monitor temperatures in destination cities. You decide to use a Windows gadget so you can see current temperatures in Celsius on your desktop.

To complete this Independent Challenge, you need an Internet connection. You also need permission to add gadgets to the Windows Desktop. If you are working in a computer lab, check with your instructor or technical support person.

a. Start your computer, log on to Windows 7 if necessary, then click the Start button, open the All Programs menu, then click Desktop Gadget Gallery.
b. Double-click the Weather gadget, then close the Gallery window.
c. Move the pointer over the Weather gadget on the desktop, then notice the small buttons that appear on its right side.
d. Click the Larger size button (the middle button).
e. Click the Options button (the third button down) to open the weather options window.
f. In the Select current location text box, type Juneau, Alaska, then click the Search button.
g. Verify that the window shows the current location as "Juneau, Alaska."
h. Click the Celsius option button, then click OK.
i. To close the gadget, point to the gadget, then click the Close button (the top button).
j. Write Peter a memo outlining how you can use the Windows Weather gadget to help keep pets safe, then exit Windows.

Real Life Independent Challenge

As a professional photographer, you often evaluate pictures. You decide to explore a Windows Desktop gadget that will let you display a slide show on your desktop using photos you choose.

To complete this Independent Challenge, you need an Internet connection. You also need permission to add gadgets to the Windows Desktop. If you are working in a computer lab, check with your instructor or technical support person.

a. Start your computer, log on to Windows 7 if necessary, click the Start button, open the All Programs menu, then click Desktop Gadget Gallery.
b. Double-click the Slide Show gadget, then close the Gallery window.
c. Move the pointer over the Slide Show gadget on the desktop, then notice the small buttons that appear on its right side.
d. Click the Larger size button (the second button down).
e. Click the Options button (the third button down) to open the Slide Show options window.
f. Click the Folder list arrow and click the My Pictures folder. If you do not have pictures on your computer, click the Sample Pictures folder.
g. Click the Show each picture list arrow and select a duration.
h. Click the Transition between pictures list arrow and select a transition.
i. If you want the pictures to be in random order, click the Shuffle pictures check box.
j. Click OK.

Advanced Challenge Exercise

- Place the mouse pointer over the Slide Show window, then right-click.
- Point to Opacity and left-click an opacity level, then move the mouse pointer over the desktop. Adjust the opacity to the level you prefer.
- Drag the gadget to the desktop location you choose.

k. View your slide show, click the Slide Show window's Close button, then exit Windows.

Visual Workshop

As owner of Icons Plus, an icon design business, you decide to customize your desktop and resize your Help window to better suit your needs as you work with Paint. Organize your screen as shown in Figure A-25. Note the position of the Recycle Bin, the location of the Paint window, and the size and location of the Help and Support window. Write a paragraph summarizing how you used clicking and dragging to make your screen look like Figure A-25. Then exit Windows.

FIGURE A-25

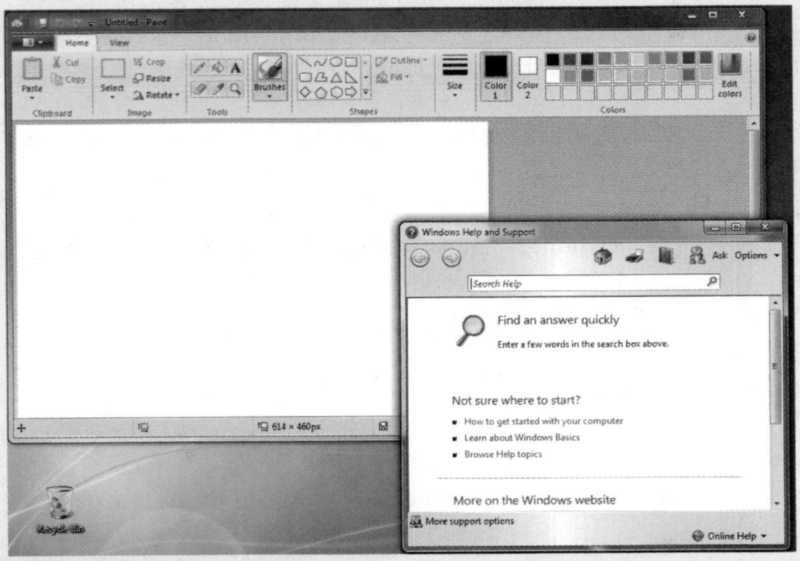

UNIT B
Windows 7

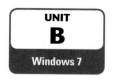

Understanding File Management

Files You Will Need:
No files needed.

To work with the folders and files on your computer, you need to understand how your computer stores them. You should also know how to organize them so you can always find the information you need. These skills are called **file management** skills. When you create a document and save it as a file, it is important that you save the file in a place where you can find it later. To keep your computer files organized, you will need to copy, move, and rename them. When you have files you don't need any more, it's a good idea to move or delete them so your computer has only current files. Your supervisor, Evelyn Swazey, asks you to learn how to manage your computer files so you can begin creating and organizing documents for the upcoming Oceania tours.

OBJECTIVES

- Understand folders and files
- Create and save a file
- Explore the files and folders on your computer
- Change file and folder views
- Open, edit, and save files
- Copy files
- Move and rename files
- Search for files, folders, and programs
- Delete and restore files

Understanding Folders and Files

As you work with your computer programs, you create and save files, such as letters, drawings, or budgets. When you save files, you usually save them inside folders, which are storage areas on your computer. You use folders to group related files, as with paper folders in a file cabinet. The files and folders on your computer are organized in a **file hierarchy**, a system that arranges files and folders in different levels, like the branches of a tree. Figure B-1 shows a sample file hierarchy. Evelyn asks you to look at some important facts about files and folders to help you store your Oceania tour files.

DETAILS

Use the following guidelines as you organize files using your computer's file hierarchy:

- **Use folders and subfolders to organize files**
  As you work with your computer, you can add folders to your hierarchy and rename them to help you organize your work. You should give folders unique names that help you easily identify them. You can also create **subfolders**, which are folders that are inside of other folders. Windows comes with several existing folders, such as My Documents, My Music, and My Pictures, that you can use as a starting point.

QUICK TIP
You can also start Windows Explorer by clicking the Windows Explorer button on the taskbar.

- **View files in windows**
  You view your computer contents by opening a **window**, like the one in Figure B-2. A window is divided into sections. The **Navigation pane** on the left side of the window shows the folder structure on your computer. When you click a folder in the Navigation pane, you see its contents in the **File list** on the right side. The **Details pane** at the bottom of the window provides information about selected files in the File list. A window actually opens in an accessory program called **Windows Explorer**, although the program name does not appear on the window. You can open this program from the Start menu, or just double-click a folder to open its window and view its contents.

- **Understand file addresses**
  A window also contains an **Address bar**, an area just below the title bar that shows the location, or address, of the files that appear in the File list. An **address** is a sequence of folder names separated by the ▸ symbol that describes a file's location in the file hierarchy. An address shows the folder with the highest hierarchy level on the left and steps through each hierarchy level toward the right, sometimes called a **path**. For example, the My Documents folder might contain a subfolder named Notes. In this case, the Address bar would show My Documents ▸ Notes. Each location between the ▸ symbols represents a level in the file hierarchy.

QUICK TIP
Remember that you single-click a folder or subfolder in the Address bar to show its contents. But in the File list, you double-click a subfolder to open it.

- **Navigate upward and downward using the Address bar and File list**
  You can use the Address bar and the File list to move up or down in the hierarchy one or more levels at a time. To **navigate upward** in your computer's hierarchy, you can click a folder or subfolder name in the Address bar. For example, in Figure B-2, you would move up in the hierarchy by clicking once on Users in the Address bar. Then the File list would show the subfolders and files inside the Users folder. To **navigate downward** in the hierarchy, double-click a subfolder in the File list. The path in the Address bar then shows the path to that subfolder.

- **Navigate upward and downward using the Navigation pane**
  You can also use the Navigation pane to navigate among folders. Move the mouse pointer over the Navigation pane, then click the small triangles or to the left of a folder name to show ▷ or hide ◢ the folder's contents under the folder name. Subfolders appear indented under the folders that contain them, showing that they are inside that folder. Figure B-2 shows a folder named Users in the Navigation pane. The subfolders Katharine, Public, and Your User Name are inside the Users folder.

FIGURE B-1: Sample folder and file hierarchy

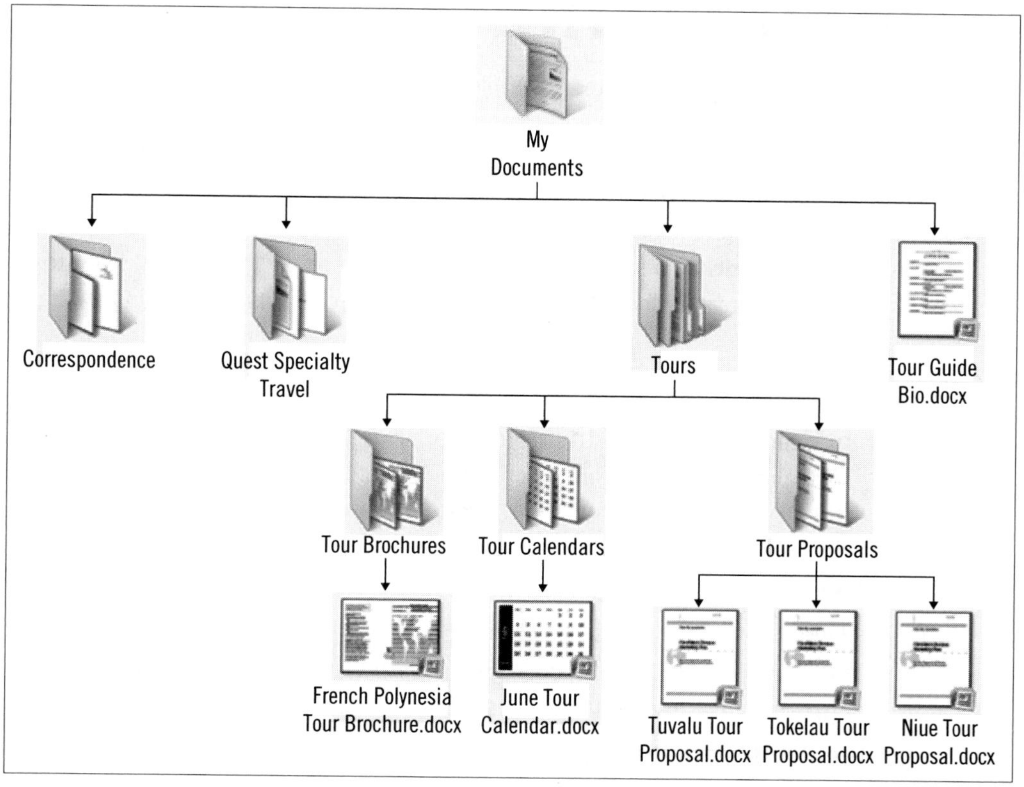

FIGURE B-2: Windows Explorer window

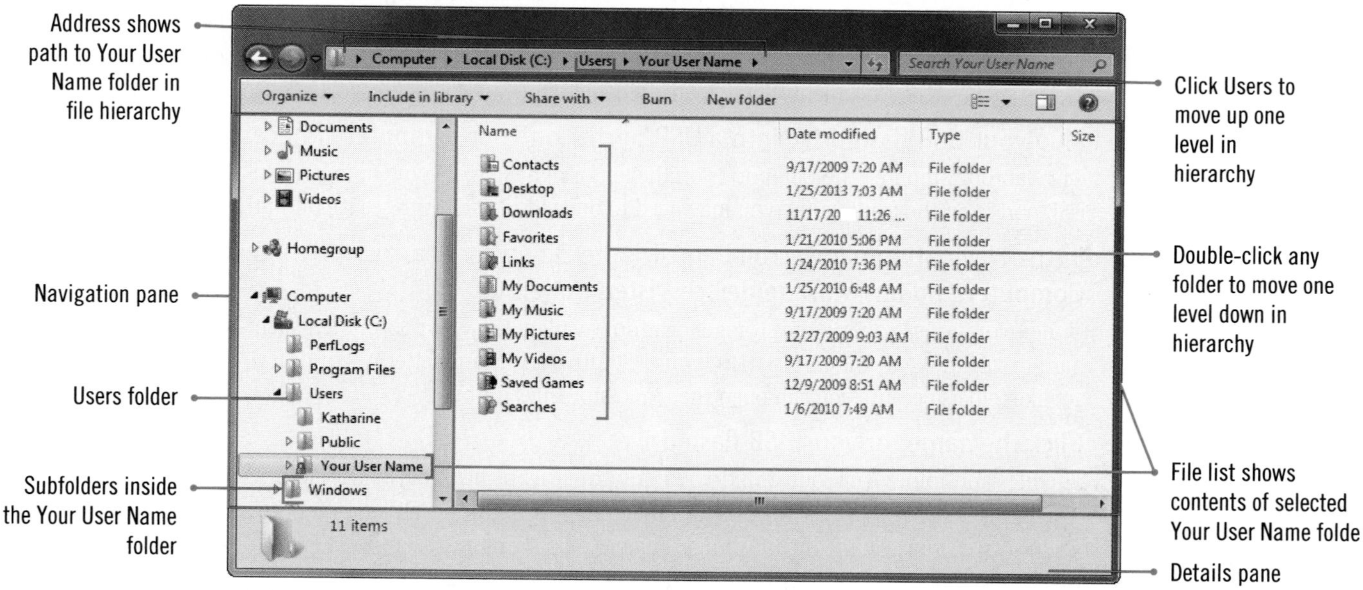

Plan your file organization

As you manage your files, you should plan how you want to organize them. First, identify the types of files you work with, such as images, music, and reports. Think about the content, such as personal, business, clients, or projects. Then think of a folder organization that will help you find them later. For example, use subfolders in the My Pictures folder to separate family photos from business photos or to group them by year. In the My Documents folder, you might group personal files in one subfolder and business files in another subfolder. Then create additional subfolders to further separate sets of files. You can always move files among folders and rename folders. You should periodically reevaluate your folder structure to make sure that it continues to meet your needs.

UNIT B Windows 7

Creating and Saving a File

After you start a program and create a new file, the file exists only in your computer's **random access memory (RAM)**, which is a temporary storage location. RAM only contains information when your computer is on. When you turn off your computer, it automatically clears the contents of RAM. So you need to save a new file onto a storage device that permanently stores the file so that you can open, change, and use it later. One important storage device is your computer's hard disk built into your computer. Another popular option is a **USB flash drive**, a small, portable storage device. Evelyn asks you to use the WordPad accessory program to create a short summary of an Oceania tour planning meeting and save it.

STEPS

1. **Start Windows if necessary, click the Start button on the taskbar, point to All Programs, click Accessories, then click WordPad**

   The WordPad program opens. Near the top of the screen you see the Ribbon containing command buttons, similar to those you used in Paint in Unit A. The Home tab appears in front. A new, blank document appears in the document window. The blinking insertion point shows you where the next character you type will appear.

2. **Type Meeting Notes, October 11, then press [Enter]**

   WordPad inserts a new blank line and places the insertion point at the beginning of the next line.

3. **Type The 2013 tour will visit:, press [Enter], type Australia, press [Enter], type Micronesia, press [Enter], type New Zealand, press [Enter], then type your name; see Figure B-3**

4. **Click the WordPad button on the upper-left side of the window below the title bar, then click Save on the WordPad menu**

   The first time you save a file using the Save button, the Save As dialog box opens. Use this dialog box to name the document file and choose a storage location for it. The Save As dialog box has many of the same elements as a Windows Explorer window, including an Address bar, a Navigation pane, and a File list. Below the Address bar, the **toolbar** contains command buttons you can click to perform actions. In the Address bar, you can see that WordPad chose the Documents library (which includes the My Documents folder) as the storage location.

5. **Plug your USB flash drive into a USB port on your computer, if necessary**

   On a laptop computer, the USB port is on the left or right side of your computer. On a desktop computer, the USB port is on the front panel (you may need to open a small door to see it), or on the back panel.

6. **In the Navigation pane scroll bar, click the Down scroll arrow as needed to see Computer and any storage devices listed under it**

   Under Computer, you see the storage locations available on your computer, such as Local Disk (C:) (your hard drive) and Removable Disk (H:) (your USB drive name and letter might differ). These storage locations act like folders because you can open them and store files in them.

7. **Click the name for your USB flash drive**

   The files and folders on your USB drive, if any, appear in the File list. The Address bar shows the location where the file will be saved, which is now Computer > Removable Disk (H:) (or the name of your drive). You need to give your document a meaningful name so you can find it later.

8. **Click in the Filename text box to select the default name Document, type Oceania Meeting, compare your screen to Figure B-4, then click Save**

   The document is saved as a file on your USB flash drive. The filename Oceania Meeting.rtf appears in the title bar at the top of the window. The ".rtf" at the end of the filename is the file extension. A **file extension** is a three- or four-letter sequence, preceded by a period, that identifies the file as a particular type of document, in this case Rich Text Format, to your computer. The WordPad program creates files using the RTF format. Windows adds the .rtf file extension automatically after you click Save.

9. **Click the Close button on the WordPad window**

   The WordPad program closes. Your meeting minutes are now saved on your USB flash drive.

TROUBLE

If you make a typing mistake, press [Backspace] to delete the character to the left of the insertion point.

TROUBLE

If you don't have a USB flash drive, save the document in the My Documents folder instead.

TROUBLE

If your Save As dialog box or title bar does not show the .rtf file extension, open any Windows Explorer window, click Organize in the toolbar, click Folder and search options, click the View tab, then under Files and Folders, click to remove the check mark from Hide extensions for known file types.

FIGURE B-3: **Saving a document**

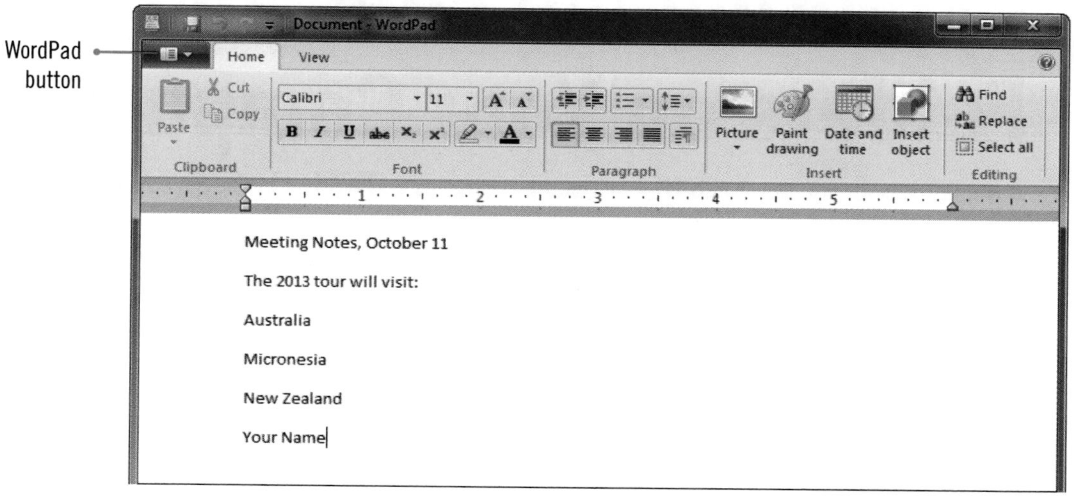

FIGURE B-4: **Save As dialog box**

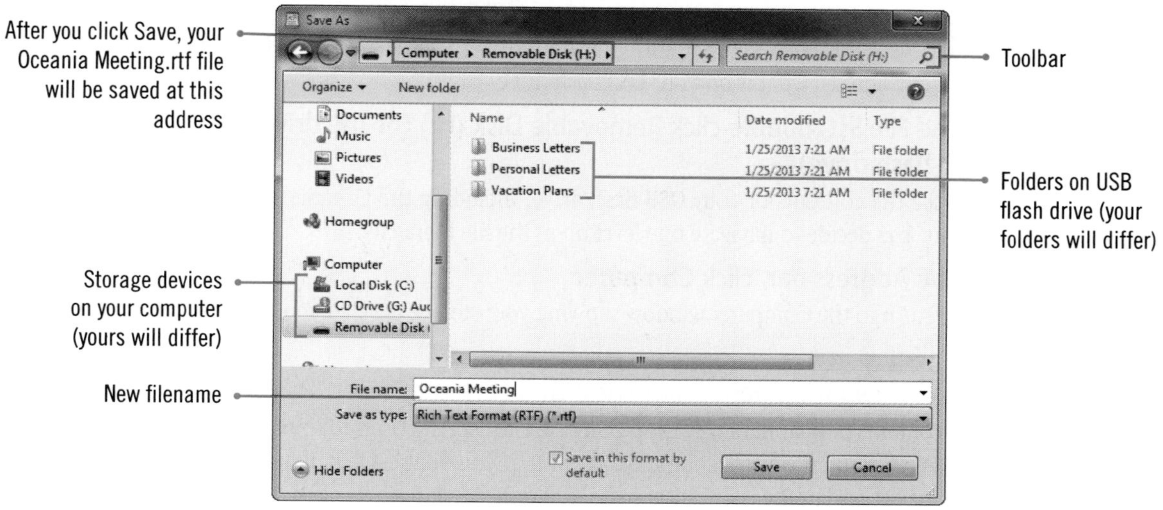

Using Windows 7 libraries

The Navigation pane contains not only files and folders, but also Libraries. A **library** gathers files and folders from different locations on your computer and displays them in one location. For example, you might have pictures in several different folders on your storage devices. You can add these folder locations to your Pictures library. Then when you want to see all your pictures, you open your Pictures library, instead of several different folders. The picture files stay in their original locations, but their names appear in the Pictures library. A library is not a folder that stores files, but rather a way of viewing similar types of documents that you have stored in multiple locations on your computer. Figure B-5 shows the four libraries that come with Windows 7: Documents, Music, Pictures, and Videos. To help you distinguish between library locations and actual folder locations, library names differ from actual folder names. For example, the My Documents folder is on your hard drive, but the library name is Documents. To add a location to a library, click the blue locations link (at the top of the File list) in the library you want to add to, click the Add button, navigate to the folder location you want to add, then click Include folder. If you delete a file or folder from a library, you delete them from their source locations. If you delete a library, you do not delete the files in it. The Documents Library that comes with Windows already has the My Documents folder listed as a save location. So if you save a document to the Documents library, it is automatically saved to your My Documents folder.

FIGURE B-5: **Libraries**

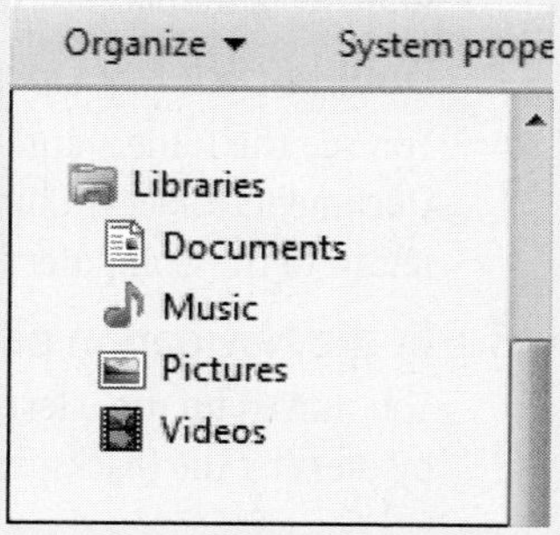

Exploring the Files and Folders on Your Computer

In the last lesson, you navigated to your USB flash drive as you worked in the Save As dialog box. But even if you're not saving a document, you will want to examine your computer and its existing folder and file structure. That way, you'll know where to save files as you work with Windows application programs. In a Windows Explorer window, you can navigate through your computer contents using the File list, the Address bar, and the Navigation pane. As you prepare for the Oceania tours, you look at the files and folders on your computer.

STEPS

TROUBLE
If you don't see the colored bar, click the More Options list arrow on the menu bar, then click Tiles.

TROUBLE
If you do not have a USB flash drive, click the Documents library in the Navigation pane instead.

QUICK TIP
Click the Back button, to the left of the Address bar, to return to the window you last viewed. In the Address bar, click ▸ to the right of a folder name to see a list of the subfolders. If the folder is open, its name appears in bold.

1. **Click the Start button on the taskbar, then click Computer**
   Your computer's storage devices appear in a window, as shown in Figure B-6, including hard drives; devices with removable storage, such as CD and DVD drives or USB flash drives; and portable devices such as personal digital assistants (PDAs). Table B-1 lists examples of different drive types. A colored bar shows you how much space has been taken up on your hard drive. You decide to move down a level in your computer's hierarchy and see what is on your USB flash drive.
2. **In the File list, double-click Removable Disk (H:) (or the drive name and letter for your USB flash drive)**
   You see the contents of your USB flash drive, including the Oceania Meeting.rtf file you saved in the last lesson. You decide to navigate one level up in the file hierarchy.
3. **In the Address bar, click Computer**
   You return to the Computer window showing your storage devices. You decide to look at the contents of your hard drive.
4. **In the Navigation pane, click Local Disk (C:)**
   The contents of your hard drive appear in the File list. The Users folder contains a subfolder for each user who has a user account on this computer. Recall that you double-click items in the File list to open them. In the Address bar and in the Navigation pane, you only need to single-click.
5. **In the File list, double-click the Users folder**
   You see folders for each user registered on your computer. You might see a folder with your user account name on it. Each user's folder contains that person's documents. User folder names are the log-in names that were entered when your computer was set up. When a user logs in, the computer allows that user access to the folder with the same user name. If you are using a computer with more than one user, you might not have permission to view other users' folders. There is also a Public folder that any user can open.
6. **Double-click the folder with your user name on it**
   Depending on how your computer is set up, this folder might be labeled with your name; however, if you are using a computer in a lab or a public location, your folder might be called Student or Computer User or something similar. You see a list of folders, such as My Documents, My Music, and others. See Figure B-7.
7. **Double-click My Documents**
   You see the folders and documents you can open and work with. In the Address bar, the path to the My Documents folder is Computer ▸ Local Disk (C:) ▸ Users ▸ Your User Name ▸ My Documents. You decide to return to the Computer window.
8. **In the Navigation pane, click Computer**
   You moved up three levels in your hierarchy. You can also move one level up at a time in your file hierarchy by pressing the [Backspace] key on your keyboard. You once again see your computer's storage devices.

FIGURE B-6: **Computer window showing storage devices**

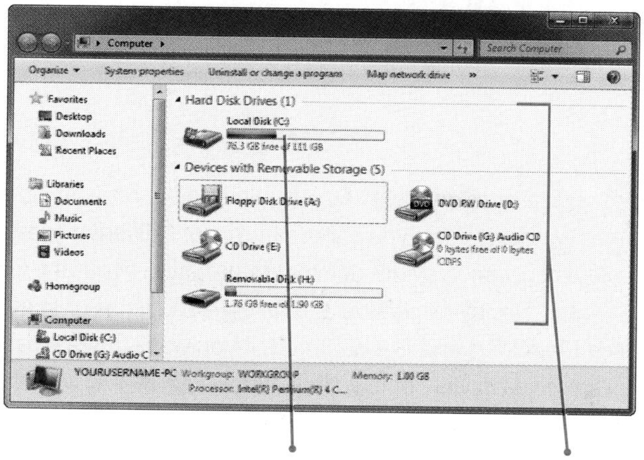

FIGURE B-7: **Your User Name folder**

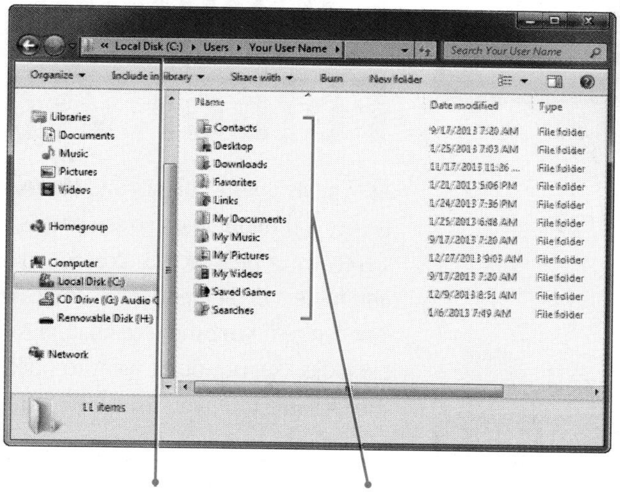

TABLE B-1: **Drive names and icons**

drive type	drive icon	drive name
hard drive		C:
CD drive		Next available drive letter, such as D:
DVD drive		Next available drive letter, such as E:
USB flash drive		Next available drive letter, such as F, G:, or H:

Sharing information with homegroups and libraries

Windows 7 lets you create a **homegroup**, a named set of computers that can share information. If your computer is in a homegroup with other Windows 7 computers, you can share libraries and printers with those computers. Click Start, then click Control Panel. Under Network and Internet, click Choose homegroup and sharing options. Click to place a check mark next to the libraries and printers you want to share, then click Save changes. To share libraries that you have created on your computer with others in your homegroup, click Start, click your user name, then in the Navigation pane, click the library you want to share, click Share with on the toolbar, then click the sharing option you want, as shown in Figure B-8.

FIGURE B-8: **Sharing a library**

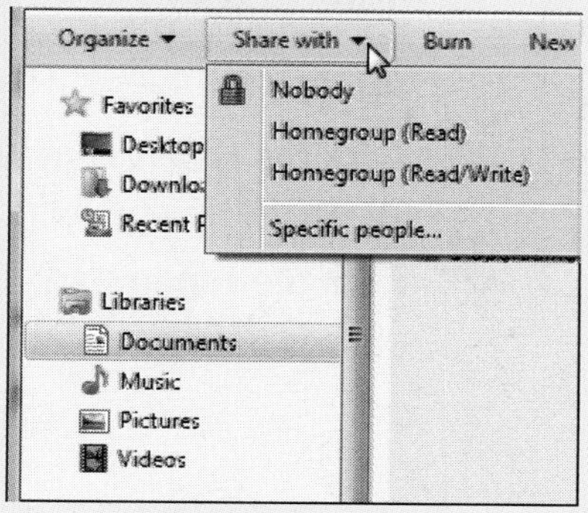

UNIT B
Windows 7

Changing File and Folder Views

As you view your folders and files, you might want to see as many items as possible in a window. At other times, you might want to see details about each item. Windows 7 lets you choose from eight different **views**, which are appearance choices for your folder contents. Each view provides different information about the files and folders in different ways. You can list your folders and files by using several different-sized icons or in lists. You can also **sort** them to change the order in which the folders and files are listed. If you want to see what a file looks like, but don't want to open the file, you can see a preview of it in the window. As you plan the Oceania tour, you review picture files in various views.

STEPS

1. **In the Navigation pane, under Libraries, click Pictures, then in the File list, double-click the Sample Pictures folder**
   You opened the Sample Pictures folder, which is inside your Pictures library.
2. **In the toolbar, click the More options list arrow next to the Change your view icon**
   The list of available views appears in a shortcut menu. See Figure B-9.
3. **Click Large Icons**
   In this view, the pictures appear as large-sized icons in the File list, as shown in Figure B-10. For image files, this view is very helpful. You can click any view name or you can drag a slider control to move through each of the available views.
4. **Click the Change your view More options list arrow again, point to the slider, then drag it so it's next to Details**
   As you drag, Live Preview shows you how each view looks in your folder. In Details view, you can see filenames, the date that files were created or modified, and other information. In Details view, you can also control the order in which the folders and files appear. In the Name column heading, you see a small triangle Name. This indicates that the sample pictures are in alphabetical order (A, B, C,...).
5. **Click the Name column heading**
   The items now appear in descending (Z, Y, X,...) order. The icon in the column header changes to Name.
6. **Click the Show the preview pane button in the toolbar**
   The Preview pane opens on the right side of the screen. The **Preview pane** is an area on the right side of a window that shows you what a selected file looks like without opening it. It is especially useful for document files so you can see the first few paragraphs of a large document.
7. **Click the name of your USB flash drive in the Navigation pane, then click the Oceania Meeting.rtf filename in the File list**
   A preview of the Oceania Meeting file you created earlier in this unit appears in the Preview pane. The WordPad file is not open, but you can still see its contents. The Details pane gives you information about the selected file. See Figure B-11.
8. **Click the Hide the preview pane button**
   The Preview pane closes.
9. **Click the window's Close button**

QUICK TIP
You can also click the Change your view button (not its list arrow) repeatedly to cycle through five of the eight views.

QUICK TIP
Click a column heading a second time to reverse the order.

QUICK TIP
The Navigation pane also contains Favorites, which are links to folders you use frequently. To add a folder to your Favorites list, open the folder in the File list. Right-click the Favorites link in the Navigation pane, then left-click Add current location to Favorites.

FIGURE B-9: **More options shortcut menu showing views**

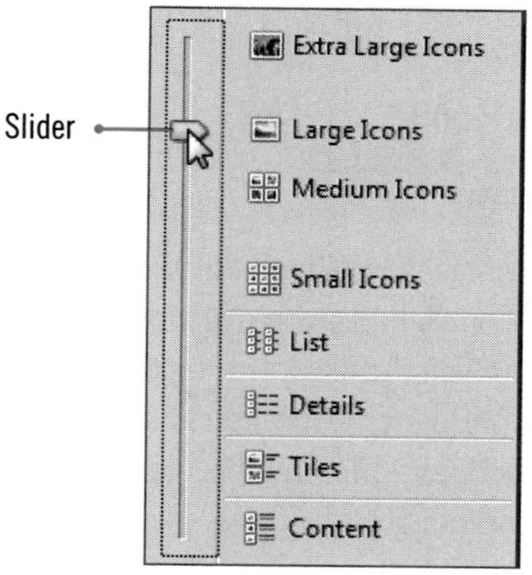

FIGURE B-10: **Sample pictures library as large icons**

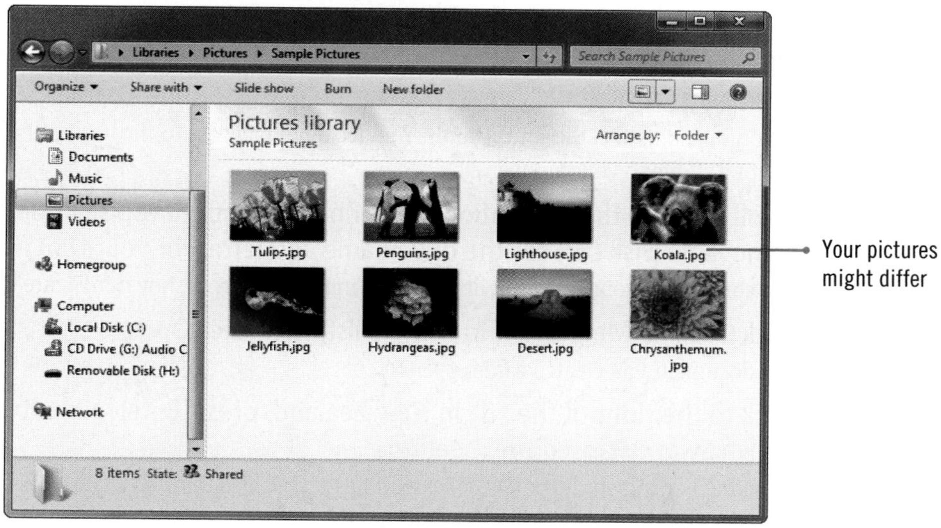

FIGURE B-11: **Preview of selected Oceania Meeting.rtf file**

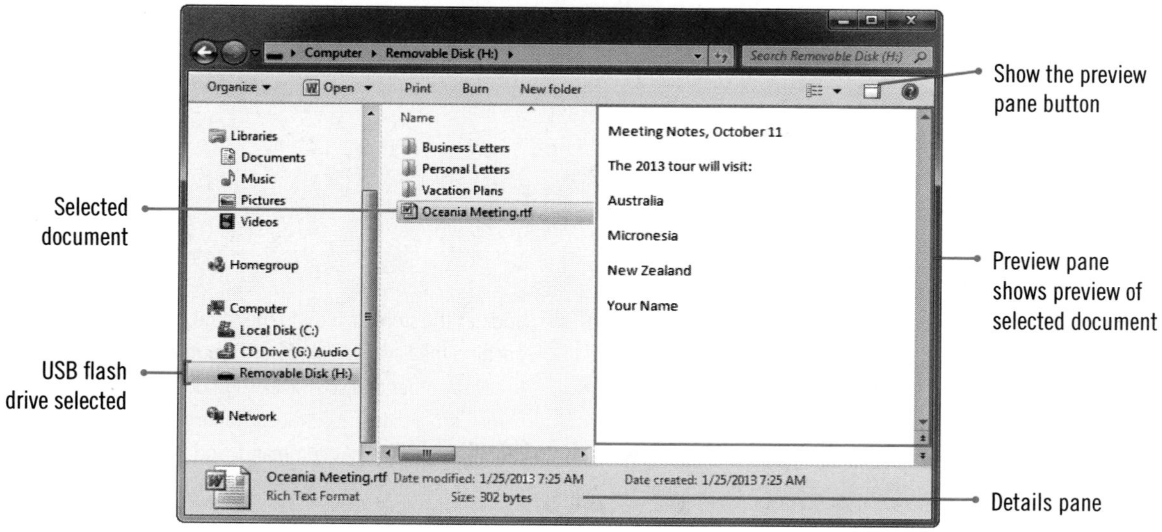

UNIT B Windows 7

Opening, Editing, and Saving Files

Once you have created a file and saved it with a name in a folder on a storage device, you can easily open it and **edit** (make changes to) it. For example, you might want to add or delete text to a document, or change the color in a drawing. Then you save the file again so that it contains your latest changes. Usually you save a file with the same filename and in the same location as the original, which replaces the existing file with the latest, updated version. When you save a file you have changed, you use the Save command. Evelyn asks you to complete the meeting notes.

STEPS

1. **Click the Start button on the taskbar, point to All Programs, click the Accessories folder, then click WordPad**

   If you use WordPad frequently, it's name might appear on the left side of the Start menu. If it does, you can click it there to open it.

2. **Click the WordPad button, then click Open**

   The Open dialog box opens. It has the same sections as the Save As dialog box and the Windows Explorer windows you used earlier in this unit. You decide to navigate to the location where you saved your Oceania Meeting.rtf file so you can open it.

3. **Scroll down in the Navigation pane if necessary until you see Computer, then click Removable Disk (H:) (or the drive name and letter for your USB flash drive)**

   The contents of your USB flash drive appear in the File list, as shown in Figure B-12.

4. **Click Oceania Meeting.rtf in the File list, then click Open**

   The document you created earlier opens.

5. **Click to the right of the "d" in New Zealand, press [Enter], then type Evelyn Swazey closed the meeting.**

   The edited document includes the text you just typed. See Figure B-13.

6. **Click the WordPad button, then click Save, as shown in Figure B-14**

   WordPad saves the document with your most recent changes, using the filename and location you specified when you saved it for the first time. When you save an existing file, the Save As dialog box does not open.

7. **Click, then click Exit**

TROUBLE

If you are not using a USB flash drive, click an appropriate storage location in the Navigation pane.

QUICK TIP

You can also double-click the filename in the File list to open the file.

QUICK TIP

Instead of using the WordPad menu and Save command to save a document, you can also click the Save button in the Quick Access toolbar at the top of the WordPad window.

Comparing Save and Save As

The WordPad menu has two save command options—Save and Save As. When you first save a file, the Save As dialog box opens (whether you choose Save or Save As). Here you can select the drive and folder where you want to save the file and enter its filename. If you edit a previously saved file, you can save the file to the same location with the same filename using the Save command. The Save command updates the stored file using the same location and filename without opening the Save As dialog box. In some situations, you might want to save another copy of the existing document using a different filename or in a different storage location. To do this, open the document, use the Save As command, and then navigate to a different location, and/or edit the name of the file.

FIGURE B-12: **Navigating in the Open dialog box**

The folders on your drive will differ

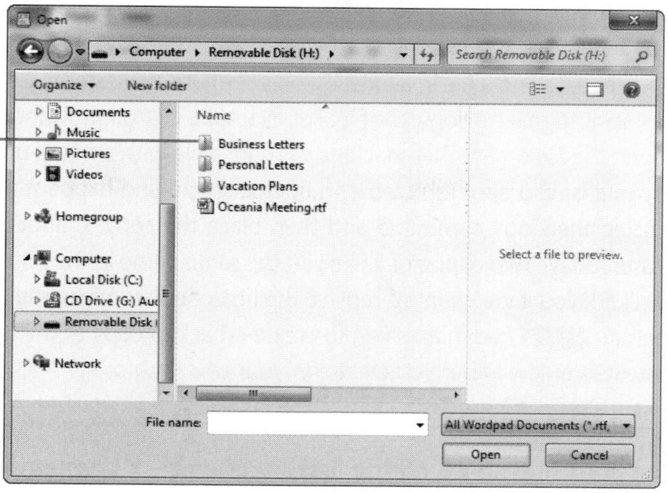

FIGURE B-13: **Edited document**

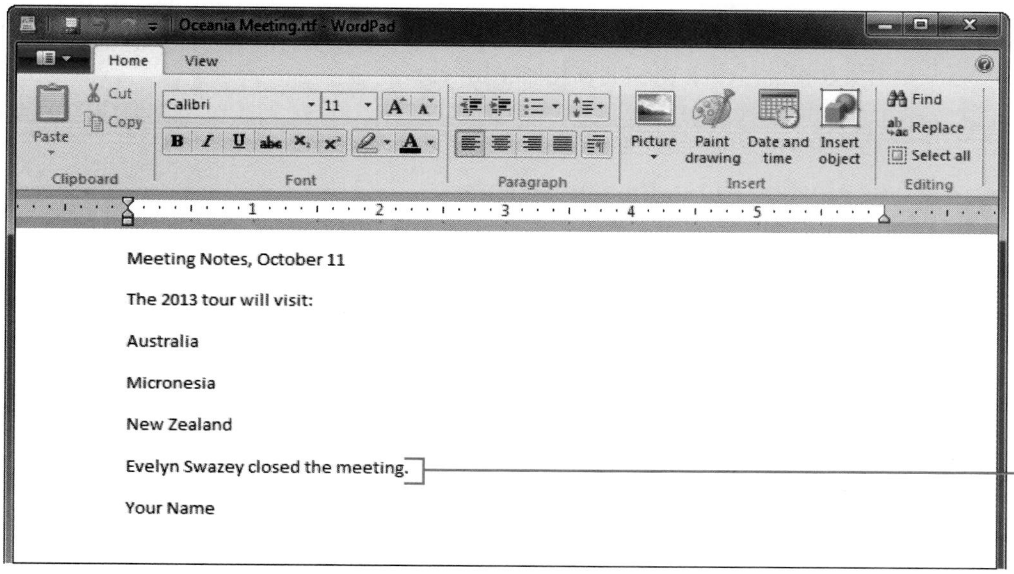

Added text

FIGURE B-14: **Saving a revised document**

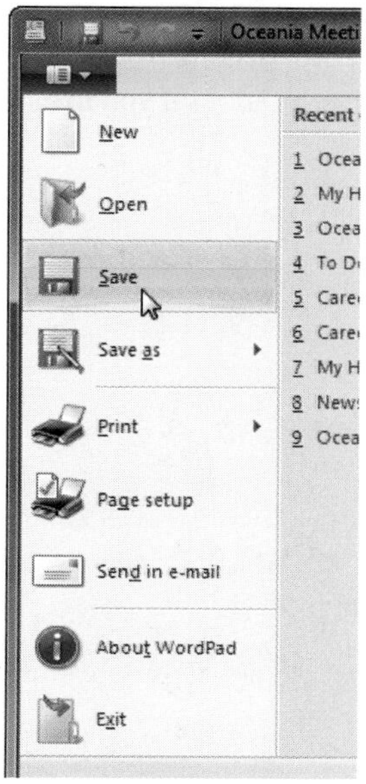

UNIT B
Windows 7

Copying Files

As you have learned, saving a file in a location on your hard drive stores it so you can open it later. But sometimes you will want to make a copy of a file. For example, you might want to put a copy on a USB flash drive so you can open the file on another machine or share a file with a friend or colleague. Or you might want to create a copy as a **backup**, or replacement, in case something happens to your original file. You copy files and folders using the Copy command and then place the copy in another location using the Paste command. You cannot have two copies of a file with the same name in the same folder. If you attempt to do this, Windows 7 will ask you if you want to replace the first one then gives you a chance to give the second copy a different name. Evelyn asks you to create a backup copy of the meeting notes document you created and paste it in a new folder you create on your USB flash drive.

STEPS

1. **Click the Start button on the taskbar, then click Computer**
2. **In the File list, double-click Removable Disk (H:) (or the drive name and letter for your USB flash drive)**
   First you create the new folder Evelyn needs.
3. **In the toolbar, click the New folder button**
   A new folder appears in the File list, with its name, New folder, selected. Because the folder name is selected, any text you type replaces the selected text as the folder name.
4. **Type Meeting Notes, then press [Enter]**
   You named the new folder Meeting Notes. Next, you copy your original Oceania Meeting.rtf file.
5. **In the File list, click the Oceania Meeting.rtf document you saved earlier, click the Organize button on the toolbar, then click Copy, as shown in Figure B-15**
   When you use the Copy command, Windows 7 places a duplicate copy of the file in an area of your computer's random access memory called the **clipboard**, ready to paste, or place, in a new location. Copying and pasting a file leaves the file in its original location. The copied file remains on the clipboard until you copy something else or end your Windows 7 session.
6. **In the File list, double-click the Meeting Notes folder**
   The folder opens.
7. **Click the Organize button on the toolbar, then click Paste**
   A copy of your Oceania Meeting.rtf file is pasted into your new Meeting Notes folder. See Figure B-16. You now have two copies of the Oceania Meeting.rtf file: one on your USB flash drive in the main folder, and a copy of the file in a folder called Meeting Notes on your USB flash drive. The file remains on the clipboard so you can paste it again to other locations if you like.

QUICK TIP
You can also copy a file by right-clicking the file in the File list and then clicking Copy. To use the keyboard, press and hold [Ctrl] and press [C], then release both keys.

QUICK TIP
To paste using the keyboard, press and hold [Ctrl] and press [V], then release both keys.

FIGURE B-15: **Copying a file**

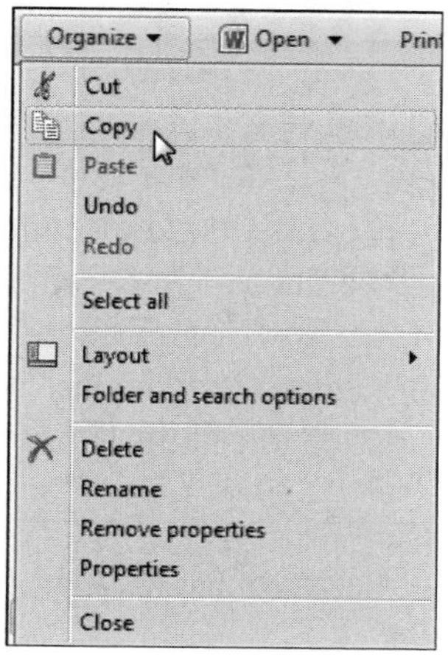

FIGURE B-16: **Duplicate file pasted into Meeting Notes folder**

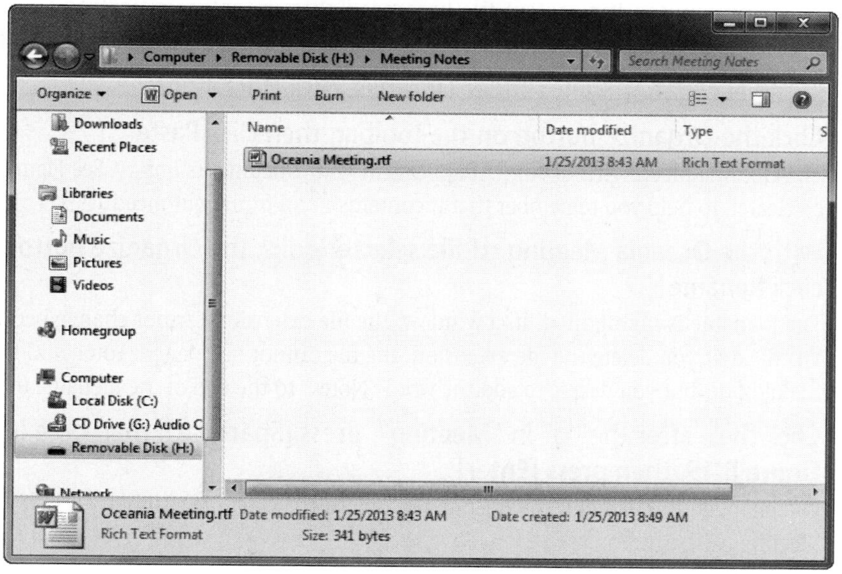

Copying files using Send to

You can also copy and paste a file to an external storage device using the Send to command. In a window, right-click the file you want to copy, point to Send to, then in the shortcut menu, click the name of the device where you want to send a copy of the file. This leaves the original file on your hard drive and creates a copy on the external device, all with just one command. See Table B-2 for a short summary of other shortcut menu commands.

TABLE B-2: **Selected Send to menu commands**

menu option	use to	menu option	use to
Compressed (zipped) folder	Create a new compressed (smaller) file with a .zip file extension	Documents	Copy the file to the Documents library
Desktop (create shortcut)	Create a shortcut (link) for the file on the desktop	DVD RW Drive (D:)	Copy the file to your computer's DVD drive
Mail recipient	Create an e-mail with the file attached to it (only if you have an e-mail program on your computer)	Removable Disk (H:)	Copy the file to your removable disk (H:)

UNIT B
Windows 7

Moving and Renaming Files

As you work with files, you might need to move files or folders to another location. You can move one or more files or folders. You might move them to a different folder on the same drive or a different drive. When you **move** a file, the file is transferred to the new location and no longer exists in its original location. You can move a file using the Cut and Paste commands. After you create a file, you might find that the original name you gave the file isn't clear anymore, so you can rename it to make it more descriptive or accurate. You decide to move your original Oceania Meeting.rtf document to your Documents library. After you move it, you decide to edit the filename so it better describes the file contents.

STEPS

QUICK TIP
You can also cut a file by right-clicking the file in the File list and then clicking Cut. To use the keyboard, press and hold [Ctrl] and press [X], then release both keys.

QUICK TIP
You can also paste a file by right-clicking an empty area in the File list and then clicking Paste. To use the keyboard, press and hold [Ctrl] and press [V], then release both keys.

1. **In the Address bar, click Removable Disk (H:) (or the drive name and letter for your USB flash drive)**
2. **Click the Oceania Meeting.rtf document to select it**
3. **Click the Organize button on the toolbar, then click Cut**
   The icon representing the cut file becomes lighter in color, indicating you have cut it, as shown in Figure B-17. You navigate to your Documents library, in preparation for pasting the cut document there.
4. **In the Navigation Pane, under Libraries, click Documents**
5. **Click the Organize button on the toolbar, then click Paste**
   The Oceania Meeting.rtf document appears in your Documents library. See Figure B-18. The filename could be clearer, to help you remember that it contains notes from your meeting.
6. **With the Oceania Meeting.rtf file selected, click the Organize button on the toolbar, then click Rename**
   The filename is highlighted. In a window, the file extension cannot change because it identifies the file to WordPad. If you delete the file extension, the file cannot be opened. You could type a new name to replace the old one, but you decide to add the word "Notes" to the end of the filename instead.
7. **Click the I after the "g" in "Meeting", press [Spacebar], then type Notes, as shown in Figure B-19, then press [Enter]**
   You changed the name of the document copy in the Documents library. The filename now reads Oceania Meeting Notes.rtf.
8. **Close the window**

FIGURE B-17: **Cutting a file**

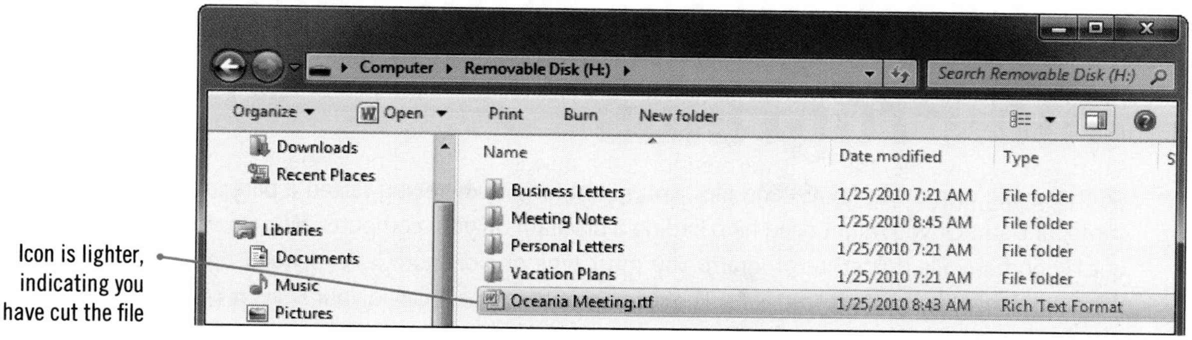

FIGURE B-18: **Pasted file in Documents library**

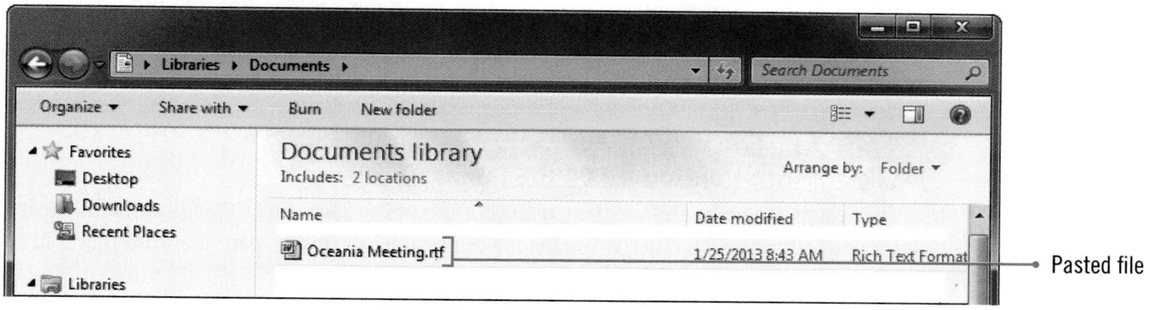

FIGURE B-19: **Renaming a file**

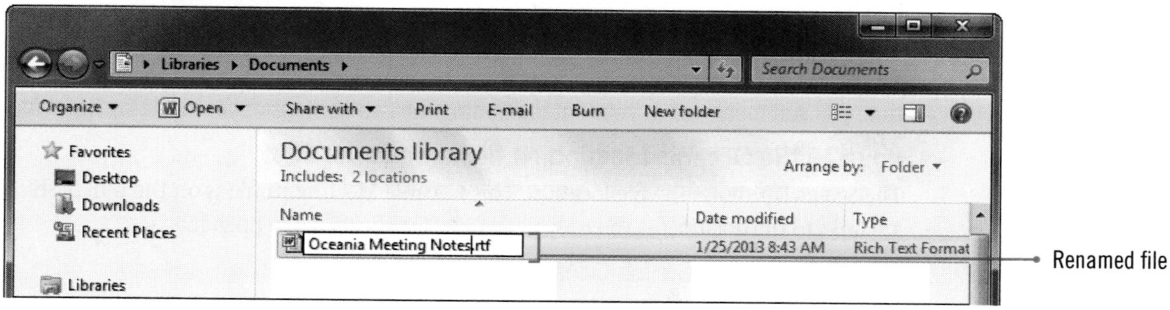

Using drag and drop to copy or move files to new locations

You can also use the mouse to copy a file and place the copy in a new location. **Drag and drop** is a technique in which you use your pointing device to drag a file or folder into a different folder and then drop it, or let go of the mouse button, to place it in that folder. Using drag and drop does not copy your file to the clipboard. If you drag and drop a file to a folder on another drive, Windows *copies* the file. See Figure B-20. However, if you drag and drop a file to a folder on the same drive, Windows 7 *moves* the file into that folder instead. If you want to move a file to another drive, hold down [Shift] while you drag and drop. If you want to copy a file to another folder on the same drive, hold down [Ctrl] while you drag and drop.

FIGURE B-20: **Copying a file using drag and drop**

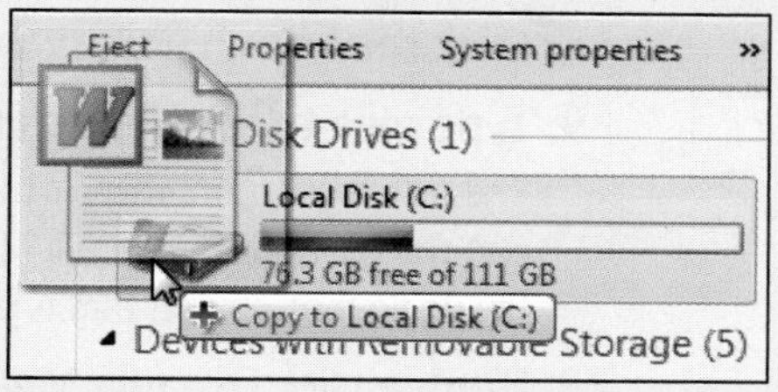

UNIT B
Windows 7

Searching for Files, Folders, and Programs

After copying or moving folders and files, you might forget where you stored a particular folder or file, its name, or both. Or you might need help finding a program on your computer. **Windows Search** helps you quickly find any file, folder, or program. You must type one or more letter sequences or words that help Windows 7 identify the item you want. The search text you type is called your **search criteria.** Your search criteria can be a filename, part of a filename, or any other characters you choose. Windows 7 will find files with that information in its name or with that information inside the file. For example, if you type "word," Windows 7 will find the program Microsoft Word, any documents with "word" in its title, or any document with "word" inside the file. To search your entire computer, including its attached drives, you can use the Search box on the Start menu. To search within a particular folder, you can use the Search box in a Windows Explorer window. You want to locate the copy of the Oceania Meeting Notes.rtf document so you can print it for a colleague.

STEPS

1. **Click the Start button on the taskbar**
   The Search programs and files box at the bottom of the Start menu already contains the insertion point, ready for you to type search criteria. You begin your search by typing a part of a word that is in the filename.
2. **Type me**
   Even before you finish typing the word "meeting", the Start menu lists all programs, files, and Control Panel items that have the letters "me" in their title or somewhere inside the file or the file properties. See Figure B-21. Your search results will differ, depending on the programs and files on your computer. **File properties** are details that Windows stores about a file. Windows arranges the search results into categories.
3. **Type e**
   The search results narrow to only the files that contain "mee". The search results become more specific every time you add more text to your criteria finding the two versions of your meeting notes file. See Figure B-22.
4. **Point to the Oceania Meeting.rtf filename under Files**
   The ScreenTip shows the file location. This Oceania Meeting.rtf file is on the USB flash drive. The filenames are links to the document. You only need to single-click a file to open it.
5. **Under Documents, click Oceania Meeting Notes.rtf**
   The file opens in WordPad.
6. **Click the Close button in the program window's title bar**
   You can search in a folder or on a drive using the search box in any Windows Explorer window.
7. **Click , click Computer, in the Navigation pane click Removable Disk (H:) (or the drive name and letter for your USB flash drive)**
8. **Click the Search Removable Disk (H:) text box, to the right of the Address bar**
9. **Type mee to list all files and folders on your USB flash drive that contain "mee"**
   The search criterion, mee, is highlighted in the filenames. The results include the folder called Meeting Notes and the file named Oceania Meeting.rtf. Because you navigated to your USB flash drive, Windows only lists the document version that is on that drive. See Figure B-23.
10. **Double-click Oceania Meeting.rtf in the File list to open the document file in WordPad, view the file, close WordPad, then close the Windows Explorer window**

QUICK TIP
Search text is not case sensitive. Typing lowercase "mee", you will still find items that start with "Mee" or "mee".

TROUBLE
Your file might open in another program on your computer that reads RTF files. You can continue with the lesson.

TROUBLE
If you do not have a USB flash drive, click another storage location in the Navigation pane.

FIGURE B-21: **Searching on criterion "me"**

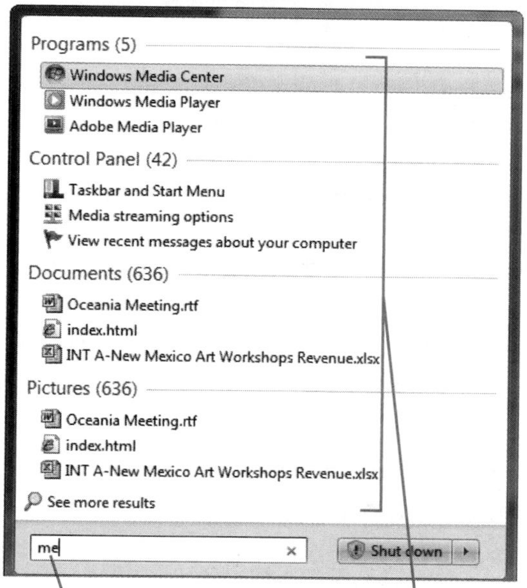

FIGURE B-22: **Searching on criterion "mee"**

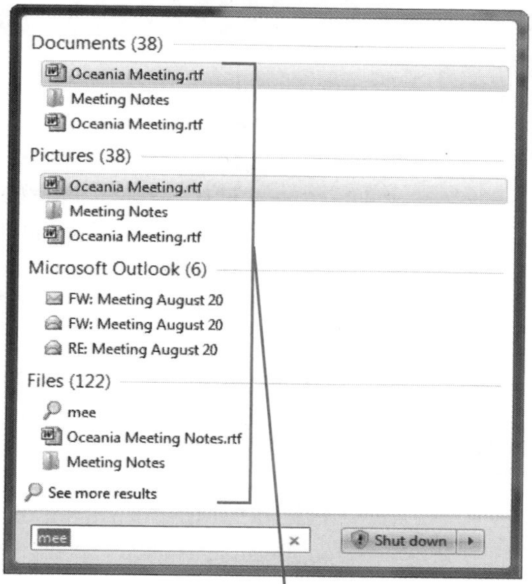

FIGURE B-23: **Searching using the Search Computer text box in folder window**

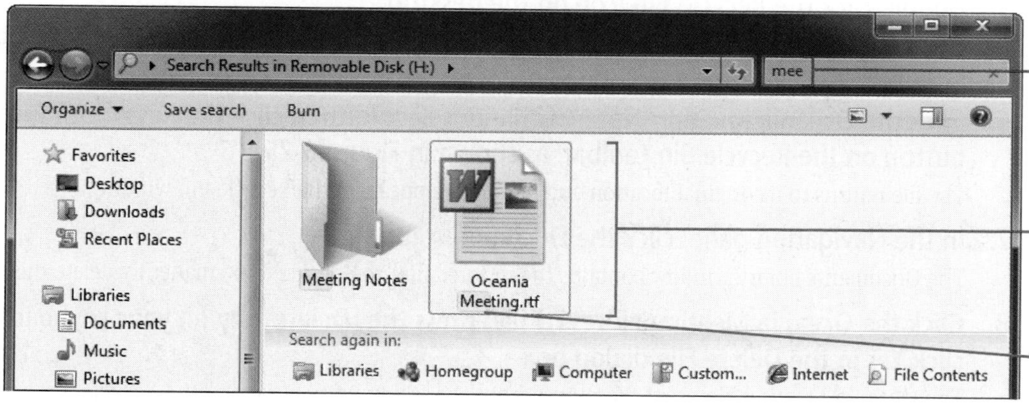

Performing more advanced searches

To locate all files that have the same file extension (such as .rtf), type the file extension as your search criterion. If you want to locate files created by a certain person, use the first name, last name, or first and last name as your search criteria. If you want to locate files created on a certain date, type the date (for example, 7/9/2012) as your search criterion. If you remember the title in a document, type the title as your search criterion. If you have created e-mail contacts in your Contacts folder, you can type the person's name to find his or her e-mail address.

UNIT
B
Windows 7

Deleting and Restoring Files

If you no longer need a folder or file, you can delete (or remove) it from the storage device. By regularly deleting files and folders you no longer need and emptying the Recycle Bin, you free up valuable storage space on your computer. This also keeps your computer uncluttered. Windows 7 places folders and files you delete from your hard drive in the Recycle Bin. If you delete a folder, Windows 7 removes the folder as well as all files and subfolders stored in it. If you later discover that you need a deleted file or folder, you can restore it to its original location, but only if you have not yet emptied the Recycle Bin. Emptying the Recycle Bin permanently removes the deleted folders and files from your computer. However, files and folders you delete from a removable drive, such as a USB flash drive, do not go to the Recycle Bin. They are immediately and permanently deleted and cannot be restored. You delete the meeting notes copy saved in the Documents library and then restore it.

STEPS

1. **Click the Start button on the taskbar, then click Documents**
   Your Documents library opens.
2. **Click Oceania Meeting Notes.rtf to select it, click the Organize button on the toolbar, then click Delete**
   The Delete File dialog box opens so you can confirm the deletion, as shown in Figure B-24.
3. **Click Yes**
   You deleted the file from the Documents library. Windows moved it into the Recycle Bin.
4. **Click the Minimize button on the window's title bar and examine the Recycle Bin icon**
   The Recycle Bin icon appears to contain crumpled paper. This tells you that the Recycle Bin contains deleted folders and files.
5. **Double-click the Recycle Bin icon on the desktop**
   The Recycle Bin window opens and displays any previously deleted folders and files, including the Oceania Meeting Notes.rtf file.
6. **Click the Oceania Meeting Notes.rtf file to select it, then click the Restore this item button on the Recycle Bin toolbar, as shown in Figure B-25**
   The file returns to its original location and no longer appears in the Recycle Bin window.
7. **In the Navigation pane, click the Documents library**
   The Documents library window contains the restored file. You decide to permanently delete this file.
8. **Click the Oceania Meeting Notes.rtf file, press the [Delete] key on your keyboard, then click Yes in the Delete File dialog box**
   The Oceania Meeting Notes.rtf file moves from the Documents library to the Recycle Bin. You decide to permanently delete all documents in the Recycle Bin.
   NOTE: If you are using a computer that belongs to someone else, or that is in a computer lab, make sure you have permission to empty the Recycle Bin before proceeding with the next step.
9. **Minimize the window, double-click the Recycle Bin, click the Empty the Recycle Bin button on the toolbar, click Yes in the dialog box, then close all open windows**

QUICK TIP
If the Recycle Bin icon does not contain crumpled paper, then it is empty.

QUICK TIP
To delete a file completely in one action, click the file to select it, press and hold [Shift], then press [Delete]. A message will ask if you want to permanently delete the file. If you click Yes, Windows deletes the file without sending it to the Recycle Bin. Use caution, however, because you cannot restore the file.

FIGURE B-24: **Delete File dialog box**

FIGURE B-25: **Restoring a file from the Recycle Bin**

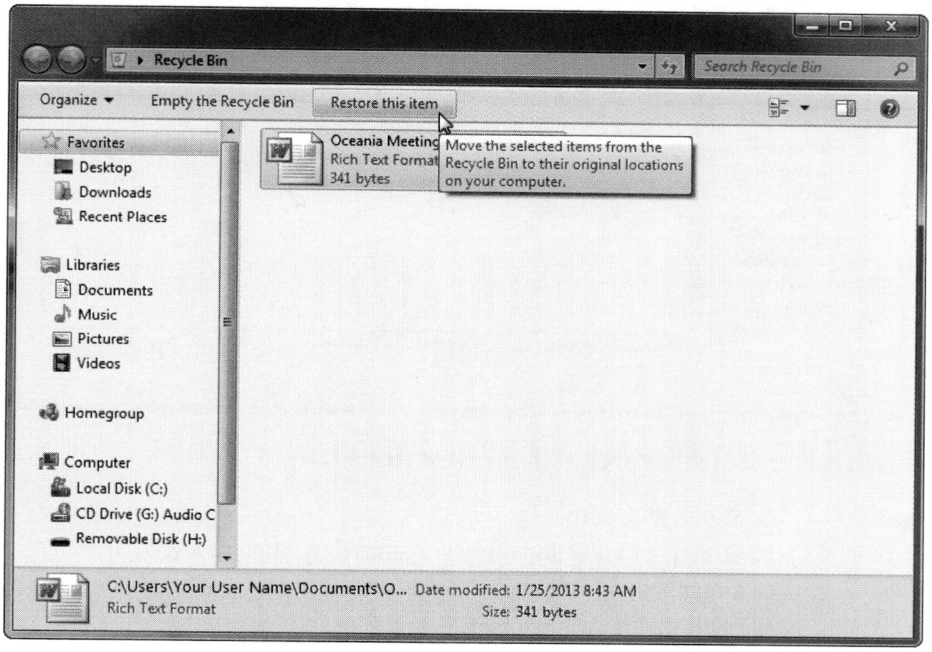

Selecting more than one file

You might want to select a group of files or folders in order to cut, copy, or delete them all at once. To select a group of items that are next to each other in a window, click the first item in the group, press and hold [Shift], then click the last item in the group. Both items you click and all the items between them become selected. To select files that are not next to each other, click the first file, press and hold [Ctrl], then click the other items you want to select as a group. Then you can copy, cut, or delete the group of files or folders you selected.

Practice

Concepts Review

For current SAM information, including versions and content details, visit SAM Central (http://samcentral.course.com). If you have a SAM user profile, you may have access to hands-on instruction, practice, and assessment of the skills covered in this unit. Since various versions of SAM are supported throughout the life of this text, check with your instructor for the correct instructions and URL/Web site for accessing assignments.

Label the elements of the Windows 7 window shown in Figure B-26.

FIGURE B-26

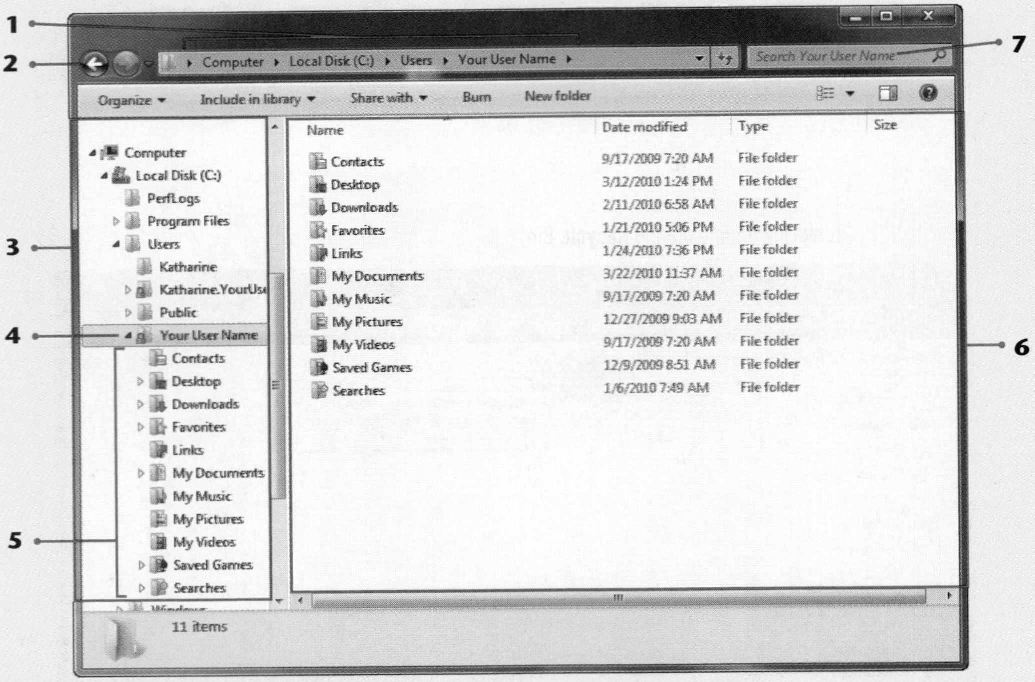

Match each term with the statement that best describes it.

8. File management
9. File extension
10. Address bar
11. Path
12. Library
13. Toolbar
14. File hierarchy

a. Shows file's path
b. Structure of files and folders organized in different levels
c. Describes a file's location in the file hierarchy
d. Skills that help you organize your files and folders
e. Contains buttons in a Windows Explorer window
f. A three- or four-letter sequence, preceded by a period, that identifies the type of file
g. Gathers files and folders from different computer locations

Select the best answer from the list of choices.

15. The way your files appear in the Details window is determined by the:
a. Path.
b. View.
c. Subfolder.
d. Criterion.

16. When you move a file:
a. It remains in its original location.
b. It is no longer in its original location.
c. It is copied to another location.
d. It is no longer in your file hierarchy.

17. The text you type in the Search programs and files box on the Start menu is called:
a. Search criteria.
b. RAM.
c. Sorting.
d. Clipboard.

18. Which of the following is not a window section?
- **a.** Address bar
- **b.** File list
- **c.** Navigation pane
- **d.** Clipboard

19. Which part of a window lets you see a file's contents without opening the file?
- **a.** File list
- **b.** Preview pane
- **c.** Navigation pane
- **d.** Address bar

20. In a file hierarchy, a folder inside another folder is called a:
- **a.** Subfolder.
- **b.** Internal hard disk.
- **c.** Clipboard.
- **d.** Path.

21. After you delete a file from your hard disk, it is automatically placed in the:
- **a.** USB flash drive.
- **b.** Clipboard.
- **c.** Recycle bin.
- **d.** Search box.

22. When you copy a file, it is automatically placed on the:
- **a.** Preview pane.
- **b.** My Documents folder.
- **c.** Hierarchy.
- **d.** Clipboard.

Skills Review

1. Understand folders and files.
- **a.** Assume that you sell books as a home business. How would you organize your folders and files using a file hierarchy? How would you use folders and subfolders? Draw a diagram and write a short paragraph explaining your answer.

2. Create and save a file.
- **a.** Connect your USB flash drive to a USB port on your computer, then open WordPad from the All Programs menu.
- **b.** Type **Marketing Plan: Oceania Tours** as the title, then start a new line.
- **c.** Type your name, then press [Enter] twice.
- **d.** Create the following list:

  Brochures
  Direct e-mail
  Web ads
  Travel conventions
- **e.** Save the WordPad file with the filename **Oceania Marketing Plan.rtf** on your USB flash drive.
- **f.** View the filename in the WordPad title bar, then close WordPad.

3. Explore the files and folders on your computer.
- **a.** Open a Windows Explorer window that shows the contents of your computer.
- **b.** Use the File list to navigate to your USB flash drive. (If you do not have a USB flash drive, navigate to your Documents library using the Navigation pane.)
- **c.** Use the Address bar to navigate to Computer again.
- **d.** Use the Navigation pane to navigate to your hard drive.
- **e.** Use the File list to open the Users folder, and then open the folder that represents your user name.
- **f.** Open the My Documents folder. (*Hint*: The path is Local Disk (C:) ▸ Users ▸ [Your User Name] ▸ My Documents.)
- **g.** Use the Navigation pane to navigate back to your computer contents.

4. Change file and folder views.
- **a.** Navigate to your USB flash drive using the method of your choice.
- **b.** View its contents as large icons.
- **c.** Use the View slider to view the drive contents in all the other seven views.
- **d.** Use the Change your view button to cycle through the five available views.
- **e.** Open the Preview pane, then click a file and view its preview. Repeat with two more files.
- **f.** Close the Preview pane.

Skills Review (continued)

5. **Open, edit, and save files.**
   - **a.** Open WordPad.
   - **b.** Use the Open dialog box to open the Oceania Marketing Plan.rtf document you created.
   - **c.** After the text "Travel conventions," add a line with the text **Canadian magazines**.
   - **d.** Save the document and close WordPad.
6. **Copy files.**
   - **a.** In the Windows Explorer window, navigate to your USB flash drive if necessary.
   - **b.** Copy the Oceania Marketing Plan.rtf document.
   - **c.** Create a new folder named **Marketing** on your USB flash drive, then open the folder. (If you don't have a USB flash drive, create the folder in your Documents library.)
   - **d.** Paste the document copy in the new folder.
7. **Move and rename files.**
   - **a.** Navigate to your USB flash drive.
   - **b.** Select the original Oceania Marketing Plan.rtf document, then cut it.
   - **c.** Navigate to your Documents library and paste the file there.
   - **d.** Rename the file **Oceania Marketing Plan - Backup.rtf**.
8. **Search for files, folders, and programs.**
   - **a.** Use the Search programs and files box on the Start menu to enter the search criterion **ma**.
   - **b.** Change your search criterion so it reads **mar**.
   - **c.** Open the backup copy of your Oceania Marketing Plan document from the Start menu, then close WordPad.
   - **d.** In Windows Explorer, navigate to your Documents library, then use the criterion **mar** in the Search Documents box.
   - **e.** Open the backup copy of the Oceania Marketing Plan document from the File list, then close WordPad.
9. **Delete and restore files.**
   - **a.** Navigate to your Documents library if necessary.
   - **b.** Delete the Oceania Marketing Plan - Backup.rtf file.
   - **c.** Open the Recycle Bin, and restore the document to its original location, navigate to your Documents library, then move the Oceania Marketing Plan - Backup file to your USB flash drive.

Independent Challenge 1

To meet the needs of pet owners in your town, you have opened a pet-sitting business named PetCare. Customers hire you to care for their pets in their own homes when the pet owners go on vacation. To promote your new business, you want to develop a newspaper ad and a flyer.

- **a.** Connect your USB flash drive to your computer, if necessary.
- **b.** Create a new folder named **PetCare** on your USB flash drive.
- **c.** In the PetCare folder, create two subfolders named **Advertising** and **Flyers**.
- **d.** Use WordPad to create a short ad for your local newspaper that describes your business:
  - Use the name of the business as the title for your document.
  - Write a short paragraph about the business. Include a fictitious location, street address, and phone number.
  - After the paragraph, type your name.
- **e.** Save the WordPad document with the filename **Newspaper Ad** in the Advertising folder, then close the document and exit WordPad.
- **f.** Open a Windows Explorer window, and navigate to the Advertising folder.
- **g.** View the contents in at least three different views, then choose the view option that you prefer.
- **h.** Copy the Newspaper Ad.rtf file, and paste a copy in the Flyers folder.
- **i.** Rename the copy **Newspaper Ad Backup.rtf**.
- **j.** Close the folder.

Independent Challenge 2

As a freelance editor for several national publishers, you depend on your computer to meet critical deadlines. Whenever you encounter a computer problem, you contact a computer consultant who helps you resolve the problem. This consultant asked you to document, or keep records of, your computer's current settings.

a. Connect your USB flash drive to your computer, if necessary.
b. Open the Computer window so that you can view information on your drives and other installed hardware.
c. View the window contents using three different views, then choose the one you prefer.
d. Open WordPad and create a document with the title **My Hardware Documentation** and your name on separate lines.
e. List the names of the hard drive (or drives), devices with removable storage, and any other hardware devices, installed on the computer you are using. Also include the total size and amount of free space on your hard drive(s) and removable storage drive(s). (*Hint*: If you need to check the Computer window for this information, use the taskbar button for the Computer window to view your drives, then use the WordPad taskbar button to return to WordPad.)

Advanced Challenge Exercise

- Navigate your computer's file hierarchy, and determine its various levels.
- On paper, draw a diagram showing your file hierarchy, starting with Computer at the top, and going down at least four levels if available.

f. Save the WordPad document with the filename **My Hardware Documentation** on your USB flash drive.
g. Preview your document, print your WordPad document, then close WordPad.

Independent Challenge 3

You are an attorney at Lopez, Rickland, and Willgor, a large law firm. You participate in your firm's community outreach program by speaking at career days in area high schools. You teach students about career opportunities available in the field of law. You want to create a folder structure on your USB flash drive to store the files for each session.

a. Connect your USB flash drive to your computer, then open the window for your USB flash drive.
b. Create a folder named **Career Days**.
c. In the Career Days folder, create a subfolder named **Mather High**.

Advanced Challenge Exercise

- In the Mather High folder, create subfolders named **Class Outline** and **Visual Aids**.
- Rename the Visual Aids folder **Class Handouts**.
- Create a new folder named **Interactive Presentations** in the Class Handouts subfolder.

d. Close the Mather High window.
e. Use WordPad to create a document with the title **Career Areas** and your name on separate lines, and the following list of items:
Current Opportunities:
Attorney
Corrections Officer
Forensic Scientist
Paralegal
Judge
f. Save the WordPad document with the filename **Careers Listing.rtf** in the Mather High folder. (*Hint:* After you switch to your USB flash drive in the Save As dialog box, open the Career Days folder, then open the Mather High folder before saving the file.)
g. Close WordPad.

Independent Challenge 3 (continued)

h. Open WordPad and the Careers Listing document again, then add **Court Reporter** to the bottom of the list, then save the file and close WordPad.
i. Using pencil and paper, draw a diagram of your new folder structure.
j. Use the Start menu to search your computer using the search criterion **car**. Locate the Careers Listing.rtf document in the list, and use the link to open the file.
k. Close the file.

Real Life Independent Challenge

Think of a hobby or volunteer activity that you do now, or one that you would like to do. You will use your computer to help you manage your plans or ideas for this activity.

a. Using paper and a pencil, sketch a folder structure using at least two subfolders that you could create on your USB flash drive to contain your documents for this activity.
b. Connect your USB flash drive to your computer, then open the window for your USB flash drive.
c. Create the folder structure for your activity, using your sketch as a reference.
d. Think of at least three tasks that you can do to further your work in your chosen activity.
e. Open WordPad and create a document with the title **Next Steps** at the top of the page and your name on the next line.
f. List the three tasks, then save the file in one of the folders you created on your USB flash drive, using the title **To Do.rtf**.
g. Close WordPad, then open a Windows Explorer window for the folder where you stored the document.
h. Create a copy of the file, give the copy a new name, then place a copy of the document in your Documents library.
i. Delete the document copy from your Documents library.
j. Open the Recycle Bin window, and restore the document to the Documents library.

Visual Workshop

You are a technical support specialist at Emergency Services. The company supplies medical staff members to hospital emergency rooms in Los Angeles. You need to respond to your company's employee questions quickly and thoroughly. You decide that it is time to evaluate and reorganize the folder structure on your computer. That way, you'll be able to respond more quickly to staff requests. Create the folder structure shown in Figure B-27 on your USB flash drive. As you work, use WordPad to prepare a simple outline of the steps you follow to create the folder structure. Add your name to the document, and store it in an appropriate location.

FIGURE B-27

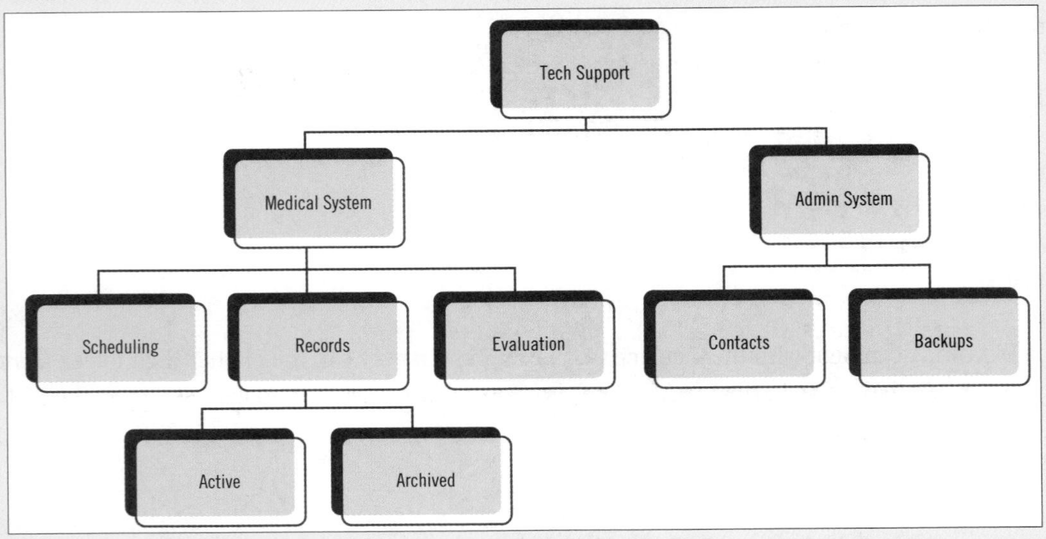

UNIT
A
Office 2010

Getting Started with Microsoft Office 2010

Files You Will Need:

OFFICE A-1.xlsx

Microsoft Office 2010 is a group of software programs designed to help you create documents, collaborate with coworkers, and track and analyze information. Each program is designed so you can work quickly and efficiently to create professional-looking results. You use different Office programs to accomplish specific tasks, such as writing a letter or producing a sales presentation, yet all the programs have a similar look and feel. Once you become familiar with one program, you'll find it easy to transfer your knowledge to the others. This unit introduces you to the most frequently used programs in Office, as well as common features they all share.

OBJECTIVES

- Understand the Office 2010 suite
- Start and exit an Office program
- View the Office 2010 user interface
- Create and save a file
- Open a file and save it with a new name
- View and print your work
- Get Help and close a file

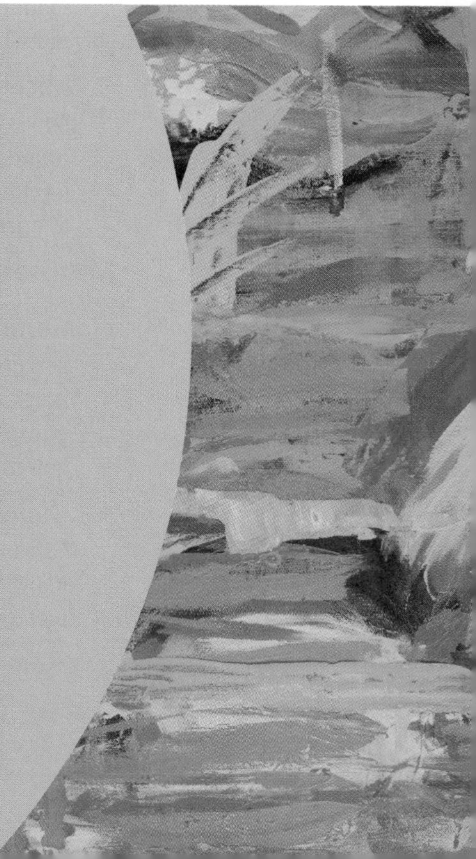

UNIT
A
Office 2010

Understanding the Office 2010 Suite

Microsoft Office 2010 features an intuitive, context-sensitive user interface, so you can get up to speed faster and use advanced features with greater ease. The programs in Office are bundled together in a group called a **suite** (although you can also purchase them separately). The Office suite is available in several configurations, but all include Word, Excel, and PowerPoint. Other configurations include Access, Outlook, Publisher, and other programs. Each program in Office is best suited for completing specific types of tasks, though there is some overlap in capabilities.

DETAILS

The Office programs covered in this book include:

- **Microsoft Word 2010**
  When you need to create any kind of text-based document, such as a memo, newsletter, or multipage report, Word is the program to use. You can easily make your documents look great by inserting eye-catching graphics and using formatting tools such as themes, which are available in most Office programs. **Themes** are predesigned combinations of color and formatting attributes you can apply to a document. The Word document shown in Figure A-1 was formatted with the Solstice theme.
- **Microsoft Excel 2010**
  Excel is the perfect solution when you need to work with numeric values and make calculations. It puts the power of formulas, functions, charts, and other analytical tools into the hands of every user, so you can analyze sales projections, calculate loan payments, and present your findings in style. The Excel worksheet shown in Figure A-1 tracks personal expenses. Because Excel automatically recalculates results whenever a value changes, the information is always up to date. A chart illustrates how the monthly expenses are broken down.
- **Microsoft PowerPoint 2010**
  Using PowerPoint, it's easy to create powerful presentations complete with graphics, transitions, and even a soundtrack. Using professionally designed themes and clip art, you can quickly and easily create dynamic slide shows such as the one shown in Figure A-1.
- **Microsoft Access 2010**
  Access helps you keep track of large amounts of quantitative data, such as product inventories or employee records. The form shown in Figure A-1 was created for a grocery store inventory database. Employees use the form to enter data about each item. Using Access enables employees to quickly find specific information such as price and quantity without hunting through store shelves and stockrooms.

Microsoft Office has benefits beyond the power of each program, including:

- **Common user interface: Improving business processes**
  Because the Office suite programs have a similar **interface**, or look and feel, your experience using one program's tools makes it easy to learn those in the other programs. In addition, Office documents are **compatible** with one another, meaning that you can easily incorporate, or **integrate**, an Excel chart into a PowerPoint slide, or an Access table into a Word document.
- **Collaboration: Simplifying how people work together**
  Office recognizes the way people do business today, and supports the emphasis on communication and knowledge sharing within companies and across the globe. All Office programs include the capability to incorporate feedback—called **online collaboration**—across the Internet or a company network.

FIGURE A-1: Microsoft Office 2010 documents

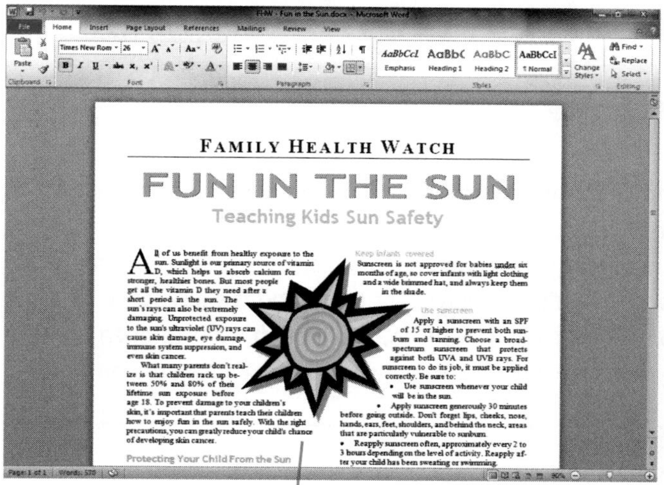

Newsletter created in Word

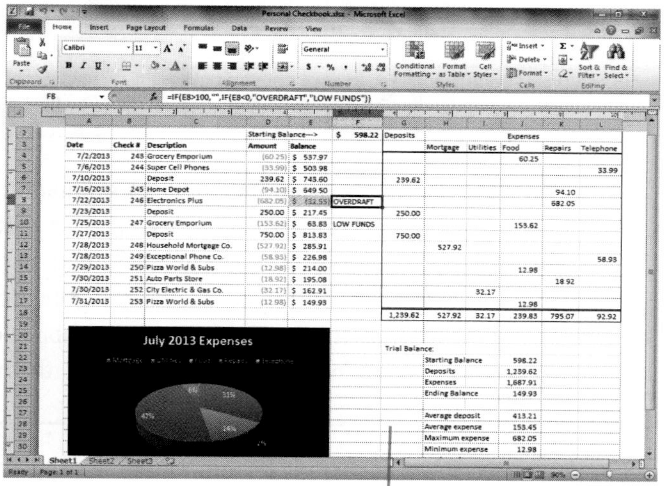

Checkbook register created in Excel

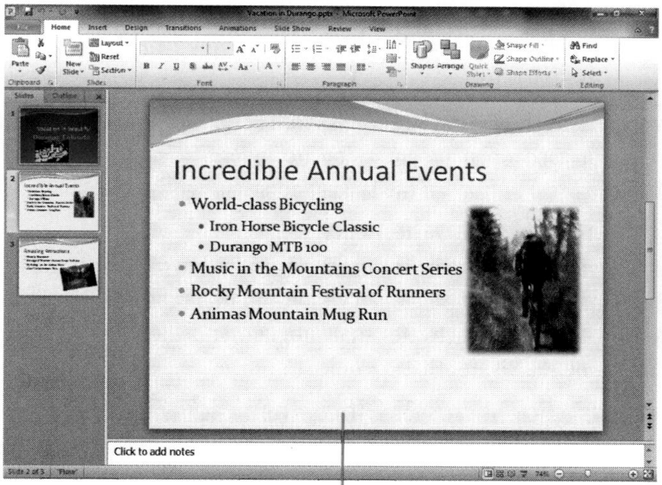

Tourism presentation created in PowerPoint

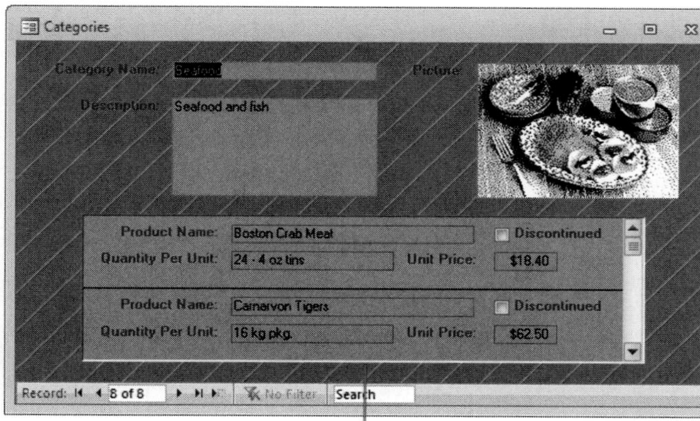

Store inventory form created in Access

Deciding which program to use

Every Office program includes tools that go far beyond what you might expect. For example, although Excel is primarily designed for making calculations, you can use it to create a database. So when you're planning a project, how do you decide which Office program to use? The general rule of thumb is to use the program best suited for your intended task, and make use of supporting tools in the program if you need them. Word is best for creating text-based documents, Excel is best for making mathematical calculations, PowerPoint is best for preparing presentations, and Access is best for managing quantitative data. Although the capabilities of Office are so vast that you *could* create an inventory in Excel or a budget in Word, you'll find greater flexibility and efficiency by using the program designed for the task. And remember, you can always create a file in one program, and then insert it in a document in another program when you need to, such as including sales projections (Excel) in a memo (Word).

UNIT A
Office 2010

Starting and Exiting an Office Program

The first step in using an Office program is to open, or **launch**, it on your computer. The easiest ways to launch a program are to click the Start button on the Windows taskbar or to double-click an icon on your desktop. You can have multiple programs open on your computer simultaneously, and you can move between open programs by clicking the desired program or document button on the taskbar or by using the [Alt][Tab] keyboard shortcut combination. When working, you'll often want to open multiple programs in Office and switch among them as you work. Begin by launching a few Office programs now.

STEPS

QUICK TIP
You can also launch a program by double-clicking a desktop icon or clicking the program name on the Start menu.

QUICK TIP
It is not necessary to close one program before opening another.

QUICK TIP
As you work in Windows, your computer adapts to your activities. You may notice that after clicking the Start button, the name of the program you want to open appears in the Start menu above All Programs; if so, you can click it to start the program.

TROUBLE
If you don't have Access installed on your computer, proceed to the next lesson.

1. **Click the Start button on the taskbar**
   The Start menu opens. If the taskbar is hidden, you can display it by pointing to the bottom of the screen. Depending on your taskbar property settings, the taskbar may be displayed at all times, or only when you point to that area of the screen. For more information, or to change your taskbar properties, consult your instructor or technical support person.
2. **Click All Programs, scroll down if necessary in the All Programs menu, click Microsoft Office as shown in Figure A-2, then click Microsoft Word 2010**
   Word 2010 starts, and the program window opens on your screen.
3. **Click on the taskbar, click All Programs, click Microsoft Office, then click Microsoft Excel 2010**
   Excel 2010 starts, and the program window opens, as shown in Figure A-3. Word is no longer visible, but it remains open. The taskbar displays a button for each open program and document. Because this Excel document is **active**, or in front and available, the Excel button on the taskbar appears slightly lighter.
4. **Point to the Word program button on the taskbar, then click**
   The Word program window is now in front. When the Aero feature is turned on in Windows 7, pointing to a program button on the taskbar displays a thumbnail version of each open window in that program above the program button. Clicking a program button on the taskbar activates that program and the most recently active document. Clicking a thumbnail of a document activates that document.
5. **Click on the taskbar, click All Programs, click Microsoft Office, then click Microsoft PowerPoint 2010**
   PowerPoint 2010 starts and becomes the active program.
6. **Click the Excel program button on the taskbar**
   Excel is now the active program.
7. **Click on the taskbar, click All Programs, click Microsoft Office, then click Microsoft Access 2010**
   Access 2010 starts and becomes the active program. Now all four Office programs are open at the same time.
8. **Click Exit on the navigation bar in the Access program window, as shown in Figure A-4**
   Access closes, leaving Excel active and Word and PowerPoint open.

Using shortcut keys to move between Office programs

As an alternative to the Windows taskbar, you can use a keyboard shortcut to move among open Office programs. The [Alt][Tab] keyboard combination lets you either switch quickly to the next open program or file or choose one from a gallery. To switch immediately to the next open program or file, press [Alt][Tab]. To choose from all open programs and files, press and hold [Alt], then press and release [Tab] without releasing [Alt]. A gallery opens on screen, displaying the filename and a thumbnail image of each open program and file, as well as of the desktop. Each time you press [Tab] while holding [Alt], the selection cycles to the next open file or location. Release [Alt] when the program, file, or location you want to activate is selected.

FIGURE A-2: Start menu

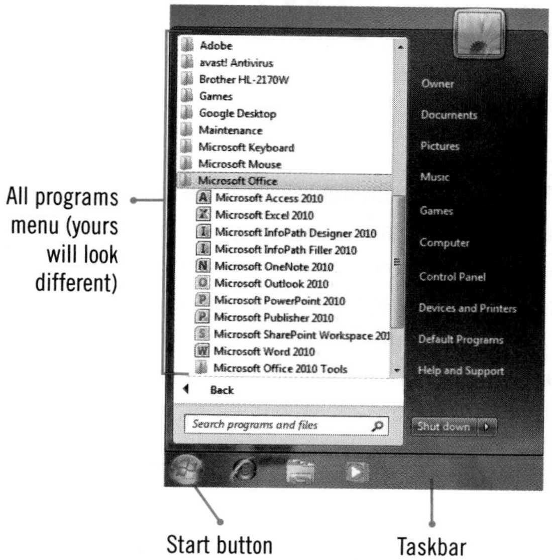

FIGURE A-3: Excel program window and Windows taskbar

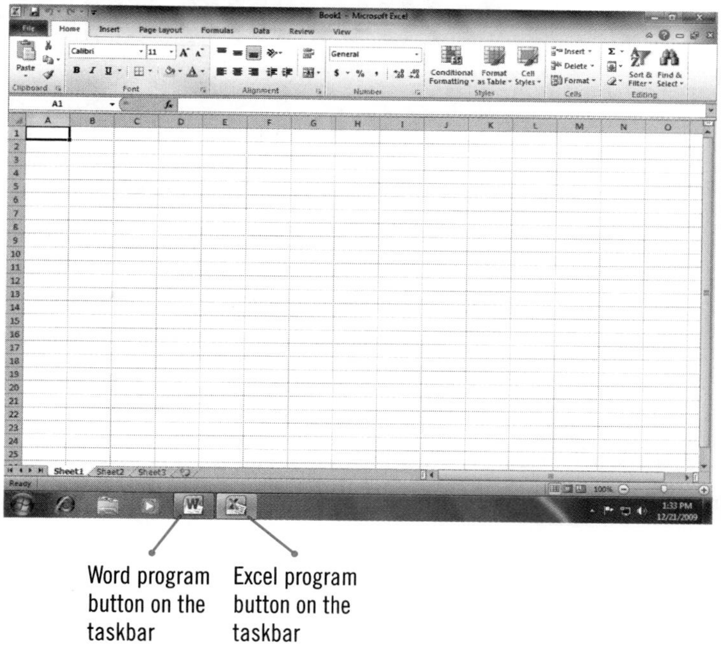

FIGURE A-4: Access program window

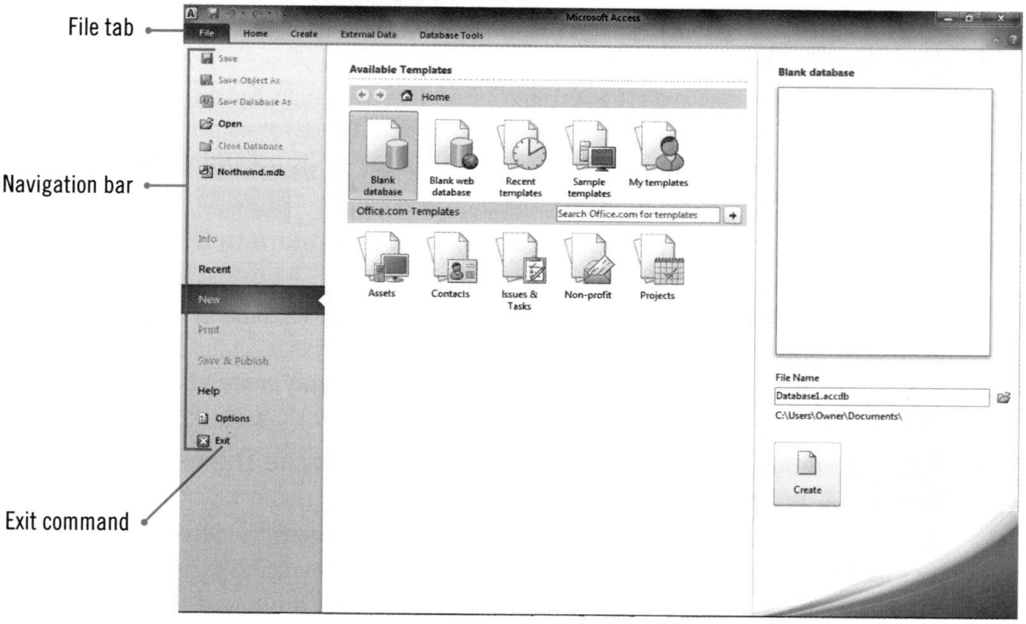

Windows Live and Microsoft Office Web Apps

All Office programs include the capability to incorporate feedback—called online collaboration—across the Internet or a company network. Using **cloud computing** (work done in a virtual environment), you can take advantage of Web programs called Microsoft Office Web Apps, which are simplified versions of the programs found in the Microsoft Office 2010 suite. Because these programs are online, they take up no computer disk space and are accessed using Windows Live SkyDrive, a free service from Microsoft. Using Windows Live SkyDrive, you and your colleagues can create and store documents in a "cloud" and make the documents available to whomever you grant access. To use Windows Live SkyDrive, you need a free Windows Live ID, which you obtain at the Windows Live Web site. You can find more information in the "Working with Windows Live and Office Web Apps" appendix.

UNIT A
Office 2010

Viewing the Office 2010 User Interface

One of the benefits of using Office is that the programs have much in common, making them easy to learn and making it simple to move from one to another. Individual Office programs have always shared many features, but the innovations in the Office 2010 user interface mean even greater similarity among them all. That means you can also use your knowledge of one program to get up to speed in another. A **user interface** is a collective term for all the ways you interact with a software program. The user interface in Office 2010 provides intuitive ways to choose commands, work with files, and navigate in the program window. Familiarize yourself with some of the common interface elements in Office by examining the PowerPoint program window.

STEPS

QUICK TIP
In addition to the standard tabs on the Ribbon, **contextual tabs** open when needed to complete a specific task; they appear in an accent color and close when no longer needed. To minimize the display of the buttons and commands on tabs, click the Minimize the Ribbon button on the right end of the Ribbon.

1. **Click the PowerPoint program button on the taskbar**
   PowerPoint becomes the active program. Refer to Figure A-5 to identify common elements of the Office user interface. The **document window** occupies most of the screen. In PowerPoint, a blank slide appears in the document window, so you can build your slide show. At the top of every Office program window is a **title bar** that displays the document name and program name. Below the title bar is the **Ribbon**, which displays commands you're likely to need for the current task. Commands are organized onto **tabs**. The tab names appear at the top of the Ribbon, and the active tab appears in front. The Ribbon in every Office program includes tabs specific to the program, but all Office programs include a File tab and Home tab on the left end of the Ribbon.

2. **Click the File tab**
   The File tab opens, displaying **Backstage view**. The navigation bar on the left side of Backstage view contains commands to perform actions common to most Office programs, such as opening a file, saving a file, and closing the current program. Just above the File tab is the **Quick Access toolbar**, which also includes buttons for common Office commands.

3. **Click the File tab again to close Backstage view and return to the document window, then click the Design tab on the Ribbon**
   To display a different tab, you click the tab on the Ribbon. Each tab contains related commands arranged into **groups** to make features easy to find. On the Design tab, the Themes group displays available design themes in a **gallery**, or visual collection of choices you can browse. Many groups contain a **dialog box launcher**, an icon you can click to open a dialog box or task pane from which to choose related commands.

QUICK TIP
Live Preview is available in many galleries and menus throughout Office.

4. **Move the mouse pointer over the Angles theme in the Themes group as shown in Figure A-6, but do not click the mouse button**
   The Angles theme is temporarily applied to the slide in the document window. However, because you did not click the theme, you did not permanently change the slide. With the **Live Preview** feature, you can point to a choice, see the results right in the document, and then decide if you want to make the change.

QUICK TIP
If you accidentally click a theme, click the Undo button on the Quick Access toolbar.

5. **Move away from the Ribbon and towards the slide**
   If you had clicked the Angles theme, it would be applied to this slide. Instead, the slide remains unchanged.

QUICK TIP
You can also use the Zoom button in the Zoom group on the View tab to enlarge or reduce a document's appearance.

6. **Point to the Zoom slider on the status bar, then drag to the right until the Zoom level reads 166%**
   The slide display is enlarged. Zoom tools are located on the status bar. You can drag the slider or click the Zoom In or Zoom Out buttons to zoom in or out on an area of interest. **Zooming in**, or choosing a higher percentage, makes a document appear bigger on screen, but less of it fits on the screen at once; **zooming out**, or choosing a lower percentage, lets you see more of the document but at a reduced size.

7. **Drag on the status bar to the left until the Zoom level reads 73%**

FIGURE A-5: PowerPoint program window

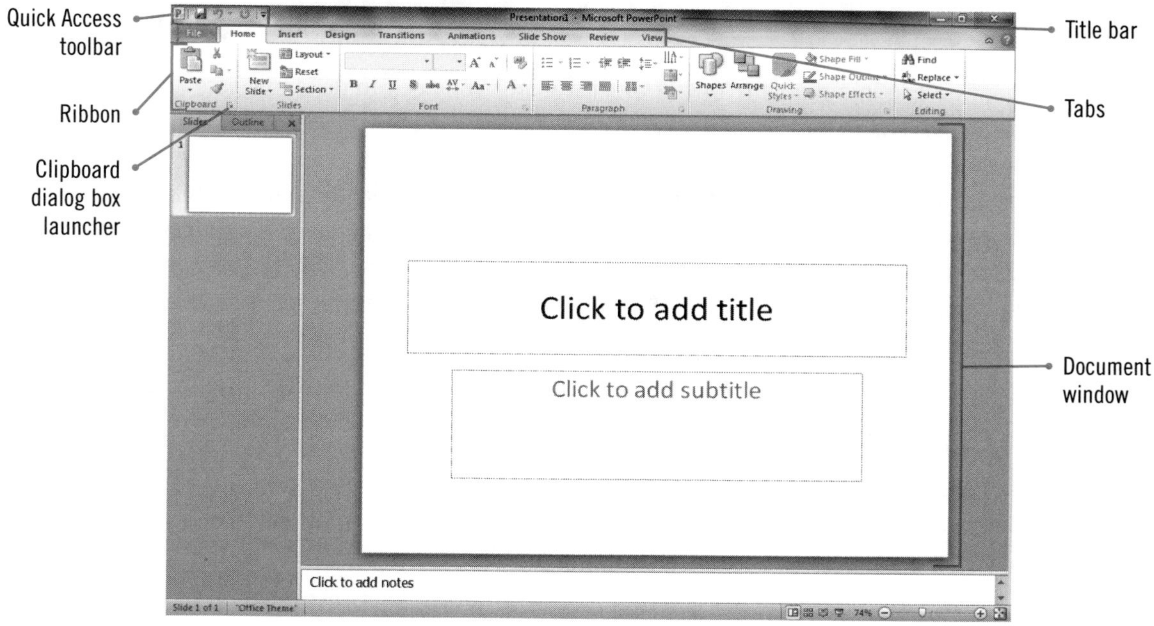

FIGURE A-6: Viewing a theme with Live Preview

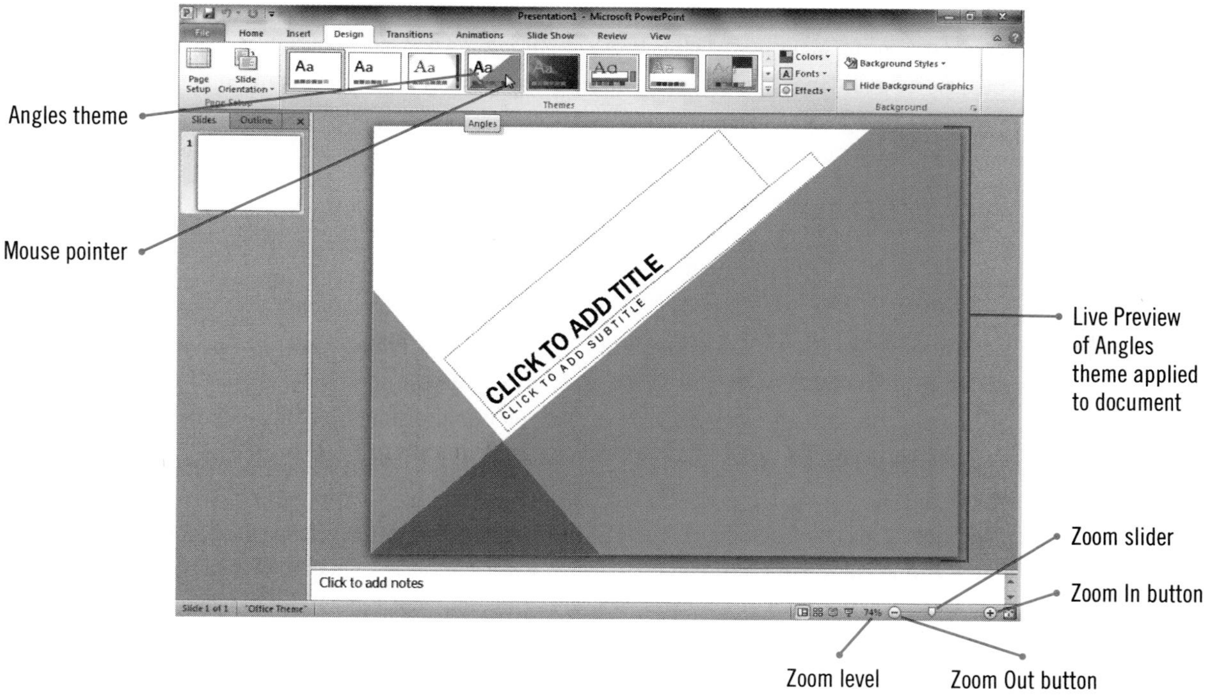

Using Backstage view

Backstage view in each Microsoft Office program offers "one stop shopping" for many commonly performed tasks, such as opening and saving a file, printing and previewing a document, defining document properties, sharing information, and exiting a program.

Backstage view opens when you click the File tab in any Office program, and while features such as the Ribbon, Mini toolbar, and Live Preview all help you work *in* your documents, the File tab and Backstage view help you work *with* your documents.

UNIT
A
Office 2010

Creating and Saving a File

When working in a program, one of the first things you need to do is to create and save a file. A **file** is a stored collection of data. Saving a file enables you to work on a project now, then put it away and work on it again later. In some Office programs, including Word, Excel, and PowerPoint, a new file is automatically created when you start the program, so all you have to do is enter some data and save it. In Access, you must expressly create a file before you enter any data. You should give your files meaningful names and save them in an appropriate location so that they're easy to find. Use Word to familiarize yourself with the process of creating and saving a document. First you'll type some notes about a possible location for a corporate meeting, then you'll save the information for later use.

STEPS

1. **Click the Word program button on the taskbar**
2. **Type Locations for Corporate Meeting, then press [Enter] twice**
   The text appears in the document window, and the **insertion point** blinks on a new blank line. The insertion point indicates where the next typed text will appear.
3. **Type Las Vegas, NV, press [Enter], type Orlando, FL, press [Enter], type Boston, MA, press [Enter] twice, then type your name**
   Compare your document to Figure A-7.
4. **Click the Save button on the Quick Access toolbar**
   Because this is the first time you are saving this document, the Save As dialog box opens, as shown in Figure A-8. The Save As dialog box includes options for assigning a filename and storage location. Once you save a file for the first time, clicking saves any changes to the file *without* opening the Save As dialog box, because no additional information is needed. The Address bar in the Save As dialog box displays the default location for saving the file, but you can change it to any location. The File name field contains a suggested name for the document based on text in the file, but you can enter a different name.
5. **Type OF A-Potential Corporate Meeting Locations**
   The text you type replaces the highlighted text. (The "OF A-" in the filename indicates that the file is created in Office Unit A. You will see similar designations throughout this book when files are named. For example, a file named in Excel Unit B would begin with "EX B-" .)
6. **In the Save As dialog box, use the Address bar or Navigation Pane to navigate to the drive and folder where you store your Data Files**
   Many students store files on a flash drive, but you can also store files on your computer, a network drive, or any storage device indicated by your instructor or technical support person.
7. **Click Save**
   The Save As dialog box closes, the new file is saved to the location you specified, then the name of the document appears in the title bar, as shown in Figure A-9. (You may or may not see the file extension ".docx" after the filename.) See Table A-1 for a description of the different types of files you create in Office, and the file extensions associated with each.

QUICK TIP
A filename can be up to 255 characters, including a file extension, and can include upper- or lowercase characters and spaces, but not ?, ", /, \, <, >, *, |, or :.

QUICK TIP
Saving a file to the Desktop creates a desktop icon that you can double-click to both launch a program and open a document.

QUICK TIP
To create a new blank file when a file is open, click the File tab, click New on the navigation bar, then click Create near the bottom of the document preview pane.

TABLE A-1: Common filenames and default file extensions

file created in	is called a	and has the default extension
Word	document	.docx
Excel	workbook	.xlsx
PowerPoint	presentation	.pptx
Access	database	.accdb

FIGURE A-7: **Document created in Word**

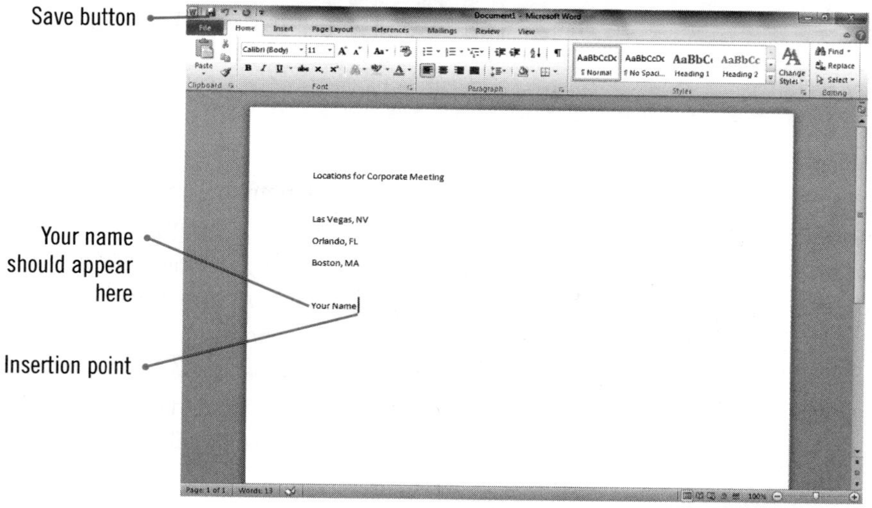

FIGURE A-8: **Save As dialog box**

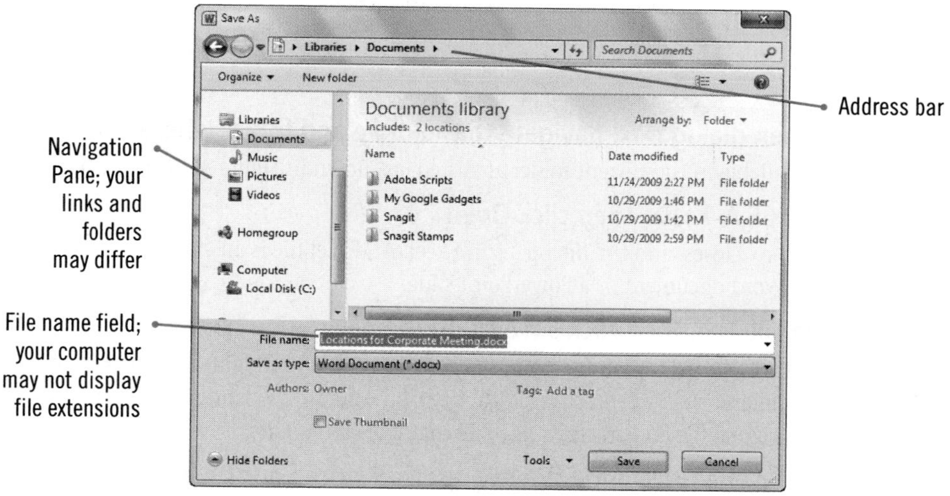

FIGURE A-9: **Saved and named Word document**

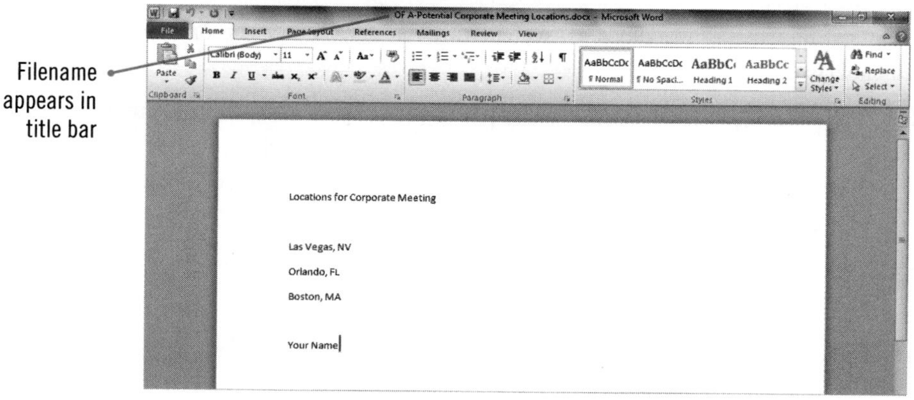

Using the Office Clipboard

You can use the Office Clipboard to cut and copy items from one Office program and paste them into others. The Office Clipboard can store a maximum of 24 items. To access it, open the Office Clipboard task pane by clicking the dialog box launcher in the Clipboard group on the Home tab. Each time you copy a selection, it is saved in the Office Clipboard. Each entry in the Office Clipboard includes an icon that tells you the program it was created in. To paste an entry, click in the document where you want it to appear, then click the item in the Office Clipboard. To delete an item from the Office Clipboard, right-click the item, then click Delete.

UNIT A
Office 2010

Opening a File and Saving It with a New Name

In many cases as you work in Office, you start with a blank document, but often you need to use an existing file. It might be a file you or a coworker created earlier as a work in progress, or it could be a complete document that you want to use as the basis for another. For example, you might want to create a budget for this year using the budget you created last year; you could type in all the categories and information from scratch, or you could open last year's budget, save it with a new name, and just make changes to update it for the current year. By opening the existing file and saving it with the Save As command, you create a duplicate that you can modify to your heart's content, while the original file remains intact. Use Excel to open an existing workbook file, and save it with a new name so the original remains unchanged.

STEPS

QUICK TIP
Click Recent on the navigation bar to display a list of recent workbooks; click a file in the list to open it.

TROUBLE
Click Enable Editing on the Protected View bar near the top of your document window if prompted.

QUICK TIP
The Save As command works identically in all Office programs, except Access; in Access, this command lets you save a copy of the current database object, such as a table or form, with a new name, but not a copy of the entire database.

1. **Click the Excel program button on the taskbar, click the File tab, then click Open on the navigation bar**

   The Open dialog box opens, where you can navigate to any drive or folder accessible to your computer to locate a file.

2. **In the Open dialog box, navigate to the drive and folder where you store your Data Files**

   The files available in the current folder are listed, as shown in Figure A-10. This folder contains one file.

3. **Click OFFICE A-1.xlsx, then click Open**

   The dialog box closes, and the file opens in Excel. An Excel file is an electronic spreadsheet, so it looks different from a Word document or a PowerPoint slide.

4. **Click the File tab, then click Save As on the navigation bar**

   The Save As dialog box opens, and the current filename is highlighted in the File name text box. Using the Save As command enables you to create a copy of the current, existing file with a new name. This action preserves the original file and creates a new file that you can modify.

5. **Navigate to the drive and folder where you store your Data Files if necessary, type OF A-Budget for Corporate Meeting in the File name text box, as shown in Figure A-11, then click Save**

   A copy of the existing workbook is created with the new name. The original file, Office A-1.xlsx, closes automatically.

6. **Click cell A19, type your name, then press [Enter], as shown in Figure A-12**

   In Excel, you enter data in cells, which are formed by the intersection of a row and a column. Cell A19 is at the intersection of column A and row 19. When you press [Enter], the cell pointer moves to cell A20.

7. **Click the Save button on the Quick Access toolbar**

   Your name appears in the workbook, and your changes to the file are saved.

Working in Compatibility Mode

Not everyone upgrades to the newest version of Office. As a general rule, new software versions are **backward compatible**, meaning that documents saved by an older version can be read by newer software. To open documents created in older Office versions, Office 2010 includes a feature called Compatibility Mode. When you use Office 2010 to open a file created in an earlier version of Office, "Compatibility Mode" appears in the title bar, letting you know the file was created in an earlier but usable version of the program. If you are working with someone who may not be using the newest version of the software, you can avoid possible incompatibility problems by saving your file in another, earlier format. To do this in an Office program, click the File tab, click Save As on the navigation bar, click the Save as type list arrow in the Save As dialog box, then click an option on the list. For example, if you're working in Excel, click Excel 97-2003 Workbook format in the Save as type list to save an Excel file so that it can be opened in Excel 97 or Excel 2003.

FIGURE A-10: **Open dialog box**

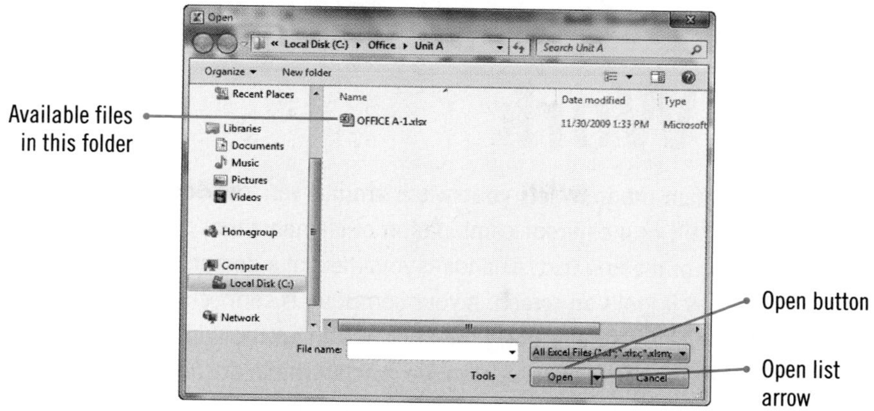

FIGURE A-11: **Save As dialog box**

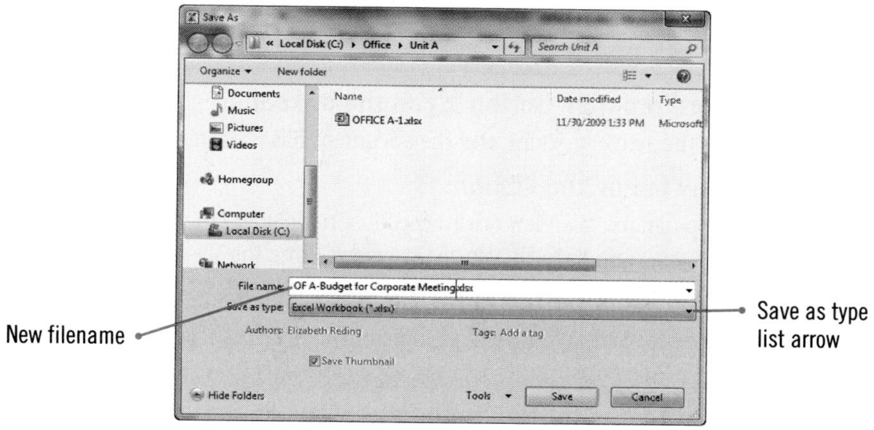

FIGURE A-12: **Your name added to the workbook**

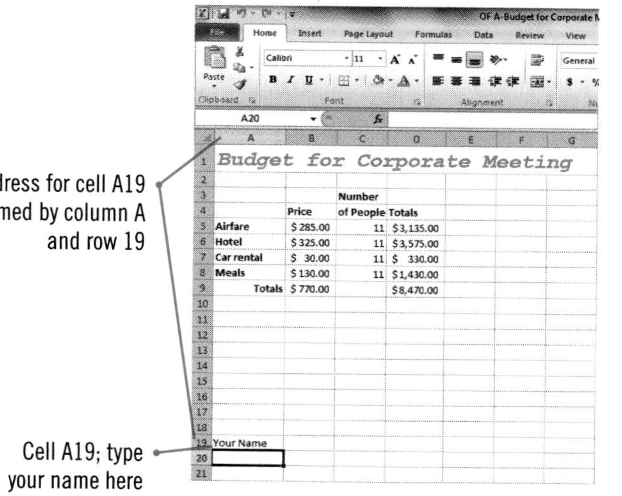

Exploring File Open options

You might have noticed that the Open button on the Open dialog box includes an arrow. In a dialog box, if a button includes an arrow you can click the button to invoke the command, or you can click the arrow to choose from a list of related commands. The Open list arrow includes several related commands, including Open Read-Only and Open as Copy. Clicking Open Read-Only opens a file that you can only save with a new name; you cannot save changes to the original file. Clicking Open as Copy creates a copy of the file already saved and named with the word "Copy" in the title. Like the Save As command, these commands provide additional ways to use copies of existing files while ensuring that original files do not get changed by mistake.

UNIT A
Office 2010

Viewing and Printing Your Work

Each Microsoft Office program lets you switch among various **views** of the document window to show more or fewer details or a different combination of elements that make it easier to complete certain tasks, such as formatting or reading text. Changing your view of a document does not affect the file in any way, it affects only the way it looks on screen. If your computer is connected to a printer or a print server, you can easily print any Office document using the Print button on the Print tab in Backstage view. Printing can be as simple as **previewing** the document to see exactly what a document will look like when it is printed and then clicking the Print button. Or, you can customize the print job by printing only selected pages or making other choices. Experiment with changing your view of a Word document, and then preview and print your work.

STEPS

1. **Click the Word program button on the taskbar**
   Word becomes the active program, and the document fills the screen.
2. **Click the View tab on the Ribbon**
   In most Office programs, the View tab on the Ribbon includes groups and commands for changing your view of the current document. You can also change views using the View buttons on the status bar.
3. **Click the Web Layout button in the Document Views group on the View tab**
   The view changes to Web Layout view, as shown in Figure A-13. This view shows how the document will look if you save it as a Web page.
4. **Click the Print Layout button on the View tab**
   You return to Print Layout view, the default view in Word.
5. **Click the File tab, then click Print on the navigation bar**
   The Print tab opens in Backstage view. The preview pane on the right side of the window automatically displays a preview of how your document will look when printed, showing the entire page on screen at once. Compare your screen to Figure A-14. Options in the Settings section enable you to change settings such as margins, orientation, and paper size before printing. To change a setting, click it, and then click the new setting you want. For instance, to change from Letter paper size to Legal, click Letter in the Settings section, then click Legal on the menu that opens. The document preview is updated as you change the settings. You also can use the Settings section to change which pages to print and even the number of pages you print on each sheet of printed paper. If you have multiple printers from which to choose, you can change from one installed printer to another by clicking the current printer in the Printer section, then clicking the name of the installed printer you want to use. The Print section contains the Print button and also enables you to select the number of copies of the document to print.
6. **Click the Print button in the Print section**
   A copy of the document prints, and Backstage view closes.

QUICK TIP
You can add the Quick Print button to the Quick Access toolbar by clicking the Customize Quick Access Toolbar button, then clicking Quick Print. The Quick Print button prints one copy of your document using the default settings.

Customizing the Quick Access toolbar

You can customize the Quick Access toolbar to display your favorite commands. To do so, click the Customize Quick Access Toolbar button in the title bar, then click the command you want to add. If you don't see the command in the list, click More Commands to open the Quick Access Toolbar tab of the current program's Options dialog box. In the Options dialog box, use the Choose commands from list to choose a category, click the desired command in the list on the left, click Add to add it to the Quick Access toolbar, then click OK. To remove a button from the toolbar, click the name in the list on the right in the Options dialog box, then click Remove. To add a command to the Quick Access toolbar on the fly, simply right-click the button on the Ribbon, then click Add to Quick Access Toolbar on the shortcut menu. To move the Quick Access toolbar below the Ribbon, click the Customize Quick Access Toolbar button, and then click Show Below the Ribbon.

FIGURE A-13: **Web Layout view**

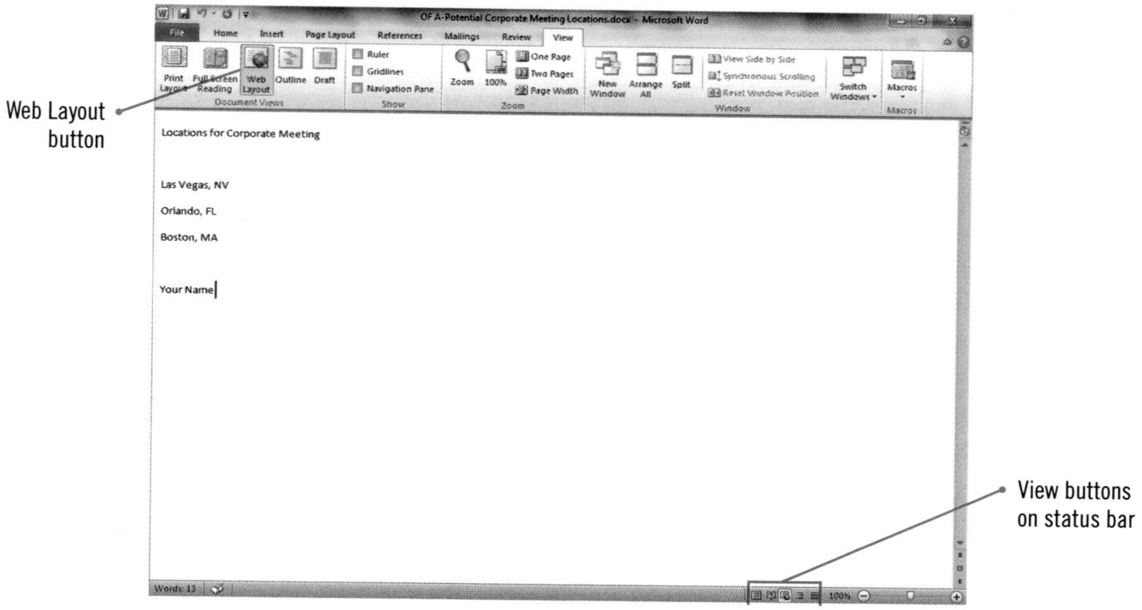

FIGURE A-14: **Print tab in Backstage view**

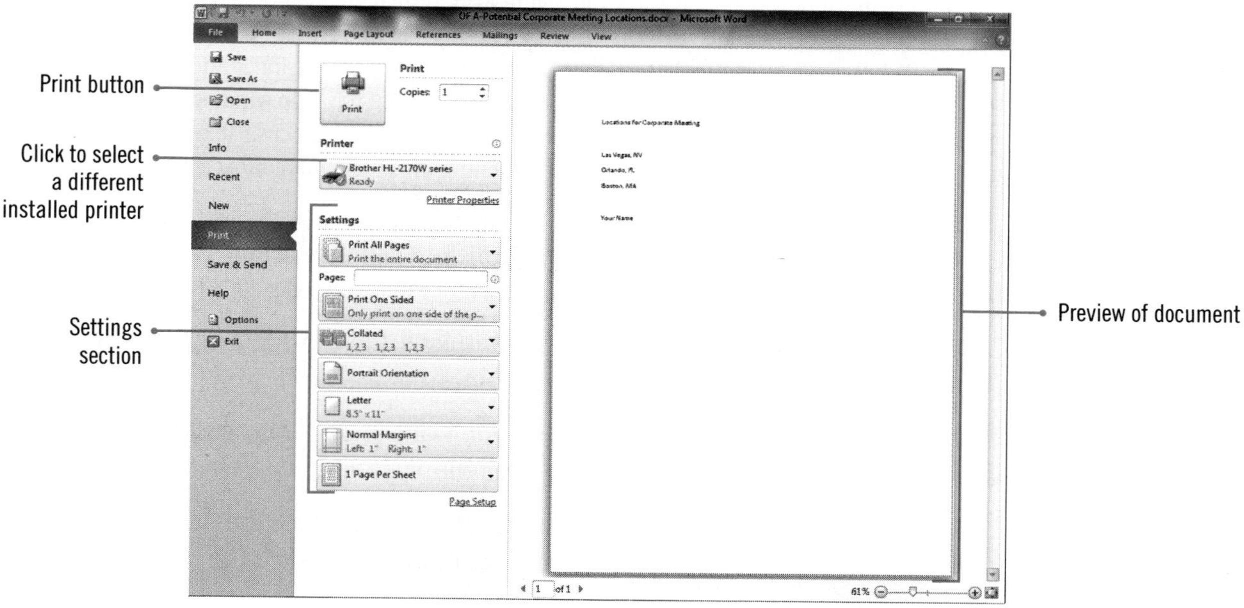

Creating a screen capture

A **screen capture** is a digital image of your screen, as if you took a picture of it with a camera. For instance, you might want to take a screen capture if an error message occurs and you want Technical Support to see exactly what's on the screen. You can create a screen capture using features found in Windows 7 or Office 2010. Windows 7 comes with the Snipping Tool, a separate program designed to capture whole screens or portions of screens. To open the Snipping Tool, click it on the Start menu or click All Programs, click Accessories, then click Snipping Tool. After opening the Snipping Tool, drag the pointer on the screen to select the area of the screen you want to capture. When you release the mouse button, the screen capture opens in the Snipping Tool window, and you can save, copy, or send it in an e-mail. In Word, Excel, and PowerPoint 2010, you can capture screens or portions of screens and insert them in the current document using the Screenshot button on the Insert tab. And finally, you can create a screen capture by pressing [PrtScn]. (Keyboards differ, but you may find the [PrtScn] button in or near your keyboard's function keys.) Pressing this key places a digital image of your screen in the Windows temporary storage area known as the **Clipboard**. Open the document where you want the screen capture to appear, click the Home tab on the Ribbon (if necessary), then click the Paste button on the Home tab. The screen capture is pasted into the document.

Getting Help and Closing a File

You can get comprehensive help at any time by pressing [F1] in an Office program. You can also get help in the form of a ScreenTip by pointing to almost any icon in the program window. When you're finished working in an Office document, you have a few choices regarding ending your work session. You can close a file or exit a program by using the File tab or by clicking a button on the title bar. Closing a file leaves a program running, while exiting a program closes all the open files in that program as well as the program itself. In all cases, Office reminds you if you try to close a file or exit a program and your document contains unsaved changes. Explore the Help system in Microsoft Office, and then close your documents and exit any open programs.

STEPS

TROUBLE
If the Table of Contents pane doesn't appear on the left in the Help window, click the Show Table of Contents button on the Help toolbar to show it.

QUICK TIP
You can also open the Help window by clicking the Microsoft Office Word Help button to the right of the tabs on the Ribbon.

QUICK TIP
You can print the entire current topic by clicking the Print button on the Help toolbar, then clicking Print in the Print dialog box.

1. **Point to the Zoom button on the View tab of the Ribbon**
   A ScreenTip appears that describes how the Zoom button works and explains where to find other zoom controls.
2. **Press [F1]**
   The Word Help window opens, as shown in Figure A-15, displaying the home page for help in Word on the right and the Table of Contents pane on the left. In both panes of the Help window, each entry is a hyperlink you can click to open a list of related topics. The Help window also includes a toolbar of useful Help commands and a Search field. The connection status at the bottom of the Help window indicates that the connection to Office.com is active. Office.com supplements the help content available on your computer with a wide variety of up-to-date topics, templates, and training. If you are not connected to the Internet, the Help window displays only the help content available on your computer.
3. **Click the Creating documents link in the Table of Contents pane**
   The icon next to Creating documents changes, and a list of subtopics expands beneath the topic.
4. **Click the Create a document link in the subtopics list in the Table of Contents pane**
   The topic opens in the right pane of the Help window, as shown in Figure A-16.
5. **Click Delete a document under "What do you want to do?" in the right pane**
   The link leads to information about deleting a document.
6. **Click the Accessibility link in the Table of Contents pane, click the Accessibility features in Word link, read the information in the right pane, then click the Help window Close button**
7. **Click the File tab, then click Close on the navigation bar; if a dialog box opens asking whether you want to save your changes, click Save**
   The Potential Corporate Meeting Locations document closes, leaving the Word program open.
8. **Click the File tab, then click Exit on the navigation bar**
   Word closes, and the Excel program window is active.
9. **Click the File tab, click Exit on the navigation bar to exit Excel, click the PowerPoint program button on the taskbar if necessary, click the File tab, then click Exit on the navigation bar to exit PowerPoint**
   Excel and PowerPoint both close.

FIGURE A-15: **Word Help window**

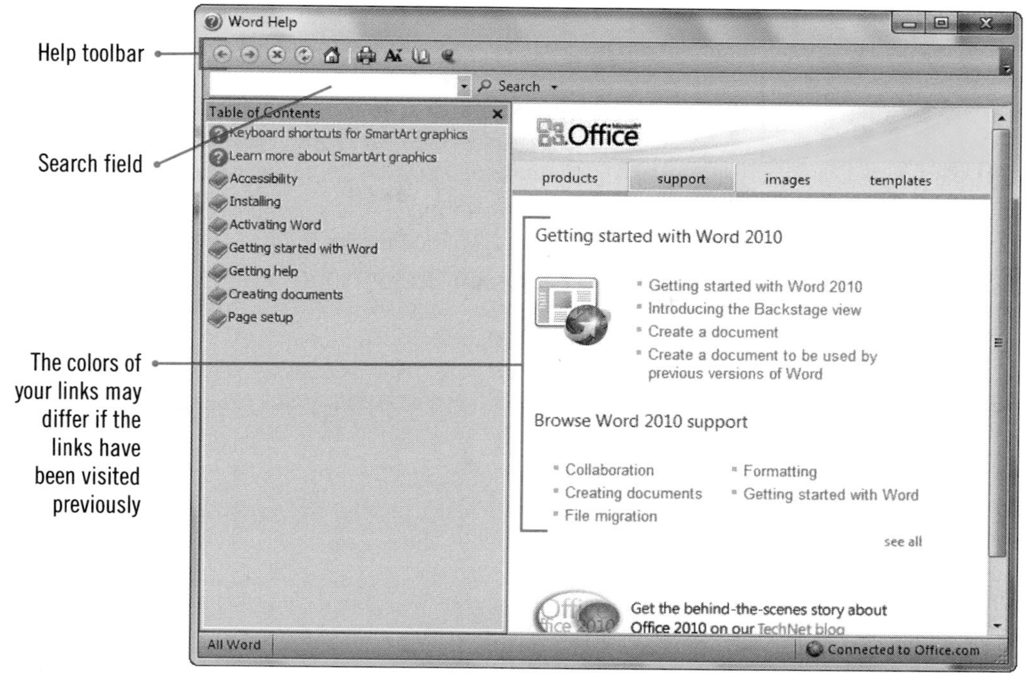

FIGURE A-16: **Create a document Help topic**

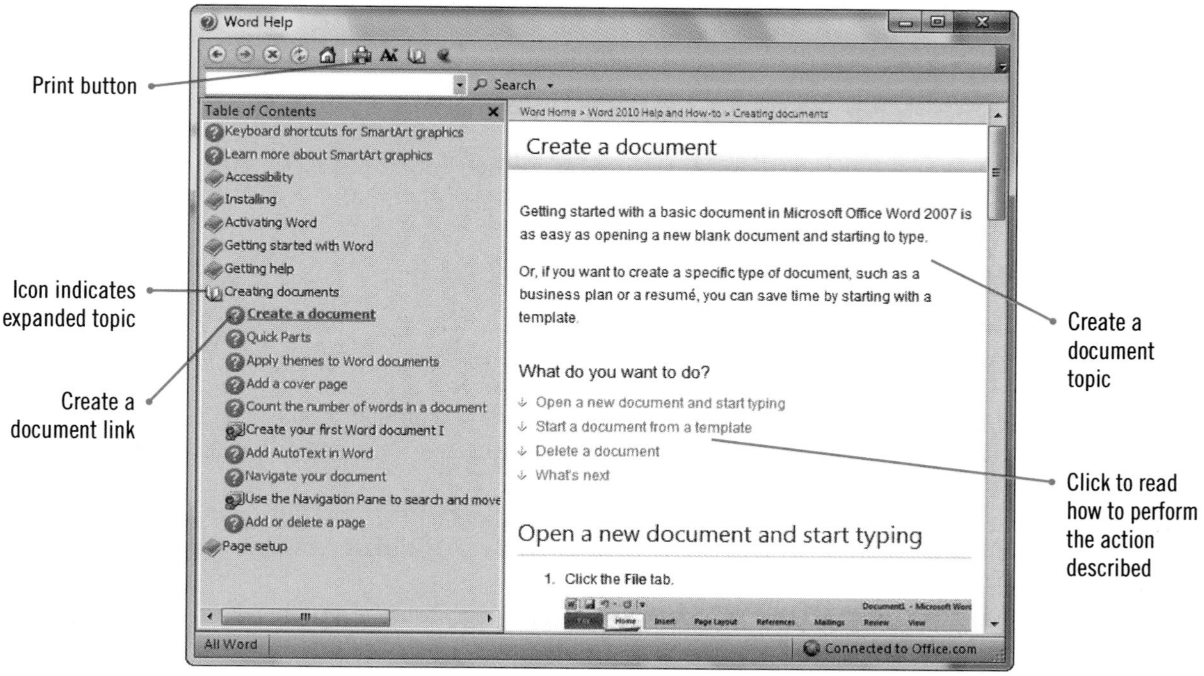

Recovering a document

Each Office program has a built-in recovery feature that allows you to open and save files that were open at the time of an interruption such as a power failure. When you restart the program(s) after an interruption, the Document Recovery task pane opens on the left side of your screen displaying both original and recovered versions of the files that were open. If you're not sure which file to open (original or recovered), it's usually better to open the recovered file because it will contain the latest information. You can, however, open and review all versions of the file that were recovered and save the best one. Each file listed in the Document Recovery task pane displays a list arrow with options that allow you to open the file, save it as is, delete it, or show repairs made to it during recovery.

Practice

Concepts Review

For current SAM information, including versions and content details, visit SAM Central (http://www.cengage.com/samcentral). If you have a SAM user profile, you may have access to hands-on instruction, practice, and assessment of the skills covered in this unit. Since various versions of SAM are supported throughout the life of this text, check with your instructor for the correct instructions and URL/Web site for accessing assignments.

Label the elements of the program window shown in Figure A-17.

FIGURE A-17

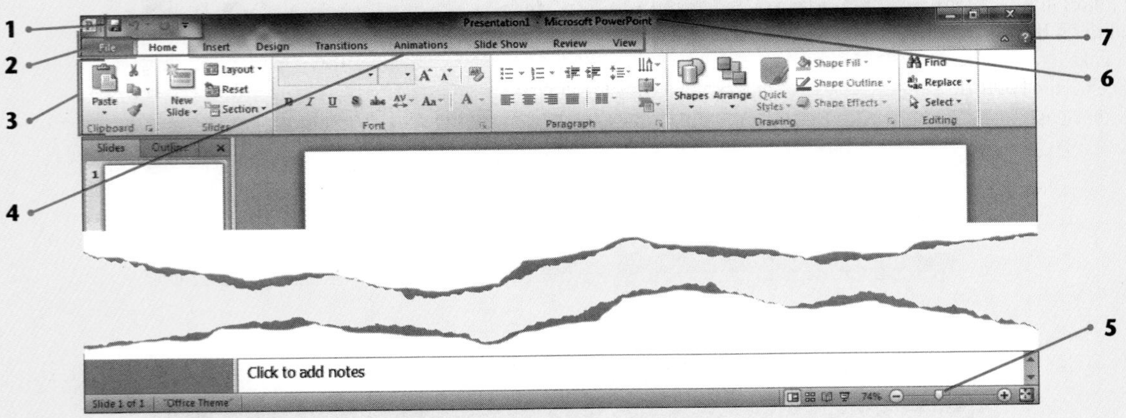

Match each project with the program for which it is best suited.

8. Microsoft Access
9. Microsoft Excel
10. Microsoft Word
11. Microsoft PowerPoint

a. Corporate convention budget with expense projections
b. Business cover letter for a job application
c. Department store inventory
d. Presentation for city council meeting

Independent Challenge 1

You just accepted an administrative position with a local independently owned produce vendor that has recently invested in computers and is now considering purchasing Microsoft Office for the company. You are asked to propose ways Office might help the business. You produce your document in Word.

a. Start Word, then save the document as **OF A-Microsoft Office Document** in the drive and folder where you store your Data Files.

b. Type **Microsoft Word**, press [Enter] twice, type **Microsoft Excel**, press [Enter] twice, type **Microsoft PowerPoint**, press [Enter] twice, type **Microsoft Access**, press [Enter] twice, then type your name.

c. Click the line beneath each program name, type at least two tasks suited to that program (each separated by a comma), then press [Enter].

Advanced Challenge Exercise

ACE

- Press the [PrtScn] button to create a screen capture.
- Click after your name, press [Enter] to move to a blank line below your name, then click the Paste button in the Clipboard group on the Home tab.

d. Save the document, then submit your work to your instructor as directed.

e. Exit Word.

UNIT
A
Access 2010

Getting Started with Access 2010

Files You Will Need:

QuestTravel-A.accdb
RealEstate-A.accdb
Recycle-A.accdb
BusinessContacts-A.accdb
Basketball-A.accdb

In this unit, you will learn the purpose, advantages, and terminology of Microsoft Access 2010, the relational database program in the Microsoft Office 2010 suite of software. You will create and relate tables, the basic building blocks of an Access relational database. You'll also navigate, enter, update, preview, and print data. Samantha Hooper is the tour developer for United States group travel at Quest Specialty Travel (QST), a tour company that specializes in customized group travel packages. Samantha uses Access to store, maintain, and analyze customer and tour information.

OBJECTIVES

- Understand relational databases
- Explore a database
- Create a database
- Create a table
- Create primary keys
- Relate two tables
- Enter data
- Edit data

UNIT
A
Access 2010

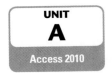

Understanding Relational Databases

Microsoft Access 2010 is relational database software that runs on the Windows operating system. You use **relational database software** to manage data that is organized into lists, such as information about customers, products, vendors, employees, projects, or sales. Many small companies track customer, inventory, and sales information in a spreadsheet program such as Microsoft Excel. Although Excel offers some list management features, Access provides many more tools and advantages for managing data. The advantages are mainly due to the "relational" nature of the lists that Access manages. Table A-1 compares the two programs. You and Samantha Hooper review the advantages of database software over spreadsheets for managing lists of information.

DETAILS

The advantages of using Access for database management include:

- **Duplicate data is minimized**
  Figures A-1 and A-2 compare how you might store sales data in a single Excel spreadsheet list versus three related Access tables. With Access, you do not have to reenter information such as a customer's name and address or tour name every time a sale is made, because lists can be linked, or "related," in relational database software.
- **Information is more accurate, reliable, and consistent because duplicate data is minimized**
  The relational nature of data stored in an Access database allows you to minimize duplicate data entry, which creates more accurate, reliable, and consistent information. For example, customer data in a Customers table is entered only once, not every time a customer makes a purchase.
- **Data entry is faster and easier using Access forms**
  Data entry forms (screen layouts) make data entry faster, easier, and more accurate than entering data in a spreadsheet.
- **Information can be viewed and sorted in many ways using Access queries, forms, and reports**
  In Access, you can save queries (questions about the data), data entry forms, and reports, allowing you to use them over and over without performing extra work to recreate a particular view of the data.
- **Information is more secure using Access passwords and security features**
  Access databases can be encrypted and password protected.
- **Several users can share and edit information at the same time**
  Unlike spreadsheets or word-processing documents, more than one person can enter, update, and analyze data in an Access database at the same time.

FIGURE A-1: **Using a spreadsheet to organize sales data**

Customer information is duplicated each time that customer makes a purchase
Tour information is duplicated each time that tour is purchased

	A	B	C	D	E	F	G	H	I
1	CustNo	FName	LName	SalesNo	SaleDate	TourName	TourStartDate	City	Cost
2	1	Gracita	Mayberry	13	11-Jul-12	Red Reef Scuba	07/24/2012	Islamadora	$1,500.00
3	2	Jacob	Alman	14	11-Jul-12	Red Reef Scuba	07/24/2012	Islamadora	$1,500.00
4	3	Julia	Bouchart	15	11-Jul-12	Red Reef Scuba	07/24/2012	Islamadora	$1,500.00
5	3	Julia	Bouchart	81	11-Jun-12	Piper-Heitman Wedding	06/17/2012	Captiva	$825.00
6	4	Kayla	Browning	5	01-Jun-12	American Heritage Tour	09/11/2012	Philadelphia	$1,200.00
7	4	Kayla	Browning	82	11-May-12	Red Reef Scuba	07/24/2012	Islamadora	$1,500.00
8	5	Samantha	Braven	16	11-Jul-12	Bright Lights Expo	12/19/2012	Branson	$200.00
9	5	Samantha	Braven	83	11-Jul-12	Red Reef Scuba	07/24/2012	Islamadora	$1,500.00
10	6	Kristen	Collins	1	30-Apr-12	Ames Ski Club	01/20/2013	Breckenridge	$850.00
11	6	Kristen	Collins	4	01-Jun-12	Yosemite National Park Great Cleanup	08/07/2012	Sacramento	$1,100.00
12	6	Kristen	Collins	8	07-Jul-12	Bright Lights Expo	12/19/2012	Branson	$200.00
13	6	Kristen	Collins	84	01-Jun-12	American Heritage Tour	09/11/2012	Philadelphia	$1,200.00

FIGURE A-2: **Using a relational database to organize sales data**

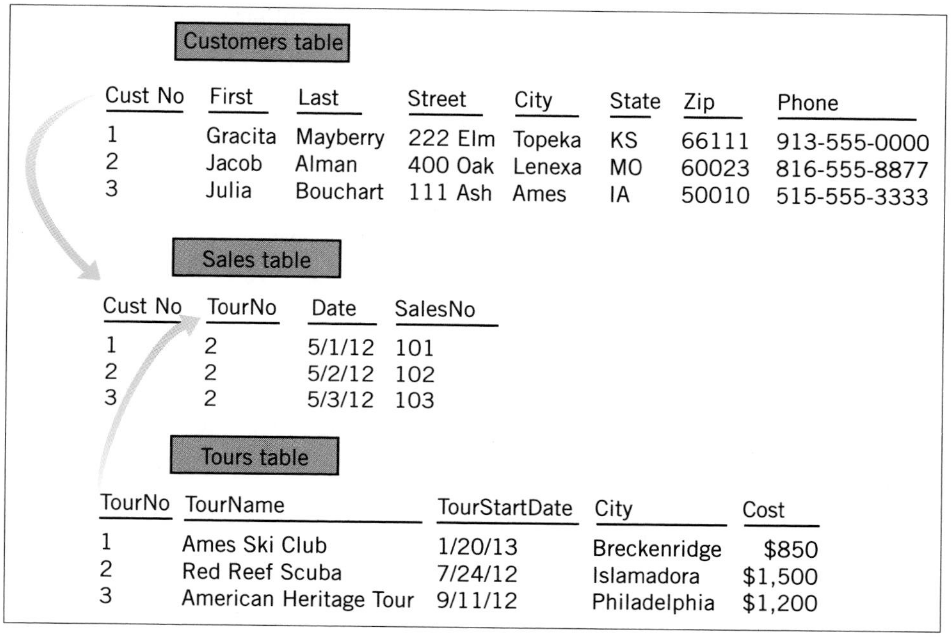

Customers table

Cust No	First	Last	Street	City	State	Zip	Phone
1	Gracita	Mayberry	222 Elm	Topeka	KS	66111	913-555-0000
2	Jacob	Alman	400 Oak	Lenexa	MO	60023	816-555-8877
3	Julia	Bouchart	111 Ash	Ames	IA	50010	515-555-3333

Sales table

Cust No	TourNo	Date	SalesNo
1	2	5/1/12	101
2	2	5/2/12	102
3	2	5/3/12	103

Tours table

TourNo	TourName	TourStartDate	City	Cost
1	Ames Ski Club	1/20/13	Breckenridge	$850
2	Red Reef Scuba	7/24/12	Islamadora	$1,500
3	American Heritage Tour	9/11/12	Philadelphia	$1,200

TABLE A-1: **Comparing Excel to Access**

feature	Excel	Access
Layout	Provides a natural tabular layout for easy data entry	Provides a natural tabular layout as well as the ability to create customized data entry screens called forms
Storage	Restricted to a file's limitations	Virtually unlimited when coupled with the ability to use Microsoft SQL Server to store data
Linked tables	Manages single lists of information—no relational database capabilities	Relates lists of information to reduce data redundancy and create a relational database
Reporting	Limited	Provides the ability to create an unlimited number of reports
Security	Limited to file security options such as marking the file "read-only" or protecting a range of cells	When used with SQL Server, provides extensive security down to the user and data level
Multiuser capabilities	Not allowed	Allows multiple users to simultaneously enter and update data
Data entry	Provides limited data entry screens	Provides the ability to create an unlimited number of data entry forms

UNIT
A
Access 2010

Exploring a Database

You can start Access from the Start menu, from an Access shortcut icon, from a pinned program on the taskbar, or by double-clicking an Access database file on your computer. When you start the Access program from the Start menu, Access displays a window that allows you to open an existing database or create a new one from a template or as a blank database. Samantha Hooper has developed a database called QuestTravel-A, which contains tour information. She asks you to start Access and review this database.

STEPS

TROUBLE
If a yellow Security Warning bar appears below the Ribbon, click Enable Content.

TROUBLE
If the Navigation Pane is not open, click the Shutter Bar Open/Close button « to open it and view the database objects.

1. **Start Access from the Start menu**
   Access starts, as shown in Figure A-3. This window helps you open an existing database, create a new database from a template, or create a new blank database. At this point, if you click the Home, Create, External Data, or Database Tools tabs, no options would be available because Access is running, but no database is open.

2. **Click the Open button, navigate to the drive and folder where you store your Data Files, click the QuestTravel-A.accdb database file, click Open, then click the Maximize button if the Access window is not already maximized**
   The QuestTravel-A.accdb database contains five tables of data named Customers, Sales, States, TourCategories, and Tours. It also contains four queries, two forms, and two reports. Each of these items (table, query, form, and report) is a different type of **object** in an Access database and is displayed in the **Navigation Pane**. The purpose of each object is defined in Table A-2. To learn about an Access database, you explore its objects.

3. **In the Navigation Pane, double-click the Tours table to open it, then double-click the Customers table to open it**
   The Tours and Customers tables open to display the data they store. A **table** is the fundamental building block of a relational database because it stores all of the data.

4. **In the Navigation Pane, double-click the TourSales query to open it, double-click any occurrence of Heritage (as in American Heritage Tour), type Legacy, then click any other row**
   A **query** selects a subset of data from one or more tables. In this case, the TourSales query selects data from the Tours, Sales, and Customers tables. Editing data in one object changes it in every other object of the database, which demonstrates the power and productivity of a relational database.

5. **Double-click the TourEntryForm to open it, double-click Tour in "American Legacy Tour", type Rally, then click any name in the middle part of the window**
   An Access **form** is a data entry screen. Users prefer forms for data entry rather than tables and queries because the information can be presented in an easy-to-use layout.

6. **Double-click the TourSales report to open it**
   An Access **report** is a professional printout. A report is for printing purposes only, not data entry. As shown in Figure A-4, the edits made to the American Legacy Rally tour name have carried through to the report.

7. **Click the File tab, then click Exit**
   Exiting Access closes the database on which you are working. If you made any changes to the database that should be saved, Access would remind you to do so before closing. Changes to data, such as the edits you made to the American Legacy Rally tour, are automatically saved as you work.

FIGURE A-3: **Opening Microsoft Access 2010 window**

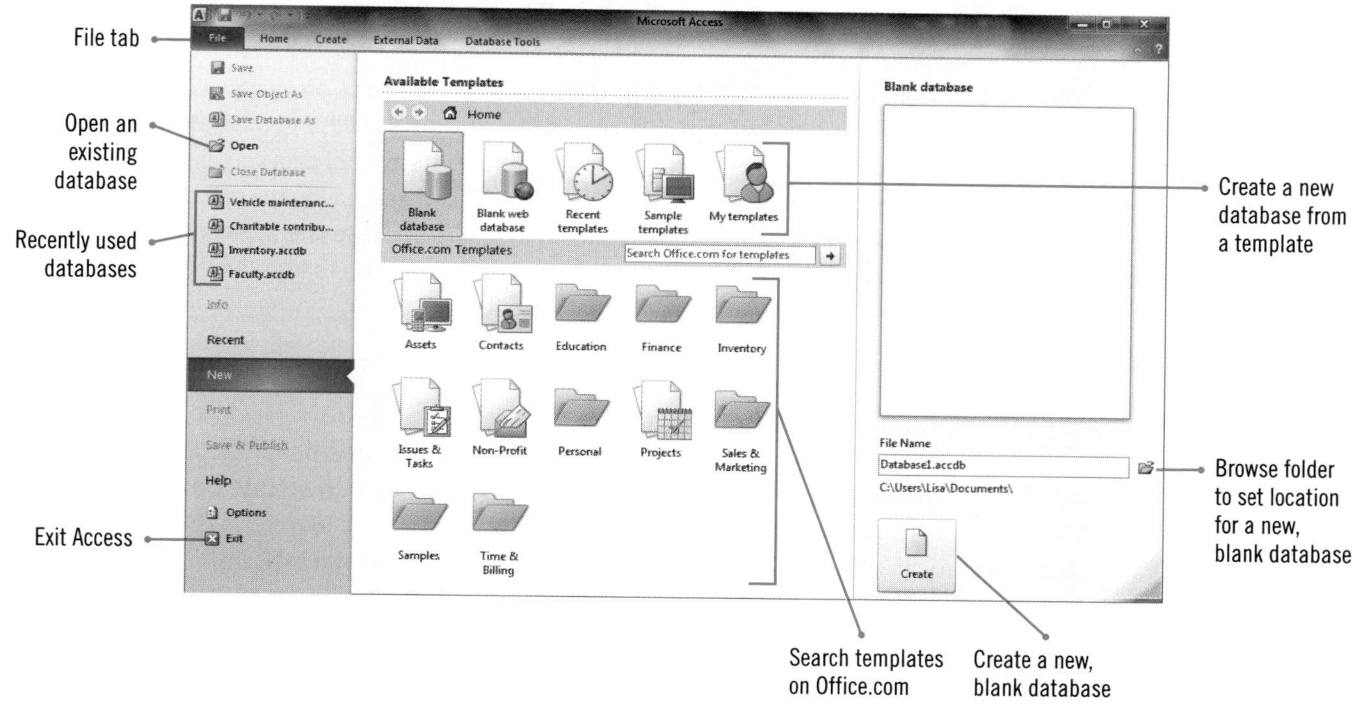
File tab
Open an existing database
Recently used databases
Exit Access
Create a new database from a template
Browse folder to set location for a new, blank database
Search templates on Office.com
Create a new, blank database

FIGURE A-4: **Objects in the QuestTravel-A database**

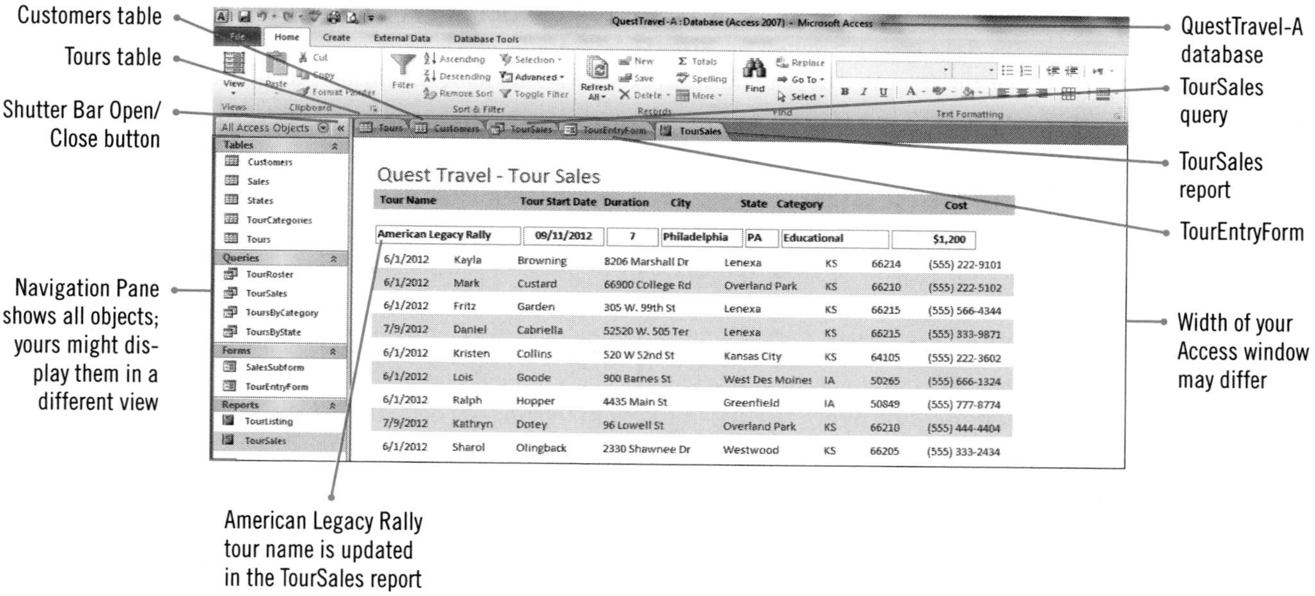
Customers table
Tours table
Shutter Bar Open/ Close button
Navigation Pane shows all objects; yours might display them in a different view
QuestTravel-A database
TourSales query
TourSales report
TourEntryForm
Width of your Access window may differ
American Legacy Rally tour name is updated in the TourSales report

TABLE A-2: **Access objects and their purpose**

object	Navigation Pane icon	purpose
Table		Contains all of the raw data within the database in a spreadsheet-like view; tables are linked with a common field to create a relational database, which minimizes redundant data
Query		Allows you to select a subset of fields or records from one or more tables; queries are created when you have a question about the data
Form		Provides an easy-to-use data entry screen
Report		Provides a professional printout of data that can contain enhancements such as headers, footers, graphics, and calculations on groups of records

UNIT
A
Access 2010

Creating a Database

You can create a database using an Access **template**, a sample database provided within the Microsoft Access program, or you can start with a blank database to create a database from scratch. Your decision depends on whether Access has a template that closely resembles the type of data you plan to manage. If it does, building your own database from a template might be faster than creating the database from scratch. Regardless of which method you use, you can always modify the database later, tailoring it to meet your specific needs. Samantha Hooper reasons that the best way for you to learn Access is to start a new database from scratch, so she asks you to create a database that will track customer communication.

STEPS

1. **Start Access**
2. **Click the Browse folder button to the right of the File Name box, navigate to the drive and folder where you store your Data Files, type Quest in the File name box, click OK, then click the Create button**

   A new, blank database file with a single table named Table1 is created as shown in Figure A-5. While you might be tempted to start entering data into the table, a better way to build a table is to first define the columns, or **fields**, of data that the table will store. **Table Design View** provides the most options for defining fields.
3. **Click the View button on the Fields tab to switch to Design View, type Customers as the table name, then click OK**

   The table name changes from Table1 to Customers, and you are positioned in Table Design View, a window you use to name and define the fields of a table. Access created a field named ID with an AutoNumber data type. The **data type** is a significant characteristic of a field because it determines what type of data the field can store, such as text, dates, or numbers. See Table A-3 for more information about data types.
4. **Type CustID to rename ID to CustID, press the [↓] to move to the first blank Field Name cell, type FirstName, press [↓], type LastName, press [↓], type Phone, press [↓], type Birthday, then press [↓]**

   Be sure to separate the first and last names so that you can easily sort, find, and filter on either part of the name later. The Birthday field will only contain dates, so you should change its data type from Text (the default data type) to Date/Time.
5. **Click Text in the Birthday row, click the list arrow, then click Date/Time**

   With these five fields properly defined for the new Customers table, as shown in Figure A-6, you're ready to enter data. You switch back to Datasheet View to enter or edit data. **Datasheet View** is a spreadsheet-like view of the data in a table. A **datasheet** is a grid that displays fields as columns and records as rows. The new **field names** you just defined are listed at the top of each column.
6. **Click the View button to switch to Datasheet View, click Yes when prompted to save the table, press [Tab] to move to the FirstName field, type your first name, press [Tab] to move to the LastName field, type your last name, press [Tab] to move to the Phone field, type 111-222-3333, press [Tab], type 1/32/80, and press [Tab]**

   Because 1/32/80 is not a valid date, Access does not allow you to make that entry and displays an error message as shown in Figure A-7. This shows that setting the best data type for each field before entering data helps prevent data entry errors.
7. **Edit the Birthday entry for the first record to 1/31/80, press [Tab], enter two more sample records containing reasonable data, right-click the Customers table tab, then click Close to close the Customers table**

TROUBLE

Tab through the CustID field rather than typing a value. The CustID value automatically increments to the next number.

FIGURE A-5: Creating a database with a new table

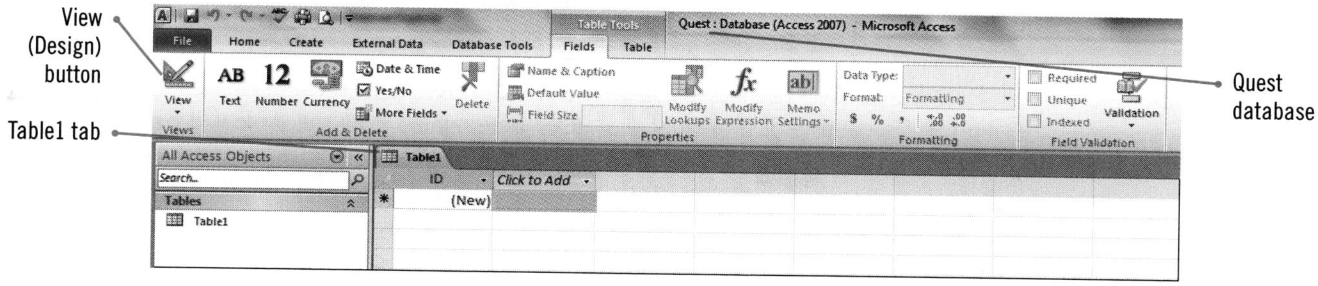
View (Design) button
Table1 tab
Quest database

FIGURE A-6: Defining field names and data types for the Customers table in Table Design View

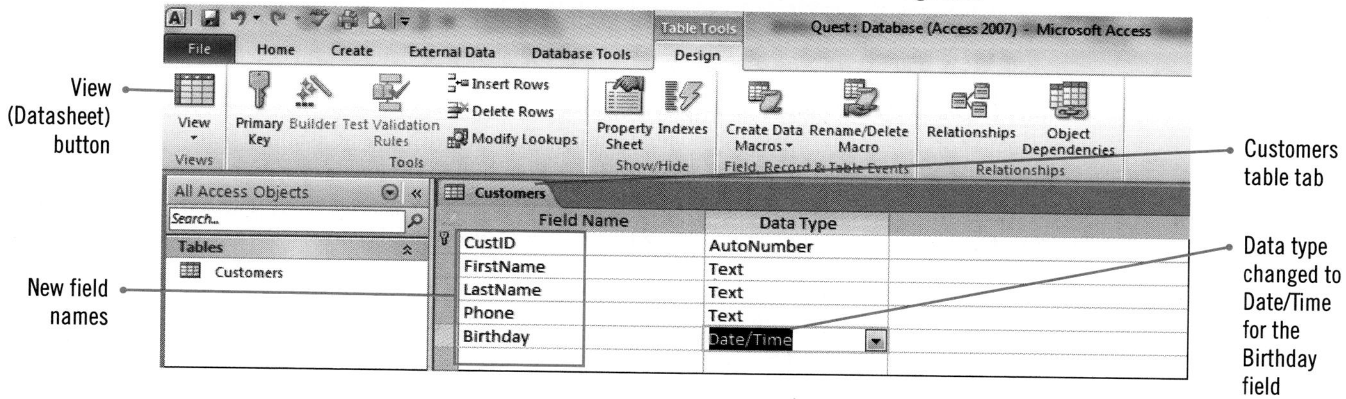
View (Datasheet) button
New field names
Customers table tab
Data type changed to Date/Time for the Birthday field

FIGURE A-7: Entering your first record in the Customers table

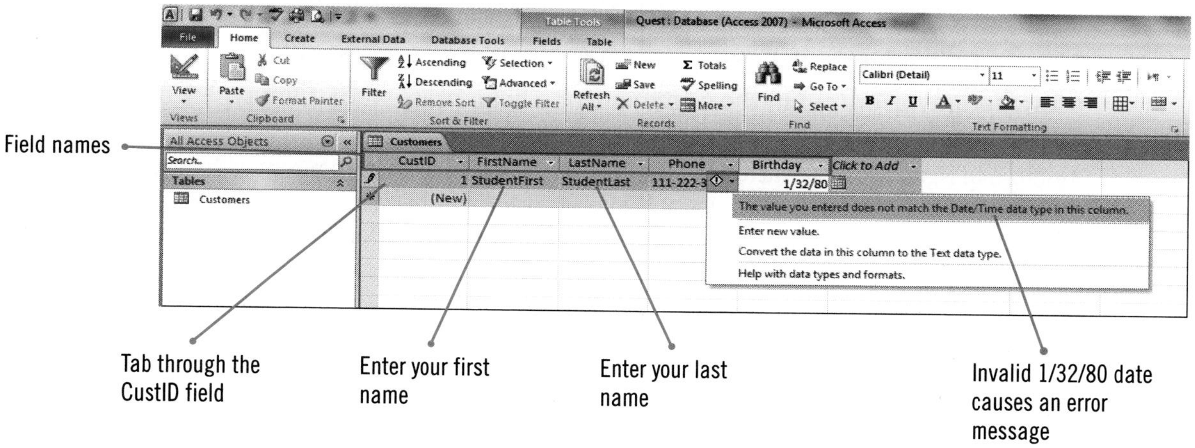
Field names
Tab through the CustID field
Enter your first name
Enter your last name
Invalid 1/32/80 date causes an error message

TABLE A-3: Data types

data type	description of data
Text	Text or numbers not used in calculations such as a name, zip code, or phone number
Memo	Lengthy text greater than 255 characters, such as comments or notes
Number	Numeric data that can be used in calculations, such as quantities
Date/Time	Dates and times
Currency	Monetary values
AutoNumber	Sequential integers controlled by Access
Yes/No	Only two values: Yes or No
Attachment	External files such as .jpg images, spreadsheets, and documents
Hyperlink	Web and e-mail addresses

UNIT
A
Access 2010

Creating a Table

After creating your database and first table, you need to create new, related tables to build a relational database. Creating a table consists of these essential tasks: determining how the table will participate in the relational database, meaningful naming of each field in the table, selecting an appropriate data type for each field, and naming the table. Samantha Hooper asks you to create another table to store customer comments. The new table will be related to the Customers table so each customer's comments are linked to each customer.

STEPS

1. **Click the Create tab on the Ribbon, then click the Table Design button in the Tables group**

   Design View is a view in which you create and manipulate the structure of an object.

2. **Enter the field names and data types as shown in Figure A-8**

   The Comments table will contain four fields. CommentID is set with an AutoNumber data type so each record is automatically numbered by Access. The Comment field has a Memo data type so a large comment can be recorded. CommentDate is a Date/Time field to identify the date of the comment. CustID has a Number data type and will be used to link the Comments table to the Customers table later.

3. **Click the Home tab, click the View button to switch to Datasheet View, click Yes when prompted to save the table, type Comments as the table name, click OK, then click No when prompted to create a primary key**

   A **primary key field** contains unique data for each record. You'll identify a primary key field for the Comments table later. For now, you'll enter the first record in the Comments table in Datasheet View. A **record** is a row of data in a table. Refer to Table A-4 for a summary of important database terminology.

4. **Press [Tab] to move to the Comment field, type Interested in future tours to Australia, press [Tab], type 1/7/13 in the CommentDate field, press [Tab], then type 1 in the CustID field**

   As shown in Figure A-9, you entered 1 in the CustID field to connect this comment with the customer in the Customers table that has a CustID value of 1. Knowing which CustID value to enter for each comment is difficult. After you properly relate the tables (a task you have not yet performed), Access can make it easier to associate comments and customers.

5. **Right-click the Comments table tab, then click Close**

Creating a table in Datasheet View

In Access 2010, you can create a new table in Datasheet View using commands on the Fields tab of the Ribbon. You can also enter data in Datasheet View. Entering data in Datasheet View *before* finishing field design activities can introduce a wide variety of data entry errors, such as entering textual data in what should be defined as a Number or Date/Time field. If you design your tables using Table Design View, you avoid the temptation of entering data before you finish defining fields, which helps minimize many types of common data entry errors.

FIGURE A-8: Creating the Comments table

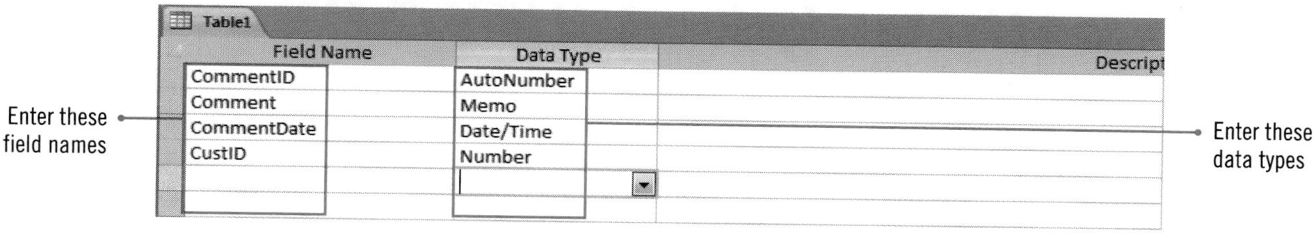

FIGURE A-9: Entering the first record in the Comments table

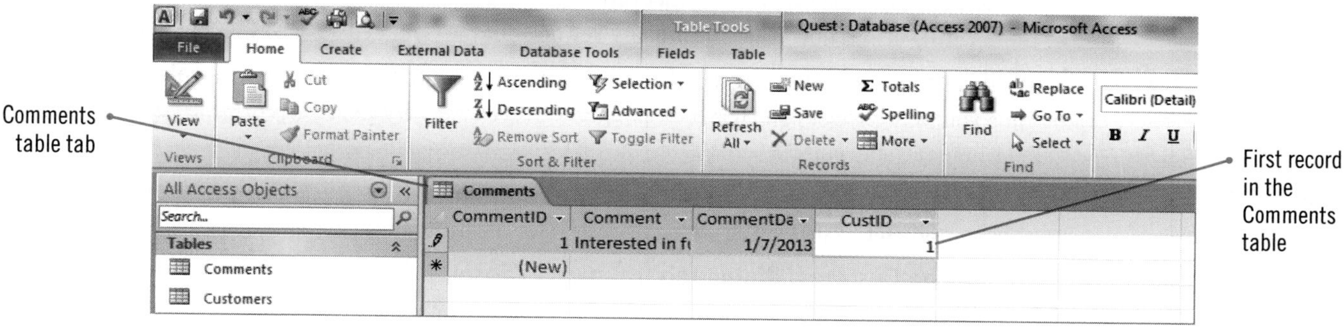

TABLE A-4: Important database terminology

term	description
Field	A specific piece or category of data such as a first name, last name, city, state, or phone number
Record	A group of related fields that describes a person, place, thing, or transaction such as a customer, location, product, or sale
Key field	A field that contains unique information for each record, such as a customer number for a customer
Table	A collection of records for a single subject such as Customers, Products, or Sales
Relational database	Multiple tables that are linked together to address a business process such as managing tours, sales, and customers at Quest Specialty Travel
Objects	The parts of an Access database that help you view, edit, manage, and analyze the data: **tables**, **queries**, **forms**, **reports**, **macros**, and **modules**

UNIT A

Access 2010

Creating Primary Keys

The primary key field of a table serves two important purposes. First, it contains data that uniquely identifies each record. No two records can have the exact same entry in the field designated as the primary key field. Secondly, the primary key field helps relate one table to another in a **one-to-many relationship**, where one record from one table is related to many records in the second table. For example, one record in the Customers table can be related to many records in the Comments table. (One customer can have many comments.) The primary key field is always on the "one" side of a one-to-many relationship between two tables. Samantha Hooper asks you to check that a primary key field has been appropriately identified for each table in the new Quest database.

STEPS

1. **Right-click the Comments table in the Navigation Pane, then click Design View**
   Table Design View for the Comments table opens. The field with the AutoNumber data type is generally the best candidate for the primary key field in a table because it automatically contains a unique number for each record.

2. **Click the CommentID field if it is not already selected, then click the Primary Key button in the Tools group on the Design tab**
   The CommentID field is now set as the primary key field for the Comments table as shown in Figure A-10.

3. **Right-click the Comments table tab, click Close, then click Yes to save the table**
   Any time you must save design changes to an Access object such as a table, Access displays a dialog box to remind you to save the object.

4. **Right-click the Customers table in the Navigation Pane, then click Design View**
   Access has already set CustID as the primary key field for the Customers table as shown in Figure A-11.

5. **Right-click the Customers table tab, then click Close**
   You were not prompted to save the Customers table because you made no design changes. Now that you're sure that each table in the Quest database has an appropriate primary key field, you're ready to link the tables. The primary key field plays a critical role in this relationship.

TROUBLE

Make sure the Design tab is selected on the Ribbon.

QUICK TIP

You can also click the Save button on the Quick Access toolbar to save a table.

FIGURE A-10: **Creating a primary key field for the Comments table**

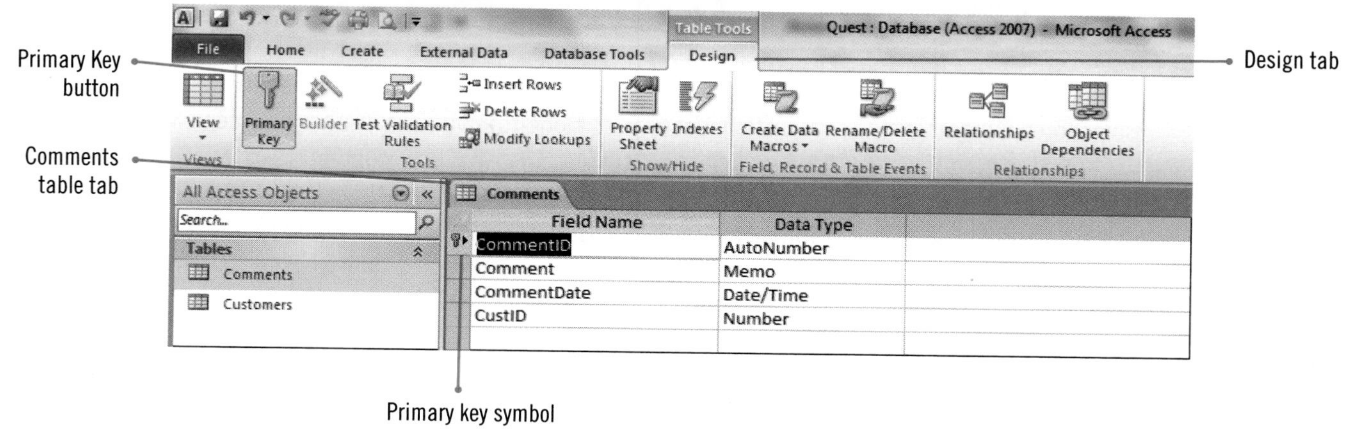

FIGURE A-11: **Confirming the primary key field for the Customers table**

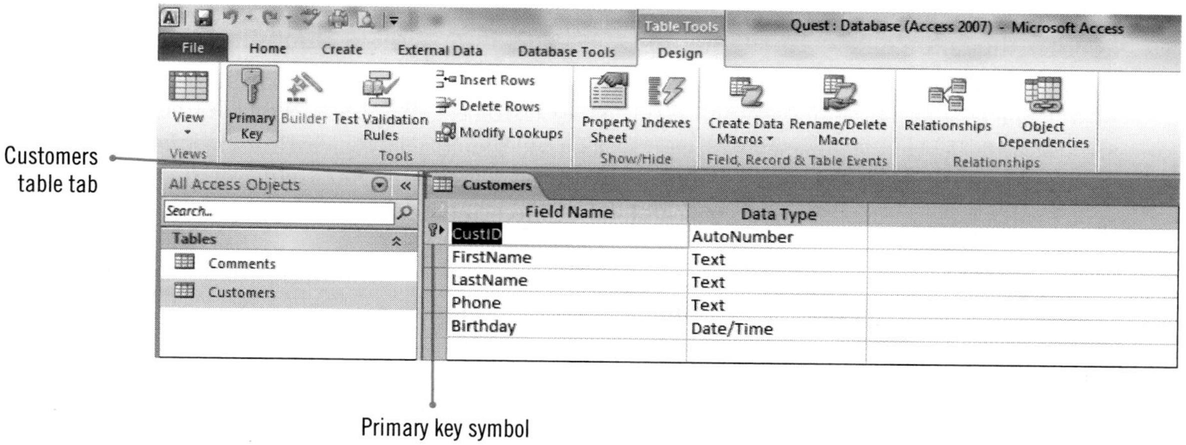

Learning about field properties

Properties are the characteristics that define the field. Two properties are required for every field: Field Name and Data Type. Many other properties, such as Field Size, Format, Caption, and Default Value, are defined in the Field Properties pane in the lower half of a table's Design View. As you add more property entries, you are generally restricting the amount or type of data that can be entered in the field, which increases data entry accuracy. For example, you might change the Field Size property for a State field to 2 to eliminate an incorrect entry such as FLL. Field properties change depending on the data type of the selected field. For example, date fields do not have a Field Size property because Access controls the size of fields with a Date/Time data type.

UNIT
A
Access 2010

Relating Two Tables

After you create tables and set primary key fields, you must link the tables together in one-to-many relationships to enjoy the benefits of a relational database. A one-to-many relationship between two tables means that one record from the first table is related to many records in the second table. You use a common field to make this connection. The common field is always the primary key field in the table on the "one" side of the relationship. Samantha Hooper explains that she has new comments to enter into the Quest database. To easily identify which customer is related to each comment, you define a one-to-many relationship between the Customers and Comments tables.

STEPS

TROUBLE
If the Show Table dialog box doesn't appear, click the Show Table button on the Design tab.

QUICK TIP
Drag a table's title bar to move the field list.

TROUBLE
If you need to delete an incorrect relationship, right-click a relationship line, then click Delete.

QUICK TIP
To print the Relationships window, click the Relationship Report button on the Design tab, then click Print.

1. **Click the Database Tools tab on the Ribbon, then click the Relationships button**

2. **In the Show Table dialog box, double-click Customers, double-click Comments, then click Close**

   Each table is represented by a small **field list** window that displays the table's field names. A key symbol identifies the primary key field in each table. To relate the two tables in a one-to-many relationship, you connect them using the common field, which is always the primary key field on the "one" side of the relationship.

3. **Drag CustID in the Customers field list to the CustID field in the Comments field list**

   The Edit Relationships dialog box opens as shown in Figure A-12. **Referential integrity**, a set of Access rules that governs data entry, helps ensure data accuracy.

4. **Click the Enforce Referential Integrity check box in the Edit Relationships dialog box, then click Create**

   The **one-to-many line** shows the link between the CustID field of the Customers table (the "one" side) and the CustID field of the Comments table (the "many" side, indicated by the **infinity symbol**), as shown in Figure A-13. The linking field on the "many" side is called the **foreign key field**. Now that these tables are related, it is much easier to enter comments for the correct customer.

5. **Click the Close button on the Design tab, click Yes to save changes, then double-click the Customers table in the Navigation Pane to open it in Datasheet View**

   When you relate two tables in a one-to-many relationship, expand buttons ⊞ appear to the left of each record in the table on the "one" side of the relationship. In this case, this is the Customers table.

6. **Click the expand button ⊞ to the left of the first record, then drag the ✛ pointer to widen the Comment field**

   A **subdatasheet** shows the related comment records for each customer. In other words, the subdatasheet shows the records on the "many" side of a one-to-many relationship. The expand button ⊞ also changed to the collapse button ⊟ for the first customer. Widening the Comment field allows you to see the entire entry in the Comments subdatasheet. Now the task of entering comments for the right customer is much more straightforward.

7. **Enter two more comments as shown in Figure A-14**

   Interestingly, the CustID field in the Comments table (the foreign key field) is not displayed in the subdatasheet. Behind the scenes, Access is entering the correct CustID value in the Comments table, which is the glue that ties each comment to the right customer.

8. **Close the Customers table, then click Yes if prompted to save changes**

FIGURE A-12: **Edit Relationships dialog box**

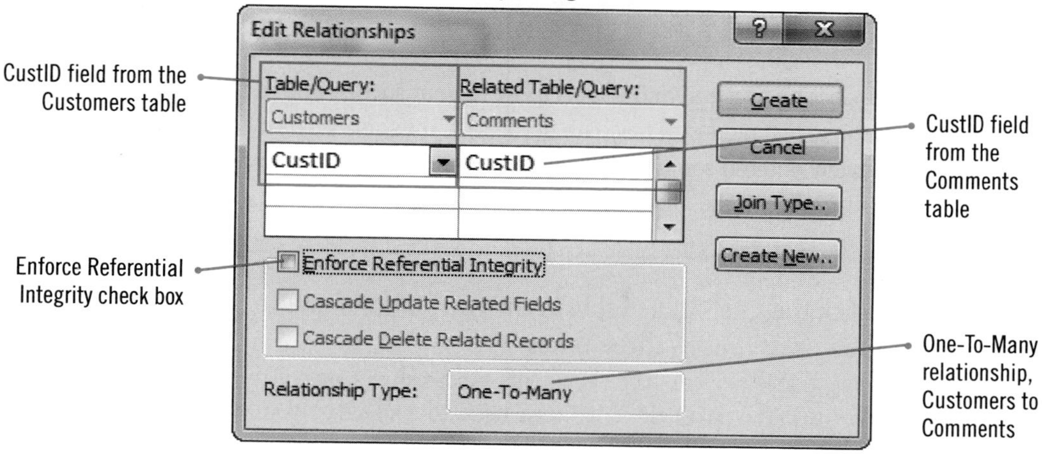

FIGURE A-13: **Linking the Customers and Comments tables**

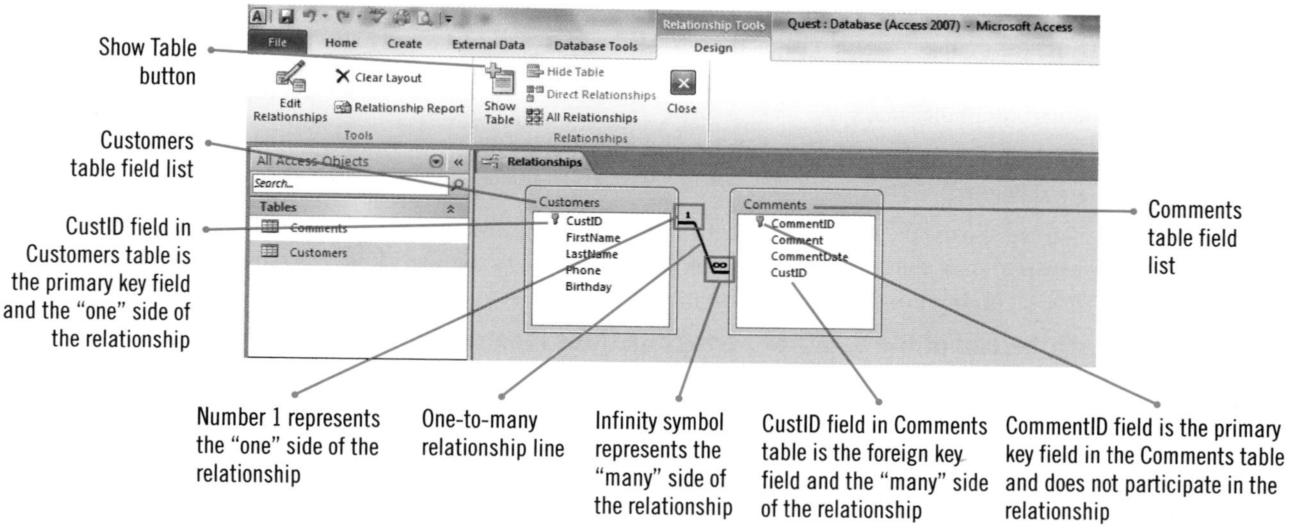

FIGURE A-14: **Entering comments using the subdatasheet**

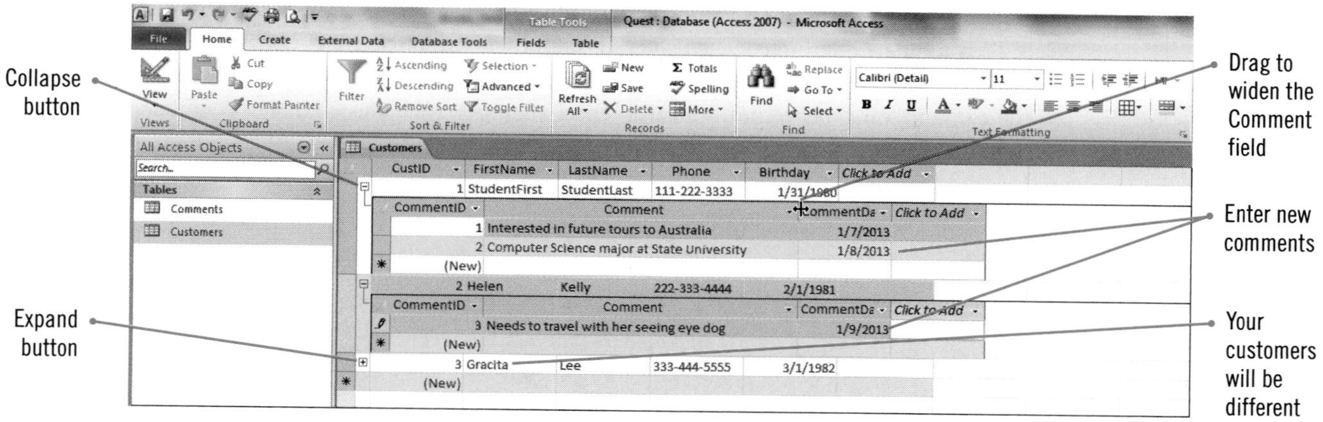

Enforcing referential integrity

Referential integrity is a set of rules that helps reduce invalid entries and orphan records. An **orphan record** is a record in the "many" table that doesn't have a matching entry in the linking field of the "one" table. With referential integrity enforced on a one-to-many relationship, you cannot enter a value in a foreign key field of the "many" table that does not have a match in the linking field of the "one" table. Referential integrity also prevents you from deleting a record in the "one" table if a matching entry exists in the foreign key field of the "many" table. You should enforce referential integrity on all one-to-many relationships if possible. If you are working with a database that already contains orphan records, you cannot enforce referential integrity on that relationship.

UNIT

A

Access 2010

Entering Data

Your skill in navigating and entering data is a key to your success with a relational database. You use either mouse or keystroke techniques to navigate the data in the table's datasheet. Even though you have already successfully entered some data, Samantha Hooper asks you to master this essential skill by entering several more customers in the Quest database.

STEPS

1. **Double-click the Customers table in the Navigation Pane to open it, press [Tab] three times, then press [Enter] three times**

   The Customers table reopens. The Comments subdatasheets are collapsed. Both the [Tab] and [Enter] keys move the focus to the next field. The **focus** refers to which data you would edit if you started typing. The record that has the focus is highlighted in light blue. The field name that has the focus is highlighted in light orange. When you navigate to the last field of the record, pressing [Tab] or [Enter] advances the focus to the first field of the next record. You can also use the Next record ▶ and Previous record ◀ **navigation buttons** on the navigation bar in the lower-left corner of the datasheet to navigate the records. The **Current record** text box on the navigation bar tells you the number of the current record as well as the total number of records in the datasheet.

2. **Click the FirstName field of the fourth record to position the insertion point to enter a new record**

   You can also use the New (blank) record button on the navigation bar to move to a new record. You enter new records at the end of the datasheet. You learn how to sort and reorder records later. A complete list of navigation keystrokes is shown in Table A-5.

3. **At the end of the datasheet, enter the three records shown in Figure A-15**

   The **edit record symbol** shown in Figure A-16 appears to the left of the record you are currently editing. When you move to a different record, Access saves the data. Therefore, Access never prompts you to save *data* because it performs that task automatically. Saving data automatically allows Access databases to be **multiuser** databases, which means that more than one person can enter and edit data in the same database at the same time.

   Your CustID values might differ from those in Figure A-16. Because the CustID field is an **AutoNumber** field, Access automatically enters the next consecutive number into the field as it creates the record. If you delete a record or are interrupted when entering a record, Access discards the value in the AutoNumber field and does not reuse it. AutoNumber values do not represent the number of records in your table. Instead, they provide a unique value per record, similar to check numbers. Each check number is unique, and does not represent the number of checks you have written.

QUICK TIP

Access databases are multiuser with one important limitation: two users cannot edit the same *record* at the same time. In that case, a message explains that the second user must wait until the first user moves to a different record.

Changing from Navigation mode to Edit mode

If you navigate to another area of the datasheet by clicking with the mouse pointer instead of pressing [Tab] or [Enter], you change from **Navigation mode** to Edit mode. In **Edit mode**, Access assumes that you are trying to make changes to the current field value, so keystrokes such as [Ctrl][End], [Ctrl][Home], [←], and [→] move the insertion point within the field. To return to Navigation mode, press [Tab] or [Enter] (thus moving the focus to the next field), or press [↑] or [↓] (thus moving the focus to a different record).

FIGURE A-15: Three records to add to the Customers table

CustID	FirstName	LastName	Phone	Birthday
[Tab]	Nicolas	McNeil	444-555-6666	4/1/1983
[Tab]	Toby	Stanton	555-666-7777	5/1/1984
[Tab]	Renada	Champ	666-777-8888	6/1/1985

FIGURE A-16: New records in the Customers table

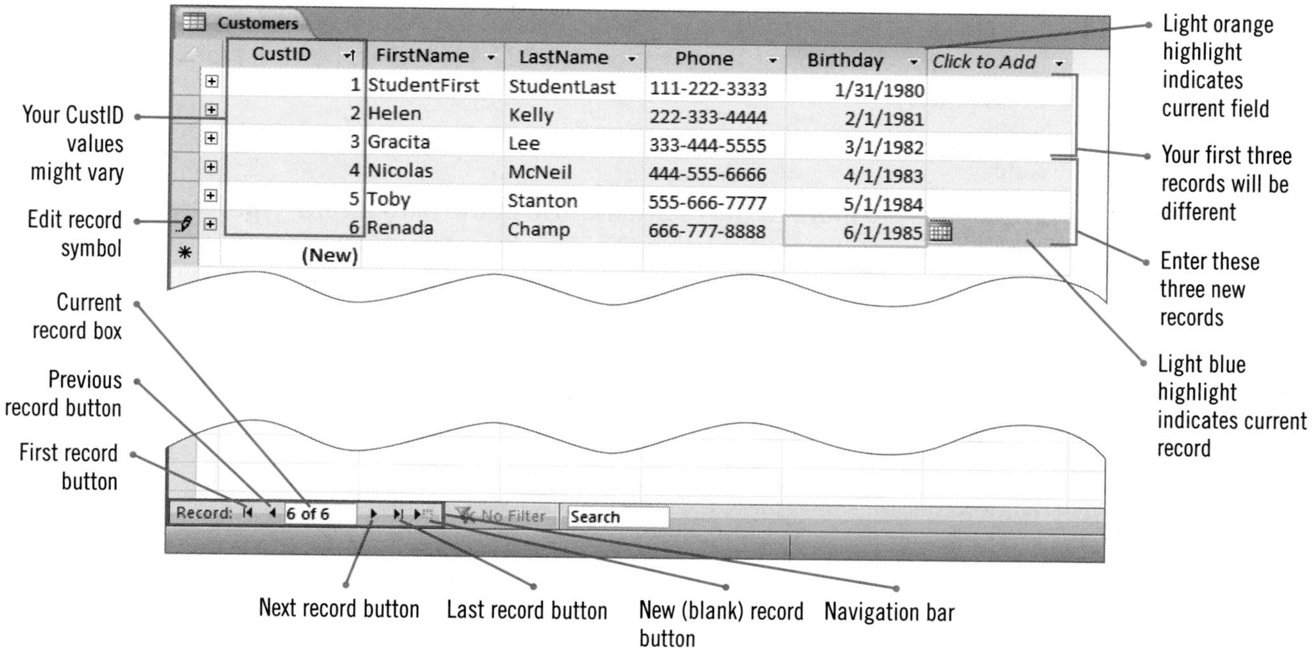

TABLE A-5: Navigation mode keyboard shortcuts

shortcut key	moves to the
[Tab], [Enter], or [→]	Next field of the current record
[Shift][Tab] or [←]	Previous field of the current record
[Home]	First field of the current record
[End]	Last field of the current record
[Ctrl][Home] or [F5]	First field of the first record
[Ctrl][End]	Last field of the last record
[↑]	Current field of the previous record
[↓]	Current field of the next record

Windows Live

Using **cloud computing** (work done in a virtual environment), you can take advantage of Windows Live SkyDrive, a free service from Microsoft. Using Windows Live SkyDrive, you and your colleagues can store files in a "cloud" and retrieve them anytime you are connected to the Internet. That way, you can access files containing data whenever you need them. To use Windows Live SkyDrive, you need a free Windows Live ID, which you obtain at the Windows Live Web site. You can find more information and projects in the "Working with Windows Live and Microsoft Office Web Apps" appendix.

UNIT
A
Access 2010

Editing Data

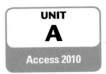

Updating information in a database is another critical data management task. To change the contents of an existing record, navigate to the field you want to change and type the new information. You can delete unwanted data by clicking the field and using [Backspace] or [Delete] to delete text to the left or right of the insertion point. Other data entry keystrokes are summarized in Table A-6. Samantha Hooper asks you to correct two records in the Customers table.

STEPS

QUICK TIP
The ScreenTip for the Undo button displays the action you can undo.

1. **Double-click the name in the FirstName field of the second record, type Jesse, press [Enter], type Siren, press [Enter], type 111-222-4444, press [Enter], type 2/15/81, then press [Enter]**
   You changed the name, telephone number, and birthdate of the second customer. You'll also change the third customer.
2. **Press [Enter] to move to the FirstName field of the third record, type Naresh, press [Enter], type Kast, press [Enter], type 111-222-5555, then press [Esc]**
   Pressing [Esc] once removes the current field's editing changes, so the Phone value changes back to the previous entry. Pressing [Esc] twice removes all changes to the current record. When you move to another record, Access saves your edits, so you can no longer use [Esc] to remove editing changes to the current record. You can, however, click the Undo button on the Quick Access toolbar to undo changes to a previous record.
3. **Retype 111-222-5555, press [Enter], click the Calendar icon, then click March 15, 1982 as shown in Figure A-17**
   When you are working in the Birthday field, which has a Date/Time data type, you can enter a date from the keyboard or use the **Calendar Picker**, a pop-up calendar to find and select a date.
4. **Click the record selector for the last record (the one for Renada Champ), click the Delete button in the Records group on the Home tab, then click Yes**
   A message warns that you cannot undo a record deletion. The Undo button is dimmed, indicating that you cannot use it. The Customers table now has five records, as shown in Figure A-18. Keep in mind that your CustID values might differ from those in the figure because they are controlled by Access.
5. **Click the File tab, click Print, click Print Preview to review the printout of the Customers table before printing, click the Print button, click OK, then click the Close Print Preview button**
6. **Click the File tab, click Exit to close the Quest.accdb database and Access 2010, then click Yes if prompted to save design changes to the Customers table**

Resizing and moving datasheet columns

You can resize the width of a field in a datasheet by dragging the **column separator**, the thin line that separates the field names to the left or right. The pointer changes to ✛ as you make the field wider or narrower. Release the mouse button when you have resized the field. To adjust the column width to accommodate the widest entry in the field, double-click the column separator. To move a column, click the field name to select the entire column, then drag the field name left or right.

FIGURE A-17: **Editing customer records**

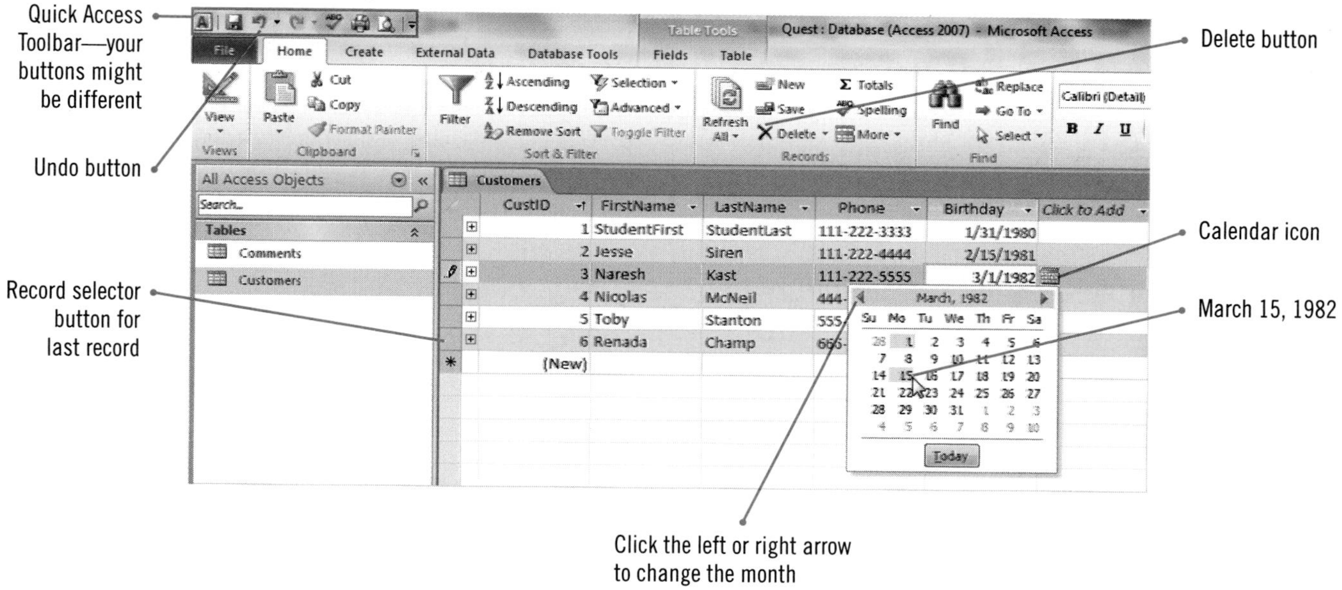
Quick Access Toolbar—your buttons might be different
Undo button
Record selector button for last record
Delete button
Calendar icon
March 15, 1982
Click the left or right arrow to change the month

FIGURE A-18: **Final Customers datasheet**

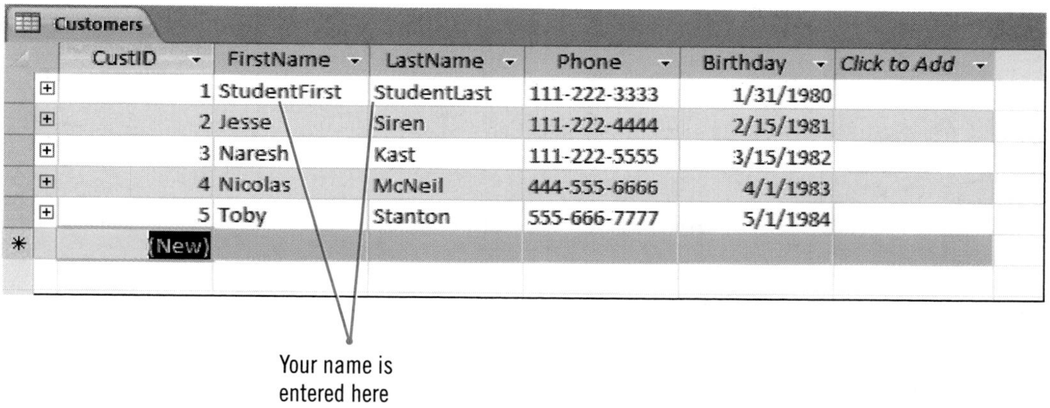
Customers
Your name is entered here

TABLE A-6: **Edit mode keyboard shortcuts**

editing keystroke	action
[Backspace]	Deletes one character to the left of the insertion point
[Delete]	Deletes one character to the right of the insertion point
[F2]	Switches between Edit and Navigation mode
[Esc]	Undoes the change to the current field
[Esc][Esc]	Undoes all changes to the current record
[F7]	Starts the spell-check feature
[Ctrl][']	Inserts the value from the same field in the previous record into the current field
[Ctrl][;]	Inserts the current date in a Date field

Practice

Concepts Review

For current SAM information, including versions and content details, visit SAM Central (http://www.cengage.com/samcentral). If you have a SAM user profile, you may have access to hands-on instruction, practice, and assessment of the skills covered in this unit. Since various versions of SAM are supported throughout the life of this text, check with your instructor for the correct instructions and URL/Web site for accessing assignments.

Label each element of the Access window shown in Figure A-19.

FIGURE A-19

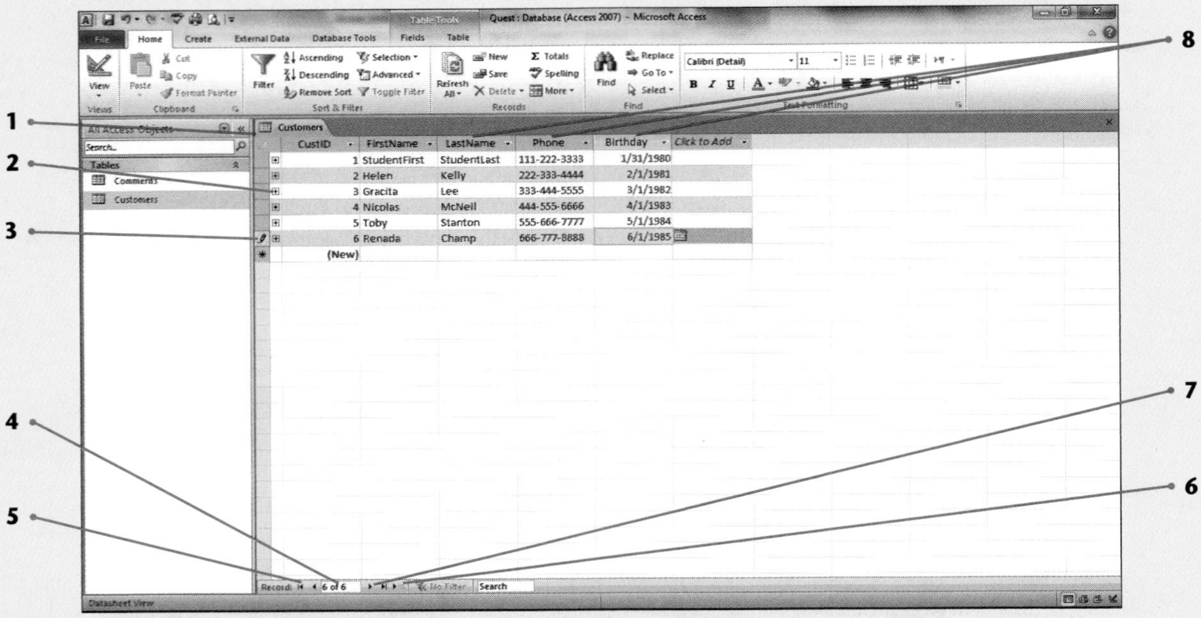

Match each term with the statement that best describes it.

9. Table	**a.** A subset of data from one or more tables
10. Query	**b.** A collection of records for a single subject, such as all the customer records
11. Field	**c.** A professional printout of database information
12. Record	**d.** A spreadsheet-like grid that displays fields as columns and records as rows
13. Datasheet	**e.** A group of related fields for one item, such as all of the information for one customer
14. Form	**f.** A category of information in a table, such as a company name, city, or state
15. Report	**g.** An easy-to-use data entry screen

Select the best answer from the list of choices.

16. Which of the following is *not* a typical benefit of relational databases?

a. More accurate data
b. Faster information retrieval
c. More common than spreadsheets
d. Minimized duplicate data entry

17. Which of the following is *not* an advantage of managing data with relational database software such as Access versus spreadsheet software such as Excel?

a. Allows multiple users to enter data simultaneously
b. Provides data entry forms
c. Reduces duplicate data entry
d. Uses a single table to store all data

18. The object that creates a professional printout of data that includes headers, footers, and graphics is the:

a. Query.
b. Report.
c. Table.
d. Form.

19. The object that contains all of the database data is the:

a. Report.
b. Page.
c. Form.
d. Table.

20. When you create a new database, which object is created first?

a. Query
b. Module
c. Table
d. Form

Skills Review

Access 2010

1. Understand relational databases.

a. Identify five advantages of managing database information in Access versus using a spreadsheet.
b. Create a sentence to explain how the terms *field*, *record*, *table*, and *relational database* relate to one another.

2. Explore a database.

a. Start Access.
b. Open the RealEstate-A.accdb database from the drive and folder where you store your Data Files. Enable content if a Security Warning message appears.
c. Open each of the three tables to study the data they contain. On a sheet of paper, complete Table A-7.
d. Double-click the ListingsByRealtor query in the Navigation Pane to open it. Change any occurrence of Gordon Matusek to your name. Move to another record to save your changes.
e. Double-click the RealtorsMainForm in the Navigation Pane to open it. Use the navigation buttons to navigate through the 11 realtors to observe each realtor's listings.
f. Double-click the RealtorListingReport in the Navigation Pane to open it. Scroll through the report to make sure your name is positioned correctly. The report is currently sorted in ascending order by realtor first names.
g. Close the RealEstate-A database, and then close Access 2010.

TABLE A-7

table name	number of records	number of fields

3. Create a database.

a. Start Access, use the Browse folder button to navigate to the drive and folder where you store your Data Files, type **RealEstateMarketing** as the File Name, click OK, and then click Create to create a new database named RealEstateMarketing.accdb.

Skills Review (continued)

b. Switch to Table Design View, name the table **Prospects**, then enter the following fields and data types:

field name	data type
ProspectID	**AutoNumber**
ProspectFirst	**Text**
ProspectLast	**Text**
Phone	**Text**
Email	**Hyperlink**
Street	**Text**
City	**Text**
State	**Text**
Zip	**Text**

c. Save the table, switch to Datasheet View, and enter two records using your name in the first record and your professor's name in the second. Tab through the ProspectID field, an AutoNumber field.

d. Enter **OK** (Oklahoma) as the value in the State field for both records. Use school or fictitious (rather than personal) data for all other field data, and be sure to fill out each record completely.

e. Widen each column in the Prospects table so that all data is visible, then save and close the Prospects table.

4. Create a table.

a. Click the Create tab on the Ribbon, click Table Design, then create a new table with the following two fields and data types:

field name	data type
StateAbbrev	**Text**
StateName	**Text**

b. Save the table with the name **States**. Click No when asked if you want Access to create the primary key field.

5. Create primary keys.

a. In Table Design View of the States table, set the StateAbbrev as the primary key field.

b. Save the States table and open it in Datasheet View.

c. Enter one state record, using **OK** for the StateAbbrev value and **Oklahoma** for the StateName value to match the State value of OK that you entered for both records in the Prospects table.

d. Close the States table.

6. Relate two tables.

a. From the Database Tools tab, open the Relationships window.

b. Add the States then the Prospects table to the Relationships window.

c. Drag the bottom edge of the Prospects table to expand the field list to display all of the fields.

d. Drag the StateAbbrev field from the States table to the State field of the Prospects table.

e. In the Edit Relationships dialog box, click the Enforce Referential Integrity check box, then click Create. Your Relationships window should look similar to Figure A-20. If you connect the wrong fields by mistake, right-click the line connecting the two fields, click Delete, then try again.

f. Close the Relationships window, and save changes when prompted.

FIGURE A-20

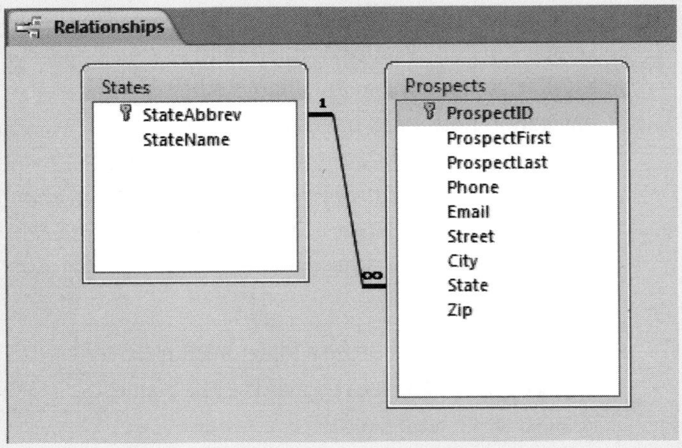

Skills Review (continued)

7. Enter data.

a. Open the States table and enter the following records:

StateAbbrev field	StateName field	StateAbbrev field	StateName field
CO	Colorado	NE	Nebraska
IA	Iowa	TX	Texas
KS	Kansas	WI	Wisconsin
MO	Missouri		

b. Add a few more state records using the correct two-character abbreviation for the state and the properly spelled state name.

c. Close and reopen the States table. Notice that Access sorts the records by the values in the primary key field, the StateAbbrev field.

8. Edit data.

a. Click the Expand button for the OK record to see the two related records from the Prospects table.

b. Enter two more prospects in the OK subdatasheet using any fictitious but realistic data as shown in Figure A-21. Notice that you are not required to enter a value for the State field, the foreign key field in the subdatasheet.

c. If required by your instructor, print the States datasheet and the Prospects datasheet.

d. Click the File tab, then click Exit to close all open objects as well as the RealEstateMarketing.accdb database and Access 2010. If prompted to save any design changes, click Yes.

FIGURE A-21

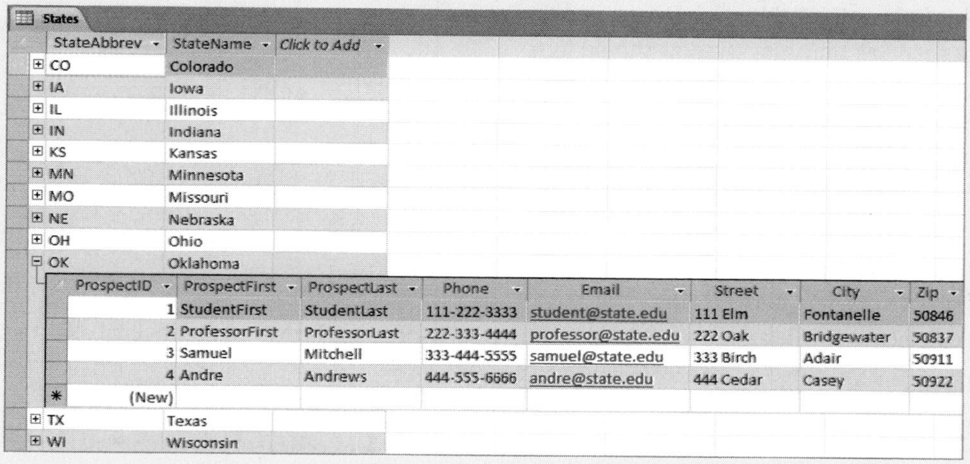

States

StateAbbrev	StateName	Click to Add
CO	Colorado	
IA	Iowa	
IL	Illinois	
IN	Indiana	
KS	Kansas	
MN	Minnesota	
MO	Missouri	
NE	Nebraska	
OH	Ohio	
OK	Oklahoma	
TX	Texas	
WI	Wisconsin	

ProspectID	ProspectFirst	ProspectLast	Phone	Email	Street	City	Zip
1	StudentFirst	StudentLast	111-222-3333	student@state.edu	111 Elm	Fontanelle	50846
2	ProfessorFirst	ProfessorLast	222-333-4444	professor@state.edu	222 Oak	Bridgewater	50837
3	Samuel	Mitchell	333-444-5555	samuel@state.edu	333 Birch	Adair	50911
4	Andre	Andrews	444-555-6666	andre@state.edu	444 Cedar	Casey	50922
(New)							

Independent Challenge 1

Review the following twelve examples of database tables:

- Telephone directory
- College course offerings
- Restaurant menu
- Cookbook
- Movie listing
- Islands of the Caribbean
- Encyclopedia
- Shopping catalog
- International product inventory
- Party guest list
- Members of the U.S. House of Representatives
- Ancient wonders of the world

In a Word document, complete the following tasks.

a. For each example, build a Word table with four to five columns. In the first row, identify four to five field names that you would expect to find in the table.

b. In the second and third rows of each table, enter two possible records. The first table, Telephone Directory, is completed in Figure A-22 as an example to follow.

FIGURE A-22

Table: Telephone Directory

FirstName	LastName	Street	Zip	Phone
Marco	Lopez	100 Main Street	88715	555-612-3312
Christopher	Stafford	253 Maple Lane	77824	555-612-1179

Independent Challenge 2

You are working with several civic groups to coordinate a community-wide cleanup effort. You have started a database called Recycle-A, which tracks the different clubs, their trash deposits, and the trash collection centers that are participating.

a. Start Access, then open the Recycle-A.accdb database from the drive and folder where you store your Data Files. Enable content if prompted.

b. Open each table's datasheet to study the number of fields and records per table. Notice that there are no expand buttons to the left of any records because relationships have not yet been established between these tables.

c. In a Word document, recreate and complete the table shown in Table A-8.

TABLE A-8

table name	number of fields	number of records

d. Close all table datasheets, then open the Relationships window and create the one-to-many relationships shown in Figure A-23. Click the Show Table button to add the field lists for each table to the Relationships window, and drag the title bars of the field lists to position them as shown in Figure A-23.

e. Be sure to enforce referential integrity on all relationships. If you create an incorrect relationship, right-click the line linking the fields, click Delete, and try again. Your final Relationships window should look like Figure A-23.

f. If required by your instructor, click the Relationship Report button on the Design tab, then click Print to print a copy of the Relationships for Recycle-A report. To close the report, right-click the Relationships for Recycle-A tab and click Close. Click No when prompted to save changes to the report.

FIGURE A-23

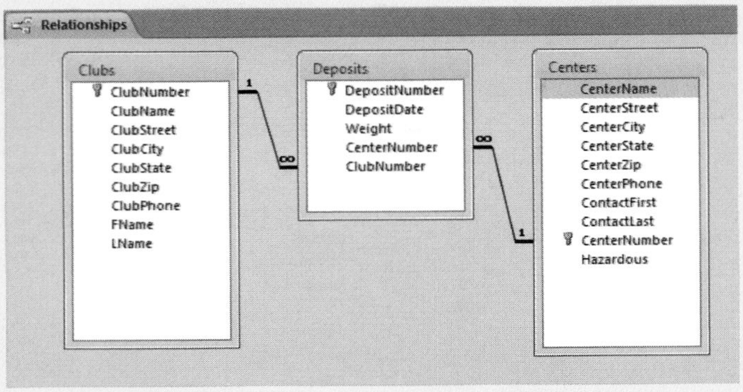

g. Save your changes to the Relationships window, if necessary, close the Recycle-A.accdb database, then exit Access 2010.

Independent Challenge 3

This Independent Challenge requires an Internet connection.

If you have a SAM 2010 user profile, an autogradable SAM version of this assignment may be available at http://www.cengage.com/sam2010. Check with your instructor to confirm that this assignment is available in SAM. To use the SAM version of this assignment, log into the SAM 2010 Web site and download the instruction and start files.

You are working for an advertising agency that provides advertising media for small and large businesses in the midwestern United States. You have started a database called BusinessContacts-A, which tracks your company's customers.

a. Start Access and open the BusinessContacts-A.accdb database from the drive and folder where you store your Data Files. Enable content if prompted.

b. Add a new record to the Customers table, using your own first and last names, $7,788.99 in the YTDSales field, and any reasonable entries for the rest of the fields.

c. Edit the Sprint Systems record (the first record). The Company name should be Embarq Corporation, and the Street value should be 2244 College St.

d. Delete the record for St Luke's Hospital (record 20), then close the Customers table.

e. Create a new table with two fields, State2 and StateName. Assign both fields a Text data type. The State2 field will contain the two-letter abbreviation for state names. The StateName field will contain the full state name.

f. Set the State2 field as the primary key field, then save the table as States.

Independent Challenge 3 (continued)

g. Enter at least three records into the States table, making sure that all of the states used in the Customers datasheet are entered in the States table. This includes *KS Kansas, MO Missouri,* and any other state you entered in Step b when you added a new record to the Customers table.

h. Close all open tables. Open the Relationships window, add both the States and Customers field lists to the window, then expand the size of the Customers field list so that all fields are visible.

i. Build a one-to-many relationship between the States and Customers tables by dragging the State2 field from the States table to the State field of the Customers table to create a one-to-many relationship between the two tables. Enforce referential integrity on the relationship. If you are unable to enforce referential integrity, it means that a value in the State field of the Customers table doesn't have a perfect match in the State2 field of the States table. Open both datasheets, making sure every state in the Customers table is also represented in the States table, close all datasheets, then reestablish the one-to-many relationship between the two tables with referential integrity.

j. Close the Relationships window and save your changes.

Advanced Challenge Exercise

ACE

- Use your favorite search engine to research the two-character abbreviations for the 13 provinces of Canada using the Web search criteria of **provinces of Canada postcodes**.
- Enter the 13 records into the States table, entering the two-character abbreviation in the State2 field and the province name in the StateName field. Note that all 13 entries are different from the 50 states in the United States. Close the States table.
- Right-click the States table in the Navigation Pane and click Rename. Enter **StatesProvinces** as the new table name.
- Reopen the Relationships window, click the Show Table button, double-click StatesProvinces, and click Close. The relationship between the StatesProvinces table and the Customers table has remained intact, but when you rename a table after establishing relationships, review the Relationships window to make sure all tables are visible.
- Click the Relationship Report button on the Design tab, then click Print to print the report.
- Right-click the Relationships for BusinessContacts-A tab, then click Close. Click Yes to save the report, then click OK to name the report Relationships for BusinessContacts-A.
- Close the Relationships window, saving changes as prompted.

k. Close the BusinessContacts-A.accdb database, and exit Access 2010.

Real Life Independent Challenge

This Independent Challenge requires an Internet connection.

Now that you've learned about Microsoft Access and relational databases, brainstorm how you might use an Access database in your daily life or career. Start by visiting the Microsoft Web site, and explore what's new about Access 2010.

a. Using your favorite search engine, look up the keywords *benefits of a relational database* or *benefits of Microsoft Access* to find articles that discuss the benefits of organizing data in a relational database.

b. Read several articles about the benefits of organizing data in a relational database such as Access, identifying three distinct benefits. Use a Word document to record those three benefits. Also, copy and paste the Web site address of the article you are referencing for each benefit you have identified.

c. In addition, as you read the articles that describe relational database benefits, list any terminology unfamiliar to you, identifying at least five new terms.

d. Using a search engine or a Web site that provides a computer glossary such as *www.whatis.com* or *www.webopedia.com*, look up the definition of the new terms, and enter both the term and the definition of the term in your document as well as the Web site address where your definition was found.

e. Finally, based on your research and growing understanding of Access 2010, list three ways you could use an Access database to organize, enhance, or support the activities and responsibilities of your daily life or career. Type your name at the top of the document, and submit it to your instructor as requested.

Visual Workshop

Open the Basketball-A.accdb database from the drive and folder where you store your Data Files, enable content if prompted, then open the Offense query datasheet, which lists offensive statistics by player by game. Modify any of the Kelsey Douglas records to contain your first and last names, then move to a new record, observing the power of a relational database to modify every occurrence of that name throughout the database. Close the Offense query, then open the Players table, shown in Figure A-24. Note that your name will be listed in alphabetical order based on the current sort field, PLast. Print the Players datasheet if requested by your instructor, then close the Players table, exit the Basketball-A.accdb database, and exit Access.

FIGURE A-24

Players

	PFirst	PLast	Height	PlayerNo	GradYear	Position	HomeTown	HomeState	Lettered
⊞	Kristen	Czyenski	73	35	2015	F	Omaha	NE	☐
⊞	Denise	Franco	72	42	2016	F	Antigua	WI	☑
⊞	Sydney	Freesen	68	4	2014	G	Panora	IA	☐
⊞	Theresa	Grant	73	22	2013	F	McKinney	TX	☐
⊞	Megan	Hile	74	45	2015	F	Cumberland	IA	☑
⊞	Amy	Hodel	72	21	2014	F	Oakbrook	IL	☑
⊞	Ellyse	Howard	70	12	2016	G	Osseo	MN	☑
⊞	Jamie	Johnson	75	52	2016	F	Belleville	IL	☐
⊞	Sandy	Robins	65	23	2013	G	Anita	IA	☐
⊞	StudentFirst	StudentLast	69	5	2015	G	Linden	IA	☑
⊞	Ashley	Sydnes	75	30	2013	F	Salina	KS	☐
⊞	Morgan	Tyler	71	51	2014	G	Roseau	MN	☐
⊞	Abbey	Walker	76	32	2014	C	Fargo	ND	☐
*			0	0					■

UNIT

B

Access 2010

Building and Using Queries

Files You Will Need:

QuestTravel-B.accdb
Recycle-B.accdb
Membership-B.accdb
Congress-B.accdb
Vet-B.accdb
Baseball-B.accdb

You build queries in an Access database to ask "questions" about data, such as which adventure tours are scheduled for July or what types of tours take place in Florida. Queries present the answer in a datasheet, which you can sort, filter, and format. Because queries are stored in the database, they can be used multiple times. Each time a query is opened, it displays a current view of the latest updates to the database. Samantha Hooper, tour developer for U.S. group travel at Quest Specialty Travel, has several questions about the customer and tour information in the Quest database. You'll develop queries to provide Samantha with up-to-date answers.

OBJECTIVES

- Use the Query Wizard
- Work with data in a query
- Use Query Design View
- Sort and find data
- Filter data
- Apply AND criteria
- Apply OR criteria
- Format a datasheet

UNIT B

Access 2010

Using the Query Wizard

A **query** allows you to select a subset of fields and records from one or more tables and then present the selected data as a single datasheet. A major benefit of working with data through a query is that you can focus on only the information you need to answer your question, rather than navigating the fields and records from many large tables. You can enter, edit, and navigate data in a query datasheet just like a table datasheet. However, keep in mind that Access data is physically stored only in tables, even though you can view and edit it through other Access objects such as queries and forms. Because a query doesn't physically store the data, a query datasheet is sometimes called a **logical view** of the data. Technically, a query is a set of **SQL (Structured Query Language)** instructions, but because you can use Access query tools such as Query Design View, you are not required to know SQL to build or use Access queries. You use the Simple Query Wizard to build a query that displays a few fields from the Tours and Customers tables in one datasheet.

STEPS

1. **Start Access, open the QuestTravel-B.accdb database, enable content if prompted, then maximize the window**

   Access provides several tools to create a new query. One way is to use the **Simple Query Wizard**, which prompts you for information it needs to create a new query.

> **TROUBLE**
> If a Microsoft Access Security Notice dialog box opens, click the Open button.

2. **Click the Create tab on the Ribbon, click the Query Wizard button in the Queries group, then click OK to start the Simple Query Wizard**

   The first Simple Query Wizard dialog box opens, prompting you to select the fields you want to view in the new query.

3. **Click the Tables/Queries list arrow, click Table: Tours, double-click TourName, double-click City, double-click Category, then double-click Cost**

   So far, you've selected four fields from the Tours table to display basic tour information in this query. You also want to add the first and last name fields from the Customers table so you know which customers purchased each tour.

> **TROUBLE**
> Click the Remove Single Field button < if you need to remove a field from the Selected Fields list.

4. **Click the Tables/Queries list arrow, click Table: Customers, double-click FName, then double-click LName**

   You've selected four fields from the Tours table and two from the Customers table for your new query, as shown in Figure B-1.

5. **Click Next, click Next to select Detail, select Tours Query in the title text box, type TourCustomers as the name of the query, then click Finish**

   The TourCustomers datasheet opens, displaying four fields from the Tours table and two from the Customers table as shown in Figure B-2. The query can show which customers have purchased which tours because of the one-to-many table relationships established in the Relationships window.

FIGURE B-1: **Selecting fields using the Simple Query Wizard**

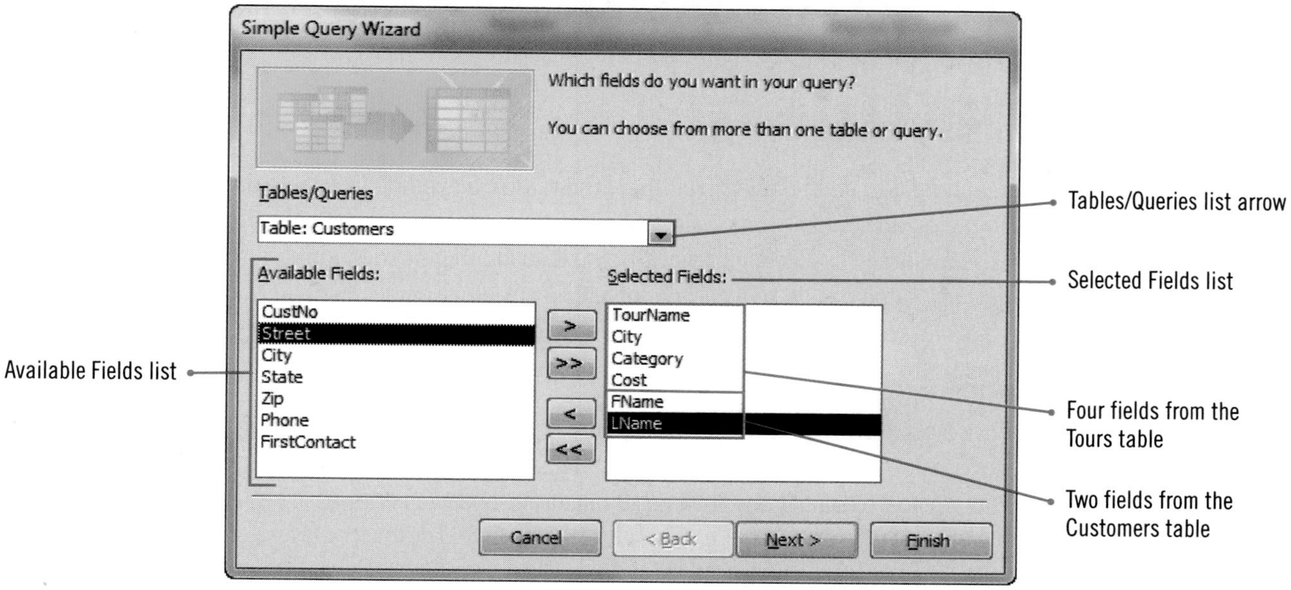

FIGURE B-2: **TourCustomers datasheet**

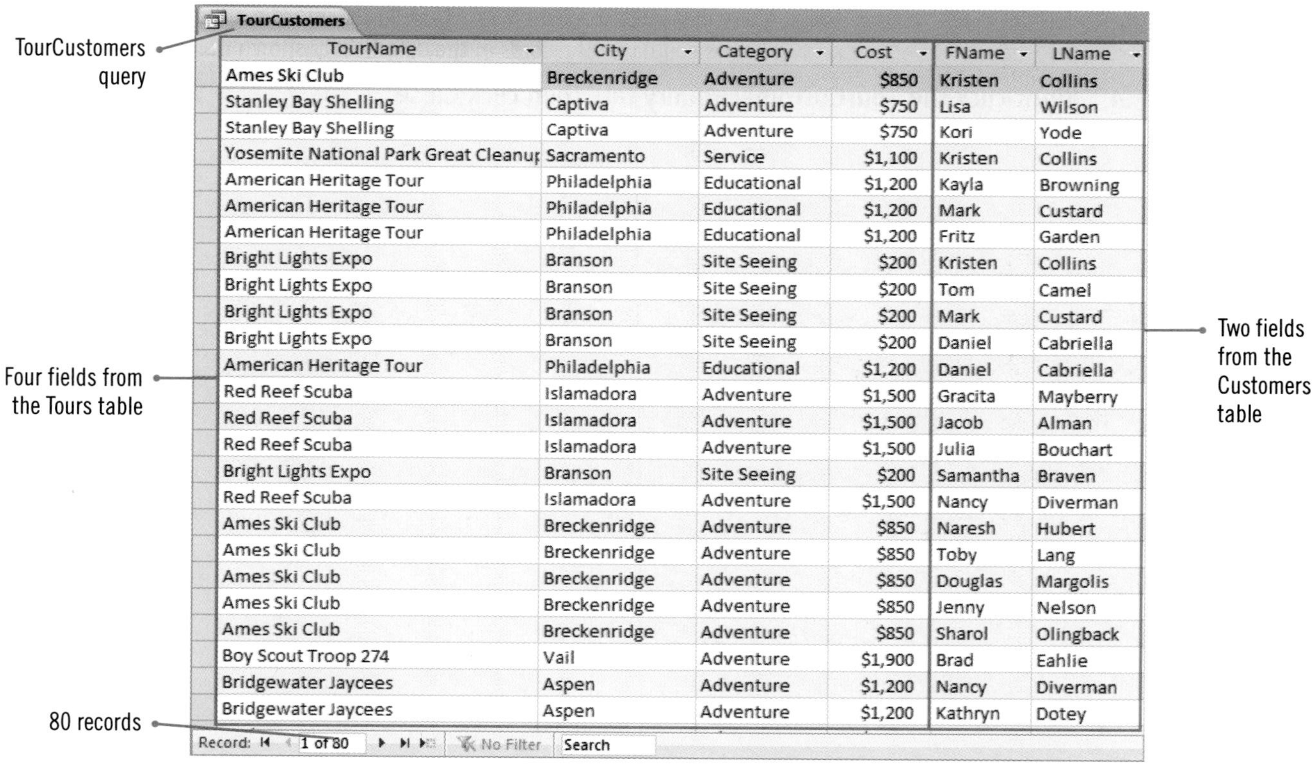

TourName	City	Category	Cost	FName	LName
Ames Ski Club	Breckenridge	Adventure	$850	Kristen	Collins
Stanley Bay Shelling	Captiva	Adventure	$750	Lisa	Wilson
Stanley Bay Shelling	Captiva	Adventure	$750	Kori	Yode
Yosemite National Park Great Cleanup	Sacramento	Service	$1,100	Kristen	Collins
American Heritage Tour	Philadelphia	Educational	$1,200	Kayla	Browning
American Heritage Tour	Philadelphia	Educational	$1,200	Mark	Custard
American Heritage Tour	Philadelphia	Educational	$1,200	Fritz	Garden
Bright Lights Expo	Branson	Site Seeing	$200	Kristen	Collins
Bright Lights Expo	Branson	Site Seeing	$200	Tom	Camel
Bright Lights Expo	Branson	Site Seeing	$200	Mark	Custard
Bright Lights Expo	Branson	Site Seeing	$200	Daniel	Cabriella
American Heritage Tour	Philadelphia	Educational	$1,200	Daniel	Cabriella
Red Reef Scuba	Islamadora	Adventure	$1,500	Gracita	Mayberry
Red Reef Scuba	Islamadora	Adventure	$1,500	Jacob	Alman
Red Reef Scuba	Islamadora	Adventure	$1,500	Julia	Bouchart
Bright Lights Expo	Branson	Site Seeing	$200	Samantha	Braven
Red Reef Scuba	Islamadora	Adventure	$1,500	Nancy	Diverman
Ames Ski Club	Breckenridge	Adventure	$850	Naresh	Hubert
Ames Ski Club	Breckenridge	Adventure	$850	Toby	Lang
Ames Ski Club	Breckenridge	Adventure	$850	Douglas	Margolis
Ames Ski Club	Breckenridge	Adventure	$850	Jenny	Nelson
Ames Ski Club	Breckenridge	Adventure	$850	Sharol	Olingback
Boy Scout Troop 274	Vail	Adventure	$1,900	Brad	Eahlie
Bridgewater Jaycees	Aspen	Adventure	$1,200	Nancy	Diverman
Bridgewater Jaycees	Aspen	Adventure	$1,200	Kathryn	Dotey

UNIT
B
Access 2010

Working with Data in a Query

You enter and edit data in a query datasheet the same way you do in a table datasheet. Because all data is stored in tables, any edits you make in a query datasheet are permanently stored in the underlying tables, and are automatically updated in all views of the data in other queries, forms, and reports. You want to change the name of two tours and update one customer name. You can use the TourCustomers query datasheet to make these edits.

STEPS

1. **Double-click Stanley in the Stanley Bay Shelling tour name in either the second or third record, type Princess, then click any other record**

   All occurrences of Stanley Bay Shelling automatically update to Princess Bay Shelling because this tour name value is stored only once in the Tours table (see Figure B-3). The tour name is selected from the Tours table and displayed in the TourCustomers query for each customer who purchased this tour.

2. **Double-click Cabriella in the LName field, type Dodds, then click any other record**

   All occurrences of Cabriella automatically update to Dodds because this last name value is stored only once in the Customers table. This name is selected from the Customers table and displayed in the TourCustomers query for each tour this customer purchased.

3. **Click the record selector button to the left of the first record, click the Home tab, click the Delete button in the Records group, then click Yes**

   You can delete records from a query datasheet the same way you delete them from a table datasheet. Notice that the navigation bar now indicates you have 79 records in the datasheet as shown in Figure B-4.

4. **Right-click the TourCustomers query tab, then click Close**

FIGURE B-3: **Working with data in a query datasheet**

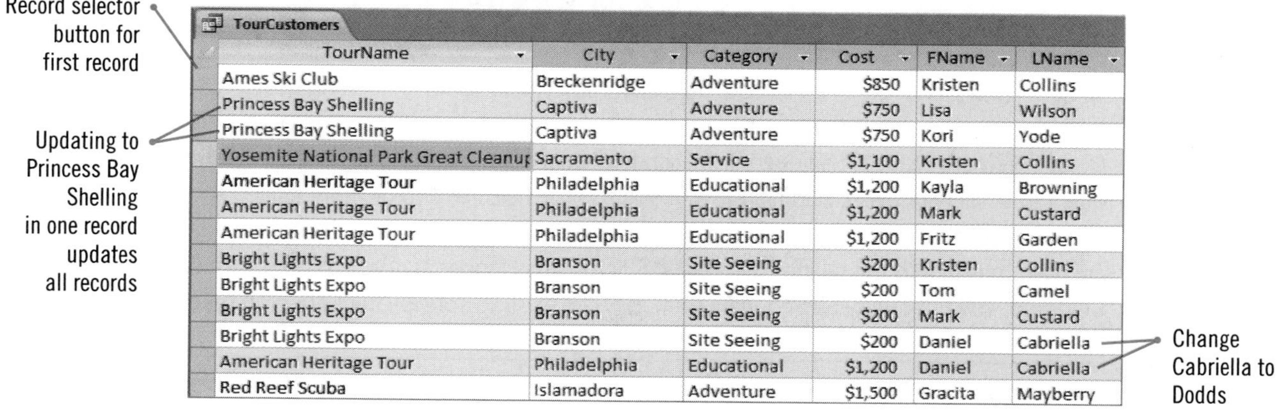

TourName	City	Category	Cost	FName	LName
Ames Ski Club	Breckenridge	Adventure	$850	Kristen	Collins
Princess Bay Shelling	Captiva	Adventure	$750	Lisa	Wilson
Princess Bay Shelling	Captiva	Adventure	$750	Kori	Yode
Yosemite National Park Great Cleanup	Sacramento	Service	$1,100	Kristen	Collins
American Heritage Tour	Philadelphia	Educational	$1,200	Kayla	Browning
American Heritage Tour	Philadelphia	Educational	$1,200	Mark	Custard
American Heritage Tour	Philadelphia	Educational	$1,200	Fritz	Garden
Bright Lights Expo	Branson	Site Seeing	$200	Kristen	Collins
Bright Lights Expo	Branson	Site Seeing	$200	Tom	Camel
Bright Lights Expo	Branson	Site Seeing	$200	Mark	Custard
Bright Lights Expo	Branson	Site Seeing	$200	Daniel	Cabriella
American Heritage Tour	Philadelphia	Educational	$1,200	Daniel	Cabriella
Red Reef Scuba	Islamadora	Adventure	$1,500	Gracita	Mayberry

FIGURE B-4: **Final TourCustomers datasheet**

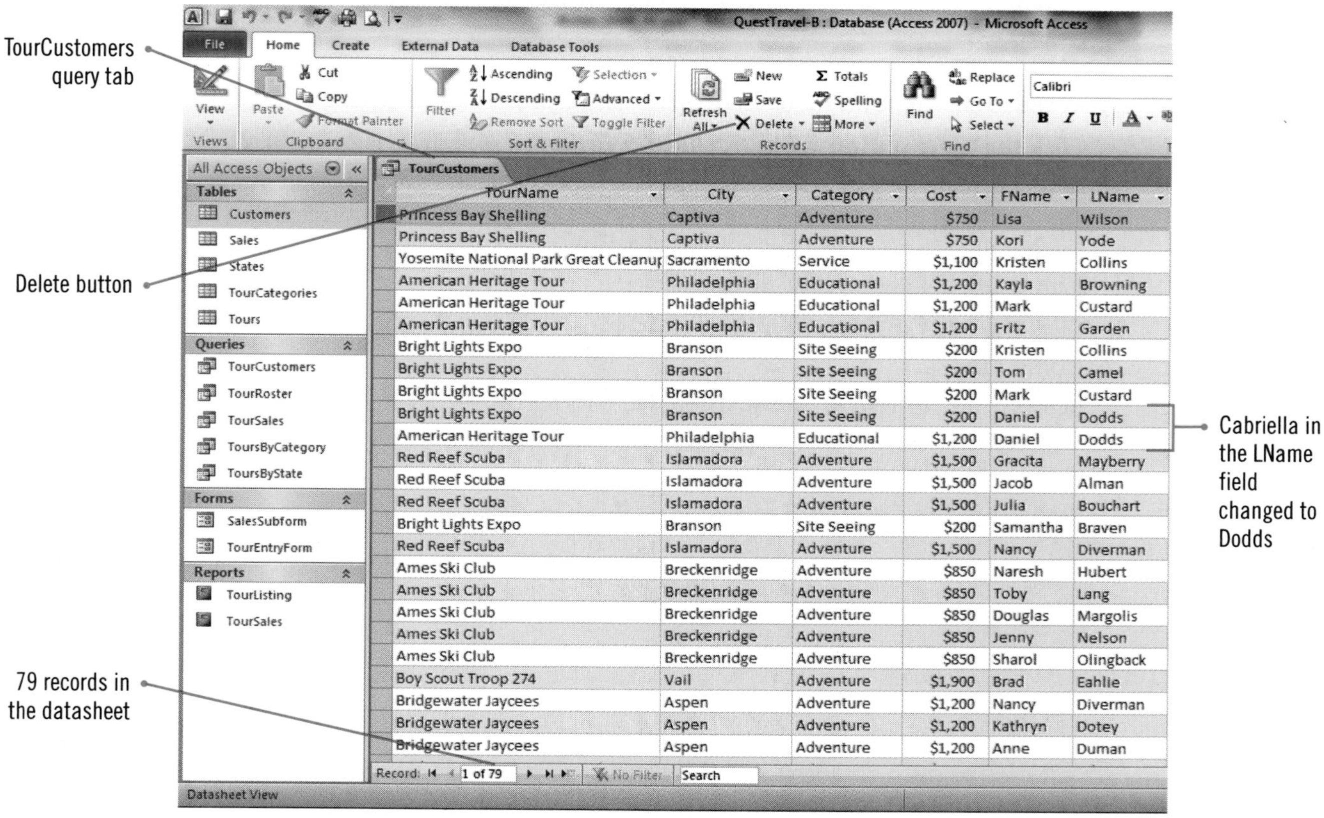

TourName	City	Category	Cost	FName	LName
Princess Bay Shelling	Captiva	Adventure	$750	Lisa	Wilson
Princess Bay Shelling	Captiva	Adventure	$750	Kori	Yode
Yosemite National Park Great Cleanup	Sacramento	Service	$1,100	Kristen	Collins
American Heritage Tour	Philadelphia	Educational	$1,200	Kayla	Browning
American Heritage Tour	Philadelphia	Educational	$1,200	Mark	Custard
American Heritage Tour	Philadelphia	Educational	$1,200	Fritz	Garden
Bright Lights Expo	Branson	Site Seeing	$200	Kristen	Collins
Bright Lights Expo	Branson	Site Seeing	$200	Tom	Camel
Bright Lights Expo	Branson	Site Seeing	$200	Mark	Custard
Bright Lights Expo	Branson	Site Seeing	$200	Daniel	Dodds
American Heritage Tour	Philadelphia	Educational	$1,200	Daniel	Dodds
Red Reef Scuba	Islamadora	Adventure	$1,500	Gracita	Mayberry
Red Reef Scuba	Islamadora	Adventure	$1,500	Jacob	Alman
Red Reef Scuba	Islamadora	Adventure	$1,500	Julia	Bouchart
Bright Lights Expo	Branson	Site Seeing	$200	Samantha	Braven
Red Reef Scuba	Islamadora	Adventure	$1,500	Nancy	Diverman
Ames Ski Club	Breckenridge	Adventure	$850	Naresh	Hubert
Ames Ski Club	Breckenridge	Adventure	$850	Toby	Lang
Ames Ski Club	Breckenridge	Adventure	$850	Douglas	Margolis
Ames Ski Club	Breckenridge	Adventure	$850	Jenny	Nelson
Ames Ski Club	Breckenridge	Adventure	$850	Sharol	Olingback
Boy Scout Troop 274	Vail	Adventure	$1,900	Brad	Eahlie
Bridgewater Jaycees	Aspen	Adventure	$1,200	Nancy	Diverman
Bridgewater Jaycees	Aspen	Adventure	$1,200	Kathryn	Dotey
Bridgewater Jaycees	Aspen	Adventure	$1,200	Anne	Duman

Access 2010

UNIT **B** Access 2010

Using Query Design View

You use **Query Design View** to add, delete, or move the fields in an existing query, to specify sort orders, or to add **criteria** to limit the number of records shown in the resulting datasheet. You can also use Query Design View to create a new query from scratch. Query Design View presents the fields you can use for that query in small windows called field lists. If you use the fields of two or more related tables in the query, the relationship between two tables is displayed with a **join line** (also called a **link line**) identifying which fields are used to establish the relationship. Samantha Hooper asks you to print a list of Adventure tours in Colorado. You use Query Design View to modify the existing ToursByState query to meet her request.

STEPS

1. **Double-click the ToursByState query in the Navigation Pane to review the datasheet**
   The ToursByState query contains the StateName field from the States table, and the TourName, TourStartDate, and Cost fields from the Tours table.
2. **Click the View button in the Views group to switch to Query Design View**
   Query Design View displays the tables used in the query in the upper pane of the window. The link line shows that one record in the States table may be related to many records in the Tours table. The lower pane of the window, called the **query design grid** (or query grid for short) displays the field names, sort orders, and criteria used within the query.
3. **Click the first Criteria cell for the StateName field, then type Colorado as shown in Figure B-5**
   Criteria are limiting conditions you set in the query design grid. In this case, the condition limits the selected records to only those with "Colorado" in the StateName field.

   > **QUICK TIP**
   > Query criteria are not case sensitive, so Colorado equals COLORADO equals colorado.

4. **Click the View button in the Results group to switch to Datasheet View**
   Now only six records are selected, because only six of the tours have "Colorado" in the StateName field, as shown in Figure B-6. Remember that this query contains two ascending sort orders: StateName and TourName. Because all of the records have the same StateName, they are further sorted by the TourName values. You want to save this query with a different name.
5. **Click the File tab, click Save Object As, type ColoradoTours, click OK, then click the Home tab**
   In Access, the **Save command** on the File tab saves the current object, and the **Save Object As command** saves the current object with a new name. Recall that Access saves *data* automatically as you move from record to record.
6. **Right-click the ColoradoTours query tab, then click Close**

FIGURE B-5: ToursByState query in Design View

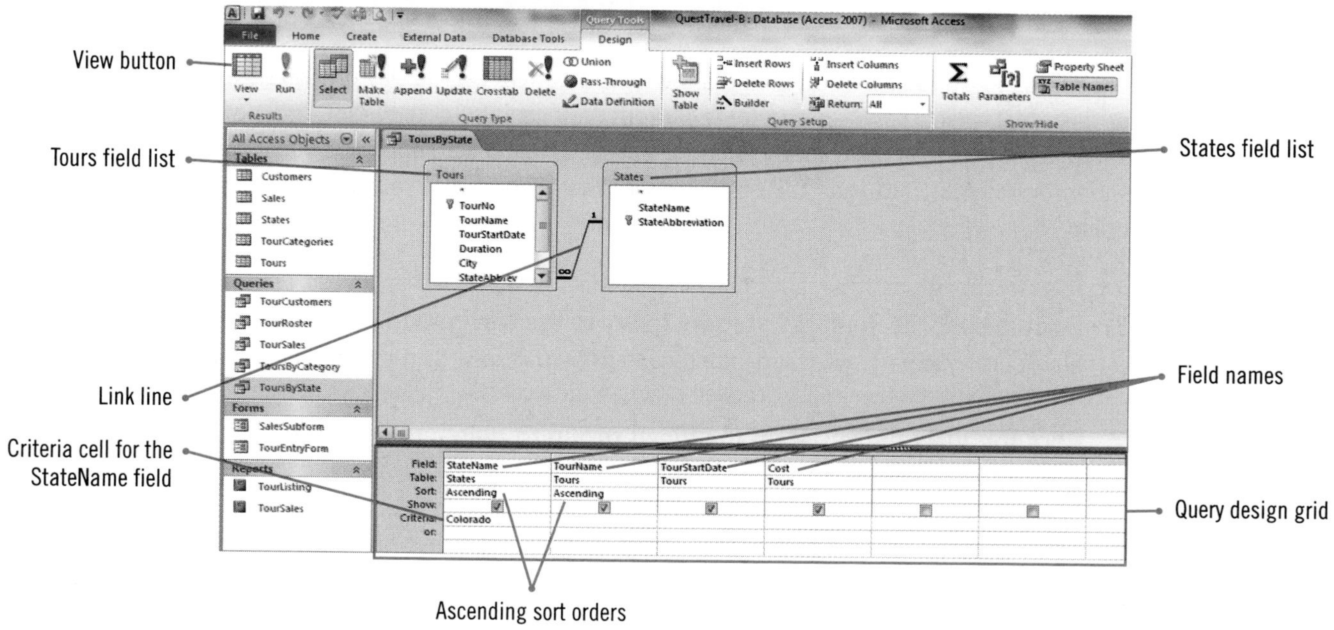
View button
Tours field list
States field list
Link line
Field names
Criteria cell for the StateName field
Query design grid
Ascending sort orders
Field: StateName TourName TourStartDate Cost
Table: States Tours Tours Tours
Sort: Ascending Ascending
Criteria: Colorado

FIGURE B-6: ToursByState datasheet with Colorado criterion

Only six Colorado records are selected
TourName values displayed in ascending order
ToursByState
StateName TourName TourStartDate Cost
Colorado Ames Ski Club 01/20/2013 $850
Colorado Boy Scout Troop 274 01/31/2013 $1,900
Colorado Bridgewater Jaycees 03/05/2013 $1,200
Colorado Eagle Hiking Club 07/07/2012 $695
Colorado Franklin Family Reunion 03/29/2013 $700
Colorado Team Discovery 07/17/2012 $550

Adding or deleting a table in a query

You might want to add a table's field list to the upper pane of Query Design View in order to select fields from that table for the query. To add a new table to Query Design View, click the Show Table button on the Design tab, then add the desired table(s). To delete an unneeded table from Query Design View, click its title bar, then press [Delete].

UNIT
B
Access 2010

Sorting and Finding Data

The Access sort and find features are handy tools that help you quickly organize and find data in a table or query datasheet. Besides using these buttons, you can also click the list arrow on the field name in a datasheet, and then click a sorting option. Samantha Hooper asks you to provide a list of tours sorted by TourStartDate, and then by Duration. You'll modify the ToursByCategory query to answer this query.

STEPS

1. **Double-click the ToursByCategory query in the Navigation Pane to open its datasheet**
   The ToursByCategory query currently sorts tours by Category, then by TourName. You'll add the Duration field to this query, then change the sort order for the records.

2. **Click the View button in the Views group to switch to Design View, then double-click the Duration field in the Tours field list**
   When you double-click a field in a field list, Access inserts it in the next available position in the query design grid. You can also select a field, and then drag it to a specific column of the query grid. To select a field in the query grid, you click its field selector. The **field selector** is the thin gray bar above each field in the query grid. If you want to delete a field from a query, click its field selector, then press [Delete]. Deleting a field from a query does not delete it from the underlying table; the field is only deleted from the query's logical view of the data.
   Currently, the ToursByCategory query is sorted by Category and then by TourName. Access evaluates sort specifications from left to right. You want to sort this query first by TourStartDate then by Duration.

3. **Click Ascending in the Category Sort cell, click the list arrow, click (not sorted), click Ascending in the TourName Sort cell, click the list arrow, click (not sorted), double-click the TourStartDate Sort cell to specify an Ascending sort, then double-click the Duration Sort cell to specify an Ascending sort**
   The records are now set to be sorted in ascending order, first by TourStartDate, then by the values in the Duration field, as shown in Figure B-7. Because sort orders always work left to right, you sometimes need to rearrange the fields before applying a sort order that uses more than one field. To move a field in the query design grid, click its field selector, then drag it left or right.

4. **Click the View button in the Results group to display the query datasheet**
   The new datasheet shows the Duration field in the fifth column. The records are now sorted in ascending order by the TourStartDate field. If two records have the same TourStartDate, they are further sorted by Duration. You can also sort directly in the datasheet using the Ascending and Descending buttons on the Home tab, but to specify multiple sort orders on nonconsecutive fields, it's best to use Query Design View.
   Your next task is to replace all occurrences of "Site Seeing" with "Cultural" in the Category field.

5. **Click the Find button on the Home tab, type Site Seeing in the Find What box, click the Replace tab, click in the Replace With box, then type Cultural**
   The Find and Replace dialog box is shown in Figure B-8.

> **TROUBLE**
> If your find-and-replace effort did not work correctly, click the Undo button and repeat Steps 5 and 6.

6. **Click the Replace All button in the Find and Replace dialog box, click Yes to continue, then click Cancel to close the Find and Replace dialog box**
   Access replaced all occurrences of "Site Seeing" with "Cultural" in the Category field, as shown in Figure B-9.

7. **Right-click the ToursByCategory query tab, click Close, then click Yes if prompted to save changes**

FIGURE B-7: **Changing sort orders for the ToursByCategory query**

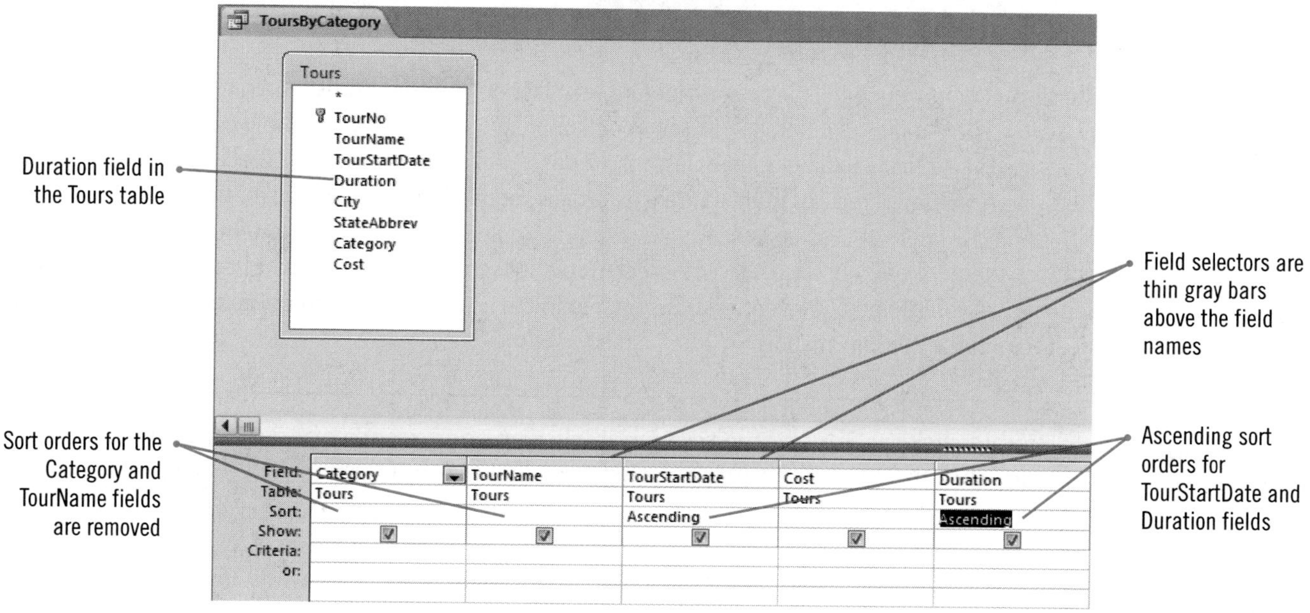

FIGURE B-8: **Find and Replace dialog box**

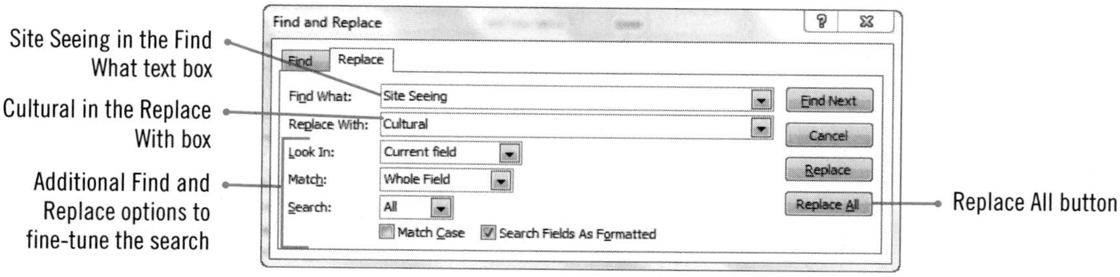

FIGURE B-9: **Final ToursByCategory datasheet with new sort orders**

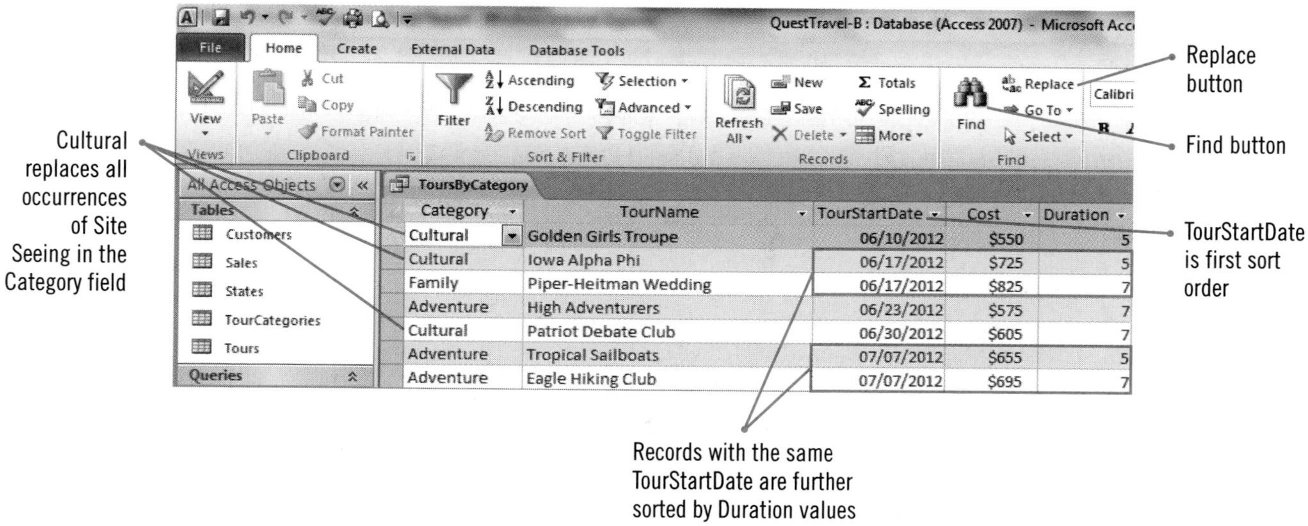

UNIT
B
Access 2010

Filtering Data

Filtering a table or query datasheet temporarily displays only those records that match given criteria. Recall that criteria are limiting conditions you set. For example, you might want to show only tours in the state of Florida, or only tours with a duration of less than 7 days. While filters provide a quick and easy way to display a temporary subset of records in the current datasheet, they are not as powerful or flexible as queries. Most importantly, a query is a saved object within the database, whereas filters are temporary because Access removes them when you close the datasheet. Table B-1 compares filters and queries. Samantha Hooper asks you to find all Adventure tours offered in the month of July. You can filter the Tours table datasheet to provide this information.

STEPS

QUICK TIP
You can also apply a sort or filter by clicking the Sort and filter arrow to the right of the field name and choosing the sort order or filter values you want.

1. **Double-click the Tours table to open it, click any occurrence of Adventure in the Category field, click the Selection button in the Sort & Filter group, then click Equals "Adventure"**

   Eighteen records are selected, some of which are shown in Figure B-10. A filter icon appears to the right of the Category field. Filtering by the selected field value, called **Filter By Selection**, is a fast and easy way to filter the records for an exact match. To filter for comparative data (for example, where TourStartDate is *equal to* or *greater than* 7/1/2012), you must use the **Filter By Form** feature.

2. **Click the Advanced button in the Sort & Filter group, then click Filter By Form**

   The Filter by Form window opens. The previous Filter By Selection criterion, "Adventure" in the Category field, is still in the grid. Access distinguishes between text and numeric entries by placing "quotation marks" around text criteria.

QUICK TIP
If you need to clear previous criteria, click the Advanced button, then click Clear All Filters.

3. **Click the TourStartDate cell, then type 7/*/2012 as shown in Figure B-11**

   Filter by Form also allows you to apply two or more criteria at the same time. An asterisk (*) in the day position of the date criterion works as a wildcard, selecting any date in the month of July (the 7th month) in the year 2012.

QUICK TIP
Be sure to remove existing filters before applying a new filter, or the new filter will apply to the current subset of records instead of the entire datasheet.

4. **Click the Toggle Filter button in the Sort & Filter group**

   The datasheet selects nine records that match both filter criteria, as shown in Figure B-12. Note that filter icons appear next to the TourStartDate and Category field names as both fields are involved in the filter.

5. **Close the Tours datasheet, then click Yes when prompted to save the changes**

   Saving changes to the datasheet saves the last sort order and column width changes. Filters are not saved.

Using wildcard characters

To search for a pattern, you can use a **wildcard** character to represent any character in the condition entry. Use a question mark (?) to search for any single character, and an asterisk (*) to search for any number of characters. Wildcard characters are often used with the **Like operator**. For example, the criterion Like "12/*/13" would find all dates in December of 2013, and the criterion Like "F*" would find all entries that start with the letter F.

FIGURE B-10: Filtering the Tours table

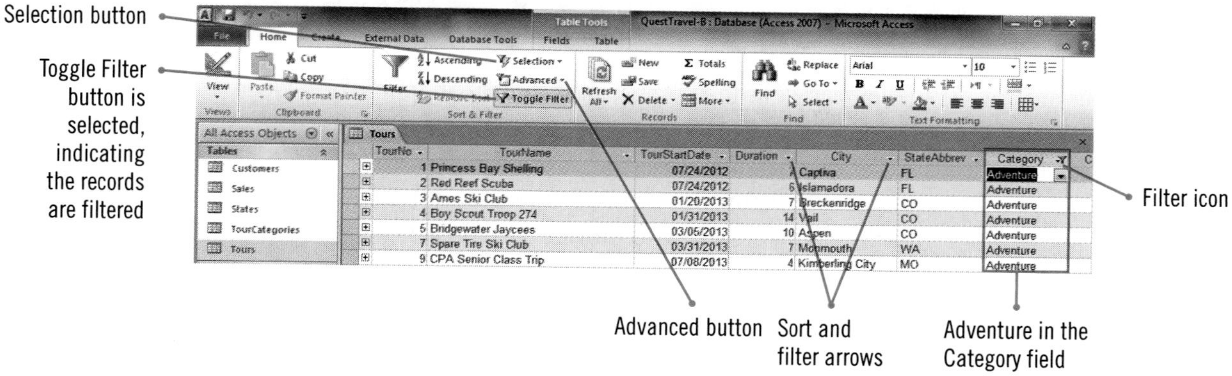
Selection button
Toggle Filter button is selected, indicating the records are filtered
Filter icon
Advanced button
Sort and filter arrows
Adventure in the Category field

FIGURE B-11: Filtering by Form criteria

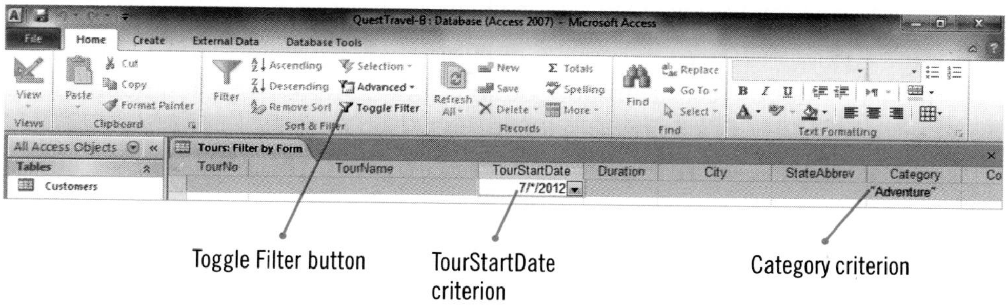
Toggle Filter button
TourStartDate criterion
Category criterion

FIGURE B-12: Results of filtering by form

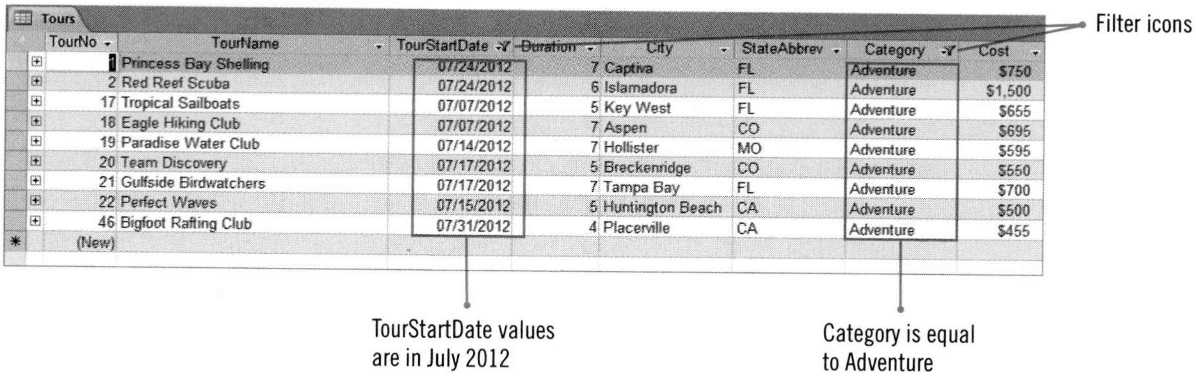
Filter icons
TourStartDate values are in July 2012
Category is equal to Adventure

TABLE B-1: Filters vs. queries

characteristics	filters	queries
Are saved as an object in the database	No	Yes
Can be used to select a subset of records in a datasheet	Yes	Yes
Can be used to select a subset of fields in a datasheet	No	Yes
Resulting datasheet used to enter and edit data	Yes	Yes
Resulting datasheet used to sort, filter, and find records	Yes	Yes
Commonly used as the source of data for a form or report	No	Yes
Can calculate sums, averages, counts, and other types of summary statistics across records	No	Yes
Can be used to create calculated fields	No	Yes

UNIT B

Access 2010

Applying AND Criteria

As you have seen, you can limit the number of records that appear on a query datasheet by entering criteria in Query Design View. Criteria are tests, or limiting conditions, for which the record must be true to be selected for the query datasheet. To create **AND criteria**, which means that all criteria must be true to select the record, enter two or more criteria on the same Criteria row of the query design grid. Samantha Hooper asks you to provide a list of all family tours in the state of Florida with a duration equal to or less than 7 days. Use Query Design View to create the query with AND criteria to meet her request.

STEPS

1. **Click the Create tab on the Ribbon, click the Query Design button in the Queries group, double-click Tours, then click Close in the Show Table dialog box**

   You want four fields from the Tours table in this query.

2. **Drag the lower edge of the Tours field list down to display all of the fields, double-click TourName, double-click Duration, double-click StateAbbrev, then double-click Category to add these fields to the query grid**

   First add criteria to select only those records in Florida. Because you are using the StateAbbrev field, you need to use the two-letter state abbreviation for Florida, FL, as the Criteria entry.

3. **Click the first Criteria cell for the StateAbbrev field, type FL, then click the View button to display the results**

   Querying for only those tours in the state of Florida selects 11 records. Next, you add criteria to select only those records in the Family category.

4. **Click the View button to switch to Design View, click the first Criteria cell for the Category field, type Family, then click**

   Criteria added to the same line of the query design grid are AND criteria. When entered on the same line, each criterion must be true for the record to appear in the resulting datasheet. Querying for both FL and Family tours selects three records with durations of 8, 7, and 3 days. Every time you add AND criteria, you *narrow* the number of records that are selected because the record must be true for *all* criteria.

5. **Click , click the first Criteria cell for the Duration field, then type <=7 as shown in Figure B-13**

   Access assists you with **criteria syntax**, rules that specify how to enter criteria. Access automatically adds "quotation marks" around text criteria in Text fields ("FL" and "Family") and pound signs (#) around date criteria in Date/Time fields. The criteria in Number, Currency, and Yes/No fields are not surrounded by any characters. See Table B-2 for more information about comparison operators such as > (greater than).

TROUBLE

If your datasheet doesn't match Figure B-14, return to Query Design View and compare your criteria to that of Figure B-13.

6. **Click to display the query datasheet**

   The third AND criterion further narrows the number of records selected to two, as shown in Figure B-14.

7. **Click the Save button on the Quick Access toolbar, type FamilyFL as the query name, click OK, then close the query**

   The query is saved with the new name, FamilyFL, as a new object in the QuestTravel-B database.

Searching for blank fields

Is Null and Is Not Null are two other types of common criteria. The **Is Null** criterion finds all records where no entry has been made in the field. **Is Not Null** finds all records where there is any entry in the field, even if the entry is 0. Primary key fields cannot have a null entry.

FIGURE B-13: **Query Design View with AND criteria**

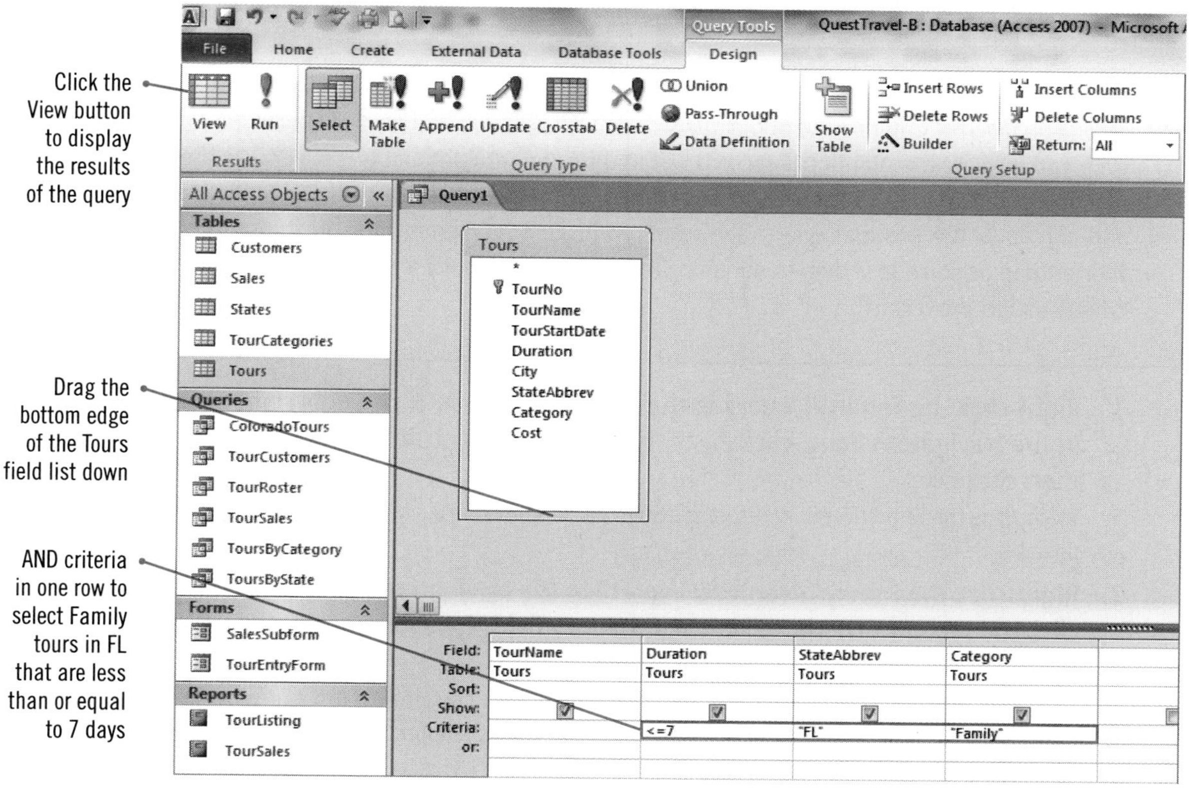
Click the View button to display the results of the query
Drag the bottom edge of the Tours field list down
AND criteria in one row to select Family tours in FL that are less than or equal to 7 days

FIGURE B-14: **Final datasheet of FamilyFL query**

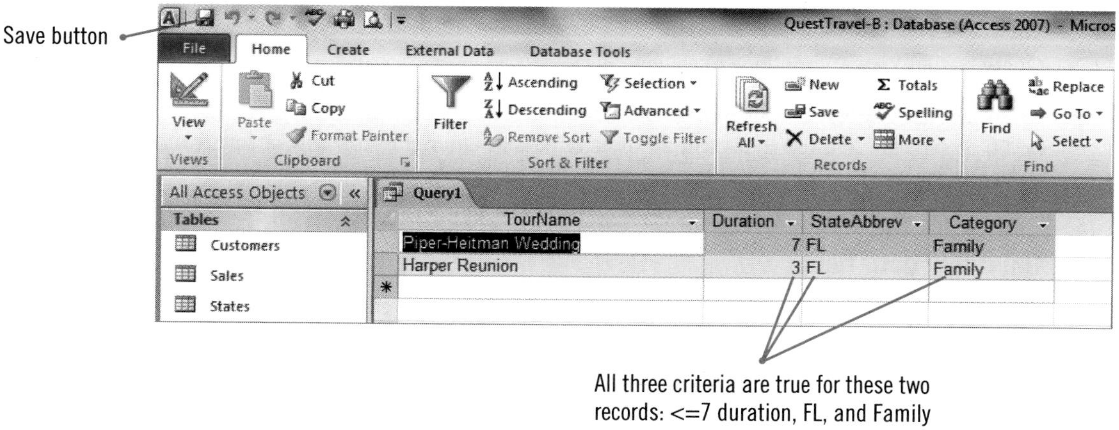
Save button
All three criteria are true for these two records: <=7 duration, FL, and Family

TABLE B-2: **Comparison operators**

operator	description	expression	meaning
>	Greater than	>500	Numbers greater than 500
>=	Greater than or equal to	>=500	Numbers greater than or equal to 500
<	Less than	<"Braveheart"	Names from A to Braveheart, but not Braveheart
<=	Less than or equal to	<="Bridgewater"	Names from A through Bridgewater, inclusive
<>	Not equal to	<>"Fontanelle"	Any name except for Fontanelle

Applying OR Criteria

You use **OR criteria** when any one criterion must be true in order for the record to be selected. Enter OR criteria on *different* Criteria rows of the query design grid. As you add rows of OR criteria to the query design grid, you *increase* the number of records selected for the resulting datasheet because the record needs to match *only one* of the Criteria rows to be selected for the datasheet. Samantha Hooper asks you to add criteria to the previous query. She wants to include Adventure tours in the state of Florida that are shorter than or equal to 7 days in duration. To do this, you modify a copy of the FamilyFL query to use OR criteria to add the records.

STEPS

1. **Right-click the FamilyFL query in the Navigation Pane, click Copy, right-click a blank spot in the Navigation Pane, click Paste, type FamilyAdventureFL in the Paste As dialog box, then click OK**

   By copying the FamilyFL query before starting your modifications, you avoid changing the FamilyFL query by mistake.

2. **Right-click the FamilyAdventureFL query in the Navigation Pane, click Design View, click the second Criteria cell in the Category field, type Adventure, then click the View button to display the query datasheet**

   The query selected 20 records including all of the tours with Adventure in the Category field. Note that some of the Duration values are greater than 7 and some of the StateAbbrev values are not FL. Because each row of the query grid is evaluated separately, all Adventure tours are selected regardless of criteria in any other row. In other words, the criteria in one row have no effect on the criteria of other rows. To make sure that the Adventure tours are also in Florida and have a duration of less than or equal to 7 days, you need to modify the second row of the query grid (the "or" row) to specify that criteria.

> **QUICK TIP**
> The Datasheet, Design, and other view buttons are also located in the lower-right corner of the Access window.

3. **Click the View button, click the second Criteria cell in the Duration field, type <=7, click the second Criteria cell in the StateAbbrev field, then type FL**

   Query Design View should look like Figure B-15.

4. **Click to display the query datasheet**

   Seven records are selected that meet all three criteria as entered in row one *or* row two of the query grid, as shown in Figure B-16.

5. **Right-click the FamilyAdventureFL query tab, click Close, then click Yes to save and close the query datasheet**

FIGURE B-15: **Query Design View with OR criteria**

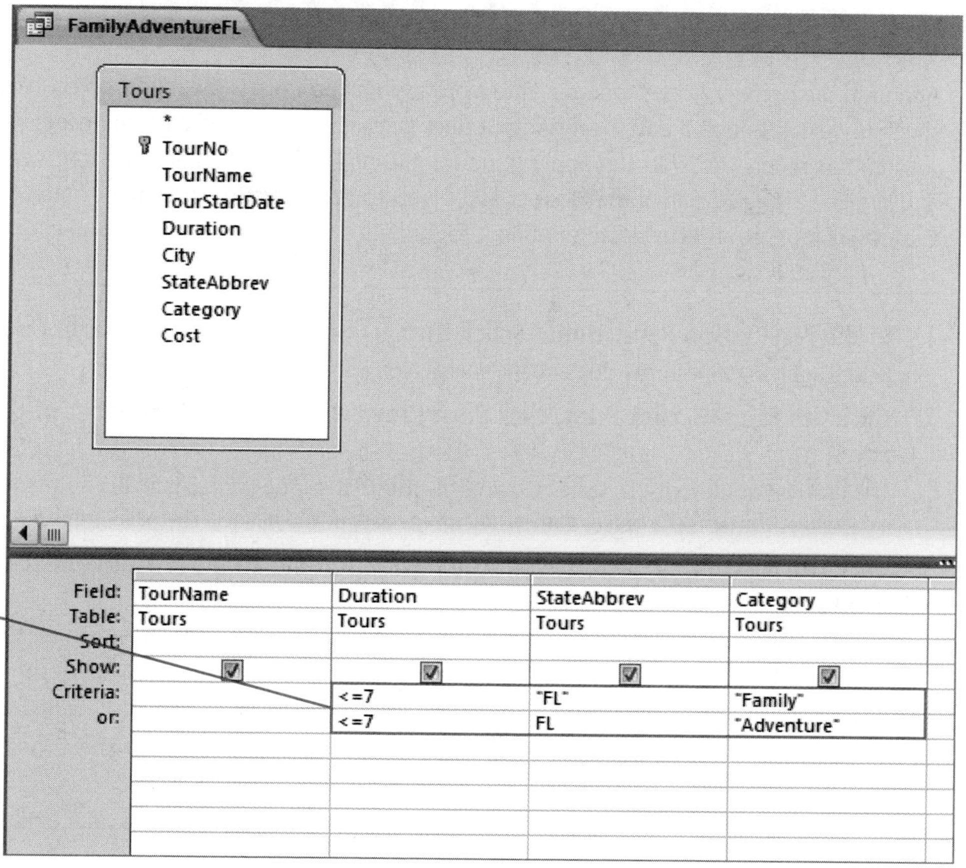

OR criteria in two rows to select both Family and Adventure tours in FL with a Duration less than or equal to 7 days

FIGURE B-16: **Final datasheet of the FamilyAdventureFL query**

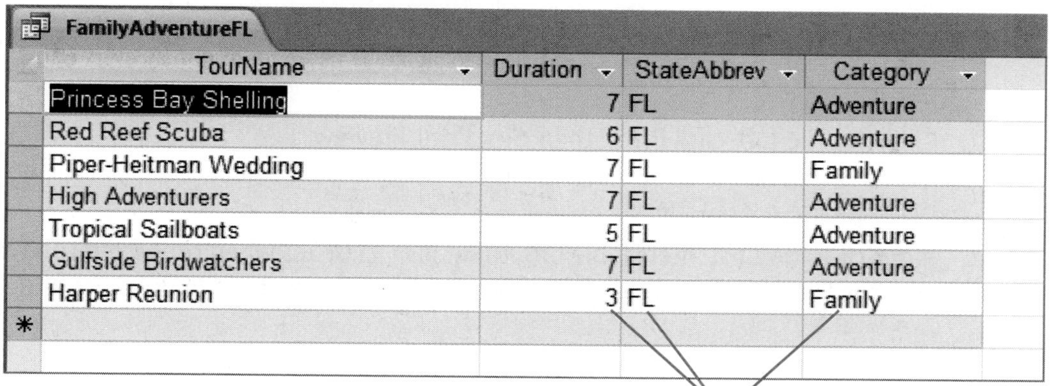

FamilyAdventureFL

TourName	Duration	StateAbbrev	Category
Princess Bay Shelling	7	FL	Adventure
Red Reef Scuba	6	FL	Adventure
Piper-Heitman Wedding	7	FL	Family
High Adventurers	7	FL	Adventure
Tropical Sailboats	5	FL	Adventure
Gulfside Birdwatchers	7	FL	Adventure
Harper Reunion	3	FL	Family

All three criteria are true for either row:
<=7 duration, FL, and Family
or
<=7 duration, FL, and Adventure

UNIT B

Access 2010

Formatting a Datasheet

Although the primary Access tool to create a professional printout is the report object, you can print a datasheet as well. Although a datasheet printout does not allow you to add custom headers, footers, images, or subtotals as reports do, you can apply some formatting, such as changing the font size, font face, colors, and gridlines. Samantha Hooper asked you to print a list of customers. You decide to format the Customers table datasheet before printing it for her.

STEPS

1. **In the Navigation Pane, double-click the Customers table to open it in Datasheet View**
   Before applying new formatting enhancements, you preview the default printout.
2. **Click the File tab, click Print, click Print Preview, then click the header of the printout to zoom in**
   The preview window displays the layout of the printout, as shown in Figure B-17. By default, the printout of a datasheet contains the object name and current date in the header. The page number is in the footer.
3. **Click the Next Page button in the navigation bar to move to the next page of the printout**
   The last two fields print on the second page because the first is not wide enough to accommodate them. You decide to switch the report to landscape orientation so that all of the fields print on one page, and then increase the size of the font before printing to make the text easier to read.
4. **Click the Landscape button in the Page Layout group, then click the Close Print Preview button**
   You return to Datasheet View where you can make font face, font size, font color, gridline color, and background color choices.
5. **Click the Font list arrow Calibri in the Text Formatting group, click Times New Roman, click the Font Size list arrow 11, then click 12**
   With the larger font size applied, you need to resize some columns to accommodate the widest entries.
6. **Use the ✛ pointer to double-click the field separator between the Street and City field names, then double-click the field separator between the Phone and FirstContact field names**
   Double-clicking the field separators widens the column as necessary to display every entry in that field, as shown in Figure B-18.
7. **Click the File tab, click Print, then click Print Preview**
   All of the fields now fit across a page in landscape orientation. The printout is still two pages, but with the larger font size, it is easier to read.
8. **Right-click the Customers table tab, click Close, click Yes when prompted to save changes, click the File tab, then click Exit to close the QuestTravel-B.accdb database and Access 2010**

QUICK TIP

If you need a printout of this datasheet, click the Print button on the Print Preview tab, then click OK.

FIGURE B-17: **Preview of Customers datasheet**

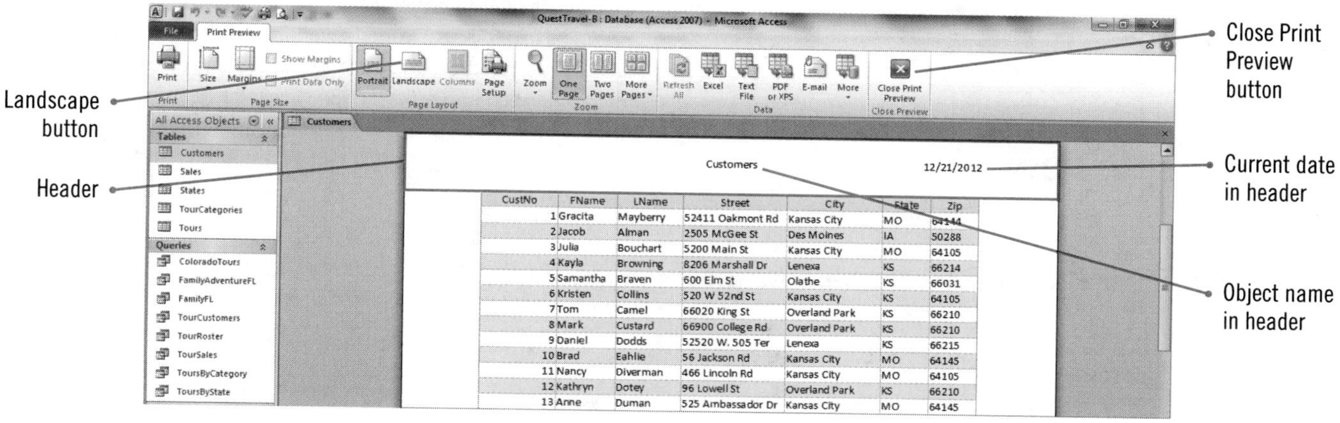

Landscape button
Header
Close Print Preview button
Current date in header
Object name in header

FIGURE B-18: **Formatting the Customers datasheet**

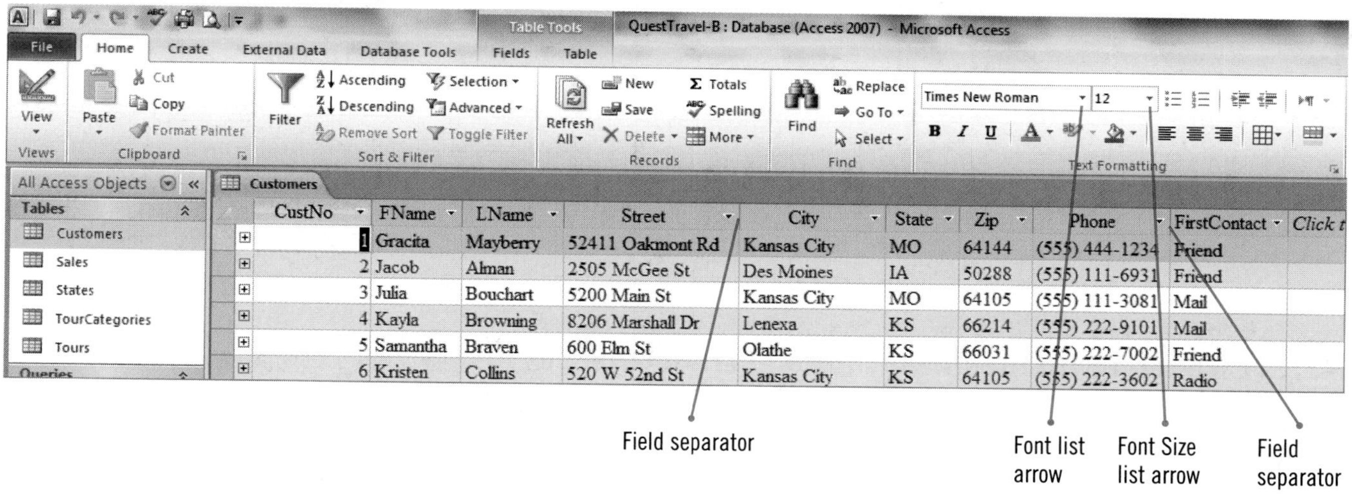

Field separator
Font list arrow
Font Size list arrow
Field separator

Practice

Concepts Review

For current SAM information, including versions and content details, visit SAM Central (http://www.cengage.com/samcentral). If you have a SAM user profile, you may have access to hands-on instruction, practice, and assessment of the skills covered in this unit. Since various versions of SAM are supported throughout the life of this text, check with your instructor for the correct instructions and URL/Web site for accessing assignments.

Label each element of the Access window shown in Figure B-19.

FIGURE B-19

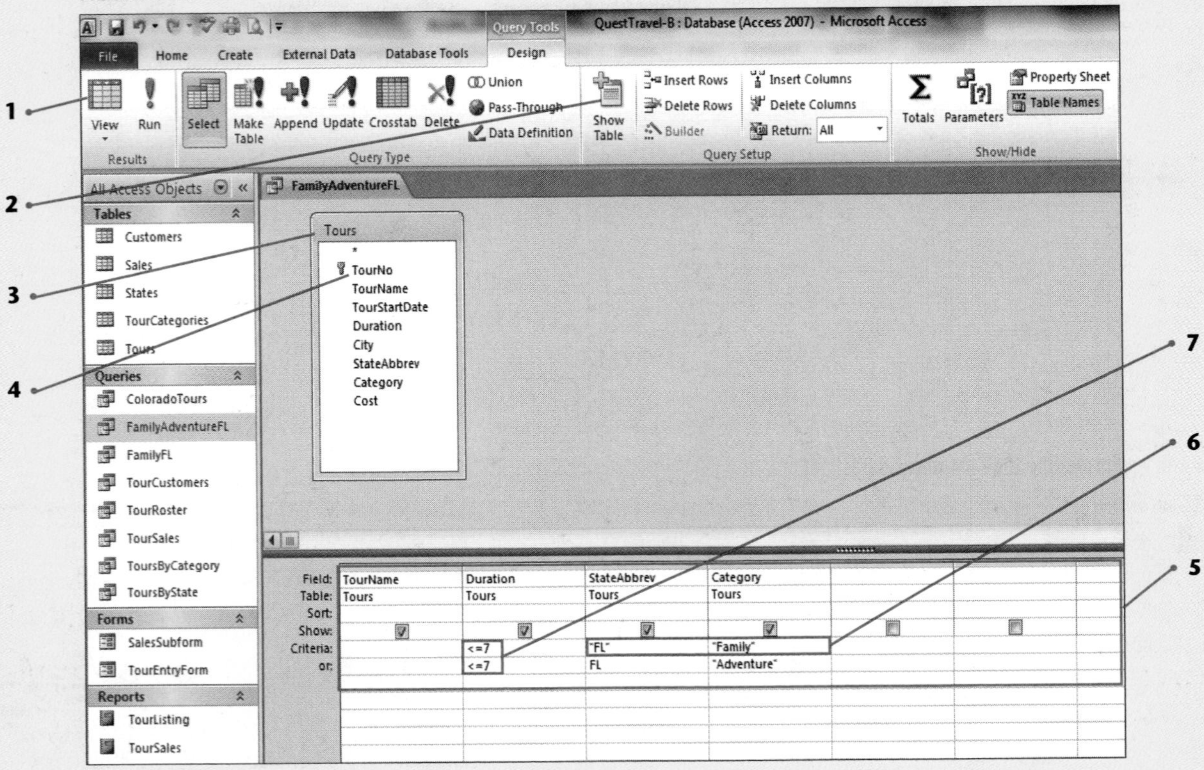

Match each term with the statement that best describes it.

8. **Query grid**
9. **Criteria**
10. **Filter**
11. **Syntax**
12. **Field lists**
13. **Sorting**
14. **Wildcard**
15. **Is Null**

a. Creates a temporary subset of records
b. Small windows that display field names
c. Rules that determine how criteria are entered
d. Limiting conditions used to restrict the number of records that are selected in a query
e. Used to search for a pattern of characters
f. Criterion that finds all records where no entry has been made in the field
g. The lower pane in Query Design View
h. Putting records in ascending or descending order based on the values of a field

Select the best answer from the list of choices.

16. AND criteria:
- **a.** Must all be true for the record to be selected.
- **b.** Determine sort orders.
- **c.** Determine fields selected for a query.
- **d.** Help set link lines between tables in a query.

17. SQL stands for which of the following?
- **a.** Standard Query Language
- **b.** Special Query Listing
- **c.** Structured Query Language
- **d.** Simple Query Listing

18. A query is sometimes called a logical view of data because:
- **a.** You can create queries with the Logical Query Wizard.
- **b.** Queries do not store data, they only display a view of data.
- **c.** Queries contain logical criteria.
- **d.** Query naming conventions are logical.

19. Which of the following describes OR criteria?
- **a.** Selecting a subset of fields and/or records to view as a datasheet from one or more tables
- **b.** Using two or more rows of the query grid to select only those records that meet given criteria
- **c.** Reorganizing the records in either ascending or descending order based on the contents of one or more fields
- **d.** Using multiple fields in the query design grid

20. Which of the following is *not* true about a query?
- **a.** A query can be used to create calculated fields.
- **b.** A query can be used to create summary statistics.
- **c.** A query can be used to enter and edit data.
- **d.** A query is the same thing as a filter.

Skills Review

1. Use the Query Wizard.
- **a.** Open the Recycle-B.accdb database from the drive and folder where you store your Data Files. Enable content if prompted.
- **b.** Create a new query using the Simple Query Wizard. Select the CenterName field from the Centers table, the DepositDate and Weight fields from the Deposits table, and the ClubName field from the Clubs table. Select Detail, and enter **CenterDeposits** as the name of the query.
- **c.** Open the query in Datasheet View, change any record with the Big Trash Can CenterName value to a center name that includes your last name.

2. Work with data in a query.
- **a.** Delete the first record.
- **b.** Change any occurrence of Lions in the ClubName field to **Lions of Okoboji**.
- **c.** Click any value in the DepositDate field, then click the Descending button in the Sort & Filter group on the Home tab to sort the records in descending order on the DepositDate field.
- **d.** Use the Calendar Picker to choose the date of **1/9/2013** for the first record.
- **e.** Save and close the CenterDeposits query.

3. Use Query Design View.
- **a.** Click the Create tab, click the Query Design button, double-click Clubs, double-click Deposits, and then click Close to add the Clubs and Deposits tables to Query Design View.
- **b.** Drag the bottom edge of the Clubs table down to display all of the field names.

Skills Review (continued)

c. Add the following fields from the Clubs table to the query design grid in the following order: FName, LName, ClubName. Add the following fields from the Deposits table in the following order: DepositNumber, DepositDate, Weight. View the results in Datasheet View observing the number of records that are selected.

d. In Design View, enter criteria to display only those records with a Weight value of **greater than or equal to 100**, then observe the number of records that are selected.

e. Save the query with the name **100PlusDeposits**, and close it.

4. Sort and find data.

a. Open the CenterDeposits query in Datasheet View to observe how the records are currently sorted (in descending order based on the DepositDate field).

b. In Query Design View, choose an ascending sort order for the CenterName and DepositDate fields. (*Note*: Queries that are created with the Query Wizard do not show the 1 and infinity symbols on the link lines between the tables. However, the one-to-many relationships between these tables are still intact.)

c. Display the query in Datasheet View noting how the records have been resorted.

d. Click any value in the ClubName field, then use the Find and Replace dialog box to find all occurrences of **Patriots**, and replace them with **Kansas City Patriots**.

5. Filter data.

a. Filter the CenterDeposits datasheet for only those records where the ClubName equals **Kansas City Patriots**.

b. Apply an advanced filter by form and use wildcard characters to further narrow the records so that only the deposits made in the year 2012 are selected.

c. If requested by your instructor, print the filtered CenterDeposits datasheet.

d. Save and close the CenterDeposits query.

6. Apply AND criteria.

a. Open the 100PlusDeposits query in Query Design View.

b. Modify the criteria to select all of the listings with a ClubName of **Ice Kings** and a Weight value of greater than or equal to 100.

c. In the results, edit Tara in any occurrence in the FName field to your initials.

d. If requested by your instructor, print the 100PlusDeposits query.

7. Apply OR criteria.

a. Open the 100PlusDeposits query in Query Design View.

b. Add criteria to include the records with **Jaycees** as the ClubName with a Weight value **greater than or equal to 100** to the existing selections so that both the Ice Kings and Jaycees large deposit records are selected.

c. Save the 100PlusDeposits query, then switch to Datasheet View.

8. Format a datasheet.

a. In the 100PlusDeposits datasheet, apply an Arial Narrow font and a 14-point font size.

b. Resize all columns so that all data and field names are visible. See Figure B-20.

c. Save the 100PlusDeposits query.

d. If requested by your instructor, print the datasheet.

e. Close the 100PlusDeposits query and the Recycle-B.accdb database, then exit Access 2010.

FIGURE B-20

100PlusDeposits

	FName	LName	ClubName	DepositNumber	DepositDate	Weight
	Francis	Weaver	Jaycees	25	8/21/2012	105
	Francis	Weaver	Jaycees	59	3/7/2011	200
	Francis	Weaver	Jaycees	63	4/23/2011	105
	Francis	Weaver	Jaycees	75	7/9/2011	200
	Francis	Weaver	Jaycees	82	1/31/2010	100
	Francis	Weaver	Jaycees	99	3/6/2010	200
	SI	Block	Ice Kings	6	2/23/2012	100
	SI	Block	Ice Kings	42	1/31/2011	100
	SI	Block	Ice Kings	46	2/14/2011	185
	SI	Block	Ice Kings	50	2/19/2011	185
	SI	Block	Ice Kings	60	3/8/2011	145
	SI	Block	Ice Kings	61	4/20/2011	115
	SI	Block	Ice Kings	67	5/2/2011	105
	SI	Block	Ice Kings	86	2/14/2010	200
	SI	Block	Ice Kings	94	2/27/2010	100
*				(New)		

Independent Challenge 1

You have built an Access database to track member-ship in a community service club. The database tracks member names and addresses as well as their status in the club, which moves from rank to rank as the members contribute increased hours of service to the community.

a. Start Access, open the Membership-B.accdb database from the drive and folder where you store your Data Files, enable content if prompted, then open the Activities, Members, and Zips tables to review their datasheets.

b. In the Zips table, click the expand button to the left of the 64131, Overland Park, KS, record to display the two members linked to that zip code. Click the expand button to the left of the Gabriel Hammer record to display the two activity records linked to Gabriel.

c. Close all three datasheets, click the Database Tools tab, then click the Relationships button. The Relationships window also shows you that one record in the Zips table is related to many records in the Members table through the common ZipCode field, and that one record in the Members table is related to many records in the Activities table through the common MemberNo field.

d. Close the Relationships window.

e. In Query Design View, build a query with the following fields: FirstName and LastName from the Members table, and ActivityDate and HoursWorked from the Activities table.

f. View the datasheet, observe the number of records selected, then return to Query Design View.

g. Add criteria to select only those records where the ActivityDate is in March of 2012. (*Hint*: Use a wildcard character in the day position of the date criterion.) Apply an ascending sort order to the LastName and ActivityDate fields, then view the datasheet.

h. Enter your name in the first record, widen all columns so that all data and field names are visible, and save the query with the name **March2012** as shown in Figure B-21.

i. If requested by your instructor, print the datasheet.

j. Close the March2012 query and the Membership-B.accdb database, then exit Access 2010.

FIGURE B-21

March2012

FirstName	LastName	ActivityDate	HoursWorked
StudentFirst	StudentLast	3/29/2012	4
Golga	Collins	3/31/2012	8
Martha	Duman	3/27/2012	4
Allie	Eahlie	3/29/2012	4
Jana	Eckert	3/29/2012	5
Quentin	Garden	3/29/2012	4
Quentin	Garden	3/30/2012	8
Loraine	Goode	3/29/2012	5
Gabriel	Hammer	3/29/2012	5
Jeremiah	Hopper	3/27/2012	4
Helen	Hubert	3/29/2012	5
Heidi	Kalvert	3/29/2012	4
Harvey	Mackintosh	3/30/2012	4
Jon	Maxim	3/30/2012	4
Micah	Mayberry	3/29/2012	4
Patch	Mullins	3/30/2012	8
Patch	Mullins	3/31/2012	8
Young	Nelson	3/30/2012	10
Mallory	Olson	3/31/2012	8
Su	Vogue	3/30/2012	8
Sherry	Walker	3/29/2012	4
Taney	Wilson	3/30/2012	8
*			

Independent Challenge 2

You work for a nonprofit agency that relies on grant money from the federal government. To keep in touch with elected members of Congress, you have developed an Access database with contact information for the House of Representatives. The director of the agency has asked you to create several state lists of representatives. You will use queries to extract this information.

SAM

If you have a SAM 2010 user profile, an autogradable SAM version of this assignment may be available at http://www.cengage.com/sam2010. Check with your instructor to confirm that this assignment is available in SAM. To use the SAM version of this assignment, log into the SAM 2010 Web site and download the instruction and start files.

a. Start Access, open the Congress-B.accdb database from the drive and folder where you store your Data Files, then enable content if prompted.

b. Open the Representatives and the States tables. Notice that one state is related to many representatives as evidenced by the expand buttons to the left of the records in the States tables.

Independent Challenge 2 (continued)

c. Close both datasheets, then using Query Design View, create a query with the StateAbbrev, StateName, and Capital fields from the States table (in that order) as well as the LName field from the Representatives table.
d. Sort the records in ascending order on the StateName field, then the LName field.
e. Add criteria to select the representatives from North Carolina or South Carolina. Use the StateAbbrev field to enter your criteria, using the two-character state abbreviations of NC and SC.
f. Save the query with the name **Carolinas**, view the results, then change the last name of Boehlert to your last name. Resize the columns as needed to view all the data and field names.
g. Print the datasheet if requested by your instructor, then save and close it.
h. Close the Congress-B.accdb database, then exit Access 2010.

Independent Challenge 3

You have built an Access database to track the veterinarians and clinics in your area.

a. Start Access, open the Vet-B.accdb database from the drive and folder where you store your Data Files, and enable content if prompted.
b. Open the Vets table and then the Clinics table to review the data in both datasheets.
c. Click the expand button next to the Veterinary Specialists record in the Clinics table, then add your name as a new record to the Vets subdatasheet.
d. Close both datasheets.
e. Using the Simple Query Wizard, select the VetLast and VetFirst fields from the Vets table, and select the ClinicName and Phone fields from the Clinics table. Title the query **ClinicListing**, then view the datasheet.
f. Find the single occurrence of Cooper in the VetLast field, and replace it with **Chen**.
g. Update any occurrence of Leawood Animal Clinic in the ClinicName field by changing Leawood to **Emergency**.
h. In Query Design View, add criteria to select only Emergency Animal Clinic or Veterinary Specialists in the ClinicName field, then view the results.

Advanced Challenge Exercise

- In Query Design View, move the ClinicName field to the first column, then add an ascending sort order on the ClinicName and VetLast fields.
- Display the ClinicListing query in Datasheet View, resize the fields as shown in Figure B-22, then print the datasheet if requested by your instructor.
- Return to Query Design View of the ClinicListing query. Notice the link line between the tables. This link line was created by the Simple Query Wizard.
- Save and close the ClinicListing query then open the Relationships window. Notice the link line between the tables. In a Word document, explain the difference in appearance and meaning of the link line between the Vets and Clinics tables in the Relationships window with that of Query Design View.

i. If you have not already done so, save and close the ClinicListing datasheet, then close the Vet-B.accdb database and exit Access 2010.

FIGURE B-22

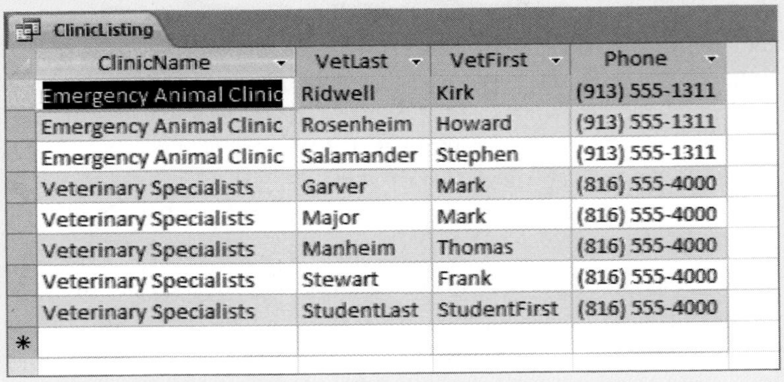
ClinicListing

ClinicName	VetLast	VetFirst	Phone
Emergency Animal Clinic	Ridwell	Kirk	(913) 555-1311
Emergency Animal Clinic	Rosenheim	Howard	(913) 555-1311
Emergency Animal Clinic	Salamander	Stephen	(913) 555-1311
Veterinary Specialists	Garver	Mark	(816) 555-4000
Veterinary Specialists	Major	Mark	(816) 555-4000
Veterinary Specialists	Manheim	Thomas	(816) 555-4000
Veterinary Specialists	Stewart	Frank	(816) 555-4000
Veterinary Specialists	StudentLast	StudentFirst	(816) 555-4000

Real Life Independent Challenge

An Access database is an excellent tool to help record and track job opportunities. For this exercise you'll create a database from scratch that you can use to enter, edit, and query data in pursuit of a new job or career.

a. Create a new database named **Jobs.accdb**.

b. Create a table named **Positions** with the following field names, data types, and descriptions:

field name	data type	description
PositionID	**AutoNumber**	**Primary key field**
Title	**Text**	**Title of position such as Accountant, Assistant Court Clerk, or Director of Finance**
CareerArea	**Text**	**Area of the career field such as Accounting, Information Systems, Retail, or Landscaping**
AnnualSalary	**Currency**	**Annual salary**
Desirability	**Number**	**Desirability rating of 1 = low to 5 = high to show how desirable the position is to you**
EmployerID	**Number**	**Foreign key field to the Employers table**

c. Create a table named **Employers** with the following field names, data types, and descriptions:

field name	data type	description
EmployerID	**AutoNumber**	**Primary key field**
CompanyName	**Text**	**Company name of the employer**
EmpStreet	**Text**	**Employer's street address**
EmpCity	**Text**	**Employer's city**
EmpState	**Text**	**Employer's state**
EmpZip	**Text**	**Employer's zip code**
EmpPhone	**Text**	**Employer's phone, including area code**

d. Be sure to set EmployerID as the primary key field in the Employers table and the PositionID as the primary key field in the Positions table.

e. Link the Employers and Positions table together in a one-to-many relationship using the common EmployerID field. One employer record will be linked to many position records. Be sure to enforce referential integrity.

f. Using any valid source of potential employer data, enter five records into the Employers table.

g. Using any valid source of job information, enter five records into the Positions table by using the subdatasheets from within the Employers datasheet. Because one employer may have many positions, all five of your Positions records may be linked to the same employer, you may have one position record per employer, or any other combination.

h. Build a query that selects CompanyName from the Employers table, and the Title, CareerArea, AnnualSalary, and Desirability fields from the Positions table. Sort the records in descending order based on Desirability. Save the query as **JobList**, and print it if requested by your instructor.

i. Close the JobList datasheet, then close the Jobs.accdb database and exit Access 2010.

Visual Workshop

Open the Baseball-B.accdb database from the drive and folder where you store your Data Files, and enable content if prompted. Create a query based on the Players and Teams tables as shown in Figure B-23. Criteria has been added to select only those records where the PlayerPosition field values are equal to 1 or 2 (representing pitchers and catchers). An ascending sort order has been added to the TeamName and PlayerPosition fields. Save the query with the name **PitchersAndCatchers**, then compare the results to Figure B-23, making changes as necessary. Change the name of Roy Campanella to your name before printing the datasheet if requested by your instructor. Close the query and the Baseball-B.accdb database, then exit Access 2010.

FIGURE B-23

PitchersAndCatchers

TeamName	PlayerLast	PlayerFirst	Position
Brooklyn Beetles	Campanella	Roy	1
Brooklyn Beetles	Young	Cycylie	2
Mayfair Monarchs	Durocher	Luis	1
Mayfair Monarchs	Mathewson	Carl	2
Rocky's Rockets	Spalding	Andrew	1
Rocky's Rockets	Koufax	Sanford	2
Snapping Turtles	Ford	Charles	1
Snapping Turtles	Perry	Greg	2

UNIT
C
Access 2010

Using Forms

Files You Will Need:

QuestTravel-C.accdb
QuestLogo.bmp
RealEstate-C.accdb
ForSale.bmp
QuestDives-C.accdb
Membership-C.accdb
PeoplePower.bmp
Recycle-C.accdb
JobSearch-C.accdb
Baseball-C.accdb

Although you can enter and edit data on datasheets, most database designers develop and build forms as the primary method for users to interact with a database. In a datasheet, sometimes you have to scroll left or right to see all of the fields, which is inconvenient and time consuming. A form solves these problems by allowing you to organize the fields on the screen in any arrangement. A form also supports graphical elements such as pictures, buttons, and tabs, which make data entry faster and more accurate. In addition, forms provide a layer of database security and make the database much easier to use. Samantha Hooper, a tour developer at Quest Specialty Travel, asks you to create forms to make tour information easier to access, enter, and update.

OBJECTIVES

- Use the Form Wizard
- Create a split form
- Use Form Layout View
- Add fields to a form
- Modify form controls
- Create calculations
- Modify tab order
- Insert an image

UNIT
C
Access 2010

Using the Form Wizard

A **form** is an Access database object that allows you to arrange the fields of a record in any layout so you can enter, edit, and delete records. A form provides an easy-to-use data entry and navigation screen. Forms provide many productivity and security benefits for the **user**, who is primarily interested in entering, editing, and analyzing the data in the database. As the **database designer**, the person responsible for building and maintaining tables, queries, forms, and reports, you also need direct access to all database objects, and you use the Navigation Pane for this purpose. Not all users should be able to access all the objects in a database—imagine how disastrous it would be if someone accidentally deleted an entire table of data. You can add a layer of security to your database with well-designed forms. Samantha Hooper asks you to build a form to enter and maintain tour information.

STEPS

1. **Start Access, open the QuestTravel-C.accdb database from the drive and folder where you store your Data Files, then enable content if prompted**

   You can use many methods to create a new form, but the Form Wizard is a fast and popular tool to get started. The **Form Wizard** prompts you for information it needs to create a form, such as the fields, layout, and title for the form.

2. **Click the Create tab on the Ribbon, then click the Form Wizard button in the Forms group**

   The Form Wizard starts, prompting you to select the fields for this form. You want to create a form to enter and update data in the Tours table.

3. **Click the Tables/Queries list arrow, click Table: Tours, then click the Select All Fields button >>**

   You could now select fields from other tables, if necessary, but in this case, you have all of the fields you need.

4. **Click Next, click the Columnar option button, click Next, type Tours Entry Form as the title, then click Finish**

   The Tours Entry Form opens in **Form View**, as shown in Figure C-1. The three different form views are summarized in Table C-1. Each item on the form is called a **control**. Field names are shown as label controls in the first column of the form. A **label** displays fixed text that doesn't change as you navigate from record to record. Labels usually describe other controls on the form such as text boxes that show field values. A label control is also often used in headers or footers. Field values are displayed in text box and combo box controls in the second column of the form. A **text box** is the most common type of control used to display field values. You enter, edit, find, sort, and filter data by working with the data in a text box control. The Category field value is displayed in a combo box control. A **combo box** is a combination of two controls: a text box and a list. You click the arrow button on a combo box control to display a list of values, or you can edit data directly in the combo box itself.

> **QUICK TIP**
> Always click a value in a field to identify which field you want to sort or filter before clicking a sort or filter button.

5. **Click Princess Bay Shelling in the TourName text box, click the Ascending button in the Sort & Filter group, then click the Next record button ▶ in the navigation bar to move to the second record**

   The Ames Ski Club is the second record when the records are sorted in ascending order on the TourName field. Information about the current record number and total number of records appears in the navigation bar, just as it does in a datasheet.

6. **Edit Ames Ski Club to Story County Ski Club**

   Your screen should look like Figure C-2. Forms displayed in Form View are the primary tool used to enter, edit, and delete data in an Access database.

7. **Right-click the Tours Entry Form tab, then click Close**

   When a form is closed, Access automatically saves any edits made to the current record.

FIGURE C-1: **Tours Entry Form in Form View**

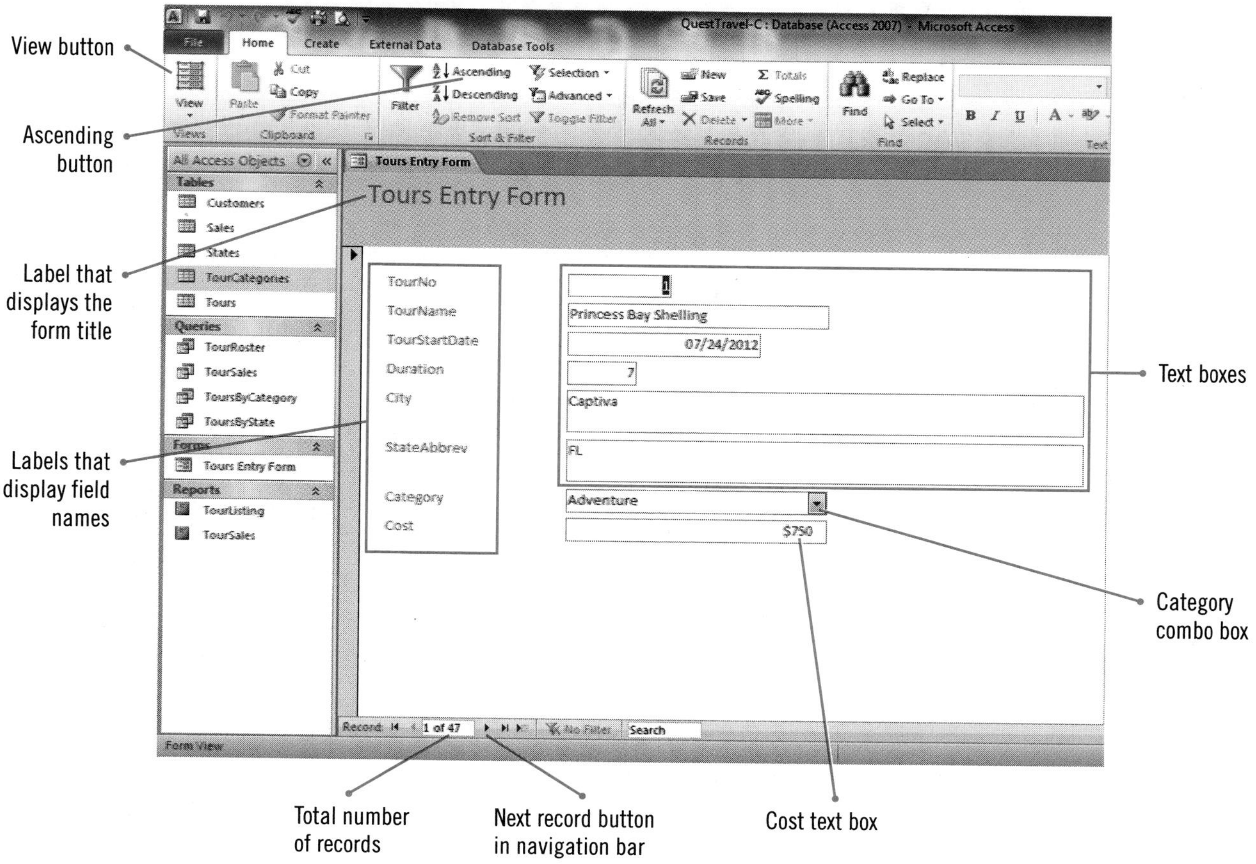

FIGURE C-2: **Editing data in a text box**

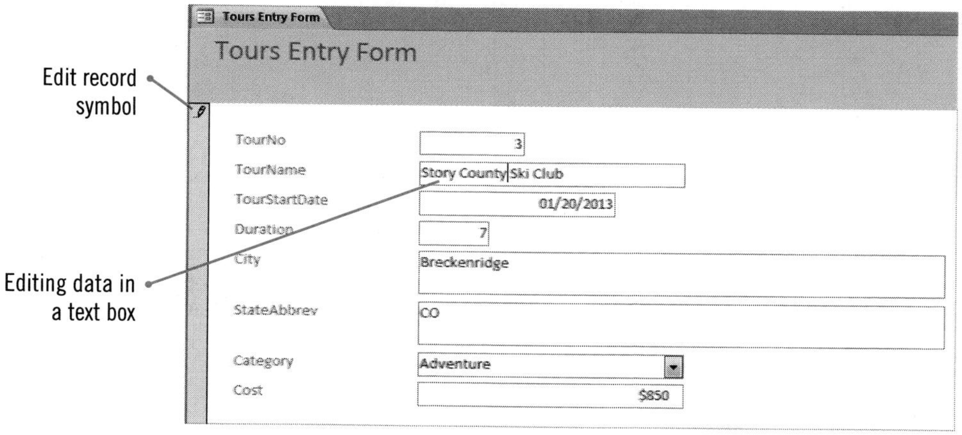

TABLE C-1: **Form views**

view	primary purpose
Form	To view, enter, edit, and delete data
Layout	To modify the size, position, or formatting of controls; shows data as you modify the form, making it the tool of choice when you want to change the appearance and usability of the form while viewing live data
Design	To modify the form header, detail, and footer section, or to access the complete range of controls and form properties; Design View does not display data

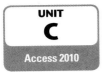

Creating a Split Form

In addition to the Form Wizard, you should be familiar with several other form creation tools. Table C-2 identifies those tools and the purpose for each. Samantha Hooper asks you to create another form to manage customer data. You'll work with the Split Form tool for this task.

STEPS

1. **Click the Customers table in the Navigation Pane, click the Create tab, click the More Forms button, then click Split Form**
   The Customers data appears in a split form as shown in Figure C-3. The benefit of a **split form** is that the upper pane allows you to display the fields of one record in any arrangement, and the lower pane maintains a datasheet view of the first few records, which you can navigate very quickly. The two panes of the split form are always synchronized. In other words, if you edit, sort, or filter records in the upper pane, the lower pane is automatically updated, and vice versa. The navigation bar shows that there are 37 total records.

2. **Click MO in the State text box in the upper pane, click the Home tab, click the Selection button in the Sort & Filter group, then click Does Not Equal "MO"**
   Twenty-six records are filtered where the State field is not equal to MO. You also need to change a value in the Jacob Alman record.

> **TROUBLE**
> Make sure you edit the record in the lower pane.

3. **In the lower pane, click Des Moines in the City field of the first record, edit the entry to read West Des Moines, click any other record in the lower pane, then click Jacob in the lower pane**
   Moving from record to record also automatically saves data, regardless of whether you are working in the upper or lower pane. Note that "West Des Moines" is the entry in the City field in both the upper and lower panes as shown in Figure C-4.

4. **Click the record selector for the Kristen Collins record in the lower pane, then click the Delete button in the Records group on the Home tab**
   A message appears indicating that you cannot delete this record because it contains related records in the Sales table. This is a benefit of referential integrity on the one-to-many relationships between the Customers, Sales, and Tours tables. Referential integrity prevents the creation of orphan records, records on the *many* side of a relationship (in this case, the Sales table), that do not have a match in the *one* side (in this case, the Customers table).

5. **Click OK, right-click the Customers form tab, click Close, click Yes when prompted to save changes, then click OK to save the form with the name Customers**

TABLE C-2: Form creation tools

tool	icon	creates a form:
Form		with one click based on the selected table or query
Form Design		from scratch with access to advanced design changes in Form Design View
Blank Form		with no controls starting in Form Layout View
Form Wizard		by answering a series of questions provided by the Form Wizard dialog boxes
Navigation		used to navigate or move between different areas of the database
More Forms		based on Multiple Items, Datasheet, Split Form, Modal Dialog, PivotChart, or PivotTable arrangements
Split Form		where the upper half displays data the fields of one record in any arrangement, and the lower half displays data as a datasheet

FIGURE C-3: **Customers table in a split form**

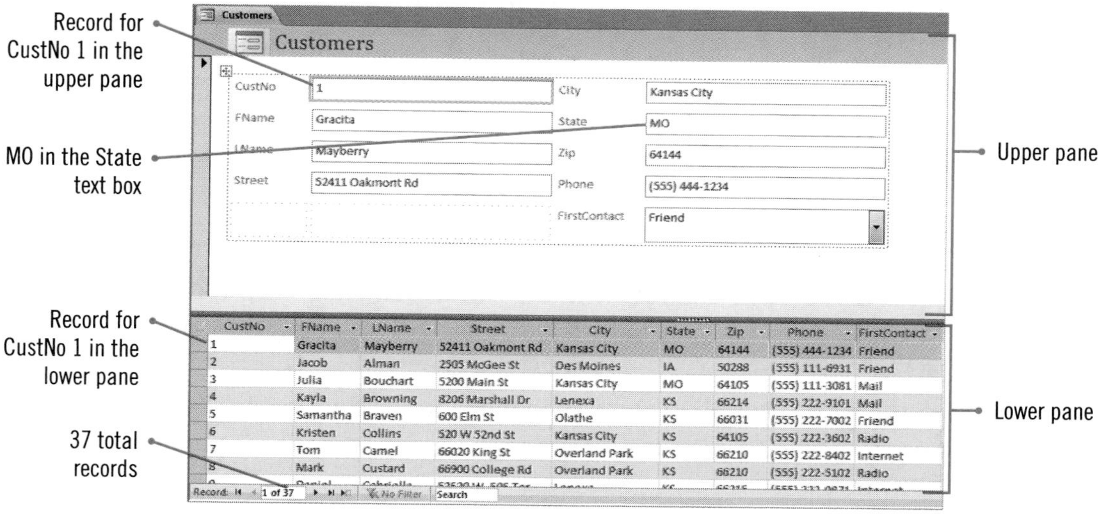
Record for CustNo 1 in the upper pane
MO in the State text box
Record for CustNo 1 in the lower pane
37 total records
Upper pane
Lower pane

FIGURE C-4: **Editing data in a split form**

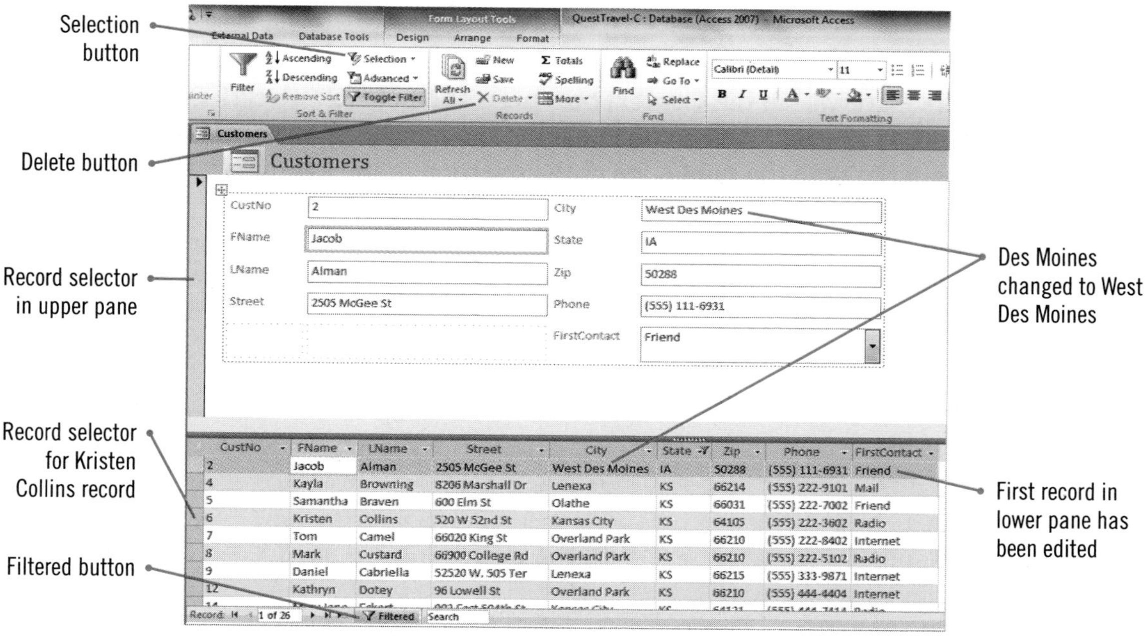
Selection button
Delete button
Record selector in upper pane
Record selector for Kristen Collins record
Filtered button
Des Moines changed to West Des Moines
First record in lower pane has been edited

UNIT C

Access 2010

Using Form Layout View

Layout View lets you make some design changes to a form while you are browsing the data. For example, you can move and resize controls, add or delete a field in the form, or change formatting characteristics such as fonts and colors. Samantha Hooper asks you to make several design changes to the Tours Entry Form. You can make these changes in Layout View.

STEPS

1. **Right-click the Tours Entry Form in the Navigation Pane, then click Layout View**
   In Layout View, you can move through the records, but you cannot enter or edit the data as you can in Form View.

2. **Click the Next record button twice to move to the third record, Bigfoot Rafting Club**
   You often use Layout View to make minor design changes such as editing labels and changing formatting characteristics.

> **TROUBLE**
> If your third record is not Bigfoot Rafting Club, sort the records in ascending order on the TourName field.

3. **Click the TourNo label to select it, click between the words Tour and No, then press [Spacebar]**
   You also want to edit a few more labels.

4. **Continue editing the labels as shown in Figure C-5**
   You also want to change the text color of the first two labels, Tour No and Tour Name, to red to make them more visible.

> **TROUBLE**
> Be sure to modify the *labels in the left column* instead of the text boxes on the right.

5. **Click the Tour No label, click the Home tab, click the Font Color button A, click the Tour Name label, then click A**
   Often, you want to apply the same formatting enhancement to multiple controls. For example, you decide to narrow the City and State Abbrev text boxes. Select the text boxes at the same time to make the same change to both.

6. **Click Placerville in the City text box, press and hold [Shift], click CA in the State Abbrev text box to select the two text boxes at the same time, release [Shift], then use the ↔ pointer to drag the right edge of the selection to the left to make the text boxes approximately half as wide**
   Layout View for the Tours Entry Form should look like Figure C-6. Mouse pointers in Form Layout and Form Design View are very important as they indicate what happens when you drag the mouse. Mouse pointers are described in Table C-3.

> **TROUBLE**
> Be sure to modify the *text boxes in the right column* instead of the labels on the left.

TABLE C-3: Mouse pointer shapes

shape	when does this shape appear?	action
↖	When you point to any unselected control on the form (the default mouse pointer)	Single-clicking with this mouse pointer *selects* a control
✥	When you point to the upper-left corner or edge of a selected control in Form Design View or the middle of the control in Form Layout View	Dragging with this mouse pointer *moves* the selected control(s)
↕, ↔, ⤡, ⤢	When you point to any sizing handle (except the larger one in the upper-left corner in Form Design View)	Dragging with one of these mouse pointers *resizes* the control

FIGURE C-5: **Using Layout View to modify form labels on the Tours Entry Form**

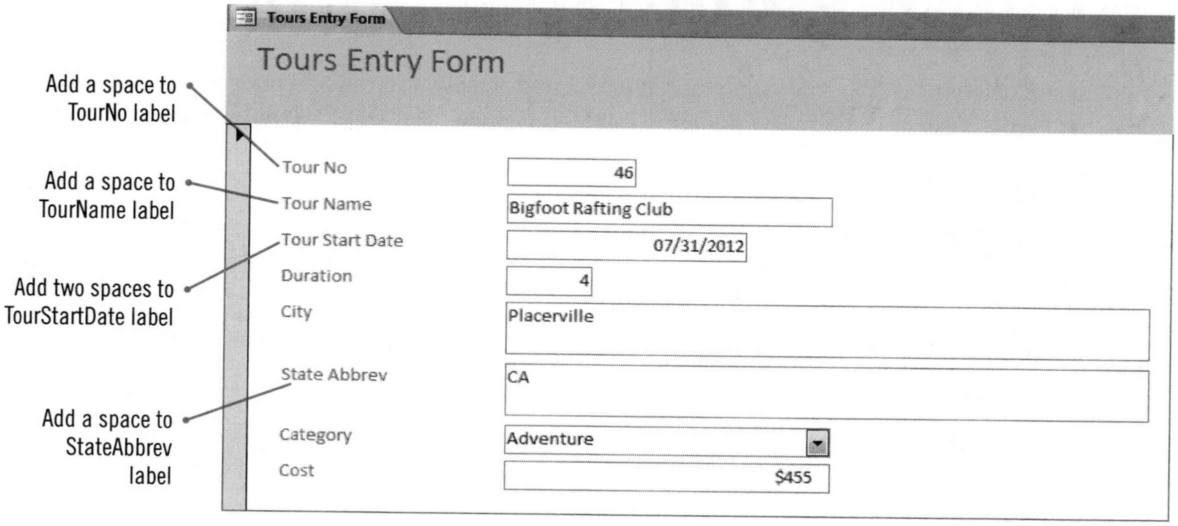

Add a space to TourNo label
Add a space to TourName label
Add two spaces to TourStartDate label
Add a space to StateAbbrev label
Tours Entry Form
Tours Entry Form
Tour No
46
Tour Name
Bigfoot Rafting Club
Tour Start Date
07/31/2012
Duration
4
City
Placerville
State Abbrev
CA
Category
Adventure
Cost
$455

FIGURE C-6: **Layout View for the Tours Entry Form**

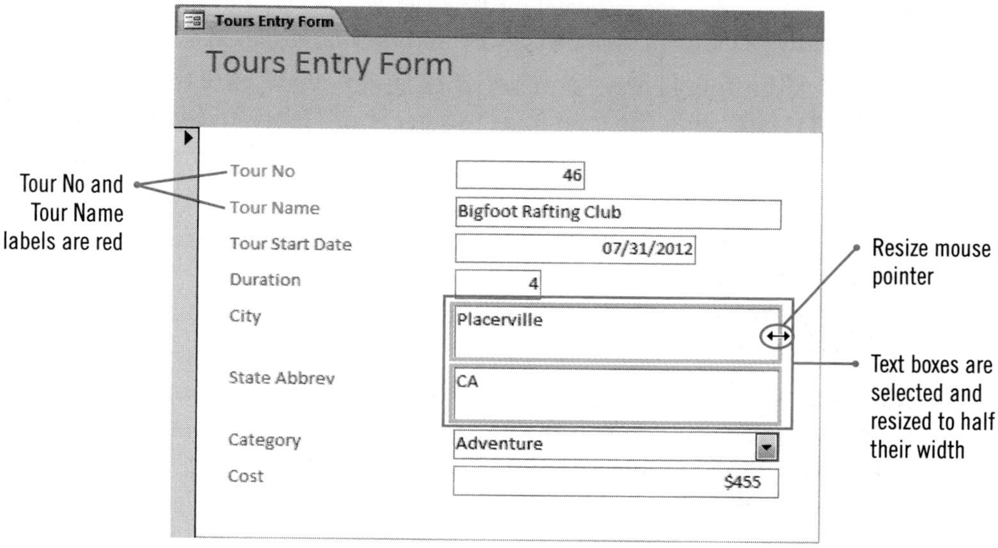

Tour No and Tour Name labels are red
Resize mouse pointer
Text boxes are selected and resized to half their width
Tours Entry Form
Tours Entry Form
Tour No
46
Tour Name
Bigfoot Rafting Club
Tour Start Date
07/31/2012
Duration
4
City
Placerville
State Abbrev
CA
Category
Adventure
Cost
$455

Access 2010

UNIT C
Access 2010

Adding Fields to a Form

Adding and deleting fields in an existing form is a common activity. You can add or delete fields in a form in either Layout View or Design View using the Field List window. The **Field List window** lists the database tables and the fields they contain. To add a field to the form, drag it from the Field List to the desired location on the form. To delete a field on a form, click the field to select it, then press the [Delete] key. Deleting a field from a form does not delete it from the underlying table nor does it have any effect on the data contained in the field. You can toggle the Field List on and off using the Add Existing Fields button on the Design tab. Samantha Hooper asks you to add the tour description from the TourCategories table to the Tours Entry Form. You can use Layout View and the Field List window to accomplish this goal.

STEPS

1. **Click the Design tab on the Ribbon, click the Add Existing Fields button in the Tools group, then click the Show all tables link in the Field List window if the Field List window does not look like Figure C-7**

   The Field List window opens in Layout View, as shown in Figure C-7. Notice that the Field List is divided into sections. The upper section shows the tables currently used by the form, the middle section shows related tables, and the lower section shows other tables. The expand/collapse button to the left of the table names allows you to expand (show) the fields within the table or collapse (hide) them. The Description field is in the TourCategories table in the middle section.

QUICK TIP
If you make a mistake, click the Undo button and try again.

2. **Click the expand button to the left of the TourCategories table, drag the Description field to the form, then use the pointer to drag the new Description combo box and label below the Cost controls**

   When you add a new field to a form, two controls are usually generated: a label and a text box. The label contains the field name and the text box displays the contents of the field. The TourCategories table moved from the middle to the top section of the Field List. You also want to align and size the new controls with others already on the form. Form Design View works best for alignment activities.

3. **Right-click the Tours Entry Form tab, click Design View, click the Description label, press and hold [Shift], click the Cost label to select both labels, release [Shift], click the Arrange tab, click the Align button in the Sizing & Ordering group, then click Left**

   Now resize the labels.

4. **With the two labels still selected, click the Size/Space button in the Sizing & Ordering group, then click To Widest**

   With the new controls in position, you want to enter a new record. You must switch to Form View to edit, enter, or delete data.

TROUBLE
Don't worry if your Tour No value doesn't match Figure C-8. It is an AutoNumber value, controlled by Access.

5. **Click the Home tab, click the View button to switch to Form View, click the New (blank) record button in the navigation bar, click the TourName text box, then enter a new record in the updated form, as shown in Figure C-8**

   Note that when you select a value in the Category combo box, the Description automatically updates. This is due to the one-to-many relationship between the TourCategories and Tours tables in the Relationships window.

FIGURE C-7: **Field List in Form Layout View**

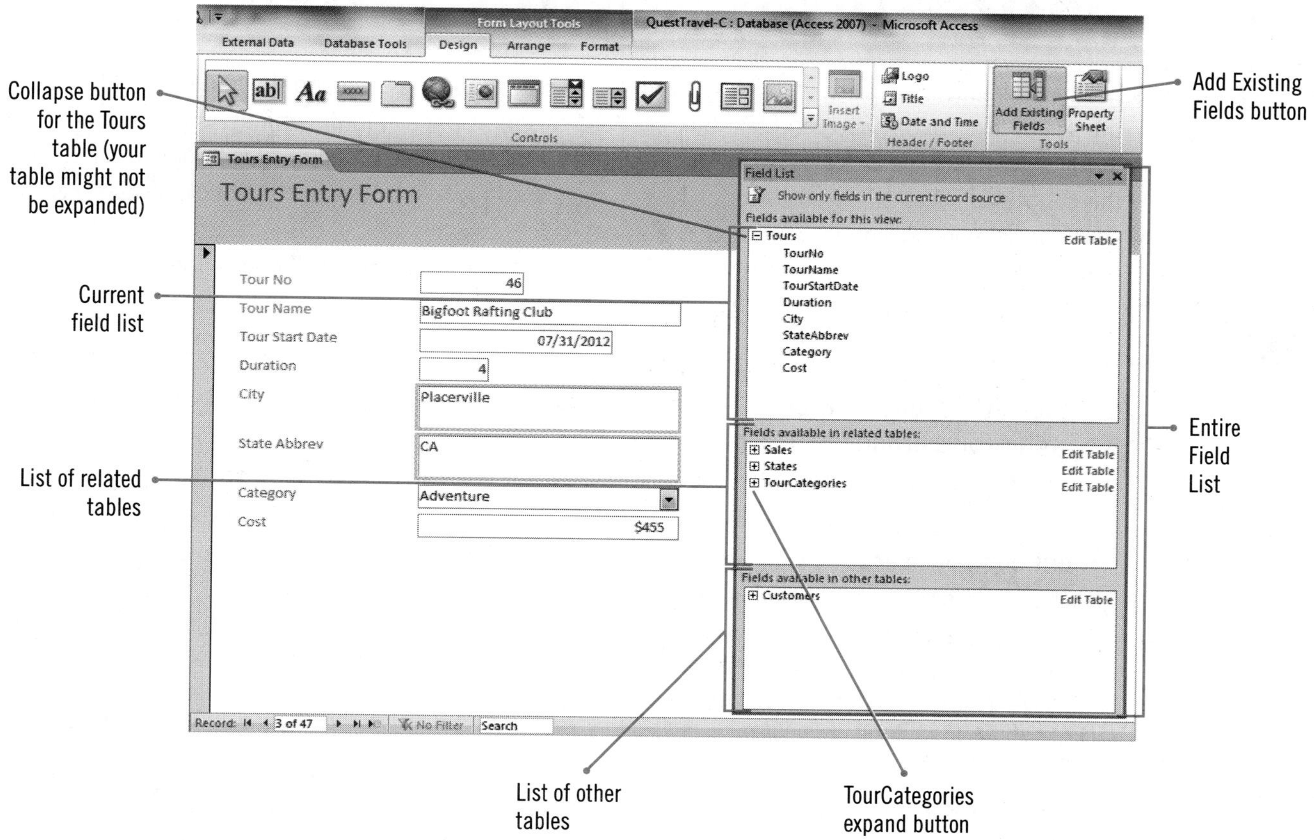

FIGURE C-8: **Entering a record in the updated Tours Entry Form in Form View**

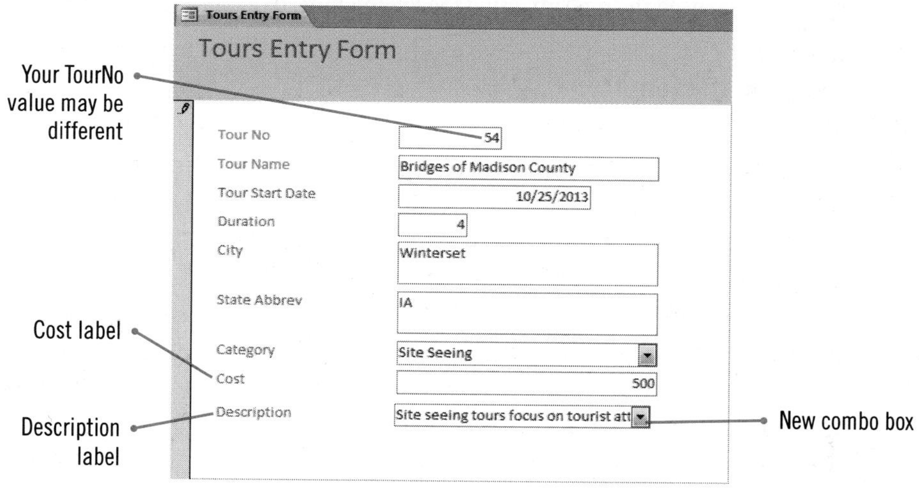

Bound versus unbound controls

Controls are either bound or unbound. **Bound controls** display values from a field such as text boxes and combo boxes. **Unbound controls** do not display data, but rather serve to describe data or enhance the appearance of the form. Labels are the most common type of unbound control, but other types include lines, images, tabs, and command buttons. Another way to distinguish bound from unbound controls is to observe the form as you move from record to record. Because bound controls display data, their contents change as you move through the records, displaying the entry in the field of the current record. Unbound controls such as labels and lines do not change as you move through the records in a form.

UNIT
C
Access 2010

Modifying Form Controls

You have already made many modifications to form controls such as changing the font color of labels and the size of text boxes. Labels and text boxes are the two most popular form controls. Other common controls are listed in Table C-4. When you modify controls, you change their **properties** (characteristics). All of the control characteristics you can modify are stored in the control's **Property Sheet**. Because Quest offers more adventure tours than any other type of tour, you decide to use the Property Sheet of the Category field to modify the default value to be "Adventure." You also use the Property Sheet to make other control modifications to better size and align the controls.

STEPS

1. **Click the Layout View button on the Home tab, then click the Property Sheet button in the Tools group**

   The Property Sheet window opens, showing you all of the properties for the selected item.

2. **Click the Category combo box, click the Data tab in the Property Sheet window (if it is not already selected), click the Default Value box, type Adventure, then press [Enter]**

   The Property Sheet should look like Figure C-9. Access often helps you with the **syntax** (rules) of entering property values. In this case, Access added quotation marks around "Adventure" to indicate that the default entry is text. Properties are categorized in the Property Sheet with the Format, Data, Event, and Other tabs. The All tab is a complete list of all the control's properties. You can use the Property Sheet to make all control modifications, although you'll probably find that some changes are easier to make using the Ribbon. The Property Sheet changes as you modify a control using the Ribbon.

> **TROUBLE**
> Be sure to click the Tour No label on the left, not the TourNo text box on the right.

3. **Click the Format tab of the Property Sheet, click the Tour No label in the form to select it, click the Home tab on the Ribbon, then click the Align Text Right button in the Text Formatting group**

   Notice that the **Text Align property** in the Property Sheet is automatically updated from Left to Right even though you changed the property using the Ribbon instead of directly in the Property Sheet.

4. **Click the Tour Name label, press and hold [Shift], then click every other label in the first column on the form**

   With all the labels selected, you can modify their Text Align property at the same time.

> **TROUBLE**
> You may need to click the Align Text Right button twice.

5. **Click the Align Text Right button in the Text Formatting group**

   Don't be overwhelmed by the number of properties available for each control on the form or the number of ways to modify each property. Over time, you will learn about most of these properties. At this point, it's only important to know the purpose of the Property Sheet and understand that properties are modified in various ways.

6. **Click the Save button on the Quick Access toolbar, click the Form View button on the Design tab, click the New (blank) record button in the navigation bar, then enter the record shown in Figure C-10**

   For new records, "Adventure" is provided as the default value for the Category combo box, but you can change it by typing a new value or selecting one from the list. With the labels right-aligned, they are much closer to the data in the text boxes that they describe.

FIGURE C-9: **Using the Property Sheet**

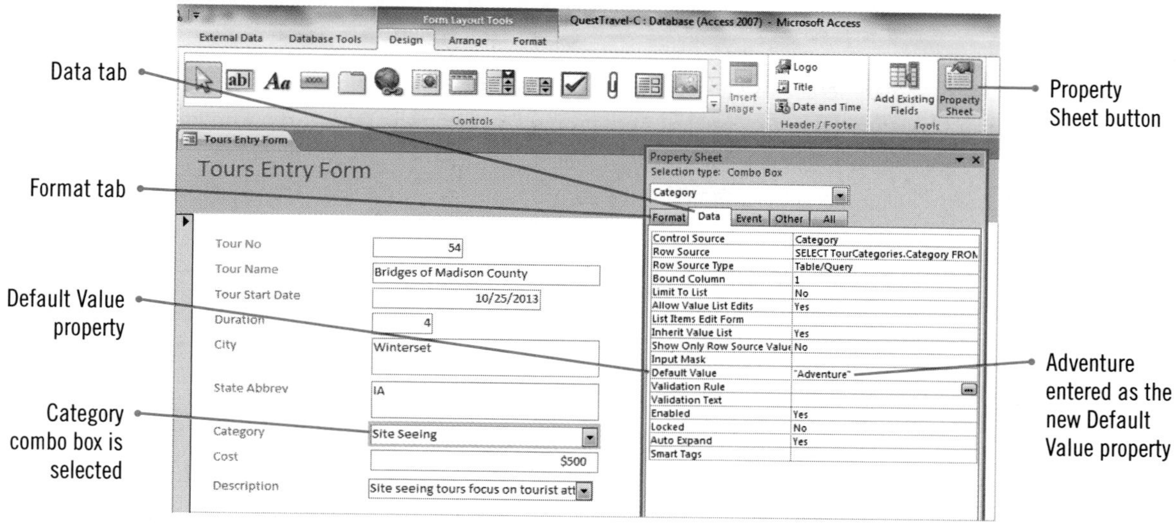

FIGURE C-10: **Modified Tours Entry Form**

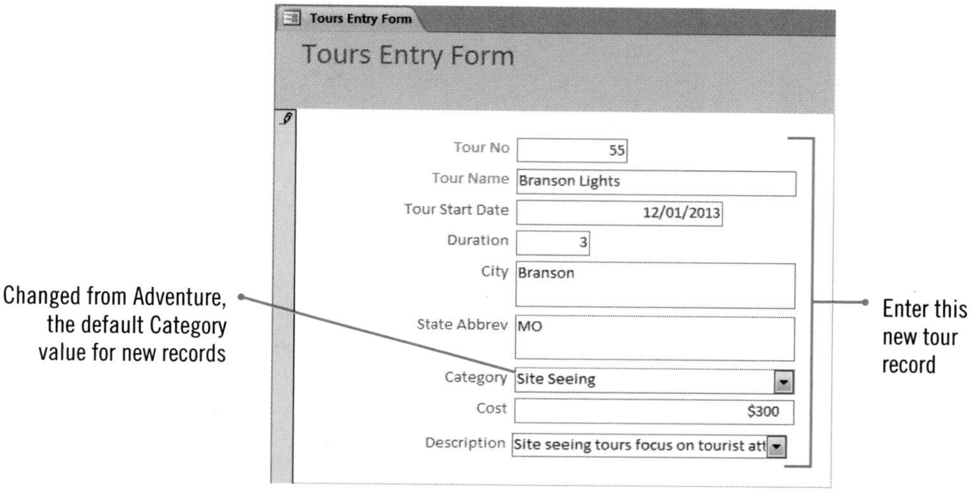

TABLE C-4: **Common form controls**

name	used to	bound	unbound
Label	Provide consistent descriptive text as you navigate from record to record; the label is the most common type of unbound control and can also be used as a hyperlink to another database object, external file, or Web page		x
Text box	Display, edit, or enter data for each record from an underlying record source; the text box is the most common type of bound control	x	
List box	Display a list of possible data entries	x	
Combo box	Display a list of possible data entries for a field, and provide a text box for an entry from the keyboard; combines the list box and text box controls	x	
Tab control	Create a three-dimensional aspect on a form		x
Check box	Display "yes" or "no" answers for a field; if the box is checked, it means "yes"	x	
Toggle button	Display "yes" or "no" answers for a field; if the button is pressed, it means "yes"	x	
Option button	Display a choice for a field	x	
Option group	Display and organize choices (usually presented as option buttons) for a field	x	
Line and Rectangle	Draw lines and rectangles on the form		x
Command button	Provide an easy way to initiate a command or run a macro		x

UNIT C

Access 2010

Creating Calculations

Text boxes are generally used to display data from underlying fields. The connection between the text box and field is defined by the **Control Source property** on the Data tab of the Property Sheet for that text box. A text box control can also display a calculation. To create a calculation in a text box, you enter an expression instead of a field name in the Control Source property. An **expression** is a combination of field names, operators (such as +, –, /, and *), and functions (such as Sum, Count, or Avg) that result in a single value. Sample expressions are shown in Table C-5. Samantha Hooper asks you to add a text box to the Tours Entry Form to calculate the tour end date. You can add a text box in Form Design View to accomplish this.

STEPS

1. **Right-click the Tours Entry Form tab, then click Design View**

   You want to add the tour end date calculation just below the Duration text box. First you'll resize the City and StateAbbrev fields.

2. **Click the City label, press and hold [Shift], click the City text box, click the StateAbbrev label, click the StateAbbrev text box to select the four controls together, release [Shift], click the Arrange tab, click the Size/Space button, then click To Shortest**

   With the City and StateAbbrev fields resized, you're ready to move them to make room for the new control to calculate the tour end date.

QUICK TIP

You can also press an arrow key to move a selected control.

3. **Click a blank spot on the form to deselect the four controls, click the StateAbbrev text box, use the pointer to move it down, click the City text box, then use the pointer to move it down**

   To add the calculation to determine the tour end date (the tour start date plus the duration), start by adding a new text box to the form between the Duration and City text boxes.

TROUBLE

If you position the new text box incorrectly, click Undo on the Quick Access toolbar and try again.

4. **Click the Design tab, click the Text Box button in the Controls group, then click between the Duration and City text boxes to insert the new text box**

   Adding a new text box automatically adds a new label to the left of the text box.

TROUBLE

The initial number in your label is based on previous work done to the form, so it might vary.

5. **Double-click the new Text22 label on the left, type Tour End Date, then press [Enter]**

   With the label updated to correctly identify the text box to the right, you're ready to enter the expression to calculate the tour end date.

6. **Click the new text box to select it, click the Data tab of the Property Sheet, click the Control Source property, type =[TourStartDate]+[Duration], then press [Enter] to update the form as shown in Figure C-11**

   All expressions entered in a control start with an equal sign (=). When referencing a field name within an expression, [square brackets]—(not parentheses) and not {curly braces}—surround the field name. In an expression, you must type the field name exactly as it was created in Table Design View, but you do not need to match the capitalization.

7. **Click the View button to switch to Form View, click the value in the Tour Name text box, click the Ascending button, select 7 in the Duration text box, type 5, then press [Enter]**

   Note that the tour end date, calculated by an expression, automatically changed to five days after the tour start date to reflect the new duration value. The updated Tours Entry Form with the tour date end calculation for the American Heritage Tour is shown in Figure C-12.

FIGURE C-11: Adding a text box to calculate a value

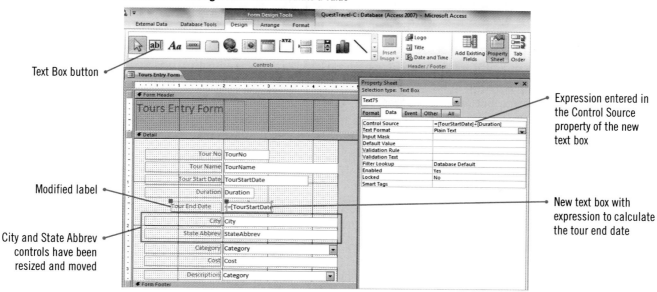

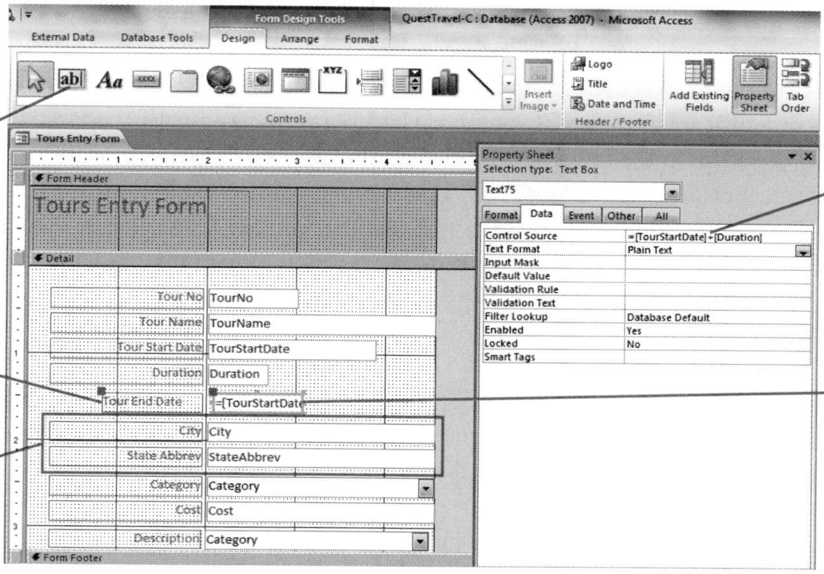
Text Box button
Modified label
City and State Abbrev controls have been resized and moved
Expression entered in the Control Source property of the new text box
New text box with expression to calculate the tour end date

FIGURE C-12: Displaying the results of a calculation in Form View

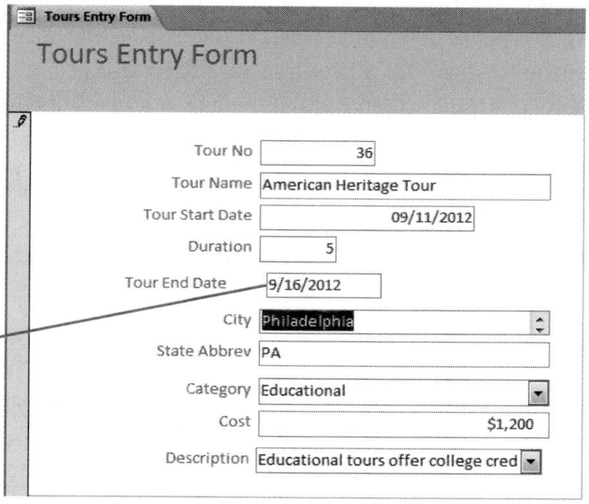
Tour End Date is calculated with the expression =[TourStartDate]+[Duration]

TABLE C-5: Sample expressions

sample expression	description
=Sum([Salary])	Uses the **Sum function** to add the values in the Salary field
=[Price] * 1.05	Multiplies the Price field by 1.05 (adds 5% to the Price field)
=[Subtotal] + [Shipping]	Adds the value of the Subtotal field to the value of the Shipping field
=Avg([Freight])	Uses the **Avg function** to display an average of the values in the Freight field
=Date()	Uses the **Date function** to display the current date in the form of mm-dd-yy
="Page " &[Page]	Displays the word Page, a space, and the result of the [Page] field, an Access field that contains the current page number
=[FirstName]& " " &[LastName]	Displays the value of the FirstName and LastName fields in one control, separated by a space
=Left([ProductNumber],2)	Uses the **Left function** to display the first two characters in the ProductNumber field

Modifying Tab Order

After positioning all of the controls on the form, you should check the tab order and tab stops. **Tab order** is the order the focus moves as you press [Tab] in Form View. A **tab stop** refers to whether a control can receive the focus in the first place. By default, the tab stop property for all text boxes and combo boxes is set to Yes, but some text boxes, such as those that contain expressions, will not be used for data entry. Therefore, the tab stop property for a text box that contains a calculation should be set to No. Unbound controls such as labels and lines do not have a tab stop property because they cannot be used to enter or edit data. You plan to check the tab order of the Tours Entry Form, then change tab stops and tab order as necessary.

STEPS

1. **Press [Tab] enough times to move through several records, watching the focus move through the bound controls of the form**

   Because the tour end date text box is a calculated field, you don't want it to receive the focus. To prevent the Tour End Date text box from receiving the focus, you set its tab stop property to No using its Property Sheet. You can work with the Property Sheet in either Layout or Design View.

> **QUICK TIP**
> You can also switch between views using the View buttons in the lower-right corner of the window.

2. **Right-click the Tours Entry Form tab, click Design View, click the Tour End Date text box, click the Other tab in the Property Sheet, double-click the Tab Stop property to toggle it from Yes to No, then change the Name property to TourEndDate as shown in Figure C-13**

   The Other tab of the Property Sheet contains the properties you need to change the tab stop and tab order. The **Tab Stop property** determines whether the field accepts focus, and the **Tab Index property** indicates the numeric tab order for all controls on the form that have the Tab Stop property set to Yes. The **Name property** on the Other tab is also important as it identifies the name of the control, which is used in other areas of the database. To review your tab stop changes, return to Form View.

> **QUICK TIP**
> In Form Design View, press [Ctrl][.] to switch to Form View. In Form View, press [Ctrl][,] to switch to Form Design View.

3. **Click the View button on the Design tab to switch to Form View, then press [Tab] nine times to move to the next record**

   Now that the tab stop has been removed from the TourEndDate text box, the tab order flows correctly from the top to the bottom of the form, but skips the calculated field. To review the tab order for the entire form in one dialog box, you must switch to Form Design View.

> **TROUBLE**
> If the order of your fields does not match those in Figure C-14, move a field by clicking the field selector and then dragging the field.

4. **Right-click the Tours Entry Form tab, click Design View, then click the Tab Order button in the Tools group to open the Tab Order dialog box as shown in Figure C-14**

   The Tab Order dialog box allows you to view and change the tab order by dragging fields up or down using the field selectors to the left of the field names. Moving fields up and down in this list also renumbers the Tab Index property for the controls in their respective Property Sheets.

5. **Click OK to close the Tab Order dialog box, click the Property Sheet button to toggle it off, then click the Save button on the Quick Access toolbar to save your work**

FIGURE C-13: **Using the Property Sheet to set tab properties**

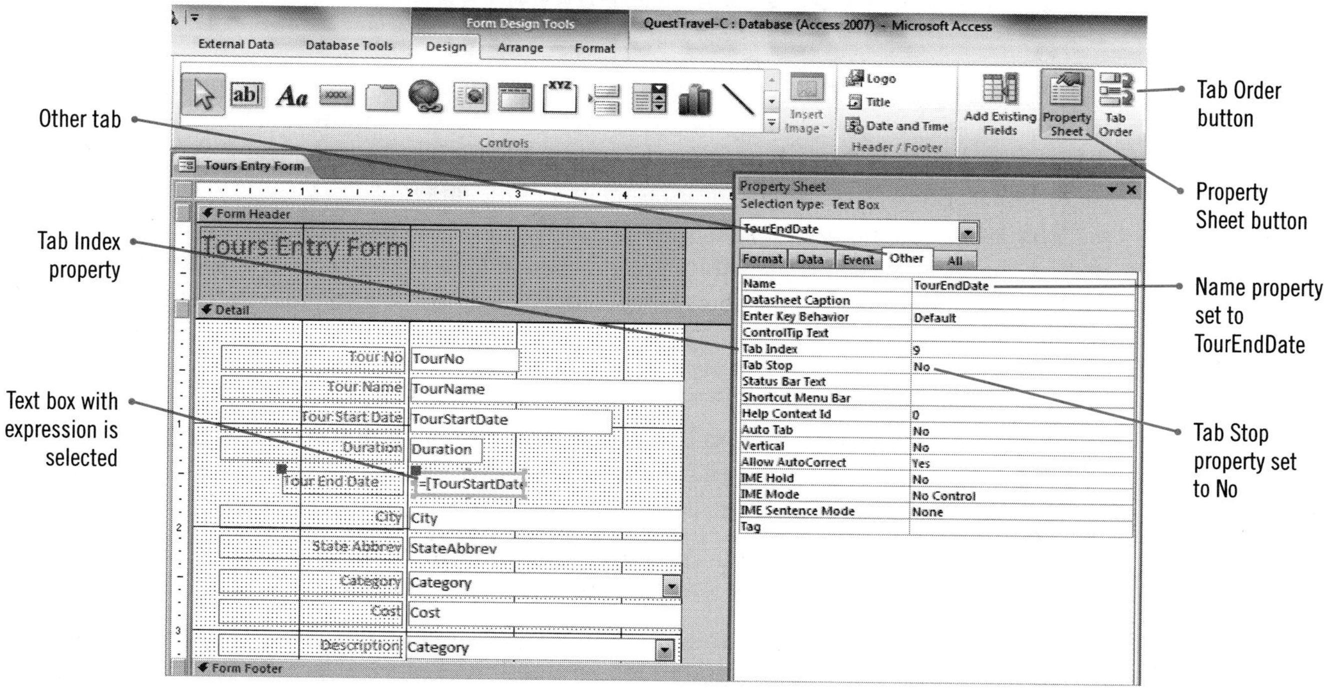
Other tab
Tab Index property
Text box with expression is selected
Tab Order button
Property Sheet button
Name property set to TourEndDate
Tab Stop property set to No

FIGURE C-14: **Tab Order dialog box**

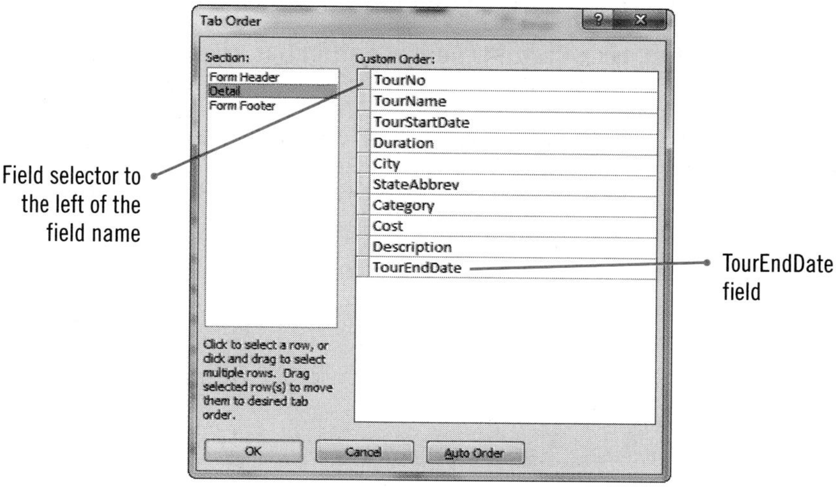
Field selector to the left of the field name
TourEndDate field

UNIT C

Access 2010

Inserting an Image

Graphic images, such as pictures, logos, or clip art, can add style and professionalism to a form. The form section in which you place the images is significant. **Form sections** determine where controls are displayed and printed; they are described in Table C-6. For example, if you add a company logo to the Form Header section, the image appears at the top of the form in Form View as well as at the top of a printout. If you add the same image to the Detail section, it prints next to each record in the printout because the Detail section is printed for every record. Samantha Hooper suggests that you add the Quest logo to the top of the Tours Entry Form. You can add the control in either Layout or Design View, but if you want to place it in the Form Header section, you have to work in Design View.

STEPS

1. **Click the Form Header section bar, click the Insert Image button in the Controls group, click Browse, then navigate to the drive and folder where you store your Data Files**
   The Insert Picture dialog box opens, prompting you for the location of the image.
2. **Double-click QuestLogo.bmp, then click the right side of the Form Header section**
   The QuestLogo image is added to the right side of the Form Header. You want to resize it to about 1.5" × 1.5".
3. **With the QuestLogo image still selected, use the ↘ pointer to drag the lower-right corner of the image up and to the left so that it is about 1.5" × 1.5", then drag the top edge of the Detail section up using the ✛ pointer as shown in Figure C-15**
   When an image or control is selected in Design View, you can use **sizing handles**, which are small squares at the corner of the selection box. Drag a handle to resize the image or control. With the form completed, you open it in Form View to observe the changes.
4. **Click the Save button on the Quick Access toolbar, then click the View button to switch to Form View**
   You decide to add one more record with your final Tours Entry Form.
5. **Enter the new record shown in Figure C-16, using your last name in the TourName field**
   Now print only this single new record.
6. **Click the File tab, click Print in the navigation bar, click Print, click the Selected Record(s) option button, then click OK**
7. **Close the Tours Entry Form, click Yes if prompted to save it, close the QuestTravel-C.accdb database, then exit Access 2010**

TROUBLE

The lower-right corner of the image touches the top edge of the Detail section. To resize the Quest logo, click it to select it.

TABLE C-6: **Form sections**

section	controls placed in this section print:
Form Header	Only once at the top of the first page of the printout
Detail	Once for every record
Form Footer	Only once at the end of the last page of the printout

FIGURE C-15: **Adding an image to the Form Header section**

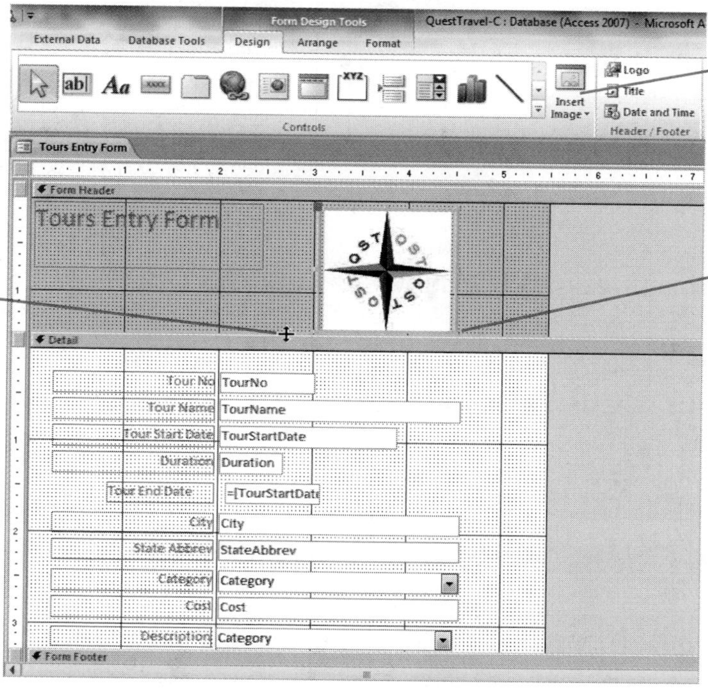

FIGURE C-16: **Final Tours Entry Form with new record**

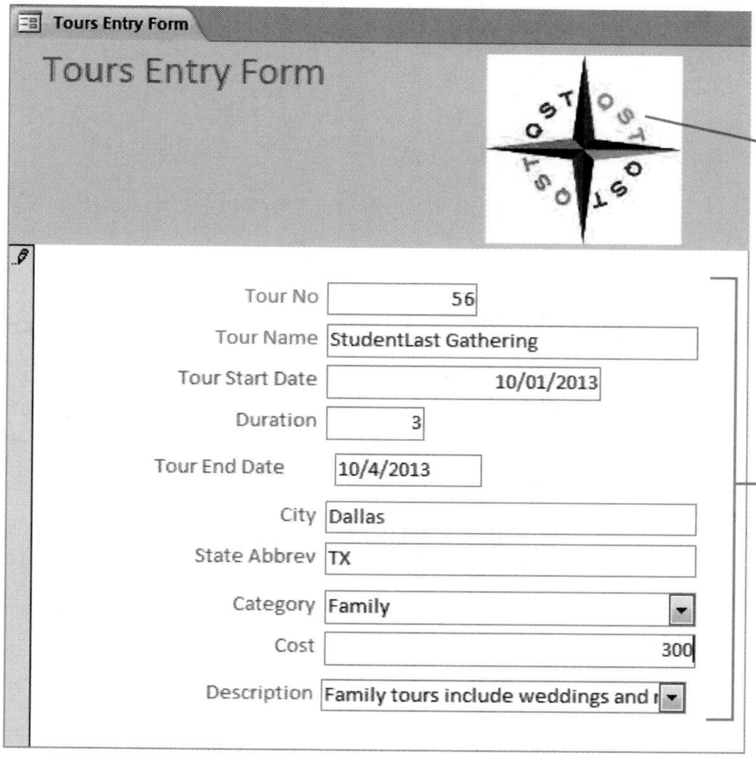

Practice

Concepts Review

For current SAM information, including versions and content details, visit SAM Central (http://www.cengage.com/samcentral). If you have a SAM user profile, you may have access to hands-on instruction, practice, and assessment of the skills covered in this unit. Since various versions of SAM are supported throughout the life of this text, check with your instructor for the correct instructions and URL/Web site for accessing assignments.

Label each element of Form Design View shown in Figure C-17.

FIGURE C-17

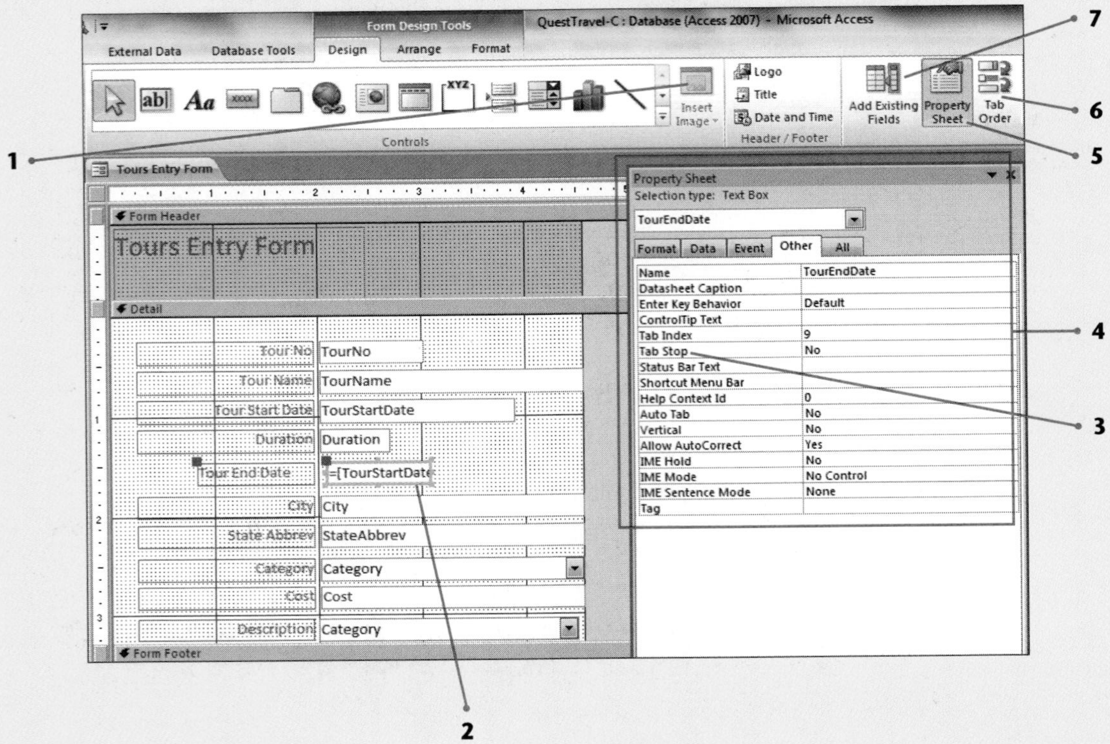

Match each term with the statement that best describes it.

8. Bound control
9. Calculated control
10. Detail section
11. Database designer
12. Tab order
13. Form Footer section

a. The way the focus moves from one bound control to the next in Form View
b. Created by entering an expression in a text box
c. Controls placed here print once for every record in the underlying record source
d. Used on a form to display data from a field
e. Controls placed here print only once at the end of the printout
f. Responsible for building and maintaining tables, queries, forms, and reports

Select the best answer from the list of choices.

14. Every element on a form is called a(n):

a. Control.
b. Item.
c. Tool.
d. Property.

15. Which of the following is probably *not* a graphic image?

a. Logo
b. Clip art
c. Calculation
d. Picture

16. The most common bound control is the:

- **a.** Label.
- **b.** Combo box.
- **c.** List box.
- **d.** Text box.

17. The most common unbound control is the:

- **a.** Command button.
- **b.** Label.
- **c.** Text box.
- **d.** Combo box.

18. Which form view *cannot* be used to view data?

- **a.** Layout
- **b.** Preview
- **c.** Design
- **d.** Datasheet

19. Which property helps you set tab order?

- **a.** Control Source
- **b.** Tab Index
- **c.** ControlTip
- **d.** Default

20. When you enter a calculation in a text box, the first character is a(n):

- **a.** Equal sign, =
- **b.** Left square bracket, [
- **c.** Left parenthesis, (
- **d.** Asterisk, *

Skills Review

1. Use the Form Wizard.

- **a.** Start Access and open the RealEstate-C.accdb database from the drive and folder where you store your Data Files. Enable content if prompted.
- **b.** Click the Create tab, then use the Form Wizard to create a form based on all of the fields in the Realtors table. Use a Columnar layout, and type **Realtor Entry Form** to title the form.
- **c.** Add a new record with your name. Note that the RealtorNo field is an AutoNumber field that is automatically incremented as you enter your first and last names. Enter your school's telephone number for the RPhone field value, and enter **4** as the AgencyNo field value.
- **d.** Save and close the Realtor Entry Form.

2. Create a split form.

- **a.** Click the Realtors table in the Navigation Pane, click the Create tab, click the More Forms button, then click Split Form.
- **b.** Switch to Form View, then navigate to the RealtorNo 11 (Rob Zacharias) record in either the upper or lower pane of the split form.
- **c.** Click the record selector in either the upper or lower pane for RealtorNo 11 (Rob Zacharias) and click the Delete button in the Records group to delete this realtor. Click Yes when prompted.
- **d.** Navigate to the RealtorNo 5 (Jane Ann Welch) record in either the upper or lower pane of the split form. Change Welch to **Rockaway**.
- **e.** Click the record selector in either the upper or lower pane for RealtorNo 5, Jane Ann Rockaway, and click the Delete button in the Records group. A message appears explaining why this record cannot be deleted. In a written document, explain the concept of an "orphan record" and how it applies to this situation. Click OK.
- **f.** Right-click the Realtors form tab, click Close, click Yes when prompted to save changes, and type **Realtors Split Form** as the name of the form.

3. Use Form Layout View.

- **a.** Open the Realtor Entry Form in Layout View.
- **b.** Modify the labels on the left to read: **Realtor Number**, **Realtor First Name**, **Realtor Last Name**, **Realtor Phone**, and **Agency Number**.
- **c.** Modify the text color of the labels to black.
- **d.** Resize the RFirst, RLast, and RPhone text boxes on the right to be the same width as the RealtorNo and AgencyNo text boxes.
- **e.** Save the Realtor Entry Form.

Skills Review (continued)

4. **Add fields to a form.**
   a. Open the Field List window, show all the tables, then expand the field list for the Agencies table.
   b. Drag the AgencyName field to the form, then move the AgencyName label and combo box to below the Agency Number controls.
   c. Modify the AgencyName label to read **Agency Name**.
   d. Modify the text color of the Agency Name label to black.
   e. Save the form and close the Field List window.
5. **Modify form controls.**
   a. In Layout View, use the Align Text Right button on the Home tab to right-align each of the labels in the left column.
   b. Switch to Form View, then use the Agency Name combo box to change the Agency Name to **Marvin and Pam Realtors** for Realtor Number 1.
   c. If the combo box is not wide enough to display the entire entry for Marvin and Pam Realtors, switch back to Layout View and widen the combo box as much as needed to display the entire entry in the combo box.
6. **Create calculations.**
   a. Switch to Form Design View, then add a text box below the Realtor Entry Form label in the Form Header section. Delete the extra label that is created when you add a new text box.
   b. Widen the text box to be almost as wide as the entire form, then enter the following expression into the text box, which will add the words **Information for** to the realtor's first name, a space, and then the realtor's last name.
   ="Information for "&[RFirst]&" "&[RLast]
   c. Save the form, then view it in Form View. Be sure the new text box correctly displays spaces in the text. Return to Design View to edit the expression as needed.
   d. In Form View, change the Realtor Last Name in the first record from Matusek to **King**.
   e. Tab to the Realtor Phone text box, observing the automatic change to the expression in the Form Header section.
7. **Modify tab order.**
   a. Switch to Form Design View, then open the Property Sheet window.
   b. Select the new text box with the expression in the Form Header section, then change the Tab Stop property from Yes to No.
   c. Select the RealtorNo text box in the Detail section, then change the Tab Stop property from Yes to No. (AutoNumber fields cannot be edited, so they do not need to be in the tab order.)
   d. Close the Property Sheet.
   e. Save the form and view it in Form View. Tab through the form to make sure that the tab order is sequential. Use the Tab Order button on the Design tab in Form Design View to modify tab order, if necessary.
8. **Insert an image.**
   a. Switch to Design View, and click the Form Header section bar.
   b. Add the ForSale.bmp image to the right side of the Form Header, then resize the image to be about 1.5" × 1.5".
   c. Remove extra blank area in the Form Header section by dragging the top edge of the Detail section up as far as possible.
   d. Save the form, then switch to Form View. Move through the records, observing the calculated field from record to record to make sure it is calculating correctly.
   e. Find the record with your name as shown in Figure C-18, and then print only that record if requested by your instructor.
   f. Close the Realtor Entry Form, close the RealEstate-C.accdb database, then exit Access.

FIGURE C-18

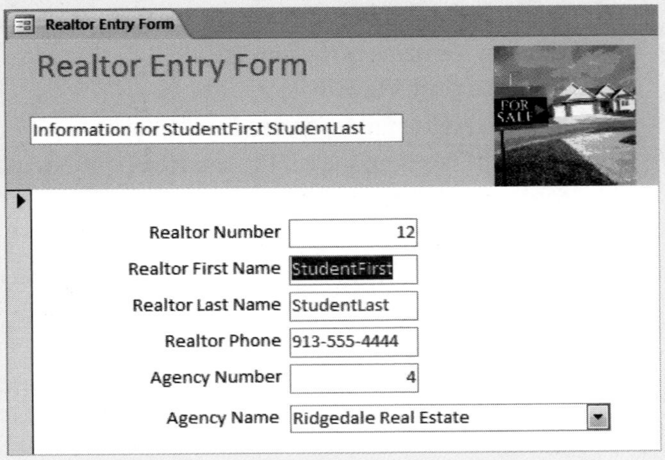

Independent Challenge 1

As the manager of the scuba divers branch of the Quest Specialty Travel tour company, you have developed a database to help manage scuba dives. In this exercise, you'll create a data entry form to manage the dive trips.

If you have a SAM 2010 user profile, an autogradable SAM version of this assignment may be available at http://www.cengage.com/sam2010. Check with your instructor to confirm that this assignment is available in SAM. To use the SAM version of this assignment, log into the SAM 2010 Web site and download the instruction and start files.

a. Start Access, then open the QuestDives-C.accdb database from the drive and folder where you store your Data Files. Enable content if prompted.

b. Using the Form Wizard, create a form that includes all the fields in the DiveTrips table and uses the Columnar layout, then type **Dive Trip Entry** as the title of the form.

c. Switch to Layout View, then delete the ID text box and label.

d. Using Form Design View, select all of the text boxes except the last one for TripReport, and resize them to the shortest size using the To Shortest option on the Size/Space button on the Arrange tab.

e. Using Form Design View, resize the Location, City, State/Province, Country, Lodging, and TripReport text boxes to be no wider than the Rating text box.

f. Using Form Design View and Form Layout View, move, edit, format, and align the labels and text boxes as shown in Figure C-19. Note that there are spaces between the words in the labels, the labels are right-aligned, and the text boxes are left-aligned. Use a Light Blue color for the labels and a Dark Blue for the text in the text boxes.

g. In Form View, enter the Trip Report record as shown in Figure C-19, using your own name instead of Enter Your Name.

h. Save the form, then print only the first record with your name, if requested by your instructor.

i. Close the Dive Trip Entry form, close the QuestDives-C.accdb database, then exit Access 2010.

FIGURE C-19

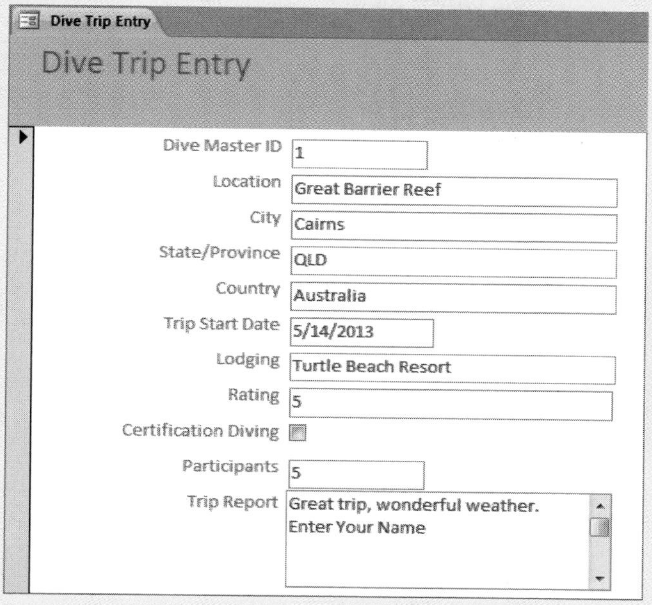

Independent Challenge 2

You have built an Access database to track membership in a community service club. The database tracks member names and addresses as well as their status in the club, which moves from rank to rank as the members contribute increased hours of service to the community.

a. Start Access, then open the Membership-C.accdb database from the drive and folder where you store your Data Files. Enable content if prompted.

b. Using the Form Wizard, create a form based on all of the fields of the Members table and only the DuesOwed field in the Status table.

c. View the data by Members, use a Columnar layout, then enter **Member Information** as the title of the form.

d. Enter a new record with your name and the school name, address, and phone number of your school. Give yourself a StatusNo entry of **1**. In the DuesPaid field, enter **75**. DuesOwed automatically displays 100 because that value is pulled from the Status table and is based on the entry in the StatusNo field, which links the Members table to the Status table.

e. In Layout View, add a text box to the form and move it below the DuesOwed text box.

f. Open the Property Sheet for the new text box, and in the Control Source property of the new text box, enter the expression that calculates the balance between DuesOwed and DuesPaid: **=[DuesOwed]-[DuesPaid]**.

g. Open the Property Sheet for the new label, and change the Caption property for the new label to **Balance**.

Independent Challenge 2 (continued)

h. Right-align all of the labels in the first column.
i. Set the Tab Stop property for the text box that contains the calculated Balance to **No**, then close the Property Sheet.

Advanced Challenge Exercise

ACE

- Switch to Form Design View, then drag the right edge of the form to the 7" mark on the horizontal ruler.
- Resize the last three text boxes that contain DuesPaid, DuesOwed, and the expression to calculate the Balance to be the same size as the new Balance text box, and right-align all data within the three text boxes.
- Open the Property Sheet for the text box that contains the expression, and change the Format property on the Format tab to Currency. Close the Property Sheet.
- Click a blank spot to the right of the text boxes, click the Insert Image button, browse for the PeoplePower.bmp image, then insert it to the right of the Company text box.
- Move and resize the controls as necessary to accommodate the picture, save the form, find the record with your name, and change the DuesPaid value to **85** as shown in Figure C-20.

FIGURE C-20

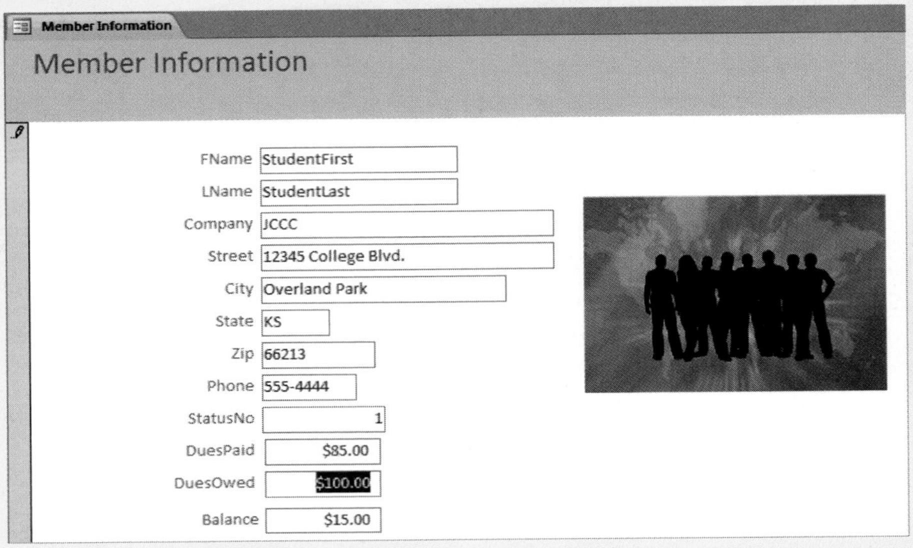

j. Print only the record with your name, if requested by your instructor.
k. Save and close the Member Information form, then close the Membership-C.accdb database and exit Access 2010.

Independent Challenge 3

You have built an Access database to organize the deposits at a recycling center. Various clubs regularly deposit recyclable material, which is measured in pounds when the deposits are made.

a. Open the Recycle-C.accdb database from the drive and folder where you store your Data Files. Enable content if prompted.
b. Using the Form Wizard, create a form based on all of the fields in the DepositList query. View the data by Deposits, use the Columnar layout, and title the form **Deposit Listing**.
c. Switch to Layout View, then make each label bold.
d. Switch to Form Design View and resize the CenterName and ClubName text boxes so they are the same height and width as the Weight text box.
e. Switch to Layout View and modify the DepositNumber and DepositDate labels so they read **Deposit Number** and **Deposit Date**. Modify the CenterName and ClubName labels so they read **Center Name** and **Club Name** as shown in Figure C-21.

FIGURE C-21

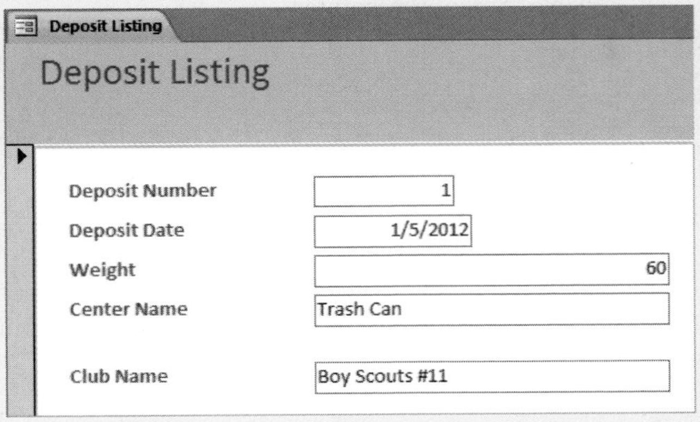

Independent Challenge 3 (continued)

f. Switch to Form View, find and change any entry of Jaycees in the ClubName field to your last name, then print a deposit record with your name if requested by your instructor.

Advanced Challenge Exercise

- Using Form View of the Deposit Listing form, filter for all records with your last name in the ClubName field.
- Using Form View of the Deposit Listing form, sort the filtered records in descending order on the DepositDate field.
- Preview, then print the first record of the filtered and sorted records, if requested by your instructor.

g. Save and close the Deposit Listing form, close the Recycle-C.accdb database, then exit Access.

Real Life Independent Challenge

One way you can use an Access database on your own is to record and track your job search efforts. In this exercise, you will develop a form to help you enter data into your job-tracking database.

a. Open the JobSearch-C.accdb database from the drive and folder where you store your Data Files. Enable content if prompted.

b. Click the Create tab, then use the Form Wizard to create a new form based on all the fields of both the Employers and Positions tables.

c. View the data by Employers, use a Datasheet layout, accept the default names for the form and subform, then open the form to view information.

d. Use Layout View and Design View to modify the form labels, text box positions, and sizes as shown in Figure C-22. Note that the columns within the subform have been resized to display all of the data in the subform.

e. Change the CompanyName of IBM in the first record to **Your Last Name's Software**, and if instructed to create a printout, print only that record.

f. Save and close the Employers form, close the JobSearch-C.accdb database, then exit Access.

FIGURE C-22

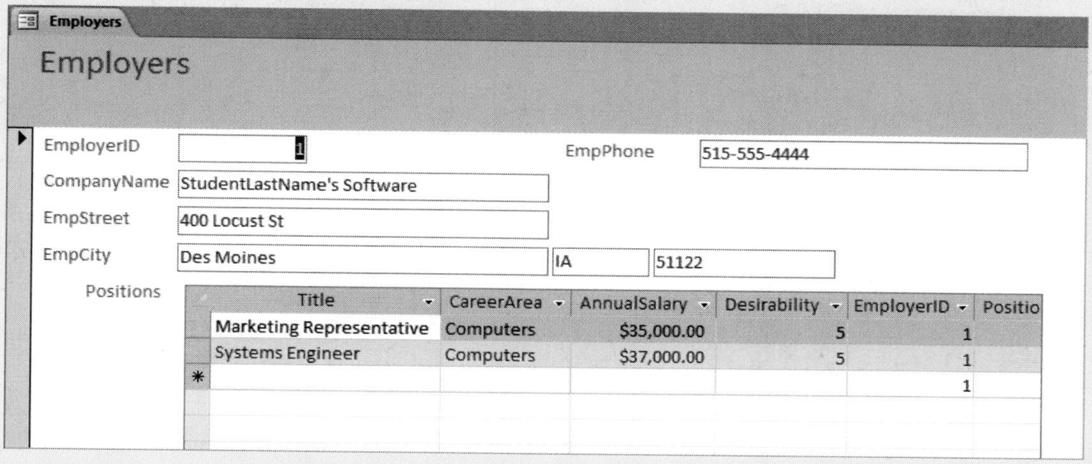
Employers
Employers
EmployerID
1
EmpPhone
515-555-4444
CompanyName
StudentLastName's Software
EmpStreet
400 Locust St
EmpCity
Des Moines
IA
51122
Positions
Title
CareerArea
AnnualSalary
Desirability
EmployerID
Positio
Marketing Representative
Computers
$35,000.00
5
1
Systems Engineer
Computers
$37,000.00
5
1
1

Visual Workshop

Open the Baseball-C.accdb database, enable content if prompted, then use the Split Form tool to create the form as shown in Figure C-23 based on the Players table. Resize the PlayerLast text box as shown. Modify the labels as shown. View the data in Form View, and sort the records in ascending order by last name. Change the name of Henry Aaron in the first record to **Your Name**, and if instructed to create a printout, print only that record. Save and close the Players form, close the Baseball-C.accdb database, then exit Access.

FIGURE C-23

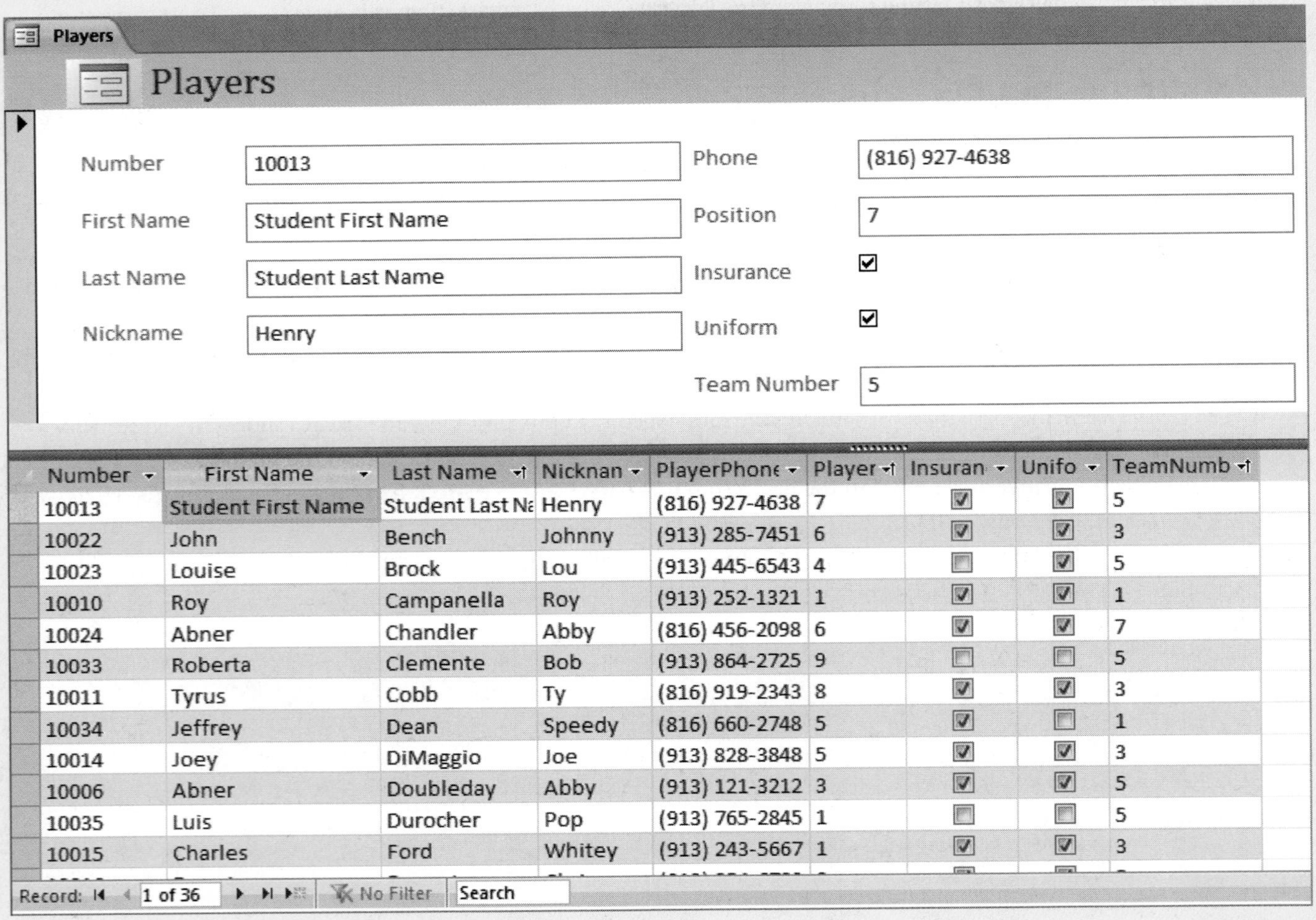

UNIT D Access 2010

Using Reports

Files You Will Need:

QuestTravel-D.accdb
RealEstate-D.accdb
Conventions-D.accdb
Membership-D.accdb
Recycle-D.accdb
JobSearch-D.accdb
Basketball-D.accdb

A **report** is an Access object used to create professional-looking printouts. Although you can print a datasheet or form, reports are the primary object you use to print database content because they provide the most formatting, layout, and summary options. For example, a report might include formatting embellishments such as multiple fonts and colors, extra graphical elements such as clip art and lines, and multiple headers and footers. Reports are also very powerful data analysis tools. A report can calculate subtotals, averages, counts, or other statistics for groups of records. Samantha Hooper, a tour developer at Quest Specialty Travel, asks you to produce some reports to help her share and analyze data.

OBJECTIVES

- Use the Report Wizard
- Use Report Layout View
- Review report sections
- Apply group and sort orders
- Add subtotals and counts
- Resize and align controls
- Format a report
- Create mailing labels

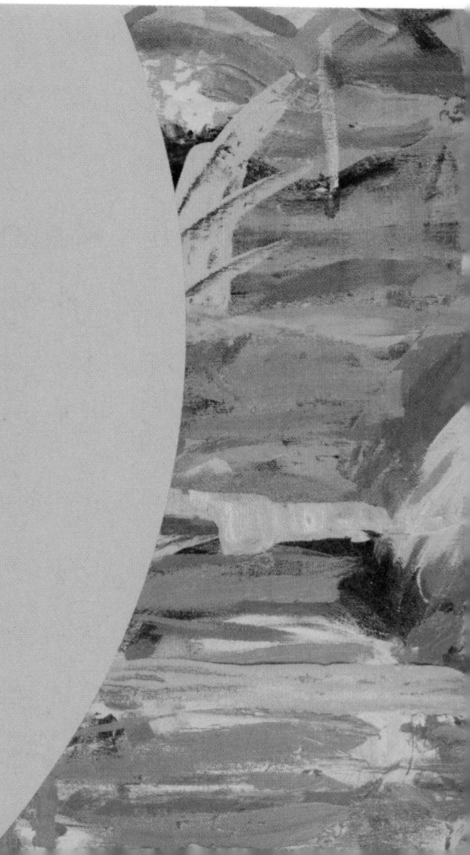

UNIT
D
Access 2010

Using the Report Wizard

You can create reports in Access by using the **Report Wizard**, a tool that asks questions to guide you through the initial development of the report, similar to the Form Wizard. Your responses to the Report Wizard determine the record source, style, and layout of the report. The **record source** is the table or query that defines the fields and records displayed on the report. The Report Wizard also helps you sort, group, and analyze the records. You use the Report Wizard to create a report to display the tours within each state.

STEPS

1. **Start Access, open the QuestTravel-D.accdb database, enable content if prompted, click the Create tab on the Ribbon, then click the Report Wizard button in the Reports group**
   The Report Wizard starts, prompting you to select the fields you want on the report. You can select fields from one or more tables or queries.

> **TROUBLE**
> If you select a field by mistake, click the unwanted field in the Selected Fields list, then click the Remove Field button [<].

2. **Click the Tables/Queries list arrow, click Table: States, double-click the StateName field, click the Tables/Queries list arrow, click Table: Tours, click the Select All Fields button [>>], click StateAbbrev in the Selected Fields list, then click the Remove Field button [<]**
   By selecting the StateName field from the States table, and all fields from the Tours table except the StateAbbrev field, you have all of the fields you need for the report as shown in Figure D-1. You selected the full state name stored in the States table instead of the two-letter state abbreviation used in the Tours table.
3. **Click Next, then click by States if it is not already selected**
   Choosing "by States" groups together the records for each state. In addition to record-grouping options, the Report Wizard later asks if you want to sort the records within each group. You can use the Report Wizard to specify up to four fields to sort in either ascending or descending order.

> **QUICK TIP**
> Click Back to review previous dialog boxes within a wizard.

4. **Click Next, click Next again to include no additional grouping levels, click the first sort list arrow, click TourStartDate, then click Next**
   The last questions in the Report Wizard deal with report appearance and creating a report title.
5. **Click the Stepped option button, click the Landscape option button, click Next, type Tours by State for the report title, then click Finish**
   The Tours by State report opens in **Print Preview**, which displays the report as it appears when printed, as shown in Figure D-2. The records are grouped by state, the first state being California, and then sorted in ascending order by the TourStartDate field within each state. Reports are **read-only** objects, meaning that they read and display data but cannot be used to change (write to) data. As you change data using tables, queries, or forms, reports constantly display those up-to-date edits just like all of the other Access objects.
6. **Scroll down to see the second grouping section on the report for the state of Colorado, then click the Next Page button [▶] in the navigation bar to see the second page of the report**
   Even in **landscape orientation** (11" wide by 8.5" tall as opposed to **portrait orientation**, which is 8.5" wide by 11" tall), the fields on the Tours by State report may not neatly fit on one sheet of paper. The labels in the column headings and the data in the columns need to be resized to improve the layout. Depending on your monitor, you might need to scroll to the right to display all the fields on this page.

FIGURE D-1: **Selecting fields for a report using the Report Wizard**

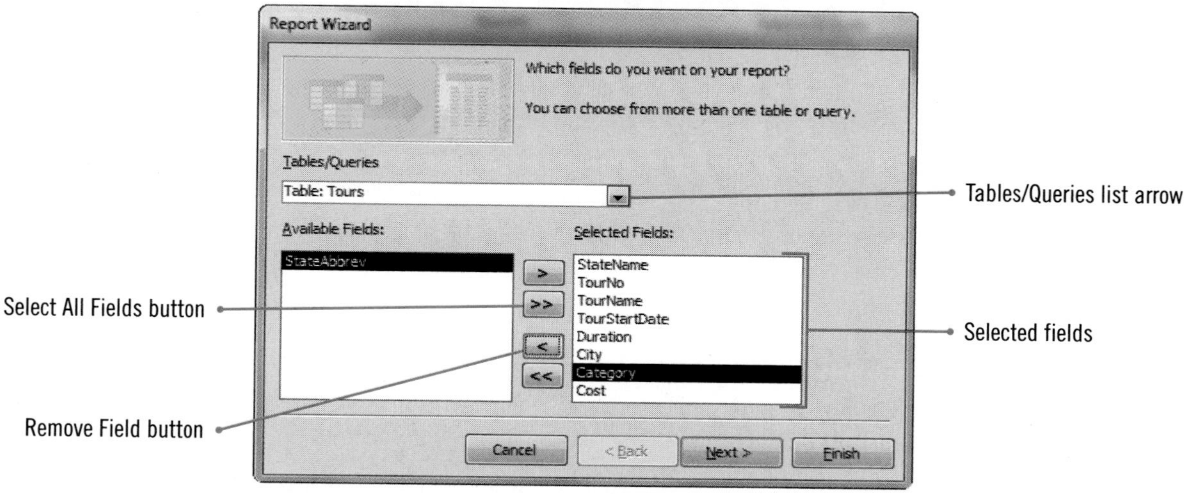

FIGURE D-2: **Tours by State report in Print Preview**

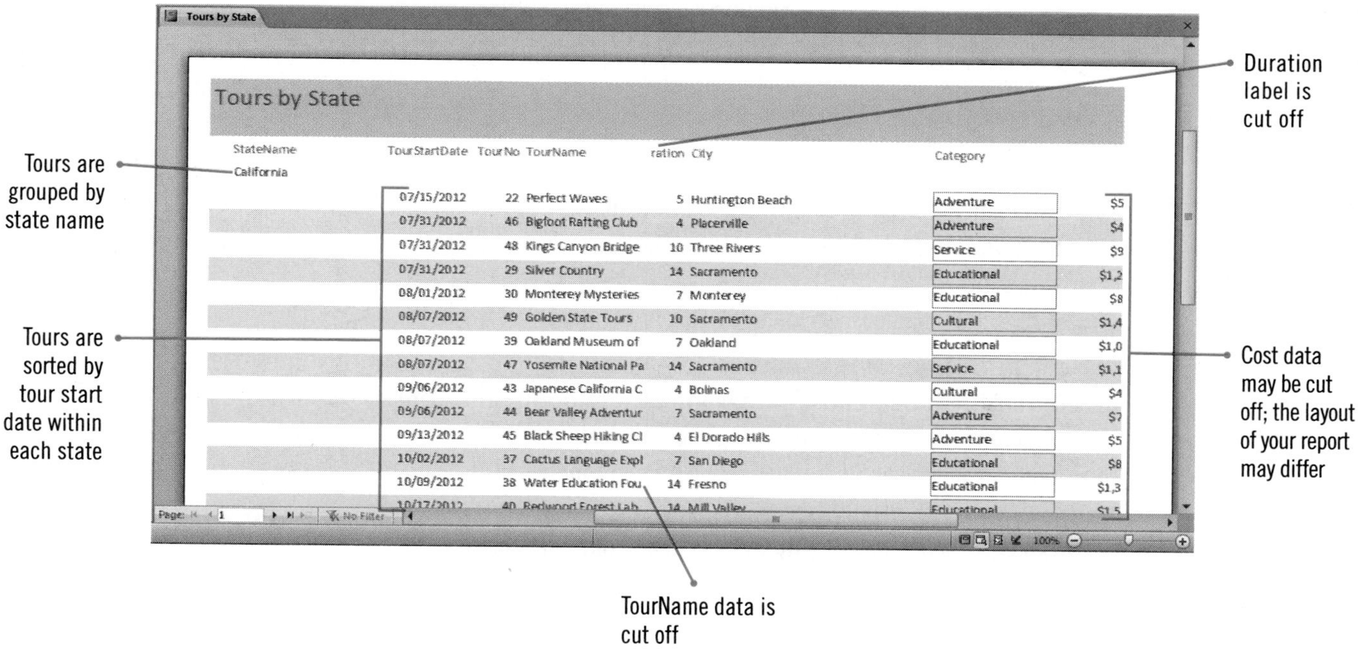

UNIT
D
Access 2010

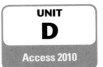

Using Report Layout View

Like forms, reports have multiple views that you use for various report-building and report-viewing activities. While some tasks can be accomplished in more than one view, each view has a primary purpose to make your work with reports as easy and efficient as possible. The different report views are summarized in Table D-1. Samantha Hooper asks you to modify the Tours by State report so that all of the fields fit comfortably across one piece of paper in landscape orientation. You'll use Report Layout View to achieve this goal.

STEPS

1. **Right-click the Tours by State report tab, then click Layout View**
   Layout View opens and applies a grid to the report that helps you resize, move, and position controls. You decide to narrow the City column to make room for the Cost data.
2. **Click Sacramento (or any City value), then use the ↔ pointer to drag the right edge of the City column to the left to narrow it to about half of its current size as shown in Figure D-3**
   By narrowing the City column, you create extra space in the report.
3. **Click any value in the Cost column, use the pointer to drag the Cost values to the left of the Category column, click the Cost label, then use to move the Cost label to the left of the Category label**
   All the columns are now within the boundaries of a single piece of paper in landscape orientation. You also notice that centering some data would make it easier to read.
4. **Click any value in the TourNo column, click the Home tab, click the Center button in the Text Formatting group, click the TourNo label, then click again**
   The TourName column and Duration label could use a little more space.
5. **Use ↔ to resize the TourStartDate, TourNo, and TourName columns and their labels to the left, then use ↔ to resize the Category, Cost, City, and Duration columns and their labels to the right**
   Now the report has enough room to resize the TourName column and the Duration label.
6. **Resize the TourName column so that all of the data is visible, paying special attention to the longest value, Yosemite National Park Great Cleanup, then resize the Duration label to display the complete text**
   You can also rename labels in Report Layout View.
7. **Click the StateName label, click between the words State and Name, press the [Spacebar] so that the label reads State Name, then modify the TourStartDate, TourNo, and TourName labels to contain spaces as well**
   Modifying labels in this way helps make a report more readable and professional.
8. **Continue resizing the columns so that all of the data is visible, paying special attention to the longest value so your report looks like Figure D-4**
   All of the labels are positioned in the Page Header section so that they appear only once per page. The text box controls are positioned in the Detail section. Depending on your monitor, you might need to scroll to display all the columns in Report Layout View.

QUICK TIP
Resizing with ↔ instead of moving with maintains the vertical alignment of the controls.

QUICK TIP
Using the Undo button arrow, you can undo many actions in Layout View.

FIGURE D-3: Modifying the column width in Report Layout View

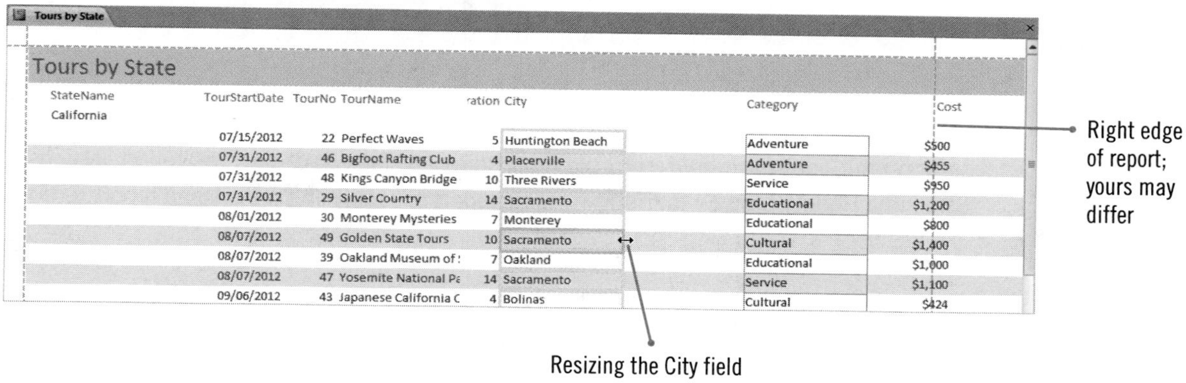
Tours by State
Right edge of report; yours may differ
Resizing the City field

FIGURE D-4: Final Tours by State report in Report Layout View

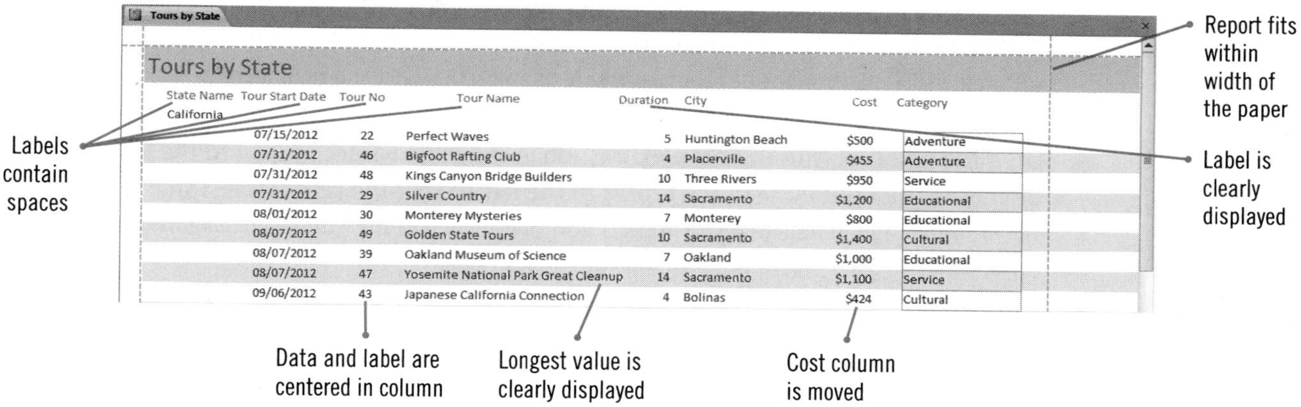
Tours by State
Labels contain spaces
Report fits within width of the paper
Label is clearly displayed
Data and label are centered in column
Longest value is clearly displayed
Cost column is moved

TABLE D-1: Report views

view	primary purpose
Report View	To quickly review the report without page breaks
Print Preview	To review each page of an entire report as it will appear if printed
Layout View	To modify the size, position, or formatting of controls; shows live data as you modify the report, making it the tool of choice when you want to change the appearance and positioning of controls on a report while also reviewing live data
Design View	To work with report sections or to access the complete range of controls and report properties; Design View does not display data

UNIT
D
Access 2010

Reviewing Report Sections

Report **sections** determine where and how often controls in that section print in the final report. For example, controls in the Report Header section print only once at the beginning of the report, but controls in the Detail section print once for every record the report displays. Table D-2 describes report sections. You and Samantha Hooper preview the Tours by State report to review and understand report sections.

STEPS

TROUBLE
You may need to zoom in and out several times by clicking the report to position it where you want.

QUICK TIP
Pointing to the error indicator displays a message about the error.

QUICK TIP
You can also use the View buttons in the lower-right corner of a report to switch views.

1. **Right-click the Tours by State tab, click Print Preview, click the First Page button in the navigation bar if you need to see the first page of the report, then click in the middle of the top edge of the report to zoom in to 100% if needed as shown in Figure D-5**
   The first page contains four sections: Report Header, Page Header, StateAbbreviation Header, and Detail section.
2. **Click the Next Page button on the navigation bar to move to the second page**
   The second page of the report may not contain data. The report may be too wide to fit on a single sheet of paper. You'll fix the report width in Report Design View.
3. **Right-click the Tours by State tab, click Design View, scroll to the far right using the bottom horizontal scroll bar, drag the right edge of the report to the 11" mark on the horizontal ruler, point to the error indicator in the upper-left corner of the report, then drag the right edge of the report as far as you can to the left as shown in Figure D-6**
   In Report Design View, you can work with the report sections and make modifications to the report that you cannot make in other views, such as narrowing the width. Report Design View does not display any data, though. For your report to fit on one page in landscape orientation, you need to move all of the controls within the 10.5" mark on the horizontal **ruler** to allow for 0.25" left and right margins. The **error indicator** in the upper-left corner of the report indicates that the report is too wide to fit on one piece of paper.
4. **Drag the text box with the page expression in the Page Footer section to the left about 1", then drag the right edge of the report to the left so that the report is less than 10.5" wide**
   The error indicator automatically disappears now that the report fits within the margins of a single piece of paper. To review your modifications, show the report in Print Preview.
5. **Right-click the Tours by State tab, click Print Preview, click the report to zoom in and out to examine the page, then click twice on the navigation bar to navigate to the last page as shown in Figure D-7**
   The last page of the report, page 3, shows how the Page Header and Page Footer sections border all pages (except the first page where the Report Header is at the top of the page). It also shows how the Group Header, tied to the StateName field, prints once per state, and how the tours within each state are created by the Detail section. Previewing each page of the report also helps you confirm that no blank pages are created.

TABLE D-2: **Report sections**

section	where does this section print?
Report Header	At the top of the first page
Page Header	At the top of every page (but below the Report Header on the first page)
Group Header	Before every group of records
Detail	Once for every record
Group Footer	After every group of records
Page Footer	At the bottom of every page
Report Footer	At the end of the report

FIGURE D-5: Tours by State report in Report View

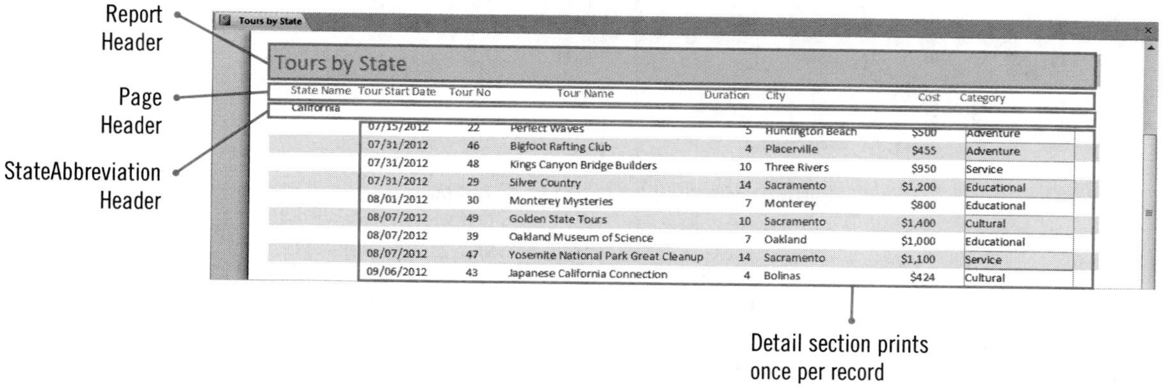

Report Header

Page Header

StateAbbreviation Header

Tours by State

State Name	Tour Start Date	Tour No	Tour Name	Duration	City	Cost	Category
California							
	07/15/2012	22	Perfect Waves	5	Huntington Beach	$500	Adventure
	07/31/2012	46	Bigfoot Rafting Club	4	Placerville	$455	Adventure
	07/31/2012	48	Kings Canyon Bridge Builders	10	Three Rivers	$950	Service
	07/31/2012	29	Silver Country	14	Sacramento	$1,200	Educational
	08/01/2012	30	Monterey Mysteries	7	Monterey	$800	Educational
	08/07/2012	49	Golden State Tours	10	Sacramento	$1,400	Cultural
	08/07/2012	39	Oakland Museum of Science	7	Oakland	$1,000	Educational
	08/07/2012	47	Yosemite National Park Great Cleanup	14	Sacramento	$1,100	Service
	09/06/2012	43	Japanese California Connection	4	Bolinas	$424	Cultural

Detail section prints once per record

FIGURE D-6: Tours by State report in Design View

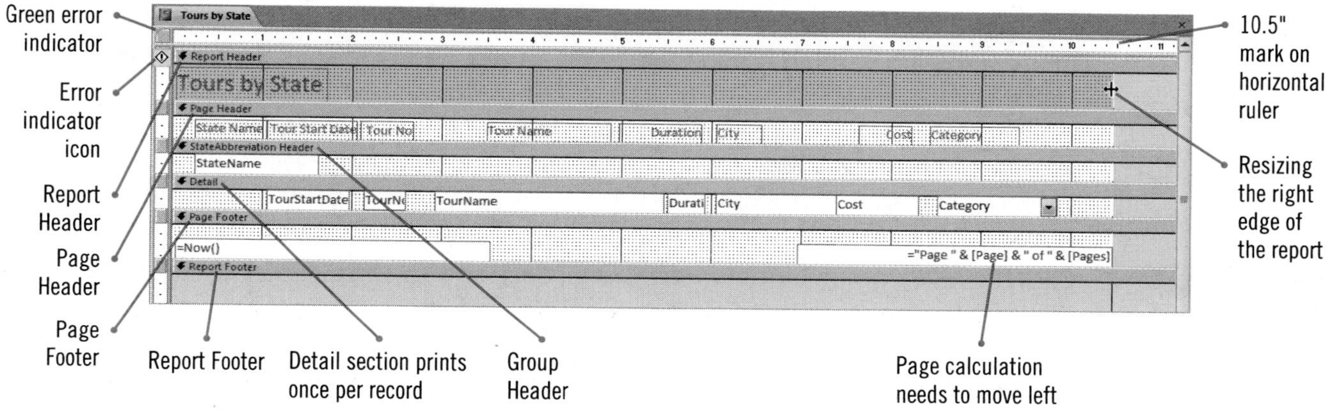

Green error indicator

Error indicator icon

Report Header

Page Header

Page Footer

Report Footer

Detail section prints once per record

Group Header

Page calculation needs to move left

10.5" mark on horizontal ruler

Resizing the right edge of the report

FIGURE D-7: Tours by State report in Print Preview

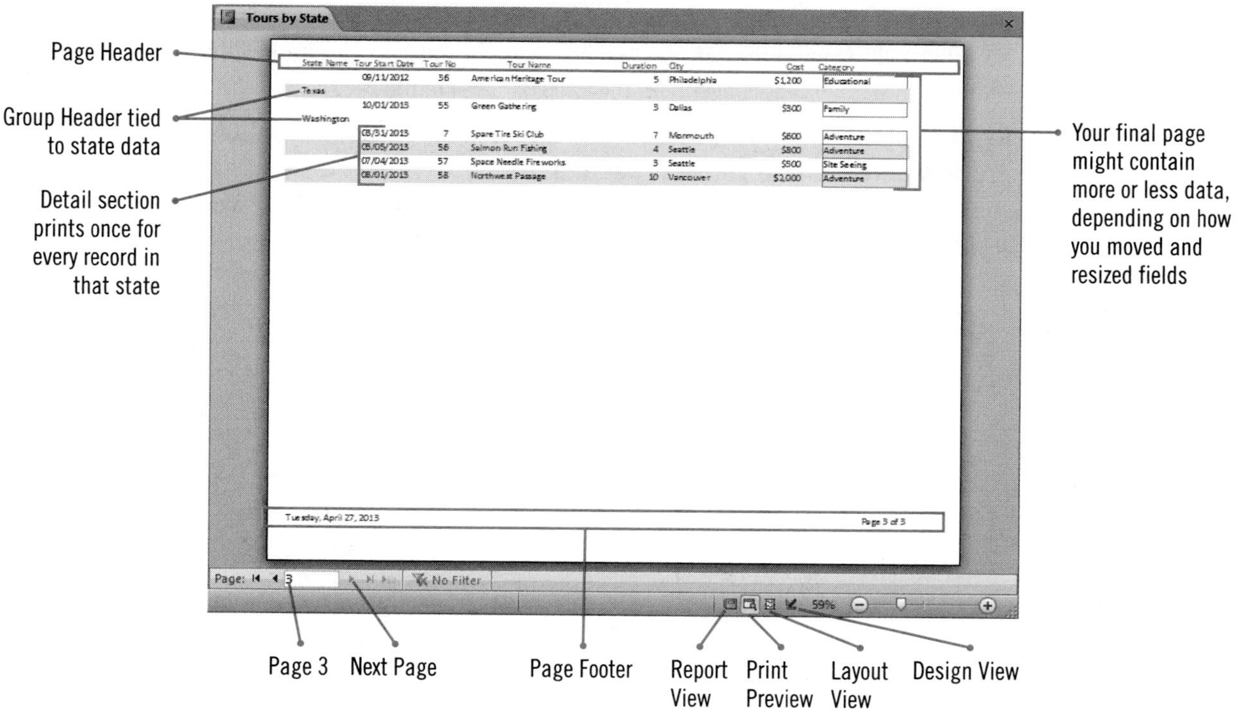

Page Header

Group Header tied to state data

Detail section prints once for every record in that state

Page 3   Next Page   Page Footer   Report View   Print Preview   Layout View   Design View

Your final page might contain more or less data, depending on how you moved and resized fields

Using Reports

Applying Group and Sort Orders

Grouping means to sort records by a particular field *plus* provide a header and/or footer section before or after each group of sorted records. For example, if you group records by the StateName field, the Group Header is called the StateName Header and the Group Footer is called the StateName Footer. The StateName Header section appears once for each state in the report, immediately before the records in that state. The StateName Footer section also appears once for each state in the report, immediately after the records for that state. The records in the Tours by State report are currently grouped by the StateAbbreviation field. Samantha Hooper asks you to further group the records by the Category field (Adventure, Educational, and Family, for example) within each state.

STEPS

1. **Close Print Preview to return to Report Design View, then click the Group & Sort button in the Grouping & Totals group to open the Group, Sort, and Total pane as shown in Figure D-8**

   To change sorting or grouping options for a report, you need to work in Report Design View. Currently, the records are grouped by the StateAbbreviation field and further sorted by the TourStartDate field. To add the Category field as a grouping field within each state, you work with the Group, Sort, and Total pane. Depending on your monitor, you might need to scroll to the right to display all the controls in Report Design View.

> **QUICK TIP**
> The More Options button becomes the Less Options button when clicked.

2. **Click the Add a group button in the Group, Sort, and Total pane, click Category, click the Move up button so that Category is positioned between StateAbbreviation and TourStartDate, then click the More Options button to display the Category group options**

   A Category Header section is added to Report Design View just below the StateAbbreviation Header section. To print category information only once within each state, you move the Category control from the Detail section to the Category Header section.

> **TROUBLE**
> Use the Move up and Move down buttons as needed to make sure your Group, Sort, and Total pane looks exactly like Figure D-9.

3. **Right-click the Category combo box in the Detail section, click Cut on the shortcut menu, right-click the Category Header section, click Paste, then drag the Category combo box to the right to position it as shown in Figure D-9**

   Now that you've moved the Category combo box to the Category Header, it will print only once per category within each state. You no longer need the Category label in the Page Header section.

4. **Right-click the Category label in the Page Header section, click Cut, then switch to Print Preview and zoom to 100% as needed**

   The Tours by State report should look similar to Figure D-10. Notice that the values in the Category field now appear once per category, before the records in each category are listed.

FIGURE D-8: Group, Sort, and Total pane

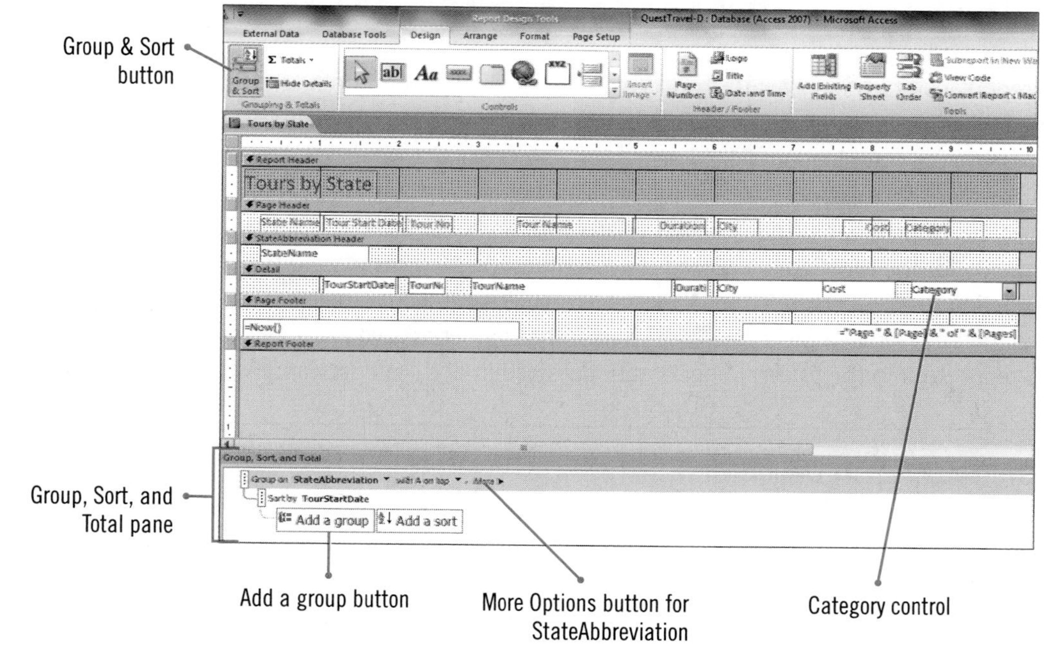
Group & Sort button
Group, Sort, and Total pane
Add a group button
More Options button for StateAbbreviation
Category control
Tours by State

FIGURE D-9: Tours by State report with new Category Header section

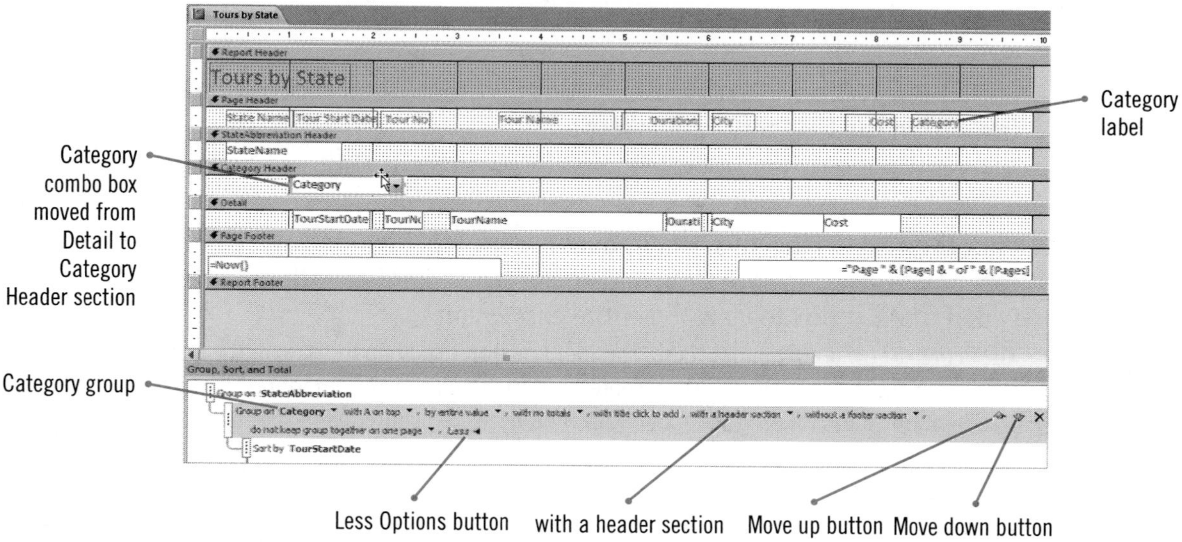
Category label
Category combo box moved from Detail to Category Header section
Category group
Less Options button
with a header section
Move up button
Move down button
Tours by State

FIGURE D-10: Tours by State report grouped by state and category

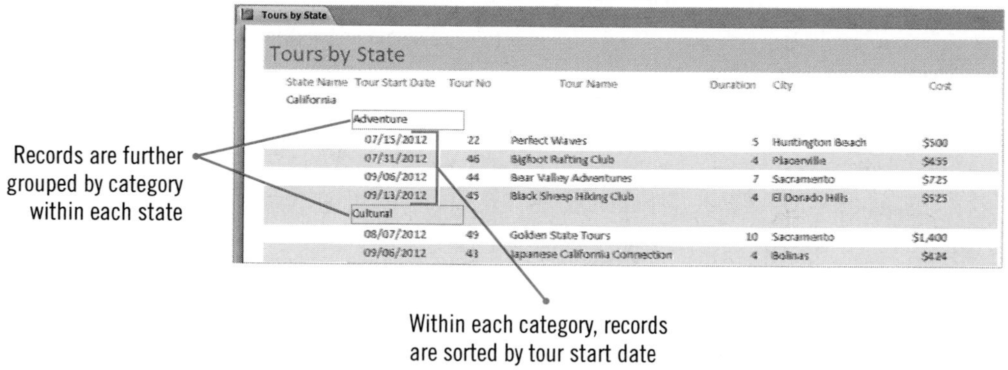
Records are further grouped by category within each state
Within each category, records are sorted by tour start date
Tours by State

UNIT D
Access 2010

Adding Subtotals and Counts

In a report, you create a **calculation** by entering an expression into a text box. When a report is previewed or printed, the expression is evaluated and the resulting calculation is placed on the report. An **expression** is a combination of field names, operators (such as +, –, /, and *), and functions that result in a single value. A **function** is a built-in formula, such as Sum or Count, that helps you quickly create a calculation. Notice that every expression starts with an equal sign (=), and when it uses a function, the arguments for the function are placed in (parentheses). **Arguments** are the pieces of information that the function needs to create the final answer. When an argument is a field name, the field name must be surrounded by [square brackets]. Samantha Hooper asks you to add a calculation to the Tours by State report to sum the total number of tour days within each category and within each state.

STEPS

1. **Switch to Report Design View**

   A logical place to add subtotals for each group is immediately after the group in the Group Footer section. You need to use the Group, Sort, and Total pane to open the Group Footer sections for both the Category and StateAbbreviation fields.

TROUBLE

Click Category in the Group, Sort, and Total pane to display the grouping options.

2. **Click the More Options button for the StateAbbreviation field in the Group, Sort, and Total pane, click the without a footer section list arrow, click with a footer section, then do the same for the Category field as shown in Figure D-11**

   With the StateAbbreviation and Category Footer sections open, you're ready to add controls to calculate the total number of tour days within each category and state. You can use a text box control with an expression to make this calculation.

3. **Click the Text Box button in the Controls group, then click just below the Duration text box in the Category Footer section**

   Adding a new text box automatically adds a new label to its left. First, you modify the label to identify the information, then you modify the text box to contain the correct expression to sum the number of tour days.

TROUBLE

Depending on your activity in Report Design View, you may see a different number in the Text##: label.

4. **Click the Text19 label to select it, double-click Text19, type Total days:, click the Unbound text box to select it, click Unbound again, type =Sum([Duration]), press [Enter], then widen the text box to view the entire expression**

   The expression =Sum([Duration]) uses the Sum function to add up the days in the Duration field. Because the expression is entered in the Category Footer section, it will sum all Duration values for that category. To sum the Duration values for each state, the expression needs to be inserted in the StateAbbreviation Footer.

QUICK TIP

Pasting the expression in the Report Footer section would subtotal the duration values for the entire report.

5. **Right-click the =Sum([Duration]) text box, click Copy, right-click the StateAbbreviation Footer section, click Paste, then press [→] enough times to position the controls in the StateAbbreviation Footer section just below those in the Category Footer section as shown in Figure D-12**

   With the expression in the StateAbbreviation Footer section, you're ready to preview your work.

6. **Switch to Print Preview, then position the report so you can see all of the Colorado tours on the second page**

   As shown in Figure D-13, 43 tour days are totaled for the Adventure category, and 7 for the Family category, which is a total of 50 tour days for the state of Colorado. The summary data would look better if it were aligned more directly under the individual Duration values. You resize and align controls in the next lesson.

FIGURE D-11: Opening group footer sections

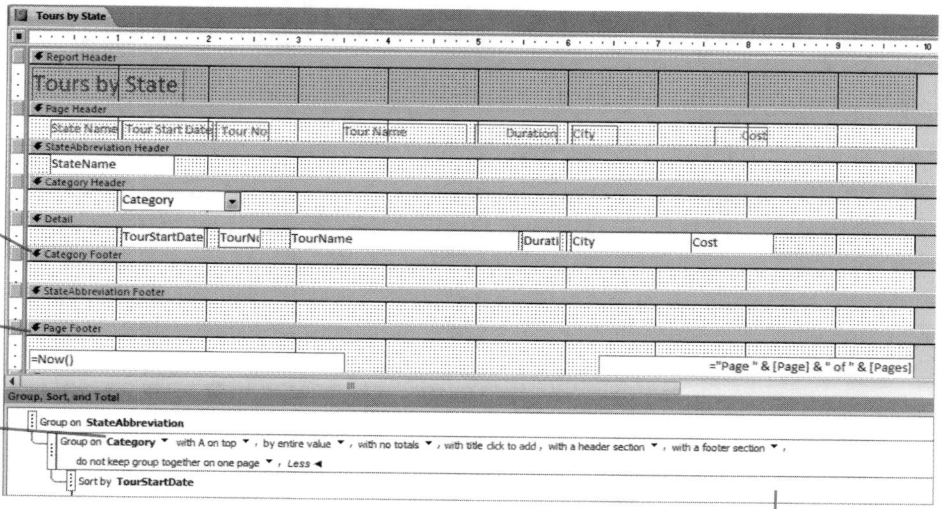
Category Footer section
StateAbbreviation Footer section
Category group within each state
Footer section added for the Category field

FIGURE D-12: Adding subtotals to group footer sections

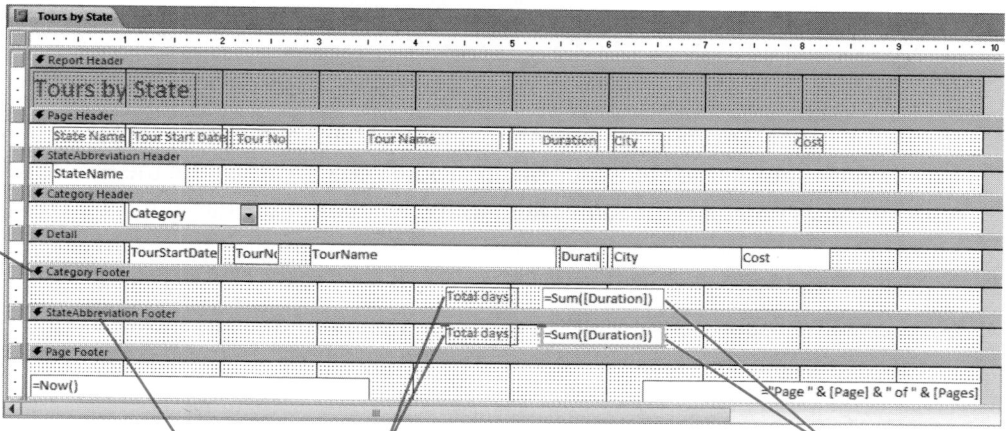
Category Footer
StateAbbreviation Footer
New labels to describe information
New text boxes to calculate total number of tour days

FIGURE D-13: Previewing the new group footer calculations

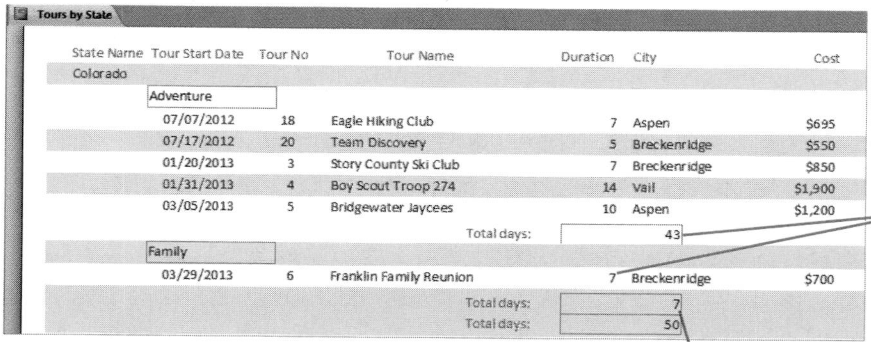
Sum of Duration for each category in Category Footer section
Sum of Duration in StateAbbreviation Footer for all Colorado tours

UNIT D Access 2010

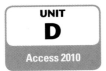

Resizing and Aligning Controls

After you add information to the appropriate section of a report, you might also want to align the data in precise columns and rows to make the information easier to read. There are two different types of **alignment** commands. You can left-, right-, or center-align a control *within its own border* using the Align Text Left, Center, and Align Text Right buttons on the Home tab. You can also align the edges of controls *with respect to one another* using the Left, Right, Top, and Bottom commands on the Align button of the Arrange tab in Report Design View. You decide to resize and align several controls in the report to improve the readability of the Tours by State report. Layout View is a good choice for these tasks.

STEPS

1. **Switch to Layout View, then click the Group & Sort button to toggle off the Group, Sort, and Total pane**
   You decide to align the expressions that subtotal the number of tour days for each category within the Duration column.
2. **Click the Total days text box in the Category Footer, click the Home tab, click the Center button in the Text Formatting group, then use the ↔ pointer to resize the text box so that the data is aligned in the Duration column as shown in Figure D-14**
   With the calculation formatted as desired in the Category Footer, you can quickly apply those modifications to the calculation in the StateAbbreviation Footer as well.
3. **Scroll down the report far enough to find the StateAbbreviation Footer section, click the Total days text box in the StateAbbreviation Footer, click, then use the ↔ pointer to resize the text box so that it is the same width as the text box in the Category Footer section**
   With both expressions centered and aligned, they are easier to read on the report. For longer or more complex numbers, you can right-align the values so that they align on the decimal point.
4. **Scroll the report so you can see all of the Colorado tours as shown in Figure D-15**
   You can apply resize, alignment, or formatting commands to more than one control at a time. Table D-3 provides techniques for selecting more than one control at a time in Report Design View.

TROUBLE

If you make a mistake, click the Undo button on the Quick Access toolbar.

Precisely moving and resizing controls

You can move and resize controls using the mouse, but you can move controls more precisely using the keyboard. Pressing the arrow keys while holding [Ctrl] moves selected controls one **pixel** (**picture element**) at a time in the direction of the arrow. Pressing the arrow keys while holding [Shift] resizes selected controls one pixel at a time.

FIGURE D-14: Resizing controls in Layout View

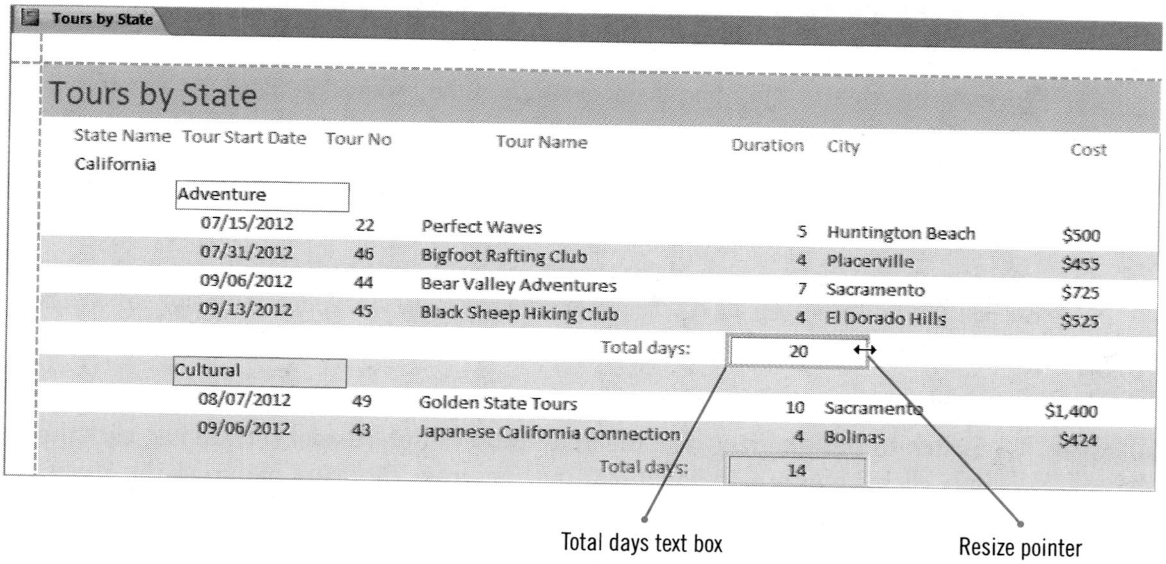
Tours by State
Tours by State
State Name Tour Start Date Tour No Tour Name Duration City Cost
California
Adventure
07/15/2012 22 Perfect Waves 5 Huntington Beach $500
07/31/2012 46 Bigfoot Rafting Club 4 Placerville $455
09/06/2012 44 Bear Valley Adventures 7 Sacramento $725
09/13/2012 45 Black Sheep Hiking Club 4 El Dorado Hills $525
Total days: 20
Cultural
08/07/2012 49 Golden State Tours 10 Sacramento $1,400
09/06/2012 43 Japanese California Connection 4 Bolinas $424
Total days: 14
Total days text box
Resize pointer

FIGURE D-15: Reviewing the widened and aligned controls

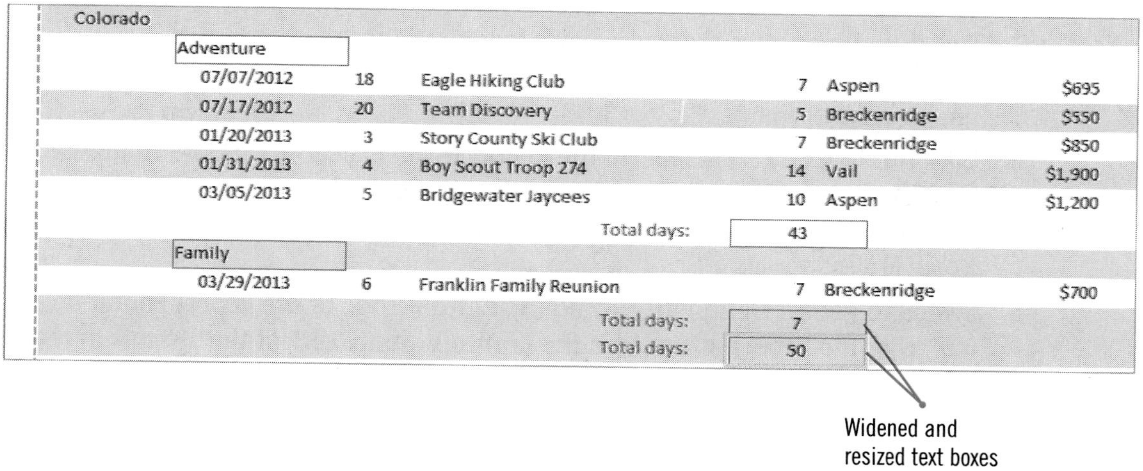
Colorado
Adventure
07/07/2012 18 Eagle Hiking Club 7 Aspen $695
07/17/2012 20 Team Discovery 5 Breckenridge $550
01/20/2013 3 Story County Ski Club 7 Breckenridge $850
01/31/2013 4 Boy Scout Troop 274 14 Vail $1,900
03/05/2013 5 Bridgewater Jaycees 10 Aspen $1,200
Total days: 43
Family
03/29/2013 6 Franklin Family Reunion 7 Breckenridge $700
Total days: 7
Total days: 50
Widened and
resized text boxes

TABLE D-3: Selecting more than one control at a time in Report Design View

technique	description
Click, [Shift]+click	Click a control, then press and hold [Shift] while clicking other controls; each one is selected
Drag a selection box	Drag a selection box (an outline box you create by dragging the pointer in Report Design View); every control that is in or is touched by the edges of the box is selected
Click in the ruler	Click in either the horizontal or vertical ruler to select all controls that intersect the selection line
Drag in the ruler	Drag through either the horizontal or vertical ruler to select all controls that intersect the selection line as it is dragged through the ruler

UNIT D
Access 2010

Formatting a Report

Formatting refers to enhancing the appearance of the information. Table D-4 lists several of the most popular formatting commands found on the Format tab when you are working in Report Design View. Although the Report Wizard automatically applies many formatting embellishments, you often want to improve the appearance of the report to fit your particular needs. When reviewing the Tours by State report with Samantha, you decide to change the background color of some of the report sections to make the data easier to read. Your first change will be to shade each StateAbbreviation Header and Footer section (rather than alternating sections, the format initially provided by the Report Wizard). To make changes to entire report sections, you must work in Report Design View.

STEPS

QUICK TIP
The quick keystroke for Undo is [Ctrl][Z]. The quick keystroke for Redo is [Ctrl][Y].

1. **Switch to Design View, click the StateAbbreviation Header section bar, click the Format tab, click the Alternate Row Color button arrow, click No Color, click the Shape Fill button, then click the Maroon 2 color square as shown in Figure D-16**
   Make a similar modification by applying a different fill color to the Category Header section.
2. **Click the Category Header section bar, click the Alternate Row Color button arrow, click No Color, click the Shape Fill button, click the Green 2 color square (just to the right of Maroon 2 in the Standard Colors section)**
   When you use the Alternate Row Color and Shape Fill buttons, you're actually modifying the **Back Color** and **Alternate Back Color** properties in the Property Sheet of the section or control you selected. Background shades can help differentiate parts of the report, but be careful with dark colors as they may print as solid black on some printers and fax machines.
3. **Switch to Layout View to review your modifications**
   The state and category sections are much clearer, but you decide to make one more modification to emphasize the report title.
4. **Click the Tours by State label in the Report Header section, click the Home tab, then click the Bold button B in the Text Formatting group**
   The report in Layout View should look like Figure D-17. You also want to add a label to the Report Footer section to identify yourself.
5. **Switch to Report Design View, drag the bottom edge of the Report Footer down about 0.5", click the Label button Aa in the Controls group, click at the 1" mark in the Report Footer, type Created by your name, press [Enter], click the Home tab, then click B in the Text Formatting group**
6. **Save, preview, and print the Tours by State report if required, then close it**

FIGURE D-16: **Formatting section backgrounds**

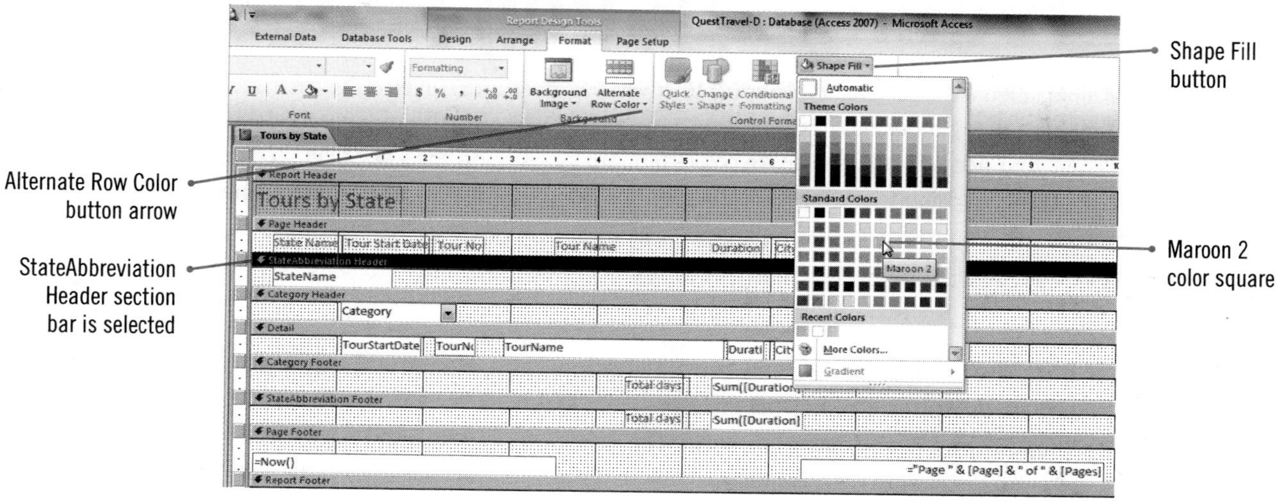

FIGURE D-17: **Final formatted Tours by State report**

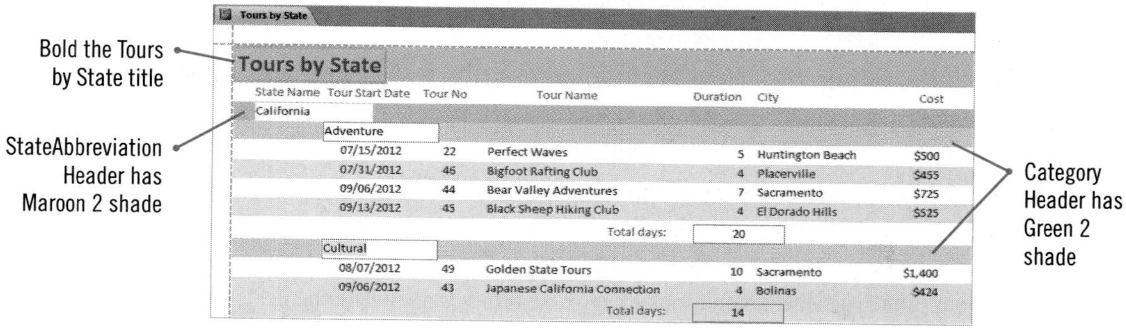

TABLE D-4: **Useful formatting commands**

button	button name	description
	Bold	Toggles bold on or off for the selected control(s)
	Italic	Toggles italics on or off for the selected control(s)
	Underline	Toggles underline on or off for the selected control(s)
	Align Text Left	Left-aligns the selected control(s) within its own border
	Center	Centers the selected control(s) within its own border
	Align Text Right	Right-aligns the selected control(s) within its own border
Shape Fill	**Shape Fill**	Changes the background color of the selected control(s)
	Alternate Row Color	Changes the background color of alternate records in the selected section
	Font Color	Changes the text color of the selected control(s)
Shape Outline	**Shape Outline** **Line Thickness option** **Line Type option**	Changes the border color of the selected control(s) Changes the border style of the selected control(s) Changes the special visual effect of the selected control(s)

UNIT
D
Access 2010

Creating Mailing Labels

Mailing labels are often created to apply to envelopes, postcards, or letters when assembling a mass mailing. They have many other business purposes too, such as using them on paper file folders or name tags. Any data in your Access database can be converted into labels using the **Label Wizard**, a special report wizard that precisely positions and sizes information for hundreds of standard business labels. Samantha Hooper asks you to create mailing labels for all of the addresses in the Customers table. You use the Label Wizard to handle this request.

STEPS

1. **Click the Customers table in the Navigation Pane, click the Create tab, then click the Labels button in the Reports group**
   The first Label Wizard dialog box opens. The Filter by manufacturer list box provides over 30 manufacturers of labels. Because Avery is the most common, it is the default choice. With the manufacturer selected, your next task is to choose the product number of the labels you will feed through the printer. The label list box is the best source for this information. In this case, you'll be using Avery 5160 labels, a common type of sheet labels used for mailings and other purposes.
2. **Scroll through the Product numbers, then click 5160 as shown in Figure D-18**
   Note that by selecting a product number, you also specify the dimensions of the label and number of columns.
3. **Click Next, then click Next again to accept the default font and color choices**
   The third question of the Label Wizard asks how you want to construct your label. You'll add the fields from the Customers table in a standard mailing format.
4. **Double-click FName, press [Spacebar], double-click LName, press [Enter], double-click Street, press [Enter], double-click City, type comma and press [Spacebar], double-click State, press [Spacebar], then double-click Zip**
   If your prototype label doesn't look exactly like Figure D-19, delete the fields and try again. Be careful to put a space between the FName and LName fields in the first row, a comma and a space between the City and State fields, and a space between the State and Zip fields.
5. **Click Next, double-click LName to select it as a sorting field, click Next, click Finish to accept the name Labels Customers for the new report, then click OK if prompted**
   A portion of the new report is shown in Figure D-20. It is generally a good idea to print the first page of the report on standard paper to make sure everything is aligned correctly before printing on labels.
6. **Click the Print button on the Print Preview tab, click the From box, type 1, click the To box, type 1, then click OK if a printout is desired**
7. **Close the Labels Customers report, close the QuestTravel-D.accdb database, then exit Access 2010**

QUICK TIP
To include your name on the printout, first change Jacob Alman's name to your own in the Customers table, then close and open the report again.

FIGURE D-18: Label Wizard dialog box

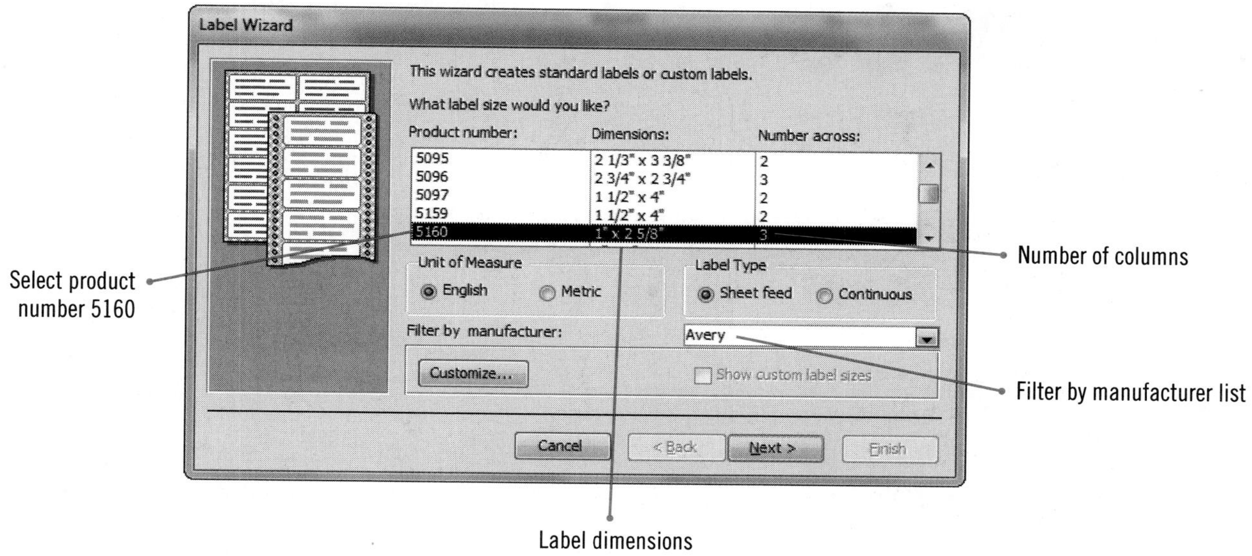

FIGURE D-19: Building a prototype label

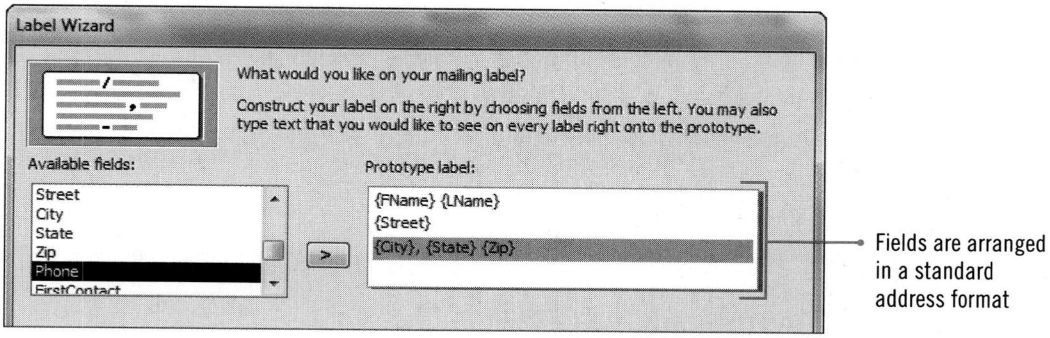

FIGURE D-20: Labels Customers report

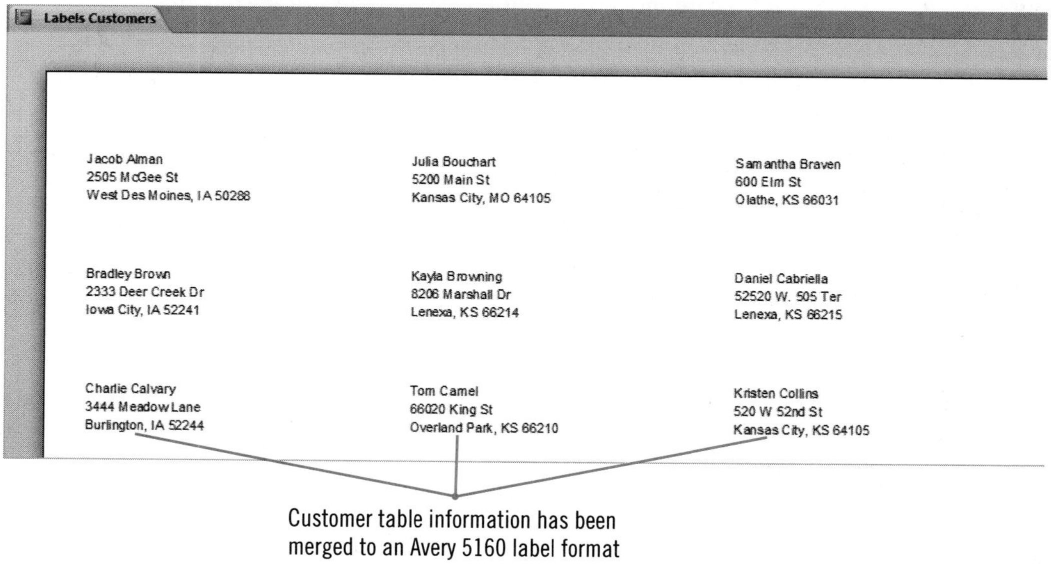

Practice

Concepts Review

For current SAM information, including versions and content details, visit SAM Central (http://www.cengage.com/samcentral). If you have a SAM user profile, you may have access to hands-on instruction, practice, and assessment of the skills covered in this unit. Since various versions of SAM are supported throughout the life of this text, check with your instructor for the correct instructions and URL/Web site for accessing assignments.

Label each element of the Report Design View window shown in Figure D-21.

FIGURE D-21

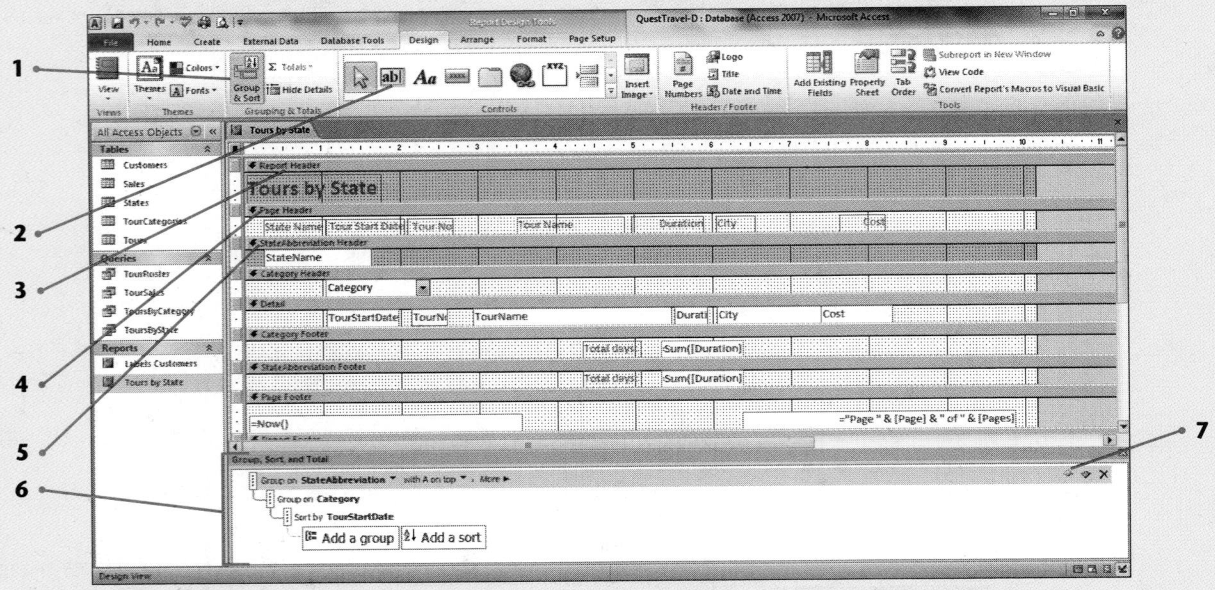

Match each term with the statement that best describes it.

8. **Expression**
9. **Section**
10. **Detail section**
11. **Record source**
12. **Formatting**
13. **Grouping**
14. **Alignment**

- **a.** Left, center, or right are common choices
- **b.** Prints once for every record
- **c.** Used to identify which fields and records are passed to the report
- **d.** Sorting records *plus* providing a header or footer section
- **e.** Determines how controls are positioned on the report
- **f.** A combination of field names, operators, and functions that results in a single value
- **g.** Enhancing the appearance of information displayed in the report

Select the best answer from the list of choices.

15. Which of the following is *not* a valid report view?

- **a.** Print Preview
- **b.** Design View
- **c.** Layout View
- **d.** Section View

16. Which type of control is most commonly placed in the Detail section?

a. Image
b. Line
c. Label
d. Text box

17. A title for a report would most commonly be placed in which report section?

a. Report Header
b. Detail
c. Group Footer
d. Report Footer

18. A calculated expression that presents page numbering information would probably be placed in which report section?

a. Report Header
b. Group Footer
c. Detail
d. Page Footer

19. Which of the following expressions counts the number of records using the FirstName field?

a. =Count([FirstName])
b. =Count(FirstName)
c. =Count[FirstName]
d. =Count{FirstName}

20. To align the edges of several controls with each other, you use the alignment commands on the:

a. Formatting tab.
b. Print Preview tab.
c. Design tab.
d. Arrange tab.

Skills Review

1. Use the Report Wizard.

a. Start Access and open the RealEstate-D.accdb database from the drive and folder where you store your Data Files. Enable content if prompted.
b. Use the Report Wizard to create a report based on the RLast and RPhone fields from the Realtors table, and the Type, SqFt, BR, Bath, and Asking fields from the Listings table.
c. View the data by Realtors, do not add any more grouping levels, and sort the records in descending order by the Asking field.
d. Use a Stepped layout and a Landscape orientation. Title the report **Realtor Listings**.
e. Preview the first page of the new report. Notice whether any fields or field names need more space.

2. Use Report Layout View.

a. Switch to Layout View.
b. Narrow the RLast and RPhone columns enough so they are only as wide as necessary.
c. Modify the RLast label to read **Realtor**, the RPhone label to read **Phone**, the SqFt label to read **Square Feet**, the BR label to read **Bedrooms**, and the Bath label to read **Baths**.
d. Switch to Print Preview, and view each page of the report.

3. Review report sections.

a. Switch to Report Design View.
b. Drag the text box that contains the Page calculation in the lower-right corner of the Page Footer section to the left so that it is to the left of the 9" mark on the horizontal ruler.
c. Drag the right edge of the entire report to the left so it ends within the 10.5" mark on the horizontal ruler.

4. Apply group and sort orders.

a. Open the Group, Sort, and Total pane.
b. Add the Type field as a grouping field between the RealtorNo grouping field and Asking sort field.
c. Cut and paste the Type combo box from its current position in the Detail section to the Type Header section.
d. Move the Type combo box in the Type Header section so its left edge is at about the 1" mark on the horizontal ruler.
e. Delete the Type label in the Page Header section.
f. Switch to Layout View, and move the Asking column—the data and label—closer to the Square Feet column.
g. Select the Type text box, and right-align the information in the text box.

Skills Review (continued)

5. **Add subtotals and counts.**
   a. Switch to Report Design View, then open the RealtorNo Footer section.
   b. Add a text box control to the RealtorNo Footer section, just below the Asking text box in the Detail section. Change the label to read **Subtotal:**, and enter the expression **=Sum([Asking])** in the text box.
   c. Drag the bottom edge of the Report Footer down about 0.25" to add space to the Report Footer.
   d. Copy and paste the new expression in the RealtorNo Footer section to the Report Footer section. Position the controls as directly under the controls in the RealtorNo Footer section as possible.
   e. Modify the label in the Report Footer section to read **Grand Total:**.
   f. Preview the last page of the report to view both the new subtotals in the RealtorNo Footer section as well as in the Report Footer section.
6. **Resize and align controls.**
   a. Switch to Layout View, close the Group, Sort, and Total pane if it is open, and move to the last page of the report to view the Subtotal and Grand Total calculations.
   b. Right-align the text within the Subtotal and Grand Total labels. Move the labels so that their right edges are aligned.
   c. Move the labels and text boxes as needed so that the calculations are positioned directly under the Asking column. Also make sure that the right edges of text boxes that contain the calculations are aligned with the right edge of the Asking column. (*Hint*: If you want to precisely align the right edges of two controls, you need to switch to Report Design View, select both controls at the same time, click the Align button on the Arrange tab, and then click Right to right-align the right edges of the selected controls. Or you can use your mouse or arrow keys to move the right edges of the controls in Layout View.)
   d. Save the report.
7. **Format a report.**
   a. Switch to Report Design View, and change the Alternate Row Color of the Detail section to No Color.
   b. Change the Alternate Row Color of the Type Header section to No Color.
   c. Change the Alternate Row Color of the RealtorNo Header section to No Color, and change the Shape Fill color of the RealtorNo Header section to Green 2.
   d. Select the RLast text box in the RealtorNo Header section, and change the Shape Fill color to Green 2 to match the RealtorNo Header section. Apply the same Green 2 background color to the RPhone text box.
   e. Bold the title of the report, the **Realtor Listings** label in the Report Header.
   f. Double-click a sizing handle on the label in the Report Header to expand it to accommodate the entire label. Be sure to double-click a sizing handle of the label, not the label itself, which opens the Property Sheet.
   g. Change the font color of each label in the Page Header section to black.
   h. Save and preview the report in Report View. It should look like Figure D-22.
   i. In Report Design View, add a label to the left side of the Report Footer section with your name.
   j. Return to Print Preview, print the report if requested by your instructor, then close the Realtor Listings report.

FIGURE D-22

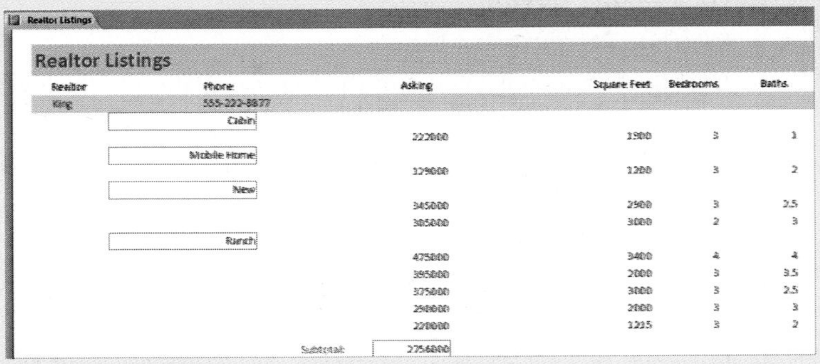

8. **Create mailing labels.**
   a. Click the Agencies table in the Navigation Pane, then start the Label Wizard.
   b. Choose Avery 5160 labels and the default text appearance choices.
   c. Build a prototype label with the AgencyName on the first line, Street on the second line, and City, State, and Zip on the third line with a comma and space between City and State, and a space between State and Zip.
   d. Sort by AgencyName, and name the report **Labels Agencies**.

Skills Review (continued)

e. Preview then close the report. Click OK if a warning dialog box appears regarding horizontal space.

f. If your instructor asks you to print the Labels Agencies report, open the Agencies table and change the name of Four Lakes Realtors to **YourLastName Realtors**. Close the Agencies table, reopen the Labels Agencies report, then print it.

g. Close the Labels Agencies report, close the RealEstate-D.accdb database, then exit Access 2010.

Independent Challenge 1

As the office manager of an international convention planning company, you have created a database to track convention, enrollment, and company data. Your goal is to create a report of up-to-date attendee enrollments.

SAM

If you have a SAM 2010 user profile, an autogradable SAM version of this assignment may be available at http://www.cengage.com/sam2010. Check with your instructor to confirm that this assignment is available in SAM. To use the SAM version of this assignment, log into the SAM 2010 Web site and download the instruction and start files.

a. Start Access, then open the Conventions-D.accdb database from the drive and folder where you store your Data Files. Enable content if prompted.

b. Use the Report Wizard to create a report with the AttendeeFirst and AttendeeLast fields from the Attendees table, the CompanyName field from the Companies table, and the ConventionName and CountryName from the Conventions table.

c. View your data by Conventions, do not add any more grouping levels, and sort in ascending order by CompanyName, then AttendeeLast.

d. Use the Block layout and Portrait orientation, then name the report **Convention Listing**.

e. In Layout View, change the labels in the Page Header section from ConventionName to **Convention**, CountryName to **Country**, CompanyName to **Company**, and AttendeeLast to **Attendee**. Delete the AttendeeFirst label.

f. Open the Group, Sort, and Total pane, then use the More Options button to open the CompanyName field's Group Header and Group Footer sections.

g. In Report Design View, expand the ConventionNo Header section about 0.5", then use Cut and Paste to move the ConventionName text box from the Detail section to the ConventionNo Header section. Left-align the ConventionName text box with the Convention label in the Page Header section. Drag the top edge of the CompanyName Header section up to close the extra space in the ConventionNo Header.

h. Expand the CompanyName Header section about 0.25". Drag the CompanyName text box to the bottom of the CompanyName Header section. Use Cut and Paste to move the CountryName text box from the Detail section to the ConventionNo Header section and position it directly above the CompanyName text box in the CompanyName Header section.

i. Delete the Country and CompanyName labels in the Page Header section.

j. In Layout View, scroll through the entire report and widen the ConventionName and CompanyName text boxes as necessary to show all of the data. Be careful, however, to not expand the report beyond the width of the portrait orientation of the report.

k. In Design View, expand the CompanyName Footer, and enter an expression in a new text box to count the values in the AttendeeLast field, **=Count([AttendeeLast])**. Position the new text box directly below the AttendeeLast text box.

l. Modify the new label in the Company Name Footer to read **Count:**. Format the text color of the label to black.

m. Change the color of the report title and the labels in the Page Header section to black. Preview the report. The subtotal count for the first convention should be 21.

n. If required to print the report, switch to Report Design View, add your name as a label to the Report Header section, then print the first page.

o. Save and close the Convention Listing report, close the Conventions-D.accdb database, then exit Access 2010.

Independent Challenge 2

You have built an Access database to track membership in a community service club. The database tracks member names and addresses as well as their status in the club, which moves from rank to rank as the members contribute increased hours of service to the community.

a. Start Access and open the Membership-D.accdb database from the drive and folder where you store your Data Files. Enable content if prompted.

b. Open the Members table, find and change the name of Traci Kalvert to your name, then close the Members table.

c. Use the Report Wizard to create a report using the Status and DuesOwed fields from the Status table, and the FName, LName, and DuesPaid fields from the Members table.

d. View the data by Status. Do not add any more grouping fields, and sort the records in ascending order by LName.

e. Use a Stepped layout and Portrait orientation, title the report **Dues Report**, then preview the report.

f. Switch to Report Design View, then use the Group, Sort, and Total pane to open the StatusNo Footer section.

g. Add a text box to the StatusNo Footer section, just below the DuesPaid text box. Change the label to **Count:** and the expression in the text box to **=Count([DuesPaid])**.

h. Expand the StatusNo Footer section as necessary, and add a second text box to the StatusNo Footer section, just below the first. Change the label to **Subtotal:** and the expression in the text box to **=Sum([DuesPaid])**.

i. Move, resize, and align the controls in the StatusNo Footer section as needed so they are positioned directly under the DuesPaid text box in the Detail section.

Advanced Challenge Exercise

- Open the Property Sheet for the =Sum([DuesPaid]) text box. On the Format tab, set the Format property to Currency and the Decimal Places property to 2.
- Expand the StatusNo Footer section as necessary, and add a third text box to the StatusNo Footer section, just below the second. Change the label to **Balance:**.
- Change the text box expression to **=Count([LName])*[DuesOwed]–Sum([DuesPaid])**. This expression counts the number of values in the LName field, and multiplies it by the DuesOwed field. From that value, the sum of the DuesPaid field is subtracted. This calculates the balance between dues owed and dues paid.
- Open the Property Sheet for the text box with the balance calculation. On the Format tab, set the Format property to Currency and the Decimal Places property to 2.

j. Align the right edges of the DuesPaid text box in the Detail section and all text boxes in the StatusNo Footer section.

k. Save, then preview the Dues Report, print the first page of the Dues Report if requested by your instructor, then close it.

l. Close the Membership-D.accdb database, then exit Access.

Independent Challenge 3

You have built an Access database to organize the deposits at a recycling center. Various clubs regularly deposit recyclable material, which is measured in pounds when the deposits are made.

a. Start Access and open the Recycle-D.accdb database from the drive and folder where you store your Data Files. Enable content if prompted.

b. Open the Centers table, change **Trash Can** to **YourLastName Recycling**, then close the table.

c. Use the Report Wizard to create a report with the CenterName field from the Centers table, the Deposit Date and Weight from the Deposits table, and the ClubName field from the Clubs table.

d. View the data by Centers, do not add any more grouping levels, and sort the records in ascending order by DepositDate.

e. Use a Stepped layout and a Portrait orientation, then title the report **Deposit Listing**.

f. In Layout View, center the Weight label and Weight data. Resize any other labels to display all of their text.

g. Add spaces to the labels so that CenterName becomes **Center Name**, DepositDate becomes **Deposit Date**, and ClubName becomes **Club Name**.

Independent Challenge 3 (continued)

h. In Report Design View, open the Group, Sort, and Total pane and add a CenterNumber Footer section.
i. Add a text box to the CenterNumber Footer section just below the Weight text box with the expression **=Sum([Weight])**.
j. Rename the new label to be **Total Center Weight:** and move it to the left as needed so that it doesn't overlap the text box.
k. Resize and align the edges of the =Sum([Weight]) text box in the CenterNumber Footer section with the Weight text box in the Detail section. Center the data in the =Sum([Weight]) text box.
l. Expand the Report Footer section, then copy and paste the =Sum([Weight]) text box from the CenterNumber Footer section to the Report Footer section.
m. Move and align the controls in the Report Footer section with their counterparts in the CenterNumber Footer section.
n. Change the label in the Report Footer section to **Grand Total Weight:**.
o. Drag the top edges of every section bar up as far as possible to remove extra blank space in the report, then preview the last page of the report as shown in Figure D-23. Your spacing may be a bit different, but the Center subtotals and grand total should match.
p. Save and close the Deposit Listing report, close the Recycle-D.accdb database, then exit Access.

FIGURE D-23

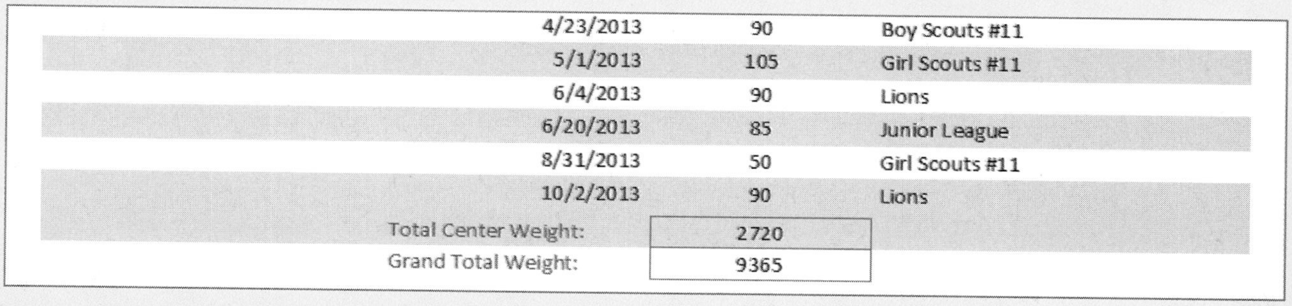

	4/23/2013	90	Boy Scouts #11
	5/1/2013	105	Girl Scouts #11
	6/4/2013	90	Lions
	6/20/2013	85	Junior League
	8/31/2013	50	Girl Scouts #11
	10/2/2013	90	Lions
Total Center Weight:		2720	
Grand Total Weight:		9365	

Real Life Independent Challenge

One way you can use an Access database on your own is to record and track your job search efforts. In this exercise, you create a report to help read and analyze data into your job-tracking database.

a. Start Access and open the JobSearch-D.accdb database from the drive and folder where you store your Data Files. Enable content if prompted.
b. Open the Employers table, and enter five more records to identify five more potential employers.
c. Use subdatasheets in the Employers table to enter five more potential jobs. You may enter all five jobs for one employer, one job for five different employers, or any combination thereof. Be sure to check the spelling of all data entered.
d. Use the Report Wizard to create a report that lists all fields from the Employers table except for EmployerID, and all fields from the Positions table except for the Desirability, EmployerID, and PositionID fields.
e. View the data by Employers, do not add any more grouping levels, and do not add any sort orders.
f. Use a Block layout and a Landscape orientation, then title the report **Job Openings**.
g. In Layout View, revise the labels in the Page Header section from CompanyName to **Company**, EmpStreet to **Street**, EmpCity to **City**, EmpState to **State**, EmpZip to **Zip**, EmpPhone to **Phone**, CareerArea to **Area**, and AnnualSalary to **Salary**.
h. In Layout View, resize the columns so that all data fits on one landscape piece of paper.
i. In Report Design View, move the Page expression in the Page Footer section and the right edge of the report to the left, within the 10.5" mark on the horizontal ruler.
j. Preview and save the Job Openings report, then print it if requested by your instructor.
k. Close the Job Openings report, close the JobSearch-D.accdb database, then exit Access 2010.

Visual Workshop

Open the Basketball-D.accdb database from the drive and folder where you store your Data Files and enable content if prompted. Open the Players table, enter your own name instead of Kelsey Douglas, then close the table. Your goal is to create the report shown in Figure D-24. Use the Report Wizard, and select the PFirst, PLast, HomeTown, and HomeState fields from the Players table. Select the FieldGoals, 3Pointers, and FreeThrows fields from the Stats table. View the data by Players, do not add any more grouping levels, and do not add any more sorting levels. Use a Block layout and a Portrait orientation, then title the report **Scoring Report**. In Layout View, resize all of the columns so that they fit on a single piece of portrait paper, and change the labels in the Page Header section as shown. In Report Design View, move the page calculation in the Page Footer section within the margins of the report, and drag the right edge of the report to the left to eliminate blank pages. Open the PlayerNo Footer section and add text boxes with expressions to sum the FieldGoals, 3Pointers, and FreeThrow fields. Move, modify, and resize all controls as needed.

FIGURE D-24

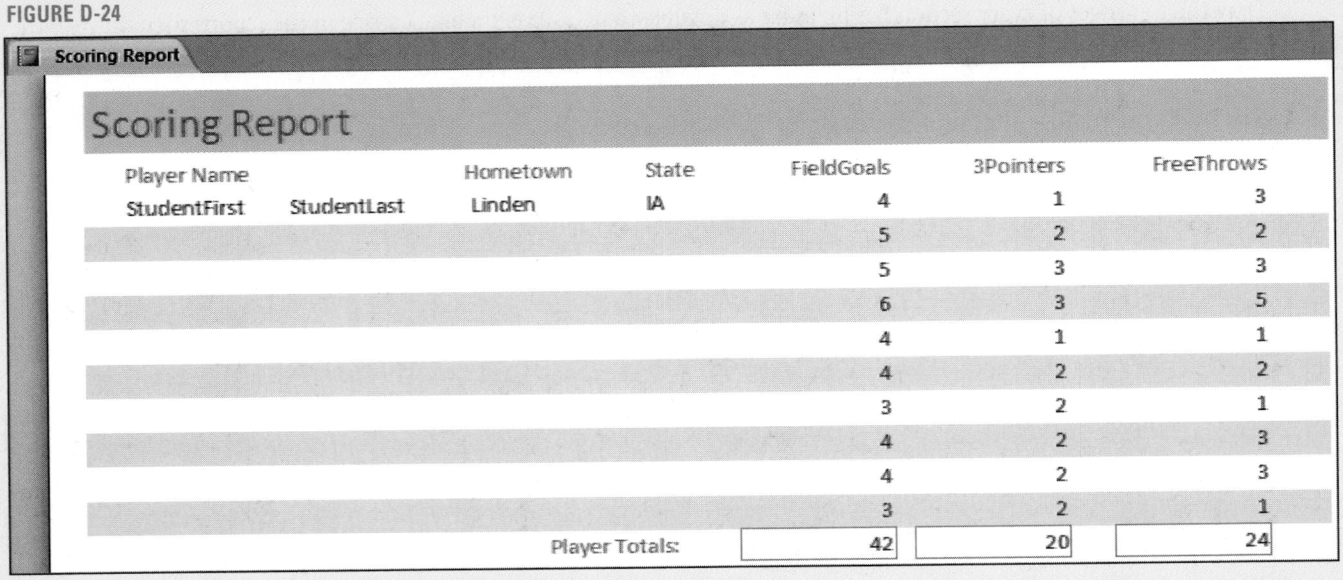
Scoring Report

Scoring Report

Player Name		Hometown	State	FieldGoals	3Pointers	FreeThrows
StudentFirst	StudentLast	Linden	IA	4	1	3
				5	2	2
				5	3	3
				6	3	5
				4	1	1
				4	2	2
				3	2	1
				4	2	3
				4	2	3
				3	2	1
		Player Totals:		42	20	24

UNIT
E
Access 2010

Modifying the Database Structure

Files You Will Need:

QuestTravel-E.accdb
GMayberry.jpg
Member1.jpg
JobSearch-E.accdb
Training-E.accdb

In this unit, you refine a database by adding a new table to an existing database and then linking tables using one-to-many relationships to create a relational database. You work with fields that have different data types, including Text, Number, Currency, Date/Time, and Yes/No, to define the data stored in the database. You create and use Attachment fields to store images. You also modify table and field properties to format and validate data. Working with Samantha Hooper, the tour developer for U.S. group travel at Quest Specialty Travel, you are developing an Access database to track the tours, customers, sales, and payments for this division. The database consists of multiple tables that you link, modify, and enhance to create a relational database.

OBJECTIVES

- Examine relational databases
- Design related tables
- Create one-to-many relationships
- Create Lookup fields
- Modify Text fields
- Modify Number and Currency fields
- Modify Date/Time fields
- Modify validation properties
- Create Attachment fields

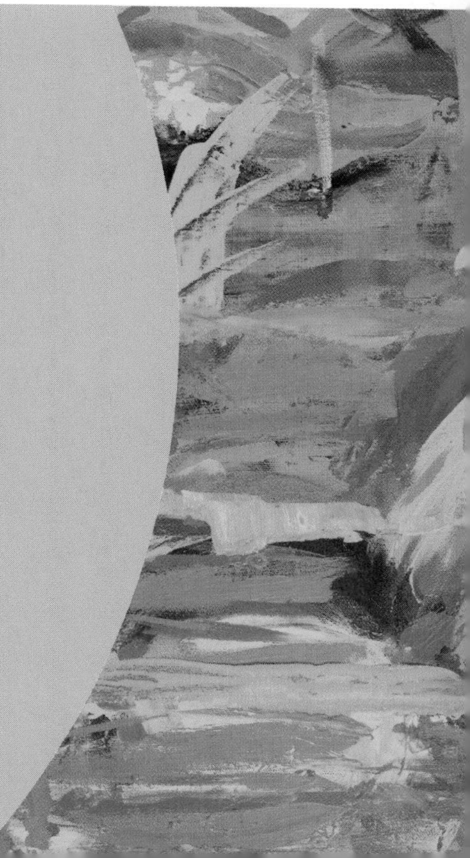

Examining Relational Databases

The purpose of a relational database is to organize and store data in a way that minimizes redundancy and maximizes your flexibility when querying and analyzing data. To accomplish these goals, a relational database uses related tables rather than a single large table of data. At one time, the Sales department at Quest Specialty Travel tracked information about their tour sales and payments using a single Access table called Sales, shown in Figure E-1. This created data redundancy problems because of the duplicate tour, customer, and payment information entered into a single table. You decide to study the principles of relational database design to help Quest Specialty Travel reorganize these fields into a correctly designed relational database.

DETAILS

To redesign a list into a relational database, follow these principles:

- **Design each table to contain fields that describe only one subject**
  Currently, the table in Figure E-1 contains four subjects—tours, sales, customers, and payments—which creates redundant data. For example, the customer's name must be reentered every time that customer purchases a tour or makes a payment. The problems of redundant data include extra data-entry work, more data-entry inconsistencies and errors, larger physical storage requirements, and limitations on your ability to search for, analyze, and report on the data. You minimize these problems by implementing a properly designed relational database.

- **Identify a primary key field for each table**
  A **primary key field** is a field that contains unique information for each record. For example, in a customer table, the customer number field usually serves this purpose. Although using the customer's last name as the primary key field might work in a small database, names are generally a poor choice for a primary key field because the primary key could not accommodate two customers who have the same name.

- **Build one-to-many relationships**
  To tie the information from one table to another, a field must be common to each table. This linking field is the primary key field on the "one" side of the relationship and the **foreign key field** on the "many" side of the relationship. For example, a CustomerNo field acting as the primary key field in the Customers table would link to a CustomerNo foreign key field in a Sales table to join one customer to many sales. You are not required to give the linking field the same name in the "one" and "many" tables.

  The revised design for the database is shown in Figure E-2. One customer can purchase many tours, so the Customers and Sales tables have a one-to-many relationship based on the linking CustNo field. One tour can have many sales, so the Tours and Sales tables also have a one-to-many relationship based on the common TourID field (named TourNo in the Tours table). And one sale may have many payments, creating a one-to-many relationship based on the common SalesNo field.

FIGURE E-1: **Single Sales table – redundant data**

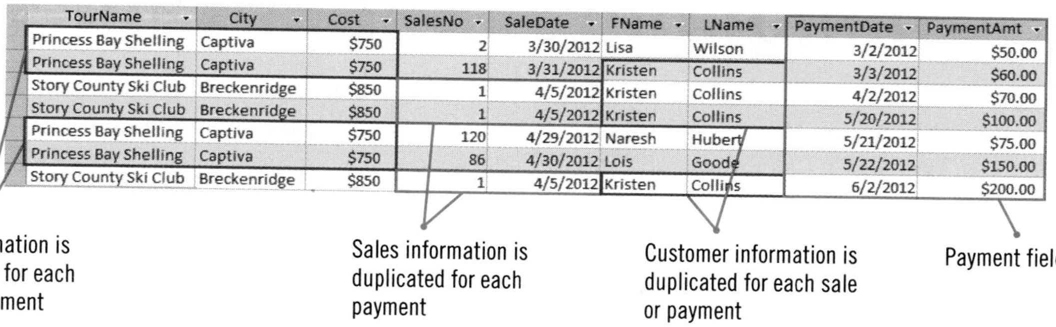

TourName	City	Cost	SalesNo	SaleDate	FName	LName	PaymentDate	PaymentAmt
Princess Bay Shelling	Captiva	$750	2	3/30/2012	Lisa	Wilson	3/2/2012	$50.00
Princess Bay Shelling	Captiva	$750	118	3/31/2012	Kristen	Collins	3/3/2012	$60.00
Story County Ski Club	Breckenridge	$850	1	4/5/2012	Kristen	Collins	4/2/2012	$70.00
Story County Ski Club	Breckenridge	$850	1	4/5/2012	Kristen	Collins	5/20/2012	$100.00
Princess Bay Shelling	Captiva	$750	120	4/29/2012	Naresh	Hubert	5/21/2012	$75.00
Princess Bay Shelling	Captiva	$750	86	4/30/2012	Lois	Goode	5/22/2012	$150.00
Story County Ski Club	Breckenridge	$850	1	4/5/2012	Kristen	Collins	6/2/2012	$200.00

Tour information is duplicated for each sale or payment
Sales information is duplicated for each payment
Customer information is duplicated for each sale or payment
Payment fields

FIGURE E-2: **Related tables reduce redundant data**

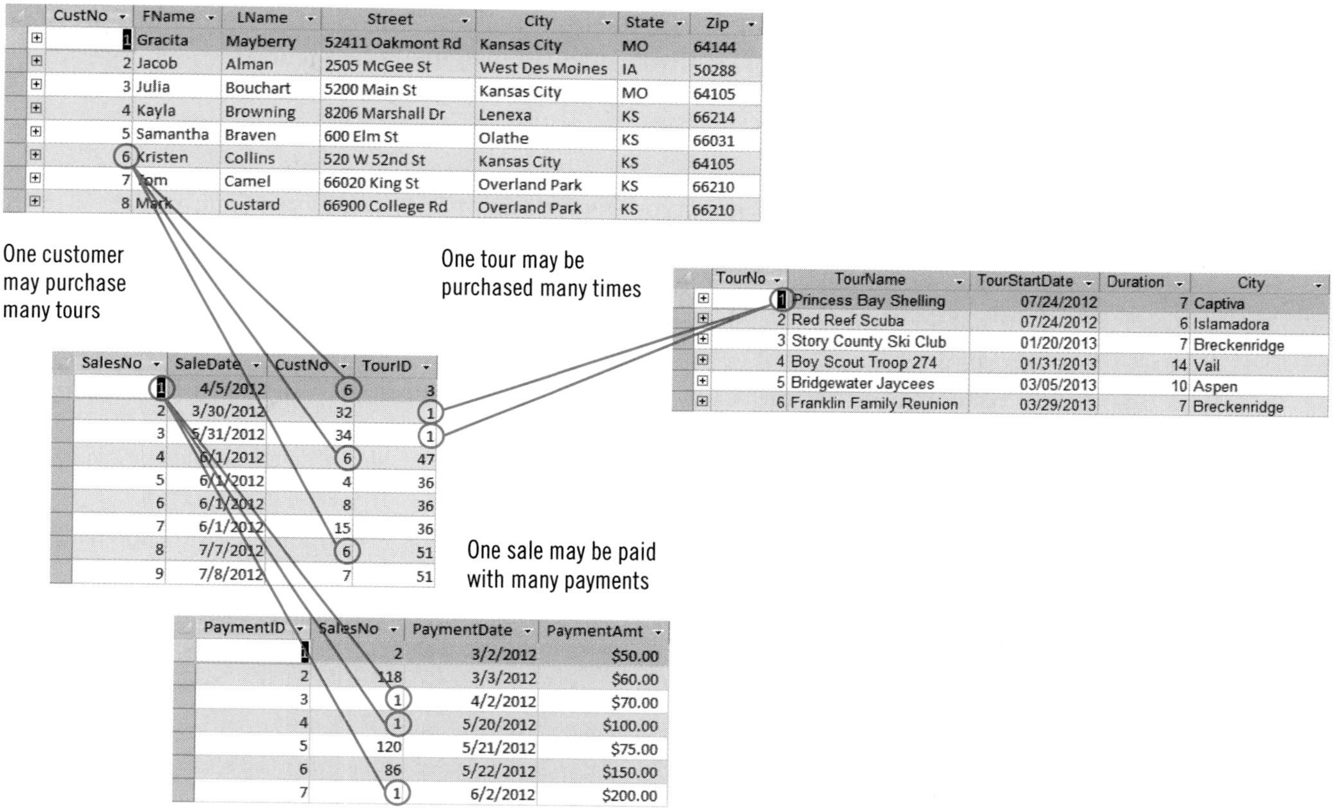

CustNo	FName	LName	Street	City	State	Zip
1	Gracita	Mayberry	52411 Oakmont Rd	Kansas City	MO	64144
2	Jacob	Alman	2505 McGee St	West Des Moines	IA	50288
3	Julia	Bouchart	5200 Main St	Kansas City	MO	64105
4	Kayla	Browning	8206 Marshall Dr	Lenexa	KS	66214
5	Samantha	Braven	600 Elm St	Olathe	KS	66031
6	Kristen	Collins	520 W 52nd St	Kansas City	KS	64105
7	Tom	Camel	66020 King St	Overland Park	KS	66210
8	Mark	Custard	66900 College Rd	Overland Park	KS	66210

TourNo	TourName	TourStartDate	Duration	City
1	Princess Bay Shelling	07/24/2012	7	Captiva
2	Red Reef Scuba	07/24/2012	6	Islamadora
3	Story County Ski Club	01/20/2013	7	Breckenridge
4	Boy Scout Troop 274	01/31/2013	14	Vail
5	Bridgewater Jaycees	03/05/2013	10	Aspen
6	Franklin Family Reunion	03/29/2013	7	Breckenridge

SalesNo	SaleDate	CustNo	TourID
1	4/5/2012	6	3
2	3/30/2012	32	1
3	3/31/2012	34	1
4	6/1/2012	6	47
5	6/1/2012	4	36
6	6/1/2012	8	36
7	6/1/2012	15	36
8	7/7/2012	6	51
9	7/8/2012	7	51

PaymentID	SalesNo	PaymentDate	PaymentAmt
1	2	3/2/2012	$50.00
2	118	3/3/2012	$60.00
3	1	4/2/2012	$70.00
4	1	5/20/2012	$100.00
5	120	5/21/2012	$75.00
6	86	5/22/2012	$150.00
7	1	6/2/2012	$200.00

One customer may purchase many tours
One tour may be purchased many times
One sale may be paid with many payments

Using many-to-many relationships

As you design your database, you might find that two tables have a **many-to-many relationship**. To join them, you must establish a third table called a **junction table**, which contains two foreign key fields to serve on the "many" side of separate one-to-many relationships with the two original tables. The Customers and Tours tables have a many-to-many relationship because one customer can purchase many tours and one tour can have many customers purchase it. The Sales table serves as the junction table to link the three tables together.

UNIT E

Access 2010

Designing Related Tables

After you develop a valid relational database design, you are ready to define the tables in Access. Using **Table Design View**, you can specify all characteristics of a table including field names, data types, field descriptions, field properties, Lookup properties, and primary key field designations. Using the new database design, you are ready to create the Payments table for Quest Specialty Travel.

STEPS

1. **Start Access, open the QuestTravel-E.accdb database, then enable content if prompted**
   The Customers, Sales, and Tours tables have already been created in the database. You need to create the Payments table.

2. **Click the Create tab on the Ribbon, then click the Table Design button in the Tables group**
   Table Design View opens, where you can enter field names and specify data types and field properties for the new table. Field names should be as short as possible, but long enough to be descriptive. The field name you enter in Table Design View is used as the default name for the field in all later queries, forms, and reports.

> **QUICK TIP**
> When specifying field data types, you can type the first letter of the data type to quickly select it.

3. **Type PaymentNo, press [Enter], click the Data Type list arrow, click AutoNumber, press [Tab], type Primary key field for the Payments table, then press [Enter]**
   The AutoNumber data type automatically assigns the next available integer in the sequence to each new record. This data type is often used as the primary key field for a table because it always contains a unique value for each record.

4. **Type the other field names, data types, and descriptions as shown in Figure E-3**
   Field descriptions entered in Table Design View are optional, but they are helpful in that they provide further information about the field.

> **TROUBLE**
> If you set the wrong field as the primary key field, click the Primary Key field button again to toggle it off.

5. **Click PaymentNo in the Field Name column, then click the Primary Key button in the Tools group**
   A **key symbol** appears to the left of PaymentNo to indicate that this field is defined as the primary key field for this table. Primary key fields have two roles: they uniquely define each record, and they may also serve as the "one" side of a one-to-many relationship between two tables. Table E-1 describes common examples of one-to-many relationships.

> **QUICK TIP**
> To delete or rename an existing table, right-click it in the Navigation Pane, then click Delete or Rename.

6. **Click the Save button on the Quick Access toolbar, type Payments in the Table Name text box, click OK, then close the table**
   The Payments table is now displayed as a table object in the QuestTravel-E.accdb database Navigation Pane, as shown in Figure E-4.

Specifying the foreign key field data type

A foreign key field in the "many" table must have the same data type (Text or Number) as the primary key it is related to in the "one" table. An exception to this rule is when the primary key field in the "one" table has an AutoNumber data type. In this case, the linking foreign key field in the "many" table must have a Number data type. Also note that a Number field used as a foreign key field must have a Long Integer Field Size property to match the Field Size property of the AutoNumber primary key field.

FIGURE E-3: **Table Design View for the new Payments table**

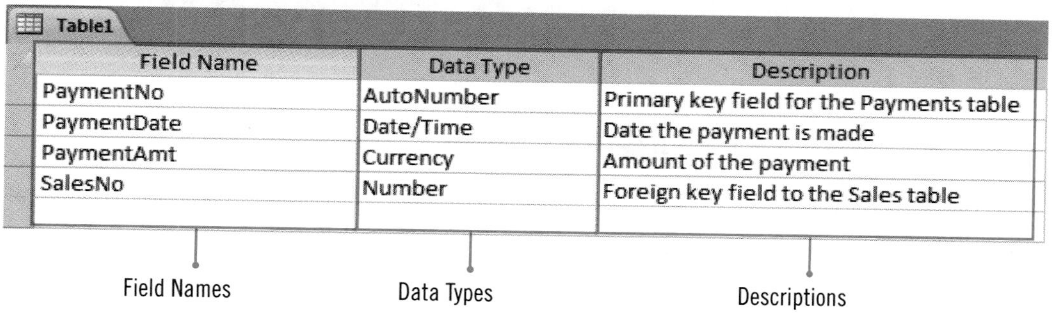

Table1
Field Name
Data Type
Description
PaymentNo
AutoNumber
Primary key field for the Payments table
PaymentDate
Date/Time
Date the payment is made
PaymentAmt
Currency
Amount of the payment
SalesNo
Number
Foreign key field to the Sales table
Field Names
Data Types
Descriptions

FIGURE E-4: **Payments table in the QuestTravel-E database Navigation Pane**

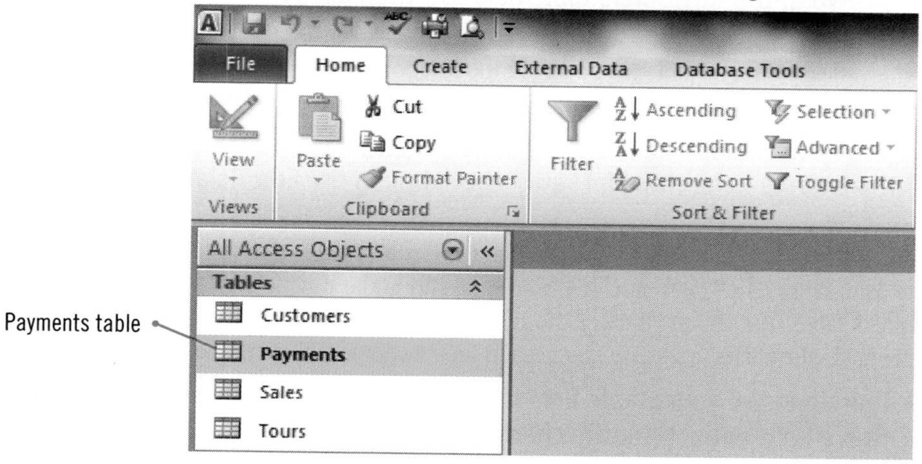

TABLE E-1: **Common one-to-many relationships**

table on "one" side	table on "many" side	linking field	description
Products	Sales	ProductID	A ProductID field must have a unique entry in a Products table, but it is listed many times in a Sales table
Students	Enrollments	StudentID	A StudentID field must have a unique entry in a Students table, but it is listed many times in an Enrollments table as the student enrolls in multiple classes
Employees	Promotions	EmployeeID	An EmployeeID field must have a unique entry in an Employees table, but it is listed many times in a Promotions table as the employee is promoted over time

Creating One-to-Many Relationships

After creating the tables you need, you link them together in appropriate one-to-many relationships using the primary key field in the "one" table and the foreign key field in the "many" table. To avoid rework, be sure that your table relationships are finished before building queries, forms, or reports using fields from multiple tables. You are ready to define the one-to-many relationships between the tables of the QuestTravel-E.accdb database.

STEPS

QUICK TIP
Drag the table's title bar to move the field list.

1. **Click the Database Tools tab on the Ribbon, click the Relationships button, click the Show Table button, double-click Customers, double-click Sales, double-click Tours, double-click Payments, then close the Show Table dialog box**

   The four table field lists appear in the Relationships window. The primary key fields are identified with a small key symbol to the left of the field name. With all of the field lists in the Relationships window, you're ready to link them in proper one-to-many relationships.

QUICK TIP
Drag the bottom border of the field list to display all of the fields.

2. **Click CustNo in the Customers table field list, then drag it to the CustNo field in the Sales table field list**

   Dragging a field from one table to another in the Relationships window links the two tables by the selected fields and opens the Edit Relationships dialog box, as shown in Figure E-5. Recall that referential integrity helps ensure data accuracy.

TROUBLE
Right-click a relationship line, then click Delete if you need to delete a relationship and start over.

3. **Click the Enforce Referential Integrity check box in the Edit Relationships dialog box, then click Create**

   The **one-to-many line** shows the link between the CustNo field of the Customers table and the CustNo field of the Sales table. The "one" side of the relationship is the unique CustNo value for each record in the Customers table. The "many" side of the relationship is identified by an infinity symbol pointing to the CustNo field in the Sales table. You also need to link the Tours table to the Sales table.

4. **Click TourNo in the Tours table field list, drag it to TourID in the Sales table field list, click the Enforce Referential Integrity check box, then click Create**

   Finally, you need to link the Payments table to the Sales table.

5. **Click SalesNo in the Sales table field list, drag it to SalesNo in the Payments table field list, click the Enforce Referential Integrity check box, click Create, then drag the Tours title bar down so all links are clear**

   The updated Relationships window should look like Figure E-6.

TROUBLE
Click the Landscape button on the Print Preview tab if the report is too wide for portrait orientation.

6. **Click the Relationship Report button in the Tools group, click the Print button on the Print Preview tab, then click OK**

   A printout of the Relationships window, called the **Relationships report**, shows how your relational database is designed and includes table names, field names, primary key fields, and one-to-many relationship lines. This printout is helpful as you later create queries, forms, and reports that use fields from multiple tables. Note that it is not necessary to directly link each table to every other table.

7. **Right-click the Relationships for QuestTravel-E report tab, click Close, click Yes to save the report, then click OK to accept the default report name**

   The Relationships for QuestTravel-E report is saved in your database, as shown in the Navigation Pane.

8. **Close the Relationships window, then click Yes if prompted to save changes**

FIGURE E-5: **Edit Relationships dialog box**

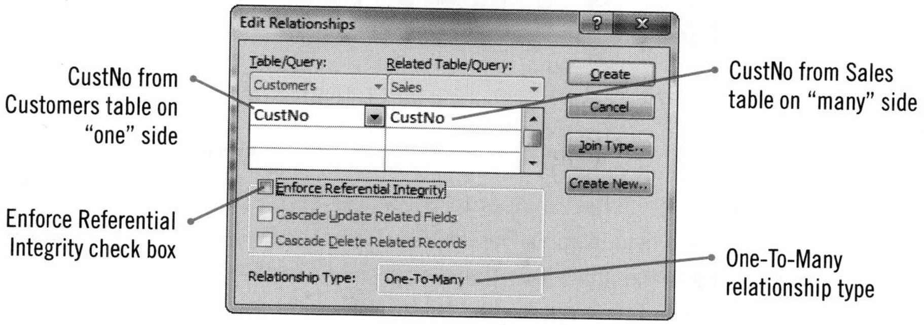

FIGURE E-6: **Final Relationships window**

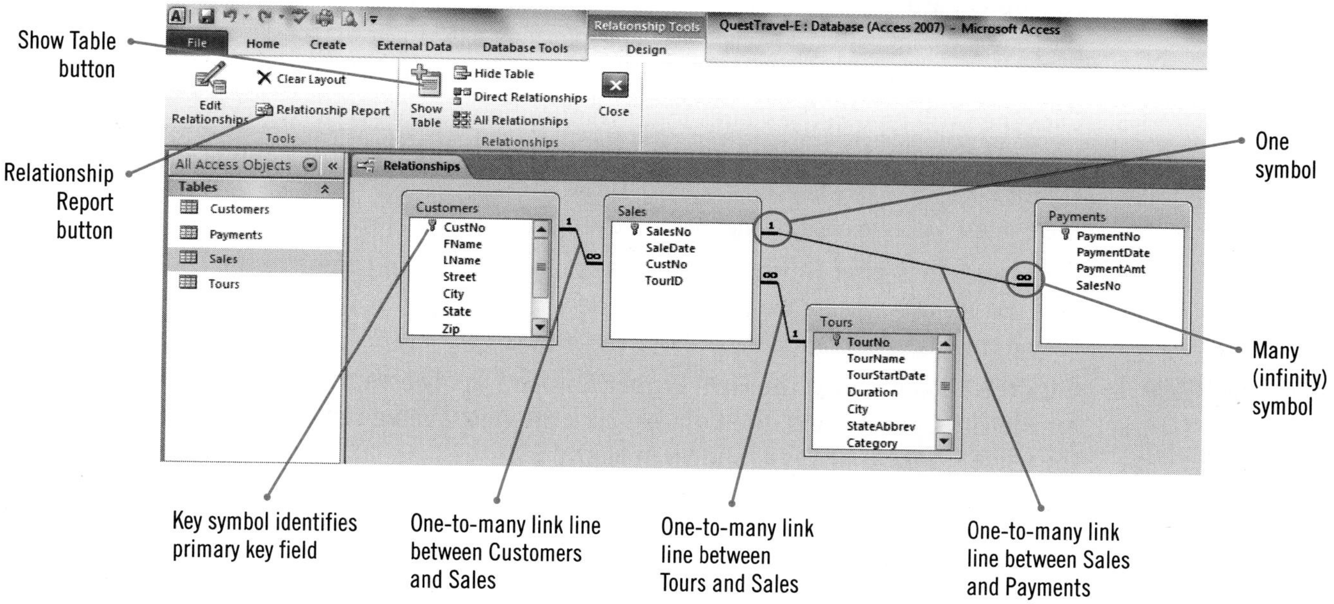

More on enforcing referential integrity

Recall that referential integrity is a set of rules to help ensure that no orphan records are entered or created in the database. An **orphan record** is a record in the "many" table (also called the **child table**) that doesn't have a matching entry in the linking field of the "one" table (also called the **parent table**). Referential integrity prevents orphan records in multiple ways. Referential integrity will not allow you to make an entry in the foreign key field of the child table that does not have a matching value in the linking field of the parent table. Referential integrity also prevents you from deleting a record in the parent table that has related records in the child table. You should enforce referential integrity on all one-to-many relationships if possible. Unfortunately, if you are working with a database that already contains orphan records, you cannot enforce this powerful set of rules unless you find and fix the data so that orphan records no longer exist. The process of removing and fixing orphan records is commonly called "scrubbing the database."

UNIT E
Access 2010

Creating Lookup Fields

A **Lookup field** is a field that contains Lookup properties. **Lookup properties** are field properties that supply a drop-down list of values for a field. The values can be stored in another table or directly stored in the **Row Source** Lookup property of the field. Fields that are good candidates for Lookup properties are those that contain a defined set of appropriate values such as State, Gender, or Department. You can set Lookup properties for a field in Table Design View using the **Lookup Wizard.** The FirstContact field in the Customers table identifies how the customer first made contact with Quest Specialty Travel such as being referred by a friend (Friend), finding the company through the Internet (Internet), or responding to a radio advertisement (Radio). Because the FirstContact field has only a handful of valid entries, it is a good Lookup field candidate.

STEPS

1. **Right-click the Customers table in the Navigation Pane, then click Design View**
   The Lookup Wizard is included in the Data Type list.
2. **Click the Text data type for the FirstContact field, click the Data Type list arrow, then click Lookup Wizard**
   The Lookup Wizard starts and prompts you for information about where the Lookup column will get its values.
3. **Click the I will type in the values that I want option button, click Next, click the first cell in the Col1 column, type Friend, press [Tab], then type the rest of the values as shown in Figure E-7**
   These are the values to populate the Lookup value drop-down list for the FirstContact field.
4. **Click Next, then click Finish to accept the default label and complete the Lookup Wizard**
   Note that the data type for the FirstContact field is still Text. The Lookup Wizard is a process for setting Lookup property values for a field, not a data type itself.
5. **Click the Lookup tab in the Field Properties pane to observe the new Lookup properties for the FirstContact field, then double-click the Allow Value List Edits property to change the value from No to Yes as shown in Figure E-8**
   The Lookup Wizard helped you enter the correct Lookup properties for the FirstContact field, but you can always enter or edit them directly, too. The Row Source property stores the values that are provided in the drop-down list for a Lookup field. The **Limit To List** Lookup property determines whether you can enter a new value into a field with other Lookup properties, or whether the entries are limited to the drop-down list.
6. **Click the View button to switch to Datasheet View, click Yes when prompted to save the table, press [Tab] eight times to move to the FirstContact field, then click the FirstContact list arrow as shown in Figure E-9**
   The FirstContact field now provides a list of four values for this field. To edit the list in Datasheet View, click the **Edit List Items button** below the list.
7. **Close the Customers table**

QUICK TIP
The Property Update Options button helps you propagate field property changes everywhere a field is used in the database.

Creating multivalued fields

Multivalued fields allow you to make more than one choice from a drop-down list for a field. As a database designer, multivalued fields allow you to select and store more than one choice without having to create a more advanced database design. To create a multivalued field, enter Yes in the **Allow Multiple Values** Lookup property. This feature is only available for an Access database created or saved in the Access 2007 file format.

FIGURE E-7: **Entering a list of values in the Lookup Wizard**

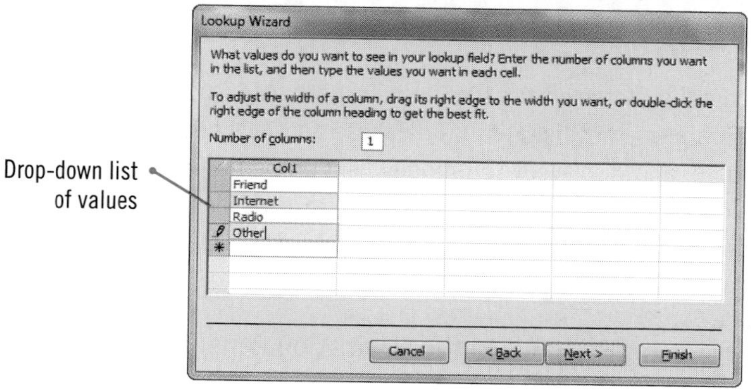

FIGURE E-8: **Viewing Lookup properties**

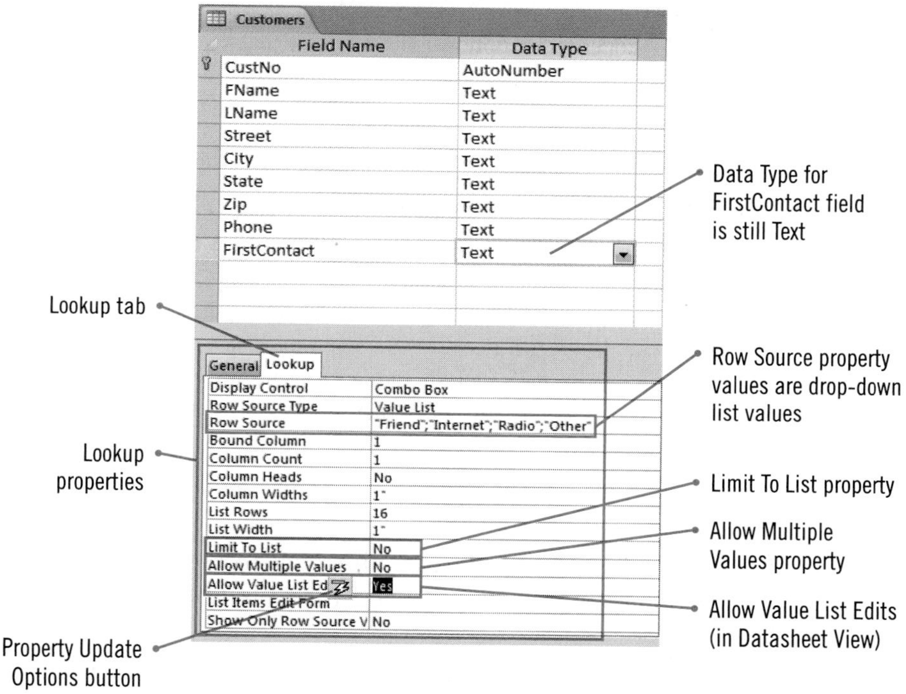

FIGURE E-9: **Using a Lookup field in a datasheet**

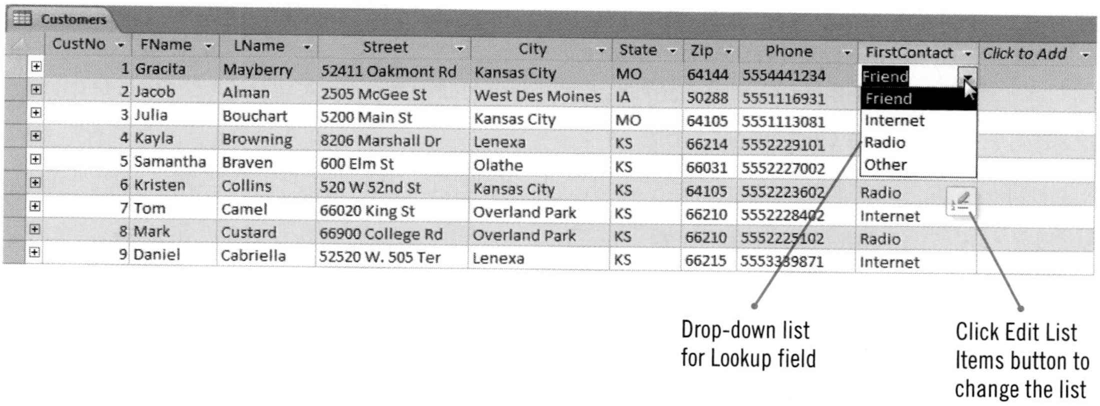

UNIT
E
Access 2010

Modifying Text Fields

Field properties are the characteristics that describe each field, such as Field Size, Default Value, Caption, or Row Source. These properties help ensure database accuracy and clarity because they restrict the way data is entered, stored, and displayed. You modify field properties in Table Design View. See Table E-2 for more information on Text field properties. After reviewing the Customers table with Samantha Hooper, you decide to change field properties for several Text fields in that table.

STEPS

1. **Right-click the Customers table in the Navigation Pane, then click Design View on the shortcut menu**

   The Customers table opens in Design View. The field properties appear on the General tab on the lower half of the Table Design View window and apply to the selected field. Field properties change depending on the field's data type. For example, when you select a field with a Text data type, one visible property is the **Field Size property**, which determines the number of characters you can enter in the field. However, when you select a field with a Date/Time data type, Access controls the size of the data, so the Field Size property is not displayed. Many field properties are optional, but for those that require an entry, Access provides a default value.

2. **Press [↓] to move through each field while viewing the field properties in the lower half of the window**

   The **field selector button** to the left of the field indicates which field is currently selected.

3. **Click the FirstContact field name, double-click 255 in the Field Size property text box, type 8, click the Save button on the Quick Access toolbar, then click Yes**

   The maximum and the default value for the Field Size property for a Text field is 255. In general, however, you want to make the Field Size property for Text fields only as large as needed to accommodate the longest entry. You can increase the size later if necessary. In some cases, shortening the Field Size property helps prevent typographical errors. For example, you should set the Field Size property for a State field that stores two-letter state abbreviations to 2 to prevent errors such as TXX. For the FirstContact field, your longest entry is "Internet"—8 characters.

4. **Change the Field Size property to 30 for the FName and LName fields, click , then click Yes**

   No existing entries are greater than 30 characters for either of these fields, so no data is lost. The **Input Mask** property provides a visual guide for users as they enter data. It also helps determine what types of values can be entered into a field.

5. **Click the Phone field name, click the Input Mask property text box, click the Build button [...], click the Phone Number input mask, click Next, click Next, then click Finish**

   Table Design View of the Customers table should look like Figure E-10, which shows the Input Mask property entered for the Phone field.

6. **Right-click the Customers table tab, click Datasheet View, click Yes to save the table, press [Tab] enough times to move to the Phone field for the first record, type 5554441234, then press [Enter]**

   The Phone Input Mask property creates an easy-to-use visual guide to facilitate accurate data entry.

7. **Close the Customers table**

> **TROUBLE**
> If the Input Mask Wizard is not installed on your computer, you can complete this step by typing !(999) 000-0000;;_ directly into the Input Mask property for the Phone field.

FIGURE E-10: **Changing Text field properties**

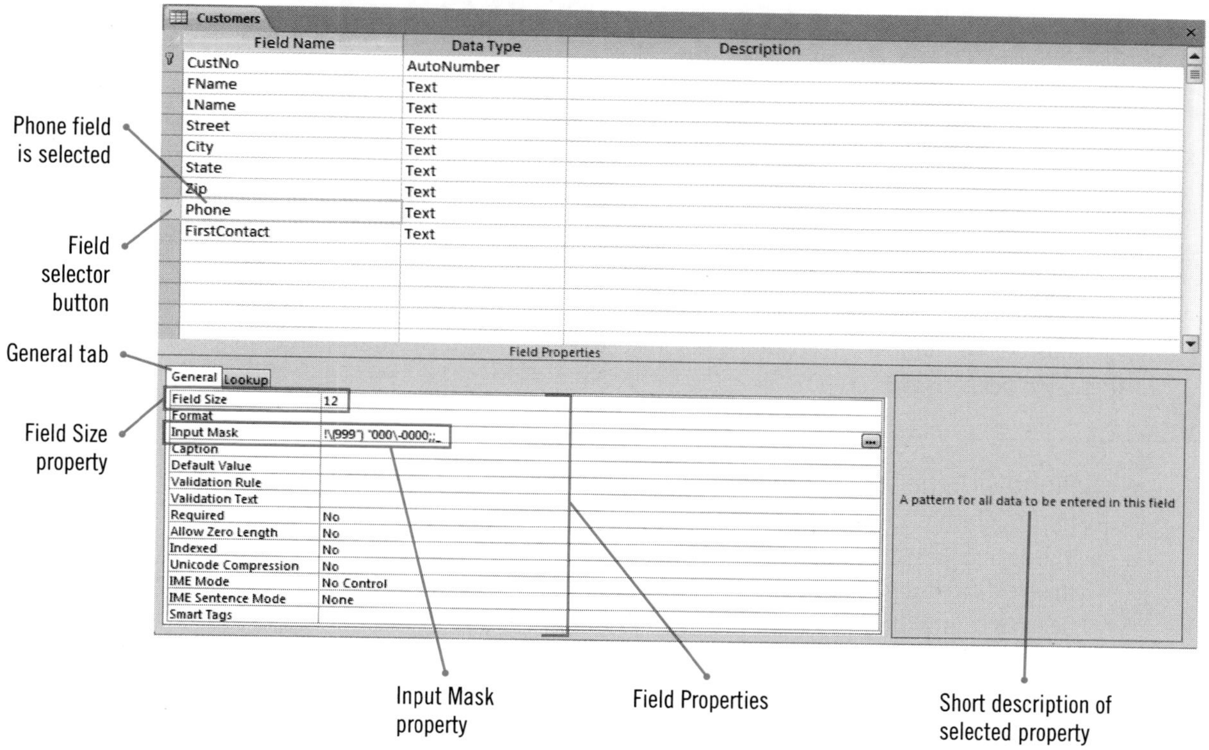

TABLE E-2: **Common Text field properties**

property	description	sample field	sample property entry
Field Size	Controls how many characters can be entered into the field	State	2
Format	Controls how information will be displayed and printed	State	> (displays all characters in uppercase)
Input Mask	Provides a pattern for data to be entered	Phone	!(999) 000-0000;1;_
Caption	Describes the field in the first row of a datasheet, form, or report; if the Caption property is not entered, the field name is used to label the field	EmpNo	Employee Number
Default Value	Displays a value that is automatically entered in the given field for new records	City	Des Moines
Required	Determines if an entry is required for this field	LastName	Yes

Working with the Input Mask property

The Input Mask property provides a pattern for data to be entered, using three parts separated by semicolons. The first part provides a pattern for what type of data can be entered. For example, 9 represents an optional number, 0 a required number, ? an optional letter, and L a required letter. The second part determines whether all displayed characters (such as dashes in a phone number) are stored in the field. For the second part of the input mask, a 0 entry stores all characters such as 555-7722, and a 1 entry stores only the entered data, 5557722. The third part of the input mask determines which character Access uses to guide the user through the mask. Common choices are the asterisk (*), underscore (_), or pound sign (#).

UNIT
E
Access 2010

Modifying Number and Currency Fields

Although some properties for Number and Currency fields are the same as the properties of Text fields, each data type has its own list of valid properties. Number and Currency fields have similar properties because they both contain numeric values. Currency fields store values that represent money, and Number fields store values that represent values such as quantities, measurements, and scores. The Tours table contains both a Number field (Duration) and a Currency field (Cost). You want to modify the properties of these two fields.

STEPS

1. **Right-click the Tours table in the Navigation Pane, click Design View on the shortcut menu, then click the Duration field name**

   The default Field Size property for a Number field is **Long Integer**. See Table E-3 for more information on the Field Size property and other common properties for a Number field. Access sets the size of Currency fields to control the way numbers are rounded in calculations, so the Field Size property isn't available for Currency fields.

2. **Click Long Integer in the Field Size property text box, click the Field Size list arrow, then click Byte**

   Choosing a **Byte** value for the Field Size property allows entries from 0 to 255, so it greatly restricts the possible values and the storage requirements for the Duration field.

3. **Click the Cost field name, click Auto in the Decimal Places property text box, click the Decimal Places list arrow, click 0, then press [Enter]**

   Your Table Design View should look like Figure E-11. Because all of Quest's tours are priced at a round dollar value, you do not need to display cents in the Cost field.

4. **Save the table, then switch to Datasheet View**

   Because none of the current entries in the Duration field is greater than 255, which is the maximum value allowed by a Number field with a Byte Field Size property, you don't lose any data. You want to test the new property changes.

5. **Press [Tab] three times to move to the Duration field for the first record, type 800, then press [Tab]**

   Because 800 is larger than what the Byte Field Size property allows (0–255), an Access error message appears indicating that the value isn't valid for this field.

6. **Press [Esc] twice to remove the inappropriate entry in the Duration field, then press [Tab] four times to move to the Cost field**

   The Cost field is set to display zero digits after the decimal point.

7. **Type 750.25 in the Cost field of the first record, press [↓], then click $750 in the Cost field of the first record to see the full entry**

   Although the Decimal Places property for the Cost field specifies that entries in the field are *formatted* to display zero digits after the decimal point, 750.25 is the actual value stored in the field. Modifying the Decimal Places property does not change the actual data. Rather, the Decimal Places property only changes the way the data is *presented*.

8. **Close the Tours table**

FIGURE E-11: **Changing Currency and Number field properties**

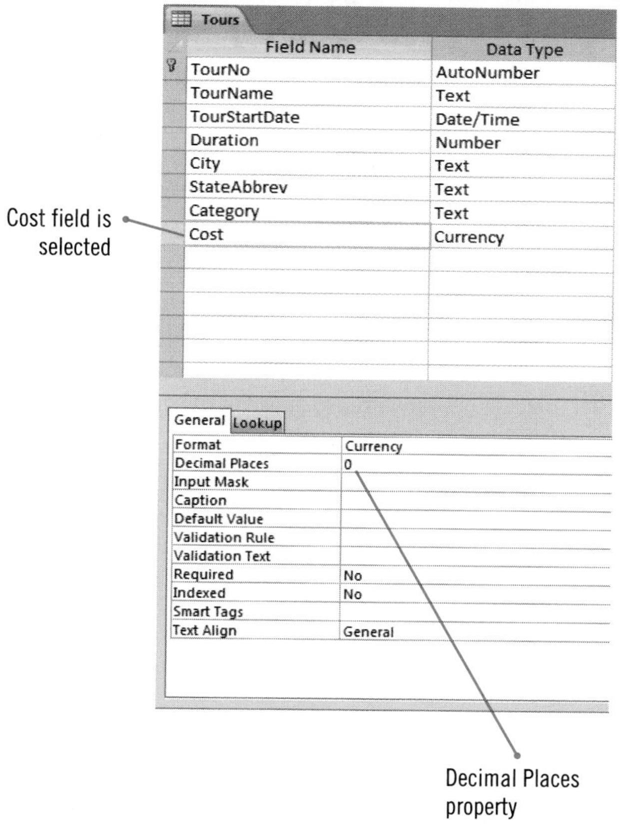

TABLE E-3: **Common Number field properties**

property	description
Field Size	Determines the largest number that can be entered in the field, as well as the type of data (e.g., integer or fraction)
Byte	Stores numbers from 0 to 255 (no fractions)
Integer	Stores numbers from –32,768 to 32,767 (no fractions)
Long Integer	Stores numbers from –2,147,483,648 to 2,147,483,647 (no fractions)
Single	Stores numbers (including fractions with six digits to the right of the decimal point) times 10 to the –38th to +38th power
Double	Stores numbers (including fractions with over 10 digits to the right of the decimal point) in the range of 10 to the –324th to +324th power
Decimal Places	The number of digits displayed to the right of the decimal point

Modifying fields in Datasheet View

When you work in Table *Datasheet* View, the Fields tab on the Ribbon provides many options to modify fields and field properties. For example, you can add and delete fields, change a field name or data type, and modify many field properties such as Caption, Default Value, and Format. Table *Design* View, however, gives you full access to *all* field properties such as all of the Lookup properties.

UNIT
E
Access 2010

Modifying Date/Time Fields

Many properties of the Date/Time field, such as Input Mask, Caption, and Default Value, work the same way as they do in fields with a Text or Number data type. One difference, however, is the **Format** property, which helps you format dates in various ways such as January 25, 2013; 25-Jan-13; or 01/25/2013. You want to change the format of Date/Time fields in the Tours table to display two digits for the month and day values and four digits for the year, as in 05/05/2013.

STEPS

1. **Right-click the Tours table in the Navigation Pane, click Design View on the shortcut menu, then click the TourStartDate field name**

   You want the tour start dates to appear with two digits for the month and day, such as 07/05/2013, instead of the default presentation of dates, 7/5/2013.

> **QUICK TIP**
> Click any property box, then press [F1] to open the Microsoft Access Help window to the page that describes that property (or enter the property name in the Search box).

2. **Click the Format property box, then click the Format list arrow**

   Although several predefined Date/Time formats are available, none matches the format you want. To define a custom format, enter symbols that represent how you want the date to appear.

3. **Type mm/dd/yyyy then press [Enter]**

   The updated Format property for the TourStartDate field shown in Figure E-12 sets the date to appear with two digits for the month, two digits for the day, and four digits for the year. The parts of the date are separated by forward slashes.

4. **Save the table, display the datasheet, then click the New (blank) record button on the navigation bar**

   To test the new Format property for the TourStartDate field, you can add a new record to the table.

> **QUICK TIP**
> Access assumes that years entered with two digits from 30 to 99 refer to the years 1930 through 1999, and 00 to 29 refers to the years 2000 through 2029. To enter a year before 1930 or after 2029, enter all four digits of the year.

5. **Press [Tab] to move to the TourName field, type Missouri Eagles, press [Tab], type 9/1/13, press [Tab], type 7, press [Tab], type Hollister, press [Tab], type MO, press [Tab], type Adventure, press [Tab], then type 700**

   The new record you entered into the Tours table should look like Figure E-13. The Format property for the TourStartDate field makes the entry appear as 09/01/2013, as desired.

FIGURE E-12: **Changing Date/Time field properties**

TourStartDate field is selected

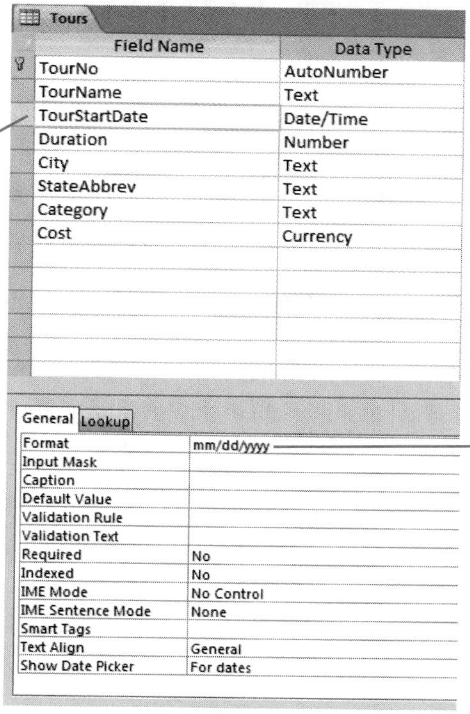

Field Name	Data Type
TourNo	AutoNumber
TourName	Text
TourStartDate	Date/Time
Duration	Number
City	Text
StateAbbrev	Text
Category	Text
Cost	Currency

General	Lookup
Format	mm/dd/yyyy
Input Mask	
Caption	
Default Value	
Validation Rule	
Validation Text	
Required	No
Indexed	No
IME Mode	No Control
IME Sentence Mode	None
Smart Tags	
Text Align	General
Show Date Picker	For dates

Custom Format property

FIGURE E-13: **Testing the Format property**

TourNo	TourName	TourStartDate	Duration	City	StateAbbrev	Category	Cost
49	Golden State Tours	08/07/2012	10	Sacramento	CA	Cultural	$1,400
51	Bright Lights Expo	12/19/2012	3	Branson	MO	Site Seeing	$200
52	Missouri Bald Eagle Watc	08/31/2012	7	Hollister	MO	Adventure	$700
53	Bridges of Madison Count	10/25/2013	4	Winterset	IA	Site Seeing	$500
54	Branson Lights	12/01/2013	3	Branson	MO	Site Seeing	$300
55	Green Gathering	10/01/2013	3	Dallas	TX	Family	$300
56	Salmon Run Fishing	05/05/2013	4	Seattle	WA	Adventure	$800
57	Space Needle Fireworks	07/04/2013	3	Seattle	WA	Site Seeing	$500
58	Northwest Passage	08/01/2013	10	Vancouver	WA	Adventure	$2,000
59	Missouri Eagles	09/01/2013	7	Hollister	MO	Adventure	700
(New)							

Custom mm/dd/yyyy Format property applied to TourStartDate field

Using Smart Tags

Smart Tags are buttons that automatically appear in certain conditions. They provide a small menu of options to help you work with the task at hand. Access provides the **Property Update Options** Smart Tag to help you quickly apply property changes to other objects of the database that use the field. The **Error Indicator** Smart Tag helps identify potential design errors. For example, if you are working in Report Design View and the report is too wide for the paper, the Error Indicator appears in the upper-left corner by the report selector button to alert you to the problem.

UNIT E

Access 2010

Modifying Validation Properties

The **Validation Rule** property determines what entries a field can accept. For example, a validation rule for a Date/Time field might require date entries on or after 6/1/2012. A validation rule for a Currency field might indicate that valid entries fall between $0 and $1,500. You use the **Validation Text** property to display an explanatory message when a user tries to enter data that breaks the validation rule. Therefore, the Validation Rule and Validation Text field properties help you prevent unreasonable data from being entered into the database. Samantha Hooper reminds you that all new Quest tours start on or after June 1, 2012. You can use the validation properties to establish this rule for the TourStartDate field in the Tours table.

STEPS

1. **Click the View button on the Home tab to return to Design View, click the TourStartDate field if it isn't already selected, click the Validation Rule property box, then type >=6/1/2012**

   This entry forces all dates in the TourStartDate field to be greater than or equal to 6/1/2012. See Table E-4 for more examples of Validation Rule expressions. The Validation Text property provides a helpful message to the user when the entry in the field breaks the rule entered in the Validation Rule property.

2. **Click the Validation Text box, then type Date must be on or after 6/1/2012**

   Design View of the Tours table should now look like Figure E-14. Access modifies a property to include additional syntax by changing the entry in the Validation Rule property to >=#6/1/2012#. Pound signs (#) are used to surround date criteria.

3. **Save the table, then click Yes when asked to test the existing data with new data integrity rules**

   Because no dates in the TourStartDate field are earlier than 6/1/2012, Access finds no date errors in the current data and saves the table. You now want to test that the Validation Rule and Validation Text properties work when entering data in the datasheet.

4. **Click the View button to display the datasheet, press [Tab] twice to move to the TourStartDate field, type 5/1/12, then press [Tab]**

   Because you tried to enter a date that was not true for the Validation Rule property for the TourStartDate field, a dialog box opens and displays the Validation Text entry, as shown in Figure E-15.

5. **Click OK to close the validation message**

   You now know that the Validation Rule and Validation Text properties work properly.

6. **Press [Esc] to reject the invalid date entry in the TourStartDate field**

7. **Close the Tours table**

FIGURE E-14: Entering Validation properties

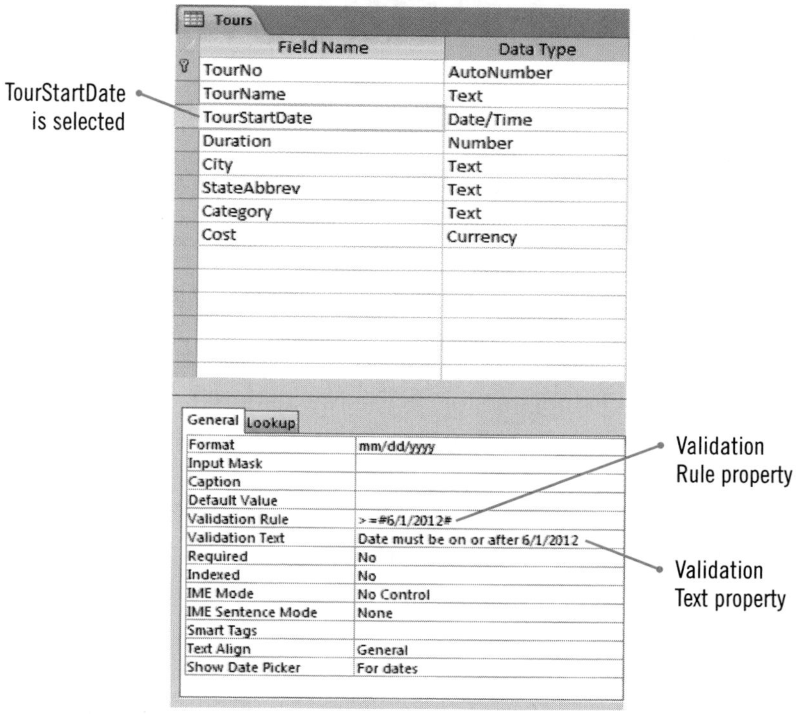
TourStartDate is selected
Tours
Field Name
Data Type
TourNo
AutoNumber
TourName
Text
TourStartDate
Date/Time
Duration
Number
City
Text
StateAbbrev
Text
Category
Text
Cost
Currency
General
Lookup
Format
mm/dd/yyyy
Input Mask
Caption
Default Value
Validation Rule
>=#6/1/2012#
Validation Text
Date must be on or after 6/1/2012
Required
No
Indexed
No
IME Mode
No Control
IME Sentence Mode
None
Smart Tags
Text Align
General
Show Date Picker
For dates
Validation Rule property
Validation Text property

FIGURE E-15: Validation Text message

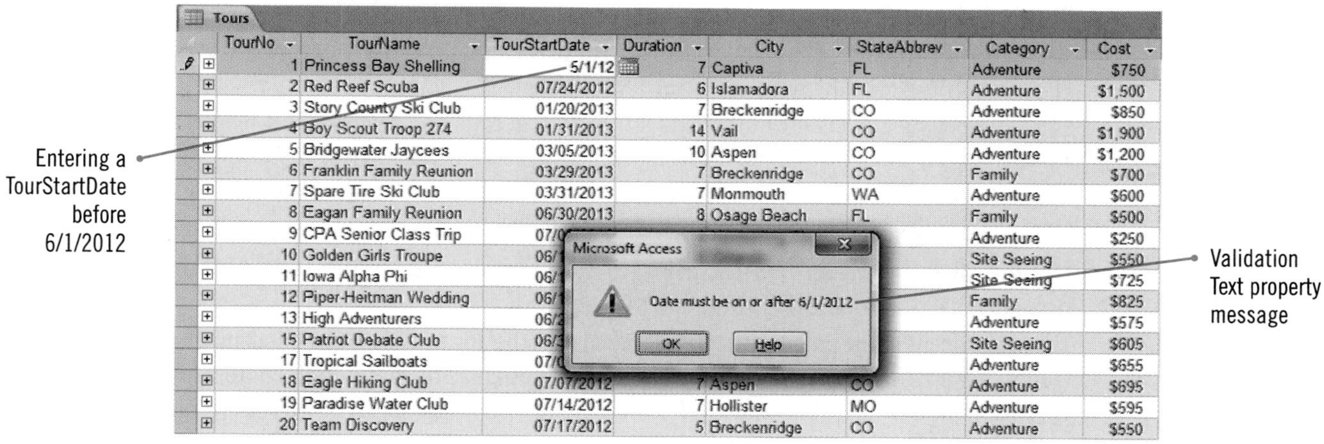
Entering a TourStartDate before 6/1/2012
Tours
TourNo
TourName
TourStartDate
Duration
City
StateAbbrev
Category
Cost
5/1/12
Microsoft Access
Date must be on or after 6/1/2012
OK
Help
Validation Text property message

TABLE E-4: Validation Rule expressions

data type	validation rule expression	description
Number or Currency	>0	The number must be positive
Number or Currency	>10 And <100	The number must be greater than 10 and less than 100
Number or Currency	10 Or 20 Or 30	The number must be 10, 20, or 30
Text	"IA" Or "NE" Or "MO"	The entry must be IA, NE, or MO
Date/Time	>=#7/1/93#	The date must be on or after 7/1/1993
Date/Time	>#1/1/10# And <#1/1/12#	The date must be greater than 1/1/2010 and less than 1/1/2012

UNIT E

Access 2010

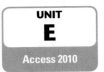

Creating Attachment Fields

An **Attachment field** allows you to attach an external file such as a Word document, PowerPoint presentation, Excel workbook, or image file to a record. Earlier versions of Access allowed you to link or embed external data using the **OLE** (object linking and embedding) data type. The Attachment data type is superior to OLE because it stores data more efficiently, stores more file formats such as JPEG images, and requires no additional software to view the files from within Access. Samantha Hooper asks you to incorporate images on forms and reports to help describe and market each tour. You can use an Attachment field to store JPEG images for customer photo identification.

STEPS

1. **Right-click the Customers table in the Navigation Pane, then click Design View**

   You can insert a new field anywhere in the list.

2. **Click the Street field selector, click the Insert Rows button on the Design tab, click the Field Name cell, type Photo, press [Tab], click the Data Type list arrow, then click Attachment as shown in Figure E-16**

   Now that you created the new Attachment field named Photo, you're ready to add data to it in Datasheet View.

3. **Click the Save button on the Quick Access toolbar, click the View button on the Design tab to switch to Datasheet View, then press [Tab] three times to move to the new Photo field**

   An Attachment field cell displays a small paper clip icon with the number of files attached to the field in parentheses. You have not attached any files to this field yet, so each record shows zero (0) file attachments. You can attach files to this field directly from Datasheet View.

4. **Right-click the attachment icon for the first record, click Manage Attachments on the shortcut menu, click Add, navigate to the drive and folder where you store your Data Files, double-click GMayberry.jpg, then click OK**

   The GMayberry.jpg file is now included with the first record, and the datasheet reflects that one (1) file is attached to the Photo field of the first record. You can add more than one file attachment to the same field. For example, you might add other pictures of this customer to this Photo Attachment field. You can view file attachments directly from the datasheet, form, or report.

5. **Double-click the attachment icon for the first record to open the Attachments dialog box shown in Figure E-17, then click Open**

   The image opens in the program that is associated with the .jpg extension on your computer such as Windows Photo Viewer. The **.jpg** file extension is short for **JPEG**, an acronym for Joint Photographic Experts Group. This association defines the standards for the compression algorithms that make JPEG files very efficient to use in databases and on Web pages.

6. **Close the window that displays the GMayberry.jpg image, click Cancel in the Attachments dialog box, close the Customers table, close the QuestTravel-E.accdb database, then exit Access**

FIGURE E-16: **Adding an Attachment field**

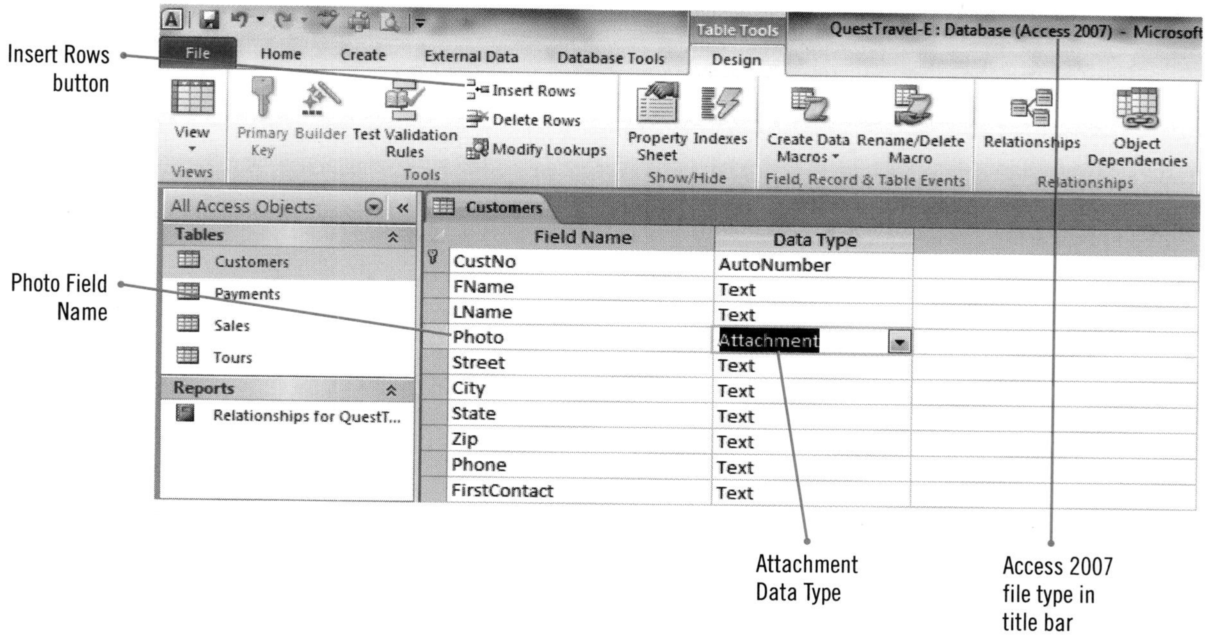

FIGURE E-17: **Opening an attached file**

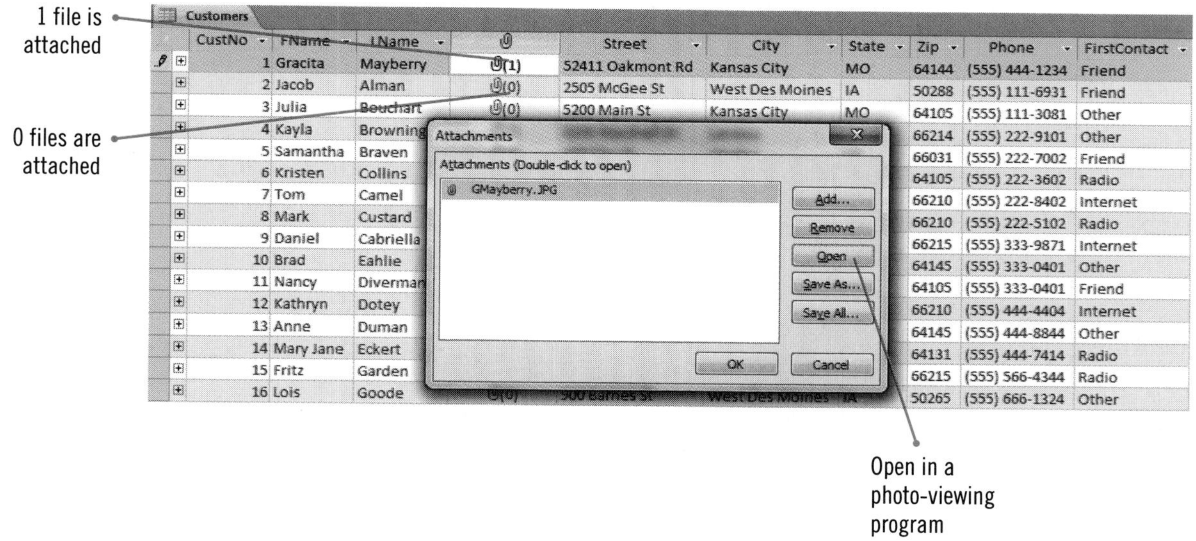

Working with database file types

When you create a new database in Microsoft Office Access 2010, Access gives the file an **.accdb** extension, and saves it as an Access 2007 database file type. This is why (Access 2007) is shown in the title bar of a database opened in Access 2010. Saving the database as an Access 2007 file type allows users of Access 2007 and 2010 to share the same database. Access 2007 databases are *not* readable by earlier versions of Access, however, such as Access 2000, Access 2002 (XP), or Access 2003. If you need to share your database with people using Access 2000, 2002, or 2003, you can use the Save As command on the Office button menu to save the database with an Access 2000 file type, which applies an **.mdb** file extension to the database. Databases with an Access 2000 file type can be used by any version of Access from Access 2000 through 2010, but some features such as multivalued fields and Attachment fields are only available when working with an Access 2007 database.

Practice

Concepts Review

For current SAM information, including versions and content details, visit SAM Central (http://www.cengage.com/samcentral). If you have a SAM user profile, you may have access to hands-on instruction, practice, and assessment of the skills covered in this unit. Since various versions of SAM are supported throughout the life of this text, check with your instructor for the correct instructions and URL/Web site for accessing assignments.

Identify each element of the Relationships window shown in Figure E-18.

FIGURE E-18

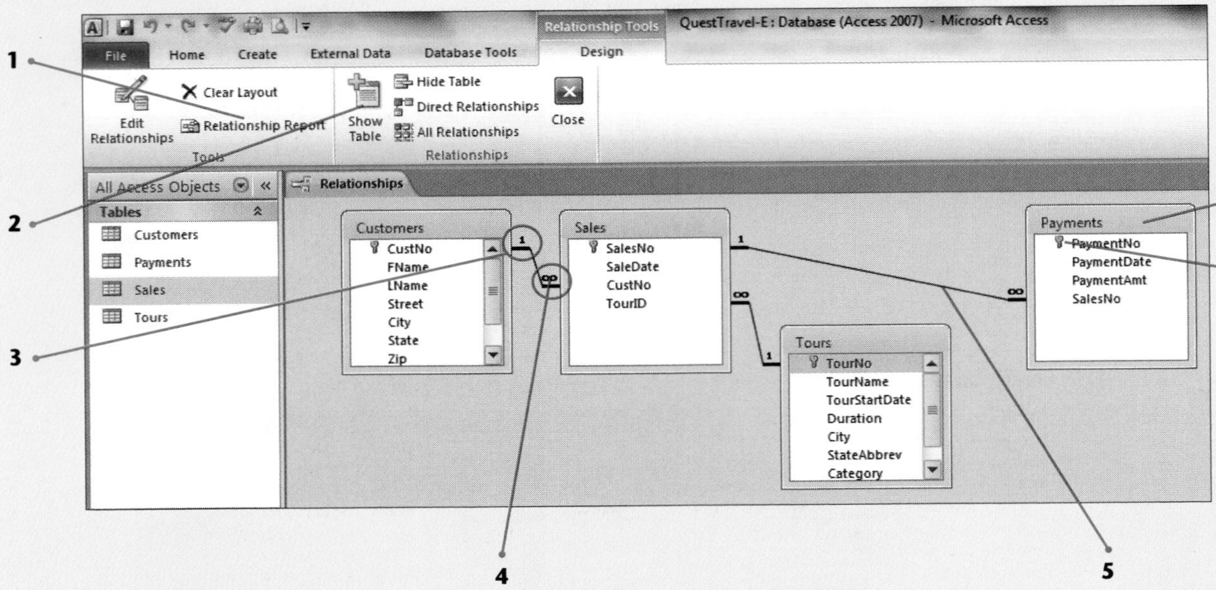

Match each term with the statement that best describes it.

8. **Primary key field**
9. **Validation Rule**
10. **Table Design View**
11. **Row Source**
12. **Limit to List**
13. **Input Mask**
14. **Lookup properties**
15. **Multivalued field**
16. **Attachment field**

a. Field that allows you to store external files such as a Word document, PowerPoint presentation, Excel workbook, or JPEG image
b. Field that holds unique information for each record in the table
c. Field that allows you to make more than one choice from a drop-down list
d. Determines whether you can enter a new value into a field
e. Field properties that allow you to supply a drop-down list of values for a field
f. Access window where all characteristics of a table, such as field names and field properties, are defined
g. Field property that provides a visual guide as you enter data
h. Field property that prevents unreasonable data entries for a field
i. Lookup property that determines where the Lookup field gets its list of values

Select the best answer from the list of choices.

17. Which of the following problems most clearly indicates that you need to redesign your database?
  a. The Input Mask Wizard has not been used.
  b. There is duplicated data in several records of a table.
  c. Not all fields have Validation Rule properties.
  d. Referential integrity is enforced on table relationships.

18. Which of the following is *not* done in Table Design View?
  a. Specifying the primary key field
  b. Setting Field Size properties
  c. Defining Field data types
  d. Creating file attachments

19. What is the purpose of enforcing referential integrity?
  a. To prevent incorrect entries in the primary key field
  b. To require an entry for each field of each record
  c. To prevent orphan records from being created
  d. To force the application of meaningful validation rules

20. To create a many-to-many relationship between two tables, you must create:
  a. A junction table.
  b. Two primary key fields in each table.
  c. Two one-to-one relationships between the two tables, with referential integrity enforced.
  d. Foreign key fields in each table.

21. The linking field in the "many" table is called the:
  a. Primary key field.
  b. Attachment field.
  c. Child field.
  d. Foreign key field.

22. The default filename extension for a database created in Access 2010 is:
  a. .acc10.
  b. .accdb.
  c. .mdb.
  d. .mdb10.

23. If the primary key field in the "one" table is an AutoNumber data type, the linking field in the "many" table will have which data type?
  a. AutoNumber
  b. Number
  c. Text
  d. Attachment

24. Which symbol is used to identify the "many" field in a one-to-many relationship in the Relationships window?
  a. Arrow
  b. Key
  c. Infinity
  d. Triangle

25. The process of removing and fixing orphan records is commonly called:
  a. Relating tables.
  b. Designing a relational database.
  c. Analyzing performance.
  d. Scrubbing the database.

Skills Review

1. Examine relational databases.

a. List the fields needed to create an Access relational database to manage volunteer hours for the members of a philanthropic club or community service organization.

b. Identify fields that would contain duplicate values if all of the fields were stored in a single table.

c. Group the fields into subject matter tables, then identify the primary key field for each table.

d. Assume that your database contains two tables: Members and ServiceRecords. If you did not identify these two tables earlier, regroup the fields within these two table names, then identify the primary key field for each table, the foreign key field in the ServiceRecords table, and how the tables would be related using a one-to-many relationship.

2. Design related tables.

a. Start Access 2010, then create a new database named **Service-E** in the drive and folder where you store your data files.

b. Use Table Design View to create a new table with the name **Members** and the field names and data types shown in Figure E-19.

FIGURE E-19

field name	data type
MemberNo	AutoNumber
FirstName	Text
LastName	Text
City	Text
Phone	Text
Email	Hyperlink
Birthdate	Date/Time
Gender	Text

c. Specify MemberNo as the primary key field, save the Members table, then close it.

d. Use Table Design View to create a new table named **ServiceHours** with the field names and data types shown in Figure E-20.

FIGURE E-20

field name	data type
ServiceNo	AutoNumber
MemberNo	Number
ServiceDate	Date/Time
Location	Text
Description	Text
ServiceHours	Number
ServiceValue	Currency

e. Identify ServiceNo as the primary key field, save the ServiceHours table, then close it.

3. **Create one-to-many relationships.**
   a. Open the Relationships window, double-click Members, then double-click ServiceHours to add the two tables to the Relationships window. Close the Show Table dialog box.
   b. Resize all field lists as necessary so that all fields are visible, then drag the MemberNo field from the Members table to the MemberNo field in the ServiceHours table.
   c. Enforce referential integrity, and create the one-to-many relationship between Members and ServiceHours. See Figure E-21.

FIGURE E-21

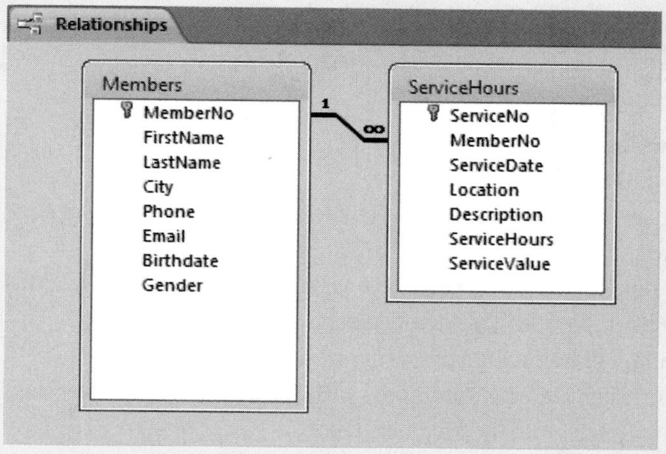

   d. Create a Relationships report for the Service-E database, add your name as a label to the Report Header section of the report in Report Design View, then print the report, if requested by your instructor.
   e. Save and close the Relationships report with the default name, Relationships for Service-E, then save and close the Relationships window.
4. **Create Lookup fields.**
   a. Open the Members table in Design View, then start the Lookup Wizard for the Gender field.
   b. Select the option that allows you to enter your own values, then enter **Female, Male,** and **Unknown** as the values for the Lookup column.
   c. Use the default **Gender** label, then finish the Lookup Wizard.
   d. Save and close the Members table.
5. **Modify Text fields.**
   a. Open the Members table in Design View.
   b. Use the Input Mask Wizard to create an Input Mask property for the Phone field. Choose the Phone Number Input Mask. Accept the other default options provided by the Input Mask Wizard. (*Hint*: If the Input Mask Wizard is not installed on your computer, type **!(999) 000-0000;;_** for the Input Mask property for the Phone field.)
   c. Change the Field Size property of the FirstName, LastName, and City fields to **30**. Change the Field Size property of the Phone field to **10**. Change the Field Size property of the Gender field to **6**. Save the Members table.
   d. Open the Members table in Datasheet View, and enter a new record with your name in the FirstName and LastName fields and your school's City and Phone field values. Enter your school e-mail address, **1/1/1995** for the Birthdate field, and an appropriate choice for the Gender field.

Skills Review (continued)

6. **Modify Number and Currency fields.**
   a. Open the ServiceHours table in Design View.
   b. Change the Decimal Places property of the ServiceHours field to **0**.
   c. Change the Decimal Places property of the ServiceValue field to **2**.
   d. Save and close the ServiceHours table.
7. **Modify Date/Time fields.**
   a. Open the ServiceHours table in Design View.
   b. Change the Format property of the ServiceDate field to **mm/dd/yyyy**.
   c. Save and close the ServiceHours table.
   d. Open the Members table in Design View.
   e. Change the Format property of the Birthdate field to **mm/dd/yyyy**.
   f. Save and close the Members table.
8. **Modify validation properties.**
   a. Open the Members table in Design View.
   b. Click the Birthdate field name, click the Validation Rule text box, then type **<1/1/2000**. (Note that Access automatically adds pound signs around date criteria in the Validation Rule property.)
   c. Click the Validation Text box, then type **Birthdate must be before 1/1/2000**.
   d. Save and accept the changes, then open the Members table in Datasheet View.
   e. Test the Validation Text and Validation Rule properties by tabbing to the Birthdate field and entering a date after 1/1/2000 such as 1/1/2001. Click OK when prompted with the Validation Text message, press [Esc] to remove the invalid Birthdate field entry, then close the Members table.
9. **Create Attachment fields.**
   a. Open the Members table in Design View, then add a new field after the Gender field with the field name **Photo** and an Attachment data type. Save the table.
   b. Display the Members table in Datasheet View, then attach a .jpg file of yourself to the record. If you do not have a .jpg file of yourself, use the **Member1.jpg** file provided in the drive and folder where you store your Data Files.
   c. Close the Members table.
   d. Use the Form Wizard to create a form based on all of the fields in the Members table. Use a Columnar layout, and title the form **Member Entry Form**.
   e. If requested by your instructor, print the first record in the Members Entry Form that shows the picture you just entered in the Photo field, then close the form.
   f. Close the Service-E.accdb database, then exit Access.

Independent Challenge 1

As the manager of a music store's instrument rental program, you decide to create a database to track rentals to schoolchildren. The fields you need to track are organized with four tables: Instruments, Rentals, Customers, and Schools.

a. Start Access, then create a new blank database called **Music-E** in the folder where you store your Data Files.

b. Use Table Design View or the Fields tab on the Ribbon of Table Datasheet View to create the four tables in the MusicStore-E database using the information shown in Figure E-22. The primary key field for each table is identified with bold text.

c. Enter **>1/1/2011** as the Validation Rule property for the RentalStartDate field of the Rentals table. This change allows only dates later than 1/1/2011, the start date for this business, to be entered into this field.

d. Enter **Rental start dates must be after January 1, 2011** as the Validation Text property to the RentalStartDate field of the Rentals table. Note that Access adds pound signs (#) to the date criteria entered in the Validation Rule as soon as you enter the Validation Text property.

e. Save and close the Rentals table.

f. Open the Relationships window, add the Instruments, Rentals, Customers, and Schools tables to the window, and create one-to-many relationships as shown in Figure E-23. Be sure to enforce referential integrity on each relationship.

g. Preview the Relationships report, add your name as a label to the Report Header section, then print the report, if requested by your instructor, making sure that all fields of each table are visible.

h. Save the Relationships report with the default name, and close it. Save and close the Relationships window.

i. Close the Music-E.accdb database, then exit Access.

FIGURE E-22

table	field name	data type
Rentals	**RentalNo**	**AutoNumber**
	CustNo	Number
	SerialNo	Text
	RentalStartDate	Date/Time
Customers	FirstName	Text
	LastName	Text
	Street	Text
	City	Text
	State	Text
	Zip	Text
	CustNo	**AutoNumber**
	SchoolCode	Text
Instruments	Description	Text
	SerialNo	**Text**
	MonthlyFee	Currency
Schools	SchoolName	Text
	SchoolCode	**Text**

FIGURE E-23

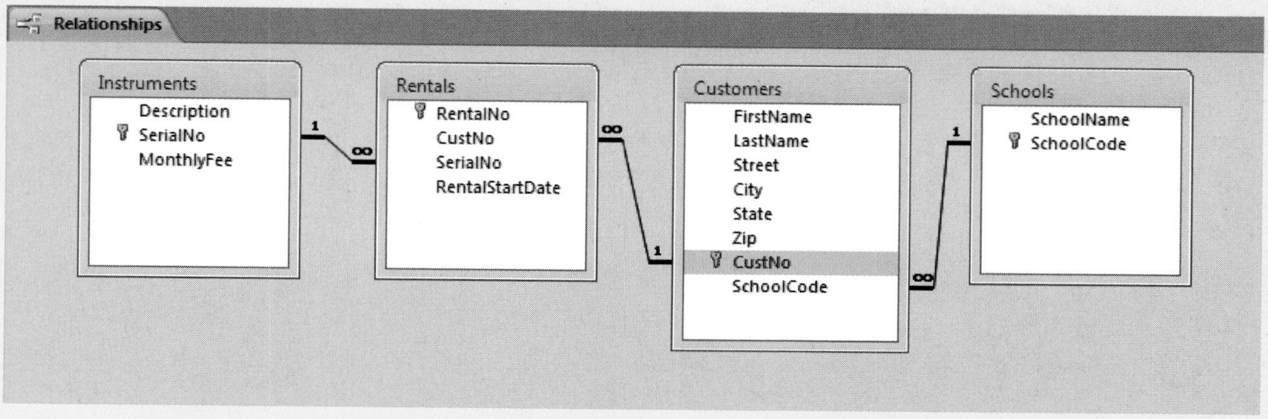

Independent Challenge 2

You want to create a database that documents blood bank donations by the employees of your company. You want to track information such as employee name, department, blood type, date of donation, and the hospital where the employee chooses to receive the donation. You also want to track basic hospital information, such as the hospital name and address.

a. Start Access, then create a new database called **BloodDrive-E** in the drive and folder where you store your Data Files.

b. Create an **Employees** table with fields and appropriate data types to record the automatic employee ID, employee first name, employee last name, and blood type. Make the employee ID field the primary key field.

c. Add Lookup properties to the blood type field in the Employees table to provide only valid blood type entries of **A+**, **A–**, **B+**, **B–**, **O+**, **O–**, **AB+**, and **AB–** for this field.

d. Create a **Donations** table with fields and appropriate data types to record an automatic donation ID, date of the donation, and an employee ID field to serve as a foreign key field. Make the donation ID the primary key field.

e. Create a **Hospitals** table with fields and appropriate data types to record a hospital code, donation ID (foreign key field), hospital name, street, city, state, and zip. Make the hospital code field the primary key field.

f. In the Relationships window, create a one-to-many relationship with referential integrity between the Employees and Donations table, using the common EmployeeID field.

g. In the Relationships window, create a one-to-many relationship with referential integrity between the Donations and Hospitals table, using the common DonationID field. The final Relationships window is shown in Figure E-24. (Your field names might differ.)

h. Preview the Relationships report, add your name as a label to the Report Header section, then print the report if requested by your instructor, making sure that all fields of each table are visible.

i. Save the Relationships report with the default name, and close it. Save and close the Relationships window.

j. Close BloodDrive-E.accdb, then exit Access.

FIGURE E-24

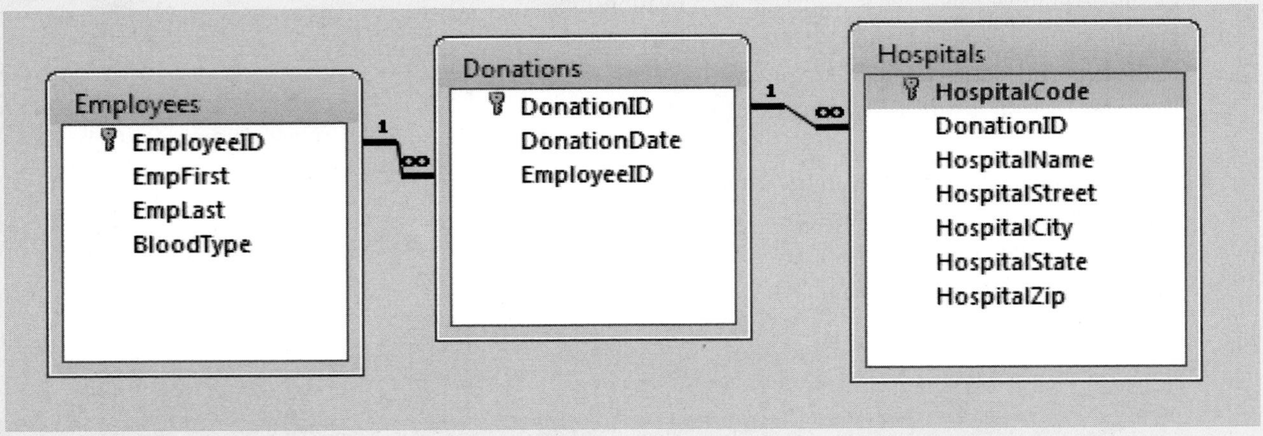

Independent Challenge 3

This Independent Challenge requires an Internet connection.

You're a member and manager of a recreational baseball team and decide to create an Access database to manage player information, games, and batting statistics.

a. Start Access, then create a new database called **Baseball-E** in the drive and folder where you store your Data Files.

b. Create a **Players** table with fields and appropriate data types to record the player first name, last name, and uniform number. Make the uniform number field the primary key field.

c. Create a **Games** table with fields and appropriate data types to record an automatic game number, date of the game, opponent's name, home score, and visitor score. Make the game number field the primary key field.

d. Create an **AtBats** table with fields and appropriate data types to record hits, at bats, the game number, and the uniform number of each player. The game number and uniform number fields will both be foreign key fields. This table does not need a primary key field.

e. In the Relationships window, create a one-to-many relationship with referential integrity between the Games and AtBats table, using the common game number field.

f. In the Relationships window, create a one-to-many relationship with referential integrity between the Players and AtBats table, using the common uniform number field. The final Relationships window is shown in Figure E-25. (Your field names might differ.)

FIGURE E-25

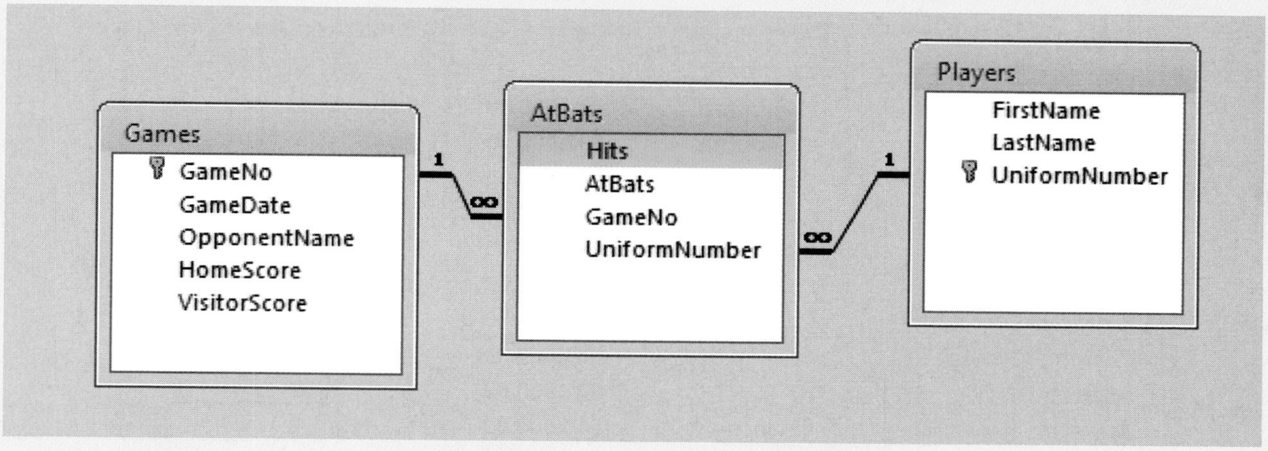

g. Preview the Relationships report, add your name as a label to the Report Header section, then print the report, if requested by your instructor, making sure that all fields of each table are visible.

h. Save the Relationships report with the default name, and close it. Save and close the Relationships window.

Advanced Challenge Exercise

ACE

- Enter your own name into the Players table, using **1** as the value for the UniformNumber field. Using an Internet search tool, find the roster for a baseball team in your area, and enter eight more baseball players into the Players table. Close the Players table.
- Research the games that this team has previously played, and enter one game record into the Games table. Close the Games table.
- Open the Players table and use subdatasheets to enter Hits and AtBats for GameNo 1 for each of the nine players. Your entries need not represent a real game, but they should be realistic. (*Hint*: Most players bat three or four times per game. A player cannot have more hits in a game than at bats.) In other words, each player will have one record in its subdatasheet that represents that player's batting statistics for GameNo 1.

i. Close the Baseball-E.accdb database, then exit Access.

Real Life Independent Challenge

An Access database can help record and track your job search efforts. In this exercise, you will modify two fields in the Positions table in your JobSearch database with Lookup properties to make data entry easier, more efficient, and more accurate.

a. Start Access, open the JobSearch-E.accdb database from the drive and folder where you store your Data Files, then enable content if prompted.

b. Open the Positions table in Design View. Click the EmployerID field, then start the Lookup Wizard.

c. In this situation, you want the EmployerID field in the Positions table to look up both the EmployerID and the CompanyName fields from the Employers table, so leave the "I want the lookup field to get the values from another table or query" option button selected.

d. The Employers table contains the fields you need. Select both the EmployerID field and the CompanyName field. Sort the records in ascending order by the CompanyName field.

e. Deselect the "Hide key column" check box so that you can see the data in both the EmployerID and CompanyName fields.

f. Choose EmployerID as the field to store values in and EmployerID as the label for the Lookup field. Click Yes when prompted to save relationships.

g. Save the table, and test the EmployerID field in Datasheet View. You should see both the EmployerID field as well as the CompanyName field in the drop-down list as shown in Figure E-26.

FIGURE E-26

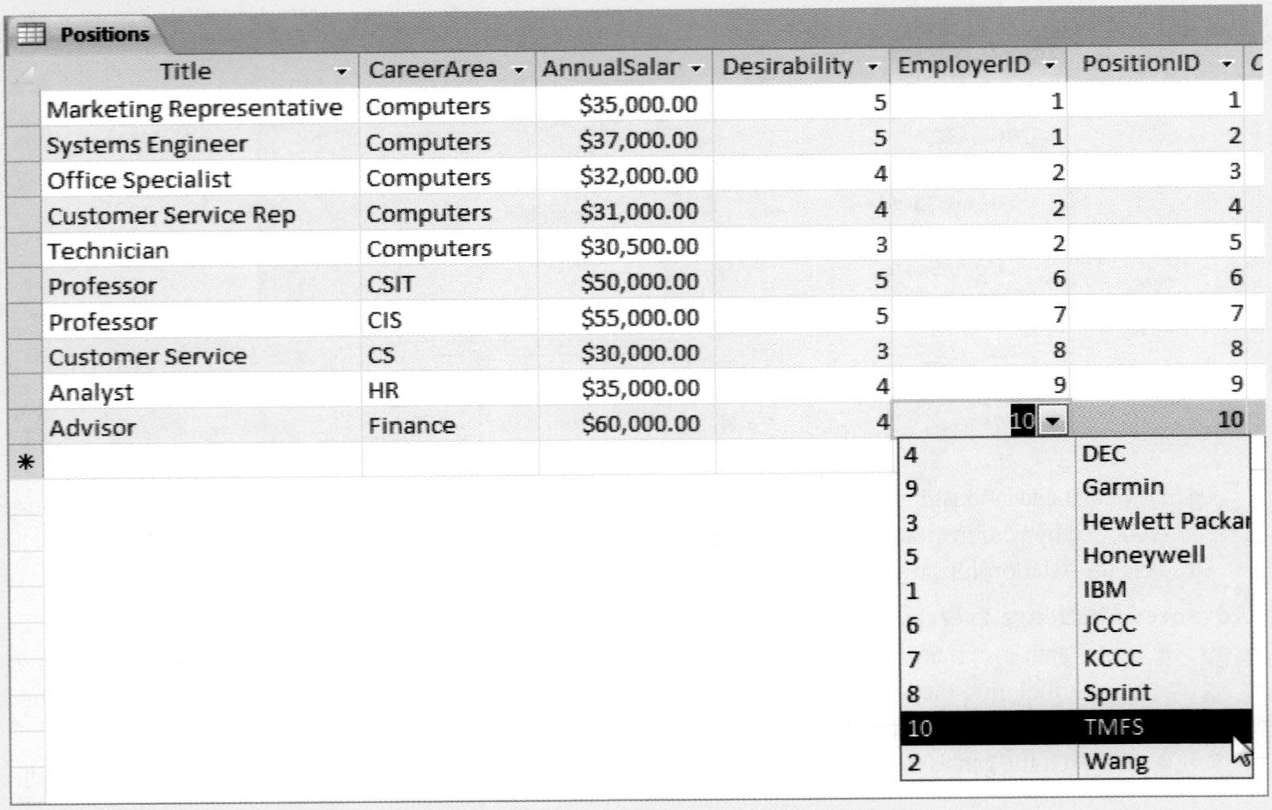

Positions

Title	CareerArea	AnnualSalar	Desirability	EmployerID	PositionID
Marketing Representative	Computers	$35,000.00	5	1	1
Systems Engineer	Computers	$37,000.00	5	1	2
Office Specialist	Computers	$32,000.00	4	2	3
Customer Service Rep	Computers	$31,000.00	4	2	4
Technician	Computers	$30,500.00	3	2	5
Professor	CSIT	$50,000.00	5	6	6
Professor	CIS	$55,000.00	5	7	7
Customer Service	CS	$30,000.00	3	8	8
Analyst	HR	$35,000.00	4	9	9
Advisor	Finance	$60,000.00	4	10	10

4	DEC
9	Garmin
3	Hewlett Packar
5	Honeywell
1	IBM
6	JCCC
7	KCCC
8	Sprint
10	TMFS
2	Wang

Real Life Independent Challenge (continued)

h. Return to Design View, click the Desirability field, and start the Lookup Wizard. This field stores the values 1 through 5 as a desirability rating. You will manually enter those values so choose the "I will type in the values that I want" option button.

i. Enter **1**, **2**, **3**, **4**, and **5** in the Col1 column, and accept the Desirability label for the Lookup field.

j. Save the table, and test the Desirability field in Datasheet View. You should see a drop-down list with the values 1, 2, 3, 4, and 5 in the list as shown in Figure E-27.

FIGURE E-27

Positions

	Title	CareerArea	AnnualSalar	Desirability	EmployerID	PositionID
	Marketing Representative	Computers	$35,000.00	5	1	1
	Systems Engineer	Computers	$37,000.00	5	1	2
	Office Specialist	Computers	$32,000.00	4	2	3
	Customer Service Rep	Computers	$31,000.00	4	2	4
	Technician	Computers	$30,500.00	3	2	5
	Professor	CSIT	$50,000.00	5	6	6
	Professor	CIS	$55,000.00	5	7	7
	Customer Service	CS	$30,000.00	3	8	8
	Analyst	HR	$35,000.00	4	9	9
	Advisor	Finance	$60,000.00	4	10	10
*						(New)

Drop-down list: 1, 2, 3, 4, 5

Real Life Independent Challenge (continued)

k. Return to Design View and modify the Limit To List Lookup property on the Lookup tab in the Field Properties pane for both the Desirability as well as the EmployerID fields to Yes.

l. Save the table, and test the Desirability and EmployerID fields. You should not be able to make any entries in those fields that are not presented in the list.

m. Close the Positions table, and open the Relationships window.

n. Double-click the link line created by the Lookup Wizard between the Employers and Positions tables, click Enforce Referential Integrity, then click OK. Your Relationships window should look like Figure E-28.

FIGURE E-28

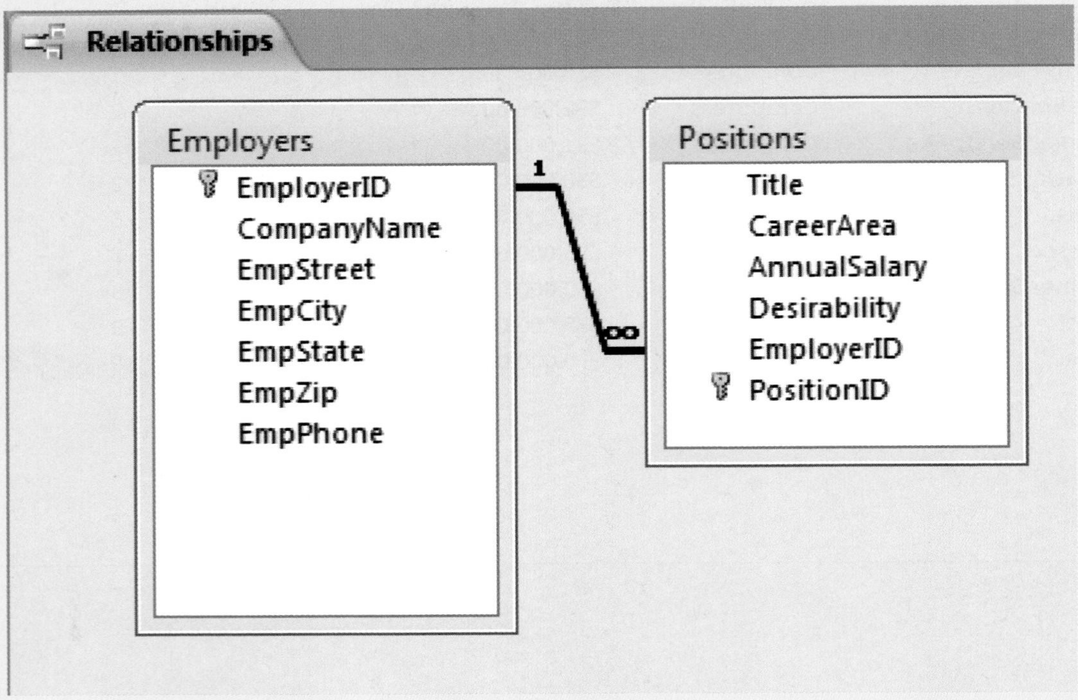

Real Life Independent Challenge (continued)

Advanced Challenge Exercise

- Use the Form Wizard to create a form/subform with all of the fields from both the Employers and Positions tables.
- View the data by Employers, and use a Datasheet layout for the subform.
- Title the form **Employers Entry Form** and the subform **Positions Subform**. View the form in Form View.
- In Form Design View, use your skills to move, resize, align, and edit the controls as shown in Figure E-29.
- Add a new record to the subform for the first company, IBM. Use realistic but fictitious data. Note that the EmployerID and PositionID values are automatically entered.

FIGURE E-29

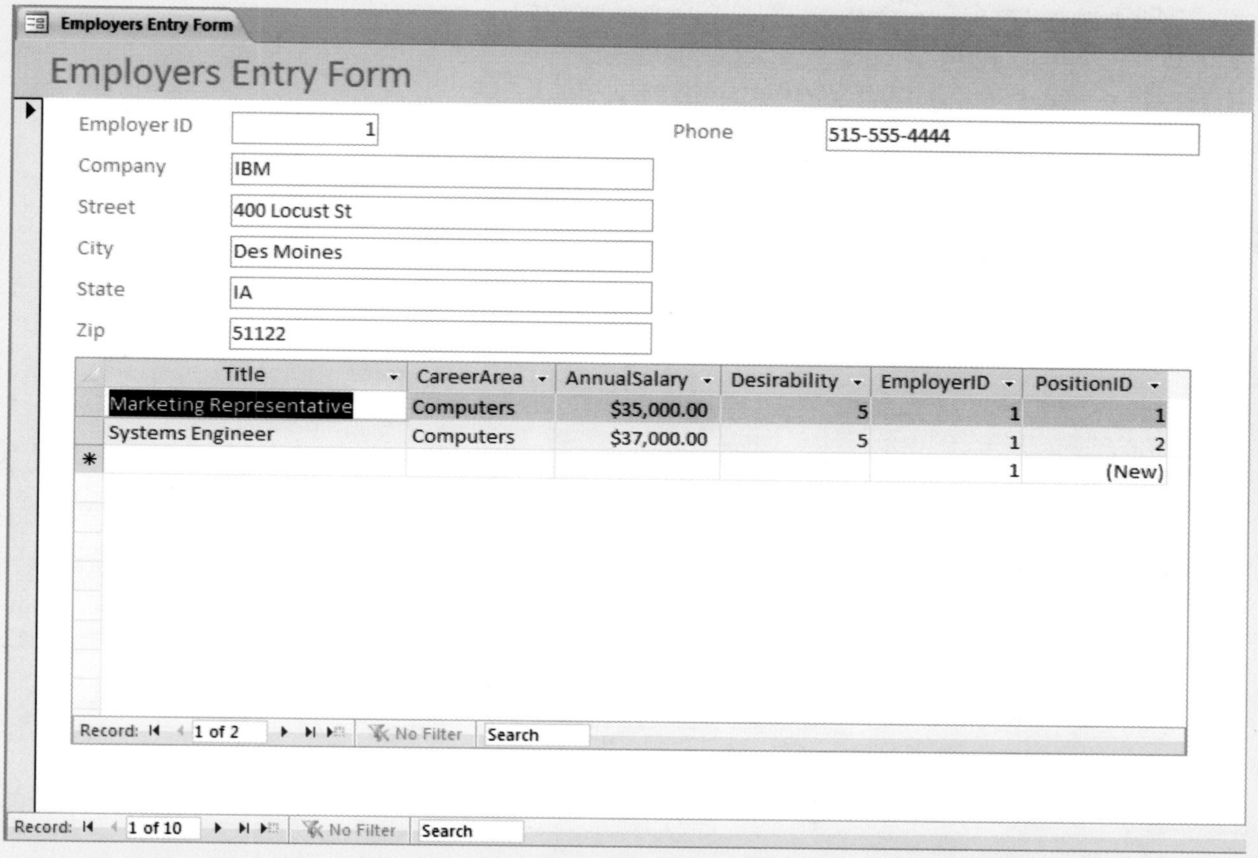

o. Save and close the Relationships window. Save and close the JobSearch-E.accdb database, and exit Access.

Visual Workshop

Open the Training-E.accdb database from the drive and folder where you store your Data Files, then enable content if prompted. Create a new table called **Vendors** using the Table Design View shown in Figure E-30 to determine field names and data types. Make the following property changes: Change the Field Size property of the VState field to **2**, the VZip field to **9**, and VPhone field to **10**. Change the Field Size property of the VendorName, VStreet, and VCity fields to **30**. Apply a Phone Number Input Mask to the VPhone field. Be sure to specify that the VendorID field is the primary key field. Relate the tables in the Training-E database as shown in Figure E-31, then view the Relationships report in landscape view. Move the tables in the Relationships window as needed so that the relationships printout fits on a single piece of paper. Add your name as a label to the Report Header section to document the Relationships report.

FIGURE E-30

Vendors

Field Name	Data Type
VendorID	AutoNumber
VendorName	Text
VStreet	Text
VCity	Text
VState	Text
VZip	Text
VPhone	Text

FIGURE E-31

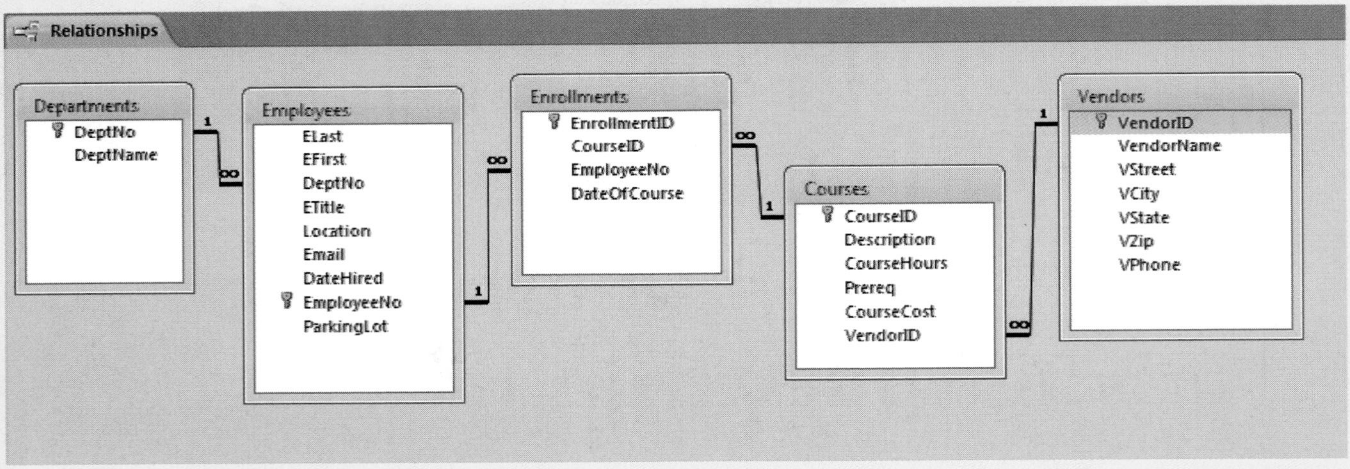

UNIT F
Access 2010

Improving Queries

Files You Will Need:

QuestTravel-F.accdb
Service-F.accdb
MusicStore-F.accdb
RealEstate-F.accdb
Scholarship-F.accdb
Training-F.accdb

Queries are database objects that organize fields from one or more tables into a single datasheet. A **select query**, the most common type of query, retrieves fields from related tables and displays records in a datasheet. Select queries are used to select only certain records from a database. They can also sort records, calculate new fields of data, or calculate statistics such as the sum or average of a given field. You can also present data selected by a query in PivotTable View or PivotChart View. These views display information about summarized groups of records in a crosstabular report or graph. The Quest database has been updated to contain more customers, tours, and sales. You help Samantha Hooper, a Quest tour developer for U.S. travel, create queries to analyze this information.

OBJECTIVES

- Create multitable queries
- Apply sorts and view SQL
- Develop AND criteria
- Develop OR criteria
- Create calculated fields
- Build summary queries
- Build crosstab queries
- Build PivotTables and PivotCharts

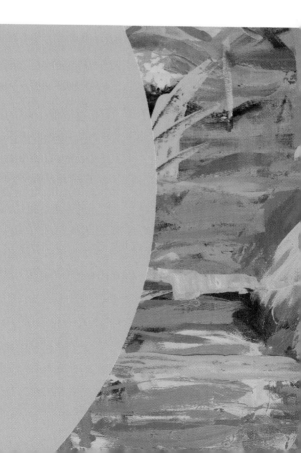

UNIT F

Access 2010

Creating Multitable Queries

You can create multitable queries by using the Simple Query Wizard, or you can start from scratch in Query Design View. **Query Design View** gives you more options for selecting and presenting information. When you open (or **run**) a query, the fields and records that you selected for the query are presented in **Query Datasheet View**, also called a logical view of the data. You can enter, edit, and delete data in the datasheet of a **select query**, the most common type of query, which selects fields and records from one or more tables. Samantha Hooper asks you to create a query to analyze customer payments. You select fields from the Customers, Tours, Sales, and Payments tables to answer this question.

STEPS

1. **Start Access, open the QuestTravel-F.accdb database from the drive and folder where you store your Data Files, then enable content if prompted**
2. **Click the Create tab on the Ribbon, then click the Query Design button in the Queries group**
   The Show Table dialog box opens and lists all the tables in the database.
3. **Double-click Customers, double-click Sales, double-click Tours, double-click Payments, then click Close**
   Recall that the upper pane of Query Design View displays the fields for each of the selected tables in field lists. The name of the table is shown in the field list title bar. Primary key fields are identified with a small key icon. Relationships between tables are displayed with **one-to-many join lines** that connect the linking fields. You select the fields you want by adding them to the query design grid.

> **TROUBLE**
> If you add a table to Query Design View twice by mistake, click the title bar of the extra field list, then press [Delete].

4. **Double-click FName field in the Customers table field list to add this field to the first column of the query design grid, double-click LName, double-click TourName in the Tours field list, double-click Cost in the Tours field list, double-click PaymentDate in the Payments field list, then double-click PaymentAmt as shown in Figure F-1**
   When you *double-click* a field in a field list, it is automatically added as the next field in the query grid. When you *drag* a field to the query design grid, any existing fields move to the right to accommodate the new field.

> **TROUBLE**
> Drag the bottom edge of the Tours field list down to resize it.

5. **Click the View button in the Results group to run the query and display the query datasheet**
   The resulting datasheet looks like Figure F-2. The datasheet shows the six fields selected in Query Design View: FName and LName from the Customers table, TourName and Cost from the Tours table, and PaymentDate and PaymentAmt from the Payments table. The datasheet displays 80 records because 80 different payments have been made. Some of the payments are from the same customer. For example, Christine Collins has made payments on multiple tours. The American Heritage Tour is also repeated because it has been sold to many customers who have made many payments. Christine's last name has changed to Rogers.
6. **Double-click any occurrence of Collins, type Rogers, then click another record**
   Because Christine's data is physically stored in only one record in the Customers table (but selected multiple times in this query because Christine has made many payments), changing any occurrence of her last name automatically updates all other selections of that data in this query, and throughout all other queries, forms, and reports in the database, too.

FIGURE F-1: **Query design view with six fields in the query design grid**

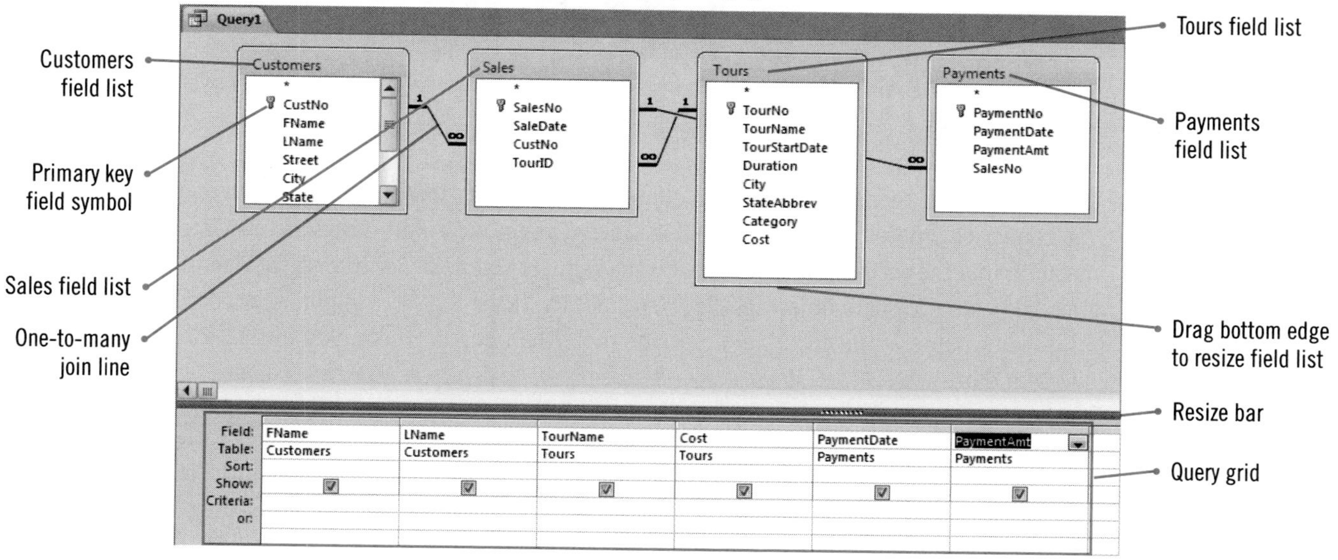
Customers field list
Primary key field symbol
Sales field list
One-to-many join line
Tours field list
Payments field list
Drag bottom edge to resize field list
Resize bar
Query grid
Query1
Customers
CustNo
FName
LName
Street
City
State
Sales
SalesNo
SaleDate
CustNo
TourID
Tours
TourNo
TourName
TourStartDate
Duration
City
StateAbbrev
Category
Cost
Payments
PaymentNo
PaymentDate
PaymentAmt
SalesNo
Field: FName, LName, TourName, Cost, PaymentDate, PaymentAmt
Table: Customers, Customers, Tours, Tours, Payments, Payments
Sort:
Show:
Criteria:
or:

FIGURE F-2: **Query datasheet showing related information**

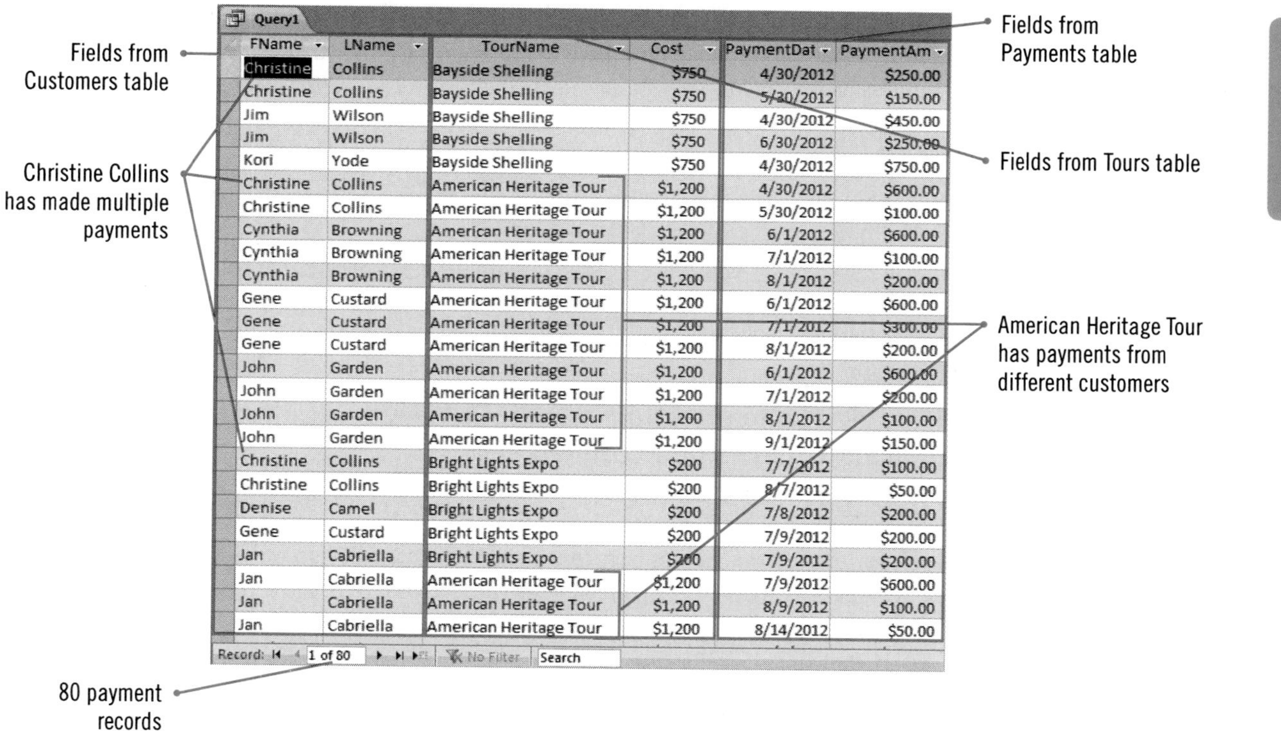
Fields from Customers table
Christine Collins has made multiple payments
80 payment records
Fields from Payments table
Fields from Tours table
American Heritage Tour has payments from different customers
Query1
Record: 1 of 80
No Filter
Search

FName	LName	TourName	Cost	PaymentDat	PaymentAm
Christine	Collins	Bayside Shelling	$750	4/30/2012	$250.00
Christine	Collins	Bayside Shelling	$750	5/30/2012	$150.00
Jim	Wilson	Bayside Shelling	$750	4/30/2012	$450.00
Jim	Wilson	Bayside Shelling	$750	6/30/2012	$250.00
Kori	Yode	Bayside Shelling	$750	4/30/2012	$750.00
Christine	Collins	American Heritage Tour	$1,200	4/30/2012	$600.00
Christine	Collins	American Heritage Tour	$1,200	5/30/2012	$100.00
Cynthia	Browning	American Heritage Tour	$1,200	6/1/2012	$600.00
Cynthia	Browning	American Heritage Tour	$1,200	7/1/2012	$100.00
Cynthia	Browning	American Heritage Tour	$1,200	8/1/2012	$200.00
Gene	Custard	American Heritage Tour	$1,200	6/1/2012	$600.00
Gene	Custard	American Heritage Tour	$1,200	7/1/2012	$300.00
Gene	Custard	American Heritage Tour	$1,200	8/1/2012	$200.00
John	Garden	American Heritage Tour	$1,200	6/1/2012	$600.00
John	Garden	American Heritage Tour	$1,200	7/1/2012	$200.00
John	Garden	American Heritage Tour	$1,200	8/1/2012	$100.00
John	Garden	American Heritage Tour	$1,200	9/1/2012	$150.00
Christine	Collins	Bright Lights Expo	$200	7/7/2012	$100.00
Christine	Collins	Bright Lights Expo	$200	8/7/2012	$50.00
Denise	Camel	Bright Lights Expo	$200	7/8/2012	$200.00
Gene	Custard	Bright Lights Expo	$200	7/9/2012	$200.00
Jan	Cabriella	Bright Lights Expo	$200	7/9/2012	$200.00
Jan	Cabriella	American Heritage Tour	$1,200	7/9/2012	$600.00
Jan	Cabriella	American Heritage Tour	$1,200	8/9/2012	$100.00
Jan	Cabriella	American Heritage Tour	$1,200	8/14/2012	$50.00

Deleting a field from the query grid

If you add the wrong field to the query design grid, you can delete it by clicking the field selector, a thin gray bar above each field name, then pressing [Delete]. Deleting a field from the query design grid removes it from the logical view of this query's datasheet, but does not delete the field from the database. A field is defined and the field's contents are stored in a table object only.

UNIT F

Access 2010

Applying Sorts and Viewing SQL

Sorting refers to reordering records in either ascending or descending order based on the values in a field. You can specify more than one sort field in Query Design View. Sort orders are evaluated from left to right, meaning that the sort field on the far left is the primary sort field. Sort orders defined in Query Design View are saved with the query object. You want to list the records in alphabetical order based on the customer's last name. If the customer has made more than one payment, you further sort the records by the payment date.

STEPS

1. **Click the View button on the Home tab to return to Query Design View**
   To sort the records by last name then by payment date, the LName field must be the primary sort field, and the PaymentDate field must be the secondary sort field.
2. **Click the LName field Sort cell in the query design grid, click the Sort list arrow, click Ascending, click the PaymentDate field Sort cell in the query design grid, click the Sort list arrow, then click Ascending**
   The resulting query design grid should look like Figure F-3.
3. **Click the View button in the Results group to display the query datasheet**
   The records of the datasheet are now listed in ascending order based on the values in the LName field. When the same value appears in the LName field, the records are further sorted by the secondary sort field, PaymentDate, as shown in Figure F-4. Jill Alman made two payments, one on 7/11/2012 and the next on 7/23/2012.
4. **Click the Save button on the Quick Access toolbar, type CustomerPayments in the Save As dialog box, then click OK**
   When you save a query, you save a logical view of the data, a selection of fields and records from underlying tables. Technically, when you save a query, you are saving a set of instructions written in **Structured Query Language (SQL)**, which selects the data from tables. You can view the SQL code for any query by switching to **SQL View**.
5. **Click the View button list arrow, click SQL View, then click in the lower part of the SQL window to deselect the code**
   The SQL statements shown in Figure F-5 determine what fields are selected after the **SELECT** keyword, how the tables are joined after the **FROM** keyword, and how the resulting records are sorted after the **ORDER BY** keyword. Fortunately, you do not have to write or understand SQL to use Access or select data from multiple tables. The easy-to-use Query Design View gives you a way to select and sort data from underlying tables without being an SQL programmer.
6. **Close the CustomerPayments query**

QUICK TIP
You can resize the columns of a datasheet by pointing to the right column border that separates the field names, then dragging left or right to resize the columns. Double-click ✥ to automatically adjust the column width to fit the widest entry.

QUICK TIP
SQL keywords such as SELECT or FROM should not be used as field names.

FIGURE F-3: **Specifying multiple sort orders in Query Design View**

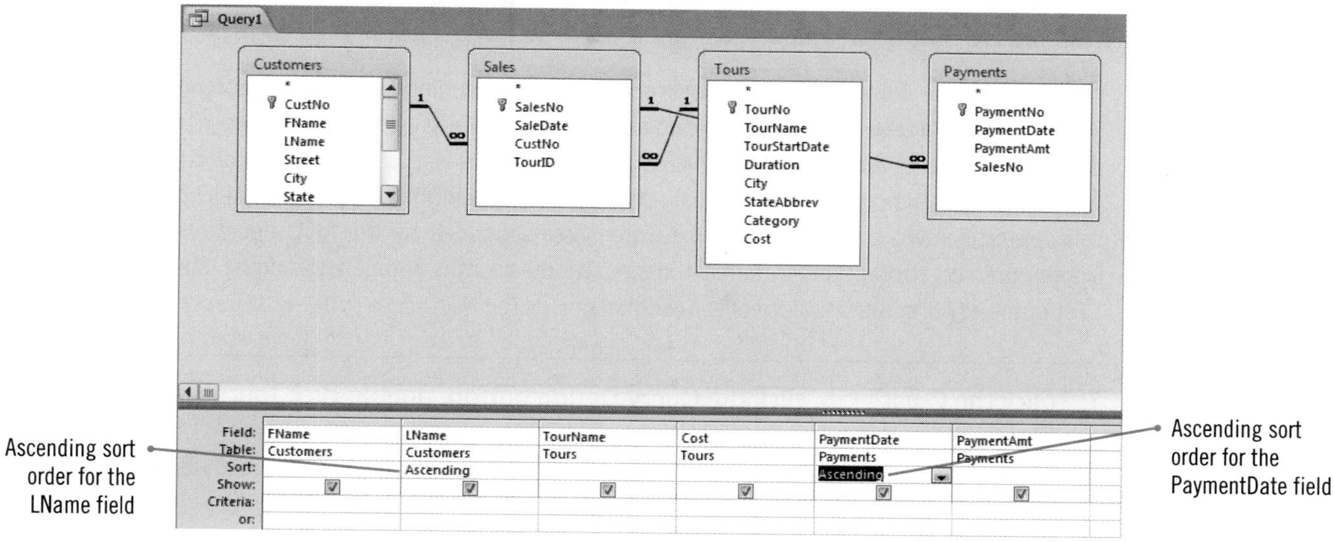
Query1
Customers
CustNo
FName
LName
Street
City
State
Sales
SalesNo
SaleDate
CustNo
TourID
Tours
TourNo
TourName
TourStartDate
Duration
City
StateAbbrev
Category
Cost
Payments
PaymentNo
PaymentDate
PaymentAmt
SalesNo
Field:
Table:
Sort:
Show:
Criteria:
or:
FName
Customers
LName
Customers
Ascending
TourName
Tours
Cost
Tours
PaymentDate
Payments
Ascending
PaymentAmt
Payments
Ascending sort order for the LName field
Ascending sort order for the PaymentDate field

FIGURE F-4: **Records sorted by LName, then by PaymentDate**

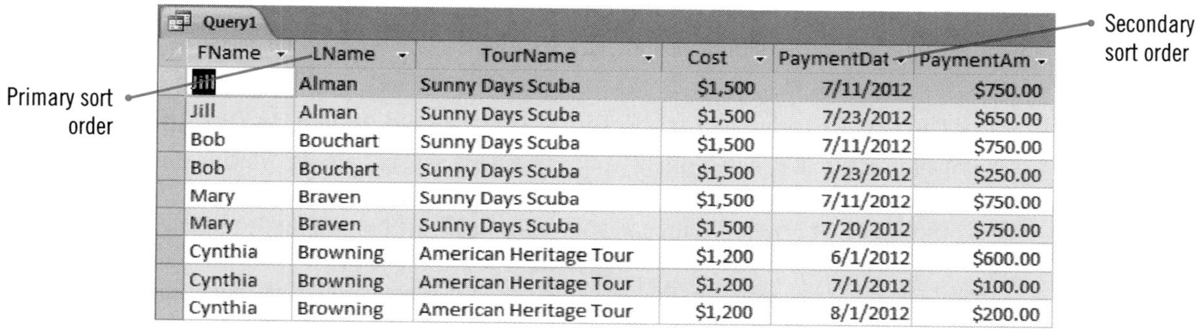
Query1
Primary sort order
Secondary sort order

FName	LName	TourName	Cost	PaymentDat	PaymentAm
Jill	Alman	Sunny Days Scuba	$1,500	7/11/2012	$750.00
Jill	Alman	Sunny Days Scuba	$1,500	7/23/2012	$650.00
Bob	Bouchart	Sunny Days Scuba	$1,500	7/11/2012	$750.00
Bob	Bouchart	Sunny Days Scuba	$1,500	7/23/2012	$250.00
Mary	Braven	Sunny Days Scuba	$1,500	7/11/2012	$750.00
Mary	Braven	Sunny Days Scuba	$1,500	7/20/2012	$750.00
Cynthia	Browning	American Heritage Tour	$1,200	6/1/2012	$600.00
Cynthia	Browning	American Heritage Tour	$1,200	7/1/2012	$100.00
Cynthia	Browning	American Heritage Tour	$1,200	8/1/2012	$200.00

FIGURE F-5: **SQL View**

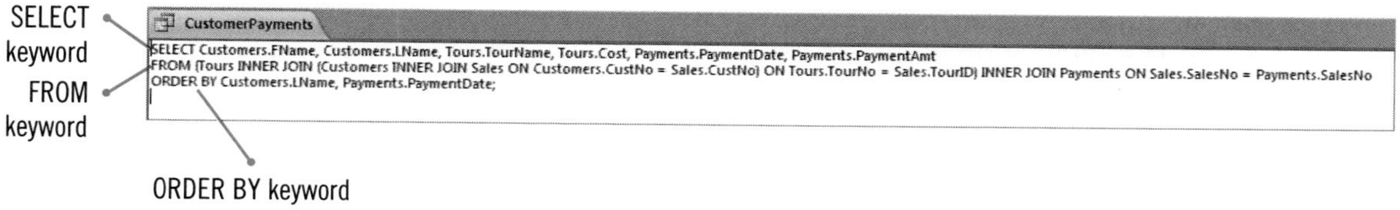
CustomerPayments
SELECT Customers.FName, Customers.LName, Tours.TourName, Tours.Cost, Payments.PaymentDate, Payments.PaymentAmt
FROM (Tours INNER JOIN (Customers INNER JOIN Sales ON Customers.CustNo = Sales.CustNo) ON Tours.TourNo = Sales.TourID) INNER JOIN Payments ON Sales.SalesNo = Payments.SalesNo
ORDER BY Customers.LName, Payments.PaymentDate;
SELECT keyword
FROM keyword
ORDER BY keyword

Specifying a sort order different from the field order in the datasheet

If your database has several customers with the same last name, you can include a secondary sort on the first name field to distinguish the customers. If you want to display the fields in a different order from which they are sorted, you can use the solution shown in Figure F-6. Add a field to the query design grid twice, once to select for the datasheet, and once to use as a sort order. Use the Show check box to unselect the field used as a sort order.

FIGURE F-6: **Sorting on a field that is not displayed**

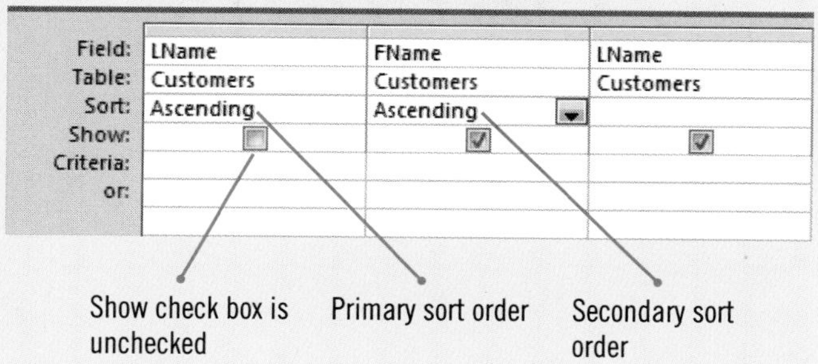
Field:
Table:
Sort:
Show:
Criteria:
or:
LName
Customers
Ascending
FName
Customers
Ascending
LName
Customers
Show check box is unchecked
Primary sort order
Secondary sort order

Access 2010

UNIT
F
Access 2010

Developing AND Criteria

You can limit the number of records that appear on the resulting datasheet by entering criteria in Query Design View. **Criteria** are tests, or limiting conditions, that must be true for the record to be selected for a datasheet. To create **AND criteria**, which means the query selects a record only if *all* criteria are true, enter two or more criteria on the same Criteria row of the query design grid. To create AND criteria for the same field, enter the two criteria in the *same* Criteria cell separated by the AND operator. Samantha Hooper predicts strong sales for family tours during the months of June and August. She asks you to create a list of the existing tours that meet those criteria.

STEPS

1. **Click the Create tab, click the Query Design button, double-click Tours, then click the Close button**

   To query for family tours, you need to add the Category field to the query grid. In addition, you want to know the tour name and start date.

2. **Resize the Tours field list to display all fields, double-click the TourName field, double-click the TourStartDate field, then double-click the Category field**

   To find tours in the Family category, you need to add a criterion for this field in the query grid.

3. **Click the first Criteria cell for the Category field, then type family**

   To find all tours in the month of June, use the asterisk (*) wildcard character in the day portion of the TourStartDate criterion.

4. **Click the first Criteria cell for the TourStartDate field, type 6/*/2012, then press [↓]**

   As shown in Figure F-7, Access assists you with criteria syntax, rules by which criteria need to be entered. Access automatically adds quotation marks around text criteria in Text fields such as "family" in the Category field. The criteria in Number, Currency, and Yes/No fields are not surrounded by any characters. Access also adds the Like operator to the TourStartDate field criterion because it includes the asterisk wildcard character. (Access uses the Like operator to find values in a field that match the pattern you specify.) See Table F-1 for more information on common Access comparison operators and criteria syntax.

5. **Click the Save button on the Quick Access toolbar, type FamilyJune in the Save As dialog box, click OK, then click the View button to view the query results**

   The query results are shown in Figure F-8.

6. **Close the FamilyJune datasheet**

QUICK TIP

Criteria are not case sensitive, so *family*, *Family*, and *FAMILY* are equivalent criteria entries.

FIGURE F-7: **Entering AND criteria on the same row**

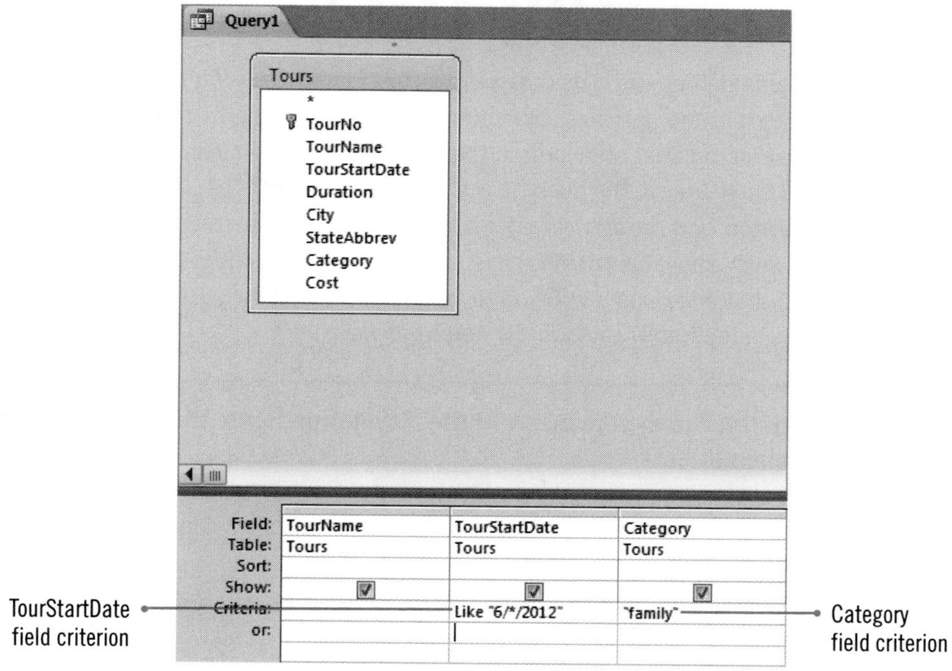

FIGURE F-8: **Datasheet for FamilyJune records**

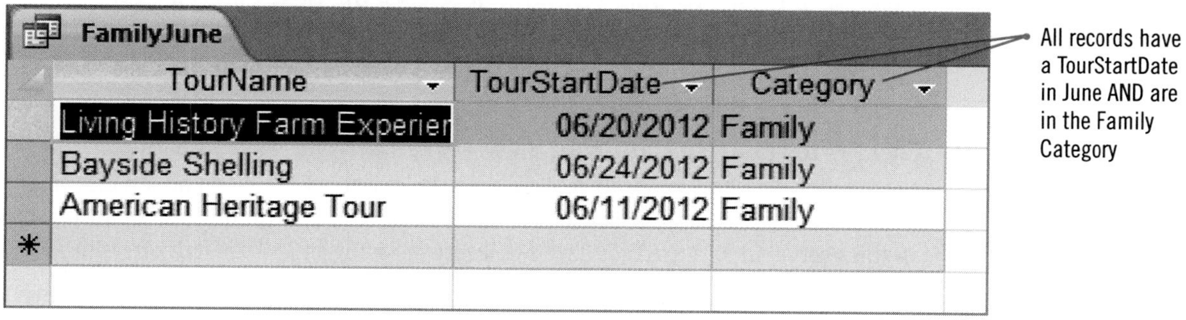

TABLE F-1: **Common comparison operators**

operator	description	example	result
>	Greater than	>50	Value exceeds 50
>=	Greater than or equal to	>=50	Value is 50 or greater
<	Less than	<50	Value is less than 50
<=	Less than or equal to	<=50	Value is 50 or less
<>	Not equal to	<>50	Value is any number other than 50
Between...And	Finds values between two numbers or dates	Between #2/2/2012# And #2/2/2013#	Dates between 2/2/2012 and 2/2/2013, inclusive
In	Finds a value that is one of a list	In ("IA","KS","NE")	Value equals IA or KS or NE
Null	Finds records that have no entry in a particular field	Null	No value has been entered in a field
Is Not Null	Finds records that have any entry in a particular field	Is Not Null	Any value has been entered in a field
Like	Finds records that match the criterion	Like "A*"	Value starts with A
Not	Finds records that do not match the criterion	Not 2	Numbers other than 2

UNIT
F
Access 2010

Developing OR Criteria

In a query, criteria define which records are selected for the resulting datasheet. AND criteria *narrow* the number of records in the datasheet by requiring that a record be true for multiple criteria. However, **OR criteria** *expand* the number of records in the datasheet because a record needs to be true for *only one* of the criteria. OR criteria mean the query selects records where *any one* criterion is true. You enter OR criteria in the query design grid on *different* criteria rows. Because each criteria row of the query design grid is evaluated separately, more OR criteria entries in the query grid produce more records for the resulting datasheet. Samantha Hooper asks you to modify the FamilyJune query to expand the number of records to include tours in the Family category for August as well.

STEPS

1. **Right-click the FamilyJune query in the Navigation Pane, then click Design View on the shortcut menu**
   To add OR criteria, you have to enter criteria in the next available "or" row of the query design grid. By default, the query grid displays eight rows for additional OR criteria, but you can add even more rows using the Insert Rows button on the Design tab.
2. **In the TourStartDate column, click the next Criteria cell, type 8/*/2012, then click the View button to display the datasheet**
   The datasheet expands from 3 to 12 records because all tours offered in August were added to the datasheet. To select only those August tours in the Family category, you need to add more criteria to Query Design View.
3. **Click to return to Query Design View, click the next Category Criteria cell, type family, then click elsewhere in the grid as shown in Figure F-9**
   Each criteria row is evaluated separately, which is why you must put the same "family" criterion for the Category field in *both* rows of the query design grid.
4. **Click to return to Datasheet View**
   The resulting datasheet selects six records, as shown in Figure F-10. When no sort order is applied, the records are sorted by the primary key field of the first table in the query (in this case, TourNo, which is not selected for this query). All of the records have a Category of Family and a TourStartDate value in June or August.
5. **Click the File tab, click Save Object As, type FamilyJuneAugust, click OK, then click the Home tab**
   The FamilyJuneAugust query is saved as a new query object.
6. **Close the FamilyJuneAugust query**
   The QuestTravel-F.accdb Navigation Pane displays the three queries you created plus the StateAnalysis query that was already in the database.

QUICK TIP
To rename an existing object, right-click it in the Navigation Pane, then choose Rename on the shortcut menu.

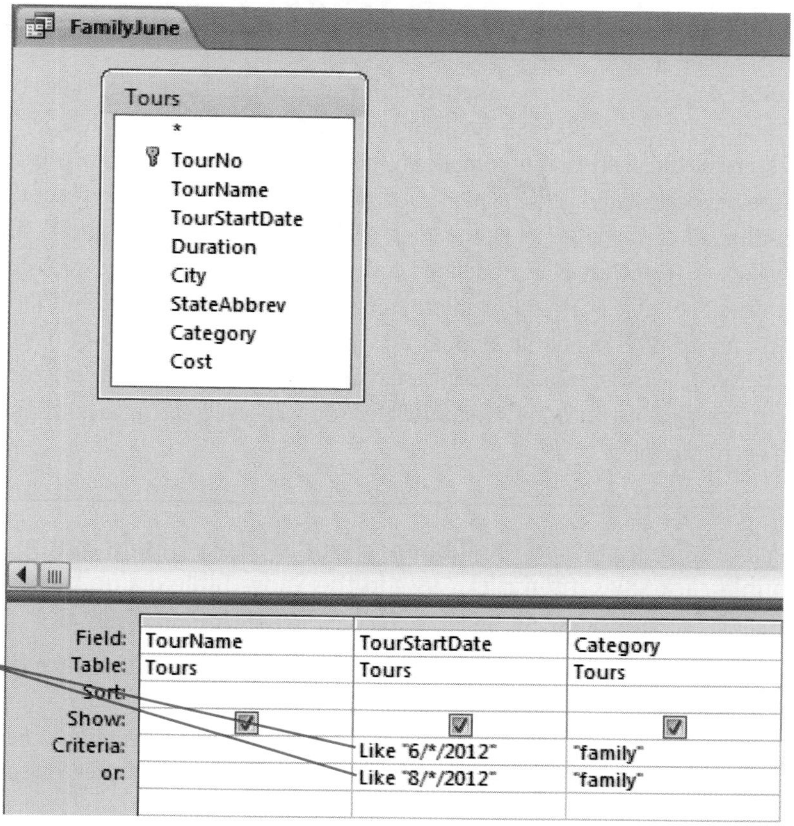

FIGURE F-9: Entering OR criteria on different rows

OR criteria is
entered on
different rows

Field:	TourName	TourStartDate	Category
Table:	Tours	Tours	Tours
Sort:			
Show:	☑	☑	☑
Criteria:		Like "6/*/2012"	"family"
or:		Like "8/*/2012"	"family"

FIGURE F-10: OR criteria adds more records to the datasheet

FamilyJune

Family tours
offered in June
and August

TourName	TourStartDate	Category
Shelling Expeditions	08/17/2012	Family
Living History Farm Experier	06/20/2012	Family
State Fair Campout	08/20/2012	Family
Table Rock Lake Days	08/20/2012	Family
Bayside Shelling	06/24/2012	Family
American Heritage Tour	06/11/2012	Family

Using wildcard characters in query criteria

To search for a pattern, use a **wildcard** character to represent any character in the criteria entry. Use a **question mark (?)** to search for any single character and an **asterisk (*)** to search for any number of characters. Wildcard characters are often used with the Like operator. For example, the criterion Like "10/*/2010" finds all dates in October of 2010, and the criterion Like "F*" finds all entries that start with the letter *F*.

UNIT F

Access 2010

Creating Calculated Fields

A **calculated field** is a field of data that can be created based on the values of other fields. For example, you can calculate the value for a Tax field by multiplying the value of the Sales field by a percentage. To create a calculated field and automatically populate every record with the correct value for that field, define the new calculated field in Query Design View using an expression that describes the calculation. An **expression** is a combination of field names, operators (such as +, –, /, and *), and functions that result in a single value. A **function** is a predefined formula that returns a value such as a subtotal, count, or the current date. See Table F-2 for more information on arithmetic operators and Table F-3 for more information on functions. Samantha Hooper asks you to find the number of days between the sale and the tour's start date. To determine this information, you can create a calculated field called LeadTime that subtracts the SaleDate from the TourStartDate. You will also create a calculation to determine the commission on each tour sale.

STEPS

1. **Click the Create tab on the Ribbon, click the Query Design button, double-click Tours, double-click Sales, then click Close in the Show Table dialog box**
   First, you add the fields to the grid that you want to display in the query.
2. **Double-click the TourName field, double-click the TourStartDate field, double-click the Cost field, then double-click the SaleDate field**
   You create a calculated field in the Field cell of the design grid by entering a new descriptive field name followed by a colon, then an expression. Field names you use in an expression must be surrounded by square brackets.
3. **Click the blank Field cell in the fifth column, type LeadTime:[TourStartDate]-[SaleDate], then drag the ✛ pointer on the right edge of the fifth column selector to the right to display the entire entry**
   You create another calculated field to determine the commission paid on each sale, which is calculated as 11% of the Cost field.
4. **Click the blank Field cell in the sixth column, then type Commission:[Cost]*0.11 as shown in Figure F-11**
   You view the datasheet to see the resulting calculated fields.
5. **Click the View button, press [Tab], type 7/26/12 in the TourStartDate field for the first record, press [Tab], type 1000 in the Cost field for the first record, then press [↓]**
   The resulting datasheet, with two calculated fields, is shown in Figure F-12. The LeadTime field is calculated correctly, showing the number of days between the TourStartDate and the SaleDate. The Commission field is also calculated correctly, multiplying the Cost value by 11%. Any change to a field value that is used in an expression for a calculated field automatically updates the result as the data is edited.
6. **Click the Save button on the Quick Access toolbar, type LeadTimesAndCommissions in the Save As dialog box, click OK, then close the datasheet**

QUICK TIP
To display a long entry in a field cell, you can also right-click the cell, then click Zoom.

TABLE F-2: **Arithmetic operators**

operator	description
+	Addition
–	Subtraction
*	Multiplication
/	Division
^	Exponentiation

FIGURE F-11: **Creating calculated fields**

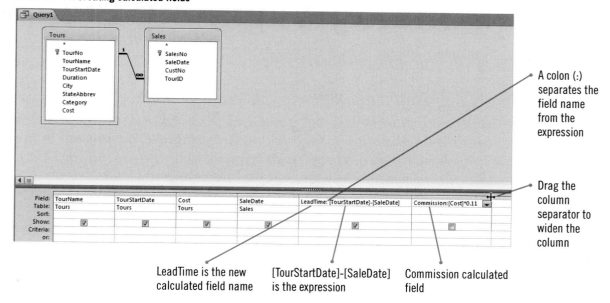

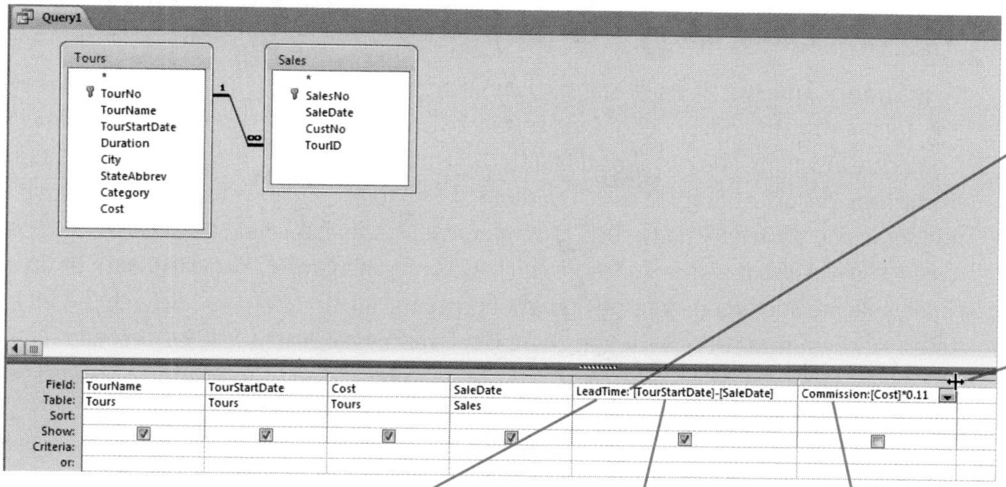

FIGURE F-12: **Viewing and testing the calculated fields**

TourName	TourStartDate	Cost	SaleDate	LeadTime	Commission
Bayside Shelling	07/26/2012	$1,000	4/30/2012	87	110
Bayside Shelling	07/26/2012	$1,000	5/1/2012	86	110
Bayside Shelling	07/26/2012	$1,000	5/2/2012	85	110
Sunny Days Scuba	07/24/2012	$1,500	7/11/2012	13	165
Sunny Days Scuba	07/24/2012	$1,500	7/14/2012	10	165
Sunny Days Scuba	07/24/2012	$1,500	7/16/2012	8	165
Sunny Days Scuba	07/24/2012	$1,500	7/17/2012	7	165
Sunny Days Scuba	07/24/2012	$1,500	7/18/2012	6	165
Cyclone Ski Club	01/20/2013	$850	7/11/2012	193	93.5
Cyclone Ski Club	01/20/2013	$850	7/12/2012	192	93.5
Cyclone Ski Club	01/20/2013	$850	7/30/2012	174	93.5
Cyclone Ski Club	01/20/2013	$850	7/13/2012	191	93.5
Cyclone Ski Club	01/20/2013	$850	8/13/2012	160	93.5
Boy Scout Troop 6	01/31/2013	$1,900	7/14/2012	201	209

TABLE F-3: **Common functions**

function	sample expression and description
DATE	DATE()-[BirthDate] Calculates the number of days between today and the date in the BirthDate field; Access expressions are not case sensitive, so DATE()-[BirthDate] is equivalent to date()-[birthdate] and DATE()-[BIRTHDATE]; therefore, use capitalization in expressions in any way that makes the expression easier to read
PMT	PMT([Rate],[Term],[Loan]) Calculates the monthly payment on a loan where the Rate field contains the monthly interest rate, the Term field contains the number of monthly payments, and the Loan field contains the total amount financed
LEFT	LEFT([LastName],2) Returns the first two characters of the entry in the LastName field
RIGHT	RIGHT([PartNo],3) Returns the last three characters of the entry in the PartNo field
LEN	LEN([Description]) Returns the number of characters in the Description field

UNIT
F
Access 2010

Building Summary Queries

A **summary query** calculates statistics about groups of records. To create a summary query, you add the Total row to the query design grid to specify how you want to group and calculate the statistics using aggregate functions. You can also add a Total row to the bottom of any table or query datasheet. **Aggregate functions** calculate a statistic such as a subtotal, count, or average on a field in a group of records. You can use some aggregate functions, such as Sum or Avg (Average), only on fields with Number or Currency data types. You can also use other functions, such as Min (Minimum), Max (Maximum), or Count, on Text fields. Table F-4 provides more information on aggregate functions. A key difference between the statistics displayed by a summary query and those displayed by calculated fields is that summary queries provide calculations that describe a *group of records*, whereas calculated fields provide a new field of information for *each record*. Samantha Hooper asks you to calculate total sales per tour category. You can use the Total row and build a summary query to provide these statistics.

STEPS

1. **Click the Create tab on the Ribbon, click the Query Design button, double-click Sales, double-click Tours, then click Close in the Show Table dialog box**
   It doesn't matter in what order you add the field lists to Query Design View, but it's important to move and resize the field lists as necessary to clearly see all field names and relationships.
2. **Double-click the SalesNo field in the Sales field list, double-click the Category field in the Tours field list, double-click the Cost field in the Tours field list, then click the View button to view the datasheet**
   Forty-three records are displayed, representing all 43 records in the Sales table. You can add a Total row to any datasheet.
3. **Click the Totals button in the Records group, click the Total cell below the Cost field, click the Total list arrow, click Sum, then widen the Cost column to display the entire total**
   The Total row is added to the bottom of the datasheet and displays the sum total of the Cost field, $37,950. Other Total row statistics you can select include Average, Count, Maximum, Minimum, Standard Deviation, and Variance. To create subtotals per Category, you need to modify the query in Query Design View.
4. **Click the View button to return to Query Design View, click the Totals button in the Show/Hide group, click Group By in the SalesNo column, click the list arrow, click Count, click Group By in the Cost column, click the list arrow, then click Sum**
   The Total row is added to the query grid below the Table row. To calculate summary statistics for each category, the Category field is the Group By field, as shown in Figure F-13.
5. **Click to display the datasheet, widen each column as necessary to view all field names, click in the Total row for the SumOfCost field, click the list arrow, click Sum, then click another row in the datasheet to remove the selection**
   The Adventure category leads all others with a count of 25 sales totaling $24,250. The total revenue for all sales is $37,950, as shown in Figure F-14.
6. **Click the Save button on the Quick Access toolbar, type CategorySummary, click OK, then close the datasheet**

FIGURE F-13: **Summary query in Design View**

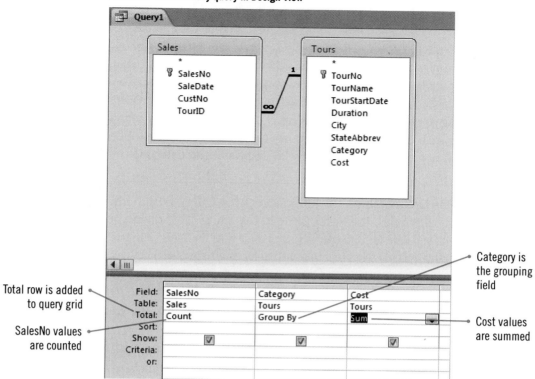

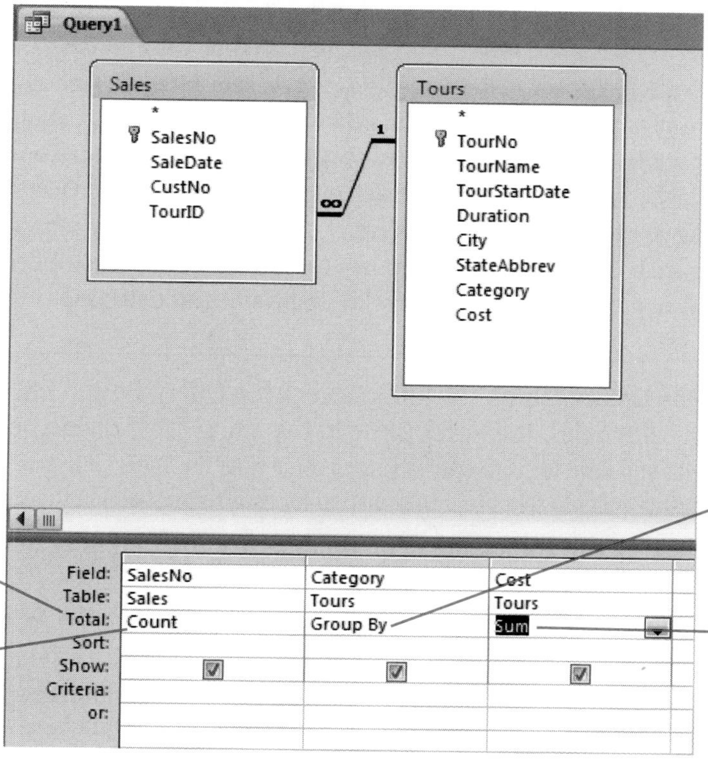

FIGURE F-14: **Summary query datasheet**

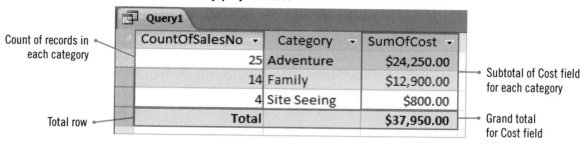

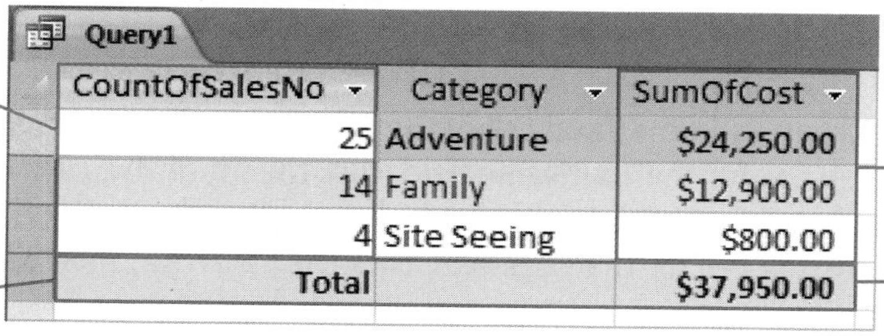

TABLE F-4: **Aggregate functions**

aggregate function	used to find the
Sum	Total of values in a field
Avg	Average of values in a field
Min	Minimum value in a field
Max	Maximum value in a field
Count	Number of values in a field (not counting null values)
StDev	Standard deviation of values in a field
Var	Variance of values in a field
First	Field value from the first record in a table or query
Last	Field value from the last record in a table or query

Building Crosstab Queries

A **crosstab query** generally uses three fields to calculate a statistic such as a sum or average of one field by grouping records according to a second field in a column heading position and a third field used in a row heading position. You can use the **Crosstab Query Wizard** to guide you through the steps of creating a crosstab query, or you can build the crosstab query from scratch using Query Design View. Samantha Hooper asks you to continue your analysis of costs per category by summarizing the cost values for each tour within each category. A crosstab query works well for this request because you want to subtotal the Cost field as summarized by two other fields, TourName and Category.

STEPS

1. **Click the Create tab on the Ribbon, click the Query Design button, double-click Tours, double-click Sales, then click Close in the Show Table dialog box**

   The fields you need for your crosstab query come from the Tours table, but you also need to include the Sales table in this query to select tour information for each record (sale) in the Sales table.

2. **Double-click the TourName field, double-click the Category field, then double-click the Cost field**

   The first step in creating a crosstab query is to create a select query with the three fields you want to use in the crosstabular report.

3. **Click the View button to review the unsummarized datasheet of 43 records, then click the View button to return to Query Design View**

   To summarize these 43 records in a crosstabular report, you need to change the current select query into a crosstab query.

4. **Click the Crosstab button in the Query Type group**

   Note that two new rows are added to the query grid—the Total row and the Crosstab row. The **Total row** helps you determine which fields group or summarize the records, and the **Crosstab row** identifies which of the three positions each field takes in the crosstab report: Row Heading, Column Heading, or Value. The **Value field** is typically a numeric field, such as Cost, that can be summed or averaged.

5. **Click Group By in the Total cell of the Cost field, click the list arrow, click Sum, click the Crosstab cell for the TourName field, click the list arrow, click Row Heading, click the Crosstab cell for the Category field, click the list arrow, click Column Heading, click the Crosstab cell for the Cost field, click the list arrow, then click Value**

   The completed Query Design View should look like Figure F-15. Note the choices made in the Total and Crosstab rows of the query grid.

6. **Click to review the crosstab datasheet**

   The final crosstab datasheet is shown in Figure F-16. The datasheet summarizes all 43 sales records by the Category field used as the column headings and by the TourName field used in the row heading position. Although you can switch the row and column heading fields without changing the numeric information on the crosstab datasheet, you should generally place the field with the most entries (in this case TourName) in the row heading position so that the printout is taller than it is wide.

7. **Click the Save button on the Quick Access toolbar, type TourCrosstab as the query name, click OK, then close the datasheet**

   Crosstab queries appear with a crosstab icon to the left of the query name in the Navigation Pane.

FIGURE F-15: **Query Design View of a crosstab query**

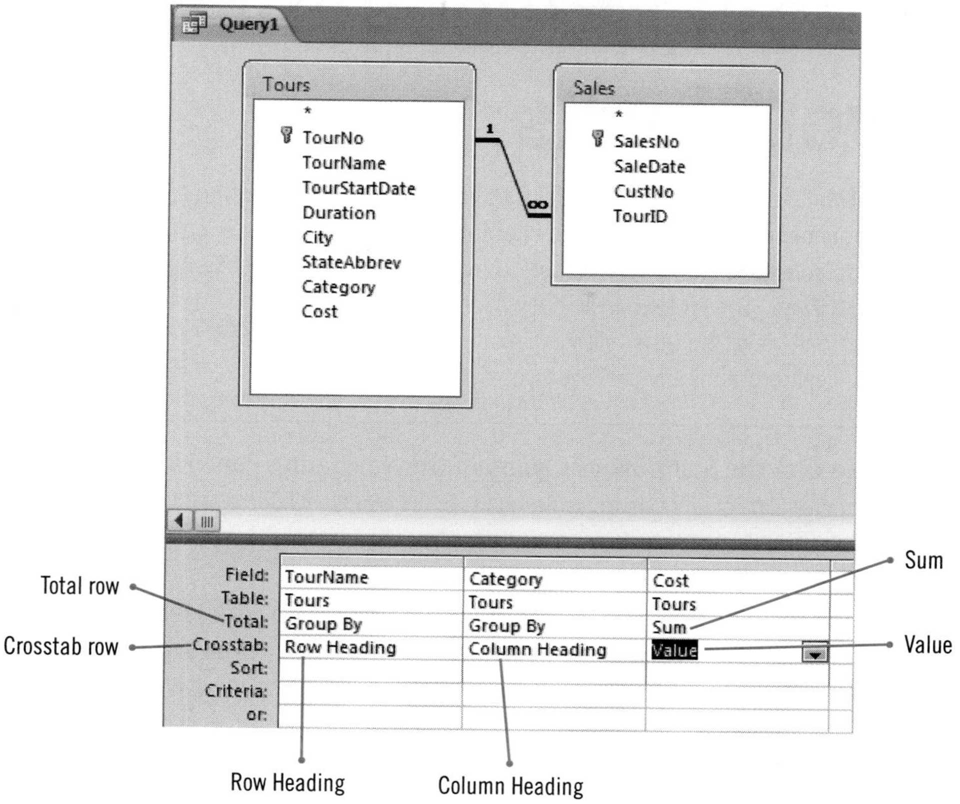

FIGURE F-16: **Crosstab query datasheet**

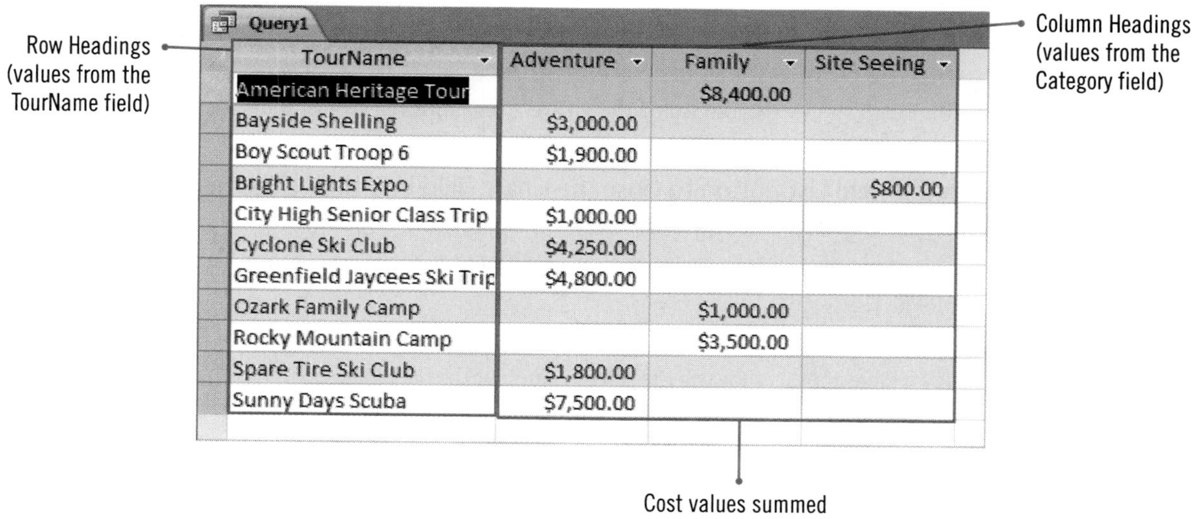

TourName	Adventure	Family	Site Seeing
American Heritage Tour		$8,400.00	
Bayside Shelling	$3,000.00		
Boy Scout Troop 6	$1,900.00		
Bright Lights Expo			$800.00
City High Senior Class Trip	$1,000.00		
Cyclone Ski Club	$4,250.00		
Greenfield Jaycees Ski Trip	$4,800.00		
Ozark Family Camp		$1,000.00	
Rocky Mountain Camp		$3,500.00	
Spare Tire Ski Club	$1,800.00		
Sunny Days Scuba	$7,500.00		

Using query wizards

Four query wizards are available to help you build queries including the Simple (which creates a select query), Crosstab, Find Duplicates, and Find Unmatched Query Wizards. Use the **Find Duplicates Query Wizard** to determine whether a table contains duplicate values in one or more fields. Use the **Find Unmatched Query Wizard** to find records in one table that do not have related records in another table. To use the query wizards, click the Query Wizard button on the Create tab.

UNIT
F
Access 2010

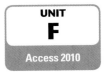

Building PivotTables and PivotCharts

A **PivotTable** calculates a statistic, such as a sum or average, by grouping records like a crosstab query with the additional benefit of allowing you to filter the data. A **PivotChart** is a graphical presentation of the data in the PivotTable. You build a PivotTable using **PivotTable View**. Similarly, you design PivotCharts in **PivotChart View**. The PivotChart and PivotTable Views are bound to one another so that when you make a change in one view, the other view is updated automatically. Samantha Hooper asks you to use PivotChart View to graphically present an analysis of tour sales.

STEPS

1. **Double-click the StateAnalysis query in the Navigation Pane to open its datasheet**
   You can view data of any existing table, query, or form in PivotTable and PivotChart views. StateAnalysis contains the customer name, customer state, tour name, and cost of the tour. Analyzing which tours are the most popular in various states will help focus marketing expenses.

2. **Click the View button arrow on the Home tab, then click PivotChart View**
   In PivotChart View, you drag a field from the Chart Field List to a **drop area**, a position on the chart where you want the field to appear. The fields in the **Chart Field List** are the fields in the underlying object, in this case, the StateAnalysis query. The relationship between drop areas on a PivotChart, PivotTable, and crosstab query are summarized in Table F-5.

> **TROUBLE**
> You may need to move the Chart Field List by dragging its title bar to see all drop areas.

3. **Drag TourName from the Chart Field List to the Drop Category Fields Here drop area near the bottom of the window**
   When you successfully drag a field to a drop area, the drop area displays a blue border. The TourName field values will appear on the x-axis, also called the **category axis**. To remove a field, drag it out of the PivotChart window.

> **TROUBLE**
> If the PivotChart doesn't appear, switch to Datasheet View and back to PivotChart View to refresh it.

4. **Drag State from the Chart Field List to the Drop Series Fields Here drop area, then drag Cost to the Drop Data Fields Here drop area**
   On this chart, the y-axis, also called the **value axis**, sums the cost of tours for each state. The colors of the bars represent different states but are not identified until you add a legend.

5. **Click the Field List button to close the Chart Field List, then click the Legend button in the Show/Hide group to toggle the Legend button on**
   The legend identifies which color represents each state as shown in Figure F-17. To view the information as a PivotTable, you change the view.

6. **Click the View button arrow on the Design tab, then click PivotTable View**
   The PivotTable appears showing the actual values for the data graphed in the PivotChart. PivotTables are very similar in structure to crosstab queries, but they also allow you to move and filter the data. For example, you can filter by both the State and TourName. You want to find out which tours are popular for customers from Iowa (IA) and Missouri (MO).

7. **Click the State field list arrow, click the KS check box to uncheck it, then click OK**
   The filtered PivotTable should look like Figure F-18. If you were to switch to PivotChart View at this time, it would also be filtered to show only MO and IA customers.

8. **Save and close the StateAnalysis query, close the QuestTravel-F.accdb database, and exit Access**

FIGURE F-17: **PivotChart View**

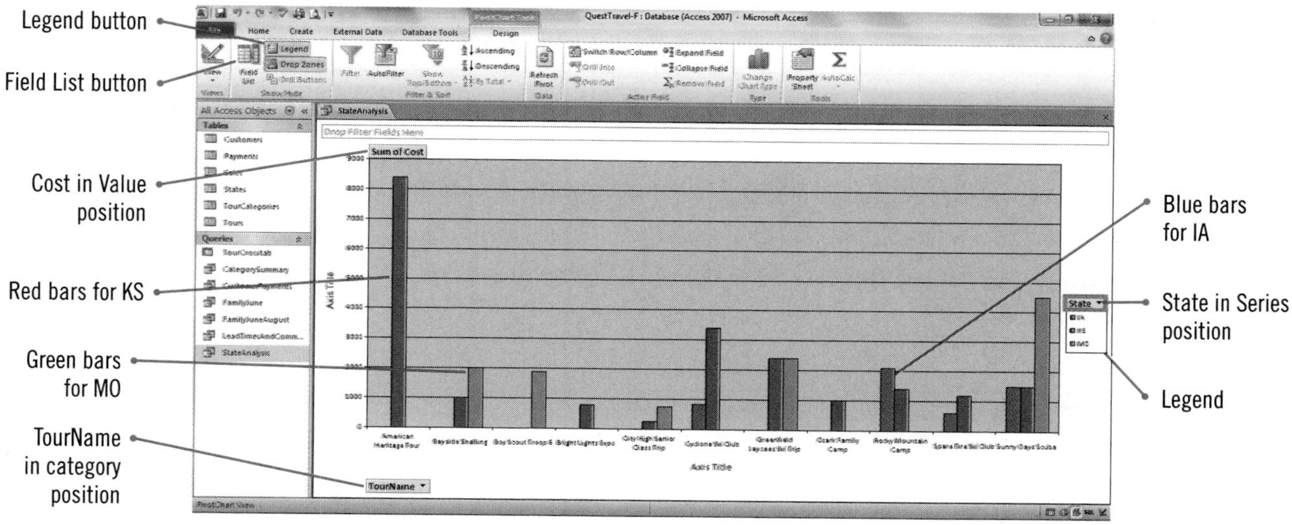

FIGURE F-18: **PivotTable View filtered for IA and MO customers**

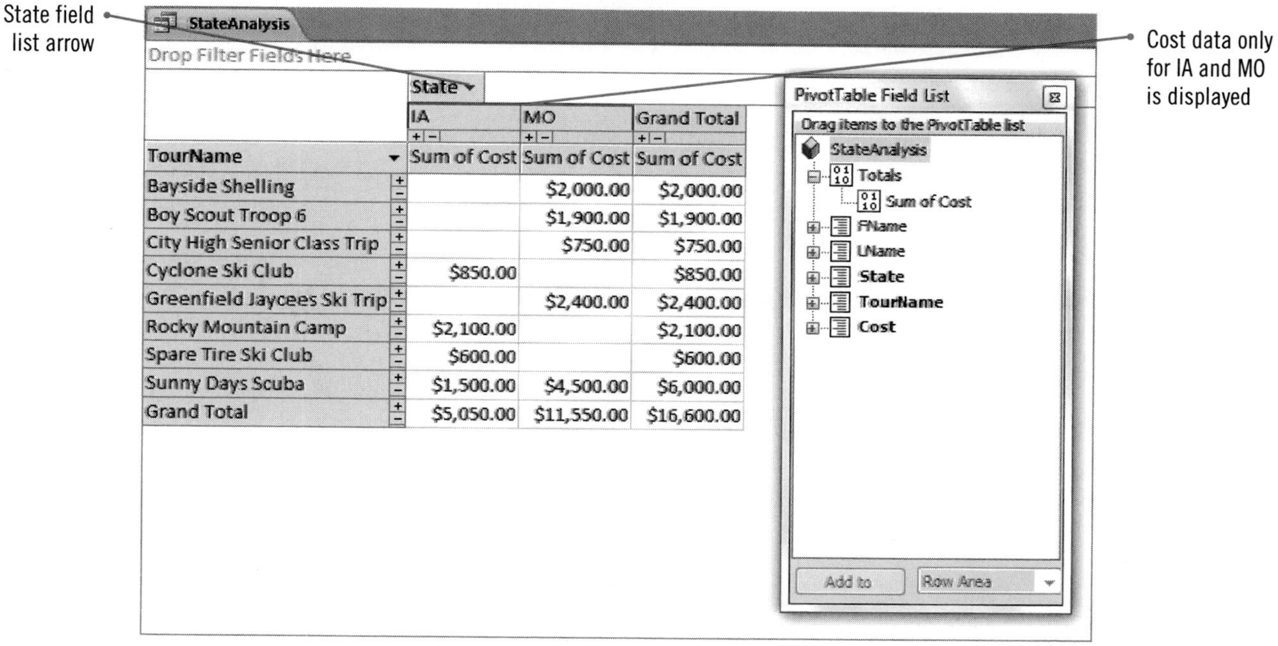

TourName	IA Sum of Cost	MO Sum of Cost	Grand Total Sum of Cost
Bayside Shelling		$2,000.00	$2,000.00
Boy Scout Troop 6		$1,900.00	$1,900.00
City High Senior Class Trip		$750.00	$750.00
Cyclone Ski Club	$850.00		$850.00
Greenfield Jaycees Ski Trip		$2,400.00	$2,400.00
Rocky Mountain Camp	$2,100.00		$2,100.00
Spare Tire Ski Club	$600.00		$600.00
Sunny Days Scuba	$1,500.00	$4,500.00	$6,000.00
Grand Total	$5,050.00	$11,550.00	$16,600.00

TABLE F-5: **PivotTable and PivotChart drop areas**

drop area on PivotTable	drop area on PivotChart	crosstab query field position
Filter Field	Filter Field	(NA)
Row Field	Category Field	Row Heading
Column Field	Series Field	Column Heading
Totals or Detail Field	Data Field	Value

Practice

Concepts Review

For current SAM information, including versions and content details, visit SAM Central (http://www.cengage.com/samcentral). If you have a SAM user profile, you may have access to hands-on instruction, practice, and assessment of the skills covered in this unit. Since various versions of SAM are supported throughout the life of this text, check with your instructor for the correct instructions and URL/Web site for accessing assignments.

Identify each element of Query Design View shown in Figure F-19.

FIGURE F-19

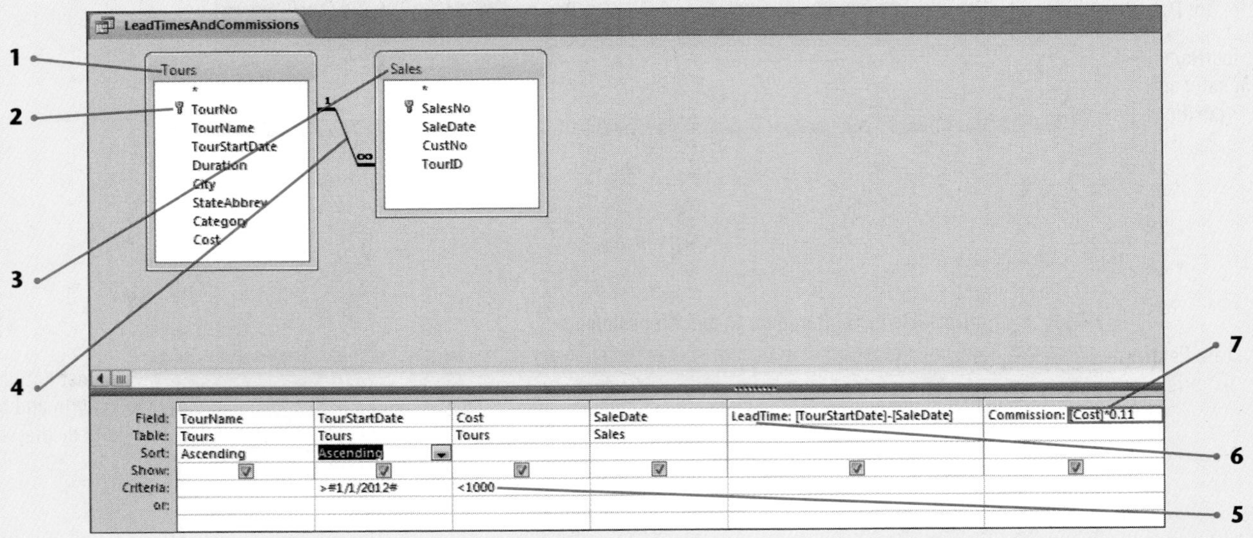

Match each term with the statement that best describes its function.

8. **PivotChart**
9. **Select query**
10. **Wildcard character**
11. **AND criteria**
12. **Sorting**
13. **OR criteria**

a. Graphical presentation of data
b. Placing the records of a datasheet in a certain order
c. Entered on more than one row of the query design grid
d. Asterisk (*) or question mark (?) used in query criteria
e. Retrieves fields from related tables and displays records in a datasheet
f. Entered on one row of the query design grid

Select the best answer from the list of choices.

14. The query datasheet can best be described as a:
- **a.** Logical view of the selected data from underlying tables.
- **b.** Duplication of the data in the underlying table's datasheet.
- **c.** Separate file of data.
- **d.** Second copy of the data in the underlying tables.

15. Queries may *not* be used to:
- **a.** Calculate new fields of data.
- **b.** Enter or update data.
- **c.** Set the primary key field for a table.
- **d.** Sort records.

16. When you update data in a table that is also selected in a query:
- **a.** You must relink the query to the table to refresh the data.
- **b.** The updated data is automatically displayed in the query.
- **c.** You must also update the data in the query datasheet.
- **d.** You can choose whether to update the data in the query.

17. Which of the following is *not* an aggregate function available to a summary query?
- **a.** Avg
- **b.** Count
- **c.** Subtotal
- **d.** Max

18. The order in which records in a query are sorted is determined by:
- **a.** The order in which the fields are defined in the underlying table.
- **b.** The importance of the information in the field.
- **c.** The alphabetic order of the field names.
- **d.** The left-to-right position of the fields in the query design grid that contain a sort order choice.

19. The presentation of data in a crosstab query is most similar to:
- **a.** PivotTable View.
- **b.** Table Datasheet View.
- **c.** PivotChart View.
- **d.** Layout View.

20. A crosstab query is generally constructed with how many fields?
- **a.** 1
- **b.** 2
- **c.** 3
- **d.** More than 5

21. In a crosstab query, which field is the most likely candidate for the Value position?
- **a.** FName
- **b.** Cost
- **c.** Department
- **d.** Country

Skills Review

1. **Create multitable queries.**
   a. Start Access and open the **Service-F.accdb** database from the drive and folder where you store your Data Files, and enable content if prompted.
   b. Create a new select query in Query Design View using the Names and Zips tables.
   c. Add the following fields to the query design grid in this order:
      - FirstName, LastName, and Street from the Names table
      - City, State, and Zip from the Zips table
   d. In Datasheet View, replace the LastName value in the Martin Chen record with your last name.
   e. Save the query as **AddressList**, print the datasheet if requested by your instructor, then close the query.
2. **Apply sorts and view SQL.**
   a. Open the AddressList query in Query Design View.
   b. Drag the FirstName field from the Names field list to the third column in the query design grid to make the first three fields in the query design grid FirstName, LastName, and FirstName.
   c. Add an ascending sort to the second and third fields in the query design grid, and uncheck the Show check box in the third column. The query is now sorted in ascending order by LastName, then by FirstName, though the order of the fields in the resulting datasheet still appears as FirstName, LastName.
   d. Use Save Object As to save the query as **SortedAddressList**, view the datasheet, print the datasheet if requested by your instructor, then close the query.
3. **Develop AND criteria.**
   a. Open the SortedAddressList query in Design View.
   b. Type **C*** (the asterisk is a wildcard) in the LastName field Criteria cell to choose all people whose last name starts with *C*. Access assists you with the syntax for this type of criterion and enters Like "C*" in the cell when you click elsewhere in the query design grid.
   c. Enter **KS** as the AND criterion for the State field. Be sure to enter the criterion on the same line in the query design grid as the Like "C*" criterion.
   d. View the datasheet. It should select only those people from Kansas with a last name that starts with the letter *C*.
   e. Enter your own home town in the City field of the first record to uniquely identify the printout.
   f. Use Save Object As to save the query as **KansasC**, print the datasheet if requested by your instructor, then close the query.
4. **Develop OR criteria.**
   a. Open the KansasC query in Query Design View.
   b. Enter **D*** in the second Criteria row (the or row) of the LastName field.
   c. Enter **KS** as the criterion in the second Criteria row (the or row) of the State field so that those people from KS with a last name that starts with the letter *D* are added to this query.
   d. Use Save Object As to save the query as **KansasCD**, view the datasheet, print the datasheet if requested by your instructor, then close the query.
5. **Create calculated fields.**
   a. Create a new select query in Query Design View using only the Names table.
   b. Add the following fields to the query design grid in this order: FirstName, LastName, Birthday.
   c. Create a calculated field called Age in the fourth column of the query design grid by entering the expression: **Age: Int((Now()-[Birthday])/365)** to determine the age of each person in years based on the information in the Birthday field. The Now() function returns today's date. Now()-[Birthday] determines the number of days a person has lived. Dividing that value by 365 determines the number of years a person has lived. The Int() function is used to return the integer portion of the answer. So if a person has lived 23.5 years, Int(23.5) = 23.
   d. Sort the query in descending order on the calculated Age field.
   e. Save the query with the name **AgeCalculation**, view the datasheet, print the datasheet if requested by your instructor, then close the query.

Skills Review (continued)

6. Build summary queries.

a. Create a new select query in Query Design View using the Names and Activities tables.

b. Add the following fields: FirstName and LastName from the Names table, and Hours from the Activities table.

c. Add the Total row to the query design grid, then change the aggregate function for the Hours field from Group By to Sum.

d. Sort in descending order by Hours.

e. Save the query as **HoursSummary**, view the datasheet, widen all columns so that all data is clearly visible, print the datasheet if requested by your instructor, then save and close the query.

7. Build crosstab queries.

a. Use Query Design View to create a select query with the City and State fields from the Zips table and the Dues field from the Names table. Save the query as **DuesCrosstab**, then view the datasheet.

b. Return to Query Design View, then click the Crosstab button to add the Total and Crosstab rows to the query design grid.

c. Specify City as the crosstab row heading, State as the crosstab column heading, and Dues as the summed value field within the crosstab datasheet.

d. View the datasheet as shown in Figure F-20, print the datasheet if requested by your instructor, then save and close the DuesCrosstab query.

FIGURE F-20

DuesCrosstab

City	IA	KS	MO
Blue Springs			$50.00
Bridgewater	$50.00		
Buehler		$50.00	
Des Moines	$25.00		
Dripping Springs		$25.00	
Flat Hills		$50.00	
Fontanelle	$50.00		
Greenfield	$50.00		
Kansas City		$50.00	$100.00
Langguth		$25.00	
Leawood			$50.00
Lee's Summit			$75.00
Lenexa		$25.00	
Manawatta		$25.00	
Manhattan		$25.00	
Overland Park		$100.00	
Red Bridge		$425.00	
Running Deer			$25.00
Shawnee		$200.00	
Student City		$100.00	

8. Build PivotTables and PivotCharts.

a. Create a select query with the State field from the Zips table and the CharterMember and Dues fields from the Names table. Save it as **DuesPivot**, then run the query.

b. Switch to PivotChart View, and open the Chart Field List if it is not already displayed.

c. Drag the State field to the Drop Category Fields Here drop area, the CharterMember field to the Drop Series Fields Here drop area, and the Dues field to the Drop Data Fields Here drop area. Refresh the PivotChart by switching to Datasheet View then back to PivotChart View if needed.

d. Close the field list, display the legend, then print the PivotChart if requested by your instructor, which should look like Figure F-21.

e. Switch to PivotTable View, remove KS from the State list to filter for only the states of Iowa (IA) and Missouri (MO), then print the PivotTable if requested by your instructor.

FIGURE F-21

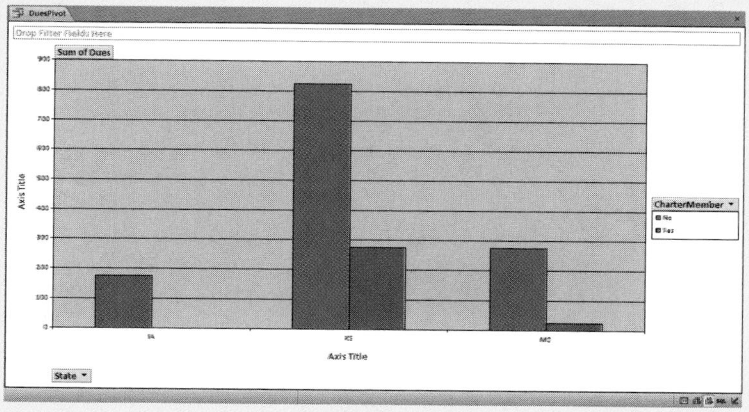

f. Save and close the DuesPivot query, close the Service-F.accdb database, then exit Access.

Independent Challenge 1

As the manager of a music store's instrument rental program, you have created a database to track rentals to schoolchildren. Now that several rentals have been made, you want to query the database for several different datasheet printouts to analyze school information.

a. Start Access and open the **MusicStore-F.accdb** database from the drive and folder where you store your Data Files, and enable content if prompted.

b. In Query Design View, create a query with the following fields in the following order:
- SchoolName field from the Schools table
- RentalDate field from the Rentals table
- Description field from the Instruments table

(*Hint*: Although you don't use any fields from the Customers table, you need to add the Customers table to this query to make the connection between the Schools table and the Rentals table.)

c. Sort in ascending order by SchoolName, then in ascending order by RentalDate.

d. Save the query as **SchoolRentals**, view the datasheet, replace **Lincoln Elementary** with your elementary school name, then print the datasheet if requested by your instructor.

e. Modify the SchoolRentals query by deleting the Description field. Use the Totals button to group the records by SchoolName and to count the RentalDate field. Print the datasheet if requested by your instructor, then use Save Object As to save the query as **SchoolCount**. Close the datasheet.

f. Create a crosstab query named **SchoolCrosstab** selecting the SchoolRentals query in the Show Table dialog box to display the SchoolRentals query's field list. Use Description as the row heading position and SchoolName in the column heading position. Count the RentalDate field.

g. Save, view, print (if requested by your instructor), and close the SchoolCrosstab query.

h. Modify the SchoolRentals query so that only those schools with the word **Elementary** in the SchoolName field are displayed. (*Hint*: You have to use wildcard characters in the criteria.)

i. Use Save Object As to save the query as **ElementaryRentals**, then view, print (if requested by your instructor), and close the datasheet.

j. Close the MusicStore-F.accdb database, then exit Access.

Independent Challenge 2

As the manager of a music store's instrument rental program, you have created a database to track rentals to schoolchildren. You can use queries to analyze customer and rental information.

a. Start Access and open the **MusicStore-F.accdb** database from the drive and folder where you store your Data Files, and enable content if prompted.

b. In Query Design View, create a query with the following fields in the following order:
- Description and MonthlyFee fields from the Instruments table
- LastName, Zip, and City fields from the Customers table

(*Hint*: Although you don't need any fields from the Rentals table in this query's datasheet, you need to add the Rentals table to this query to make the connection between the Customers table and the Instruments table.)

c. Add the Zip field to the first column of the query grid, and specify an ascending sort order for this field. Uncheck the Show check box for the first Zip field so that it does not appear in the datasheet.

d. Specify an ascending sort order for the Description field.

e. Save the query as **ZipAnalysis**.

f. View the datasheet, replace Johnson with **your last name** in the LastName field, then print (if requested by your instructor) and close the datasheet.

g. Modify the ZipAnalysis query by adding criteria to find the records where the Description is equal to **viola**.

h. Use Save Object As to save this query as **Violas**.

Advanced Challenge Exercise

ACE

- Modify the Violas query with AND criteria to further specify that the City must be **Des Moines**.
- Use Save Object As to save this query as **DesMoinesViolas**, then view the results.
- Modify the DesMoinesViolas query with OR criteria that find all violas or violins in Des Moines.
- Use Save Object As to save this query as **DesMoinesV2**, then view and close the query.
- In Query Design View, create a crosstab query that uses the Description field from the Instruments table for the column headings, the SchoolName field from the Schools table for the row headings, and that sums the MonthlyFee field from the Instruments table. Note that the Rentals and Customers field lists are necessary in this query to connect the Instruments and Schools tables.
- Save the crosstab query as **RentalCrosstab**, view the datasheet, then print the datasheet in landscape orientation if requested by your instructor, narrowing the margins so that it fits on one page.

i. Close the MusicStore-F.accdb database, then exit Access.

Independent Challenge 3

As a real estate agent, you use an Access database to track residential real estate listings in your area. You can use queries to answer questions about the real estate properties and to analyze home values.

a. Start Access and open the **RealEstate-F.accdb** database from the drive and folder where you store your Data Files, and enable content if prompted.

b. In Query Design View, create a query with the following fields in the following order:
- AgencyName from the Agencies table
- RFirst and RLast from the Realtors table
- SqFt and Asking from the Listings table

c. Sort the records in descending order by the Asking field.

d. Save the query as **AskingPrice**, view the datasheet, enter your own last name instead of Dell for the most expensive listing, then print the datasheet if requested by your instructor.

e. In Query Design View, modify the AskingPrice query by creating a calculated field that determines price per square foot. The new calculated field's name should be **SquareFootCost**, and the expression should be the asking price divided by the square foot field, or **[Asking]/[SqFt]**.

f. Remove any former sort orders, sort the records in descending order based on the SquareFootCost calculated field, and view the datasheet. Save and close the AskingPrice query.

g. Reopen the AskingPrice query in Query Design View, right-click the calculated SquareFootCost field, click Properties, then change the Format property to Currency.

Advanced Challenge Exercise

- In Design View of the AskingPrice query, delete the RFirst, RLast, and SqFt fields.
- Use the Save Object As feature to save the query as **CostSummary**.
- View the datasheet, then change the Sun and Ski Realtors agency name to your last name followed by **Realtors**.
- In Design View, add the Total row, then sum the Asking field and use the Avg (Average) aggregate function for the SquareFootCost calculated field.
- In Datasheet View, add the Total row and display the sum of the Asking field. Widen all columns as needed as shown in Figure F-22.
- Save and print the query, then close it.

FIGURE F-22

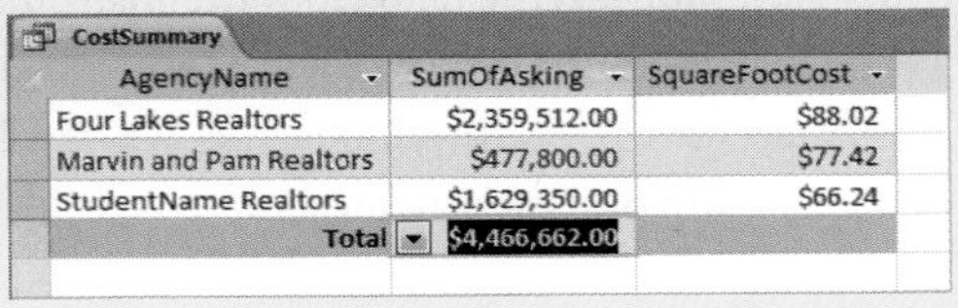
CostSummary

AgencyName	SumOfAsking	SquareFootCost
Four Lakes Realtors	$2,359,512.00	$88.02
Marvin and Pam Realtors	$477,800.00	$77.42
StudentName Realtors	$1,629,350.00	$66.24
Total	$4,466,662.00	

h. Close the RealEstate-F.accdb database, then exit Access.

Real Life Independent Challenge

One way to use Access in your real life is in a community service project. You're working with the local high school guidance counselor to help him with an Access database used to record college scholarship opportunities. You help him with the database by creating several queries.

This Independent Challenge requires an Internet connection.

a. Start Access and open the **Scholarships-F.accdb** database from the drive and folder where you store your Data Files.

b. Conduct research on the Internet or at your school to find at least five new scholarships relevant to your major and enter them into the Scholarships table.

c. Conduct research on the Internet or at your school to find at least one new scholarship relevant to a Business major as well as a Science major, and enter the two records into the Scholarships table.

d. Create a query called **Business** that displays all records in the Business major.

e. Add OR criteria to the Business query to also select all scholarships in the Science major named **BusinessOrScience**.

f. Create a query that selects the ScholarshipName, DueDate, and Amount from the Scholarships table, and sorts the records in ascending order by DueDate, then descending order by Amount. Name the query **ScholarshipMasterList**.

Advanced Challenge Exercise

- View the ScholarshipMasterList query in PivotTable view, then drag the Amount field to the Drop Totals or Detail Fields Here area, the ScholarshipName field to the Drop Row Fields Here area, and the DueDate By Month field to the Drop Filter Fields Here area.
- Filter the PivotTable for only those scholarships in the year **2014**, a portion of which are shown in Figure F-23.

g. Save and close the ScholarshipMasterList query, close the Scholarships-F.accdb database, then exit Access.

FIGURE F-23

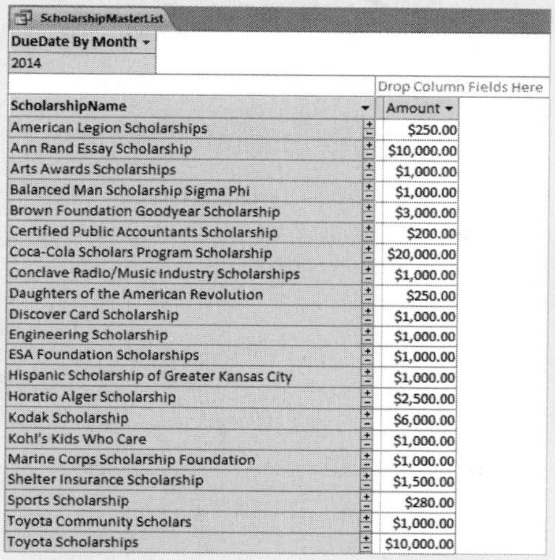

ScholarshipMasterList

DueDate By Month
2014

Drop Column Fields Here

ScholarshipName	Amount
American Legion Scholarships	$250.00
Ann Rand Essay Scholarship	$10,000.00
Arts Awards Scholarships	$1,000.00
Balanced Man Scholarship Sigma Phi	$1,000.00
Brown Foundation Goodyear Scholarship	$3,000.00
Certified Public Accountants Scholarship	$200.00
Coca-Cola Scholars Program Scholarship	$20,000.00
Conclave Radio/Music Industry Scholarships	$1,000.00
Daughters of the American Revolution	$250.00
Discover Card Scholarship	$1,000.00
Engineering Scholarship	$1,000.00
ESA Foundation Scholarships	$1,000.00
Hispanic Scholarship of Greater Kansas City	$1,000.00
Horatio Alger Scholarship	$2,500.00
Kodak Scholarship	$6,000.00
Kohl's Kids Who Care	$1,000.00
Marine Corps Scholarship Foundation	$1,000.00
Shelter Insurance Scholarship	$1,500.00
Sports Scholarship	$280.00
Toyota Community Scholars	$1,000.00
Toyota Scholarships	$10,000.00

Visual Workshop

Open the **Training-F.accdb** database from the drive and folder where you store your Data Files, and enable content if prompted. In Query Design View, create a new select query with the DeptName field from the Departments table, the CourseCost field from the Courses table, and the Description field from the Courses table. Save the query with the name **CourseAnalysis,** display it in PivotTable view as shown in Figure F-24. Save the query, then print it if requested by your instructor.

FIGURE F-24

CourseAnalysis

Drop Filter Fields Here

Drop Column Fielc

Description	DeptName	CourseCost
⊟ Access Case Problems	Accounting	$200.00
		$200.00
	Engineering	$200.00
	Executive	$200.00
	Legal	$200.00
		$200.00
		$200.00
	Marketing	$200.00
	Operations	$200.00
	Training	$200.00
	Total	
⊟ Computer Fundamentals	Accounting	$200.00
	Engineering	$200.00
	Executive	$200.00
	Human Resources	$200.00
		$200.00
	Information Systems	$200.00
	Legal	$200.00
		$200.00
		$200.00
		$200.00
	Marketing	$200.00
		$200.00
		$200.00

UNIT G

Access 2010

Enhancing Forms

Files You Will Need:

QuestTravel-G.accdb
Service-G.accdb
MusicStore-G.accdb
RealEstate-G.accdb
Scholarships-G.accdb
Baseball-G.accdb

A **form** is a database object designed to make data easy to find, enter, and edit. You create forms by using **controls** such as labels, text boxes, combo boxes, and command buttons, which help you manipulate data more quickly and reliably than working in a datasheet. A form that contains a **subform** allows you to work with related records in an easy-to-use screen arrangement. For example, using a form/subform combination, you can display customer data and all of the orders placed by that customer at the same time. Samantha Hooper wants to improve the usability of the forms in the QuestTravel database. You will build and improve forms by working with subforms, combo boxes, option groups, and command buttons to enter, find, and filter data.

OBJECTIVES

- Use Form Design View
- Add subforms
- Align control edges
- Add a combo box for data entry
- Add a combo box to find records
- Add command buttons
- Add option groups
- Add tab controls

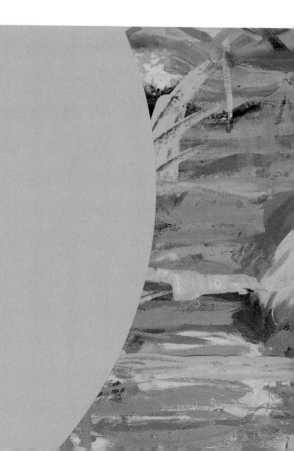

UNIT
G
Access 2010

Using Form Design View

Design View of a form is devoted to working with the detailed structure of a form. The purpose of Design View is to provide full access to all of the modifications you can make to the form. Samantha Hooper has asked you to create a customer entry form. You create this form from scratch in Form Design View.

STEPS

QUICK TIP
Click the Build button in the Record Source property to build or edit a query as the record source for this form.

TROUBLE
You may need to scroll or resize the Field List to see the Gender field.

TROUBLE
Be sure to select the bound controls on the right, not the labels on the left.

1. **Start Access, then open the QuestTravel-G.accdb database from the drive and folder where you store your Data Files, enable content if prompted, click the Create tab on the Ribbon, then click the Form Design button in the Forms group**

   A blank form in Design View is displayed. Your first step is to connect the blank form to an underlying **record source**, a table or query that contains the data you want to display on the form. The fields in the record source populate the Field List. The Customers table should be the record source for the CustomerEntry form.

2. **Double-click the form selector button to open the form's Property Sheet, click the Data tab, click the Record Source list arrow, then click Customers**

   With the record source selected, you're ready to add controls to the form. Recall that bound controls such as text boxes and combo boxes display data from the record source, and unbound controls such as labels, lines, and command buttons clarify information for the person using the form.

3. **Click the Add Existing Fields button in the Tools group to open the Field List, click CustNo in the Field List, press and hold [Shift], click Gender in the Field List, then drag the selection to the form at about the 1" mark on the horizontal ruler**

   The fields of the Customers table are added to the form as shown in Figure G-1. The State, FirstContact, and Gender fields are added as combo boxes because they have Lookup properties. The other fields are text boxes with the exception of the Photo field, which is an Attachment data type. Labels are created for each bound control and are captioned with the field name. You can rearrange the controls by moving them.

4. **Click the form to deselect all controls, click the Phone text box, press and hold [Ctrl], click the FirstContact combo box, Email text box, Photo box, and Gender combo box to add them to the selection, then release [Ctrl]**

   Selected controls will move as a group.

5. **Drag the selected controls up and to the right to position them about 0.25" to the right of the name and address controls, then click the View button to switch to Form View**

   The new form in Form View is shown in Figure G-2.

6. **Click the Save button on the Quick Access toolbar, type CustomerEntry as the form name, click OK, then close the CustomerEntry form**

FIGURE G-1: **Adding fields in Form Design View**

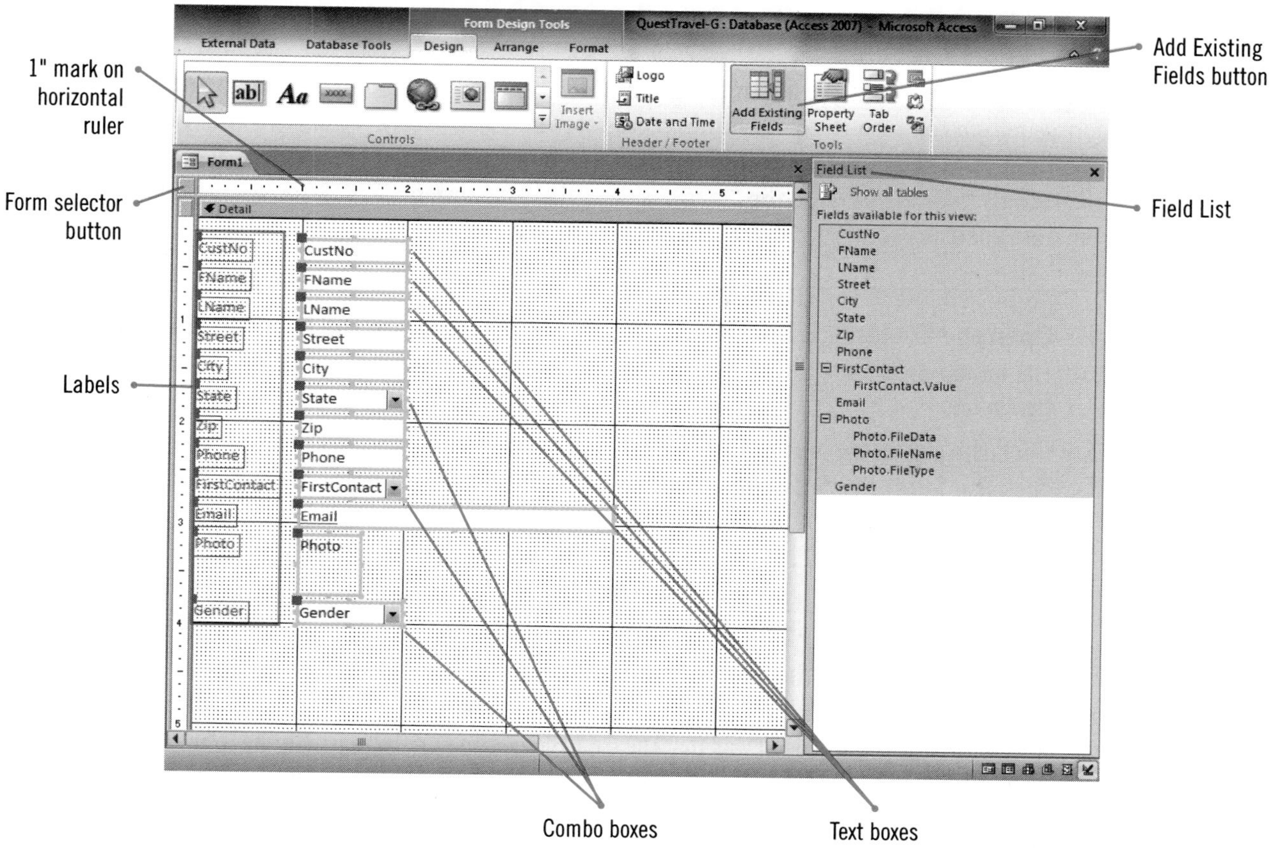

FIGURE G-2: **New form in Form View**

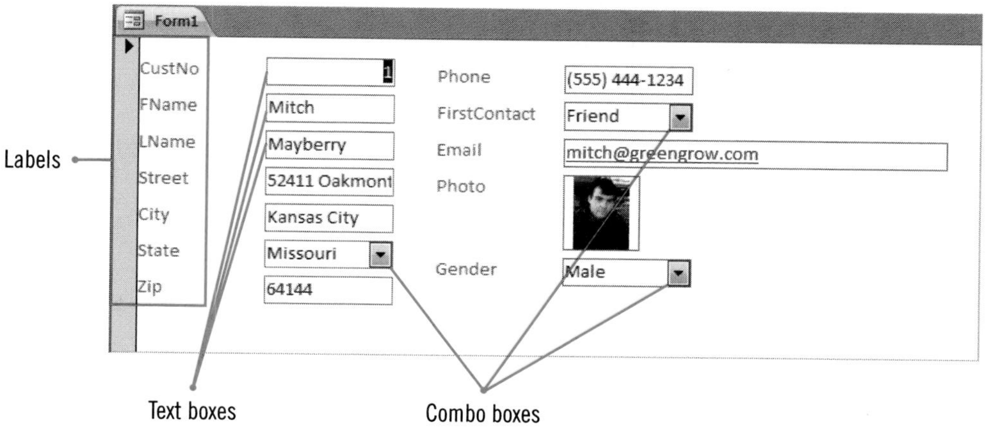

Access 2010

UNIT G

Access 2010

Adding Subforms

A **subform** is a form within a form. The form that contains the subform is called the **main form**. A main form/subform combination displays the records of two tables that are related in a one-to-many relationship. The main form shows data from the table on the "one" side of the relationship, and the subform shows the records from the table on the "many" side of the relationship. You decide to add a subform to the CustomerEntry form to show related sales for each customer.

STEPS

1. **Open the CustomerEntry form in Design View, then close the Field List if it is open**

   The button for adding a subform control is in the second row of buttons in the Controls group on the Design tab.

2. **Click the down arrow button in the Controls group to scroll the list of form controls, click the Subform/Subreport button as shown in Figure G-3, then click below the Zip label in the form**

   The subform control has an associated wizard that helps you add the control to the report.

3. **Click Next to use existing Tables and Queries as the data for the subform, click the Tables/Queries list arrow, click Query: SalesInfo, click the Select All Fields button >>, click Next, click Next to accept the option Show SalesInfo for each record in Customers using CustNo, then click Finish to accept SalesInfo subform as the name for the new subform control**

   A form **layout** is the general way that the data and controls are arranged on the form. By default, subforms display their controls in a columnar layout in Design View, but their **Default View property** is set to Datasheet. See Table G-1 for a description of form layouts. The difference in form layout is apparent when you view the form in Form View.

4. **Click the View button to switch to Form View, then navigate to CustNo 6, Christine Rogers, who has purchased four tours**

   The sales for each customer appear in the subform as a datasheet as you move through the records of the main form. The main form and subform are linked by the common CustNo field. Resize the columns of the subform to make the information easier to read.

5. **Point to the line between field names and use the ↔ pointer to resize the column widths of the subform as shown in Figure G-4**

   The CustomerEntry form displays two navigation bars. The inside bar is for the subform records, and the outside bar is for the main form records.

6. **Right-click the CustomerEntry form tab, click Close, then click Yes when prompted to save changes to both form objects**

TROUBLE

If the SubForm Wizard doesn't start, click the More button in the Controls group then click Use Control Wizards to toggle it on.

QUICK TIP

Double-click the line between field names to automatically adjust the width of the column to the widest field entry.

Linking the form and subform

If the form and subform do not appear to be correctly linked, examine the subform's property sheet, paying special attention to the **Link Child Fields** and **Link Master Fields** properties on the Data tab. These properties tell you which field serves as the link between the main form and subform.

FIGURE G-3: Adding the subform control

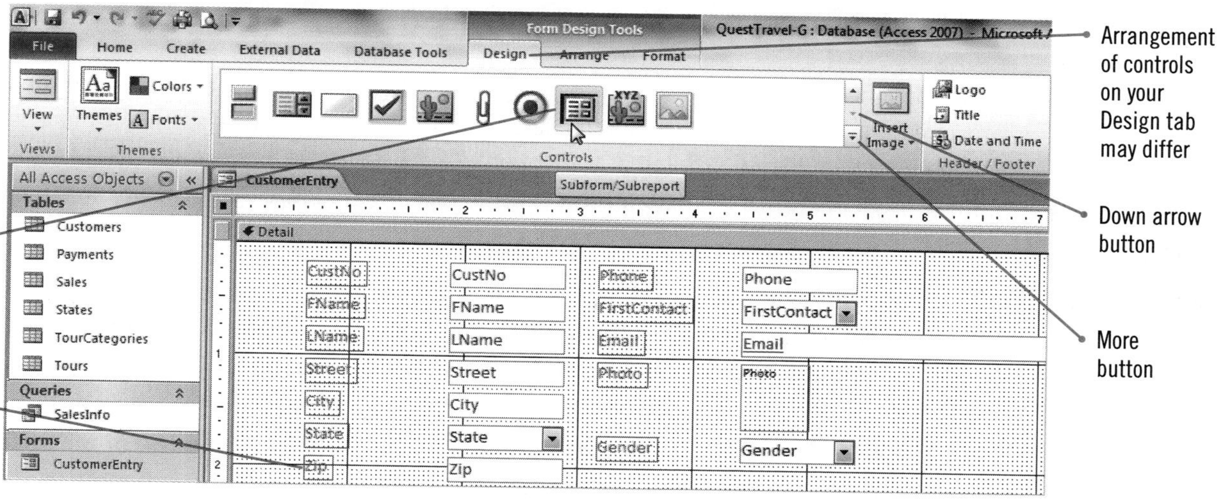

Arrangement of controls on your Design tab may differ
Down arrow button
More button
Subform/ Subreport button
Zip label

FIGURE G-4: Final CustomerEntry form and SalesInfo subform

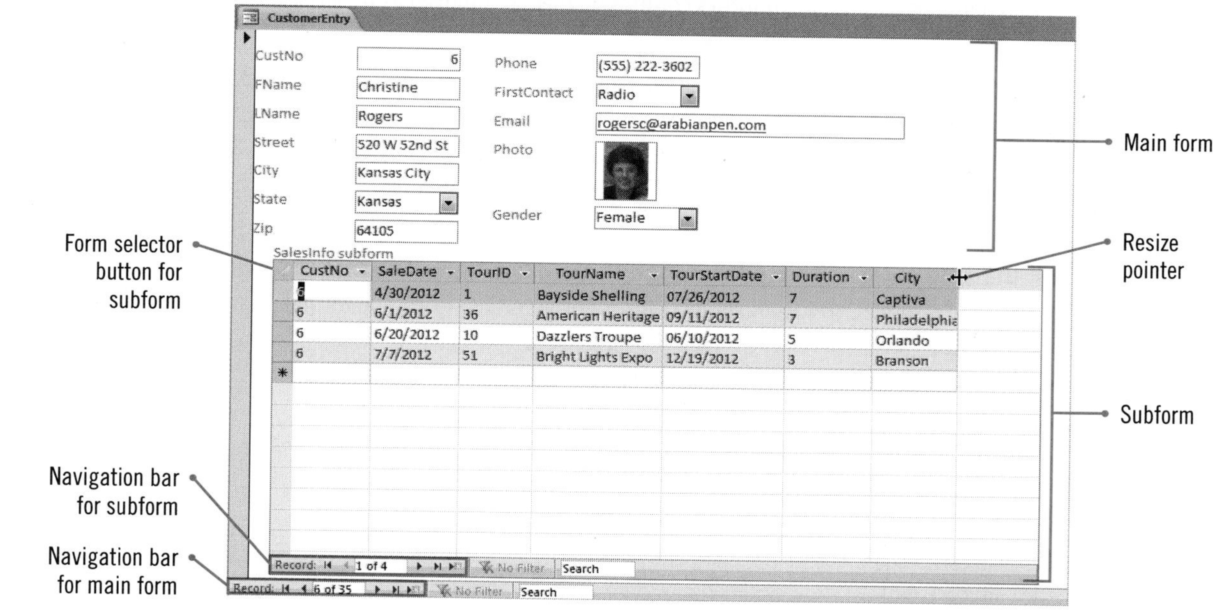

Main form
Resize pointer
Subform
Form selector button for subform
Navigation bar for subform
Navigation bar for main form

Access 2010

TABLE G-1: Form layouts

layout	description
Columnar	Default view for main forms; each field appears on a separate row with a label to its left
Tabular	Each field appears as an individual column, and each record is presented as a row
Datasheet	Default view for subforms; fields and records are displayed as they appear in a table or query datasheet
PivotTable	Fields are organized in a PivotTable arrangement
PivotChart	Fields are organized in a PivotChart arrangement

UNIT G

Access 2010

Aligning Control Edges

Well-designed forms are logical, easy to read, and easy to use. Aligning the edges of controls can make a big difference in form usability. To align the left, right, top, or bottom edges of two or more controls, use the Align button on the Arrange tab of the Ribbon. Samantha Hooper asks you to align and rearrange the controls in the main form to make it easier to read, and to resize the Photo box so it is much larger.

STEPS

QUICK TIP

To select multiple controls, click the first control, then press and hold either [Ctrl] or [Shift] to add more controls to the selection.

1. **Right-click the CustomerEntry form in the Navigation Pane, click Design View, click the CustNo label in the main form, press and hold [Shift] while clicking the other labels in the first column, click the Arrange tab, click the Align button, then click Right**

   Aligning the right edges of these labels makes them easier to read and closer to the data they describe.

2. **Click the CustNo text box, press and hold [Shift] while clicking the other text boxes and combo box in the second column, then drag a middle-left sizing handle to the left**

   Leave only a small amount of space between the labels in the first column and the bound controls in the second column as shown in Figure G-5.

3. **Select all of the labels in the third column of the main form, click the Align button in the Sizing & Ordering group, click Right, then press [←] six times**

   Leave only a small amount of space between the bound controls of the second column with the labels in the third column. With the main form's controls aligned and moved as far left as possible, you resize the Email text box.

4. **Click the Email text box, then drag the middle-right sizing handle to the left to about the 5" mark on the horizontal ruler**

   You delete the Photo label, and move and resize the Photo box to make it much larger.

TROUBLE

The Undo button will undo multiple actions in Form Design View.

5. **Click the Photo label, press [Delete], click the Photo box to select it, use the to move it to the upper-right corner of the form, use the to drag the lower-left sizing handle to fill the space, click the Home tab, then click the View button to view the changes**

   The final CustomerEntry form should look like Figure G-6. Continue to make additional enhancements in Form Design View as needed to match the figure.

6. **Save and close the CustomerEntry form**

FIGURE G-5: **Aligning and resizing controls**

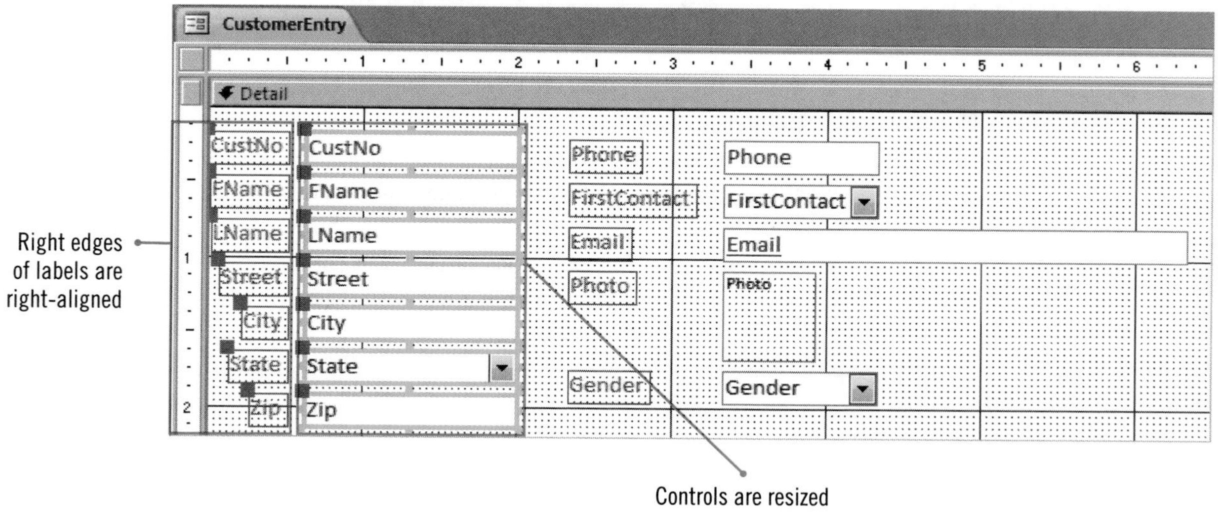

FIGURE G-6: **Final CustomerEntry form**

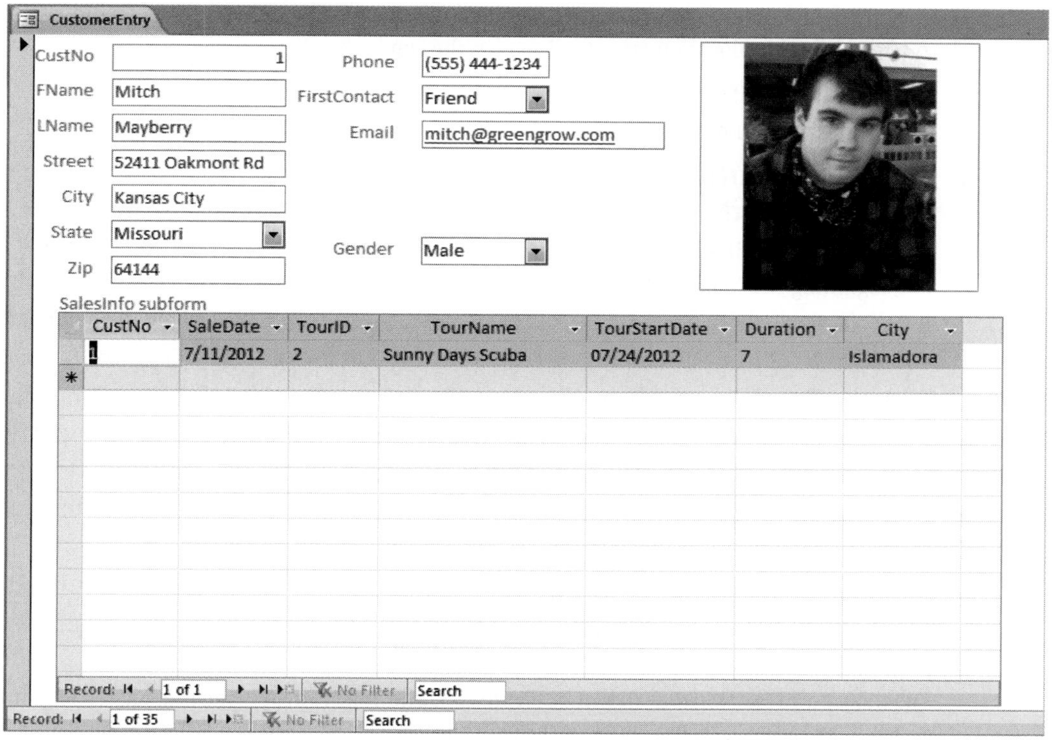

Adding a Combo Box for Data Entry

If a finite set of values can be identified for a field, using a combo box instead of a text box control on a form allows the user to select and enter data faster and more accurately. Both the **list box** and **combo box** controls provide a list of values from where the user can choose an entry. A combo box also allows the user to type an entry from the keyboard; therefore, it is a "combination" of the list box and text box controls. You can create a combo box by using the **Combo Box Wizard**, or you can change an existing text box or list box into a combo box. Fields with Lookup properties are automatically created as combo boxes on new forms. Foreign key fields are also good candidates for combo boxes. Samantha Hooper asks you to change the TourID field in the subform of the CustomerEntry form into a combo box so that users can choose the tour from a list when a customer purchases a new tour.

STEPS

1. **Open the CustomerEntry form in Design View, right-click the TourID text box in the subform, point to Change To, then click Combo Box**

   Now that the control has been changed from a text box to a combo box, you are ready to populate the list with the appropriate duration values.

> **QUICK TIP**
> For more information on any property, click the property then press [F1].

2. **Click the Property Sheet button in the Tools group, click the Data tab in the Property Sheet, click the Row Source property box, then click the Build button**

   Clicking the Build button for the **Row Source** property opens the Query Builder window, which allows you to select the field values you want to display in the combo box list.

> **QUICK TIP**
> The Edit List Items dialog box also allows you to specify a default value.

3. **Double-click Tours, then click Close in the Show Table dialog box**

   Because the most common tour duration is 7 days, you'll set 7 as the default value.

4. **Double-click TourNo in the Tours field list to add it to the first column of the query grid, double-click TourName, click the Sort list arrow for the TourName field, click Ascending, click the Close button on the Design tab, then click Yes to save the changes**

   The beginning of a SELECT statement is displayed in the Row Source property as shown in Figure G-7. This is an SQL (Structured Query Language) statement and can be modified by clicking the Build button. If you save the query with a name, you can use the query name in the Row Source property.

> **QUICK TIP**
> The title bar of the Property Sheet identifies the name of the control with which you are currently working.

5. **With the TourID combo box still selected, click the Format tab of the Property Sheet, click the Column Count property, change 1 to 2, click the Column Widths property, type 0.5;2, save the form, then display it in Form View**

   Entering 0.5;2 sets the width of the first column to 0.5 inches and the width of the second column to 2 inches. To test the new combo box, you add a sales record in the subform.

6. **Click the TourID list arrow in the second record in the subform, scroll as needed and click Black Sheep Hiking Club on the list, press [Tab], enter 8/1/13 as the SaleDate value, then press [→]**

   The new record is entered as shown in Figure G-8. The TourID field is the foreign key field in the Sales table, and it is linked to tour information through the TourNo primary key field in the Tours table. Selecting a specific TourID automatically fills in the correct Tour fields for that TourID number.

FIGURE G-7: **Changing TourID into a combo box**

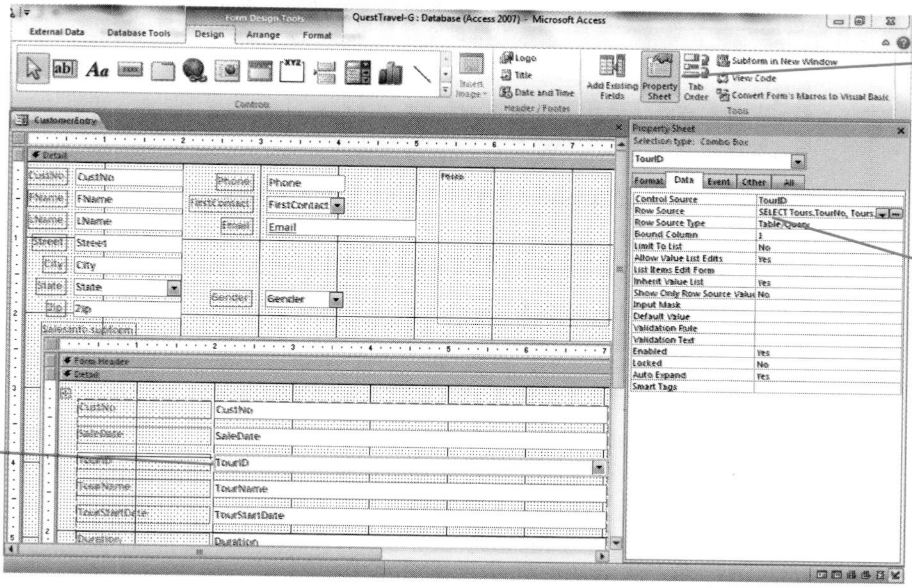
Property Sheet button
SELECT statement in Row Source
TourID text box changed into a combo box

FIGURE G-8: **Using the TourID combo box to enter a new record**

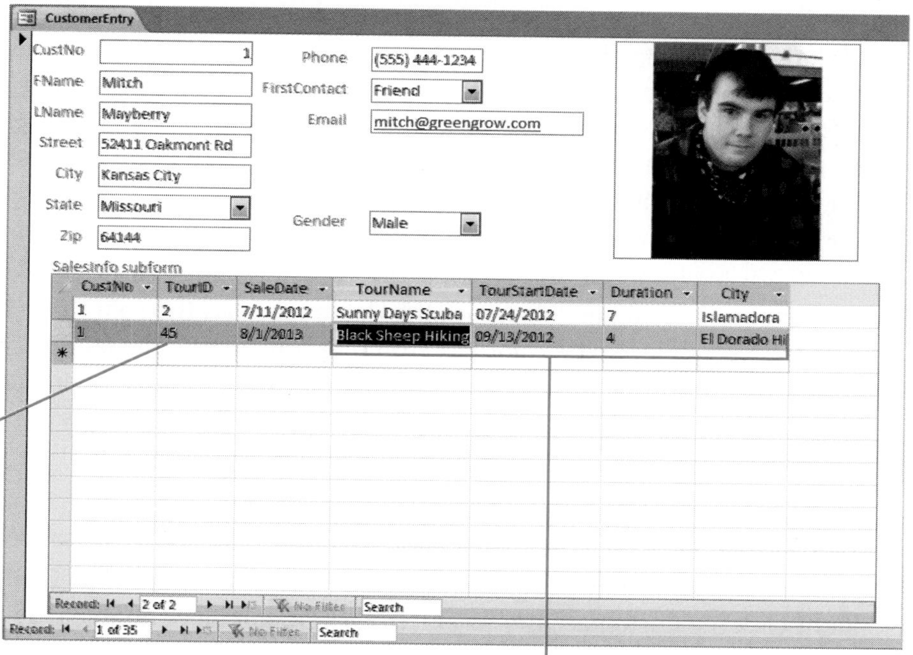
TourID is the foreign key field in the Sales table
Tour table values are automatically populated due to relationship with Sales table

Choosing between a combo box and a list box

The list box and combo box controls are very similar, but the combo box is more popular for two reasons. While both provide a list of values from which the user can choose to make an entry in a field, the combo box also allows the user to make a unique entry from the keyboard (unless the **Limit To List** property is set to Yes). More importantly, however, most users like the drop-down list action of the combo box.

Adding a Combo Box to Find Records

Most combo boxes are used to enter data; however, you can also use a combo box to find records. Often, controls used for navigation are placed in the Form Header section to make them easy to find. **Sections** determine where controls appear on the screen and print on paper. See Table G-2 for more information on form sections. You decide to add a combo box to the Form Header section to quickly locate customers in the CustomerEntry form.

STEPS

1. **Right-click the CustomerEntry form tab, click Design View, close the Property Sheet if it is open, then click the Title button in the Header/Footer group on the Design tab**
   The Form Header section opens and displays a label captioned with the name of the form. You modify the label and then add the combo box to find customers.
2. **Click between the words Customer and Entry in the label in the Form Header, press the [Spacebar], then use the ↔ pointer to drag the middle-right sizing handle to the left to about the 3" mark on the horizontal ruler**
   With the header open and space provided, you add a combo box to find records to the right side of the Form Header section.
3. **Click the Combo Box button in the Controls group, click in the Form Header at about the 5" mark on the horizontal ruler, click the Find a record option button in the Combo Box Wizard, click Next, double-click LName, double-click FName, click Next, click Next to accept the column widths and hide the key column, type Find Customer: as the label for the combo box, then click Finish**
   The new combo box is placed in the Form Header section as shown in Figure G-9. The accompanying label is hard to read because of the text color. You modify the label and widen the combo box.
4. **Click the Find Customer: label, click the Home tab, click the Font Color button arrow, click the Dark Blue, Text 2 color box (top row, fourth from the left), click the Unbound combo box, use the ↔ pointer to drag the middle-right sizing handle to the right edge of the form to widen the combo box, then click the View button**
   You test the combo box.
5. **Click the Find Customer: list arrow, then click Custard**
   The combo box works to find the customer named Custard as intended, but the combo box list entries are not in alphabetical order. You fix this in Form Design View by working with the Property Sheet of the combo box.
6. **Right-click the CustomerEntry form tab, click Design View, double-click the edge of the Unbound combo box in the Form Header to open its Property Sheet, click the Data tab, click SELECT in the Row Source property, then click the Build button for the Row Source property**
   The Query Builder opens, allowing you to modify the fields or sort order of the values in the combo box list.
7. **Click Ascending in the Sort cell for LName, click Ascending in the Sort cell for FName, click the Close button on the Design tab, click Yes when prompted to save changes, click the View button, then click the Find Customer: list arrow**
   This time, the combo box list is sorted in ascending order by last name, then by first name as shown in Figure G-10.
8. **Click Custard to test the combo box again, then save and close the CustomerEntry form**

QUICK TIP
To modify the number of items displayed in the list, use the **List Rows** property on the Format tab.

FIGURE G-9: **Adding a combo box to find records**

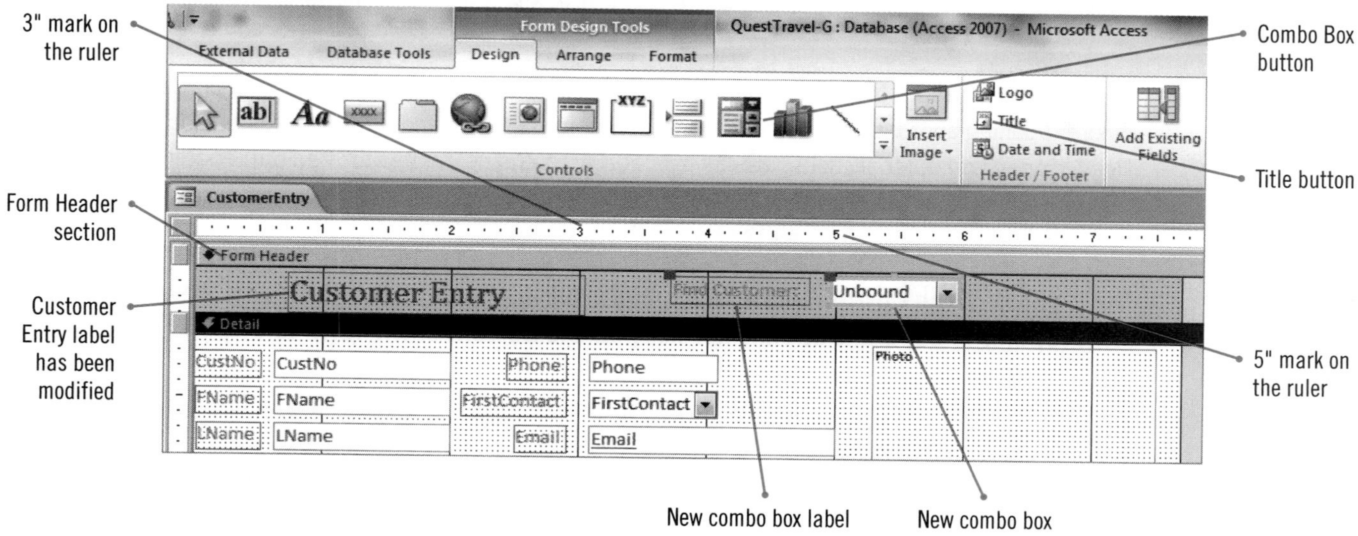
3" mark on the ruler
Form Header section
Customer Entry label has been modified
Combo Box button
Title button
5" mark on the ruler
New combo box label
New combo box

FIGURE G-10: **Final combo box used to find customers**

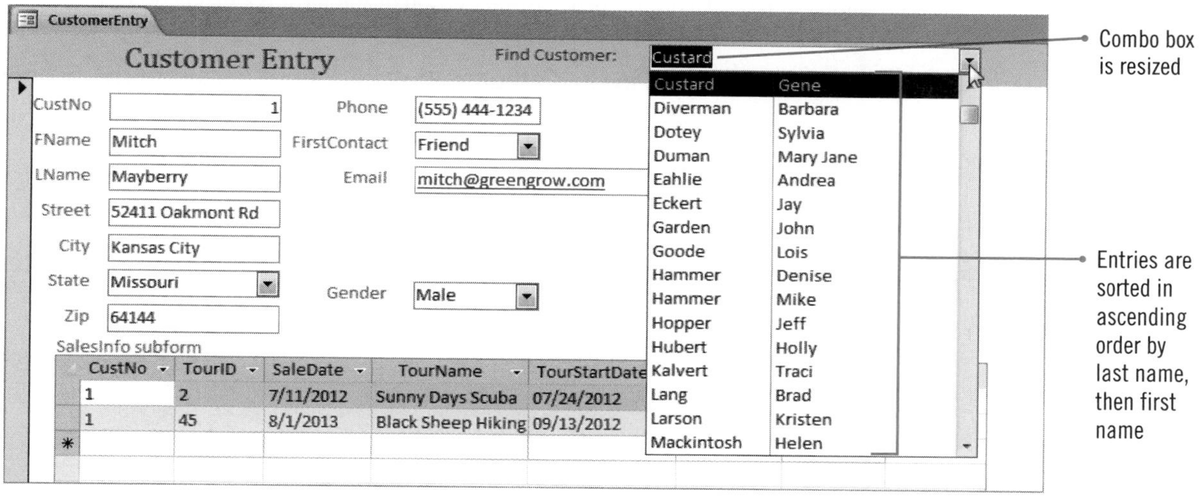
Combo box is resized
Entries are sorted in ascending order by last name, then first name

TABLE G-2: **Form sections**

section	description
Detail	Appears once for every record
Form Header	Appears at the top of the form and often contains command buttons or a label with the title of the form
Form Footer	Appears at the bottom of the form and often contains command buttons or a label with instructions on how to use the form
Page Header	Appears at the top of a printed form with information such as page numbers or dates
Page Footer	Appears at the bottom of a printed form with information such as page numbers or dates

UNIT
G
Access 2010

Adding Command Buttons

You use a **command button** to perform a common action in Form View such as printing the current record, opening another form, or closing the current form. Command buttons are often added to the Form Header or Form Footer sections. You add a command button to the Form Footer section of the CustomerEntry form to help other Quest Specialty Travel employees print the current record.

STEPS

TROUBLE
You may have to drag the Form Footer section bar down before you can select the sizing handles on the bottom of the subform.

1. **Right-click the CustomerEntry form in the Navigation Pane, click Design View, close the Property Sheet if it is open, then scroll to the bottom of the form to display the Form Footer section**
   Good form design minimizes extra work for the user. Therefore you'll resize the subform and shorten the form to eliminate vertical scrolling before adding a command button to the Form Footer.
2. **Click the edge of the subform to select it, drag the lower-middle sizing handle up using the ↕ pointer to resize the subform to about half of its current size, then use the ✢ pointer to drag the top edge of the Form Footer section up to remove the blank space as shown in Figure G-11**
   With the form shortened, you're ready to add a command button to the Form Footer to print the current record.
3. **Click the Button button in the Controls group, then click in the Form Footer at the 1" mark**
   The Command Button Wizard opens, listing over 30 of the most popular actions for the command button, organized within six categories as shown in Figure G-12.
4. **Click Record Operations in the Categories list, click Print Record in the Actions list, click Next, click Next to accept the default picture, type PrintRecord as the button name, then click Finish**
   Adding this command button to print only the current record helps avoid creating a printout that prints *every* record.
5. **Click the View button, click the Print button you added in the Form Footer section, then click OK to confirm that only one record prints**
6. **Save and close the CustomerEntry form**

FIGURE G-11: **Resizing the subform to eliminate scrolling**

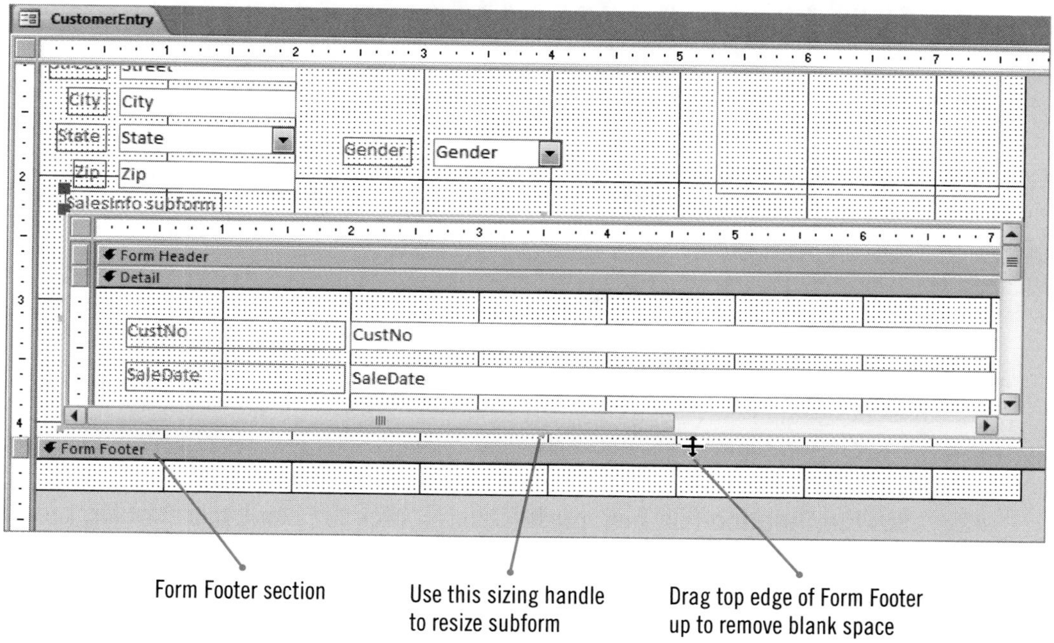

FIGURE G-12: **Command Button Wizard**

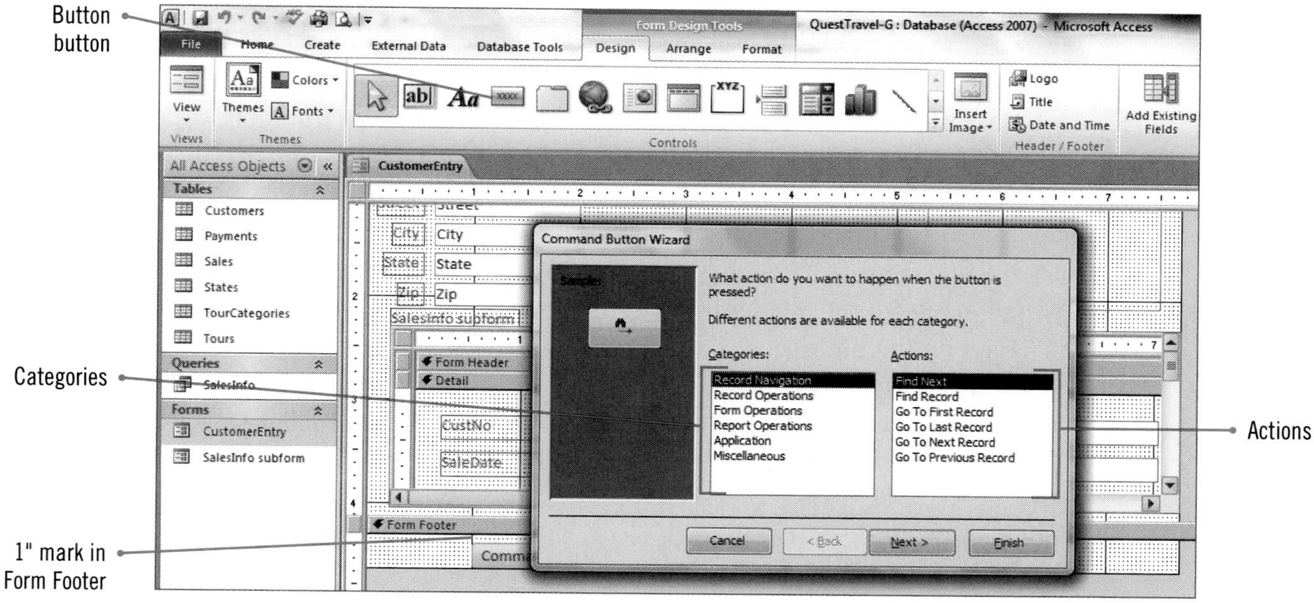

Access 2010

UNIT
G
Access 2010

Adding Option Groups

An **option group** is a bound control used in place of a text box when only a few values are available for a field. You add **option button** controls within the option group box to give the user a way to select a specific value for the field. Option buttons within an option group are mutually exclusive; only one can be chosen at a time. Samantha Hooper asks you to build a new form to view tours and sales information. You decide to use an option group to work with the data in the Duration field.

STEPS

1. **Click the Tours table in the Navigation Pane, click the Create tab, then click the Form button in the Forms group**
   A form/subform combination is displayed in Layout View, showing tour information in the main form and sales records in the subform. You delete the Duration text box and resize the controls to provide room for an option group.
2. **Click the Duration text box, press [Delete], click the blank placeholder, press [Delete], click the right edge of any text box, then use the ↔ pointer to drag the right edge of the controls to the left so they are about half as wide**
   You add the Duration field back to the form as an option group control using the blank space on the right that you created.
3. **Right-click the Tours tab, click Design View, click the Option Group button in the Controls group, then click to the right of the TourNo text box**
   The Option Group Wizard starts and prompts for labels. All the tours sold by Quest Specialty Travel have a duration of 3, 4, 5, 7, 10, or 14 days, so the labels and values will describe this data.
4. **Enter the Label Names as shown in Figure G-13, click Next, click the No, I don't want a default option button, click Next, then enter the Values to correspond with their labels as shown in Figure G-13**
   The Values are the actual data that are entered into the field and correspond with the **Option Value property** of each option button. The Label Names are clarifying text.

   > **TROUBLE**
   > Figure G-13 shows the completed Label Names and Values in the Option Group Wizard at the end of Step 4.

5. **Click Next, click the Store the value in this field list arrow, click Duration, click Next, click Next to accept Option buttons in an Etched style, type Duration as the caption, then click Finish**
   View and work with the new option group in Form View.
6. **Click the View button to switch to Form View, click the Next record button in the navigation bar for the main form twice to move to the Cyclone Ski Club tour, then click the 5 days option button**
   Your screen should look like Figure G-14. You changed the duration of this tour from 7 to 5 days. To add more option buttons to this option group later, work in Form Design View and use the Option Button button on the Design tab to add the new option button to the option group. Modify the value represented by that option button by opening the option button's Property Sheet and changing the Option Value property.
7. **Right-click the Tours form tab, click Close, click Yes when prompted to save changes, then click OK to accept Tours as the form name**

FIGURE G-13: **Option Group Label Names and Values**

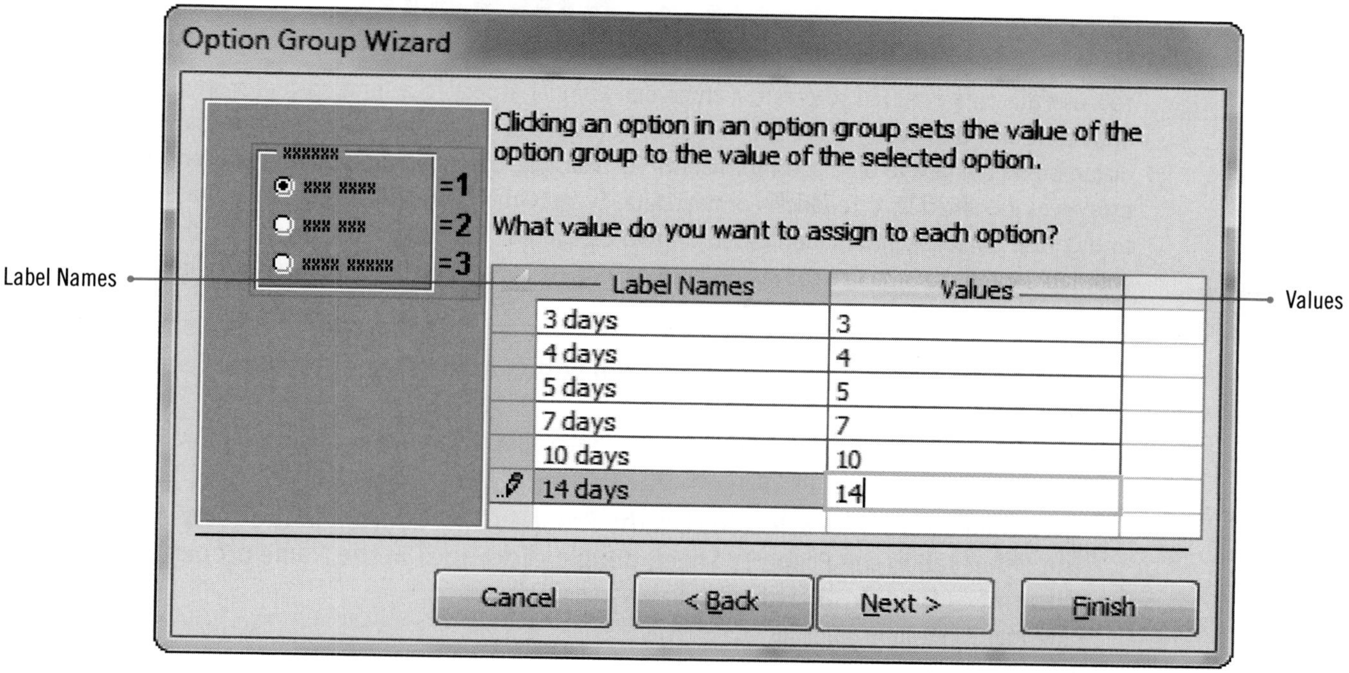

Option Group Wizard
Clicking an option in an option group sets the value of the option group to the value of the selected option.
What value do you want to assign to each option?
Label Names
Values
3 days
3
4 days
4
5 days
5
7 days
7
10 days
10
14 days
14
Cancel
< Back
Next >
Finish
Label Names
Values

FIGURE G-14: **Tours form with option group for Duration field**

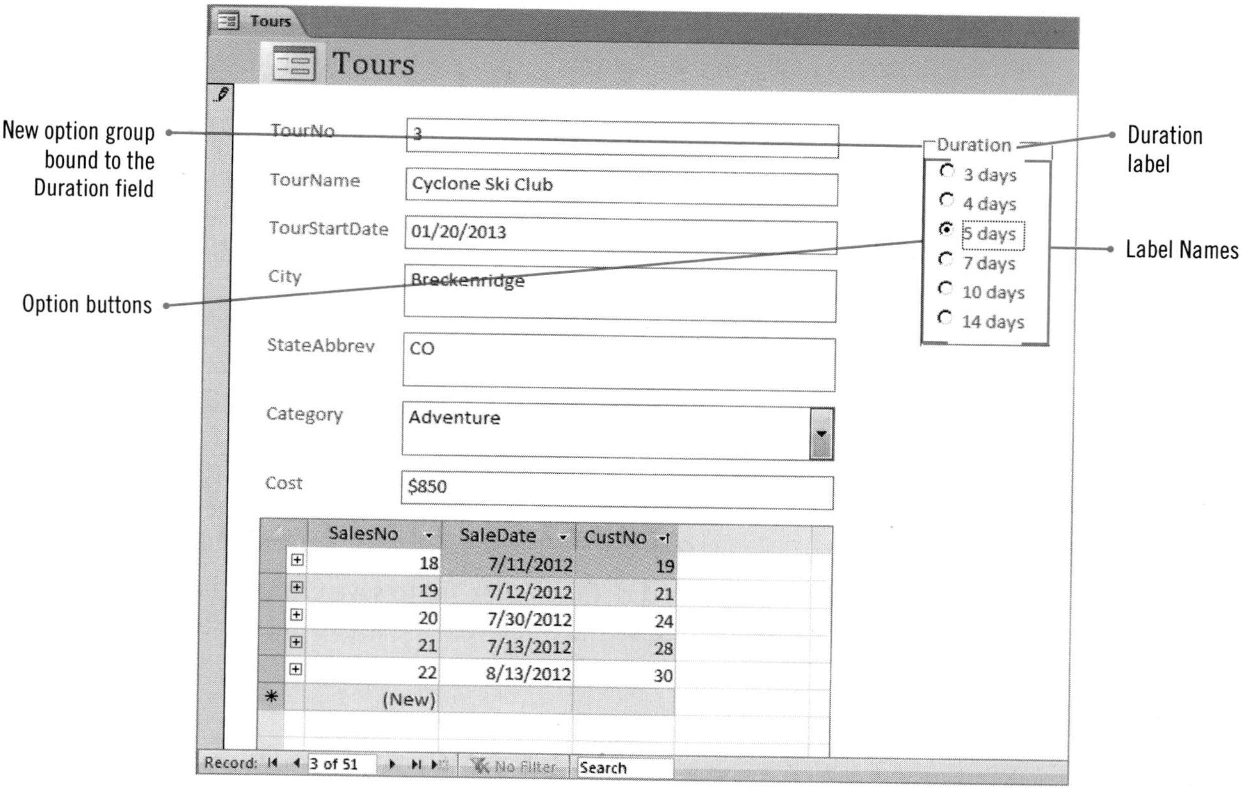

Tours
New option group bound to the Duration field
Option buttons
Duration label
Label Names
TourNo
3
TourName
Cyclone Ski Club
TourStartDate
01/20/2013
City
Breckenridge
StateAbbrev
CO
Category
Adventure
Cost
$850
Duration
3 days
4 days
5 days
7 days
10 days
14 days
SalesNo
SaleDate
CustNo
18
7/11/2012
19
19
7/12/2012
21
20
7/30/2012
24
21
7/13/2012
28
22
8/13/2012
30
(New)
Record: 3 of 51
No Filter
Search

Protecting data

You may not want to allow all users who view a form to change all the data that appears on that form. You can design forms to limit access to certain fields by changing the Enabled and Locked properties of a control. The **Enabled property** specifies whether a control can have the focus in Form View. The **Locked property** specifies whether you can edit data in a control in Form View.

UNIT G

Access 2010

Adding Tab Controls

You use the **tab control** to create a three-dimensional aspect to a form so that many controls can be organized and displayed by clicking the tabs. You have already used tab controls because many Access dialog boxes use tabs to organize information. For example, the Property Sheet uses tab controls to organize properties identified by categories: Format, Data, Event, Other, and All. Samantha Hooper asks you to organize database information based on two categories: Tours and Customers. You create a new form with tab controls to organize command buttons for easy access to tour and customer information.

STEPS

1. **Click the Create tab, click the Blank Form button in the Forms group, click the Tab Control button, then click the form**

   A new tab control is automatically positioned in the upper-left corner of the new form with two tabs. You rename the tabs to clarify their purpose.

2. **Click the Page1 tab to select it, click the Property Sheet button in the Tools group, click the Other tab in the Property Sheet, double-click Page1 in the Name property, type Customers, then press [Enter]**

   Give Page2 a meaningful name.

3. **Click Page2 to open its Property Sheet, click the Other tab (if it is not already selected), double-click Page2 in the Name property text box, type Tours, then press [Enter]**

   Now that the tab names are meaningful, you're ready to add controls to each page. In this case, you add command buttons to each page.

4. **Click the Customers tab, click the Button button in the Controls group, click in the middle of the Customers page, click the Form Operations category, click the Open Form action, click Next, click CustomerEntry, click Next, then click Finish**

   You add a command button to the Tours tab to open the Tours form.

5. **Click the Tours tab, click the Button button, click in the middle of the Tours page, click the Form Operations category, click the Open Form action, click Next, click Tours, click Next, then click Finish**

   Your new form should look like Figure G-15. To test your command buttons you must switch to Form View.

6. **Click the View button, click the command button on the Tours tab, click the Form1 form tab, click the Customers tab, click the command button on the Customers tab, then click the Form1 form tab again**

   Your screen should look like Figure G-16. The two command buttons opened the CustomerEntry and Tours forms. You would use the new form to make database objects (tables, queries, forms, and reports) that deal with the subjects of Customers and Tours much easier to find. Therefore you name the new form "Navigation."

7. **Right-click the Form1 form tab, click Close, click Yes to save changes, type Navigation as the form name, click OK, then close the QuestTravel-G.accdb database**

QUICK TIP

To add or delete a page, right-click a tab and choose Insert Page or Delete Page.

FIGURE G-15: **Adding command buttons to a tab control**

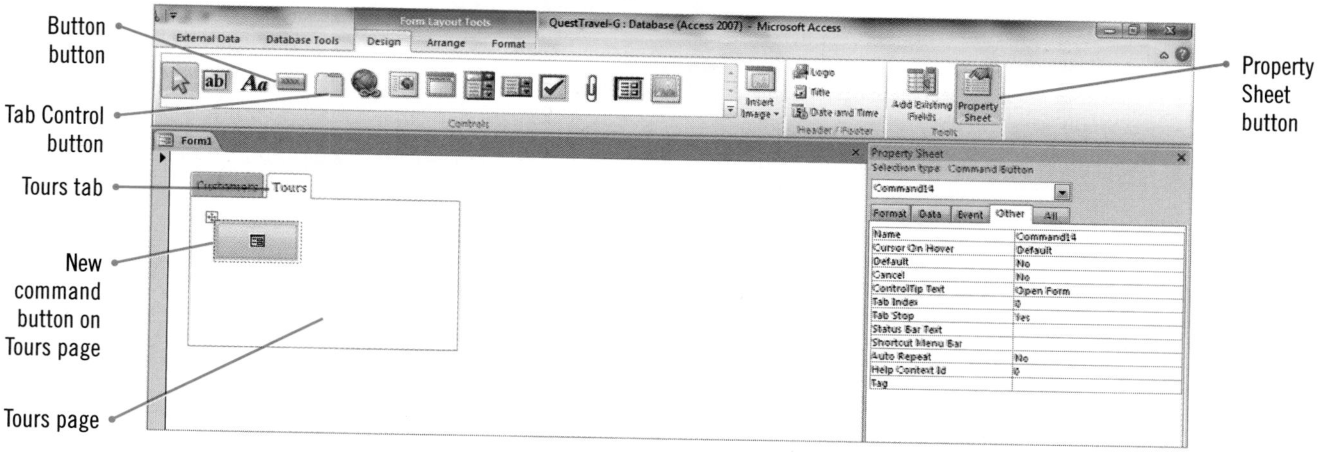
Button button
Tab Control button
Tours tab
New command button on Tours page
Tours page
Property Sheet button

FIGURE G-16: **Navigation form**

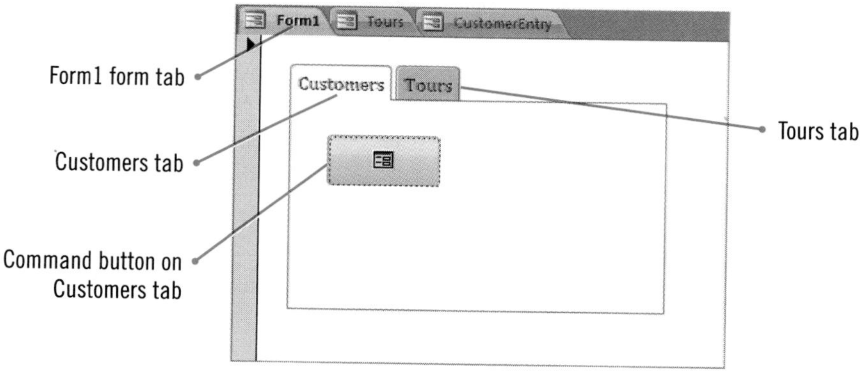
Form1 form tab
Customers tab
Command button on Customers tab
Tours tab

Access 2010

Practice

Concepts Review

For current SAM information, including versions and content details, visit SAM Central (http://www.cengage.com/samcentral). If you have a SAM user profile, you may have access to hands-on instruction, practice, and assessment of the skills covered in this unit. Since various versions of SAM are supported throughout the life of this text, check with your instructor for the correct instructions and URL/Web site for accessing assignments.

Identify each element of Form Design View shown in Figure G-17.

FIGURE G-17

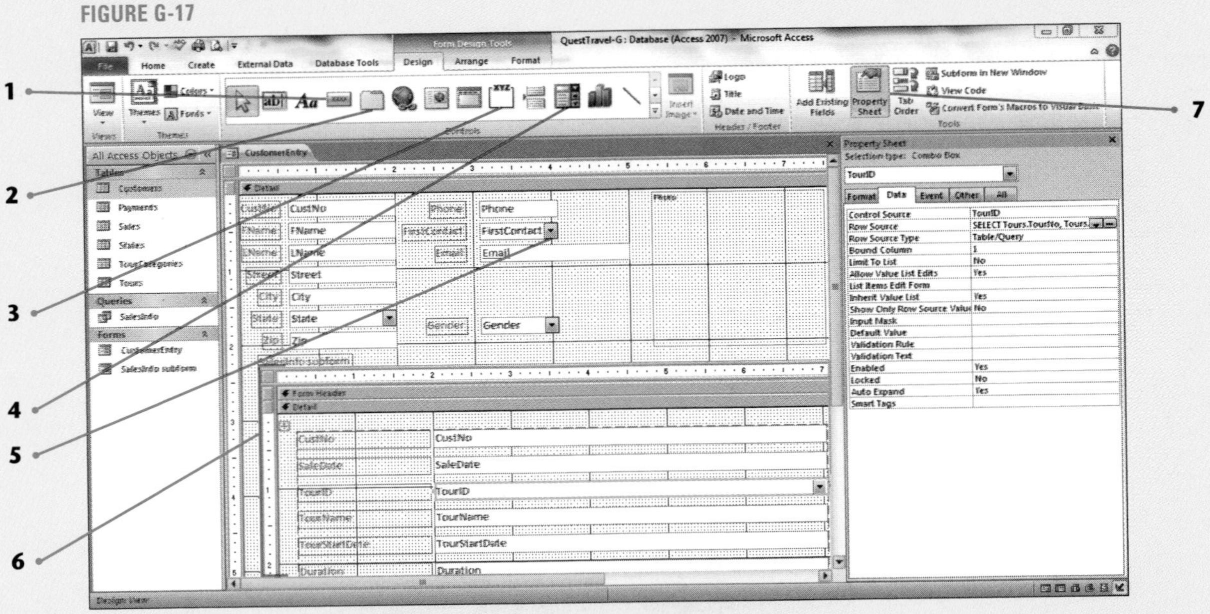

Match each term with the statement that best describes its function.

8. Command button
9. Subform
10. Tab control
11. Option group
12. Combo box

a. A bound control that displays a few mutually exclusive entries for a field
b. A bound control that is really both a list box and a text box
c. A control that shows records that are related to one record shown in the main form
d. An unbound control that executes an action when it is clicked
e. A control that provides a three-dimensional aspect to a form used to organize other controls

Select the best answer from the list of choices.

13. Which control works best to display three choices—1, 2, or 3—for a Rating field?

- **a.** Option group
- **b.** Text box
- **c.** Label
- **d.** Command button

14. Which control would you use to initiate a print action?

- **a.** Option group
- **b.** Text box
- **c.** Command button
- **d.** List box

15. Which control would you use to display a drop-down list of 50 states?

- **a.** Check box
- **b.** Combo box
- **c.** Field label
- **d.** List box

16. To view many related records within a form, use a:

- **a.** Subform.
- **b.** Design template.
- **c.** List box.
- **d.** Link control.

17. Which of the following form properties defines the fields and records that appear on a form?

- **a.** Record Source
- **b.** Row Source
- **c.** Default View
- **d.** List Items Edit Form

18. Which is a popular layout for a main form?

- **a.** Datasheet
- **b.** Columnar
- **c.** Global
- **d.** PivotTable

19. Which is a popular layout for a subform?

- **a.** Columnar
- **b.** Global
- **c.** PivotTable
- **d.** Datasheet

20. To align controls on their left edges, first:

- **a.** Click the Layout tab on the Ribbon.
- **b.** Click the Design tab on the Ribbon.
- **c.** Select the controls whose edges you want to align.
- **d.** Align the data within the controls.

21. Which control is most commonly used within an option group?

- **a.** Command button
- **b.** Option button
- **c.** Toggle button
- **d.** Check box

Skills Review

1. Use Form Design View.

- **a.** Start Access and open the Service-G.accdb database from the drive and folder where you store your Data Files. Enable content if prompted.
- **b.** Create a new form in Form Design View, open the Property Sheet for the new form, and choose Members as the Record Source.
- **c.** Open the Field List, then add all fields from the Members table to Form Design View.
- **d.** Move the Birthday, Initiation, MemberNo, CharterMember, and Status controls to a second column, just to the right of the FirstName, LastName, Street, and Zip fields at about the 4" mark on the horizontal ruler.
- **e.** Save the form with the name **MemberActivity**.

2. Add subforms.

- **a.** In Form Design View of the MemberActivity form, use the SubForm Wizard to create a subform below the Zip label at about the 2.25" mark on the vertical ruler.
- **b.** Use all three fields in the Activities table for the subform. Show Activities for each record in Members using MemberNo, and name the subform **Activities**.
- **c.** Drag the bottom edge of the form up to just below the subform control.
- **d.** View the MemberActivity form in Form View, and move through several records. Note that the form could probably be improved with better alignment, and that the Street text box is too narrow.

Skills Review (continued)

3. Align control edges.

- **a.** Switch to Form Design View, then edit the FirstName, LastName, CharterMember, and MemberNo labels to read **First Name**, **Last Name**, **Charter Member**, and **Member No**.
- **b.** Select the four labels in the first column (First Name, Last Name, Street, and Zip) together, and align their right edges.
- **c.** Move only the Charter Member label between the Member No and Status labels, position the Charter Member label to the left of the check box, then select the five labels in the third column (Birthday, Initiation, Member No, Charter Member, and Status) together, and align their right edges.
- **d.** Select the First Name label, the FirstName text box, the Birthday label, and the Birthday text box together. Align their top edges.
- **e.** Select the Last Name label, the LastName text box, the Initiation label, and the Initiation text box together. Align their top edges.
- **f.** Select the Street label, the Street text box, the MemberNo label, and the MemberNo text box together. Align their top edges.
- **g.** Select the Zip label, the Zip text box, the Charter Member label, and the Charter Member check box together. Align their top edges.
- **h.** Resize the Street and Zip text boxes to be about twice as wide as their current width.
- **i.** Select the FirstName text box, the LastName text box, the Street text box, and the Zip text box together. Align their left edges. Align the left edges of the Member No text box, Charter Member check box, and Status combo box controls.
- **j.** Save the MemberActivity form.

4. Add a combo box for data entry.

- **a.** In Form Design View, right-click the Zip text box, and change it to a combo box control.
- **b.** In the Property Sheet of the new combo box, click the Row Source property, then click the Build button.
- **c.** Select only the Zips table for the query, and then double-click the Zip field and the City field to add them to the query grid.
- **d.** Close the Query Builder window, and save the changes.
- **e.** On the Format tab of the Property Sheet, change the Column Count property to **2** and the Column Widths property to **0.5;1**.
- **f.** Close the Property Sheet, then save and view the MemberActivity form in Form View.
- **g.** In the first record for Micah Mayberry, change the Zip to **64153** using the new combo box. Change Micah's first and last name to your own.

5. Add a combo box to find records.

- **a.** Display the MemberActivity form in Design View.
- **b.** Open the Form Header section by clicking the Title button in the Header/Footer section on the Design tab.
- **c.** Modify the label to read **Member Activity**, then narrow the width of the label to be only as wide as needed.
- **d.** Add a combo box to the right side of the Form Header, and choose the "Find a record on my form…" option in the Combo Box Wizard.
- **e.** Choose the MemberNo, LastName, and FirstName fields in that order.
- **f.** Hide the key column.
- **g.** Label the combo box **FIND MEMBER:**.
- **h.** Move and widen the new combo box to be at least 2" wide, change the FIND MEMBER: label text color to black so it is easier to read, save the MemberActivity form, then view it in Form View.
- **i.** Use the FIND MEMBER combo box to find the Mildred Custard record. Notice that the entries in the combo box are not alphabetized on last name.
- **j.** Return to Form Design View, and use the Row Source property and Build button for the combo box to open the Query Builder to add an ascending sort order to the LastName and FirstName fields.
- **k.** Close the Query Builder, saving changes. View the MemberActivity form in Form View, and find the record for Bart Bouchart. Note that the entries in the combo box list are now sorted in ascending order first by the LastName field, then by the FirstName field.

Skills Review (continued)

6. **Add command buttons.**
   a. Display the MemberActivity form in Design View.
   b. Move and resize controls so that the entire form—Form Header, Detail, and Form Footer section—are clearly visible on the screen without scrolling.
   c. Use the Command Button Wizard to add a command button to the middle of the Form Footer section.
   d. Choose the Print Record action from the Record Operations category.
   e. Choose text for the button, type **Print Current Record**, then name the button **PrintButton**.
   f. Use the Command Button Wizard to add a command button to the right side of the Form Footer section.
   g. Choose the Close Form action from the Form Operations category.
   h. Choose text for the button, type **Close**, then name the button **CloseButton**.
   i. Select both command buttons then align their top edges.
   j. Save the form, display it in Form View, find your record, and, if requested by your instructor, print your record using the new Print Current Record command button.
   k. Close the MemberActivity form using the new Close command button.
7. **Add option groups.**
   a. Open the MemberActivity form in Form Design View.
   b. Because the initiation dues are always $25 or $50, the Initiation field is a good candidate for an option group control. Delete the existing Initiation text box and label. Move the MemberNo, CharterMember, and Status controls down if you need to make room for the option group.
   c. Click the Option Group button in the Controls group on the Design tab, then click the form where the Initiation text box was formerly positioned.
   d. Type **$25** and **$50** for Label Names, do not choose a default value, and enter **25** and **50** for corresponding Values.
   e. Store the value in the Initiation field, use option buttons, use etched style, and caption the option group **Initiation Fee:**.
   f. Move and align the Birthday controls below the Zip combo box, and move the Initiation option group and other controls as needed to clearly see all controls.
   g. Save the MemberActivity form, and view it in Form View, use the FIND MEMBER: combo box to find the record with your name, then change the Initiation Fee to **$25** using the new option group. The final form should look similar to Figure G-18.
   h. Use the Close command button to close the MemberActivity form.

FIGURE G-18

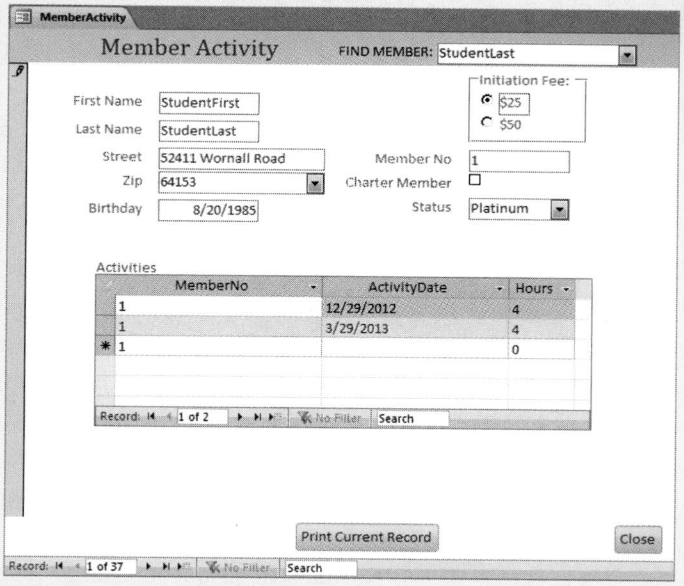

8. **Add tab controls.**
   a. Create a new blank form, and add a tab control to it.
   b. Open the Property Sheet, and use the Name property to rename Page1 to **Member Info** and Page2 to **Activity Info**.
   c. Right-click the Activity Info tab, click Insert Page, and use the Name property to rename the third page to **Dues Info**.
   d. On the Member Info tab, add a command button with the Preview Report action from the Report Operations category. Choose the MemberListing report, choose Text on the button, type **Preview Member Listing Report** as the text, and name the button **MemberListingButton**.

Skills Review (continued)

e. On the Activity Info tab, add a command button with the Open Form action from the Form Operations category. Choose the MemberActivity form, choose to open the form and show all the records, choose Text on the button, type **Open Member Activity Form** as the text, and name the button **MemberActivityButton**.

f. On the Activity Info tab, add a second command button with the Preview Report action from the Report Operations category. Choose the ActivityAnalysis report, choose Text on the button, type **Preview Activity Analysis Report** as the text, and name the button **ActivityAnalysisButton**.

g. Widen the command buttons on the Activity Info tab as needed so that all of the text on the command buttons is clearly visible as shown in Figure G-19.

h. On the Dues Info tab, add a command button with the Preview Report action from the Report Operations category. Choose the DuesAnalysis report, choose Text on the button, type **Preview Dues Analysis Report** as the text, and name the button **DuesAnalysisButton**.

i. Save the form with the name **Navigation**, then view it in Form View.

j. Test each button on each tab of the Navigation form to make sure it works as intended.

k. Close all open objects, then close the Service-G.accdb database.

FIGURE G-19

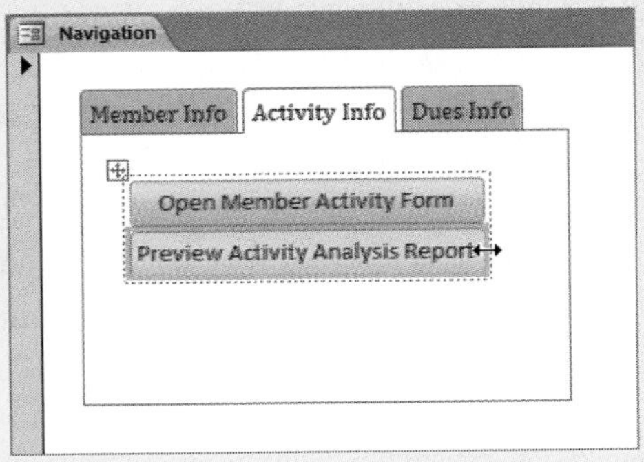

Independent Challenge 1

As the manager of a music store's instrument rental program, you have created a database to track instrument rentals to schoolchildren. You want to build an enhanced form for data entry.

a. Start Access, then open the database MusicStore-G.accdb from the drive and folder where you store your Data Files. Enable content if prompted.

b. Using the Form Wizard, create a new form based on all of the fields in the Customers and Rentals tables.

c. View the data by Customers, choose a Datasheet layout for the subform, then accept the default form titles of **Customers** for the main form and **Rentals Subform** for the subform.

d. Add another record to the rental subform for Amanda Smith by typing **888335** as the SerialNo entry and **10/1/13** as the RentalDate entry. Note that no entry is necessary in the RentalNo field because it is an AutoNumber field. No entry is necessary in the CustNo field as it is the foreign key field that connects the main form to the subform and is automatically populated when the forms are in this arrangement.

e. Change Amanda Smith's name to your own.

Advanced Challenge Exercise

- Open the Customers form in Design View.
- Right-align the text within each label control in the first column of the main form. (*Hint*: Use the Align Text Right button on the Home tab.)
- Narrow the CustNo and SchoolNo text boxes to about half of their current width, then move them to the right of the FirstName and LastName text boxes.
- Modify the FirstName, LastName, CustNo, and SchoolNo labels to read First Name, Last Name, Cust No, and School No.
- Delete the RentalNo and CustNo fields from the subform.

Independent Challenge 1 (continued)

- Open the Field List, and drag the Description field from the Instruments table to the subform above the existing text boxes. (*Hint*: Show all tables, then look in the Fields available in related tables section of the Field List.)
- Continue moving and resizing fields as needed so that your form in Form View looks like Figure G-20.

FIGURE G-20

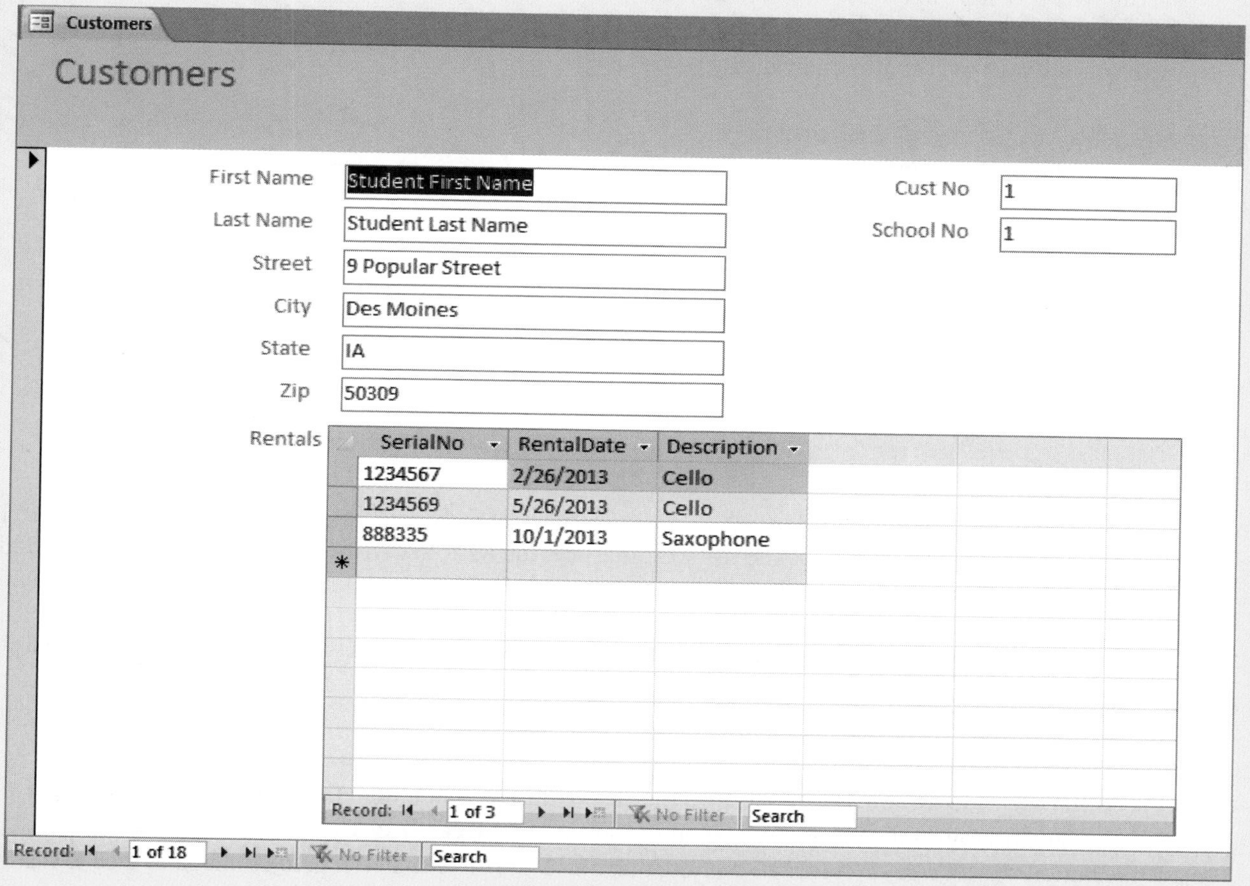

f. Save and close the Customers form, close the MusicStore-G.accdb database, then exit Access.

Independent Challenge 2

As the manager of a community effort to provide better access to residential real estate listings across a regional area, you have developed a database to track listings by realtor and real estate agency. You want to develop a form/subform system to see all listings within each realtor as well as within each real estate agency.

a. Start Access, then open the database RealEstate-G.accdb from the drive and folder where you store your Data Files. Enable content if prompted.

b. Using the Form Wizard, create a new form based on all of the fields in the Agencies, Realtors, and Listings tables.

c. View the data by Agencies, choose a Datasheet layout for each of the subforms, and accept the default titles of **Agencies**, **Realtors Subform**, and **Listings Subform**.

d. In Form Design View, use the Combo Box Wizard to add a combo box to the Form Header to find a record. Choose the AgencyName field, hide the key field, and enter the label **FIND AGENCY:**.

e. Change the text color of the FIND AGENCY: label to black, and widen the combo box to about twice its current size.

f. Add a command button to a blank spot on the main form to print the current record. Use the Print Record action from the Record Operations category. Use a picture on the button, and give the button the meaningful name of **PrintButton**.

Independent Challenge 2 (continued)

Advanced Challenge Exercise

- Use your skills to modify, move, resize, align text, and align control edges as shown in Figure G-21. (*Hint*: When you create a form with the Form Wizard, you may have to use the Remove Layout button on the Arrange tab in Form Design View in order to work with each control individually.)

FIGURE G-21

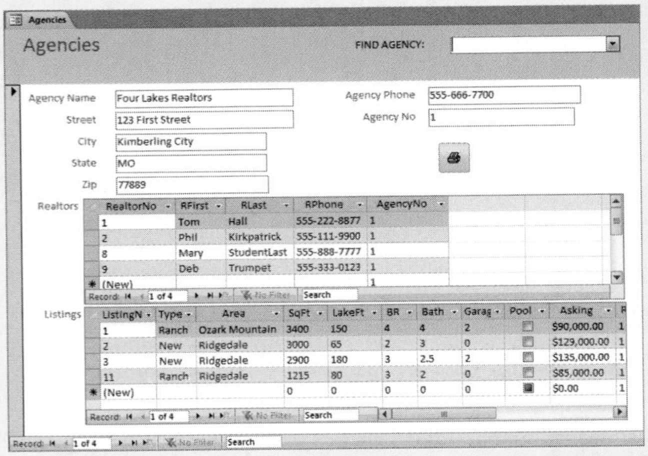

g. Save the form, view it in Form View, then use the combo box to find Side by Side Realtors.

h. Resize the columns of the subforms to view as much data as possible, change Jessica Polar's name in the first record of the Realtor's subform to your own, then print only the current record using the new command button if requested by your instructor.

i. Close the Agencies form, close the RealEstate-G.accdb database, and exit Access.

Independent Challenge 3

As the manager of a community effort to provide better access to residential real estate listings across a regional area, you have developed a database to track listings by realtor and real estate agency. You want to develop a navigation form to help find queries and reports in your database much faster.

a. Start Access, then open the database RealEstate-G.accdb from the drive and folder where you store your Data Files. Enable content if prompted.

b. Create a new blank form, and add a tab control to it.

c. Open the Property Sheet, and use the Name property to rename Page1 to **Realtors** and Page2 to **Listings**.

d. On the Realtors tab, add a command button with the Preview Report action from the Report Operations category. Choose the CurrentRealtors report, choose Text on the button, type **Preview Current Realtors** as the text, and name the button **cmdCurrentRealtors**. Note that *cmd* is the three-character prefix sometimes used to name command buttons.

e. On the Listings tab, add a command button with the Run Query action from the Miscellaneous category. Choose the AllListings query, choose Text on the button, type **Open All Listings query** as the text, and name the button **cmdAllListings**.

f. On the Listings tab, add a second command button with the Preview Report action from the Report Operations category. Choose the ListingReport report, choose Text on the button, type **Preview Listing Report** as the text, and name the button **cmdListingReport**.

g. Save the form with the name **Real Estate Navigation System**, then view it in Form View. The new form with the Listings tab selected should look like Figure G-22.

h. Test each command button on each tab on both the Realtors and Listings tabs.

i. Close all open objects, then close the RealEstate-G.accdb database and exit Access.

FIGURE G-22

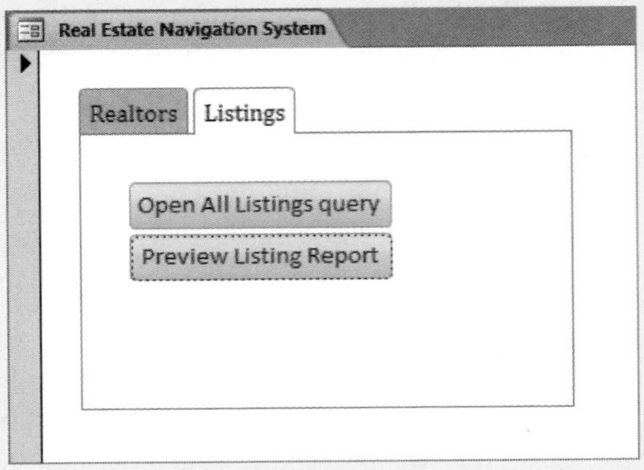

Real Life Independent Challenge

You have created an Access database to help manage college scholarship opportunities. You can keep the database updated more efficiently by creating some easy-to-use forms.

a. Start Access and open the Scholarships-G.accdb database from the drive and folder where you store your Data Files. Enable content if prompted.

b. Create a split form for the Scholarships table. Save and name the form **Scholarships**.

c. In Form Design View, use the Combo Box Wizard to add a combo box to the Form Header section to find a scholarship based on the ScholarshipName field. Hide the key column, and use the label **FIND SCHOLARSHIP:**.

d. Switch between Form View and Form Design View to test the new combo box control. In Form Design View, widen the combo box as necessary so that all of the scholarship names in the list are clearly visible. Change the color of the FIND SCHOLARSHIP: text to black.

e. In Form Design View, change the combo box's List Rows property (on the Format tab) to **50** and use the Build button to modify the Row Source property to add an ascending sort order based on the ScholarshipName field.

f. Save the form, and in Form View, use the combo box to find the Papa Johns Scholarship. Change **Papa Johns** to your name as shown in Figure G-23, then, if requested by your instructor, print only that record by using the Selected Record(s) option on the Print dialog box.

g. Save and close the Scholarships form, close the Scholarships-G.accdb database, then exit Access.

FIGURE G-23

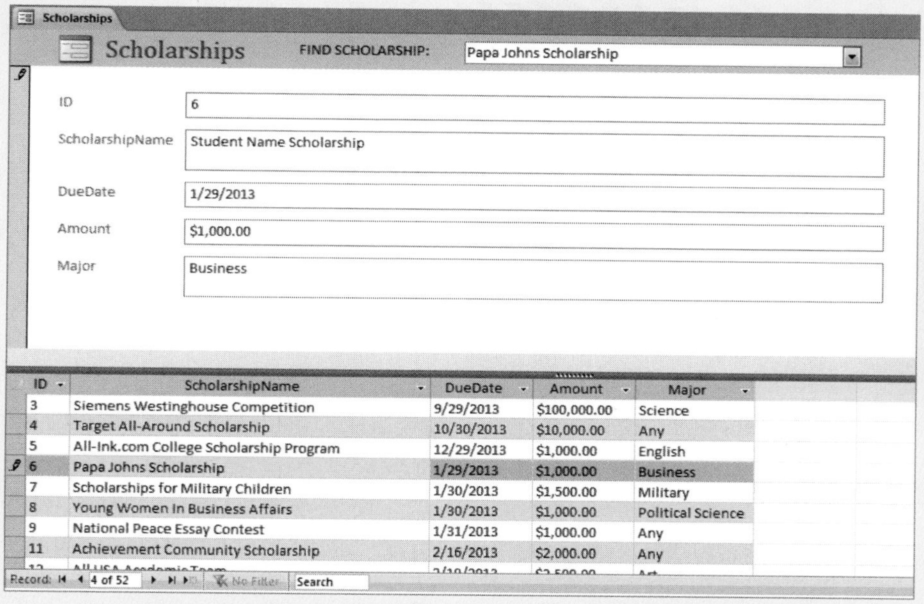

Visual Workshop

Open the Baseball-G.accdb database from the drive and folder where you store your Data Files. Enable content if prompted. Use Form Design View to create a form based on the Players table named **PlayerEntry**. Use your skills to modify, move, resize, align text, and align control edges as shown in Figure G-24. Note that both the PlayerPosition as well as the TeamNo fields are presented as option groups. The values that correspond with each Position label can be found in the Field Description of the PlayerPosition field in Table Design View of the Players table. The values that correspond with each Team label can be found by reviewing the TeamNo and TeamName fields of the Teams table.

FIGURE G-24

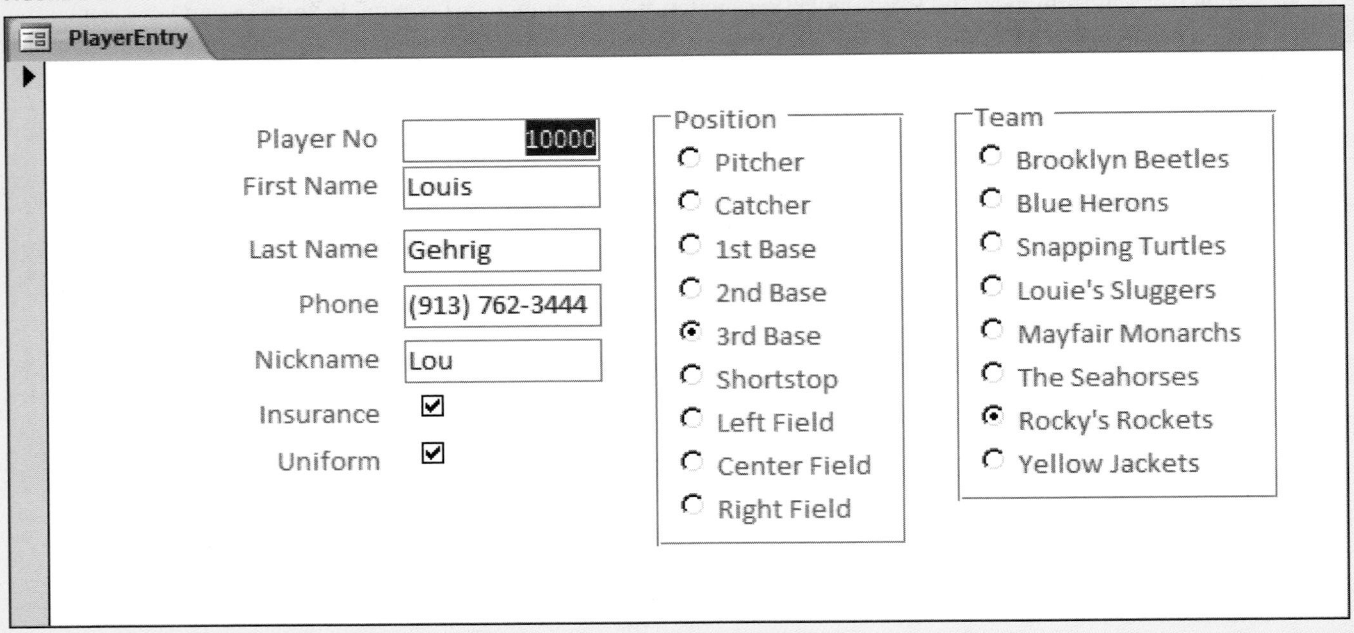

UNIT
H
Access 2010

Analyzing Data with Reports

Files You Will Need:

QuestTravel-H.accdb
RealEstate-H.accdb
MusicStore-H.accdb
Scholarships-H.accdb
Baseball-H.accdb

Although you can print data in forms and datasheets, **reports** give you more control over how data is printed and greater flexibility in presenting summary information. To create a report, you include text boxes to display data and use calculations and labels, lines, and graphics to clarify the data. Using additional report design skills, such as building summary reports and parameter reports and applying conditional formatting, you can create reports that not only present well but also analyze and clarify Quest Specialty Travel information.

OBJECTIVES

- Use Report Design View
- Create parameter reports
- Apply conditional formatting
- Add lines
- Use the Format Painter and themes
- Add subreports
- Modify section properties
- Create summary reports

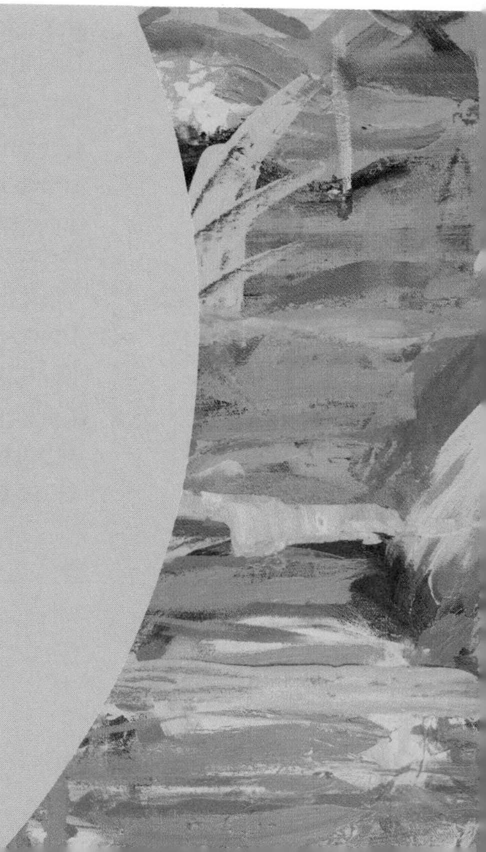

UNIT H

Access 2010

Using Report Design View

Report Design View allows you to work with a complete range of report, section, and control properties. Because Report Design View gives you full control of all aspects of a report, it is well worth your time to master. Samantha Hooper asks you to build a report that shows all tours grouped by category and sorted in descending order by cost. You use Report Design View to build this report.

STEPS

1. Start Access, open the QuestTravel-H.accdb database from the drive and folder where you store your Data Files, enable content if prompted, click the Create tab, then click the Report Design button in the Reports group

The first step to building a report in Report Design View is identifying the record source.

2. Click the Property Sheet button in the Tools group, click the Data tab, click the Record Source list arrow, then click Tours

With the record source identified, you're ready to add controls to the report. To build a report that shows tours grouped by category, you'll need to add a Category Header section. See Table H-1 for a review of report sections.

3. Scroll down in the report to view the Page Footer section, use the ↕ pointer to drag the top edge of the Page Footer section up to about the 1" mark on the vertical ruler, then click the Group & Sort button on the Design tab to open the Group, Sort, and Total pane if it is not already open

The Group, Sort, and Total pane gives you the ability to specify grouping and sorting fields and open group headers and footers.

> **TROUBLE**
> If you select the wrong group or sort field, change it by using the Group on or Sort by list arrows.

4. Click the Add a group button in the Group, Sort, and Total pane, click Category, click the Add a sort button in the Group, Sort, and Total pane, click Cost, click the from smallest to largest arrow button, then click from largest to smallest as shown in Figure H-1

With the grouping and sorting fields specified, you're ready to add controls to the report.

5. Click the Add Existing Fields button in the Tools group, click TourNo in the Field List, press and hold [Shift] as you click Cost in the Field List to select all fields in the Tours table, drag the selected fields to the Detail section of the report, then close the Field List window

Use cut and paste to move the Category controls to the Category Header section.

6. Click the report to remove the current selection, right-click the Category combo box, click Cut on the shortcut menu, right-click the Category Header section, then click Paste on the shortcut menu

You decide that the data is self-explanatory and doesn't need descriptive labels. Delete the labels, and position the text boxes across the page to finalize the report.

> **TROUBLE**
> Be sure to delete the labels on the left and move the text boxes on the right.

7. Click then press [Delete] to delete each label in the first column of the Detail section, then move and resize the remaining text boxes and shorten the Detail section as shown in Figure H-2

8. Click the Save button on the Quick Access toolbar, type ToursByCategory as the new report name, click OK, preview the first page of the report as shown in Figure H-3, then close the report

FIGURE H-1: **Creating a report in Report Design View**

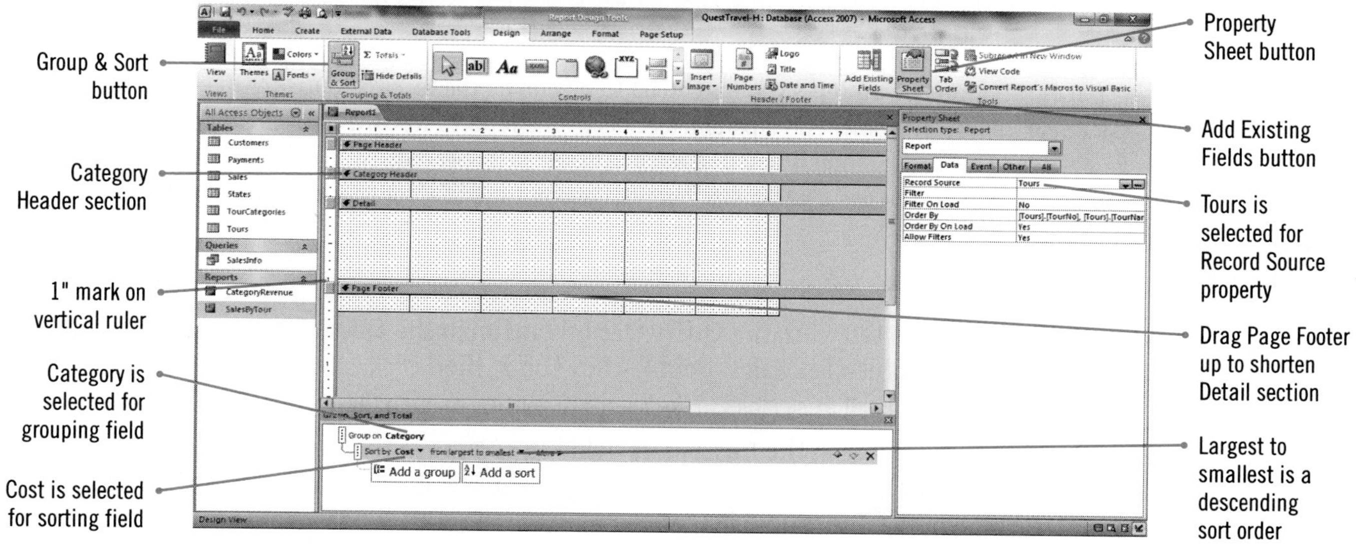

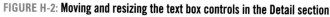

FIGURE H-2: **Moving and resizing the text box controls in the Detail section**

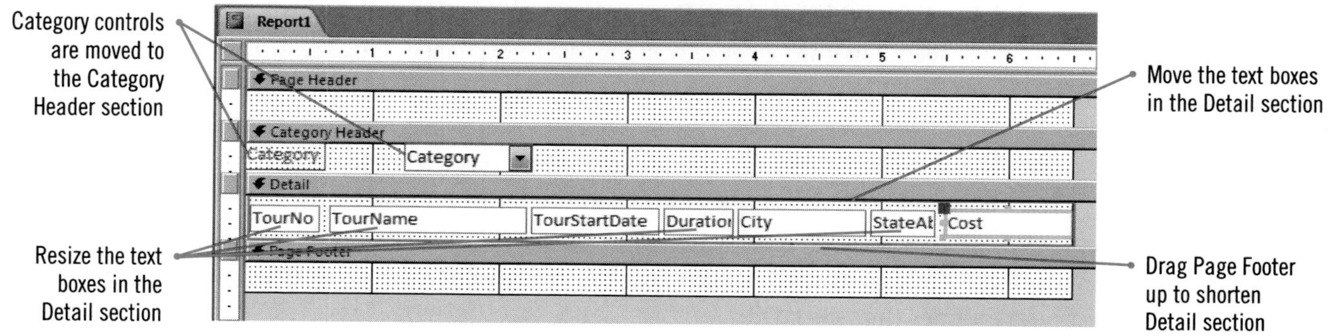

FIGURE H-3: **Previewing the ToursByCategory report**

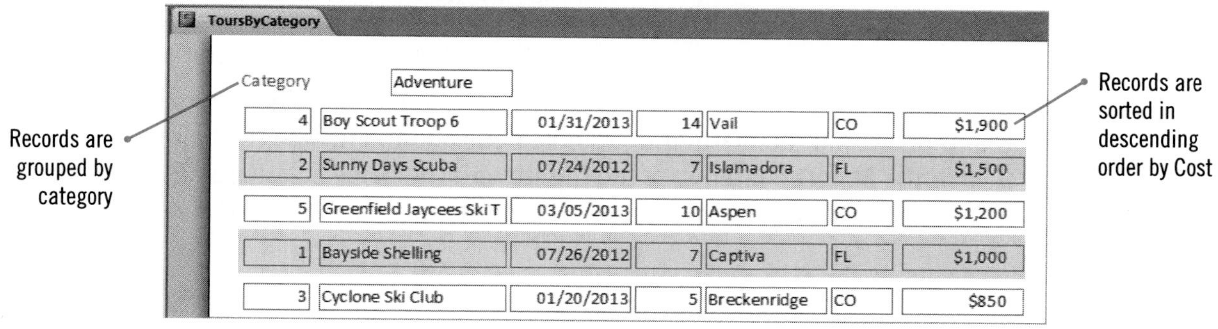

TABLE H-1: **Review of report sections**

section	where does this section print?	what is this section most commonly used for?
Report Header	At the top of the first page of the report	To print a title or logo
Page Header	At the top of every page (but below the Report Header on page 1)	To print titles, dates, or page numbers
Group Header	Before every group of records	To display the grouping field value
Detail	Once for every record	To display data for every record
Group Footer	After every group of records	To calculate summary statistics on groups of records
Page Footer	At the bottom of every page	To print dates or page numbers

UNIT H

Access 2010

Creating Parameter Reports

A **parameter report** prompts you for criteria to determine the records to use for the report. To create a parameter report, you base it on a parameter query. The report's **Record Source** property determines on what table or query the report is based. Samantha Hooper requests a report that shows all tour sales for a given period. You use a parameter query to prompt the user for the dates, then build the report on that query.

STEPS

1. **Click the Create tab, click the Query Design button in the Queries group, double-click Customers, double-click Sales, double-click Tours, then click Close**
   You want fields from all three tables in the report, so you add them to the query.
2. **Double-click FName in the Customers field list, LName in the Customers field list, SaleDate in the Sales field list, resize the Tours field list, then double-click Cost and TourName in the Tours field list**
   To select only those tours sold in a given period, you add parameter criteria to the SaleDate field.
3. **Click the Criteria cell for the SaleDate field, type Between [Enter start date] and [Enter end date], then widen the SaleDate column to see the entire entry as shown in Figure H-4**
   To test the query, run it and enter dates in the parameter prompts. **Parameter criteria** are text entered in [square brackets] that prompts the user for criteria each time the query is run. In this case, the user will be prompted for the start and end date.
4. **Click the View button on the Design tab to run the query, type 7/1/12 in the Enter start date box, click OK, type 7/31/12 in the Enter end date box, then click OK**
   Twenty-six records are displayed in the datasheet, each with a SaleDate value in July 2012.
5. **Click the Save button on the Quick Access toolbar, type SalesParameter as the new query name, then click OK**
   You use the Report button on the Create tab to quickly build a report on the SalesParameter query.
6. **Click the SalesParameter query in the Navigation Pane, click the Create tab, then click the Report button in the Reports group**
   The report is displayed in Layout View with records in July 2012. You decide to preview and save the report.
7. **Close the SalesParameter query, work in Layout and Design View to narrow the report so that it fits within the margins of a single page and to increase the height of the calculated field in the Report Footer, save the report with the name SalesParameter, then preview it as shown in Figure H-5, entering 7/1/12 as the start date and 7/31/12 as the end date**

QUICK TIP
Use Design View to narrow the report by dragging the right edge of the report to the left.

FIGURE H-4: **Creating parameter criteria in a query**

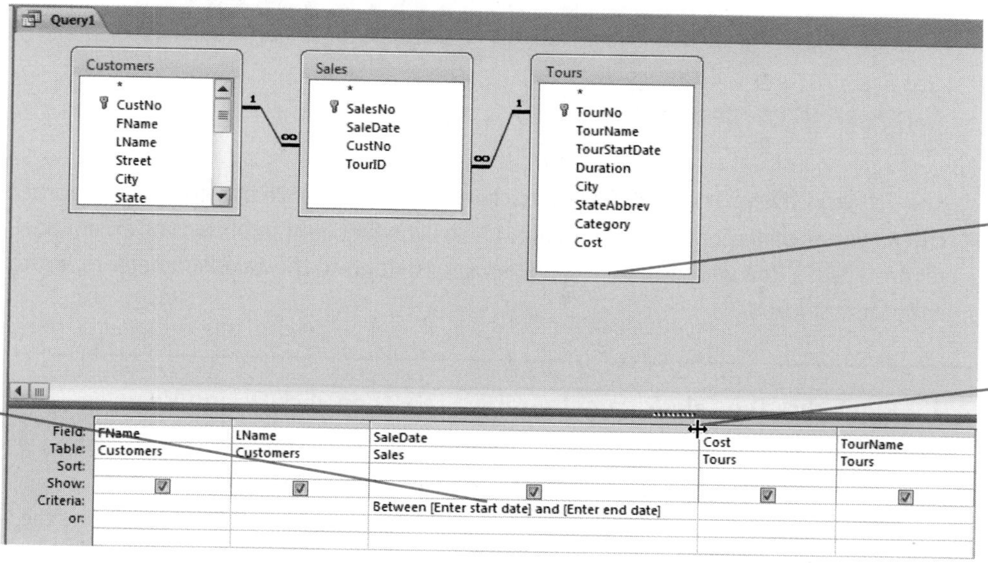

FIGURE H-5: **Previewing the SalesParameter report**

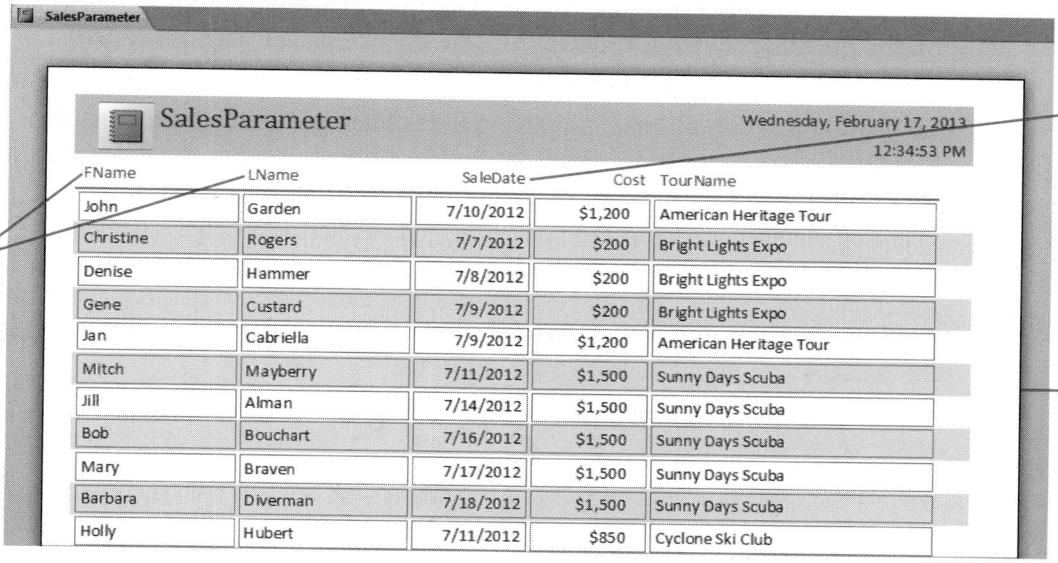

Parameter criteria

In Query Design View, you must enter parameter criteria within [square brackets]. The parameter criterion you entered appears as a prompt in the Enter Parameter Value dialog box. The entry you make in the Enter Parameter Value box is used as the final criterion for the field that contains the parameter criteria.

UNIT
H
Access 2010

Applying Conditional Formatting

Conditional formatting allows you to change the appearance of a control on a form or report based on criteria you specify. Conditional formatting helps you highlight important or exceptional data on a form or report. You want to apply conditional formatting to the SalesParameter report to emphasize different tour cost levels.

STEPS

1. **Right-click the SalesParameter report tab, then click Design View**
2. **Click the Cost text box in the Detail section, click the Format tab, then click the Conditional Formatting button in the Control Formatting group**
   The Conditional Formatting Rules Manager dialog box opens, asking you to define the conditional formatting rules. You want Cost values between 500 and 1000 to be formatted with a yellow background color.
3. **Click New Rule, click the text box to the right of the between arrow, type 500, click the and box, type 999, click the Background color button arrow, click the Yellow box on the bottom row, then click OK**
   You add the second conditional formatting rule to format cost values greater than or equal to 1000 with a light green background color.
4. **Click New Rule, click the between list arrow, click greater than or equal to, click the value box, type 1000, click the Background color button arrow, click the Light Green box on the bottom row, then click OK**
   The Conditional Formatting dialog box with two rules should look like Figure H-6.
5. **Click OK in the Conditional Formatting Rules Manager dialog box, right-click the SalesParameter report tab, click Print Preview, type 8/1/12 in the Enter start date box, click OK, type 8/31/12 in the Enter end date box, then click OK**
   Conditional formatting rules applied a yellow background color to the Cost text box for two tours because the Cost value is between 500 and 1000 as shown in Figure H-7. Conditional formatting applied a green background color to the Cost text box for one tour because the Cost value is greater than 1000. Default formatting was applied to the Cost text box for two tours because they do not meet any of the conditions in the Conditional Formatting Rules Manager dialog box.
6. **Save then close the SalesParameter report**

QUICK TIP

You can add up to three conditional formats for any combination of selected controls.

FIGURE H-6: **Conditional Formatting Rules Manager dialog box**

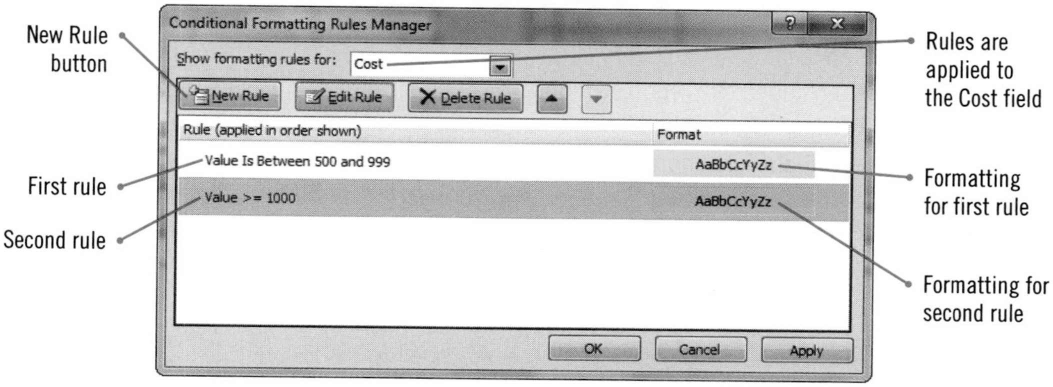
New Rule button
First rule
Second rule
Rules are applied to the Cost field
Formatting for first rule
Formatting for second rule
Conditional Formatting Rules Manager
Show formatting rules for: Cost
New Rule
Edit Rule
Delete Rule
Rule (applied in order shown)
Format
Value Is Between 500 and 999
AaBbCcYyZz
Value >= 1000
AaBbCcYyZz
OK
Cancel
Apply

FIGURE H-7: **Conditional formatting applied to SalesParameter report**

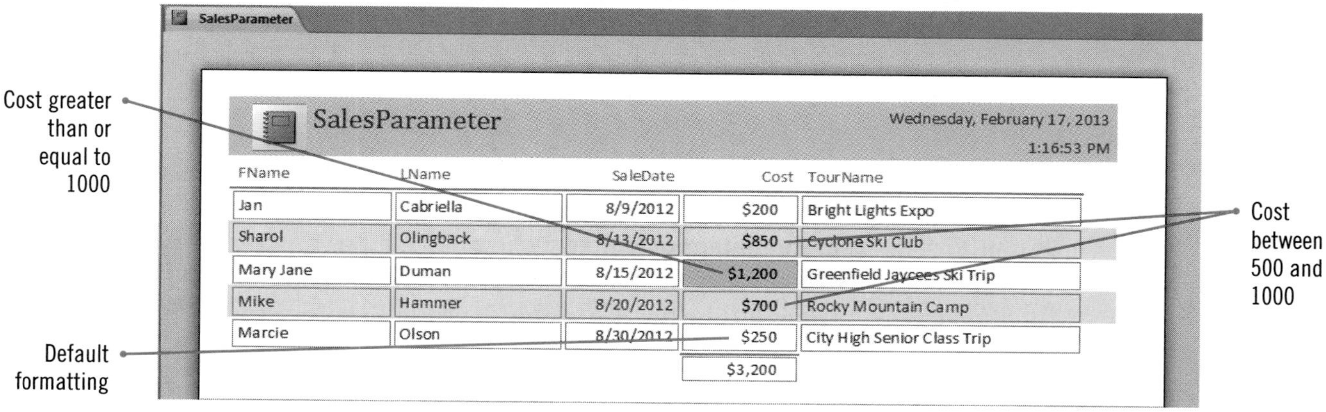
Cost greater than or equal to 1000
Default formatting
Cost between 500 and 1000
SalesParameter
SalesParameter
Wednesday, February 17, 2013
1:16:53 PM
FName LName SaleDate Cost TourName
Jan Cabriella 8/9/2012 $200 Bright Lights Expo
Sharol Olingback 8/13/2012 $850 Cyclone Ski Club
Mary Jane Duman 8/15/2012 $1,200 Greenfield Jaycees Ski Trip
Mike Hammer 8/20/2012 $700 Rocky Mountain Camp
Marcie Olson 8/30/2012 $250 City High Senior Class Trip
$3,200

Conditional formatting using data bars

A new feature of Access 2010 allows you to compare the values of one column to another with small data bars. To use this feature, use the "Compare to other records" rule type option in the New Formatting Rule dialog box as shown in Figure H-8.

FIGURE H-8: **Conditional formatting with data bars**

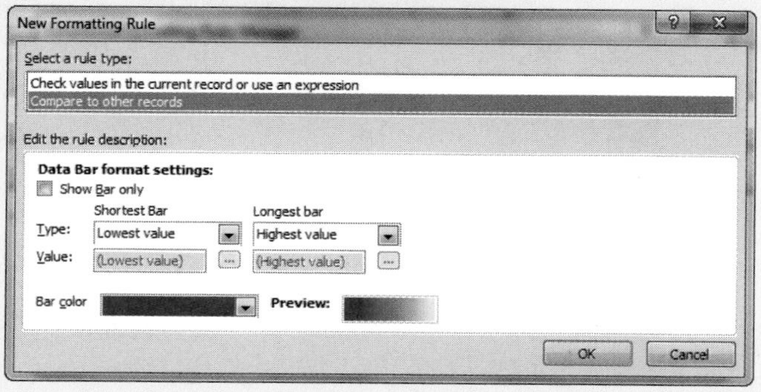
New Formatting Rule
Select a rule type:
Check values in the current record or use an expression
Compare to other records
Edit the rule description:
Data Bar format settings:
Show Bar only
Shortest Bar
Longest bar
Type:
Lowest value
Highest value
Value:
(Lowest value)
(Highest value)
Bar color
Preview:
OK
Cancel

UNIT
H
Access 2010

Adding Lines

Lines are often added to a report to highlight or enhance the clarity of information. For example, you might want to separate the report header and page header information from the rest of the report with a horizontal line. You can also use short lines to indicate subtotals and grand totals. Samantha Hooper likes the data on the CategoryRevenue report, which has already been created in the QuestTravel-H database, but she asks you to enhance the report by adding a grand total calculation and separating the categories more clearly. Lines will help clarify the information.

STEPS

1. **Double-click the CategoryRevenue report in the Navigation Pane to open it in Report View, then scroll to the end of the report**

   The report needs lines separating the tour categories and a grand total calculation on the last page of the report. You use Report Design View to make these improvements.

2. **Right-click the CategoryRevenue report tab, click Design View, right-click the =Sum([Revenue]) text box in the Category Footer section, click Copy, right-click the Report Footer section, click Paste, press [→] enough times to position the expression directly under the one in the Category Footer, click Subtotal: in the Report Footer section to select it, double-click Subtotal: in the label to select it, type Grand Total:, then press [Enter]**

   The =Sum([Revenue]) expression in the Report Footer section will sum the Revenue values in the entire report, whereas the same expression in the Category Footer section sums Revenue values in each category. With the calculations in place, you add clarifying lines.

QUICK TIP
Lines can be difficult to find in Report Design View. See the "Line troubles" box in this lesson for tips on working with lines.

3. **Click the down arrow button in the Controls group to show the second row of controls, click the Line button, press and hold [Shift], drag from the upper-left edge of =Sum([Revenue]) in the Category Footer section to its upper-right edge, press [Ctrl][C] to copy the line, click the Report Footer section, press [Ctrl][V] two times to paste the line twice, then move the lines just below the =Sum([Revenue]) expression in the Report Footer section**

   Pressing [Shift] while drawing a line makes sure that the line remains perfectly horizontal or vertical. The single line above the calculation in the Category Footer section indicates that the calculation is a subtotal. Double lines below the calculation in the Report Footer section indicate a grand total. You also want to add a line to visually separate the categories.

4. **Click the down arrow button in the Controls group, click the Line button, press and hold [Shift], then drag along the bottom of the Category Footer section**

   The final CategoryRevenue report in Report Design View is shown in Figure H-9.

5. **Right-click the CategoryRevenue report tab, click Print Preview, then navigate to the last page of the report**

   The last page of the CategoryRevenue report shown in Figure H-10 displays the Category Footer section line as well as the subtotal and grand total lines.

FIGURE H-9: **Adding lines to a report**

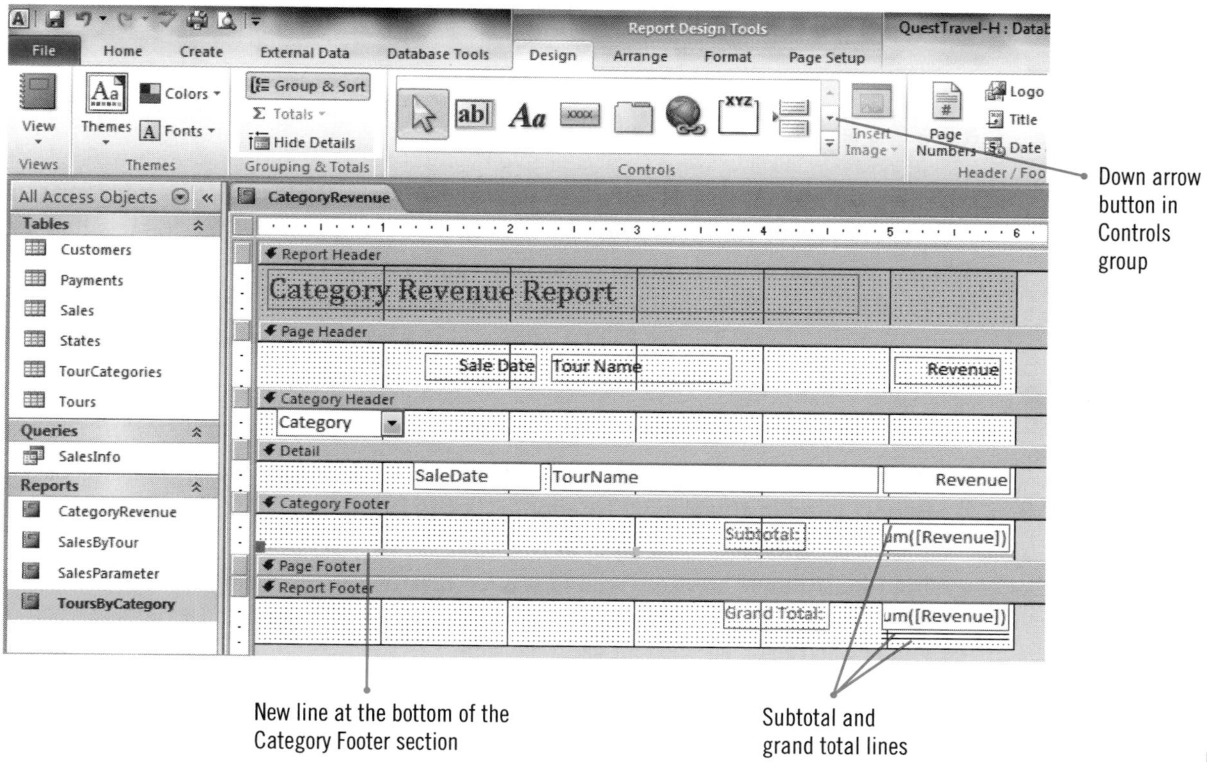

FIGURE H-10: **Previewing the last page of the CategoryRevenue report**

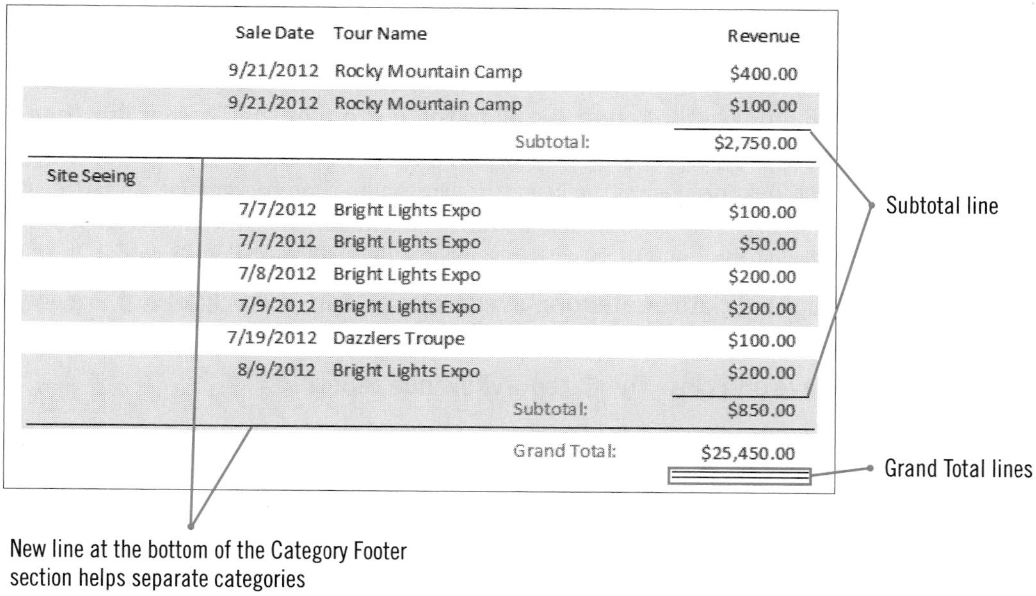
Sale Date
Tour Name
Revenue
9/21/2012 Rocky Mountain Camp $400.00
9/21/2012 Rocky Mountain Camp $100.00
Subtotal: $2,750.00
Site Seeing
7/7/2012 Bright Lights Expo $100.00
7/7/2012 Bright Lights Expo $50.00
7/8/2012 Bright Lights Expo $200.00
7/9/2012 Bright Lights Expo $200.00
7/19/2012 Dazzlers Troupe $100.00
8/9/2012 Bright Lights Expo $200.00
Subtotal: $850.00
Grand Total: $25,450.00
Subtotal line
Grand Total lines
New line at the bottom of the Category Footer section helps separate categories

Line troubles

Sometimes lines are difficult to find in Report Design View because they are placed against the edge of a section or the edge of other controls. To find lines that are positioned next to the edge of a section, drag the section bar to expand the section and expose the line. Recall that to draw a perfectly horizontal line, you hold [Shift] while creating or resizing the line. It is easy to accidentally widen a line beyond the report margins, thus creating extra unwanted pages in your printout. To fix this problem, narrow any controls that extend beyond the margins of the printout, and drag the right edge of the report to the left. Note that the default left and right margins for an 8.5 × 11-inch sheet of paper are often .25 inches each, so a report in portrait orientation must be no wider than 8 inches, and a report in landscape orientation must be no wider than 10.5 inches.

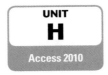

Using the Format Painter and Themes

The **Format Painter** is a tool you use to copy multiple formatting properties from one control to another in Design or Layout View for forms and reports. **Themes** are predefined formats that you apply to the database to set all of the formatting enhancements such as font, color, and alignment on all forms and reports. You think the CategoryRevenue report can be improved with a few formatting embellishments. You can use the Format Painter to quickly change the characteristics of labels in the Page Header section, then apply a built-in theme to the entire report.

STEPS

1. **Right-click the CategoryRevenue report tab, click Design View, click the Category Revenue Report label in the Report Header, click the Home tab, click the Format Painter button, then click the Sale Date label in the Page Header section**

   The Format Painter applied several formatting characteristics including font face, font color, and font size from the label in the Report Header section to the Sale Date label in the Page Header section. You like the new font face and color, but the font size is too large.

2. **Click the Sale Date label, click the Font Size list arrow 18 in the Text Formatting group, click 12, double-click the Format Painter button, click the Tour Name label in the Page Header section, click the Revenue label in the Page Header section, then press [Esc] to release the Format Painter pointer**

   Now that you've mastered the Format Painter, you're ready to see how themes affect the formatting of the report.

> **QUICK TIP**
> The selected theme is automatically applied to all forms and reports in the database.

3. **Click the Design tab, click the Themes button, point to several themes to observe the changes in the report, scroll to the bottom of the Themes list, then click Trek (first column, last row) as shown in Figure H-11**

   The Trek theme gives the Report Header section a tan background. All text now has a consistent font face, controls in the same section are the same font size, and all controls have complementary font colors. You preview the report to review the changes as they will appear on a printout.

4. **Right-click the CategoryRevenue report tab, then click Print Preview**

   The first page of the CategoryRevenue report is shown in Figure H-12.

5. **Save and close the CategoryRevenue report**

FIGURE H-11: **Applying a theme to a report**

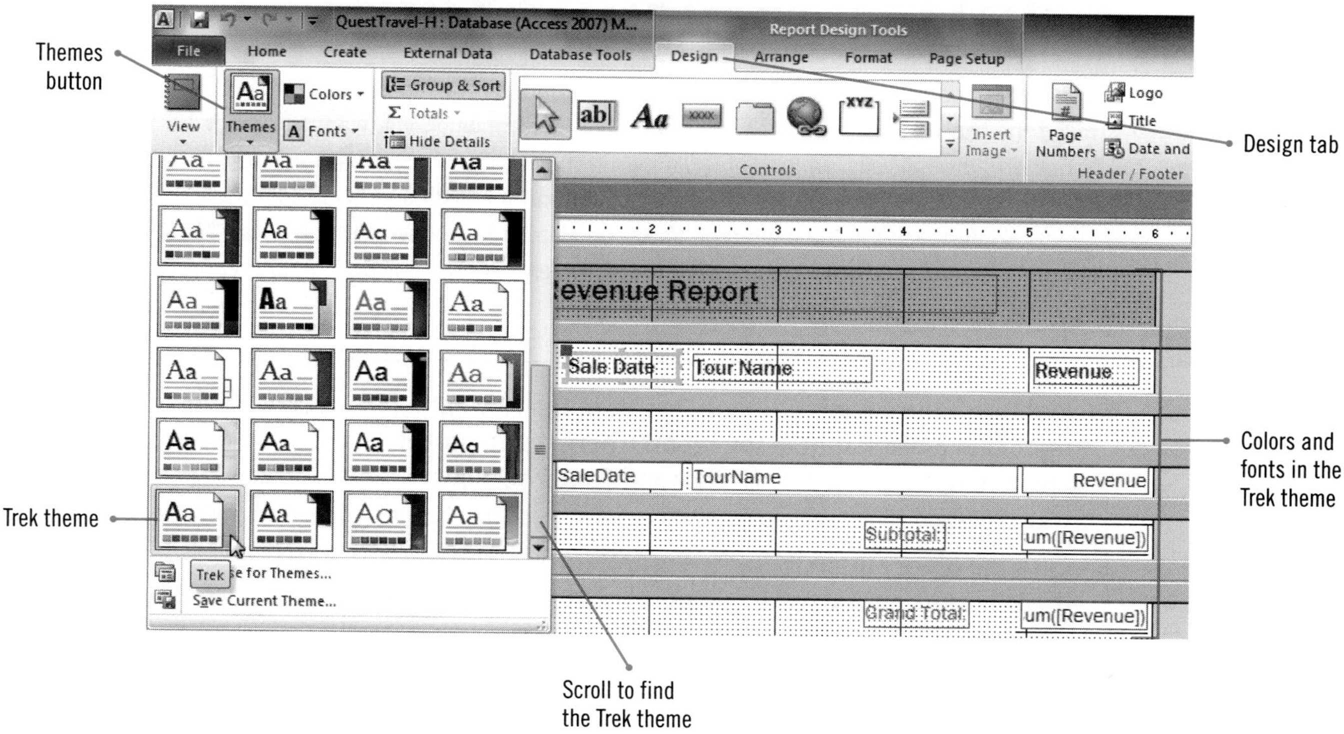
Themes button
Design tab
Colors and fonts in the Trek theme
Trek theme
Scroll to find the Trek theme

FIGURE H-12: **Print Preview of Trek theme applied to the CategoryRevenue report**

Category Revenue Report

	Sale Date	Tour Name	Revenue
Adventure			
	4/30/2012	Bayside Shelling	$150.00
	4/30/2012	Bayside Shelling	$250.00
	5/1/2012	Bayside Shelling	$450.00
	5/1/2012	Bayside Shelling	$250.00
	5/2/2012	Bayside Shelling	$750.00
	6/2/2012	Greenfield Jaycees Ski Trip	$100.00
	6/2/2012	Greenfield Jaycees Ski Trip	$200.00
	6/2/2012	Greenfield Jaycees Ski Trip	$600.00
	7/11/2012	Sunny Days Scuba	$750.00
	7/11/2012	Cyclone Ski Club	$450.00
	7/11/2012	Cyclone Ski Club	$100.00
	7/11/2012	Sunny Days Scuba	$550.00
	7/12/2012	Cyclone Ski Club	$450.00

UNIT H

Access 2010

Adding Subreports

A **subreport** control displays a report within another report. The report that contains the subreport control is called the **main report**. You can use a subreport control when you want to change the order in which information automatically prints. For example, if you want report totals (generally found in the Report Footer section, which prints on the last page) to print on the first page, you could use a subreport to place grand total information in the main report's Report Header section, which prints first. You want the CategoryRevenue report to automatically print at the end of the ToursByCategory report. You use a subreport in the Report Footer section to accomplish this.

STEPS

1. **Right-click the ToursByCategory report in the Navigation Pane, click Design View, right-click a blank spot in the report, then click Report Header/Footer on the shortcut menu to open the Report Header and Footer sections**

   With the Report Footer section open, you're ready to add the CategoryRevenue subreport.

2. **Click the More button in the Controls group, click the Subform/Subreport button, then click the left side of the Report Footer to start the SubReport Wizard as shown in Figure H-13**

   The first question of the SubReport Wizard asks what data you want to use for the subreport.

3. **Click the Use an existing report or form option button in the SubReport Wizard, click CategoryRevenue if it is not already selected, click Next, click None when asked how you want the reports to be linked, click Next, then click Finish to accept the default label**

   The Report Footer section contains the CategoryRevenue report as a subreport. Therefore, the CategoryRevenue report will print after the ToursByCategory report prints. You don't need the label that accompanies the subreport so you delete it.

> **TROUBLE**
> You may need to move the subreport control to see the CategoryRevenue label.

4. **Click the new CategoryRevenue label associated with the subreport, then press [Delete]**

   Report Design View should look similar to Figure H-14. Preview your changes.

5. **Right-click the ToursByCategory report tab, click Print Preview, then navigate through the pages of the report**

   The ToursByCategory report fills the first two pages. The CategoryRevenue subreport starts at the top of page three.

6. **Save and close the ToursByCategory report**

FIGURE H-13: **SubReport Wizard dialog box**

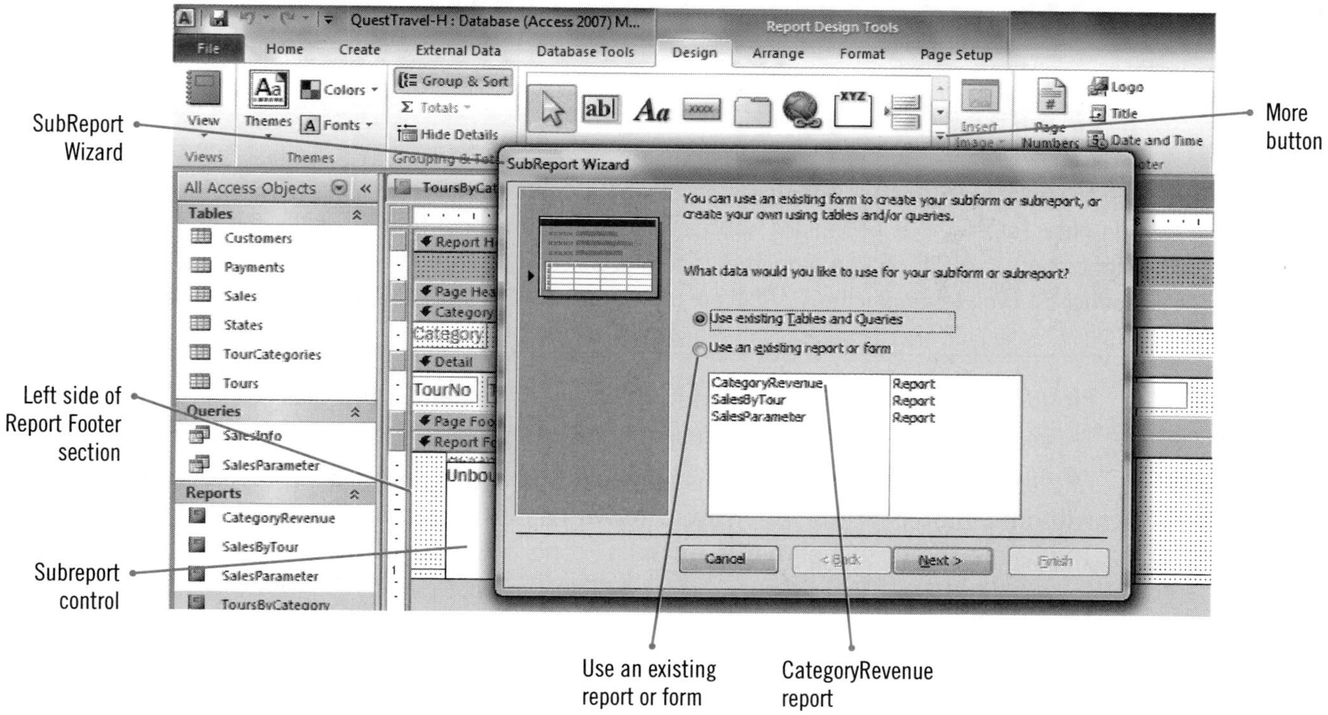
SubReport Wizard
Left side of Report Footer section
Subreport control
More button
Use an existing report or form
CategoryRevenue report

FIGURE H-14: **Subreport in Report Design View**

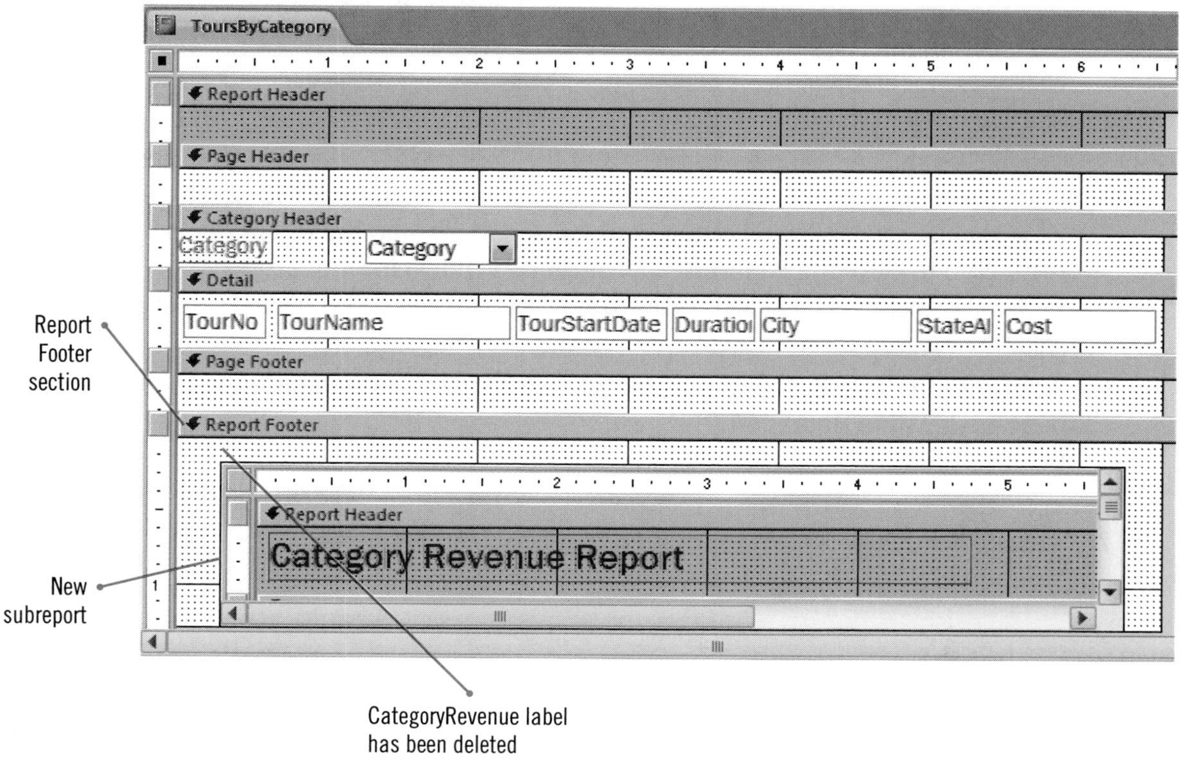
Report Footer section
New subreport
CategoryRevenue label has been deleted

UNIT
H
Access 2010

Modifying Section Properties

Report **section properties**, the characteristics that define each section, can be modified to improve report printouts. For example, you might want each new Group Header to print at the top of a page. Or, you might want to modify section properties to format that section with a background color. Samantha Hooper asks you to modify the SalesByTour report so that each tour prints at the top of a page.

STEPS

1. **Right-click the SalesByTour report in the Navigation Pane, then click Design View**

   To force each new category to start printing at the top of a page, you open and modify the TourName Footer.

2. **Click the TourName More Options button in the Group, Sort, and Total pane, click the without a footer section list arrow, click with a footer section, then double-click the TourName Footer section bar to open its Property Sheet**

   You modify the **Force New Page** property of the TourName Footer section to force each tour to start printing at the top of a new page.

3. **In the Property Sheet, click the Format tab, click the Force New Page property list arrow, then click After Section as shown in Figure H-15**

   You also move the Report Header controls into the Page Header so they print at the top of every page. First you need to create space in the upper half of the Page Header section to hold the controls.

4. **Drag the top edge of the TourName Header down to expand it to about twice its height, click the vertical ruler to the left of the TourName label in the Page Header section, click the Arrange tab, click the Remove Layout button, then use the ✥ pointer to move the labels in the Page Header section down to the bottom of the Page Header section**

   With space available in the top half of the Page Header section, you cut and paste the controls from the Report Header section to that new space.

5. **Drag down the vertical ruler to the left of the Report Header section to select all controls in that section, click the Home tab, click the Cut button in the Clipboard group, click the Page Header section bar, click the Paste button, then drag the top of the Page Header section up to close the Report Header section as shown in Figure H-16**

   Preview the report to make sure that each page contains the new header information and that each tour prints at the top of its own page.

6. **Right-click the SalesByTour report tab, click Print Preview, then navigate to the second page as shown in Figure H-17**

   Each tour now starts printing at the top of a new page, and the former Report Header section controls now print at the top of each page too, because they were moved to the Page Header section.

7. **Save and close the SalesByTour report**

FIGURE H-15: Changing section properties

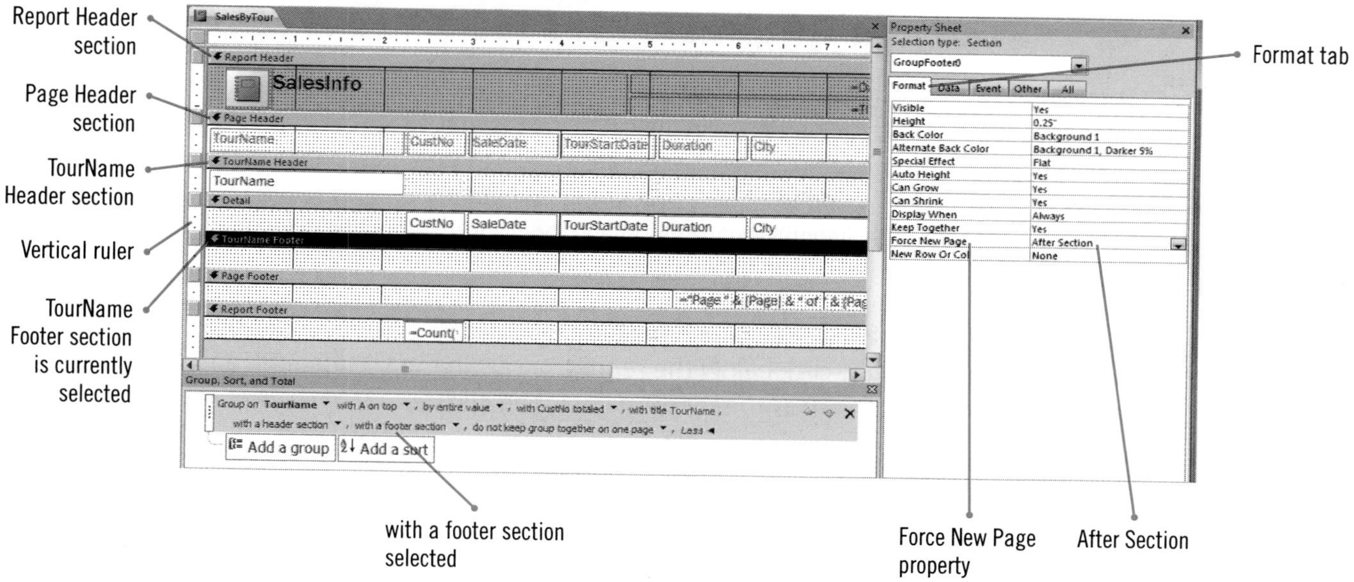

FIGURE H-16: Moving controls from the Report Header to the Page Header

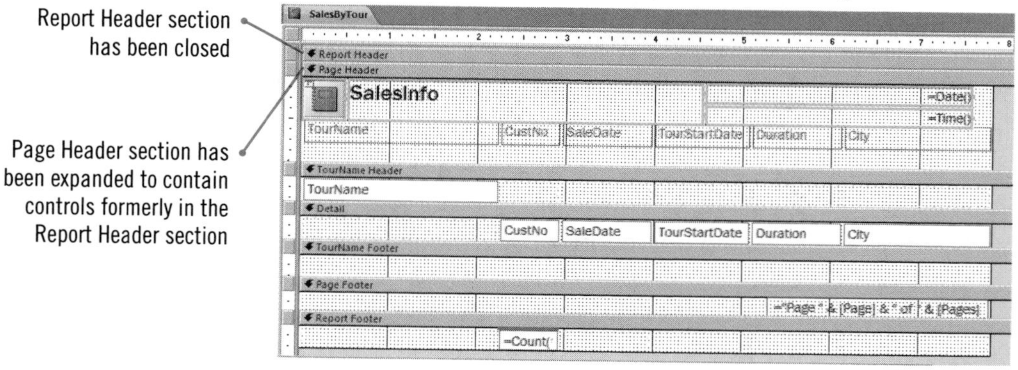

FIGURE H-17: Second page of the SalesByTour report

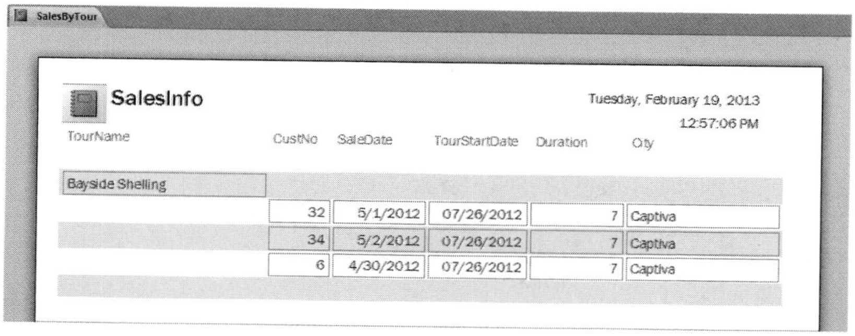

UNIT
H
Access 2010

Creating Summary Reports

Summary reports are reports that show statistics on groups of records rather than detailed information. You create summary reports by using Access functions such as Sum, Count, or Avg in expressions that calculate the desired statistic. These expressions are entered in text boxes most commonly placed in the Group Footer section. Samantha Hooper asks for a report to summarize the revenue for each tour category. You create a copy of the CategoryRevenue report and modify it to satisfy this request.

STEPS

1. **Right-click the CategoryRevenue report in the Navigation Pane, click Copy on the shortcut menu, right-click below the report objects in the Navigation Pane, click Paste, type CategorySummary as the report name, then click OK**

   Summary reports may contain controls in the Group Header and Group Footer sections, but because they provide summary statistics instead of details, they do not contain controls in the Detail section. You delete the controls in the Detail section and close it.

2. **Right-click the CategorySummary report in the Navigation Pane, click Design View, click the vertical ruler to the left of the Detail section to select all controls in the Detail section, press [Delete], then drag the top of the Category Footer section up to close the Detail section**

   You can also delete the labels in the Page Header section.

3. **Click the vertical ruler to the left of the Page Header section to select all controls in the Page Header section, press [Delete], then drag the top of the Category Header section up to close the Page Header section**

   Because the Page Header and Page Footer sections do not contain any controls, those section bars can be toggled off to simplify Report Design View.

4. **Right-click any blank spot on the report, then click Page Header/Footer on the shortcut menu to remove the Page Header and Page Footer section bars**

   With the unneeded controls and sections removed as shown in Figure H-18, you preview the final summary report.

5. **Right-click the CategorySummary report tab, then click Print Preview**

   The summarized revenue for each category is shown in the one-page summary report in Figure H-19.

6. **Save and close the CategorySummary report, then close QuestTravel-H.accdb and exit Access**

FIGURE H-18: **Design View of the CategorySummary report**

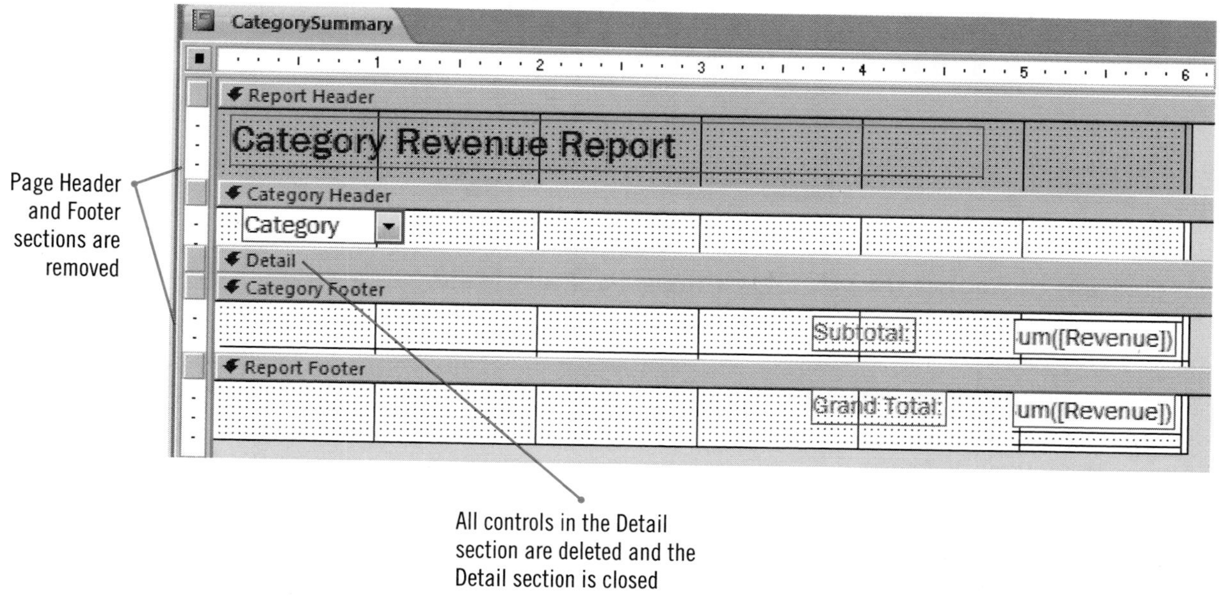

FIGURE H-19: **Preview of the CategorySummary report**

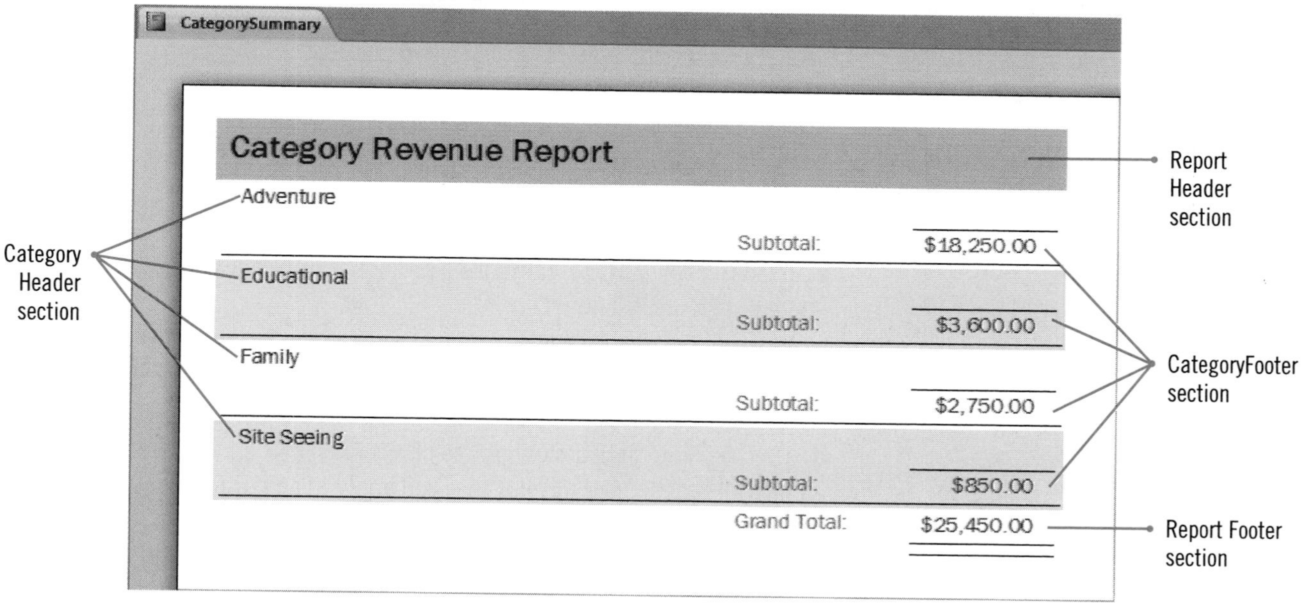

Access 2010

Practice

For current SAM information, including versions and content details, visit SAM Central (http://www.cengage.com/samcentral). If you have a SAM user profile, you may have access to hands-on instruction, practice, and assessment of the skills covered in this unit. Since various versions of SAM are supported throughout the life of this text, check with your instructor for the correct instructions and URL/Web site for accessing assignments.

Concepts Review

Identify each element of Report Design View shown in Figure H-20.

FIGURE H-20

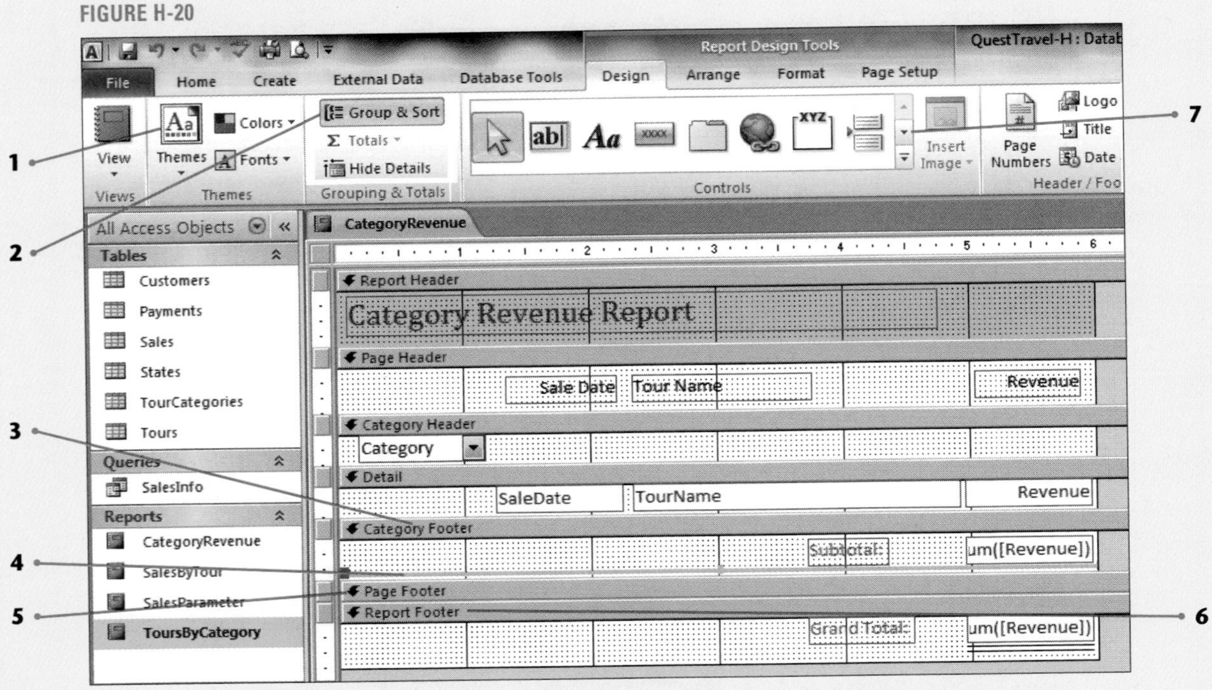

Match each term with the statement that best describes its function.

8. **Summary report**
9. **Parameter report**
10. **Conditional formatting**
11. **Format Painter**
12. **Theme**

a. Used to copy multiple formatting properties from one control to another in Report Design View

b. Prompts the user for the criteria for selecting the records for the report

c. A way to change the appearance of a control on a form or report based on criteria you specify

d. Used to show statistics on groups of records

e. Provides predefined formats that you apply to an entire form or report

Select the best answer from the list of choices.

13. Which control would you use to visually separate groups of records on a report?

a. Line

b. Option group

c. Bound Object Frame

d. Image

14. Which property would you use to force each group of records to print at the top of the next page?

a. Paginate

b. Display When

c. Calculate

d. Force New Page

15. What feature allows you to apply the formatting characteristics of one control to another?

a. AutoContent Wizard

b. Format Painter

c. Report Layout Wizard

d. Theme

16. Which key do you press when creating a line to make it perfectly horizontal?

a. [Ctrl]

b. [Shift]

c. [Alt]

d. [Home]

17. Which feature allows you to apply the same formatting characteristics to all the controls in a report at once?

a. Format Wizard

b. Themes

c. AutoPainting

d. Palletizing

18. In a report, an expression used to calculate values is entered in which type of control?

a. Text Box

b. Combo Box

c. Label

d. Command Button

19. Which section most often contains calculations for groups of records?

a. Page Header

b. Page Footer

c. Detail

d. Group Footer

20. Which control would you use to combine two reports?

a. Subreport

b. Combo Box

c. List Box

d. Group & Sort Control

Skills Review

1. Use Report Design View.

- **a.** Open the RealEstate-H.accdb database from the drive and folder where you store your Data Files and enable content if prompted.
- **b.** Open the RealtorList query, and then change the RLast value for Mary Logan to your last name. Close the query.
- **c.** Create a new report in Report Design View based on the RealtorList query.
- **d.** Select AgencyName as a grouping field and RLast as a sort field.
- **e.** Add the AgencyName field to the AgencyName Header. Delete the accompanying AgencyName label, position the AgencyName text box on the left side of the AgencyName Header, and resize it to be about 3" wide.
- **f.** Add the RealtorNo, RFirst, RLast, and RPhone fields to the Detail section. Delete all labels and position the text boxes horizontally across the top of the Detail section.
- **g.** Drag the top edge of the Page Footer section up to remove the blank space in the Detail section.
- **h.** Save the report with the name **RealtorList**, then preview it as shown in Figure H-21. The width and spacing of the controls in your report may differ.
- **i.** Close the RealtorList report.

FIGURE H-21

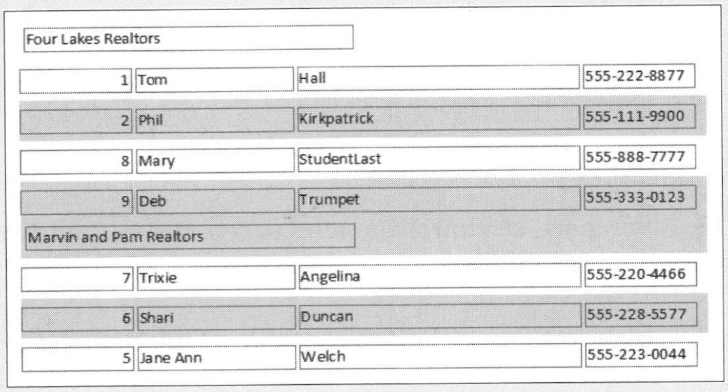

2. Create parameter reports.

- **a.** Create a query in Query Design View, including the RFirst, RLast, and RPhone fields from the Realtors table. Include the Type, Area, SqFt, and Asking fields from the Listings table.
- **b.** In the Asking field, include the following parameter criteria: **<[Enter maximum asking price]**.
- **c.** Test the query by switching to Datasheet View, enter **200000** in the Enter maximum asking price box, then click OK. The query should display 21 records, all with an AskingPrice of less than $200,000. Save the query as **AskingParameter**, then close it.
- **d.** Click the AskingParameter query in the Navigation Pane, then click Report on the Create tab. Enter **250000** in the Enter maximum asking price box, then click OK.
- **e.** Work in Layout View to narrow each column to be only as wide as necessary, and to fit all columns across a single sheet of paper in portrait orientation.
- **f.** In Report Design View, add a label with your name to the Report Header section.
- **g.** Drag the right edge of the report to the left to make sure the report is no wider than 8 inches. This may include moving controls in the Page Footer or Report Footer to the left as well.
- **h.** Preview the report again, entering **250000** in the prompt, then print it if requested by your instructor.
- **i.** Save the report with the name **AskingParameter**, then close it.

3. Apply conditional formatting.

a. Open the AskingParameter report in Report Design View, click the Asking text box, then open the Conditional Formatting Rules Manager dialog box.

b. Add a rule to format all Asking field values between **0** and **99999** with a light green background color.

c. Add a rule to format all Asking field values between **100000** and **199999** with a yellow background color.

d. Add a rule to format all Asking field values greater than or equal to **200000** with a red background color.

e. Test the report in Print Preview, entering a value of **400000** when prompted.

4. Add lines.

a. Open the AskingParameter report in Design View, then use the Group, Sort, and Total pane to add a sort order. Sort the fields in descending (largest to smallest) order on the Asking field.

b. Add a label to the Report Footer section directly to the left of the =Sum([Asking]) label. Modify the label to read **Grand Total:**.

c. Expand the vertical size of the Report Footer section to about twice its current height.

d. Draw one short horizontal line just above the =Sum([Asking]) calculation in the Report Footer section, then copy and paste the line twice. Reposition both lines to just below the =Sum([Asking]) calculation to indicate a grand total.

e. Save the report, then preview the changes using a value of **150000** when prompted.

f. Resize the text box containing the Grand Total calculation, if necessary, then save the report.

5. Use the Format Painter and themes.

a. Open the AskingParameter Report in Layout View. Enter **250000** when prompted.

b. Change the AskingParameter label in the Report Header section to **Asking Price Analysis**.

c. Apply an Angles theme (first row, third column) to the report. Resize the columns and the calculated field in the Report Footer as necessary.

d. Change the font color of the RFirst label in the Page Header section to Automatic (black).

e. Use the Format Painter to copy the format from the RFirst label to the RLast, RPhone, Type, and Area labels in the Page Header section.

f. Change the font color of the SqFt label in the Page Header section to Automatic (black).

g. Use the Format Painter to copy the format from the SqFt label to the Asking label.

h. Save and close the AskingParameter report.

Skills Review (continued)

6. Add subreports.

a. Open the ListingReport in Layout View, and resize any text boxes that are not wide enough to show all data. Be careful to not extend the right edge of the report beyond one sheet of paper.

b. Open the RealtorList report in Layout View, and resize any text boxes that are not wide enough to show all data. Again be careful to not extend the right edge of the report beyond one sheet of paper. Save and close the RealtorList report.

c. Display the ListingReport in Design View. In the Report Footer section, add the RealtorList report as a subreport using the SubReport Wizard. Choose None when asked to link the main form to the subform, and accept the default name of RealtorList.

d. Delete the extra RealtorList label in the Report Footer.

e. Preview each page of the report to make sure all data is clearly visible. Widen any controls that do not clearly display information, again being careful not to extend the report beyond the right margin.

f. Narrow the width of the report if necessary in Report Design View, then save and close it.

7. Modify section properties.

a. In Report Design View of the ListingReport, modify the Realtors.RealtorNo Footer section's Force New Page property to After Section. (*Note*: The RealtorNo field is included in two tables, Realtors and Listings. Access uses the *tablename.fieldname* convention to specify that the RealtorNo grouping field is from the Realtors table.)

b. Open the Page Footer section, and add a label, **Created by Your Name**.

c. Save and preview the ListingReport to make sure that the new section property forces each new realtor group of records to print on their own page as shown in Figure H-22. Also check that a label identifying you as the report creator appears at the bottom of each page.

d. Close the ListingReport.

FIGURE H-22

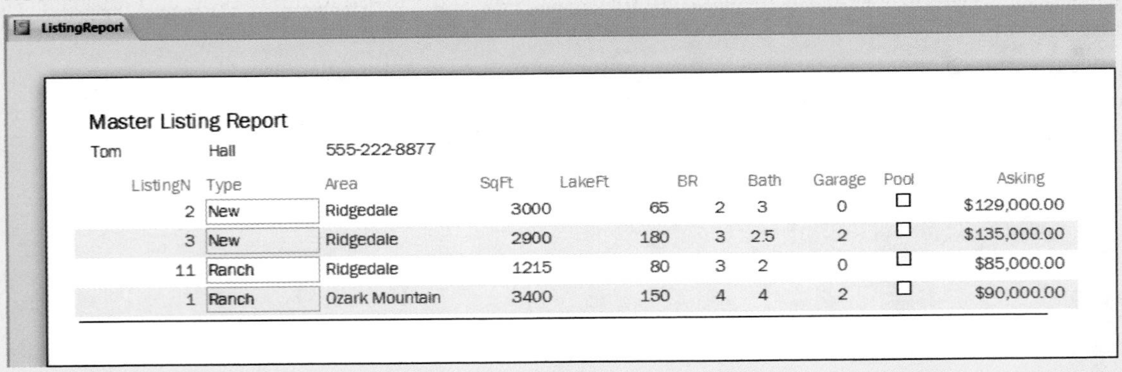

ListingReport
Master Listing Report
Tom
Hall
555-222-8877

ListingN	Type	Area	SqFt	LakeFt	BR	Bath	Garage	Pool	Asking
2	New	Ridgedale	3000	65	2	3	0	☐	$129,000.00
3	New	Ridgedale	2900	180	3	2.5	2	☐	$135,000.00
11	Ranch	Ridgedale	1215	80	3	2	0	☐	$85,000.00
1	Ranch	Ozark Mountain	3400	150	4	4	2	☐	$90,000.00

Skills Review (continued)

8. Create summary reports.

a. Right-click the ListingReport, click Copy, right-click the Navigation Pane, click Paste, then type **ListingSummary**.

b. Open the ListingSummary report in Design View, delete the subreport from the Report Footer, all the controls in the Detail section, and all the labels in the Realtors.RealtorNo Header section. (*Note*: Be careful not to delete the three text boxes for RFirst, RLast, and RPhone in the Realtors.RealtorNo Header section.)

c. Close the extra space in the Detail and Realtors.RealtorNo Header sections.

d. Expand the size of the Realtors.RealtorNo Footer section, move the line to the bottom of that section, then add a text box to the right side of the section with the following expression: **=Sum([Asking])**.

e. Modify the new label to read **Subtotal of Asking Price:**, then move and resize the controls as needed.

f. Open the Property Sheet for the =Sum([Asking]) text box, click the Format tab, then choose Currency for the Format property, and 0 for the Decimal Places property.

g. Copy the =Sum([Asking]) text box to the Report Footer section, move it directly under the =Sum([Asking]) text box in the Realtors.RealtorNo Footer section, then change the label to be **Grand Total:**.

h. Draw two lines under the =Sum([Asking]) text box in the Report Footer section to indicate a grand total.

i. Change the Force New Page property of the Realtors.RealtorNo Footer section to None.

j. Preview the report. Switch to Portrait orientation, and resize sections and move controls in Design View so the report matches Figure H-23, then save and close the report.

k. Close the RealEstate-H.accdb database, and exit Access.

FIGURE H-23

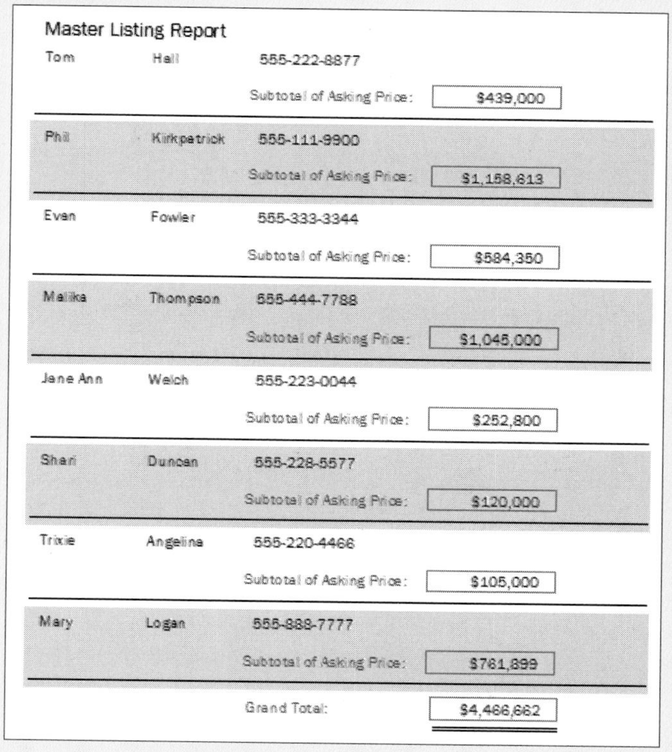

Master Listing Report
Tom Hall 555-222-8877
Subtotal of Asking Price: $439,000
Phil Kirkpatrick 555-111-9900
Subtotal of Asking Price: $1,168,813
Evan Fowler 555-333-3344
Subtotal of Asking Price: $584,350
Malika Thompson 555-444-7788
Subtotal of Asking Price: $1,045,000
Jane Ann Welch 555-223-0044
Subtotal of Asking Price: $252,800
Shari Duncan 555-228-5577
Subtotal of Asking Price: $120,000
Trixie Angelina 555-220-4466
Subtotal of Asking Price: $105,000
Mary Logan 555-888-7777
Subtotal of Asking Price: $761,899
Grand Total: $4,466,862

Independent Challenge 1

As the manager of a music store's instrument rental program, you created a database to track instrument rentals to schoolchildren. Now that several instruments have been rented, you need to create a report listing the rental transactions for each instrument.

a. Start Access, open the MusicStore-H.accdb database from the drive and folder where you store your Data Files, and enable content if prompted.

b. Use the Report Wizard to create a report based on the FirstName and LastName fields in the Customers table, the RentalDate field from the Rentals table, and the Description and MonthlyFee fields from the Instruments table.

c. View the data by Instruments, do not add any more grouping levels, sort the data from newest to oldest by RentalDate, use a Stepped layout and Portrait orientation, and title the report **Instrument Rental Report**.

d. Open the report in Design View, change the first grouping level from SerialNo to Description so that all instruments with the same description are grouped together, and open the Description Footer section.

e. Add a new text box to the Description Footer section with the expression **=Count([LastName])**. Change the label to **Customers:**.

f. Change the Force New Page property of the Description Footer section to After Section.

g. Add your name as a label to the Report Header section, and use the Format Painter to copy the formatting from the Instrument Rental Report label to your name. Double-click a corner sizing handle of the label with your name to resize it.

h. Save and preview the report as shown in Figure H-24.

i. Move, resize, and align controls as needed to match Figure H-24, then print the report if requested by your instructor.

j. Save and close the Instrument Rental Report, close the MusicStore-H.accdb database, then exit Access.

FIGURE H-24

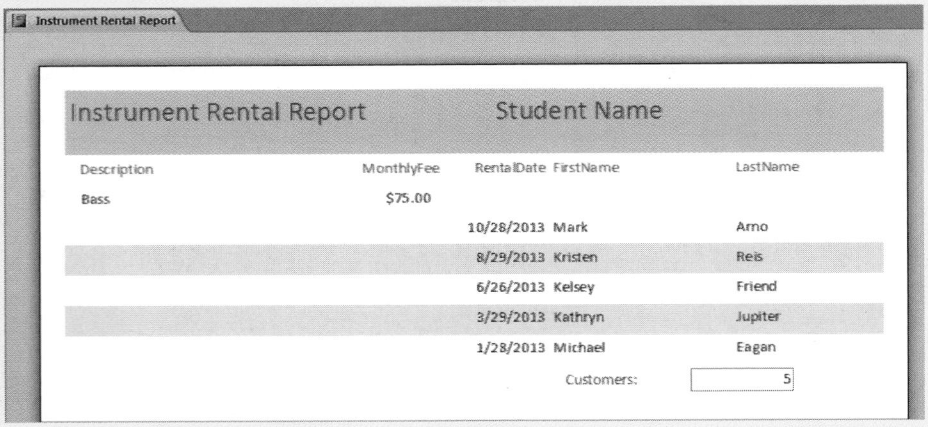

Independent Challenge 2

As the manager of a music store's instrument rental program, you have created a database to track instrument rentals to schoolchildren. Now that the rental program is underway, you need to create a summary report that shows how many instruments have been rented by each school.

a. Start Access, open the MusicStore-H.accdb database from the drive and folder where you store your Data Files, and enable content if prompted.

b. Build a query in Query Design View with the following fields: SchoolName from the Schools table, and RentalDate from the Rentals table. (*Hint*: Include the Customers table to build the proper relationships between the Schools and the Rentals table.) Save the query with the name **SchoolSummary**, then close it.

c. Create a new report in Report Design View. Use the SchoolSummary query as Record Source property.

d. Add SchoolName as a grouping field, and add the SchoolName field to the left side of the SchoolName Header section. Delete the SchoolName label, and widen the SchoolName text box to about 2".

e. Add a text box to the right side of the SchoolName Header section with the expression **=Count([RentalDate])**. Delete the accompanying label.

f. Align the top edges of the two text boxes in the SchoolName Header.

g. Drag the top edge of the Page Footer section up to completely close the Detail section.

h. Add a label to the Page Header section with your name. Format the label with an Arial Black font and 14-point font size. If necessary, resize the label to display all the text.

i. Use the Format Painter to copy the formatting from the label with your name to the SchoolName text box and the =Count([RentalDate]) expression. Resize the text boxes in the SchoolName Header section as necessary to show all information in each box.

j. Save the report with the name **SchoolSummary**, then preview it as shown in Figure H-25.

k. Close the SchoolSummary report, close the MusicStore-H.accdb database, then exit Access.

FIGURE H-25

Student Name	
Blackbob School Elementary	8
Blue Eye Elementary	6
Naish Middle School	6
South High School	6
Thomas Jefferson Elementary	12

Independent Challenge 3

As the manager of a music store's instrument rental program, you have created a database to track instrument rentals to schoolchildren. Now that the rental program is underway, you need to create a parameter report for each instrument type.

a. Start Access, open the MusicStore-H.accdb database from the drive and folder where you store your Data Files, and enable content if prompted.

b. Create a query with the RentalDate field from the Rentals table, the Description and MonthlyFee fields from the Instruments table, and the FirstName and LastName fields from the Customers table.

c. Enter the parameter criteria **Between [Enter start date] And [Enter end date]** for the RentalDate field and **[Enter instrument type such as cello]** for the Description field.

d. Save the query with the name **RentalParameter** and close it.

e. Use the Report Wizard to create a report on all fields in the RentalParameter query. View the data by Instruments, do not add any more grouping levels, sort the records in ascending order by RentalDate, and use an Outline layout and a Portrait orientation. Title the report **Instrument Info**.

f. To respond to the prompts, enter **1/1/13** for the start date and **6/30/13** for the end date. Enter **viola** for the instrument type prompt.

g. In Report Design View, apply the Essential theme. If necessary, resize the report title in the Report Header to display all the text.

h. Add your name as a label to the Report Header section. Format it with a color and size so that it is clearly visible.

Advanced Challenge Exercise

- Add spaces between all words in the labels in the Description Header section: MonthlyFee, RentalDate, FirstName, and LastName. Be sure to change the MonthlyFee *label* control and not the MonthlyFee *text box* control.
- Add a Description Footer section.
- Add a text box to the Description Footer section that contains the expression **=Count([LastName])*[MonthlyFee]**. Change the accompanying label to read **Monthly Revenue:**, then move the text box with the expression below the LastName text box.
- Open the Property Sheet for the expression. On the Format tab, change the Format property to Currency and the Decimal Places property to 0.

i. Display the report for RentalDates **1/1/13** through **6/30/13**, instrument type **violin**. If you completed all of the Advanced Challenge Exercise steps, your report should look like Figure H-26.

j. Save the Instrument Info report, print it if requested by your instructor, close the MusicStore-H.accdb database, then exit Access.

FIGURE H-26

Real Life Independent Challenge

You have created an Access database to help manage college scholarship opportunities. You analyze scholarships by building a report with conditional formatting.

a. Start Access and open the Scholarships-H.accdb database from the drive and folder where you store your Data Files. Enable content if prompted.

b. Use the Report Wizard to create a report based on the Scholarships table. Include all of the fields. Add Major then Amount as the grouping levels, then click the Grouping Options button in the Report Wizard. Choose 5000s as the Grouping interval for the Amount field. Sort the records by DueDate in a descending order. Use a Stepped layout and a Landscape orientation. Title the report **ScholarshipsByMajor**.

c. Preview the report, then add your name as a label next to the report title.

d. In Layout View, add spaces to the ScholarshipsByMajor, DueDate, and ScholarshipName labels to read Scholarships By Major, Due Date, and Scholarship Name.

e. Narrow the columns to fit on a single sheet of paper, then drag the right edge of the report to the left in Report Design View.

f. Expand the Page Header section to about twice its height, move the labels to the bottom of the Page Header section, move the labels from the Report Header section to the top of the Page Header section, then close up the Report Header section.

g. Open the Major Footer section, then change the Force New Page property of the Major Footer section to After Section.

h. Preview the fourth page of the report for the Engineering major as shown in Figure H-27.

i. Save and close the ScholarshipsByMajor report and the Scholarships-H.accdb database.

FIGURE H-27

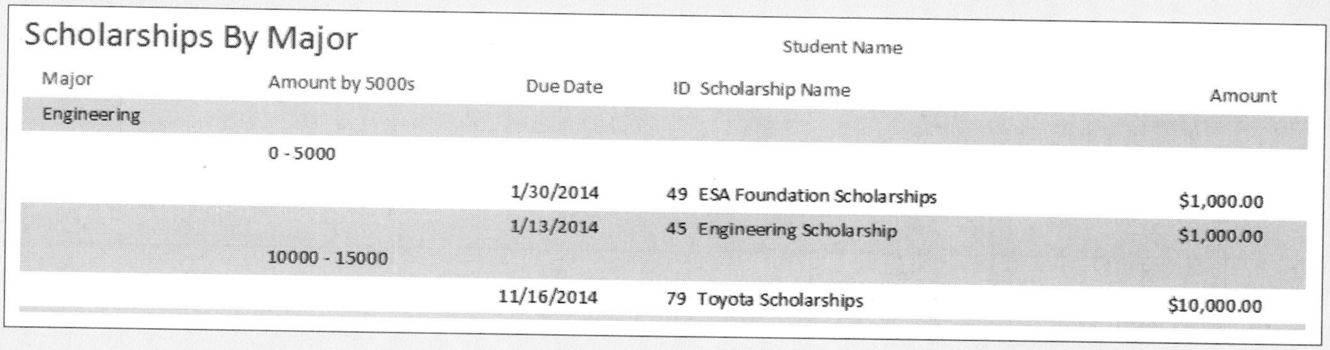

Scholarships By Major — Student Name

Major	Amount by 5000s	Due Date	ID	Scholarship Name	Amount
Engineering					
	0 - 5000				
		1/30/2014	49	ESA Foundation Scholarships	$1,000.00
		1/13/2014	45	Engineering Scholarship	$1,000.00
	10000 - 15000				
		11/16/2014	79	Toyota Scholarships	$10,000.00

Visual Workshop

Open the Baseball-H.accdb database from the drive and folder where you store your Data Files and enable content if prompted. Using the Report Wizard, build a report on the PlayerLName field from the Players table, and the AtBats and Hits fields from the Player Stats table. View the data by Players, do not add any more grouping or sorting fields, and use a Stepped layout and Portrait orientation. Enter **BattingAverage** as the name of the report. In Report Design View, add a new text box to the right of the Hits text box in the Detail section with the expression **=[Hits]/[AtBats]**. Cut the accompanying label, paste it in the Page Header section, move it above the expression, and change the caption to **Batting Average**. Click the =[Hits]/[AtBats] expression, and apply a conditional format so that if the value is greater than or equal to 0.5, the background color is yellow. Add a label to the Report Header with your name, edit the labels, and align the controls as shown in Figure H-28. Save the BattingAverage report, then close it.

FIGURE H-28

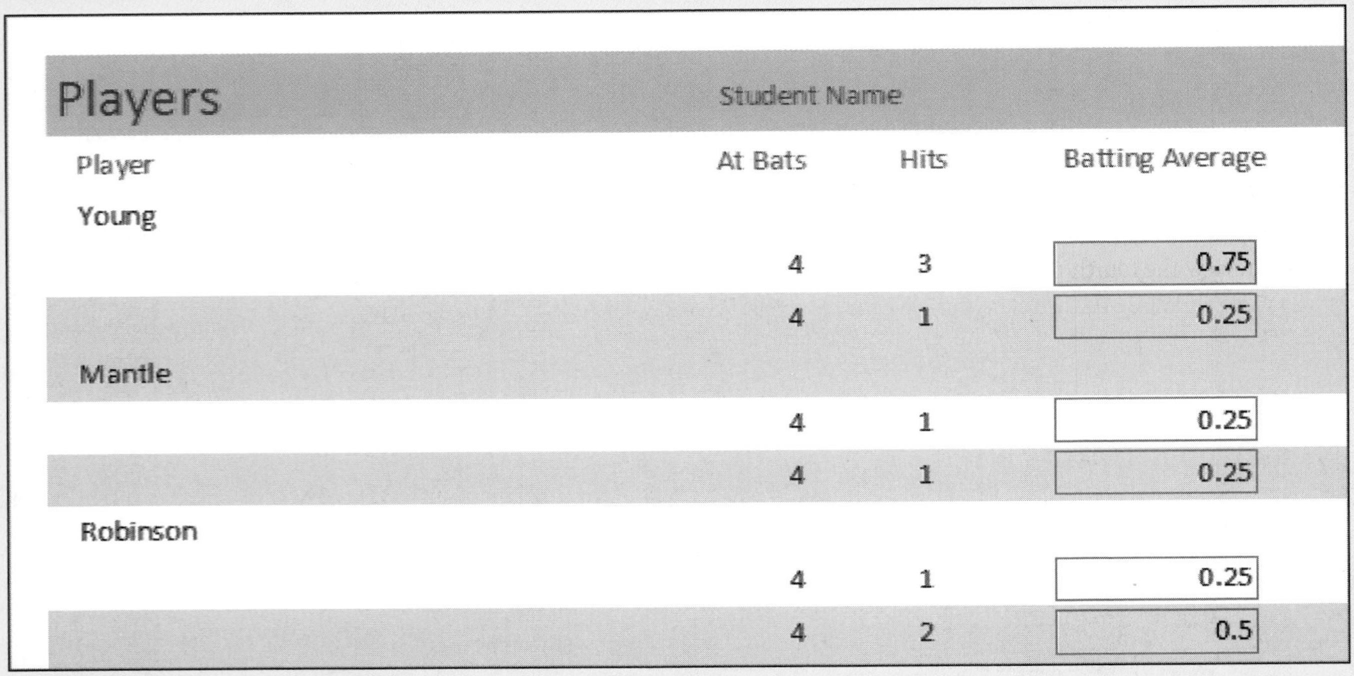

Players Student Name

Player	At Bats	Hits	Batting Average
Young			
	4	3	0.75
	4	1	0.25
Mantle			
	4	1	0.25
	4	1	0.25
Robinson			
	4	1	0.25
	4	2	0.5

UNIT I
Access 2010

Importing and Exporting Data

Files You Will Need:

- Education-I.accdb
- DepartmentData.xlsx
- CourseMaterials.xlsx
- Machinery-I.accdb
- MachineryEmp.xlsx
- Vendors.xlsx
- Basketball-I.accdb
- 2013-2014Schedule.xlsx
- Languages-I.accdb

Access can share data with many other Microsoft Office programs. For example, you can import data from an Excel workbook into an Access database or go the other way and export data from Access to Excel. You may want to merge Access data into a Word document to create a mass mailing. Or you may want to share data from your Access database using Outlook e-mail messages. At Quest Specialty Travel, Jacob Thomas, director of staff development, has asked you to develop an Access database that tracks professional staff continuing education. First you will explore the Access templates for creating a new database. Then you will work with Access tools that allow you to share Access data with other software programs so that each Quest department can have the necessary data in a format they can use.

OBJECTIVES

- Use database templates
- Use Application Parts
- Import data from Excel
- Link data
- Export data to Excel
- Publish data to Word
- Merge data with Word
- Collect data with Outlook

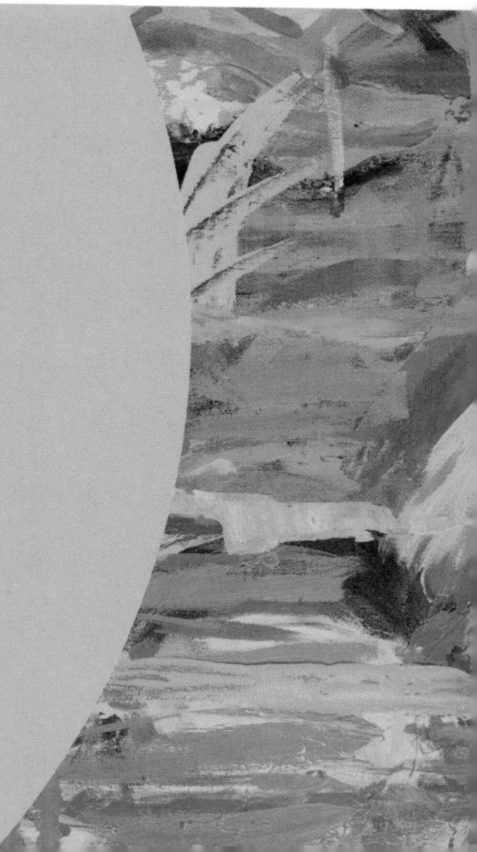

UNIT I

Access 2010

Using Database Templates

A **database template** is a tool that you use to quickly create a new database based on a particular subject such as assets, contacts, events, or projects. When you install Access 2010 on your computer, Microsoft provides many database templates for you to use. Additional templates are available from Microsoft Office Online, where they are organized by category such as business, personal, and education. Jacob Thomas, director of staff development, asks you to develop a new Access database to track the continuing education of Quest employees. You explore Microsoft database templates to learn more about Access.

STEPS

> **TROUBLE**
> If you don't see the Education folder, use the Search box to search for the Student database.

> **TROUBLE**
> The Browse button looks like a yellow folder on the far-right side of the window, to the right of the database path.

> **QUICK TIP**
> To review the video later, open the Getting Started form.

1. **Start Access 2010**

   As shown in Figure I-1, Microsoft provides many templates to help you create a new database. **Online templates** are available to download from the Microsoft Office Online Web site. Templates change over time as more are added and enhancements to existing templates are provided by Microsoft. The database you want to create should track employees and the continuing education courses they have completed, so you will explore the Education template category.

2. **Click the Education folder, click Student database, click the Browse icon, navigate to the drive and folder where you store your Data Files, click OK, then click Download**

   The template builds a new database named Student database that includes several sample tables, queries, forms, reports, macros, and a module object. You can use or modify these objects to meet your needs. A Getting Started window opens to provide video support for the database.

3. **Close the Access help window, close the Getting Started window, then enable content if prompted and close the Getting Started window again to explore the actual database as shown in Figure I-2**

   The Student List form is automatically opened, and the other objects in the database are presented in the Navigation Pane.

4. **Right-click the Student List form tab, click Close, then double-click the Student Details form in the Navigation Pane**

   Objects created by database templates are rich in functionality and can be modified for your specific needs or analyzed to learn more about Access.

5. **Close the Student Details form, then double-click the Guardian Details form to open it**

   If you wanted to use this database, your next step would be to enter sample data and continue exploring the other objects in the database. Because this database is designed for a traditional school rather than a corporate educational environment, you won't be using it at Quest. However, you can still learn a great deal by exploring the objects that the template created.

6. **Close the Guardian Details form**

FIGURE I-1: **Available Templates**

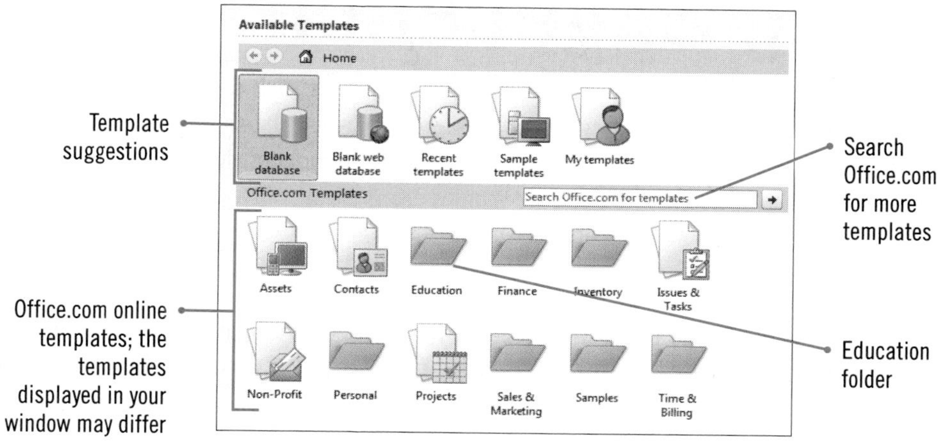
Template suggestions
Search Office.com for more templates
Office.com online templates; the templates displayed in your window may differ
Education folder

FIGURE I-2: **Student database template**

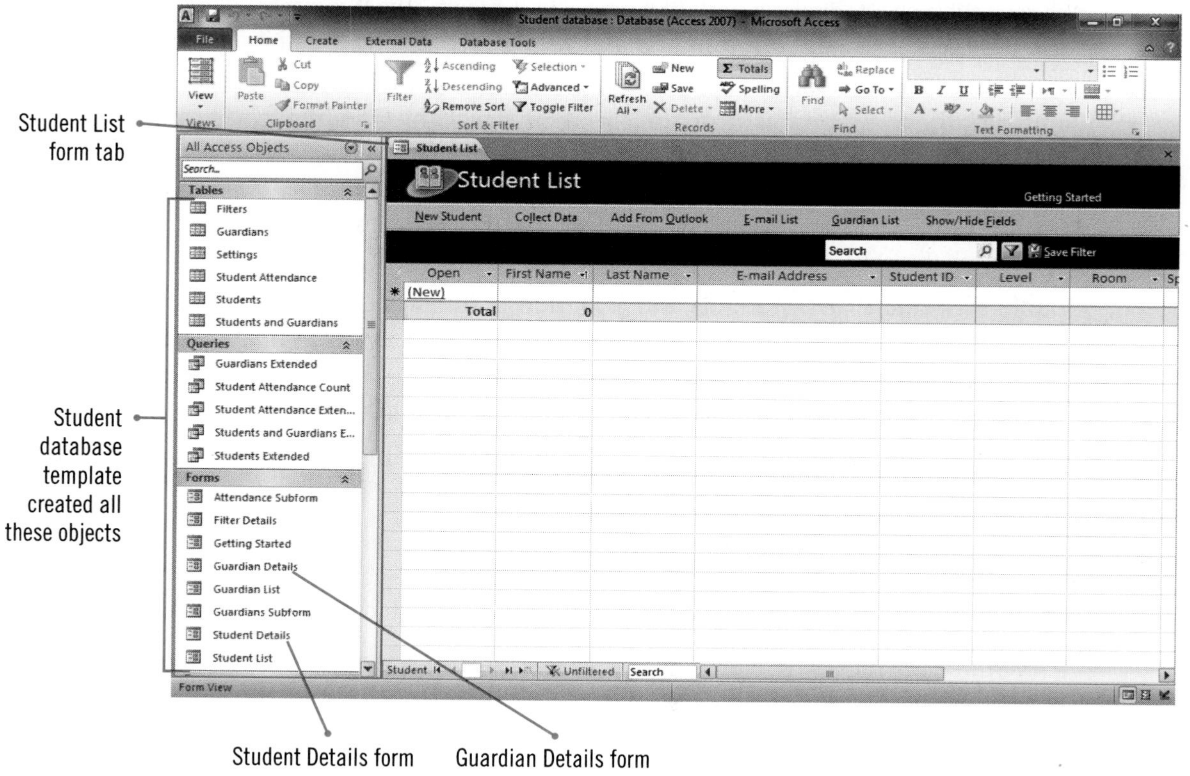
Student List form tab
Student database template created all these objects
Student Details form
Guardian Details form

Using Application Parts

Application Parts are object templates that create objects such as tables and forms. Application Parts include several **table templates**, tools you can use to quickly create a single table in a database, and **form templates** to help you create forms. As with database templates, Microsoft is constantly updating and improving this part of Access. You continue your study of templates by exploring the Access 2010 Application Parts in the new Students database.

STEPS

> **TROUBLE**
> After you click the Create tab, you might need to enable content and close the Getting Started window.

1. **Click the Create tab, then click the Application Parts button as shown in Figure I-3, click Comments, click the There is no relationship option button, then click Create**

   Access creates a new table named Comments that you can modify and relate to the other tables in the database as needed. You also want to explore the form templates.

2. **Close the Getting Started window, close the Student List form, click the Application Parts button in the Templates group, click Msgbox, close the Getting Started window and the Student List form, click Yes if prompted to close all open objects, then double-click the new MessageBox form in the Navigation Pane to open it**

   Every time you create a new object using the Application Parts button, the database reopens, which loads the Getting Started and Student List forms. A sample message box form is created with three standard command buttons. To use this form, you would further modify it in Layout View to meet your specific needs.

   Note that some database and Application Parts templates create objects that are compatible with the Web. Web-compatible objects display a small Web symbol in their icon. The Web symbol means that if you published this database to a **Microsoft SharePoint server**, users could access this form using only a Web browser such as Internet Explorer, Safari, or Firefox.

3. **Right-click the MessageBox form tab, click Close, click the Database Tools tab, then click the Relationships button**

   When you use a database or table template, you need to check the Relationships window to make sure the tables participate in a meaningful relational database. The Student database template did not create relationships between the tables. You'll connect four of the main tables.

4. **Double-click Guardians, Students and Guardians, Students, and Student Attendance, click Close, then resize the Guardians and Students field lists to view as many fields as possible**

   With the four field lists for the main tables in the database positioned in the Relationships window so that you can see all of the fields, you will build the one-to-many relationships between the tables.

5. **Drag the ID field from the Guardians table to the GuardianID field in the Students and Guardians table, click the Enforce Referential Integrity check box, then click Create**

> **TROUBLE**
> Be sure to use the exact fields shown in Figure I-4 to create the relationships. If you make a mistake, right-click the relationship, click Delete, and try again.

6. **Create the other two relationships as shown in Figure I-4**

   Note that in this database, the linking fields do not have the same name in both the "one" and "many" tables. Also recall that referential integrity helps prevent orphan records—records in the "many" table that don't have a matching record in the "one" table.

7. **Save and close the Relationships window, continue studying the tables and other objects of the Student database as desired, then close the database and exit Access 2010**

   Access database templates and Application Parts provide powerful tools to build databases and objects quickly. Templates are also an exciting way to learn more about Access features and possibilities.

FIGURE I-3: Application Parts list

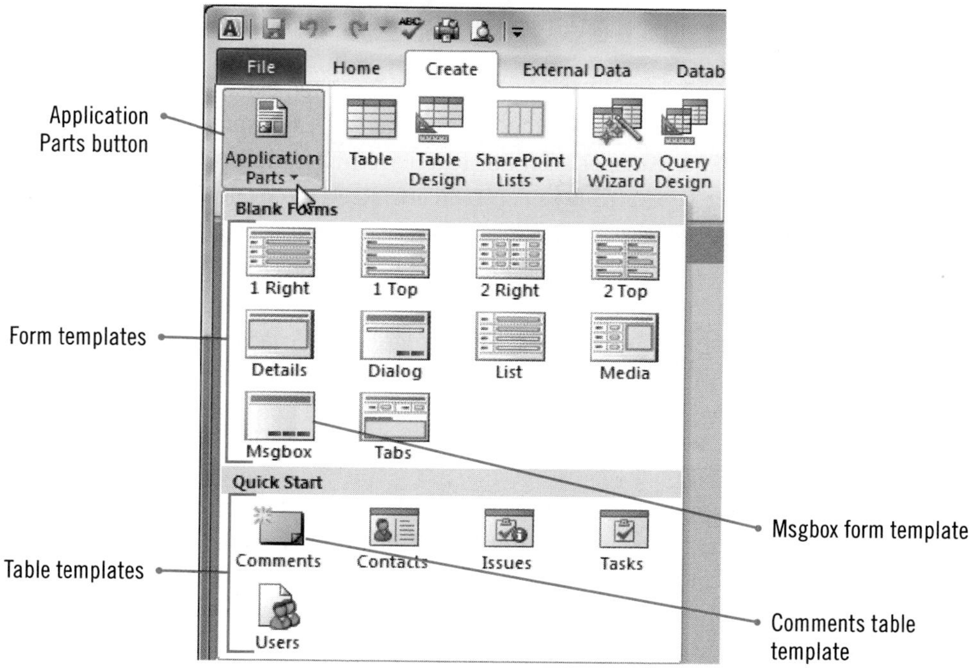

FIGURE I-4: Major relationships for the Student database

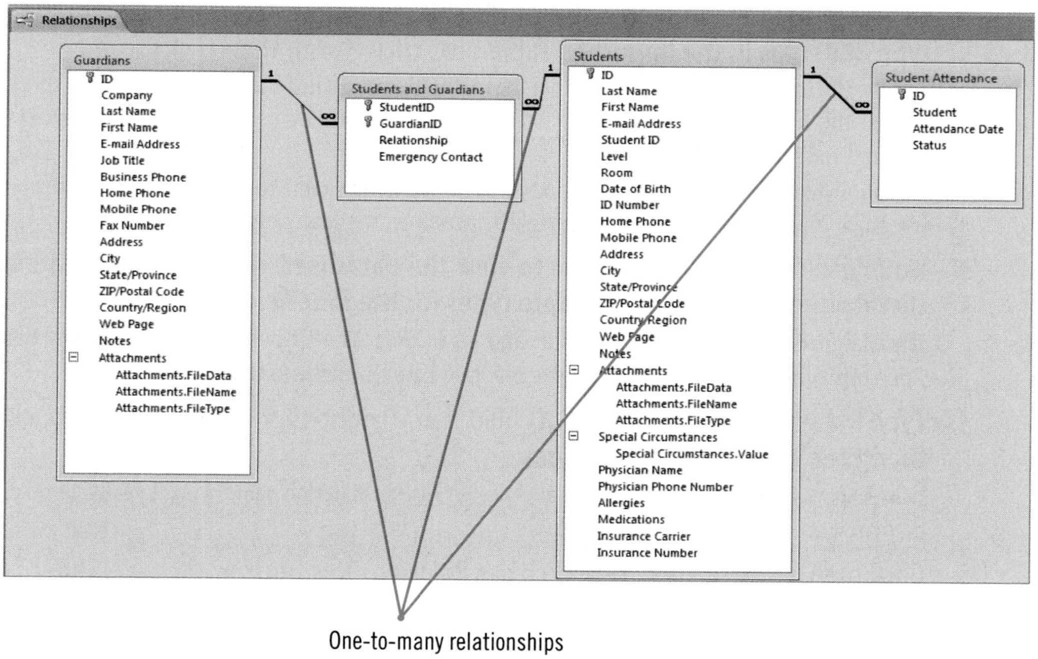

Referential integrity cascade options

When connecting tables in one-to-many relationships, apply referential integrity whenever possible. This feature prevents orphan records from being created in the database and lets you select cascade options. **Cascade Update Related Fields** means that if a value in the primary key field (the field on the "one" side of a one-to-many relationship) is modified, all values in the foreign key field (the field on the "many" side of a one-to-many relationship) are automatically updated as well. **Cascade Delete Related Records** means that if a record in the "one" side of a one-to-many relationship is deleted, all related records in the "many" table are also deleted. Because both of these options automatically change or delete data in the "many" table behind the scenes, they should be used carefully. Often these features are not employed as standard options, but are used temporarily to correct a problem in the database.

UNIT
I
Access 2010

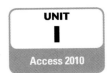

Importing Data from Excel

Importing enables you to quickly copy data from an external file into an Access database. You can import data from many sources such as another Access database, Excel spreadsheet, SharePoint site, Outlook e-mail, or text files in an HTML, XML, or delimited text file format. A **delimited text file** stores one record on each line. Field values are separated by a common character, the **delimiter**, such as a comma, tab, or dash. A **CSV (comma-separated values)** file is a common example of a delimited text file. An **XML file** is a text file containing **Extensible Markup Language (XML)** tags that identify field names and data. One of the most common file formats from which to import data into an Access database is **Microsoft Excel**, the spreadsheet program in the Microsoft Office suite. Jacob Thomas gives you an Excel spreadsheet that contains a list of supplemental materials used for various courses, and asks you to import the information in the new internal training database.

STEPS

1. **Start Access, open the Education-I.accdb database from the drive and folder where you store your Data Files, enable content if prompted, click the External Data tab, click the Excel button in the Import & Link group, click the Browse button, navigate to the drive and folder where you store your Data Files, double-click CourseMaterials.xlsx, then click OK**

   The **Import Spreadsheet Wizard** dialog box opens, as shown in Figure I-5, guiding you through the steps of importing Excel data into an Access database.

2. **Click Next, click the First Row Contains Column Headings check box, click Next, click Next to accept the default field options, click Next to allow Access to add a primary key field, type Materials in the Import to Table box, click Finish, then click Close**

   To save the import steps so that they can be easily repeated, click the Save import steps check box on the last step of the import process. You run a saved import process by using the **Saved Imports** button on the External Data tab.

   You review the imported records and relate the Materials table to the Courses table in a one-to-many relationship. One course can be related to many records in the Materials table.

3. **Double-click the Materials table to view the datasheet, right-click the Materials tab, then click Design View to view the data types for the four fields**

   The Materials table contains four fields and 45 records. The ID field is the primary key field for this table. CourseID will be used as the foreign key field to relate this table to the Courses table.

4. **Type MaterialID to replace the ID field name, right-click the Materials tab, click Close, then click Yes to save the changes**

   Now that you've examined the data and design of the Materials table, you're ready to relate it in a one-to-many relationship with the Courses table.

5. **Click the Database Tools tab, click the Relationships button, click the Show Table button, double-click Materials, click Close, drag the CourseID field in the Courses table to the CourseID field in the Materials table, click the Enforce Referential Integrity check box, then click Create**

   The final Relationships window is shown in Figure I-6. One employee record is related to many enrollments. One course record is related to many enrollments and also to many materials.

6. **Click the Close button, then click Yes to save the changes to the database relationships**

FIGURE I-5: Import Spreadsheet Wizard

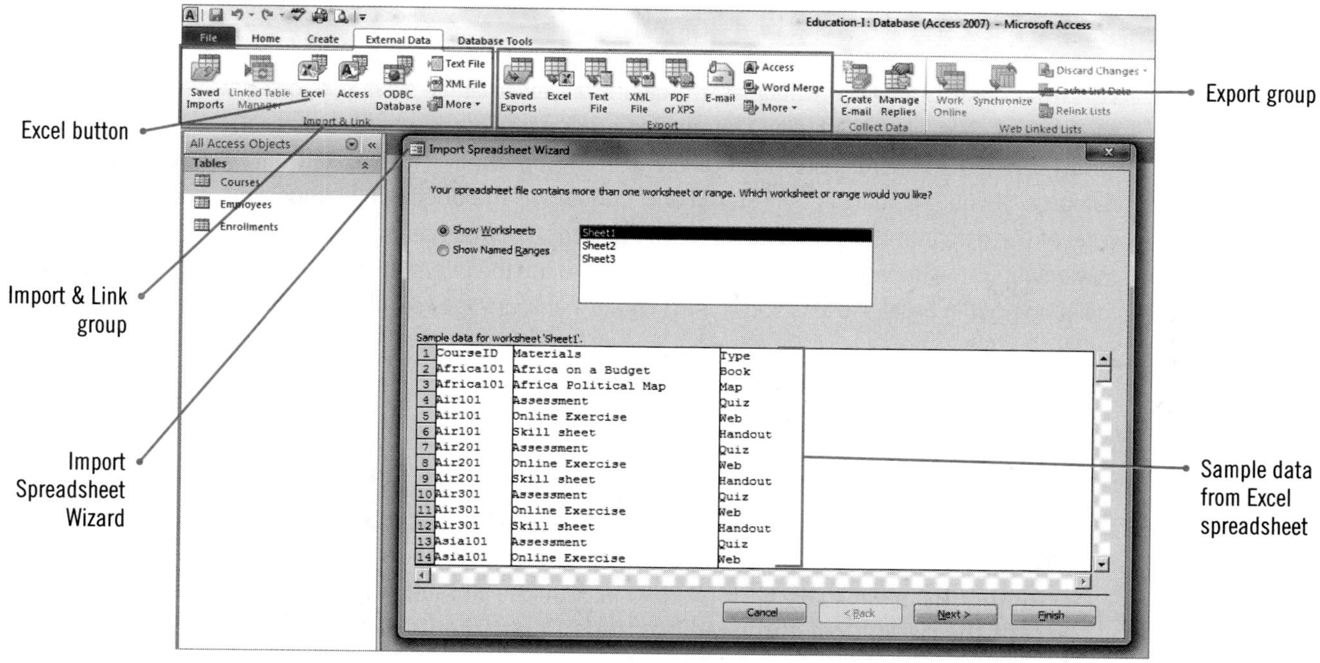

FIGURE I-6: Relationships window with imported Materials table

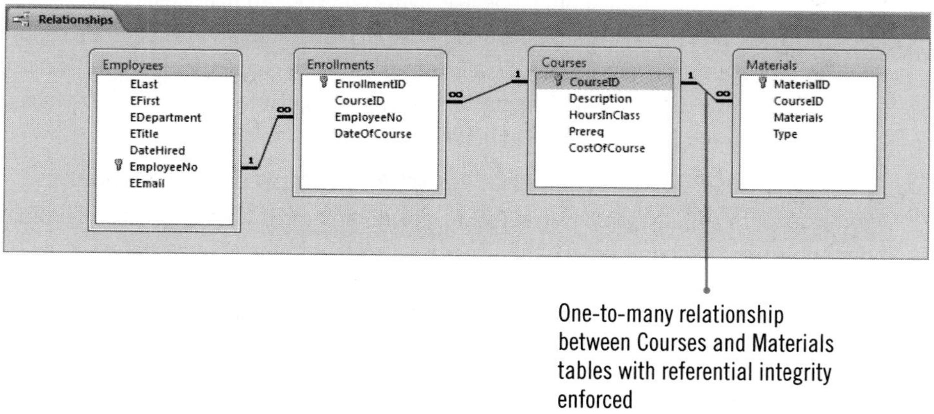

Access 2010

UNIT I

Access 2010

Linking Data

Linking connects an Access database to data in an external file such as another Access database, Excel spreadsheet, text file, HTML file, XML file, or other data sources that support **ODBC (open database connectivity)** standards. Linking is different from importing in that linked data is not copied into the database. If you link, data is only stored and updated in the original file. Importing, in contrast, makes a copy of the data in the Access database. Jacob Thomas has created a small spreadsheet with information about the departments at Quest. He wants to use the information in the Education-I database while maintaining it in Excel. He asks you to help create a link to this Excel file from the Education-I database.

STEPS

1. **Click the External Data tab, then click the Excel button in the Import & Link group**

   The Get External Data - Excel Spreadsheet dialog box opens, as shown in Figure I-7. This dialog box allows you to choose whether you want to import, append, or link to the data source.

2. **Click Browse, navigate to the drive and folder where you store your Data Files, double-click DepartmentData.xlsx, click the Link to the data source by creating a linked table option button, click OK, click Next to accept the default range selection, click Next to accept the default column headings, type Departments as the linked table name, click Finish, then click OK**

   The **Link Spreadsheet Wizard** guides you through the process of linking to a spreadsheet. The linked Departments table appears in the Navigation Pane with a linking Excel icon, as shown in Figure I-8. Like any other table, in order for the linked table to work with the rest of a database, a one-to-many relationship between it and another table should be created.

3. **Click the Database Tools tab, click the Relationships button, click the Show Table button, double-click Departments, then click Close**

   The Dept field in the Departments table is used to create a one-to-many relationship with the EDepartment field in the Employees table. One department may be related to many employees.

4. **Drag the Departments field list near the Employees table, drag the Dept field in the Departments table to the EDepartment field in the Employees table, then click Create in the Edit Relationships dialog box**

   Your Relationships window should look like Figure I-9. A one-to-many relationship is established between the Departments and Employees tables, but because referential integrity is not enforced, the one and many symbols do not appear on the link line. You cannot establish referential integrity when one of the tables is a linked table. Now that the linked Departments table is related to the rest of the database, it can participate in queries, forms, and reports that select fields from multiple tables.

5. **Click the Close button, then click Yes when prompted to save changes**

   You work with a linked table just as you work with any other table. The data in a linked table can be edited through either the source program (in this case, Excel) or in the Access database, even though the data is only physically stored in the original source file.

FIGURE I-7: **Get External Data – Excel Spreadsheet dialog box**

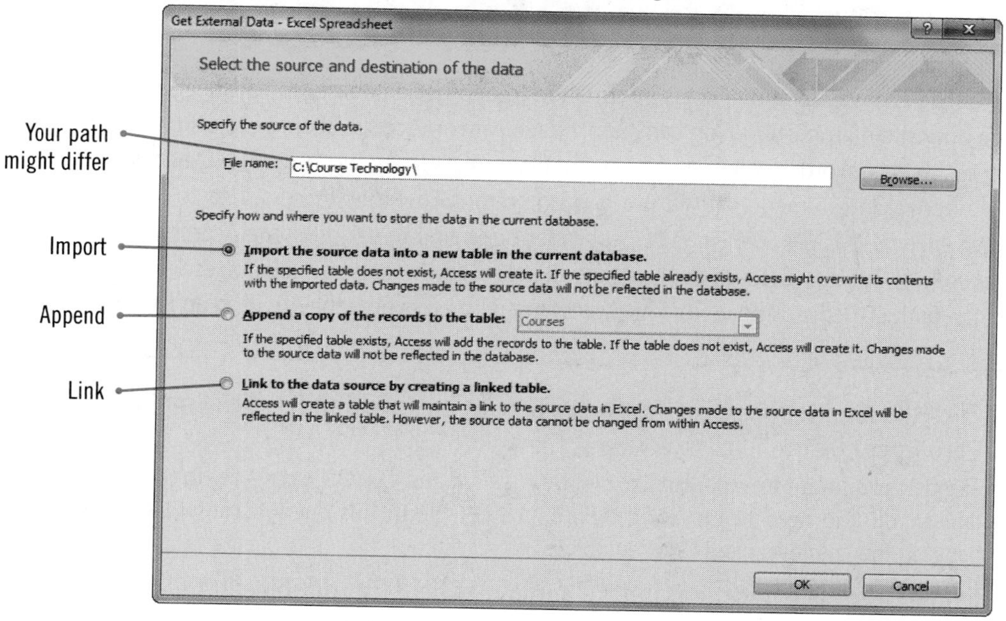

FIGURE I-8: **Departments table is linked from Excel**

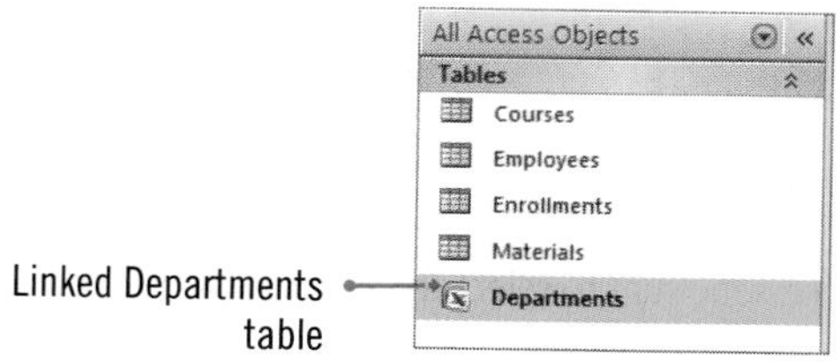

FIGURE I-9: **Relationships window with linked Departments table**

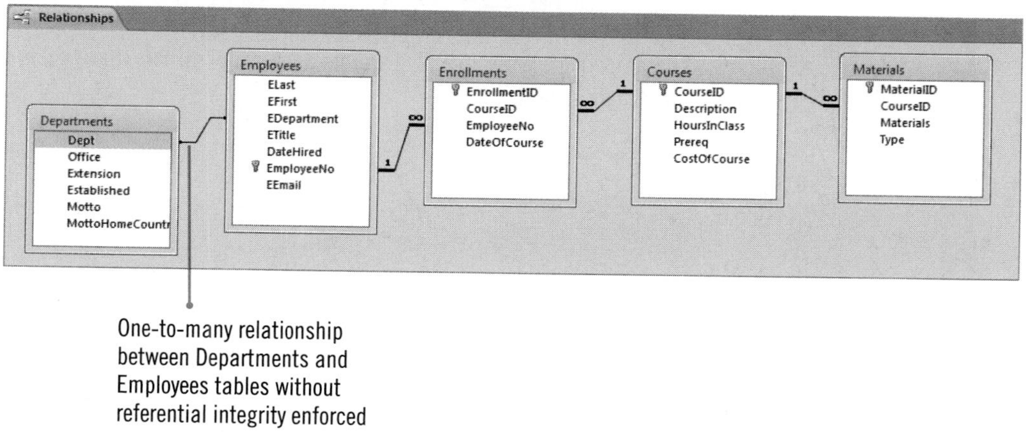

Access 2010

UNIT
I
Access 2010

Exporting Data to Excel

Exporting is a way to copy Access information to another database, spreadsheet, or file format. Exporting is the opposite of importing. You can export data from an Access database to other file types, such as those used by Excel or Word, and in several general file formats including text, HTML, and XML. Given the popularity of analyzing numeric data in Excel, it is common to export Access data to an Excel spreadsheet for further analysis. The Finance Department asks you to export some Access data to an Excel spreadsheet so they can use Excel to analyze how increases in the cost of the courses would affect departments. You can gather the fields needed in an Access query, then export the query to an Excel spreadsheet.

STEPS

1. **Click the Create tab, click the Query Design button, double-click Employees, double-click Enrollments, double-click Courses, then click Close**

   The fields you want to export to Excel—EDepartment and CostOfCourse—are in the Employees and Courses tables. You also need to include the Enrollments table in this query because it provides the connection between the Employees and Courses tables.

2. **Double-click EDepartment in the Employees field list, double-click CostOfCourse in the Courses field list, click the Sort cell for the EDepartment field, click the Sort cell list arrow, click Ascending, then click the View button to display the query datasheet**

   The resulting datasheet has 403 records. You want to summarize the costs by department before exporting this to Excel.

3. **Click the View button to return to Design View, click the Totals button in the Show/Hide group, click Group By for the CostOfCourse field, click the Group By list arrow, click Sum, click to display the query datasheet, then widen the SumOfCostOfCourse column as shown in Figure I-10**

   Save the query with a meaningful name to prepare to export it to Excel.

4. **Click the Save button on the Quick Access toolbar, type DepartmentCosts, click OK, right-click the DepartmentCosts tab, then click Close**

   Before you start an export process, be sure to select the object you want to export in the Navigation Pane.

> **QUICK TIP**
> To quickly export an object, right-click it in the Navigation Pane, point to Export, then click the file type for the export.

5. **Click the DepartmentCosts query in the Navigation Pane (if it is not already selected), click the External Data tab, click the Excel button in the Export group, click Browse, navigate to the drive and folder where you store your Data Files, click Save, click OK, then click Close**

   The data in the DepartmentCosts query has now been exported to an Excel spreadsheet file named DepartmentCosts and saved in the drive and folder where you store your Data Files. As with imports, you can save and then repeat the export process by saving the export steps when prompted by the last dialog box in the Export Wizard. Run the saved export process using the **Saved Exports** button on the External Data tab or by assigning the export process to an Outlook task.

   Access can work with data in a wide variety of file formats. Other file formats that Access can import from, link with, and export to are listed in Table I-1.

FIGURE I-10: New query selects and summarizes data to be exported to Excel

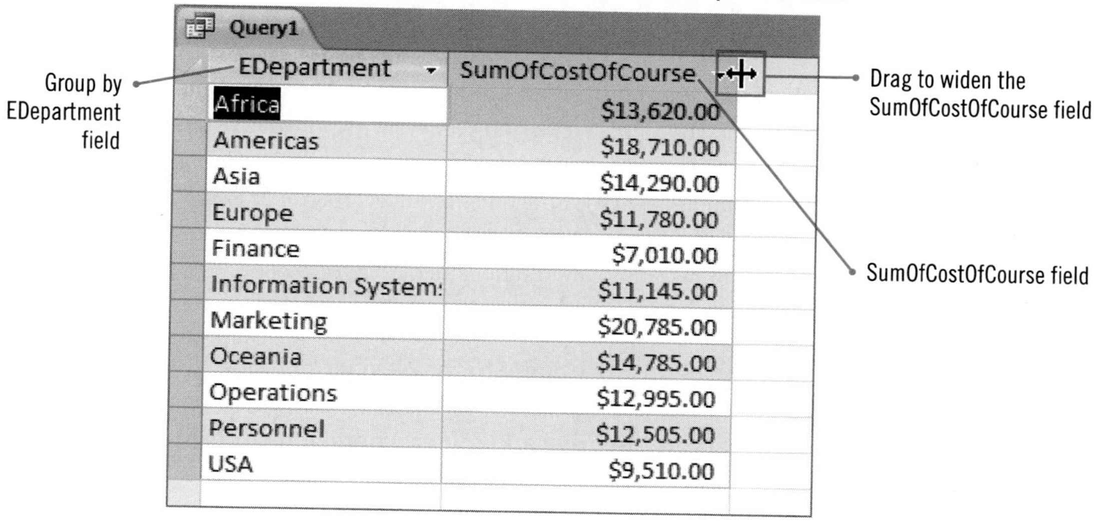

TABLE I-1: File formats that Access can link to, import, and export

file format	import	link	export
Access	Yes	Yes	Yes
Excel	Yes	Yes	Yes
Word	No	No	Yes
SharePoint site	Yes	Yes	Yes
E-mail file attachments	No	No	Yes
Outlook folder	Yes	Yes	No
ODBC database (such as SQL Server)	Yes	Yes	Yes
dBASE	Yes	Yes	Yes
HTML document	Yes	Yes	Yes
PDF or XPS file	No	No	Yes
Text file (delimited or fixed width)	Yes	Yes	Yes
XML file	Yes	No	Yes

UNIT
I
Access 2010

Publishing Data to Word

Microsoft Word, the word-processing program in the Microsoft Office suite, is a premier program for entering, editing, and formatting text. You can easily export data from an Access table, query, form, or report into a Word document. This is helpful when you want to use Word's superior text-editing features to combine the information in a Word document with Access data. You have been asked to write a memo to the management committee describing departmental costs for continuing education. You export an Access query with this data to a Word document where you finish the memo.

STEPS

1. **Click the DepartmentCosts query in the Navigation Pane (if it is not already selected), click the External Data tab, click the More button in the Export group, click Word, click Browse, navigate to the drive and folder where you store your Data Files, click Save, click OK, then click Close**

   The data in the DepartmentCosts query is exported as an **RTF (Rich Text Format)** file, which can be opened and edited in Word.

2. **Start Word, then open DepartmentCosts.rtf from the drive and folder where you store your Data Files**

   Currently, the document contains only a table of information, the data you exported from the DepartmentCosts query. Use Word to add the memo information.

3. **Press [Enter], then type the following text, pressing [Tab] after typing each colon:**

   To: Management Committee

   From: Your Name

   Re: Analysis of Continuing Education Courses

   Date: Today's date

   The following information shows the overall cost for continuing education subtotaled by department. The information shows that the Americas and Marketing departments are the highest consumers of continuing education.

4. **Proofread your document, which should now look like Figure I-11, then preview and print it**

   The **word wrap** feature in Word determines when a line of text extends into the right margin of the page and automatically forces the text to the next line without you needing to press [Enter]. This allows you to enter and edit large paragraphs of text in Word very efficiently.

5. **Save and close the document, then exit Word**

   In addition to exporting data, Table I-2 lists other techniques you can use to copy Access data to other applications.

FIGURE I-11: Final Word document

To: Management Committee

From: Student Name

Re: Analysis of Continuing Education Courses

Date: Today's date

The following information shows the overall cost for continuing education subtotaled by department. The information shows that the Americas and Marketing Departments are the highest consumers of continuing education.

EDepartment	SumOfCostOfCourse
Africa	$13,620.00
Americas	$18,710.00
Asia	$14,290.00
Europe	$11,780.00
Finance	$7,010.00
Information Systems	$11,145.00
Marketing	$20,785.00
Oceania	$14,785.00
Operations	$12,995.00
Personnel	$12,505.00
USA	$9,510.00

TABLE I-2: Techniques to copy Access data to other applications

technique	button or menu option	description
Drag and drop	Resize Access window so that the target location (Word or Excel, for example) can also be seen on the screen	With both windows visible, drag the Access table, query, form, or report object icon from the Access window to the target (Excel or Word) window
Export	Use the buttons on the Export section of the External Data tab	Copy information from an Access object into a different file format
Office Clipboard	Copy and Paste	Click the Copy button to copy selected data to the Office Clipboard (the Office Clipboard can hold multiple items); open a Word document or Excel spreadsheet, click where you want to paste the data, then click the Paste button

UNIT I
Access 2010

Merging Data with Word

Another way to export Access data is to merge it to a Word document as the data source for a mail-merge process. In a **mail merge**, data from an Access table or query is combined into a Word form letter, label, or envelope to create mass mailing documents. Jacob Thomas wants to send Quest employees a letter announcing two new continuing education courses. You merge Access data to a Word document to customize a letter to each employee.

STEPS

1. **Click the Employees table in the Navigation Pane, click the External Data tab, then click the Word Merge button in the Export group**
   The **Microsoft Word Mail Merge Wizard** dialog box opens asking whether you want to link to an existing document or create a new one.

2. **Click the Create a new document and then link the data to it option button, click OK, then maximize the Word window**
   Word starts and opens the **Mail Merge task pane**, which steps you through the mail-merge process. Before you merge the Access data with the Word document, you must create the **main document**, the Word document that contains the standard text for each letter in the mail-merge process.

> **TROUBLE**
> The "Next" links are at the bottom of the Mail Merge task pane.

3. **Type the standard text shown in Figure I-12, click the Next: Starting document link in the bottom of the Mail Merge task pane, click the Next: Select recipients link to use the current document, click the Next: Write your letter link to use the existing list of names, press [Tab] after To: in the letter, then click the Insert Merge Field button in the Write & Insert Fields group on the Mailings tab**
   The Insert Merge Field dialog box lists all of the fields in the original data source, the Employees table. You use the Insert Merge Field dialog box to insert **merge fields**, codes that are replaced with the values in the field that the code represents when the mail merge is processed.

> **TROUBLE**
> You cannot type the merge codes directly into the document. You must use the Insert Merge Field dialog box.

4. **Double-click EFirst, double-click ELast, click Close, click between the EFirst and ELast codes, then press [Spacebar] to insert a space between the codes as shown in Figure I-13**
   With the main document and merge fields inserted, you are ready to complete the mail merge.

5. **Click the Next: Preview your letters link in the Mail Merge task pane, click the Next: Complete the merge link to complete the merge, click the Edit individual letters link to view the letters on the screen, then click OK to complete the merge**
   The mail-merge process combines the EFirst and ELast field values from the Employees table with the main document, creating a 24-page document as shown in the Word status bar. Each page is a customized letter for each record in the Employees table. The first page is a letter to Ron Dawson. "Ron" is the field value for the EFirst field in the first record in the Employees table, and "Dawson" is the field value for the ELast field.

6. **Press [Page Down] several times to view several pages of the final merged document, then close the merged document, Letters1, without saving it**
   You generally don't need to save the final, large merged document. Saving the one-page main document, however, is a good idea in case you need to repeat the merge process.

> **TROUBLE**
> The main document may display the data from the first record in the Access employees table, Ron Dawson, instead of the merge codes.

7. **Click the Save button on the Quick Access toolbar, navigate to the drive and folder where you store your Data Files, enter Employees in the File name text box, click Save, then close Word**

FIGURE I-12: **Creating the main document in Word**

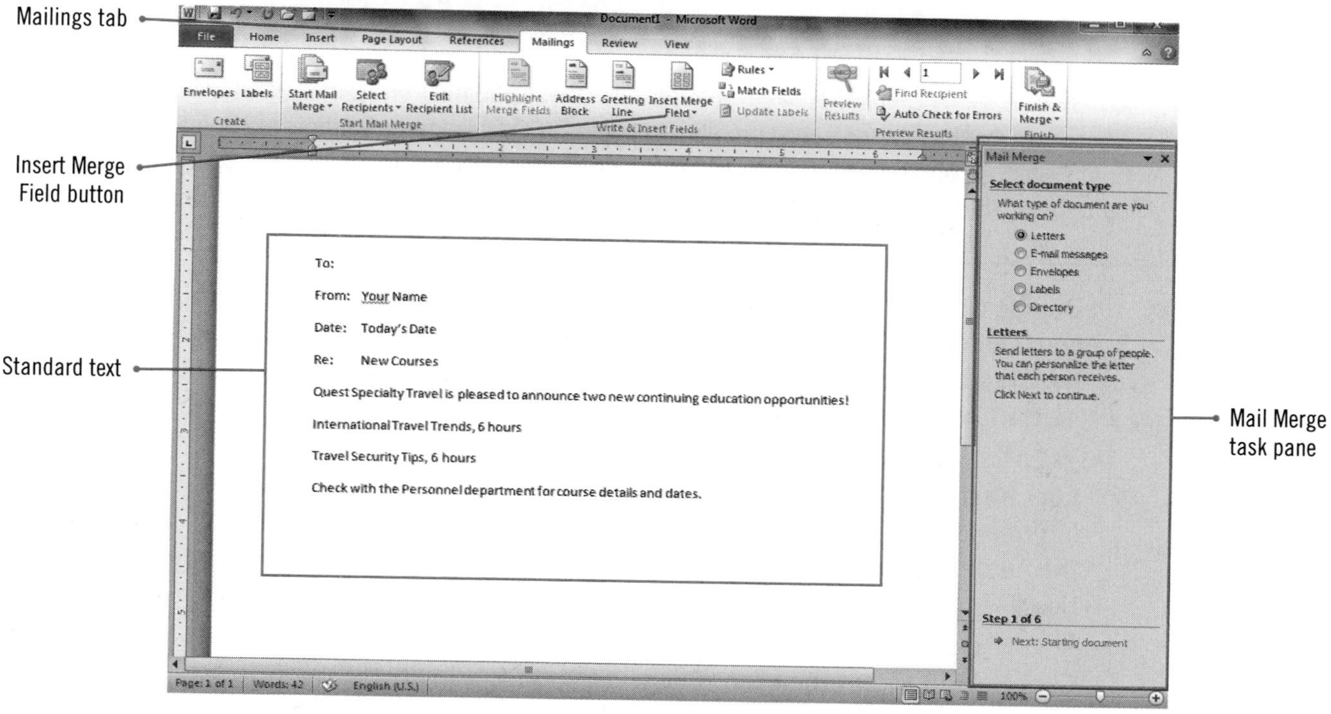

FIGURE I-13: **Inserting merge fields**

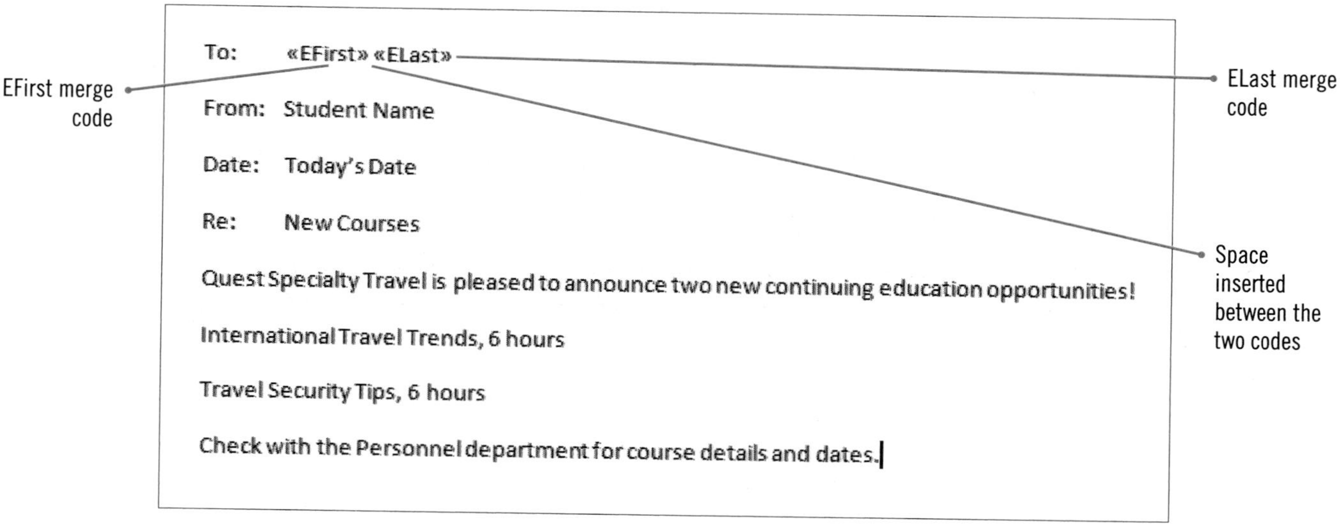

Collecting Data with Outlook

Access data can be collected and entered into the database from e-mail messages using Outlook. **Microsoft Outlook** is the e-mail program in Microsoft Office, a fast electronic method to share information. Jacob Thomas asks you to make sure all employee information in the Education database is up to date. You will distribute this information and collect updates using Outlook e-mail messages.

STEPS

> **TROUBLE**
> This lesson requires that you have a valid Outlook e-mail address to both send and receive e-mail, and Outlook 2010 or later installed and configured on the computer you are using. If not, read but do not perform the following steps.

1. **Double-click the Employees table in the Navigation Pane, tab to the EE-mail field, enter your Outlook e-mail address, close the Employees table, click the External Data tab, click the Create E-mail button in the Collect Data group, then read the steps in the wizard**
   An **Outlook data collection wizard** helps you through the steps of collecting Access data through Outlook e-mail.
2. **Click Next, click Next to accept an HTML form message, click the Update existing information option button, click Next, click the Select All Fields button >>, click Next, click the Automatically process replies and add data to Employees check box, then click Next**
   Now that you've specified how to send and process the e-mail, the wizard asks about the recipients' e-mail addresses.
3. **Click Next to accept the EE-mail field in the current table, click Next to accept the default subject and introduction text, click Next to create the e-mail messages, click Next to see the e-mail addresses that are selected, click the Select All check box to clear it, click the check box for the e-mail address you entered in Step 1, then click Send**
   To view the e-mail that has been sent, you would open Outlook and display the Sent Items folder. The e-mail message includes the employee data for the first record in the Employees table as shown in Figure I-14.
4. **Complete the Outlook portion of this lesson by starting Outlook, double-click the e-mail message in your Inbox that you sent from Access in Step 1 to open it, click Reply, enter your name in the ELast and EFirst fields, then click Send**
   If you cannot complete the Outlook portion of this lesson, you can still review the settings on your e-mail data collection processes using the Manage Replies button.
5. **Return to the Education-I database, then click the Manage Replies button in the Collect Data group**
   The Manage Data Collection Messages dialog box opens in Access to provide details of the data collection process as shown in Figure I-15. In Outlook, a folder named **Access Data Collection Replies** collects and helps you manage the e-mails initiated by Access and responses to them.

> **TROUBLE**
> Note that the update to the database won't be instantaneous. The time required to process the e-mail and update the database will vary from system to system.

6. **Click Close to close the Manage Data Collection Messages dialog box, and if you completed the task to update the record via an Outlook e-mail in Step 4, double-click the Employees table to review the first record**
   If you completed all of the steps, you used Access to send an e-mail that contained Access data from the first record of the Employees table. You used Outlook to respond to that e-mail, editing both the EFirst and ELast fields. You then returned to Access, opened the Employees table, and made sure that the edits you made to the first record in the Employees table in an Outlook e-mail message were automatically applied in the Access database, as shown in Figure I-16.
7. **Close the Employees table, close the Education-I.accdb database, then close Access 2010 and Outlook**

FIGURE I-14: Reviewing e-mails sent in Outlook

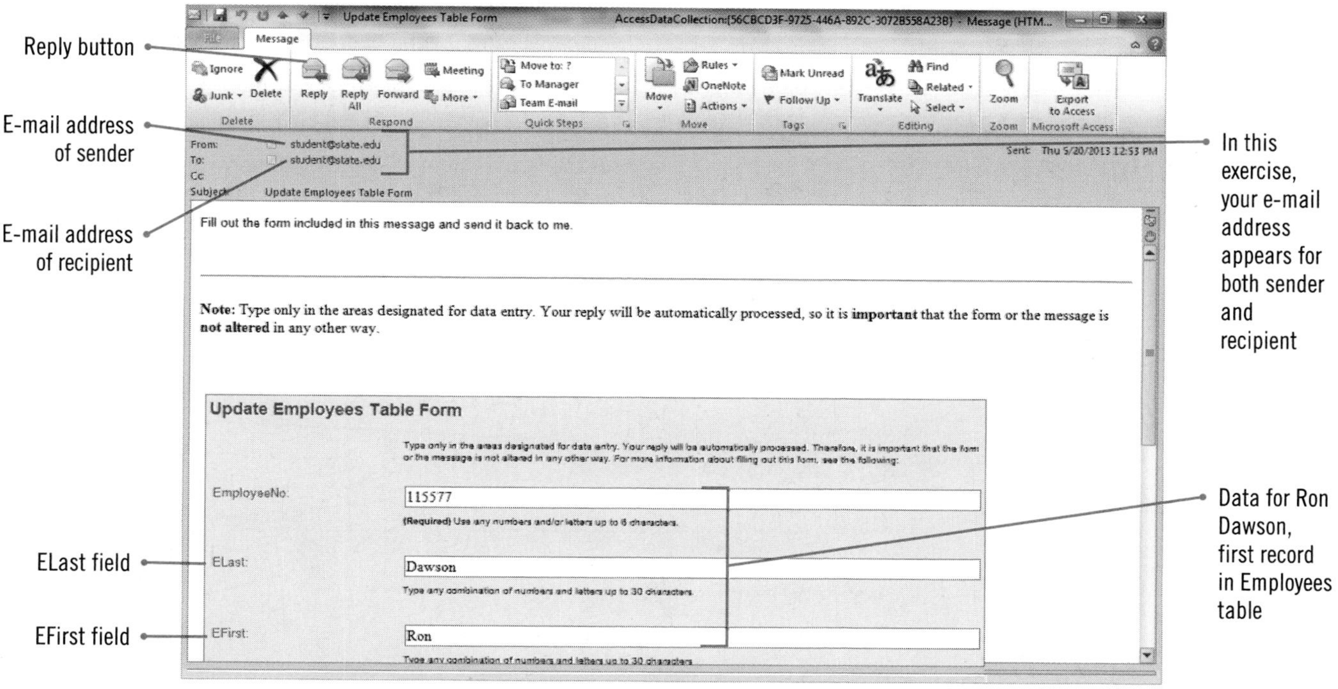

FIGURE I-15: Manage Data Collection Messages dialog box

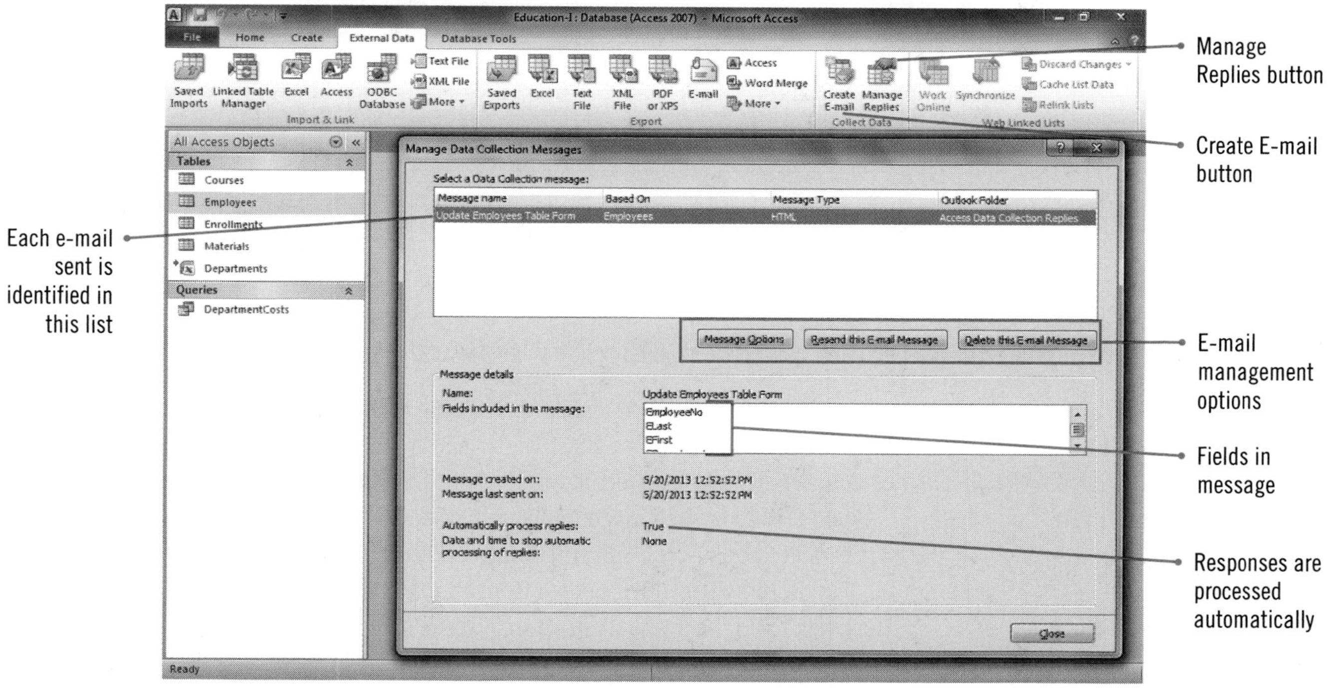

FIGURE I-16: Employees table updates

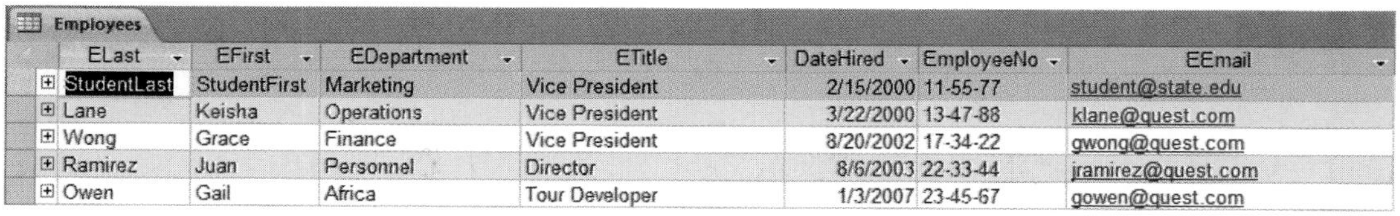

Employees

ELast	EFirst	EDepartment	ETitle	DateHired	EmployeeNo	EEmail
StudentLast	StudentFirst	Marketing	Vice President	2/15/2000	11-55-77	student@state.edu
Lane	Keisha	Operations	Vice President	3/22/2000	13-47-88	klane@quest.com
Wong	Grace	Finance	Vice President	8/20/2002	17-34-22	gwong@quest.com
Ramirez	Juan	Personnel	Director	8/6/2003	22-33-44	jramirez@quest.com
Owen	Gail	Africa	Tour Developer	1/3/2007	23-45-67	gowen@quest.com

Practice

Concepts Review

For current SAM information, including versions and content details, visit SAM Central (http://www.cengage.com/samcentral). If you have a SAM user profile, you may have access to hands-on instruction, practice, and assessment of the skills covered in this unit. Since various versions of SAM are supported throughout the life of this text, check with your instructor for the correct instructions and URL/Web site for accessing assignments.

Identify each element of the database window shown in Figure I-17.

FIGURE I-17

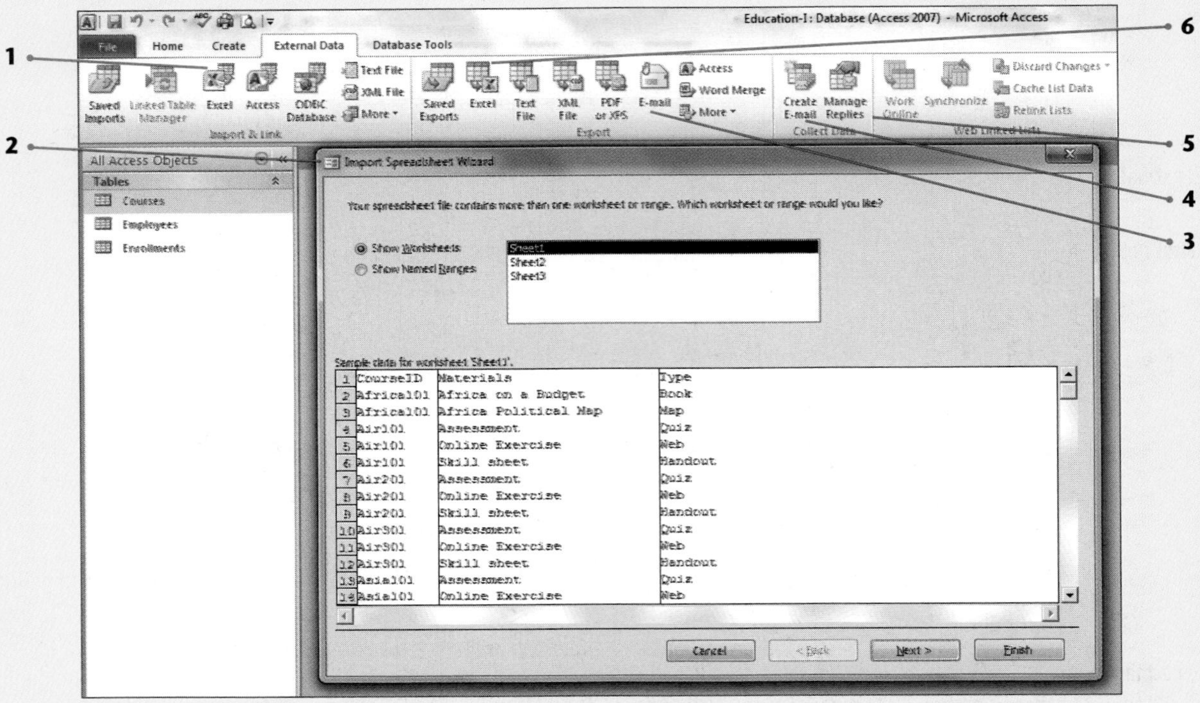

Match each term with the statement that best describes its function.

7. **Exporting**
8. **Main document**
9. **Linking**
10. **Delimited text file**
11. **Mail merge**
12. **Importing**
13. **Database template**
14. **Table template**

- **a.** A tool used to quickly create a single table within an existing database
- **b.** A file used to determine how a letter and Access data will be combined
- **c.** A file that stores one record on each line, with the field values separated by a common character such as a comma, tab, or dash
- **d.** A way to copy Access information to another database, spreadsheet, or file format
- **e.** The process of converting data from an external source into an Access database
- **f.** A way to connect to data in an external source without copying it
- **g.** A tool used to quickly create a new database based on a particular subject such as assets, contacts, events, or projects
- **h.** To combine data from an Access table or query into a Word form letter, label, or envelope to create mass mailing documents

Select the best answer from the list of choices.

15. Which of the following is *not* true about database templates?

a. Microsoft provides online templates in areas such as business and personal database applications.
b. They create multiple database objects.
c. They analyze the data on your computer and suggest database applications.
d. They cover a wide range of subjects including assets, contacts, events, or projects.

16. Which of the following is *not* true of exporting?

a. Access data can be exported into Excel.
b. Access data can be exported to Word.
c. Exporting retains a link between the original and target data files.
d. Exporting creates a copy of data.

17. Which of the following is *not* a file format that Access can import?

a. Excel
b. Access
c. HTML
d. Word

18. Which of the following software products would most likely be used to help electronically merge Access data to a list of e-mail addresses?

a. Word
b. Access
c. Outlook
d. Excel

19. Which is *not* true about enforcing referential integrity?

a. It is required for all one-to-many relationships.
b. It prevents records from being deleted in the "one" side of a one-to-many relationship that have matching records on the "many" side.
c. It prevents records from being created in the "many" side of a one-to-many relationship that do not have a matching record on the "one" side.
d. It prevents orphan records.

20. Which of the following is *not* true about linking?

a. Linking copies data from one data file to another.
b. Access can link to data in an HTML file.
c. Access can link to data in an Excel spreadsheet.
d. You can edit linked data in Access.

21. How does an imported table differ from a table created in Access?

a. They do not differ.
b. The imported table is merely a link to the original source data.
c. There is no data in an imported table.
d. The imported table displays an imported table icon.

Skills Review

1. Use database templates.

a. Start Access 2010 and use the Assets database template within Office.com to build a new Access database with the name **Assets-I**. Save the new database in the drive and folder where you store your Data Files. (*Hint*: This step requires that you are connected to the Internet to download online templates.)

b. Click the New User link in the Login dialog box, enter your e-mail and full name, click Save & Close, click your name, then click Login.

c. In the Main form, click all of the tabs—Current Assets, Retired Assets, Users, Report Center, and Getting Started—to explore the database.

d. Right-click the Main form tab, then click Close.

e. Expand the Navigation Pane, then explore several other tables, queries, forms, and reports to familiarize yourself with the database created by the Assets template. Note that each of the objects in this database displays the Web-compatible icon, showing that if this database were published to a Microsoft SharePoint server, users could access each object using a browser such as Internet Explorer, Safari, or Firefox.

f. Close all objects but leave the new Assets-I.accdb database open.

2. Use Application Parts.

a. Use the Issues table template in Application Parts to create a new table in the Assets-I.accdb database named Issues.

b. Creating a new table with the Application Parts automatically closes and reopens the database, so you are presented with the initial Login dialog box each time you use Application Parts. When prompted with the Login dialog box, click your name and then click Login.

c. Click Next to accept the relationship of one Assets record to many Issues records, then click Create to accept the other default options on the relationship.

d. Note that the new Issues table also sports the Web-compatible icon. Double-click the Issues table to open and study it in Datasheet View.

e. Close all open objects, then use the Application Parts feature to create a new Dialog form.

f. When prompted with the Login dialog box, click your name and click Login.

g. Double-click the new Web-compatible Dialog form in the Navigation Pane to view it.

h. Return to the Main form, then explore the links in the Help Videos and Get more help sections as desired.

i. Close all open objects, then close the Assets-I.accdb database.

3. Import data from Excel.

a. Open the Machinery-I.accdb database from the drive and folder where you store your Data Files. Enable content if prompted.

b. Import the MachineryEmp.xlsx spreadsheet, which contains employee information, from the drive and folder where you store your Data Files to a new table in the current database, using the Import Spreadsheet Wizard to import the data. Make sure that the first row is specified as the column headings.

c. Choose the EmployeeNo field as the primary key, and import the data to a table named **Employees**. Do not save the import steps.

d. In Table Design View for the Employees table, change the Data Type of the EmployeeNo field to Number. Save the table and click Yes when prompted. The EmployeeNo field values are from 1 to 6. No data will be lost. Close the Employees table.

4. Link data from Excel.

a. Link to the Vendors.xlsx Excel file stored on the drive and folder where you store your Data Files.

b. In the Link Spreadsheet Wizard, specify that the first row contains column headings.

c. Name the linked table **Vendors**.

Skills Review (continued)

d. Open the Relationships window, and display all five field lists in the window. Link the tables together with one-to-many relationships, as shown in Figure I-18. Be sure to enforce referential integrity on all relationships except for the relationship between Products and the linked Vendors table.

e. Save and close the Relationships window.

5. Export data to Excel.

a. Open the Products table to view the datasheet, then close it.

b. Export the Products table data to an Excel spreadsheet named **Products.xlsx**. Save the spreadsheet to the drive and folder where you store your Data Files. Do not save the export steps.

FIGURE I-18

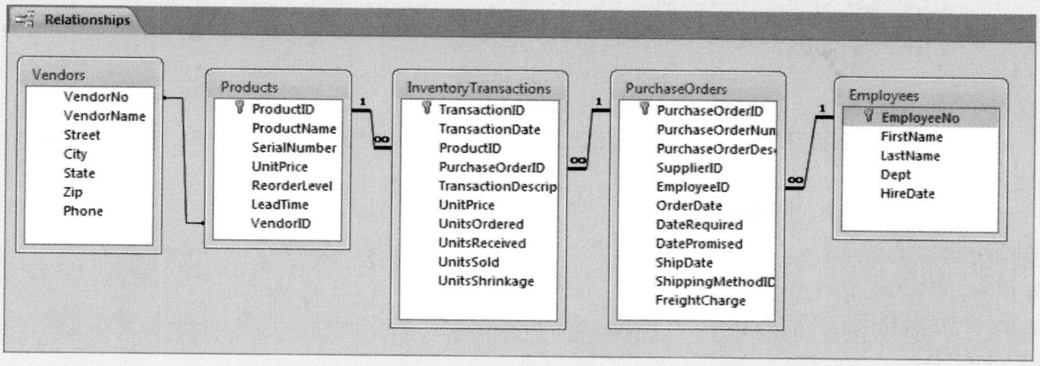

6. Publish data to Word.

a. In the Machinery-I.accdb database, export the Products table to a Word document named **Products.rtf**. Save the Products.rtf file in the drive and folder where you store your Data Files. Do not save the export steps.

b. Start Word, open the Products.rtf document from the drive and folder where you store your Data Files. Press [Enter] twice, press [Ctrl][Home] to return to the top of the document, then type the following text:

INTERNAL MEMO

From: **Your Name**

To: **Sales Staff**

Date: **Today's date**

Do not forget to mention the long lead times on the Back Hoe, Thatcher, and Biodegrader to customers. We usually do not keep these items in stock.

c. Proofread the document, then save and print it. Close the document, then exit Word.

7. Merge data with Word.

a. In the Machinery-I.accdb database, merge the data from the Employees table to a Word document.

b. Use the "Create a new document and then link the data to it" option in the Microsoft Word Mail Merge Wizard dialog box. In the Word document, enter the following text as the main document for the mail merge.

Date: **Today's date**

To:

From: **Your Name**

Re: **CPR Training**

The annual CPR Training session will be held on Friday, February 26, 2013. Please sign up for this important event in the lunchroom. Friends and family over 18 years old are also welcome.

c. To the right of **To:**, press [Tab] to position the insertion point at the location for the first merge field.

d. Click the Next links at the bottom of the Mail Merge task pane to move to Step 4 of 6, click the Insert Merge Field button, then use the Insert Merge Field dialog box to add the FirstName and LastName fields to the main document.

e. Close the Insert Merge Field dialog box, and insert a space between the <<FirstName>> and <<LastName>> merge codes.

f. Complete the mail-merge process to merge all records in the Employees table to the letter.

Skills Review (continued)

g. Print the last page of the merged document if required by your instructor (the letter to Don Balch), then close the six-page final merged document without saving changes.

h. Save the main document with the name **CPR.docx**, then exit Word.

8. **Collect data with Outlook.**

   (*Note:* Steps 8a-8h require that you have a valid Outlook e-mail address to both send and receive e-mail, and Outlook 2010 or later installed and configured on the computer you are using. If not, read but do not perform the following steps.)

   a. In the Machinery-I database, click the Products table in the Navigation Pane, then click the Create E-mail button on the External Data tab.

   b. Choose HTML Form, choose to Collect new information only, select all fields from the Products form, and choose to automatically process replies and add data to Products.

   c. Choose to Enter the e-mail addresses in Microsoft Outlook, accept the default Subject and Introduction text, and click Create.

   d. Enter your Outlook e-mail address, and click Send.

   e. Open Outlook, double-click the new message that you sent yourself through Access, click Reply, and enter a new record using the form as follows:

      Product Name: **Wood Chipper**
      Serial Number: **12345**
      Unit Price: **99.95**
      Reorder Level: **10**
      Lead Time: **20**
      VendorID: **1**

   f. When you have the e-mail form filled out, click Send.

   g. Return to the Machinery-I.accdb database and open the Products table to make sure that the new record for the Wood Chipper was automatically added to the database. Note that the time required to update the database varies between systems so you may have to wait a few seconds before the new record is entered.

   h. Once you have confirmed that the Products table has been successfully updated, close the Machinery-I.accdb database and exit Access 2010 and Outlook.

Independent Challenge 1

As the manager of a women's college basketball team, you have created a database called Basketball-I that tracks the players, games, and player statistics. You want to link to an Excel file that contains information on the player's course load. You also want to export a report to a Word document in order to add a paragraph of descriptive text.

a. Open the database Basketball-I.accdb from the drive and folder where you store your Data Files. Enable content if prompted.

b. In the Relationships window, connect the Games and Stats tables with a one-to-many relationship based on the common GameNo field. Connect the Players and Stats tables with a one-to-many relationship based on the common PlayerNo field. Be sure to enforce referential integrity on both relationships. Save and close the Relationships window.

c. Export the Player Statistics report to Word with the name **Player Statistics.rtf**. Save the Player Statistics.rtf document in the drive and folder where you store your Data Files. Do not save the export steps.

d. Start Word and open the Player Statistics.rtf document.

e. Press [Enter] three times to enter three blank lines at the top of the document, then press [Ctrl][Home] to position the insertion point at the top of the document.

f. Type your name on the first line of the document, enter today's date as the second line, then write a sentence or two that explains the Player Statistics data that follows. Save, print, and close the Player Statistics document.

g. Exit Word. Close the Basketball-I.accdb database, then exit Access.

Independent Challenge 2

As the manager of a women's college basketball team, you have created a database called Basketball-I that tracks the players, games, and player statistics. The 2013-2014 basketball schedule has been provided to you as an Excel spreadsheet file. You will import that data and append it to the current Games table.

a. Open the database Basketball-I.accdb from the drive and folder where you store your Data Files. Enable content if prompted.

b. If the relationships haven't already been established in this database, create relationships as described in Step b of Independent Challenge 1.

c. Open the Games table to observe the datasheet. It currently contains 22 records with scores for the 2012-2013 basketball season.

d. Start Excel and open the 2013-2014Schedule.xlsx file from the drive and folder where you store your Data Files. Note that it contains 22 rows of data indicating the opponent, mascot, home or away status, and date of the games for the 2013-2014 season. You have been told that the data will import more precisely if it is identified with the same field names as have already been established in the Games table in Access, so you'll insert those field names as a header row in the Excel spreadsheet.

e. Click anywhere in row 1 of the 2013-2014Schedule.xlsx spreadsheet, click the Insert button in the Cells group, and click Insert Sheet Rows to insert a new blank row.

f. In the new blank row 1, enter the field names that correspond to the field names in the Games table for the same data above each column: **Opponent**, **Mascot**, **Home-Away**, and **GameDate**. Be careful to enter the names precisely as shown.

g. Save and close the 2013-2014Schedule.xlsx spreadsheet, exit Excel, and return to the Basketball-I.accdb database.

h. Close the Games table, click the External Data tab, click the Excel button on the Import & Link group, browse for the 2013-2014Schedule.xlsx spreadsheet in your data files, and choose the Append a copy of the records to the table option button. Be sure that Games is selected as the table to use for the append process.

i. Follow the steps of the Import Spreadsheet Wizard process through completion (do not save the import steps), then open the Games table. It should contain the original 22 records for the 2012-2013 season plus 22 more from the 2013-2014Schedule.xlsx spreadsheet with default values of 0 for both the HomeScore and OpponentScore fields.

j. Change the Opponent value in the first record to your last name's College, then print the first page of the Games table if requested by your instructor.

k. Save and close the Games table, close the Basketball-I.accdb database, then exit Access.

Independent Challenge 3

You have been asked by a small private school to build a database to track library books. You decide to explore Microsoft database templates to see if there is a tool that could help you get started.

a. Create a new database using the Lending library database template from the Personal category of online templates. Enable content if prompted. Name the database **Lending library.accdb**, and store it in the drive and folder where you store your Data Files.

b. Read and then close the Access Help window. Enable content, if prompted, then close the Asset List form.

Independent Challenge 3 (continued)

c. Review the Relationships window. Rearrange the field lists as shown in Figure I-19, then print the Relationships report. Save the report with the default name, **Relationships for Lending library**, then close it.

FIGURE I-19

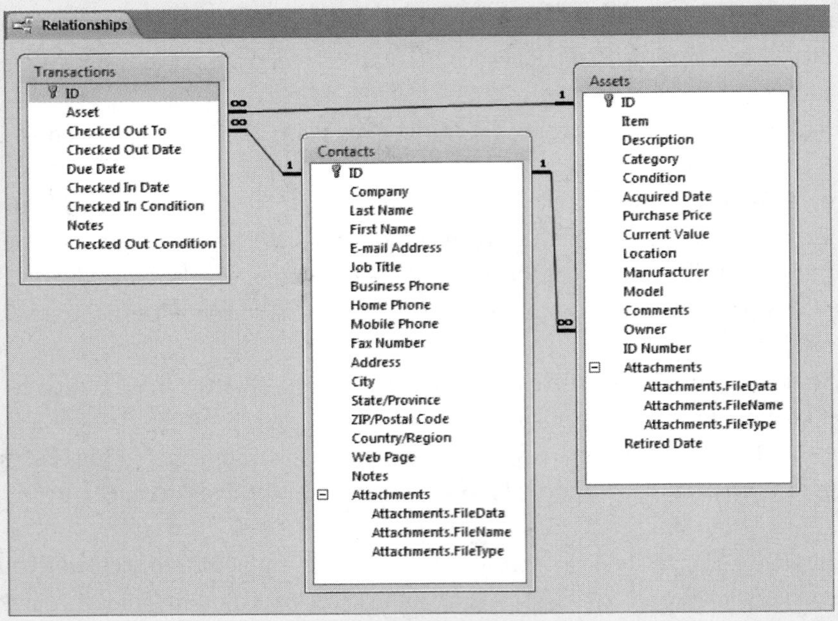

d. Save and close the Relationships window.

e. Expand the Contacts group in the Navigation Pane, double-click the Contact Details form to open it, then enter your name in the First Name and Last Name text boxes. Enter fictional but reasonable data for each field, but do not enter anything for the Notes field. Close the Contacts Details form.

Advanced Challenge Exercise

- Click the Lending library title bar in the Navigation Pane, then choose Object Type.
- In Design View of the Assets table, select the Category field, then delete the existing entry in the Default Value property.
- For the Category field, change the Row Source property on the Lookup tab to **Book;Movie;Music**.
- Select the Location field, then change the Row Source property on the Lookup tab to **East;Midwest;West**.
- Save the table, then display it in Datasheet View and test the lookup properties for the Category and Location fields.
- Save and close the Assets table, and explore the other forms and reports created by the Lending Library database template as desired.

f. Close the Lending library.accdb database, then exit Access.

Real Life Independent Challenge

This Independent Challenge requires an Internet connection.

Learning common phrases in a variety of foreign languages is extremely valuable if you travel or interact with people from other countries. As a volunteer with the foreign student exchange program at your college, you have created a database that documents the primary and secondary languages used by foreign countries. The database also includes a table of common words and phrases that you can use to practice basic conversation skills.

a. Open the Languages-I.accdb database from the drive and folder where you store your Data Files. Enable content if prompted.

Real Life Independent Challenge (continued)

b. Open the datasheets for each of the three tables to familiarize yourself with the fields and records. The Primary and Secondary fields in the Countries table represent the primary and secondary languages for that country. Close the datasheets for each of the three tables.

c. Open the Relationships window, and create a one-to-many relationship between the Languages and Countries table using the LanguageID field in the Languages table and the Primary field in the Countries table. Enforce referential integrity on the relationship.

d. Create a one-to-many relationship between the Languages and Countries tables using the LanguageID field in the Languages table and the Secondary field in the Countries table. Click No when prompted to edit the existing relationship, and enforce referential integrity on the new relationship. The field list for the Languages table will appear twice in the Relationships window with Languages_1 as the title for the second field list as shown in Figure I-20. The Words table is used for reference and does not have a direct relationship to the other tables.

e. Create a Relationships report, then display it in Design View.

f. Add a label to the Report Header section with your name, change the font color of the new label to black, then save the report with the name **Relationships for Language-I**.

g. Print the report if requested by your instructor, and close it.

h. Save and close the Relationships window.

i. Connect to the Internet and go to www.ask.com, www.about.com, or any search engine. Your goal is to find a Web site that translates English to other languages, and to print the home page of that Web site.

j. Add a new field to the Words table with a new language that isn't already represented. Use the Web site to translate the existing three words into the new language. Add three new words or phrases to the Words table, making sure that the translation is made in all of the represented languages: English, French, Spanish, German, Italian, Portuguese, Polish, and the new language you added.

k. Print the updated datasheet for the Words table, close the Words table, close the Languages-I.accdb database, then exit Access.

FIGURE I-20

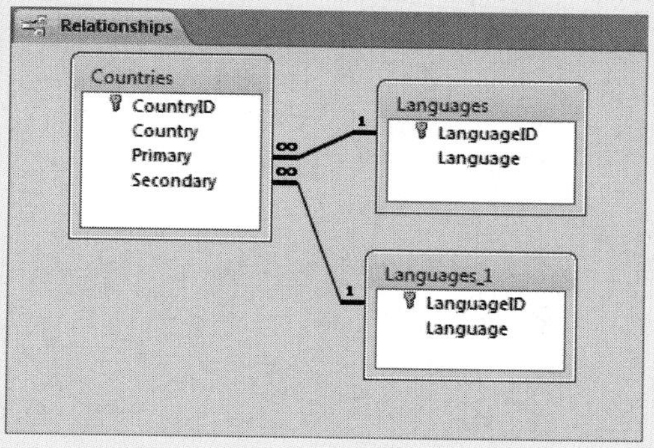

Access 2010

Visual Workshop

Start Access and open the Basketball-I.accdb database from the drive and folder where you store your Data Files. Enable content if prompted. Merge the information from the Players table to a form letter. The first page of the merged document is shown in Figure I-21. Notice that the player's first and last names have been merged to the first line and that the player's first name is merged a second time in the first sentence of the letter. Be very careful to correctly add spaces as needed around the merge fields. Print the last page of the merged document if requested by your instructor, close the 13-page final merged document without saving it, save the main document as **Champs.docx**, then close it.

FIGURE I-21

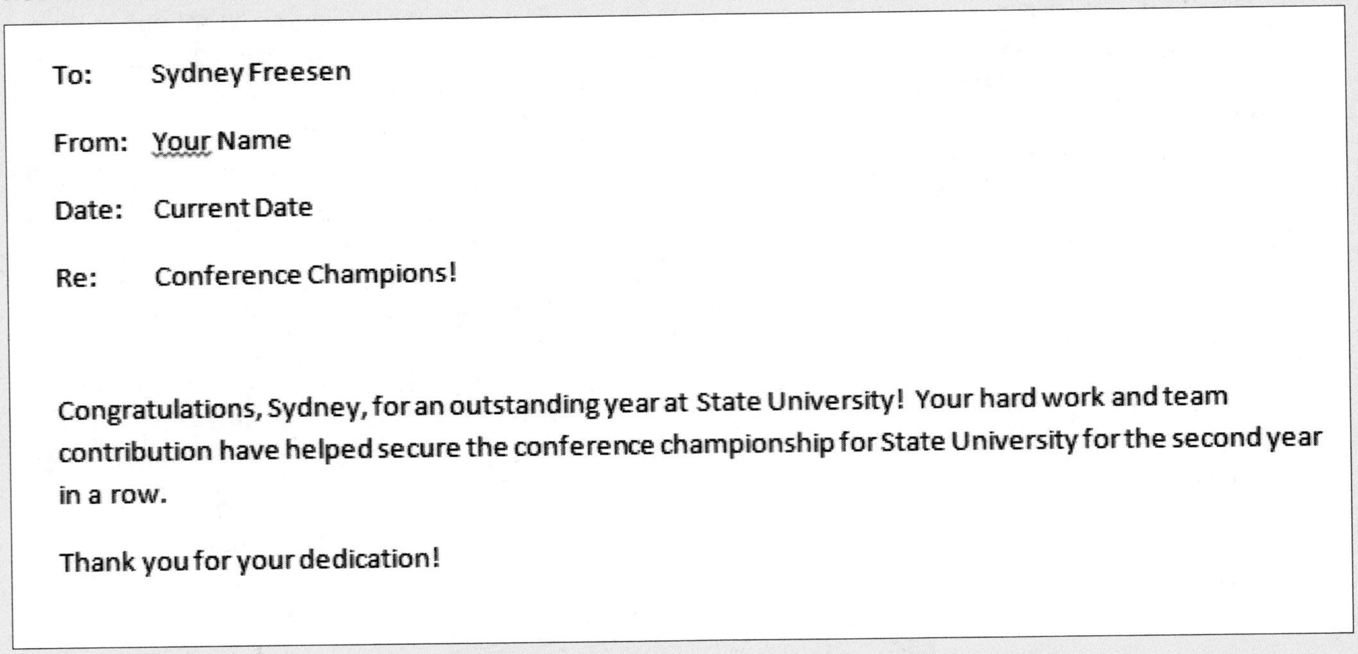

To: Sydney Freesen

From: Your Name

Date: Current Date

Re: Conference Champions!

Congratulations, Sydney, for an outstanding year at State University! Your hard work and team contribution have helped secure the conference championship for State University for the second year in a row.

Thank you for your dedication!

UNIT J
Access 2010

Analyzing Database Design Using Northwind

Files You Will Need:

Northwind.mdb
Education-J.accdb
Basketball-J.accdb
RealEstate-J.accdb
JobSearch-J.accdb
QuestDives-J.accdb

Over time, hundreds of hours are often spent designing and modifying Access database files as users discover new ways to analyze and apply the data. One of the best ways to teach yourself advanced database skills is to study a well-developed database. Microsoft provides a fully developed database example called **Northwind**, which illustrates many advanced database techniques that you can apply to your own development needs. You work with Jacob Thomas, director of staff development at Quest Specialty Travel, to examine the Microsoft Northwind database and determine what features and techniques could be applied to improve the Education database.

OBJECTIVES

- Normalize data
- Analyze relationships
- Evaluate tables
- Improve fields
- Use subqueries
- Modify joins
- Analyze forms
- Analyze reports

UNIT J

Access 2010

Normalizing Data

Normalizing data means to structure it for a relational database. A normalized database reduces inaccurate and redundant data, decreases storage requirements, improves database speed and performance, and simplifies overall database maintenance. It also helps you create accurate queries, forms, and reports. Jacob Thomas asks you to study the Northwind database to learn techniques you could use to improve the Education-J database.

STEPS

1. **Start Access, open the Northwind.mdb database from the drive and folder where you store your Data Files, enable content if prompted, then click OK if the Welcome to Northwind Traders window opens**

   Northwind.mdb, a database in the Access 2000 file format, was provided by Microsoft with Access 2000, Access 2002, and Access 2003 to help you learn about relational databases and Access. Access 2010 can open and work with an Access database in a 2000 or 2002-2003 file format.

2. **Double-click the Categories table in the Navigation Pane, press [Tab] to move from one field to another, note the number of records in the Current Record box, close the datasheet, then open, observe, and close each of the seven other tables**

   A clue that data might need to be better normalized is repeating data in any field. The tables of the Northwind database contain few fields with unnecessary repeating data. You look for repeating data in the fields of the Education-J database.

3. **Start a second session of Access, then open the Education-J.accdb database from the drive and folder where you store your Data Files, enabling content if prompted**

4. **Double-click the Employees table in the Navigation Pane**

   The Department and Title fields both contain repeating data. You decide to further normalize the Department data by creating a Departments table that uses a one-to-many relationship to the Employees table.

5. **Close the Employees datasheet, click the Create tab, click the Table Design button in the Tables group, type Department as the field name, press [Tab], click the Primary Key button in the Tools group, save the table with the name Departments, then close it**

6. **Double-click the new Departments table in the Navigation Pane, then enter the values shown in Figure J-1**

7. **Save and close the Departments datasheet, right-click the Employees table in the Navigation Pane, then click Design View**

   You can use the Lookup Wizard to establish the Department field in the Employees table as the foreign key field linked to the Department field in the Departments table.

8. **Click the Department field in the Data Type column, click the list arrow in the Text Data Type cell, click Lookup Wizard, click Next to look up values in a table, click Table: Departments, click Next, double-click Department as the selected field, click Next, click the first sort arrow, click Department, click Next, click Next, click Finish, then click Yes**

9. **Click the View button to switch to Datasheet View, click any record in the Department field, then click the field list arrow as shown in Figure J-2**

   The Departments and Employees tables are now linked in a one-to-many relationship, which provides the valid Department choices for the Department field in the Employees table. Now data entry for that field will be faster, more consistent, and more accurate.

FIGURE J-1: **Departments datasheet**

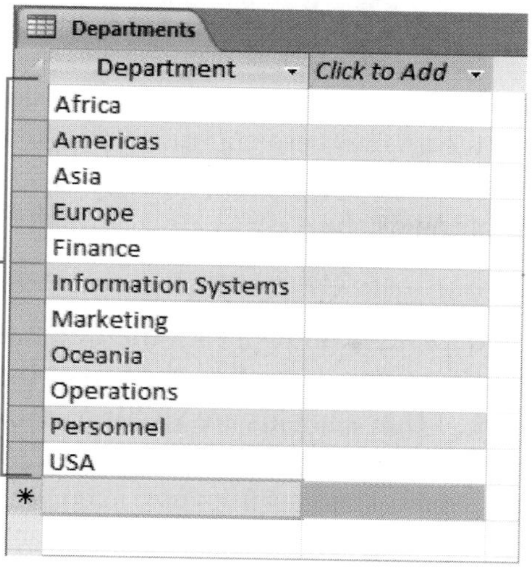
Departments
Department
Click to Add
Africa
Americas
Asia
Europe
Finance
Information Systems
Marketing
Oceania
Operations
Personnel
USA
Enter these values in the Department field

FIGURE J-2: **Department field of the Employees datasheet**

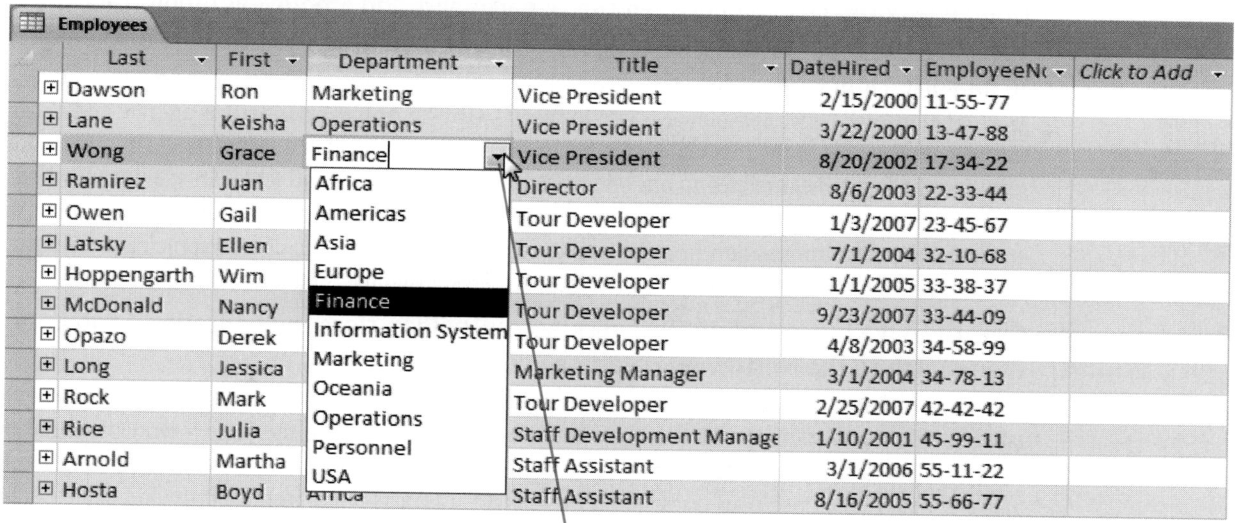
Employees
Last
First
Department
Title
DateHired
EmployeeN
Click to Add
Dawson Ron Marketing Vice President 2/15/2000 11-55-77
Lane Keisha Operations Vice President 3/22/2000 13-47-88
Wong Grace Finance Vice President 8/20/2002 17-34-22
Ramirez Juan Director 8/6/2003 22-33-44
Owen Gail Tour Developer 1/3/2007 23-45-67
Latsky Ellen Tour Developer 7/1/2004 32-10-68
Hoppengarth Wim Tour Developer 1/1/2005 33-38-37
McDonald Nancy Tour Developer 9/23/2007 33-44-09
Opazo Derek Tour Developer 4/8/2003 34-58-99
Long Jessica Marketing Manager 3/1/2004 34-78-13
Rock Mark Tour Developer 2/25/2007 42-42-42
Rice Julia Staff Development Manage 1/10/2001 45-99-11
Arnold Martha Staff Assistant 3/1/2006 55-11-22
Hosta Boyd Staff Assistant 8/16/2005 55-66-77
Africa
Americas
Asia
Europe
Finance
Information System
Marketing
Oceania
Operations
Personnel
USA
Click the Department list arrow to display the values in the Department field

Understanding third normal form

The process of normalization can be broken down into degrees, which include **first normal form (1NF)**, a single two-dimensional table with rows and columns; **second normal form (2NF)**, where redundant data in the original table is extracted, placed in a new table, and related to the original table; and **third normal form (3NF)**, where calculated fields (also called derived fields) such as totals or taxes are removed. In an Access database, calculated fields can be created "on the fly" using a query, which means that the information in the calculation is automatically produced and is always accurate based on the latest updates to the database. Strive to create databases that adhere to the rules of third normal form.

UNIT J

Access 2010

Analyzing Relationships

The relationships between tables determine the health and effectiveness of a database. The Relationships window shows how well the data has been normalized. You study the Relationships window of the Northwind database to see if you can apply the techniques used with the relationships of Northwind to the relationships of the Education-J database.

STEPS

QUICK TIP
Move field lists by dragging their title bars.

1. **In the Northwind database window, click the Database Tools tab, click the Relationships button, maximize the window, scroll to the top of the window as needed, then resize and move the field lists so that all fields are visible as shown in Figure J-3**
   Notice that all of the relationships between the tables are one-to-many relationships with referential integrity enforced. Recall that referential integrity helps prevent orphan records—records in the "many" (child) table that do not link to a matching record in the "one" (parent) table.

2. **Switch to the Education-J database window, close the Employees datasheet, click the Database Tools tab, click the Relationships button, then click All Relationships**
   The Lookup Wizard created a one-to-many relationship between the Departments and Employees tables using the common Department field, but you still need to add referential integrity to the relationship. Recall that you may enforce referential integrity on a relationship if orphan records do not exist in the "many" table.

TROUBLE
If you could not enforce referential integrity, that means you made a data-entry error in the Departments table. Open the Departments table in Datasheet View, edit your data to match Figure J-1, then redo Step 3.

3. **Double-click the link line between the Departments and Employees tables, click the Enforce Referential Integrity check box, click OK, then drag the title bars of the field lists to look like Figure J-4**
   Most relationships between tables are "one-to-many." **One-to-one relationships** are rare and occur when the primary key field of the first table is related to the primary key field of a second table. In other words, one record in the first table is related to one and only one record in the second table. An example of when a one-to-one relationship would be appropriate is when you want to separate sensitive information such as emergency contact information from an employee table that stores basic demographic data. One employee record would be linked to one record stored in the emergency contacts table.

4. **Click the Save button on the Quick Access toolbar, close the Education-J database, then switch to the Northwind database window**
   A **many-to-many relationship** cannot be created directly between two tables in Access. However, two tables have a many-to-many relationship when they are both related to the same intermediate table, called the **junction table**, with one-to-many relationships. Note that the Employees and Shippers tables have a many-to-many relationship, as do the Employees and Customers tables in the Northwind database. In each case, the Orders table is the junction table.

   Also note that the Order Details table has a **multifield primary key** that consists of the OrderID and ProductID fields. In other words, an OrderID value can be listed multiple times in the Order Details table, and a ProductID value can be listed multiple times in the Order Details table. But the combination of a particular OrderID value plus a ProductID value should be unique for each record.

FIGURE J-3: **Northwind.mdb relationships**

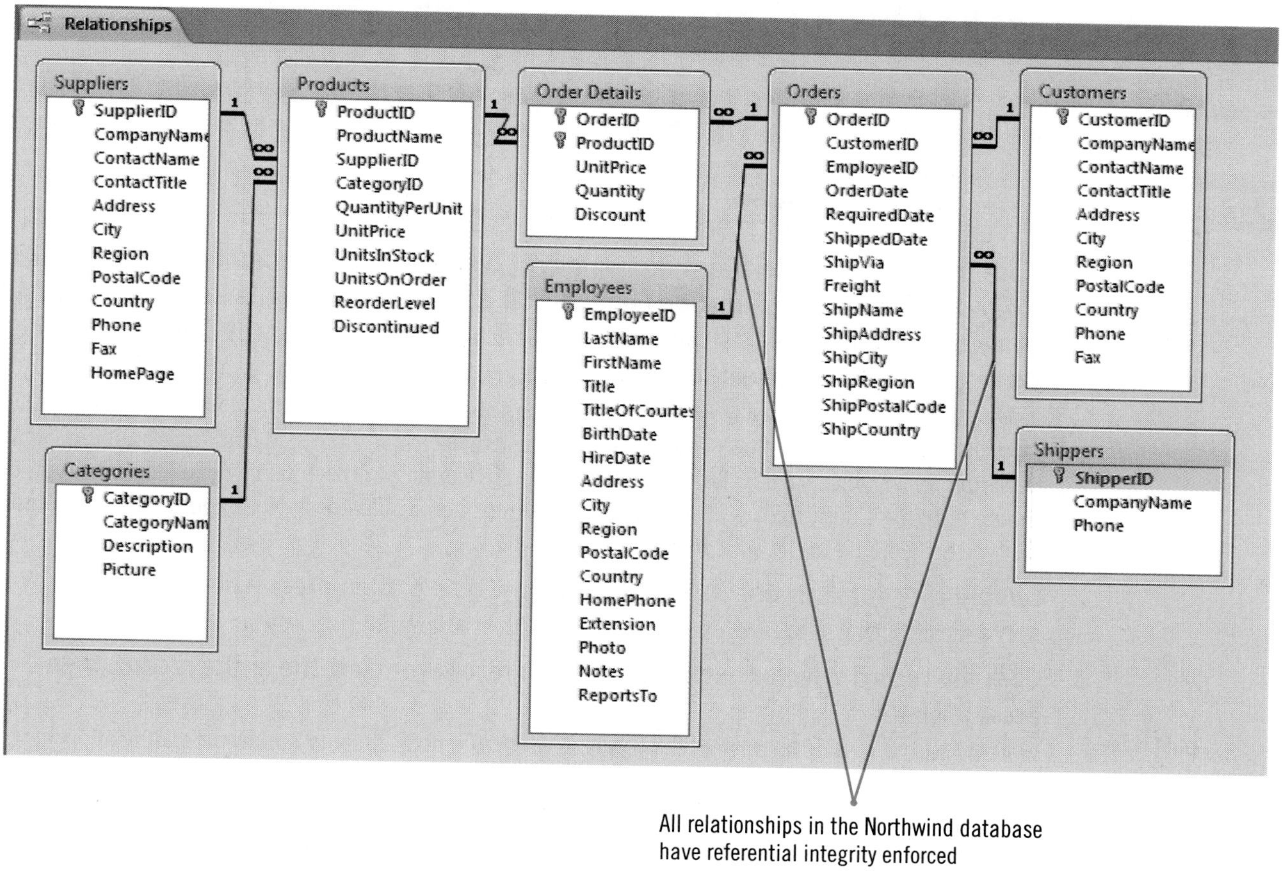

FIGURE J-4: **Education-J.accdb relationships**

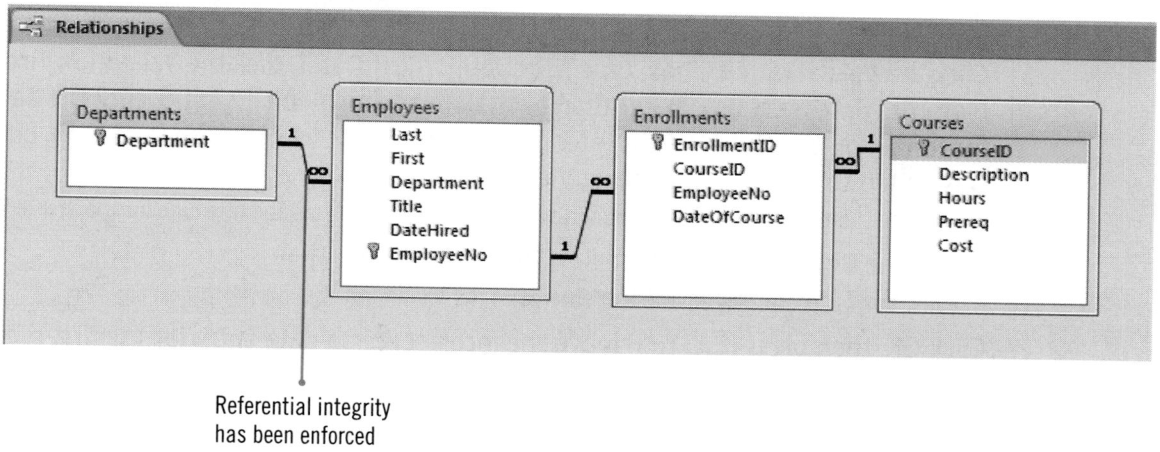

Access 2010

UNIT J

Access 2010

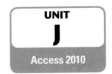

Evaluating Tables

Access offers several table features that make analyzing existing data and producing results, such as datasheet subtotals, much easier and faster. You review the tables of the Northwind database to analyze data and to study table properties.

STEPS

1. **Close the Northwind Relationships window, save the layout if prompted, double-click the Products table in the Navigation Pane, click the Totals button in the Records group on the Home tab, scroll to the Units In Stock field, click the Total cell for the Units In Stock field at the end of the datasheet, click the list arrow, then click Sum as shown in Figure J-5**

   A subtotal of the units in stock, 3119, appears in the Total cell for the Units In Stock field. As shown in the Totals list, a numeric field allows you to calculate the Average, Sum, Count, Maximum, Minimum, Standard Deviation, or Variance statistic for the field. If you were working in the Total cell of a Text field, you could choose only the Count statistic. Notice that the Current Record box displays the word "Totals" to indicate that you are working in the Total row.

2. **Double-click Totals in the Current Record box, type 6, then press [Enter]**

   Access moves the focus to the Units In Stock field of the sixth record.

3. **Click the record selector button of the sixth record to select the entire record, then press [Delete]**

   Working with a well-defined relational database with referential integrity enforced on all relationships, you are prevented from deleting a record in a "one" (parent) table if the record is related to many records in a "many" (child) table. In this case, the sixth record in the Products table is related to several records in the Order Details table, and therefore it cannot be deleted. Next, you examine table properties.

4. **Click OK, close the Products table, click Yes to save changes to the layout, right-click the Employees table, click Design View, then click the Property Sheet button in the Show/Hide group to open the Property Sheet**

   The Property Sheet for a table controls characteristics for the entire table object, such as an expanded description of the table, default view, and validation rules that use more than one field. In this case, you can prevent data-entry errors by specifying that the HireDate field value is greater than the BirthDate field value. Because two fields are used in the Validation Rule expression, you should enter the rule in the table Property Sheet instead of in the Validation Rule property of an individual field.

5. **Click the Validation Rule box, type [HireDate]>[BirthDate], click the Validation Text box, type Hire date must be greater than birth date as shown in Figure J-6, click the Save button on the Quick Access toolbar, click Yes, then click the View button on the Design tab to switch to Datasheet View**

   Test the new table validation rule by entering a birth date greater than the hire date for the first record.

6. **Tab to the Birth Date field, type 5/5/2010, then press [↓]**

   A dialog box opens, displaying the text entered in the Validation Text property.

7. **Click OK, then press [Esc] to remove the incorrect birth date entry for the first record**

FIGURE J-5: **Products datasheet with Total row**

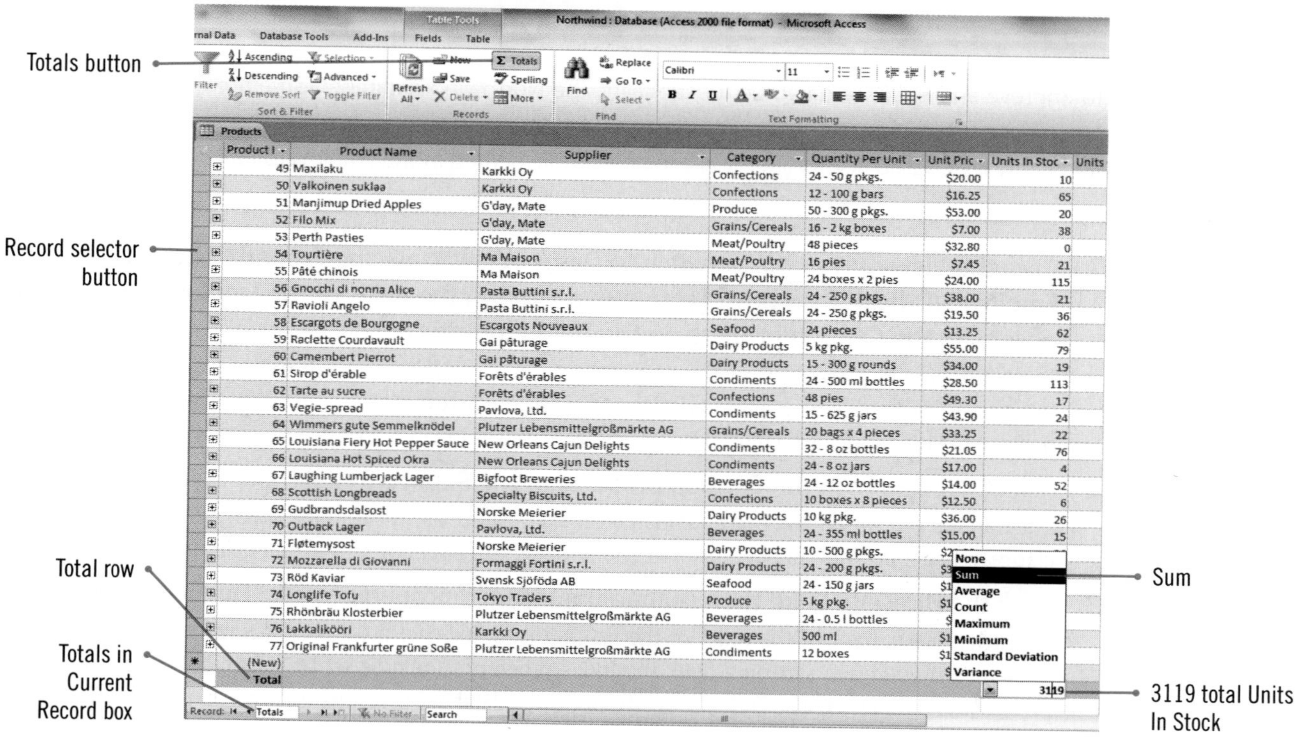

FIGURE J-6: **Property Sheet for Employees table**

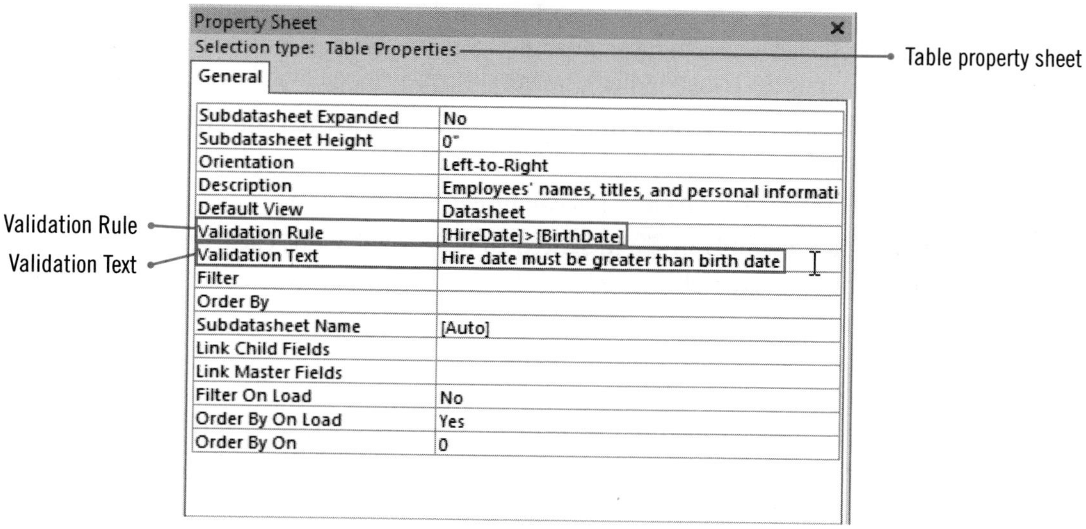

Improving Fields

To improve and enhance database functionality, the Northwind database also employs several useful field properties, such as Caption, Allow Zero Length, and Index. You review the Northwind database to study how lesser-used field properties have been implemented in the Employees table.

STEPS

1. **Click the View button to switch to Design View, close the Property Sheet, click the EmployeeID field, then press [↓] to move through the fields of the Employees table while observing the Caption property in the Field Properties pane**

   The Northwind database uses the Caption property on all fields that consist of two words, such as HireDate, to separate the words with a space, as in Hire Date. The **Caption** property text is displayed as the default field name at the top of the field column in datasheets as well as in labels that describe fields on forms and reports.

2. **Select Reports To in the Caption property of the ReportsTo field, then type Manager**

   The Caption property doesn't have to match the field name. Use the Caption property any time you want to clarify or better describe a field for the users, but prefer not to change the actual field name.

3. **Click the HireDate field, then change the Indexed property to Yes (Duplicates OK)**

   An **index** keeps track of the order of the values in the indexed field as data is being entered and edited. Therefore, if you often sort on a field, the Index property should be set to Yes so that Access can sort and present the data faster. The Index property improves database performance when a field is often used for sorting because it creates the index for the sort order as data is being entered, rather than building the index from scratch when the field is used for sorting. Fields that are not often used for sort orders should have their Index property set to No because creating and maintaining indexes is a productivity drain on the database. You can sort on any field at any time, whether the Index property is set to Yes or No.

4. **Click the HomePhone field and examine the Allow Zero Length property**

   Currently, the **Allow Zero Length** property is set to No, meaning zero-length strings ("") are not allowed. A zero-length string is an *intentional* "nothing" entry (as opposed to a **null** entry, which also means that the field contains nothing, but doesn't indicate intent). Zero-length strings are valuable when you want to show that the "nothing" entry is on purpose. For example, some employees might intentionally *not* want to provide a home phone number. In those instances, a zero-length string entry is appropriate. Note that you query for zero-length strings using "" criteria, whereas you query for null values using the operator **Is Null**.

5. **Double-click the Allow Zero Length property to switch the choice from No to Yes as shown in Figure J-7**

   With the field changes in place, you test them in Datasheet View.

6. **Click the View button to switch to Datasheet View, click Yes to save the table, tab to the Home Phone field, enter "" (two quotation marks without a space), tab to the Extension field, enter "", then press [Tab]**

   An error message appears, as shown in Figure J-8, indicating that you cannot enter a zero-length string in the Extension field.

7. **Click OK to acknowledge the error message, press [Esc], press [Tab] three more times to observe the Manager caption for the ReportsTo field, then close the Employees table**

QUICK TIP
A description of the current property is displayed in the lower-right corner of Table Design View.

FIGURE J-7: **Changing field properties in the Employees table**

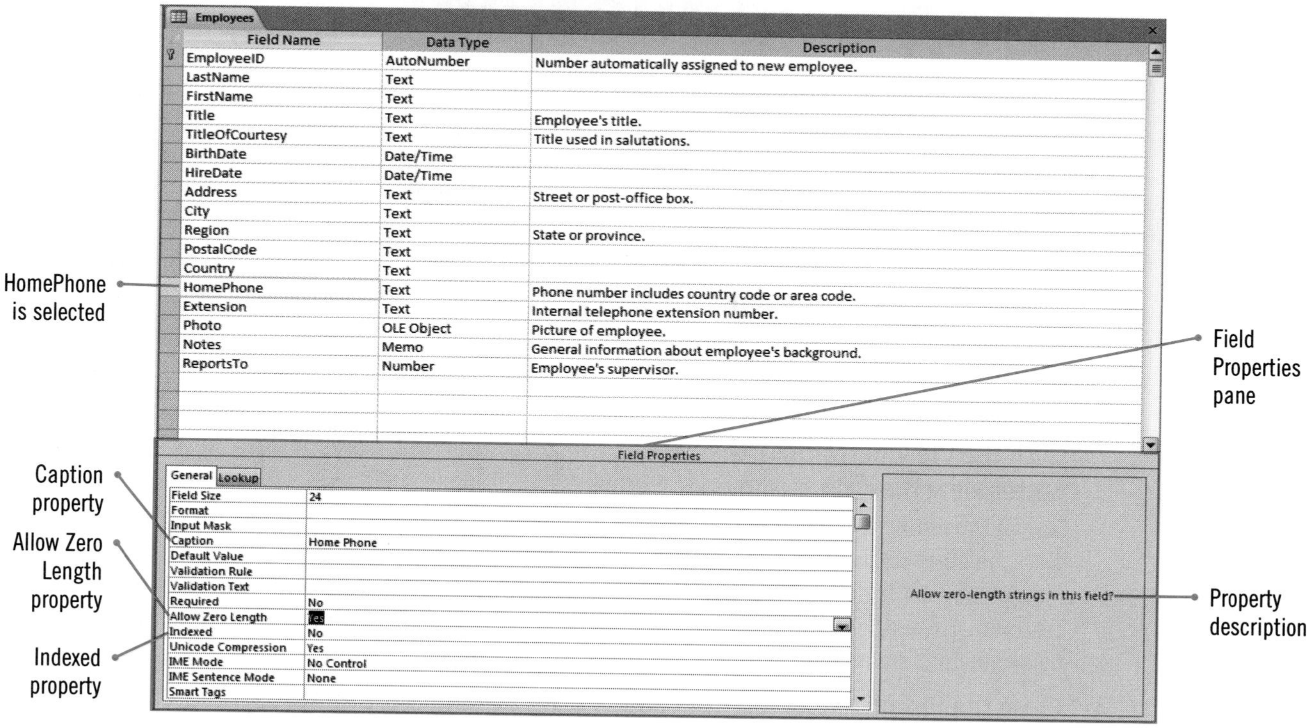

FIGURE J-8: **Testing field properties in the Employees table**

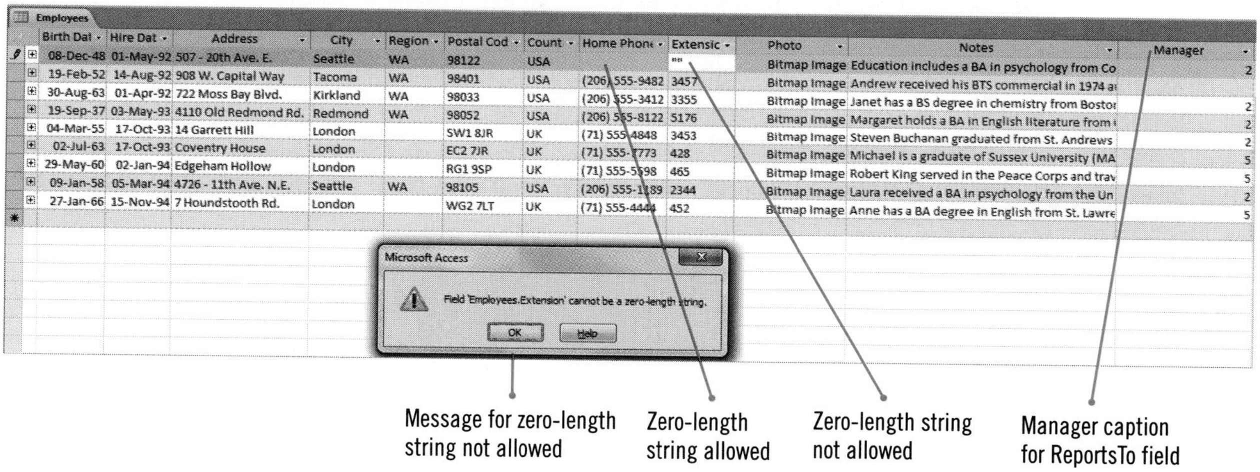

Access 2010

Using Memo fields

Use Memo fields when you need to store more than 256 characters in a field, which is the maximum Field Size value for a Text field. Fields that store comments, reviews, notes, or other ongoing conversational information are good candidates for the Memo data type. Set the **Append Only** property to Yes to allow users to add data to a Memo field, but not to change or remove existing data. The Append Only property is available for Memo fields in Access 2007 databases created in Access 2007 or Access 2010.

UNIT
J
Access 2010

Using Subqueries

The Northwind database contains several interesting queries that demonstrate advanced query techniques, such as grouping on more than one field, using functions in calculated fields, and developing subqueries, which you might not have studied yet. You work in the Northwind database to study how to use advanced query techniques, including subqueries.

STEPS

1. **Double-click the Product Sales for 1995 query to view the datasheet**
   This query summarizes product sales by product name for the year 1995. The datasheet includes 77 records, and each record represents one product name. The third column summarizes product sales for the product name. To analyze the construction of the query, switch to Design View.

2. **Click the View button, then resize the panes in the Query Design View window to better view the data as shown in Figure J-9**
   Several interesting techniques have been used in the construction of this query. The records are grouped by both the CategoryName and the ProductName fields. A calculated field, ProductSales, is computed by first multiplying the UnitPrice field from the Order Details table by the Quantity field, then subtracting the Discount. The result of this calculation is subtotaled using the Sum function. In addition, the ShippedDate field contains criteria so that only those sales between the dates of 1/1/1995 and 12/31/1995 are selected.

3. **Close the Product Sales for 1995 query, saving changes if prompted, then double-click the Category Sales for 1995 query in the Navigation Pane to open the query datasheet**
   This query contains only eight records because the sales are summarized (grouped) by the Category field and there are only eight unique categories. The CategorySales field summarizes total sales by category. To see how this query was constructed, switch to Design View.

4. **Click to switch to Design View, then resize the field list and the panes in the Query Design View window to display all of the fields**
   Note that the field list for the query is based on the Product Sales for 1995 query, as shown in Figure J-10. When a query is based on another query's field list, the field list is called a **subquery**. In this case, the Category Sales for 1995 query used the Product Sales for 1995 as its subquery to avoid having to re-create the long ProductSales calculated field.

5. **Close the Category Sales for 1995 query, then click No if you are asked to save changes**

FIGURE J-9: **Design View of the Product Sales for 1995 query**

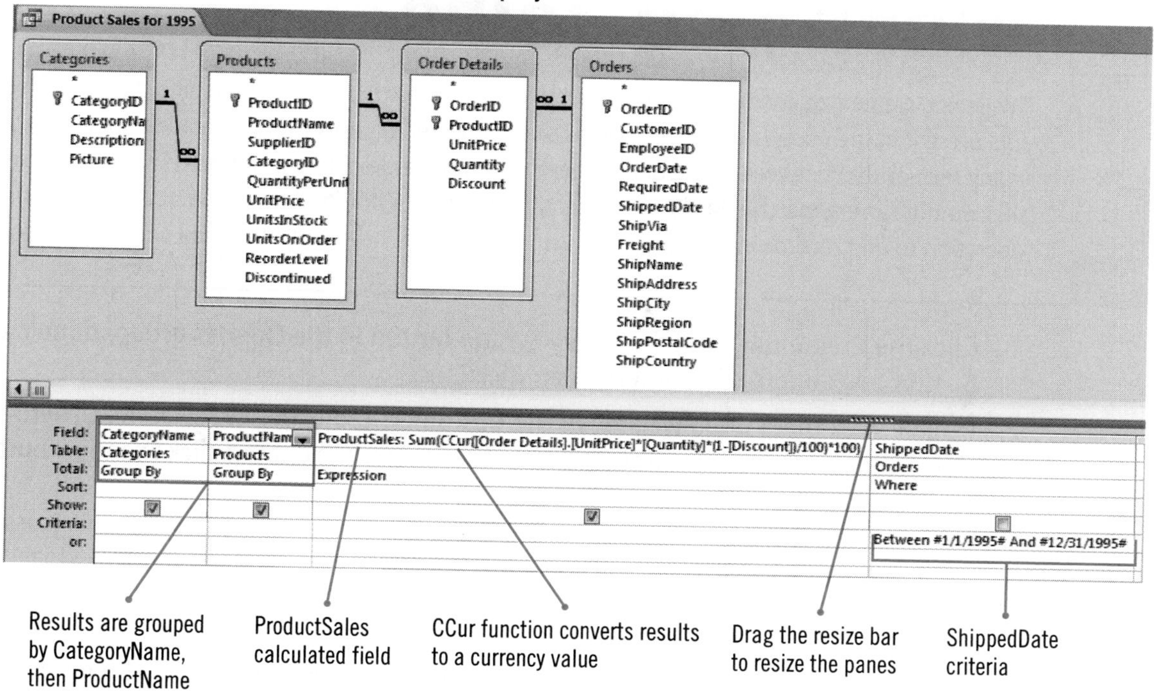

FIGURE J-10: **Using the Product Sales for 1995 query as a subquery**

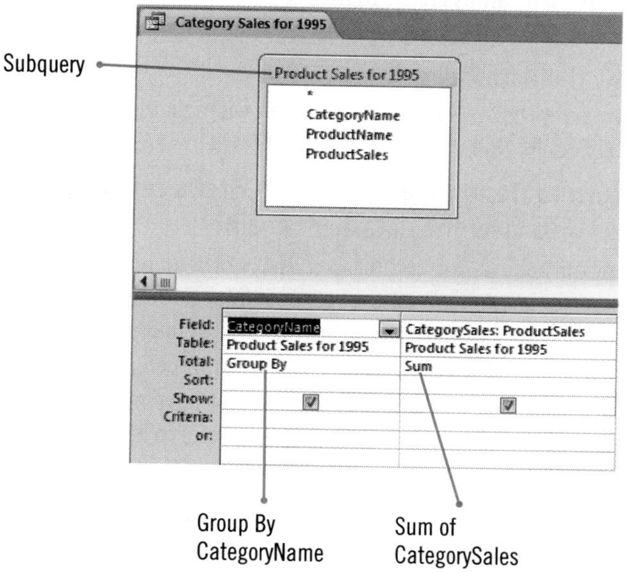

Access 2010

UNIT J
Access 2010

Modifying Joins

When you create a query based on multiple tables, only records that have matching data in each of the field lists present in the query are selected. This is due to the default **inner join** operation applied to the one-to-many relationship between two tables. Other join types are described in Table J-1. They help select records that do not have a match in a related table. You use the Northwind database and modify the join operation to find records in the Customers table that do not have a matching record in the Orders table.

STEPS

1. **Click the Create tab, click the Query Design button in the Queries group, double-click Customers, double-click Orders, then click Close**

2. **Double-click the CompanyName in the Customers table, double-click the OrderDate in the Orders table, double-click Freight in the Orders table, then click the View button to view the datasheet**

   This query selects 830 records using the default inner join between the tables. An inner join means that records are selected only if a matching value is present in both tables. Therefore, any records in the Customers table that did not have a related record in the Orders table would not be selected. You modify the join operation to find those customers.

3. **Click the View button to switch to Design View, then double-click the middle of the one-to-many relationship line between the tables to open the Join Properties dialog box shown in Figure J-11**

   The Join Properties dialog box provides information regarding how the two tables are joined and also allows you to change from the default inner join (option 1) to a left outer join (2) or right outer join (3).

> **QUICK TIP**
> Use SQL View of a query to view the SQL for an inner, left, or right join.

4. **Click the 2 option button, click OK, then resize the field lists so that you can see all the fields as shown in Figure J-12**

   The arrow pointing to the Orders table indicates that the join line has been modified to be a left outer join. With join operations, "left" always refers to the "one" table of a one-to-many relationship regardless of where the table is physically positioned in Query Design View.

5. **Click to view the datasheet**

   The datasheet now shows 832 records, two more than when an inner join operation was used. To find the two new records quickly, use Is Null criteria.

6. **Click to return to Design View, click the Criteria cell for the OrderDate field, type Is Null, then click to view the datasheet again**

   The datasheet now only shows two records as shown in Figure J-13, the two customers who do not have any matching order records. Left outer joins are very useful for finding records on the "one" side of a relationship (parent records) that do not have matching records on the "many" side (child records).

   When referential integrity is enforced on a relationship before data is entered, it is impossible to create records on the "many" side of a relationship that do not have matching records on the "one" side (orphan records). Therefore, a right outer join operation is very useful to help find orphan records in a poorly designed database, but a right outer join operation would not be useful in the Northwind database because referential integrity has been applied on all relationships since the tables were created.

7. **Save the query as CustomersWithoutOrders, then close the query and the Northwind.mdb database**

FIGURE J-11: **Join Properties dialog box**

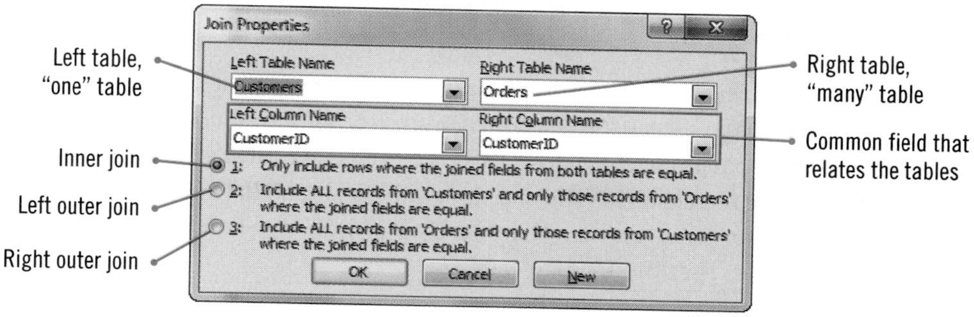

FIGURE J-12: **Left outer join line**

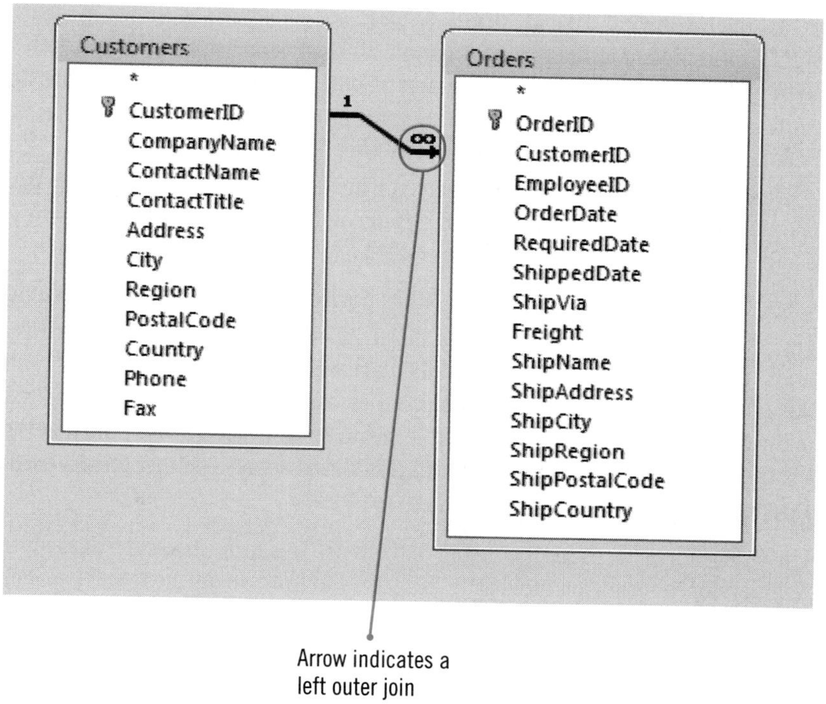

FIGURE J-13: **Customers without orders**

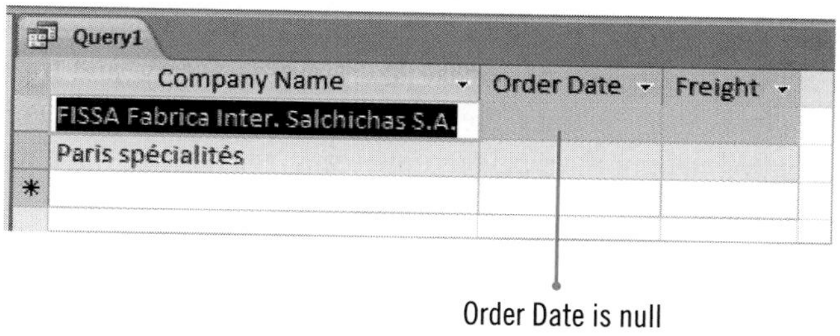

TABLE J-1: **Join operations**

join operation	description
inner	Default join; selects records from two related tables in a query that have matching values in a field common to both tables
left outer	Selects all the records from the left table (the "one" table in a one-to-many relationship) even if the "one" table doesn't have matching records in the related "many" table
right outer	Selects all the records from the right table (the "many" table in a one-to-many relationship) even if the "many" table doesn't have matching records in the related "one" table

Analyzing Forms

Database developers create forms to provide a fast and easy-to-use interface for database users. In a fully developed database, users generally do not work with individual objects or the Navigation Pane. Rather, they use forms to guide all of their activities. The Northwind database provides several examples of sophisticated forms used to easily navigate and work with the data in the underlying database. You examine Northwind forms to gain an understanding of how well-designed forms could be applied to the databases at Quest Specialty Travel.

STEPS

TROUBLE

If you click the "Don't show this screen again" check box on the Startup form, you will not see the splash screen when you open the Northwind database.

1. **Reopen the Northwind.mdb database**

   When the Northwind database opens, a splash screen appears as shown in Figure J-14. A **splash screen** is a special form used to announce information. To create a splash screen, you create a new form in Form Design View with the labels, graphics, and command buttons desired, plus you set the **Border Style** property of the form to None. You also set the following form properties to No: **Record Selectors**, **Navigation Buttons**, **Scroll Bars** (Neither), **Control Box**, **Min Max Buttons** (None).

   To automatically load the splash screen when the database opens, set the **Display Form option** in the Current Database category of the Options dialog box to the name of the form you want to open when the database starts. In this case, the name of the splash screen form is Startup.

2. **Click OK, then double-click the Main Switchboard form in the Navigation Pane**

   The Main Switchboard form opens as shown in Figure J-15. A **switchboard** is a special form used to help users navigate throughout the rest of the database. A switchboard contains command buttons to give users fast and easy access to the database objects they use. A switchboard form is created in Form Design View using many of the same form properties used to create a splash screen. Also note that the Record Source property for the splash screen and switchboard forms is not used because neither form is used for data entry.

3. **Click the Orders command button**

   The Orders form opens for the first of 830 orders. This form shows the attractiveness and sophistication of a well-developed form. You modify the first order to learn about the form's capabilities.

4. **Click the Bill To: combo box arrow, click Around the Horn, click the Salesperson combo box arrow, click King, Robert, click the Spegesild list arrow (the first product in the order), click Steeleye Stout, press [Tab], type 20 for the Quantity value, press [Tab], enter 50% for the Discount value, then press [Tab]**

   The first order in the Orders form should look like Figure J-16. The Orders form is a traditional Access form in that it is used to enter and edit data. The form uses combo boxes and calculations (in the extended price, subtotal, and total text boxes) to make data entry fast, easy, and accurate. Also notice the Print Invoice command button used to print the current record, the current invoice. Well-designed forms contain a command button to print the *current* record because the regular Print button will print *all* records (in this case, all 830 orders).

5. **Right-click the Orders tab, then click Close**

   Northwind contains many other forms you can explore later to learn more about form design and construction.

FIGURE J-14: Northwind splash screen form, Startup

FIGURE J-15: Northwind switchboard form, Main Switchboard

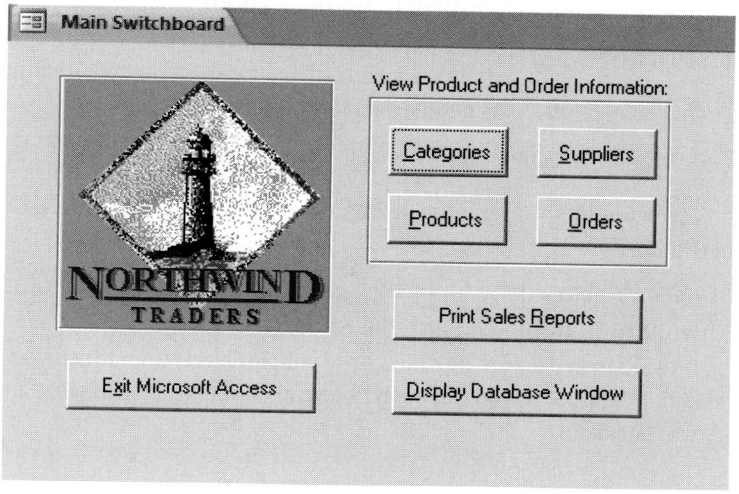

FIGURE J-16: Northwind Orders form

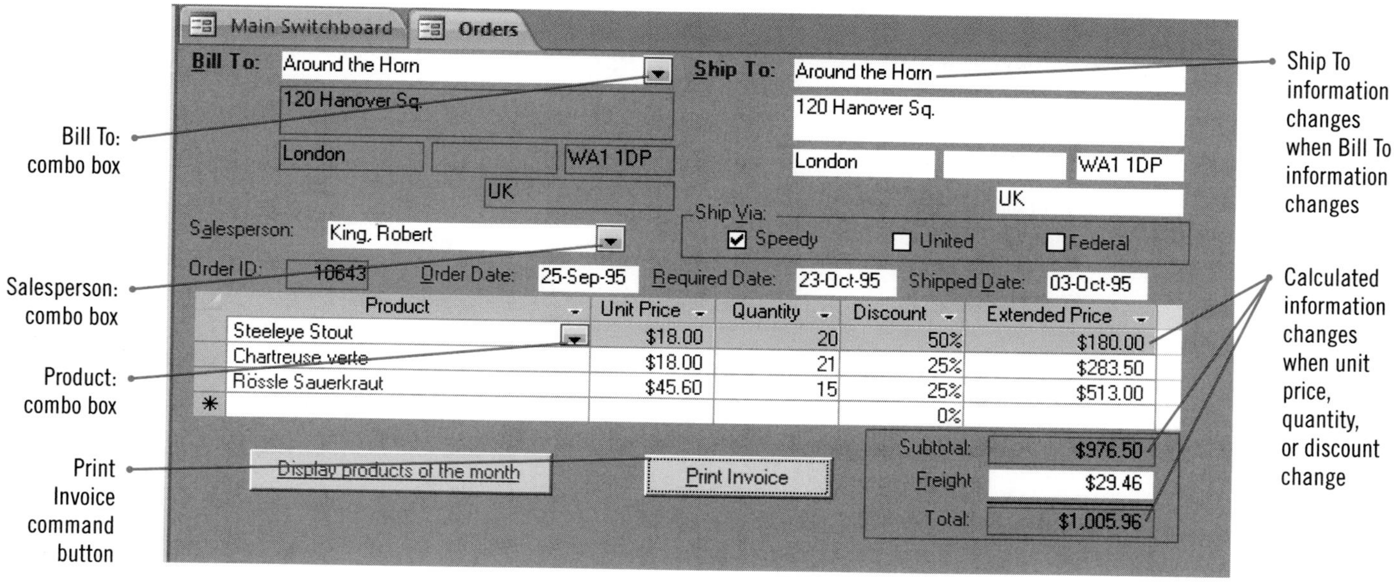

UNIT
J
Access 2010

Analyzing Reports

In a fully developed database, the database designer creates reports for the printed information needs of the users. In a well-designed database, the user can select what data they want the report to display by making choices in a dialog box or by using parameter criteria in a query on which the report is based. You study some reports in the Northwind database to gain new ideas and skills.

STEPS

QUICK TIP

The Record Source property of a report identifies the recordset (table or query) on which the report is based.

1. **Click the Print Sales Reports command button on the Main Switchboard form**

   A form, the Sales Reports dialog box shown in Figure J-17, opens. A **dialog box** is a type of form used to make choices to modify the contents of another query, form, or report. In this case, the selections you make in the Sales Reports dialog box will help you create a specific report.

2. **Click the Sales by Category option button to enable the Category list box**

   In a well-designed form, controls are often enabled and disabled based on choices the user makes. In this case, the Category list box is enabled only if the Sales by Category option button is selected. You will learn how to modify a form to respond to user interaction when you work with Visual Basic for Applications (VBA.)

3. **Click the Employee Sales by Country option button, click Preview, type 1/1/1995 in the Beginning Date text box, click OK, type 12/31/1995 in the Ending Date text box, click OK, then click the report to display it at 100% zoom, if necessary**

   The Employee Sales by Country report opens in Print Preview, as shown in Figure J-18. It is based on the Employee Sales by Country query, which contains parameter criteria that prompted you for the beginning and ending dates to select the desired data for this report.

   The Employee Sales by Country report presents several advanced report techniques including a calculated date expression in the Report Header section, multiple grouping levels, and a watermark effect. The watermark effect is achieved by specifying the desired watermark image, in this case Confidential.bmp, in the report's **Picture** property.

4. **Right-click the Employee Sales by Category report tab, click Close All, then close the Northwind.mdb database and exit Access**

   The Northwind.mdb database provides many sample objects from which you can learn a great deal. Microsoft provided this database so you can analyze several objects and techniques, and apply what you learn to your own Access databases.

FIGURE J-17: **Sales Reports dialog box**

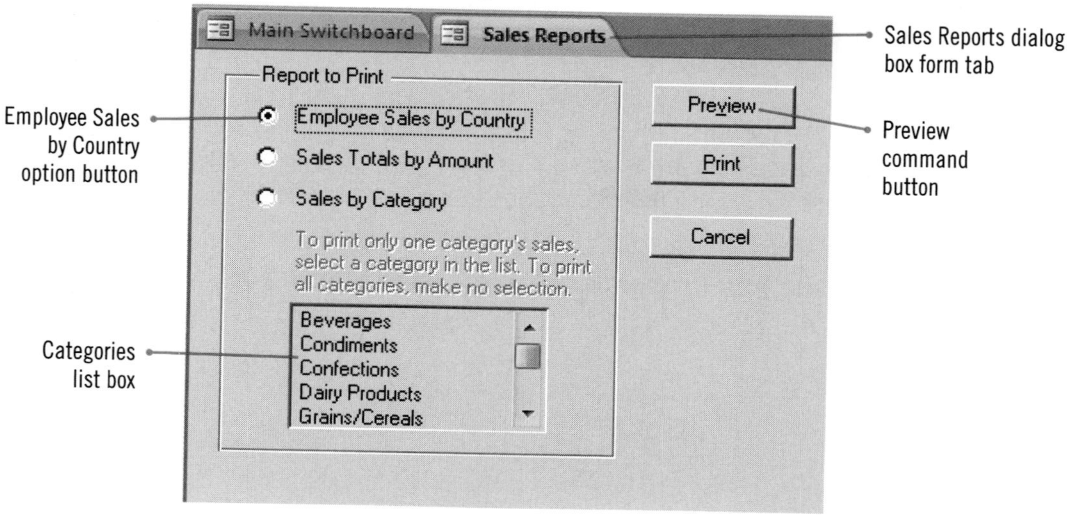

FIGURE J-18: **Employee Sales by Country report**

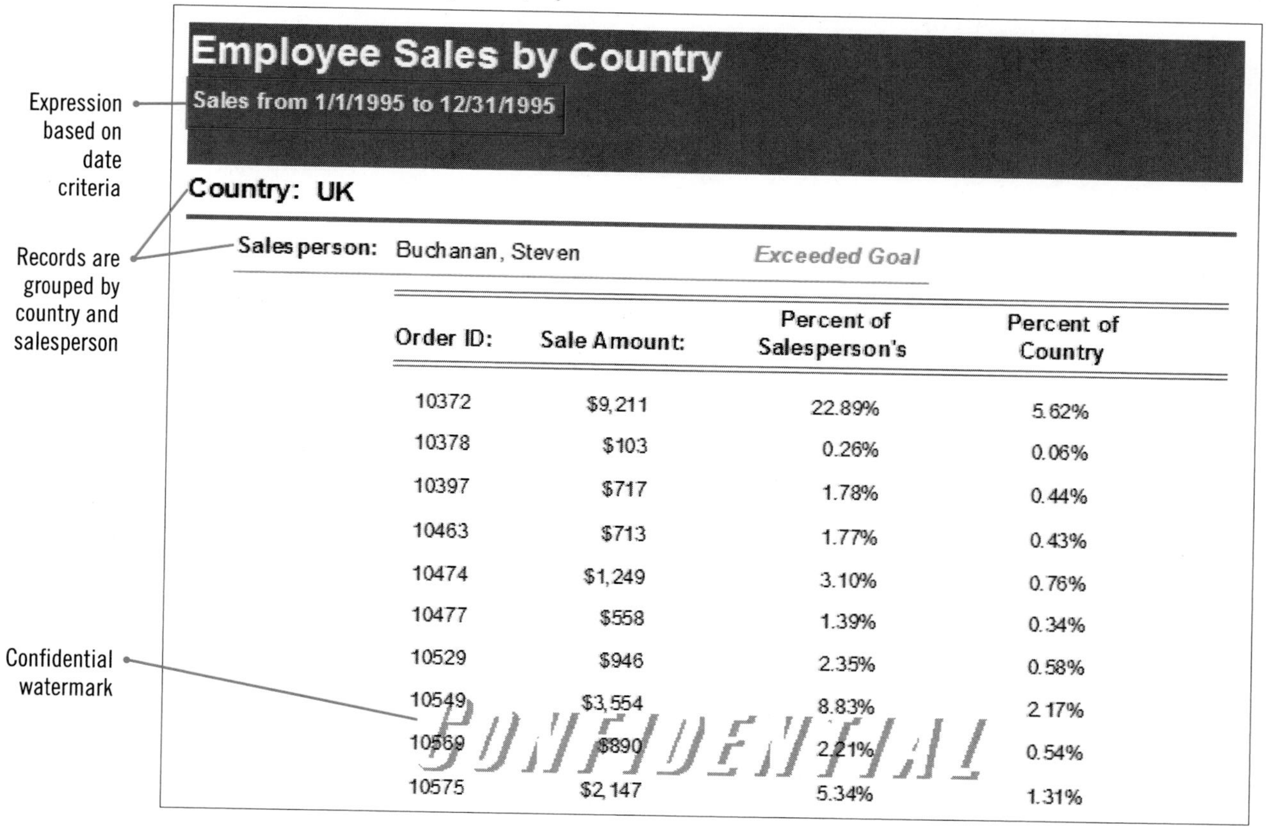

Practice

Concepts Review

For current SAM information, including versions and content details, visit SAM Central (http://www.cengage.com/samcentral). If you have a SAM user profile, you may have access to hands-on instruction, practice, and assessment of the skills covered in this unit. Since various versions of SAM are supported throughout the life of this text, check with your instructor for the correct instructions and URL/Web site for accessing assignments.

Identify each element of the Join Properties dialog box in Figure J-19.

FIGURE J-19

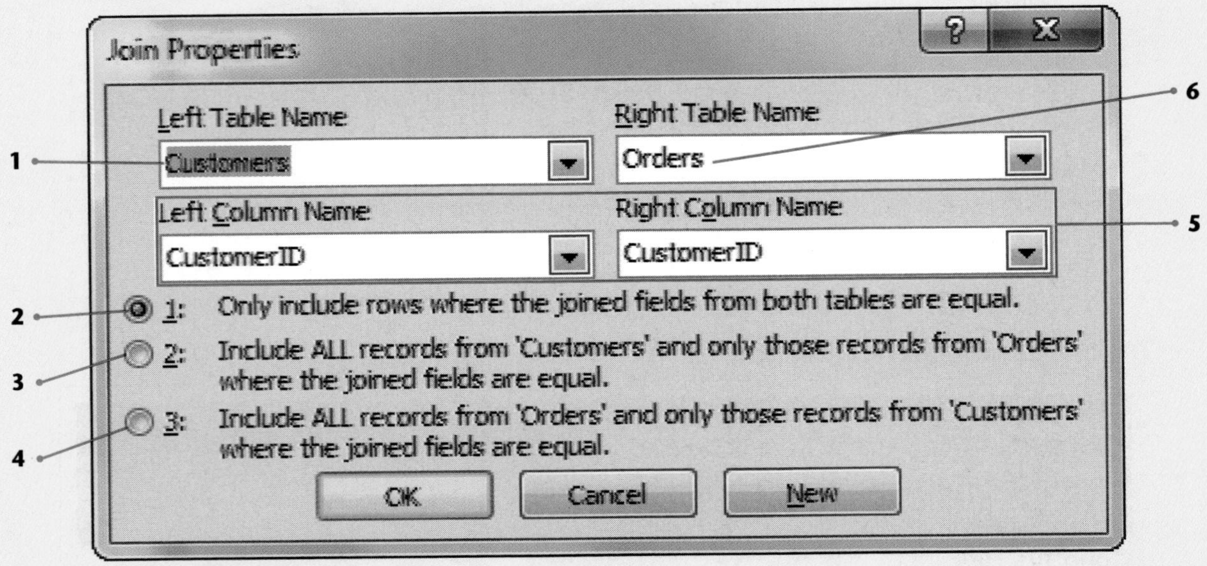

Match each term with the statement that best describes its function.

7. **Normalization**
8. **Caption**
9. **Index**
10. **Subquery**
11. **Zero-length string**

a. An *intentional* "nothing" entry

b. Displayed as the default field name at the top of the field column in datasheets as well as in labels that describe fields on forms and reports

c. Keeps track of the order of the values in the indexed field as data is entered and edited

d. Created when a query is based on another query's field list

e. The process of structuring data into a well-formed relational database

Select the best answer from the list of choices.

12. Which of the following is *not* a benefit of a well-designed relational database?

a. Reduces redundant data
b. Improves reporting flexibility
c. Is easier to create than a single-table database
d. Has lower overall storage requirements

13. First normal form can be described as:

a. Any collection of data in any form.
b. A single two-dimensional table with rows and columns.
c. A series of queries and subqueries.
d. A well-functioning, fully developed relational database.

14. Which of the following activities occurs during the creation of second normal form?

a. Calculated fields are removed from tables.
b. Additional calculated fields are added to tables.
c. Redundant data is removed from one table, and relationships are created.
d. One-to-one relationships are examined and eliminated.

15. Which of the following activities occurs during the creation of third normal form?

a. Calculated fields are removed from tables.
b. Additional calculated fields are added to tables.
c. Redundant data is removed from one table, and relationships are created.
d. One-to-one relationships are examined and eliminated.

16. One-to-one relationships occur when:

a. The foreign key field of the first table is related to the primary key field of a second table.
b. The foreign key field of the first table is related to the foreign key field of a second table.
c. The primary key field of the first table is related to the foreign key field of a second table.
d. The primary key field of the first table is related to the primary key field of a second table.

17. A multifield primary key consists of:

a. One field.
b. An AutoNumber field.
c. A primary key field that also serves as a foreign key field.
d. Two or more fields.

18. Which of the following is *not* true for the Caption property?

a. It is the default field name at the top of the field column in datasheets.
b. The value of the Caption property is the default label that describes a field on a report.
c. The value of the Caption property is the default label that describes a field on a form.
d. It is used instead of the field name when you build expressions.

19. Which of the following fields would most likely be used for an index?

a. MiddleName
b. ApartmentNumber
c. LastName
d. FirstName

20. Which of the following phrases best describes the need for both null values and zero-length strings?

a. They represent two different conditions.
b. Having two different choices for "nothing" clarifies data entry.
c. Null values speed up calculations.
d. They look different on a query datasheet.

Skills Review

1. Normalize data.

a. Start Access, open the Education-J.accdb database from the drive and folder where you store your Data Files, and enable content if prompted.

b. Double-click the Employees table to view its datasheet. Notice the repeated data in the Title field. Close the Employees datasheet. You will build a lookup table to better manage the values in the Title field.

c. Click the Create tab, click Table Design, then create a table with one field, **TitleName**. Give it a Text data type, and set it as the primary key field.

d. Save the table with the name **Titles**, and enter the data in the datasheet shown in Figure J-20. Be very careful to type the data exactly as shown. Save and close the Titles table when you are finished.

e. Open the Employees table in Design View, click the Title field, then choose Lookup Wizard using the Data Type list arrow.

f. Choose the "I want the lookup column to look up the values..." option, click Next, choose Table: Titles, select the TitleName field for the list and specify an ascending sort order on the TitleName field, accept the column widths, accept the Title label, click the Enable Data Integrity check box, finish the Lookup Wizard, then click Yes to save the table. (If you were unable to enforce referential integrity, it means you've made a data-entry error in the Titles table. Open the Titles table in Datasheet View, and check your data against the values in Figure J-20, then redo Step f.)

FIGURE J-20

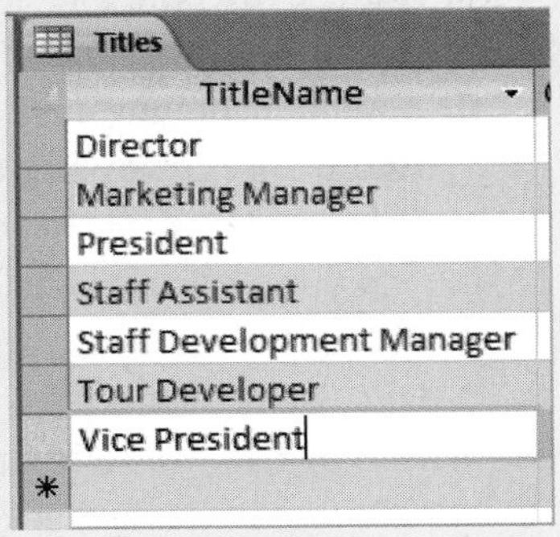

g. Close Table Design View for the Employees table, open the Relationships window, click the All Relationships button, then drag the title bar of the field lists to match Figure J-21.

FIGURE J-21

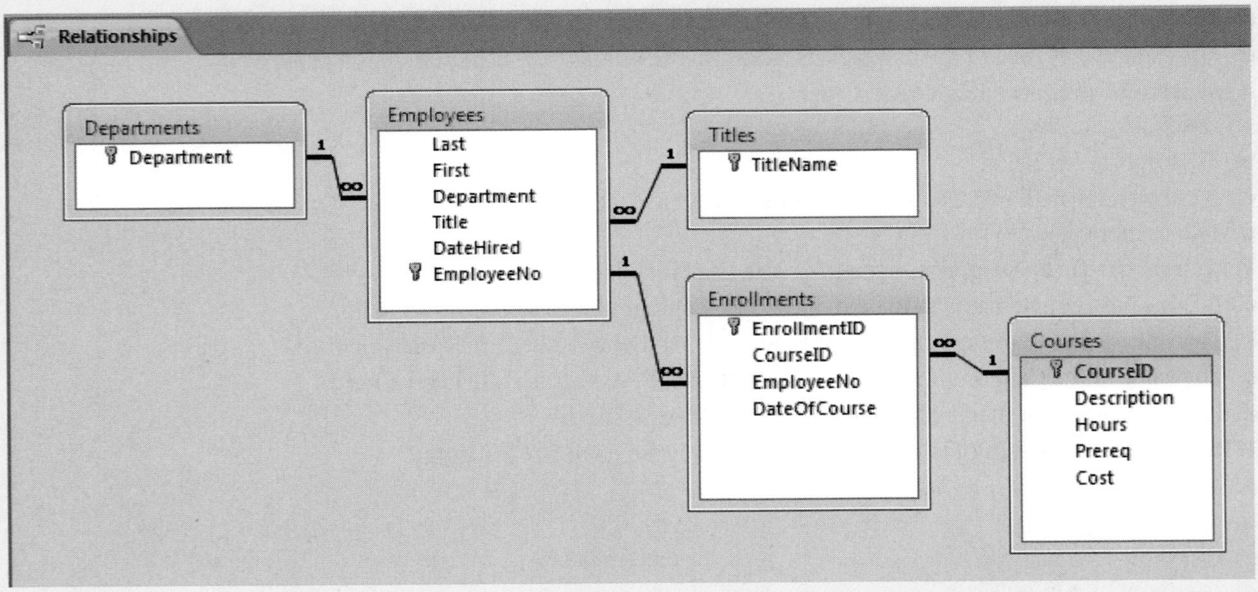

h. Save and close the Relationships window, then close the Education-J.accdb database.

2. Analyze relationships.

a. Open the Northwind.mdb database from the drive and folder where you store your Data Files, and enable content if prompted.

b. Click OK to close the splash screen, click the Database Tools tab, then click the Relationships button.

c. It is easy to see that all of the relationships are one-to-many relationships with referential enforced due to the presence of the "1" and "infinity" symbols. When two parent tables both have a one-to-many relationship with the same child table, they are said to have a many-to-many relationship with each other. This database has five many-to-many relationships. Use the following table to identify the tables involved. One many-to-many relationship is provided as an example.

Table 1	Junction Table	Table 2
Employees	Orders	Customers

d. If requested by your instructor, create a Relationships report. Use landscape orientation so that the report is only one page long, and insert your name as a label in the Report Header using black text and a 12-point font size. Save and close the report using the default name, **Relationships for Northwind**.

e. Save and close the Relationships window.

3. Evaluate tables.

a. Open the datasheet for the Order Details table.

b. Tab to the Quantity field, then click the Totals button to open the Total row at the end of the datasheet.

c. Use the Total row to find the Sum of the Quantity field, 51335, which represents the total quantity of products sold for this database.

d. Save and close the Order Details table.

4. Improve fields.

a. Open the Products table in Design View.

b. Change the Caption property for the Unit Price field to **Retail Price**.

c. At the end of the field list, add a new field named **StandardQuantity** with a Number data type and a Caption property of **Standard Quantity**.

d. At the end of the field list, add a new field named **UnitOfMeasure** with a Text data type and a Caption property of **Unit of Measure**.

e. Save the table, then display it in Datasheet View.

f. Enter the correct information into the new Standard Quantity and Unit of Measure fields for the first two records. (Base this on the information currently provided in the Quantity Per Unit field; for example, 10 is the Standard Quantity for the first record, and boxes × 20 bags is the Unit of Measure.)

g. Explain the benefits of separating quantities from their units of measure. (*Hint*: Think about how you find, filter, sort, and calculate data.) If these benefits were significant to your company, you would want to convert the rest of the data from the Quantity Per Unit field to the new Standard Quantity and Unit of Measure fields, too. Once all of the new data was in place, you could delete the original Quantity Per Unit field.

h. Close the Products table datasheet.

Skills Review (continued)

5. **Use subqueries.**
   a. Click the Create tab, then click the Query Design button.
   b. Double-click Orders, Order Details, and Products, then click Close.
   c. Double-click the OrderDate field in the Orders table, the Quantity and UnitPrice fields in the Order Details table, and the ProductName field in the Products table.
   d. In the fifth column, enter the following calculated field:
   GrossRevenue:[Quantity]*[Products].[UnitPrice]
   Because the UnitPrice field is given the same name in two tables present in this query, you use [TableName].[FieldName] syntax to specify which table supplies these fields.
   e. Save the query with the name **GrossRevenue**, then close it.
   f. Click the Create tab, then click the Query Design button.
   g. Click the Queries tab in the Show Table dialog box, double-click GrossRevenue, then click Close.
   h. Double-click the Product Name and GrossRevenue fields, then click the Totals button.
   i. Change Group By in the GrossRevenue field to Sum.
   j. Open the Property Sheet for the GrossRevenue field, change the Format property to Currency, change the Caption property to **Total Gross Revenue**, then view the resulting datasheet.
   k. Save the query with the name **GrossRevenueByProduct**, then close it.
6. **Modify joins.**
   a. Open the Suppliers table in Datasheet View, and enter a record using your own last name as the company name. Enter realistic but fictitious data for the rest of the record, then close the Suppliers table.
   b. Click the Create tab, click the Query Design button, double-click Suppliers, double-click Products, then click Close.
   c. Double-click CompanyName from the Suppliers table, and ProductName from the Products table. Add an ascending sort order for both fields, then view the datasheet. Note that there are 77 records in the datasheet.
   d. Return to Query Design View, then change the join properties to option 2, which will select all Suppliers records even if they don't have matching data in the Products table.
   e. View the datasheet, and note it now contains 78 records.
   f. Return to Query Design View, and add **Is Null** criteria to the ProductName field.
   g. View the datasheet noting that the only supplier without matching product records is the one you entered in Step a. That tells you that every other supplier in the database is related to at least one record in the Products table.
   h. Save the query with the name **SuppliersWithoutProducts**, then close it.
7. **Analyze forms.**
   a. Open the Customer Orders form in Form View.
   b. Notice that this form contains customer information in the main form and in two subforms. The first subform is for order information, and the second subform shows order details. Navigate to the fourth record, which shows the orders for the company named Around the Horn.
   c. Click the Order ID value 10383 in the upper subform, and notice that the order details automatically change in the lower subform as you move from order to order.
   d. Explore the form by moving through customer and order records, then ask yourself this question: How would this form be used? As navigation, information, data entry, or as a dialog box that specifies criteria for a query, form, or report?
   e. After you're done exploring the Customer Orders form, close it.
8. **Analyze reports.**
   a. Double-click the Sales by Year report.
   b. The Sales by Year Dialog form appears. Enter **1/1/95** in the Enter beginning date text box, enter **6/30/95** in the Enter ending date text box, then click OK.
   c. The Sales by Year report for the first two quarters of 1995 appears, indicating that 186 orders were shipped during this period. A subreport is used in the ShippedDate Header section to provide summary information for the entire report before the Detail section prints.
   d. Close the Sales by Year report, close the Northwind database, and exit Access.

Independent Challenge 1

As the manager of a basketball team, you have created an Access database called Basketball-J.accdb to track players, games, and statistics. You have recently learned how to create lookup tables to better control the values of a field that contain repeated data and to apply your new skills to your database.

a. Start Access, open the Basketball-J.accdb database from the drive and folder where you store your Data Files, and enable content if prompted.

b. Double-click the Players table to view its datasheet. Notice the repeated data in the Position and HomeState fields. You will build lookup tables to better describe and manage the values in those fields. Close the Players datasheet.

c. Click the Create tab, click Table Design, then create a two-field database with the field names **PositionDescription** and **PositionID**. Both fields should have a Text data type. Set PositionID as the primary key field. Save the table with the name **Positions**, and enter the data in the datasheet shown in Figure J-22. Save and close the Positions table.

d. Open the Players table in Design View, click the Position field, then choose Lookup Wizard using the Data Type list arrow.

e. Choose the "I want the lookup column to look up the values..." option, choose Table: Positions, choose both fields, choose PositionDescription for an ascending sort order, do not hide the key column, choose PositionID as the field that uniquely identifies the row, accept the Position label, click the Enable Data Integrity check box, finish the Lookup Wizard, then click Yes to save the table. Close the Players table.

f. Repeat Step c creating a **States** table instead of a Positions table using the field names and data shown in Figure J-23. Make the State2 field the primary key field, then close the States table.

g. Repeat Step d by using the Lookup Wizard with the HomeState field in the Player table to look up data in the States table. Choose both fields, sort in ascending order by the StateName field, do not hide the key column, choose State2 as the field that uniquely identifies the row, accept the HomeState label, click the Enable Data Integrity check box, finish the Lookup Wizard, then click Yes to save the table. Close the Players table.

h. Open the Relationships window, click the All Relationships button to make sure you're viewing all relationships. The final Relationships window should look like Figure J-24.

i. Create a Relationships report with the default name **Relationships for Basketball-J**. If requested by your instructor, print the report, then close it.

j. Save and close the Relationships window, close the Basketball-J.accdb database, then exit Access.

FIGURE J-22

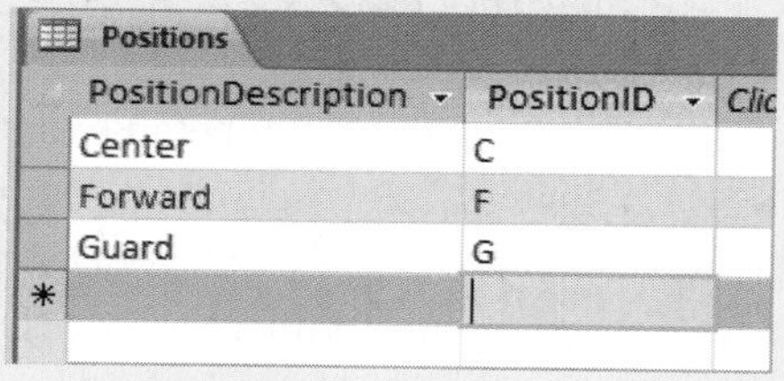

Positions

PositionDescription	PositionID
Center	C
Forward	F
Guard	G

FIGURE J-23

States

StateName	State2
Iowa	IA
Illinois	IL
Kansas	KS
Minnesota	MN
North Dakota	ND
Nebraska	NE
Texas	TX
Wisconsin	WI

FIGURE J-24

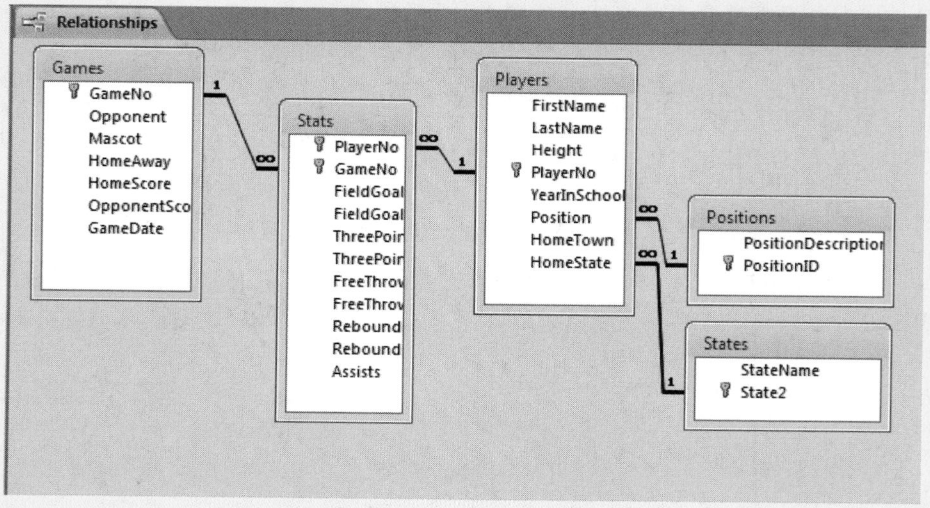

Access 2010

Independent Challenge 2

You have been asked to create a query that displays employees as well as their manager in the same datasheet. Because each employee, regardless of title and rank, is entered as a record in the Employees table, you know that you will need to relate each record in the Employees table to another record in the same table to show the employee–manager relationship. You will work in the Northwind database to learn how to join a table to itself in order to answer this challenge.

a. Start Access, open the Northwind.mdb database from the drive and folder where you store your Data Files, enable content if prompted, and click OK if prompted with the splash screen.

b. Click the Create tab, click the Query Design button, double-click Employees, double-click Employees table a second time, click Close, right-click the Employees_1 field list, click Properties, select Employees_1 in the Alias text box, type **Managers**, press [Enter], then close the Property Sheet. The Employees table relates to itself through the EmployeeID and ReportsTo fields because each employee record reports to another employee whose EmployeeID value has been entered in the ReportsTo field.

c. Resize the panes and the field lists so that you can see all fields, then drag the EmployeeID field in the Managers field list to the ReportsTo field in the Employees field list. In other words, one Manager can be related to many employees.

d. Double-click the LastName field, then double-click the FirstName field in the Managers field list.

e. Double-click the LastName field, then double-click the FirstName field in the Employees field list.

f. Add an ascending sort order on both LastName fields as shown in Figure J-25.

g. Display the query datasheet, then widen each column to display all data. The datasheet shows that three employees report to Buchanan and five report to Fuller.

h. Save the query as **ManagerList**, close the query, then close the Northwind database and exit Access.

FIGURE J-25

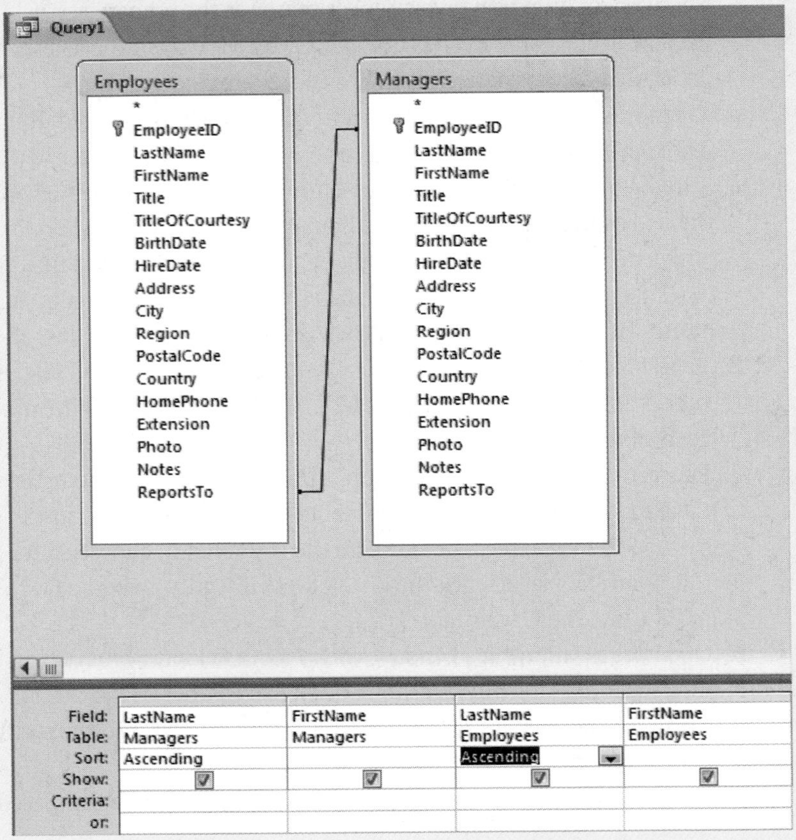

Independent Challenge 3

As the manager of a regional real estate information system, you've been asked to enhance the database to keep track of offers for each real estate listing. To do this you will need to create a new table to track the offers, and relate it to the rest of the database in an appropriate one-to-many relationship.

a. Start Access, open the RealEstate-J.accdb database from the drive and folder where you store your Data Files, and enable content if prompted.

b. Create a table named **Offers** with the fields, data types, descriptions, and primary key shown in Figure J-26.

FIGURE J-26

Offers

Field Name	Data Type	
OfferID	AutoNumber	primary key field
ListingNo	Number	foreign key field to Listings table
OfferDate	Date/Time	date of offer
OfferAmount	Currency	dollar value of the offer
Buyer	Text	last name or company name of entity making the offer
Accepted	Yes/No	was offer accepted? yes or no
DateAccepted	Date/Time	date the offer was accepted

Independent Challenge 3 (continued)

Advanced Challenge Exercise

ACE

- Use the Lookup Wizard on the ListingNo field in the Offers table to connect the Offers table to the Listings table. Select all the fields from the Listings table, sort in ascending order on the Type, Area, and SqFt fields, hide the key column, store the value in the ListingNo field, accept the ListingNo label for the lookup field, enable data integrity, and finish the wizard. Save the table when prompted.
- In Table Design View, on the Lookup tab for the ListingNo field, change the value for the Column Heads property from No to Yes.
- In Table Design View, on the Lookup tab for the ListingNo field, change the value for the List Rows property from 16 to **100**.
- Save the table, click Yes when asked to check the data, then display it in Datasheet View.
- Enter the record shown in the first row of Figure J-27, using the new combo box for the ListingNo field as shown.

FIGURE J-27

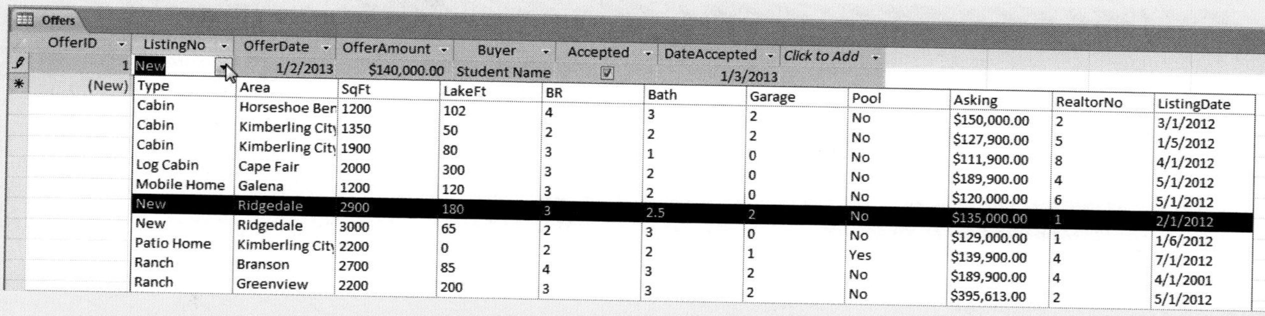
Offers

OfferID	ListingNo	OfferDate	OfferAmount	Buyer	Accepted	DateAccepted	Click to Add
1	New	1/2/2013	$140,000.00	Student Name	☑	1/3/2013	
(New)							

Type	Area	SqFt	LakeFt	BR	Bath	Garage	Pool	Asking	RealtorNo	ListingDate
Cabin	Horseshoe Ber	1200	102	4	3	2	No	$150,000.00	2	3/1/2012
Cabin	Kimberling City	1350	50	2	2	2	No	$127,900.00	5	1/5/2012
Cabin	Kimberling City	1900	80	3	1	0	No	$111,900.00	8	4/1/2012
Log Cabin	Cape Fair	2000	300	3	2	0	No	$189,900.00	4	5/1/2012
Mobile Home	Galena	1200	120	3	2	0	No	$120,000.00	6	5/1/2012
New	Ridgedale	2900	180	3	2.5	2	No	$135,000.00	1	2/1/2012
New	Ridgedale	3000	65	2	3	0	No	$129,000.00	1	1/6/2012
Patio Home	Kimberling City	2200	0	2	2	1	Yes	$139,900.00	4	7/1/2012
Ranch	Branson	2700	85	4	3	2	No	$189,900.00	4	4/1/2001
Ranch	Greenview	2200	200	3	3	2	No	$395,613.00	2	5/1/2012

c. Close the Offers table, close the RealEstate-J.accdb database, then exit Access.

Real Life Independent Challenge

An Access database can help record and track your job search efforts. In this exercise, you will work with a database that tracks employers and job positions to better normalize and present the data.

a. Start Access, open the JobSearch-J.accdb database from the drive and folder where you store your Data Files, and enable content if prompted.

b. Open both the Employers and Positions tables in Datasheet View to review the data. One employer may offer many positions, so the tables are related by the common EmployerID field. You decide to add Lookup properties to the EmployerID field in the Positions table to better identify each employer in this view.

c. Close both table datasheets, open the Relationships window, right-click the join line between the Employers and Positions tables, then click Delete. Click Yes to confirm you want to delete the relationship. Before you can start the Lookup Wizard on the EmployerID field in the Positions table, all existing relationships must be deleted.

d. Close the Relationships window, then open the Positions table in Design View.

e. Start the Lookup Wizard for the EmployerID field to lookup values in the Employers table. Select all fields, sort in ascending order on the CompanyName field, hide the key column, select EmployerID if asked to select the field containing the value you want to store, use the EmployerID label, enable data integrity, finish the wizard, then save the table.

f. Display the Positions table in Datasheet View, then test the new Lookup properties on the EmployerID field by changing the EmployerID for both of the "Professor" positions to **JCCC**.

g. Close the Positions table, then start a new query in Query Design View. Add both the Employers and Positions tables.

h. Add the CompanyName field from the Employers table, and the Title and CareerArea fields from the Positions table.

i. Modify the join line to include all records from Employers, then view the datasheet.

j. Save the query with the name **EmployerPositions**, then close it.

k. Close the JobSearch-J.accdb database, then exit Access.

Visual Workshop

Start Access, open the QuestDives-J.accdb database from the drive and folder where you store your Data Files, and enable content if prompted. Add Lookup properties to the DiveMasterID field of the DiveTrips table to achieve the result shown in Figure J-28, which looks up every value from the DiveMasters table for the lookup list and sorts the information on the LName field. First you'll have to delete the existing relationship between the DiveMasters and DiveTrips tables. You'll also want to modify the Lookup properties of the DiveMasterID field so that Column Heads is set to Yes and List Rows is set to 100. Also, be sure that referential integrity is enforced on the final relationship between the DiveMasters and DiveTrips tables.

FIGURE J-28

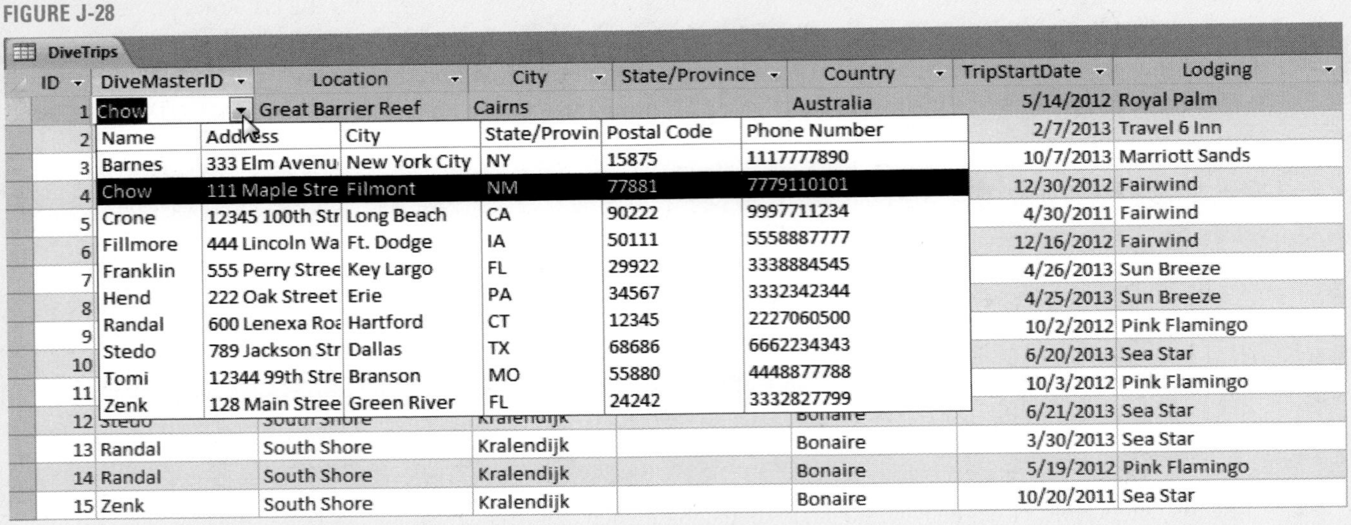
DiveTrips
ID | DiveMasterID | Location | City | State/Province | Country | TripStartDate | Lodging
1 | Chow | Great Barrier Reef | Cairns | | Australia | 5/14/2012 | Royal Palm
Name | Address | City | State/Provin | Postal Code | Phone Number
Barnes | 333 Elm Avenu | New York City | NY | 15875 | 1117777890
Chow | 111 Maple Stre | Filmont | NM | 77881 | 7779110101
Crone | 12345 100th Str | Long Beach | CA | 90222 | 9997711234
Fillmore | 444 Lincoln Wa | Ft. Dodge | IA | 50111 | 5558887777
Franklin | 555 Perry Stree | Key Largo | FL | 29922 | 3338884545
Hend | 222 Oak Street | Erie | PA | 34567 | 3332342344
Randal | 600 Lenexa Ro | Hartford | CT | 12345 | 2227060500
Stedo | 789 Jackson Str | Dallas | TX | 68686 | 6662234343
Tomi | 12344 99th Stre | Branson | MO | 55880 | 4448877788
Zenk | 128 Main Stree | Green River | FL | 24242 | 3332827799
2/7/2013 Travel 6 Inn
10/7/2013 Marriott Sands
12/30/2012 Fairwind
4/30/2011 Fairwind
12/16/2012 Fairwind
4/26/2013 Sun Breeze
4/25/2013 Sun Breeze
10/2/2012 Pink Flamingo
6/20/2013 Sea Star
10/3/2012 Pink Flamingo
6/21/2013 Sea Star
13 | Randal | South Shore | Kralendijk | | Bonaire | 3/30/2013 | Sea Star
14 | Randal | South Shore | Kralendijk | | Bonaire | 5/19/2012 | Pink Flamingo
15 | Zenk | South Shore | Kralendijk | | Bonaire | 10/20/2011 | Sea Star

UNIT K

Access 2010

Creating Advanced Queries

Files You Will Need:

Education-K.accdb
Seminar-K.accdb
Basketball-K.accdb
Chocolate-K.accdb

Queries are database objects that answer questions about the data. The most common query is the **Select query**, which selects fields and records that match specific criteria and displays them in a datasheet. Select queries, including all of their variations such as summary, crosstab, top values, and parameter queries, constitute the majority of queries you will create. Another very powerful type of query is the action query. Unlike Select queries that only *select* data, an **action query** *changes* all of the selected records when it is run. Access provides four types of action queries: Delete, Update, Append, and Make Table. You use advanced query techniques to help Jacob Thomas handle the requests for information about data stored in the Education database.

OBJECTIVES

- Query for top values
- Create a parameter query
- Modify query properties
- Create a Make Table query
- Create an Append query
- Create a Delete query
- Create an Update query
- Specify join properties
- Find unmatched records

Querying for Top Values

After you enter a large number of records into a database, you want to select only the most significant records by choosing a subset of the highest or lowest values from a sorted query. Use the **Top Values** feature in Query Design View to specify a number or percentage of sorted records that you want to display in the query's datasheet. Employee attendance at continuing education classes has grown at Quest Specialty Travel. To help plan future classes, Jacob Thomas wants a listing of the top five classes, sorted in descending order by the number of attendees for each class. You can create a summary query to find and sort the total number of attendees for each class, then use the Top Values feature to find the five most attended classes.

DETAILS

1. **Start Access, open the Education-K.accdb database, enable content if prompted, click the Create tab, then click the Query Design button in the Queries group**
   You need fields from both the Enrollments and Courses tables.

TROUBLE
If you add a table's field list to Query Design View twice by mistake, click the title bar of the extra field list, then press [Delete].

2. **Double-click Enrollments, double-click Courses, then click Close in the Show Table dialog box**
   Query Design View displays the field lists of the two related tables in the upper pane of the query window.
3. **Double-click EnrollmentID in the Enrollments field list, double-click Description in the Courses field list, then click the View button to switch to Datasheet View**
   The datasheet shows 443 total records. You want to know how many people took each course, so you need to group the records by the Description field and count the EnrollmentID field.
4. **Click the View button to switch to Query Design View, click the Totals button in the Show/Hide group, click Group By for the EnrollmentID field, click the Group By list arrow, then click Count**
   Sorting is required in order to find the top values.

QUICK TIP
Click the Datasheet View button as you design a query to view the datasheet at that point in development.

5. **Click the EnrollmentID field Sort cell, click the EnrollmentID field Sort list arrow, then click Descending**
   Your screen should look like Figure K-1. Choosing a descending sort order lists the courses with the highest count value (the most attended courses) at the top of the datasheet.
6. **Click the Top Values list arrow in the Query Setup group**
   The number or percentage specified in the Top Values list box determines which records the query returns, starting with the first record on the sorted datasheet. This is why you *must sort* your records before you use the Top Values feature. See Table K-1 for more information on Top Values options.
7. **Click 5, click to display the resulting datasheet, then widen the first column to show the complete field name**
   Your screen should look like Figure K-2. The datasheet shows the six most attended continuing education courses. The query selected the top six, rather than top five courses because there was a tie for fifth place. Both the USA Hiking Tours I and USA Biking Tours II courses had 18 attendees.
8. **Click the Save button on the Quick Access toolbar, type TopCourses, click OK, then close the datasheet**
   As with all queries, if you enter additional enrollment records into this database, the count statistics in the TopCourses query are automatically updated.

FIGURE K-1: **Designing a summary query for top values**

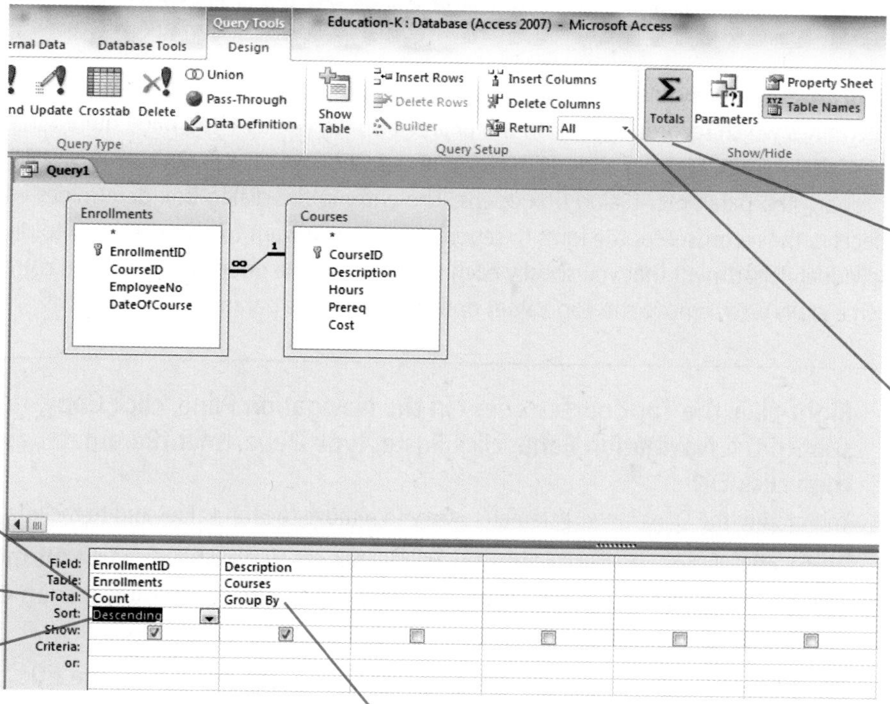

FIGURE K-2: **Top Values datasheet**

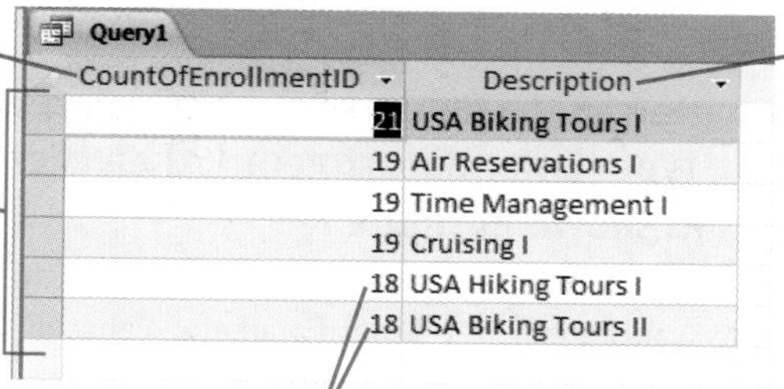

TABLE K-1: **Top Values options**

action	displays
Click 5, 25, or 100 from the Top Values list	Top 5, 25, or 100 records
Enter a number, such as 10, in the Top Values text box	Top 10, or whatever value is entered, records
Click 5% or 25% from the Top Values list	Top 5 percent or 25 percent of records
Enter a percentage, such as 10%, in the Top Values text box	Top 10%, or whatever percentage is entered, of records
Click All	All records

Creating a Parameter Query

A **parameter query** displays a dialog box that prompts you for field criteria. Your entry in the dialog box determines which records appear on the final datasheet, just as if you had entered that criteria directly in the query design grid. You can also build a form or report based on a parameter query. When you open the form or report, the parameter dialog box opens. The entry in the dialog box determines which records the query selects in the recordset for the form or report. You want to create a query to display the courses for an individual department that you specify each time you run the query. To do so, you copy the TopCourses query then modify it to remove the Top Values option and include parameter prompts.

STEPS

1. **Right-click the TopCourses query in the Navigation Pane, click Copy, right-click a blank spot in the Navigation Pane, click Paste, type DepartmentParameter as the Query Name, then click OK**

   You modify the DepartmentParameter query to remove the top values and to include the parameter prompt.

2. **Right-click DepartmentParameter, click Design View on the shortcut menu, click the Show Table button in the Query Setup group, double-click Employees, then click Close**

   The Employees table contains the Department field needed for this query.

3. **Drag the title bar of the Courses field list to the left, then drag the title bar of the Enrollments field list to the right so that the relationship lines do not cross behind a field list**

   You are not required to rearrange the field lists of a query, but doing so can help clarify the relationships between them.

4. **Double-click the Department field in the Employees field list, click the Top Values list arrow in the Query Setup group, click All, then click the View button to display the datasheet**

   The query now counts the EnrollmentID field for records grouped by Description as well as Department. Because you only want to query for one department at a time, however, you need to add parameter criteria to the Department field.

> **QUICK TIP**
> To enter a long criterion, right-click the Criteria cell, then click Zoom.

5. **Click the View button to return to Query Design View, click the Department field Criteria cell, type [Enter department:], then click to display the Enter Parameter Value dialog box as shown in Figure K-3**

   In Query Design View, you must enter parameter criteria within [square brackets]. The parameter criterion you enter appears as a prompt in the Enter Parameter Value dialog box. The entry you make in the Enter Parameter Value box is used as the final criterion for the field that contains the parameter criterion. You can combine logical operators such as greater than (>) or less than (<) as well as wildcard characters such as an asterisk (*) with parameter criteria to create flexible search options. See Table K-2 for more examples of parameter criteria.

> **QUICK TIP**
> Query criteria are not case sensitive, so "marketing", "Marketing", and "MARKETING" all yield the same results.

6. **Type Marketing in the Enter department: text box, then click OK**

   Only those records with "Marketing" in the Department field are displayed, a portion of which are shown in Figure K-4. The records are still sorted in descending order by the CountOfEnrollmentID field, and they are grouped by the Description field.

7. **Save and close the DepartmentParameter query**

FIGURE K-3: **Using parameter criteria for the Department field**

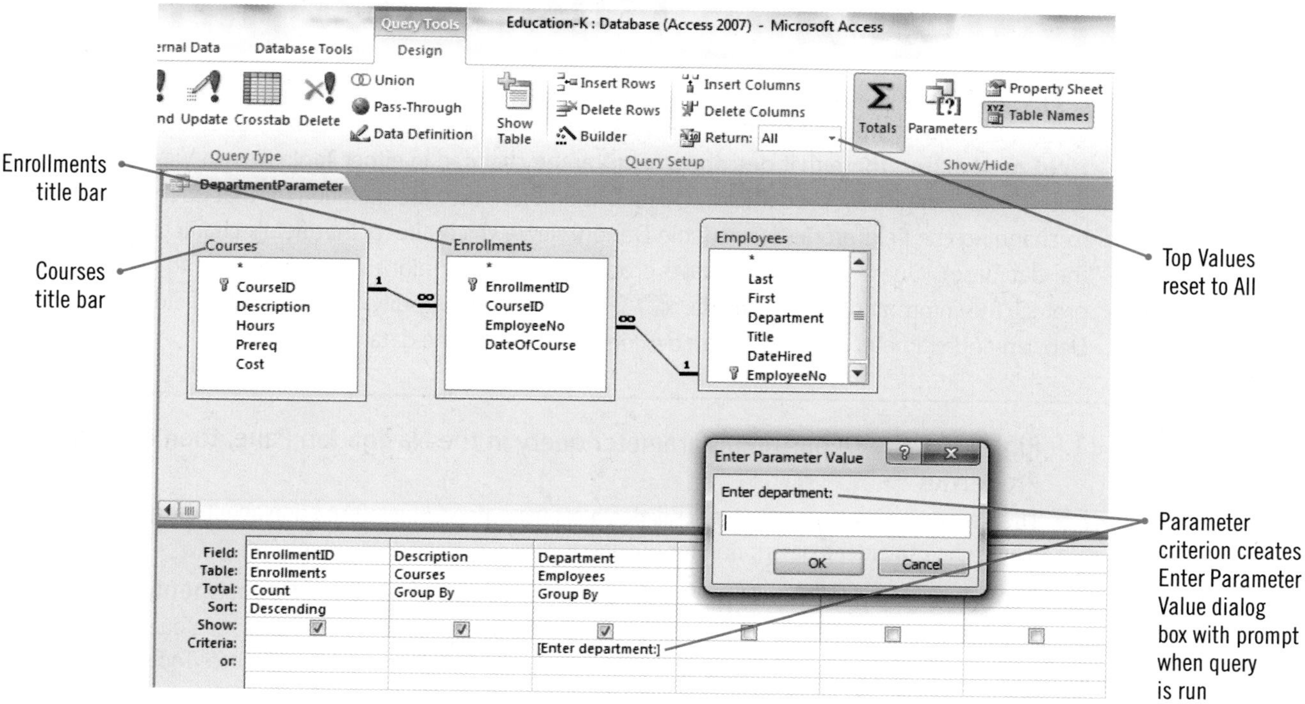

FIGURE K-4: **Datasheet for parameter query when Department equals Marketing**

TABLE K-2: **Examples of parameter criteria**

field data type	parameter criteria	description
Date/Time	>=[Enter start date:]	Searches for dates on or after the entered date
Date/Time	>=[Enter start date:] and <=[Enter end date:]	Prompts you for two date entries and searches for dates on or after the first date and on or before the second date
Text	Like [Enter the first character of the last name:] & "*"	Searches for any name that begins with the entered character
Text	Like "*" & [Enter any character(s) to search by:] & "*"	Searches for words that contain the entered characters anywhere in the field

UNIT
K
Access 2010

Modifying Query Properties

Properties are characteristics that define the appearance and behavior of items in the database such as objects, fields, sections, and controls. You can view the properties for an item by opening its Property Sheet. **Field properties**, those that describe a field, can be changed in either Table Design View or Query Design View. If you change field properties in Query Design View, they are modified for that query only (as opposed to changing the field properties in Table Design View, which affects that field's characteristics throughout the database). Query objects also have properties that you might want to modify to better describe or protect the information they provide. You want to modify the query and field properties of the DepartmentParameter query to better describe and present the data.

STEPS

1. **Right-click the DepartmentParameter query in the Navigation Pane, then click Object Properties**

   The DepartmentParameter Properties dialog box opens, providing information about the query and a text box where you can enter a description for the query.

2. **Type Counts enrollments per course description, prompts for Department, then click OK**

   The **Description** property allows you to better document the purpose or author of a query. The Description property also appears on **Database Documenter** reports, a feature on the Database Tools tab that helps you create reports with information about the database.

> **TROUBLE**
> The title bar of the Property Sheet always indicates which item's properties are shown. If it shows anything other than "Query Properties," click a blank spot beside the field lists to display query properties.

3. **Right-click the DepartmentParameter query in the Navigation Pane, click Design View on the shortcut menu, then click the Property Sheet button in the Show/Hide group**

   The Property Sheet opens, as shown in Figure K-5. View the Property Sheet for the query in Query Design View to see a complete list of the query's properties including the Description property that you modified earlier. The **Recordset Type** property determines if and how records displayed by a query are locked and has two common choices: Snapshot and Dynaset. **Snapshot** locks the recordset (which prevents it from being updated). **Dynaset** is the default value and allows updates to data. Because a summary query's datasheet summarizes several records, you cannot update the data in a summary query regardless of the Recordset Type property value. For regular Select queries, you can specify Snapshot in the Recordset Type property to give users read (but not write) access to that datasheet.

   To change the field name, you modify the field's **Caption** property in the Property Sheet for field properties. When you click a property in a Property Sheet, a short description of the property appears in the status bar. Press [F1] to open Access Help for a longer description of the selected property.

4. **Click the EnrollmentID field, click the Caption property in the Property Sheet, type Total Enrollment, click the View button, type Marketing as the parameter value, then click OK**

   The Total Enrollment Caption clarifies the first column of data as shown in Figure K-6.

5. **Save and close the DepartmentParameter query**

FIGURE K-5: **Query Property Sheet**

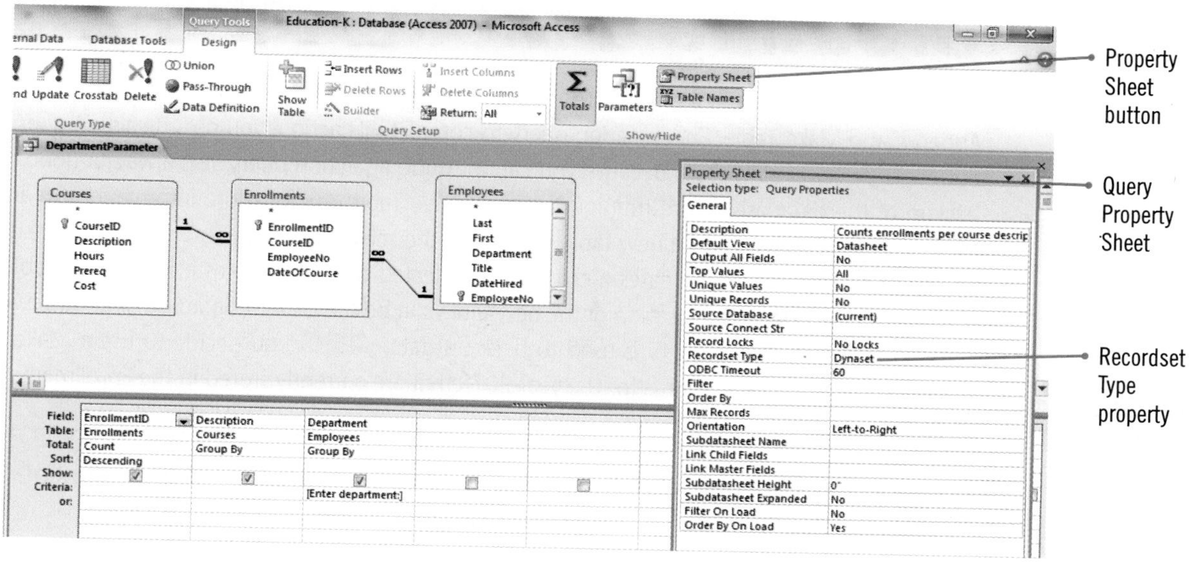

FIGURE K-6: **Final DepartmentParameter datasheet**

Total Enrollment	Description	Department
3	USA Biking Tours I	Marketing
3	Car Rentals I	Marketing
3	Cruising I	Marketing
3	Ecological Tours I	Marketing
2	Customer Service Skills I	Marketing
2	African Travel II	Marketing
2	African Travel III	Marketing
2	Air Reservations I	Marketing
2	Air Reservations II	Marketing
2	Air Reservations III	Marketing
2	Bus Travel I	Marketing

Access 2010

UNIT
K
Access 2010

Creating a Make Table Query

An **action query** *changes* many records in one process. The four types of action queries are Delete, Update, Append, and Make Table. For an action query to complete its action, you run the action query using the Run button in Query Design View. Because you cannot undo an action query, it is always a good idea to create a backup of the database before running the query. See Table K-3 for more information on action queries. A **Make Table query** creates a new table of data for the selected datasheet. The Make Table query works like an export feature in that it creates a copy of the selected data and pastes it into a new table in a database specified by the query. The location of the new table can be the current database or another Access database. Sometimes a Make Table query is used to back up data. You decide to use a Make Table query to archive the first quarter's records for the year 2012 that are currently stored in the Enrollments table.

STEPS

1. **Click the Create tab, click the Query Design button, double-click Enrollments in the Show Table dialog box, click Close, then close the Property Sheet if it is open**
2. **Double-click the * (asterisk) at the top of the Enrollments field list**
   Adding the asterisk to the query design grid includes in the grid all of the fields in that table. Later, if you add new fields to the Enrollments table, they are also added to this query.
3. **Double-click the DateOfCourse field to add it to the second column of the query grid, click the DateOfCourse field Criteria cell, type >=1/1/2012 and <=3/31/2012, click the DateOfCourse field Show check box to uncheck it, then use the resize pointer ✛ to widen the DateOfCourse column to view the entire Criteria entry as shown in Figure K-7**
   Before changing this query into a Make Table query, it is always a good idea to view the selected data.
4. **Click the View button to switch to Datasheet View, click any entry in the DateOfCourse field, then click the Descending button in the Sort & Filter group**
   Sorting the records in descending order based on the values in the DateOfCourse field allows you to confirm that no records after the first quarter of 2012 appear in the datasheet.
5. **Click the View button to return to Design View, click the Make Table button in the Query Type group, type ArchiveEnrollments in the Table Name text box, then click OK**
   The Make Table query is ready, but the new table has not yet been created. Action queries do not change data until you click the Run button. All action query icons include an exclamation point to remind you that they *change* data when you run them. To prevent running an action query accidentally, use the Datasheet View button to *view* the selected records, and use the Run button only when you want to run the action.
6. **Click the Run button in the Results group, click Yes when prompted that you are about to paste 180 rows, then save the query with the name MakeArchiveEnrollments and close it**
   When you run an action query, Access prompts you with an "Are you sure?" message before actually updating the data. The Undo button cannot undo changes made by action queries.
7. **Double-click the ArchiveEnrollments table in the Navigation Pane to view the new table's datasheet**
   All 180 records are pasted into the new table, as shown in Figure K-8.
8. **Close the ArchiveEnrollments table**

QUICK TIP
Access automatically adds pound signs (#) around the date criteria in a date field.

QUICK TIP
Double-clicking an action query in the Navigation Pane runs the query.

FIGURE K-7: **Setting up a Make Table query**

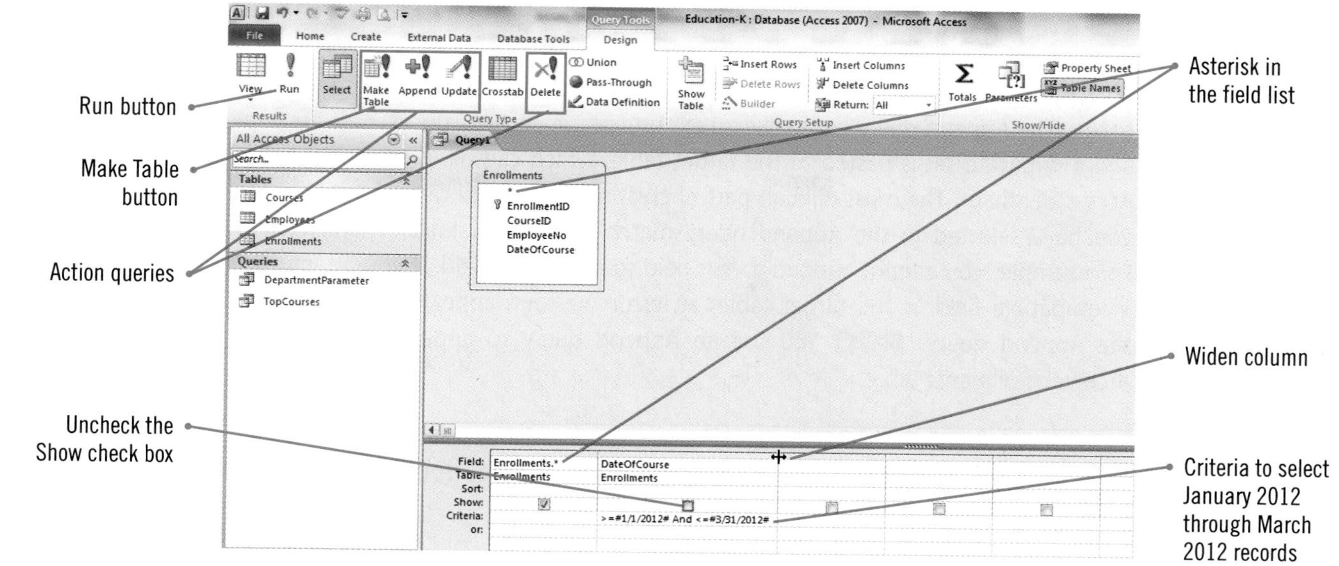

Run button
Make Table button
Action queries
Uncheck the Show check box
Asterisk in the field list
Widen column
Criteria to select January 2012 through March 2012 records

FIGURE K-8: **ArchiveEnrollments table**

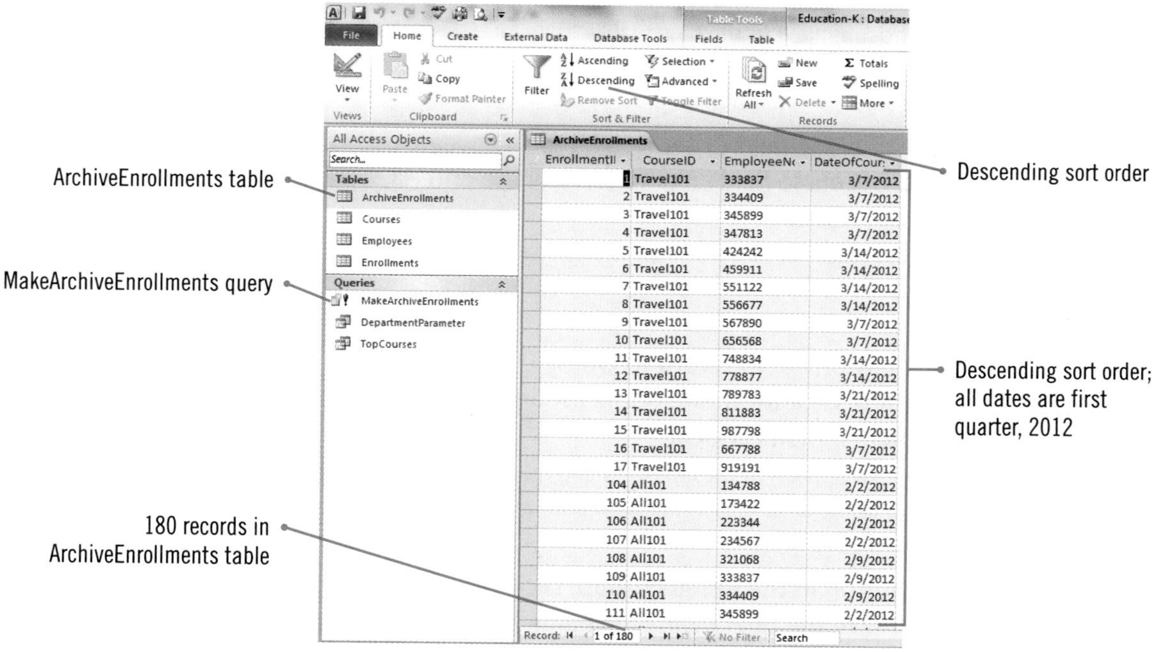

ArchiveEnrollments table
MakeArchiveEnrollments query
180 records in ArchiveEnrollments table
Descending sort order
Descending sort order; all dates are first quarter, 2012

TABLE K-3: **Action queries**

action query	query icon	description	example
Delete		Deletes a group of records from one or more tables	Remove products that are discontinued or for which there are no orders
Update		Makes global changes to a group of records in one or more tables	Raise prices by 10 percent for all products
Append		Adds a group of records from one or more tables to the end of another table	Append the employee address table from one division of the company to the address table from another division of the company
Make Table		Creates a new table from data in one or more tables	Export records to another Access database or make a backup copy of a table

Creating an Append Query

An **Append query** adds selected records to an existing table. The existing table is called the **target table**. The Append query works like an export feature because the records are copied from one location and a duplicate set is pasted to the target table, which can be in the current database or in any other Access database. The most difficult part of creating an Append query is making sure that all of the fields you have selected in the Append query match fields with similar characteristics in the target table. For example, you cannot append a Text field to a Number field. If you attempt to append a field to an incompatible field in the target table, an error message appears allowing you to cancel and correct the Append query. You use an Append query to append the records in April 2012 to the ArchiveEnrollments table.

STEPS

1. **Click the Create tab, click the Query Design button, double-click Enrollments in the Show Table dialog box, then click Close**
2. **Double-click the title bar in the Enrollments table's field list, then drag the highlighted fields to the first column of the query design grid**

   Double-clicking the title bar of the field list selects all of the fields, allowing you to add them to the query grid very quickly. To successfully append records to a table, you need to identify how each field in the query is connected to an existing field in the target table. Therefore, the technique of adding all of the fields to the query grid by using the asterisk does not work when you append records, because using the asterisk doesn't list each field in a separate column in the query grid.
3. **Click the DateOfCourse field Criteria cell, type Between 4/1/12 and 4/30/12, use ✛ to widen the DateOfCourse field column to view the criteria, then click the View button to display the datasheet**

   The datasheet should show 111 records with an April date in the DateOfCourse field. **Between...and** criteria select all records between the two dates, including the two dates. Between...and operators work the same way as the >= and <= operators.
4. **Click the View button to return to Query Design View, click the Append button in the Query Type group, click the Table Name list arrow in the Append dialog box, click ArchiveEnrollments, then click OK**

   The **Append To row** appears in the query design grid as shown in Figure K-9 to show how the fields in the query match fields in the target table, ArchiveEnrollments. You can now click the Run button to append the selected records to the table.
5. **Click the Run button in the Results group, click Yes to confirm that you want to append 111 rows, then save the query with the name AppendArchiveEnrollments and close it**
6. **Double-click the ArchiveEnrollments table in the Navigation Pane, click any entry in the DateOfCourse field, then click the Descending button**

   The 111 April records are appended to the ArchiveEnrollments table, which previously had 180 records and now has a new total of 291 records, as shown in Figure K-10.
7. **Save and close the ArchiveEnrollments table**

FIGURE K-9: Creating an Append query

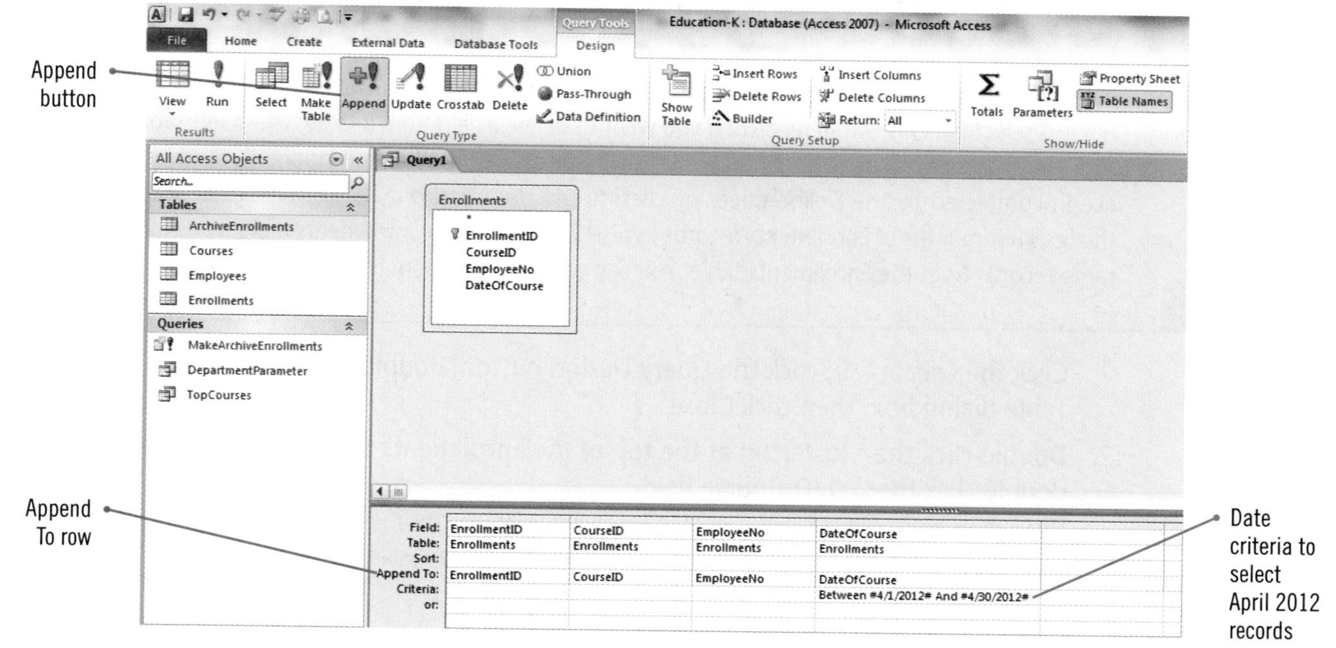
Append button
Append To row
Date criteria to select April 2012 records

FIGURE K-10: ArchiveEnrollments table with appended records

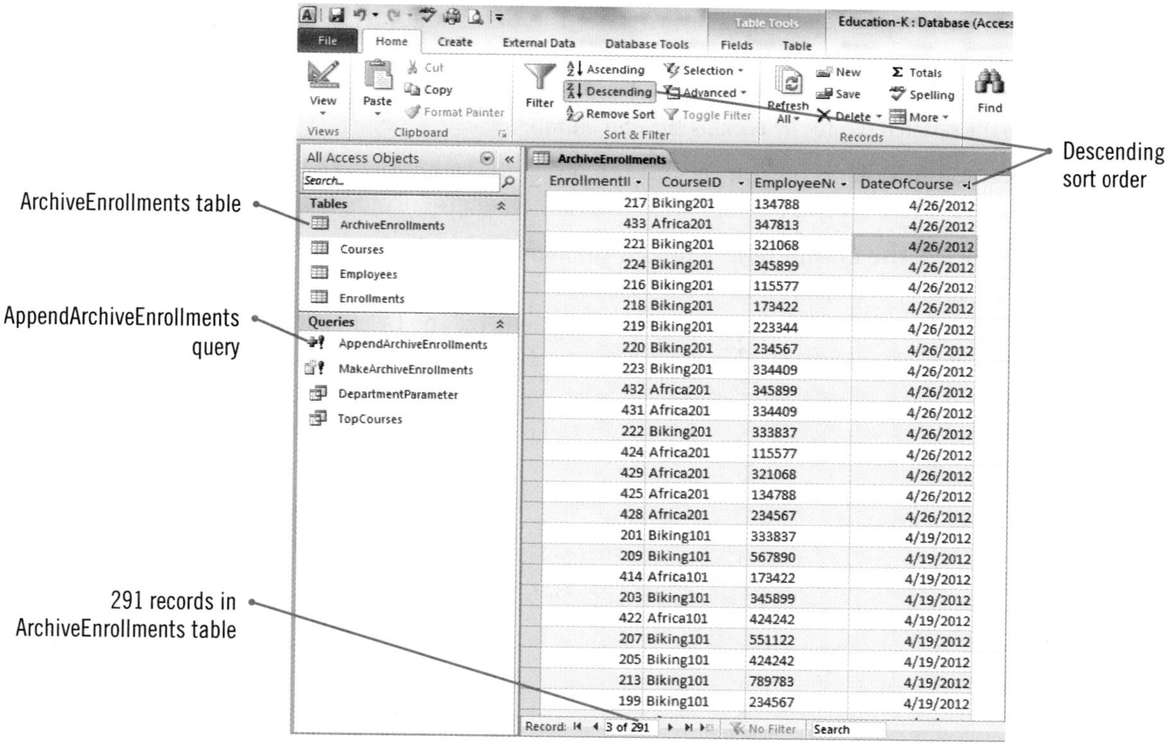
ArchiveEnrollments table
AppendArchiveEnrollments query
291 records in ArchiveEnrollments table
Descending sort order

1900 versus 2000 dates

If you type only two digits of a date, Access assumes that the digits 00 through 29 are for the years 2000 through 2029. If you type 30 through 99, Access assumes the years refer to 1930 through 1999. If you want to specify years outside these ranges, you must type all four digits of the year.

UNIT K
Access 2010

Creating a Delete Query

A **Delete query** deletes a group of records from one or more tables. Delete queries delete entire records, not just selected fields within records. If you want to delete a field from a table, you open Table Design View, click the field name, then click the Delete Rows button. As in all action queries, you cannot reverse the action completed by the Delete query by clicking the Undo button. Now that you have archived the first four months of Enrollments records for 2012 in the ArchiveEnrollments table, you want to delete the same records from the Enrollments table. You can use a Delete query to accomplish this task.

STEPS

1. **Click the Create tab, click the Query Design button, double-click Enrollments in the Show Table dialog box, then click Close**
2. **Double-click the * (asterisk) at the top of the Enrollments table's field list, then double-click the DateOfCourse field**
   Using the asterisk adds all fields from the Enrollments table to the first column of the query design grid. You add the DateOfCourse field to the second column of the query design grid so you can enter limiting criteria for this field.
3. **Click the DateOfCourse field Criteria cell, type Between 1/1/12 and 4/30/12, then use ↔ to widen the DateOfCourse field column to view the criteria**
   Before you run a Delete query, check the selected records to make sure that you have selected the same 291 records that you previously added to the ArchiveEnrollments table.
4. **Click the View button to confirm that the datasheet has 291 records, click the View button to return to Design View, then click the Delete button in the Query Type group**
   Your screen should look like Figure K-11. The **Delete row** now appears in the query design grid. You can delete the selected records by clicking the Run button.
5. **Click the Run button on the Design tab, click Yes to confirm that you want to delete 291 rows, then save the query with the name DeleteEnrollments and close it**
6. **Double-click the Enrollments table in the Navigation Pane, click any entry in the DateOfCourse field, then click the Ascending button in the Sort & Filter group**
   The records should start in May, as shown in Figure K-12. The Delete query deleted all records from the Enrollments table with dates between 1/1/2010 and 4/30/2010.
7. **Save and close the Enrollments table**

FIGURE K-11: **Creating a Delete query**

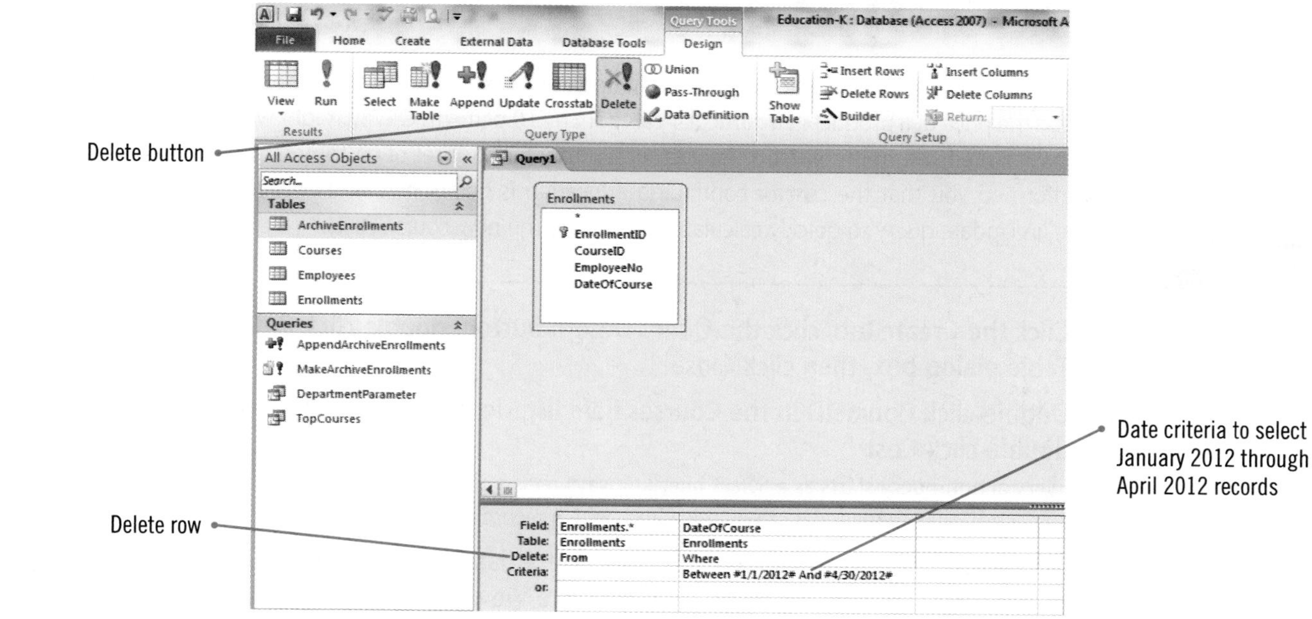
Delete button
Delete row
Date criteria to select January 2012 through April 2012 records

FIGURE K-12: **Final Enrollments table after deleting 291 records**

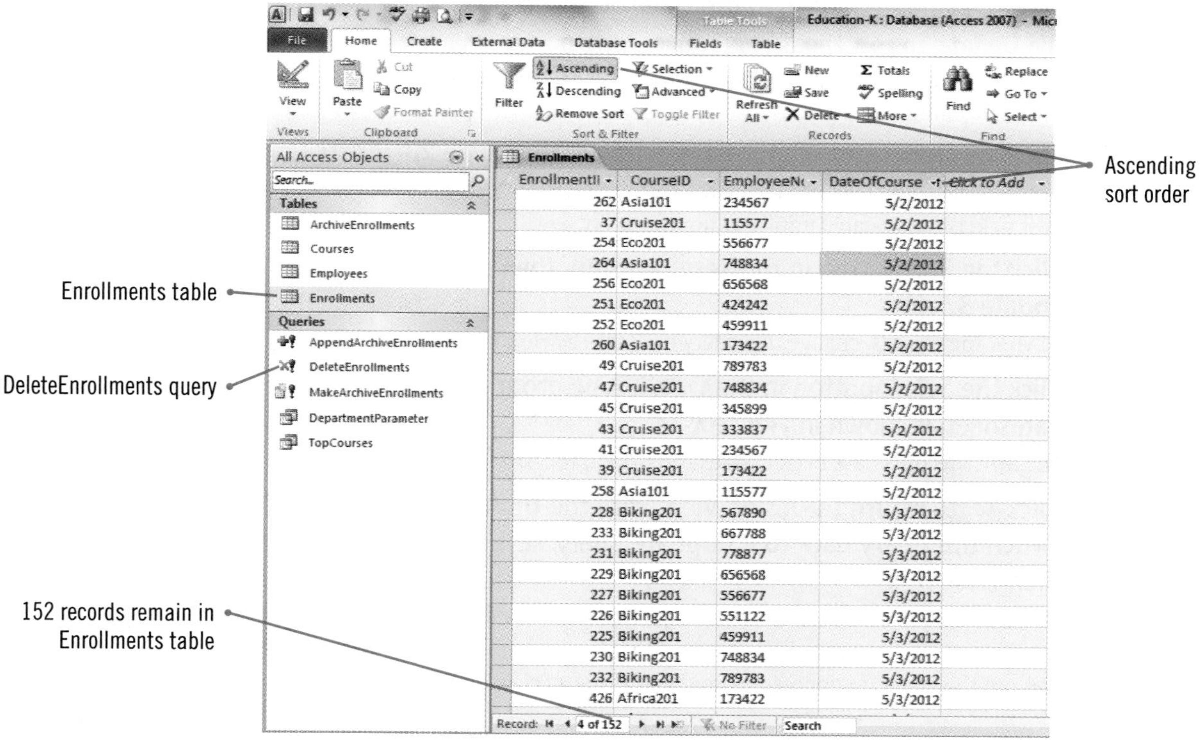
Enrollments table
DeleteEnrollments query
152 records remain in Enrollments table
Ascending sort order

Reviewing referential integrity

Recall that you can establish, or enforce, **referential integrity** between two tables when joining tables in the Relationships window. Referential integrity applies a set of rules to the relationship that ensures that no orphaned records currently exist, are added to, or are created in the database. A table has an **orphan record** when information in the foreign key field of the "many" table doesn't have a matching entry in the primary key field of the "one" table. The term "orphan" comes from the analogy that the "one" table contains **parent records**, and the "many" table contains **child records**. Referential integrity means that a Delete query would not be able to delete records in the "one" (parent) table that has related records in the "many" (child) table.

Creating an Update Query

An **Update query** is a type of action query that updates the values in a field. For example, you might want to increase the price of a product in a particular category by 10 percent. Or you might want to update information such as assigned sales representative, region, or territory for a subset of customers. Jacob Thomas has just informed you that the cost of continuing education is being increased by $20 for each class. You can create an Update query to quickly calculate and update the new course costs.

STEPS

1. **Click the Create tab, click the Query Design button, double-click Courses in the Show Table dialog box, then click Close**
2. **Double-click CourseID in the Courses field list, double-click Description, then double-click Cost**

   Every action query starts as a Select query. Always review the datasheet of the Select query before initiating any action that changes data to double-check which records are affected.
3. **Click the View button to display the query datasheet, note that the values in all three of the Africa courses are $450, then click the View button to return to Design View**

   After selecting the records you want to update and reviewing the values in the Cost field, you're ready to change this Select query into an Update query.
4. **Click the Update button in the Query Type group**

   The **Update To row** appears in the query design grid. To update the values in the Cost field by $20, you need to enter the appropriate expression in the Update To cell for the Cost field to add $20 to the current Cost field value.
5. **Click the Update To cell for the Cost field, then type 20+[Cost]**

   Your screen should look like Figure K-13. The expression adds 20 to the current value of the Cost field, but the Cost field is not updated until you run the query.
6. **Click the Run button in the Results group, then click Yes to confirm that you want to update 32 rows**

   To view the records, change this query back into a Select query, then view the datasheet.
7. **Click the Select button in the Query Type group, then click to display the query datasheet as shown in Figure K-14**

   The Africa records have been updated from $450 to $470. All other Cost values have increased by $20 as well.
8. **Click to return to Design View, click the Update button in the Query Type group to switch this query back to an Update query, save the query with the name UpdateCost, then close it**

   Often, you do not need to save action queries, because after the data has been updated, you generally won't use the same query again. Keep in mind that if you double-click an action query from the Navigation Pane, you run the query (as opposed to double-clicking a Select query, which opens its datasheet).

TROUBLE

Be sure to enter the expression for the Cost field, *not* for the CourseID or Description fields.

FIGURE K-13: **Setting up an Update query**

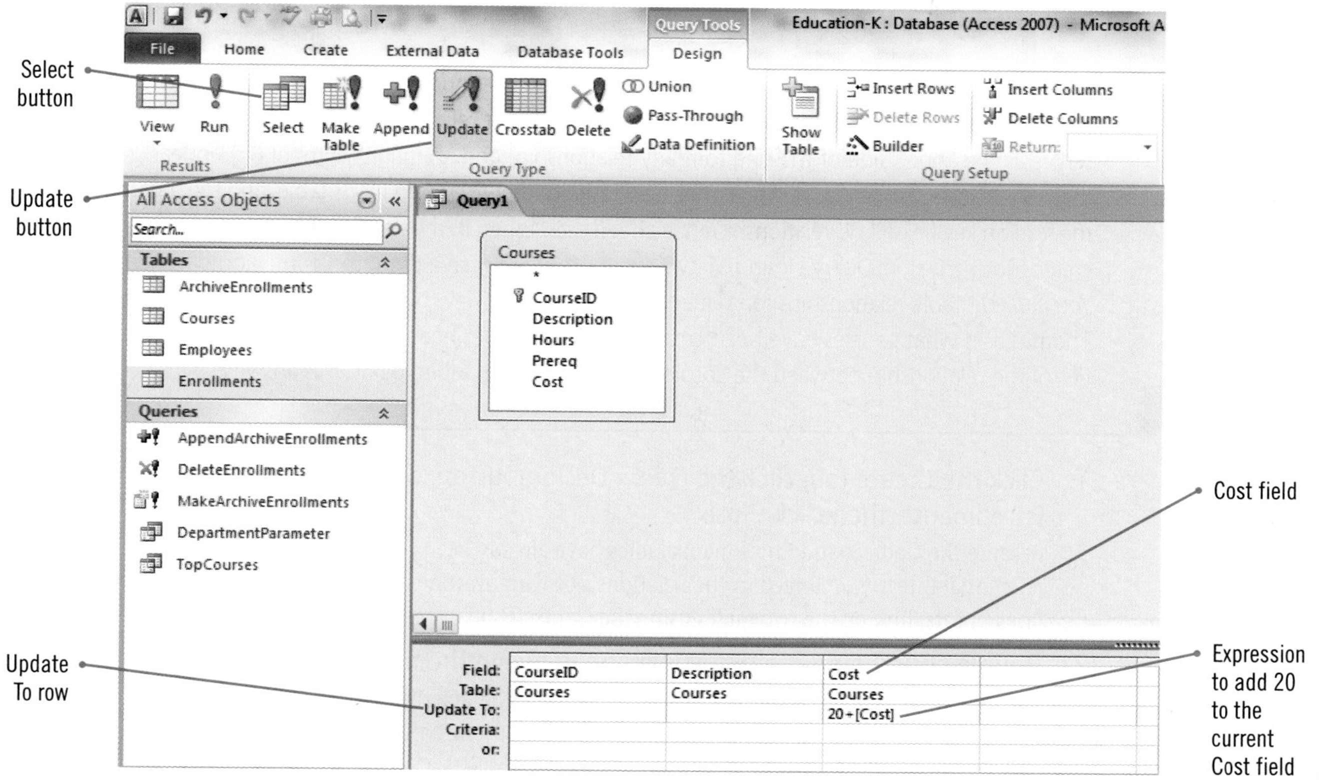

FIGURE K-14: **Updated Cost values**

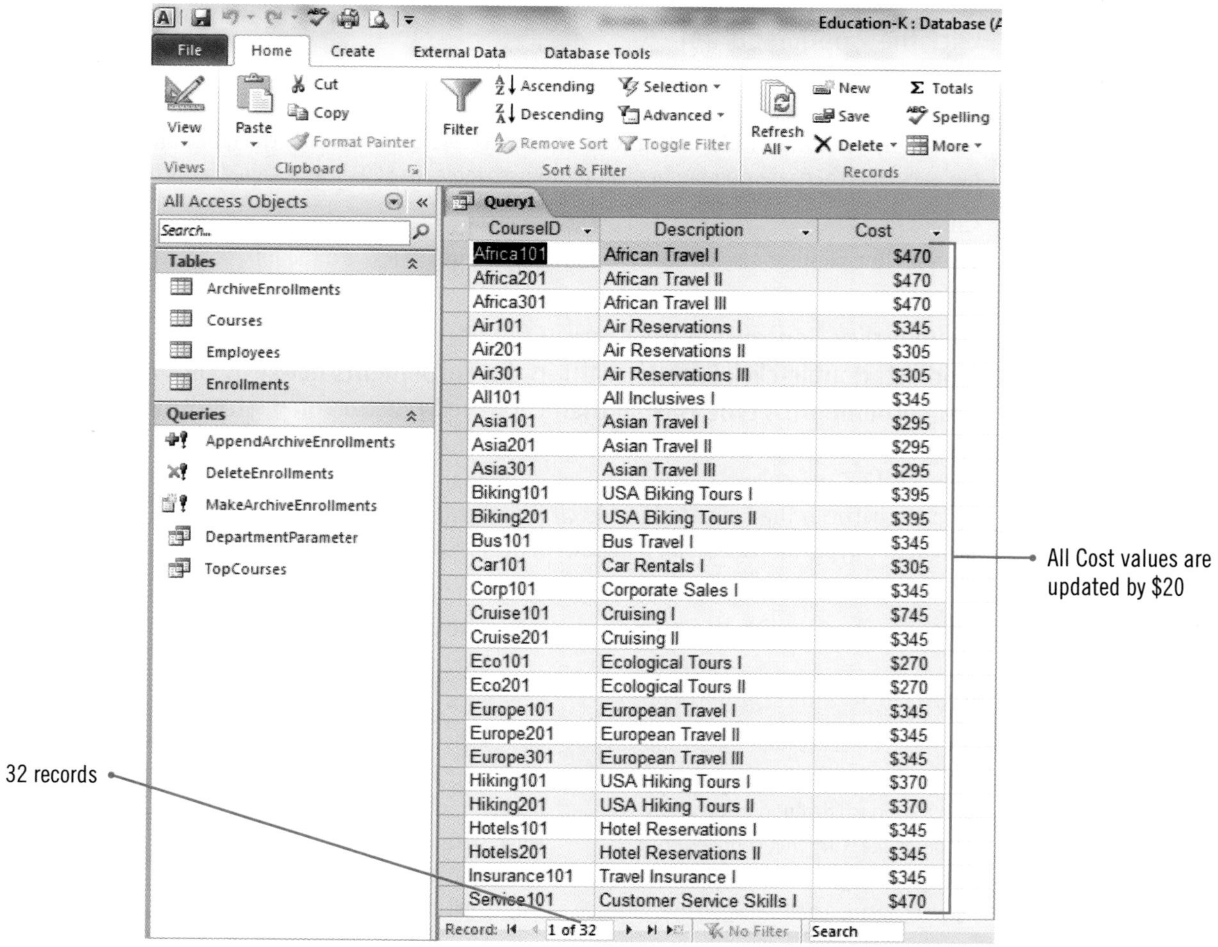

Specifying Join Properties

When you use the Relationships window to define table relationships, the tables are joined in the same way in Query Design View. If referential integrity is enforced on a relationship, a "1" appears next to the field that serves as the "one" side of the one-to-many relationship, and an infinity symbol (∞) appears next to the field that serves as the "many" side. The "one" field is the primary key field for its table, and the "many" field is called the foreign key field. If no relationships have been established in the Relationships window, Access automatically creates **join lines** in Query Design View if the linking fields have the same name and data type in two tables. You can edit table relationships for a query in Query Design View by double-clicking the join line. Jacob Thomas asks what courses have been created that have never been attended. You can modify the join properties of the relationship between the Enrollments and Courses table to find this answer.

STEPS

1. **Click the Create tab, click the Query Design button, double-click Courses, double-click Enrollments, then click Close**

   Because the Courses and Enrollments tables have already been related with a one-to-many relationship with referential integrity enforced in the Relationships window (one course can have many enrollments), the join line appears, linking the two tables using the CourseID field common to both.

2. **Double-click the one-to-many join line between the field lists**

   The Join Properties dialog box opens and displays the characteristics for the join, as shown in Figure K-15. The dialog box shows that option 1 is selected, the default join type, which means that the query displays only records where joined fields from *both* tables are equal. In **SQL (Structured Query Language)**, this is called an **inner join**. This means that if the Courses table has any records for which there are no matching Enrollments records, those courses do not appear in the resulting datasheet.

3. **Click the 2 option button**

   By choosing option 2, you are specifying that you want to see *all* of the records in the Courses table (the "one," or parent table), even if the Enrollments table (the "many," or child table) does not contain matching records. In SQL, this is called a **left join**. Option 3 selects all records in the Enrollments (the "many," or child table) even if there are no matches in the Courses table. In SQL, this is called a **right join**.

4. **Click OK**

   The join line's appearance changes, as shown in Figure K-16. With the join property set, you add fields to the query grid.

5. **Double-click CourseID in the Courses field list, double-click Description in the Courses field list, double-click EnrollmentID in the Enrollments field list, click the Criteria cell for the EnrollmentID, type Is Null, then click the View button to display the datasheet**

   The query finds 17 courses that currently have no matching records in the Enrollments table, as shown in Figure K-17. These courses contain a null (nothing) value in the EnrollmentID field. Changing the join property between the tables to include *all* records from the Courses table selects these records because the default join type, the inner join, requires a matching record in both tables to display a record in the resulting datasheet.

6. **Save the query with the name CoursesWithoutEnrollments, then close it**

TROUBLE

Double-click the middle portion of the join line, not the "one" or "many" symbols, to open the Join Properties dialog box.

QUICK TIP

To view the Relationships window from within Query Design View, right-click to the right of the field lists, then click Relationships.

Null and zero-length string values

The term **null** describes a field value that does not exist because it has never been entered. In a datasheet, null values look the same as a zero-length string value but have a different purpose. A **zero-length string** value is a *deliberate* entry that contains no characters. You enter a zero-length string by typing two quotation marks ("") with no space between them. A null value, on the other hand, indicates *unknown* data. By using null and zero-length string values appropriately, you can later query for the records that match one or the other condition. To query for zero-length string values, enter two quotation marks ("") as the criterion. To query for null values, use **Is Null** as the criterion. To query for another value other than a null value, use **Is Not Null** as the criterion.

FIGURE K-15: **Join Properties dialog box**

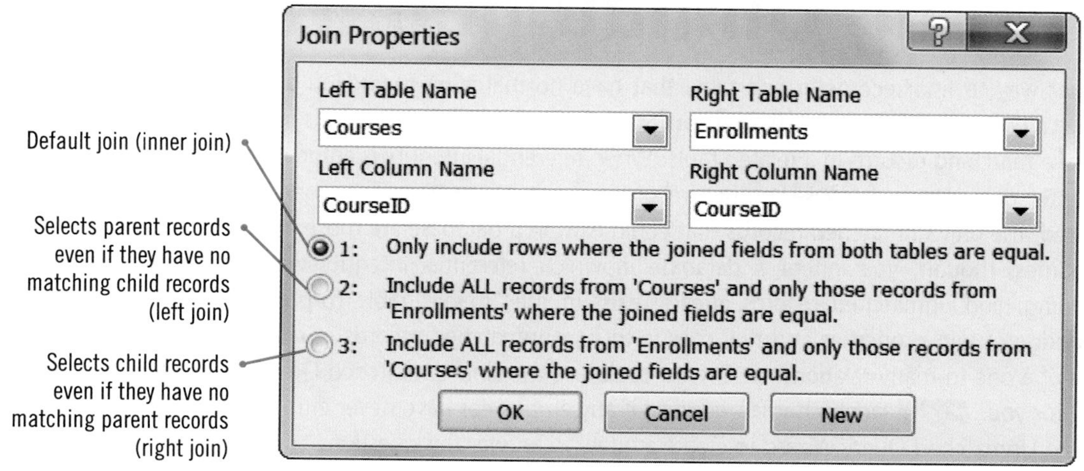
Join Properties
Left Table Name
Courses
Right Table Name
Enrollments
Left Column Name
CourseID
Right Column Name
CourseID
1: Only include rows where the joined fields from both tables are equal.
2: Include ALL records from 'Courses' and only those records from 'Enrollments' where the joined fields are equal.
3: Include ALL records from 'Enrollments' and only those records from 'Courses' where the joined fields are equal.
OK
Cancel
New
Default join (inner join)
Selects parent records even if they have no matching child records (left join)
Selects child records even if they have no matching parent records (right join)

FIGURE K-16: **Left join symbol**

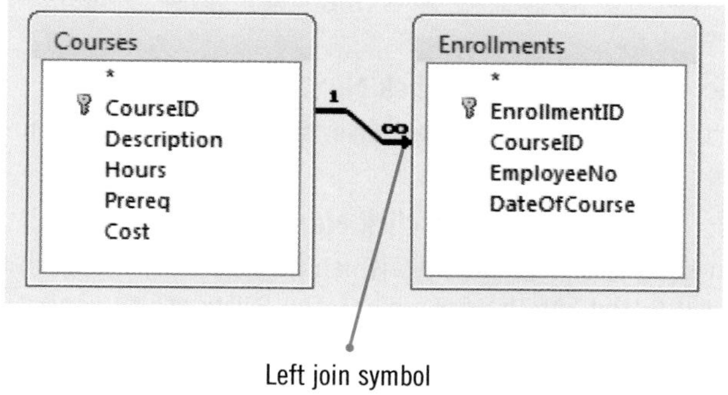
Courses
*
CourseID
Description
Hours
Prereq
Cost
Enrollments
*
EnrollmentID
CourseID
EmployeeNo
DateOfCourse
1
∞
Left join symbol

FIGURE K-17: **Courses with no matching enrollments**

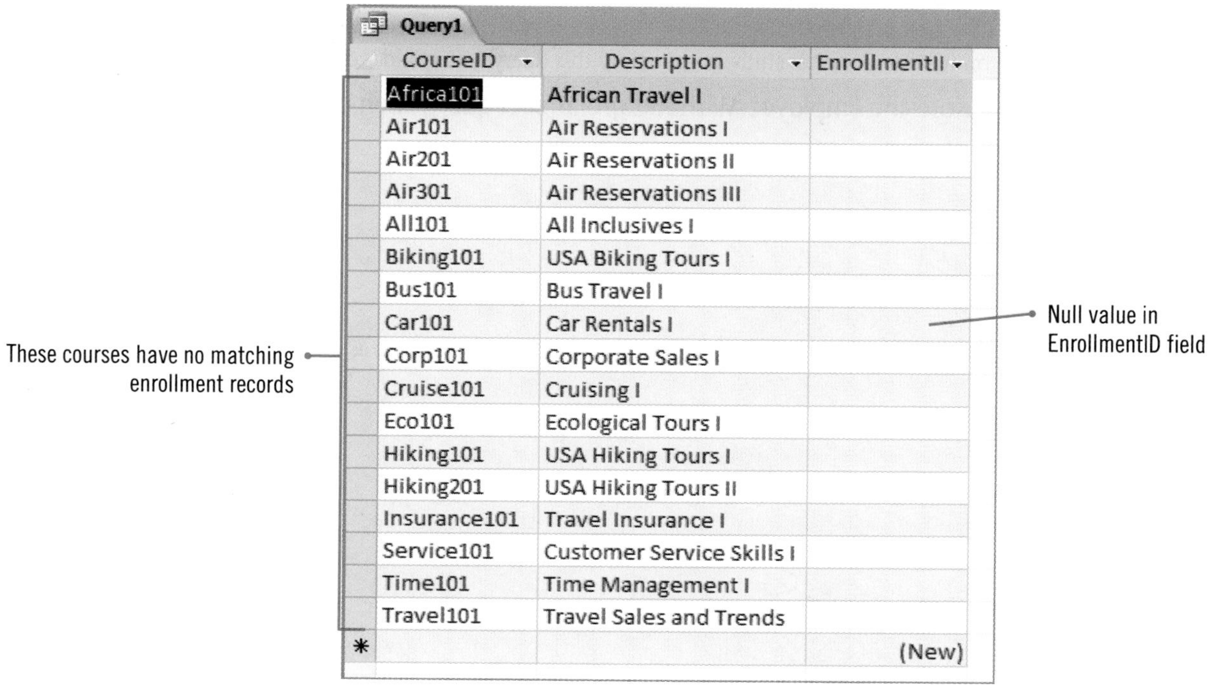
Query1
These courses have no matching enrollment records
Null value in EnrollmentID field

CourseID	Description	EnrollmentI
Africa101	African Travel I	
Air101	Air Reservations I	
Air201	Air Reservations II	
Air301	Air Reservations III	
All101	All Inclusives I	
Biking101	USA Biking Tours I	
Bus101	Bus Travel I	
Car101	Car Rentals I	
Corp101	Corporate Sales I	
Cruise101	Cruising I	
Eco101	Ecological Tours I	
Hiking101	USA Hiking Tours I	
Hiking201	USA Hiking Tours II	
Insurance101	Travel Insurance I	
Service101	Customer Service Skills I	
Time101	Time Management I	
Travel101	Travel Sales and Trends	
*		(New)

UNIT
K
Access 2010

Finding Unmatched Records

Another way to find records in one table that have no matching records in another is to use the **Find Unmatched Query Wizard**. A **find unmatched query** is a query that finds records in one table that do not have matching records in a related table. When referential integrity is enforced on a relationship before you enter data into a database, orphan records cannot be created. Therefore, with referential integrity enforced, the only unmatched records that could exist in a database are those in the "one" (parent) table. Sometimes, though, you inherit a database in which referential integrity was not imposed from the beginning, and unmatched records already exist in the "many" table (orphans). You could use your knowledge of join properties and null criteria to find unmatched records in either the "one" or "many" tables of a one-to-many relationship. Or you could use the Find Unmatched Query Wizard to structure the query for you. Jacob Thomas wonders if any employees have never enrolled in a class. You can use the Find Unmatched Query Wizard to create a query to answer this question.

STEPS

1. **Click the Create tab, click the Query Wizard button, click Find Unmatched Query Wizard, then click OK**
   The Find Unmatched Query Wizard starts, prompting you to select the table or query that may contain no related records.
2. **Click Table: Employees, then click Next**
   You want to find which employees have no enrollments, so you select the Enrollments table as the related table.
3. **Click Table: Enrollments, then click Next**
   The next question asks you to identify which field is common to both tables. Because the Employees table is already related to the Enrollments table in the Relationships window via the common EmployeeNo field, those fields are already selected as the matching fields, as shown in Figure K-18.
4. **Click Next**
   Now you must select the fields from the Employees table that you want to display in the query datasheet.
5. **Click the Select All Fields button >>**
6. **Click Next, type EmployeesWithoutEnrollments, then click Finish**
   The final datasheet is shown in Figure K-19. One employee who was recently hired has not yet enrolled in any class. To complete any further study or to modify this query, you could work in Query Design View.
7. **Save and close the EmployeesWithoutEnrollments query, then close the Education-K.accdb database**

FIGURE K-18: **Using the Find Unmatched Query Wizard**

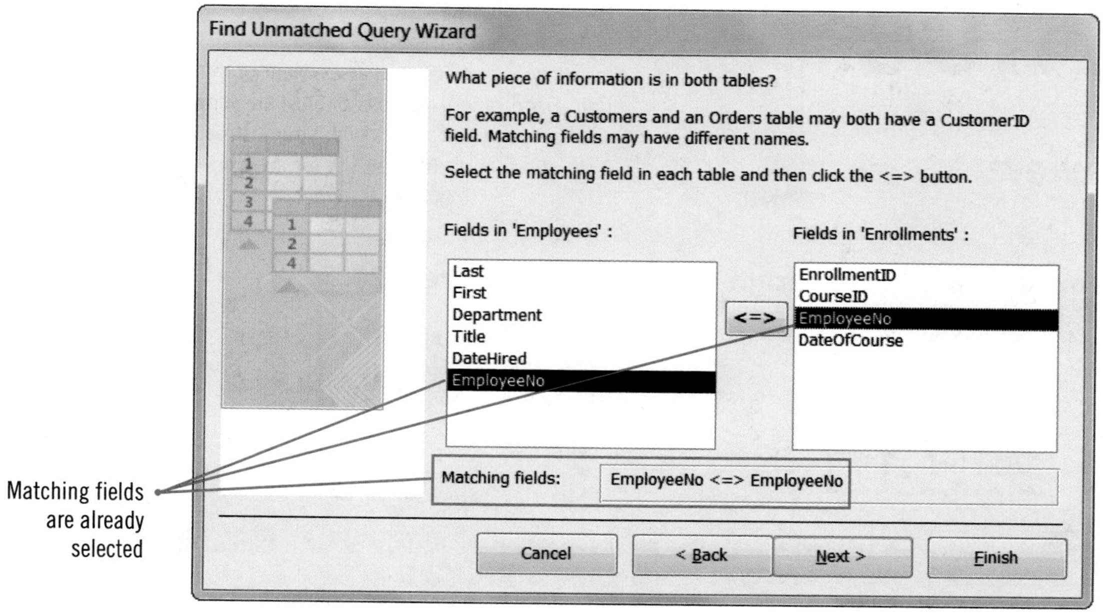

FIGURE K-19: **Employees without matching enrollment records**

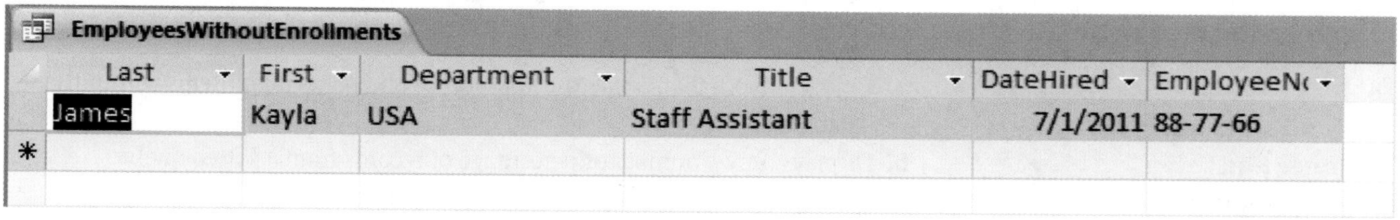
EmployeesWithoutEnrollments
Last
First
Department
Title
DateHired
EmployeeN(
James
Kayla
USA
Staff Assistant
7/1/2011
88-77-66

Find Duplicates Query Wizard

The Find Duplicates Query Wizard is another query wizard that is only available from the New Query dialog box. As you would suspect, the **Find Duplicates Query Wizard** helps you find duplicate values in a field, which can assist in finding and correcting potential data entry errors. For example, if you suspect that the same customer has been entered with two different names in your Customers table, you could use the Find Duplicates Query Wizard to find records with duplicate values in the Street or Phone field. After you isolated the records with the same values in a field, you could then edit incorrect data and delete redundant records.

Practice

Concepts Review

For current SAM information, including versions and content details, visit SAM Central (http://www.cengage.com/samcentral). If you have a SAM user profile, you may have access to hands-on instruction, practice, and assessment of the skills covered in this unit. Since various versions of SAM are supported throughout the life of this text, check with your instructor for the correct instructions and URL/Web site for accessing assignments.

Identify each element of the Query Design View shown in Figure K-20.

FIGURE K-20

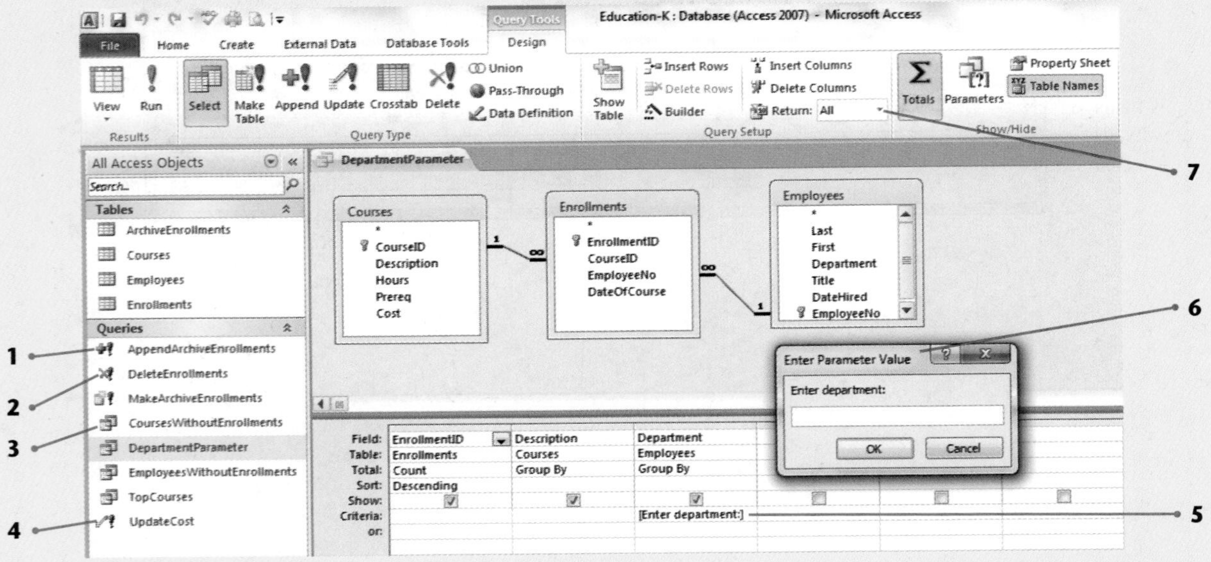

Match each term with the statement that best describes its function.

8. **Null**
9. **Top Values query**
10. **Inner join**
11. **Action query**
12. **Properties**
13. **Parameter**

a. Characteristics that define the appearance and behavior of items within the database
b. Displays only a number or percentage of records from a sorted query
c. Displays a dialog box prompting you for criteria
d. Means that the query displays only records where joined fields from both tables are equal
e. Makes changes to data
f. A field value that does not exist

Select the best answer from the list of choices.

14. Which join type selects all records from the "one" (parent) table?

- **a.** Inner
- **b.** Central
- **c.** Left
- **d.** Right

15. Which of the following is a valid parameter criterion entry in the query design grid?

- **a.** >=[Type minimum value here:]
- **b.** >=(Type minimum value here:)
- **c.** >=Type minimum value here:
- **d.** >={Type minimum value here: }

16. You *cannot* use the Top Values feature to:

- **a.** Select the bottom 10 percent of records.
- **b.** Display a subset of records.
- **c.** Show the top 30 records.
- **d.** Update a field's value by 5 percent.

17. Which of the following is *not* an action query?

- **a.** Union query
- **b.** Make table query
- **c.** Delete query
- **d.** Append query

18. Which of the following precautions should you take before running a Delete query?

- **a.** Check the resulting datasheet to make sure the query selects the right records.
- **b.** Have a current backup of the database.
- **c.** Understand the relationships between the records you are about to delete in the database.
- **d.** All of the above.

19. When querying tables in a one-to-many relationship with referential integrity enforced, which records appear (by default) on the resulting datasheet?

- **a.** All records from both tables will appear at all times.
- **b.** All records from the "one" table, and only those with matching values from the "many" side.
- **c.** Only those with matching values in both tables.
- **d.** All records from the "many" table, and only those with nonmatching values from the "one" side.

Skills Review

1. Query for top values.

- **a.** Start Access, then open the Seminar-K.accdb database from the drive and folder where you store your Data Files. Enable content if prompted.
- **b.** Create a new query in Query Design View with the EventName field from the Events table and the RegistrationFee field from the Registration table.
- **c.** Add the RegistrationFee field a second time, then click the Totals button. In the Total row of the query grid, Group By the EventName field, Sum the first RegistrationFee field, then Count the second RegistrationFee field.
- **d.** Sort in descending order by the summed RegistrationFee field.
- **e.** Enter **3** in the Top Values list box to display the top three seminars in the datasheet, then view the datasheet.
- **f.** Save the query as **Top3Revenue**, then close the datasheet.

2. Create a parameter query.

- **a.** Create a new query in Query Design View with the AttendeeLastName field from the Attendees table, the RegistrationDate field from the Registration table, and the EventName field from the Events table.
- **b.** Add the parameter criteria **Between [Enter Start Date:] and [Enter End Date:]** in the Criteria cell for the RegistrationDate field.
- **c.** Specify an ascending sort order on the RegistrationDate field.
- **d.** Click the Datasheet View button, then enter **5/1/13** as the start date and **5/31/13** as the end date to find everyone who has attended a seminar in May 2013. You should view five records.
- **e.** Save the query as **RegistrationDateParameter**, then close it.

3. Modify query properties.

- **a.** Right-click the RegistrationDateParameter query in the Navigation Pane, click Object Properties, then add the following description: **Prompts for a starting and ending registration date. Created by Your Name.**

Skills Review (continued)

b. Close the RegistrationDateParameter Properties dialog box, then open the RegistrationDateParameter query in Query Design View.

c. Right-click the RegistrationDate field, then click Properties on the shortcut menu to open the Property Sheet for the Field Properties. Enter **Date of Registration** for the Caption property, change the Format property to Medium Date, then close the Property Sheet.

d. View the datasheet for records between **5/1/13** and **5/31/13**, then widen the fields as needed to view the caption and the Medium Date format applied to the RegistrationDate field.

e. Change Skorija to your last name, then print the RegistrationDateParameter datasheet if requested by your instructor.

f. Save and close the RegistrationDateParameter query.

4. Create a Make Table query.

a. Create a new query in Query Design View, and select all the fields from the Registration table by double-clicking the Registration field list's title bar and dragging the selected fields to the query design grid.

b. Enter **<=3/31/2013** in the Criteria cell for the RegistrationDate field to find those records in which the RegistrationDate is on or before 3/31/2013.

c. View the datasheet. It should display 23 records.

d. In Query Design View, change the query into a Make Table query that creates a new table in the current database. Give the new table the name **BackupRegistration**.

e. Run the query to paste 23 rows into the BackupRegistration table.

f. Save the Make Table query with the name **MakeBackupRegistration**, then close it.

g. Open the BackupRegistration table, view the 23 records to confirm that the Make Table query worked correctly, then close the table.

5. Create an Append query.

a. Create a new query in Query Design View, and select all the fields from the Registration table by double-clicking the Registration field list's title bar and dragging the selected fields to the query design grid.

b. Enter **>=4/1/13 and <=4/30/13** in the Criteria cell for the RegistrationDate field to find those records in which the RegistrationDate is in April 2013.

c. View the datasheet, which should display one record.

d. In Query Design View, change the query into an Append query that appends records to the BackupRegistration table.

e. Run the query to append the row into the BackupRegistration table.

f. Save the Append query with the name **AppendBackupRegistration**, then close it.

g. Open the BackupRegistration table to confirm that it now contains the additional April record for a total of 24 records, then close the table.

6. Create a Delete query.

a. Create a new query in Query Design View, and select all the fields from the Registration table by double-clicking the Registration field list's title bar and dragging the selected fields to the query design grid.

b. Enter **<5/1/2013** in the Criteria cell for the RegistrationDate field to find those records in which the RegistrationDate is before May 1, 2013.

c. View the datasheet, which should display 24 records, the same 24 records you added to the BackupRegistration table.

d. In Query Design View, change the query into a Delete query.

e. Run the query to delete 24 records from the Registration table.

f. Save the query with the name **DeleteRegistration** then close it.

g. Open the Registration table in Datasheet View to confirm that it contains only five records, all with RegistrationDate values greater than or equal to 5/1/2013, then close the table.

7. Create an Update query.

a. Create a query in Query Design View, and select all the fields from the Registration table by double-clicking the Registration field list's title bar and dragging the selected fields to the query design grid.

b. Sort the records in descending order on the RegistrationFee field, then view the datasheet, which should display five records. Note the values in the RegistrationFee field.

   c. In Query Design View, change the query to an Update query, then enter **[RegistrationFee]*2** in the RegistrationFee field Update To cell to double the RegistrationFee value in each record.
   d. Run the query to update the five records.
   e. Save the query with the name **UpdateRegistrationFee**, then close it.
   f. Open the Registration table to confirm that the RegistrationFee for the five records has doubled, then close it.

8. **Specify join properties.**
   a. Create a new query in Query Design View with the following fields: AttendeeFirstName and AttendeeLastName from the Attendees table, and EventID and RegistrationFee from the Registration table.
   b. Double-click the join line between the Attendees and Registration tables to open the Join Properties dialog box. Click the 2 option button to include *all* records from Attendees and only those records from Registration where the joined fields are equal.
   c. View the datasheet, add your own first and last name as the last record, but do not enter anything in the EventID or RegistrationFee fields for your record.
   d. In Query Design View, add **Is Null** criteria to either field from the Registration table to select only those names who have never registered for an event.
   e. Save this query as **PeopleWithoutRegistrations**, then view, print (if requested by your instructor), and close the query.

9. **Find unmatched queries.**
   a. Start the Find Unmatched Query Wizard.
   b. Select the Events table, and then the Registration table to indicate that you want to view the Events records that have no related records in the Registration table.
   c. Specify that the two tables are related by the EventID field.
   d. Select all of the fields from the Events table in the query results.
   e. Name the query **EventsWithoutRegistrations**, then view the results. Change one of the entries in the Location field to **Your Name College**, as shown in Figure K-21.
   f. Print the EventsWithoutRegistrations query, then close the query, close the Seminar-K.accdb database, and exit Access.

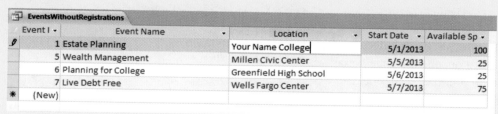

FIGURE K-21

EventsWithoutRegistrations

Event I	Event Name	Location	Start Date	Available Sp
1	Estate Planning	Your Name College	5/1/2013	100
5	Wealth Management	Millen Civic Center	5/5/2013	25
6	Planning for College	Greenfield High School	5/6/2013	25
7	Live Debt Free	Wells Fargo Center	5/7/2013	75
(New)				

Independent Challenge 1

As the manager of a college women's basketball team, you want to create several queries using the Basketball-K database.

a. Start Access, then open the Basketball-K.accdb database from the drive and folder where you store your Data Files. Enable content if prompted.

b. Create a query in Query Design View with the FirstName and LastName fields from the Players table, the FG (field goal), 3P (three pointer), and FT (free throw) fields from the Stats table, and the Opponent and GameDate fields from the Games table.

c. Enter **Between [Enter start date:] and [Enter end date:]** in the Criteria cell for the GameDate field.

d. View the datasheet for all of the records between **12/1/2012** and **12/31/2012**. It should display 18 records.

e. Save the query with the name **StatsParameter**, change Lindsey Swift's name to your own, then print the datasheet if requested by your instructor.

f. In Query Design View of the StatsParameter query, insert a new calculated field named **TotalPoints** between the FT and Opponent field with the expression **TotalPoints:[FG]*2+[3P]*3+[FT]**, then sort the records in descending order on the TotalPoints field.

g. Apply the 25% Top Values option, and view the datasheet for all of the records between **12/1/2012** and **12/31/2012**. It should display five records.

h. Use the Save Object As feature to save the revised query as **StatsParameterTopValues**. Print the datasheet if requested by your instructor, then close it.

i. Create a new query in Query Design View with the Opponent, Mascot, HomeScore, and OpponentScore fields from the Games table, then add a new calculated field as the last field with the following field name and expression: **WinRatio:[HomeScore]/[OpponentScore]**.

j. View the datasheet to make sure that the WinRatio field calculates properly, and widen all columns as necessary to see all of the data. Because the home score is generally greater than the opponent score, most values are greater than 1.

Advanced Challenge Exercise

- In Query Design View, change the Format property of the WinRatio field to Percent and the Decimal Places property to 0.
- View the datasheet, a portion of which is shown in Figure K-22.

FIGURE K-22

Query1

Opponent	Mascot	HomeScore	OpponentScore	WinRatio
Iowa	Hawkeyes	81	65	125%
Creighton	Bluejays	106	60	177%
Northern Illinoi	Huskies	65	60	108%
Louisiana Tech	Red Raiders	69	89	78%
Drake	Bulldogs	80	60	133%
Northern Iowa	Panthers	38	73	52%
Buffalo	Bulls	50	55	91%
Oklahoma	Sooners	53	60	88%
Texas	Longhorns	57	60	95%
Kansas	Jayhawks	74	58	128%
Colorado	Buffaloes	90	84	107%
Texas A&M	Aggies	77	60	128%

k. Save the query as **WinPercentage**, change the first opponent's name (Iowa) and mascot to your own name and a mascot of your choice, print the WinPercentage datasheet if requested by your instructor, and close the WinPercentage query.

l. Close the Basketball-K.accdb database, then exit Access.

Independent Challenge 2

As the manager of a college women's basketball team, you want to enhance the Basketball-K database by creating several action queries.

a. Start Access, then open the Basketball-K.accdb database from the drive and folder where you store your Data Files. Enable content if prompted.

b. Create a new query in Query Design View, and select all the fields from the Stats table by double-clicking the field list's title bar and dragging the selected fields to the query design grid.

c. Add criteria to find all of the records with the GameNo field equal to **1**, **2**, or **3**, then view the datasheet. It should display 26 records.

d. In Query Design View, change the query to a Make Table query to paste the records into a table in the current database called **Stats123**.

e. Run the query to paste the 26 rows, save the query with the name **MakeStatsBackup**, then close it.

f. Open the datasheet for the Stats123 table to confirm that it contains 26 records, then close it.

g. In Query Design View, create another new query that includes all of the fields from the Stats table by double-clicking the field list's title bar and dragging the selected fields to the query design grid.

h. Add criteria to find all of the statistics for those records with the GameNo field equal to **4** or **5**, then view the datasheet. It should display 12 records.

i. In Query Design View, change the query to an Append query to append the records to the Stats123 table.

j. Run the query to append the 12 rows, save it with the name **AppendStatsBackup**, then close it.

k. Right-click the Stats123 table in the Navigation Pane, click Rename, then edit the name to **Stats12345**.

l. Open the Stats12345 table to make sure it contains 38 records, print it if requested by your instructor, then close the Stats12345 table.

m. Close the Basketball-K.accdb database, then exit Access.

Independent Challenge 3

As the manager of a college women's basketball team, you want to query the Basketball-K database to find specific information about each player.

a. Start Access, then open the Basketball-K.accdb database from the drive and folder where you store your Data Files. Enable content if prompted.

b. Create a query in Query Design View using the Players and Stats tables. Resize the field lists to view all of the fields in each table.

c. Double-click the join line to open the Join Properties dialog box, then change the join properties to option 2 to include *all* records from Players and only those from Stats where the joined fields are equal.

d. Add the FirstName and LastName fields from the Players table and the Assists field from the Stats table.

e. Type **Is Null** in the Criteria cell for the Assists field, as shown in Figure K-23, then view the datasheet to find those players who have never recorded an Assist value in the Stats table. It should display one record.

f. Change the last name to your own last name.

g. Print the datasheet if requested by your instructor, save the query as **NoAssists**, then close the query.

h. Close Basketball-K.accdb, then exit Access.

FIGURE K-23

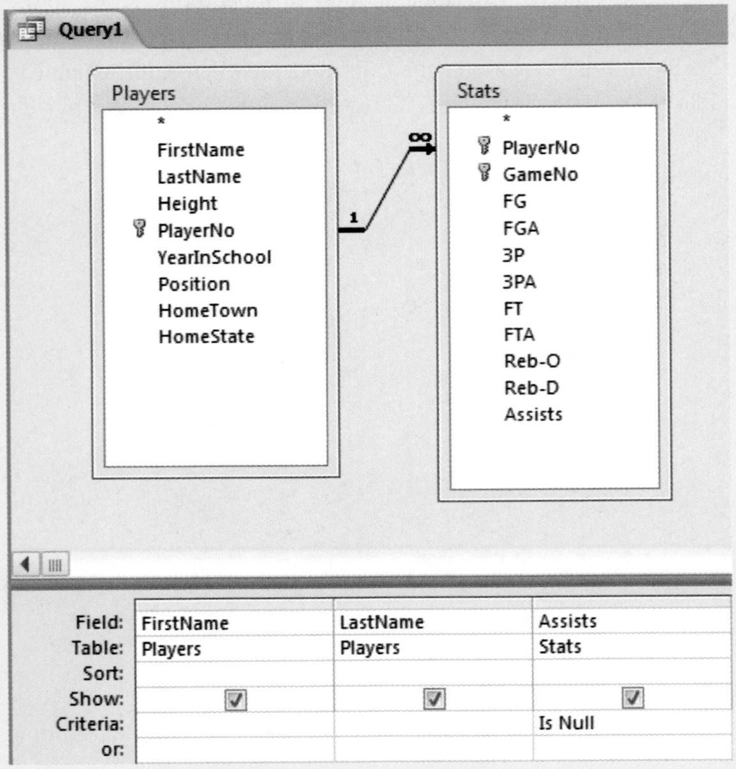

Real Life Independent Challenge

This Independent Challenge requires an Internet connection.

One way to use Access to support your personal interests is to track the activities of a club or hobby. For example, suppose you belong to a culinary club that specializes in cooking with chocolate. The club collects information on international chocolate factories and museums and asks you to help build a database to organize the information.

a. Start Access, then open the Chocolate-K.accdb database from the drive and folder where you store your Data Files. Enable content if prompted.

b. Open the Countries table, then add two more country records, allowing the CountryID field to automatically increment because it is an AutoNumber data type. Close the Countries table.

c. Create a query in Query Design View with the Country field from the Countries table, and the PlaceName, City, and State fields from the ChocolatePlaces query.

d. Name the query **PlacesOfInterest**, double-click the join line between the Countries and ChocolatePlaces tables, then choose the 2 option that includes *all* records from the Countries table.

e. Save and view the PlacesOfInterest query. Expand each column to show all of the data.

f. Print the PlacesOfInterest query if requested by your instructor, then close it.

Advanced Challenge Exercise

ACE

- Using the Internet, research a chocolate-related place of interest (a factory or museum) for one of the countries you entered in Step b.
- Open the Countries table, and use the Subdatasheet for the country you selected to enter the data for the chocolate-related place of interest. Enter **F** for factory or **M** for museum in the FactoryorMuseum field.
- Close the Countries table, and open the PlacesOfInterest query in Design View. Modify the link line to option 1, so that records that have a match in both tables are selected.
- Save and open the PlacesOfInterest query in Datasheet View as shown in Figure K-24, and print the resulting datasheet if requested by your instructor. Note that the last record will show the unique data you entered.

g. Close Chocolate-K.accdb, then exit Access.

FIGURE K-24

PlacesOfInterest

Country	PlaceName	City	State
Germany	Lindt factory	Aachen	
Germany	Imhoff Stollwerk Chocolate Museum	Cologne	
Switzerland	Lindt factory	Kilchberg	
Switzerland	Museum del Cioccolato Alprose	Caslano	Canton Ticino
Switzerland	Nestle	Broc	Canton Fribourg
France	Lindt Factory	Oloron	
France	Atelier Musee du Chocolat, Biarritz	Biarritz	
Italy	Lindt Factory	Induno	
Italy	Lindt Factory	Luserna	
Italy	Museo Storico della Perugina	Perugia	
Italy	Museo del Cioccolato Antia Norba	Norma	Latina Province
Austria	Lindt Factory	Gloggnitz	
USA	Lindt Factory	San Leandro	CA
USA	Lindt Factory	Stratham	NH
Belgium	Musee du Cacao et du Chocolat	Brussels	
Great Britian	Cadbury World	Bourneville	
Japan	Shiroi Koibito Park	Sapporo	
*			

Visual Workshop

As the manager of a college women's basketball team, you want to create a query from the Basketball-K.accdb database with the fields from the Players, Stats, and Games tables as shown. The query is a parameter query that prompts the user for a start and end date using the GameDate field from the Games table. Figure K-25 shows the datasheet where the start date of **11/13/2012** and end date of **11/16/2012** are used. Also note that the records are sorted in ascending order first by GameDate, and then by LastName. Save and name the query **Rebounds**, then print the datasheet if requested by your instructor. Be sure to change one player's name to your own if you haven't previously done this to identify your printout.

FIGURE K-25

Rebounds

GameDate	FirstName	LastName	Reb-O	Reb-D	TotalRebounds
11/13/2012	Kristen	Czyenski	2	2	4
11/13/2012	Denise	Franco	2	3	5
11/13/2012	Theresa	Grant	1	3	4
11/13/2012	Megan	Hile	1	2	3
11/13/2012	Amy	Hodel	5	3	8
11/13/2012	Ellyse	Howard	1	2	3
11/13/2012	Jamie	Johnson	0	1	1
11/13/2012	Student First	Student Last	1	2	3
11/13/2012	Morgan	Tyler	4	6	10
11/16/2012	Kristen	Czyenski	3	2	5
11/16/2012	Denise	Franco	5	3	8
11/16/2012	Sydney	Freesen	2	3	5
11/16/2012	Theresa	Grant	3	3	6
11/16/2012	Megan	Hile	1	5	6
11/16/2012	Amy	Hodel	1	4	5
11/16/2012	Ellyse	Howard	3	3	6
11/16/2012	Sandy	Robins	0	1	1
11/16/2012	Student First	Student Last	2	2	4
11/16/2012	Morgan	Tyler	3	6	9
11/16/2012	Abbey	Walker	2	4	6

UNIT L
Access 2010

Creating Advanced Reports

Files You Will Need:

Education-L.accdb
RealEstate-L.accdb
Basketball-L.accdb

In this unit you will learn techniques to make sure that the data in your reports are logical and clear using advanced formatting, grouping, and print layout features. You will also learn how to graphically display data in a variety of chart types such as pie, bar, and line charts. Jacob Thomas, coordinator of training at Quest Specialty Travel, wants to enhance existing reports to more professionally and clearly present the information in the Education-L database.

OBJECTIVES

- Apply advanced formatting
- Control layout
- Set advanced print layout
- Create charts
- Modify charts
- Apply chart types
- Create multicolumn reports
- Use domain functions

UNIT L

Access 2010

Applying Advanced Formatting

Each control on a report has formatting properties such as Text Align, Width, and Format that you can modify using the Ribbon or Property Sheet. For example, the **Format property** provides several ways to format dates (19-Jun-13, 6/19/2013, or Friday, June 19, 2013), and numbers can be formatted as Currency ($77.25), Percent (52%), or Standard (890). You review the Departmental Summary Report to identify and correct formatting problems.

STEPS

1. **Start Access, open the Education-L.accdb database from the drive and folder where you store your Data Files, enable content if prompted, double-click DeptSummary in the Navigation Pane, then scroll so your screen looks like Figure L-1**
   Some of the information is not displayed correctly and subtotals are not formatted properly.
2. **Right-click the report, click Design View, click the Department label in the Page Header section, click the ⊞ symbol to the left of the Department label to select the grouped controls, click the Arrange tab, then click the Remove Layout button in the Table group**
   Often, Access Form and Report Wizards will group controls together, which helps you work with them as a group in Layout View. Ungrouping controls allows you to work with them individually. With the controls ungrouped, you build an expression to calculate the entire employee name in one text box.

TROUBLE
Be sure to include a space after the comma to separate the parts of the name.

3. **Click a blank spot on the report to remove the selection, click the First label in the Page Header section, press [Delete], click the EFirst text box in the EmployeeNo Header section, press [Delete], double-click the border of the Last label to open its Property Sheet, modify the Caption property on the Format tab to Name, click the ELast text box in the EmployeeNo Header section to select it, use ↔ to drag the right edge of the ELast text box to about the 3.5" mark on the horizontal ruler to widen it, then modify the Control Source property of ELast to =[ELast]&", "&[EFirst]**
   The name expression requires less horizontal space and looks professional. Now widen the date controls.

TROUBLE
Drag the title bar of the Property Sheet to move it as needed.

4. **Click the Date label in the Page Header section, press and hold [Shift], click the DateOfCourse text box in the Detail section, release [Shift], use ↔ to drag the left edge of the controls to about the 3.5" mark on the horizontal ruler to widen them, click the Home tab, then click the Center button in the Text Formatting group twice**
   You also want to change the subtotal values so that they align directly under the columns they represent (Hours or Cost). In addition, you want all Cost values to be formatted as currency (with dollar signs).

TROUBLE
If Currency isn't available for the Format property, click another property then try again.

5. **Click the 7.75" mark on the horizontal ruler to select all controls in the Cost column (see Figure L-2), click the Align Text Right button twice, click the Arrange tab, click the Align button, click Right, press and hold [Shift], click the Cost label in the Page Header section to deselect it, release [Shift], click the Format tab in the Property Sheet, click the Format list arrow, click Currency, click the Decimal Places list arrow, then click 0**
   With the Cost column formatted properly, you work on the Hours column.
6. **Click the 7" mark on the horizontal ruler to select all controls in the Hours column, click the Arrange tab, click the Align button, click Right, click the Home tab, click the Align Text Right button twice, press and hold [Shift], click the Hours label in the Page Header section, release [Shift], click the Format list arrow in the Property Sheet, click Standard, click the Decimal Places list arrow, then click 0**
7. **Right-click the DeptSummary report tab, click Report View, scroll to match Figure L-3, then save and close the report**

FIGURE L-1: **Reviewing problems with the Departmental Summary Report**

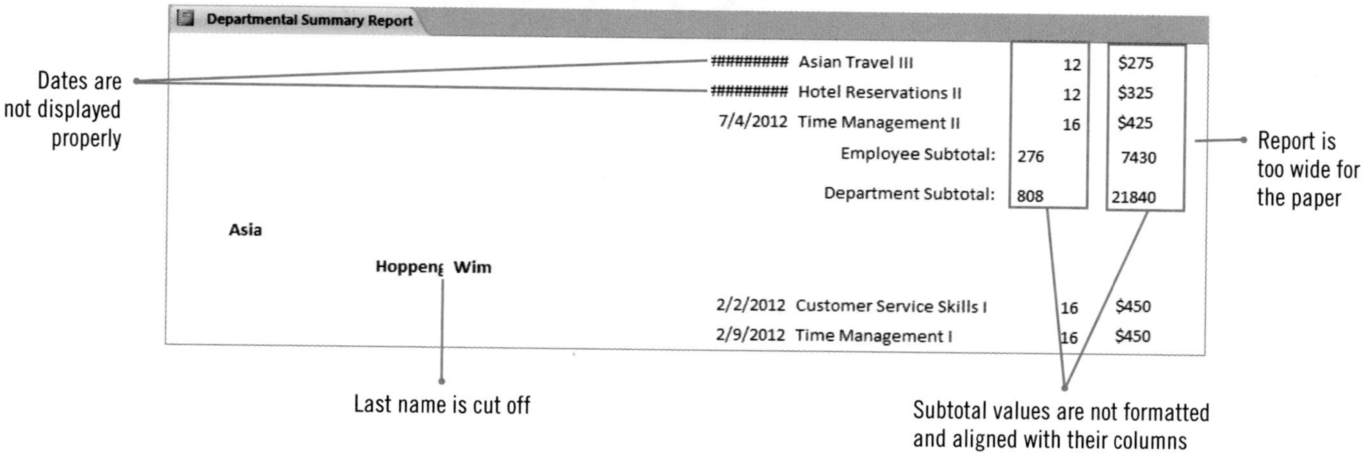

FIGURE L-2: **Formatting and aligning controls in Report Design View**

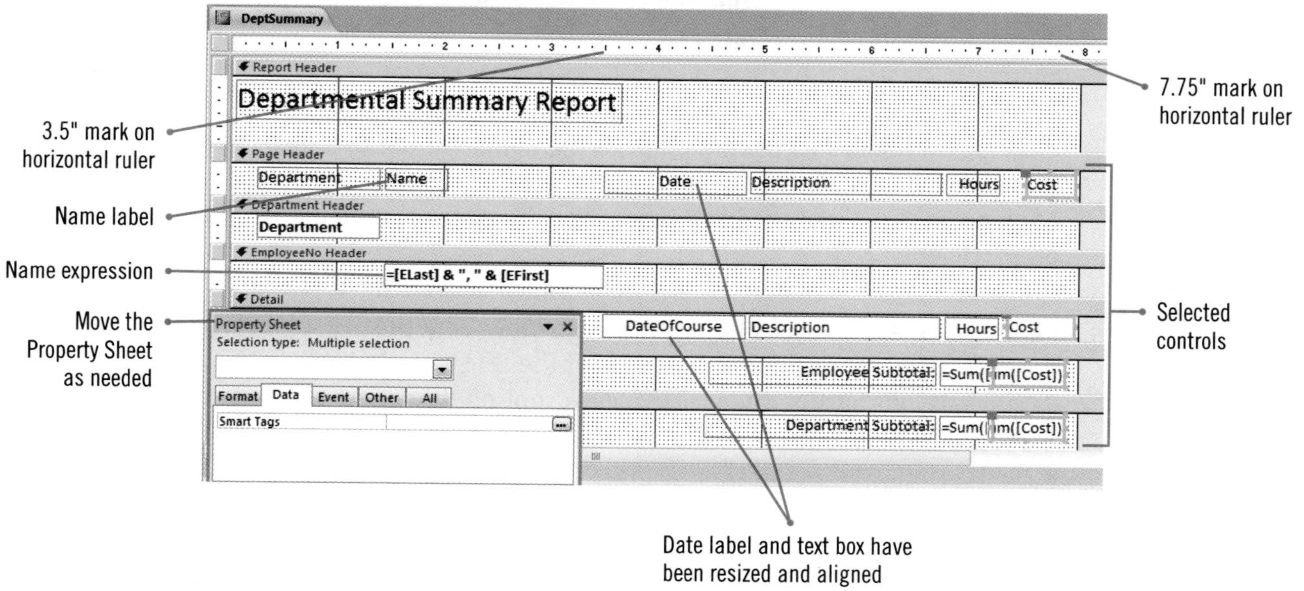

FIGURE L-3: **Reviewing the Departmental Summary Report**

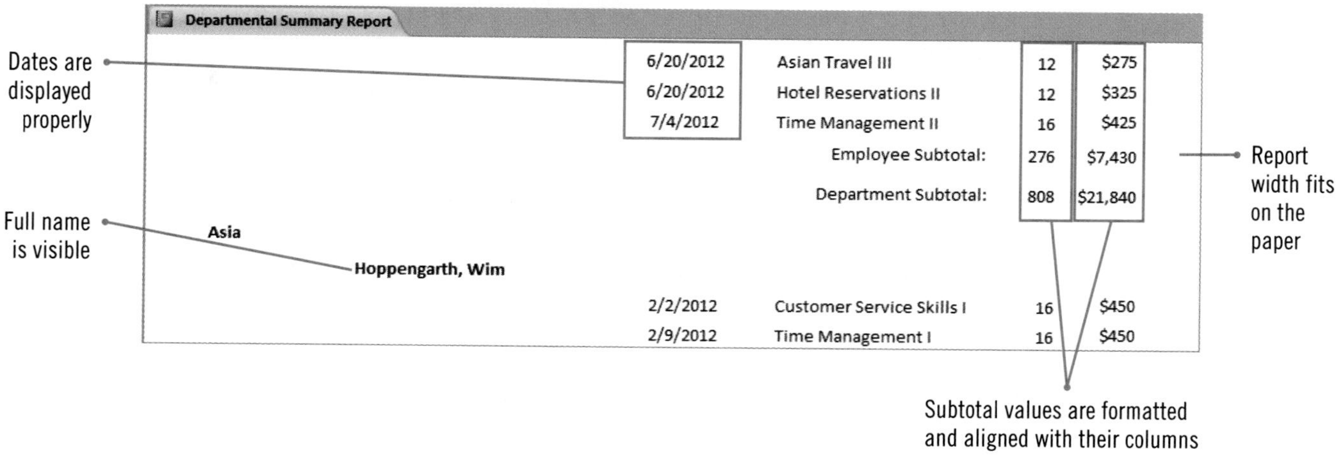

UNIT
L
Access 2010

Controlling Layout

Layout in Access forms and reports refers to connecting controls as a set so that when you move or resize them in Layout or Design View, the action you take on one control applies to all controls in the group. When you create a report using the Report button or Report Wizard, many of the controls are automatically grouped together in a layout. To productively work in Report Design View, you may need to remove the layout of existing controls or group controls in new layouts for your own purposes. Jacob Thomas asks you to create a new employee listing report.

STEPS

1. **Click the Employees table in the Navigation Pane, click the Create tab, click the Report button, then close the Property Sheet if it is open**
   The Report button creates a report on the selected table or query and displays it in Layout View. Controls that are grouped together in the same layout can be resized easily in Layout View.
2. **Click Dawson in the ELast column, use ↔ to drag the right edge of the column to the left, click Ron in the EFirst column, use ↔ to drag the right edge of the column to the left, and continue resizing the columns so that they all fit within the right border of the report as shown in Figure L-4**
   Controls in the same layout move to provide space for the control you are moving. You move the EFirst column to the first column of the report.
3. **Click Ron in the EFirst column, point to the middle of the text box and use ✥ to drag the column to the left of Dawson in the ELast column, click the EFirst label, use ✥ to drag the label to the left of the ELast label, click the blank column placeholder, then press [Delete]**
   To individually move controls, you must remove the layout in Design View.
4. **Right-click the Employees tab, click Design View, click the EFirst label to select it, click the ✥ symbol in the upper-left corner of the EFirst label, click the Arrange tab, click the Remove Layout button, then click a blank spot on the report to deselect the controls**
   You open a Department Header section and move the Department text box to that section.
5. **Click the Design tab, click the Group & Sort button to open the Group, Sort, and Total pane, click the Add a group button, click Department, right-click the Department text box in the Detail section, click Cut, right-click the Department Header section, then click Paste**
   With the Department Header section in place, you make a few more modifications to the report to finish it.
6. **Click the Department label in the Page Header section, press [Delete], move the Page expression in the Page Footer section to the left, then drag the right edge of the report as far left as possible as shown in Figure L-5**
   For now, you decide to connect the ELast and EFirst controls together in a layout so they can be moved and resized as a group.
7. **Click the EFirst label in the Page Header section, press and hold [Shift], click the EFirst text box in the Detail section, click the ELast label in the Page Header section, click the ELast text box in the Detail section, release [Shift], click the Arrange tab, click the Tabular button in the Table group, then drag the four controls to the right to fill the blank space**
   See Table L-1 for more information on layouts you can apply to a group of selected controls. You might also notice other formatting embellishments you would like to make at a later time, but for now, save, preview, and close the report.
8. **Click the Save button on the Quick Access toolbar, click OK to accept Employees as the report name, right-click the Employees report tab, click Print Preview to review the Employees report, then close it**
   Advanced sizing, moving, formatting, and aligning skills are at the heart of report design.

TROUBLE

The ✥ might be superimposed on the ELast label.

FIGURE L-4: **Resizing controls in the same layout in Report Layout View**

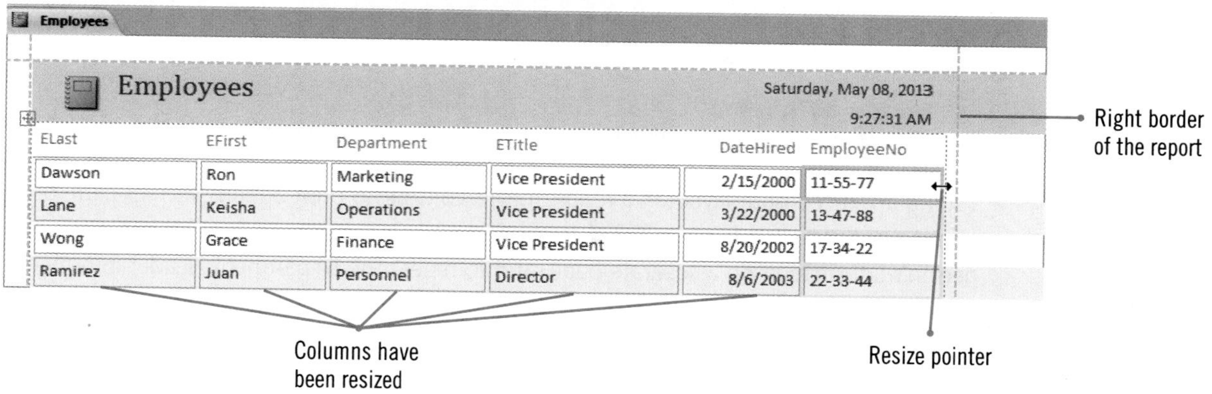

FIGURE L-5: **Working with individual controls in Report Design View**

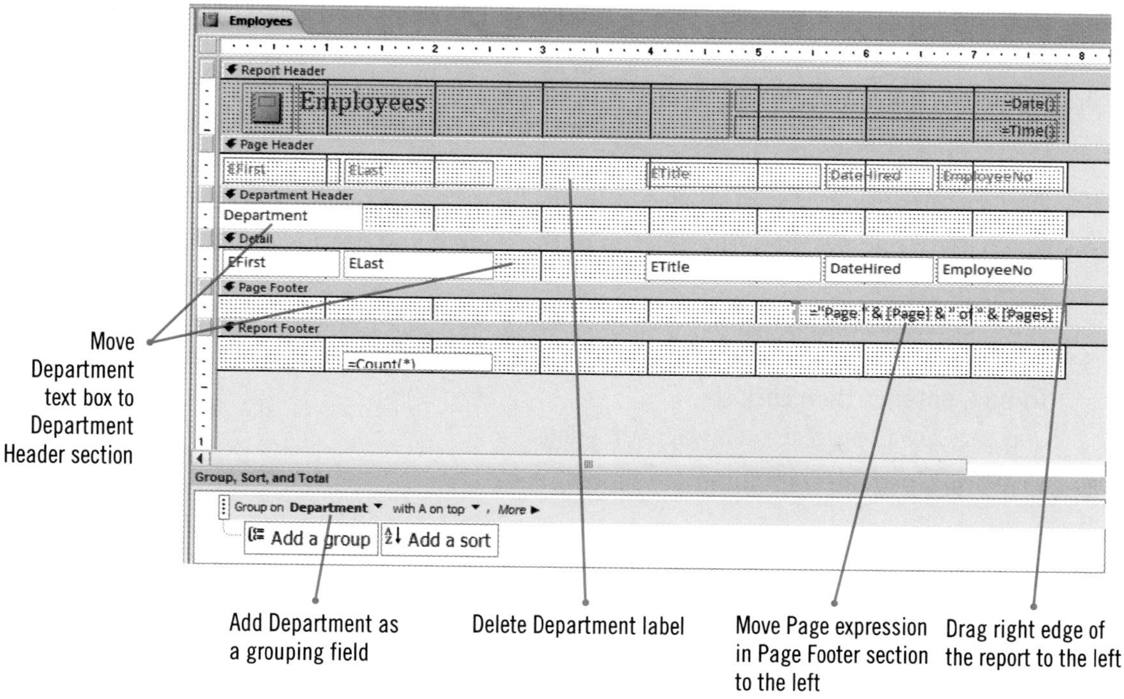

TABLE L-1: **Layouts**

layout	description
Stacked	Labels are positioned to the left of the text box; most often used in forms
Tabular	Labels are positioned across the top in the Page Header section forming columns of data with text boxes positioned in the Detail section; most often used in reports

UNIT
L
Access 2010

Setting Advanced Print Layout

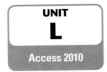

Setting advanced print layout in a report means controlling print options such as page breaks, margins, or printing only selected pages. In the Departmental Summary Report, Jacob asks you to print each person's information on a separate page, and to repeat the Department Header information at the top of each page.

STEPS

1. **Right-click the DeptSummary report in the Navigation Pane, click Design View, double-click the Department Header section bar to open its Property Sheet, double-click the Repeat Section property to change the property from No to Yes, then double-click the Force New Page property to change the property from None to Before Section as shown in Figure L-6**
   The controls in the Department Header section will now repeat at the top of every page.
2. **Click the EmployeeNo Header section bar, click the Force New Page property list arrow, then click Before Section**
   Access will format the report with a page break before each EmployeeNo Header. This means each employee's records will start printing at the top of a new page.
3. **Right-click the DeptSummary report tab, click Print Preview, click the One Page button in the Zoom group, then use the navigation buttons to move through the pages of the report**
   Previewing multiple pages helps you make sure that the department name repeats at the top of every page, that each new department starts on a new page, and that each employee starts on a new page.
4. **Navigate to page 2, then click the top of the page if you need to zoom in as shown in Figure L-7**
   To print only page 2 of the report, you use the Print dialog box.
5. **Click the Print button on the Print Preview tab, click the From box, enter 2, click the To box, enter 2, then click OK**
   Only page 2 of a 24-page report is sent to the printer.
6. **Save and close the DeptSummary report**

QUICK TIP
If you want your name to be on the report, enter it as a label in the Page Footer section.

FIGURE L-6: **Working with section properties in Report Design View**

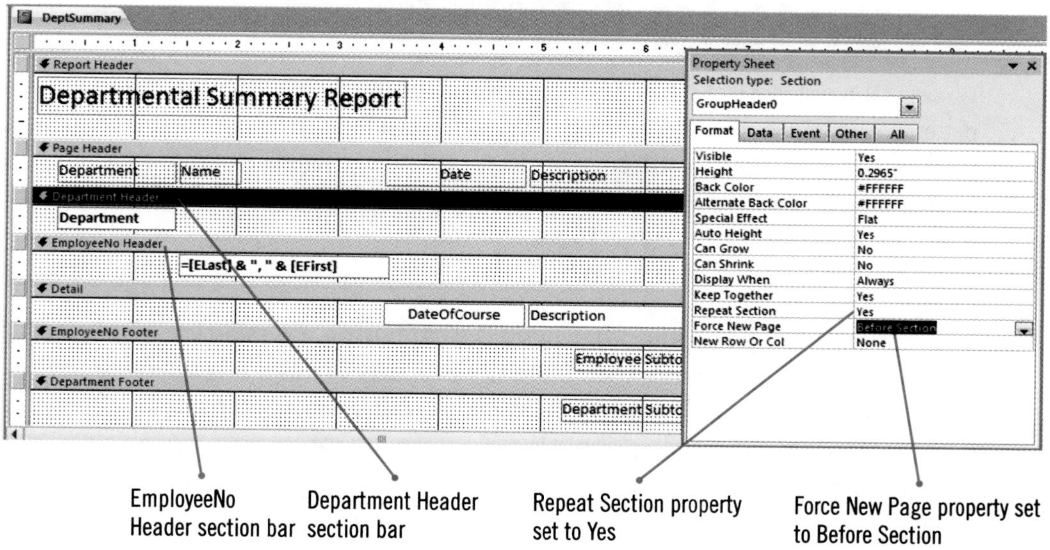

FIGURE L-7: **Previewing the final Departmental Summary Report**

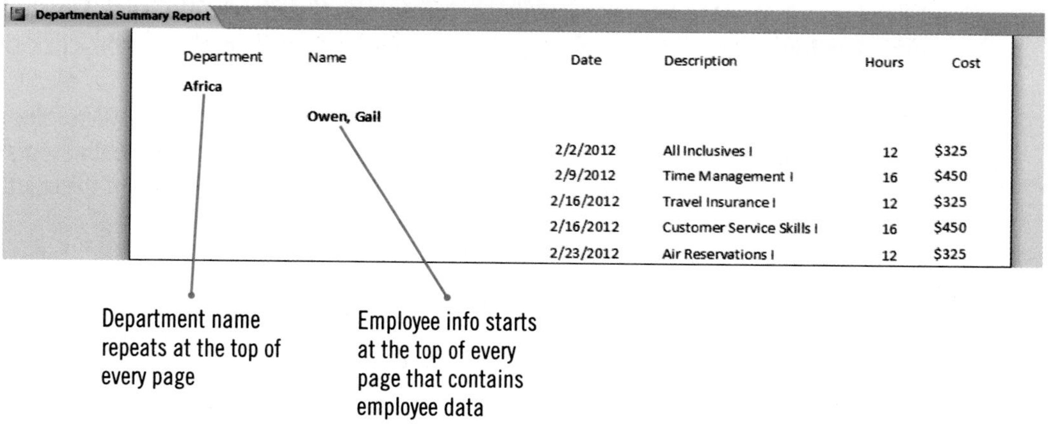

UNIT L

Access 2010

Creating Charts

Charts, also called graphs, are visual representations of numeric data that help users see comparisons, patterns, and trends in data. Charts can be inserted on a form or report. Access provides a **Chart Wizard** that helps you create the chart. Common **chart types** that determine the presentation of data on the chart such as column, pie, and line are described in Table L-2. Jacob wants you to create a chart of the total number of course registrations by department.

STEPS

1. **Click the Create tab, click the Query Design button, double-click Employees, double-click Enrollments, click Close, then close the Property Sheet if it is open**
   The first step in creating a chart is to select the data that the chart will graph.
2. **Double-click Department in the Employees field list, double-click EnrollmentID in the Enrollments field list, save the query with the name DepartmentEnrollments, then close it**
   You build a chart on a report from this query. Charts can be added to forms or reports.
3. **Click the Create tab, click the Report Design button, click the More button in the Controls group, click the Chart button in the Controls group, then click in the Detail section of the report as shown in Figure L-8**
   The Chart Wizard starts by asking which table or query holds the fields you want to add to the chart, and then asks you to select a chart type.
4. **Click the Queries option button, click Next to choose the DepartmentEnrollments query, click the Select All Fields button >>, click Next, click Next to accept Column Chart, then drag the EnrollmentID field from the Series area to the Data area as shown in Figure L-9**
   The **Data area** determines what data the chart graphs. If you drag a Number or Currency field to the Data area, the Chart Wizard automatically sums the values in the field. For Text or AutoNumber fields (such as EnrollmentID), the Chart Wizard automatically counts the values in that field.
5. **Click Next, type Department Enrollment Totals as the chart title, click Finish, use ↖↘ to drag the lower-right corner of the chart to fill the Detail section, right-click the Report1 tab, then click Print Preview**
   When charts are displayed in Design View or Layout View, they appear as a generic Microsoft chart placeholder. The chart should look similar to Figure L-10. The chart is beginning to take shape, but some of the labels on the x-axis may not have room to display all of their text depending on the size of the chart. You'll enhance this chart in the next lesson.

TABLE L-2: Common chart types

chart type	chart icon	used to show most commonly	example
Column		Comparisons of values (vertical bars)	Each vertical bar represents the annual sales for a different product for the year 2013
Bar		Comparisons of values (horizontal bars)	Each horizontal bar represents the annual sales for a different product for the year 2013
Line		Trends over time	Each point on the line represents monthly sales for one product for the year 2013
Pie		Parts of a whole	Each slice represents total quarterly sales for a company for the year 2013
Area		Cumulative totals	Each section represents monthly sales by representative, stacked to show the cumulative total sales effort for the year 2013

FIGURE L-8: Inserting a chart on a report

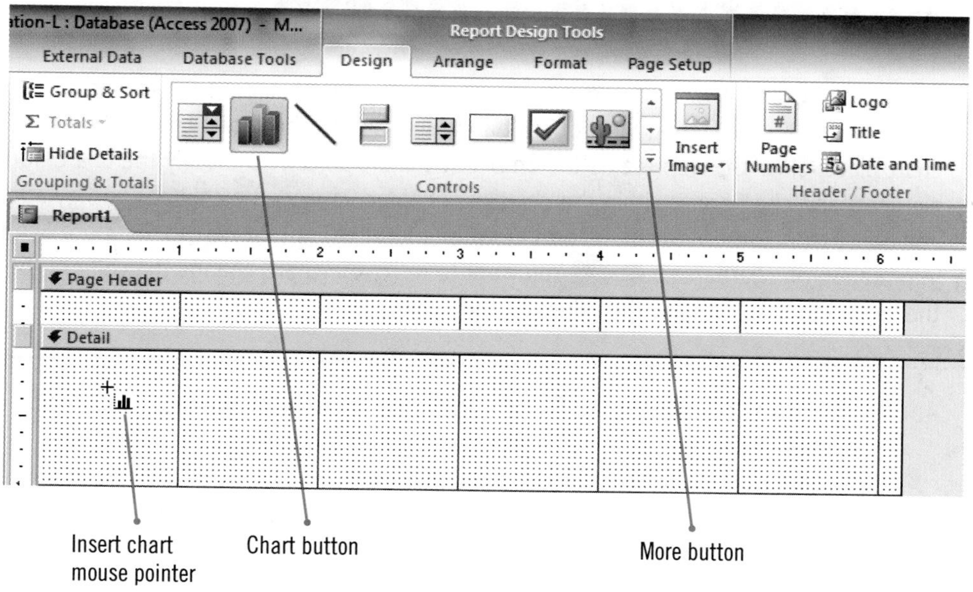

FIGURE L-9: Choosing the chart areas

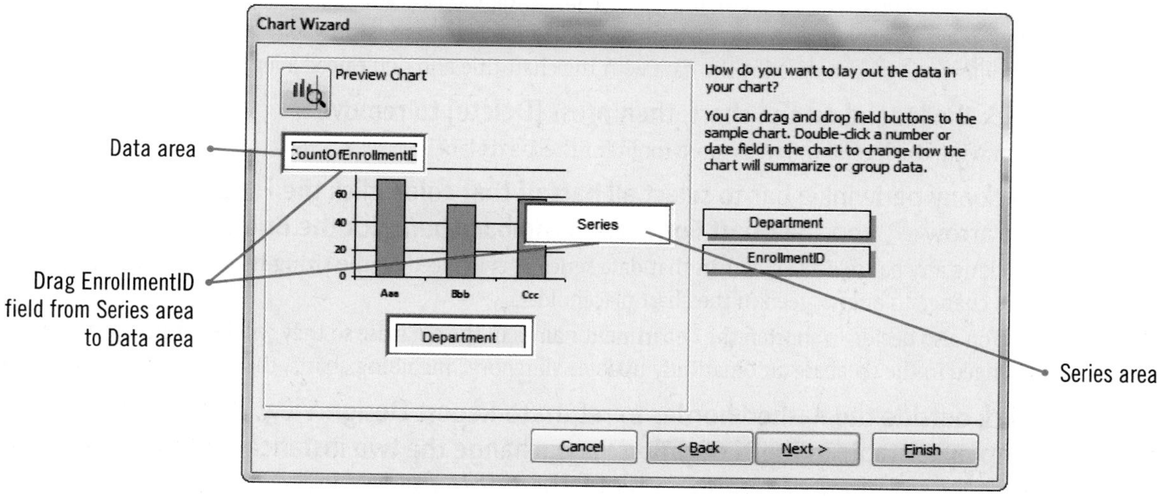

FIGURE L-10: Department Enrollment Totals column chart

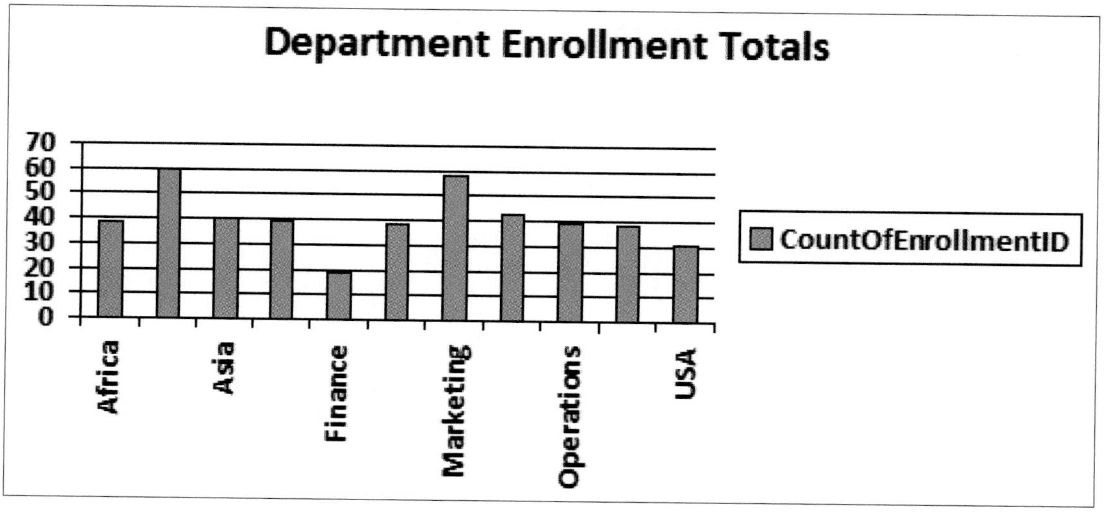

Access 2010

UNIT L

Access 2010

Modifying Charts

You modify charts in Design View of the form or report that contains the chart. Modifying a chart is challenging because Design View doesn't always show you the actual chart values, but instead, displays a chart placeholder that represents the embedded chart object. To modify the chart, you modify the chart elements and chart areas within the chart placeholder. To view the changes as they apply to the real data you are charting, return to either Form View for a form or Print Preview for a report. See Table L-3 for more information on chart areas. You want to resize the chart, change the color of the bars, and remove the legend to better display the values on the x-axis.

STEPS

1. **Right-click the report, click Design View, then close the Group, Sort, and Total pane if it is open**

   To make changes to chart elements, you open the chart in edit mode by double-clicking it. Use **edit mode** to select and modify individual chart elements such as the title, legend, bars, or axes. If you double-click the edge of the chart placeholder, you open the Property Sheet for the chart instead of opening the chart itself in edit mode.

2. **Double-click the chart**

   The hashed border of the chart placeholder control indicates that the chart is in edit mode, as shown in Figure L-11. The Chart Standard and Chart Formatting toolbars also appear when the chart is in edit mode. They may appear on one row instead of stacked. Given there is only one series of bars that count the enrollments, you can describe the data with the chart title and don't need a legend.

3. **Click the legend on the chart, then press [Delete] to remove it**

   Removing the legend provides more room for the x-axis labels.

4. **Click any periwinkle bar to select all bars of that color, click the Fill Color button list arrow on the Chart Formatting toolbar, then click the Bright Green box**

   Clicking any bar selects all bars in that data series as evidenced by the sizing handle in each of the bars. The bars change to bright green in the chart placeholder.

   You also decide to shorten the department names in the database so they will better fit on the x-axis. Data changed in the database automatically updates all reports, including charts, that are based on that data.

5. **Click outside the hashed border to return to Report Design View, double-click the Employees table in the Navigation Pane, change the two instances of Information Systems to IS in the Department field, then close the Employees table**

   Preview the updated chart.

6. **Save the report as DepartmentChart, then display it in Print Preview**

   The final chart is shown in Figure L-12.

TROUBLE

If you make a mistake, use the Undo button on the Chart Standard toolbar.

TROUBLE

If you can't see the Fill Color button on the Formatting toolbar, drag the left edge of the toolbars to position them on two rows to show all buttons.

TROUBLE

If you are prompted that the report width is greater than the page width, return to Report Design View and resize the chart and right edge of the report to fit within a width of 8".

FIGURE L-11: **Editing a chart placeholder**

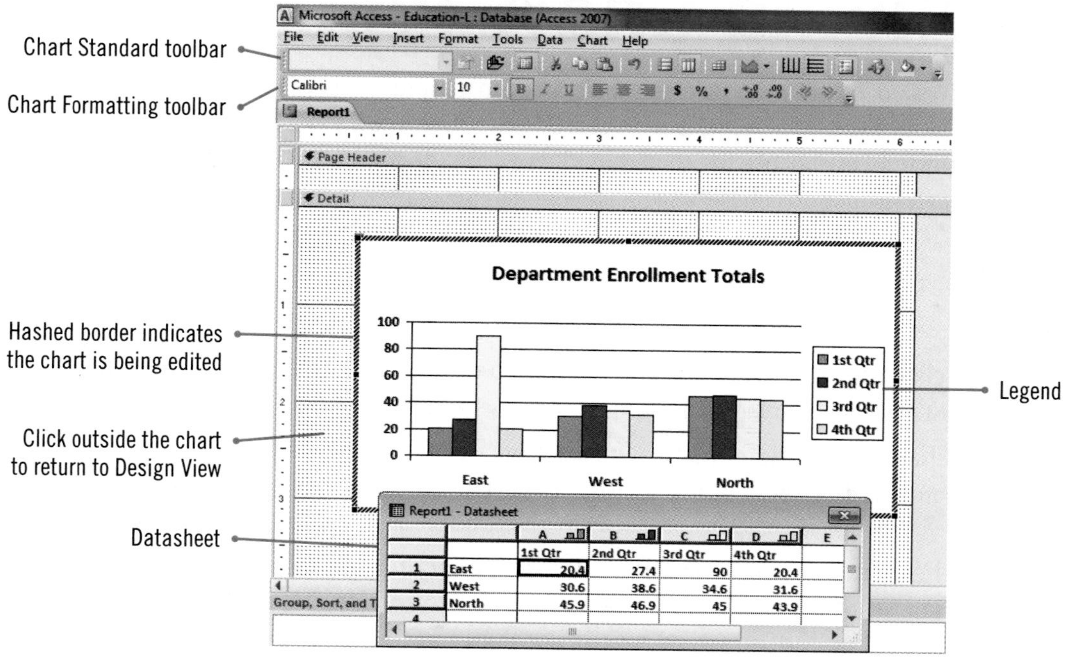

FIGURE L-12: **Final Department Enrollment Totals column chart**

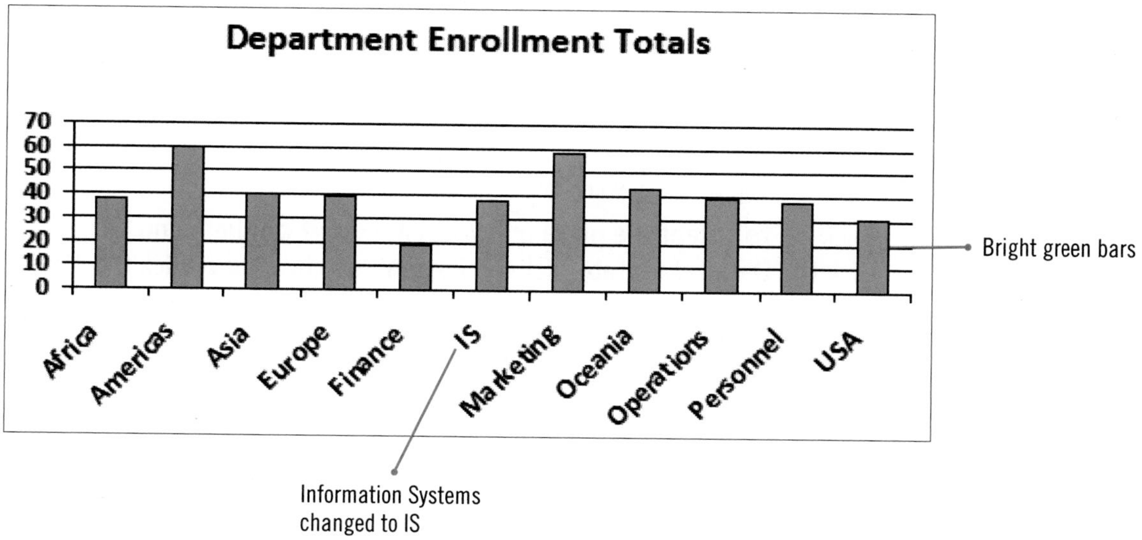

TABLE L-3: **Chart areas**

chart area	description
Data	Determines what field the bars (lines, wedges, etc.) on the chart represent
Axis	The x-axis (horizontal axis) and y-axis (vertical axis) on the chart
Series	Displays the legend when multiple series of data are graphed

UNIT
L
Access 2010

Applying Chart Types

The Chart Wizard provides 20 different chart types to choose from. While column charts are the most popular, you can also use line, area, and pie charts to effectively show some types of data. Three-dimensional effects can be used to enhance the chart, but those effects can also make it difficult to compare the sizes of bars, lines, and wedges, so choose a three-dimensional effect only if it does not detract from the point of the chart. You change the existing column chart to other chart types and subtypes to see how the data is presented.

STEPS

1. **Right-click the chart, click Design View, then double-click the chart placeholder**
   You must open the chart in edit mode to change the chart type.
2. **Click Chart on the menu bar, then click Chart Type**
   The Chart Type dialog box opens as shown in Figure L-13. All major chart types plus many chart subtypes are displayed. A button is available to preview any choice before applying that chart subtype.
3. **Click the Clustered column with a 3-D visual effect button (second row, first column in the Chart sub-type area), click and hold the Press and Hold to View Sample button, click the 3-D Column button (third row, first column in the Chart sub-type area), then click and hold the Press and Hold to View Sample button**
   A Sample box opens, presenting a rough idea of what the final chart will look like. While 3-D charts appear more interesting than 2-D chart types, the samples do not show the data more clearly, so you decide to preview other 2-D chart types.
4. **Click the Bar Chart type in the Chart type list, click and hold the Press and Hold to View Sample button, click the Line Chart type in the Chart type list, click and hold the Press and Hold to View Sample button, click the Pie Chart type in the Chart type list, click and hold the Press and Hold to View Sample button, click the Default formatting check box, then click and hold the Press and Hold to View Sample button**
   Because this chart only has one set of values that represent 100% of all enrollments, the data fits a pie chart. Other chart options help you enhance pie charts.
5. **Click OK to accept the pie chart type, click Chart on the menu bar, click Chart Options, click the Data Labels tab, click the Percentage check box, click the Titles tab, click the Chart title box, type Enrollment % by Dept, click the Legend tab, make sure the Show legend check box is selected, then click OK**
   With the modifications made to change the chart into a pie chart, you view it in Print Preview to see the final result.
6. **Click outside the hashed border to return to Report Design View, then display the report in Print Preview**
   The same departmental data, expressed as a pie chart, is shown in Figure L-14. The title of the chart is Enrollment % by Dept, but the name of the report is still DepartmentChart.
7. **Save and close the DepartmentChart report**

FIGURE L-13: **Chart Type dialog box**

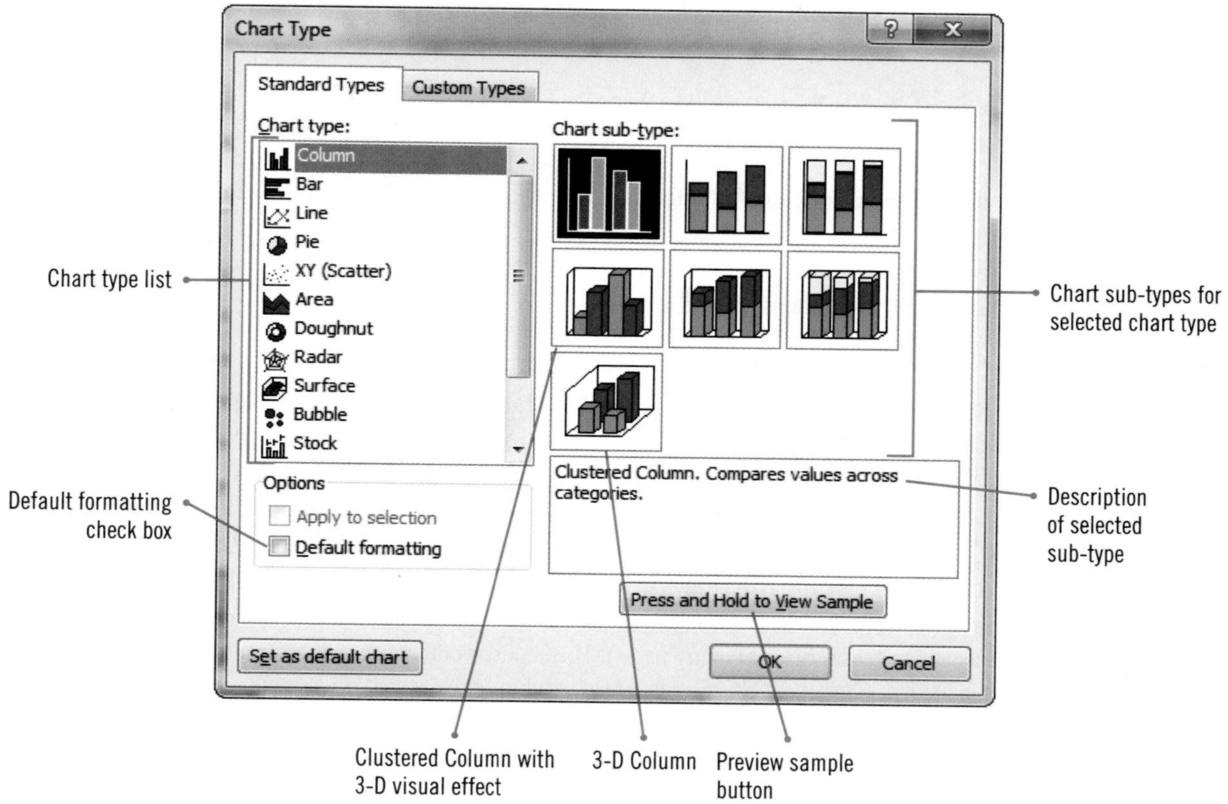

FIGURE L-14: **Department Enrollment Totals pie chart**

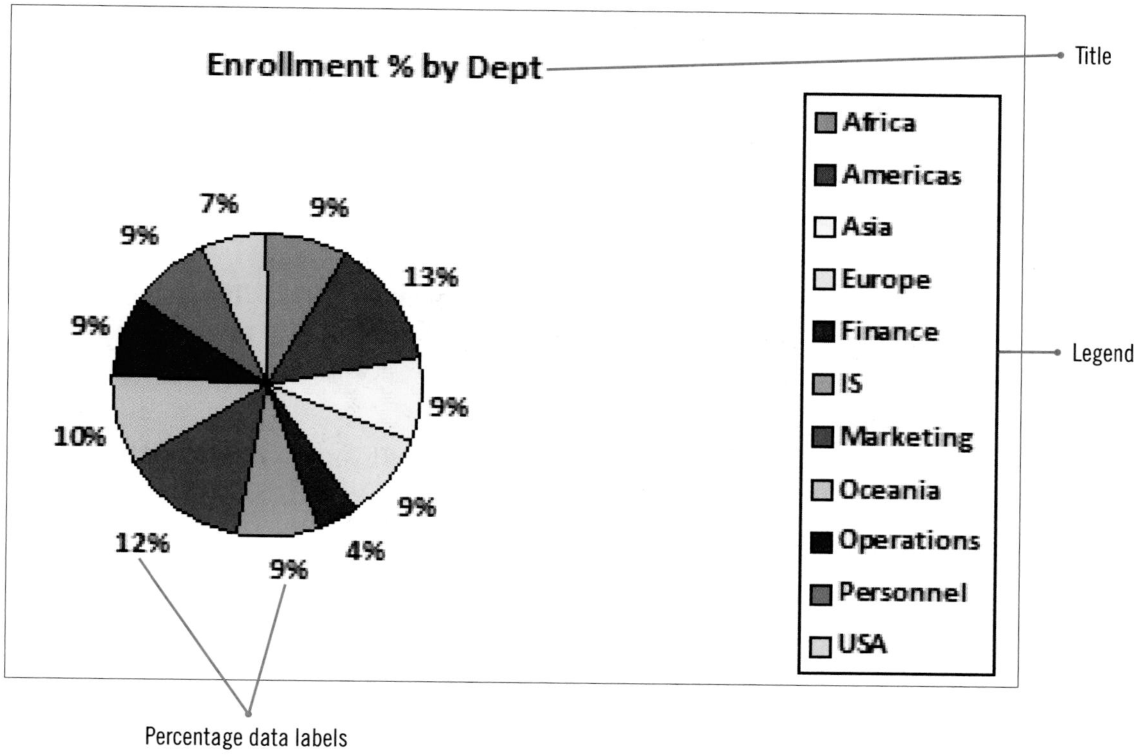

Creating Multicolumn Reports

A **multicolumn report** repeats information in more than one column on the page. To create multiple columns, you use options in the Page Setup dialog box. Samantha asks you to create a report that shows employee names sorted in ascending order for each course. A report with only a few fields is a good candidate for a multicolumn report.

STEPS

1. **Click the Create tab, click the Report Wizard button, click the Tables/Queries list arrow, click Table:Courses, double-click Description, click the Tables/Queries list arrow, click Table: Employees, double-click EFirst, double-click ELast, click Next, click Next to view the data by Courses, click Next to bypass adding any more grouping levels, click the first sort list arrow, click ELast, click Next, click Stepped, click Landscape, click Next, type Attendance List for the title, click Finish, then click the Last Page button**

   The initial report is displayed in Print Preview as a 19- or 20-page report (or twice that long if the report is too wide, which causes twice as many pages). This report would work well as a multicolumn report because only three fields are involved. You also decide to combine the names into a single expression with the employee's full name. First, delete the existing EFirst and ELast controls.

2. **Right-click the report, click Design View, click the ELast label, press [Delete], click the EFirst label, press [Delete], click the ELast text box, press [Delete], click the EFirst text box, press [Delete], click the Page expression text box in the Page Footer section, press [Delete], then drag the right edge of the report as far to the left as possible**

   You add a new text box to the Detail section with an expression that contains both the first and last names.

3. **Click the Text Box button in the Controls group, click at about the 1" mark of the Detail section to insert a new text box control, then delete the accompanying label**

4. **Click the Unbound text box to select it, click Unbound, type =[ELast]&", "&[EFirst], press [Enter], widen the new control to about 2" wide, right-click the Attendance List report tab, then click Print Preview**

   With the information clearly presented in a single, narrow column, you're ready to specify that the report print multiple columns.

5. **Click the Page Setup button, click the Columns tab, click the Number of Columns box, type 3, then click the Down, then Across option button as shown in Figure L-15**

   The content of the report is now set to print in three newspaper-style columns.

6. **Click OK**

   The final Attendance List report is shown in Figure L-16. By specifying that the report is three columns wide, the number of pages in the report is significantly reduced.

7. **Save and close the Attendance List report**

FIGURE L-15: Page Setup dialog box

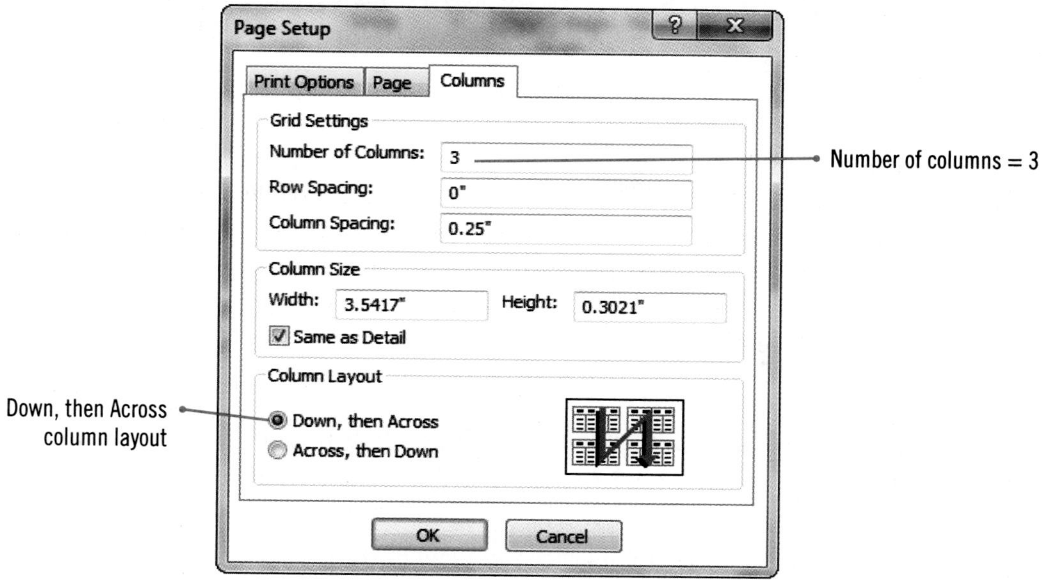

FIGURE L-16: Attendance List report in three columns

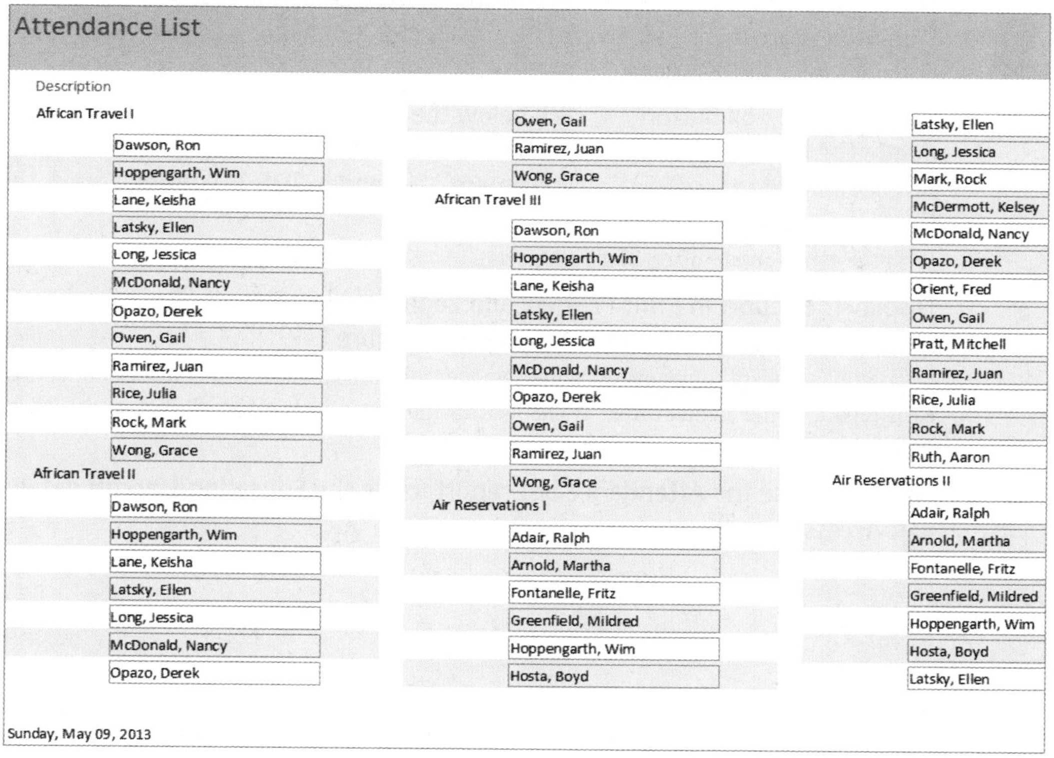

UNIT L

Access 2010

Using Domain Functions

Domain functions, also called domain aggregate functions, are used in an expression to calculate a value based on a field that is not included in the Record Source property for the form or report. Domain functions start with a "D" for "domain" such as DSum, DAvg, or DCount, and perform the same calculation as their Sum, Avg, and Count counterparts. Domain functions have two required arguments: the field that is used for the calculation and the domain name. The **domain** is the table or query that contains the field used in the calculation. A third optional argument allows you to select given records based on criteria you specify. Jacob asks you to add a standard disclaimer to the bottom of every report. This is an excellent opportunity to use the DLookup function.

STEPS

1. **Click the Create tab, click the Table Design button, then build a new table with the fields, data types, primary key field, and table name shown in Figure L-17**
   With the Disclaimers table established, you add two records of standard text used at Quest Specialty Travel.

2. **Save the Disclaimers table, click the View button, then enter the two records shown in Figure L-18**
   The first disclaimer is used with any report that contains employee information. The second is to be added to all internal reports that do not contain employee information. With the data in place, you're ready to use the DLookup function on a report to insert standard text.

3. **Save and close the Disclaimers table, right-click the Attendance List report in the Navigation Pane, click Design View, then use ✛ to drag the top of the Report Footer section down to expand the Page Footer section to about twice its current size**
   With added space in the Page Footer for a new control, you can now add a text box to return the correct disclaimer using the DLookup function.

4. **Click the Text Box button, click below the Now() text box in the Page Footer section, delete the label, click the text box to select it, click Unbound, type the expression =DLookup("[StandardText]","Disclaimers", "[StandardID]=1"), press [Enter], then widen the text box to about 3"**
   With the expression in place, you'll preview it.

5. **Display the report in Print Preview and zoom and scroll to the Page Footer to view the result of the DLookup function as shown in Figure L-19**
   By entering standard company disclaimers in one table, the same disclaimer text can be consistently added to each report. If the standard text is changed in the Disclaimers table, all reports would be automatically updated as well.

6. **Save and close the Attendance List report, close the Education-L.accdb database, then exit Access**

TROUBLE

Widen the StandardText column as needed to view all text.

TROUBLE

If you see an #Error message in the Page Footer, return to Report Design View and double-check your expression.

QUICK TIP

If you want your name to be on the report when you print it, enter your name as a label in the Page Footer section.

FIGURE L-17: New Disclaimers table

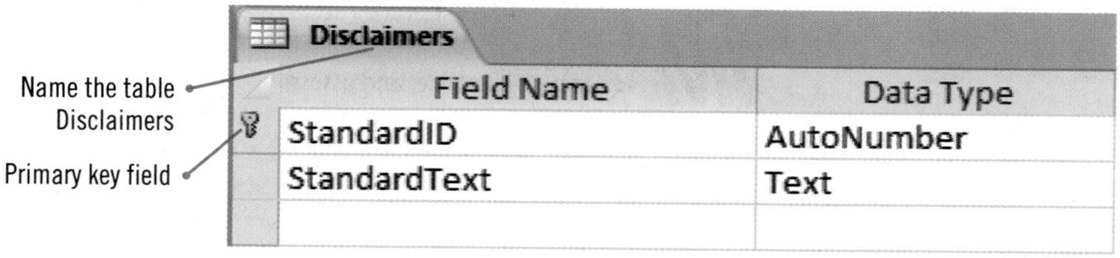

FIGURE L-18: Records in the Disclaimers table

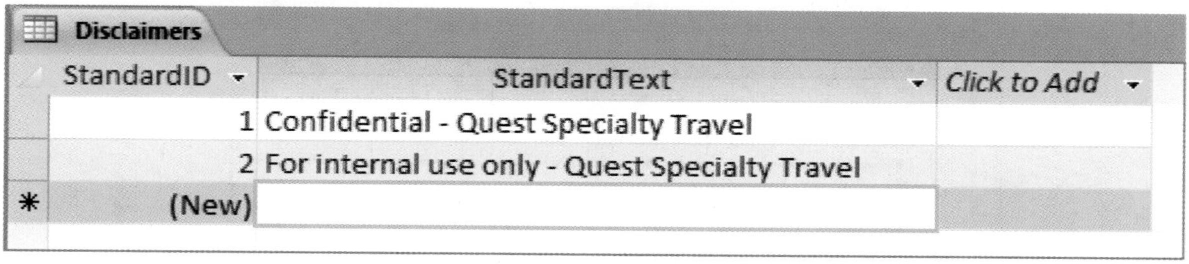

Access 2010

FIGURE L-19: Standard disclaimer in Report Footer section

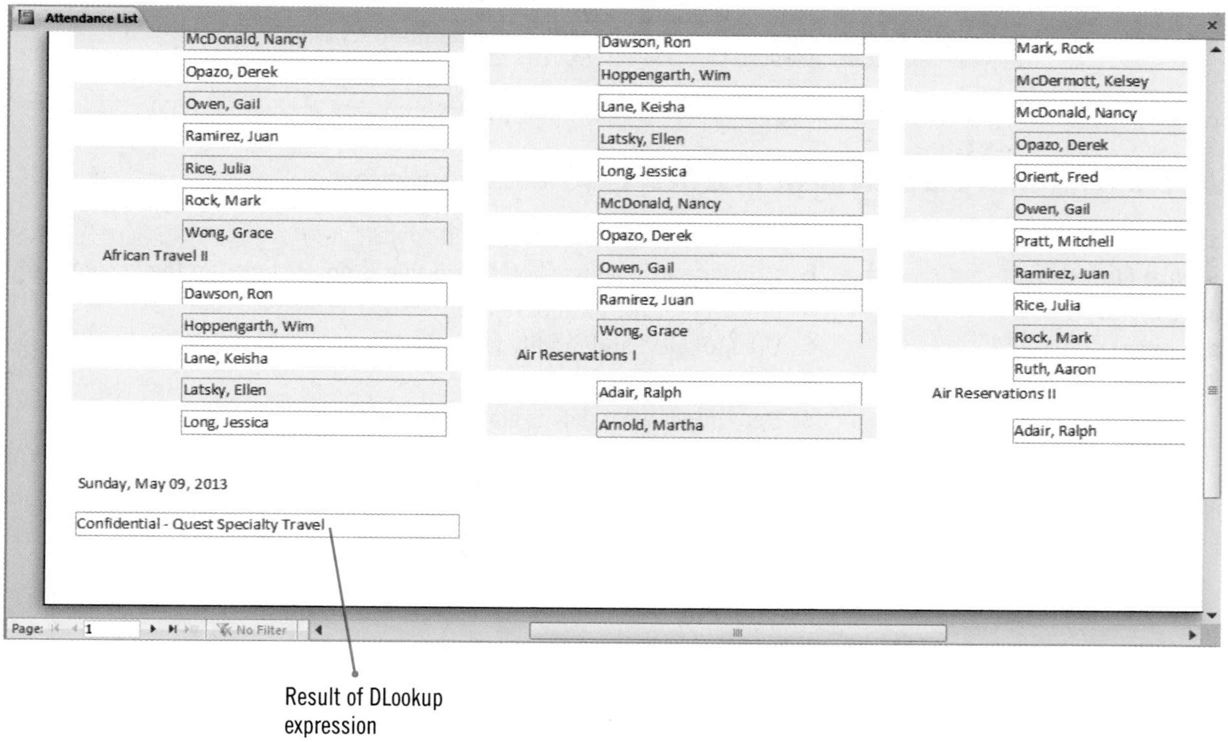

Practice

Concepts Review

For current SAM information, including versions and content details, visit SAM Central (http://www.cengage.com/samcentral). If you have a SAM user profile, you may have access to hands-on instruction, practice, and assessment of the skills covered in this unit. Since various versions of SAM are supported throughout the life of this text, check with your instructor for the correct instructions and URL/Web site for accessing assignments.

Identify each element of the Report Design View shown in Figure L-20.

FIGURE L-20

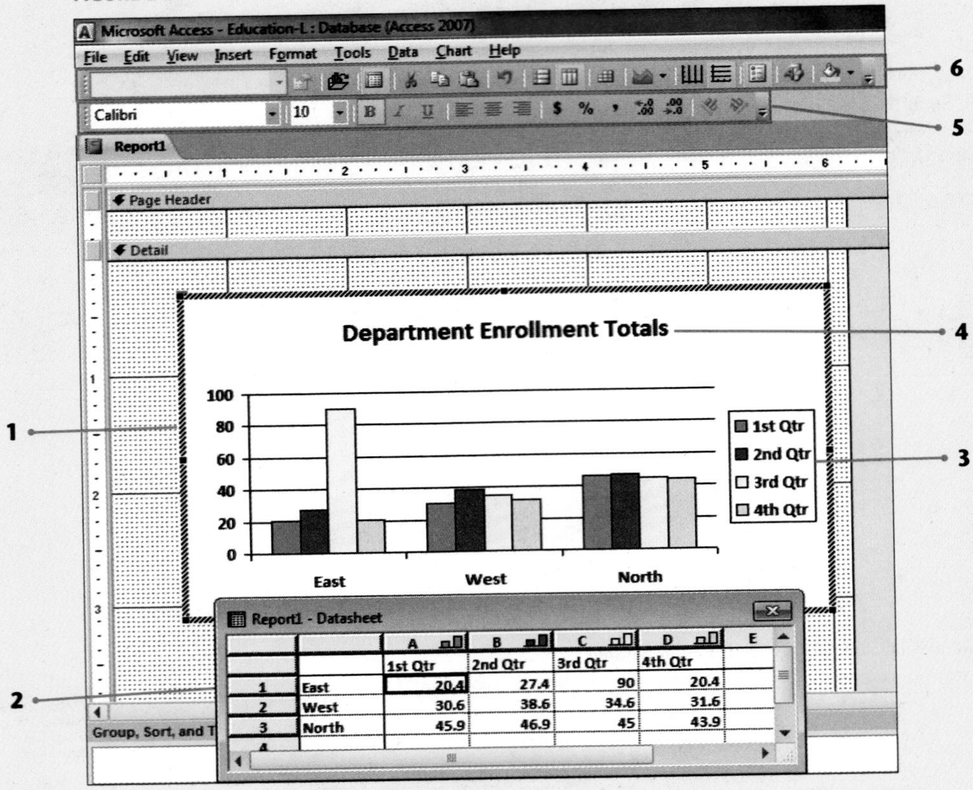

Match each term with the statement that best describes its function.

7. **Charts**
8. **Domain functions**
9. **Chart types**
10. **Data area**
11. **Edit mode**

a. Visual representations of numeric data
b. Calculate a value based on a field that is not included in the Record Source property for the form or report
c. Used to select and modify individual chart elements such as the title, legend, bars, or axes
d. Determines what data is graphed on the chart
e. Determine the presentation of data on the chart such as column, pie, and line

Select the best answer from the list of choices.

12. Which button aligns the edges of two or more selected controls?

- **a.** Align Text Right button on the Arrange tab
- **b.** Align button on the Arrange tab
- **c.** Align Text Right button on the Design tab
- **d.** Align button on the Design tab

13. To set a page break before a Group Header section on a report, you would modify the properties of the:

- **a.** Report.
- **b.** Group Header section.
- **c.** Detail section.
- **d.** Page Footer section.

14. Which control layout is common for reports?

- **a.** Stacked
- **b.** Tabular
- **c.** Datasheet
- **d.** Gridlines

15. Which dialog box allows you to specify the number of columns you want to view in a report?

- **a.** Print
- **b.** Columns
- **c.** Page Setup
- **d.** Property Sheet

16. Which type of chart is best to show an upward sales trend over several months?

- **a.** Column
- **b.** Pie
- **c.** Line
- **d.** Scatter

17. Which task can be performed on a chart *without* being in edit mode?

- **a.** Modifying the title
- **b.** Deleting the legend
- **c.** Changing bar colors
- **d.** Resizing the chart

18. Which chart area determines the field that the bars (lines, wedges, etc.) on the chart represent?

- **a.** Data
- **b.** X-axis
- **c.** Category
- **d.** Legend

19. Which chart area is used to identify the legend?

- **a.** Data
- **b.** X-axis
- **c.** Y-axis
- **d.** Series

20. Which chart type is best at showing cumulative totals?

- **a.** Column
- **b.** Area
- **c.** Bar
- **d.** Pie

21. Which chart type is best at showing parts of a whole?

- **a.** Column
- **b.** Area
- **c.** Bar
- **d.** Pie

Skills Review

1. Apply advanced formatting.

- **a.** Start Access, then open the RealEstate-L.accdb database from the drive and folder where you store your Data Files. Enable content if prompted.
- **b.** Preview the AgencyListings report, noting the format for the SqFt and Asking fields.
- **c.** In Report Design View, change the Format property for the SqFt text box in the Detail section to **Standard** and change the Decimal Places property to **0**.
- **d.** In Report Design View, change the Format property for the Asking text box in the Detail section to **Currency** and change the Decimal Places property to **0**.
- **e.** Preview the report to make sure your SqFt values appear with commas, the Asking values appear with dollar signs, and neither shows any digits to the right of the decimal place.

2. Control layout.

- **a.** Open the AgencyListings report in Design View.
- **b.** Open the Group, Sort, and Total pane, and open the AgencyName Footer section.
- **c.** Add a text box in the AgencyName Footer under the SqFt text box in the Detail section with the expression **=Sum([SqFt])**. Modify the new label to have the caption **Subtotals:**.

Skills Review (continued)

- **d.** Add a text box in the AgencyName Footer under the Asking text box in the Detail section with the expression **=Sum([Asking])**. Delete the extra label in the AgencyName Footer section.
- **e.** Format the text boxes using the Property Sheet, and align the text boxes under the fields they subtotal so that Print Preview looks similar to Figure L-21.

3. Set advanced print layout.

- **a.** Open the AgencyListings report in Design View.
- **b.** Modify the AgencyName Footer section to force a new page after that section prints.
- **c.** Preview the report to make sure each of the four agencies prints on its own page.
- **d.** Close and save the AgencyListings report.

FIGURE L-21

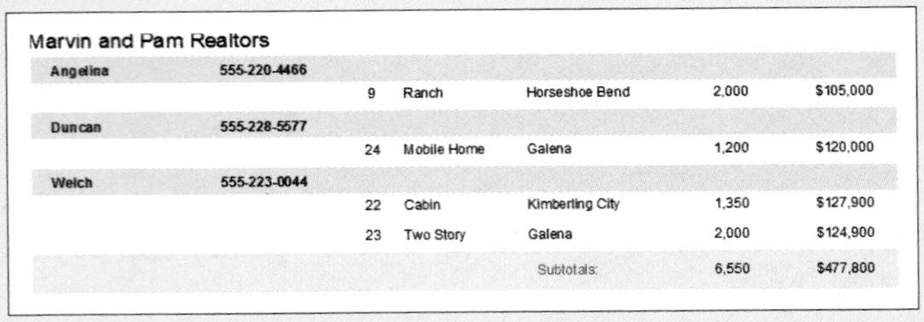
Marvin and Pam Realtors

Angelina	555-220-4466					
		9	Ranch	Horseshoe Bend	2,000	$105,000
Duncan	555-228-5577					
		24	Mobile Home	Galena	1,200	$120,000
Welch	555-223-0044					
		22	Cabin	Kimberling City	1,350	$127,900
		23	Two Story	Galena	2,000	$124,900
				Subtotals:	6,550	$477,800

4. Create charts.

- **a.** Open the Inventory query in Query Design View, then add criteria to select only the Ranch (in the Type field) records.
- **b.** Save the query with a new name as **RanchHomes**, then close it.
- **c.** Start a new report in Report Design View.
- **d.** Insert a chart in the Detail section based on the RanchHomes query.
- **e.** Choose the RLast and Asking fields for the chart, choose a Column Chart, then make sure the SumOfAsking field appears in the Data area, and move the RLast field from the Axis to the Series area.
- **f.** Title the chart **Ranch Inventory**, then preview the report to view the chart.
- **g.** Save the report with the name **RanchInventoryReport**.

5. Modify charts.

- **a.** Return to Report Design View, double-click the chart to open it in edit mode, then remove the legend.
- **b.** Double-click the y-axis values to open the Format Axis dialog box, click the Number tab, then choose the Currency format from the Category list, entering **0** for the Decimal places.
- **c.** Change the color of the periwinkle bars to red.
- **d.** Click the By Column button on the Chart Standard toolbar to switch the fields in the x-axis and legend positions.
- **e.** Return to Report Design View, then switch to Print Preview. Resize the chart as necessary so it looks like Figure L-22.

6. Apply chart types.

- **a.** Close the report, then copy and save the report with the name **RanchInventoryReport3D**.
- **b.** Switch to Report Design View, open the chart in edit mode, then change the chart type to a Clustered column with a 3-D visual effect.
- **c.** Switch between Report Design View and Print Preview, resizing the chart as needed so that all of the labels on the x-axis are displayed clearly.
- **d.** Print RanchInventoryReport3D if requested by your instructor, then save and close it.

FIGURE L-22

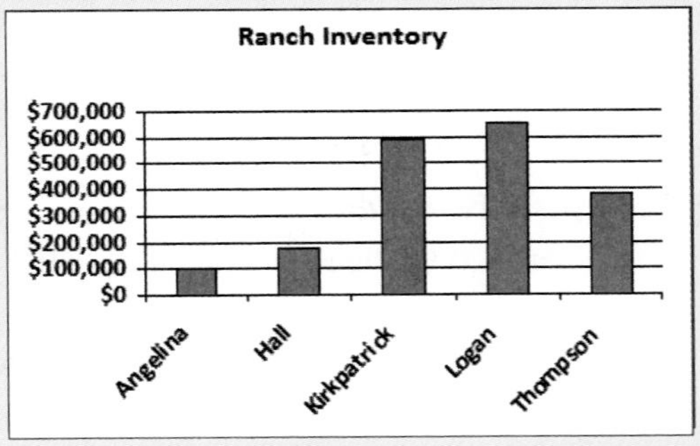

7. Create multicolumn reports.

- **a.** Use the Report Wizard to create a report with the AgencyName field from the Agencies table, the RFirst and RLast fields from the Realtors table, and the Type field from the Listings table. Be sure to select the fields from the table objects.
- **b.** View the data by Listings, add AgencyName as the grouping level, sort the records in ascending order by RLast, use a Stepped layout and a Landscape orientation, and use **Listings** as the report title.
- **c.** In Report Design View, delete the RLast and RFirst labels and text boxes.

Skills Review (continued)

- **d.** Delete the page expression in the Page Footer section, delete the Type label in the Page Header section, and delete the AgencyName label in the Page Header section. Move the Type field in the Detail section to the left to just under the AgencyName text box.
- **e.** Add a new text box to the right of the Type control in the Detail section with the following expression: **=[RLast]&", "&[RFirst]**
- **f.** Delete the label for the new text box, then widen the =[RLast]&", "&[RFirst] text box in the Detail section to be about 2" wide. Drag the right edge of the report as far as you can to the left so that the report is approximately 5" wide.
- **g.** Preview the report, and use the Page Setup dialog box to set the Number of Columns setting to **2** and the column layout to Down, then Across. It should look like Figure L-23. If you want your name to appear on the printout, change the name of Tom Hall to your own name in the Realtors table.
- **h.** Save and close the Listings report.

FIGURE L-23

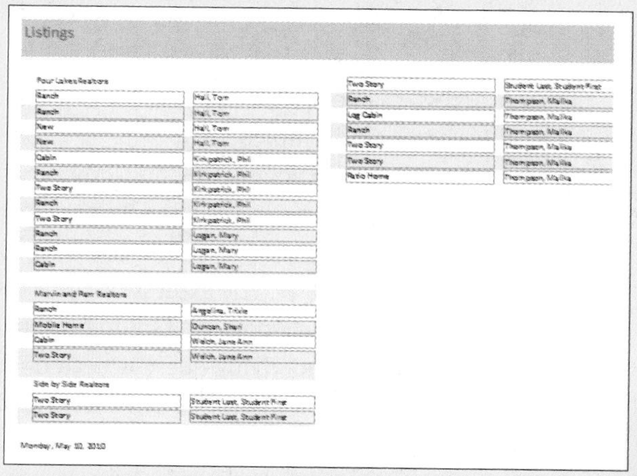

8. Use domain functions.

- **a.** Create a new table named **Legal** with two new fields: **LegalID** with an AutoNumber data type and **LegalText** with a Memo data type. Make LegalID the primary key field.
- **b.** Add one record to the table with the following entry in the LegalText field: **The realtor makes no guarantees with respect to the accuracy of the listing.** Widen the column of the LegalText field as needed. Note the value of the LegalID field for the first record, then save and close the Legal table.
- **c.** Open the ListingReport in Design View, expand the Page Footer section to about 0.5", then use a DLookup function in an expression in a text box in the Page Footer section to look up the LegalText field in the Legal table as follows: **=DLookup("[LegalText]","Legal", "LegalID=1")**. Delete the accompanying label. (Note that the number in the expression must match the value of the LegalID field for the first record that you created in Step b.)
- **d.** Preview the report, then review the Page Footer. Switch back and forth between Report Design View and Print Preview to fix and widen the text box to be about 8" wide so that it clearly displays the entire expression, then save and close the ListingReport.
- **e.** Open the Legal table, and modify the LegalText in the first record to read: The realtor **and agency make** no guarantees with respect to the accuracy of the listing.
- **f.** Preview the ListingReport again to observe the Page Footer, then print the report if requested by your instructor.
- **g.** Close the RealEstate-L.accdb database and exit Access 2010.

Independent Challenge 1

As the manager of a college women's basketball team, you want to enhance a form within the Basketball-L.accdb database to chart the home versus visiting team scores. You will build on your report creation skills to do so.

- **a.** Start Access, then open the database Basketball-L.accdb from the drive and folder where you store your Data Files. Enable content if prompted.
- **b.** Open and then maximize the GameInfo form. Page down through several records as you observe the Home and Visitor scores.
- **c.** Open the form in Form Design View, then insert a chart on the right side of the form based on the Games table. Choose the HomeScore and OpponentScore fields for the chart. Choose a Column Chart type.
- **d.** Add both the HomeScore and OpponentScore fields to the Data area, double-click the SumOfHomeScore field, select None as the summarize option, double-click the SumOfOpponentScore field, then select None as the summarize option.
- **e.** Click Next and choose GameNo as the Form Field and as the Chart Field so that the chart changes from record to record showing the HomeScore versus the OpponentScore in the chart.

Independent Challenge 1 (continued)

f. Title the chart **Scores**, and do not display a legend.

g. Open the form in Form View, and print the record for GameNo 10 as shown in Figure L-24 if requested by your instructor. To insert your name on the printout, add it as a label to the Form Header section.

h. Save the GameInfo form, close it, close the Basketball-L.accdb database, and exit Access 2007.

FIGURE L-24

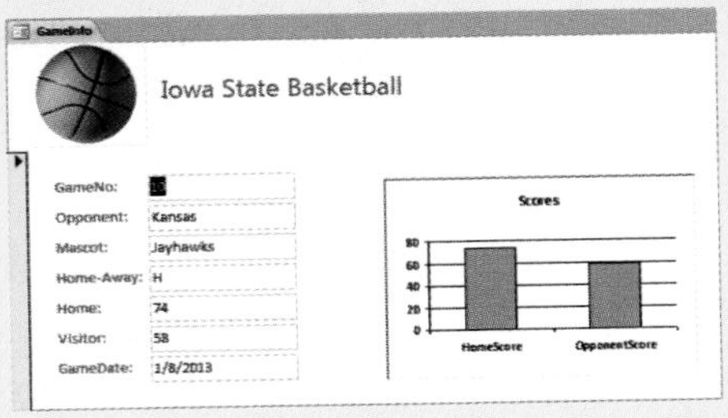

Independent Challenge 2

As the manager of a college women's basketball team, you want to build a report that shows a graph of total points per player per game.

a. Start Access, then open the database Basketball-L.accdb from the drive and folder where you store your Data Files. Enable content if prompted.

b. Open the PlayerStatistics report, and study the structure. Notice that this report has the total points per player you want to graph per game in the last column. Open the PlayerStatistics report in Report Design View.

c. Double-click the far-right text box in the Detail section, and click the Data tab in the Property Sheet to study the Control Source property. The expression =[FT]+([fg]*2)+([3p]*3) adds one-point free throws [FT] to two-point field goals [fg] to three-point three-pointers [3p] to find the player's total contribution to the score. You will calculate the total point value in the underlying query instead of on the report to make it easier to graph.

d. Click the report selector button, then click the Build button for the Record Source property, which currently displays the PlayerStats query. In the first blank column add a new field with the following expression: **TotalPts:[FT]+([fg]*2)+([3p]*3)**.

e. Save and close the PlayerStats query, then return to Design View for the PlayerStatistics report. Open the Property Sheet for the GameNo Footer section. On the Format tab, change the Force New Page property to After Section.

f. Drag the top of the Page Footer section bar down so the height of the GameNo Footer section is about 3 inches high, then insert a chart just below the existing controls in the GameNo Footer section.

g. In the Chart Wizard, choose the PlayerStats query to create the chart, choose the LastName and TotalPts fields for the chart, and choose the Column Chart type.

h. Use SumOfTotalPts in the Data area and the LastName field in the Axis area (which should be the defaults). Choose <No Field> to link the Report Fields and Chart Fields, and title the chart **Player Total Points**.

i. Widen the chart placeholder and report to be about 6" wide in Report Design View, delete the legend, then save and preview the report. The chart should look like Figure L-25.

j. Save the PlayerStatistics report, add your name as a label to the Report Header section, print the first page, then close the report.

k. Close the Basketball-L.accdb database, and exit Access 2010.

FIGURE L-25

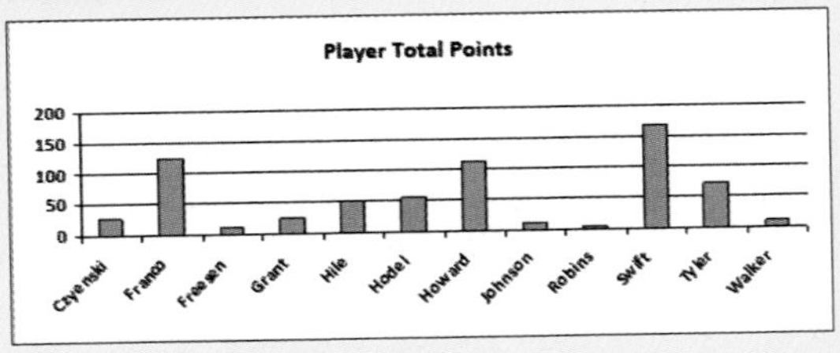

Independent Challenge 3

As the manager of a college women's basketball team, you want to create a multicolumn report from the Basketball-L.accdb database to summarize total points per game per player.

a. Start Access, then open the database Basketball-L.accdb from the drive and folder where you store your Data Files. Enable content if prompted.

b. Open the PlayerStats query in Design View. In the first blank column add a new field with the following expression (if it has not already been added): **TotalPts:[FT]+([fg]*2)+([3p]*3)**.

c. Save and close the PlayerStats query.

d. Create a new report using the Report Wizard from the PlayerStats query with the fields **Opponent**, **GameDate**, **LastName**, and **TotalPts**. View the data by Games, do not add any more grouping levels, then sort the records in descending order by TotalPts.

Independent Challenge 3 (continued)

e. Click the Summary Options button, then click the Sum check box for the TotalPts field.
f. Choose a Stepped layout and a Landscape orientation. Title the report **Point Production**, and preview it.
g. In Report Design View delete the long text box with the Summary expression in the GameNo Footer section.
h. Delete the LastName and TotalPts labels from the Page Header section.
i. Delete the page expression in the Page Footer section, then move the TotalPts and LastName text boxes in the Detail section to the left. Move any other text boxes to the left so that no control extends beyond the 4" mark on the horizontal ruler.
j. Drag the right edge of the report to the left, so that it is no wider than 4", then right-align text boxes with the subtotal for total points in the GameNo Footer and the Report Footer sections. Right-align the values within their respective controls as well. Also move and right-align the Sum and Grand Total labels closer to the text boxes they describe.
k. Preview the report, and in the Page Setup dialog box, set the report to **2** columns, and specify that the column layout go down, then across.

Advanced Challenge Exercise

ACE

- In Design View, improve the report by adding a horizontal line across the bottom of the GameNo Footer section to separate the records from game to game.
- For the GameNo Footer section, change the New Row or Col property to After Section.
- Add other formatting improvements as desired.

l. Preview the Point Production report. It should structurally look like Figure L-26. Print the first page of the report if requested by your instructor, adding your name as a label to the Report Header section if needed for the printout.
m. Close the Point Production report, close the Basketball-L.accdb database, then exit Access.

FIGURE L-26

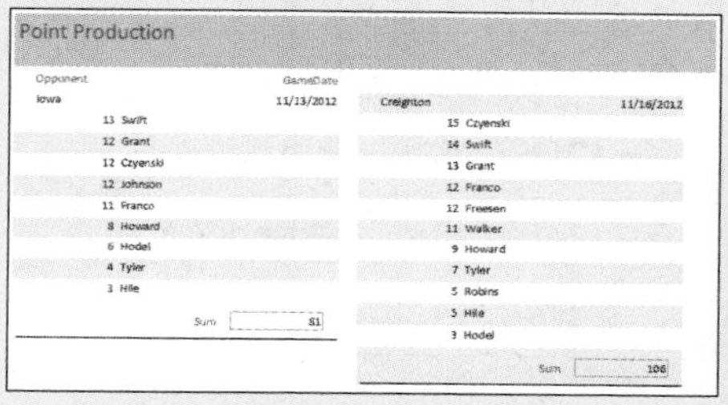

Real Life Independent Challenge

In your quest to become an Access database consultant, you want to know more about the built-in Microsoft Access templates and what you can learn about report design from these samples. In this exercise, you'll explore the reports of the Sales pipeline template.

a. Start Access 2010, then select the Sales Pipeline template from the Sales & Marketing folder. (You may find the Sales Pipeline template in the Samples folder.) Use the Browse button to specify the drive and folder where you store your Data Files, name the database **Sales**, then click Download.
b. Expand the Navigation Pane to review the objects in the database.
c. Briefly open then close each object in the Opportunities, Employees, and Customers navigation sections to study the structure of the available forms and reports. Close all open objects.
d. Open the Employees table in the Supporting Objects section, and enter your name in the Last Name and First Name fields. Enter fictitious but realistic data in the other fields. Close the Employees table.
e. Open the Customers table in the Supporting Objects section, and enter your teacher's name with other fictitious data in the first record. Close the Customers table.
f. Open the Opportunities table in the Supporting Objects section, and add a record with the title **Big Sale** entering appropriate but fictitious values in the fields. Add two more records to the Opportunities table choosing your teacher as the customer, yourself as the employee, but varying the choices in the other fields. Choose fictitious categories (1), (2), and (3) for the Category field. Close the Opportunities datasheet.
g. Open the Forecast Tracking Charts form in the Opportunities section to see how the information is being tracked. Click the Assigned To list arrow, then choose your name. Click each of the four tabs in the lower part of the form to see how the information from the Opportunity records in this database is presented.
h. If requested to print the form, add your name as a label to the Report Header section, print the form, close the Forecast Tracking Charts form, close the Sales.accdb database, and exit Access 2010.

Visual Workshop

As the manager of a college women's basketball team, you need to create a report from the Basketball-L.accdb database that lists information about each game played and subtracts the OpponentScore from the HomeScore field to calculate the number of points by which the game was won or lost in the Win/Loss column. Use the Report Wizard to start the report. Base it on the Games table, and sort the records in ascending order on the GameDate field. Use Report Layout and Design View to move, resize, align, modify, and add controls as necessary to match Figure L-27. If requested to print the report, add your name as a label to the Report Header section before printing.

FIGURE L-27

Iowa State Basketball

Game Date	Opponent	Mascot	Home-Away	Home	Opponent	Win/Loss
11/13/2012	Iowa	Hawkeyes	A	81	65	16
11/16/2012	Creighton	Bluejays	H	106	60	46
11/23/2012	Northern Illinois	Huskies	H	65	60	5
11/30/2012	Louisiana Tech	Red Raiders	A	69	89	-20
12/11/2012	Drake	Bulldogs	H	80	60	20
12/19/2012	Northern Iowa	Panthers	A	38	73	-35
12/29/2012	Buffalo	Bulls	H	50	55	-5
1/1/2013	Oklahoma	Sooners	A	53	60	-7
1/4/2013	Texas	Longhorns	H	57	60	-3

UNIT
M
Access 2010

Creating Macros

Files You Will Need:

Technology-M.accdb
Basketball-M.accdb
Patients-M.accdb
Chocolate-M.accdb

A **macro** is a database object that stores Access actions. **Actions** are the tasks that you want the macro to perform. When you run a macro, you execute the stored set of actions. Access provides over 80 actions from which to choose when creating a macro. Repetitive Access tasks such as printing several reports, or opening and maximizing a form, are good candidates for a macro. Automating routine tasks by using macros builds efficiency, accuracy, and flexibility into your database. Kayla Green, the network administrator at Quest Specialty Travel, has identified several Access tasks that are repeated on a regular basis. She has asked you to help her automate these processes with macros.

OBJECTIVES

- Understand macros
- Create a macro
- Modify actions and arguments
- Assign a macro to a command button
- Use If statements
- Work with events
- Create a data macro
- Troubleshoot macros

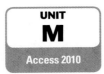

Understanding Macros

A macro object may contain one or more actions, the tasks that you want Access to perform. Actions are entered in **Macro Design View**, the window in which you build and modify macros. Each action has a specified set of arguments. **Arguments** provide additional information on how to carry out the action. For example, the OpenForm action contains six arguments, including Form Name (identifies which form to open) and View (determines whether the form should be opened in Form View or Design View). After choosing the macro action you want, the associated arguments for the action automatically appear below the macro action. You decide to study the major benefits of using macros, macro terminology, and the components of the Macro Design View before building your first macro.

DETAILS

The major benefits of using macros include:

- Saving time by automating routine tasks
- Increasing accuracy by ensuring that tasks are executed consistently
- Improving the functionality and ease of use of forms by using macros connected to command buttons
- Ensuring data accuracy in forms by using macros to respond to data entry errors
- Automating data transfers such as collecting data from Outlook
- Creating your own customized user interface

Macro terminology:

- A **macro** is an Access object that stores a series of actions to perform one or more tasks.
- Macro Design View is the window in which you create a macro. Figure M-1 shows Macro Design View with an OpenForm action. See Table M-1 for a description of the Macro Design View components.
- Each task that you want the macro to perform is called an **action**.
- Arguments are properties of an action that provide additional information on how the action should execute.
- A **conditional expression** is an expression resulting in either a true or false answer that determines whether a macro action will execute. Conditional expressions are used in If statements.
- An **event** is something that happens to a form, window, toolbar, or control—such as the click of a command button or an entry in a field—that can be used to initiate the execution of a macro.
- A **submacro** is a collection of actions within a macro object that allows you to name and create multiple, separate macros within a single macro object.

FIGURE M-1: **Macro Design View with OpenForm action**

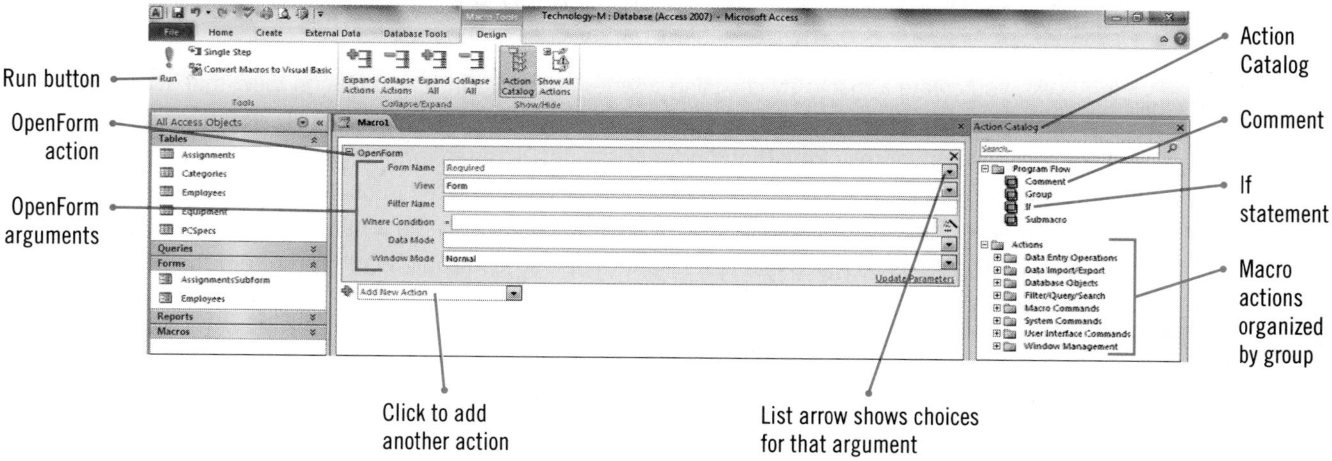
Run button
OpenForm action
OpenForm arguments
Action Catalog
Comment
If statement
Macro actions organized by group
Click to add another action
List arrow shows choices for that argument

TABLE M-1: **Macro Design View components**

component	description
Action Catalog	Lists all available macro actions organized by category. Use the Search box to narrow the number of macro actions to a particular subject.
If statement	Contains conditional expressions that are evaluated either true or false. If true, the macro action is executed. If false, the macro action is skipped. If statements in Access 2010 may contain Else If and Else clauses.
Comment	Allows you to document the macro with explanatory text.
Arguments	Lists required and optional arguments for the selected action.
Run button	Runs the selected macro.

UNIT
M
Access 2010

Creating a Macro

In Access, you create a macro by choosing a series of actions in Macro Design View that accomplishes the job you want to automate. Therefore, to become proficient with Access macros, you must be comfortable with macro actions. Some of the most common actions are listed in Table M-2. When you create a macro in other Microsoft Office products such as Word or Excel, you create Visual Basic for Applications (VBA) statements. In Access, macros do not create VBA code, but after creating a macro, you can convert it to VBA if desired. Kayla observes that users want to open the AllEquipment report from the Employees form, so she asks you to create a macro to help automate this task.

STEPS

1. **Start Access, open the Technology-M.accdb database from the drive and folder where you store your Data Files, enable content if prompted, click the Create tab, then click the Macro button**

   Macro Design View opens, ready for you to choose your first action.

> **TROUBLE**
> If you choose the wrong macro action, click the Delete button in the upper-right corner of the macro action block and try again.

2. **Click the first row's Action list arrow, type op to quickly scroll to the actions that start with the letters "op", then scroll and click OpenReport**

   The OpenReport action is now the first action in the macro, and the arguments that further define the OpenReport action appear in the action block. The **action block** organizes all of the arguments for a current action and is visually highlighted with a rectangle and gray background. You can expand or collapse the action block to view or hide details by clicking the Collapse/Expand button to the left of the action name or the Expand and Collapse buttons on the Design tab in Macro Design View.

   The **OpenReport** action has three required arguments: Report Name, View, and Window Mode. View and Window Mode have default values, but the word "Required" is shown in the Report Name argument indicating that you must select a choice. The Filter Name and Where Condition arguments are optional as indicated by their blank boxes.

3. **Click the Report Name argument list arrow, then click AllEquipment**

   All of the report objects in the Technology-M.accdb database appear in the Report Name argument list, making it easy to choose the report you want.

4. **Click the View argument list arrow, then click Print Preview**

   Your screen should look like Figure M-2. Macros can contain one or many actions. In this case, the macro has only one action.

5. **Click the Save button on the Quick Access toolbar, type PreviewAllEquipmentReport in the Macro Name text box, click OK, right-click the PreviewAllEquipmentReport macro tab, then click Close**

   The Navigation Pane lists the PreviewAllEquipmentReport object in the Macros group.

> **QUICK TIP**
> To print Macro Design View, click the File tab, click Print, click the Print button, then click OK in the Print Macro Definition dialog box.

6. **Double-click the PreviewAllEquipmentReport macro in the Navigation Pane to run the macro**

   The AllEquipment report opens in Print Preview.

7. **Close the AllEquipment report**

FIGURE M-2: **Macro Design View with OpenReport action**

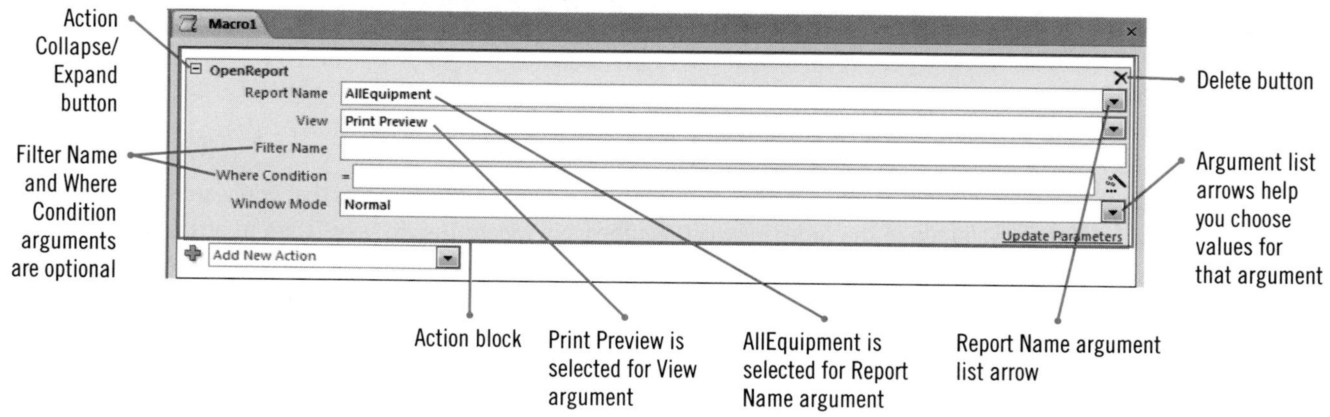

TABLE M-2: **Common macro actions**

subject area	macro action	description
Data Entry Operations	DeleteRecord	Deletes the current record
	SaveRecord	Saves the current record
Data Import/Export	ImportExportSpreadsheet	Imports or exports the spreadsheet you specify
	ImportExportText	Imports or exports the text file you specify
	EMailDatabaseObject	Sends the specified database object through Outlook with specified e-mail settings
Database Objects	OpenForm	Opens a form in Form View, Design View, Print Preview, or Datasheet View
	OpenQuery	Opens a select or crosstab query in Datasheet View, Design View, or Print Preview; runs an action query
	OpenReport	Opens a report in Design View or Print Preview, or prints the report
	OpenTable	Opens a table in Datasheet View, Design View, or Print Preview
	GoToControl	Moves the focus (where you are currently typing or clicking) to a specific field or control
	GoToRecord	Makes a specified record the current record
	SetValue	Sets the value of a field, control, or property
Filter/Query/Search	ApplyFilter	Restricts the number of records that appear in the resulting form or report by applying limiting criteria
	FindRecord	Finds the first record that meets the criteria
Macro Commands	RunCode	Runs a Visual Basic function (a series of programming statements that do a calculation or comparison and return a value)
	RunMacro	Runs a macro or attaches a macro to a custom menu command
	StopMacro	Stops the currently running macro
System Commands	Beep	Sounds a beep tone through the computer's speaker
	PrintOut	Prints the active object, such as a datasheet, report, form, or module
	SendKeys	Sends keystrokes directly to Microsoft Access or to an active Windows application
User Interface Commands	MessageBox	Displays a message box containing a warning or an informational message
	ShowToolbar	Displays or hides a given toolbar
Window Management	CloseWindow	Closes a window
	MaximizeWindow	Enlarges the active window to fill the Access window

Modifying Actions and Arguments

Macros can contain as many actions as necessary to complete the process that you want to automate. Each action is evaluated in the order in which it appears in Macro Design View, starting at the top. While some macro actions open, close, preview, or export data or objects, others are used only to make the database easier to use. **MessageBox** is a useful macro action because it displays an informational message to the user. You add a MessageBox action to the PrintAllEquipmentReport macro to display a descriptive message in a dialog box.

STEPS

1. **Right-click the PreviewAllEquipmentReport macro in the Navigation Pane, then click Design View on the shortcut menu**

   The PreviewAllEquipmentReport macro opens in Macro Design View.

2. **Click the Add New Action list arrow, type me to quickly scroll to the actions that start with the letters "me", then click MessageBox**

   Each action has its own arguments that further clarify what the action does.

3. **Click the Message argument text box in the action block, then type Click the Print button to print this report**

   The Message argument determines what text appears in the message box. By default, the Beep argument is set to "Yes" and the Type argument is set to "None".

4. **Click the Type argument list arrow in the action block, then click Information**

   The Type argument determines which icon appears in the dialog box that is created by the MessageBox action.

5. **Click the Title argument text box in the action block, then type To print this report. . .**

   Your screen should look like Figure M-3. The Title argument specifies what text is displayed in the title bar of the resulting dialog box. If you leave the Title argument empty, the title bar of the resulting dialog box displays "Microsoft Access."

6. **Save the macro, then click the Run button in the Tools group**

   If your speakers are turned on, you should hear a beep, then the message box appears, as shown in Figure M-4.

7. **Click OK in the dialog box, close the AllEquipment report, then save and close Macro Design View**

FIGURE M-3: **Adding the MessageBox action**

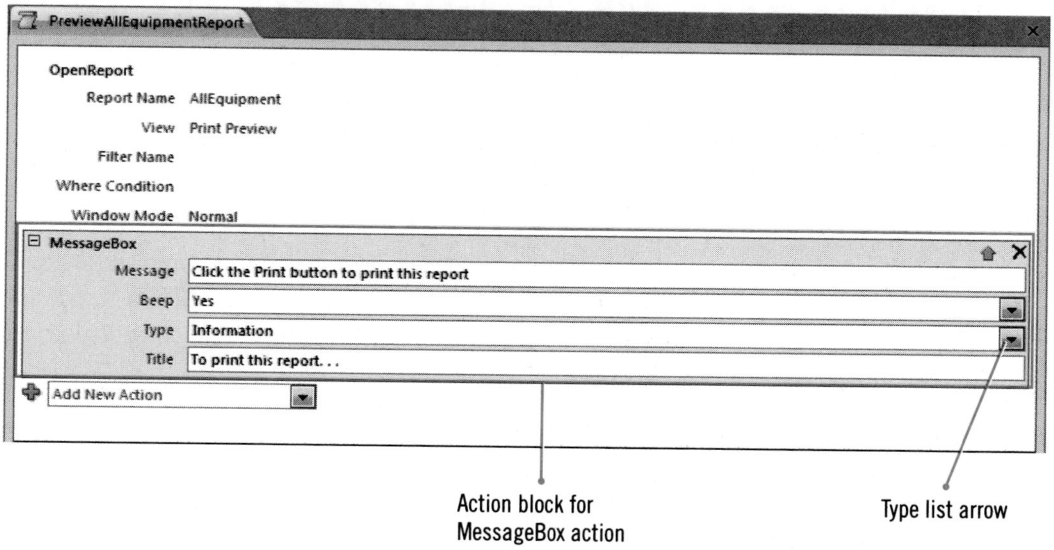

FIGURE M-4: **Dialog box created by MessageBox action**

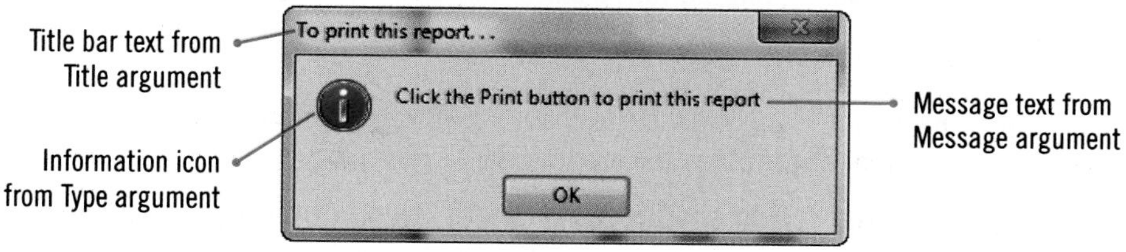

Assigning a macro to a key combination

You can assign a key combination such as [Ctrl][L] to a macro by creating a macro with the name **AutoKeys**. Enter the key combination in the Macro Names column for the first action of the associated macro. Any key combination assignments you make in the AutoKeys macro override those that Access has already specified. Therefore, check the Keyboard Shortcuts information in the Microsoft Access Help system to make sure that the AutoKey assignment that you are creating doesn't override an existing Access quick keystroke that may be used for another purpose.

UNIT M
Access 2010

Assigning a Macro to a Command Button

Access provides many ways to run a macro: clicking the Run button in Macro Design View, clicking the Run Macro button from the Database Tools tab, assigning the macro to a command button, or assigning the macro to a Ribbon or shortcut menu command. Assigning a macro to a command button on a form provides a very intuitive way for the user to access the macro's functionality. You decide to modify the Employees form to include a command button that runs the PreviewAllEquipmentReport macro.

STEPS

QUICK TIP
Be sure the Use Control Wizards button is selected. To find it, click the More button in the Controls group on the Design tab.

1. **Right-click the Employees form in the Navigation Pane, click Design View, expand the Form Footer about 0.5", click the Button button in the Controls group, then click the left side of the Form Footer section**

   The **Command Button Wizard** starts, presenting you with 28 actions on the right organized in 6 categories on the left. If you wanted the command button to open a report, you would choose the OpenReport action in the Report Operations category. In this case, however, you want to run the PreviewAllEquipmentReport macro, which not only opens a report but also presents a message. The Miscellaneous category contains an action that allows you to run an existing macro.

2. **Click Miscellaneous in the Categories list, click Run Macro in the Actions list as shown in Figure M-5, click Next, click PreviewAllEquipmentReport, click Next, click the Text option button, select Run Macro, type All Equipment Report, then click Next**

   The Command Button Wizard asks you to give the button a meaningful name.

3. **Type cmdAllEquipment, click Finish, then click the Property Sheet button in the Tools group to open the Property Sheet for the command button**

   The new command button that runs a macro has been added to the Employees form in Form Design View. Some developers give all controls three-character prefixes to make the control easier to identify in macros and VBA.

   You work with the Property Sheet to change the text color of the button to differentiate it from the button color as well as to examine how the macro was attached to the command button.

4. **Click the Format tab in the Property Sheet, scroll down and click the Fore Color list arrow, click Text Dark, then click the Event tab in the Property Sheet, noting that the On Click property contains [Embedded Macro]**

   The PreviewAllEquipment macro was attached to the **On Click property** of this command button. In other words, the macro is run when the user clicks the command button. To make sure that the new command button works as intended, you view the form in Form View and test the command button.

5. **Close the Property Sheet, click the View button to switch to Form View, click the All Equipment Report command button in the Form Footer section, click OK in the message box, then close the AllEquipment report**

   The Employees form with the new command button should look like Figure M-6. It's common to put command buttons in the Form Footer so that users have a consistent location to find them.

6. **Save and close the Employees form**

FIGURE M-5: **Adding a command button to run a macro**

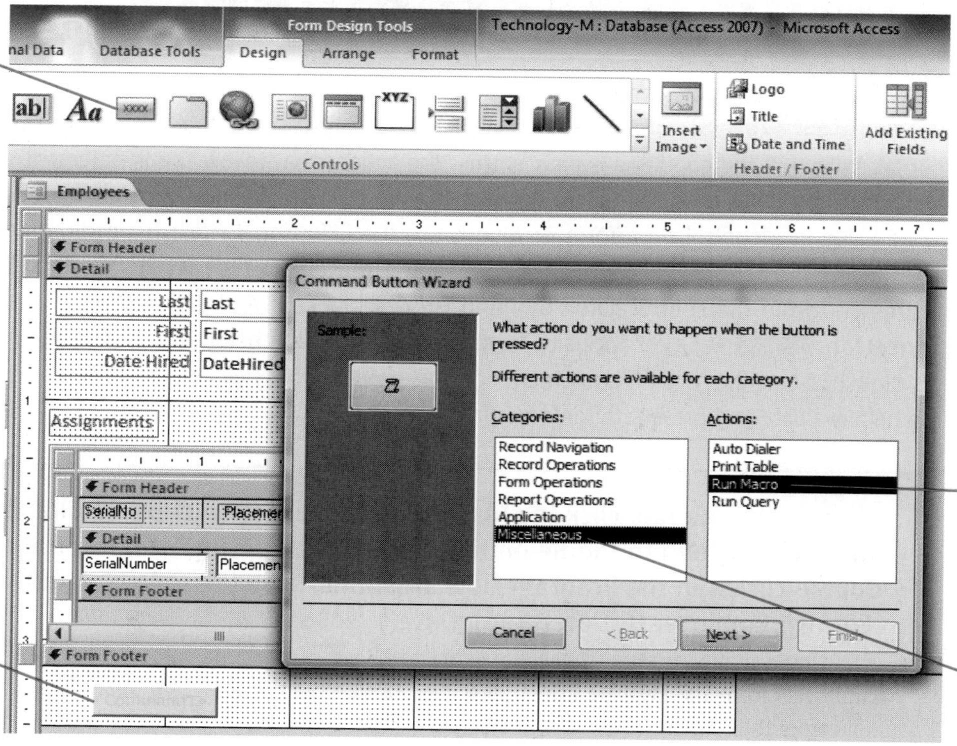

FIGURE M-6: **Employees form with new command button**

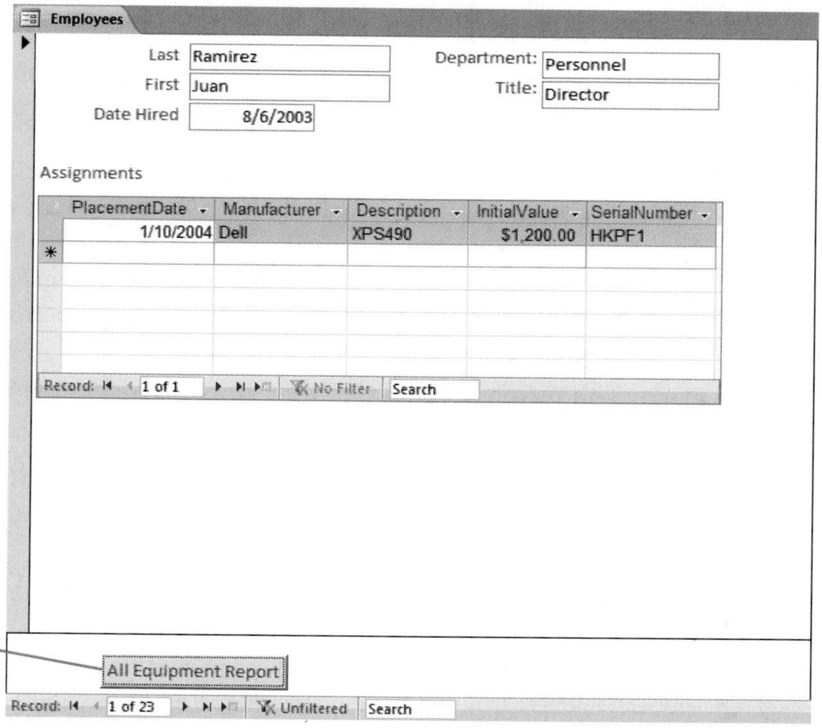

Using a trusted database and setting up a trusted folder

A **trusted database** allows you to run macros and VBA. By default, a database is not trusted. To trust a database, click the Enable Content button on the Security Warning bar each time you open a database. To permanently trust a database, store the database in a **trusted folder**.

To create a trusted folder, open the Options dialog box from the File tab, click the Trust Center, click the Trust Center Settings button, click the Trusted Locations option, click the Add new location button, then browse for and choose the folder you want to trust.

Using If Statements

An **If statement** allows you to run macro actions based on the result of a conditional expression. A **conditional expression** is an expression such as [Price]>100 or [StateName]="MO" that results in a true or false value. If the condition evaluates true, the actions that follow the If statement are executed. If the condition evaluates false, the macro skips those actions. When building a conditional expression that refers to a value in a control on a form or report, use the following syntax: [Forms]![*formname*]![*controlname*] or [Reports]![*reportname*]![*controlname*]. Separating the object type (Forms or Reports) from the object name and from the control name by using [square brackets] and exclamation points (!) is called **bang notation**. At Quest Specialty Travel, everyone who has been with the company longer than 5 years is eligible to take their old PC equipment home as soon as it has been replaced. You use a conditional macro to help evaluate and present this information in a form.

STEPS

1. **Click the Create tab, click the Macro button, click the Action Catalog button in the Show/Hide group to toggle on the Action Catalog window if it is not already visible, double-click If in the Program Flow area, then type the following in the If box: [Forms]![Employees]![DateHired]<Date()-(5*365)**

   The conditional expression shown in Figure M-7 says, "Check the value in the DateHired control on the Employees form and evaluate true if the value is earlier than 5 years from today. Evaluate false if the value is not earlier than 5 years ago."

> **QUICK TIP**
> Macro actions that require a trusted database are not shown unless you click the Show All Actions button in the Show/Hide group.

2. **Click the Add New Action list arrow in the If block, then scroll and click SetProperty**

   The **SetProperty** action has three arguments: Control Name, Property, and Value, which set the control, property, and value of that property.

3. **Click the Control Name argument text box in the Action Arguments pane, type LabelPCProgram, click the Property argument list arrow, click Visible, click the Value Property argument, then type True**

   Your screen should look like Figure M-8. The **Control Name** argument for the label is set to LabelPCProgram, which must match the **Name property** in the Property Sheet of the label that will be modified. The **Property** argument determines what property is being modified for the LabelPCProgram control. In this case, you are modifying the Visible property. The **Value** argument determines the value of the Visible property. For properties such as the Visible property that have only two choices in the Property Sheet, Yes or No, you enter a value of False for No and True for Yes.

4. **Save the macro with the name 5YearsPC, then close Macro Design View**

   Test the macro using the Employees form.

> **TROUBLE**
> Be sure Juan Ramirez with a hire date of 8/6/2003 is the current record.

5. **In the Navigation Pane, double-click the Employees form to open it**

   The record for Juan Ramirez, hired 8/6/2003, appears. Given that Juan has worked at Quest much longer than 5 years, you anticipate that the macro will display the label when it is run.

> **TROUBLE**
> Be sure the insertion point is in the main form when you run the 5YearsPC macro so it can find all of the controls to which it refers.

6. **Click the Database Tools tab, click the Run Macro button, verify that 5YearsPC is in the Macro Name text box, then click OK**

   After evaluating the HireDate field of this record and determining that this employee has been working at Quest Specialty Travel longer than 5 years, the LabelPCProgram label's Visible property was set to Yes, as shown in Figure M-9. The LabelPCProgram label's **Caption** property is "Eligible for PC Program!".

7. **Navigate through several records and note that the label remains visible for each employee even though the hire date may not be longer than 5 years ago**

   Because the macro only ran once, the label's Visible property remains Yes regardless of the current data in the HireDate field. You need a way to rerun or trigger the macro to evaluate each employee.

8. **Close the Employees form**

FIGURE M-7: **Using an If statement to set a control's Visible property**

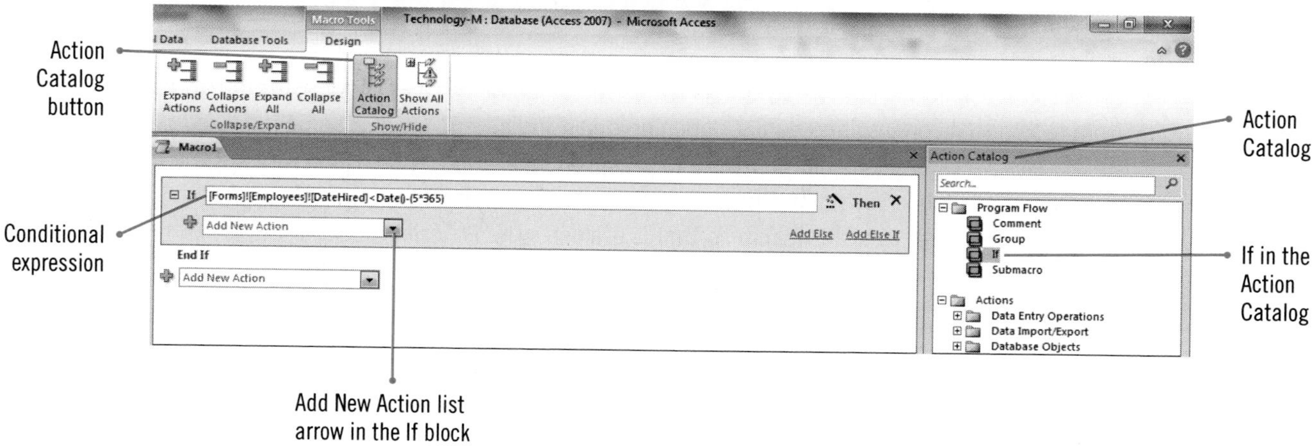

FIGURE M-8: **Entering arguments for the SetProperty action**

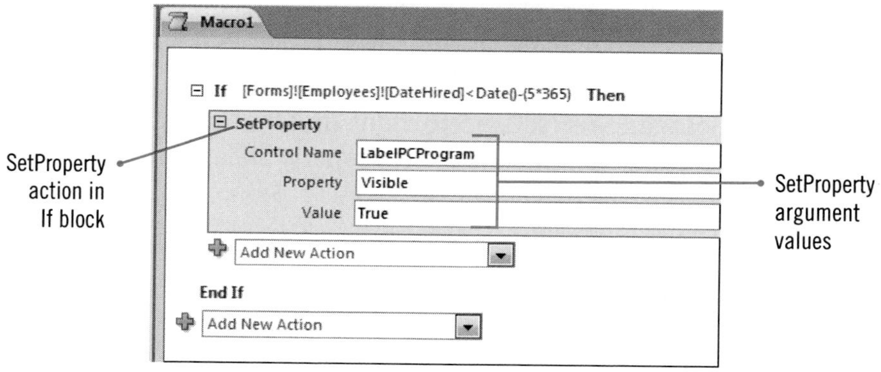

FIGURE M-9: **Running the 5YearsPC macro**

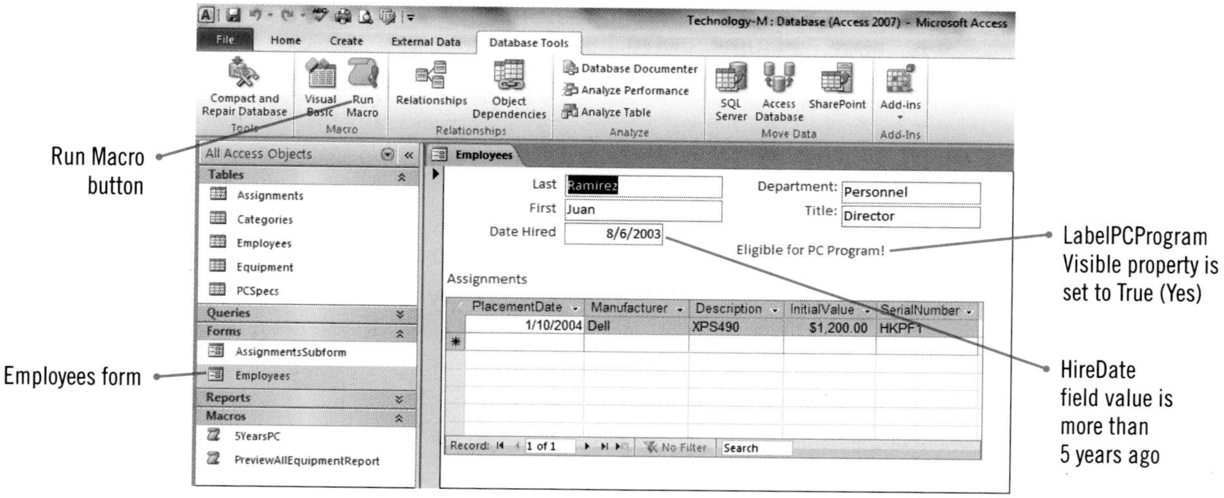

Access 2010

UNIT
M
Access 2010

Working with Events

An **event** is a specific activity that occurs within the database, such as clicking a command button, moving from record to record, editing data, or opening or closing a form. Events can be triggered by the user or by the database itself. By assigning a macro to an appropriate event rather than running the macro from the Database Tools tab or command button, you further automate and improve your database. You need to modify the 5YearsPC macro so that it evaluates the DateHired field to display or hide the label as you move from record to record.

STEPS

1. **Right-click the 5YearsPC macro in the Navigation Pane, click Design View on the shortcut menu, click anywhere in the If block to activate it, then click the Add Else link in the lower-right corner of the If block**

   The **Else** portion of an If statement allows you to run a different set of macro actions if the conditional expression evaluates False. In this case, you want to set the Value of the Visible property to False if the conditional expression evaluates False (if the HireDate is less than 5 years from today's date) so that the label does not appear if the employee is not eligible for the PC program.

> **TROUBLE**
> If your screen doesn't match Figure M-10, use the Undo button to try again.

2. **Right-click the SetProperty action block, click Copy, right-click the Else block, click Paste, select True in the Value property, then type False as shown in Figure M-10**

   With the second action edited, the macro will now turn the label's Visible property to True (Yes) *or* False (No), depending on HireDate value. You attach the macro to the event on the form that is triggered each time you move from record to record.

3. **Save and close the 5YearsPC macro, right-click the Employees form in the Navigation Pane, click Design View, then click the Property Sheet button**

   All objects, sections, and controls have a variety of events to which macros can be attached. Most event names are self-explanatory, such as the **On Click** event (which occurs when that item is clicked).

> **TROUBLE**
> Be sure you are viewing the Property Sheet for the form. If not, click the Form Selector button to select the form.

4. **Click the Event tab in the Property Sheet, click the On Current list arrow, then click 5YearsPC**

   Your screen should look like Figure M-11. The **On Current** event occurs when focus moves from one record to another, therefore the 5YearsPC macro will automatically run each time you move from record to record in the form. Test your new macro by moving through several records in Form View.

5. **Close the Property Sheet, click the View button to switch to Form View, then click the Next record button in the navigation bar for the main form several times while observing the Eligible for PC Program! label**

   For every DateHired value that is earlier than five years before today's date, the Eligible for PC Program! label is visible. If the DateHired is less than five years before today's date, the label is hidden.

6. **Save and close the Employees form**

FIGURE M-10: **Adding an Else portion to an If block**

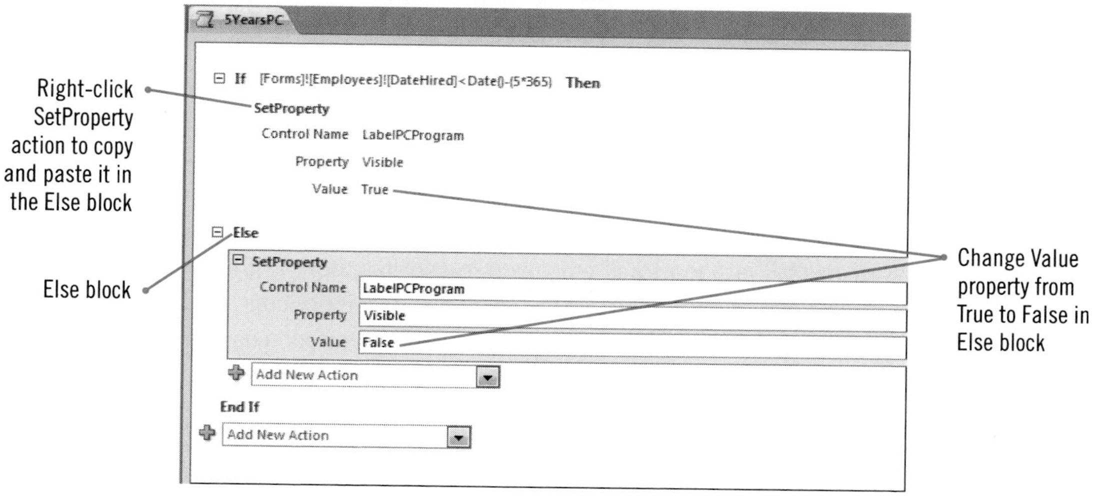

FIGURE M-11: **Attaching a macro to the On Current event of the form**

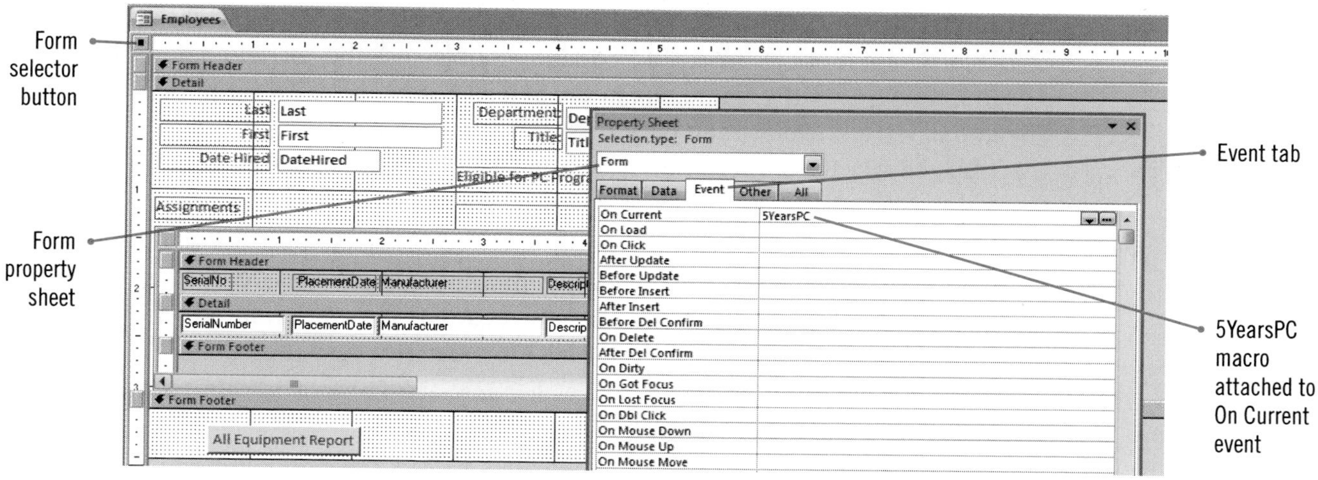

UNIT
M
Access 2010

Creating a Data Macro

A **data macro** allows you to embed macro capabilities directly in a table to add, change, or delete data based on conditions you specify. Data macros are a new feature of Access 2010. Data macros are managed directly from within tables, and do not appear in the Macros group in the Navigation Pane. You most often run a data macro based on a table event, such as modifying data or deleting a record, but you can run a data macro separately as well, similar to how you run a regular macro. Quest Specialty Travel grants 10 days of regular vacation to all employees except for those in the Africa and Asia departments, who receive 15 days due to the extra travel requirements of their positions. Kayla asks you to figure out an automatic way to assign each employee the correct number of vacation days based on their department. A data macro will work well for this task.

STEPS

1. **Double-click the Employees table in the Navigation Pane, then observe the Vacation field throughout the datasheet**
   Currently, the Vacation field contains the value of 10 for each record, or each employee.
2. **Right-click the Employees table tab, click Design View on the shortcut menu, click the Create Data Macros button in the Field, Record & Table Events group, click After Insert, then click the Action Catalog button in the Show/Hide group if the Action Catalog window is not already open**
   In this case, you chose the After Insert event, which is run after a new record is entered. See Table M-3 for more information on table events. Creating a data macro is very similar to creating a regular macro. You add the logic and macro actions needed to complete the task at hand.
3. **Double-click ForEachRecord in the Action Catalog to add a For Each Record In block, click the For Each Record In list arrow, click Employees in the list, click the Where Condition text box, type [Department]="Africa" or [Department]="Asia", double-click the EditRecord data block in the Action Catalog, double-click the SetField data action in the Action Catalog, click the Name box in the SetField block, type Vacation, click the Value box in the SetField block, then type 15 as shown in Figure M-12**
   The Default value for the Vacation field is set to 10 in Table Design View of the Employees table so all existing records should have a value of 10 in the Vacation field. Test the new data macro by adding a new record.
4. **Click the Close button, click Yes when prompted to save changes, click the View button to display the datasheet, click Yes when prompted to save changes, click the New button in the Records group, enter the new record as shown in Figure M-13, except do not enter a Vacation value, then press [Tab] to move to a new record**
   The macro is triggered by the After Insert event of the record, and the Vacation field is automatically updated to 15 for that record and all other records with Asia or Africa in the Department field as shown in Figure M-13.
5. **Right-click the Employees table tab, then click Close on the shortcut menu**
   Data is automatically saved when you move from record to record or close a database object.

QUICK TIP
You can also drag a block or action from the Action Catalog to Macro Design View.

TROUBLE
Be sure to tab to a completely new record to trigger the data macro attached to the After Insert event.

FIGURE M-12: **Creating a data macro**

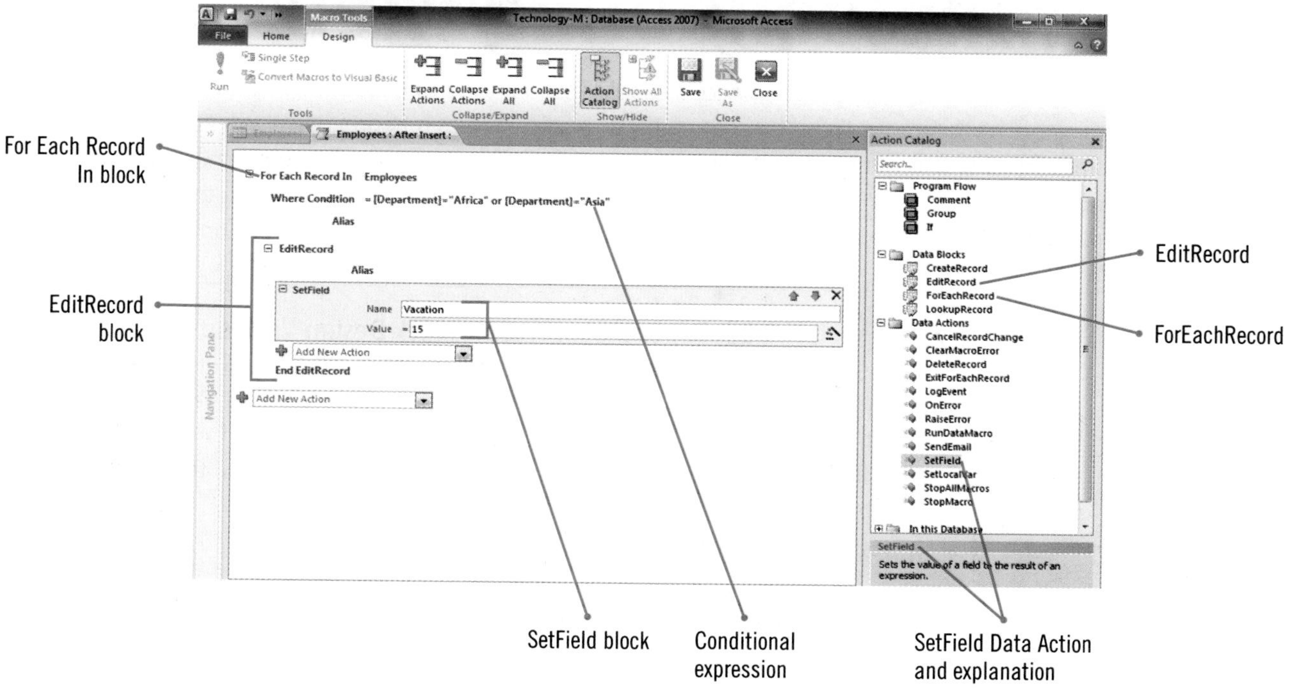

FIGURE M-13: **Running a data macro**

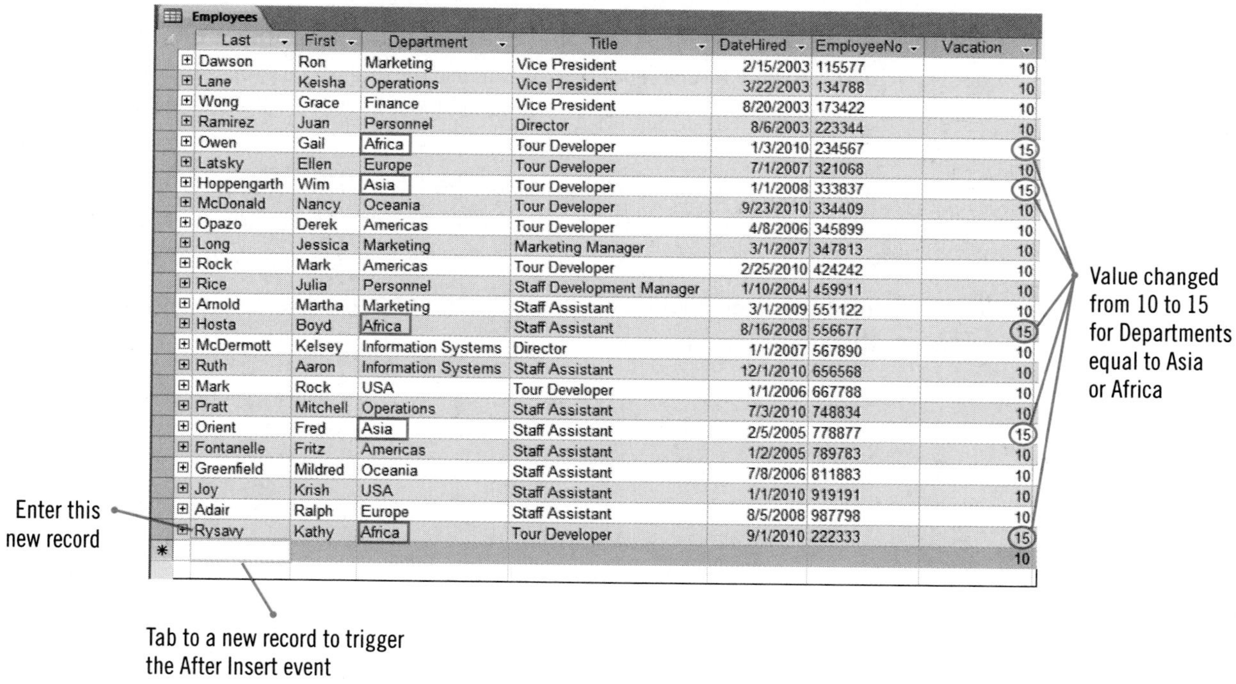

Last	First	Department	Title	DateHired	EmployeeNo	Vacation
Dawson	Ron	Marketing	Vice President	2/15/2003	115577	10
Lane	Keisha	Operations	Vice President	3/22/2003	134788	10
Wong	Grace	Finance	Vice President	8/20/2003	173422	10
Ramirez	Juan	Personnel	Director	8/6/2003	223344	10
Owen	Gail	Africa	Tour Developer	1/3/2010	234567	15
Latsky	Ellen	Europe	Tour Developer	7/1/2007	321068	10
Hoppengarth	Wim	Asia	Tour Developer	1/1/2008	333837	15
McDonald	Nancy	Oceania	Tour Developer	9/23/2010	334409	10
Opazo	Derek	Americas	Tour Developer	4/8/2006	345899	10
Long	Jessica	Marketing	Marketing Manager	3/1/2007	347813	10
Rock	Mark	Americas	Tour Developer	2/25/2010	424242	10
Rice	Julia	Personnel	Staff Development Manager	1/10/2004	459911	10
Arnold	Martha	Marketing	Staff Assistant	3/1/2009	551122	10
Hosta	Boyd	Africa	Staff Assistant	8/16/2008	556677	15
McDermott	Kelsey	Information Systems	Director	1/1/2007	567890	10
Ruth	Aaron	Information Systems	Staff Assistant	12/1/2010	656568	10
Mark	Rock	USA	Tour Developer	1/1/2006	667788	10
Pratt	Mitchell	Operations	Staff Assistant	7/3/2010	748834	10
Orient	Fred	Asia	Staff Assistant	2/5/2005	778877	15
Fontanelle	Fritz	Americas	Staff Assistant	1/2/2005	789783	10
Greenfield	Mildred	Oceania	Staff Assistant	7/8/2006	811883	10
Joy	Krish	USA	Staff Assistant	1/1/2010	919191	10
Adair	Ralph	Europe	Staff Assistant	8/5/2008	987798	10
Rysavy	Kathy	Africa	Tour Developer	9/1/2010	222333	15
*						10

TABLE M-3: **Table events**

table event	runs...
After Insert	...after a new record has been inserted into the table
After Update	...after an existing record has been changed
After Delete	...after an existing record has been deleted
Before Delete	...before a record is deleted, to help the user validate or cancel the deletion
Before Change	...before a record is changed, to help the user validate or cancel the edits

UNIT M

Access 2010

Troubleshooting Macros

When macros don't run properly, Access supplies several tools to debug them. **Debugging** means determining why the macro doesn't run correctly. It usually involves breaking down a dysfunctional macro into smaller pieces that can be individually tested. For example, you can **single step** a macro, which means to run it one line (one action) at a time to observe the effect of each specific action in the Macro Single Step dialog box. You use the PreviewAllEquipmentReport to learn debugging techniques.

STEPS

1. **Right-click the PreviewAllEquipmentReport macro, click Design View on the shortcut menu, click the Single Step button in the Tools group, then click the Run button**

   The screen should look like Figure M-14, with the Macro Single Step dialog box open. This dialog box displays information including the macro's name, the action's name, the action arguments, and whether the current action's condition is true. From the Macro Single Step dialog box, you can step into the next macro action, halt execution of the macro, or continue running the macro without single stepping.

2. **Click Step in the Macro Single Step dialog box**

   Stepping into the second action lets the first action run and pauses the macro at the second action. The Macro Single Step dialog box now displays information about the second action.

3. **Click Step**

   The second action, the MessageBox action, is executed, which displays the message box.

4. **Click OK, then close the AllEquipment report**

5. **Click the Design tab, then click the Single Step button to toggle it off**

   Another technique to help troubleshoot macros is to use the built-in prompts and Help system provided by Microsoft Access. For example, you may have questions about how to use the optional Filter Name argument for the OpenReport macro action.

6. **Click the OpenReport action block, point to the Filter Name argument to view the ScreenTip that supplies information about that argument as shown in Figure M-15**

   The redesigned Access 2010 Macro Design View window has been improved with interactive prompts.

7. **Save and close the PreviewAllEquipmentReport macro, close the Technology-M.accdb database, then exit Access**

FIGURE M-14: **Single stepping through a macro**

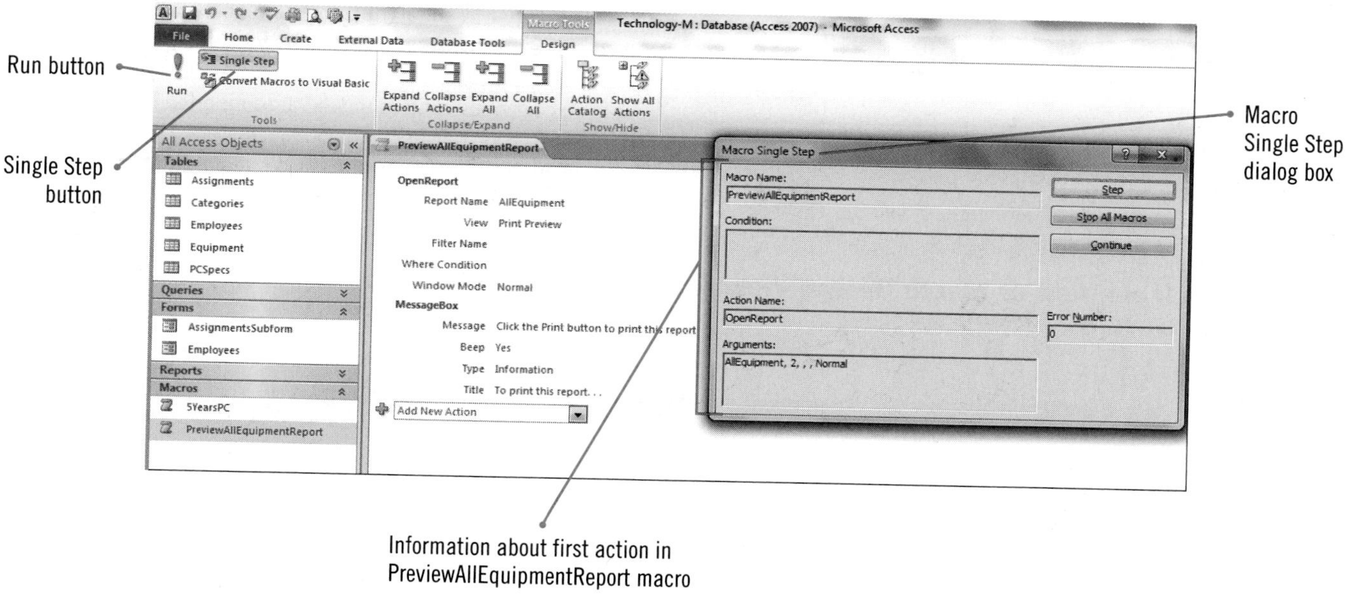
Run button
Single Step button
Macro Single Step dialog box
Information about first action in PreviewAllEquipmentReport macro

FIGURE M-15: **Viewing automatic prompts**

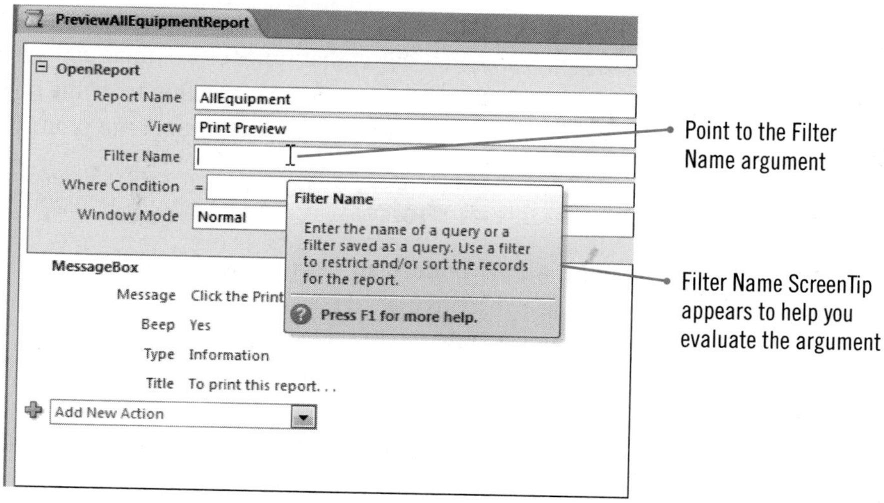
Point to the Filter Name argument
Filter Name ScreenTip appears to help you evaluate the argument

Practice

Concepts Review

For current SAM information, including versions and content details, visit SAM Central (http://www.cengage.com/samcentral). If you have a SAM user profile, you may have access to hands-on instruction, practice, and assessment of the skills covered in this unit. Since various versions of SAM are supported throughout the life of this text, check with your instructor for the correct instructions and URL/Web site for accessing assignments.

Identify each element of Macro Design View shown in Figure M-16.

FIGURE M-16

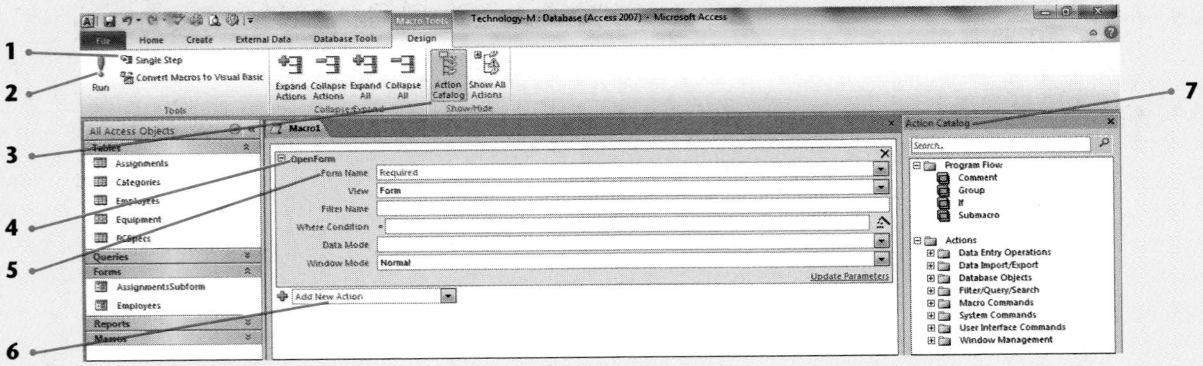

Match each term with the statement that best describes its function.

8. Action
9. Event
10. Debugging
11. Argument
12. Conditional expression
13. Macro

a. Specific action that occurs within the database, such as clicking a button or opening a form
b. Part of an If statement that evaluates as either true or false
c. Individual step that you want the Access macro to perform
d. Access object that stores one or more actions that perform one or more tasks
e. Provides additional information to define how an Access action will perform
f. Determines why a macro doesn't run properly

Select the best answer from the list of choices.

14. Which of the following is *not* a major benefit of using a macro?
- **a.** To make the database more flexible or easy to use
- **b.** To redesign the relationships among the tables of the database
- **c.** To ensure consistency in executing routine or complex tasks
- **d.** To save time by automating routine tasks

15. Which of the following best describes the process of creating an Access macro?
- **a.** Use the single-step recorder to record clicks and keystrokes as you complete a task.
- **b.** Use the macro recorder to record clicks and keystrokes as you complete a task.
- **c.** Use the Macro Wizard to determine which tasks are done most frequently.
- **d.** Open Macro Design View and add actions, arguments, and If statements to accomplish the desired task.

16. Which of the following would *not* be a way to run a macro?
- **a.** Click the Run Macro button on the Database Tools tab.
- **b.** Assign the macro to a command button on a form.
- **c.** Assign the macro to an event of a control on a form.
- **d.** Double-click a macro action within the Macro Design View window.

17. Which of the following is *not* a reason to run a macro in single-step mode?

a. You want to debug a macro that isn't working properly.

b. You want to run only a few of the actions of a macro.

c. You want to observe the effect of each macro action individually.

d. You want to change the arguments of a macro while it runs.

18. Which of the following is *not* true of conditional expressions in If statements in macros?

a. Conditional expressions allow you to skip over actions when the expression evaluates as false.

b. Conditional expressions give the macro more power and flexibility.

c. Macro If statements provide for Else and Else If clauses.

d. More macro actions are available when you are also using conditional expressions.

19. Which example illustrates the proper syntax to refer to a specific control on a form?

a. [Forms] ! [*formname*] ! [*controlname*]

b. {Forms} ! {*formname*} ! (*controlname*)

c. Forms ! formname. controlname

d. (Forms) ! (formname) ! (controlname)

20. Which event is executed every time you move from record to record in a form?

a. Next Record

b. New Record

c. On Current

d. On Move

Skills Review

1. Understand macros.

a. Start Access, then open the Basketball-M.accdb database from the drive and folder where you store your Data Files. Enable content if prompted.

b. Open the PrintMacroGroup macro in Macro Design View, then record your answers to the following questions on a sheet of paper:

- What is the name of the first submacro?
- How many macro actions are in the first submacro?
- What arguments does the first action in the first submacro contain?
- What values were chosen for these arguments?

c. Close Macro Design View for the PrintMacroGroup object.

2. Create a macro.

a. Start a new macro in Macro Design View.

b. Add the OpenQuery action.

c. Select PlayerStats as the value for the Query Name argument.

d. Select Datasheet for the View argument.

e. Select Edit for the Data Mode argument.

f. Save the macro with the name **ViewPlayerStats**.

g. Run the macro to make sure it works, close the PlayerStats query, then close the ViewPlayerStats macro.

3. Modify actions and arguments.

a. Open the ViewPlayerStats macro in Macro Design View.

b. Add a MessageBox action as the second action of the query.

c. Type **We had a great season!** for the Message argument.

d. Select Yes for the Beep argument.

e. Select Warning! for the Type argument.

f. Type **Iowa State Cyclones** for the Title argument.

g. Save the macro, then run it to make sure the MessageBox action works as intended.

h. Click OK in the dialog box created by the MessageBox action, close the PlayerStats query, then close the ViewPlayerStats macro.

i. Open the PrintMacroGroup macro object in Design View.

j. Modify the View argument for the OpenReport object of the PlayerStatistics submacro from Print to Print Preview.

k. Save and close the PrintMacroGroup macro.

Skills Review (continued)

4. Assign a macro to a command button.

- **a.** In Design View of the PlayerInformationForm, use the Command Button Wizard to add a command button to the Form Footer that runs the PlayerStatistics submacro in the PrintMacroGroup macro (PrintMacroGroup.PlayerStatistics).
- **b.** The text on the button should read **View Player Statistics**.
- **c.** The meaningful name for the button should be **cmdPlayerStatistics**.
- **d.** Test the command button in Form View, click OK in the message box, then close the PlayerStats report.
- **e.** Save and close the PlayerInformationForm.

5. Use If statements.

- **a.** Start a new macro in Macro Design View, and open the Action Catalog window if it is not already open.
- **b.** Double-click If in the Action Catalog pane to add an If block to the macro.
- **c.** Enter the following condition in the If box: **[Forms]![GameSummaryForm]![HomeScore]>[OpponentScore]**.
- **d.** Add the SetProperty action to the If block.
- **e.** Type **VictoryLabel** in the Control Name box for the SetProperty action.
- **f.** Select Visible for the Property argument for the SetProperty action.
- **g.** Enter **True** for the Value argument for the SetProperty action to indicate Yes.
- **h.** Click the Add Else link in the lower-right corner of the If block.
- **i.** Copy the existing SetProperty action, then paste it under the Else clause.
- **j.** Modify the Value property from True to **False** for the second SetProperty action.
- **k.** Save the macro with the name **VictoryCalculator**, compare it to Figure M-17, make any necessary adjustments, then close Macro Design View.

FIGURE M-17

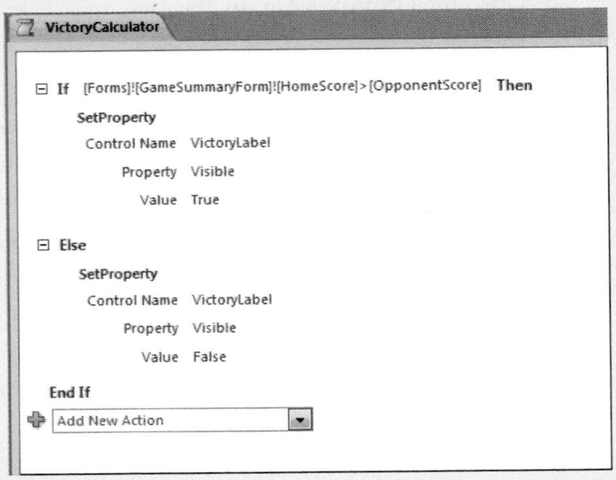

6. Work with events.

- **a.** Open the GameSummaryForm in Form Design View.
- **b.** Open the Property Sheet for the form.
- **c.** Assign the VictoryCalculator macro to the On Current event of the form.
- **d.** Close the Property Sheet, save the form, then open the GameSummaryForm in Form View.
- **e.** Navigate through the first four records. The Victory label should be visible for the first three records, but not the fourth.
- **f.** Add your name as a label in the Form Footer section to identify your printouts, print the third and fourth records if requested by your instructor, then save and close the GameSummaryForm.

7. Create a data macro.

- **a.** Open the Games table in Table Design View.
- **b.** Add a field named **RoadWin** with a Yes/No data type and the following Description: **Enter Yes if the Home-Away field is Away and the HomeScore is greater than the OpponentScore**.
- **c.** Save the Games table and switch to Datasheet View to note that the RoadWin check box is empty (No) for every record.
- **d.** Switch back to Table Design View, and create a data macro based on the After Insert event.
- **e.** Insert a ForEachRecord data block, and specify Games for the For Each Record In argument.
- **f.** The Where Condition should be: **[Home-Away]="A" and [HomeScore]>[OpponentScore]**.
- **g.** Add an EditRecord data block in the For Each Record In block, and a SetField data action. Be careful to add the EditRecord block *within* the For Each Record Block.

Skills Review (continued)

h. Enter **RoadWin** in the Name argument and **Yes** in the Value argument as shown in Figure M-18.

i. Save and close the data macro, save the Games table and switch to Datasheet View, then test the new data macro by entering a new record in the Games table as follows:

Opponent: **Tulsa**
Mascot: **Hurricanes**
Home-Away: **A**
HomeScore: **100**
OpponentScore: **50**
GameDate: **3/1/2013**

j. Tab to a new record. The six existing records where the Home-Away field is set to "A" and the HomeScore is greater than the OpponentScore should be checked. Close the Games table.

FIGURE M-18

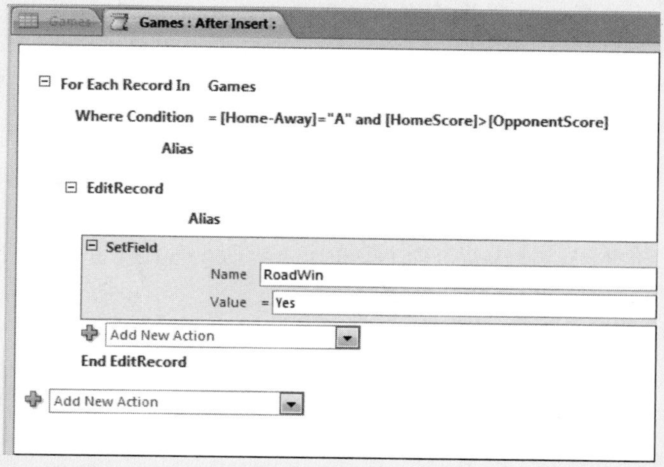

8. **Troubleshoot macros.**

a. Open the PrintMacroGroup in Macro Design View.

b. Click the Single Step button, then click the Run button.

c. Click Step twice to step through the two actions of the submacro, PlayerStatistics, then click OK in the resulting message box.

d. Close the PlayerStats report.

e. Return to Macro Design View of the PrintMacroGroup macro, and click the Single Step button on the Design tab to toggle off this feature.

f. Save and close the PrintMacroGroup macro, close the Basketball-M.accdb database, then exit Access.

Independent Challenge 1

As the manager of a doctor's clinic, you have created an Access database called Patients-M.accdb to track insurance claim reimbursements. You use macros to help automate the database.

a. Start Access, then open the database Patients-M.accdb from the drive and folder where you store your Data Files. Enable content if prompted.

b. Open Macro Design View of the CPT Form Open macro. (CPT stands for Current Procedural Terminology, which is a code that describes a medical procedure.) If the Single Step button is toggled on, click it to toggle it off.

c. On a separate sheet of paper, identify the macro actions, arguments for each action, and values for each argument.

d. In two or three sentences, explain in your own words what tasks this macro automates.

e. Close the CPT Form Open macro.

f. Open the Claim Entry Form in Form Design View. Maximize the window.

g. In the Form Footer of the Claim Entry Form are several command buttons. Open the Property Sheet of the Add CPT Code button, then click the Event tab.

h. On your paper, write the event to which the CPT Form Open macro is assigned.

i. Open the Claim Entry Form in Form View, then click the Add CPT Code button in the Form Footer.

j. On your paper, write the current record number that is displayed for you.

k. In the CPT Form, find the record for CPT Code 99243. Write down the RBRVS value for this record, then close the CPT form and Claim Entry form. (RBRVS stands for Resource-Based Relative Value System, a measurement of relative value between medical procedures.)

l. Close the Patients-M.accdb database, then exit Access.

Independent Challenge 2

As the manager of a doctor's clinic, you have created an Access database called Patients-M.accdb to track insurance claim reimbursements. You use macros to help automate the database.

- **a.** Start Access, then open the database Patients-M.accdb from the drive and folder where you store your Data Files. Enable content if prompted.
- **b.** Start a new macro in Macro Design View, and open the Action Catalog window if it is not already open.
- **c.** Double-click the Submacro entry in the Program Flow folder to add a submacro block.
- **d.** Type **Preview DOS Denied** as the first macro name, then add the OpenReport macro action.
- **e.** Select Date of Service Report — Denied for the Report Name argument, then select Print Preview for the View argument of the OpenReport action.
- **f.** Double-click the Submacro entry in the Program Flow folder to add another submacro block.
- **g.** Type **Preview DOS Fixed** as a new macro name, then add the OpenReport macro action.
- **h.** Select Date of Service Report - Fixed for the ReportName argument, then select Print Preview for the View argument of the second OpenReport action.
- **i.** Save the macro with the name **Preview Group**, then close Macro Design View.
- **j.** Using the Run Macro button on the Database Tools tab, run the Preview Group.Preview DOS Denied macro to test it, then close Print Preview.
- **k.** Using the Run Macro button on the Database Tools tab, run the Preview Group.Preview DOS Fixed macro to test it, then close Print Preview.

Advanced Challenge Exercise

ACE

- In the Preview Group macro, click the Collapse buttons to the left of the Submacro statements to collapse the two submacro blocks.
- Create two more submacros, one that previews Monthly Claims Report — Denied and the other that previews Monthly Claims Report - Fixed. Name the two macros **Preview MCR Denied** and **Preview MCR Fixed** as shown in Figure M-19.
- Save and close the Preview Group macro.
- In Design View of the Claim Entry Form, add four separate command buttons to the Form Footer of the subform to run the four submacros in Preview Group macro. (The Form Footer of the main form already includes four command buttons, so be sure to add the new command buttons to the subform.) Use the captions and meaningful names of **DOS Denied** and **cmdDOSDenied**; **DOS Fixed** and **cmdDOSFixed**; **MCR Denied** and **cmdMCRDenied**; and **MCR Fixed** and **cmdMCRFixed** to correspond with the four submacros in the Preview Group macro.
- Change the font color on the new command buttons to black.
- Select all four new command buttons in the Form Footer section of the subform and use the Size/Space and Align commands on the Arrange tab to precisely size, align, and space the buttons equally in the Form Footer section.
- Save the Claim Entry Form, switch to Form View as shown in Figure M-20, then test each of the new command buttons to make sure it opens the correct report.
- Close the Claim Entry Form.

FIGURE M-19

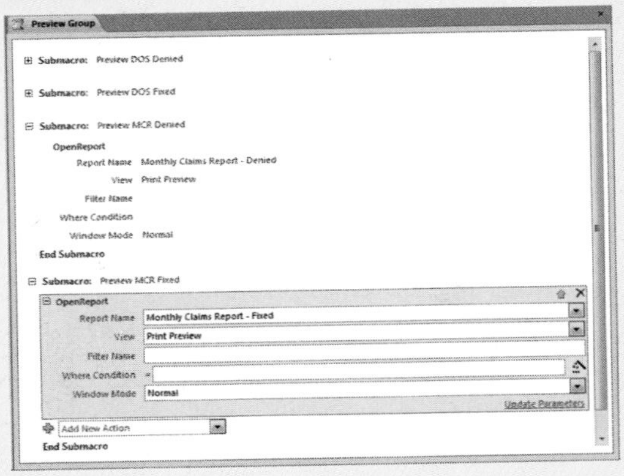

FIGURE M-20

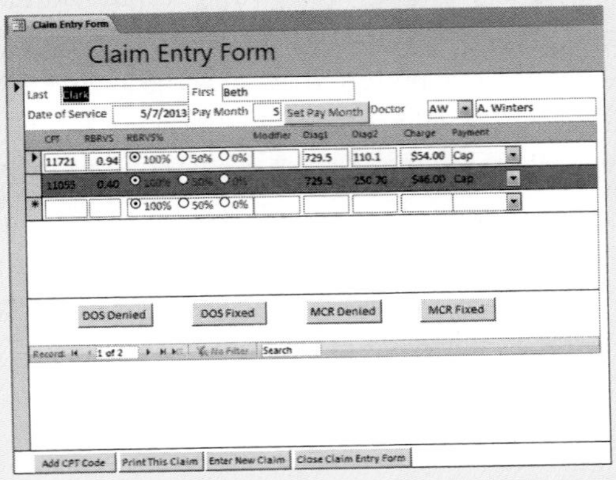

- **l.** Close the Patients-M.accdb database, then exit Access.

Independent Challenge 3

As the manager of a doctor's clinic, you have created an Access database called Patients-M.accdb to track insurance claim reimbursements. You use macros to help automate the database.

a. Start Access, then open the Patients-M.accdb database from the drive and folder where you store your Data Files.
b. Start a new macro in Macro Design View, then add an If statement.
c. Enter the following in the If box: **[Forms]![CPT Form]![RBRVS]=0**.
d. Select the SetProperty action for the first action in the If block.
e. Enter the following arguments for the SetProperty action: Control Name: **ResearchLabel**, Property: **Visible**, and Value: **True**.
f. Click the Add Else link.
g. Select the SetProperty action for the first action of the Else clause.
h. Enter the following arguments for the SetProperty action: Control Name: **ResearchLabel**, Property: **Visible**, and Value: **False**.
i. Save the macro with the name **Research** as shown in Figure M-21, then close Macro Design View.
j. Open the CPT Form in Form Design View, and open the Property Sheet for the form.
k. Assign the Research macro to the On Current event of the form.
l. Close the Property Sheet, save the form, then open the CPT Form in Form View.
m. Use the Next record button to move quickly through all 64 records in the form. Notice that the macro displays Research! only when the RBRVS value is equal to zero.
n. Save and close the CPT Form, then close the Patients-M.accdb database.

FIGURE M-21

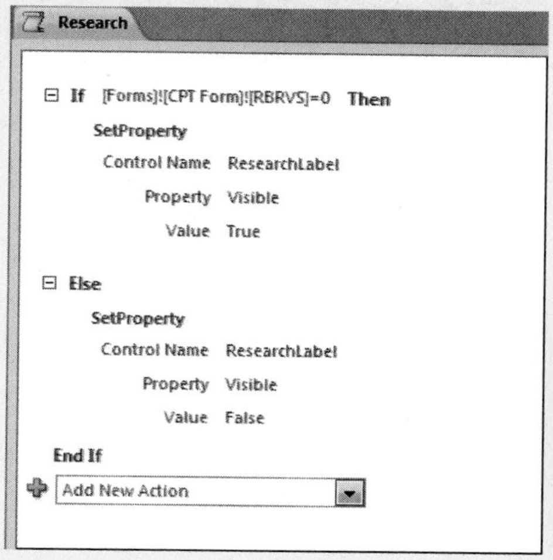

Real Life Independent Challenge

This Independent Challenge requires an Internet connection.

Suppose your culinary club is collecting information on international chocolate factories, museums, and stores, and asks you to help build a database to organize the information. You can collect some information on the Web to enter into the database, then tie the forms together with macros attached to command buttons.

a. Open the Chocolate-M.accdb database from the drive and folder where you store your Data Files, enable content if prompted, then open the Countries form in Form View.
b. Click the New (blank) record button for the main form, then type **Poland** in the Country text box.
c. In the subform for the Poland record, enter **Cadbury-Wedel Polska** in the Name field, **F** in the Type field (F for factory), **Praga** in the City field, and **Lodz** in the StateProvince field.
d. Open Macro Design View for a new macro, then add the MaximizeWindow action. Save the macro with the name **Maximize**, then close it.
e. If the Countries form is maximized, restore it, view it in Design View, add the Maximize macro to the On Load event of the Countries form, then open the Countries form in Form View to test it.
f. Save and close the Countries form.
g. Add the Maximize macro to the On Load event of the Places of Interest report, then open the Places of Interest report in Print Preview to test it.
h. Save and close the Places of Interest report.
i. Close the Chocolate-M.accdb database, then exit Access.

Visual Workshop

As the manager of a doctor's clinic, you have created an Access database called Patients-M.accdb to track insurance claim reimbursements. Develop a new macro called **QueryGroup** with the actions and argument values shown in Table M-4 and Figure M-22. Run both macros to test them by using the Run Macro button on the Database Tools tab, and debug the macros if necessary.

TABLE M-4

submacro	action	argument	argument value
Denied	OpenQuery	Query Name	Monthly Query – Denied
		View	Datasheet
		Data Mode	Edit
	MaximizeWindow		
	MessageBox	Message	These claims were denied
		Beep	Yes
		Type	Information
		Title	Denied
Fixed	OpenQuery	Query Name	Monthly Query – Fixed
		View	Datasheet
		Data Mode	Edit
	MaximizeWindow		
	MessageBox	Message	These claims were fixed
		Beep	Yes
		Type	Information
		Title	Fixed

FIGURE M-22

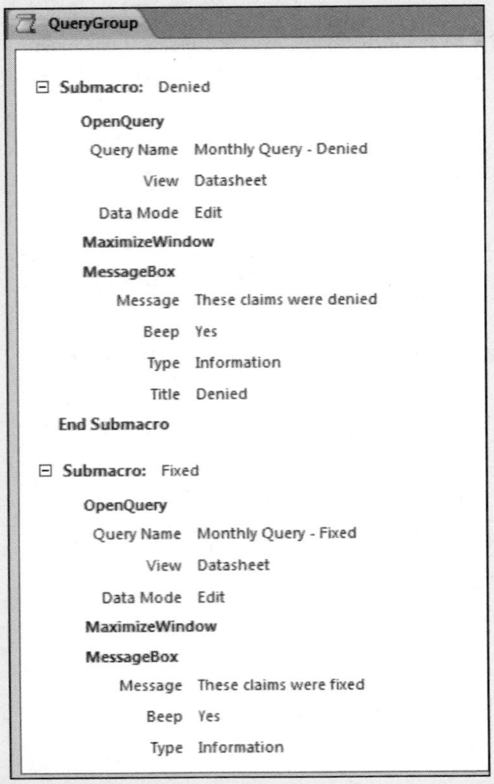

UNIT
N
Access 2010

Creating Modules and VBA

Files You Will Need:

Technology-N.accdb
Baseball-N.accdb
Patients-N.accdb
Basketball-N.accdb

Access is a robust and easy-to-use relational database program. Access provides user-friendly tools, such as wizards and Design Views, to help users quickly create reports and forms that previously took programmers hours to build. You may, however, want to automate a task or create a new function that goes beyond the capabilities of the built-in Access tools. Within each program of the Microsoft Office suite, a programming language called **Visual Basic for Applications (VBA)** is provided to help you extend the program's capabilities. In Access, VBA is stored within modules. You want to learn about VBA and create modules to enhance the capabilities of the Technology-N database for Quest Specialty Travel.

OBJECTIVES

- Understand modules and VBA
- Compare macros and modules
- Create functions
- Use If statements
- Document procedures
- Build class modules
- Modify sub procedures
- Troubleshoot modules

UNIT
N
Access 2010

Understanding Modules and VBA

A **module** is an Access object that stores Visual Basic for Applications (VBA) programming code. VBA is written in the **Visual Basic Editor (VBE)**, shown in Figure N-1. The components and text colors of the VBE are described in Table N-1. An Access database has two kinds of modules. **Standard modules** contain global code that can be executed from anywhere in the database and are displayed as module objects in the Navigation Pane. **Class modules** are stored within the form or report object itself. Class modules contain VBA code used only within that particular form or report. Before working with modules, you ask some questions about VBA.

DETAILS

The following questions and answers introduce the basics of Access modules:

- **What does a module contain?**
  A module contains VBA programming code organized in procedures. A procedure contains several lines of code, each of which is called a **statement**. Modules can also contain **comments**, text that helps explain and document the code.

- **What is a procedure?**
  A **procedure** is a series of VBA statements that performs an operation or calculates an answer. VBA has two types of procedures: functions and subs. **Declaration statements** precede procedure statements and help set rules for how the statements in the module are processed.

- **What is a function?**
  A **function** is a procedure that returns a value. Access supplies many built-in functions such as Sum, Count, Pmt, and Now that can be used in an expression in a query, form, or report to calculate a value. You might want to create a new function, however, to help perform calculations unique to your database. For example, you might create a new function called RetireDate to calculate the date an employee is eligible to retire with full benefits at your company.

- **What is a sub?**
  A **sub** (also called **sub procedure**) performs a series of VBA statements to manipulate controls and objects. Subs are generally executed when an event occurs, such as when a command button is clicked or a form is opened. Unlike a function, a sub does not return a value and cannot be used in an expression.

- **What are arguments?**
  Arguments are constants, variables, or expressions passed to a procedure that the procedure needs in order to execute. For example, the full syntax for the Sum function is Sum (*expr*), where *expr* represents the argument for the Sum function, the field that is being summed. In VBA, arguments are declared in the first line of the procedure. They are specified immediately after a procedure's name and are enclosed in parentheses. Multiple arguments are separated by commas.

- **What is an object?**
  In VBA, an **object** is any item that can be identified or manipulated, including the traditional Access objects (table, query, form, report, macro, and module) as well as other items that have properties such as controls, sections, and existing procedures.

- **What is a method?**
  A **method** is an action that an object can perform. Procedures are often written to invoke methods in response to user actions. For example, you could invoke the GoToControl method to move the focus to a specific control on a form in response to the user clicking a command button.

FIGURE N-1: **Visual Basic Editor window for a standard module**

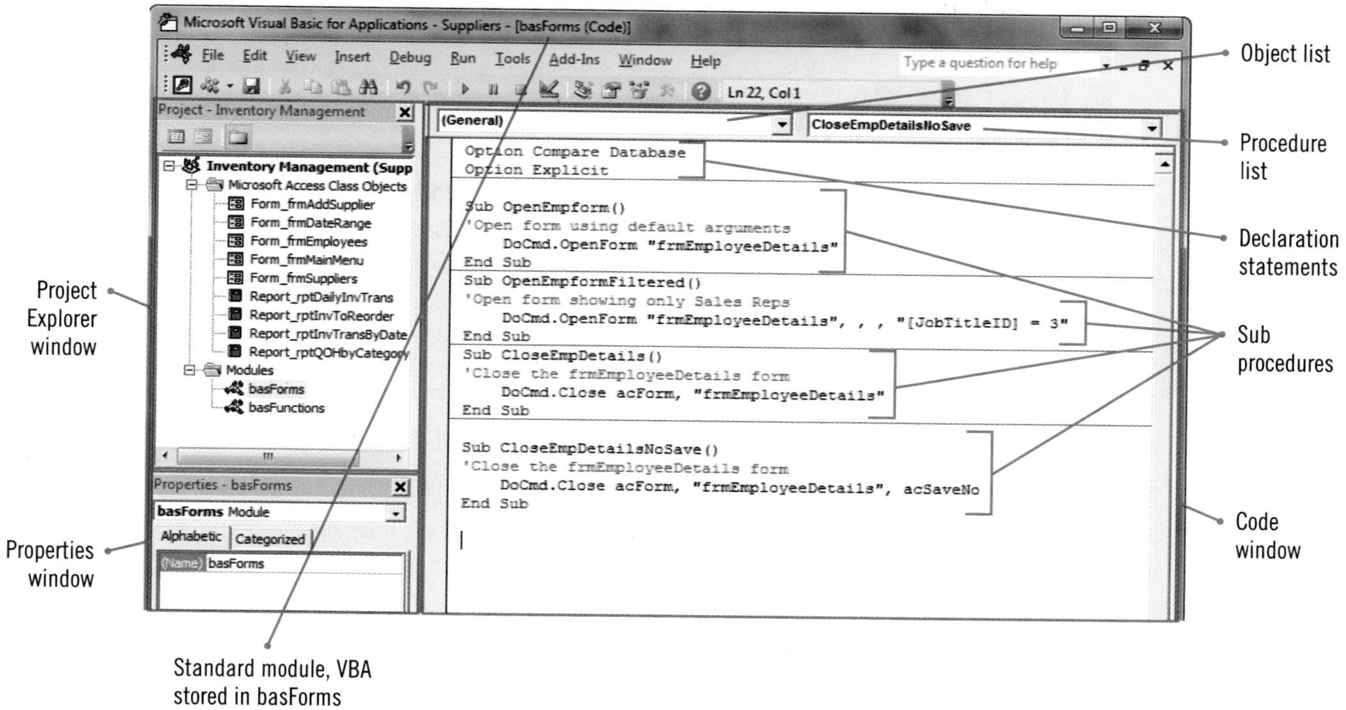

TABLE N-1: **Components and text colors for the Visual Basic Editor window**

component or color	description
Visual Basic Editor, VBE	Comprises the entire Microsoft Visual Basic program window that contains smaller windows, including the Code window and Project Explorer window
Code window	Contains the VBA for the project selected in the Project Explorer window
Project Explorer window	Displays a hierarchical list of the projects in the database; a **project** can be a module object or a form or report object that contains a class module
Declaration statements	Includes statements that apply to every procedure in the module, such as declarations for variables, constants, user-defined data types, and external procedures in a dynamic link library
Object list	In a class module, lists the objects associated with the current form or report
Procedure list	In a standard module, lists the procedures in the module; in a class module, lists events (such as Click or Dblclick)
Blue	Indicates a VBA keyword; blue words are reserved by VBA and are already assigned specific meanings
Black	Indicates normal text; black words are the unique VBA code developed by the user
Red	Indicates syntax error text; a red statement indicates that it will not execute correctly because of a syntax error (perhaps a missing parenthesis or a spelling error)
Green	Indicates comment text; any text after an apostrophe is considered documentation, or a comment, and is therefore ignored in the execution of the procedure

UNIT
N
Access 2010

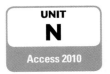

Comparing Macros and Modules

Both macros and modules help run your database more efficiently and effectively. Creating a macro or a module requires some understanding of programming concepts, an ability to follow a process through its steps, and patience. Some tasks can be accomplished by using an Access macro or by writing VBA. Guidelines can help you determine which tool is best for the task. You compare Access macros and modules by asking more questions.

DETAILS

The following questions and answers provide guidelines for using macros and modules:

- **For what types of tasks are macros best suited?**
  Macros are an easy way to handle common, repetitive, and simple tasks such as opening and closing forms, showing and hiding toolbars, and printing reports.
- **Which is easier to create, a macro or a module, and why?**
  Macros are generally easier to create because Macro Design View is more structured than the VBE. The hardest part of creating a macro is choosing the correct macro action. But once the action is selected, the arguments associated with that macro action are displayed, eliminating the need to learn any special programming syntax. To create a module, however, you must know a robust programming language, VBA, as well as the correct **syntax** (rules) for each VBA statement. In a nutshell, macros are simpler to create, but VBA is more powerful.
- **When must I use a macro?**
  You must use macros to make global, shortcut key assignments. **AutoExec** is a special macro name that automatically executes when the database first opens.
- **When must I use a module?**
  You must use modules to create unique functions. Macros cannot create functions. For instance, you might want to create a function called Commission that calculates the appropriate commission on a sale using your company's unique commission formula.

  Access error messages can be confusing to the user. But using VBA procedures, you can detect the error when it occurs and display your own message.

  Although Access 2010 macros have been enhanced to include more powerful If-Then logic, VBA is still more robust in the area of programming flow statements with tools such as nested If statements, Case statements, and multiple looping structures. Some of the most common VBA keywords, including If...Then, are shown in Table N-2. VBA keywords appear blue in the VBE code window.

  VBA code may declare **variables**, which are used to store data that can be used, modified, or displayed during the execution of the procedure.

  VBA may be used in conjunction with SQL (Structured Query Language) to select, update, append, and delete data.

  Class modules, like the one shown in Figure N-2, are stored as part of the form or report object in which they are created. If you develop forms and reports in one database and copy them to another, class module VBA automatically travels with the object that stores it.

FIGURE N-2: **Visual Basic Editor window for a class module**

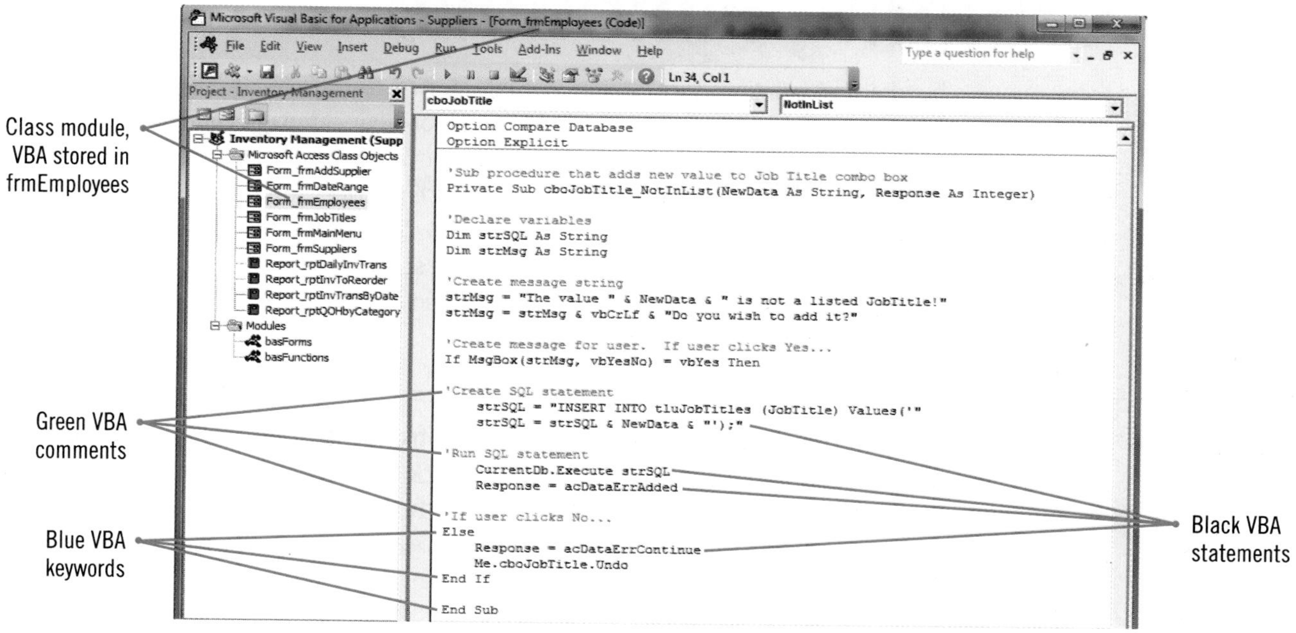

TABLE N-2: **Common VBA keywords**

statement	explanation
Function	Declares the name and arguments that create a new function procedure
End Function	When defining a new function, the End Function statement is required as the last statement to mark the end of the VBA code that defines the function
Sub	Declares the name for a new Sub procedure; **Private Sub** indicates that the Sub is accessible only to other procedures in the module where it is declared
End Sub	When defining a new sub, the End Sub statement is required as the last statement to mark the end of the VBA code that defines the sub
If...Then	Executes code (the code follows the Then statement) when the value of an expression is true (the expression follows the If statement)
End If	When creating an If...Then statement, the End If statement is required as the last statement
Const	Declares the name and value of a **constant**, an item that retains a constant value throughout the execution of the code
Option Compare Database	A declaration statement that determines the way string values (text) will be sorted
Option Explicit	A declaration statement that specifies that you must explicitly declare all variables used in all procedures; if you attempt to use an undeclared variable name, an error occurs at **compile time**, the period during which source code is translated to executable code
Dim	Declares a **variable**, a named storage location that contains data that can be modified during program execution
On Error GoTo	Upon an error in the execution of a procedure, the On Error GoTo statement specifies the location (the statement) where the procedure should continue
Select Case	Executes one of several groups of statements called a **Case** depending on the value of an expression; use the Select Case statement as an alternative to using **ElseIf** in **If...Then...Else** statements when comparing one expression to several different values
End Select	When defining a new Select Case group of statements, the End Select statement is required as the last statement to mark the end of the VBA code

UNIT N
Access 2010

Creating Functions

Access supplies hundreds of functions such as Sum, Count, IIf, First, Last, Date, and Hour. However, you might want to create a new function to calculate a value based on your company's unique business rules. You would create the new function in a standard module so that it can be used in any query, form, or report throughout the database. Quest Specialty Travel allows employees to purchase computer equipment when it is replaced. Equipment that is less than a year old will be sold to employees at 75 percent of its initial value, and equipment that is more than a year old will be sold at 50 percent of its initial value. Kayla Green, network administrator, asks you to create a new function called EmpPrice that determines the employee purchase price of replaced computer equipment.

STEPS

QUICK TIP
The Option Explicit statement appears if the Require Variable Declaration option is checked in the VBA Options dialog box. To view the default settings, click Options on the VBA Tools menu.

1. **Start Access, open the Technology-N.accdb database from the drive and folder where you store your Data Files, enable content if prompted, click the Create tab, click the Module button in the Macros & Code group, then maximize the Visual Basic window**

   Access automatically inserts the Option Compare Database declaration statement in the Code window. You will create the new EmpPrice function one step at a time.

2. **Type Function EmpPrice(StartValue), then press [Enter]**

   This statement creates a new function named EmpPrice, and states that it contains one argument, StartValue. VBA automatically adds the **End Function** statement, a required statement to mark the end of the function. Because both Function and End Function are VBA keywords, they are blue. The insertion point is positioned between the statements so that you can further define how the new EmpPrice function will calculate by entering more VBA statements.

3. **Press [Tab], type EmpPrice = StartValue * 0.5, then press [Enter]**

   Your screen should look like Figure N-3. The second statement explains how the EmpPrice function will calculate. The function will return a value that is calculated by multiplying the StartValue by 0.5. It is not necessary to indent statements, but indenting code between matching Function/End Function, Sub/End Sub, or If/End If statements enhances the program's readability. Also, it is not necessary to enter spaces around the equal sign and the asterisk used as a multiplication sign, but when you press [Enter] at the end of a VBA statement, Access automatically adds spaces as appropriate to enhance the readability of the statement.

4. **Click the Save button on the Standard toolbar, type basFunctions in the Save As dialog box, click OK, then click the upper Close button in the upper-right corner of the VBE to close the Visual Basic Editor**

   It is common for VBA programmers to use three-character prefixes to name objects and controls. This makes it easier to identify that object or control in expressions and modules. The prefix **bas** is short for Basic, and applies to global modules. Naming conventions for other objects and controls are listed in Table N-3 and used throughout the Technology-N.accdb database. You can use the new function, EmpPrice, in a query, form, or report.

5. **Click the Queries bar in the Navigation Pane to expand the Queries section if it is collapsed, right-click the qryEmpPricing query in the Navigation Pane, then click Design View on the shortcut menu**

   Now you can use the new EmpPrice function in the query to determine the employee purchase price of replaced computer equipment.

QUICK TIP
Field names used in expressions are not case sensitive, but they must exactly match the spelling of the field name as defined in Table Design View.

6. **Click the blank Field cell to the right of the InitialValue field, type Price:EmpPrice([InitialValue]), then click the View button to switch to Datasheet View**

   Your screen should look like Figure N-4. In this query, you created a new field called Price that uses the EmpPrice function. The value in the InitialValue field is used for the StartValue argument of the new EmpPrice function. The InitialValue field is multiplied by 0.5 to create the new Price field.

7. **Save then close the qryEmpPricing query**

FIGURE N-3: Creating the EmpPrice function

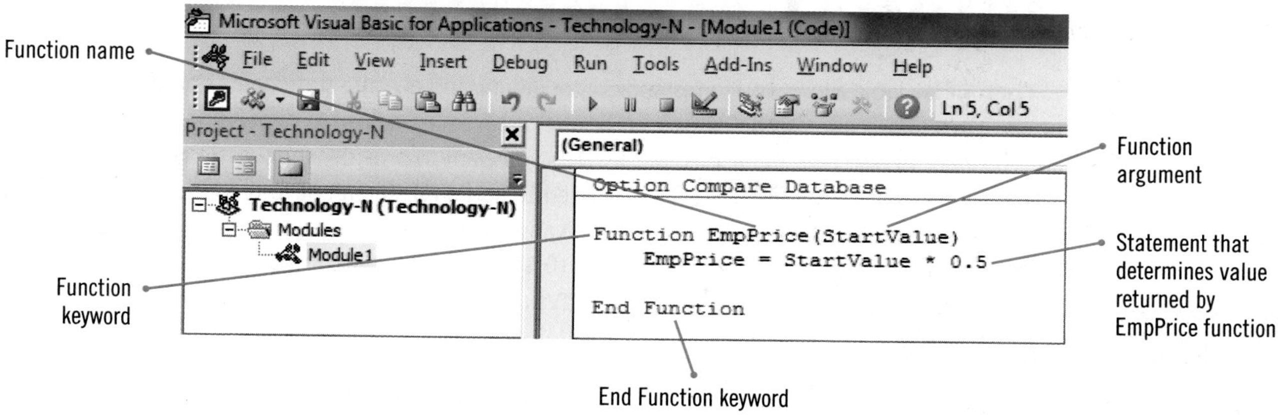

FIGURE N-4: Using the EmpPrice function in a query

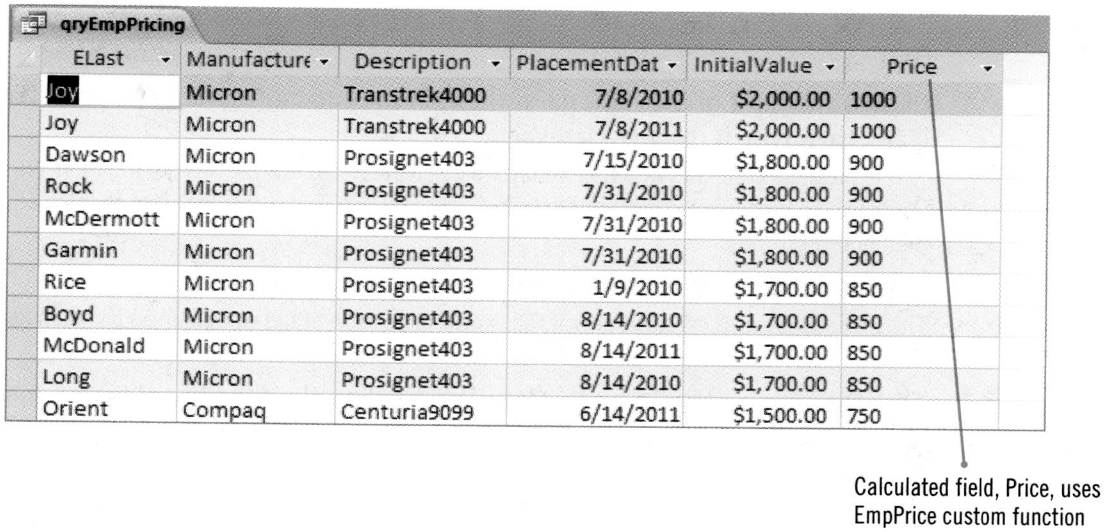

ELast	Manufacturer	Description	PlacementDat	InitialValue	Price
Joy	Micron	Transtrek4000	7/8/2010	$2,000.00	1000
Joy	Micron	Transtrek4000	7/8/2011	$2,000.00	1000
Dawson	Micron	Prosignet403	7/15/2010	$1,800.00	900
Rock	Micron	Prosignet403	7/31/2010	$1,800.00	900
McDermott	Micron	Prosignet403	7/31/2010	$1,800.00	900
Garmin	Micron	Prosignet403	7/31/2010	$1,800.00	900
Rice	Micron	Prosignet403	1/9/2010	$1,700.00	850
Boyd	Micron	Prosignet403	8/14/2010	$1,700.00	850
McDonald	Micron	Prosignet403	8/14/2011	$1,700.00	850
Long	Micron	Prosignet403	8/14/2010	$1,700.00	850
Orient	Compaq	Centuria9099	6/14/2011	$1,500.00	750

TABLE N-3: Three-character prefix naming conventions

object or control type	prefix	example
Table	tbl	tblProducts
Query	qry	qrySalesByRegion
Form	frm	frmProducts
Report	rpt	rptSalesByCategory
Macro	mcr	mcrCloseInventory
Module	bas	basRetirement
Label	lbl	lblFullName
Text Box	txt	txtLastName
Combo box	cbo	cboStates
Command button	cmd	cmdPrint

UNIT N

Access 2010

Using If Statements

If...Then...Else logic allows you to test logical conditions and execute statements only if the conditions are true. If...Then...Else code can be composed of one or several statements, depending on how many conditions you want to test, how many possible answers you want to provide, and what you want the code to do based on the results of the tests. You need to add an If statement to the EmpPrice function to test the age of the equipment, and then calculate the answer based on that age. Right now, the EmpPrice function multiplies the StartValue argument by 50% (0.5). You want to modify the EmpPrice function so that if the equipment is less than one year old, the StartValue is multiplied by 75% (0.75).

STEPS

1. **Scroll down the Navigation Pane, right-click the basFunctions module, then click Design View**

   To determine the age of the equipment, the EmpPrice function needs another argument, the purchase date of the equipment.

2. **Click just before the right parenthesis in the Function statement, type , (a comma), press [Spacebar], type DateValue, then press [↓]**

   Now that you established another argument, you can work with the argument in the definition of the function.

> **QUICK TIP**
> Indentation doesn't affect the way the function works, but does make the code easier to read.

3. **Click to the right of the right parenthesis in the Function statement, press [Enter], press [Tab], then type If (Now()–DateValue) >365 Then**

   The expression compares whether today's date, represented by the Access function **Now()**, minus the DateValue argument value is greater than 365 days (1 year). If true, this indicates that the equipment is older than one year.

4. **Indent and type the rest of the statements exactly as shown in Figure N-5**

   The **Else** statement is executed only if the expression is false (if the equipment is less than 365 days old). The **End If** statement is needed to mark the end of the If block of code.

> **TROUBLE**
> If a compile or syntax error appears, open the Visual Basic window, check your function against Figure N-5, then correct any errors.

5. **Click the Save button on the Standard toolbar, close the Visual Basic window, right-click the qryEmpPricing query in the Navigation Pane, then click Design View on the shortcut menu**

   Now that you've modified the EmpPrice function to include two arguments, you need to modify the calculated Price field expression, too.

6. **Right-click the Price field in the query design grid, click Zoom on the shortcut menu, click between the right square bracket and right parenthesis, then type ,[PlacementDate]**

   Your Zoom dialog box should look like Figure N-6. Both of the arguments used to define the EmpPrice function in the VBA code are replaced with actual field names that contain the data to be analyzed. Field names must be typed exactly as shown and surrounded by square brackets. Commas separate multiple arguments in the function.

7. **Click OK in the Zoom dialog box, then click the View button to display the datasheet**

> **TROUBLE**
> The new calculated Price field is based on the current date on your computer, so your results may vary.

8. **Click any entry in the PlacementDate field, then click the Ascending button in the Sort & Filter group as shown in Figure N-7**

   The EmpPrice function now calculates one of two different results, depending on the age of the equipment determined by the date in the PlacementDate field.

9. **Save and then close the qryEmpPricing query**

FIGURE N-5: Using an If…Then…Else structure

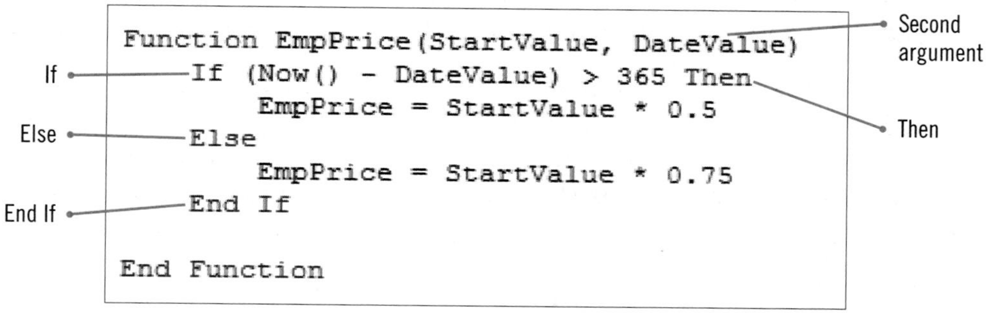
Function EmpPrice(StartValue, DateValue)
If (Now() - DateValue) > 365 Then
EmpPrice = StartValue * 0.5
Else
EmpPrice = StartValue * 0.75
End If
End Function
If
Else
End If
Second argument
Then

FIGURE N-6: Using the Zoom dialog box for long expressions

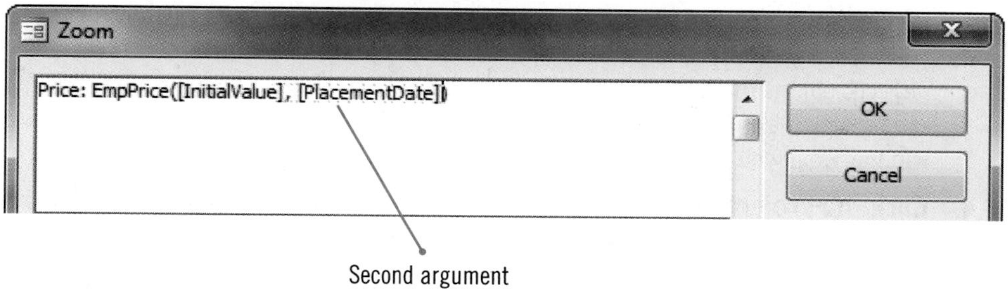
Zoom
Price: EmpPrice([InitialValue], [PlacementDate])
OK
Cancel
Second argument

Access 2010

FIGURE N-7: Price field is calculated at 50% or 75% based on age of equipment

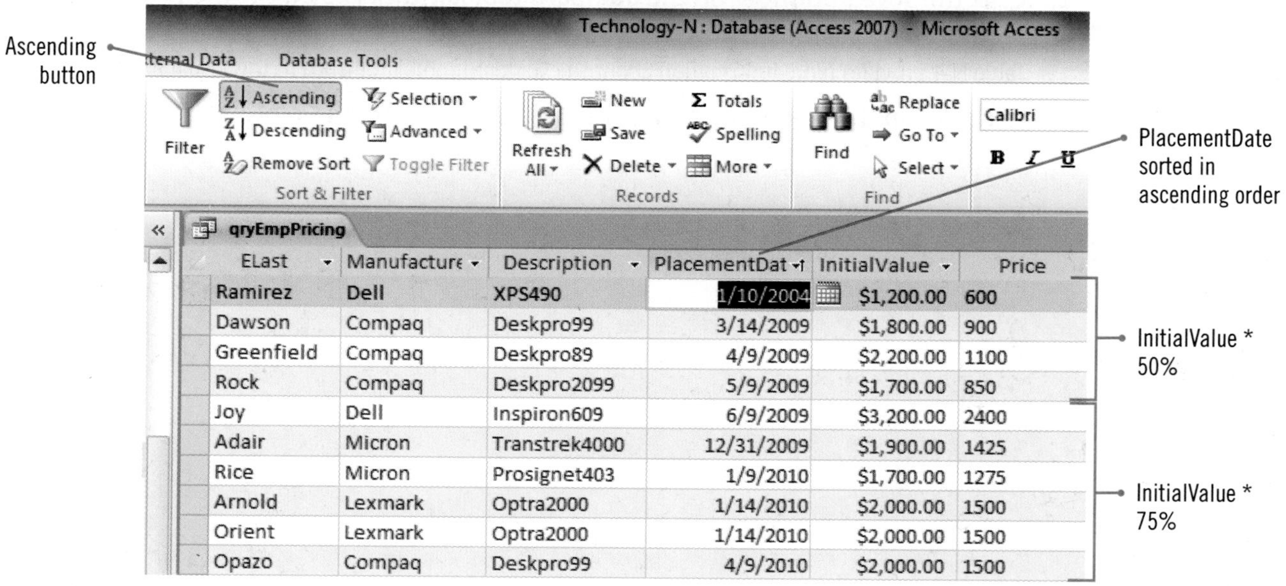
Technology-N : Database (Access 2007) - Microsoft Access
Ascending button
PlacementDate sorted in ascending order
InitialValue * 50%
InitialValue * 75%
qryEmpPricing
ELast | Manufacturer | Description | PlacementDate | InitialValue | Price
Ramirez | Dell | XPS490 | 1/10/2004 | $1,200.00 | 600
Dawson | Compaq | Deskpro99 | 3/14/2009 | $1,800.00 | 900
Greenfield | Compaq | Deskpro89 | 4/9/2009 | $2,200.00 | 1100
Rock | Compaq | Deskpro2099 | 5/9/2009 | $1,700.00 | 850
Joy | Dell | Inspiron609 | 6/9/2009 | $3,200.00 | 2400
Adair | Micron | Transtrek4000 | 12/31/2009 | $1,900.00 | 1425
Rice | Micron | Prosignet403 | 1/9/2010 | $1,700.00 | 1275
Arnold | Lexmark | Optra2000 | 1/14/2010 | $2,000.00 | 1500
Orient | Lexmark | Optra2000 | 1/14/2010 | $2,000.00 | 1500
Opazo | Compaq | Deskpro99 | 4/9/2010 | $2,000.00 | 1500

UNIT N
Access 2010

Documenting Procedures

Comment lines are statements in the code that document the code; they do not affect how the code runs. At any time, if you want to read or modify existing code, you can write the modifications much more quickly if the code is properly documented. Comment lines start with an apostrophe and are green in the VBE. You decide to document the EmpPrice function in the basFunctions module with descriptive comments. This will make it easier for you and others to follow the purpose and logic of the function later.

STEPS

QUICK TIP
You can also create comments by starting the statement with the Rem statement (for remark).

TROUBLE
Be sure to use an ' (apostrophe) and not a " (quotation mark) to begin the comment line.

1. **Right-click the basFunctions module in the Navigation Pane, then click Design View**
   The Code window for the basFunctions module opens.
2. **Click the blank line between the Option Compare Database and Function statements, press [Enter], type 'This function is called EmpPrice and has two arguments, then press [Enter]**
   As soon as you move to another statement, the comment statement becomes green.
3. **Type 'Created by Your Name on Today's Date, then press [Enter]**
   Your screen should look like Figure N-8. You can also place comments at the end of a line by entering an apostrophe to mark that the next part of the statement is a comment. Closing the Project Explorer window gives you more room for the Code window. (You use the **Project Explorer window** to switch between open projects, objects that can contain VBA code. The **utility project** contains VBA code that helps Access with certain activities such as presenting the Zoom dialog box. It automatically appears in the Project Explorer window when you use the Access features that utilize this code.)
4. **Click the Project Explorer Close button, click to the right of Then at the end of the If statement, press [Spacebar], type 'Now() returns today's date, then press [↓]**
   This comment explains that the Now() function is today's date. All comments are green, regardless of whether they are on their own line or at the end of an existing line.
5. **Click to the right of 0.5, press [Spacebar] three times, then type 'If > 1 year, multiply by 50%**
6. **Click to the right of 0.75, press [Spacebar] twice, type 'If < 1 year, multiply by 75%, then press [↓]**
   Your screen should look like Figure N-9. Each comment will turn green as soon as you move to a new statement.
7. **Click the Save button on the Standard toolbar, click File on the menu bar, click Print if requested by your instructor, then click OK**
   Table N-4 provides more information about the Standard toolbar buttons in the Visual Basic window.
8. **Click File on the menu bar, then click Close and Return to Microsoft Access**

FIGURE N-8: **Adding comments**

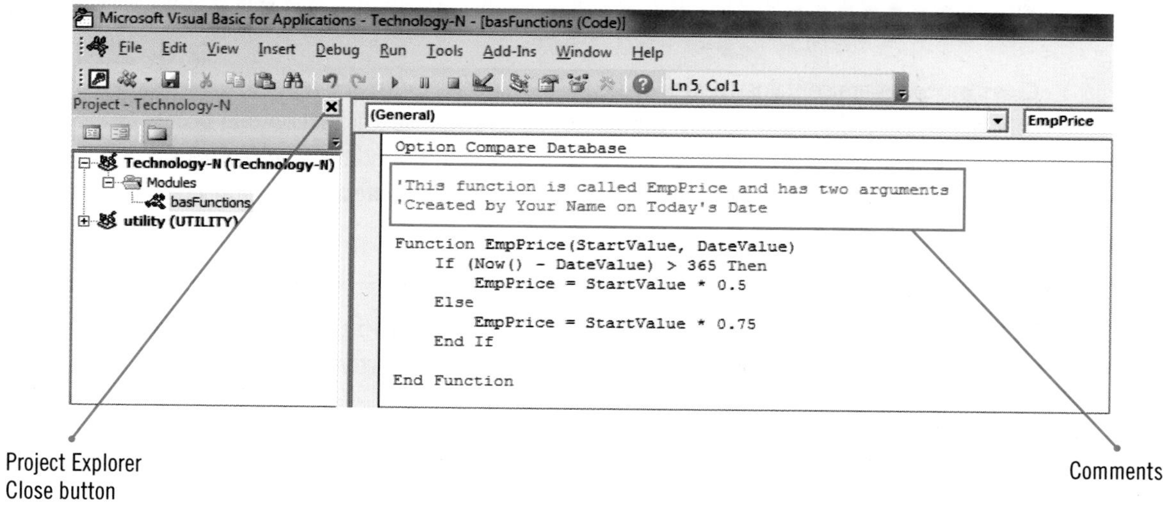

FIGURE N-9: **Adding comments at the end of a statement**

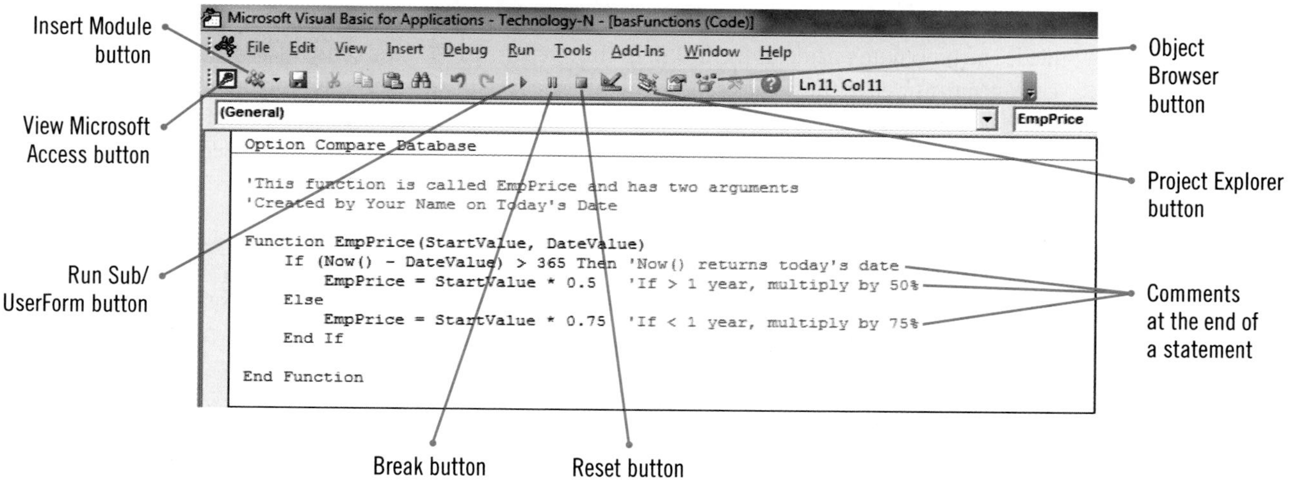

TABLE N-4: **Standard toolbar buttons in the Visual Basic window**

button name	button	description
View Microsoft Access		Switches from the active Visual Basic window to the Access window
Insert Module		Opens a new module or class module Code window, or inserts a new procedure in the current Code window
Run Sub/UserForm		Runs the current procedure if the insertion point is in a procedure, or runs the UserForm if it is active
Break		Stops the execution of a program while it's running and switches to break mode, which is the temporary suspension of program execution in which you can examine, debug, reset, step through, or continue program execution
Reset		Resets the procedure
Project Explorer		Displays the Project Explorer, which displays a hierarchical list of the currently open projects (set of modules) and their contents
Object Browser		Displays the Object Browser, which lists the defined modules and procedures as well as available methods, properties, events, constants, and other items that you can use in the code

UNIT N

Access 2010

Building Class Modules

Class modules are contained and executed within specific forms and reports. Class modules most commonly contain sub procedures and run in response to an **event**, a specific action that occurs as the result of a user action. Common events include clicking a command button, editing data, or closing a form. You examine an existing class module to understand and create sub procedures connected to events that occur on the form.

STEPS

QUICK TIP
frmEmployees has a Caption property of Employees displayed in the form tab.

1. **Double-click the frmEmployees form in the Navigation Pane to open it in Form View, then click the Branch of Service combo box list arrow to review the choices**

   The Branch of Service combo box provides a list of the branches of the armed services. For a choice to make sense, however, an employee would first need to be a veteran. You'll set the Visible property for the Branch of Service combo box to True if the Veteran check box is checked and False if the Veteran check box is not checked.

TROUBLE
If the first line of your procedure is not Private Sub chkVeteran_AfterUpdate( ), delete the stub, close the VBE, and repeat Step 2.

2. **Right-click the Employees tab, click Design View on the shortcut menu, double-click the edge of the Veteran check box to open its Property Sheet, click the Event tab in the Property Sheet, click the After Update property, click the Build button, click Code Builder, then click OK**

   The class module for the frmEmployees form opens. Because you opened the VBE from within a specific event of a specific control on the form, the **stub**, the first and last lines of the sub procedure, were automatically created. The procedure's name in the first line, chkVeteran_AfterUpdate, contains *both* the name of the control, chkVeteran, as well as the name of the event, AfterUpdate, that triggers this procedure. (Recall that the **Name property** of a control is found on the Other tab in the control's property sheet. The **After Update property** is on the Event tab.) A sub procedure that is triggered by an event is often called an **event handler**.

3. **Enter the statements shown in Figure N-10**

   When you use three-character prefixes for all controls and objects in your database, it increases the meaning and readability of your VBA. In this case, the name of the sub procedure shows that it runs on the AfterUpdate event of the chkVeteran control. (The sub runs when the Veteran check box is checked or unchecked.) The If structure contains VBA that makes the cboBranchOfService control either visible or not visible based on the value of the chkVeteran control. To test the sub procedure, you switch to Form View.

4. **Save the changes and close the VBE, click the View button to switch to Form View, click the Veteran check box for the first record several times, then navigate through several records**

   By clicking the Veteran check box in the first record, you triggered the procedure that responds to the After Update event of the Veteran check box. However, you also want the procedure to run every time you move from record to record. The **On Current** event of the form is triggered when you navigate through records.

TROUBLE
If the VBA code window appears with a yellow line, it means the code cannot be run successfully. Click the Reset button, then compare your VBA to Figure N-11.

5. **Right-click the Employees form tab, click Design View on the shortcut menu, click the Form Selector button, click the Event tab in the Property Sheet, click the On Current event property in the Property Sheet, click the Build button, click Code Builder, click OK, then copy or retype the If structure from the chkVeteran_AfterUpdate sub to the Form_Current sub as shown in Figure N-11**

   By copying the same If structure to a second sub procedure, you've created a second event handler. Now, the cboBrandOfService combo box will either be visible or not based on two different events: updating the chkVeteran check box or moving from record to record. To test the new sub procedure, you switch to Form View.

6. **Save the changes and close the VBE, click to switch to Form View, then navigate to the fifth record for Gail Owen to test the new procedures**

   Now, as you move from record to record, the Branch of Service combo box should be visible for those employees with the Veteran check box selected, and not visible if the Veteran check box is not selected.

7. **Click the Branch of Service combo box list arrow, click Army as shown in Figure N-12, then save and close the frmEmployees form**

FIGURE N-10: **Creating your first sub procedure**

```
Private Sub chkVeteran_AfterUpdate()

If chkVeteran.Value = True Then
    cboBranchOfService.Visible = True
Else
    cboBranchOfService.Visible = False
End If

End Sub
```

FIGURE N-11: **Copying the If structure to a new event handler**

```
Private Sub chkVeteran_AfterUpdate()

If chkVeteran.Value = True Then
    cboBranchOfService.Visible = True
Else
    cboBranchOfService.Visible = False
End If

End Sub

Private Sub Form_Current()

If chkVeteran.Value = True Then
    cboBranchOfService.Visible = True
Else
    cboBranchOfService.Visible = False
End If

End Sub
```

If structure copied from chkVeteran_AfterUpdate sub to Form_Current sub

FIGURE N-12: **Using the Branch of Service combo box when the Veteran check box is selected**

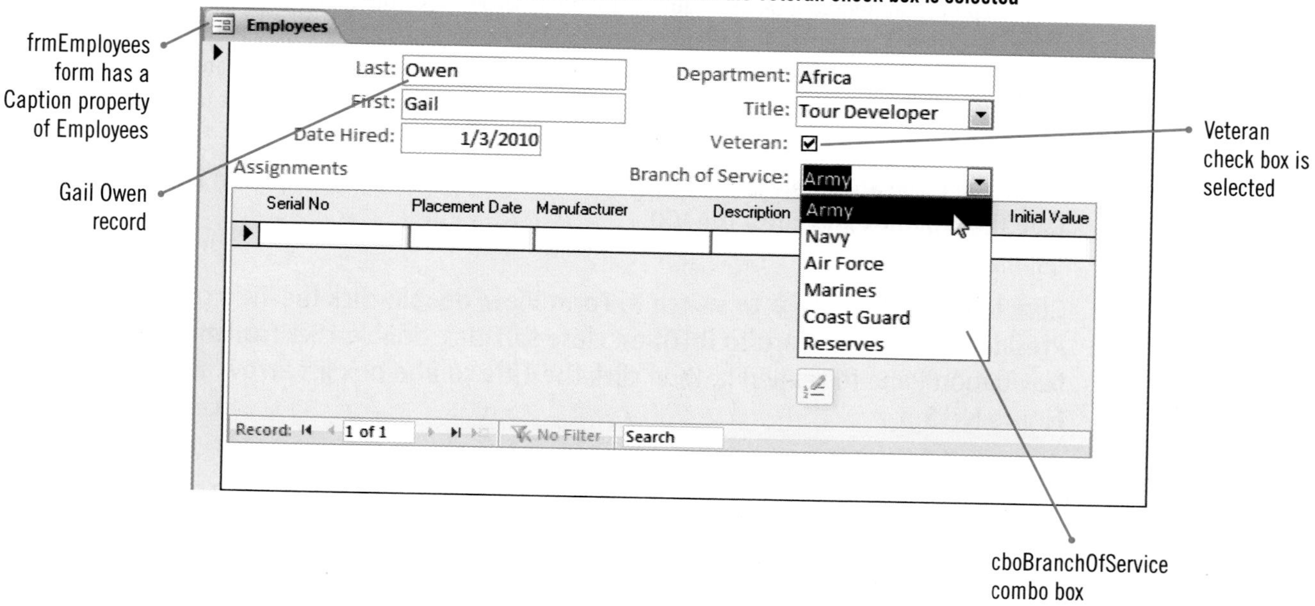

Modifying Sub Procedures

Sub procedures can be triggered on any event identified in the Property Sheet such as **On Got Focus** (when the control gets the focus), **After Update** (after a field is updated), or **On Dbl Click** (when the control is double-clicked). Not all items have the same set of event properties. For example, a text box control has both a Before Update and After Update event property, but neither of these events exists for unbound controls such as a label or command button because those controls are not used to update data. Kayla Green asks if there is a way to easily add new items to the Title combo box. You use VBA sub procedures to handle this request.

STEPS

1. **Right-click the frmEmployees form, click Design View on the shortcut menu, then double-click the edge of the ETitle combo box to open its Property Sheet**

   When entering a new employee, if the desired title is not available on the list, you want to give the user a way to add the new title. You decide to use the double-click event property of the ETitle combo box to open the tblTitles table where you can add the new title.

2. **Click the Event tab in the Property Sheet, click the On Dbl Click text box, click the Build button, click Code Builder, then click OK**

   The class module opens and creates a stub for the new procedure. The name of the new procedure is cboETitle_DblClick indicating that it is an event handler procedure that will run when the cboETitle control is double-clicked. As you type the statement, be sure to watch the screen carefully for IntelliSense programming support.

3. **Type DoCmd.Close, press [Enter], then type DoCmd. (include the period)**

   DoCmd is a VBA object that supports many methods to run common Access commands such as closing windows, opening forms, previewing reports, navigating records, and setting the value of controls. The first DoCmd statement will close the current object, frmEmployees. The second DoCmd statement will open the tblTitles table. As you write a VBA statement, visual aids that are part of **IntelliSense technology** help you complete it. For example, when you press the period (.) after the DoCmd object, a list of available methods appears. Watching the VBA window carefully and taking advantage of all IntelliSense clues as you complete a statement can greatly improve your accuracy and productivity in writing VBA.

4. **Type OpenTab, press [Tab] when OpenTable is highlighted in the IntelliSense list, press [Spacebar], type "tblTitles", then type , (comma)**

   Your sub procedure should look like Figure N-13. IntelliSense helps you fill out the rest of the statement, indicating the order of arguments needed for the method to execute (the current argument is listed in bold), and whether the argument is required or optional (optional arguments are listed in [square brackets]). Optional arguments can be skipped by typing a comma (,). Optional arguments at the end of a statement can be ignored.

5. **Press [Backspace] to delete the unneeded comma, press [↓] as shown in Figure N-14, then save the changes and close the VBE**

   Test the new procedure.

> **TROUBLE**
> Be sure to double-click the combo box and not the Title label.

6. **Click the View button to switch to Form View, double-click the Title combo box, add President as a new record to tblTitles, close tblTitles, double-click frmEmployees in the Navigation Pane to reopen it, then click the Title combo box list arrow as shown in Figure N-15**

7. **Click President as the new Title for Ron Dawson, then close frmEmployees**

   VBA is a robust and powerful programming language. It takes years of experience to appreciate the vast number of objects, events, methods, and properties that are available. With only modest programming skills, however, you can create basic sub procedures that greatly help the users enter, find, and analyze information.

FIGURE N-13: **Using IntelliSense to add a new statement**

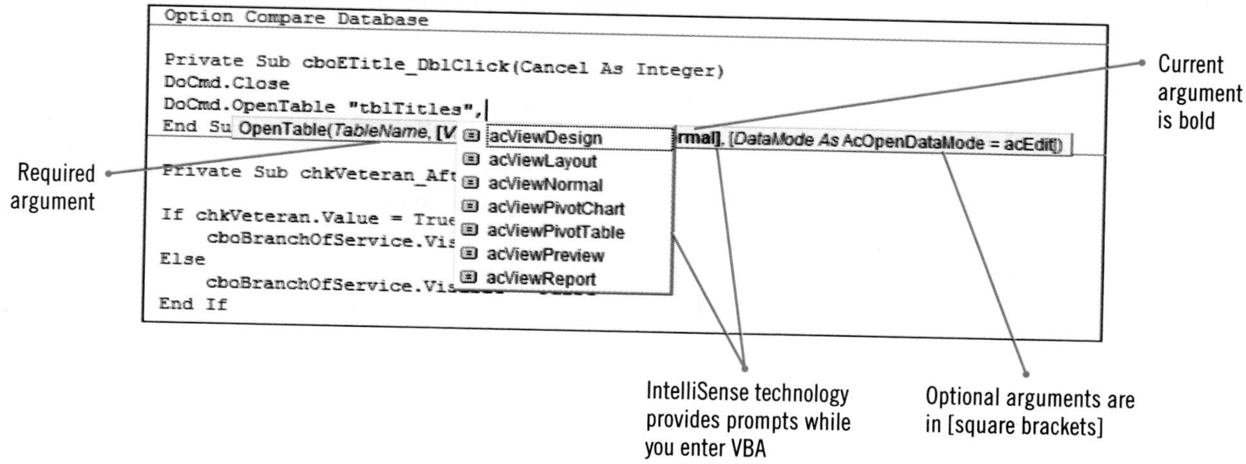

FIGURE N-14: **Final cboETitle_DblClick sub**

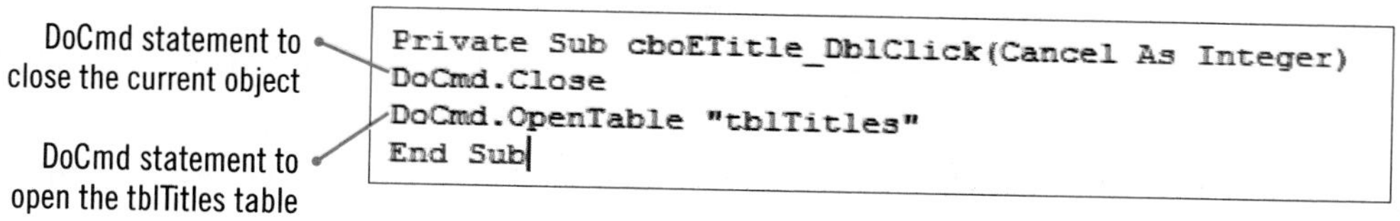

FIGURE N-15: **Updated combo box**

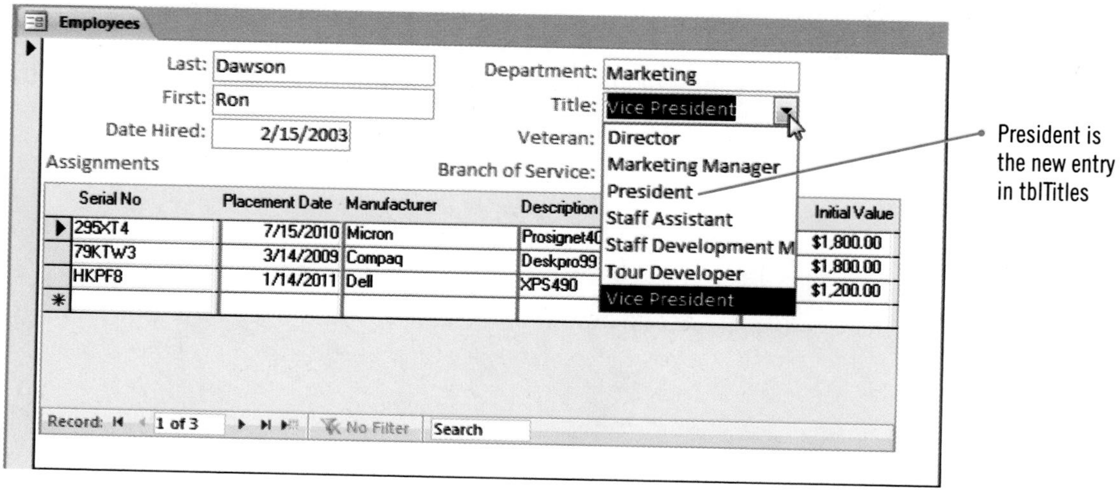

Access 2010

UNIT
N
Access 2010

Troubleshooting Modules

Access provides several techniques to help you **debug** (find and resolve) different types of VBA errors. A **syntax error** occurs immediately as you are writing a VBA statement that cannot be read by the Visual Basic Editor. This is the easiest type of error to identify because your code turns red when the syntax error occurs. **Compile-time errors** occur as a result of incorrectly constructed code and are detected as soon as you run your code or select the Compile option on the Debug menu. For example, you may have forgotten to insert an End If statement to finish an If structure. **Run-time errors** occur as incorrectly constructed code runs and include attempting an illegal operation such as dividing by zero or moving focus to a control that doesn't exist. When you encounter a run-time error, VBA will stop executing your procedure at the statement in which the error occurred and highlight the line with a yellow background in the Visual Basic Editor. **Logic errors** are the most difficult to troubleshoot because they occur when the code runs without obvious problems, but the procedure still doesn't produce the desired result. You study debugging techniques using the basFunctions module.

STEPS

1. **Right-click the basFunctions module in the Navigation Pane, click Design View, click to the right of the End If statement, press the [Spacebar], type your name, then press [↓]**
   Because the End If your name statement cannot be resolved by the Visual Basic Editor, it immediately turns red.
2. **Click OK in the Compile error message box, delete your name, then press [↓]**
   Another VBA debugging tool is to set a **breakpoint**, a bookmark that suspends execution of the procedure at that statement to allow you to examine what is happening.
3. **Click in the If statement line, click Debug on the menu bar, then click Toggle Breakpoint**
   Your screen should look like Figure N-16.
4. **Click the View Microsoft Access button on the Standard toolbar, then double-click the qryEmpPricing query in the Navigation Pane**
   When the qryEmpPricing query opens, it immediately runs the EmpPrice function. Because you set a breakpoint at the If statement, the statement is highlighted as shown in Figure N-17, indicating that the code has been suspended at that point.
5. **Click View on the menu bar, click Immediate Window, type ? DateValue, then press [Enter]**
   Your screen should look like Figure N-18. The **Immediate window** is an area where you can determine the value of any argument at the breakpoint.
6. **Click Debug on the menu bar, click Clear All Breakpoints, click the Continue button on the Standard toolbar to execute the remainder of the function, then save and close the basFunctions module**
   The qryEmpPricing query's datasheet should be visible.
7. **Close the qryEmpPricing datasheet, close the Technology-N.accdb database, then exit Access**

QUICK TIP
Click the gray bar to the left of a statement to toggle a breakpoint on and off.

QUICK TIP
Pointing to an argument in the Code window displays a ScreenTip with the argument's current value.

FIGURE N-16: **Setting a breakpoint**

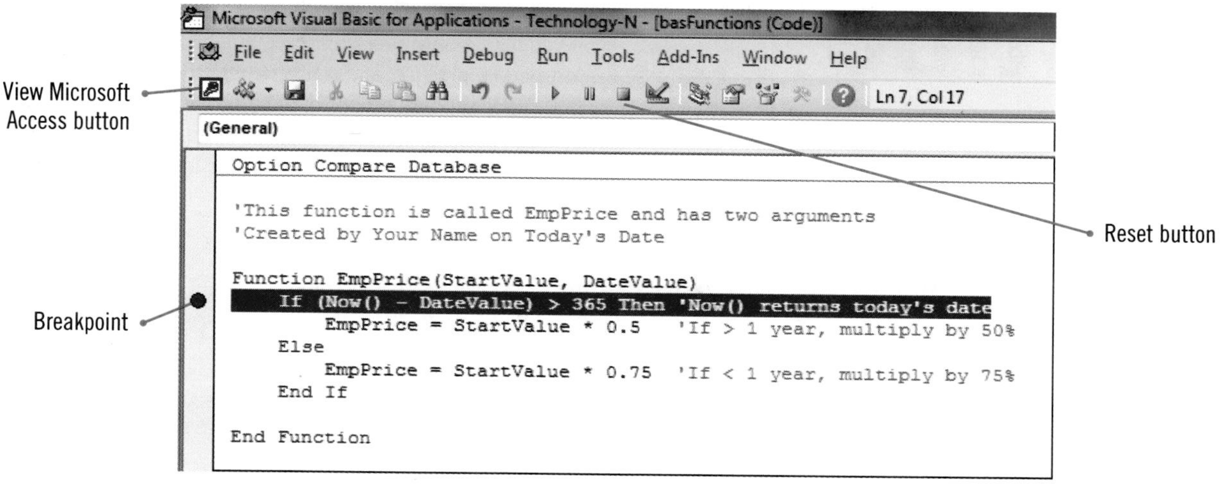
Microsoft Visual Basic for Applications - Technology-N - [basFunctions (Code)]
File Edit View Insert Debug Run Tools Add-Ins Window Help
Ln 7, Col 17
(General)
Option Compare Database
'This function is called EmpPrice and has two arguments
'Created by Your Name on Today's Date
Function EmpPrice(StartValue, DateValue)
If (Now() - DateValue) > 365 Then 'Now() returns today's date
EmpPrice = StartValue * 0.5 'If > 1 year, multiply by 50%
Else
EmpPrice = StartValue * 0.75 'If < 1 year, multiply by 75%
End If
End Function
View Microsoft Access button
Breakpoint
Reset button

FIGURE N-17: **Stopping execution at a breakpoint**

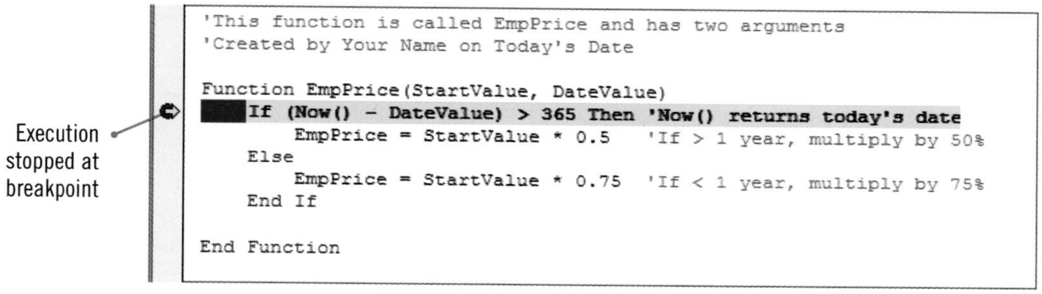
'This function is called EmpPrice and has two arguments
'Created by Your Name on Today's Date
Function EmpPrice(StartValue, DateValue)
If (Now() - DateValue) > 365 Then 'Now() returns today's date
EmpPrice = StartValue * 0.5 'If > 1 year, multiply by 50%
Else
EmpPrice = StartValue * 0.75 'If < 1 year, multiply by 75%
End If
End Function
Execution stopped at breakpoint

FIGURE N-18: **Updated combo box**

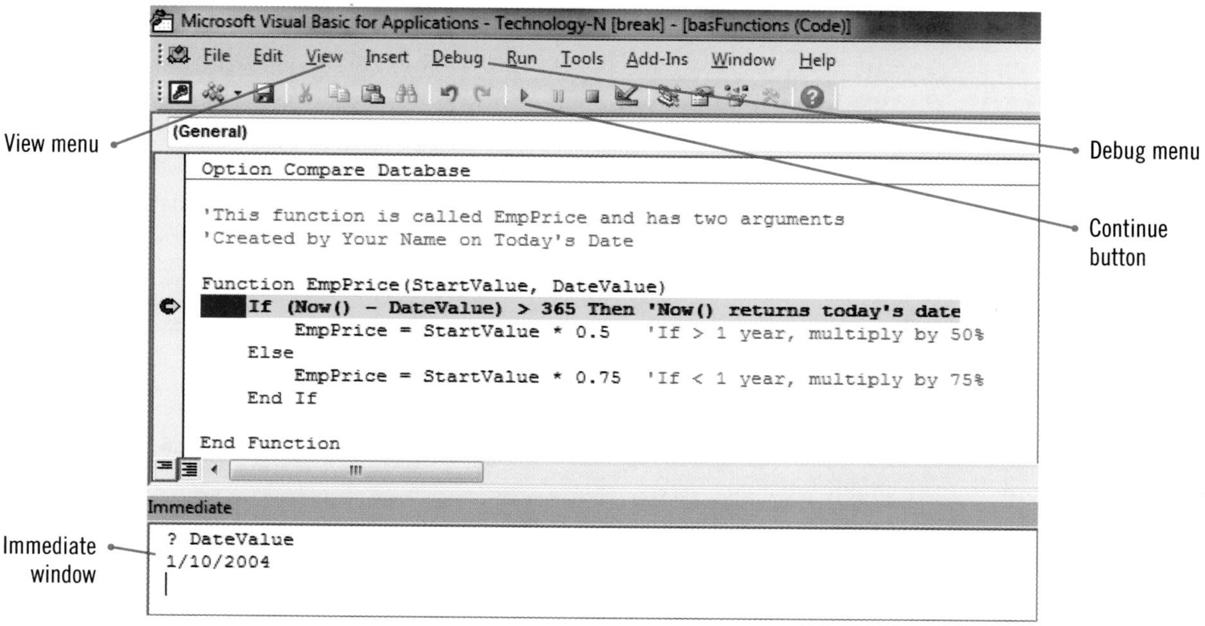
Microsoft Visual Basic for Applications - Technology-N [break] - [basFunctions (Code)]
File Edit View Insert Debug Run Tools Add-Ins Window Help
(General)
Option Compare Database
'This function is called EmpPrice and has two arguments
'Created by Your Name on Today's Date
Function EmpPrice(StartValue, DateValue)
If (Now() - DateValue) > 365 Then 'Now() returns today's date
EmpPrice = StartValue * 0.5 'If > 1 year, multiply by 50%
Else
EmpPrice = StartValue * 0.75 'If < 1 year, multiply by 75%
End If
End Function
Immediate
? DateValue
1/10/2004
View menu
Debug menu
Continue button
Immediate window

Access 2010

Practice

Concepts Review

For current SAM information, including versions and content details, visit SAM Central (http://www.cengage.com/samcentral). If you have a SAM user profile, you may have access to hands-on instruction, practice, and assessment of the skills covered in this unit. Since various versions of SAM are supported throughout the life of this text, check with your instructor for the correct instructions and URL/Web site for accessing assignments.

Identify each element of the Visual Basic window shown in Figure N-19.

FIGURE N-19

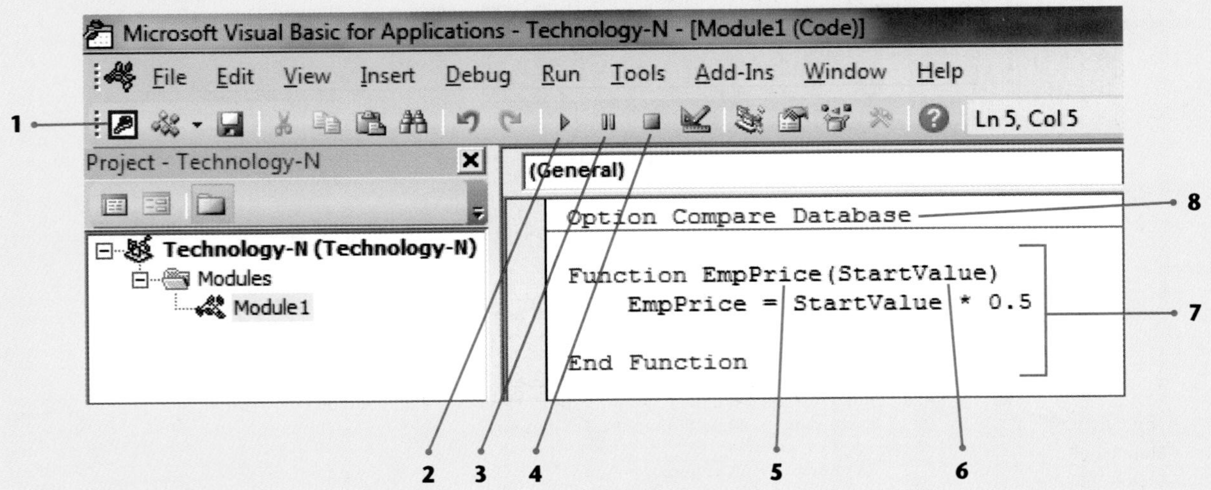

Microsoft Visual Basic for Applications - Technology-N - [Module1 (Code)]
File Edit View Insert Debug Run Tools Add-Ins Window Help
Ln 5, Col 5
Project - Technology-N
Technology-N (Technology-N)
Modules
Module1
(General)
Option Compare Database
Function EmpPrice(StartValue)
EmpPrice = StartValue * 0.5
End Function
1
2
3
4
5
6
7
8

Match each term with the statement that best describes its function.

9. **Visual Basic for Applications (VBA)**
10. **Debugging**
11. **If...Then...Else statement**
12. **Breakpoint**
13. **Function**
14. **Module**
15. **Procedure**
16. **Arguments**
17. **Class modules**

- **a.** Allows you to test a logical condition and execute commands only if the condition is true
- **b.** The programming language used in Access modules
- **c.** A line of code that automatically suspends execution of the procedure
- **d.** A process to find and resolve programming errors
- **e.** A procedure that returns a value
- **f.** Constants, variables, or expressions passed to a procedure to further define how it should execute
- **g.** Stored as part of the form or report object in which they are created
- **h.** The Access object where VBA code is stored
- **i.** A series of VBA statements that perform an operation or calculate a value

Select the best answer from the list of choices.

18. Which type of procedure returns a value?

- **a.** Function
- **b.** Sub procedure
- **c.** Sub
- **d.** Class module

19. Which of the following is *not* a reason to use modules rather than macros?

- **a.** Modules are used to create unique functions.
- **b.** Modules contain code that can work with other Microsoft Office programs.
- **c.** Modules are usually easier to write than macros.
- **d.** Modules can contain procedures that mask error messages.

20. Which of the following is *not* a type of VBA error?

a. Class action

b. Run time

c. Logic

d. Compile time

21. Which of the following is a specific action that occurs on or to an object, and is usually the result of a user action?

a. Argument

b. Event

c. Function

d. Sub

Skills Review

1. Understand modules and VBA.

a. Start Access, then open the Baseball-N.accdb (not the Basketball-N.accdb) database from the drive and folder where you store your Data Files. Enable content if prompted.

b. Open the Code window for the basFunctions module.

c. Record your answers to the following questions on a sheet of paper.

- What is the name of the function defined in this module?
- What are the names of the arguments defined in this module?
- What is the purpose of the If statement?
- What is the purpose of the End Function statement?
- Why is the End Function statement in blue?
- Why are some of the lines indented?

2. Compare macros and modules.

a. If not already opened, open the Code window for the basFunctions module.

b. Record your answers to the following questions on a sheet of paper.

- Why was a module rather than a macro used to create this procedure?
- Why is VBA generally more difficult to create than a macro?
- Identify each of the VBA keywords or keyword phrases, and explain the purpose for each.

3. Create functions.

a. If not already opened, open the Code window for the basFunctions module.

b. Create a function called **SluggingAverage** below the End Function statement of the BattingAverage function by typing the VBA statements shown in Figure N-20.

FIGURE N-20

```
Function SluggingAverage(SingleValue, DoubleValue, TripleValue, HRValue, AtBatsValue)
   SluggingAverage = (SingleValue + 2 * DoubleValue + 3 * TripleValue + 4 * HRValue) / AtBatsValue
End Function
```

In baseball, the slugging average is a popular statistic because it accounts for the power of each hit. In the regular batting average, a single, double, triple, and home run are all given the same weight. In the slugging average, each hit is multiplied by the number of bases earned (one for single, 2 for double, 3 for triple, and 4 for home run). A perfect batting average is 1 (any type of a hit each time at bat). A perfect slugging average is 4 (a home run, or 4 bases, each time at bat).

c. Save the basFunctions module, then close the Visual Basic window.

d. Use Query Design View to create a new query using the PlayerFName and PlayerLName fields from the tblPlayers table, and the AtBats field from the tblPlayerStats table.

e. Create a calculated field named **Batting** in the next available column by carefully typing the expression as follows: **Batting: BattingAverage([1Base],[2Base],[3Base],[4Base],[AtBats])**.

f. Create a second calculated field named **Slugging** in the next available column by carefully typing the expression as follows: **Slugging: SluggingAverage([1Base],[2Base],[3Base],[4Base],[AtBats])**.

g. View the datasheet, change Louis Gehrig to your first and last name, save the query with the name **qryStats**, then close qryStats.

Skills Review (continued)

4. Use If statements.

a. Open the Code window for the basFunctions module, then modify the function to add the If structure shown in Figure N-21. The If structure prevents the error caused by attempting to divide by zero. The If structure checks to see if the AtBatValue argument is equal to 0. If so, the SluggingAverage function is set to 0. Else, the SluggingAverage function is calculated.

FIGURE N-21

```
Function SluggingAverage(SingleValue, DoubleValue, TripleValue, HRValue, AtBatsValue)
If AtBatsValue = 0 Then
    SluggingAverage = 0
Else
    SluggingAverage = (SingleValue + 2 * DoubleValue + 3 * TripleValue + 4 * HRValue) / AtBatsValue
End If
End Function
```

b. Save the basFunctions module, then close the Visual Basic window.

c. Open the qryStats datasheet, then change the AtBats value to **0** for the first record to test the If statement. Both the Batting and Slugging calculated field should equal 0.

d. Close the datasheet.

5. Document procedures.

a. Open the Code window for the basFunctions module, and add the two statements above each End Function statement as shown in Figure N-22. The statements use the Format function to format the calculation as a number with three digits to the right of the decimal. The comments help clarify the statement.

FIGURE N-22

```
Function BattingAverage(SingleValue, DoubleValue, TripleValue, HRValue, AtBatsValue)
If AtBatsValue = 0 Then
    BattingAverage = 0
Else
    BattingAverage = (SingleValue + DoubleValue + TripleValue + HRValue) / AtBatsValue
End If
'Format the answer as a number with three digits to the right of the decimal point
BattingAverage = Format(BattingAverage, "0.000")
End Function

Function SluggingAverage(SingleValue, DoubleValue, TripleValue, HRValue, AtBatsValue)
If AtBatsValue = 0 Then
    SluggingAverage = 0
Else
    SluggingAverage = (SingleValue + 2 * DoubleValue + 3 * TripleValue + 4 * HRValue) / AtBatsValue
End If
'Format the answer as a number with three digits to the right of the decimal point
SluggingAverage = Format(SluggingAverage, "0.000")
End Function

'Created by (Your Name) on (Today's Date)
```

b. Add a comment at the end of the VBA code that identifies your name and today's date as shown in Figure N-22.

c. Save the changes to the basFunctions module, print the module if requested by your instructor, then close the Visual Basic window.

d. Open the qryStats query datasheet and change the AtBats value to **3** for the first record to observe how the values in the Batting and Slugging calculated fields change and how they are now formatted consistently due to the VBA statements you added to format the values.

e. Print the qryStats datasheet if requested by your instructor, then close it.

6. Build class modules.

a. Open frmPlayerEntry in Form View, then move through several records to observe the data.

b. Switch to Design View, and on the right side of the form, select the Print Current Record button.

c. Open the Property Sheet for the button, click the Event tab, click the On Click property, then click the Build button to open the class module.

d. Add a comment to the last line to show your name and the current date. Save the module, print it if requested by your instructor, then close the Visual Basic window.

7. Modify sub procedures.

a. Open the frmPlayerEntry form in Form View, move through a couple of records to observe the txtSalary text box (currently blank), then switch to Design View.

b. The base starting salary in this league is $24,000. You will add a command button with VBA to help enter the correct salary for each player. Use the Button button to add a command button below the txtSalary text box, then cancel the Command Button Wizard if it starts.

c. Open the Property Sheet for the new command button, then change the Caption property on the Format tab to **Base Salary**. Change the Name property on the Other tab to **cmdBaseSalary**.

d. On the Event tab of the Property Sheet, click the On Click property, click the Build button, click Code Builder, then click OK. The stub for the new cmdBaseSalary_Click sub is automatically created for you.

e. Enter the following statement between the Sub and End Sub statements:
txtSalary.Value = 24000

f. Save the changes, then close the Visual Basic window.

g. Close the Property Sheet, then save and open the frmPlayerEntry form in Form View.

h. Click the Base Salary command button for the first player, move to the second record, then click the Base Salary command button for the second player.

i. Save, then close the frmPlayerEntry form.

8. Troubleshoot modules.

a. Open the Code window for the basFunctions module.

b. Click anywhere in the If AtBatsValue = 0 Then statement in the BattingAverage function.

c. Click Debug on the menu bar, then click Toggle Breakpoint to set a breakpoint at this statement.

d. Save the changes, then and close the Visual Basic window and return to Microsoft Access.

e. Open the qryStats query datasheet. This action will attempt to use the BattingAverage function to calculate the value for the Batting field, which will stop and highlight the statement in the Visual Basic window where you set a breakpoint.

f. Click View on the menu bar, click Immediate Window (if not already visible), delete any previous entries in the Immediate window, type **?AtBatsValue**, then press [Enter]. At this point in the execution of the VBA, the AtBatsValue should be 3, the value for the first record.

g. Type **?SingleValue**, then press [Enter]. At this point in the execution of the VBA code, the SingleValue should be 1, the value for the first record.

h. Click Debug on the menu bar, click Clear All Breakpoints, then click the Continue button on the Standard toolbar. Close the Visual Basic window.

i. Return to the qryStats query in Datasheet View.

j. Close the qryStats query, close the Baseball-N.accdb database, then exit Access.

Independent Challenge 1

As the manager of a doctor's clinic, you have created an Access database called Patients-N.accdb to track insurance claim reimbursements and general patient health. You want to modify an existing function within this database.

a. Start Access, then open the Patients-N.accdb database from the drive and folder where you store your Data Files. Enable content if prompted.

b. Open the basBodyMassIndex module in Design View, and enter the **Option Explicit** declaration statement just below the existing Option Compare Database statement.

c. Record your answers to the following questions on a sheet of paper:

- What is the name of the function in the module?

Independent Challenge 1 (continued)

- What are the function arguments?
- What is the purpose of the Option Explicit declaration statement?

d. Edit the BMI function by adding a comment below the last line of code with your name and today's date.

e. Edit the BMI function by adding a comment above the Function statement with the following information: **'A healthy BMI is in the range of 21-24.**

f. Edit the BMI function by adding an If clause that checks to make sure the height argument is not equal to 0. The final BMI function code should look like Figure N-23.

g. Save the module, print it if requested by your instructor, then close the Visual Basic window.

h. Create a new query that includes the following fields from the tblPatients table: **PtLastName**, **PtFirstName**, **PtHeight**, **PtWeight**.

i. Create a calculated field with the following field name and expression: **BMICalculation: BMI([PTWeight], [PTHeight])**.

FIGURE N-23

```
Option Compare Database
Option Explicit

'A healthy BMI is in the range of 21-24.

Function BMI(weight, height)

If height = 0 Then
    BMI = 0
Else
    BMI = (weight * 0.4536) / (height * 0.0254) ^ 2
End If

End Function

'Student Name and current date
```

j. Save the query as **qryPatientBMI**, view the qryPatientBMI query datasheet, then test the If statement by entering **0** in the PtHeight field for the first record. Press [Tab] to move to the BMICalculation field, which should recalculate to 0.

k. Edit the first record to contain your first and last name, print the datasheet if requested by your instructor, then close the qryPatientBMI query.

l. Close the Patients-N.accdb database, then exit Access.

Independent Challenge 2

As the manager of a doctor's clinic, you have created an Access database called Patients-N.accdb to track insurance claim reimbursements. You want to study the existing sub procedures stored as class modules in the Claim Entry Form.

a. Start Access, then open the Patients-N.accdb database from the drive and folder where you store your Data Files. Enable content if prompted.

b. Open frmClaimEntryForm in Form View, then switch to Design View.

c. Open the Visual Basic window to view this class module, then record your answers to the following questions on a sheet of paper:

- What are the names of the sub procedures in this class module? (*Hint*: Be sure to scroll the window to see the complete contents.)
- What Access functions are used in the PtFirstName_AfterUpdate sub?
- How many arguments do the functions in the PtFirstName_AfterUpdate sub have?
- What do the functions in the PtFirstName_AfterUpdate sub do? (*Hint*: You may have to use the Visual Basic Help system if you are not familiar with the functions.)
- What is the purpose of the On Error command? (*Hint*: Use the Visual Basic Help system if you are not familiar with this command.)

Advanced Challenge Exercise

ACE

- Use the Property Sheet of the form to create an event handler procedure based on the On Load property. The statement will be one line using the Maximize method of the VBA DoCmd object, which will maximize the form each time it is loaded.
- Save the changes, close the Visual Basic window and the Claim Entry Form, then open frmClaimEntryForm in Form View to test the new sub.

d. Close the Visual Basic window, save and close frmClaimEntryForm, close the Patients-N.accdb database, then exit Access.

Independent Challenge 3

As the manager of a doctor's clinic, you have created an Access database called Patients-N.accdb to track insurance claim reimbursements that are fixed (paid at a predetermined fixed rate) or denied (not paid by the insurance company). You want to enhance the database with a class module.

a. Start Access, then open the Patients-N.accdb database from the drive and folder where you store your Data Files. Enable content if prompted.
b. Open frmCPT in Form Design View.
c. Use the Command Button Wizard to add a command button in the Form Header section. Choose the Add New Record action from the Record Operations category.
d. Accept **Add Record** as the text on the button, then name the button **cmdAddRecord**.
e. Use the Command Button Wizard to add a command button in the Form Header section to the right of the existing Add Record button. (*Hint*: Move and resize controls as necessary to put two command buttons in the Form Header section.)
f. Choose the Delete Record action from the Record Operations category.
g. Accept Delete Record as the text on the button, and name the button **cmdDeleteRecord**.
h. Size the two buttons to be the same height and width, and align their top edges.
i. Save and view frmCPT in Form View, then click the Add Record command button.
j. Add a new record (it will be record number 65) with a CPTCode value of **999** and an RBRVS value of **1.5**.
k. To make sure that the Delete Record button works, click the record selector for the new record you just entered, click the Delete Record command button, then click Yes to confirm the deletion. Save and close frmCPT.

Advanced Challenge Exercise

- In Design View of the frmCPT form, open the Property Sheet for the Delete Record command button, click the Event tab, then click the Build button beside [Embedded Macro]. The Command Button Wizard created the embedded macro that deletes the current record. You can convert macro objects to VBA code to learn more about VBA. To convert an embedded macro to VBA, you must first copy and paste the embedded macro actions to a new macro object.
- Press [Ctrl][A] to select all macro actions, then press [Ctrl][C] to copy all macro actions to the clipboard.
- Close the macro window, then save and close frmCPT.
- On the Create tab, open Macro Design View, then press [Ctrl][V] to paste the macro actions to the window.
- Click the Convert Macros to Visual Basic button, click Yes when prompted to save the macro, click Convert, then click OK when a dialog box indicates the conversion is finished.
- Save and close all open windows with default names if prompted. Open the Converted Macro-Macro1 VBE window. Add a comment as the last line of code in the Code window with your name and the current date, save the module, print it if requested by your instructor, then close the Visual Basic window.

l. Close the Patients-N.accdb database, then exit Access.

Real Life Independent Challenge

This Independent Challenge requires an Internet connection.

Learning a programming language is sometimes compared to learning a foreign language. Imagine how it would feel to learn a new programming language if English wasn't your primary language, or if you had another type of accessibility challenge. Advances in technology are helping to break down many barriers to those with vision, hearing, mobility, cognitive, and language issues. In this challenge, you explore the Microsoft Web site for resources to address these issues.

a. Go to www.microsoft.com/enable, then print that page. Explore the Web site.
b. After exploring the Web site for products, profiles, demos, and tutorials, write a one- or two-page, double-spaced paper describing five types of accessibility solutions that might make a positive impact on someone you know. Refer to your acquaintances as "my friend," "my cousin," and so forth as appropriate. Do not include real names.
c. Go back to www.microsoft.com/enable, then find the International link to change languages. Write down the languages for which the Microsoft Accessibility Web site is available.

Visual Workshop

As the manager of a college basketball team, you are helping the coach build meaningful statistics to compare the relative value of the players in each game. The coach has stated that one offensive rebound is worth as much to the team as two defensive rebounds, and would like you to use this rule to develop a "rebounding impact statistic" for each game. Open the Basketball-N.accdb (not the Baseball-N.accdb) database, enable content if prompted, and use Figure N-24 to develop a new function. Name the new function **ReboundImpact** in a new module called **basFunctions** to calculate this statistic. Include your name and the current date as a comment in the last row of the function.

FIGURE N-24

```
Function ReboundImpact(OffenseValue As Integer, DefenseValue As Integer) As Integer
    ReboundImpact = (OffenseValue * 2) + DefenseValue
End Function

'Your Name, Current Date
```

Create a query called **qryRebounds** with the fields shown in Figure N-25. Note that the records are sorted in ascending order on GameNo and LastName. The ReboundCalculation field is created using the following expression: **ReboundImpact([Reb-O],[Reb-D])**. Enter your own first and last name instead of Kristen Czyenski, and print the datasheet if requested by your instructor.

FIGURE N-25

qryRebounds

GameNo	FirstName	LastName	Reb-O	Reb-D	ReboundCalculation
1	StudentFirst	StudentLast	2	2	6
1	Denise	Franco	2	3	7
1	Theresa	Grant	1	3	5
1	Megan	Hile	1	2	4
1	Amy	Hodel	5	3	13
1	Ellyse	Howard	1	2	4
1	Jamie	Johnson	0	1	1
1	Lindsey	Swift	1	2	4
1	Morgan	Tyler	4	6	14
2	StudentFirst	StudentLast	3	2	8
2	Denise	Franco	5	3	13

UNIT
O
Access 2010

Building a Database Interface

Files You Will Need:

Technology-O.accdb
Basketball-O.accdb
RealEstate-O.accdb
Baltic-O.accdb

As your database grows in size and functionality, the number of objects (especially queries and reports) grows as well. As the database expands in scope and complexity, you need to build a database interface to make it easy to use for yourself and others. Kayla Green is the network administrator at Quest corporate headquarters. You have helped Kayla develop a database to document Quest computer equipment. The number of objects in the database makes it increasingly difficult to find and organize information. You will use Access tools and create a database interface to manage the growing database and make it easier to navigate for new users.

OBJECTIVES

- Work with objects
- Group objects
- Create a dialog box
- Create a pop up form
- Create a navigation form
- Create a switchboard
- Modify a switchboard
- Use the Documenter

Working with Objects

You work with objects in the **Navigation Pane**. The Navigation Pane is most commonly organized to show database objects listed by object type (tables, queries, forms, reports, macros, and modules). The Navigation Pane can also organize objects by their table association, created date, modified date, or a custom group. To copy, delete, or rename an object, you right-click it in the Navigation Pane, and then choose the desired option from the shortcut menu. Kayla Green asks you to make several queries easier to find. You decide to delete, rename, sort, and add descriptions to several queries to meet her request.

STEPS

1. **Start Access, open the Technology-O.accdb database from the drive and folder where you store your Data Files, enable content if prompted, click All Access Objects on the title bar of the Navigation Pane, then click Modified Date in the Navigate To Category section**

   In this case, the filter is still showing all of the objects in order of the most recently modified to the last modified. To further organize them, you can use other sorting and viewing options.

2. **Click All Dates in the Navigation Pane title bar, click Object Type, right-click All Access Objects in the title bar of the Navigation Pane, point to Category, point to Sort By, point to View By, then click Details**

   The **Sort By option** allows you to change the sort order of the objects in the Navigation Pane. The **View By option** changes the way the objects are displayed: with Details, as Icons, or in a List. When viewing the objects by Details, the Navigation Pane displays Date Created and Date Modified information for each table as shown in Figure O-1.

3. **Click the tblPCSpecs table, click the Database Tools tab, click the Object Dependencies button, then click OK if prompted**

   The **Object Dependencies task pane** opens, as shown in Figure O-2. Option buttons allow you to view either the objects that depend on the selected object or objects that the selected object itself depends on.

4. **Click the expand button to the left of the qryAfrica query in the Object Dependencies task pane**

   Expanding the qryAfrica query reveals that the rptAfrica report depends on the qryAfrica query. Another way to organize and manage objects is to check default database options. All default options are stored in the Access Options dialog box.

5. **Click the File tab on the Ribbon, click Options toward the bottom, then click the Current Database category as shown in Figure O-3**

   The Access Options dialog box provides many important default options and techniques to customize Access, which are summarized in Table O-1.

6. **Click the Datasheet category and several others to explore Access Options, then click Cancel to close the Access Options dialog box**

7. **Click the Close button in the upper-right corner of the Object Dependencies task pane to close it**

FIGURE O-1: **Viewing objects by Details**

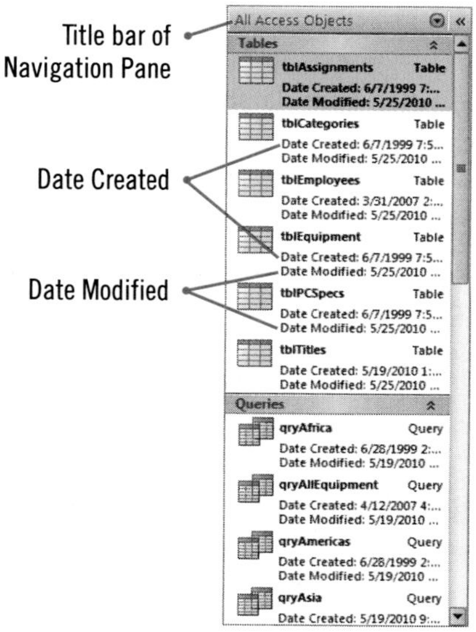
Title bar of Navigation Pane
Date Created
Date Modified

FIGURE O-2: **Object Dependencies task pane**

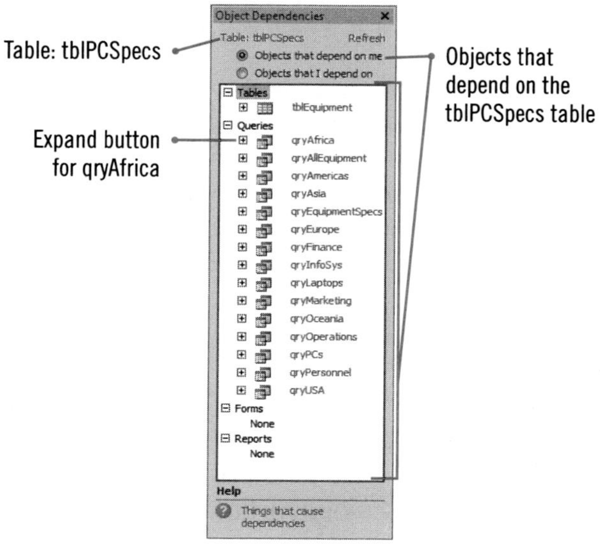
Table: tblPCSpecs
Expand button for qryAfrica
Objects that depend on the tblPCSpecs table

FIGURE O-3: **Access Options dialog box**

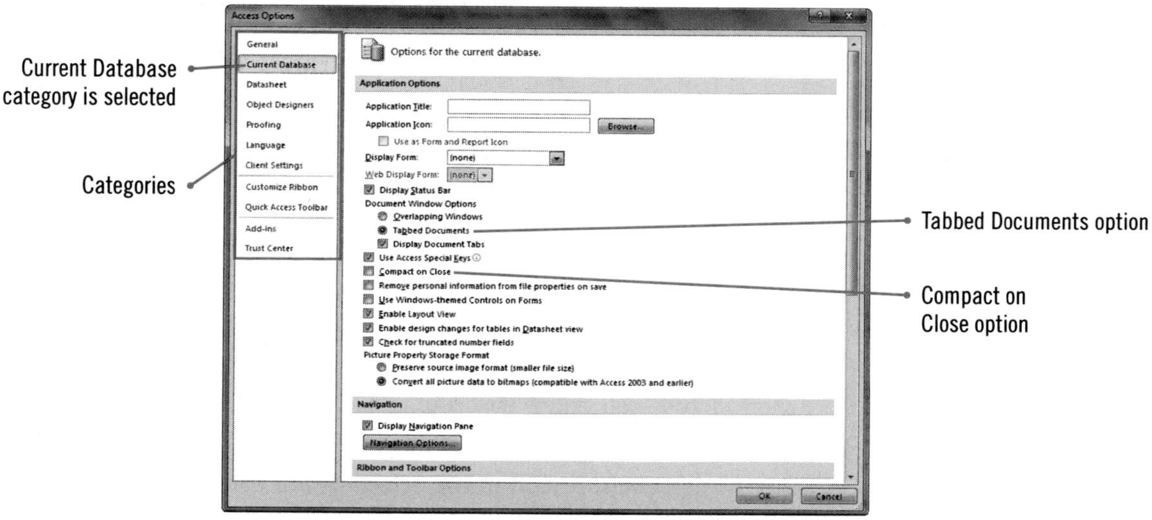
Current Database category is selected
Categories
Tabbed Documents option
Compact on Close option

TABLE O-1: **Access options**

category	description
General	Sets default interface, file format, default database folder, and user name options
Current Database	Provides for application changes such as whether the windows are overlapping or tabbed, the database compacts on close, and Layout View is enabled; also provides Navigation Pane, Ribbon, toolbar, and AutoCorrect options
Datasheet	Determines the default gridlines, cell effects, and fonts of datasheets
Object Designers	Determines default Design View settings for tables, queries, forms, and reports; also provides default error-checking options
Proofing	Sets AutoCorrect and Spelling options
Language	Sets Editing, Display, and Help languages
Client Settings	Sets defaults for cursor action when editing, display elements, printing margins, date formatting, and advanced record management options
Customize Ribbon	Provides an easy-to-use interface to modify the buttons and tabs on the Ribbon (new in Access 2010)
Quick Access Toolbar	Provides an easy-to-use interface to modify the buttons on the Quick Access toolbar
Add-ins	Provides a way to manage **add-ins**, software that works with Access to add or enhance functionality
Trust Center	Provides a way to manage trusted publishers, trusted locations, trusted documents, macro settings, and other privacy and security settings

UNIT O

Access 2010

Grouping Objects

Viewing every object in the Navigation Pane can be cumbersome when your database contains many objects. **Groups** are also used to organize objects by subject or purpose. For example, you might create a group for each department so that the forms and reports used by that department are organized together. A group consists of **shortcuts** (pointers) to the objects that belong to that group. You use these shortcuts to open the object without affecting the original location of the object. You can create more than one shortcut to the same object and place it in several groups. You add and display groups in the Navigation Pane. You organize the objects in your database by creating groups for two different departments: Travel and Operations.

STEPS

1. **Right-click All Access Objects on the Navigation Pane title bar, point to View By, click List to return to the default view, right-click All Access Objects, click Navigation Options, then click Custom Groups**

   The **Favorites** custom group is provided by default, but you can create your own custom groups, too. Objects that have not been placed in a custom group remain in the **Unassigned Objects** group.

2. **Click the Add Group button, type Travel, click the Add Group button, type Operations, then press [Enter] to create two groups as shown in Figure O-4**

   With the new groups in place, you're ready to organize objects within them.

3. **Click OK in the Navigation Options dialog box, right-click All Access Objects on the Navigation Pane title bar, point to Category, click Custom Groups, then scroll to the top of the Navigation Pane**

   Dragging an object to a group icon places a shortcut to that object within the group. A shortcut icon looks different from the actual object because it has a small blue arrow in its lower-left corner.

4. **Drag the qryAfrica query icon in the Navigation Pane to the Travel group, then drag the rptAfrica report icon to the Travel group as shown in Figure O-5**

   You have added shortcut icons representing the qryAfrica query and rptAfrica report in the Travel group. You can open or design an object by accessing it through a shortcut icon.

5. **Double-click the rptAfrica report icon in the Travel group to open the rptAfrica report, then close the report**

   You can create multiple shortcuts to the same object in different groups, and you can rename shortcuts to be more meaningful.

6. **Right-click the rptAfrica report icon in the Travel group, click Rename Shortcut, type Africa report, press [Enter], right-click the qryAfrica query icon in the Travel group, click Rename Shortcut, type Africa query, then press [Enter] to rename the objects as shown in Figure O-6**

   You can make your database interface much easier and faster for others to use by creating custom groups, adding shortcuts to those groups for only the objects that user needs, and then renaming shortcuts to be meaningful to the user.

TROUBLE

If you make a mistake, use the Delete Group or Rename Group buttons to fix it.

FIGURE O-4: **Creating custom groups in the Navigation Options dialog box**

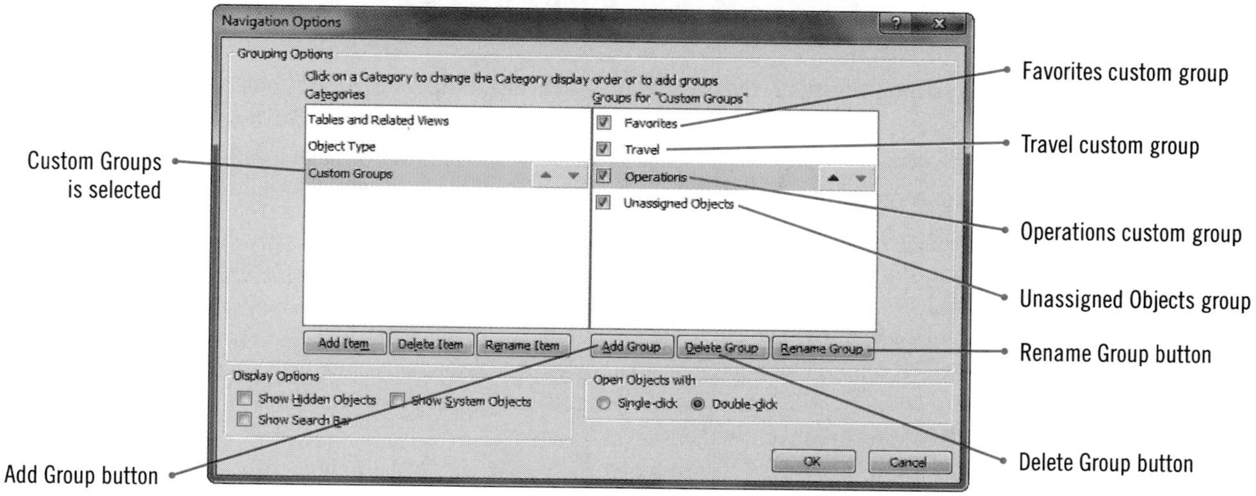

FIGURE O-5: **Navigation Pane with custom Travel and Operations groups**

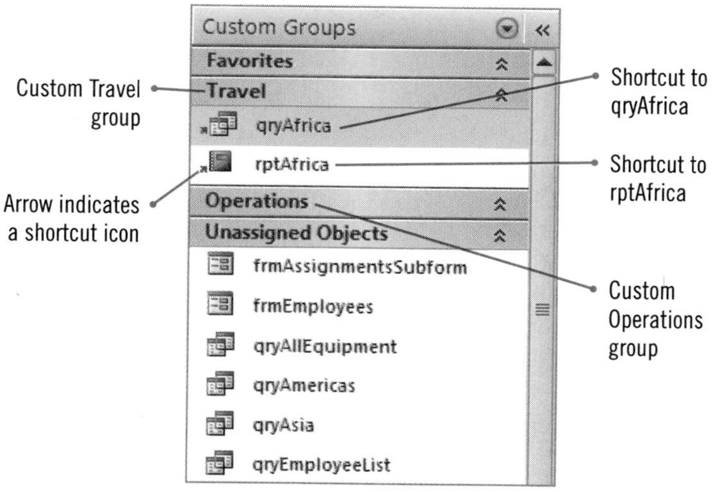

FIGURE O-6: **Navigation Pane with renamed shortcuts in custom Travel group**

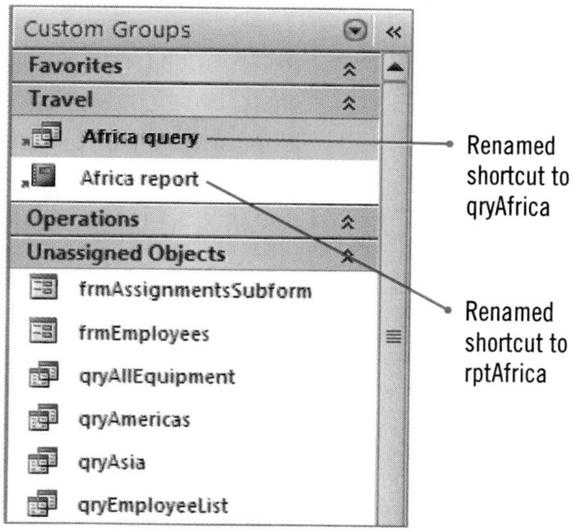

Naming objects

Object names can be 64 characters long and can include any combination of letters, numbers, spaces, and special characters, except a period (.), exclamation point (!), accent (`), or brackets ([ ]). It is helpful to keep the names as short, yet as descriptive, as possible. Short names make objects easier to reference in other places in the database, such as in the Record Source property for a form or report. Three-character prefixes such as tbl for table or qry for query provide more meaning when viewed from within an expression, Macro Design View, or a VBA module.

UNIT O
Access 2010

Creating a Dialog Box

A **dialog box** is a form used to display messages or prompt a user for a choice. Creating dialog boxes helps to simplify use of various database objects. For example, you might create a dialog box to give the user access to a list of reports the user needs to preview or print. To make a form look like a dialog box, you modify form properties that affect its appearance and borders. You want to create a dialog box to provide an easy way for Quest users to print various reports.

STEPS

1. **Click the Create tab, then click the Form Design button**
   A dialog box form is not bound to an underlying table or query, and therefore it doesn't use the form's Record Source property. You place unbound controls, such as labels and command buttons, on a dialog box to offer the user information and choices.

> **TROUBLE**
> Be sure the Use Control Wizards button is selected. To find it, click the More arrow in the Controls group on the Design tab.

2. **Click the Button button in the Controls group, then click in the upper-middle section of the form**
   The **Command Button Wizard** shown in Figure O-7 organizes over 30 of the most common command button actions within six categories.
3. **Click Report Operations in the Categories list, click Preview Report in the Actions list, click Next, click rptAfrica as the report choice, click Next, click the Text option button, press [Tab], type Africa, click Next, type cmdAfrica as the button name, then click Finish**
   The command button appears in Form Design View.

> **QUICK TIP**
> Every command button must have a unique name.

4. **Click the Button button, click below the first command button on the form, click Report Operations in the Categories list, click Preview Report in the Actions list, click Next, click rptAmericas, click Next, click the Text option button, press [Tab], type Americas, click Next, type cmdAmericas, then click Finish**
   With the command buttons in place, you modify form properties to make the form look like a dialog box.

> **TROUBLE**
> You may need to scroll the Property Sheet to find the Border Style property.

5. **Double-click the Form Selector button to open the form's Property Sheet, click the Format tab, then double-click the Border Style property to change it from Sizable to Dialog**
   The **Border Style** property determines the appearance of the outside border of the form. The **Dialog** option indicates that the form will have a thick border and may not be maximized, minimized, or resized. A dialog box does not need a record selector or navigation buttons, so you want to remove them from this form using the Record Selectors and Navigation Buttons properties.
6. **Double-click the Record Selectors property to change it from Yes to No, then double-click the Navigation Buttons property to change it from Yes to No as shown in Figure O-8**

> **QUICK TIP**
> Resize the cmdAfrica button as needed to match Figure O-9.

7. **Close the Property Sheet, save the form with the name frmDialogBox, then click the View button to switch to Form View as shown in Figure O-9**
   Note that the form has a thin dialog style border, no record selector, and no navigation buttons. Test the command buttons.
8. **Click the Americas command button**
   Clicking the Americas command button displays the Americas report. Given more time, you'd want to add command buttons for all departmental reports to frmDialogBox.
9. **Close the Americas report, then save and close the frmDialogBox form**

FIGURE O-7: **Command Button Wizard**

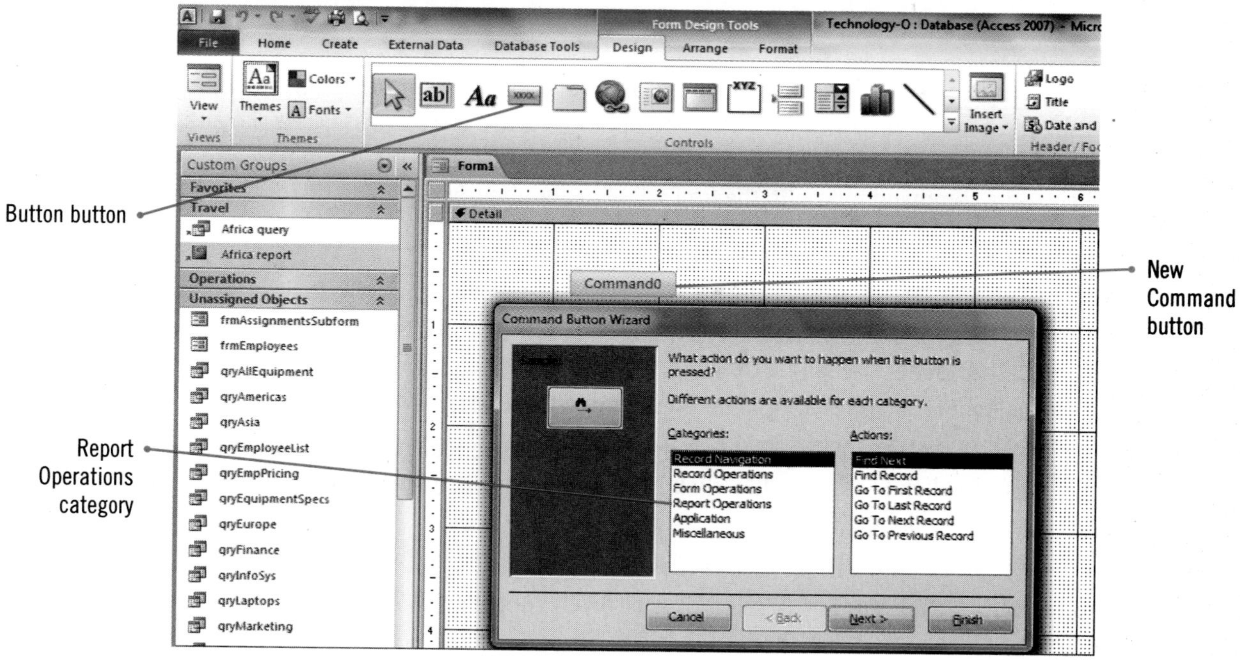

FIGURE O-8: **Setting dialog box properties**

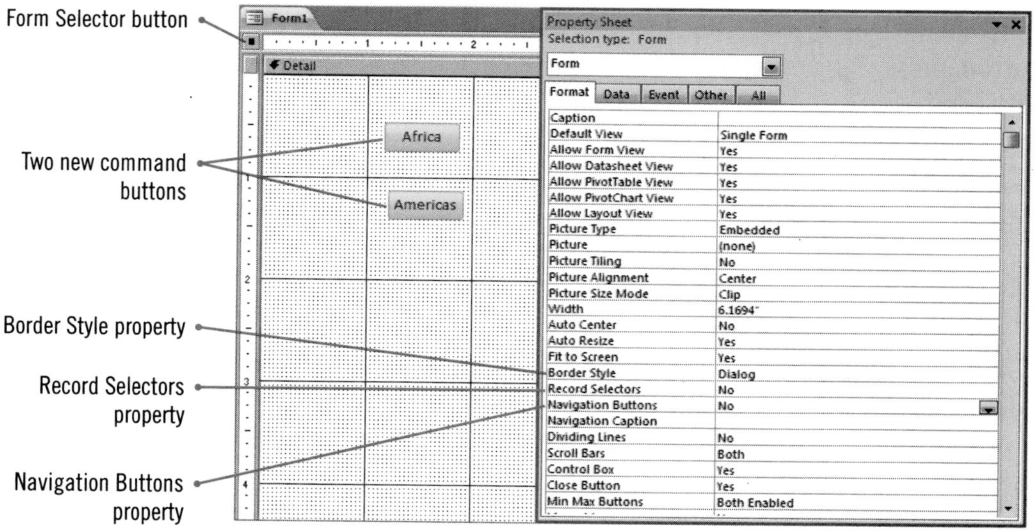

FIGURE O-9: **frmDialogBox in Form View**

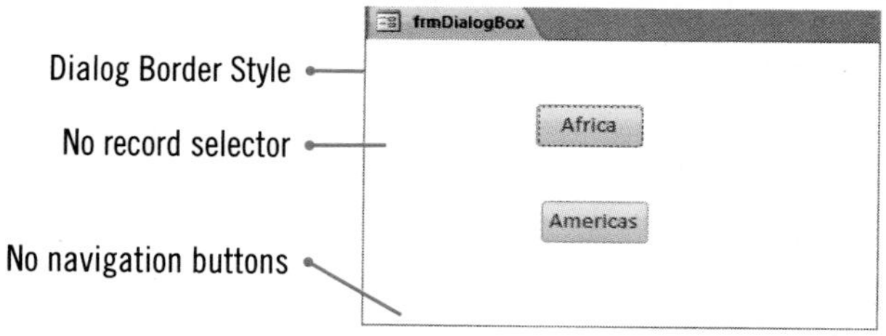

Creating a Pop Up Form

A **pop up form** is a form that stays on top of other open forms, even when another form is active. For example, you might want to create a pop up form to give the user easy access to a reference list of phone numbers or e-mail addresses. You create a pop up form to access employee department information. You add a command button to the frmDialogBox form to open the pop up form.

STEPS

1. **Click the Create tab, click the Form Design button, click the Property Sheet button, click the Data tab in the Property Sheet, click the Record Source list arrow, then scroll and click tblEmployees**
   You want to add three fields to the pop up form: EFirst, ELast, and EDepartment.

TROUBLE
If the Property Sheet remains open, close it.

2. **Click the Add Existing Fields button to open the Field List, double-click EFirst, double-click ELast, double-click EDepartment, close the Field List, then save the form as frmEmployeePopup**
   You change a regular form into a pop up form by changing its **Pop Up property**.
3. **Double-click the Form Selector button to reopen the Property Sheet for the form, click the Other tab, then double-click the Pop Up property to change it from No to Yes as shown in Figure O-10**
   You add a command button to the right side of the frmDialogBox form to open the frmEmployeePopup form.
4. **Right-click frmDialogBox in the Navigation Pane, click Design View, click the Button button in the Controls group, click to the right of the existing command buttons on the form, click the Form Operations category, click the Open Form action, click Next, click frmEmployeePopup, click Next, click Next to show all of the records, click the Text option button, press [Tab], type Employee Departments, click Next, type cmdEmployee, then click Finish**
   You need to test your pop up form.
5. **Save frmDialogBox, click the View button to switch to Form View, click the Employee Departments command button, then save and close frmEmployeePopup**
   Pop up forms are often used to display reference information. If the records were presented as a datasheet, you would be able to see much more information. You make this change by modifying the embedded macro that is triggered on the Employee Departments command button.
6. **Switch to Design View of frmDialogBox, open the Property Sheet for cmdEmployee if it is not already open, click the Event tab, click the Build button for the On Click property, click Form in the View argument, click the View list arrow, then click Datasheet as shown in Figure O-11**
   Save and test the updated macro.

QUICK TIP
The rptAmericas report has a Caption property of Americas, which is displayed in the report tab.

7. **Click the Close button, click Yes when prompted to save, close the Property Sheet, click, click the Employee Departments command button, resize and move the frmEmployeePopup window to the right, then click the Americas command button**
   The frmEmployeePopup form stayed "on top" even though you opened a report, as shown in Figure O-12. Given more time, you'd want to automatically resize and position the pop up form. You set the width of a form using the form's **Width** property. You can set the position of the form using the DoCmd.MoveSize VBA statement triggered by the form's Load property.
8. **Close the frmEmployeePopup form, close the Americas report, then save and close the frmDialogBox form**

FIGURE O-10: **Creating a pop up form**

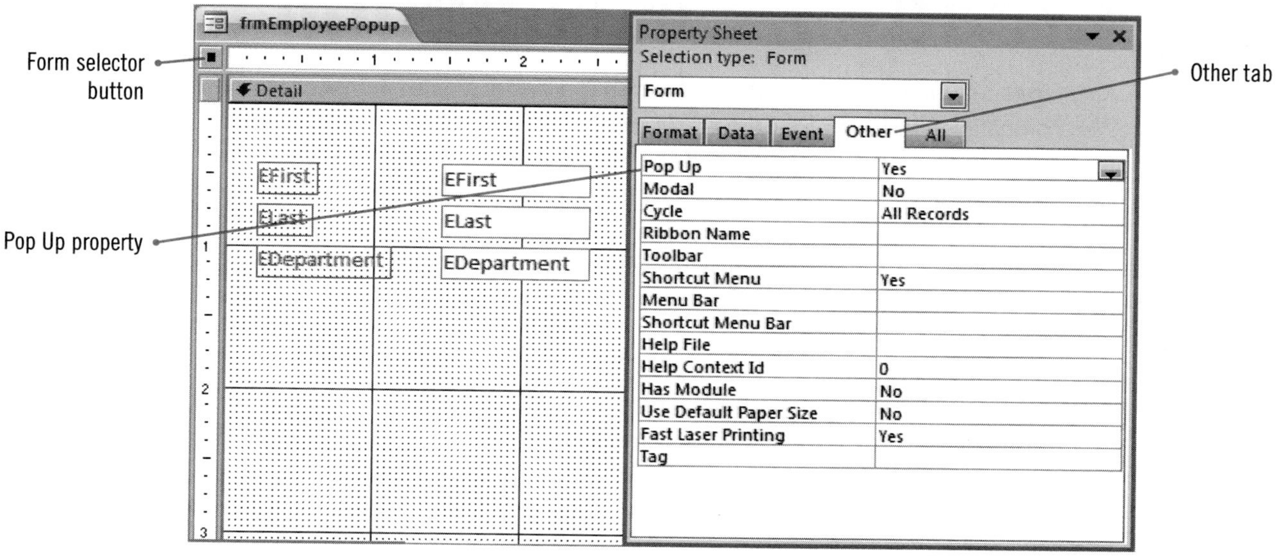

FIGURE O-11: **Changing the View argument for frmEmployeePopup**

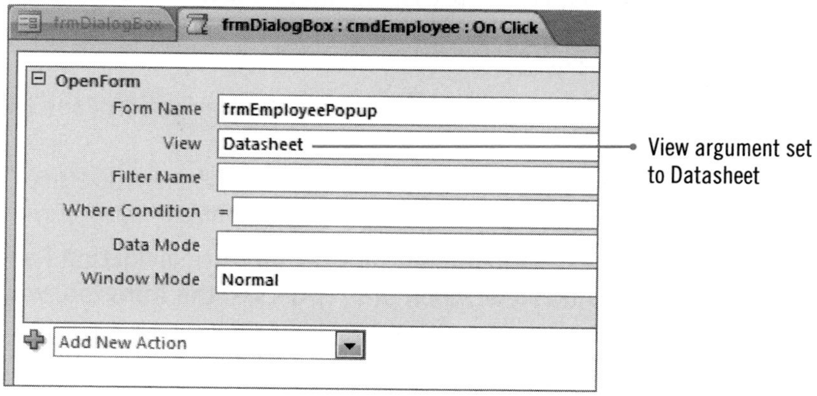

FIGURE O-12: **Working with a pop up form**

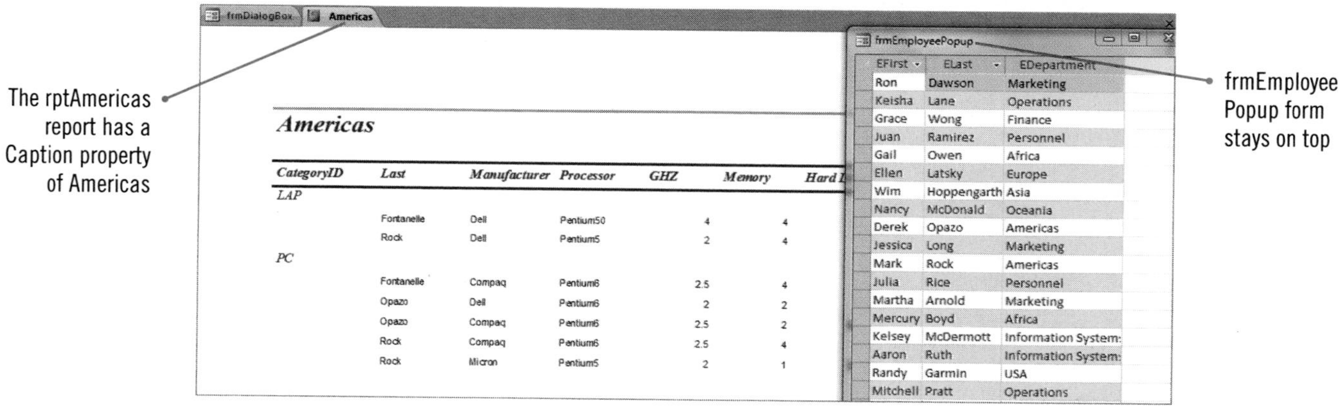

UNIT
O
Access 2010

Creating a Navigation Form

A **navigation form** is a special Access form that provides an easy-to-use database interface that is also Web compatible. Being **Web compatible** means that the form can be opened and used with Internet Explorer when the database is published to a SharePoint server. A **SharePoint server** is a special type of Microsoft Web server that allows people to share and collaborate on information using only a browser such as Internet Explorer. Navigation forms can be used with any Access database, however, even if you don't publish it to a SharePoint server. You create a navigation form to easily access forms and reports in the Technology-O database.

STEPS

1. **Click the Create tab, click the Navigation button in the Forms group, click the Horizontal Tabs option, then close the Field List window**

   Horizontal Tabs is a **navigation system style** that determines how the navigation buttons will be displayed on the form. Other navigation system styles include vertical tabs (buttons) on the left or right, or both horizontal and vertical tabs.

   The new navigation form opens in Layout View, ready for you to add the objects that you want to quickly find. To easily access the forms and reports in this database, you change the Navigation Pane to organize the objects by object type.

2. **Click Custom Groups in the Navigation Pane title bar, click Object Type, scroll the Navigation Pane, then click the Expand buttons for the Forms and Reports categories to open those parts of the Navigation Pane if they are not already visible**

   To add objects to the tabs of the new navigation forms, you can type the name of an object in the tab or drag an object to the tab.

3. **Drag the frmEmployees form from the Navigation Pane to the first tab, which displays [Add New]**

   The frmEmployees form is added as the first tab, as shown in Figure O-13, and a new tab with [Add New] is automatically created as well. The second and third tabs will display reports.

4. **Drag the rptAllEquipment report from the Navigation Pane to the second tab, which displays [Add New], then drag rptPCs to the third tab, which also displays [Add New]**

   With the objects in place, you'll rename the tabs to be less technical.

5. **Double-click the frmEmployees tab, edit it to read Employees, double-click the rptAllEquipment tab, edit it to read All Equipment, double-click the rptPCs tab, edit it to read PCs, then click the View button to display the form in Form View as shown in Figure O-14**

   Test, save, and close the new navigation form.

6. **Click the All Equipment tab, click the Employees tab, click the Save button on the Quick Access toolbar, type frmNavigation, click OK, then close frmNavigation**

FIGURE O-13: **Adding frmEmployees as the first tab of the navigation form**

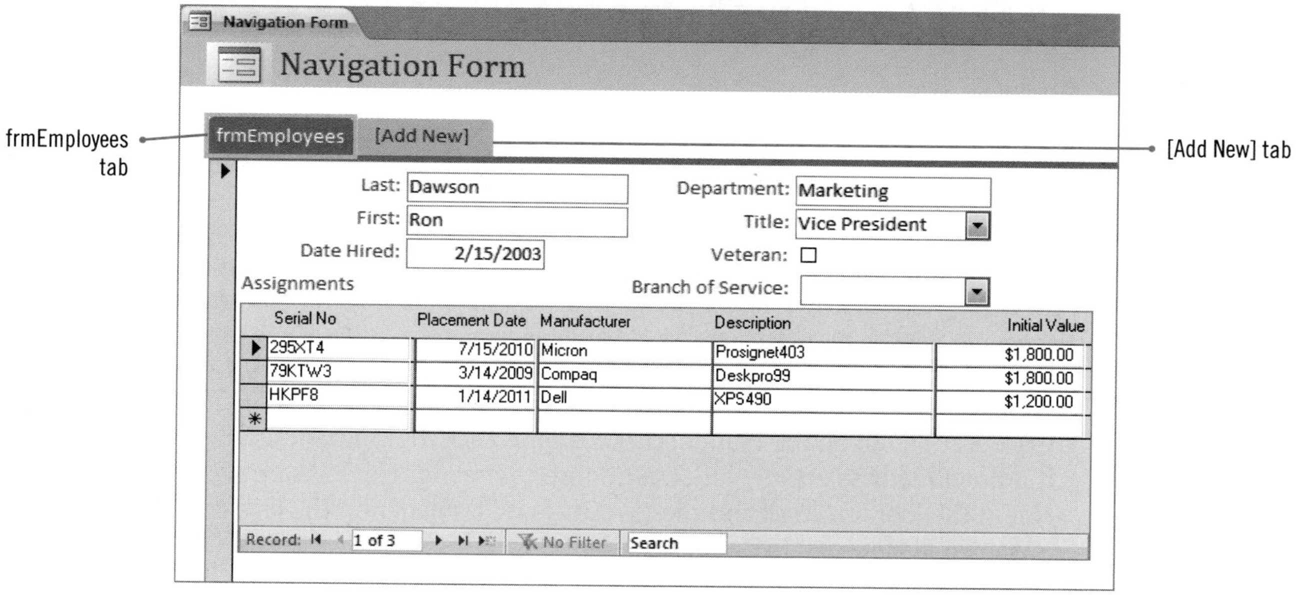

FIGURE O-14: **Final navigation form in Form View**

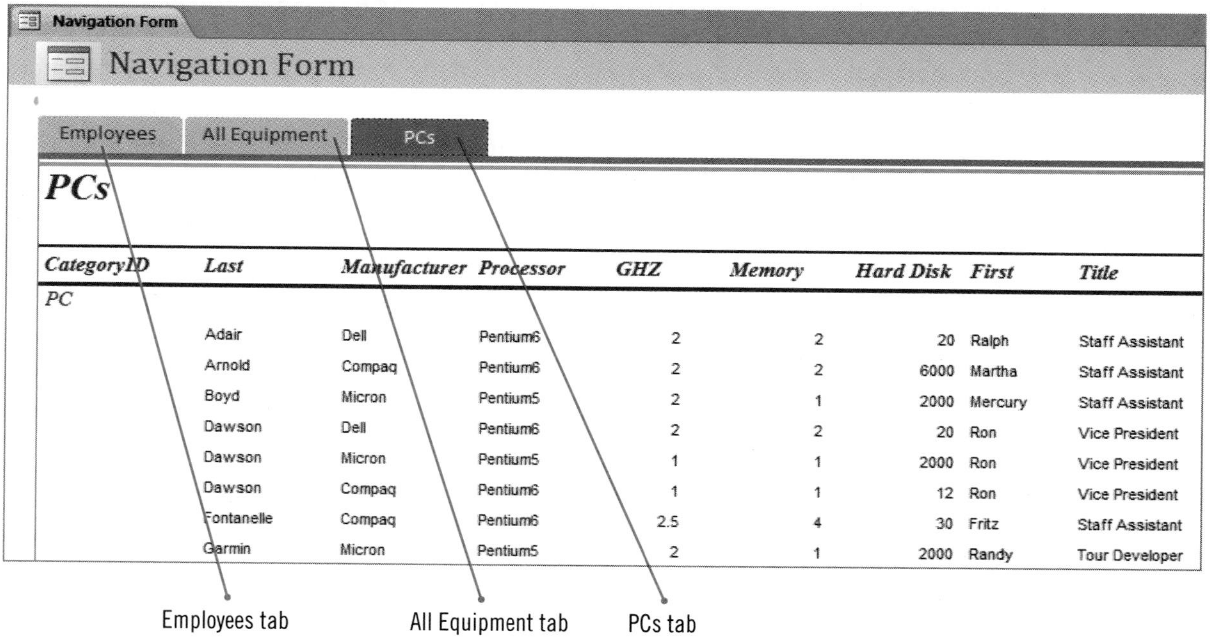

UNIT O

Access 2010

Creating a Switchboard

Given the new emphasis on Web-compatible navigation forms, Access 2010 puts less emphasis on older form navigation tools such as the switchboard. A **switchboard** is a special Access form that uses command buttons to provide an easy-to-use and secure database interface, and it was very popular with previous versions of Access. You create and modify switchboards by using an Access tool called the **Switchboard Manager**. Because your employees are already familiar with switchboard forms from older databases, you decide to create a switchboard form to serve as the opening database interface for Technology-O.accdb. Your first challenge is finding the Switchboard Manager functionality, which is no longer provided on the default Access 2010 Ribbon.

STEPS

TROUBLE

If this step is already completed on your computer, skip Step 1 and continue with Step 2.

1. **Click the File tab on the Ribbon, click Options, click the Quick Access Toolbar category (if it is not already selected), click the Choose commands from list arrow, click Commands Not in the Ribbon, scroll and click Switchboard Manager on the left, click the Add button as shown in Figure O-15, then click OK**

   With the Switchboard Manager functionality available on the Quick Access toolbar, you can use it to create a switchboard form.

2. **Click the Switchboard Manager button on the Quick Access toolbar, then click Yes when prompted to create a switchboard**

   The Switchboard Manager dialog box opens and presents the options for the first switchboard page. One switchboard page must be designated as the **default switchboard**, which links to additional switchboard pages as needed. Your switchboard page will start with two command buttons.

QUICK TIP

To rename the switchboard, edit "Main Switchboard" in the Switchboard Name text box.

3. **Click Edit, then click New**

   The Edit Switchboard Item dialog box opens, prompting you for three pieces of information: Text (a label on the switchboard form that identifies the corresponding command button), Command (which corresponds to a database action), and Switchboard (an option that changes depending on the command and further defines the command button action).

4. **Type Open Employees Form in the Text text box, click the Command list arrow, click Open Form in Edit Mode, click the Form list arrow, then click frmEmployees**

   The Edit Switchboard Item dialog box should look like Figure O-16. Opening a form in **Edit Mode** allows you to edit records, whereas **Add Mode** only allows you to add new records.

5. **Click OK to add the first command button to the switchboard, click New, type Select Reports in the Text text box, click the Command list arrow, click Open Form in Edit Mode, click the Form list arrow, click frmDialogBox, then click OK**

   The Edit Switchboard Page dialog box has two items. Each entry in this dialog box represents a command button that will appear on the final switchboard.

TROUBLE

To delete a switchboard form and start over, first delete the Switchboard Items table so you can create the switchboard from scratch.

6. **Click Close to close the Edit Switchboard Page dialog box, click Close to close the Switchboard Manager dialog box, then double-click the new Switchboard form in the Navigation Pane**

   The finished switchboard opens in Form View, as shown in Figure O-17. Note that creating a switchboard form using the Switchboard Manager also creates a table called **Switchboard Items**, which contains information the form needs.

7. **Click the Open Employees Form command button on the Switchboard, close the frmEmployees form, click the Select Reports command button, then close the frmDialogBox form**

   Switchboard forms provide a fast and easy way to help users work with only those objects they need in a database. Given more time, you'd want to add more buttons to the switchboard to access more database objects.

FIGURE O-15: **Customizing the Quick Access toolbar to include the Switchboard Manager button**

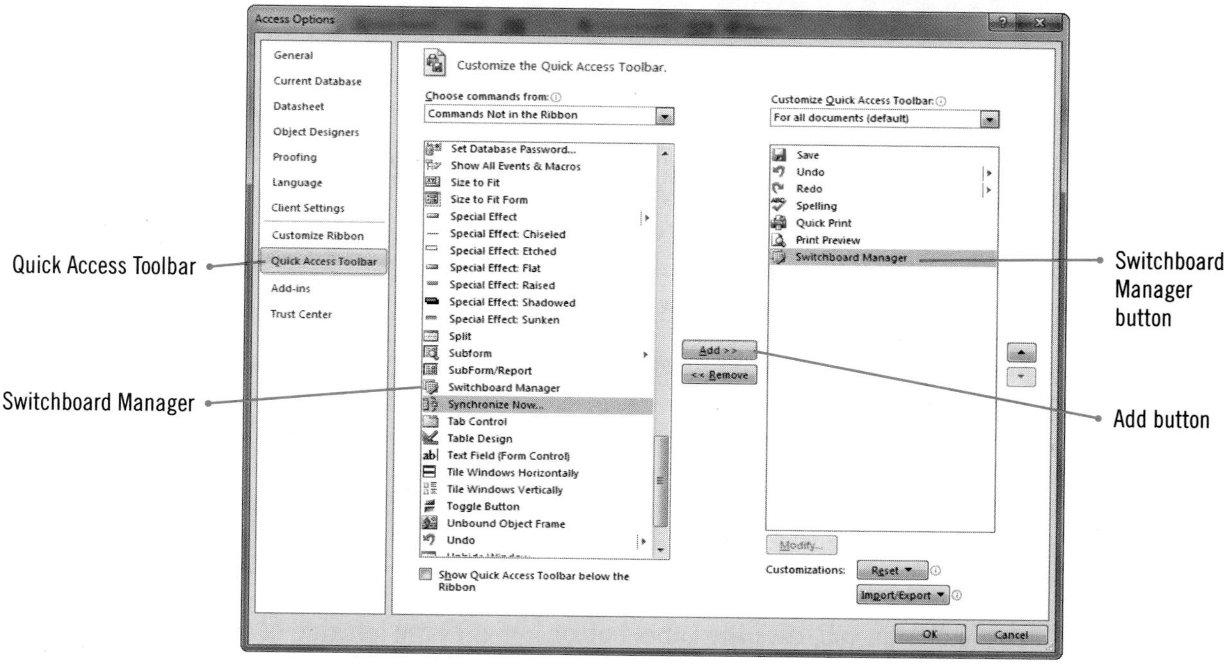
Quick Access Toolbar
Switchboard Manager
Switchboard Manager button
Add button

FIGURE O-16: **Adding an item to a switchboard page**

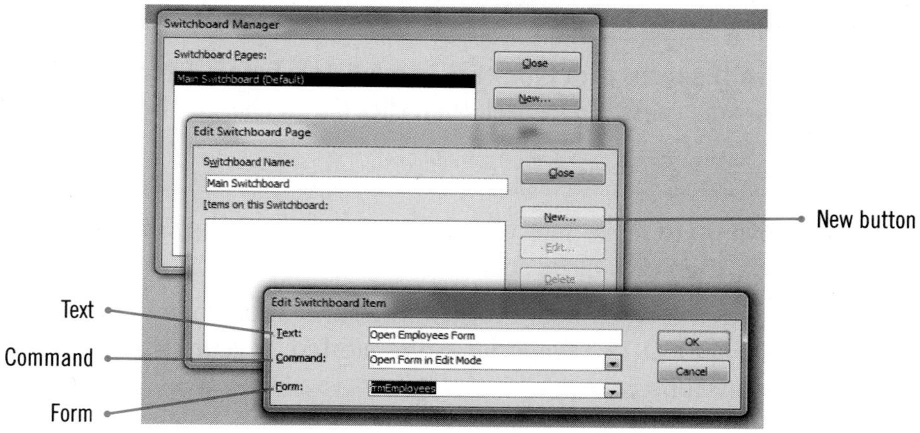
New button
Text
Command
Form

FIGURE O-17: **Switchboard form**

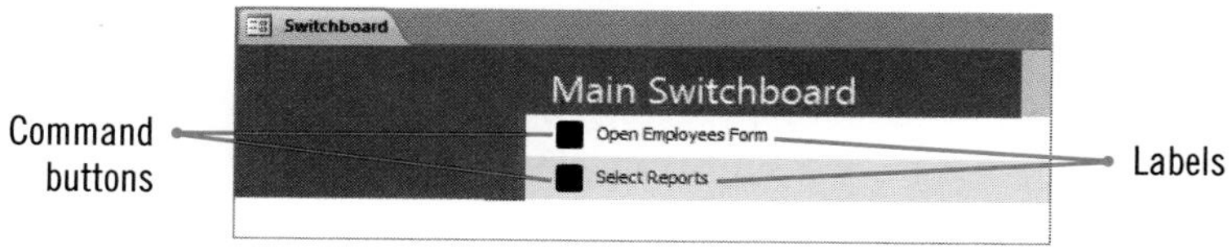
Command buttons
Labels

UNIT O
Access 2010

Modifying a Switchboard

Always use the Switchboard Manager to add, delete, move, and edit the command buttons and labels on a switchboard form. Use Form Design View to make formatting modifications such as changing form colors, adding clip art, or changing the switchboard title. Kayla Green is pleased with the steps you've taken to make the database easier to use, but she suggests changing the title, colors, and order of the command buttons to improve the switchboard. You use Form Design View to make the formatting changes and the Switchboard Manager to change the order of the buttons.

STEPS

1. **Right-click the Switchboard tab, click Design View, then click the teal rectangle on the left of the Detail section**

   The teal areas on the left and top portion of the Switchboard are rectangles. You can modify their color or shape just as you would modify any drawn object.

2. **Click the Home tab, click the Background Color button arrow, click the yellow box in the last row, click the teal rectangle in the Form Header section, click the Background Color button arrow, then click the red box in the last row**

3. **Click the Design tab, click the Label button, click the left side of the Form Header section, type your name, press [Enter], click the Home tab, click the Font Color button arrow, then click the Automatic box to change the text color to black**

   Your switchboard should look like Figure O-18. You use Form Design View to modify colors, clip art, and labels. Notice that neither the command buttons nor the text describing each command button appears in Form Design View. You use the Switchboard Manager to modify the command buttons on a switchboard.

> **TROUBLE**
> Do not delete the existing labels in the Form Header section, as this will cause an error when opening the switchboard.

4. **Save and close the Switchboard form, click the Switchboard Manager button on the Quick Access toolbar, then click Edit**

   Use the Switchboard Manager to add, delete, or modify the command buttons on the switchboard, including the text labels that describe them.

5. **Click Select Reports, click Edit, click immediately before Reports in the Text text box, type Departmental, press [Spacebar], then click OK to change the reference to Select Departmental Reports**

   You can also change the order of the command buttons from the Edit Switchboard Page dialog box.

6. **Click Move Up to make Select Departmental Reports the first item in the Switchboard, click Close, then click Close again**

7. **Double-click the Switchboard form in the Navigation Pane to open it in Form View as shown in Figure O-19, save, print it if requested by your instructor, then close the Switchboard form**

FIGURE O-18: **Modifying a switchboard in Form Design View**

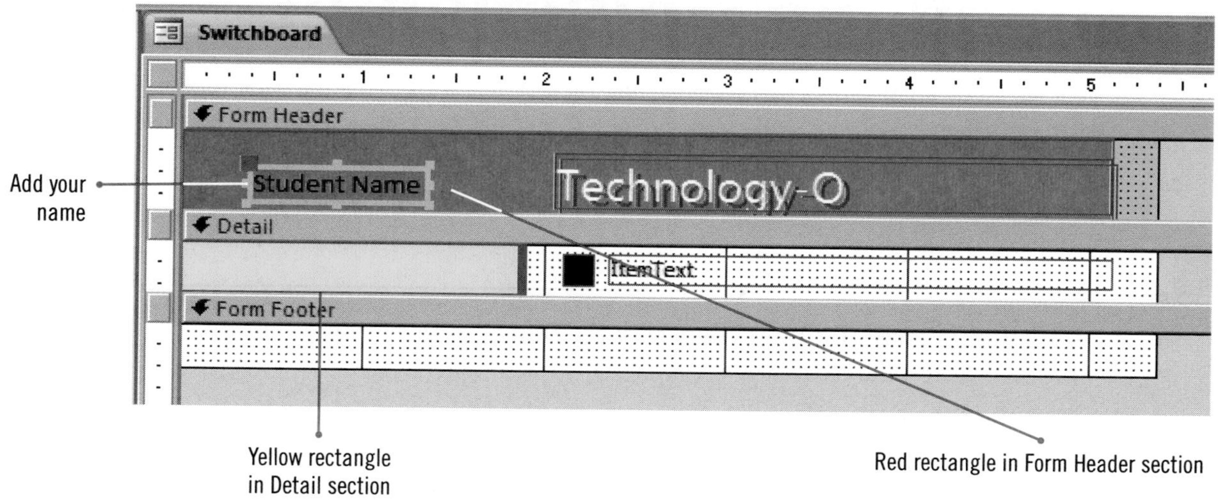

FIGURE O-19: **Final switchboard in Form View**

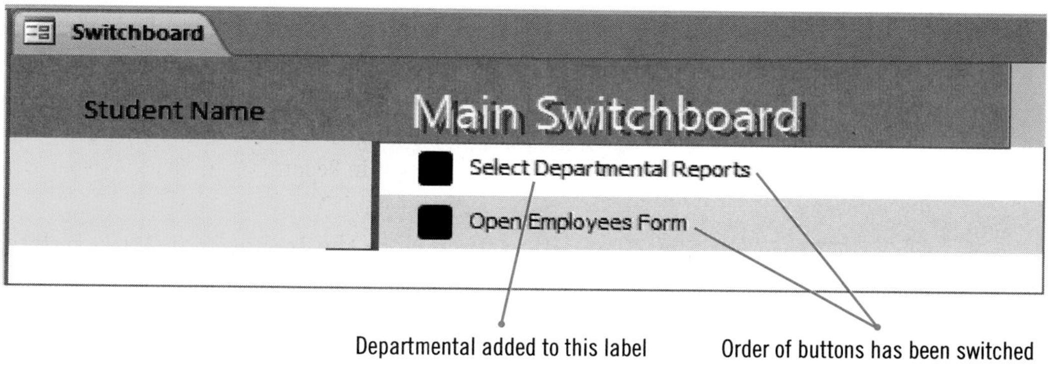

UNIT
O
Access 2010

Using the Documenter

As your Access database grows, users will naturally request new ways to use the data. Your ability to modify a database depends on your understanding of existing database objects. Access provides an analysis feature called the **Documenter** that creates reports on the properties and relationships among the objects in a database. You use the Documenter to create paper documentation that describes the Technology-O database.

STEPS

1. **Click the Database Tools tab, then click the Database Documenter button**
   The Documenter dialog box opens, displaying tabs for each object type.

2. **Click the Tables tab, then click Options in the Documenter dialog box**
   The Print Table Definition dialog box opens as shown in Figure O-20. This dialog box gives you some control over what type of documentation you will print for the table. The documentation for each object type varies slightly. For example, the documentation on forms and reports also includes information on controls and sections.

3. **Click the Names, Data Types, and Sizes option button in the Include for Fields section, click the Nothing option button in the Include for Indexes section, then click OK**
   You can select or deselect individual objects by clicking the check box to the left of each object, or you can click the Select All button to quickly select all objects of that type.

4. **Click the Select All button to select all of the tables, click the Forms tab, click the Select All button to select all of the forms, click OK, navigate to the second page, click the pointer on the report preview to zoom in, then scroll to display the table relationships as shown in Figure O-21**
   The Documenter creates a report for all of the table and form objects in the Technology-O.accdb database. The first page contains information about the first table in the database, the Switchboard Items table. The second page contains information about the second table in the database, tblAssignments.

> **QUICK TIP**
> Click the More button in the Data group on the Print Preview tab to display the report exporting options.

5. **Click the Last Page button in the navigation bar, then click the Previous Page button**
   The last part of the report contains information about the forms in the database. The properties for each control on the form are listed in two columns. Because most form controls have approximately 50 properties, the documentation to describe a form can be quite long. You can print the report or export it to a Word document, but you cannot modify a Documenter report in Report Design View or save it as an object within this database.

6. **Click the Close Print Preview button, then close the Technology-O.accdb database and exit Access**

FIGURE O-20: **Print Table Definition dialog box**

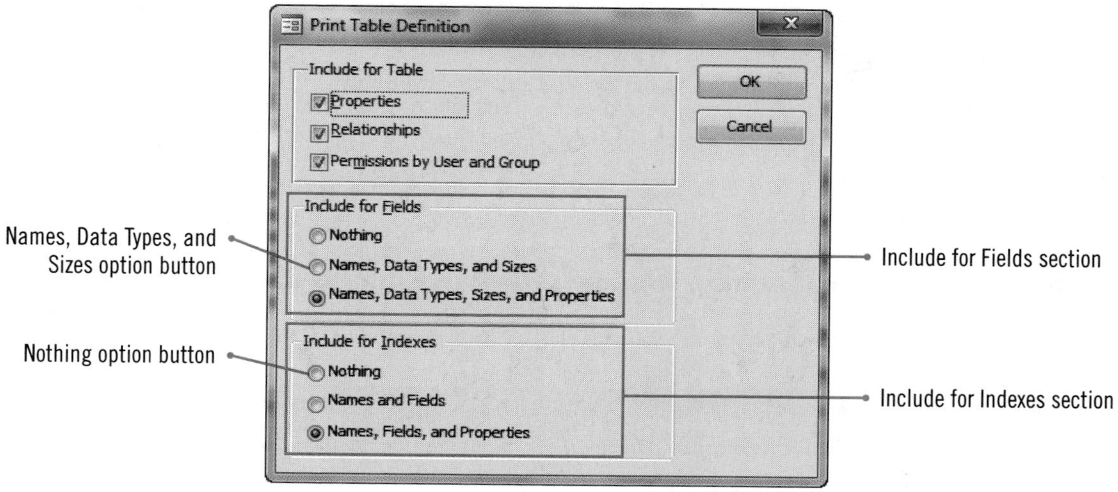

FIGURE O-21: **Object Definition report**

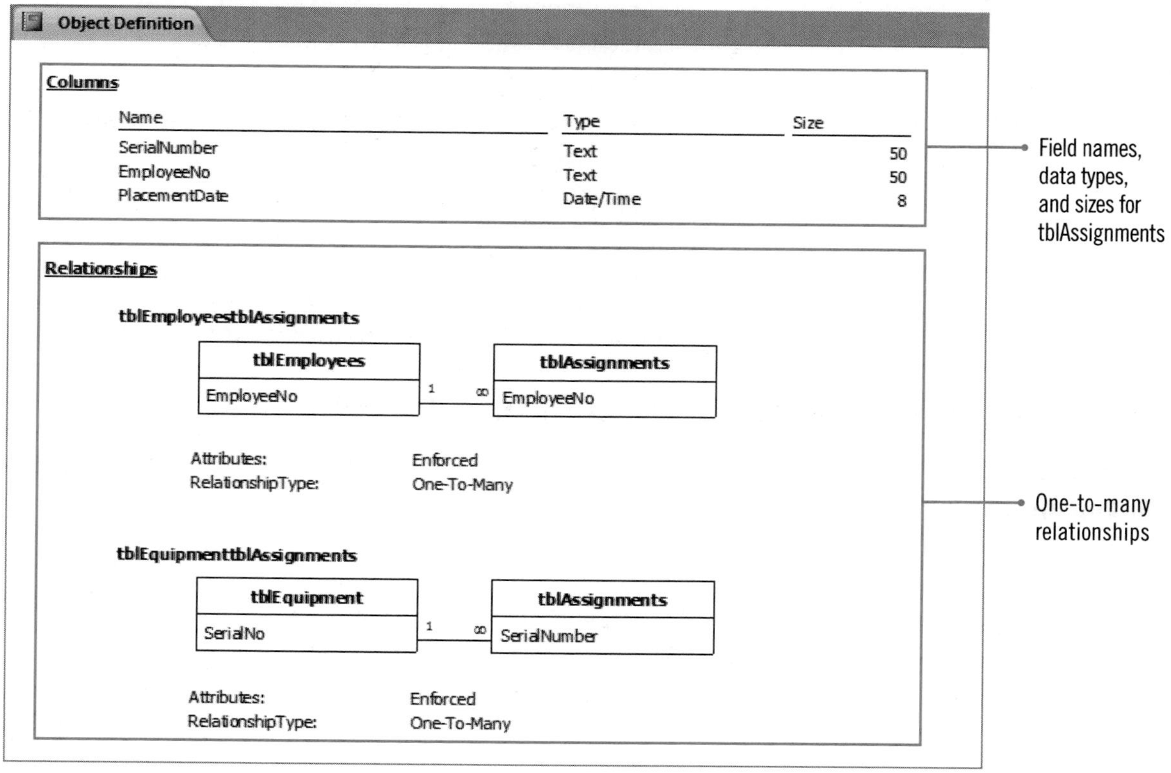

Access 2010

Practice

Concepts Review

For current SAM information, including versions and content details, visit SAM Central (http://www.cengage.com/samcentral). If you have a SAM user profile, you may have access to hands-on instruction, practice, and assessment of the skills covered in this unit. Since various versions of SAM are supported throughout the life of this text, check with your instructor for the correct instructions and URL/Web site for accessing assignments.

Identify each element of the database window shown in Figure O-22.

FIGURE O-22

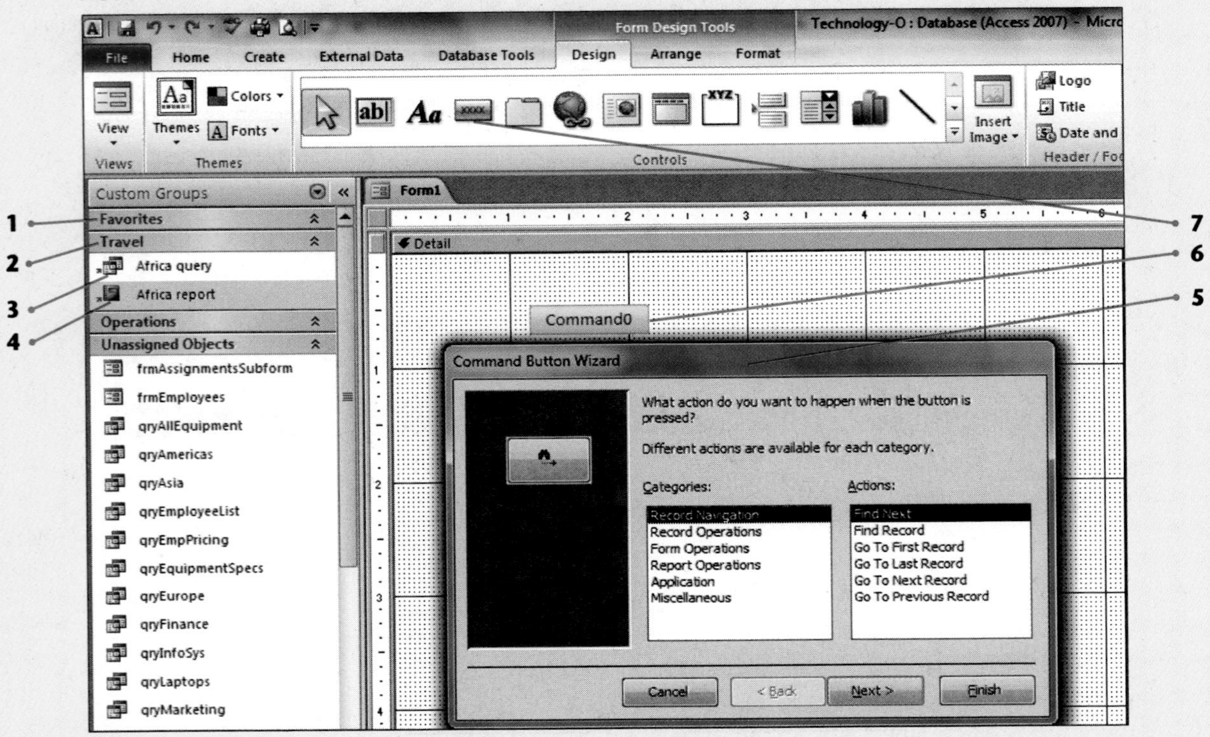

Match each term with the statement that best describes its function.

8. **Dialog box**
9. **Pop up form**
10. **Switchboard**
11. **Shortcut**
12. **Command Button Wizard**
13. **Documenter**

a. Creates reports on the properties and relationships among the objects in your database

b. Pointer to a database object

c. Stays on top of other open forms, even when another form is active

d. Uses command buttons to simplify access to database objects

e. Used to display information or prompt a user for a choice

f. Organizes over 30 of the most common command button actions within six categories

Select the best answer from the following list of choices.

14. Which View By option do you use to display the date that an object was created?
- **a.** Small Icons
- **b.** Details
- **c.** List
- **d.** Date

15. If you wanted to add a command button to a switchboard, which view or tool would you use?
- **a.** Form Design View
- **b.** Switchboard Analyzer
- **c.** Report Design View
- **d.** Switchboard Manager

16. Which item would *not* help you organize the Access objects that the Human Resources (HR) department most often uses?
- **a.** A report that lists all HR employees
- **b.** A switchboard that provides command buttons to the appropriate HR objects
- **c.** A dialog box with command buttons that reference the most commonly used HR forms and reports
- **d.** An HR group with shortcuts to the HR objects

17. A dialog box is which type of object?
- **a.** Form
- **b.** Report
- **c.** Table
- **d.** Macro

18. A switchboard is which type of object?
- **a.** Form
- **b.** Report
- **c.** Table
- **d.** Macro

19. If you want to change the color of a switchboard, which view or tool do you use?
- **a.** Form Design View
- **b.** Switchboard Documenter
- **c.** Form View
- **d.** Switchboard Manager

20. Which is *not* a valid name for an Access object?
- **a.** tblEmployees
- **b.** E1-E2
- **c.** Employees table
- **d.** E1!E2

Skills Review

1. Work with objects.
- **a.** Start Access, open the Basketball-O.accdb database from the drive and folder where you store your Data Files, and enable content if prompted.
- **b.** Using the Navigation Pane, change the view to Icon.
- **c.** Show the Object Dependencies for qryPlayerStats.
- **d.** Switch the Object Dependencies task pane to show Objects that depend on me for qryPlayerStats if it is not already selected.
- **e.** Close the Object Dependencies task pane.

2. Group objects.
- **a.** Use the Navigation Options dialog box to create a custom group named **Offense** and another named **Defense**.
- **b.** In the Navigation Pane, change the category grouping to Custom.
- **c.** Create shortcuts for the qryFieldGoalStats query and the rptPointProduction report in the Offense group.
- **d.** Rename the qryFieldGoalStats report shortcut in the Offense group to **Field Goal Stats**.
- **e.** Rename the rptPointProduction report shortcut in the Offense group to **Point Production**.

3. Create a dialog box.
- **a.** Create a new form in Form Design View.
- **b.** Add a command button to the upper-left corner of the form using the Command Button Wizard. Select Report Operations from the Categories list, select Preview Report from the Actions list, then select the rptPlayerStatistics report.
- **c.** Type **Preview Player Statistics** as the text for the button, then type **cmdPlayerStats** for the button name.
- **d.** Add a second command button below the first to preview the rptPointProduction report.
- **e.** Type **Preview Point Production** as the text for the button, then type **cmdPointProduction** for the button name.

Skills Review (continued)

f. Below the two buttons, add a label to the form with your name.

g. In the Property Sheet for the form, change the Border Style property of the form to Dialog, the Record Selectors property to No, and the Navigation Buttons property to No.

h. Close the Property Sheet, then size the buttons to be the same size and aligned on their left edges.

i. Save the form as **frmTeamReports**.

j. Open the frmTeamReports form in Form View, test the buttons, close the reports, then print the form if requested by your instructor. Your frmTeamReports form should be similar to Figure O-23.

k. Close the frmTeamReports form.

FIGURE O-23

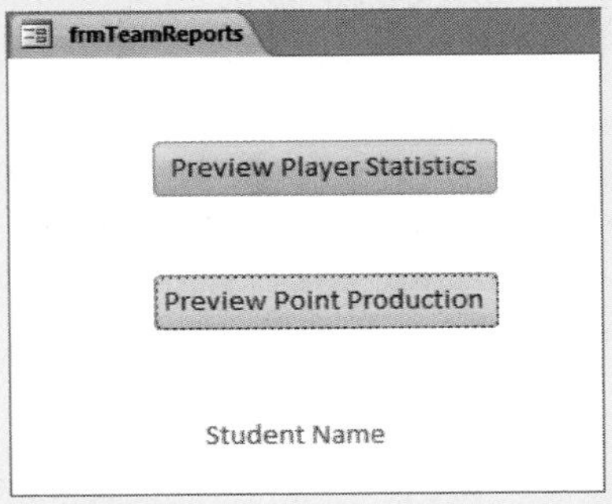

4. Create a pop up form.

a. Create a form in Form Design View, change the Record Source for the form to tblPlayers, and add the following fields to the form: FirstName, LastName, and PlayerNo.

b. Save the form with the name **frmPlayerPopup**.

c. Open the Property Sheet for the frmPlayerPopup form, change the Pop Up property on the Other tab to Yes. Change the Width property on the Format tab to 3.

d. Save, then close the frmPlayerPopup form.

e. Open the frmTeamReports form in Form Design View, then add a command button below your name using the Command Button Wizard.

f. In the Command Button Wizard, select the Form Operations category, the Open Form action, and the frmPlayerPopup form to open. The form should be opened to show all of the records.

g. Type **Open Player Popup** as the text for the button, then name the button **cmdPlayerPopup**.

h. Modify the Embedded Macro on the On Click property of the cmdPlayerPopup button so that the View property is Datasheet.

i. Save the frmTeamReports form, then open it in Form View. Click the Open Player Popup command button to test it. Test the other buttons as well. The frmPlayerPopup form should stay on top of all other forms and reports until you close it.

j. Save then close all open forms and reports.

5. Create a navigation form.

a. Create a Navigation form using the Vertical Tabs, Left style.

b. Close the Field List.

c. Add the frmGameInfo form, the frmGameSummaryForm, and the frmPlayerInformationForm to the tabs.

d. Rename the tabs **Game Info**, **Game Summary**, and **Player Information**.

e. Display the form in Form View, then test each tab.

f. Save the form with the name **frmNavigationForms**, then close it.

6. Create a switchboard.

a. Start the Switchboard Manager, and click Yes to create a new switchboard.

b. Click Edit to edit the Main Switchboard, then click New to add the first item to it.

c. Type **Select a Team Report** as the Text entry for the first command button, select Open Form in Add Mode for the Command, select frmTeamReports for the Form, then click OK to add the first command button to the switchboard.

d. Click New to add a second item to the switchboard. Type **Open Player Entry Form** as the Text entry, select Open Form in Add Mode for the Command, select frmPlayerInformationForm for the Form, then click OK to add the second command button to the switchboard.

e. Close the Edit Switchboard Page dialog box, then close the Switchboard Manager dialog box. Open the Switchboard form and click both command buttons to make sure they work. Notice that when you open the Player Entry Form in Add Mode (rather than using the Open Form in Edit Mode action within the Switchboard Manager), the navigation buttons indicate that you can only add a new record, and not edit an existing one.

f. Close all open forms, including the Switchboard form.

Skills Review (continued)

7. Modify a switchboard.

a. Open the Switchboard Manager, then click Edit to edit the Main Switchboard.

b. Click the Open Player Entry Form item, then click Edit.

c. Select Open Form in Edit Mode for the Command, select frmPlayerInformationForm for the Form, then click OK.

d. Move the Open Player Entry Form item above the Select a Team Report item, then close the Edit Switchboard Page and Switchboard Manager dialog boxes.

e. In Form Design View of the Switchboard form, add a label with your name and another label with the name of your favorite team to the Form Header section of the form. Change the text color to white for both of the labels.

f. View the modified switchboard in Form View, as shown in Figure O-24, then test the buttons. Notice the difference in the Open Player Entry Form button (the Player Entry Form opens in Edit Mode versus Add Mode).

g. Save, print (if requested by your instructor), then close the Switchboard form.

FIGURE O-24

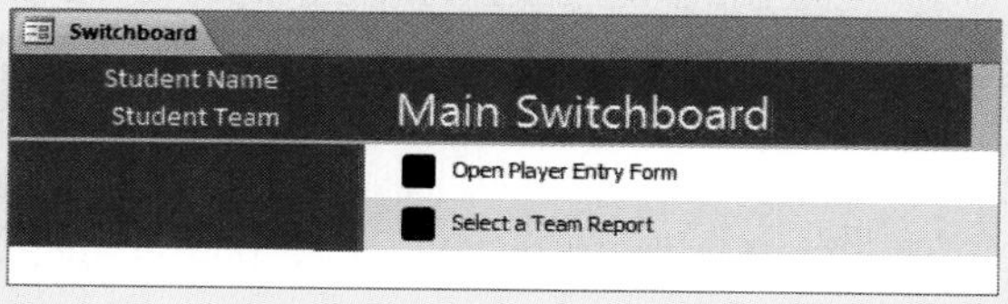

8. Use the Documenter.

a. Use the Database Documenter tool to document all tables and forms in the database.

b. Print the first two pages and the last two pages of the report.

c. Close the report created by Documenter without saving it.

d. Close the Basketball-O.accdb database, then exit Access.

Independent Challenge 1

As the manager of a real estate office, you have created a database to track local real estate agencies, agents, and property listings. You want to create a group to organize the database objects used by the realtors. You also want to document the database's relationships.

a. Start Access, open the database RealEstate-O.accdb from the drive and folder where you store your Data Files, and enable content if prompted.

b. In the Navigation Pane, create a custom group named **Realtors**.

c. View the objects in the Navigation Pane by Custom Groups, then add the following shortcuts to the Realtors group: frmListingsEntryForm, rptRealtorList report, and rptPropertyList report.

d. Test all of the shortcuts to make sure they open the object they point to, then close all open objects.

e. Start the Documenter. On the Current Database tab, click the Relationships check box, then click OK.

f. Print the Documenter's report, then close it. Write your name on the printout.

Advanced Challenge Exercise

- Create a switchboard form with the following four command buttons in the following order:

Text	**Command**	**Form or Report**
Open Agency Information Form	**Open Form in Edit Mode**	**frmAgencyInformation**
Open Listings Entry Form	**Open Form in Edit Mode**	**frmListingsEntryForm**
Open Realtor List Report	**Open Report**	**rptRealtorList**
Open Property List Report	**Open Report**	**rptPropertyList**

- Open the Switchboard, and insert a label that reads **Your Name's Real Estate Agency** on the left side of the Form Header section, and change the text color to white.
- Save, print (if requested by your instructor), then close the switchboard form. It should look like Figure O-25.

FIGURE O-25

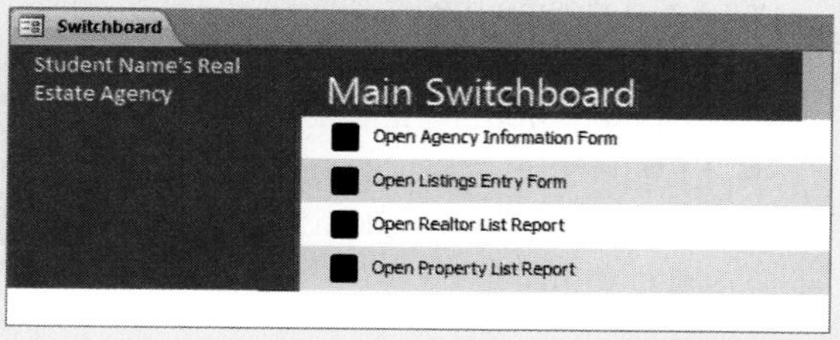

g. Close the RealEstate-O.accdb database, then exit Access.

Independent Challenge 2

As the manager of a real estate office, you have created a database to track local real estate agencies, agents, and property listings. You want to create a new dialog box to make it easier to preview the reports within your database.

a. Start Access, then open the database RealEstate-O.accdb from the drive and folder where you store your Data Files. Enable content if prompted.
b. Start a new form in Form Design View.
c. Using the Command Button Wizard, add a command button to the form. Select Report Operations from the Categories list, select Preview Report from the Actions list, then select the rptRealtorList report.
d. Type **Realtor List** as the text for the button, then type **cmdRealtorList** for the button name.
e. Using the Command Button Wizard, add a second command button below the first. Select Report Operations from the Categories list, select Preview Report from the Actions list, then select the rptPropertyList report.
f. Type **Property List** as the text for the button, then type **cmdPropertyList** for the button name.
g. Using the Command Button Wizard, add a third command button below the second. Select Form Operations from the Categories list, and select Close Form from the Actions list.
h. Type **Close** as the text for the button, then type **cmdClose** as the meaningful name for the button.
i. Add a label to the form with your name and any other formatting enhancements you desire.
j. Open the Property Sheet for the form, change the Border Style property to Dialog, the Record Selectors property to No, and the Navigation Buttons property to No.
k. Close the Property Sheet, and then save the form as **frmDialogBox**.
l. Resize all the command buttons to be the same width and aligned on the left edges.
m. Open the frmDialogBox form in Form View, test the buttons, save the form when prompted, then print the form if requested by your instructor. It should look similar to Figure O-26.
n. Close the frmDialogBox form, close the RealEstate-O.accdb database, then exit Access.

FIGURE O-26

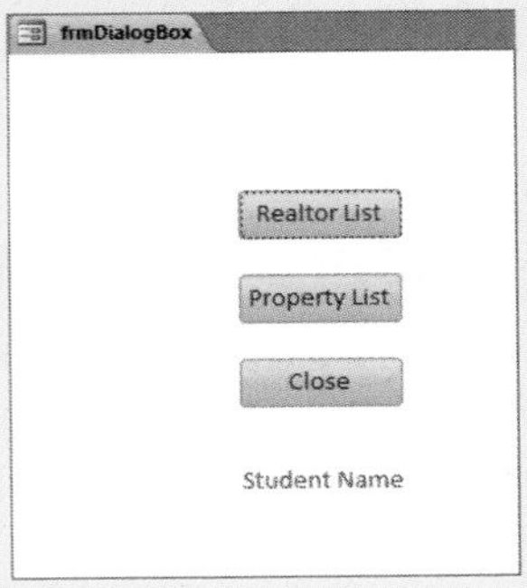

Independent Challenge 3

As the manager of a real estate office, you have created a database to track local real estate agencies, agents, and property listings. You want to create a pop up form to provide agent information. You want to add a command button to the frmListingsEntryForm to open the pop up form.

a. Start Access, then open the database RealEstate-O.accdb from the drive and folder where you store your Data Files. Enable content if prompted.
b. Use the Form Wizard to create a form with the RealtorNo, RealtorFirst, RealtorLast, and RealtorPhone fields from the Realtors table.
c. Use a Tabular layout, and type **Realtor Popup** for the form title.
d. Open the Property Sheet for the form, then change the Pop Up property to Yes.
e. Save, then close the Realtor Popup form. Rename it **frmRealtorPopup** in the Navigation Pane.
f. In Form Design View of frmListingsEntryForm, open the Form Header section about 0.5", then use the Command Button Wizard to create a command button on the right side of the Form Header.
g. Select Form Operations from the Categories list, select Open Form from the Actions list, select the frmRealtorPopup form, then open the form and show all of the records.
h. Type **Realtor Popup** as the text for the button, then type **cmdRealtorPopup** for the button name.
i. Add a label to the left side of the Form Header with your name.
j. Modify the embedded macro in the On Click property of the Realtor Popup command button by changing the View argument from Form to Datasheet.
k. Save the frmListingsEntryForm, open it in Form View, then click the Realtor Popup command button.
l. Move through the records of the frmListingsEntryForm. The frmRealtorPopup form should stay on top of all other forms.

Independent Challenge 3 (continued)

Advanced Challenge Exercise

- Create a second pop up form using the Form Wizard with all of the fields of the Agencies table except for AgencyNo.
- Use a Tabular layout, and title the form **Agency Popup**.
- Change the form's Pop Up property to Yes, then save and close the form. Rename it **frmAgencyPopup** in the Navigation Pane.
- In Design View of the frmListingsEntryForm, add another command button just below the Realtor Popup command button in the Form Header section to open the frmAgencyPopup form and show all of the records.
- Type **Agency Popup** as the text for the button, then type **cmdAgencyPopup** for the button name.
- Move, resize, and align the controls in the Form Header as needed.
- Modify the embedded macro in the On Click property of the Agency Popup command button by changing the View argument from Form to Datasheet.
- Open frmListingsEntryForm in Form View, and test both command buttons.

m. Close any open pop up forms, then print the first record in the frmListingsEntryForm if requested by your instructor.

n. Save and close all open forms, close the RealEstate-O.accdb database, then exit Access.

Real Life Independent Challenge

This Independent Challenge requires an Internet connection.

The larger your database becomes, the more important it is to document it properly so that others can also work with it successfully. Many companies require that you use an adopted set of naming standards when you create new fields, objects, and controls so that other database developers can more readily understand and modify a database they have not created. In this Real Life Independent Challenge, you will search for and report on database naming standards.

a. Connect to the Internet, go to *www.google.com*, *www.bing.com*, or your favorite search engine, then search for Web sites with the key words **Access naming conventions**. You might also try searching for the **Leszynski Naming Convention**, **object naming convention**, or **database naming convention**.

b. Find and print two different reference pages that describe naming conventions for fields, objects, or controls.

c. Find and print two different discussions of the advantages of adopting a common naming convention for all database development for your company.

Advanced Challenge Exercise

- Call two local businesses and contact a programmer in the Information Systems Department who is willing to answer questions about naming conventions. Ask whether their business employs standardized naming conventions in database development. Ask what types of database software they use. Ask what types of challenges they face in database development, maintenance, and standards. Finally, ask what type of advice they have for a future database developer. Be sure to thank them for their time and advice.

d. Write a two-page paper summarizing your findings. If using references or information from articles or interviews, be sure to reference those sources of information properly, in accordance with class instructions.

Visual Workshop

As the manager of a tourism company that promotes travel to European countries, you have created an Access database called Baltic-O.accdb that tracks events at various European cities. Create a switchboard form to give the Baltic-O users an easy-to-use interface, as shown in Figure O-27. All command buttons on the switchboard access a report for the country they reference. Be sure to add your own name as a label to the switchboard, and include any other formatting improvements that you desire.

FIGURE O-27

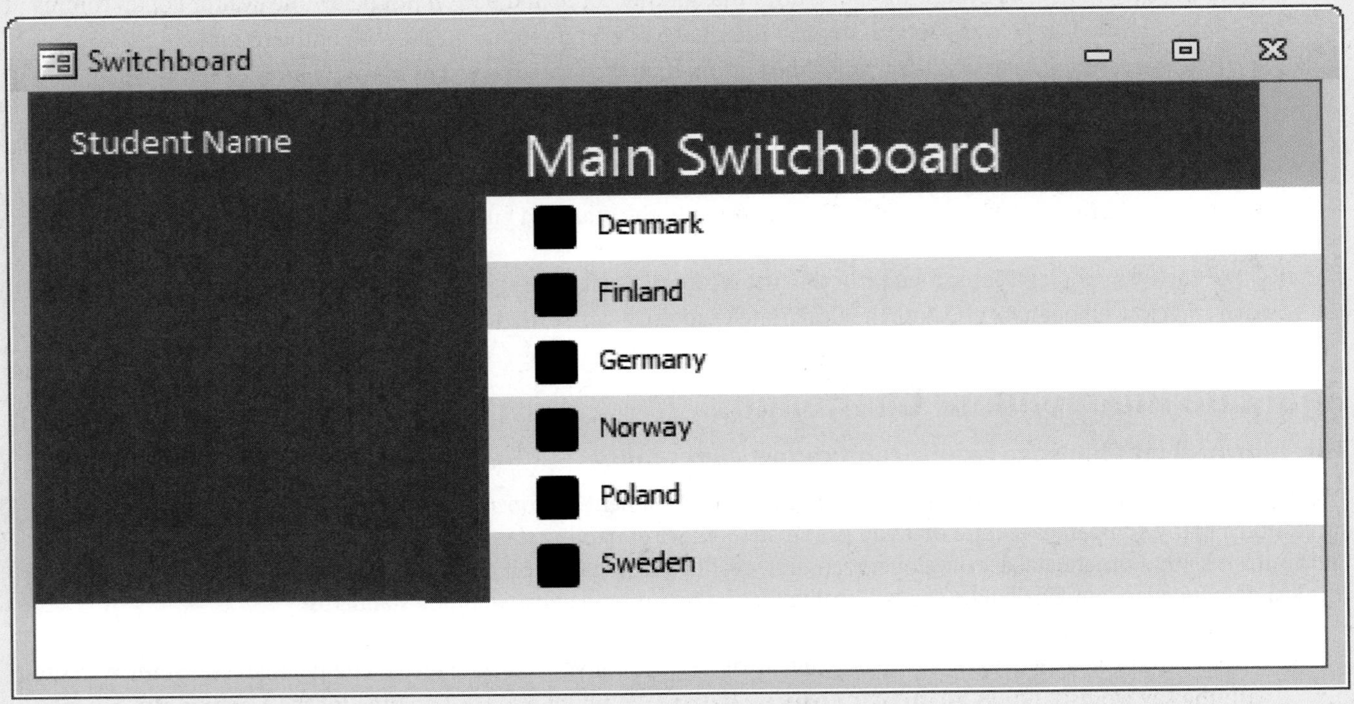

UNIT
P
Access 2010

Administering the Database

Files You Will Need:

- Technology-P.accdb
- Basketball-P.accdb
- Patients-P.accdb
- Membership-P.accdb
- MusicStore-P.accdb

Access databases are unlike the other Microsoft Office files, such as Word documents or Excel spreadsheets, in that they are typically used by multiple people and for extended periods. Therefore, spending a few hours to secure a database and improve its performance is a good investment. **Database administration** involves making the database faster, easier, more secure, and more reliable. You work with Kayla Green, network administrator at Quest Specialty Travel, to examine several administrative issues such as setting passwords, changing startup options, and analyzing database performance to protect, improve, and enhance the database.

OBJECTIVES

- Compact and repair a database
- Change startup options
- Set a database password
- Analyze database performance
- Analyze table performance
- Back up a database
- Convert a database
- Split a Database

UNIT
P
Access 2010

Compacting and Repairing a Database

Compacting and repairing a database refers to a process that Access 2010 uses to reorganize the parts of a database to eliminate wasted space on the disk storage device, which also helps prevent data integrity problems. You can compact and repair a database at any time, or you can set a database option to automatically compact and repair the database when it is closed. You and Kayla Green decide to compact and repair the Technology database, and then learn about the option to automatically compact and repair the database when it is closed.

STEPS

1. **Start Access, then open the Technology-P.accdb database from the drive and folder where you store your Data Files, enabling content if prompted**
   You can compact and repair the database at any time with an option on the File tab.
2. **Click the File tab on the Ribbon, then click the Compact & Repair Database button**
   The database is closed, the compact and repair process is completed, and the database reopened automatically.
   Compacting and repairing a database can reduce the size of the database by 10, 50, or even 75 percent because the space occupied by deleted objects and deleted data is not reused until the database is compacted. Therefore, it's a good idea to set up a regular schedule to compact and repair a database. You decide to change Access options to automatically compact the database when it is closed.
3. **Click the File tab on the Ribbon, then click Options**
   The Compact on Close feature is in the Current Database category.
4. **Click the Current Database category, then click the Compact on Close check box**
   Your screen should look like Figure P-1. Now, every time the database is closed, Access will also compact and repair it. This helps you keep the database as small and efficient as possible and protects your database from potential corruption. For other database threats and solutions, see Table P-1.
5. **Click OK to close the Access Options dialog box, then click OK when prompted to close and reopen the current database**

FIGURE P-1: **Setting the Compact on Close option**

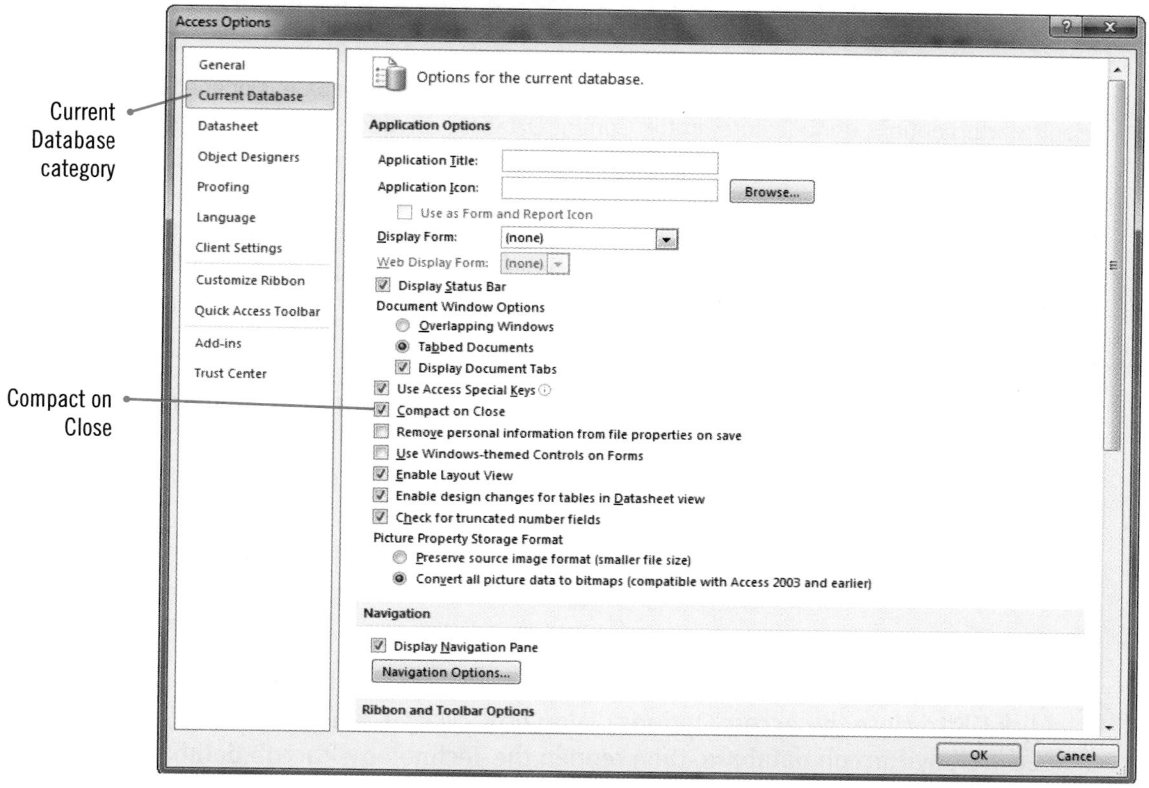

TABLE P-1: **Database threats**

incident	what can happen	appropriate actions
Virus	Viruses can cause a wide range of harm, from profane messages to corrupted files	Purchase the leading virus-checking software for each machine, and keep it updated
Power outage	Power problems such as construction accidents, **brown-outs** (dips in power often causing lights to dim), and **spikes** (surges in power) can damage the hardware, which may render the computer useless	Purchase a **UPS** (uninterruptible power supply) to maintain constant power to the file server Purchase a **surge protector** (power strip with surge protection) for each user
Theft or intentional damage	Computer thieves or other scoundrels steal or vandalize computer equipment	Place the file server in a room that can be locked after hours Use network drives for user data files, and back them up on a daily basis Use off-site storage for backups Set database passwords and encrypt the database so that files that are stolen cannot be used; use computer locks for equipment that is at risk, especially laptops

UNIT P

Access 2010

Changing Startup Options

Startup options are a series of commands that execute when the database is opened. You manage the default startup options using features in the Current Database category of the Access Options dialog box. More startup options are available through the use of **command-line options**, a special series of characters added to the end of the pathname (for example, C:\My Documents\Quest.accdb /excl), which execute a command when the file is opened. See Table P-2 for information on common startup command-line options. You want to view and set database properties and then specify that the frmEmployees form opens when the Technology-P.accdb database is opened.

STEPS

1. **Click the File tab on the Ribbon, click Options, then click Current Database if it is not already selected**

   The Access Options dialog box opens. The startup options are in the Application Options area of the Current Database category.

2. **Click the Application Title text box, then type Quest Specialty Travel**

   The Application Title database property value appears in the title bar instead of the database filename.

3. **Click the Display Form list arrow, then click frmEmployees**

   See Figure P-2. You test the Application Title and Display Form database properties.

4. **Click OK to close the Access Options dialog box, click OK when prompted, close the Technology-P.accdb database, then reopen the Technology-P.accdb database and enable content if prompted**

   The Technology-P.accdb database opens with the new application title, followed by the frmEmployees form, as shown in Figure P-3. If you want to open an Access database and bypass startup options, press and hold [Shift] while the database opens.

5. **Close the frmEmployees form**

> **QUICK TIP**
> The Enable Layout View check box allows or removes the ability to work with forms and reports in Layout View. Some database designers do not use this view, and therefore may decide to disable it.

TABLE P-2: Startup command-line options

option	effect
/excl	Opens the database for exclusive access
/ro	Opens the database for read-only access
/pwd *password*	Opens the database using the specified *password* (applies to Access 2002–2003 and earlier version databases only)
/repair	Repairs the database (in Access 2000 and 2002, compacting the database also repairs it; if you choose the Compact on Close command, you don't need the /repair option)
/convert *target database*	Converts a previous version of a database to an Access 2000 database with the *target database* name
/x *macro*	Starts Access and runs the specified *macro*
/wrkgrp *workgroup information file*	Starts Access using the specified *workgroup information file* (applies to Access 2002–2003 and earlier version databases only)

FIGURE P-2: **Setting the Display Form option**

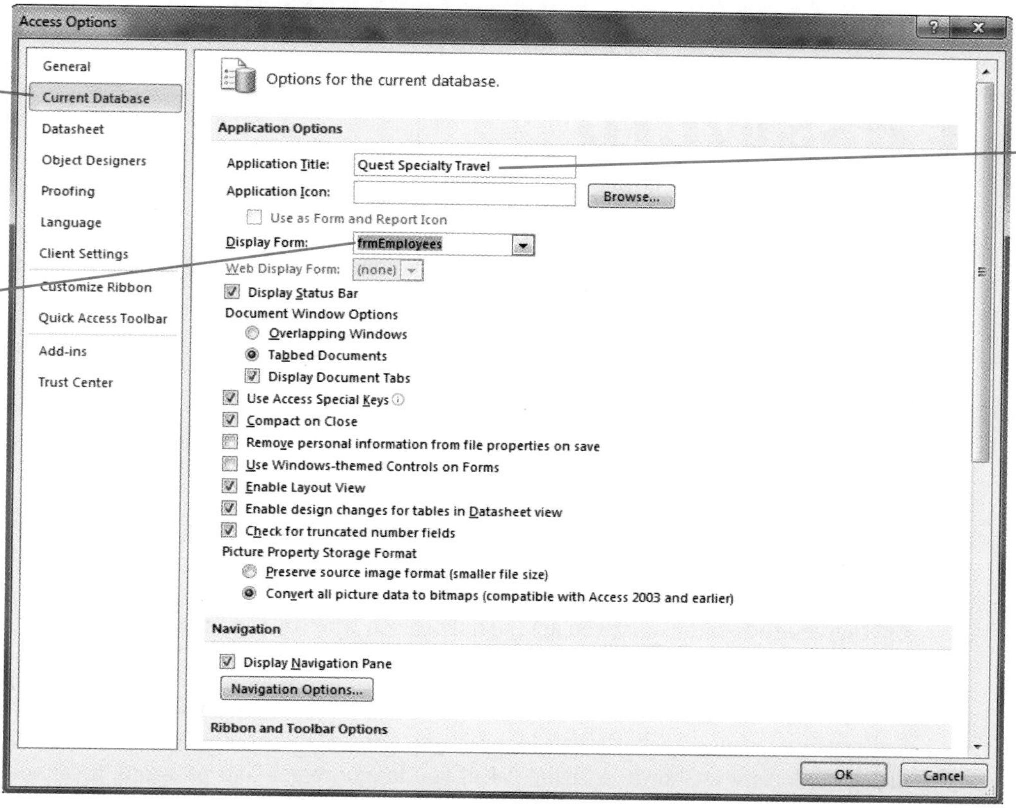

FIGURE P-3: **Form and Application Title startup options are in effect**

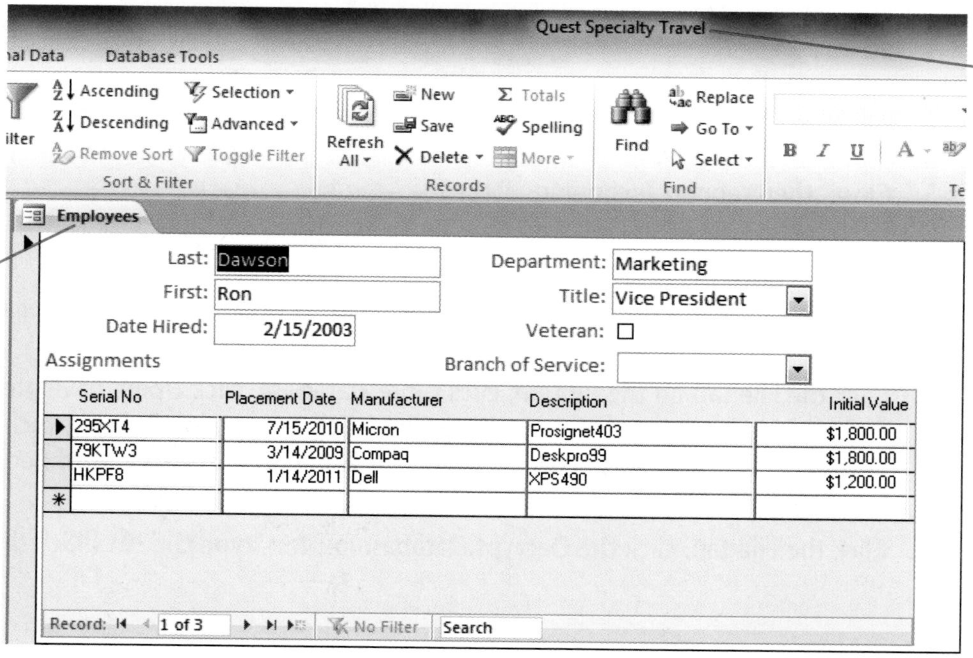

Access 2010

UNIT P

Access 2010

Setting a Database Password

A **password** is a combination of uppercase and lowercase letters, numbers, and symbols that the user must enter to open the database. Setting a database password means that anyone who doesn't know the password cannot open the database. Other ways to secure an Access database are listed in Table P-3. You apply a database password to the Technology-P.accdb database to secure its data.

STEPS

QUICK TIP
It's always a good idea to back up a database before creating a database password.

1. **Click the File tab on the Ribbon, then click Close Database**
   The Technology-P.accdb database closes, but the Access application window remains open. To set a database password, you must open the database in Exclusive mode.

2. **Click Open, navigate to the drive and folder where you store your Data Files, click Technology-P.accdb, click the Open button arrow, click Open Exclusive, then enable content if prompted**
   Exclusive mode means that you are the only person who has the database open, and others cannot open the file during this time.

3. **Click the File tab on the Ribbon, click Info, then click the Encrypt with Password button**
   Encryption means to make the data in the database unreadable by other software. The Set Database Password dialog box opens, as shown in Figure P-4. If you lose or forget your password, it cannot be recovered. For security reasons, your password does not appear as you type; for each keystroke, an asterisk appears instead. Therefore, you must enter the same password in both the Password and Verify text boxes to make sure you haven't made a typing error. Passwords are case sensitive, so Cyclones and cyclones are different.

QUICK TIP
Check to make sure the Caps Lock light is not on before entering a password.

4. **Type Go!2014!ISU in the Password text box, press [Tab], type Go!2014!ISU in the Verify text box, click OK, then click OK if prompted about row-level security**
   Passwords should be easy to remember, but not as obvious as your name, the word "password," the name of the database, or the name of your company. **Strong passwords** are longer than eight characters and use the entire keyboard including uppercase and lowercase letters, numbers, and symbols. Microsoft provides an online tool to check the strength of your password. Go to www.microsoft.com and search for password checker.

5. **Close, then reopen Technology-P.accdb**
   The Password Required dialog box opens, as shown in Figure P-5.

6. **Type Go!2014!ISU, then click OK**
   The Technology-P.accdb database opens, giving you full access to all of the objects. To remove a password, you must exclusively open a database, just as you did when you set the database password.

7. **Click the File tab on the Ribbon, click Close Database, click Open, navigate to the drive and folder where you store your Data Files, click Technology-P.accdb, click the Open button arrow, click Open Exclusive, type Go!2014!ISU in the Password Required dialog box, then click OK**

8. **Click the File tab, click the Decrypt Database button, type Go!2014!ISU, then click OK**

FIGURE P-4: **Set Database Password dialog box**

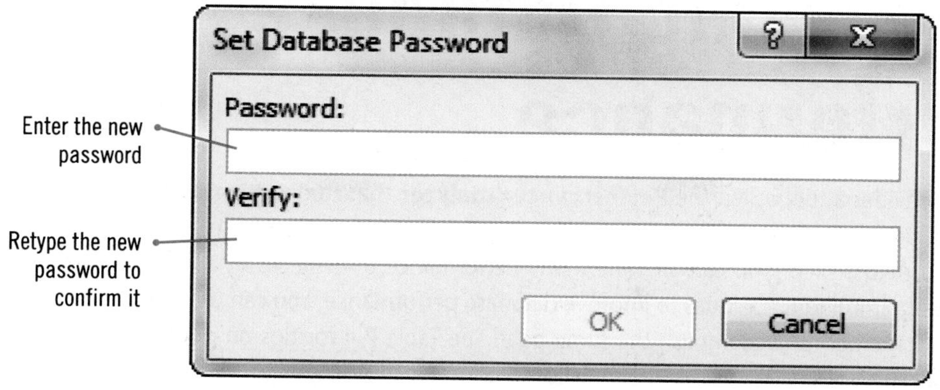

FIGURE P-5: **Password Required dialog box**

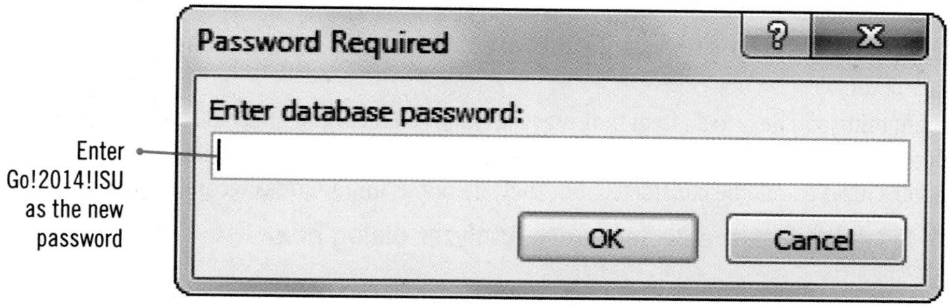

TABLE P-3: **Methods to secure an Access database**

method	description
Password	Restricts access to the database, and can be set at the database, workgroup, or VBA level
Encryption	Makes the data indecipherable to other programs
Startup options	Hides or disables certain functions when the database is opened
Show/hide objects	Shows or hides objects in the Navigation Pane; a simple way to prevent users from unintentionally deleting objects is to hide them in the database window by checking the Hidden property in the object's Property Sheet
Split a database	Separates the back-end data and the front-end objects (such as forms and reports) into two databases that work together; splitting a database allows you to give each user access to only those front-end objects they need as well as add security measures to the back-end database that contains the data

UNIT
P
Access 2010

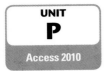

Analyzing Database Performance

Access provides a tool called the **Performance Analyzer** that studies the structure and size of your database and makes a variety of recommendations on how you can improve its performance. With adequate time and Access skills, you can alleviate many performance bottlenecks by using software tools and additional programming techniques to improve database performance. You can often purchase faster processors and more memory to accomplish the same goal. See Table P-4 for tips on optimizing the performance of your computer. You use the Database Performance Analyzer to see whether Access provides any recommendations on how to easily maintain peak performance of the Technology-P.accdb database.

STEPS

1. **Close frmEmployees, click the Database Tools tab, click the Analyze Performance button in the Analyze group, then click the All Object Types tab**

   The Performance Analyzer dialog box opens, as shown in Figure P-6. You can choose to analyze selected tables, forms, other objects, or the entire database.

2. **Click the Select All button, then click OK**

   The Performance Analyzer examines each object and presents the results in a dialog box, as shown in Figure P-7. The key shows that the analyzer gives four levels of advice regarding performance: recommendations, suggestions, ideas, and items that were fixed.

3. **Click each line in the Analysis Results area, then read each description in the Analysis Notes area**

   The light bulb icon next to an item indicates that this is an idea. The Analysis Notes section of the Performance Analyzer dialog box gives you additional information regarding the specific item. All of the Performance Analyzer's ideas should be considered, but they are not as important as recommendations and suggestions.

4. **Click Close to close the Performance Analyzer dialog box**

TABLE P-4: **Tips for optimizing performance**

degree of difficulty	tip
Easy	To free memory and other computer resources, close all applications that you don't currently need
Easy	If they can be run safely only when you need them, eliminate memory-resident programs such as complex screen savers, e-mail alert programs, and virus checkers
Easy	If you are the only person using a database, open it in Exclusive mode
Easy	Use the Compact on Close feature to regularly compact and repair your database
Moderate	Add more memory to your computer; once the database is open, memory is generally the single most important determinant of overall performance
Moderate	If others don't need to share the database, load it on your local hard drive instead of the network's file server (but be sure to back up local drives regularly, too)
Moderate	Split the database so that the data is stored on the file server, but other database objects are stored on your local (faster) hard drive
Moderate to difficult	If you are using disk compression software, stop doing so or move the database to an uncompressed drive
Moderate to difficult	Run Performance Analyzer on a regular basis, examining and appropriately acting on each recommendation, suggestion, and idea
Moderate to difficult	Make sure that all PCs are running the latest versions of Windows and Access; this might involve purchasing more software or upgrading hardware to properly support these robust software products

FIGURE P-6: **Performance Analyzer dialog box**

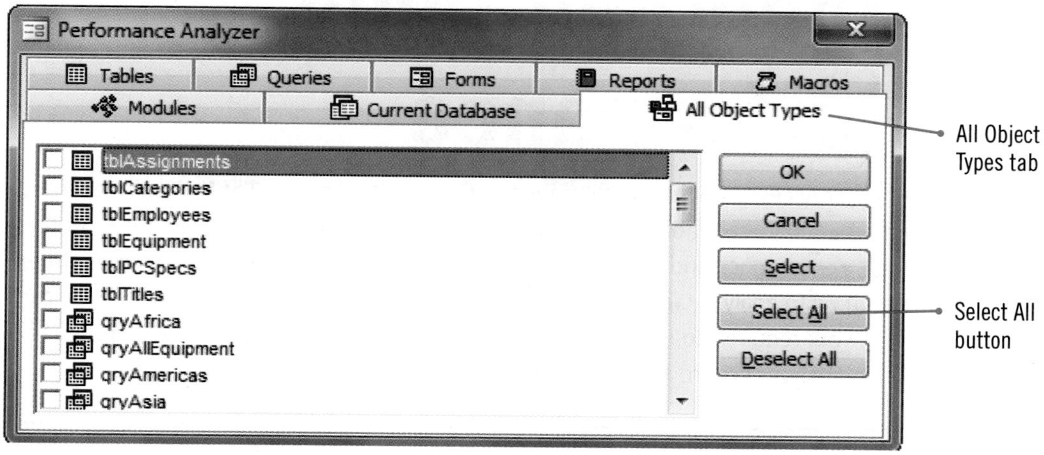

FIGURE P-7: **Performance Analyzer results**

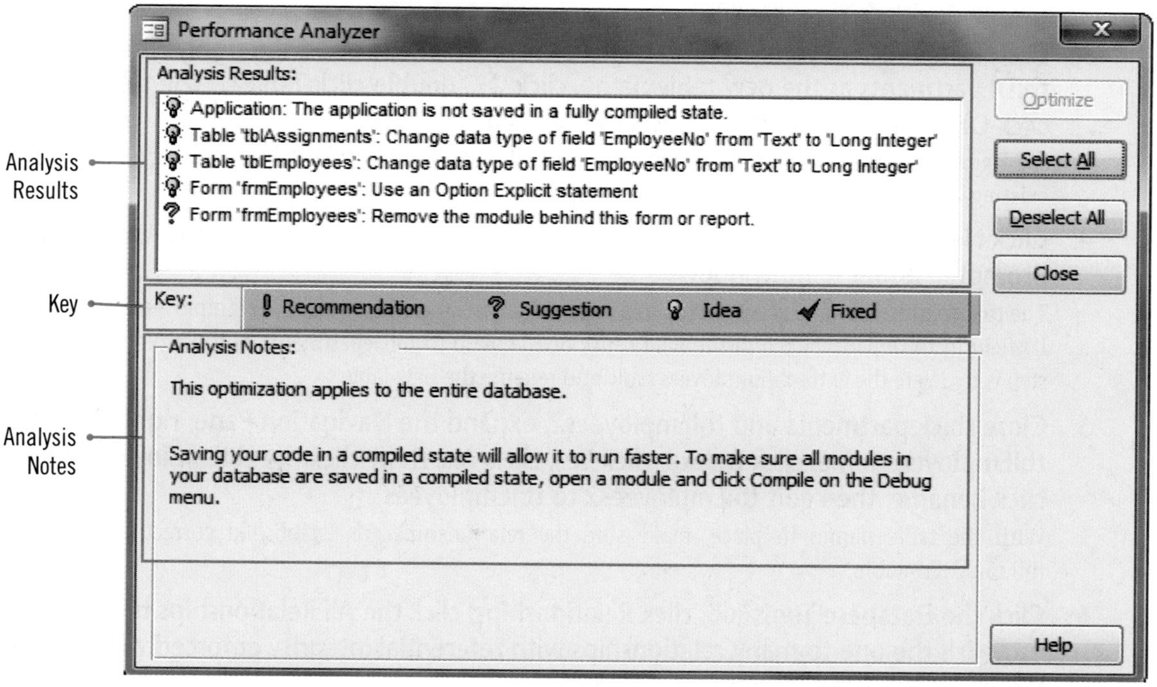

UNIT

P

Access 2010

Analyzing Table Performance

Another Access database performance analysis tool, called the **Table Analyzer Wizard**, looks for duplicate information in one table that could be separated and stored in its own table. Storing duplicate data in one table wastes space and causes database accuracy errors, yet it is a very common table design problem. The best time to analyze tables is shortly after you initially build the tables, so that you can minimize the amount of rework required to update other queries, forms, and reports that rely on the table. You use the Table Analyzer Wizard to examine the tblEmployees table.

STEPS

1. **Click the Database Tools tab, then click the Analyze Table button**

   The Table Analyzer Wizard starts, as shown in Figure P-8. The first dialog box describes the problems caused by storing duplicate data in one table. The **Show me an example** buttons give you more information by using a common example to explain the problem.

2. **Click Next, read about solving the redundant data problem, click Next, click tblEmployees in the Tables list, click Next, click the No, I want to decide option button, then click Next**

   The Table Analyzer Wizard helps you break repeated information into separate **lookup tables**. For example, the EDepartment field contains a given number of values that could be supplied by a lookup table. By using a lookup table for EDepartment data, users could not enter the same department name two or more ways (HR and Human Resources, for example).

3. **Drag EDepartment from the Table1 field list to a blank spot on the right, type tblDepartments as the new table name, click OK, double-click Table1, type tblEmployees2, click OK, then resize both field lists to see all of the fields**

   See Figure P-9. The wizard prevents you from using the names of existing tables so you do not replace any existing data.

4. **Click Next, click the No, don't create the query option button, click Finish, then click OK if prompted about tiling windows**

   The tblDepartments table is connected in a one-to-many relationship with the tblEmployees2 table using the ID field in tblDepartments and the field captioned Lookup to tblDepartments in tblEmployees2. Your next step is to delete the extra tblEmployees table and rename the new table.

5. **Close tblDepartments and tblEmployees2, expand the Navigation Pane, right-click the tblEmployees table, click Delete, click Yes, click Yes, right-click the tblEmployees2 table, click Rename, then edit tblEmployees2 to tblEmployees**

   With the table names in place, make sure the relationships are established correctly with the new tblEmployees table.

6. **Click the Database Tools tab, click Relationships, click the All Relationships button, then establish the one-to-many relationships with referential integrity enforced with the new tblEmployees table as shown in Figure P-10**

   Any time you change or modify tables, it's important to check the Relationships window to make sure that all relationships are still in place.

7. **Close the Relationships window, then click Yes when prompted to save changes**

FIGURE P-8: **Table Analyzer Wizard**

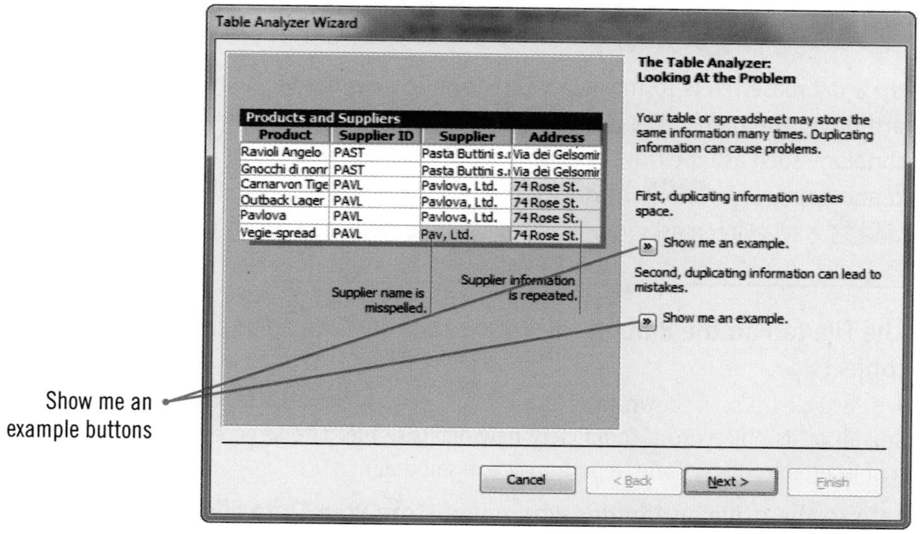

FIGURE P-9: **Creating a lookup table**

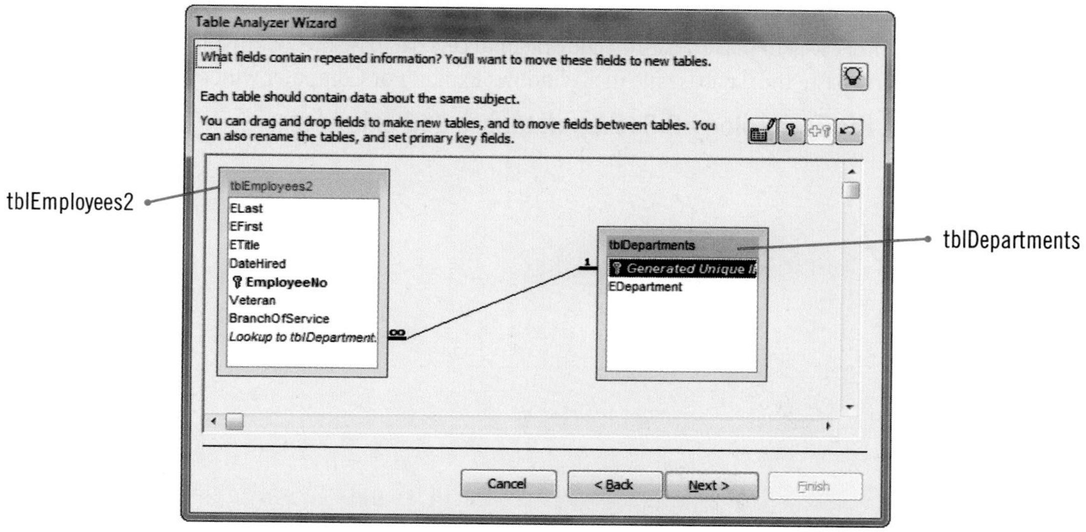

FIGURE P-10: **Establishing relationships**

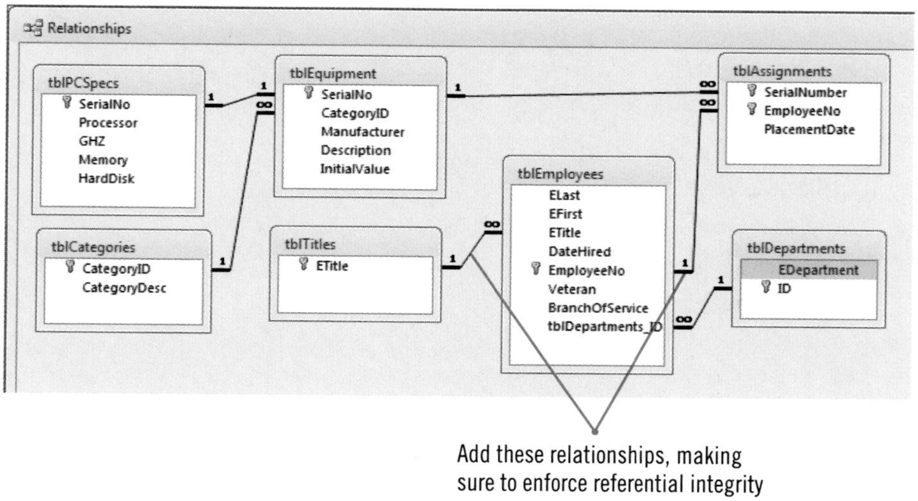

Access 2010

UNIT
P
Access 2010

Backing Up a Database

Backing up a database refers to making a copy of it in a secure location. Backups can be saved on an external hard drive, the hard drive of a second computer, or a Web server. Several years ago, portable backup technology such as tape drives or compact discs (CDs) were used. Because most users are familiar with saving and copying files to hard drives, the new technology streamlines the effort of backing up a database. Kayla Green asks you to review the methods of backing up the database.

STEPS

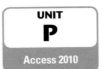

1. **Click the File tab on the Ribbon, click Save Database As, then click Yes to close all open objects**
   The Save As dialog box is shown in Figure P-11. Note that **Save Database As** saves the entire database including all of its objects to a completely new database file. The **Save Object As** option saves only the current object (table, query, form, report, macro, or module).
2. **Navigate to the drive and folder where you store your Data Files, enter Technology-P-Backup in the File name box, then click Save**
   A copy of the Technology-P.accdb database is saved in the location you selected with the name Technology-P-Backup.accdb. Access also automatically closed the Technology-P.accdb database and opened Technology-P-Backup.accdb.
   Another way to make a backup copy of an Access database file, or any file, is to use your Windows skills to copy and paste the database file in a Windows Explorer or Computer window.
3. **Close the Technology-P-Backup database and exit Access**

FIGURE P-11: Save As dialog box to backup a database

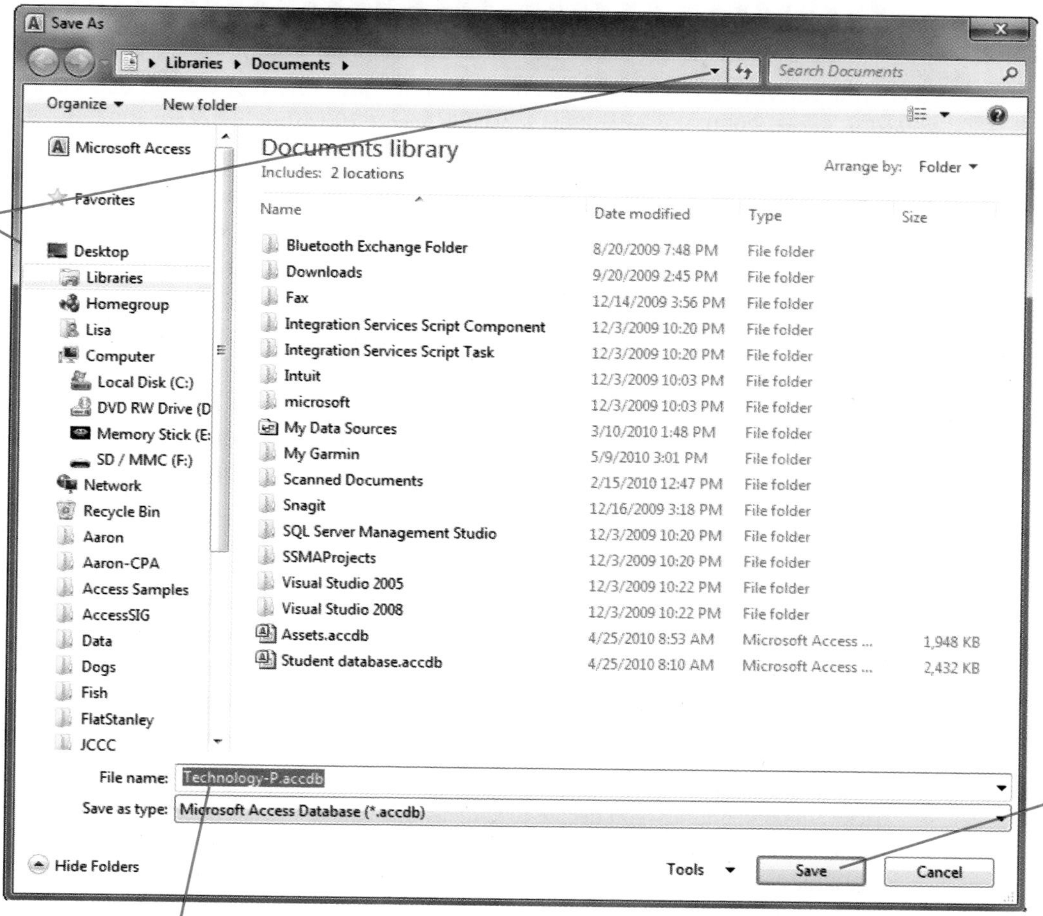
Use the Previous Locations list or folder window to navigate to your data files
Save button
Enter Technology-P-Backup in File name box

Using portable storage media

Technological advancements continue to make it easier and less expensive to store large files on portable storage devices. A few years ago, 3.5-inch disks with roughly 1 **MB** (megabyte, a million bytes) of storage capacity were common. Today, 3.5-inch disks have been replaced by a variety of inexpensive, high-capacity storage media that work with digital devices such as digital cameras, cell phones, tablet computers, and personal digital assistants (PDAs). **Secure digital (SD) cards** are quarter-sized devices that slip directly into a computer and typically store around 4 **GB** (gigabyte, 4,000 MB). **CompactFlash (CF) cards** are slightly larger, about the size of a matchbook, and store more data, around 8 GB. **USB (Universal Serial Bus) drives** (which plug into a computer's USB port), are also popular. USB drives are also called thumb drives, flash drives, and travel drives. USB devices typically store 1 GB to 10 GB of information. Larger still are **external hard drives**, sometimes as small as the size of a cell phone, that store anywhere from 20 to about 400 GB of information and connect to a computer using either a USB or FireWire port.

UNIT P
Access 2010

Converting a Database

When you **convert** a database, you change the file into one that can be opened in another version of Access. In Access 2010, the default file format is Access 2007, but in Access 2003, the default file format for a new database was Access 2000, a file format that could be seamlessly opened in Access 2000, Access 2002 (also called Access XP), or Access 2003. Therefore, Access users must now consider the version of Access they want to create ahead of time because Access 2007 databases work only with Access 2007 and Access 2010. If you want to open an Access 2007 database in Access 2000, 2002, or 2003, you need to convert it to an Access 2000 database first. The Training Department asks you to convert the Technology-P.accdb database to a version that they can open and use in Access 2000, 2002, or 2003.

STEPS

1. **Start Access, then open the Technology-P.accdb database from the drive and folder where you store your Data Files, enabling content if prompted**

2. **Click the File tab on the Ribbon, click Save & Publish, click Access 2000 Database (*.mdb), click the Save As button, then click Yes to close open objects**

   To convert a database, you must make sure that no other users are currently working with it. Because you are the sole user of this database, it is safe to start the conversion process. The Save As dialog box opens, prompting you for the name of the database.

> **TROUBLE**
> If you do not see the extensions on the filenames, click Organize on the toolbar, click Folder and search options, click the View tab, then uncheck the Hide file extensions for known file types check box.

3. **Navigate to the drive and folder where you store your Data Files, then type Technology-P-2000.mdb in the File name text box as shown in Figure P-12**

   Because Access 2000, 2002, and 2003 all work with Access 2000 databases equally well, to allow for maximum backward compatibility you decide to convert this database to an Access 2000 version database. Recall that Access 2007 databases have an **.accdb** file extension, but Access 2000 and 2002–2003 databases have the **.mdb** file extension.

   Also note that you may see two other database extensions, .ldb for older databases and .laccdb for newer databases. The **.ldb** and **.laccdb** files are temporary files that keep track of record-locking information when the database is open. They help coordinate the multiuser capabilities of an Access database so that several people can read and update the same database at the same time.

4. **Click Save, then click OK**

   A copy of the database with the name Technology-P-2000.mdb is saved to the drive and folder you specified and is opened in the Access window. You can open and use Access 2000 and 2002–2003 databases in Access 2010 just as you would open and use an Access 2007 database. Each database version has its advantages, however, which are summarized in Table P-5.

5. **Close the database and exit Access**

FIGURE P-12: **Save As dialog box to convert a database**

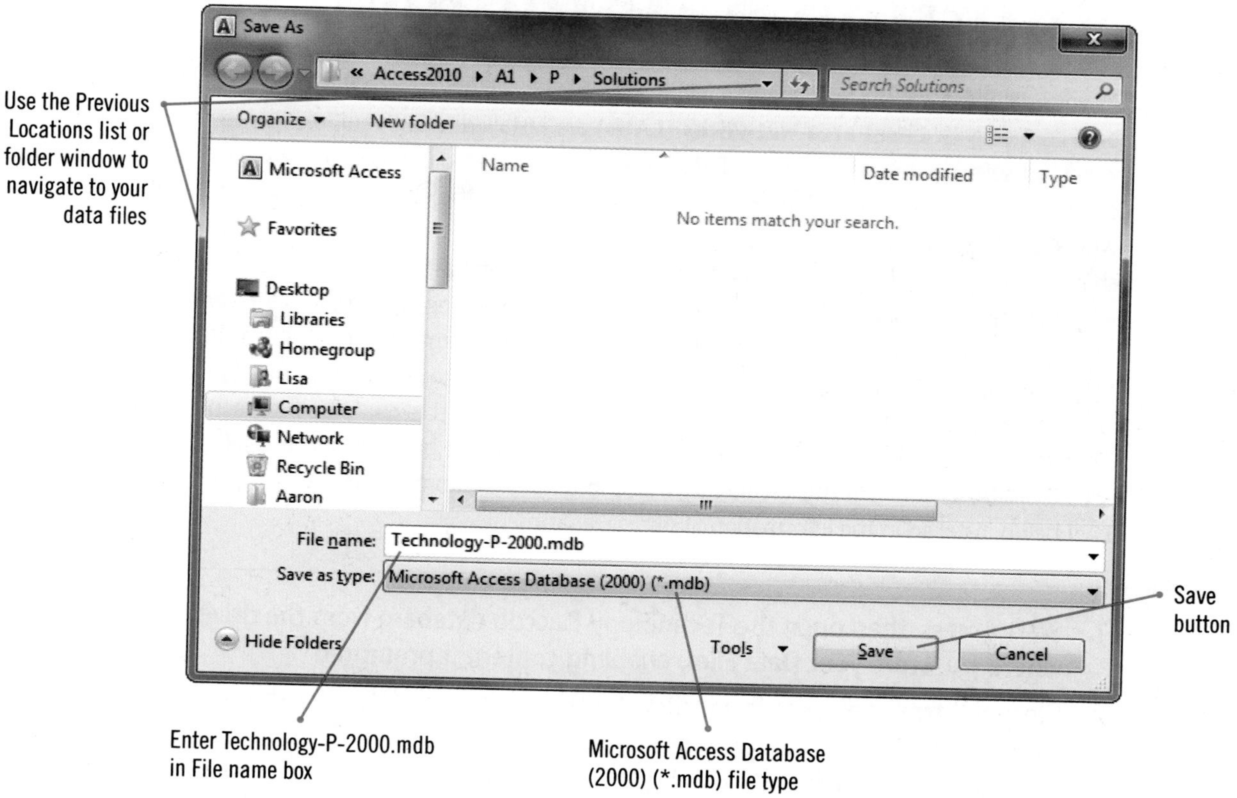
Save As
« Access2010 ▸ A1 ▸ P ▸ Solutions
Search Solutions
Organize
New folder
Microsoft Access
Favorites
Desktop
Libraries
Homegroup
Lisa
Computer
Network
Recycle Bin
Aaron
Name
Date modified
Type
No items match your search.
File name: Technology-P-2000.mdb
Save as type: Microsoft Access Database (2000) (*.mdb)
Hide Folders
Tools
Save
Cancel
Use the Previous Locations list or folder window to navigate to your data files
Save button
Enter Technology-P-2000.mdb in File name box
Microsoft Access Database (2000) (*.mdb) file type

Access 2010

TABLE P-5: **Differences between database file formats**

database file format	file extension	Access version(s) that can read this file	benefits
2000	.mdb	2000, 2002, 2003, 2007, and 2010	Most versatile if working in an environment where multiple versions of Access are still in use
2002–2003	.mdb	2002, 2003, 2007, and 2010	Provides some advanced technical advantages for large databases over the Access 2000 file format
2007	.accdb	2007 and 2010	Supports the Attachment data type Supports multivalued fields Provides excellent integration with SharePoint and Outlook Provides more robust encryption

Splitting a Database

As your database grows, more people will want to use it, which creates the need for higher levels of database connectivity. **Local area networks (LANs)** are installed to link multiple PCs so they can share hardware and software resources. After a LAN is installed, a shared database can be moved to a **file server**, a centrally located computer from which every user can access the database via the network. The more users who share the same database, however, the slower it responds. To improve the performance of a database shared among several users, you might want to **split** the database into two files: the **back-end database**, which contains the actual table objects and is stored on the file server, and the **front-end database**, which contains the other database objects (forms and reports, for example), and links to the back-end database tables. You copy the front-end database for as many users as needed because the front-end database must be located on each user's PC. You can also customize the objects contained in each front-end database. Therefore, front-end databases not only improve performance but also add a level of customization and security. You split the Technology-P.accdb database into two databases in preparation for the new LAN being installed in the Information Systems Department.

STEPS

1. **Start Access, then open the Technology-P.accdb database from the drive and folder where you store your Data Files, enabling content if prompted**

2. **Close the frmEmployees form, click the Database Tools tab, click the Access Database button in the Move Data group, read the dialog box, then click Split Database**

   Access suggests the name of Technology-P_be.accdb for the back-end database in the Create Back-end Database dialog box.

3. **Navigate to the drive and folder where you store your Data Files, click Split, then click OK**

   Technology-P.accdb has now become the front-end database, which will contain all of the Access objects except for the tables, as shown in Figure P-13. The tables have been replaced with links to the physical tables in the back-end database.

4. **Point to several linked table icons to read the path to the back-end database, right-click any of the linked table icons, then click Linked Table Manager**

   The Linked Table Manager dialog box opens, as shown in Figure P-14. This allows you to select and manually update tables. This is useful if the path to the back-end database changes and you want to reconnect the front-end and back-end database.

5. **Click Cancel**

   Linked tables work just like regular physical tables, even though the data is physically stored in another database.

6. **Close the Technology-P.accdb database and exit Access**

FIGURE P-13: **Front-end database**

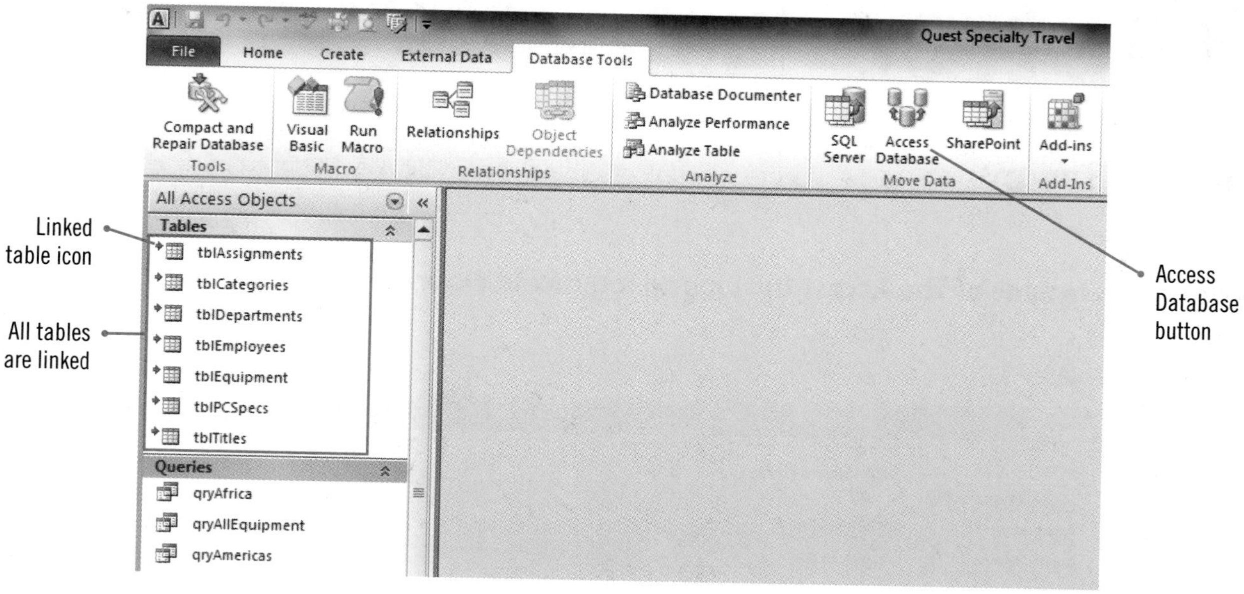

FIGURE P-14: **Linked Table Manager**

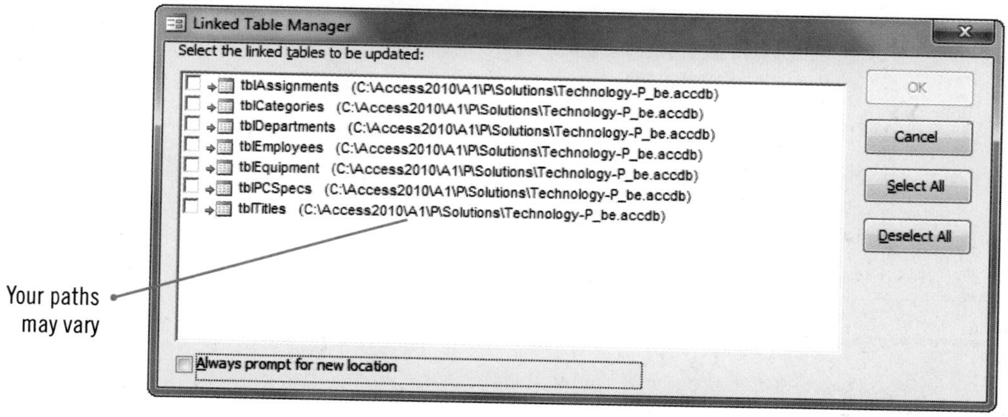

Databases and client/server computing

Splitting a database into a front-end and back-end database that work together is an excellent example of client/server computing. **Client/server computing** can be defined as two or more information systems cooperatively processing to solve a problem. In most implementations, the **client** is defined as the user's PC and the **server** is defined as the shared file server, mini computer, or mainframe computer. The server usually handles corporate-wide computing activities such as data storage and management, security, and connectivity to other networks. Within Access, client computers generally handle those tasks specific to each user, such as storing all of the queries, forms, and reports used by a particular user. Effectively managing a client/server network in which many front-end databases link to a single back-end database is a tremendous task, but the performance and security benefits are worth the effort.

Practice

Concepts Review

For current SAM information, including versions and content details, visit SAM Central (http://www.cengage.com/samcentral). If you have a SAM user profile, you may have access to hands-on instruction, practice, and assessment of the skills covered in this unit. Since various versions of SAM are supported throughout the life of this text, check with your instructor for the correct instructions and URL/Web site for accessing assignments.

Identify each element of the Access Options dialog box in Figure P-15.

FIGURE P-15

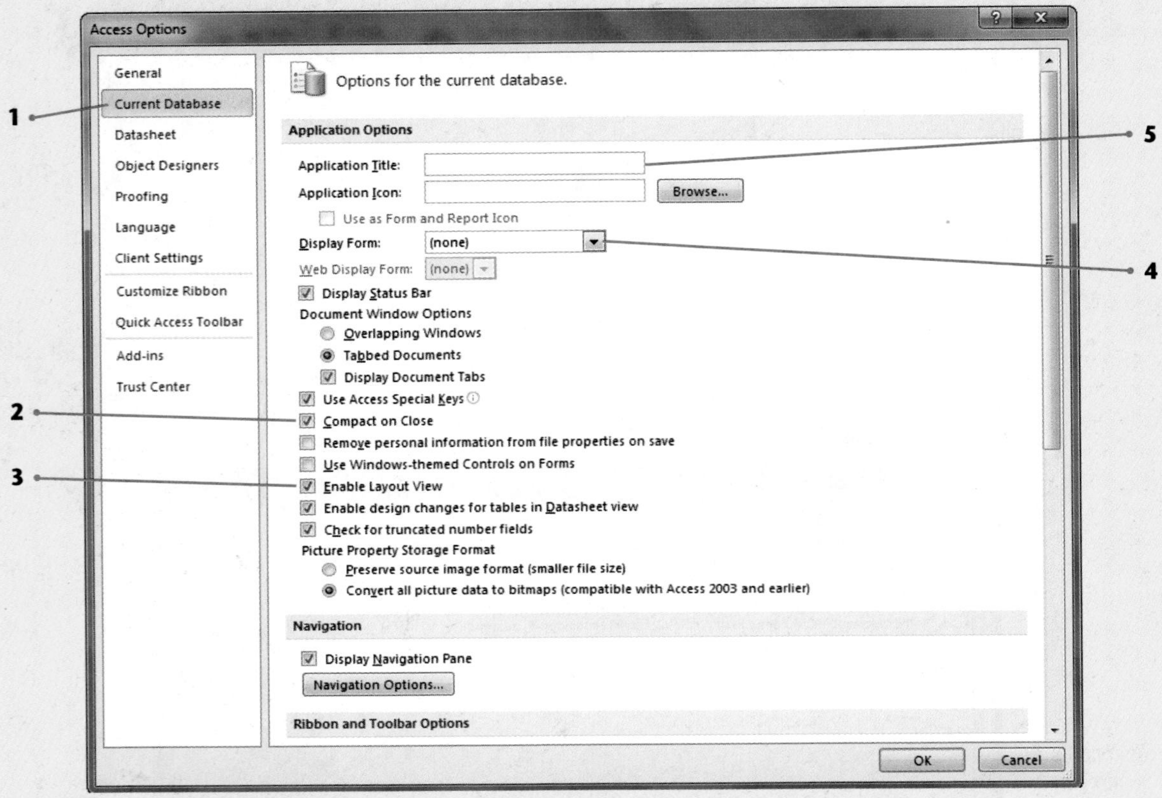

Match each term with the statement that best describes its function.

6. **Table Analyzer Wizard**
7. **Back-end database**
8. **Encrypting**
9. **Database Performance Analyzer**
10. **Exclusive mode**

a. Scrambles data so that it is indecipherable when opened by another program

b. Studies the structure and size of your database, and makes a variety of recommendations on how you can improve its speed

c. Contains database tables

d. Looks for duplicate information in one table that should be separated and stored in its own table

e. Means that no other users can have access to the database file while it's open

Select the best answer from the list of choices.

11. Changing a database file so that a previous version of Access can open it is called:
   a. Splitting.
   b. Analyzing.
   c. Converting.
   d. Encrypting.

12. Which is *not* a strong password?
   a. 1234$College=6789
   b. password
   c. 5Matthew14?
   d. Lip44Balm*!

13. Power outages can be caused by which of the following?
   a. Surges
   b. Spikes
   c. Construction accidents
   d. All of the above

14. Which character precedes a command-line option?
   a. ^
   b. /
   c. @
   d. !

Skills Review

1. **Compact and repair a database.**
   a. Start Access, open the Basketball-P.accdb database from the drive and folder where you store your Data Files, and enable content if prompted.
   b. Compact and repair the database using an option on the File tab.
   c. Open the Access Options dialog box, and check the Compact on Close option in the Current Database category.
2. **Change startup options.**
   a. Open the Access Options dialog box.
   b. Type **Iowa State Cyclones** in the Application Title text box, click the Display Form list arrow, click the frmGameInfo form, then apply the changes.
   c. Close the Basketball-P.accdb database, then reopen it to check the startup options. Notice the change in the Access title bar.
   d. Close the frmGameInfo form that automatically opened when the database was opened.
   e. Close the Basketball-P.accdb database.
3. **Set a database password.**
   a. Open the Basketball-P.accdb database in Exclusive mode.
   b. Set the database password to **b*i*g*1*2**. (*Hint*: Check to make sure the Caps Lock light is not on because passwords are case sensitive.) Click OK if prompted.
   c. Close the Basketball-P.accdb database, but leave Access open.
   d. Reopen the Basketball-P.accdb database to test the password. Close the Basketball-P.accdb database.
   e. Reopen the Basketball-P.accdb database in Exclusive mode. Type **b*i*g*1*2** as the password.
   f. Unset the database password.
   g. Close the frmGameInfo form.
4. **Analyze database performance.**
   a. On the Database Tools tab, click the Analyze Performance button.
   b. On the All Object Types tab, select all objects, then click OK.
   c. Read each of the ideas and descriptions, then close the Performance Analyzer.
5. **Analyze table performance.**
   a. On the Database Tools tab, click the Analyze Table button.
   b. Step through the wizard, choosing the tblPlayers table to analyze. Choose the No, I want to decide option button when prompted.
   c. Drag the Position field from Table1 to a blank spot in the Table Analyzer Wizard dialog box to create a new lookup table named **tblPositions**.
   d. Rename Table1 to **tblPlayers2** so that the Table Analyzer Wizard dialog box looks like Figure P-16.

FIGURE P-16

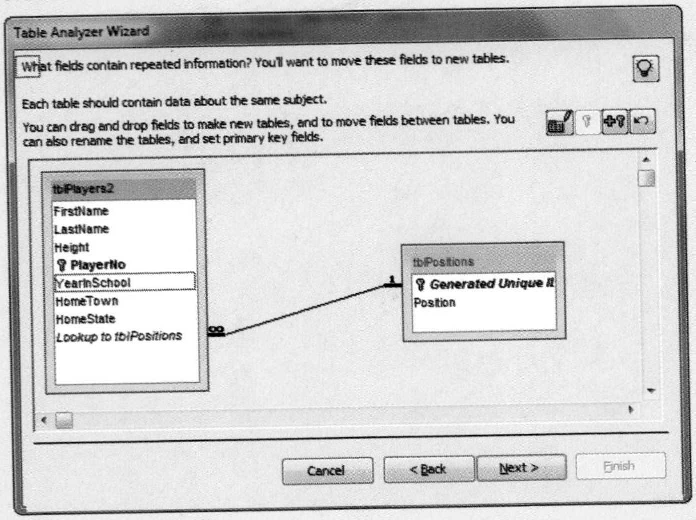

Skills Review (continued)

e. Move through the rest of the Table Analyzer Wizard, do not make any corrections, do not create a query, click Finish, then click OK if prompted at the end.
f. Close the tblPositions and tblPlayers2 tables.
g. Delete the tblPlayers table, then rename tblPlayers2 to **tblPlayers**.
h. Open the Relationships window, click the All Relationships button, then connect the tblPlayers table to the tblStats table using the common PlayerNo field. Be sure to enforce referential integrity.
i. Save and close the Relationships window.

6. **Back up a database.**
   a. Click the File tab, click Save Database As, click Yes to have Access close all open objects if prompted, then save the database backup with the name **Basketball-P-Backup.accdb** in the drive and folder where you store your Data Files.
   b. Close the Basketball-P-Backup.accdb database.
7. **Convert a database.**
   a. Start Access, open the Basketball-P.accdb database from the drive and folder where you store your Data Files, and enable content if prompted.
   b. Close frmGameInfo.
   c. Click the File tab, click Save & Publish, and save the database backup as an Access 2000 database with the name **Basketball-P-2000.mdb** in the drive and folder where you store your Data Files.
   d. Close the Basketball-P-2000.mdb database and exit Access 2010.
8. **Split a database.**
   a. Start Access, open the Basketball-P.accdb database from the drive and folder where you store your Data Files, and enable content if prompted.
   b. Close frmGameInfo.
   c. On the Database Tools tab, click the Access Database button and split the database.
   d. Name the backend database **Basketball-P_be.accdb**, and save it in the drive and folder where you store your Data Files.
   e. Close the Basketball-P.accdb database and exit Access.

Independent Challenge 1

As the manager of a doctor's clinic, you have created an Access database called Patients-P.accdb to track insurance claims. You want to set a database password and encrypt the database, as well as set options to automatically compact the database when it is closed.

a. Start Access. Open Patients-P.accdb in Exclusive mode from the drive and folder where you store your Data Files. Enable content if prompted.
b. Encrypt the database with a password.
c. Enter **4-your-health** in the Password text box and the Verify text box, then click OK.
d. Close the Patients-P.accdb database, but leave Access running.
e. Reopen the Patients-P.accdb database, enter **4-your-health** as the password, then click OK.
f. In the Access Options dialog box, check the Compact on Close option.
g. Close the database and Access.

Independent Challenge 2

As the manager of a doctor's clinic, you have created an Access database called Patients-P.accdb to track insurance claims. You want to analyze database performance.

a. Open the Patients-P.accdb database from the drive and folder where you store your Data Files, and enable content if prompted.
b. Enter **4-your-health** as the password if prompted.
c. Use the Performance Analyzer tool on the Database Tools tab to analyze all objects.
d. Click each item in the Performance Analyzer results window, and record the idea on another sheet of paper.

Advanced Challenge Exercise

- Implement each of the ideas in the Performance Analyzer results window. Apply each suggestion to the database.
- Note that the data type of the Diag1 field in the tblClaimLineItems table will be changed to Number with a Double Field Size property.
- Eventually you end up with only one suggestion: to save the application as an MDE file. To implement this suggestion, use the Make ACCDE button after you click Save & Publish on the File tab.

e. Close the Patients-P.accde database, then close Access.

Independent Challenge 3

As the manager of a community service club, you have created an Access database called Membership-P.accdb to track community service hours. You want to convert the database to an Access 2007 database and analyze table performance.

a. Start Access, then open the database Membership-P.accdb from the drive and folder where you store your Data Files.
b. Analyze table performance for the Members table. Let the wizard decide how to split the tables.
c. Rename Table1 as **Members2**, and rename Table2 as **ZipCodes**.
d. Click Next when prompted about the bold fields, do not make any corrections, and do not create a query. Click Finish, then click OK if prompted.
e. Close the Members2 and ZipCodes tables.
f. Delete the Members table, and rename the Members2 table to **Members**.
g. In the Relationships window, click the All Relationships button.
h. Link the Status and Members tables using the common StatusNo field. Enforce referential integrity on the relationship. The Relationships window should look like Figure P-17.
i. Save and close the Relationships window.
j. Close the Membership-P.accdb database, then exit Access.

FIGURE P-17

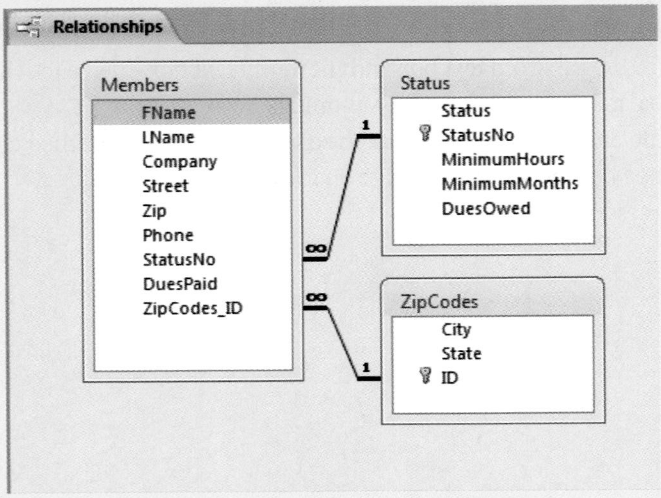

Real Life Independent Challenge

Microsoft provides extra information, templates, files, and ideas at a Web site called Tools on the Web. You have been given an opportunity to intern with an Access consultant and are considering this type of work for your career. As such, you know that you need to be familiar with all of the resources on the Web that Microsoft provides to help you work with Access. In this exercise, you'll explore the Tools on the Web services.

a. Start Access, but do not open any databases.
b. Click the Microsoft Access Help button.
c. Click the Videos link to open a page similar to the one shown in Figure P-18.
d. Choose three of the videos to watch.
e. In a Word document, write one paragraph for each of the videos summarizing the topic and new concepts and techniques that you learned.
f. Close Access and any open Access Help windows.

FIGURE P-18

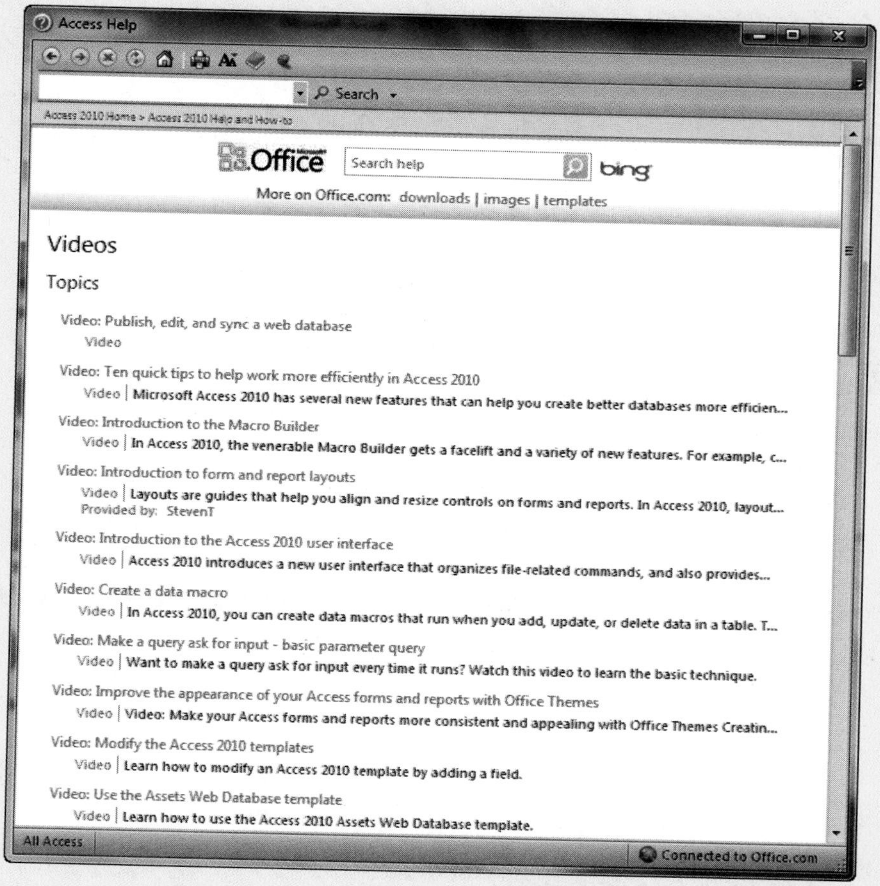

Access 2010

Visual Workshop

As the manager of a music store, you have created an Access database called MusicStore-P.accdb that tracks musical instrument rentals to schoolchildren. Use the Performance Analyzer to generate the results shown in Figure P-19 by analyzing all object types. Save the database as an MDE file, but do not implement the other ideas. In a Word document, explain why implementing the last three ideas might not be appropriate.

FIGURE P-19

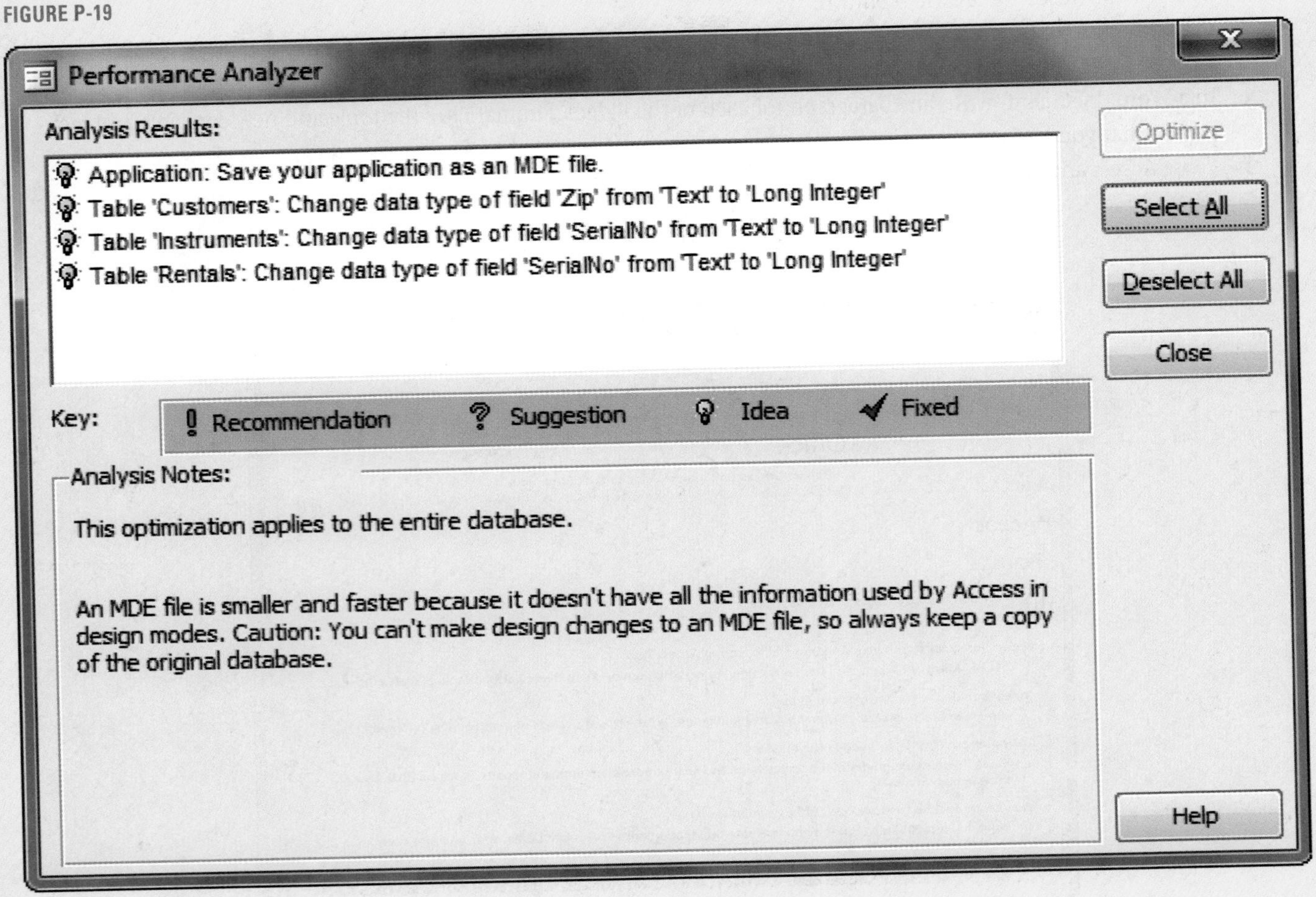

Appendix
Web Apps
Office 2010

Working with Windows Live and Office Web Apps

Files You Will Need:

WEB-1.pptx
WEB-2.xlsx

If the computer you are using has an active Internet connection, you can go to the Microsoft Windows Live Web site and access a wide variety of services and Web applications. For example, you can check your e-mail through Windows Live, network with your friends and coworkers, and use SkyDrive to store and share files. From SkyDrive, you can also use Office Web Apps to create and edit Word, PowerPoint, Excel, and OneNote files, even when you are using a computer that does not have Office 2010 installed. You work in the Vancouver branch of Quest Specialty Travel. Your supervisor, Mary Lou Jacobs, asks you to explore Windows Live and learn how she can use SkyDrive and Office Web Apps to work with her files online.

(*Note*: SkyDrive and Office Web Apps are dynamic Web pages, and might change over time, including the way they are organized and how commands are performed. The steps and figures in this appendix were accurate at the time this book was published.)

OBJECTIVES

- Explore how to work online from Windows Live
- Obtain a Windows Live ID and sign in to Windows Live
- Upload files to Windows Live
- Work with the PowerPoint Web App
- Create folders and organize files on SkyDrive
- Add people to your network and share files
- Work with the Excel Web App

Appendix
Web Apps
Office 2010

Exploring How to Work Online from Windows Live

You can use your Web browser to upload your files to Windows Live from any computer connected to the Internet. You can work on the files right in your Web browser using Office Web Apps and share your files with people in your Windows Live network. You review the concepts and services related to working online from Windows Live.

DETAILS

- **What is Windows Live?**
  Windows Live is a collection of services and Web applications that you can use to help you be more productive both personally and professionally. For example, you can use Windows Live to send and receive e-mail, to chat with friends via instant messaging, to share photos, to create a blog, and to store and edit files using SkyDrive. Table WEB-1 describes the services available on Windows Live. Windows Live is a free service that you sign up for. When you sign up, you receive a Windows Live ID, which you use to sign in to Windows Live. When you work with files on Windows Live, you are cloud computing.
- **What is Cloud Computing?**
  The term **cloud computing** refers to the process of working with files online in a Web browser. When you save files to SkyDrive on Windows Live, you are saving your files to an online location. SkyDrive is like having a personal hard drive in the cloud.
- **What is SkyDrive?**
  SkyDrive is an online storage and file sharing service. With a Windows Live account, you receive access to your own SkyDrive, which is your personal storage area on the Internet. On your SkyDrive, you are given space to store up to 25 GB of data online. Each file can be a maximum size of 50 MB. You can also use SkyDrive to access Office Web Apps, which you use to create and edit files created in Word, OneNote, PowerPoint, and Excel online in your Web browser.
- **Why use Windows Live and SkyDrive?**
  On Windows Live, you use SkyDrive to access additional storage for your files. You don't have to worry about backing up your files to a memory stick or other storage device that could be lost or damaged. Another advantage of storing your files on SkyDrive is that you can access your files from any computer that has an active Internet connection. Figure WEB-1 shows the SkyDrive Web page that appears when accessed from a Windows Live account. From SkyDrive, you can also access Office Web Apps.
- **What are Office Web Apps?**
  Office Web Apps are versions of Microsoft Word, Excel, PowerPoint, and OneNote that you can access online from your SkyDrive. An Office Web App does not include all of the features and functions included with the full Office version of its associated application. However, you can use the Office Web App from any computer that is connected to the Internet, even if Microsoft Office 2010 is not installed on that computer.
- **How do SkyDrive and Office Web Apps work together?**
  You can create a file in Office 2010 using Word, Excel, PowerPoint, or OneNote and then upload the file to your SkyDrive. You can then open the Office file saved to SkyDrive and edit it using your Web browser and the corresponding Office Web App. Figure WEB-2 shows a PowerPoint presentation open in the PowerPoint Web App. You can also use an Office Web App to create a new file, which is saved automatically to SkyDrive while you work. In addition, you can download a file created with an Office Web App and continue to work with the file in the full version of the corresponding Office application: Word, Excel, PowerPoint, or OneNote. Finally, you can create a SkyDrive network that consists of the people you want to be able to view your folders and files on your SkyDrive. You can give people permission to view and edit your files using any computer with an active Internet connection and a Web browser.

FIGURE WEB-1: **SkyDrive on Windows Live**

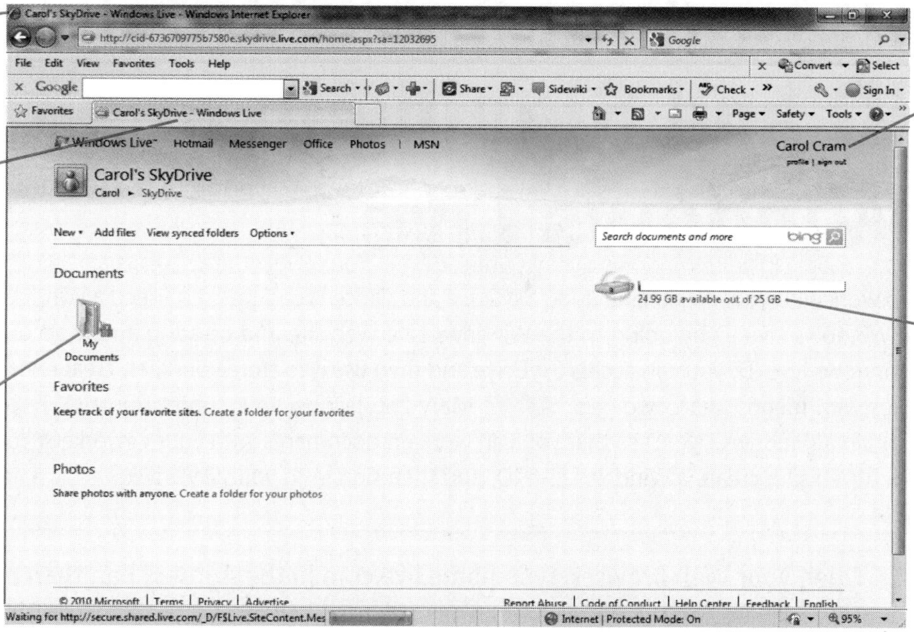
Browser window
SkyDrive - Windows Live tab
By default, one folder is available on SkyDrive; you can create additional folders
The name of the person who signed into Windows Live and SkyDrive appears here
Monitors the amount of space still available on your SkyDrive
Carol's SkyDrive
Documents
My Documents
Favorites
Photos
24.99 GB available out of 25 GB

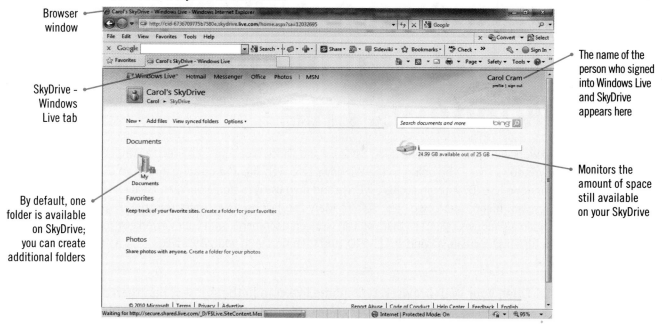

FIGURE WEB-2: **PowerPoint presentation open in the PowerPoint Web App**

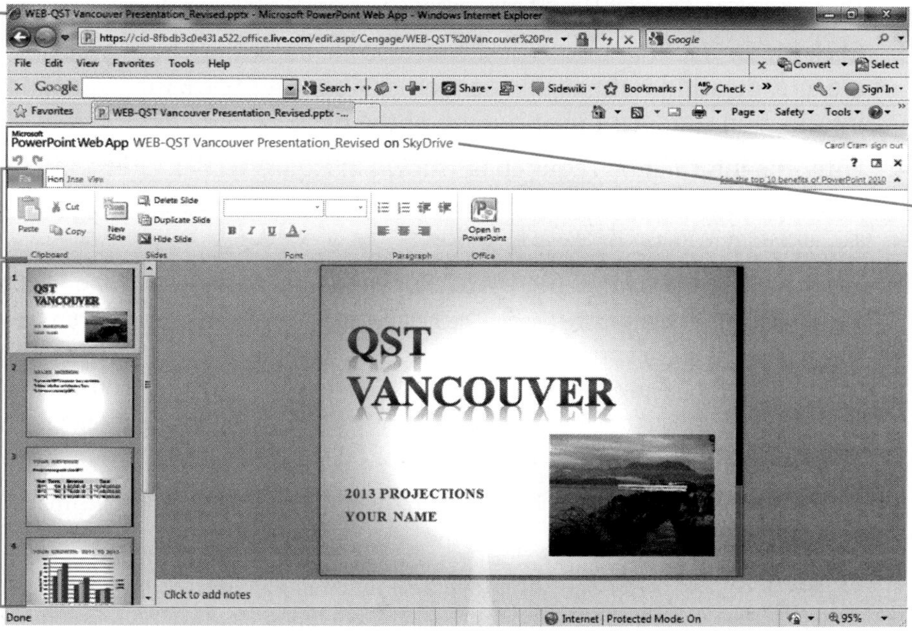
Browser window
Ribbon available in PowerPoint Web App
The presentation in PowerPoint Web App maintains the same look and feel as the same presentation in the desktop version of PowerPoint
Name of PowerPoint presentation open in PowerPoint Web App
PowerPoint Web App WEB-QST Vancouver Presentation_Revised on SkyDrive
QST VANCOUVER
2013 PROJECTIONS
YOUR NAME
Click to add notes

TABLE WEB-1: **Services available via Windows Live**

service	description
E-mail	Send and receive e-mail using a Hotmail account
Instant Messaging	Use Messenger to chat with friends, share photos, and play games
SkyDrive	Store files, work on files using Office Web Apps, and share files with people in your network
Photos	Upload and share photos with friends
People	Develop a network of friends and coworkers, then use the network to distribute information and stay in touch
Downloads	Access a variety of free programs available for download to a PC
Mobile Device	Access applications for a mobile device: text messaging, using Hotmail, networking, and sharing photos

Obtaining a Windows Live ID and Signing In to Windows Live

To work with your files online using SkyDrive and Office Web Apps, you need a Windows Live ID. You obtain a Windows Live ID by going to the Windows Live Web site and creating a new account. Once you have a Windows Live ID, you can access SkyDrive and then use it to store your files, create new files, and share your files with friends and coworkers. Mary Lou Jacobs, your supervisor at QST Vancouver, asks you to obtain a Windows Live ID so that you can work on documents with your coworkers. You go to the Windows Live Web site, create a Windows Live ID, and then sign in to your SkyDrive.

STEPS

QUICK TIP
If you already have a Windows Live ID, go to the next lesson and sign in as directed using your account.

1. **Open your Web browser, type home.live.com in the Address bar, then press [Enter]**
   The Windows Live home page opens. From this page, you can create a Windows Live account and receive your Windows Live ID.
2. **Click the Sign up button** ***(Note: You may see a Sign up link instead of a button)***
   The Create your Windows Live ID page opens.
3. **Click the Or use your own e-mail address link under the Check availability button or if you are already using Hotmail, Messenger, or Xbox LIVE, click the Sign in now link in the Information statement near the top of the page**
4. **Enter the information required, as shown in Figure WEB-3**
   If you wish, you can sign up for a Windows Live e-mail address such as yourname@live.com so that you can also access the Windows Live e-mail services.
5. **Enter the code shown at the bottom of your screen, then click the I accept button**
   The Windows Live home page opens. The name you entered when you signed up for your Windows Live ID appears in the top right corner of the window to indicate that you are signed in to Windows Live. From the Windows Live home page, you can access all the services and applications offered by Windows Live. See the Verifying your Windows Live ID box for information on finalizing your account set up.
6. **Point to Windows Live, as shown in Figure WEB-4**
   A list of options appears. SkyDrive is one of the options you can access directly from Windows Live.
7. **Click SkyDrive**
   The SkyDrive page opens. Your name appears in the top right corner, and the amount of space available is shown on the right side of the SkyDrive page. The amount of space available is monitored, as indicated by the gauge that fills with color as space is used. Using SkyDrive, you can add files to the existing folder and you can create new folders.
8. **Click sign out in the top right corner under your name, then exit the Web browser**
   You are signed out of your Windows Live account. You can sign in again directly from the Windows Live page in your browser or from within a file created with PowerPoint, Excel, Word, or OneNote.

TROUBLE
The code can be difficult to read. If you receive an error message, enter the new code that appears.

TROUBLE
Click I accept if you are asked to review and accept the Windows Live Service Agreement and Privacy Statement.

FIGURE WEB-3: **Creating a Windows Live ID**

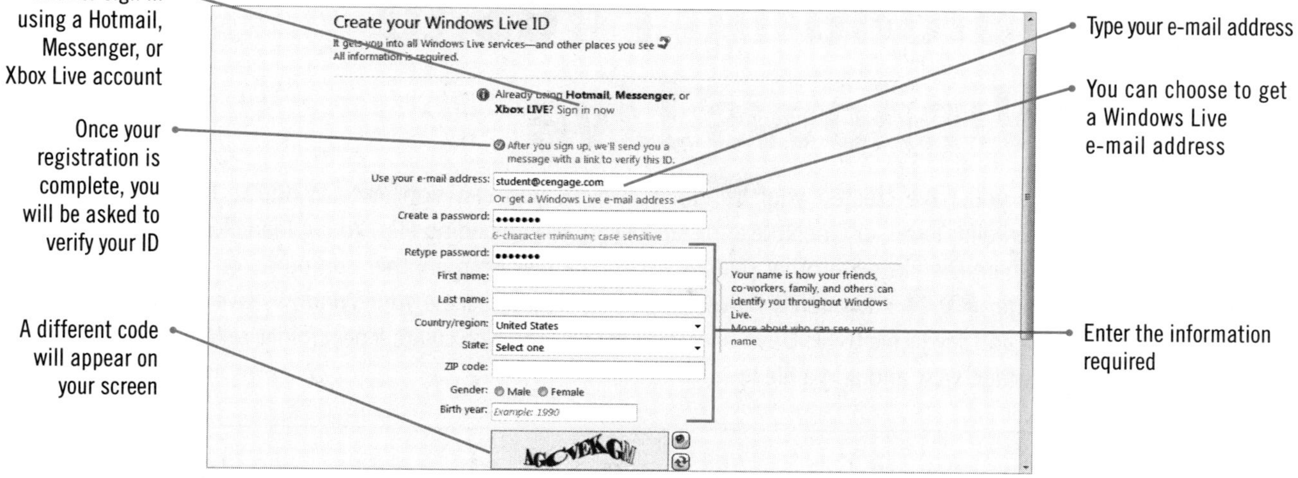

FIGURE WEB-4: **Selecting SkyDrive**

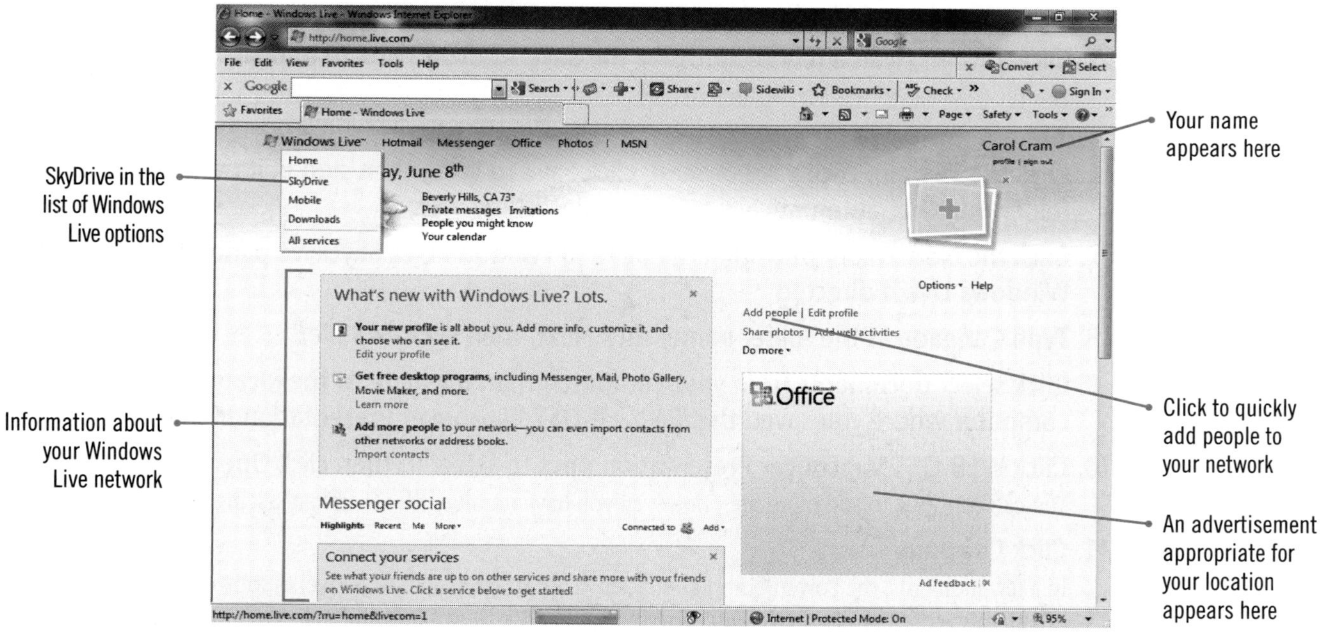

Verifying your Windows Live ID

As soon as you accept the Windows Live terms, an e-mail is sent to the e-mail address you supplied when you created your Windows Live ID. Open your e-mail program, and then open the e-mail from Microsoft with the Subject line: Confirm your e-mail address for Windows Live. Follow the simple, step-by-step instructions in the e-mail to confirm your Windows Live ID. When the confirmation is complete, you will be asked to sign in to Windows Live, using your e-mail address and password. Once signed in, you will see your Windows Live Account page.

Uploading Files to Windows Live

Once you have created your Windows Live ID, you can sign in to Windows Live directly from Word, PowerPoint, Excel, or OneNote and start saving and uploading files. You upload files to your SkyDrive so you can share the files with other people, access the files from another computer, or use SkyDrive's additional storage. You open a PowerPoint presentation, access your Windows Live account from Backstage view, and save a file to SkyDrive on Windows Live. You also create a new folder called Cengage directly from Backstage view and add a file to it.

STEPS

1. **Start PowerPoint, open the file WEB-1.pptx from the drive and folder where you store your Data Files, then save the file as WEB-QST Vancouver Presentation**
2. **Click the File tab, then click Save & Send**
   The Save & Send options available in PowerPoint are listed in Backstage view, as shown in Figure WEB-5.
3. **Click Save to Web**
4. **Click Sign In, type your e-mail address, press [Tab], type your password, then click OK**
   The My Documents folder on your SkyDrive appears in the Save to Windows Live SkyDrive information area.

   > **QUICK TIP**
   > Skip this step if the computer you are using signs you in automatically.

5. **Click Save As, wait a few seconds for the Save As dialog box to appear, then click Save**
   The file is saved to the My Documents folder on the SkyDrive that is associated with your Windows Live account. You can also create a new folder and upload files directly to SkyDrive from your hard drive.
6. **Click the File tab, click Save & Send, click Save to Web, then sign in if the My Documents folder does not automatically appear in Backstage view**
7. **Click the New Folder button in the Save to Windows Live SkyDrive pane, then sign in to Windows Live if directed**
8. **Type Cengage as the folder name, click Next, then click Add files**
9. **Click select documents from your computer, then navigate to the location on your computer where you saved the file WEB-QST Vancouver Presentation in Step 1**
10. **Click WEB-QST Vancouver Presentation.pptx to select it, then click Open**
    You can continue to add more files; however, you have no more files to upload at this time.
11. **Click Continue**
    In a few moments, the PowerPoint presentation is uploaded to your SkyDrive, as shown in Figure WEB-6. You can simply store the file on SkyDrive or you can choose to work on the presentation using the PowerPoint Web App.
12. **Click the PowerPoint icon on your taskbar to return to PowerPoint, then close the presentation and exit PowerPoint**

FIGURE WEB-5: **Save & Send options in Backstage view**

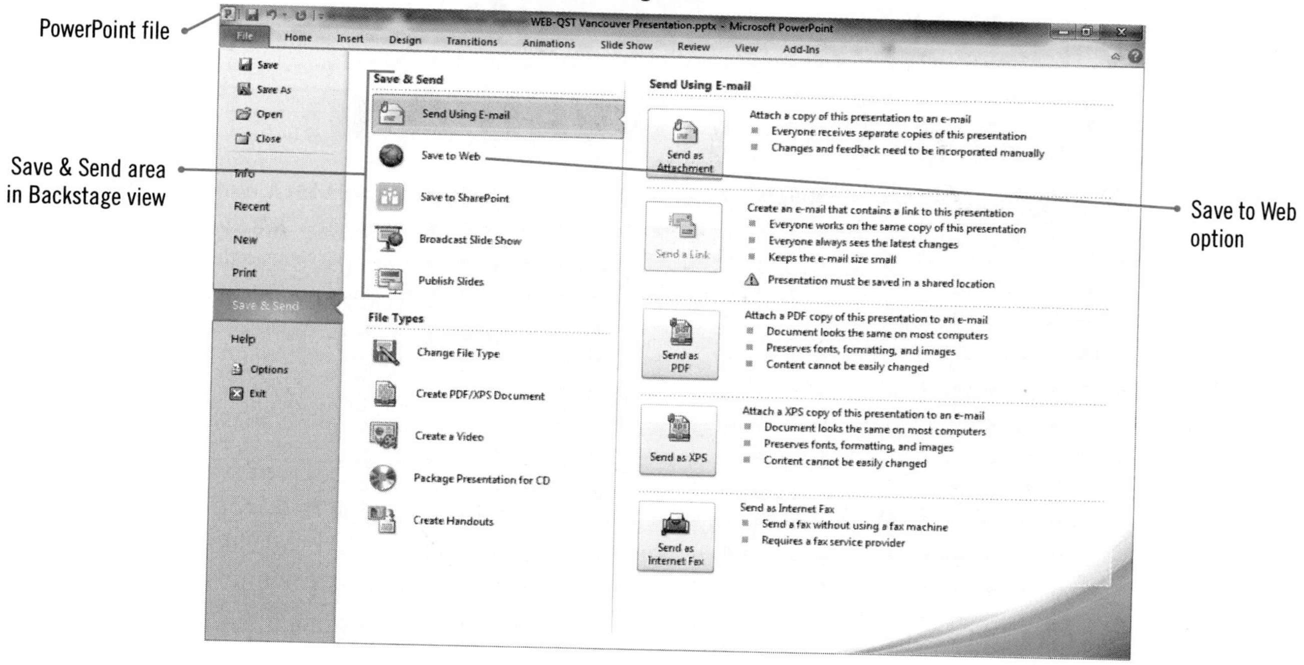
PowerPoint file
Save & Send area in Backstage view
Save to Web option

FIGURE WEB-6: **File uploaded to the Cengage folder on Windows Live**

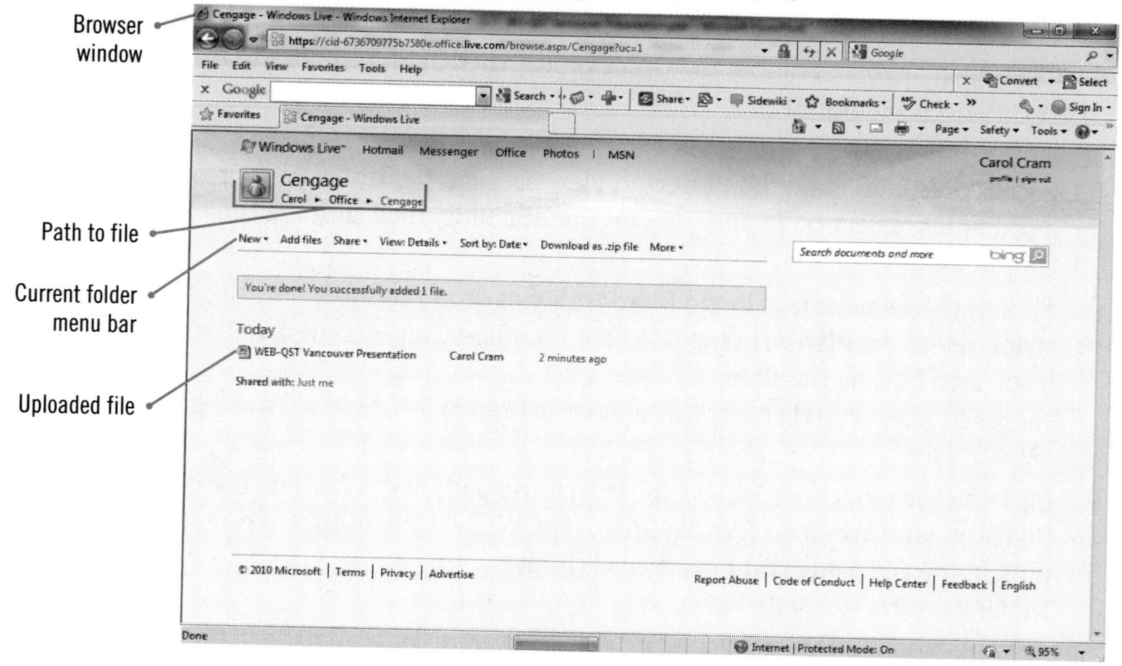
Browser window
Path to file
Current folder menu bar
Uploaded file

Working with the PowerPoint Web App

Once you have uploaded a file to SkyDrive on Windows Live, you can work on it using its corresponding Office Web App. **Office Web Apps** provide you with the tools you need to view documents online and to edit them right in your browser. You do not need to have Office programs installed on the computer you use to access SkyDrive and Office Web Apps. From SkyDrive, you can also open the document directly in the full Office application (for example, PowerPoint) if the application is installed on the computer you are using. You use the PowerPoint Web App to make some edits to the PowerPoint presentation. You then open the presentation in PowerPoint and use the full version to make additional edits.

STEPS

> **TROUBLE**
> Click the browser button on the taskbar, then click the Windows Live SkyDrive window to make it the active window.

1. **Click the WEB-QST Vancouver Presentation file in the Cengage folder on SkyDrive**
   The presentation opens in your browser window. A menu is available, which includes the options you have for working with the file.
2. **Click Edit in Browser, then if a message appears related to installing the Sign-in Assistant, click the Close button ✖ to the far right of the message**
   In a few moments, the PowerPoint presentation opens in the PowerPoint Web App, as shown in Figure WEB-7. Table WEB-2 lists the commands you can perform using the PowerPoint Web App.

> **QUICK TIP**
> The changes you make to the presentation are saved automatically on SkyDrive.

3. **Enter your name where indicated on Slide 1, click Slide 3 (New Tours) in the Slides pane, then click Delete Slide in the Slides group**
   The slide is removed from the presentation. You decide to open the file in the full version of PowerPoint on your computer so you can apply WordArt to the slide title. You work with the file in the full version of PowerPoint when you want to use functions, such as WordArt, that are not available on the PowerPoint Web App.
4. **Click Open in PowerPoint in the Office group, click OK in response to the message, then click Allow if requested**
   In a few moments, the revised version of the PowerPoint slide opens in PowerPoint on your computer.
5. **Click Enable Editing on the Protected View bar near the top of your presentation window if prompted, select QST Vancouver on the title slide, then click the Drawing Tools Format tab**

> **QUICK TIP**
> Use the ScreenTips to help you find the required WordArt style.

6. **Click the More button in the WordArt Styles group to show the selection of WordArt styles, select the WordArt style Gradient Fill - Blue-Gray, Accent 4, Reflection, then click a blank area outside the slide**
   The presentation appears in PowerPoint as shown in Figure WEB-8. Next, you save the revised version of the file to SkyDrive.
7. **Click the File tab, click Save As, notice that the path in the Address bar is to the Cengage folder on your Windows Live SkyDrive, type WEB-QST Vancouver Presentation_Revised.pptx in the File name text box, then click Save**
   The file is saved to your SkyDrive.

> **TROUBLE**
> The browser opens to the Cengage folder but the file is not visible. Follow Step 8 to open the Cengage folder and refresh thelist of files in the folder.

8. **Click the browser icon on the taskbar to open your SkyDrive page, then click Office next to your name in the SkyDrive path, view a list of recent documents, then click Cengage in the list to the left of the recent documents list to open the Cengage folder**
   Two PowerPoint files now appear in the Cengage folder.
9. **Exit the Web browser and close all tabs if prompted, then exit PowerPoint**

FIGURE WEB-7: Presentation opened in the PowerPoint Web App from Windows Live

Browser window
Name of Web App
PowerPoint Web App Ribbon
URL is the file location
QST VANCOUVER
2013 PROJECTIONS
YOUR NAME

FIGURE WEB-8: Revised PowerPoint presentation

PowerPoint title bar
PowerPoint Ribbon
Presentation title enhanced using full version of PowerPoint
Name added using PowerPoint Web App
QST VANCOUVER
2013 PROJECTIONS
YOUR NAME
Click to add notes

TABLE WEB-2: Commands on the PowerPoint Web App

tab	commands available
File	• Open in PowerPoint: select to open the file in PowerPoint on your computer • Where's the Save Button?: when you click this option, a message appears telling you that you do not need to save your presentation when you are working on it with PowerPoint Web App. The presentation is saved automatically as you work. • Print • Share • Properties • Give Feedback • Privacy • Terms of Use • Close
Home	• Clipboard group: Cut, Copy, Paste • Slides group: Add a New Slide, Delete a Slide, Duplicate a Slide, and Hide a Slide • Font group: Work with text: change the font, style, color, and size of selected text • Paragraph group: Work with paragraphs: add bullets and numbers, indent text, align text • Office group: Open the file in PowerPoint on your computer
Insert	• Insert a Picture • Insert a SmartArt diagram • Insert a link such as a link to another file on SkyDrive or to a Web page
View	• Editing view (the default) • Reading view • Slide Show view • Notes view

Creating Folders and Organizing Files on SkyDrive

As you have learned, you can sign in to SkyDrive directly from the Office applications PowerPoint, Excel, Word, and OneNote, or you can access SkyDrive directly through your Web browser. This option is useful when you are away from the computer on which you normally work or when you are using a computer that does not have Office applications installed. You can go to SkyDrive, create and organize folders, and then create or open files to work on with Office Web Apps. You access SkyDrive from your Web browser, create a new folder called Illustrated, and delete one of the PowerPoint files from the My Documents folder.

STEPS

TROUBLE
Go to Step 3 if you are already signed in.

TROUBLE
Type your Windows Live ID (your e-mail) and password, then click Sign in if prompted to do so.

1. **Open your Web browser, type home.live.com in the Address bar, then press [Enter]**
   The Windows Live home page opens. From here, you can sign in to your Windows Live account and then access SkyDrive.
2. **Sign into Windows Live as directed**
   You are signed in to your Windows Live page. From this page, you can take advantage of the many applications available on Windows Live, including SkyDrive.
3. **Point to Windows Live, then click SkyDrive**
   SkyDrive opens.
4. **Click Cengage, then point to WEB-QST Vancouver Presentation.pptx**
   A menu of options for working with the file, including a Delete button to the far right, appears to the right of the filename.
5. **Click the Delete button, then click OK**
   The file is removed from the Cengage folder on your SkyDrive. You still have a copy of the file on your computer.
6. **Point to Windows Live, then click SkyDrive**
   Your SkyDrive screen with the current selection of folders available on your SkyDrive opens, as shown in Figure WEB-9.
7. **Click New, click Folder, type Illustrated, click Next, click Office in the path under Add documents to Illustrated at the top of the window, then click View all in the list under Personal**
   You are returned to your list of folders, where you see the new Illustrated folder.
8. **Click Cengage, point to WEB-QST Vancouver Presentation_Revised.pptx, click More, click Move, then click the Illustrated folder**
9. **Click Move this file into Illustrated, as shown in Figure WEB-10**
   The file is moved to the Illustrated folder.

FIGURE WEB-9: **Folders on your SkyDrive**

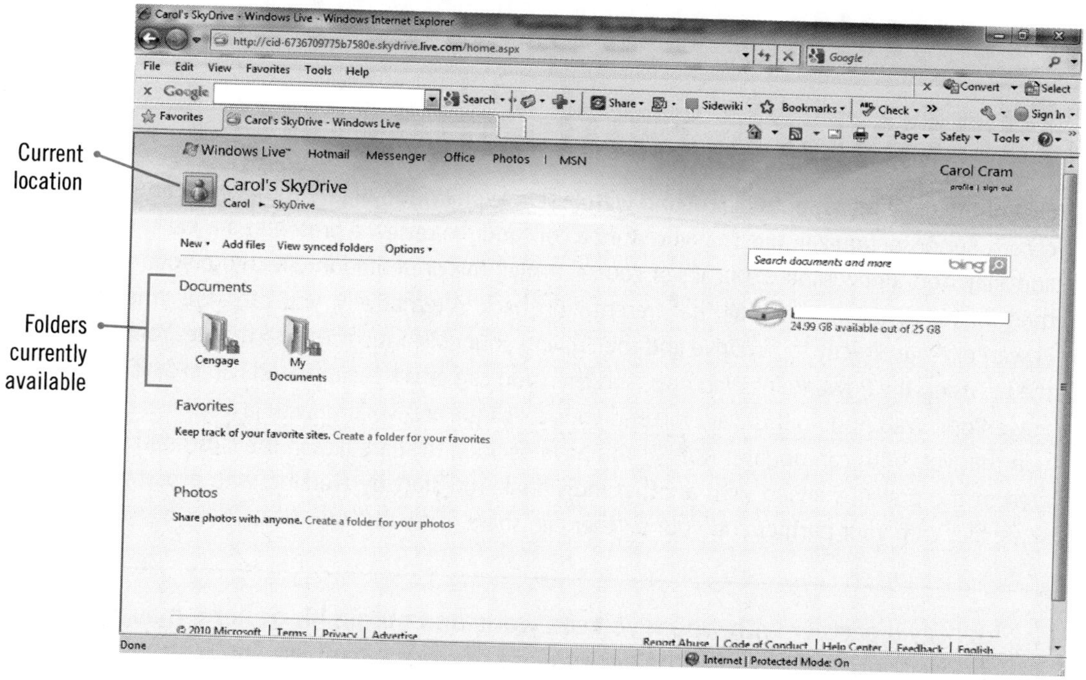

FIGURE WEB-10: **Moving a file to the Illustrated folder**

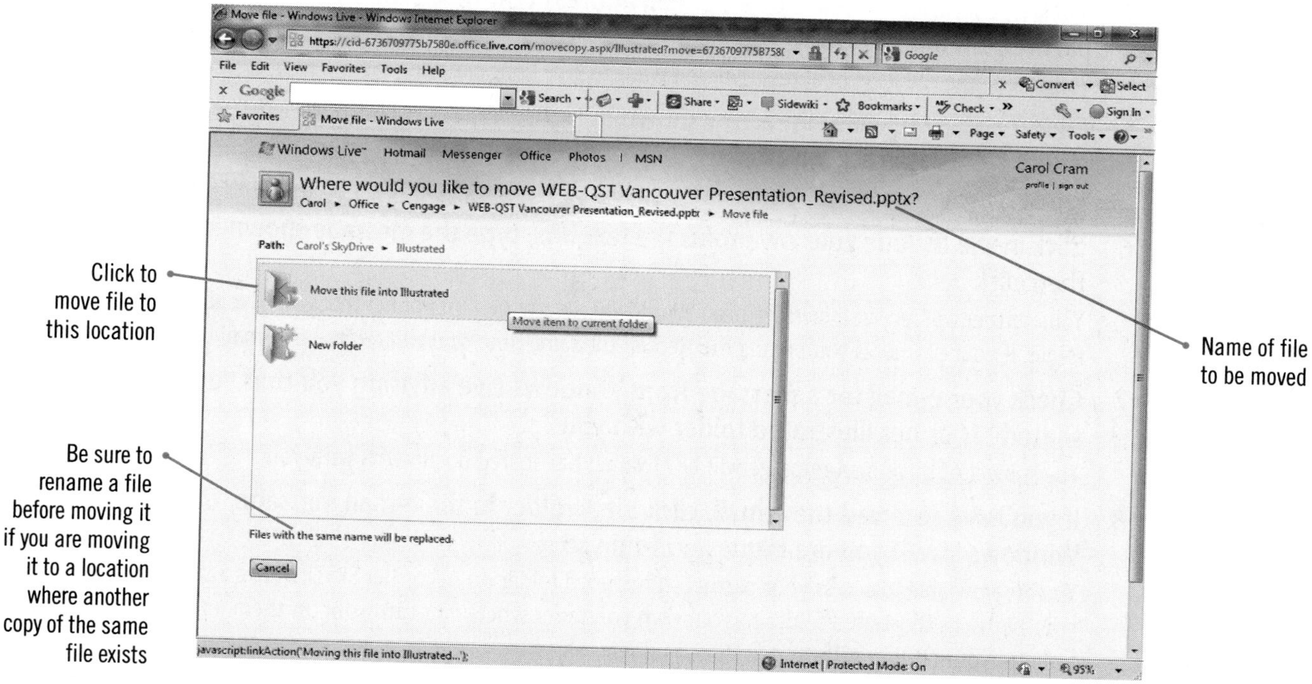

Adding People to Your Network and Sharing Files

One of the great advantages of working with SkyDrive on Windows Live is that you can share your files with others. Suppose, for example, that you want a colleague to review a presentation you created in PowerPoint and then add a new slide. You can, of course, e-mail the presentation directly to your colleague, who can then make changes and e-mail the presentation back. Alternatively, you can save time by uploading the PowerPoint file directly to SkyDrive and then giving your colleague access to the file. Your colleague can edit the file using the PowerPoint Web App, and then you can check the updated file on SkyDrive, also using the PowerPoint Web App. In this way, you and your colleague are working with just one version of the presentation that you both can update. You have decided to share files in the Illustrated folder that you created in the previous lesson with another individual. You start by working with a partner so that you can share files with your partner and your partner can share files with you.

STEPS

TROUBLE
If you cannot find a partner, read the steps so you understand how the process works.

1. **Identify a partner with whom you can work, and obtain his or her e-mail address; you can choose someone in your class or someone on your e-mail list, but it should be someone who will be completing these steps when you are**
2. **From the Illustrated folder, click Share**
3. **Click Edit permissions**

   The Edit permissions page opens. On this page, you can select the individual with whom you would like to share the contents of the Illustrated folder.
4. **Click in the Enter a name or an e-mail address text box, type the e-mail address of your partner, then press [Tab]**

   You can define the level of access that you want to give your partner.
5. **Click the Can view files list arrow shown in Figure WEB-11, click Can add, edit details, and delete files, then click Save**

   You can choose to send a notification to each individual when you grant permission to access your files.
6. **Click in the Include your own message text box, type the message shown in Figure WEB-12, then click Send**

   Your partner will receive a message from Windows Live advising him or her that you have shared your Illustrated folder. If your partner is completing the steps at the same time, you will receive an e-mail from your partner.

TROUBLE
If you do not receive a message from Windows Live, your partner has not yet completed the steps to share the Illustrated folder.

7. **Check your e-mail for a message from Windows Live advising you that your partner has shared his or her Illustrated folder with you**

   The subject of the e-mail message will be "[Name] has shared documents with you."

QUICK TIP
You will know you are on your partner's SkyDrive because you will see your partner's first name at the beginning of the SkyDrive path.

8. **If you have received the e-mail, click View folder in the e-mail message, then sign in to Windows Live if you are requested to do so**

   You are now able to access your partner's Illustrated folder on his or her SkyDrive. You can download files in your partner's Illustrated folder to your own computer where you can work on them and then upload them again to your partner's Illustrated shared folder.
9. **Exit the browser**

FIGURE WEB-11: Editing folder permissions

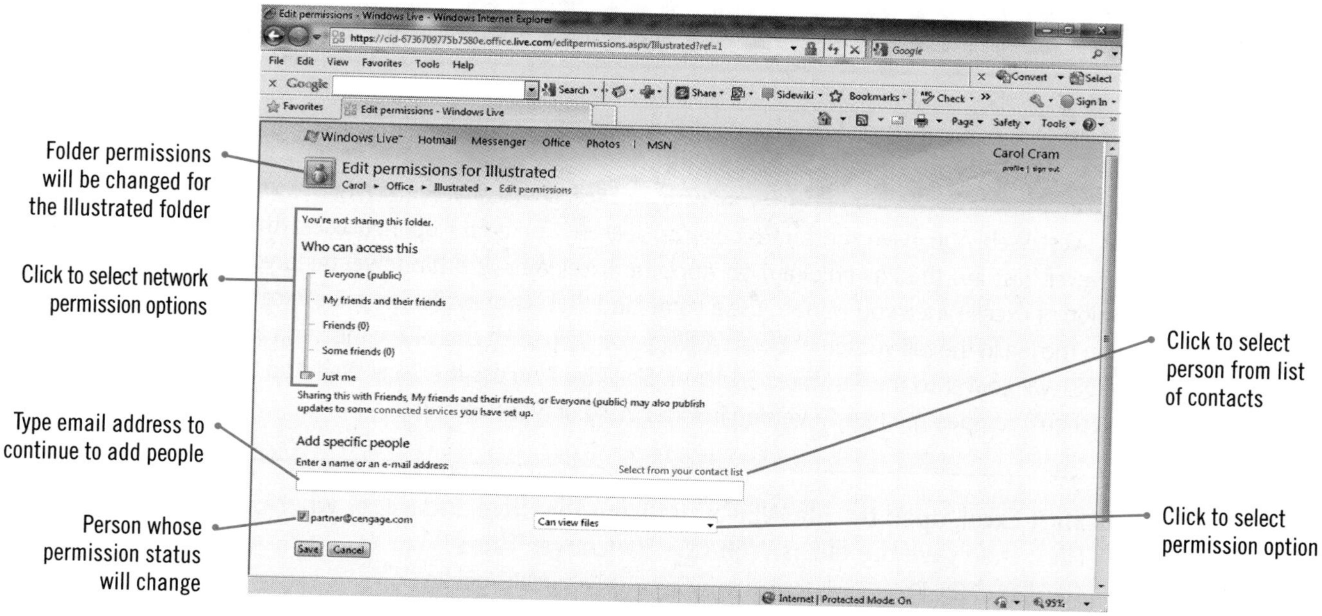

FIGURE WEB-12: Entering a message to notify a person that file sharing permission has been granted

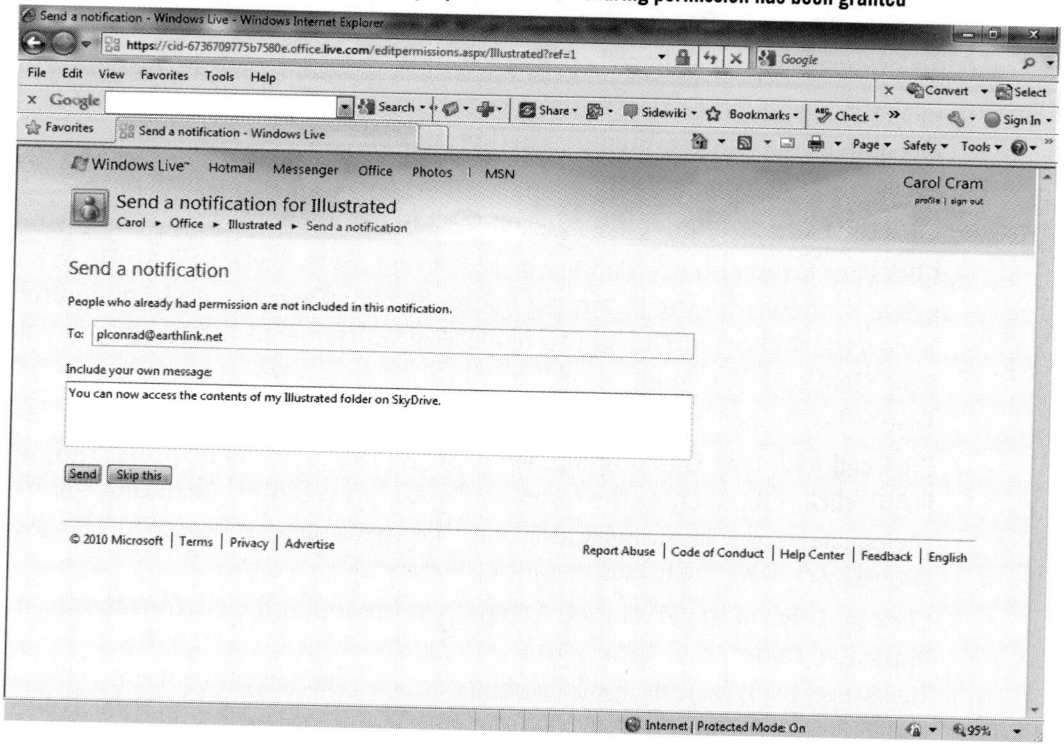

Sharing files on SkyDrive

When you share a folder with other people, the people with whom you share a folder can download the file to their computers and then make changes using the full version of the corresponding Office application. Once these changes are made, each individual can then upload the file to SkyDrive and into a folder shared with you and others. In this way, you can create a network of people with whom you share your files.

Appendix
Web Apps
Office 2010

Working with the Excel Web App

You can use the Excel Web App to work with an Excel spreadsheet on SkyDrive. Workbooks opened using the Excel Web App have the same look and feel as workbooks opened using the full version of Excel. However, just like the PowerPoint Web App, the Excel Web App has fewer features available than the full version of Excel. When you want to use a command that is not available on the Excel Web App, you need to open the file in the full version of Excel. You upload an Excel file containing a list of the tours offered by QST Vancouver to the Illustrated folder on SkyDrive. You use the Excel Web App to make some changes, and then you open the revised version in Excel 2010 on your computer.

STEPS

1. **Start Excel, open the file WEB-2.xlsx from the drive and folder where you store your Data Files, then save the file as WEB-QST Vancouver Tours**
   The data in the Excel file is formatted using the Excel table function.
2. **Click the File tab, click Save & Send, then click Save to Web**
   In a few moments, you should see three folders to which you can save spreadsheets. My Documents and Cengage are personal folder that contains files that only you can access. Illustrated is a shared folder that contains files you can share with others in your network. The Illustrated folder is shared with your partner.
3. **Click the Illustrated folder, click the Save As button, wait a few seconds for the Save As dialog box to appear, then click Save**
4. **Click the File tab, click Save & Send, click Save to Web, click the Windows Live SkyDrive link above your folders, then sign in if prompted**
   Windows Live opens to your SkyDrive.
5. **Click the Excel program button on the taskbar, then exit Excel**
6. **Click your browser button on the taskbar to return to SkyDrive if SkyDrive is not the active window, click the Illustrated folder, click the Excel file, click Edit in Browser, then review the Ribbon and its tabs to familiarize yourself with the commands you can access from the Excel Web App**
   Table WEB-3 summarizes the commands that are available.
7. **Click cell A12, type Gulf Islands Sailing, press [TAB], type 3000, press [TAB], type 10, press [TAB], click cell D3, enter the formula =B3*C3, press [Enter], then click cell A1**
   The formula is copied automatically to the remaining rows as shown in Figure WEB-13 because the data in the original Excel file was created and formatted as an Excel table.
8. **Click SkyDrive in the Excel Web App path at the top of the window to return to the Illustrated folder**
   The changes you made to the Excel spreadsheet are saved automatically on SkyDrive. You can download the file directly to your computer from SkyDrive.
9. **Point to the Excel file, click More, click Download, click Save, navigate to the location where you save the files for this book, name the file WEB-QST Vancouver Tours_Updated, click Save, then click Close in the Download complete dialog box**
   The updated version of the spreadsheet is saved on your computer and on SkyDrive.
10. **Exit the Web browser**

TROUBLE
If prompted, sign in to your Windows Live account as directed.

QUICK TIP
Alternately, you can open your Web browser and go to Windows Live to sign in to SkyDrive.

FIGURE WEB-13: **Updated table in the Excel Web App**

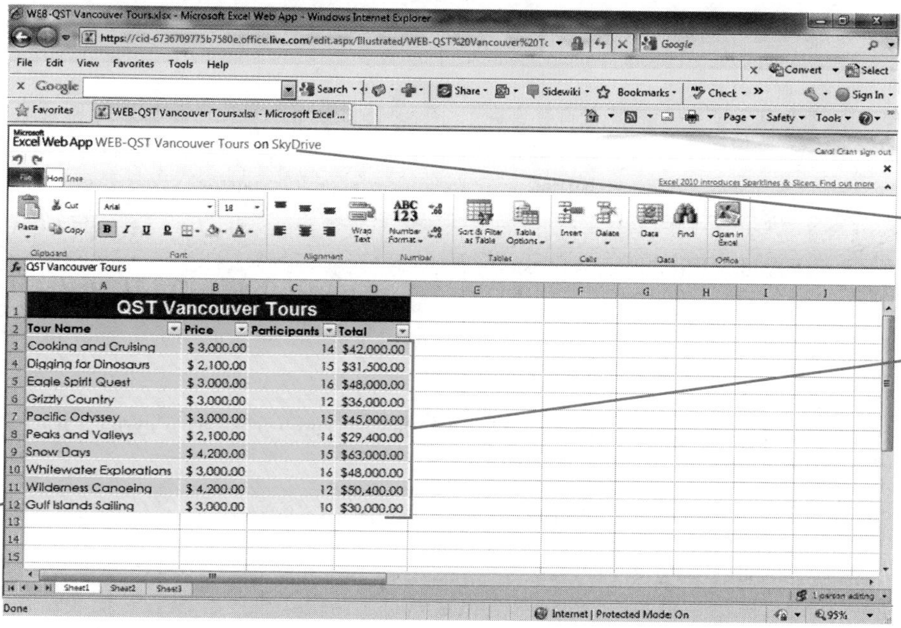
Click to return to Illustrated folder
Totals calculated based on formula in cell D3
New entry

TABLE WEB-3: **Commands on the Excel Web App**

tab	commands available
File	• Open in Excel: select to open the file in Excel on your computer • Where's the Save Button?: when you click this option, a message appears telling you that you do not need to save your spreadsheet when you are working in it with Excel Web App; the spreadsheet is saved automatically as you work • Save As • Share • Download a Snapshot: a snapshot contains only the values and the formatting; you cannot modify a snapshot • Download a Copy: the file can be opened and edited in the full version of Excel • Give Feedback • Privacy Statement • Terms of Use • Close
Home	• Clipboard group: Cut, Copy, Paste • Font group: change the font, style, color, and size of selected labels and values, as well as border styles and fill colors • Alignment group: change vertical and horizontal alignment and turn on the Wrap Text feature • Number group: change the number format and increase or decrease decimal places • Tables: sort and filter data in a table and modify Table Options • Cells: insert and delete cells • Data: refresh data and find labels or values • Office: open the file in Excel on your computer
Insert	• Insert a Table • Insert a Hyperlink to a Web page

Exploring other Office Web Apps

Two other Office Web Apps are Word and OneNote. You can share files on SkyDrive directly from Word or from OneNote using the same method you used to share files from PowerPoint and Excel. After you upload a Word or OneNote file to SkyDrive, you can work with it in its corresponding Office Web App. To familiarize yourself with the commands available in an Office Web App, open the file and then review the commands on each tab on the Ribbon. If you want to perform a task that is not available in the Office Web App, open the file in the full version of the application.

In addition to working with uploaded files, you can create files from new on SkyDrive. Simply sign in to SkyDrive and open a folder. With a folder open, click New and then select the Web App you want to use to create the new file.

Windows Live and Microsoft Office Web Apps Quick Reference

To Do This	Go Here
Access Windows Live	From the Web browser, type **home.live.com**, then click Sign In
Access SkyDrive on Windows Live	From the Windows Live home page, point to Windows Live, then click SkyDrive
Save to Windows Live from Word, PowerPoint, or Excel	File tab | Save & Send | Save to Web | Select a folder | Save As
Create a New Folder from Backstage view	File tab | Save & Send | Save to Web | New Folder button
Edit a File with a Web App	From SkyDrive, click the file, then click Edit in Browser
Open a File in a desktop version of the application from a Web App: Word, Excel, PowerPoint	Click Open in [Application] in the Office group in each Office Web App
Share files on Windows Live	From SkyDrive, click the folder containing the files to share, click Share on the menu bar, click Edit permissions, enter the e-mail address of the person to share files with, click the Can view files list arrow, click Can add, edit details, and delete files, then click Save

Glossary

.accdb The file extension that usually means the database is an Access 2007 format database.

Access Data Collection Replies A folder that collects and helps you manage the e-mails initiated by Access and responses to them.

Accessories Simple Windows programs that perform specific tasks, such as the Calculator accessory for performing calculations.

Action Each task that you want a macro to perform.

Action block In Macro Design View, the area of the window that organizes all of the arguments for a current action.

Action query A query that changes all of the selected records when it is run. Access provides four types of action queries: delete, update, append, and make table.

Active The currently available document, program, or object; on the taskbar, when more than one program is open, the button for the active program appears slightly lighter.

Active window The window you are currently using; if multiple windows are open, the window with the darker title bar.

Add Mode When creating a switchboard, an option you can specify so that users can only add new records to an object, such as a form.

Add-in Software that works with Access to add or enhance functionality.

Address A sequence of drive and folder names that describes a folder's or file's location in the file hierarchy; the highest hierarchy level is on the left, with lower hierarchy levels separated by the ▸ symbol to its right.

Address bar In a window, the white area just below the title bar that shows the file hierarchy, or address of the files that appear in the file list below it; the address appears as a series of links (separated by the ▸ symbol) you can click to navigate to other locations on your computer.

Aero A Windows 7 viewing option that shows windows as translucent objects and features subtle animations; only available on a computer that has enough memory to support Aero and on which a Windows Aero theme has been selected.

Aero Flip 3D A Windows 7 feature that lets you preview all open folders and documents without using the taskbar and that displays open windows in a stack if you press [Ctrl][⊞][Tab]; only available if using a Windows Aero theme.

Aero Peek A Windows 7 feature that lets you point to a taskbar icon representing an open program and see a thumbnail (small version) of the open file; only visible if the computer uses a Windows Aero theme.

After Update A property that specifies an action to perform after an object is updated.

Aggregate function A function such as Sum, Avg, and Count used in a summary query to calculate information about a group of records.

Alignment command A command used in Layout or Design View for a form or report to either left-, center-, or right-align a value within its control, or to align the top, bottom, right, or left edge of the control with respect to other controls.

Allow Multiple Values A lookup property in a database in the Access 2007 file format that lets you create a multivalued field.

Allow Zero Length A field property that does not allow zero-length strings (""), which are intentional "nothing" entries, such as a blank Phone Number field for an employee who does not provide a home phone number.

Alternate Back Color property A property that determines the alternating background color of the selected section in a form or report.

AND criteria Criteria placed in the same row of the query design grid. All criteria on the same row must be true for a record to appear on the resulting datasheet.

Append Only A field property available for Memo fields in Access 2007 databases. When enabled, the property allows users to add data to a Memo field, but not change or remove existing data.

Append query A query that adds selected records to an existing table, and works like an export feature because the records are copied from one location and a duplicate set is pasted within the target table.

Append To row When creating an Append query, a row that appears in the query design grid to show how the fields in the query match fields in the target table.

Application Part An object template that creates objects such as tables and forms.

Application program Any program that lets you work with files or create and edit files such as graphics, letters, financial summaries, and other useful documents, as well as view Web pages on the Internet and send and receive e-mail.

Argument Information that a function uses to create the final answer. Multiple arguments are separated by commas. All of the arguments for a function are surrounded by a single set of parentheses. Also part of a macro that provides additional information on how to carry out an action. In VBA, a constant, variable, or expression passed to a procedure that the procedure needs in order to execute.

Asterisk (*) A wildcard character you use to search for any number of characters.

Attachment field A field that allows you to attach an external file such as a Word document, PowerPoint presentation, Excel workbook, or image file to a record.

AutoExec A special macro name that automatically executes when a database opens.

AutoKeys A macro designed to be assigned a key combination (such as [Ctrl][L]).

AutoNumber A field data type in which Access enters a sequential integer for each record added into the datasheet. Numbers cannot be reused even if the record is deleted.

Avg function A built-in Access function used to calculate the average of the values in a given field.

Backup (noun) A duplicate copy of a file that is stored in another location.

Back up (verb) To create a duplicate copy of a database that is stored in a secure location.

Back Color property A property that determines the background color of the selected control or section in a form or report.

Back-end database Part of a split database that contains the actual table objects and is stored on a file server.

Backward-compatible Software feature that enables documents saved in an older version of a program to be opened in a newer version of the program.

Bang notation A format that separates the object type from an object name and from a control name by using [square brackets] and exclamation points (!).

Between...and Criteria that selects all records between the two dates, including the two dates. Between...and criteria work the same way as the >= and <= operators.

Border A window's edge; drag to resize the window.

Border Style A form property that determines the appearance of the outside border of the form.

Bound control A control used in either a form or report to display data from the underlying field; used to edit and enter new data in a form.

Breakpoint A VBA debugging tool that works like a bookmark to suspend execution of the procedure at that statement so you can examine what is happening.

Brown-out A power problem caused by a dip in power, often making the lights dim.

Byte A field size that allows entries only from 0 to 255.

Calculated field A field created in Query Design View that results from an expression of existing fields, Access functions, and arithmetic operators. For example, the entry Profit: [RetailPrice]-[WholesalePrice] in the field cell of the query design grid creates a calculated field called Profit that is the difference between the values in the RetailPrice and WholesalePrice fields.

Calculation A new value that is created by entering an expression in a text box on a form or report.

Calendar Picker A pop-up calendar from which you can choose dates for a date field.

Canvas In the Paint accessory program, the area in the center of the program window that you use to create drawings.

Caption A field property that determines the default field name at the top of the field column in datasheets as well as in labels that describe fields on forms and reports.

Cascade Delete Related Records A relationship option that means that if a record in the "one" side of a one-to-many relationship is deleted, all related records in the "many" table are also deleted.

Cascade Update Related Fields A relationship option that means that if a value in the primary key field (the field on the "one" side of a one-to-many relationship) is modified, all values in the foreign key field (the field on the "many" side of a one-to-many relationship) are automatically updated as well.

Case In VBA, a programming structure that executes one of several groups of statements depending on the value of an expression.

Case sensitive Describes a program's ability to differentiate between uppercase and lowercase letters; usually used to describe how an operating system evaluates passwords that users type to gain entry to user accounts.

Category axis On a PivotChart, the horizontal axis. Also called the x-axis.

Chart A visual representation of numeric data that helps users see comparisons, patterns, and trends in data. Also called a graph.

Chart Field List A list of fields in the underlying record source for a PivotChart.

Chart type A category of chart layouts that determines the presentation of data on the chart such as column, pie, and line.

Chart Wizard A wizard that guides you through the steps of creating a chart in Access.

Check box A box that turns an option on when checked or off when unchecked.

Child record A record contained in the "many" table in a one-to-many relationship.

Child table The "many" table in a one-to-many relationship.

Class module An Access module that is contained and executed within specific forms and reports.

Click To quickly press and release the left button on the pointing device; also called single-click.

Client In client/server computing, the user's PC.

Client/server computing Two or more information systems cooperatively processing to solve a problem.

Clipboard A location in a computer's random access memory that stores information you copy or cut.

Close button In a Windows title bar, the rightmost button; closes the open window, program, and/or document.

Cloud computing When data, applications, and resources are stored on servers accessed over the Internet or a company's internal network rather than on user's computers.

Code window Contains the VBA for the project selected in the Project Explorer window.

Column separator The thin line that separates the field names to the left or right.

Combo box A bound control used to display a list of possible entries for a field in which you can also type an entry from the keyboard. It is a "combination" of the list box and text box controls.

Combo Box Wizard A bound control used to display a list of possible entries for a field in which you can also type an entry from the keyboard.

Comma-separated values (CSV) A text file where fields are delimited, or separated, by commas.

Command An instruction to perform a task, such as opening a file or emptying the Recycle Bin.

Command button In Access, an unbound control used to provide an easy way to initiate an action. In Windows, a button you click to issue instructions to modify program objects.

Command Button Wizard A wizard that organizes over 30 of the most common command button actions within six categories.

Command-line option A special series of characters added to the end of the path to the file (for example, C:\My Documents\Quest.accdb /excl), and execute a special command when the file is opened.

Comment Text in a module that helps explain and document the code.

Comment line In VBA, a statement in the code that documents the code; it does not affect how the code runs.

Compact and repair To reorganize the pieces of the database to eliminate wasted space on the disk storage device, which also helps prevent data integrity problems.

Compact Flash (CF) card A card about the size of a matchbook that you can plug into your computer to store data.

Compatibility The ability of different programs to work together and exchange data.

Compile time The period during which source code is translated to executable code.

Compile-time error In VBA, an error that occurs as a result of incorrectly constructed code and is detected as soon as you run your code or select the Compile option on the Debug menu.

Conditional expression An expression resulting in either a true or false answer that determines whether a macro action will execute.

Conditional formatting Formatting that is based on specified criteria. For example, a text box may be conditionally formatted to display its value in red if the value is a negative number.

Constant In VBA, an object that retains a constant value throughout the execution of the code.

Control Any element on a form or report such as a label, text box, line, or combo box. Controls can be bound, unbound, or calculated.

Control Box A form property that determines whether a control box (which provides access to menu commands that let you close or minimize a form, for example) are displayed in a form.

Control Name A property that specifies the name of a control on a form or report.

Control Source property A property of a bound control in a form or report that determines the field to which the control is connected.

Convert To change the database file into one that can be opened in another version of Access.

Copy To make a duplicate copy of a file, folder, or other object that you want to store in another location.

Criteria Entries (rules and limiting conditions) that determine which records are displayed when finding or filtering records in a datasheet or form, or when building a query.

Criteria syntax Rules by which criteria need to be entered. For example, text criteria syntax requires that the criteria are surrounded by quotation marks (" "). Date criteria are surrounded by pound signs (#).

Crosstab query A query that represents data in a cross-tabular layout (fields are used for both column and row headings), similar to PivotTables in other database and spreadsheet products.

Crosstab Query Wizard A wizard used to create crosstab queries and which helps identify fields that will be used for row and column headings, and fields that will be summarized within the datasheet.

Crosstab row A row in the query design grid used to specify the column and row headings and values for the crosstab query.

CSV *See* comma-separated values.

Current record The record that has the focus or is being edited.

Data area When creating a chart, the area in the Chart Wizard that determines what data the chart graphs.

Data macro A type of macro that allows you to embed macro capabilities directly in a table to add, change, or delete data based on conditions you specify.

Data type A required property for each field that defines the type of data that can be entered in each field. Valid data types include AutoNumber, Text, Number, Currency, Date/Time, and Memo.

Database administration The task of making a database faster, easier, more secure, and more reliable.

Database designer The person responsible for building and maintaining tables, queries, forms, and reports.

Database Documenter A feature on the Database Tools tab that helps you create reports containing information about the database.

Database template A tool that can be used to quickly create a new database based on a particular subject such as assets, contacts, events, or projects.

Datasheet A spreadsheet-like grid that displays fields as columns and records as rows.

Datasheet View A view that lists the records of the object in a datasheet. Tables, queries, and most form objects have a Datasheet View.

Date function Built-in Access function used to display the current date on a form or report; enter the Date function as Date().

Debug To determine why a macro or program doesn't run correctly.

Declaration statement A type of VBA statement that precedes procedure statements and helps set rules for how the statements in the module are processed.

Default In a program window or dialog box, a value that is already set by the program; you can change the default to any valid value.

Default switchboard The switchboard page designated as the one to contain links to additional switchboard pages.

Default View property A form property that determines whether a subform automatically opens in Datasheet or Continuous Forms view.

Delete query A query that deletes a group of records from one or more tables.

Delete row When creating a Delete query, a row that appears in the query design grid to specify criteria for deleting records.

Delimited text file A text file that typically stores one record on each line, with the field values separated by a common character such as a comma, tab, or dash.

Delimiter A common character, such as a comma, tab, or dash.

Description A query property that allows you to better document the purpose or author of a query.

Design View A view in which the structure of the object can be manipulated. Every Access object (table, query, form, report, macro, and module) has a Design View.

Desktop A shaded or picture background that appears to fill the screen after a computer starts up; usually contains icons, which are small images that represent items on your computer and allow you to interact with the computer.

Desktop background The shaded area behind your desktop objects; can show colors, designs, or photographs, which you can customize.

Details pane A pane located at the bottom of a window that displays information about the selected disk, drive, folder, or file.

Device A hardware component that is part of your computer system, such as a disk drive or a pointing device.

Dialog A Border Style option that indicates a form will have a thick border and cannot be maximized, minimized, or resized.

Dialog box In Access, a special form used to display information or prompt a user for a choice. In Windows, a type of window in which you specify how you want to complete an operation. In Windows, a window with controls that lets you tell Windows how you want to complete a program command.

Dim A VBA keyword that declares a variable.

Display Form option An option in the Access Options dialog box where you can specify a form to display when a database opens.

DoCmd A VBA object that supports many methods to run common Access commands such as closing windows, opening forms, previewing reports, navigating records, and setting the value of controls.

Document window The portion of a program window in which you create the document; displays all or part of an open document.

Documents folder The folder on your hard drive used to store most of the files you create or receive from others; might contain subfolders to organize the files into smaller groups.

Documenter An Access analysis feature that creates reports on the properties and relationships among the objects in a database.

Domain The recordset (table or query) that contains the field used in a domain function calculation.

Domain function A function used to display a calculation on a form or report using a field that is not included in the Record Source property for the form or report. Also called domain aggregate function.

Double-click To quickly press and release or click the left button on the pointing device twice.

Drag To point to an object, press and hold the left button on the pointing device, move the object to a new location, and then release the left button.

Drag and drop To use a pointing device to move or copy a file or folder to a new location.

Drive A physical location on your computer where you can store files.

Drive name A name for a drive that consists of a letter followed by a colon, such as C: for the hard disk drive.

Drop area A position on a PivotChart or PivotTable where you can drag and place a field. Drop areas on a PivotTable include the Filter field, Row field, Column field, and Totals or Detail field. Drop areas on a PivotChart include the Filter field, Category field, Series field, and Data field.

Dynaset A query property that allows updates to data in a recordset.

Edit To make changes to a file.

Edit List Items button A button you click to add items to the combo box list in Form View.

Edit mode When working with Access records, the mode in which Access assumes you are trying to edit a particular field, so keystrokes such as [Ctrl][End], [Ctrl][Home], [↑], and [↓] move the insertion point within the field. When working with charts, a mode that lets you select and modify individual chart elements such as the title, legend, bars, or axes. When creating a switchboard, an option you can specify so that users can open an object, such as a form, for editing records.

Edit record symbol A pencil-like symbol that appears in the record selector box to the left of the record that is currently being edited in either a datasheet or a form.

Else The part of an If statement that allows you to run a different set of actions if the conditional expression evaluates False.

ElseIf In VBA, a keyword that executes a statement depending on the value of an expression.

Enabled property A control property that determines whether the control can have the focus in Form View.

Encryption To make the data in the database unreadable by tools other than opening the Access database itself, which is protected by a password.

End Function In VBA, a required statement to mark the end of the code that defines the new function.

End If In VBA, a statement needed to mark the end of the If block of code.

End Select When defining a new Select Case group of VBA statements, the End Select statement is required as the last statement to mark the end of the VBA code.

End Sub When defining a new sub in VBA, the End Sub statement is required as the last statement to mark the end of the VBA code that defines the sub.

Error indicator A Smart Tag that helps identify potential design errors in Report or Form Design View.

Event A specific activity that happens in a database, such as the click of a command button or an entry in a field, that can be used to initiate the execution of a macro.

Event handler A procedure that is triggered by an event. Also called an event procedure.

Exclusive mode A mode indicating that you are the only person who has the database open, and others cannot open the file during this time.

Export To copy Access information to another database, spreadsheet, or file format.

Expression A combination of values, functions, and operators that calculates to a single value. Access expressions start with an equal sign and are placed in a text box in either Form Design View or Report Design View.

Extensible Markup Language (XML) A programming language in which data can be placed in text files and structured so that most programs can read the data.

External hard drive A device that plugs into a computer and stores more data than a typical USB drive, anywhere from 20 to 200 GB of information, and connects to a computer using either a USB or FireWire port.

F

Favorites A custom group for the Navigation Pane that is provided by default.

Field In a table, a field corresponds to a column of data, a specific piece or category of data such as a first name, last name, city, state, or phone number.

Field list A list of the available fields in the table or query that the field list represents.

Field name The name given to each field in a table.

Field properties Characteristics that further define the field.

Field selector The button to the left of a field in Table Design View that indicates the currently selected field. Also the thin gray bar above each field in the query grid.

Field selector button The button to the left of a field in Table Design View that indicates which field is currently selected. Also the thin gray bar above each field in the query grid.

Field Size property A field property that determines the number of characters that can be entered in a field.

File A collection of information stored on your computer, such as a letter, video, or program.

File extension A three- or four-letter sequence, preceded by a period, at the end of a filename that identifies the file as a particular type of document; documents in the Rich Text Format have the file extension .rtf.

File hierarchy The tree-like structure of folders and files on your computer.

File list In Windows Explorer, the right section of the window; shows the contents of the folder selected in the Navigation pane on the left.

File management The ability to organize folders and files on your computer.

File properties Details that Windows stores about a file, such as the date it was created or modified.

File server A centrally located computer from which every user can access the database by using the network.

Filename A unique, descriptive name for a file that identifies the file's content.

Filter A way to temporarily display only those records that match given criteria.

Filter By Form A way to filter data that allows two or more criteria to be specified at the same time.

Filter By Selection A way to filter records for an exact match.

Find Duplicates Query Wizard A wizard used to create a query that determines whether a table contains duplicate values in one or more fields.

Find unmatched query A type of query that finds records in one table that do not have matching records in a related table.

Find Unmatched Query Wizard A wizard used to create a query that finds records in one table that doesn't have related records in another table.

First normal form (1NF) The first degree of normalization, in which a table has rows and columns with no repeating groups.

Focus The property that indicates which field would be edited if you were to start typing.

Folder An electronic container that helps you organize your computer files, like a cardboard folder on your desk; it can contain subfolders for organizing files into smaller groups.

Folder name A unique, descriptive name for a folder that helps identify the folder's contents.

Force New Page A property that forces a report section to start printing at the top of a new page.

Foreign key field In a one-to-many relationship between two tables, the foreign key field is the field in the "many" table that links the table to the primary key field in the "one" table.

Form An Access object that provides an easy-to-use data entry screen that generally shows only one record at a time.

Form template A tool you can use to quickly create a form in a database, which can be used or modified to meet your needs.

Form View View of a form object that displays data from the underlying recordset and allows you to enter and update data.

Form Wizard An Access wizard that helps you create a form.

Format Painter A tool you can use when designing and laying out forms and reports to copy formatting characteristics from one control to another.

Format property A field property that controls how information is displayed and printed.

Formatting Enhancing the appearance of the information through font, size, and color changes.

Forum An electronic gathering place on the World Wide Web where anyone can add questions and answers on issues; available on the Microsoft Answers website.

FROM A SQL keyword that determines how tables are joined.

Front-end database Part of a split database that contains the database objects other than tables (forms, reports, so forth), and links to the back-end database tables.

Function A special, predefined formula that provides a shortcut for a commonly used calculation, for example, SUM or COUNT. Also a procedure that returns a value.

Gadget An optional program you can display on your desktop that presents helpful or entertaining information, such as a clock, current news headlines, a calendar, a picture album, or a weather report.

Gallery A visual collection of choices you can browse through to make a selection. Often available with Live Preview.

Gigabyte (GB or G) One billion bytes (or one thousand megabytes).

Graphic image *See* Image.

Group (noun) In the Navigation Pane, a custom category that organizes the objects that belong to that category. On the Ribbon, a set of related commands on a tab.

Grouping A way to sort records in a particular order, as well as provide a section before and after each group of records.

Hard disk A built-in, high-capacity, high-speed storage medium for all the software, folders, and files on a computer.

Highlighted Describes the changed appearance of an item or other object, usually a change in its color, background color, and/or border; often used for an object on which you will perform an action, such as a desktop icon.

Homegroup A named group of Windows 7 computers that can share information, including libraries and printers.

Icon A small image, usually on the desktop, which represents items on your computer, such as the Recycle Bin; you can rearrange, add, and delete desktop icons.

If statement A statement in a macro that allows you to run macro actions based on the result of a conditional expression.

If...Then In VBA, a logical structure that executes code (the code follows the Then statement) when the value of an expression is true (the expression follows the If statement).

If...Then...Else In VBA, a logical structure that allows you to test logical conditions and execute statements only if the conditions are true. If...Then...Else code can be composed of one or several statements, depending on how many conditions you want to test, how many possible answers you want to provide, and what you want the code to do based on the results of the tests.

Image A nontextual piece of information such as a picture, piece of clip art, drawn object, or graph. Because images are graphical (and not numbers or letters), they are sometimes referred to as graphical images.

Immediate window In the Visual Basic Editor, a pane where you can determine the value of any argument at the breakpoint.

Import To quickly convert data from an external file into an Access database. You can import data from one Access database to another—or from many other data sources such as files created by Excel, SharePoint, Outlook, dBase, and Paradox or text files in an HTML, XML, or delimited text file format.

Import Spreadsheet Wizard A wizard that guides you through the steps of importing a spreadsheet into an Access database.

Inactive window An open window you are not currently using; if multiple windows are open, the window(s) with the dimmed title bar.

Index A field property that keeps track of the order of the values in the indexed field as data is being entered and edited. Therefore, if you often sort on a field, the Index property should be set to Yes as this theoretically speeds up the presentation of the sorted data later (because the index has already been created).

Infinity symbol The symbol that indicates the "many" side of a one-to-many relationship.

Inner join A type of relationship in which a query displays only records where joined fields from both tables are equal. This means that if a parent table has any records for which there are no matching records in the child table, those records do not appear in the resulting datasheet.

Input Mask property A field property that provides a visual guide for users as they enter data.

Insertion point In a document or filename, a blinking, vertical bar that indicates where the next character you type will appear.

Integrate To incorporate a document and parts of a document created in one program into another program; for example, to incorporate an Excel chart into a PowerPoint slide, or an Access table into a Word document.

IntelliSense technology In VBA, visual aids that appear as you write a VBA statement to help you complete it.

Interface The look and feel of a program; for example, the appearance of commands and the way they are organized in the program window.

Is Not Null A criterion that finds all records in which any entry has been made in the field.

Is Null A criterion that finds all records in which no entry has been made in the field.

.jpg The filename extension for JPEG files.

Join line The line identifying which fields establish the relationship between two related tables. Also called a link line.

JPEG Acronym for Joint Photographic Experts Group, which defines the standards for the compression algorithms that allow image files to be stored in an efficient compressed format. JPEG files use the .jpg filename extension.

Junction table A table created to establish separate one-to-many relationships to two tables that have a many-to-many relationship.

Key symbol The symbol appearing to the left of a primary key field.

Keyboard shortcut A key or a combination of keys that you press to perform a command.

Keyword A descriptive word or phrase you enter to obtain a list of results that include that word or phrase.

.laccdb The file extension for a temporary file that keeps track of record-locking information when a .accdb database is open. It helps coordinate the multiuser capabilities of an Access database so that several people can read and update the same database at the same time.

.ldb The file extension for a temporary file that keeps track of record-locking information when a .mdb database is open. It helps coordinate the multiuser capabilities of an Access database so that several people can read and update the same database at the same time.

Label An unbound control that displays text to describe and clarify other information on a form or report.

Label Wizard A report wizard that precisely positions and sizes information to print on a vast number of standard business label specifications.

Landscape orientation A way to print or view a page that is 11 inches wide by 8.5 inches tall.

Launch To open or start a program on your computer.

Layout The general arrangement in which a form displays the fields in the underlying recordset. Layout types include Columnar, Tabular, Datasheet, Chart, and PivotTable. Columnar is most popular for a form, and Datasheet is most popular for a subform. In Access forms and reports, layout also refers to connecting controls as a set so that when you move or resize them in Layout or Design View, the action you take on one control applies to all controls in the group.

Layout View An Access view that lets you make some design changes to a form or report while you are browsing the data.

Left function An Access function that returns a specified number of characters, starting with the left side of a value in a Text field.

Left join A type of relationship in which a query displays all of the records in the parent table, even if the child table does not contain matching records.

Len function Built-in Access function used to return the number of characters in a field.

Library A window that shows files and folders stored in different storage locations; default libraries in Windows 7 include the Documents, Music, Pictures, and Videos libraries.

Like operator An operator used in a query to find values in a field that match the pattern you specify.

Limit to List A combo box control property that allows you to limit the entries made by that control to those provided by the combo box list.

Link In Access, to connect an Access database to data in an external file such as another Access, dBase, or Paradox database; an Excel or other type of spreadsheet; a text file; an HTML file; or an XML file. In Windows, a shortcut for opening a Help topic or a Web site. In Windows, text or an image that you click to display another location, such as a Help topic, a Web site, or a device.

Link Child Fields A subform property that determines which field serves as the "many" link between the subform and main form.

Link line The line identifying which fields establish the relationship between two related tables.

Link Master Fields A subform property that determines which field serves as the "one" link between the main form and the subform.

Link Spreadsheet Wizard A wizard that guides you through the steps of linking to a spreadsheet.

List box In Access, a bound control that displays a list of possible choices for the user. Used mainly on forms. In Windows, a box that displays a list of options from which you can choose (you may need to scroll and adjust your view to see additional options in the list).

List Rows A control property that determines how many items can be displayed in a list, such as in a combo box.

Live Preview A feature that lets you point to a choice in a gallery or palette and see the results in the document without actually clicking the choice.

Local area network (LAN) A type of network installed to link multiple PCs together so they can share hardware and software resources.

Locked property A control property specifies whether you can edit data in a control on Form View.

Log in To select a user account name when a computer starts up, giving access to that user's files.

Log off To close all windows, programs, and documents, then display the Welcome screen.

Logic error In VBA, an error that occurs when the code runs without obvious problems, but the procedure still doesn't produce the desired result.

Logical view The datasheet of a query is sometimes called a logical view of the data because it is not a copy of the data, but rather, a selected view of data from the underlying tables.

Long Integer A field size that stores numbers from -2,147,483,648 to 2,147,483,647 as integers. Long Integer is the default field size for Number fields.

Lookup field A field that has lookup properties. Lookup properties are used to create a drop-down list of values to populate the field.

Lookup properties Field properties that allow you to supply a drop-down list of values for a field.

Lookup table A table that contains one record for each field value.

Lookup Wizard A wizard used in Table Design View that allows one field to "look up" values from another table or entered list. For example, you might use the Lookup Wizard to specify that the Customer Number field in the Sales table display the Customer Name field entry from the Customers table.

.mdb The file extension for Access 2000 and 2002–2003 databases.

Macro An Access object that stores a collection of keystrokes or commands such as those for printing several reports in a row or providing a toolbar when a form opens.

Macro Design View An Access window in which you build and modify macros.

Mail merge A way to export Microsoft Office Access data by merging it to a Word document as the data source for a mail merge process, in which data from an Access table or query is combined into a Word form letter, label, or envelope to create mass mailing documents.

Mail Merge task pane A tool in Microsoft Office Word that steps you through creating a mail merge.

Main document In a mail merge, the document used to determine how the letter and Access data are combined. This is the standard text that will be consistent for each letter created in the mail merge process.

Main form A form that contains a subform control.

Main report A report that contains a subreport control.

Make table query A query that creates a new table of data based on the recordset defined by the query. The make table query works like an export feature in that it creates a copy of the selected data and pastes it into a new table in a database specified by the query.

Many-to-many relationship The relationship between two tables in an Access database in which one record of one table relates to many records in the other table and vice versa. You cannot directly create a many-to-many relationship between two tables in Access. To relate two tables with such a relationship, you must establish a third table called junction table that creates separate one-to-many relationships with the two original tables.

Maximize button On the right side of a window's title bar, the center button of three buttons; use to expand a window so that it fills the entire screen. In a maximized screen, this button turns into a Restore button.

Maximized window A window that fills the desktop.

Megabyte (MB or M) One million bytes (or one thousand kilobytes).

Menu A list of related commands.

Menu bar A horizontal bar in a window that displays menu names, or categories of related commands.

Merge field A code in the main document of a mail merge that is replaced with the values in the field that the code represents when the mail merge is processed.

MessageBox A macro action that displays an informational message to the user.

Method An action that an object can perform. Procedures are often written to invoke methods in response to user actions.

Microsoft Answers A Microsoft website that lets you search forums, Microsoft Help files, and demonstration videos.

Microsoft Excel The spreadsheet program in the Microsoft Office suite.

Microsoft Outlook The e-mail program in Microsoft Office, a fast electronic method to share information.

Microsoft SharePoint server A server computer that runs Microsoft SharePoint, software that allows an organization to host Web pages on an intranet.

Microsoft Windows 7 An operating system.

Microsoft Word The word-processing program in the Microsoft Office suite.

Microsoft Word Mail Merge Wizard A wizard that guides you through the steps of preparing to merge Access data with a Word document.

Min Max Buttons A form property that determines whether Minimize and Maximize buttons are displayed in a form.

Minimize button On the right side of a window's title bar, the left-most button of three buttons; use to reduce a window so that it only appears as an icon on the taskbar.

Minimized window A window that is visible only as an icon on the taskbar.

Module An Access object that stores Visual Basic programming code that extends the functions of automated Access processes.

Mouse pointer A small arrow or other symbol on the screen that you move by manipulating the pointing device; also called a pointer.

Move To change the location of a file, folder, or other object by physically placing it in another location.

Multicolumn report A report that repeats the same information in more than one column across the page.

Multifield primary key A primary key that is composed of two or more fields. For example, an OrderID value can be listed multiple times in the Order Details table, and a ProductID value can be listed multiple times in the Order Details table. But the combination of a particular OrderID value plus a ProductID value should be unique for each record.

Multiuser A characteristic that means more than one person can enter and edit data in the same Access database at the same time.

Multivalued field A field that allows you to make more than one choice from a drop-down list.

Name property A property that uniquely identifies each object and control on a form or report.

Navigate To move around in your computer's folder and file hierarchy.

Navigate downward To move to a lower level in your computer's folder and file hierarchy.

Navigate upward To move to a higher level in your computer's folder and file hierarchy.

Navigation Buttons A form property that determines whether a navigation bar is displayed in a form. Navigation buttons are also buttons in the lower-left corner of a datasheet or form that allow you to quickly navigate between the records in the underlying object as well as add a new record.

Navigation form A special Access form that provides an easy-to-use database interface that is also Web compatible.

Navigation mode A mode in which Access assumes that you are trying to move between the fields and records of the datasheet (rather than edit a specific field's contents), so keystrokes such as [Ctrl][Home] and [Ctrl][End] move you to the first and last field of the datasheet.

Navigation Pane In Access, a pane in the program window that provides a way to move between objects (tables, queries, forms, reports, macros, and modules) in the database. In Windows, the Navigation pane is a pane on the left side of a window that contains links to folders and libraries on your computer; click an item in the Navigation pane to display its contents in the file list or click the ▷ or ◢ symbols to display or hide subfolders in the Navigation pane.

Navigation system style In a navigation form, a style that determines how the navigation buttons will be displayed on the form.

Normalize To structure data for a relational database.

Northwind.mdb A fully developed database example in the Access 2000 file format that illustrates many advanced database techniques you can apply to your own development needs.

Notification area An area on the right side of the Windows 7 taskbar that displays the current time as well as icons representing programs; displays pop-up messages when a program on your computer needs your attention.

Now() An Access function that displays today's date.

Null A field value that means that a value has not been entered for the field.

Null entry The state of "nothingness" in a field. Any entry such as 0 in a numeric field or a space in a text field is not null. It is common to search for empty fields by using the Null criterion in a filter or query. The Is Not Null criterion finds all records where there is an entry of any kind.

Object A table, query, form, report, macro, or module in a database. In VBA, any item that can be identified or manipulated, including the traditional Access objects (table, query, form, report, macro, module) as well as other items that have properties such as controls, sections, and existing procedures.

Object list In a VBA class module, lists the objects associated with the current form or report.

ODBC *See* open database connectivity

Office Web App Versions of the Microsoft Office applications with limited functionality that are available online from Windows Live SkyDrive. Users can view documents online and then edit them in the browser using a selection of functions. Office Web Apps are available for Word, PowerPoint, Excel, and One Note.

OLE A field data type that stores pointers that tie files, such as pictures, sound clips, or spreadsheets, created in other programs to a record.

On Click An event that occurs when an item is clicked.

On Current An event that occurs when focus moves from one record to another.

On Dbl Click An Access event that is triggered by a double-click.

On Error GoTo Upon an error in the execution of a procedure, the On Error GoTo statement specifies the location (the statement) where the procedure should continue.

On Got Focus An Access event that is triggered when a specified control gets the focus.

One-to-many line The line that appears in the Relationships window and shows which field is duplicated between two tables to serve as the linking field. The one-to-many line displays a "1" next to the field that serves as the "one" side of the relationship and displays an infinity symbol next to the field that serves as the "many" side of the relationship when referential integrity is specified for the relationship. Also called the one-to-many join line.

One-to-many relationship The relationship between two tables in an Access database in which a common field links the tables together. The linking field is called the primary key field in the "one" table of the relationship and the foreign key field in the "many" table of the relationship.

One-to-one relationship A relationship in which the primary key field of the first table is related to the primary key field of a second table. In other words, one record in the first table can be related to one and only one record in the second table.

Online collaboration The ability to incorporate feedback or share information across the Internet or a company network or intranet.

Online template A database template available to download from the Microsoft Office Online Web site.

Open database connectivity (ODBC) A collection of standards that govern how Access connects to other sources of data.

OpenReport A macro action that opens a specified report.

Operating system A program that manages the complete operation of your computer and lets you interact with it.

Option button In Access, a bound control used to display a limited list of mutually exclusive choices for a field, such as "female" or "male" for a gender field in form or report. In Windows, a small circle in a dialog box that you click to select only one of two or more related options.

Option Compare Database A VBA declaration statement that determines the way string values (text) will be sorted.

Option Explicit A VBA declaration statement that specifies that you must explicitly declare all variables used in all procedures; if you attempt to use an undeclared variable name, an error occurs at compile time.

Option group A bound control placed on a form that is used to group together several option buttons that provide a limited number of values for a field.

Option Value An option button property that determines the values entered into a field when the option button is selected.

OR criteria Criteria placed on different rows of the query design grid. A record will appear in the resulting datasheet if it is true for any single row.

ORDER BY A SQL keyword that determines how records in the query result are sorted.

Orphan record A record in the "many" table of a one-to-many relationship that doesn't have a matching entry in the linking field of the "one" table.

Outlook Data Collection Wizard A wizard that guides you through the steps of collecting Access data through Outlook e-mail.

P

Parameter criteria In a query, text entered in square brackets in Design View that prompts the user for criteria each time the query is run.

Parameter query A query that displays a dialog box to prompt users for field criteria. The entry in the dialog box determines which records appear on the final datasheet, similar to criteria entered directly in the query design grid.

Parameter report A report that prompts you for criteria to determine the records to use for the report.

Parent record A record contained in the "one" table in a one-to-many relationship.

Parent table The "one" table in a one-to-many relationship.

Password A special sequence of numbers and letters known only to selected users, that users can create to control who can access the files in their user account area; helps keep users' computer information secure.

Path The sequence of folders that describes a file location in the file hierarchy; appears in the Address bar of Windows Explorer and the Open and Save dialog boxes.

Performance Analyzer An Access tool that studies the structure and size of your database and makes a variety of recommendations on how you can improve its performance.

Picture A form and report property that determines which image is displayed in the form or report (if any).

PivotChart A graphical presentation of the data in a PivotTable.

PivotChart View The view in which you build a PivotChart.

PivotTable An arrangement of data that uses one field as a column heading, another as a row heading, and summarizes a third field, typically a Number field, in the body.

PivotTable View The view in which you build a PivotTable.

Pixel (picture element) One pixel is the measurement of one picture element on the screen.

Pmt function Built-in Access function used to calculate the monthly payment on a loan; enter the Pmt function as Pmt([Rate],[Term],[Loan]).

Point To position the tip of the mouse pointer over an object, option, or item.

Pointer *See* Mouse pointer.

Pointing device A device that lets you interact with your computer by controlling the movement of the mouse pointer on your computer screen; examples include a mouse, trackball, touchpad, pointing stick, on-screen touch pointer, or a tablet.

Pointing device action A movement you execute with your computer's pointing device to communicate with the computer; the five pointing device actions are point, click, double-click, drag, and right-click.

Pop up form A form that stays on top of other open forms, even when another form is active.

Portrait orientation A way to print or view a page that is 8.5 inches wide by 11 inches tall.

Power button 1) The physical button on your computer that turns your computer on. 2) The Start menu button or button on the right side of the Welcome screen that lets you shut down or restart your computer. Click the button arrow to log off your user account, switch to another user, or hibernate the computer to put your computer to sleep so that your computer appears off and uses very little power.

Preview pane A pane on the right side of a window that shows the actual contents of a selected file without opening a program; might not work for some types of files.

Previewing Prior to printing, seeing onscreen exactly how the printed document will look.

Primary key field A field that contains unique information for each record. A primary key field cannot contain a null entry.

Print Preview An Access view that shows you how a report or other object will print on a sheet of paper.

Private Sub A statement that indicates a sub procedure is accessible only to other procedures in the module where it is declared.

Procedure A series of VBA statements that performs an operation or calculates an answer. VBA has two types of procedures: functions and subs.

Procedure list In a VBA standard module, lists the procedures in the module; in a class module, lists events (such as Click or Dblclick).

Program A set of instructions written for a computer, such as an operating system program or an application program; also called an application.

Program window The window that opens after you start a program, showing you the tools you need to use the program and any open program documents.

Project In VBA, a module object or a form or report object that contains a class module.

Project Explorer window In the Visual Basic Editor, a window you use to switch between open projects, objects that can contain VBA code.

Property In Access, a characteristic that defines the appearance and behavior of items in the database such as objects, fields, sections, and controls. You can view the properties for an item by opening its Property Sheet. In a macro, an argument that determines what property is being modified. In Windows, a characteristic or setting of a file, folder, or other item, such as its size or the date it was created.

Property Sheet A window that displays an exhaustive list of properties for the chosen control, section, or object within the Form Design View or Report Design View.

Property Update Options A Smart Tag that applies property changes in one field to other objects of the database that use the field.

Query An Access object that provides a spreadsheet-like view of the data, similar to that in tables. It may provide the user with a subset of fields and/or records from one or more tables. Queries are created when the user has a "question" about the data in the database.

Query Datasheet View The view of a query that shows the selected fields and records as a datasheet.

Query design grid The bottom pane of the Query Design View window in which you specify the fields, sort order, and limiting criteria for the query.

Query Design View The window in which you develop queries by specifying the fields, sort order, and limiting criteria that determine which fields and records are displayed in the resulting datasheet.

Question mark (?) A wildcard character you use to search for any single character.

Quick Access toolbar A small toolbar on the left side of a Microsoft application program window's title bar, containing icons that you click to quickly perform common actions, such as saving a file.

RAM (random access memory) The storage location that is part of every computer that temporarily stores open programs and documents information while a computer is on.

Read-only An object property that indicates whether the object can read and display data, but cannot be used to change (write to) data.

Record A row of data in a table.

Record Selectors A form property that determines whether record selectors are displayed in a form.

Record source The table or query that defines the field and records displayed in a form or report.

Record Source property In a form or report, the property that determines which table or query object contains the fields and records that the form or report will display. It is the most important property of the form or report object. A bound control on a form or report has Control Source property. In this case, the Control Source property identifies the field to which the control is bound.

Recordset Type A property that determines if and how records displayed by a query are locked.

Recycle Bin A desktop object that stores folders and files you delete from your hard drive(s) and that enables you to restore them.

Referential integrity A set of Access rules that govern data entry and help ensure data accuracy.

Relational database software Software such as Access that is used to manage data organized in a relational database.

Relationship report A printout of the Relationships window that shows how a relational database is designed and includes table names, field names, primary key fields, and one-to-many relationship lines.

Removable storage Storage media that you can easily transfer from one computer to another, such as DVDs, CDs, or USB flash drives.

Report An Access object that creates a professional printout of data that may contain such enhancements as headers, footers, and calculations on groups of records.

Report Design View An Access view that allows you to work with a complete range of report, section, and control properties.

Report View An Access view that maximizes the amount of data you can see on the screen.

Report Wizard An Access wizard that helps you create a report.

Resize bar A thin gray bar that separates the field lists from the query design grid in Query Design View.

Restore Down button On the right side of a maximized window's title bar, the center of three buttons; use to reduce a window to its last non-maximized size.

Ribbon In many Microsoft application program windows, a horizontal strip near the top of the window that contains tabs (pages) of grouped command buttons that you click to interact with the program.

Rich Text Format (RTF) A file format for exporting data to a text file that can be opened and edited in Word.

Right-click To press and release the right button on the pointing device; use to display a shortcut menu with commands you issue by left-clicking them.

Right function Built-in Access function used to return the specified number of characters from the end of a field value.

Right join A type of relationship in which a query selects all records in the child table even if there are no matches in the parent table.

Row Source The Lookup property that defines the list of values for the Lookup field.

RTF *See* Rich Text Format.

Ruler A vertical or horizontal guide that both appear in Form and Report Design View to help you position controls.

Run a query To open a query and view the fields and records that you have selected for the query presented as a datasheet.

Run-time error In VBA, an error that occurs as incorrectly constructed code runs and includes attempting an illegal operation such as dividing by zero or moving focus to a control that doesn't exist. When you encounter a run-time error, VBA will stop executing your procedure at the statement in which the error occurred and highlight the line with a yellow background in the Visual Basic Editor.

Save command A command on the File tab or Quick Access toolbar that saves the current object.

Save Database As command An Access command that saves an entire database including all of its objects to a completely new database file.

Save Object As command A command on the File tab that saves the current object with a new name.

Saved Exports An option provided in Microsoft Access that lets you save export steps.

Saved Imports An option provided in Microsoft Access that lets you quickly repeat the import process by saving the import steps.

Screen capture An electronic snapshot of your screen, as if you took a picture of it with a camera, which you can paste into a document.

ScreenTip A small box that appears when you position the mouse over an object; identifies the object when you point to it.

Scroll To adjust your view to see portions of the program window that are not currently in a window.

Scroll arrow A button at each end of a scroll bar for adjusting your view in a window in small increments in that direction.

Scroll bar A vertical or horizontal bar that appears along the right or bottom side of a window when there is more content than can be displayed within the window, so that you can adjust your view.

Scroll Bars A form property that determines whether vertical, horizontal, or both scroll bars are displayed in a form.

Scroll box A box in a scroll bar that you can drag to display a different part of a window.

Search criteria Descriptive text that helps Windows identify the program, folder, file, or Web site you want to locate.

Second normal form (2NF) The second degree of normalization, in which redundant data from an original table is extracted, placed in a new table, and related to the original table.

Secure digital (SD) card A small device that slips directly into a computer, and typically stores around 256 MB.

Section A location of a form or report that contains controls. The section in which a control is placed determines where and how often the control prints.

Section properties Characteristics that define each section in a report.

Select To change the appearance of an item by clicking, double-clicking, or dragging across it, to indicate that you want to perform an action on it.

SELECT A SQL keyword that determines what fields a query selects.

Select Case In VBA, executes one of several groups of Case statements depending on the value of an expression.

Select pointer The mouse pointer shape that looks like a white arrow oriented toward the upper-left corner of the screen.

Select query The most common type of query that retrieves data from one or more linked tables and displays the results in a datasheet.

Server In client/server computing, the shared file server, mini, or mainframe computer. The server usually handles corporate-wide computing activities such as data storage and management, security, and connectivity to other networks.

SetProperty A macro action that allows you to manipulate the property value of any control on a form.

SharePoint server *See* Microsoft SharePoint server.

Shortcut In Access, a pointer to the actual database object that is identified as a shortcut by the small black arrow in the lower-left corner of the icon. You double-click a shortcut icon to open that object. In Windows, a link that gives you quick access to a particular folder, file, or Web site.

Shortcut menu A menu of context-appropriate commands for an object that opens when you right-click that object.

Show me an example A button that gives you more information on the subject at hand by using a common example to explain the issue.

Shut down To turn off your computer.

Simple Query Wizard An Access wizard that prompts you for information it needs to create a new query.

Single-click *See* Click.

Single step To run a macro one line (one action) at a time to observe the effect of each specific action in the Macro Single Step dialog box.

Sizing handles Small squares at each corner of a selected control in Access. Dragging a handle resizes the control. Also known as handles.

SkyDrive An online storage and file sharing service. Access to SkyDrive is through a Windows Live account. Up to 25 GB of data can be stored in a personal SkyDrive, with each file a maximum size of 50 MB.

Slider A shape you drag to select a setting, such as the slider on the View menu that you drag to select a view.

Smart Tag A button that provides a small menu of options and automatically appears under certain conditions to help you work with a task, such as correcting errors. For example, the AutoCorrect Options button, which helps you correct typos and update properties, and the Error Indicator button, which helps identify potential design errors in Form and Report Design View, are smart tags.

Snapshot A query property that locks the recordset (which prevents it from being updated).

Sort In Access, to reorder records in either ascending or descending order based on the values of a particular field. In Windows, to change the order of, such as the order of files or folders in a window based on criteria such as date, file size, or alphabetical by filename.

Spike A surge in power, which can cause damage to the hardware, and can render the computer useless.

Spin box A text box with up and down arrows; you can type a setting in the text box or click the arrows to increase or decrease the setting.

Splash screen A special form used to announce information.

Split form A form split into two panes; the upper pane allows you to display the fields of one record in any arrangement, and the lower pane maintains a datasheet view of the first few records.

SQL (Structured Query Language) A language that provides a standardized way to request information from a relational database system.

SQL View A query view that displays the SQL code for the query.

Standard module A type of Access module that contains global code that can be executed from anywhere in the database. Standard modules are displayed as module objects in the Navigation Pane.

Start button The round button on the left side of the Windows 7 taskbar; click it to start programs, to find and open windows that show you the contents of your computer, to get help, and to end your Windows session, and turn off your computer.

Startup option One of a series of commands that execute when the database is opened.

Statement A single line of code within a VBA procedure.

Status bar A horizontal bar at the bottom of a program window that displays simple helpful information and tips.

Strong password A password longer than eight characters that uses a combination of uppercase and lowercase letters, numbers, and symbols.

Stub In the Visual Basic window, the first and last lines of an event handler procedure.

Sub (sub procedure) A procedure that performs a series of VBA statements, but does not return a value and cannot be used in an expression like a function procedure. You use subs to manipulate controls and objects. They are generally executed when an event occurs, such as when a command button is clicked or a form is opened.

Subdatasheet A datasheet that is nested within another datasheet to show related records. The subdatasheet shows the records on the "many" side of a one-to-many relationship.

Subfolder A folder within another folder for organizing sets of related files into smaller groups.

Subform A form placed within a form that shows related records from another table or query. A subform generally displays many records at a time in a datasheet arrangement.

Submacro A collection of actions within a macro object that allows you to name and create multiple, separate macros within a single macro object.

Subquery A query based on another query's field list.

Subreport A control that displays a report within another report.

Suite A group of programs that are bundled together and share a similar interface, making it easy to transfer skills and program content among them.

Sum function A mathematical function that totals values in a field.

Summary query A query used to calculate and display information about records grouped together.

Summary report A report that calculates and displays information about records grouped together.

Surge protector A power strip with surge protection.

Switch User To lock your user account and display the Welcome screen so another user can log on.

Switchboard A special Access form that uses command buttons to provide an easy-to-use and secure database interface.

Switchboard Items A table that contains information the Switchboard form needs.

Switchboard Manager An Access tool that help you create and modify switchboards.

Syntax Rules that govern how to write programming statements so that they execute properly or how to enter property values and other information.

Syntax error In VBA, an error that occurs immediately as you are writing a VBA statement that cannot be read by the Visual Basic Editor.

T

Tab A page in an application program's Ribbon, or in a dialog box, that contains a group of related settings.

Tab control An unbound control used to create a three-dimensional aspect to a form so that other controls can be organized and shown in Form View by clicking the "tabs."

Tab Index property A form property that indicates the numeric tab order for all controls on the form that have the Tab Stop property set to Yes.

Tab order The sequence in which the controls on the form receive the focus when the user presses [Tab] or [Enter] in Form view.

Tab stop In Access, this refers to whether you can tab into a control when entering or editing data; in other words, whether the control can receive the focus.

Tab Stop property A form property that determines whether a field accepts focus.

Table A collection of records for a single subject, such as all of the customer records; the fundamental building block of a relational database because it stores all of the data.

Table Analyzer Wizard An Access tool that looks for duplicate information in one table that should be separated and stored in its own table.

Table Design View The view in which you can add, delete, or modify fields and their associated properties.

Table template A tool you can use to quickly create a single table within an existing database by providing a set of fields that describe a particular subject, such as contacts or tasks, which can be used or modified to meet your needs.

Target table The table to which an append query adds records.

Taskbar The horizontal bar at the bottom of the Windows 7 desktop; displays the Start button, the Notification area, and icons representing programs, folders, and/or files.

Template A sample file, such as a database provided within the Microsoft Access program.

Text Align property A control property that determines the alignment of text within the control.

Text box In Access, the most common type of control used to display field values. In Windows, a box in which you type text, such as the Search programs and files text box on the Start menu.

Themes Predesigned combinations of colors, fonts, and formatting attributes that you can apply to a document in any Office program.

Third normal form (3NF) The third degree of normalization, in which calculated fields (also called derived fields) such as totals or taxes are removed. Strive to create databases that adhere to the rules of third normal form.

Title bar The shaded top border of a window that displays the name of the window, folder, or file and the program name. Darker shading indicates the active window.

Toolbar In an application program, a set of buttons you can click to issue program commands.

Top Values A feature in Query Design View that lets you specify a number or percentage of sorted records that you want to display in the query's datasheet.

Total row Row in the query design grid used to specify how records should be grouped and summarized with aggregate functions.

Touch pointer A pointer on the screen for performing pointing operations with a finger if touch input is available on your computer.

Translucency The transparency feature of Windows Aero that enables you to locate content by seeing through one window to the next window.

Trusted database A database that allows you to run macros and VBA.

Trusted folder A folder specified as a trusted location for storing files.

Unassigned Objects A group for Navigation Pane objects that have not been assigned to a custom group.

Unbound A group of controls that do not display data.

Unbound control A control that does not change from record to record and exists only to clarify or enhance the appearance of the form, using elements such as labels, lines, and clip art.

Update query A type of action query that updates the values in a field.

Update To row When creating an Update query, a row that appears in the query design grid to specify criteria or an expression for updating records.

UPS (Uninterruptible Power Supply) A device that provides constant power to other devices, including computers.

USB (Universal Serial Bus) drive A device that plugs into a computer's USB port to store data. USB drives are also called thumb drives, flash drives, and travel drives. USB devices typically store 1 GB to 10 GB of information.

User The person primarily interested in entering, editing, and analyzing the data in the database.

User account A special area in a computer's operating system where users can store their own files.

User interface A collective term for all the ways you interact with a software program.

Utility project A VBA project containing code that helps Access with certain activities such as presenting the Zoom dialog box. It automatically appears in the Project Explorer window when you use the Access features that use this code.

Validation Rule A field property that helps eliminate unreasonable entries by establishing criteria for an entry before it is accepted into the database.

Validation Text A field property that determines what message appears if a user attempts to make a field entry that does not pass the validation rule for that field.

Value In a macro, an argument determines the value of a property or field.

Value axis On a PivotChart, the vertical axis. Also called the y-axis.

Value field A numeric field, such as Cost, that can be summed or averaged.

Variable In VBA, an object used to store data that can be used, modified, or displayed during the execution of the procedure.

VBA *See* Visual Basic for Applications.

VBE *See* Visual Basic Editor.

View Appearance choices for your folder contents, such as Large Icons view or Details view.

Visual Basic Editor (VBE) Comprises the entire Microsoft Visual Basic program window that contains smaller windows, including the Code window and Project Explorer window.

Visual Basic for Applications (VBA) A programming language provided with each program of the Microsoft Office suite to help you extend the program's capabilities. In Access, VBA is stored within modules.

Web compatible An object that can be opened and used with Internet Explorer when the database is published to a SharePoint server.

Welcome screen An initial startup screen that displays icons for each user account on the computer.

Width property A form property that determines the width of a form.

Wildcard A special character used in criteria to find, filter, and query data. The asterisk (*) stands for any group of characters. For example, the criteria I* in a State field criterion cell would find all records where the state entry was IA, ID, IL, IN, or Iowa. The question mark (?) wildcard stands for only one character.

Window A rectangular-shaped work area that displays a program or a collection of files, folders, and Windows tools.

Windows Aero *See* Aero.

Windows Explorer An accessory program that displays windows, allowing you to navigate your computer's file hierarchy and interact with your computer's contents.

Windows Live A collection of services and Web applications that people can access through a login. Windows Live services include access to e-mail and instant messaging, storage of files on SkyDrive, sharing and storage of photos, networking with people, downloading software, and interfacing with a mobile device.

Windows Remote Assistance A Windows Help feature that lets you connect with another computer so that users can operate your computer using an Internet connection.

Windows Search The Windows feature that lets you look for files and folders on your computer storage devices; to search, type text in the Search text box in the title bar of any open window, or click the Office button and type text in the Search programs and files text box.

Word wrap A feature in word processing programs that determines when a line of text extends into the right margin of the page and automatically forces the text to the next line without you needing to press Enter.

XML Acronym that stands for eXtensible Markup Language, which is a language used to structure, store, and send information.

XML file A text file containing XML tags that identify field names and data. *See also* Extensible Markup Language (XML)

Zero-length string A deliberate entry that contains no characters. You enter a zero-length string by typing two quotation marks ("") with no space between them.

Zooming in A feature that makes a document appear larger but shows less of it on screen at once; does not affect actual document size.

Zooming out A feature that shows more of a document on screen at once but at a reduced size; does not affect actual document size.

Index

Note: The following abbreviations have been used before page numbers: AC=Access; OFF=Office A; WEB=WebApps; WIN=Windows 7.

B

C

D

E

F

G

H

I

J

K

L

M

N

Q

R

S

T

U

V

W

X

Y

Z